The Donkey and the Boat

The Donkey and the Boat

Reinterpreting the Mediterranean Economy, 950–1180

CHRIS WICKHAM

OXFORD
UNIVERSITY PRESS

OXFORD
UNIVERSITY PRESS

Great Clarendon Street, Oxford, OX2 6DP,
United Kingdom

Oxford University Press is a department of the University of Oxford.
It furthers the University's objective of excellence in research, scholarship,
and education by publishing worldwide. Oxford is a registered trade mark of
Oxford University Press in the UK and in certain other countries

First Edition published in 2023

Published in the United States of America by Oxford University Press
198 Madison Avenue, New York, NY 10016, United States of America

British Library Cataloguing in Publication Data
Data available

Library of Congress Control Number: 2022944501

ISBN 978–0–19–885648–1

DOI: 10.1093/oso/9780198856481.001.0001

Printed and bound by
CPI Group (UK) Ltd, Croydon, CR0 4YY

For Leslie

Acknowledgements

Many people have helped me materially with the writing of this book, across the six years, 2016–22, of the book project from start to finish. I hope that I have named them all here; I have anyway tried to, helped by my email files, and I can only apologize to anyone whom I have missed out. To start with, several people read chapters or sections of this book and gave me essential critiques: Lucia Arcifa, Pamela Armstrong, Giovanna Bianchi, Lorenzo Bondioli, Leslie Brubaker (who read all of it), Sandro Carocci, Wendy Davies, Lisa Fentress, Alison Gascoigne, Sauro Gelichi, Caroline Goodson, Paolo Grillo, John Haldon, Patrizia Mainoni, Eduardo Manzano, Alessandra Molinari, Annliese Nef, Sheilagh Ogilvie, Rob Portass, Elena Salinas (who also gave me a four-hour tutorial on Andalusī ceramics which was indispensable for Chapter 5), and Stefanie Schmidt.

I am also very grateful to the people who invited me to give papers during these years, in which I had the opportunity to try out drafts, less or more finished, and got in every case very useful (often crucial) feedback in return: first of all Peter Gray and the Wiles Trust, who invited me to give the Wiles Lectures in November 2021, and the invited guests whom I brought, who turned the discussions afterwards into a brainstorming meeting, Lorenzo Bondioli, Leslie Brubaker, Sandro Carocci, Caroline Goodson, Eduardo Manzano, Alessandra Molinari, plus Bruce Campbell, who was on the spot; and, for other invitations, Maria João Branco, Maria Elena Cortese and Paola Guglielmotti, Jean-Pierre Devroey, Hugh Doherty, Stefano Gasparri, Jessica Goldberg, Stefan Heidemann, Marek Jankowiak, Rutger Kramer, Cristina La Rocca, Iñaki Martín, Elvira Migliario, Maureen Miller, Cecilia Palombo, Steffen Patzold, Pino Petralia, Walter Pohl, Sebastian Richter, Marina Rustow, Diego Santos, Jana Schulman for the Kalamazoo congress committee, Tamás Kiss, Alexis Wilkin, Simon Yarrow, and Luca Zavagno.

Particular thanks are owed to the people who helped me with the *geniza* material: Maayan Ravid and Netta Cohen, who translated for me many of Moshe Gil's translations into Hebrew; Lorenzo Bondioli, who followed up several queries on the originals, Jessica Goldberg for an array of good ideas and advice, and Marina Rustow for more advice and for giving me the run of the database behind the marvellous Princeton Geniza Project website. And, in addition to that, I thank Andreas Kaplony and his team, who run and develop the equally marvellous Arabic Papyrology Database, which makes Arabic-script documentary texts unusually accessible. Without the people in this paragraph, I could not have written Chapter 2 of this book, and the book would have been very different (and much shorter).

And I relied on very many more people for more specific help, in sending me texts (often unpublished ones), locating particularly difficult-to-find material (including photos—see the picture credits), talking to me about problems I was finding, and answering questions I sent them, often out of the blue. Again in alphabetical order, they are (or include) Paul Arthur, Rafael Azuar, Denise Bezzina, John Bintliff, David Bramoullé, Rebecca Bridgman, Federico Cantini, Claudio Capelli, Mayte Casal, Alexandra Chavarría, Ann Christys, Francesca Colangeli, Simone Collavini, Adele Curness, Koen De Groote, Federico Del Tredici, Mariette de Vos, Carolina Doménech, Laurent Feller, James Fentress, Alberto García Porras, Roland-Pierre Gayraud, Roger Gill, Sophie Gilotte, Susana Gómez, Sonia Gutiérrez, Catherine Holmes, Dario Internullo, Jeremy Johns, Anna Kelley, Fotini Kondyli, Eve Krakowski, Philippe Lefeuvre, Marie Legendre, Francisco López-Santos, Elisa Maccadanza, Tom McCaskie, Nicola Mancassola, Cristina Menghini, Antonino Meo and Paola Orecchioni and the rest of the SicTransit team, Alex Metcalfe, Nicolas Michel, Antonio Musarra, Alessandra Nardini, Elisabetta Neri, Hagit Nol, James Norrie, Elisabeth O'Connell, Vivien Prigent, Natalia Poulou, Juan Antonio Quirós, Riccardo Rao, Yossi Rapoport, Paul Reynolds, Catherine Richarté, Ana Rodríguez, Alessia Rovelli, Lucie Ryzova, Viva Sacco, Fabio Saggioro, Marco Sannazaro, Nadine Schibille, Phillipp Schofield, Valerie Scott, Simone Sestito, Petra Sijpesteijn, Andrew Small, Julia Smith, Alessandro Soddu, Lorenzo Tabarrini, Catarina Tente, Paolo Tomei, Francesca Trivellato, Marco Valenti, Anastasia Vassiliou, Joanita Vroom, Mark Whittow, Gregory Williams; and from OUP Stephanie Ireland, who encouraged this project from the start, and Cathryn Steele, Emma Slaughter, and Donald Watt, who guided it into port. Finally, I am indebted to Clare Whitton for the index.

This is over a hundred people, friends and colleagues, who were all happy to help push this project along and save me from gaps and errors. They did so without any visible concern that I might not agree with their own views. Thank you all. This is what research should be like: generous and collaborative. I shall be only too happy to repay it all in kind, now and into the future.

I have tried to keep up to date with all the regions of this book, up to at least the middle of 2021; I have not tried very hard to incorporate material from after the end of that year. I will have missed things, but from the start of 2022 onwards I won't feel guilty about it.

Birmingham
June 2022

Contents

List of Maps

Illustrations of Ceramic Types

Credits and copyright, and thanks: 1 British Museum, 2 Sworders Fine Art Auctioneers, 3 Walters Art Museum (CC-BY-SA), 4 Richard Mortel (CC-BY-NC-SA), 5 Alessandra Molinari and Paola Orecchioni, 6, 7 Viva Sacco, 8 I, Sailko (CC-BY-SA), 9 Anastasia Vassiliou and the Byzantine Museum of Argolis, 10 Giovanni Dall'Orto (CC-BY), 11, 12, 13, 14 Joanita Vroom, 15, 16 Susana Gómez Martínez, 17 Julio Navarro Palazón, 18 Giovanna Bianchi (from G. Bianchi, G. Berti, eds., *Piombino: La chiesa di Sant'Antimo sopra i canali* (All'insegna del Giglio, Florence, 2007)), 19 Museo Archeologico Ambientale, San Giovanni in Persiceto (CC-BY-NC-ND), 20 Nicola Mancassola.

List of Abbreviations

Arabic-script original documents and letters are universally cited in this book according to the conventions of the APD (see below), normally in the format P.Cair.Arab., P.Marchands, P.Mozarab, etc., in every case denoting published texts. Hebrew-script texts from the Fusṭāṭ *geniza* are, instead, cited according to their manuscript collocation, most commonly T-S (see below), but also Bodl., CUL, ENA, etc., according to the conventions of the PGP (see below); but in each case I also cite the publication, if there is one (very commonly as Gil K and Gil P; see below), and any published translation (very commonly as S; see below).

I cite in this book every published primary source together with the name of the editor (and/or translator) of the version I have used; the exceptions are *MGH* editions (see below), and those of the Archives de l'Athos (see the Bibliography under *Actes*), where I have left editors out, as the editions tend to be cited in sets and the footnotes would often become too unwieldy. They all appear in the Bibliography; so do the full citations for the monographic works listed below.

a.	*anno* (the year date)
AI	*Annales islamologiques*
AM	*Archeologia medievale*
APD	Arabic Papyrology Database, http://www.apd.gwi.uni-muenchen.de:8080/apd/project1c.jsp
ASM, Monza	Archivio di Stato di Milano, Fondo di religione, pergamene, Capitolo di S. Giovanni di Monza
ASV, SZ	Archivio di Stato di Venezia, Patrimonio, San Zaccaria, pergamene
ATM	*Arqueología y territorio medieval*
b.	*ibn*: son of (in Arabic)
BAR	*British Archaeological Reports*
BAR, I	*British Archaeological Reports, International Series*
BMFD	J. Thomas and A. Constantinides Hero (trans.), *Byzantine Monastic Foundation Documents*
bt.	*bint*: daughter of (in Arabic)
CCE	*Cahiers de la céramique égyptienne*
CDGE	C. Imperiale di S. Angelo (ed.), *Codice diplomatico della repubblica di Genova*
CDVE	Archivio di Stato di Venezia, *Codice diplomatico veneziano. Codice Lanfranchi*
d.	died
DAI	Deutsches Archäologisches Institut

DCV	R. Morozzo della Rocca and A. Lombardo (eds.), *Documenti del commercio veneziano nei secoli XI–XIII*
DCV, N	A. Lombardo and R. Morozzo della Rocca (eds.), *Nuovi documenti del commercio veneto dei sec. XI–XIII*
DOP	*Dumbarton Oaks Papers*
EHB	A. E. Laiou (ed.), *The Economic History of Byzantium*
EI[2]	*Encyclopaedia of Islam*, 2nd edn
FFS	Fusṭāṭ Fāṭimid Sgraffiato/Sgraffito
Gil K	M. Gil (ed.), *Be-malkhut Yishmaʿel bi-teḳufat ha-ge'onim*
Gil P	M. Gil (ed.), *Erets-Yishraʿel ba-teḳufah ha-Muslemit ha-rishonah*
Giovanni Scriba	*Il cartolare di Giovanni Scriba*, ed. M. Chiaudano and M. Moresco
Goitein, *MS*	S. D. Goitein, *A Mediterranean Society*
Guglielmo Cassinese	*Guglielmo Cassinese (1190–1192)*, ed. M. W. Hall et al.
JESHO	*Journal of the Economic and Social History of the Orient*
LI	A. Rovere et al. (eds.), *I libri iurium della repubblica di Genova*, 1
MEFR	*Mélanges de l'École française de Rome*
MEFRM	*Mélanges de l'École française de Rome, Moyen Âge*
MGH	*Monumenta Germaniae historica*
Oberto Scriba 1186	*Oberto Scriba de Mercato (1186)*, ed. M. Chiaudano
Oberto Scriba 1190	*Oberto Scriba de Mercato (1190)*, ed. M. Chiaudano and R. Morozzo della Rocca
PGP	Princeton Geniza Project, https://genizalab.princeton.edu/pgp-database
SRG	*Scriptores rerum germanicarum*
S	S. Simonsohn, *The Jews in Sicily*, 1
T-S	The Taylor-Schechter Genizah collection in Cambridge University library, by far the commonest location for a geniza text.

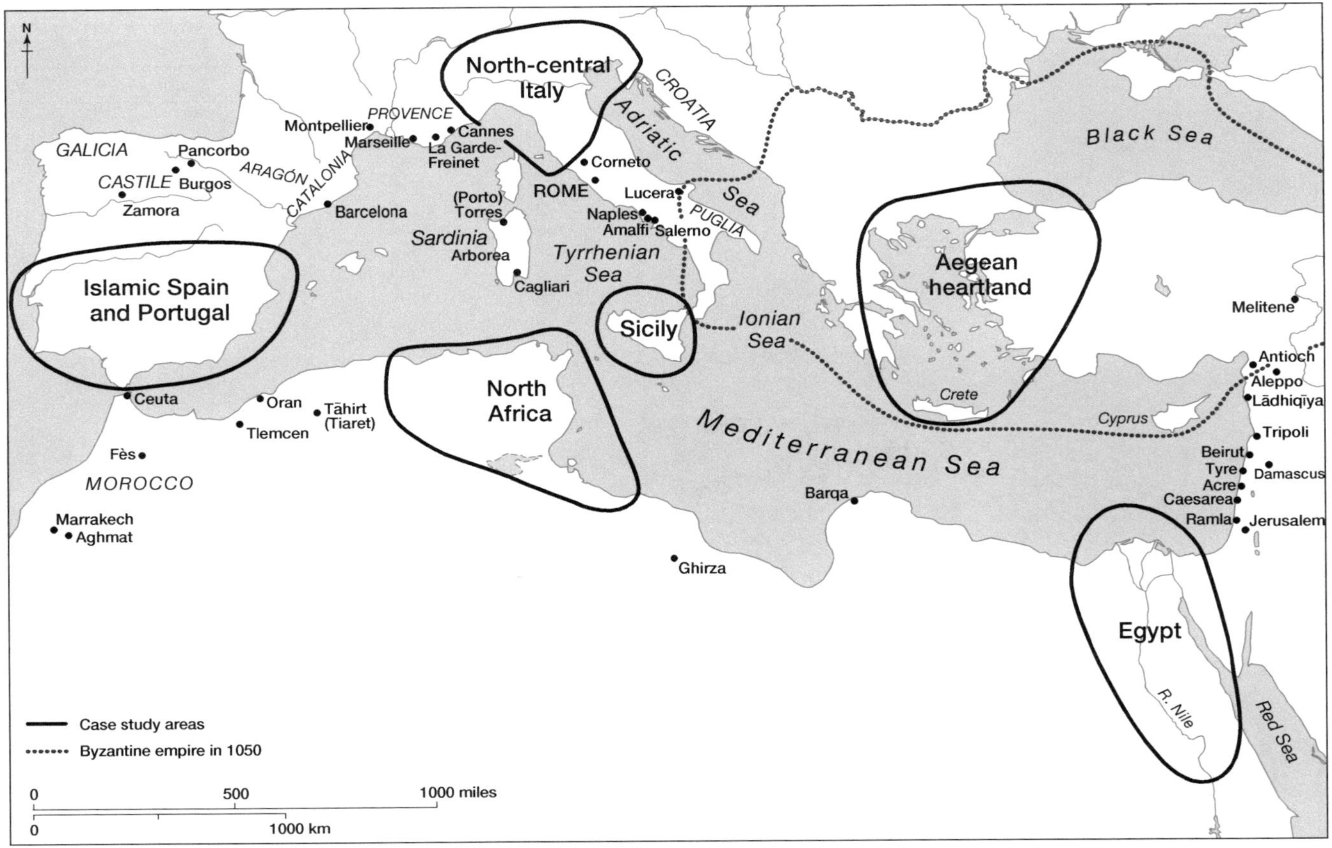

Map I. The Mediterranean: Regional case studies

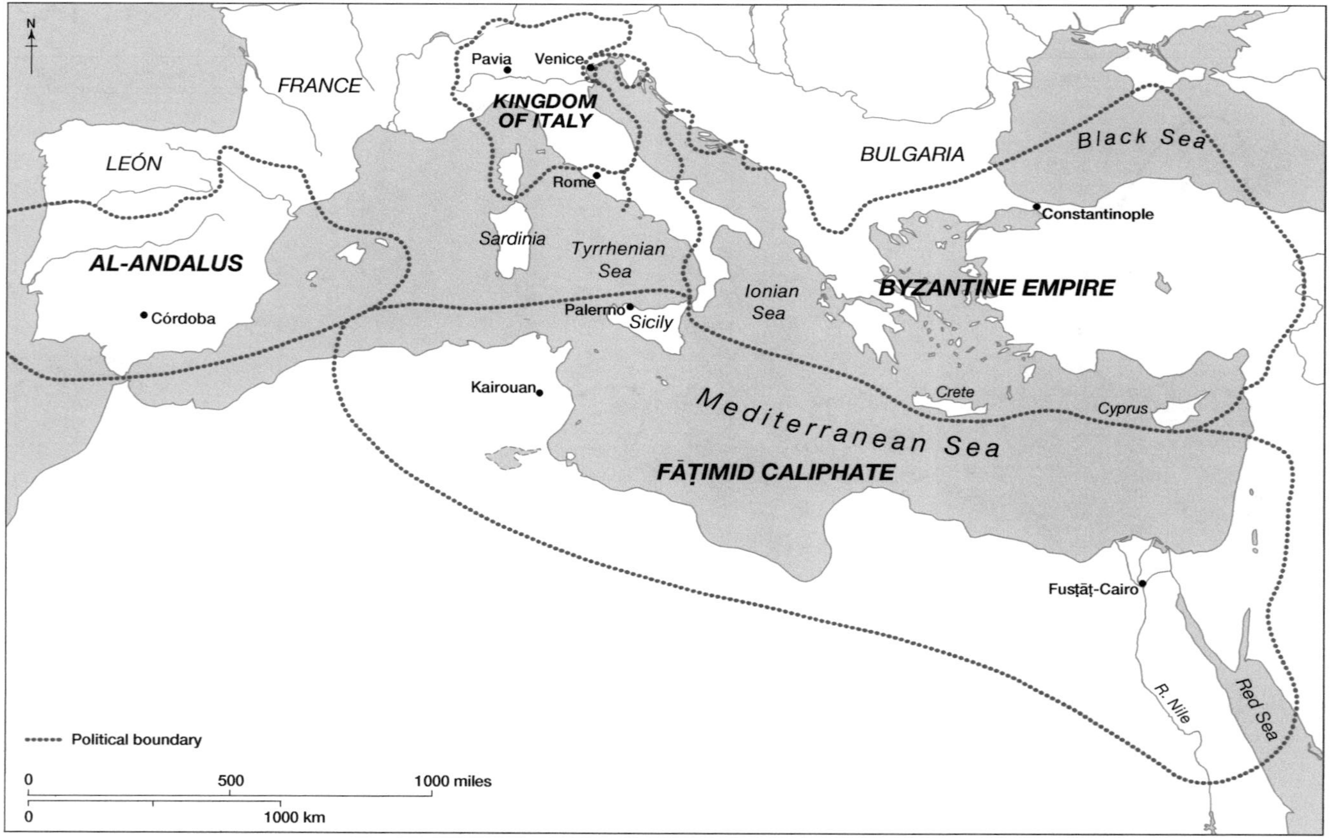

Map 2. The Mediterranean in 970: Political

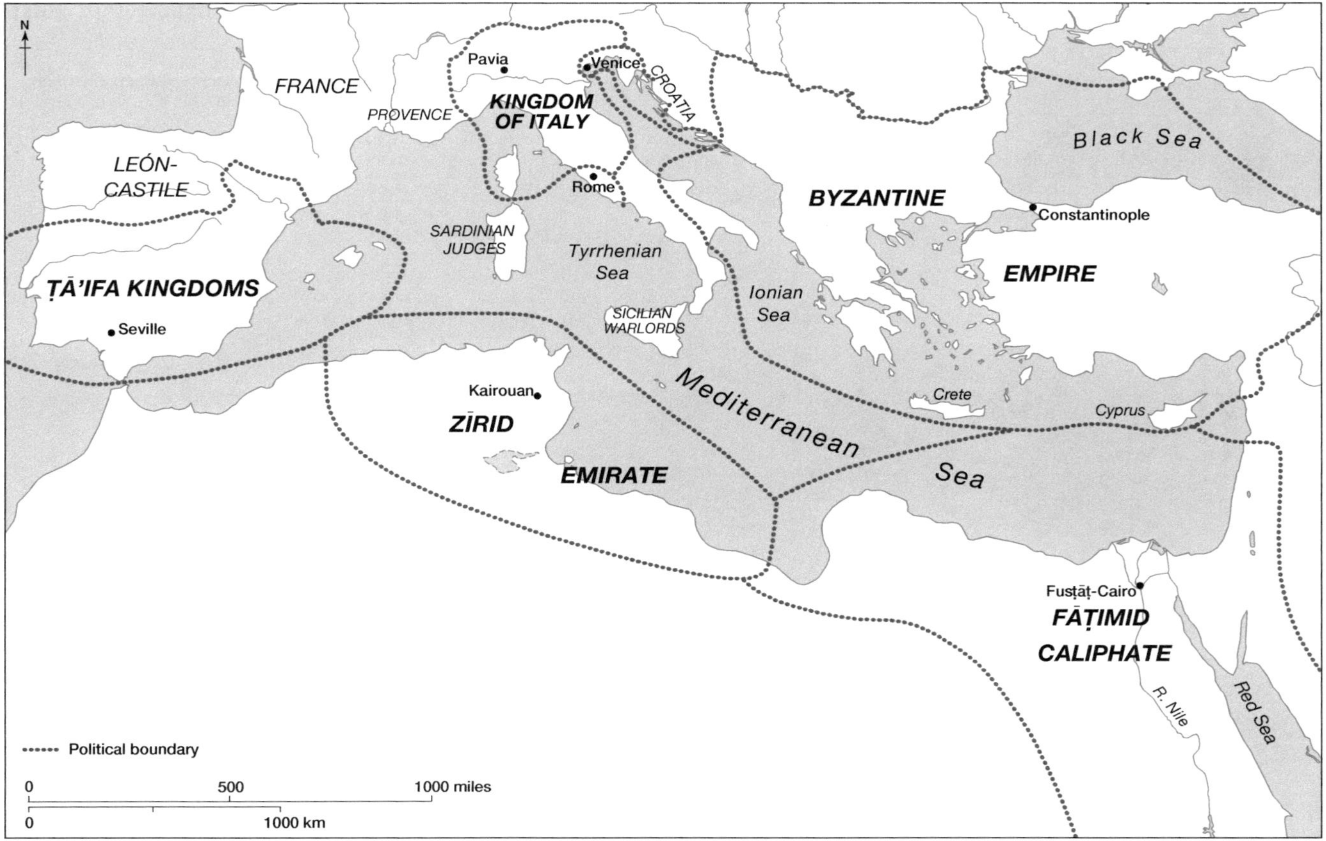

Map 3. The Mediterranean in 1050: Political

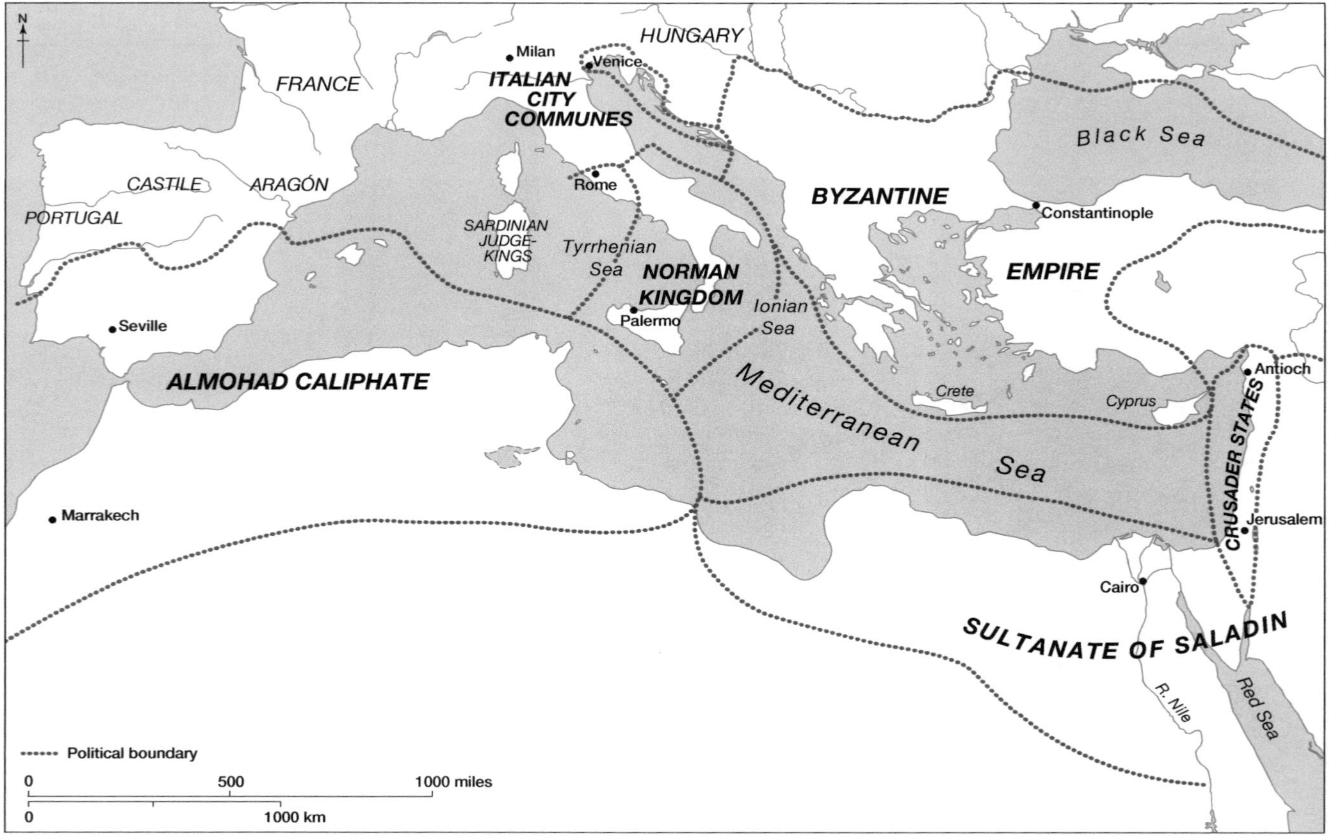

Map 4. The Mediterranean in 1180: Political

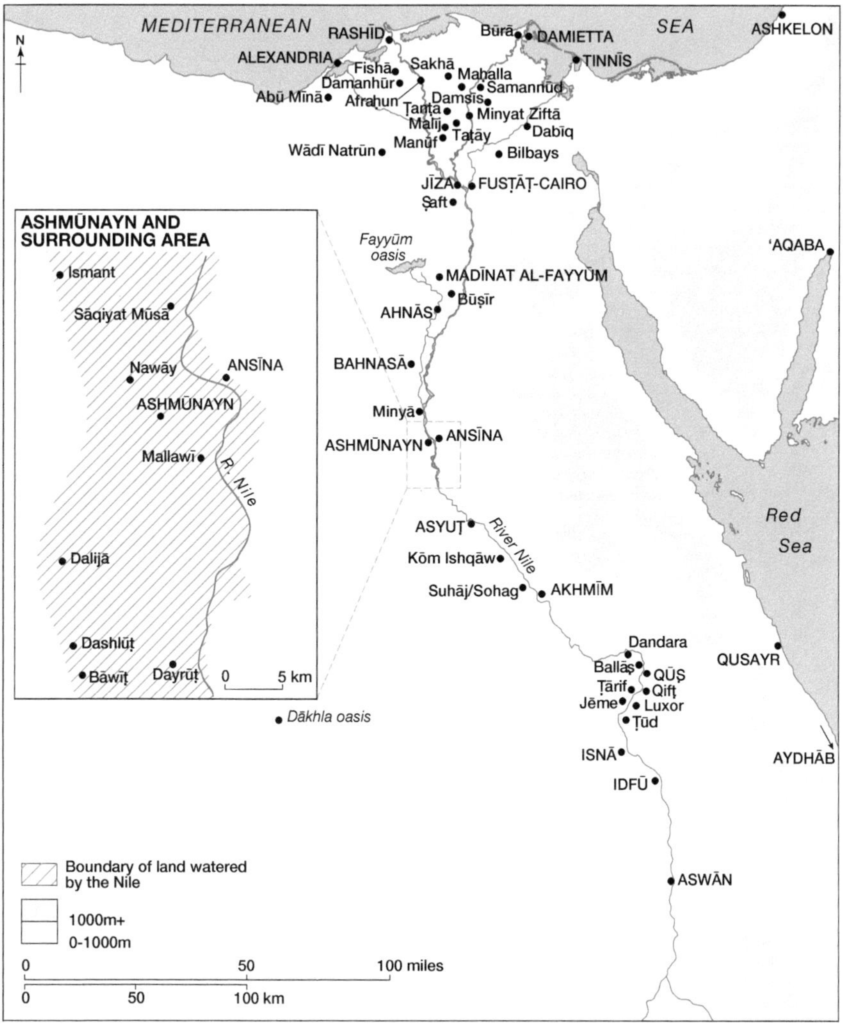

Map 5. Egypt: General

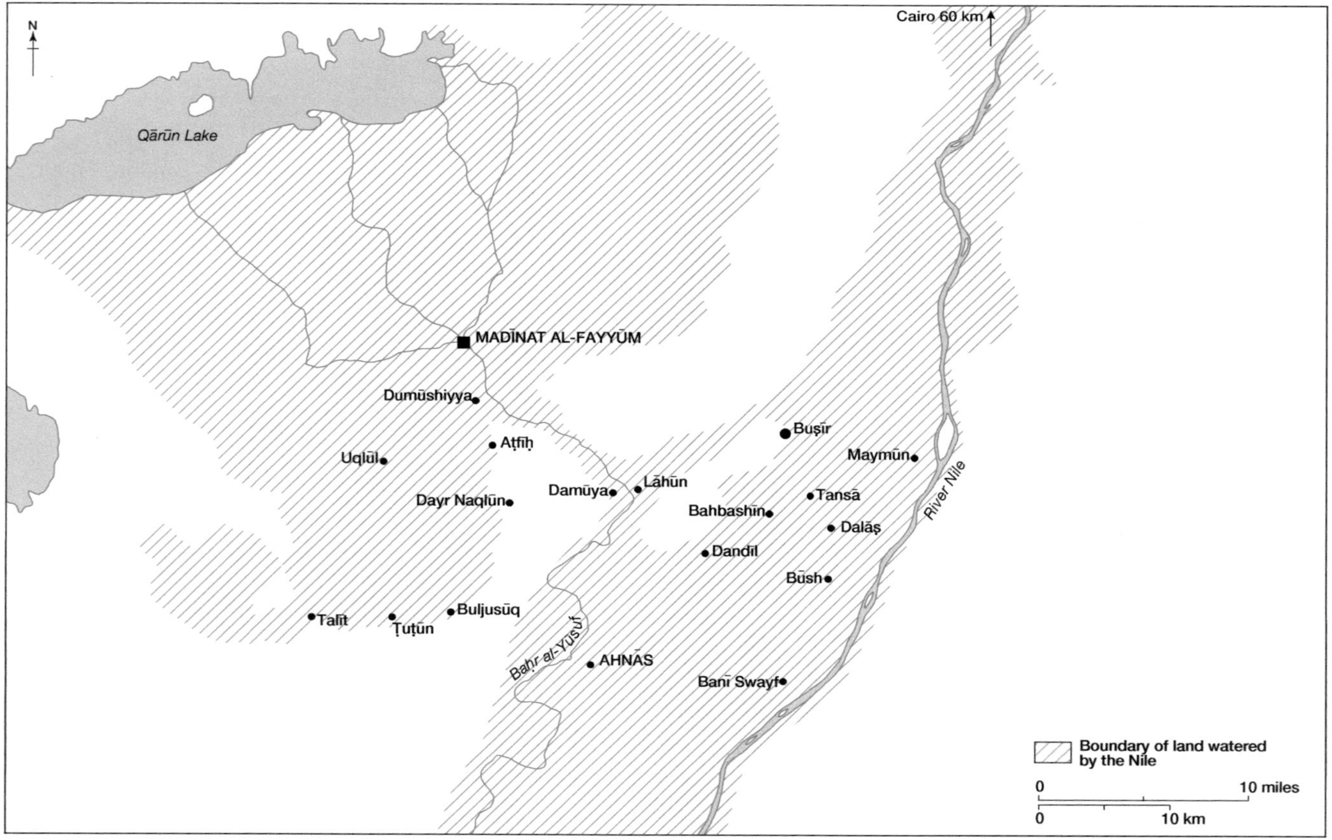

Map 6. Egypt: The Fayyūm eastwards to the Nile

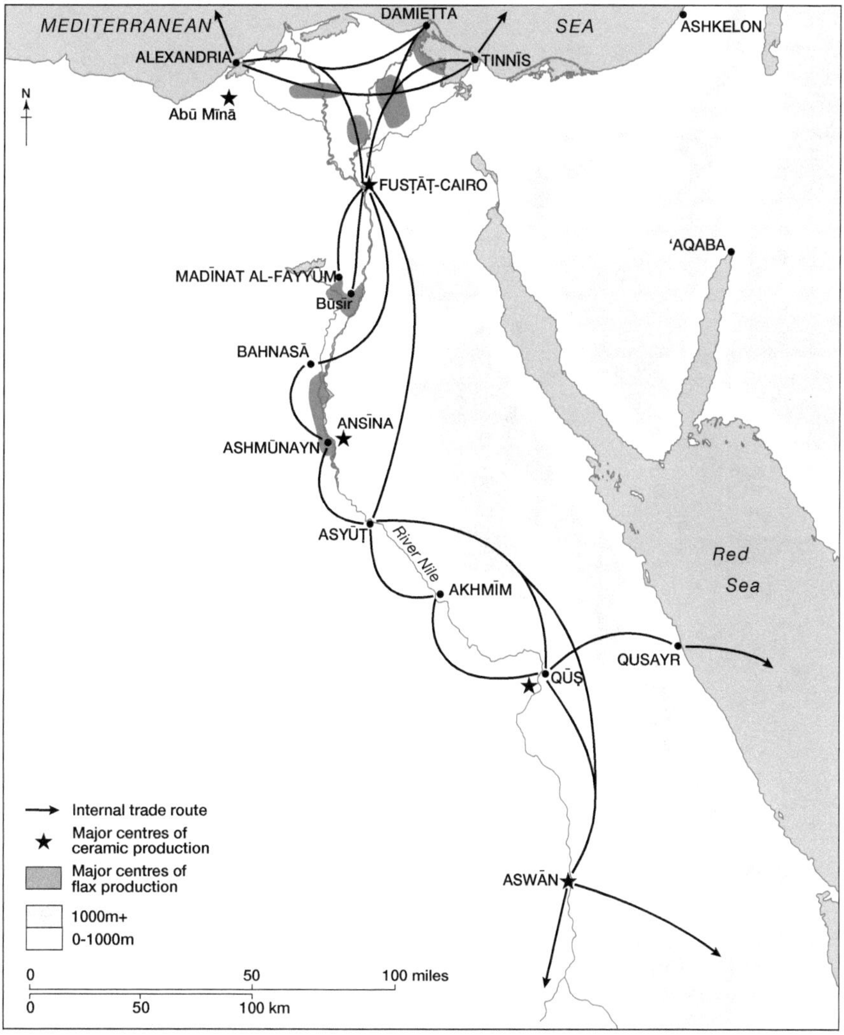

Map 7. Egypt: Internal trade routes

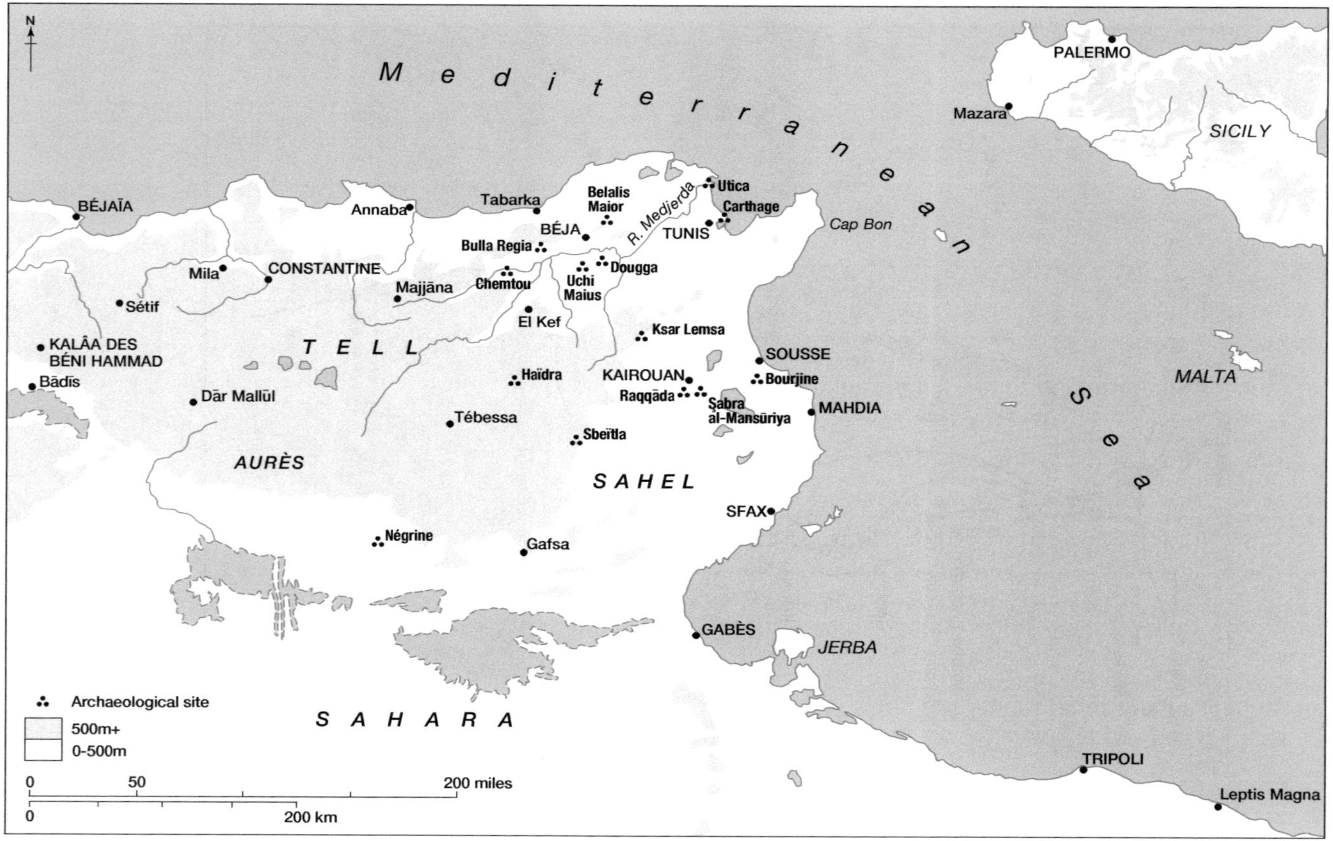

Map 8. Ifrīqiya: General

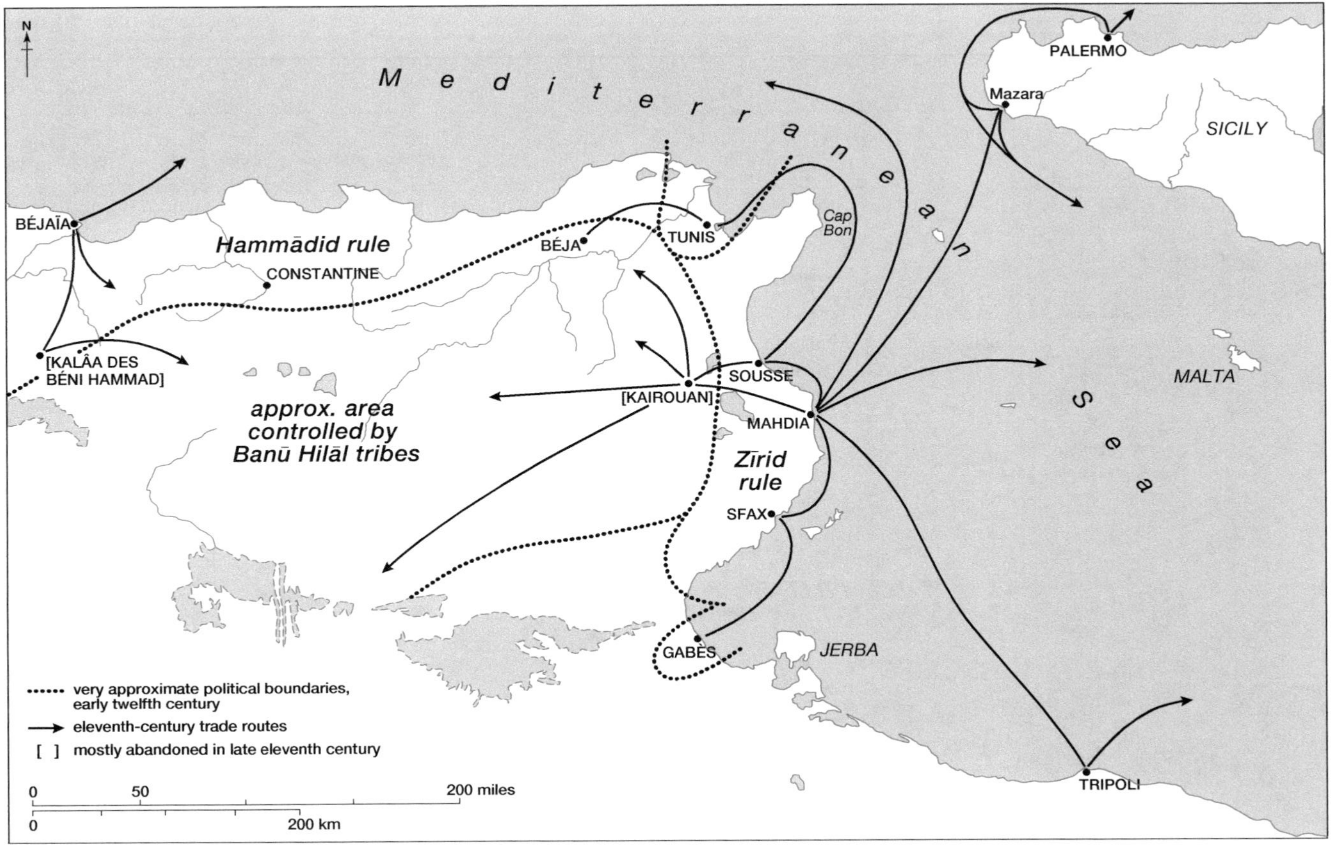

Map 9. Ifrīqiya: Political and trade routes

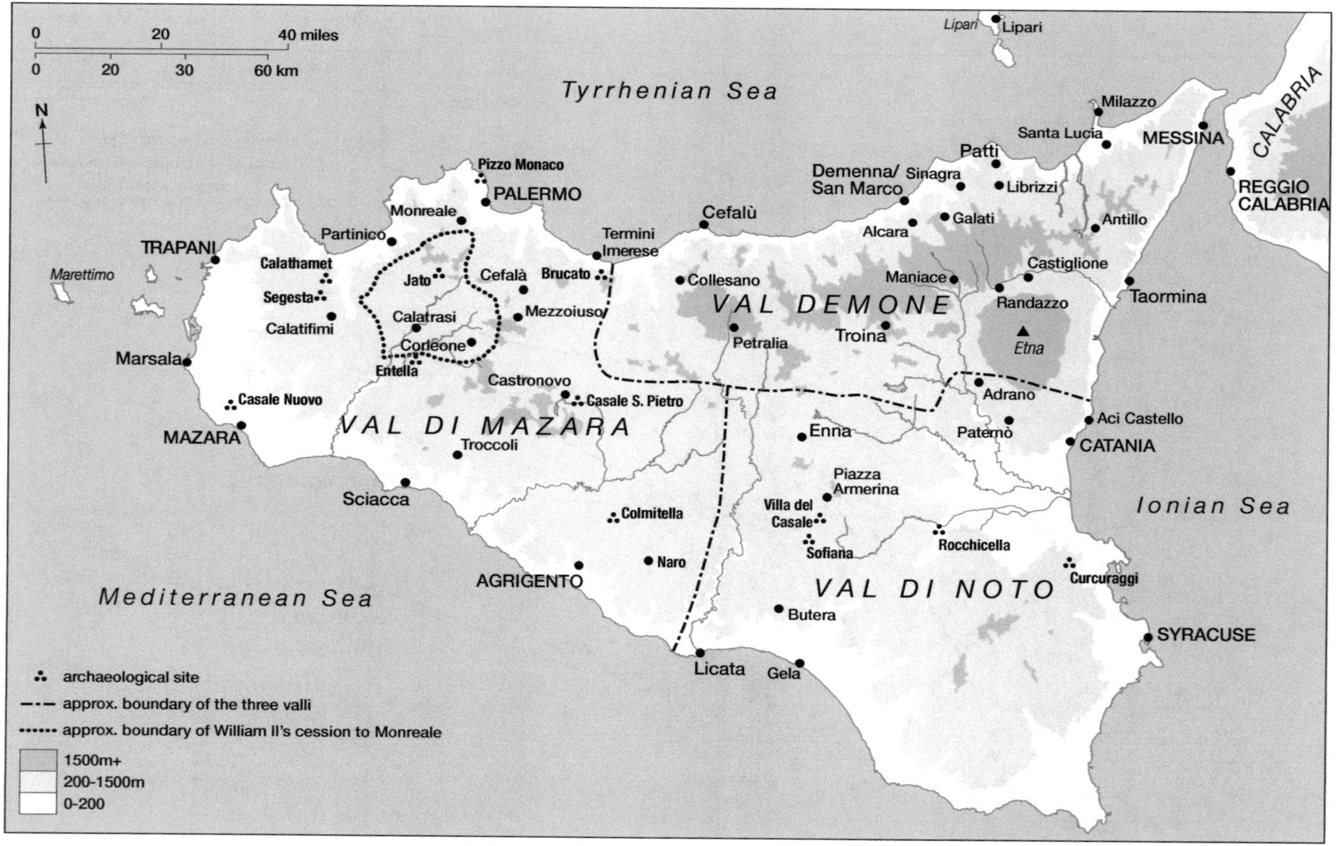

Map 10. Sicily: General

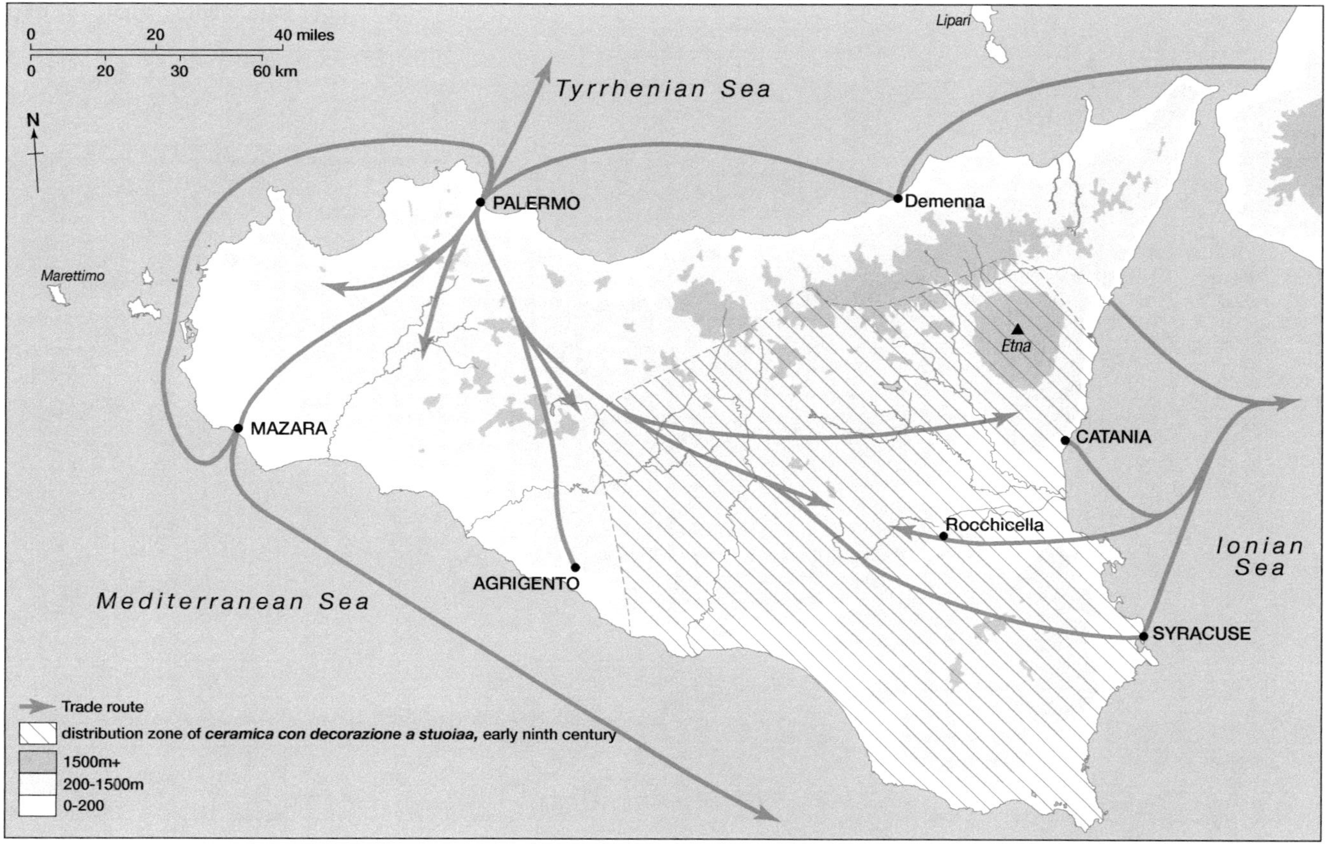

Map 11. Sicily: Trade routes, 1000

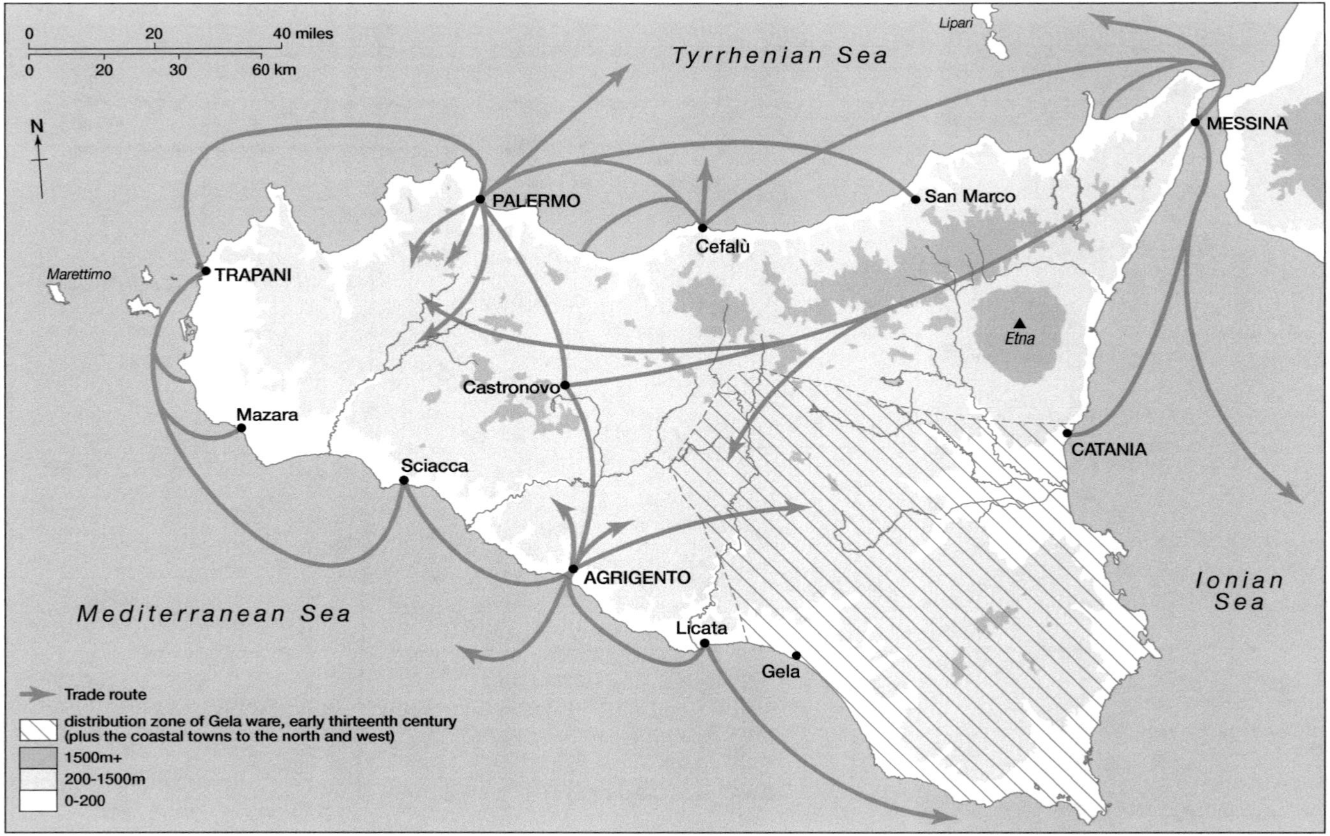

Map 12. Sicily: Trade routes, 1150

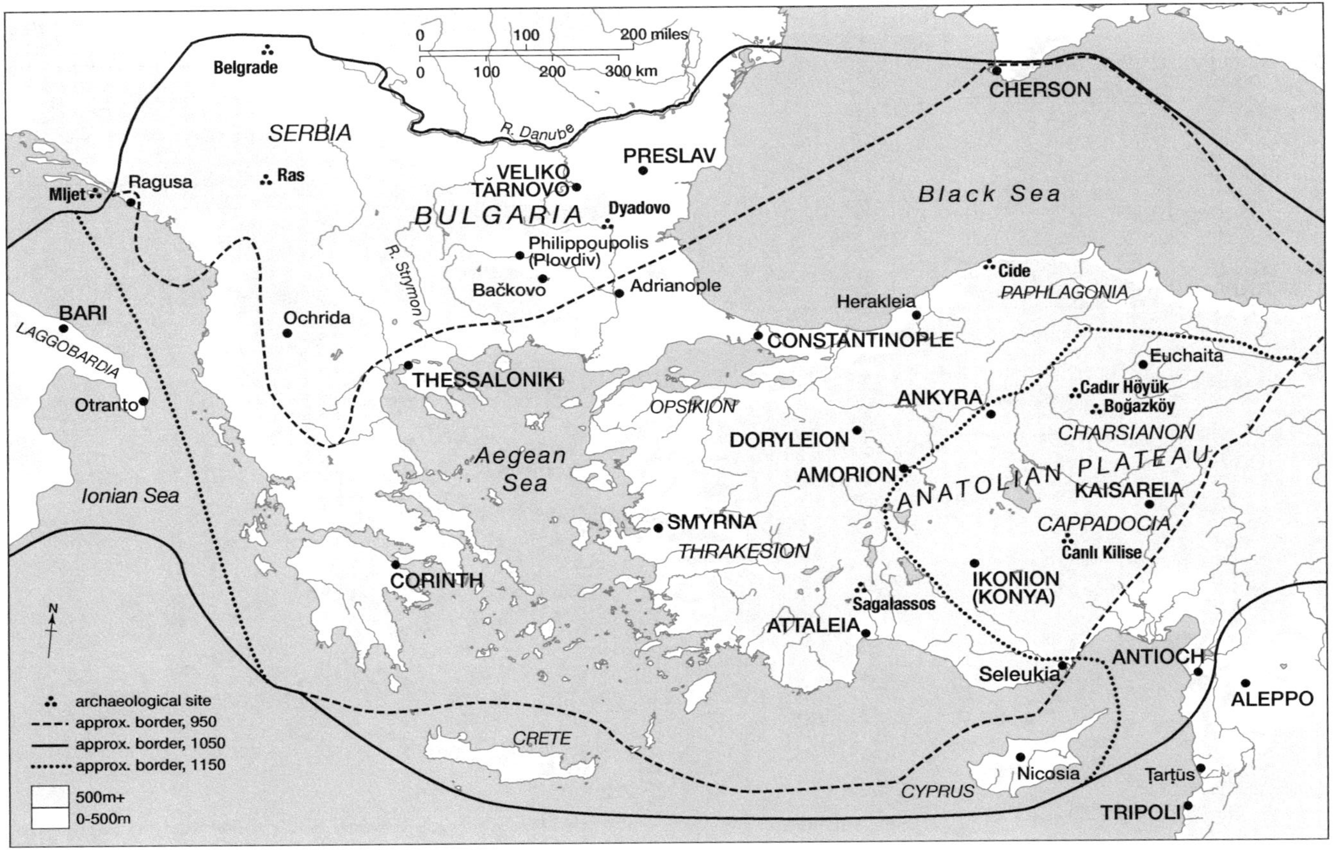

Map 13. The Byzantine Empire: Political

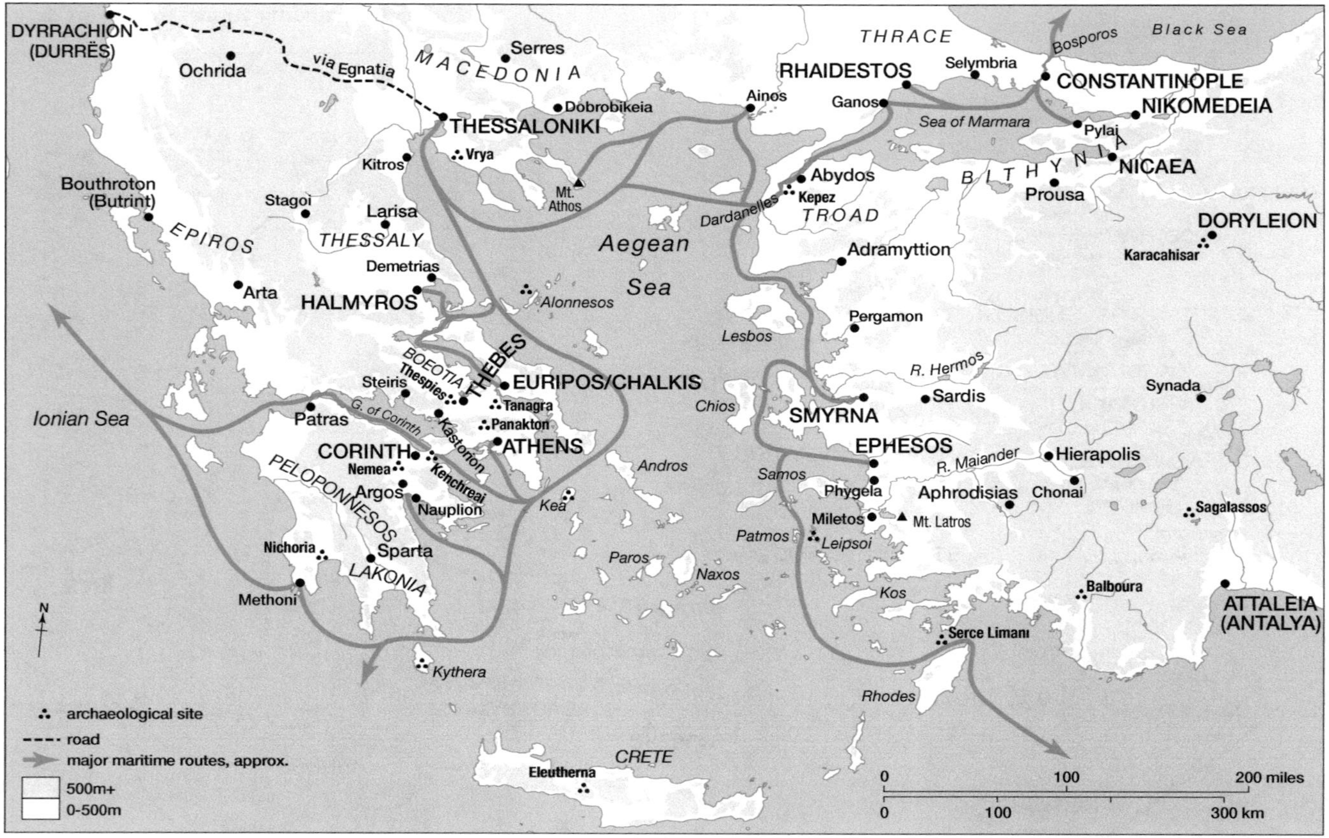

Map 14. The Aegean Sea: Trade routes, 1000

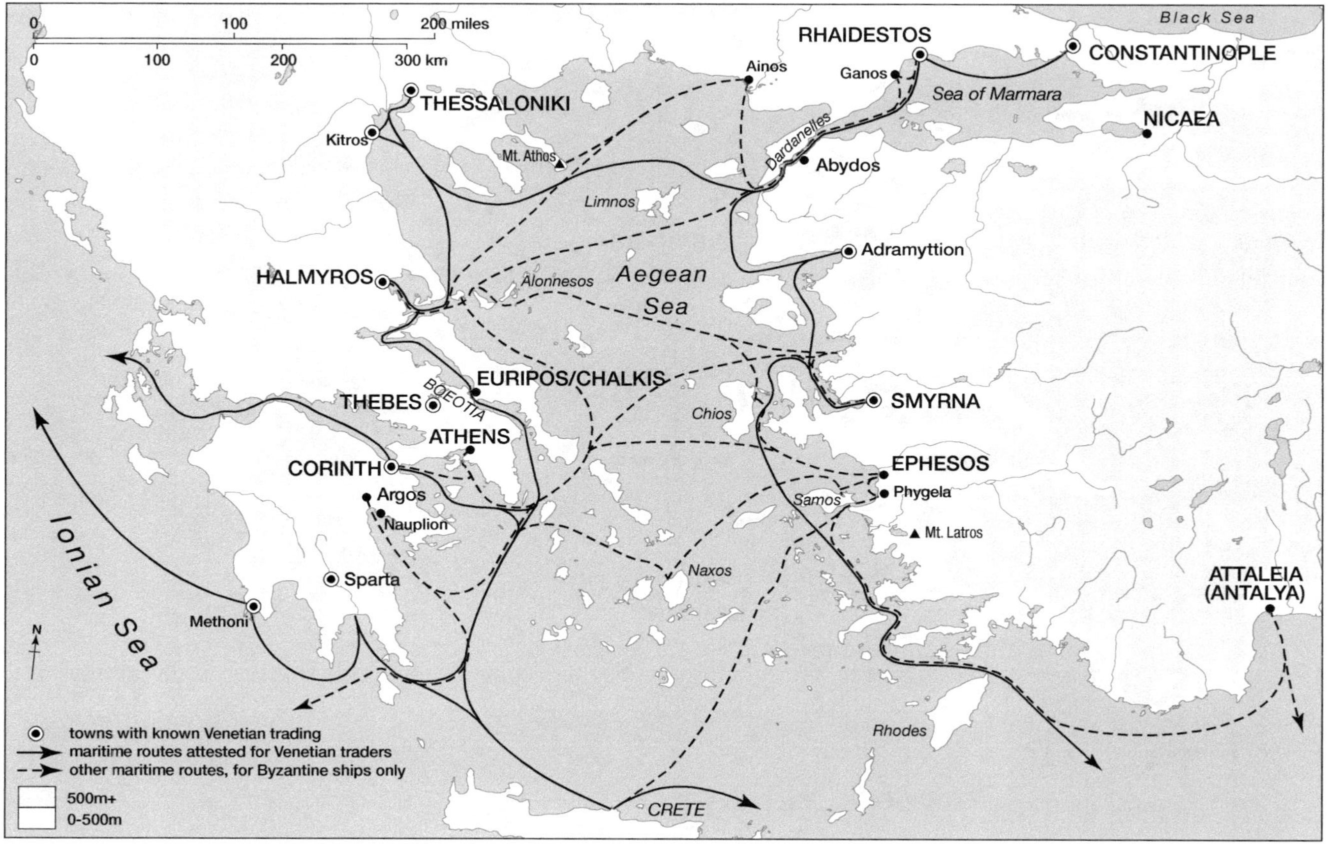

Map 15. The Aegean Sea: Trade routes, 1150

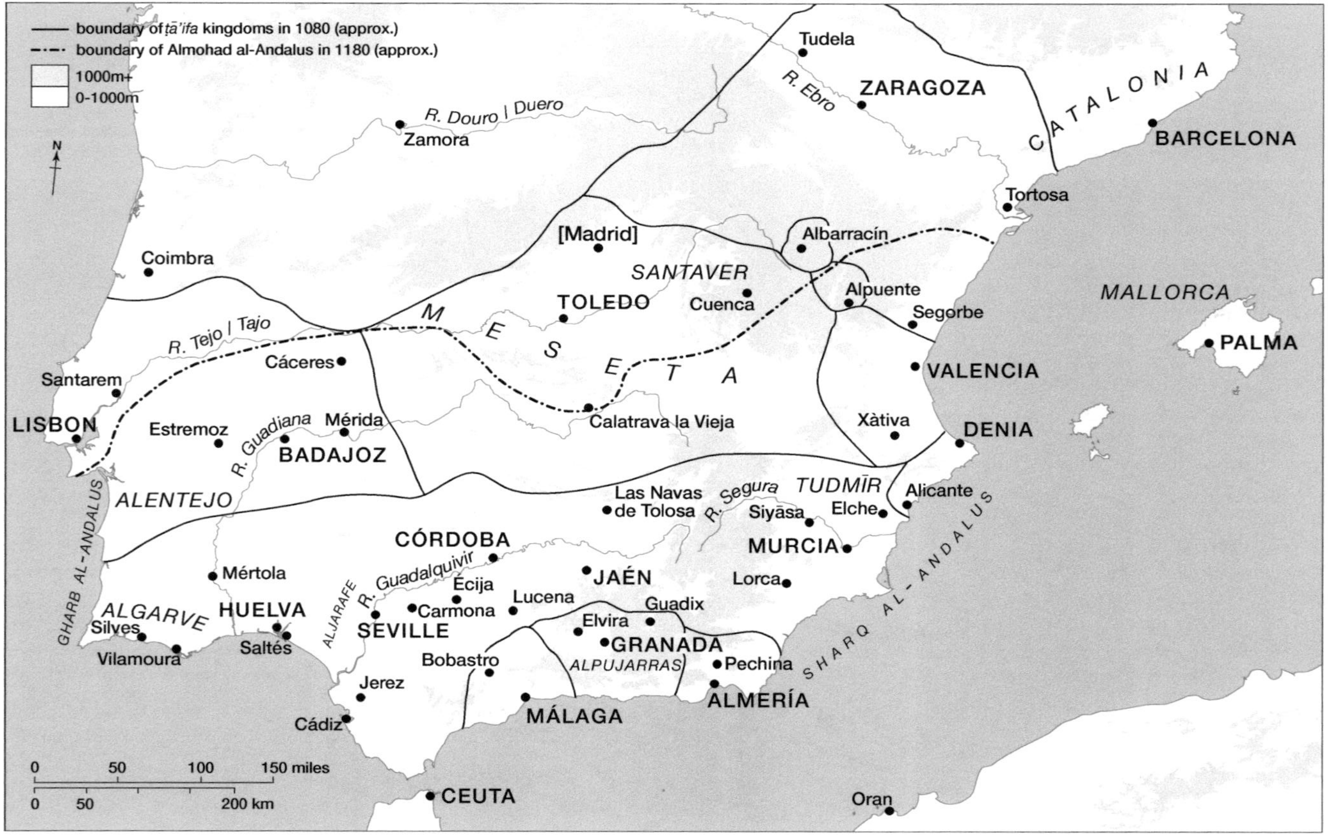

Map 16. Al-Andalus: General

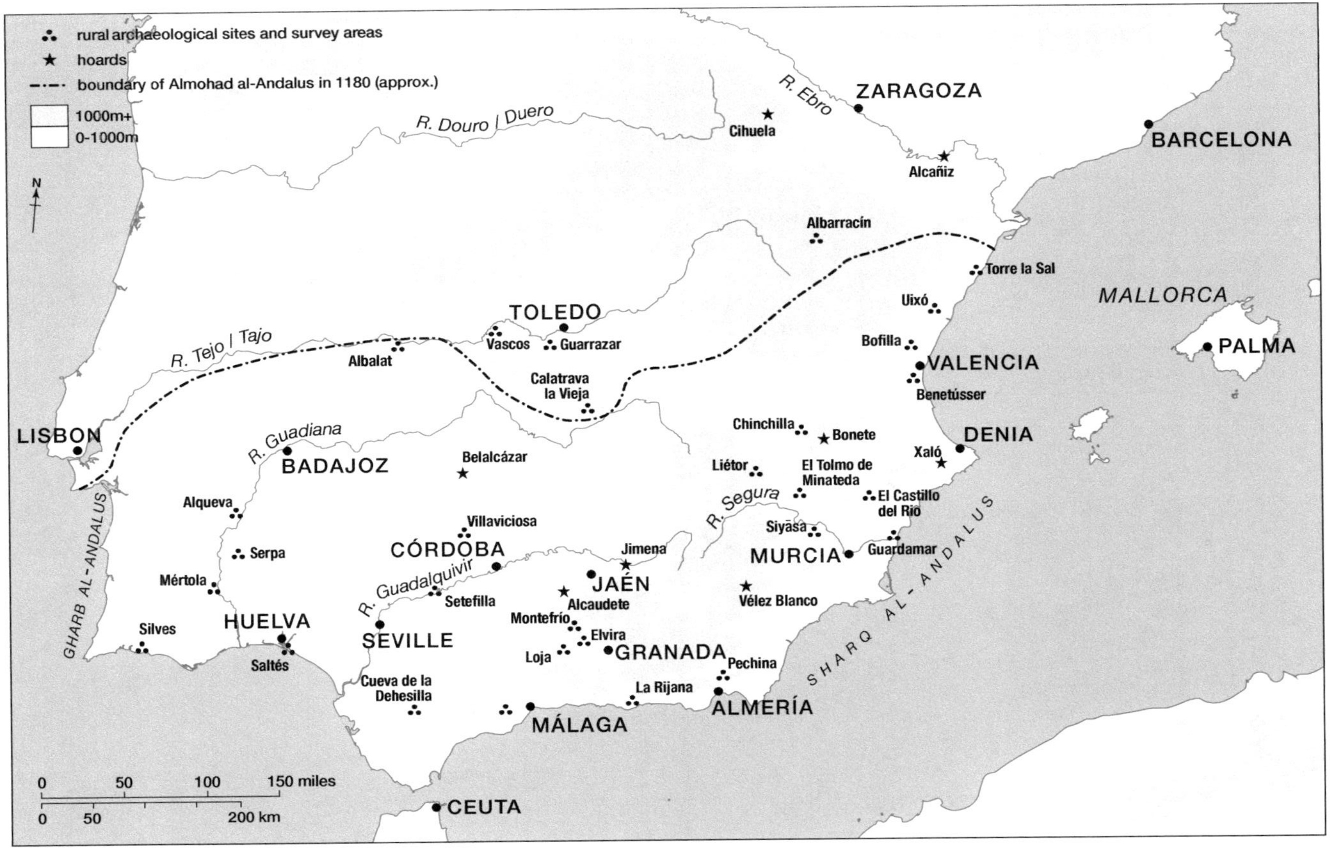

Map 17. Al-Andalus: Archaeology

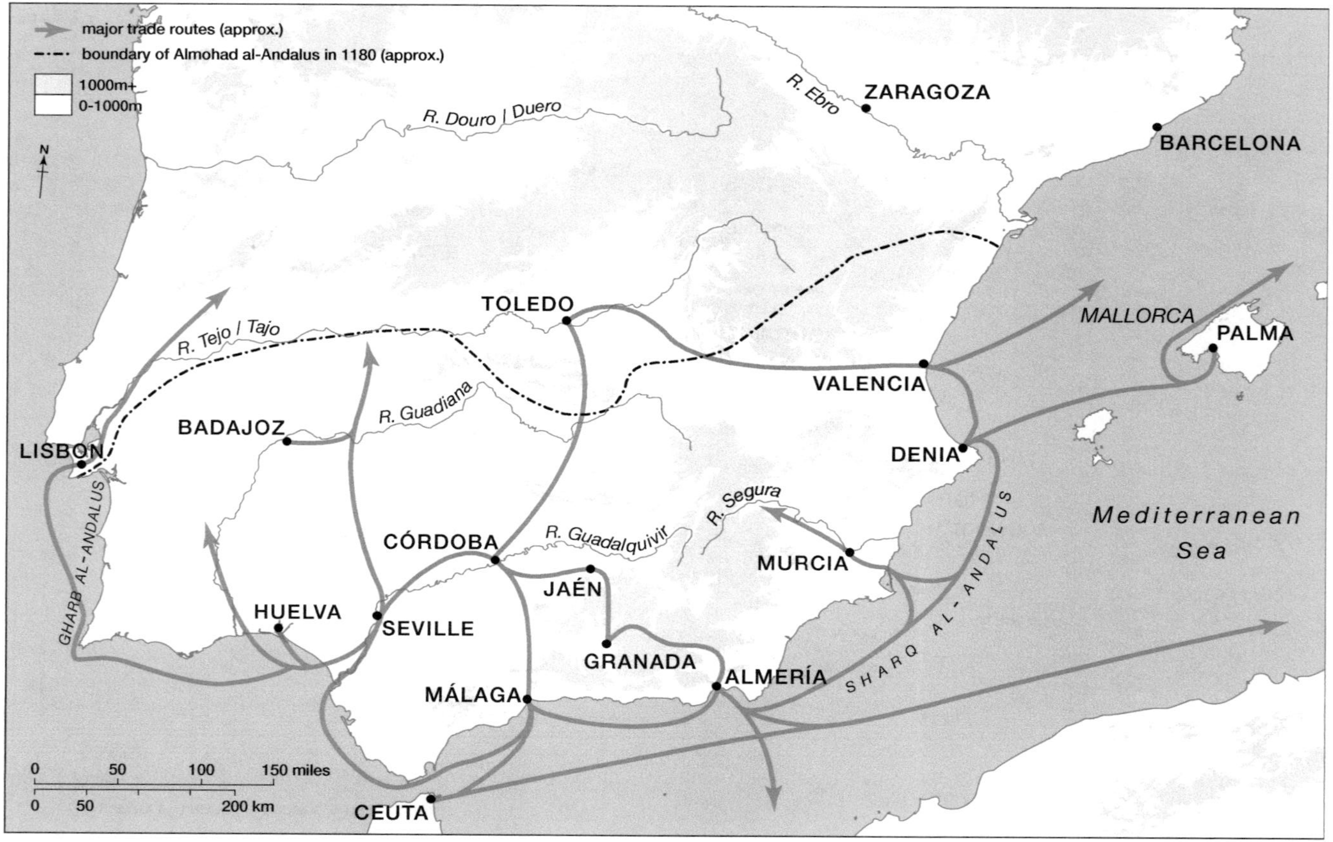

Map 18. Al-Andalus: Internal trade routes, 1100

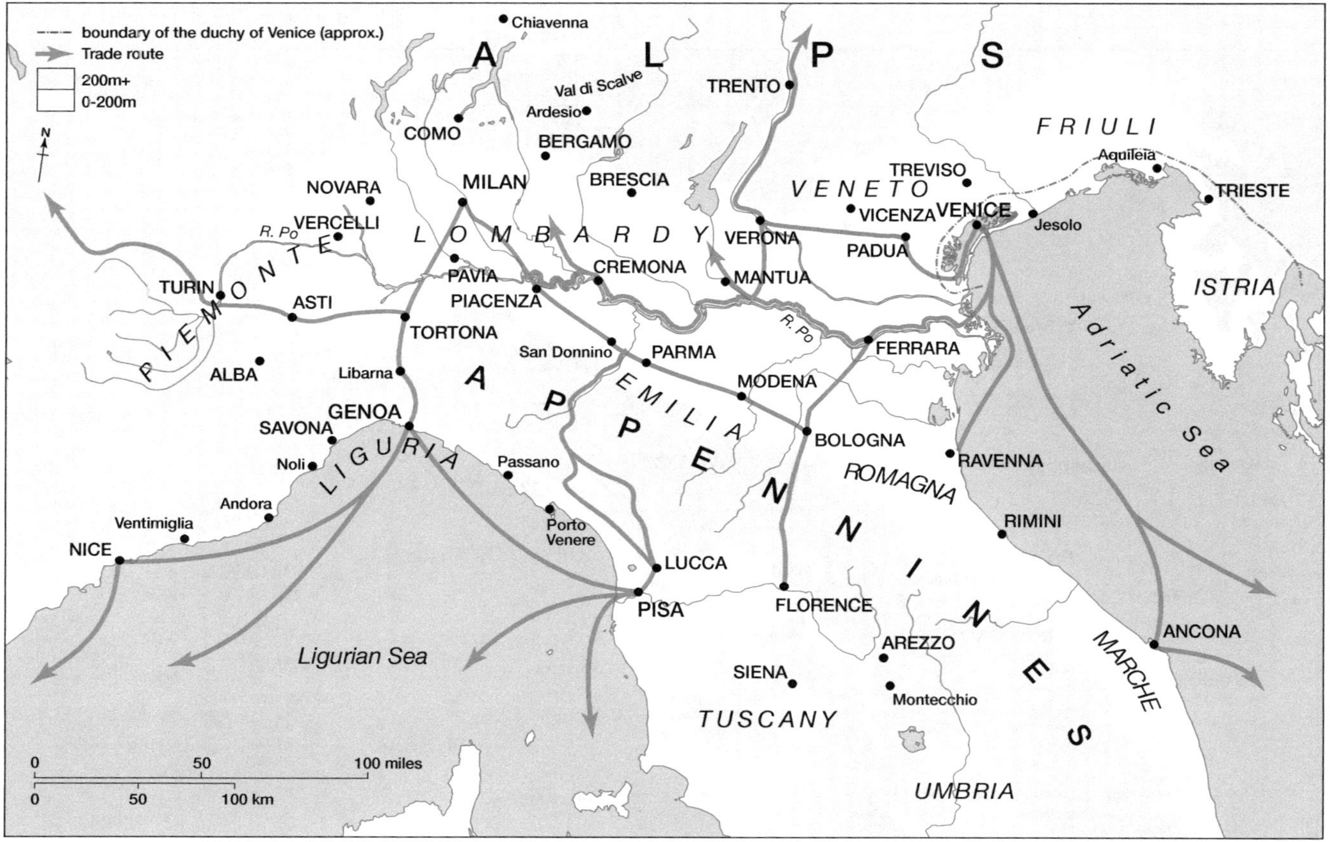

Map 19. North-central Italy: General

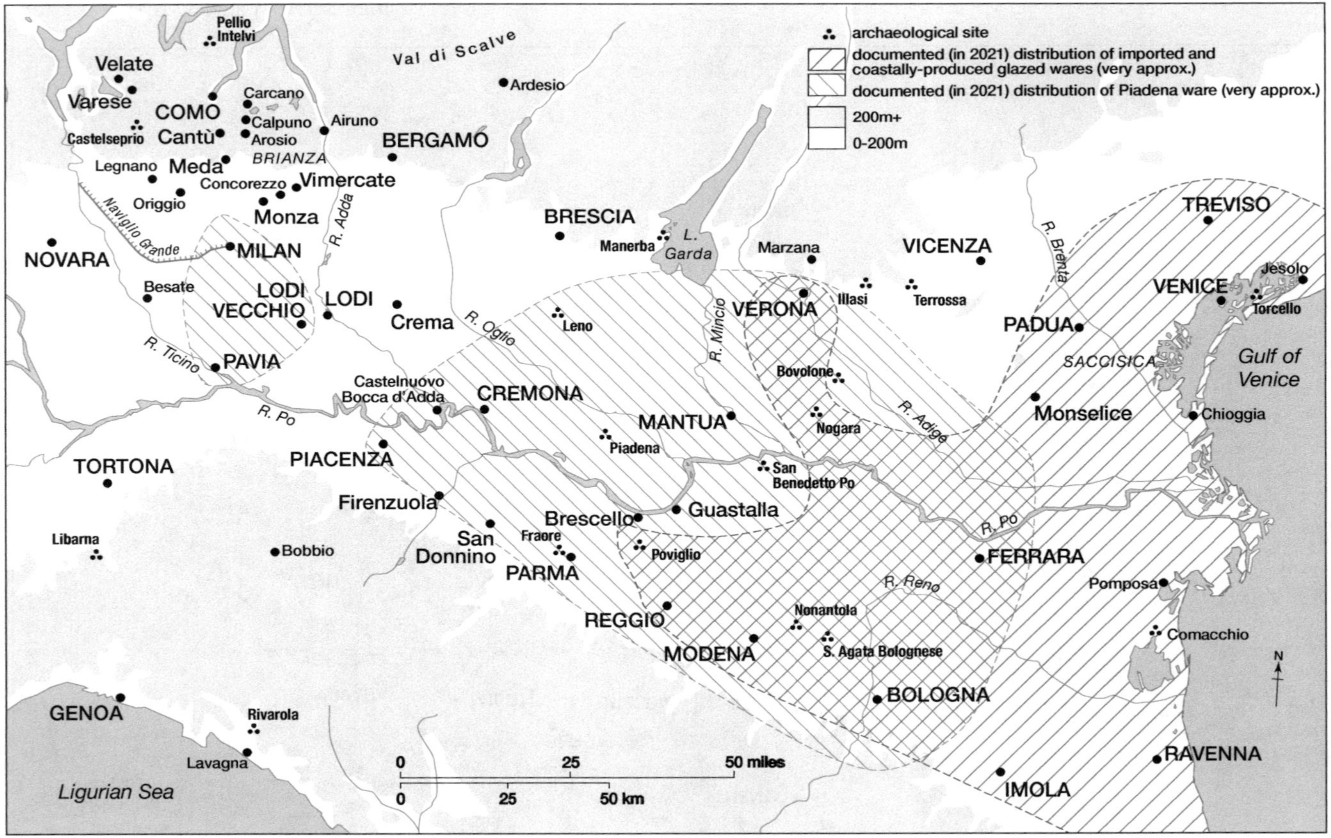

Map 20. The central and eastern Po plain

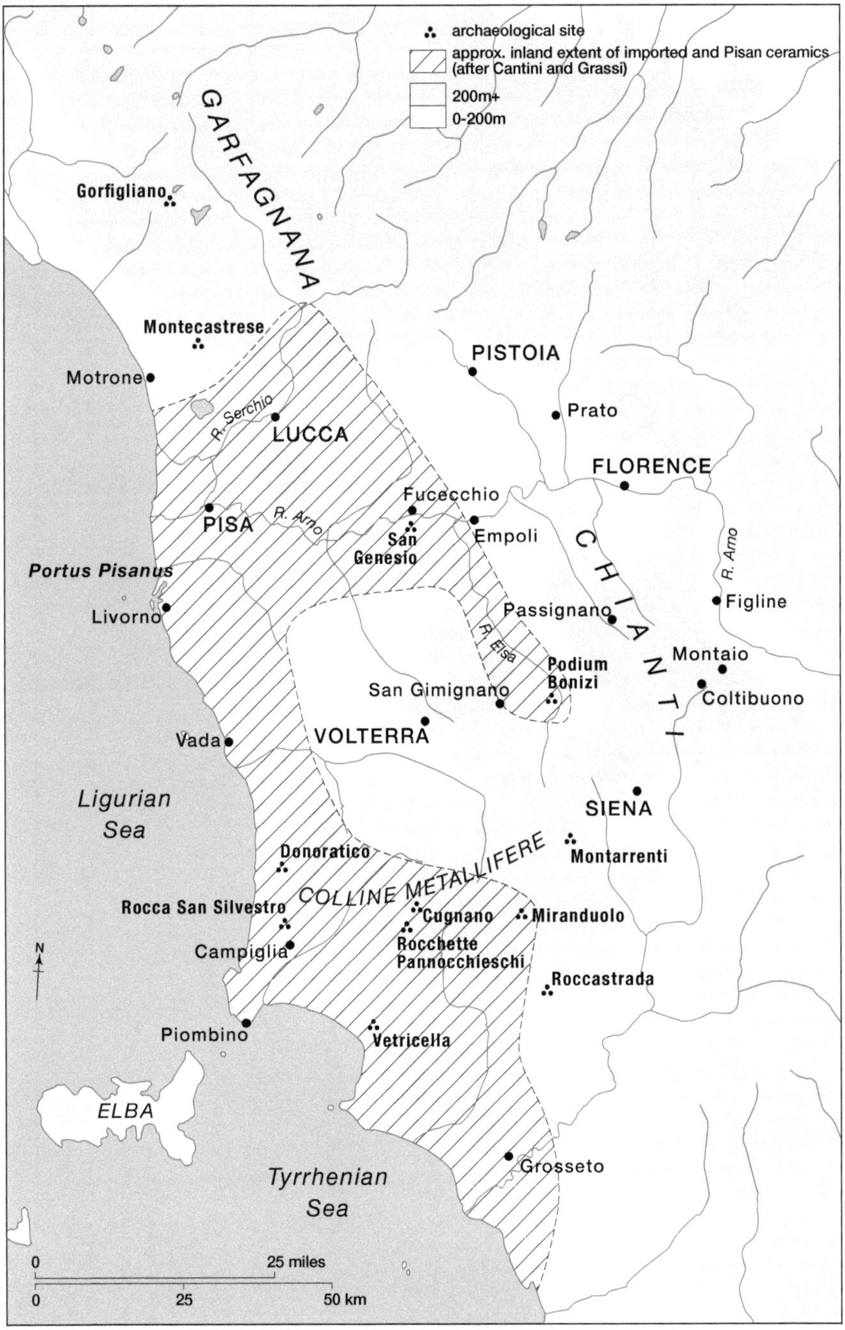

Map 21. Tuscany

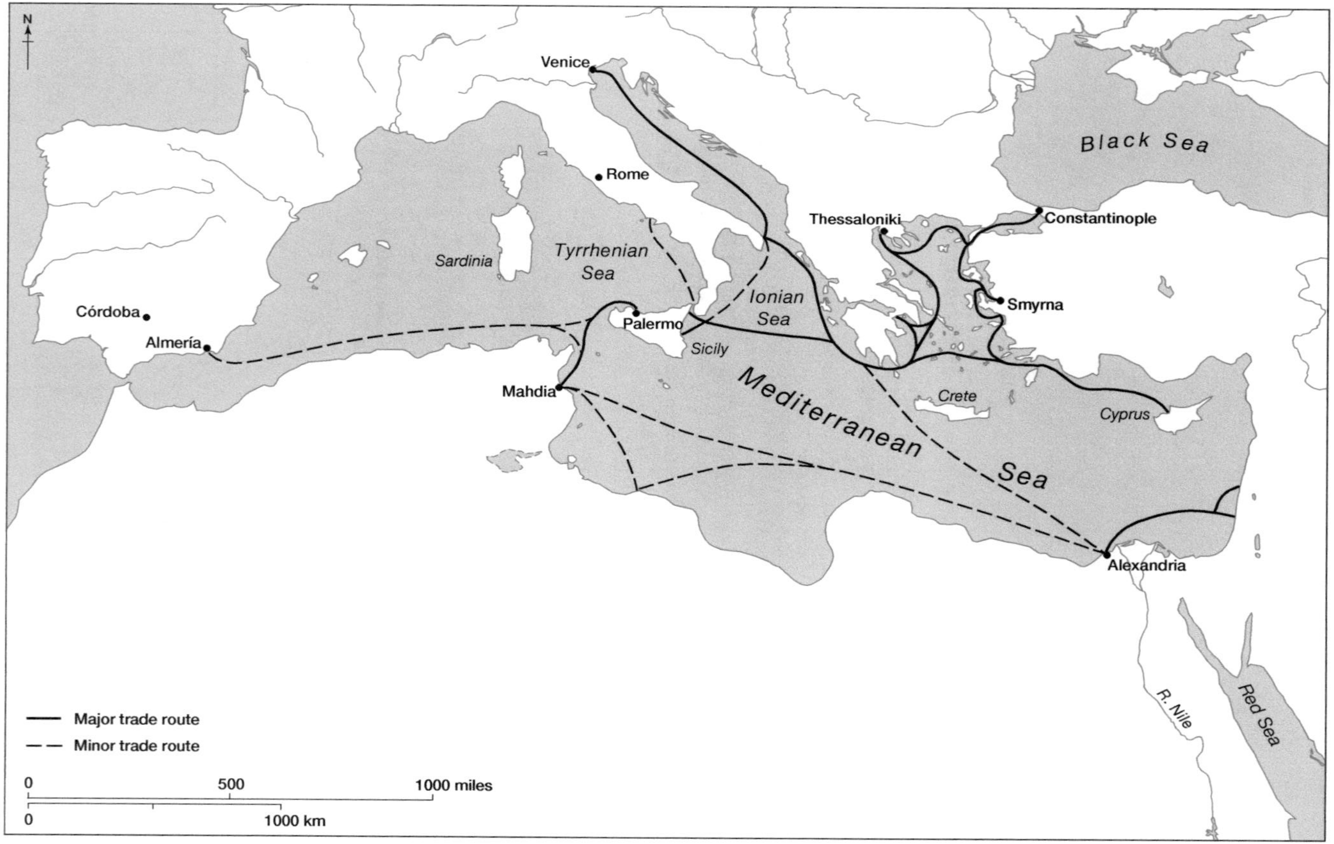

Map 22. Mediterranean trade routes, 950

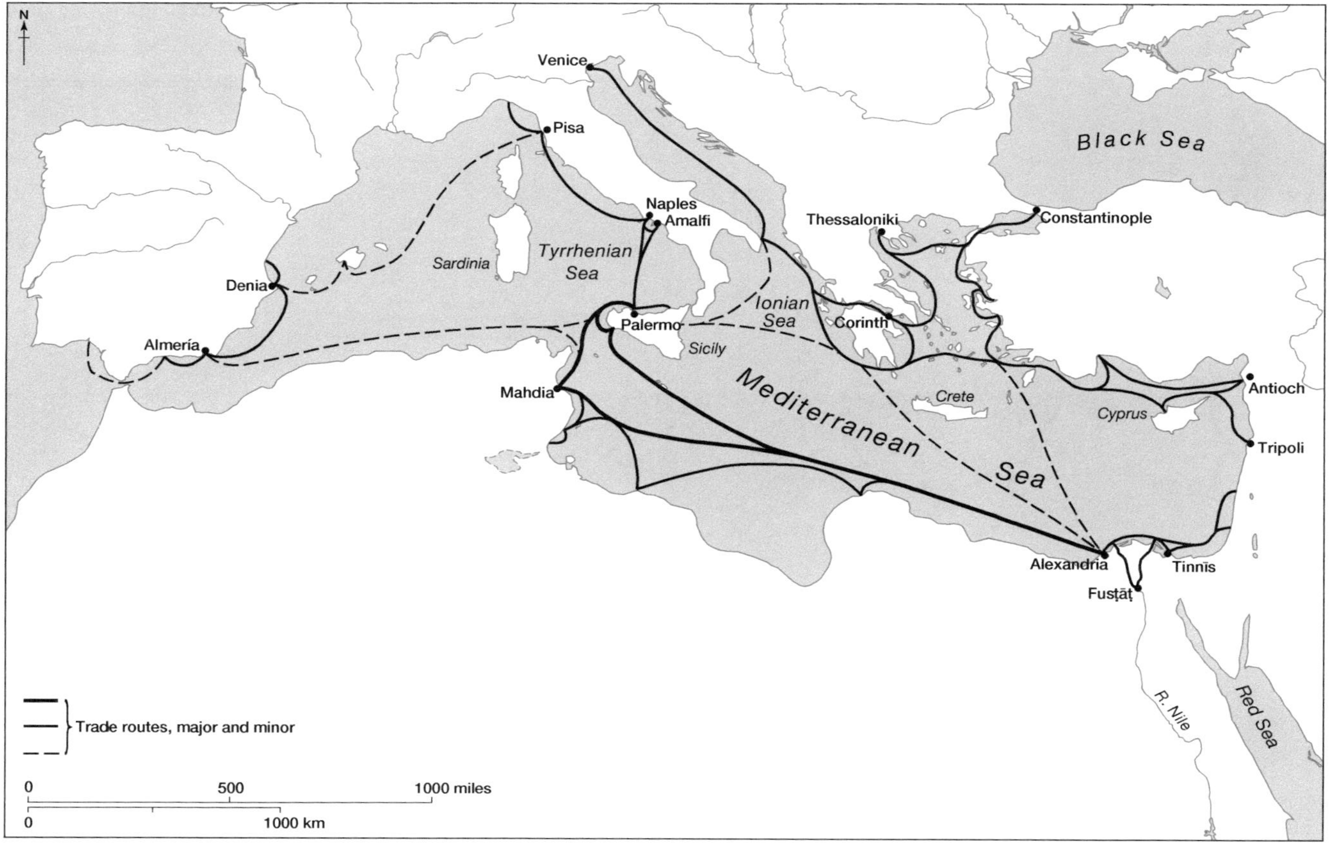

Map 23. Mediterranean trade routes, 1050

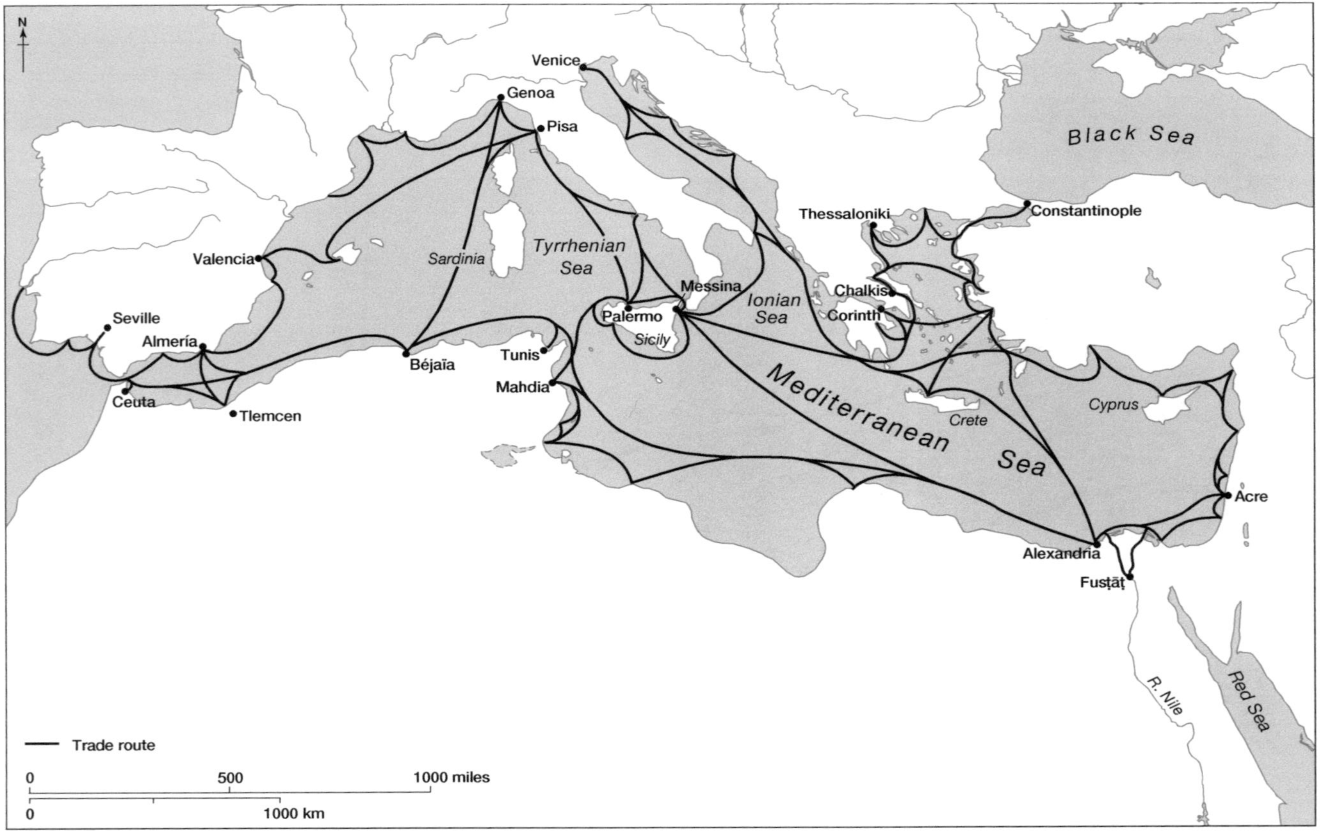

Map 24. Mediterranean trade routes, 1150

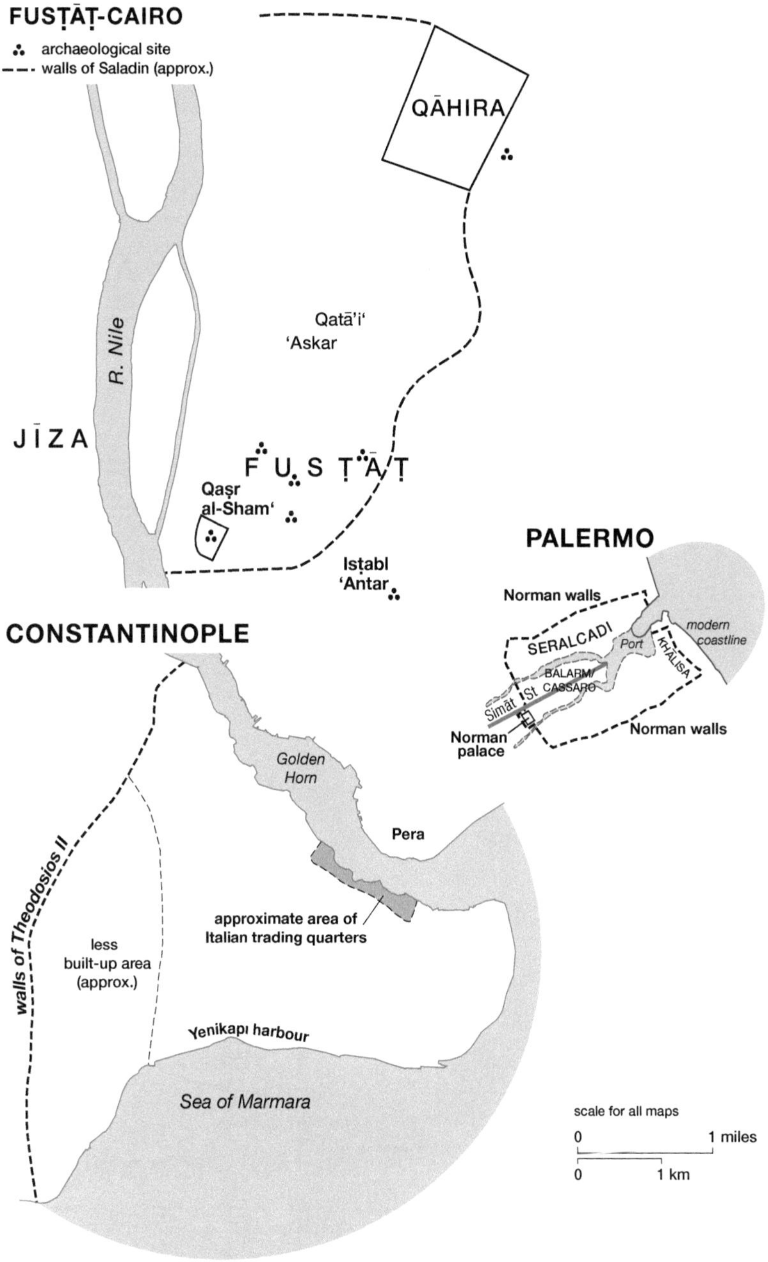

Map 25. City maps of Fusṭāṭ-Cairo, Constantinople, Palermo

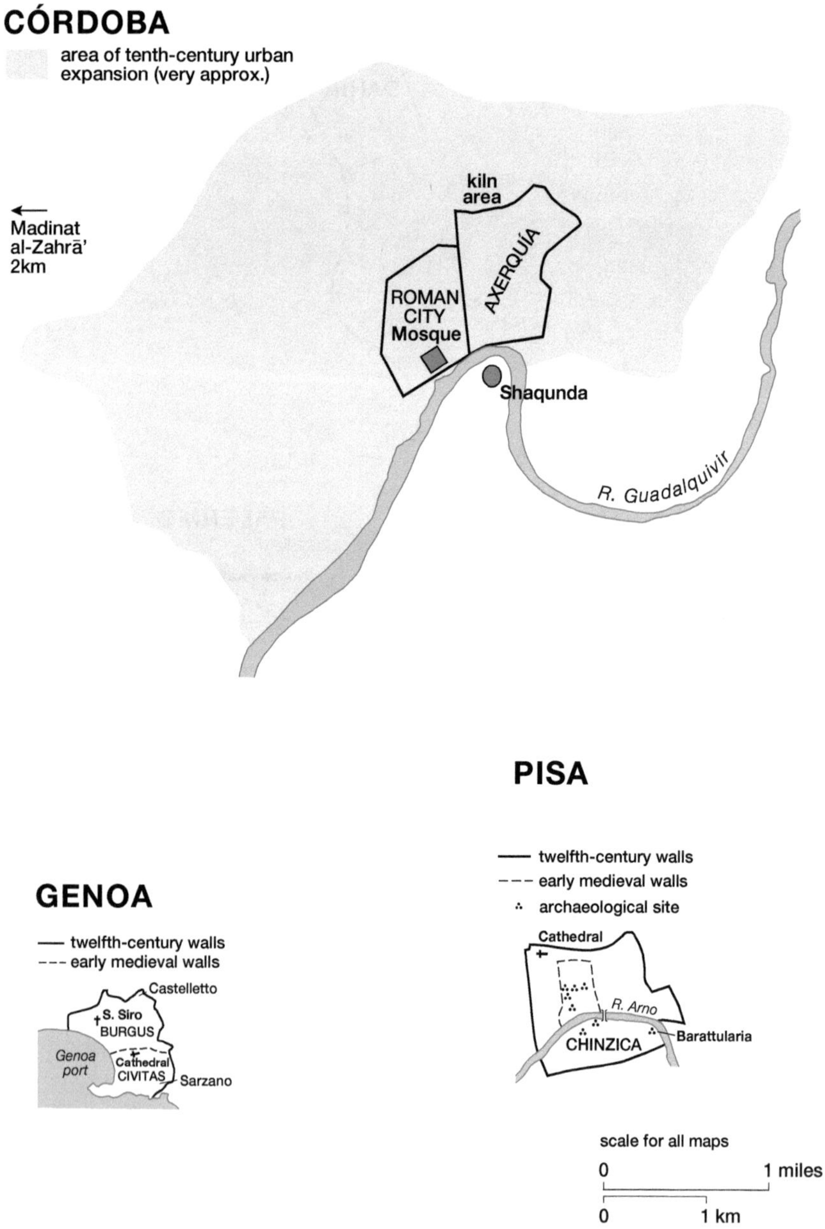
CÓRDOBA
area of tenth-century urban expansion (very approx.)
Madinat al-Zahrā' 2km
kiln area
AXERQUÍA
ROMAN CITY
Mosque
Shaqunda
R. Guadalquivir
PISA
twelfth-century walls
early medieval walls
archaeological site
Cathedral
R. Arno
CHINZICA
Barattularia
GENOA
twelfth-century walls
early medieval walls
Castelletto
S. Siro
BURGUS
Genoa port
Cathedral
CIVITAS
Sarzano
scale for all maps
0
1 miles
0
1 km

Map 26. City maps of Córdoba, Genoa, Pisa

1
Introduction

This book began with the intense dissatisfaction I felt with the traditional narratives of the 'commercial revolution' of the central middle ages in Europe and the Mediterranean, and above all of its origins. There is at least no doubt that a major economic change occurred. The period 950/1000–1300/1350 saw a considerable increase in agricultural production, in commercial exchange and markets, and in urbanization and urban production, both in north-west Europe and around the Mediterranean Sea, whether in Christian- or Muslim-ruled lands. (It did for that matter in some other parts of the world too, most obviously China, though the reasons for that coincidence in time are essentially chance.[1]) But what caused it, and what its very nature was in different places, seem to me to be widely misunderstood, even in its most basic elements. Hence my dissatisfaction. What follows is an attempt to resolve the problems I found, as they relate, specifically, to the Mediterranean and the regions bordering it, in the period of the origins of that 'revolution', up to 1180 or so.

Obviously, the book has become much more substantial than that. I had decided to start my research with Egypt, where the challenges of the *geniza* documentation, which will figure large in this book, drew me in from the beginning, influenced as I was (and am) by Jessica Goldberg's work; I did not want the material to remain as the black box which it often seems to be to outsiders to *geniza* studies, owing to the linguistic challenges it offers. And I knew that there was also Egyptian material in Arabic script, which intrigued me, as I had become convinced of the potential of the documentation for the Nile valley as a result of earlier work. I did not realize quite how much there was, however, and how much it could help me; and I did not realize how little it had been studied. My Egypt chapter rapidly became quite long as a result. And then so did every other chapter, for it turned out that in each section of the Mediterranean there was exciting and under-used material, and more and more archaeology, which needed to be set out properly, so that the experiences of each region could be properly compared with others.

I did not know what I would find anywhere, even in Italy, which I knew best. But I came to see that there were indeed enough flaws in the accepted paradigms

[1] The best current survey of the economy of Song China in a western language is McDermott and Shiba, 'Economic change in China, 960–1279'; for Chinese towns in the *longue durée*, see Zurndorfer, 'Cities and the urban economy'. Thanks to Sheilagh Ogilvie for critiquing this chapter and Chapters 7 and 8.

The Donkey and the Boat. Chris Wickham, Oxford University Press. © Chris Wickham 2023.
DOI: 10.1093/oso/9780198856481.003.0001

for economic change in the central middle ages that it would be necessary to reshape it—or to attempt to reshape it—on the basis of a new look at all the sources, without relying on the interpretations and the choices of others. These choices indeed in many cases go back to the beginnings of systematic medieval socio-economic history, whose pioneers—Marc Bloch, Henri Pirenne, Eileen Power, Roberto Lopez, Cinzio Violante, Georges Duby, to name only a few—set out compelling hypotheses based on sample explorations of empirical data, which they presumed would be tested as well as filled out by later work, but which in many cases have simply been taken as axiomatic, paradigms in the Kuhnian sense, ever since. That testing sometimes confirms their intuitions, as one would expect, for these pioneers could be brilliant historians, but sometimes radically undermines them; what we have to do is simply to go back and look properly. Hence the scale of the book, even though it only discusses a small sector of the paradigms they created.

The most approachable and influential narrative of the 'commercial revolution' remains that of Lopez back in 1971, *The Commercial Revolution of the Middle Ages*. Unlike Pirenne's *Mahomet et Charlemagne* for the early middle ages, a similar work in its wide influence, it did not create the picture in itself; but it summed one up, in a footnote-free account of under 200 pages, written with considerable narrative verve, and it is still regularly cited.[2] One could see it as, in a sense, the distillation of the medieval commercial chapters of the *Cambridge economic history of Europe*, which were still relatively recent then and had similar arguments—and which included an important contribution by Lopez himself, dating to 1952; Lopez had also, before the war, written major work on thirteenth-century Genoa, which underpinned his thought ever after. But the essentials of the story he told went back to the work of Wilhelm Heyd in 1879 and Adolf Schaube in 1906 on Mediterranean trade, now well over a century old—path-breaking in their time, but inevitably based on published sources, which were then relatively few—plus (among others) that of Raymond de Roover, the historian of banking and credit, who actually coined the term 'commercial revolution' in 1942, although he located it late in the thirteenth century.[3]

For Lopez, the 'commercial revolution' (I cut his capitals, and prefer scare quotes) was based on European demographic growth, and consequential agricultural

[2] Lopez knew the sources well, however; he had published another influential text, an excellent translated sourcebook, *Medieval trade in the Mediterranean world*, with Irving Raymond, in 1955, as well as any number of monographic books and articles. He was already using the term 'Commercial Revolution' in 1952: see his 'The trade of medieval Europe: the south', *passim*.

[3] Heyd, *Histoire du commerce* (the updated 1885 French translation, which I have used); Schaube, *Handelsgeschichte*; de Roover. 'The commercial revolution of the thirteenth century', a very sketchy characterization. Henri Pirenne was also an intermediary, although what he wrote on Mediterranean trade was fairly generic: see, e.g., *An economic and social history of medieval Europe*, pp. 26–35. *The Cambridge economic history of Europe* remains useful, despite its age: only vol. 2, on trade, has been slightly revised, in 1987.

expansion which outpaced that growth. This created surplus which could be traded, and the leaders of that trading enterprise were the Italian port cities, Venice, Genoa, and Pisa, with some prior Amalfi trade. (Lopez paid due attention to northern Europe, particularly Flanders, as one would expect, but his mental focus was always the Italian cities.) He was above all interested in the process of that trading: contracts, accounting, commercial handbooks, sea routes. He was vaguer about what was actually traded. He stated that 'agricultural progress was an essential prerequisite of the Commercial Revolution', which thus 'took off from the manor', implying clearly that agricultural products were the core of that commerce; but he also said that 'luxury products and the custom of the rich tend[ed] to play a more important role than commodities for mass consumption', and then, later, that it was iron and timber, and after that industrial products like arms and cloth, which 'Europe' (he meant Italy) exported to the east in return for silk, spices, and pepper. He had not, that is to say, thought this through; this was largely because he belonged to the wing of economic historians who focus on the organization of commerce as their major guide to economic change and complexity, rather than to those who focus on production and consumption. But one thing was clear: Italy was the prime mover here. In Italy, unlike the Islamic world, towns had the 'freedom and power that was indispensable for their progress'; Islamic towns were hobbled by not having this autonomy. Italian towns thus dominated the 'commercial revolution', even though the luxuries which supposedly were its most important element came from or through the Islamic lands.[4] Lopez was not unaware that one actually did also have to consider local trade, not least between towns and the countryside, if one wanted to develop a picture of commerce as a whole, but, although he occasionally said this explicitly, he did not develop the point.[5] One is left with the rosy image of the wharves of Venice and Genoa groaning with silks and spices taken off the argosies from the east, which is then used as a proxy for the whole economy; I exaggerate, but only a little.

Of course, there have been fifty years of economic history since Lopez, which have produced a great deal—even if the medieval economy as a historical research area is less studied than it was, and in some countries has gone out of fashion in the last generation. Monographic studies abound in every region for the rural

[4] Lopez, *The Commercial Revolution*, pp. 56–7, 93, 96. On p. 25, he even stated, bizarrely, that Islamic economic growth, although greater than that of the west in the early middle ages, was held back 'by the Arabs' traditional disinclination for political order and teamwork'. This is an unusual version of the standard Orientalist negative tropes, and may show that he was having trouble with his explanatory models. (It is hardly necessary to cite counterarguments, but Shatzmiller, 'Economic performance and economic growth in the early Islamic world', is effective here.) A recent stimulating textbook, Cortonesi and Palermo, *La prima espansione economica europea*, pp. 23–4, 31, 37, still (in 2009) makes analogous mistakes: the Arabs never innovated in their agriculture, nor did they invest. For the differing traditions of economic historians here, see among others the characterizations of Mainoni, 'Le produzioni non agricole', pp. 222–3; Cammarosano, *Economia politica classica e storia economica*, pp. 50–125.

[5] Lopez, 'The trade of medieval Europe: the south', pp. 365–8; Lopez, *The Commercial Revolution*, p. 95.

economy, and also, after 1200 in particular, for urban production and exchange. From then on too, when the 'revolution' was fully under way, trading systems have some powerful Europe-wide surveys, such as Peter Spufford's *Power and profit: the merchant in medieval Europe* (2002), which generalizes from his earlier work on coin production to produce a rich (and richly illustrated) analysis of the world of merchants, in a very long fourteenth century. By that time, there is much more evidence for how that world worked in Europe, and its main features are not controversial, with the major north-south routes linking northern Italy and Flanders, and steadily extending eastwards too, to connect with late medieval south German urbanization and Bohemian silver; the account books and occasionally letter collections of major international merchant entrepreneurs and bankers are by now easily available for inspection and study.[6] There are still major holes in our paradigm (Why was Paris so big after 1200, for example? How was it fed, what did it produce, and for whom?[7]), but historians, I think, simply assume that these holes will be filled in in the end.

More problematic for us is that both monographs and syntheses for the period after 1200 tend to take for granted the prior existence of the 'commercial revolution'. Given that it had started by the time the period of their research begins, they simply analyse its inner workings, or celebrate its results, as with many works on Italy's active urban societies. The problem of how to explain its origins seldom poses itself, except in some work on England, where the density of high-quality economic history has remained higher than for many parts of Europe.[8] Furthermore, little attention is generally given to what was happening on the southern side of the Mediterranean. One important synthesis, Janet Abu-Lughod's *Before European hegemony* (1986), does that, and in fact aims to show that European medieval commerce in the period 1250–1350 was only part of a set of interlocking networks stretching from Flanders to China, and not the largest-scale of them either. She entirely convinces, but the book is based on secondary literature, and, as with many others, mostly concerns long-distance commerce, not the regional and local economic structures which lay beneath it and determined it.[9] Otherwise,

[6] Spufford, *Power and profit*; earlier, his *Money and its use*. The Datini archive in the Archivio di Stato di Prato is the classic example of a late medieval merchant archive; see, e.g., Nigro, *Francesco di Marco Datini*. Here it is appropriate to signal the annual *Atti delle settimane di studi* of the Fondazione Datini: the go-to starting point for the study of the post-1200 economic history of Europe, although seldom useful for the period discussed here.

[7] There is no monograph on this known to me. Carpentier and Le Mené, *La France*, pp. 296–306 and Cazelles, *Nouvelle histoire*, pp. 131–49 give pointers; for one important aspect of urban food supply, milling, see now Marchandin, *Moulins et energie à Paris*, esp. pp. 34–43, 102–16, 136–41, a reference I owe to Alexis Wilkin.

[8] e.g. Britnell, *Britain and Ireland*, pp. 81–4, 118–57; Britnell, 'Commercialisation and economic development in England'; Masschaele, *Peasants, merchants*, esp. pp. 227–33. For some exceptions to this in Italy, see Chapter 6, n. 5 below.

[9] In addition to Abu-Lughod, see the briefer survey in Abulafia, 'Asia, Africa'. Economic monographs on the south of the Mediterranean are rarer, outside *geniza* studies (see n. 11 below), but Valérian, *Bougie*, is important.

in general, the Mediterranean is seen from the standpoint of the Venetians and Genoese in these books; the dominance of the sea by their ships is taken for granted, and often the assumption remains, as for Lopez, that Mediterranean-wide commerce pretty much began with them.[10]

But, actually, when Lopez rounded off his career with that synthesis, it was already out of date. Cairo only appears once in its index, but in 1967 Shelomo Goitein had already published the first volume of his *A Mediterranean society*, about the commercial activities of the communities of Jews in Fusṭāṭ, twin city to Cairo, whose Judaeo-Arabic letters and documents, above all from the eleventh and twelfth centuries, were thrown into the *geniza*—not an archive, but a huge wastepaper bin, hundreds of thousands of bits of paper—of the Ben Ezra synagogue, one of the three main synagogues of Fusṭāṭ in our period. *Geniza* scholarship has been active ever since, in the hands of Goitein's pupils and their pupils; in recent years, by far the most significant book on *geniza* economic issues in our period has been Jessica Goldberg's *Trade and institutions in the medieval Mediterranean* (2012).[11] From all this work, a clear picture of a Mediterranean-wide trade by Jewish (and, by implication in Goitein's work—in my view rightly—also Muslim) merchants could be established. It started by the late tenth century, well before the Italian cities got a look in, and was focussed on selling Egyptian flax to Muslim-ruled Sicily and Tunisia to be made into linen cloth and sold on, whether inside those two regions or back to Egypt (among other commodities, olive oil came back from Tunisia to Egypt too). It was also linked to the Levant and Spain to a lesser extent, as well as to a largely luxury trade connecting China and India with the Mediterranean, which has long been known about. This Fusṭāṭ-centred and textile-focussed trade was the dominant exchange network on the inland sea until 1100 at the earliest, and shared with that promoted by the Italian cities for some time after.

The importance of the evidence from the *geniza* has several elements which are of direct relevance for us, and which will recur throughout this book. Here, I list four. First, empirically, it shows that the Mediterranean was not just an empty space before the eleventh century, waiting for the Italians to fill, a position which has been generalized very effectively by Christophe Picard's *La mer des califes* (2015). Some historians are still capable of supposing that the Egyptian flax traders simply represented a sort of prehistory to the major period of the second great Mediterranean trade cycle (the first being that of the Roman Empire), extending from the late tenth century to the late middle ages, which could thus

[10] For example Cortonesi and Palermo, *La prima espansione economica europea*: this does not discuss the *geniza*, and the authors write as if it did not exist. Tangheroni, *Commercio e navigazione*, pp. 58–72, 356–62, although tending to write off the Islamic side of the Mediterranean after the eleventh century, at least confronts it.

[11] Goitein, *MS*, 1 (eventually five volumes appeared, plus an index volume); Goldberg, *Trade and institutions*.

still be seen as dominated by the Italians; but we have to recognize that the basic sea-trading patterns of the twelfth- and thirteenth-century Mediterranean were by no means a creation of the Italians alone. We can now better see that the Genoese and Pisans and (to a lesser extent) Venetians simply added themselves to this network by force, much as the Vikings did in the ninth-century North Sea, or as the Portuguese did in the sixteenth-century Indian Ocean.[12] Historians have shown that the Italians did indeed take over much of the trans-Mediterranean carrying trade by 1150–1200, shifting much of it northwards,[13] and it stayed that way until the Ottoman reunification of three-quarters of the Mediterranean in the fifteenth and sixteenth centuries; but the whole configuration of the trade cycle changes once one knows the *geniza* evidence. Indeed, as we shall see, Lopez and the others had the whole narrative backwards, to a large extent; notwithstanding the maritime importance of its port cities, north-central Italy not only did not have the leading economy in the Mediterranean in our period, but was actually among the last regions to develop an internally integrated production and exchange system. This is a paradox which will be explored in Chapters 6 and 7.

The other points can be set out more rapidly. Second, the *geniza* makes clear that one could develop a major-scale Mediterranean exchange network dominated, not by luxuries, but by bulk goods, bales of raw flax, bales of linen or cotton cloth, skins full of olive oil. Lopez explicitly doubted this, because transport costs were too high—even if it is hard to see how he could have said so, given his knowledge of the Genoese cloth and alum trade in the thirteenth century—but, in fact, bulk goods can be shown empirically to have been the main element of the second trade cycle throughout, and luxuries were no more than an adjunct to them. I will come back to the point later in this chapter, and throughout the book.[14] Third, it shows that any discussion of the origins of the 'commercial revolution' cannot just be about Europe; in fact, it is unlikely that they were really about Europe at all, and I shall argue that they were not. 'Europe' will not reappear here as a point of reference, in fact. It is undoubtedly true that a north-west European take-off, centred on Flanders and the region around it, began perhaps a century earlier than that of northern Italy, and that there were links between them; but these links were not causal, and in fact I would see the two developments in themselves as having partly different causes. My focus here will only be the

[12] As well as Picard, see Bramoullé, *Les Fatimides et la mer* (2020). Cahen, *Orient et Occident* (1983), a surprisingly underused book, given its quality and the high reputation of its author, partly reshapes our understanding of the twelfth century, but says less about the eleventh. The classic account of the fleets of the Italian ports as military first, commercial second, is Petralia, 'Le "navi" e i "cavalli"'.

[13] See the works of David Jacoby in the Bibliography, for a multitude of case studies; for nuancing, see Chapters 6 and 7 below.

[14] Lopez, *The Commercial Revolution*, pp. 93–4; contrast Lopez, *Studi sull'economia genovese*, or Lopez, *Genova marinara*, on Benedetto Zaccaria.

Mediterranean as a result, and I will not privilege any particular region of the Mediterranean for a priori reasons. Fourth, the different perspective of the *geniza* also poses basic questions about how we can theorize economic causes in the medieval period. What *were* the economy's prime movers? How far can we generalize about them? What, indeed, was the economic logic that characterized the medieval period? I have discussed this last issue elsewhere,[15] and I shall return to it at the end of this chapter and at the end of the book.

My focus here is a long eleventh century, very long in fact, going from *c.*950 to *c.*1180. The first date marks the rough point at which the Mediterranean trade cycle began. The second, by when it was mostly in full swing, requires more comment, because it should not be taken as over-precise. It does not matter for most of my regions whether I chose a final date of 1180 or 1200, and I have been fairly flexible about how I have treated the data for the end of the twelfth century; active internal exchange had by now visibly begun in all but one of them. It is Italy which causes problems here. I initially thought, following the assumptions of the historiography, that it would be relatively straightforward to pin down the moment when the internal productive and commercial economy of north-central Italy took a decisive upturn, to sometime in the early twelfth century at the latest, and that it would then not be necessary to go much later, as the issue of its origins would already be clear. As I researched the issue further, however, that date has receded. First, 1150 seemed like a new plausible turning point; it is, probably, for Milan and Piacenza, although the evidence is poor and indirect even for there, plus, without any doubt, the port cities. For most of the rest of the Italian north, however, we do not yet have any indication that we could say the same, so I decided to push the end date later, to 1180; even then, as we shall see in Chapter 6, it was probably later still for much of the region. But I gave up chasing it in 1180. This is because I wanted to be able to study all available documentation, documentary, literary, and archaeological alike, for the regions I was focussing on; I needed to study it all directly, as the use made of it by too much of the historiography has been distorted by prior assumptions about what the historian *ought* to be finding. Inside Italy, however, after 1150 the documentation in some cities increases exponentially, decade by decade. In Genoa, for example, there is more documentation for the period 1180–1200 than there is for the previous 250 years, and the same is nearly true for Venice as well—although Genoa and Venice, actually, are not the problem, for their commercial commitment was among the earliest and strongest in Italy, and is unusually easy to track. 1180 can stand as an end point for Italy, then, although in some parts of it, here too, I have looked later; and it is not a misleading end point for any other region either. At least, in the case of Byzantium, it allows me to sidestep the issue, which is marginal for the arguments of this

[15] Wickham, 'How did the feudal economy work?'.

book but crucial for Byzantinists, of what effect the disaster of the Fourth Crusade had on the economy of the empire after 1204.

The Mediterranean is too large, and the evidence for this period too substantial, for all its constituent regions to be properly studied in depth for this period, without creating a book of absurd length. About half of the regions around it are discussed here. I chose six as case studies, which offer complementary particularities. In order of presentation, they are Egypt; the central section of North Africa, centred on what is now Tunisia, then called Ifrīqiya; Sicily; the Byzantine Empire, particularly its Aegean heartland; al-Andalus, that is to say, Islamic Spain and Portugal; and north-central Italy, particularly the central and eastern Po plain and Tuscany. (See Map 1. Note that, throughout this book, I mean by 'regions' relatively big geographical blocks such as these; it is a convenient generalizing term, since such regions seldom coincide with single polities, ancient or modern.) The evidence, whether documentary or archaeological or both, for nearly all these regions is good enough to justify a focussed study; the exception here is Ifrīqiya, but it was too closely linked to Sicily to exclude it easily, and in fact I present the two regions together. Given the quantity of data for Italy, city by city, I have had to be more selective there, and have again gone for case studies, Venice, Genoa, Pisa, Milan, and to a lesser extent Padua, Lucca, Florence, Cremona, and Piacenza—and referring briefly to Rome as a comparator, since I had already worked on it, and since its role in the period, as a large but relatively isolated city, raises interesting questions in itself.

The main regions I have left out are Morocco, the Catalan and south French coast, Sardinia, southern mainland Italy, Croatia, and the Levant—that is to say, Syria and Palestine. These varied quite substantially in the degree to which they were integrated, either internally or externally, by exchange networks; the data for them across the period of this book are also for the most part poorer. The data for Catalonia are rich, but it was slow to move economically; the opposite is true for the Levant; only southern Italy would have matched up with the regions I chose in the evidence for its active production and exchange, but it seemed to me that the patterns it showed were sufficiently similar to those of other regions to allow me not to include it. I regret all these omissions (particularly Sardinia, terribly documented as it is for our period, but fascinatingly strange in its socio-economic structure), but they seemed to me necessary. They mean that this book is not about the Mediterranean as a whole, but, rather, the development and interconnections of a subset of the regions around the sea. But, to repeat, this imperfection seemed to me justifiable heuristically, for we will find a large amount of variation anyway. Each region has a long chapter (with one, as noted, for Ifrīqiya plus Sicily); there is then a chapter summing up how our understanding of the way the Mediterranean fitted together commercially can, or should, be refigured as a result of the empirical discussions offered here. A final chapter explores the issue of how the logic of the medieval economy worked, again in the light of these discussions.

I must confess here that the book got out of hand anyway. I thought that I would be able to rely, to a considerable extent, on previous work in the field, balanced against targeted critical investigations of specific sectors of the evidence. But I discovered at the start, as stated earlier, that this was not the case for Egypt; and in fact it was untrue elsewhere as well. Not one of the regions discussed here (or indeed any of the others) has a reliable overall economic analysis for our period, except the Byzantine Empire—even Italy, which has had by far the densest sets of discussions. Archaeological syntheses are also lacking, except for Sicily and again Byzantium. Every region also has its own historiographical *idées fixes*, which do not match up with—and in some cases are directly challenged by—the debates on other regions. That is to say, as indeed I have found for other periods, historians and archaeologists do not as a rule read enough outside the region they study, so they can get caught up in local solipsistic discussions, which are in this period very often about grand narratives of nationhood (in Italy or Spain) or of supposed regional failure (in Ifrīqiya, Sicily, Egypt, or Byzantium), and which never, in any case discussed here, actually help our understanding.[16] Indeed, many commonly held assumptions, which recur in discussions of the period, are entirely mistaken, making even good work at times unreliable.

So I found that I had to begin again, with both the documentary and the archaeological evidence, all of which needed to be contextualized, plus the added task of explaining why local debates had come to be how they are. Each chapter, therefore, has a substantial historiographical section which tries to do so. The work was in every case fascinating and rewarding; but the chapters mushroomed as a result. Should individual chapters in any book be over 50,000 words long? No, but all the substantive ones here are, and the Italian chapter is longer still. I have to apologize for this, in a general way at least; but the chapters are also quite synthetic, given that they are characterizations of the changing economic structures of whole modern countries or sets of countries across almost a quarter of a millennium, and could in nearly every case have been twice the length. I anyway seek in each to be as clear and exact as one can be, given that new research, particularly by archaeologists, can change our knowledge so rapidly. I also hope that the regional chapters will show experts on other regions that there are important features of all those discussed here which cannot be ignored in any holistic account of the medieval economy; some of them, inexplicably, have hardly featured in wider surveys before at all. You could see each of the regional analyses as aiming at being a contribution to understanding, and reinterpreting, the economic development of each of my six case studies, and, as that, they can each be read on their own. They have for that reason been written so that each is self-explanatory, even if this involves occasional repetitions—which is also aimed

[16] Cf. Wickham, 'The early middle ages and national identity', for the previous period.

at helping non-experts on each region to get more easily into the evidence and the debates. This is also why I have included in most of the regional chapters some quite detailed critiques of specific arguments which seem to me mistaken, and which might mislead outsiders: among others, about the supposed trade in potters' clay along the Nile, or the economic role of the Venetians in the twelfth-century Aegean, or the absence of amphorae in al-Andalus. But these chapters furnish, as well, the basic empirical material that underpins the final two, shorter chapters, which aim to rethink our wider paradigms for the period: in the first, for Mediterranean economic change and its drivers; in the second, for the structures of the medieval economy as a whole.

I have used, systematically, both written and archaeological sources, and they come together in individual sections of the book. It is ever clearer that one cannot write medieval economic history (as also that of the ancient world) without the evidence from archaeology. But it needs to be recognized that the two disciplines are different epistemologically: the conventions for truth criteria in each do not always match up. How they should do has not been my concern here, but it does make working with each body of data a distinct process. Added to this is the fact that archaeologists, in particular, sometimes have a habit of using document-based assumptions to develop hypotheses about their own archaeological data, which are then used to reinforce the documentary assumptions, in a circular argument: 'historians tell us that this city was destroyed in 1150, so we must date our deposits to before that moment; the fact that there are now no deposits after that moment confirms the destruction'. (If historians do not do the same in reverse, it is only because they do not read enough archaeology.) I have, therefore, sought, in nearly every case, to set up each archaeology-based argument separately from the parallel argument based on documentary or, more rarely, literary sources. Only when each is developed on its own in this way does it seem to me methodologically permissible to compare, and seek to reconcile, the results, and this has been my practice in nearly every part of the book.[17]

The written sources I have used are above all in three languages, Latin, Greek, and Arabic (occasional Coptic and Hebrew texts appear too). Latin is not a problem. My Greek is less good, and it would be disingenuous to pretend that I have not been helped by translations, where there are any; but I will stand by my interpretations of texts, which I have checked in the original at every crux. My Arabic is no longer non-existent, but it is still very poor, and dealing with the *geniza* is that much harder because the texts from it were written in 'Judaeo-Arabic', Arabic written in Hebrew script. Here I have openly used, and also cited, translations of literary texts; where there are linguistic cruxes in them which I could not resolve,

[17] The principles are set out in Wickham, 'Fonti archeologiche e fonti storiche'. I have discussed my considerable caution about literary sources elsewhere too; but the point will recur in the substantive chapters which follow.

I have sought help, and in that case acknowledge it explicitly. Arabic (including Judaeo-Arabic) and Coptic documents and letters for the most part already have line-by-line translations, which have helped me to identify the cruxes and resolve them myself. Where those translations are into modern Hebrew I have again usually sought help, and, when I have done, again acknowledge it. You cannot write any book without the help of friends and colleagues, and certainly not one like this, where there is so much for anyone to learn. But my experience of asking for linguistic help here, although it takes time, and creates many debts of gratitude which, as noted in the Acknowledgements, I shall be only too happy to repay in kind, has another dimension too: it is for me a démarche which will have to be followed by others, if we want to succeed in creating a global medieval history which is actually based on primary research, rather than on—as it only too often seems—outdated cliché. Egypt is not geographically very far away from my fullest research experiences, which are Italy-based above all, but it is already sufficiently linguistically and culturally different in our period to be challenging to an outsider. Iran would present challenges of the same type. The evidence for India, China, and Japan is even harder to penetrate. All the same, with help and collaboration we can get a long way; and this is a path which others, I am glad to see, are also walking on.[18]

* * *

The rest of this introduction sets out some of the basic starting points and approaches I have used in this book, to give a clearer guide to some of my aims. This book focusses on the movement of goods, usually through commercial exchange, but I do not wish to propose that this is the essential feature of the medieval (or any) economy. On the contrary: production and demand, both agricultural and urban, comes first, even if exchange follows on fast, linking them together, and more and more so in any expanding economy. So, although I am describing some of the same sorts of phenomena which were studied by major historians of commerce such as Henri Pirenne, Roberto Lopez, Raymond de Roover, Maurice Lombard, Marco Tangheroni, or Peter Spufford, I do not make the assumption which many of them have made, more or less explicitly, that long-distance commercial and/or financial complexity is the principal element, even sometimes the prime mover, in economic historical analysis.[19] It is in this context

[18] See, for example, Holmes and Standen, *The global middle ages*. For the possibilities and challenges of medieval global history, see most recently the important discussion in Ertl and Oschema, 'Les études médiévales après le tournant global', with ample bibliography.

[19] A sharp-eyed historiographical commentary here is Cammarosano, *Economia politica classica e storia economica*, esp. pp. 26–8, 56–63, 105–8. For a fairly recent explicit claim, see Tangheroni, *Commercio e navigazione*; he is cautious about Lopez's concept of 'commercial revolution' (pp. 127–30), but he adopts it precisely because he refuses the view that economic change derives from internal agrarian developments, and because capital investment was far higher in the commercial than in the industrial sector. Tangheroni's chosen topic was sea commerce (Milan, for example, hardly appears in the book), so he did not need to be as explicit as this, but he was too coherent a thinker not

that my two main starting points, although they are much the same as in other works of mine on the economy (I insisted on them at some length in *Framing the early middle ages*), need to be set out here as well. They would be obvious to most economists, but not all historians think this way.

The first is that the development of regional economic complexity is above all internal, based on local demand, both of landowning or official elites and of peasants, for the development of sellable products, whether agrarian or artisanal, and on the consequent local and medium-distance exchange of these products.[20] It is not based on trans-Mediterranean shipping—or, elsewhere in Eurasia, any other form of long-distance transport. Large-scale longer-distance systems could, of course, exist in the pre-industrial world. The Roman Empire was one, in that case supported by large-scale state demand; the flax export of eleventh-century Egypt was another, as we shall see in Chapters 2 and 3; later than our period, the urban economies of thirteenth- and fourteenth-century northern Italy and Flanders were also at the centre of European systems of a similar scale. But their origins were in no case driven by long-distance trade. Initially, at least, basic artisanal products such as clothing and iron tools are made close to the origin of their raw materials; then, local and regional exchange networks need to be established before one can sell goods anywhere. Even after this, one will not be able to both buy and sell interregionally on any scale unless some other region has developed a parallel set of trading goods and a similar network of regional exchange.

Furthermore, if one takes even contemporary parallels, long-distance trade recedes in importance. United States exports have only once exceeded 10 per cent of GDP in the last two centuries and have mostly been under 7 per cent; French and Italian exports only exceeded 20 per cent after 2000, and UK exports have never gone past 25 per cent (and doubtless never will again). Imports have

to do so—which I respect, while entirely disagreeing with him. Even more recent is Tognetti, 'Attività mercantili e finanziarie', pp. 24–32, which develops Tangheroni's position interestingly, but not, for me, more convincingly.

[20] 'Elite' and 'peasant' both need a gloss. I will use the word 'elite' a great deal in this book, as a wide all-purpose term. I mean by it, essentially, anyone who is living off the surplus of others: landowners (including the most status-filled lay landowners, 'aristocrats', but not restricted to them; landowning monasteries figure as elites too, and so do the smaller-scale landowners who could dominate small towns and villages), state officials who lived on salaries and legal or illegal perquisites, and the urban rich who lived off trade and the artisanal work of others. Towns contained plenty of non-elites—artisans and the poor—but, as collectivities, added to elite buying power, as they did not produce their own food. 'Peasants' are settled cultivators (plus pastoralists) who cultivate largely for subsistence (and thus do not need to buy most of their food), who do at least some agricultural work personally, and who control their own labour on the land (see further p. 674 below). They can own their land, or hold it from a landowner in return for rent—the difference in prosperity between small owners and tenants will be a feature of several discussions across this book—but both groups are peasants, and there was a grey area between them, with plenty of peasants who owned some land plots and paid rent for others (as there also was at the top end of the peasantry, when rich peasants, often members of village-level elites, accumulated enough land that they might be renting most of it out). Rural wage labourers complicate the picture, especially, in this book, in Egypt and al-Andalus, but were in our period essentially a minority, and formed part of peasant society and the peasant economy.

followed very similar paths, except for a greater UK import reliance in the nineteenth century, at the high point of the Industrial Revolution. And, as late as the end of the eighteenth century, almost all European countries probably exported only around 4 per cent outside their borders. We could not reasonably expect most of the regional economies of the central middle ages to have exported anywhere near that—maybe 1 per cent, or 2 per cent for export-orientated economies?—but however much it was (no exact figures can even be contemplated), we cannot be dealing with more than extremely low levels of interregional exchange in our period, even in the most externally orientated economies. One of the clearest figures I have seen, for fifteenth-century Sicily, is 5 per cent for the scale of cloth imports to the island, when set against local production, and cloth was one of the most imported and exported commodities; that, as we can already see, was in fact very high for the period, and it is extremely unlikely that any region came anywhere near that before 1180.[21] One result of these figures, it is worth noting, is that world-systems theories concerning the major economic developments of the modern period, which put a great deal of stress on international connections, have no real explanatory traction; the debate about them concerns a period too late in time for us to need to deal with it, but I will come back briefly to the point at the end of the book (pp. 683–4).

The questions, therefore, have to be posed at the local and regional level. Who produces? Who sells? Who buys? Where does the motor of exchange start, and what keeps it going? These questions need to be asked every time, if we wish to give form to the local and regional infrastructure of exchange. The interregional maritime network depends entirely on that infrastructure; without it, goods will not even get to the coast. If one starts with the maritime network, as historians of, say, Venice and Genoa are prone to do, it is only too common to neglect the local,

[21] See, for Sicily, Chapter 3, n. 265 below. For the contemporary figures, see Ortiz-Ospina and Beltekian, 'Trade and globalization'. I restrict myself to industrialized countries; some of the implausibly high figures in that table (50% for imports to Senegal?) must derive from the difficulties of calculating the subsistence agrarian sector, difficulties which medievalists have too. Thanks to Roger Gill for advice and references here. For a parallel argument and set of figures, from the late middle ages to the present, see Ogilvie, *Institutions and European trade*, pp. 197–202. She builds on the classic discussion by O'Brien, 'European economic development' (see p. 4 for 4% around 1790), itself building on Bairoch, *Commerce extérieur*, pp. 78–9, who is open about the hypothetical nature of any figures before 1830; but they anyway cannot, given the better data from then onwards, have been significantly higher. For Sicily, see p. 261. Fernand Braudel needs to be nodded to here as well. His lasting classic on the sixteenth century, *The Mediterranean*, esp. pp. 438–48, put more analytical weight on luxury trading than bulk trade, because the profits were higher, and because—as is well known—Braudel was fascinated by capitalist developments in themselves. He also avoided offering overall comparative figures for international versus regional-level trade; he only gives us one (ibid., p. 441), for Spain, of 3:1 internal vs external trade, but this is based on urban tolls, which will have caught only a small proportion of internal economic activity. I do not follow him here. But he knew well that agriculture was the overwhelmingly dominant element in the economy (see, e.g., ibid., p. 421). Note that his guesstimate of the percentage of wheat exported in the Mediterranean, 0.8% of total consumption, is misleadingly inflated to 8% in the English translation: see ibid., p. 423, set against Braudel, *La Méditerranée*, p. 386.

sometimes almost entirely; it is less sexy, more workaday. It gets mentioned casually and then moved on from; it is not analysed in any detail. But it is the core; we need to start from there if we want to understand the economic system as a whole.

And that brings us to the title of this book: we have to study the donkey as well as the boat. It is a cliché of ancient and medieval history that transport is far cheaper, perhaps by a ratio of 20:1, by boat than on land, and this was in general true (we indeed have occasional confirmation of it for our period).[22] Long-distance trade was overwhelmingly carried out by boat, and not only in the Mediterranean—the so-called 'silk roads' of Central Asia were of tiny importance compared with the ocean route from and around India. But goods were, in every part of the Mediterranean, moved around by donkey *first*, before they ever reached boats—even river boats, for we, of course, have to recognize the importance of rivers as routes, whenever they were navigable. Arabic letters from Egypt have many references to donkeys, and rightly so; we can assume their presence elsewhere too.[23] The point can be developed further if one looks at it from the perspective of towns. There has to be an agrarian surplus available, from either close by or farther away, for urban centres, cities or towns, to be fed.[24] That surplus may come into towns in rent or as a result of sales by country dwellers (whether larger landowners or cultivators), but it needs to be accessible for any kind of complex economy to begin to appear, and, again, in our period it came in above

[22] For one example, from the Fayyūm in Egypt, see P.Vind.Arab. I 41, where, in fact, the difference between the cost of the short donkey/mule journey to the Nile boat and the longer Nile journey itself appears to be 30:1 (see Chapter 2, n. 2 below, for the abbreviations, here and in n. 23 below). See, for the general rule, Jones, *The later Roman empire*, pp. 841–2, based on Diocletian's *Price edict*.

[23] Mitchell, *The donkey in human history*, pp. 126–41, 166–79, discusses the ubiquity of donkeys (including mules) as pack animals in the ancient and medieval periods. For Egypt, see, among many for donkeys, P.Cair.Arab. 311, 365; P.Philad.Arab. 54; P.Hamb.Arab. II 29; P.Vind.Arab. III 32, 47; P.Vente 24, Appendix 2; for mules, see, e.g., P.Marchands III 3, 9, 35, 39. Sources outside Egypt rarely give us any detailed evidence about donkeys and mules, unfortunately, even though we know they were always there in the Mediterranean (we have a few prices for Byzantium and Genoa: below, pp. 338, 544). We can add ox-carts, where the terrain allowed. Horses were, of course, used too, but were expensive; camels were less common except for desert routes, like the land routes from Ifrīqiya to Egypt or Egypt to Palestine. My book title, however, openly acknowledges a debt to Richard Bulliet's *The camel and the wheel*.

[24] Note that throughout this book I shall use 'city' and 'town' more or less as synonyms, to mean any urban centre. In Muslim-ruled political systems, the presence or absence of a bishop—a standard element in the differentiation between the two in Europe—was not of importance by now in most cases, even in relatively Christian Egypt; *madīna* was the basic word for urban centres of all types (although there were certainly places with urban features which were not called that). In Byzantium, the word *polis* had by now lost its automatic association with episcopal centres; these were as often called *kastra*, but a *kastron* not only did not have to have a bishop, but did not have to be urban at all. Among my case-study regions, only in Italy, by now, was there still a technical term (*civitas*) which distinguished political and episcopal centres from other towns, but many *civitates* were also not urban in an economic sense. I will rarely use the word 'city' for smaller urban centres, as it does not feel helpful to do so, but I will never draw any form of sharp distinction between the two words.

all by donkey.[25] Urban-made artisanal goods in return, also carried by donkey, will be sold above all locally and subregionally, in return for agricultural goods; after that, the more complex a regional economy, the more such goods will be available across the region, rather than being restricted to single localities; and then, sometimes, they can go beyond it. Interregional sales in general, however, to repeat, only constituted a very small minority of transactions in the middle ages, or indeed later, right up to the twentieth century.

So the underpinning of a complex economy was never in our period long-distance maritime trade. This was true even in eleventh-century Egypt or Sicily, or thirteenth-century northern Italy, which were, for sure, parts of a large-scale interregional trading network. The exceptions were a handful of entrepôt cities such as Venice and Genoa, or Tinnīs in Egypt (see Chapters 6 and 2 respectively); and even Venice used the medium-distance export of salt across northern Italy as a major basis for the accumulation of wealth throughout our period.[26] A maritime trade in sets of bulk goods between two regions for the most part serves as a sign of something more important: that each of their economies was sufficiently complex internally to buy on a large scale abroad and to produce enough goods to pay for it. When we can see this occurring, then we can begin to talk of an economic system which is, at least up to a point, Mediterranean-wide. But when we are looking at scale, we have to think of the donkey first; only then do we need to consider the boat.

My second, linked, starting point has already been mentioned: it is that the indicators of exchange complexity are not luxury goods, but, rather, goods that are transported in bulk. In our period, these were, among foodstuffs, wheat, wine, olive oil, and cheese (and not spices); among primary products, flax, cotton, wool, timber, and skins; among artisanal products, cloth, ironwork, leatherwork, paper, and ceramics (and not goldwork or jewellery). Only bulk goods are really significant to any economy. Luxuries always exist in stratified societies, whether simple or complex, essentially to mark elite status; expensive to make and/or hard to get, they are a small minority of commodities by definition. One can indeed say, as a rule of thumb, that if a luxury is important for an economic system, taken as a whole, then it has ceased to be a luxury. (We must again, of course, set aside single entrepôt cites such as Venice, which could grow rich on largely luxury transport.) We have to focus on bulk goods if we want to understand how the economy worked, whether internally or interregionally; as a result, I will systematically set aside luxury trade in what follows. There were semi-luxuries as

25 Another definitional note: I mean by a 'complex' regional economy, throughout this book, one with exchange networks which link villages to towns and towns to capitals, in sets of overlapping patterns of production and commercialization of different goods, which do not depend on one single centre. The more different exchange networks there are, and the more overlapping they are, plus the more social strata there are which are involved in buying and selling, the more complex the economy.

26 For Venetian salt, the basic account for our period is Hocquet, 'Le saline'. See pp. 508–9 below.

well, such as silk, which was bought by a much wider elite and was made on a considerable scale in Spain, Byzantium, and Sicily, or silver, which, although a precious metal, was a basic currency for most people and widely available; we will look at these too. But neither of them could, or did, create exchange systems on their own, except for the individual cities or mining areas which produced them. Rather, as we shall see, silk weaving, in particular, is at best an unusually well-documented proxy for quantitatively more important types of cloth production, such as linen and cotton.[27]

On the basis of these observations, I want, as set out earlier, to create a picture of how the Mediterranean exchange economies worked and changed and interlinked, across the period covered by this book. It needs to be clear at the outset that, however they did work, they did not resemble the structural dynamics of what has been called the first long trade cycle, that of the Roman Empire. That, as it developed, was structured by state (fiscal) demand, for army supply and for feeding the huge Roman capitals—Rome's own million or so inhabitants in the first century AD were not matched again in Europe and the Mediterranean until the nineteenth.[28] Wheat moved north from Africa and Egypt in taxation, so did olive oil from Spain and, later, Africa again, and these, and other products like them, taken in tax or (in the case of armaments) made or bought by the state, constituted a state-backed movement of some bulk goods which underpinned the interregional commerce of others, cloth, wine, or mass-produced good-quality ceramics, the last two identifiable archaeologically (as is the oil transport—both wine and oil travelled in ceramic amphorae), as well as any number of other commodities. And when the state disintegrated from the fifth century onwards in the western Roman Empire, or, in the case of the eastern empire, was broken in two by the seventh-century Islamic conquests, the trade cycle broke down as well.[29]

The second long trade cycle, that of the 'commercial revolution', may not have matched the scale of the first. After all, wheat and wine were grown all around the Mediterranean; they did not need to be moved much outside regions for strictly commercial purposes, except in times of local famines. The direct involvement of the state in the movement of goods, which was so much a feature of the Roman world, was also never repeated in medieval times (see pp. 628–9 below). And

[27] See, earlier, Wickham, *Framing*, pp. 696–700 (where I should have cited Chaudhuri, *Trade and civilisation*, from which I initially learned the importance of the bulk–luxury distinction, decades ago); for our period, see, e.g., Goldberg, *Trade and institutions*, pp. 18–21, 276–86.

[28] The ballpark figure of 800,000 to a million for the population of first-century Rome has been repeated often enough; see, in particular, Elio Lo Cascio's detailed calculation of the citizen population of Rome under Augustus in 'Le procedure di *recensus*', p. 36; as one alternative, Morley, 'Population size', sees the minimum as 650,000, and the maximum (which he doubts) as over a million. These uncertainties are based on actual data; we shall find that parallel calculations for the largest cities of the Mediterranean in our period, Fusṭāṭ-Cairo, Constantinople, and (briefly) Córdoba, are far more hypothetical. See, pp. 41, 279, 395–6 below.

[29] Wickham, *Framing*, Chapter 11.

only complex regional economies had much use for large-scale bulk trade at all, as just noted. But, all the same, that trade did develop again, not least because, by the twelfth century, many of the regions of the Mediterranean—Egypt and al-Andalus in particular, and northern Italy coming up fast at the very end of our period—were more complex economically than they were under the Romans, with most of the others at least matching Roman levels. This time manufactured goods, and the raw materials for them, were the main drivers of commerce, although the wine trade, visible archaeologically inside some of our regions, in particular Byzantium and Sicily, could still be highly active. From the tenth century onwards, good-quality ceramics become again, as under Rome, one proxy for these goods (although, as they consisted of hand-decorated glazed wares, not the red-slipped wares of the Roman Empire, they were less mass-produced); but we have better evidence than in the ancient world for the movement of cloth, and we will indeed find, in several regions, that the evidence for each, ceramics and cloth, matches the other. So our period saw regional economies which were often more complex internally than in the ancient world, even though the trade which linked them together was often less large-scale. That is a further empirical reason, in addition to the basic starting points just discussed, to concentrate on internal exchange developments.

My essential focus in this book is on exchange, of all types of goods. Most of the transport of bulk goods was commercial, although I do not wish to exclude the fiscal movement of goods, which did still occur, at least inside regions. This, of course, must lead us to look at urban production, and I do so, in as much detail as is possible on the basis of our data. It also means, however, that we cannot exclude agricultural production, and the general question of the extraction, and scale of distribution, of agricultural surplus, whenever there is any evidence about it. Agriculture constituted the largest part of the economy in every period and region in the world before the eighteenth century at the earliest, after all, so it cannot be sensibly excluded. It tends to be discussed by different sorts of economic historian from those who are most interested in towns and trade—there is a whole historiography on the changes in the organization and management of landed estates, which in many cases hardly alludes to how, or if, surpluses were sold; just as there is a historiography focussed on 'the merchant', which says little about where the goods merchants sold actually came from.[30] But what happened to these agricultural surpluses is of crucial importance for the arguments of this book, as towns could not exist without food supplies, and some of those rural surpluses, as with wool and flax, were the direct underpinning of urban production.

[30] Apart from Spufford, *The merchant*, which is the most up-to-date and best, examples (of varying quality) include Sapori, *Il mercante italiano*; Le Goff, *Marchands et banquiers*; *Le marchand au Moyen Âge*.

In addition, we need to look not just at urban and merchant-run exchange, but at that of the peasants themselves, the overwhelming majority of the population in every medieval region, which archaeology is beginning to tell us more about. We will find that increasingly, in most of our regions, peasants themselves had in many cases enough surplus, over and above rent, tax, and subsistence, to sell produce on their own account, and buy their own urban products, which can indeed be found increasingly widely in village-level field surveys and excavations. That contributed very directly to the breadth of urban production, and thus to the development of products which were large-scale enough to be sold elsewhere too. Knowledge of the existence of this stratum of peasants, who were prosperous enough to participate directly in commercial exchange, is a recent development in the literature for our period, moving away from the automatic assumption, normal into the 1970s at least, that peasants were so grindingly poor, so close to the boundaries of survival, that buying and selling, over the minimum necessary to pay rents or taxes in money, was beyond them, and that trade and its development hardly concerned them at all. The implications of this will underpin most of my empirical chapters, and will be discussed further as a theoretical issue in Chapter 8, when I look at how the economy of this period can be conceived as a whole. It also means that I will be less uneasy about using the word 'development', which has quite a positive ring, when discussing the increases in regional economic complexity we see in this book, than I have been in previous work.[31] That work mostly focussed on the pre-1000 period, when greater economic complexity did indeed correlate well with higher levels of surplus extraction, and thus lower levels of prosperity for the peasant majority. But after 950/1000 the situation changed, and some of the most important parameters for economic 'development' changed with it. I shall argue this further in Chapter 8 as well.

One issue that this book does not discuss is economic failure. There is a metanarrative of failure underpinning the historiography of nearly every region discussed in this book; the only exception is north-central Italy, whose medieval high point for economic complexity was reached after the period discussed here ended. This metanarrative has at least two main underpinnings. One is the implicit belief that every active economy 'fails' if its exchange activity does not develop into capitalism, which, of course, empirically, the great majority of active medieval economies did not; Italy itself would later get hit by this storyline, at some point in the late middle ages or early modern period (in the fifteenth century, it often used to be thought; now, the early seventeenth).[32] So would the Mediterranean as a whole, maybe also in the seventeenth, when it was supposedly eclipsed by the larger exchange networks which the Atlantic and the eastwards

[31] See, e.g., Wickham, *Framing*, pp. 706–7.

[32] For continuities to 1600 or so, see, e.g., Goldthwaite, *The economy of Renaissance Florence*; Franceschi and Molà, 'Regional states and economic development'; Malanima, *La fine del primato*.

route around Africa offered. This story is not interesting to me. Economies in the medieval period operated by largely different rules from today, as we shall also see at the end of the book, and the nature of their dynamics regularly changed; if elite investment moved into agriculture for a time rather than urban production, as often occurred, this would certainly affect that production, but it was a normal, not a 'failing' response to an economic logic which would stay feudal, not capitalist, for centuries. (See pp. 673–6, below for my definition of 'feudal' here.)

The second element of the metanarrative of failure is more explicit, and as a result more egregious. It concerns the supposed 'failure' of Islamic societies to build on their economic position in the early middle ages, when Egypt and the Levant were certainly far more complex economically than were any of the Mediterranean Christian lands, even Byzantium.[33] This 'failure' has been mistakenly attached to all sorts of elements, such as the absence of formal institutions such as guilds and city councils in the Islamic world, or the trend to 'feudalism' supposedly represented by giving tax-farming concessions in *iqṭāʿ* to military figures, which are (wrongly) seen as similar to fiefs—a really perplexing argument, given that fiefs, of course, precisely characterized Latin Europe, where such a 'failure' did not occur. Eliyahu Ashtor was particularly guilty of this sort of imagery in his general survey of the economies of the medieval Islamic world (1976), which unfortunately, notwithstanding his out-of-date categorizations, a moralistic teleology which by now just looks strange, and a range of factual errors, has not been replaced.[34] What lies behind this sort of explanation is simply Orientalism, in Edward Said's sense: the construction of the 'East' as an invented exotic land with no real history, just meaningless coups and court intrigue—or, in economic terms, no real development, just *sūq*s full of spices and silks and merchants drinking sherbet. But the imagery persists, and is implicit even in some recent scientific work. I reject it out of hand. In empirical terms, most Islamic regions became more economically complex across our period, not less. One, al-Andalus, for long outpaced Italy, as we shall see in Chapter 5; as for Egypt, it was as much the powerhouse of Mediterranean trade in 1180 as it was in 950/1000. Political crises hit regions, but in this period they were usually recovered from; and there was no difference between Christian- and Muslim-ruled regions in this respect. So, in general, regional economies did not 'fail'. They did, certainly, sometimes lose complexity, but, even if they did not regain it later, what matters to us is to follow the structural explanations for each change, and not either to be triumphalist about upturns or moralistic about downturns. To do that is, simply, bad history.

[33] See, e.g., Wickham, *Framing*, pp. 720–824 (it should be added that early medieval northern Francia, well away from the Mediterranean, matched the Levant).

[34] Ashtor, *A social and economic history*. For a good recent critique of the 'failure' argument, see Palombo, 'Studying trade and local economies'.

In this book, as elsewhere, I aim to be comparative; each region studied here is better understood if it is set against the similar, or differing, experiences of other regions. Without the comparative method, we cannot usefully explain; it is often very easy to falsify single-region explanations, once they are set against those other experiences.[35] Three bodies of evidence are particularly valuable here, as the information they provide is not restricted to a single region, so we can see how much incidence each has from one place to another; they act as controls for such comparisons, in the same way as Weberian ideal types do. The first is the *geniza*, which gives us a guide to the complexities and values of the interpersonal relationships underpinning regional and interregional trade in much of the Islamic Mediterranean across our period, and also to the scale of goods transported; among the regions studied here, it illuminates Egypt, Ifrīqiya, and Sicily in particular, and al-Andalus to a lesser extent. The second is the sets of Venetian and Genoese commercial documents, which begin to be rich near the end of our period; they tell us little about values, but something about relationships and plenty about scale, in Italy and Egypt for both, plus Byzantium for Venice and Sicily for Genoa. Both bodies of evidence are, of course, well-known; the second has been very extensively analysed, the first not so fully, although what has been done on the *geniza* is often remarkable, as we shall see in Chapter 2. For many people now, what 'the' Mediterranean economy is in our period could simply be delineated by a study and a comparison of both sets. But they are problematic for us in one crucial sense: they focus, almost exclusively (the Italian documents above all), on long-distance trade. They tell us much less about internal buying and selling—even if, as we shall see, one important section of the *geniza* material, not so fully studied, does illuminate that for Egypt—which, as I have argued and will argue, is the most important aspect of exchange.

The third type of evidence, however, does tell us directly about internal exchange, and, furthermore, does it for every one of our regions: this is ceramics, the most diagnostic type of archaeological find. The geographical distribution of given pottery types, particularly fine wares and amphorae, inside smaller or larger areas, or whole regions, or several regions; the scale of their production; their availability on different kinds of site, particularly village sites: all these tell us directly about economic relationships, sometimes with considerable granularity. This sort of analysis has long been done for the Roman Empire, and there are people who doubt that it can be done as effectively in our period, but the work carried out for this book persuades me that this doubt is misplaced. On the contrary, these distributions are our best guides to economic relationships, taken as a whole. (In all the regions discussed here, there is only one exception to that

[35] See, for fuller discussion of the issues involved in systematic comparison, and the role of Weberian ideal types in it, Wickham, 'Problems in doing comparative history'.

statement, the central Po plain around Milan: see pp. 594–7 below.) The question of what productions and exchange relationships ceramics are a proxy for, of course, has always to be posed, for they were not in themselves the most important commodity produced anywhere. But, as noted earlier, fine-ware distributions can be matched in enough cases with that of cloth to allow us to be reasonably optimistic that we can use them as a proxy for those of cloth elsewhere. Amphorae, for their part, in the majority of cases tell us most about the wine trade in this period, and anyway always tell us directly about the existence of a trade in foodstuffs. So I shall use ceramics as much as I can in the chapters which follow, with no apology. They are discussed in detail, precisely because this book concentrates on exchange; and also because the necessary syntheses have only been carried out in Byzantium and Sicily, so there is more to explain. In my view, indeed, we cannot usefully study the topic of this book, anywhere, if we do not have in mind what such distributions can tell us. Archaeologists will agree already; it is for me to convince historians as well.

Many of the points I have just raised were already raised in a book I finished nearly twenty years ago, *Framing the early middle ages*, which covered the years 400–800. Since this too is a comparative project, based on many of the same regions, using archaeology as much as documents, and beginning only a century and a half after that book ended (and readers will find flashbacks to 800 at several points in the book), it is worth posing the question of whether we are really dealing here with *Framing 2*. There is a sense in which this is partly true. I had so enjoyed ranging from region to region back then that I was looking forward to doing the same again, and indeed did so with equal enjoyment; this time, however—and this was part of the attraction—while discussing a period of economic upturn, unlike the downturn and sometimes full-on crisis at the end of the Roman Empire. In both cases I wanted to understand it differently, and I was (and am) sure that this was only possible if a properly comparative approach was taken. The structure of this book is, however, quite different—that was thematic; this goes region by region. This book is less wide-ranging, for it only focusses on exchange and its wider economic context and implications; it does not discuss the state, or either aristocratic or peasant society, except insofar as these tell us about wealth, and thus buying power. It is also less wide-ranging in that it only discusses the Mediterranean, and not all of it at that; northern Europe is virtually absent. There are, of course, as was stressed earlier, so many more data for the period 950–1180 than there are for 400–800 that these sorts of restriction were essential anyway. But the ultimate aim here is also quite different. In *Framing* I was, precisely, seeking to demonstrate the usefulness of the comparative method, and to explore what insights it could give us; that's been done now, and does not need a whole book to do it again. Here, rather, I am trying to explain the nature of a major economic change, the 'commercial revolution' of the second Mediterranean trade cycle. And, through that, as we shall see in Chapter 8, I want to use the solutions to this problem as a way into what, for me, is the most crucial economic question of all: how the medieval economy actually worked as a whole, and how its economic logic operated.

And that question is, actually, hard to answer. We have empirical absences which cannot easily be filled out. We know much more about the countryside in the Christian parts of the Mediterranean than we know about most towns—even in Byzantium, where the documentary record is relatively thin, outside the capital at least; in the Islamic lands it is usually the other way round. We do not have, even with the range of recent work, enough data on climatic change—and enough data with sufficient granularity, given the very wide range of microclimates in the Mediterranean, each of them with different sorts of exposure to climatic shifts—to allow us, as yet, to use it as an explanatory factor (although, here at least, I do not doubt that in a decade or so we will be able to say more about it), so climate will be for the most part left out of this book. We do not know how, when, or (sometimes) even if demographic growth started in our period, or how it related to a growth in economic complexity, in any region.[36] We cannot anyway give an accurate figure for the population of any city, let alone of any region; those offered by historians are all invented (that goes for those offered here too, although at least I am explicit about it).[37] We do not know for sure when or how far regional buying power depended on elite, or peasant, demand (although I will systematically confront this issue, at least). We do not know in any detail before 1200 at the earliest what most cities produced for wider markets, and when they started to produce it—even if here, fortunately, there are some exceptions, as we shall see in each substantive chapter. We can only guess at how it was that Egyptian peasants came to be sufficiently aware that there was enough demand for raw flax half the Mediterranean away, in Sicily and Tunisia, that it was not only worthwhile but (more vital still) safe to begin to specialize in flax cultivation. And so on. There are big gaps here, which can only be filled by guesswork.

But even if we hypothesize constructively, and then put together what we have, we face difficulties. Much of the historiography has got the basic structures of economic processes wrong for our period, and for the pre-capitalist period as a whole. It tends, still today, to see pre-capitalist (or pre-industrial, or just 'premodern') economies as basically primitive, 'backward', as they are sometimes described, unable to take advantage of the technological breakthroughs that presented themselves; or else—or, sometimes, as well as—simply potentially

[36] Most people assume that demographic growth, other things being equal, is the underpinning for commercialization, and so do I, as a starting point for research at least; but Masschaele, 'Economic take-off and the rise of markets', interestingly argues the opposite for north-west Europe. The uncertainties in our data mean that I will not always stress demography in this book, but at least we must recognize that there is normally a dialectical relationship between demographic and economic growth.

[37] The only exception is Pisa, shortly after the end of our period: see Salvatori, *La popolazione pisana*.

modern societies, running by modern economic rules, but just undermined or blocked by institutional failures, or sometimes furthered by their efficiencies, as in much New Institutional Economic history.[38] Different regions get brownie points for being more *like* modern societies; the most active economies of the pre-capitalist world get seen as handing the torch on, one to another, as each in turn 'failed', until it finally ended up in its natural home, seventeenth- or eighteenth-century England, ready for industrial society to be born. Writers here never consider properly the proposition that, in any feudal economy, such as those of the whole of central medieval Eurasia, except the remotest regions where permanent elites did not exist, economic rules for exchange and development might be differently constructed, and might not work like capitalist ones at all. It will here be argued that they were indeed differently constructed, and did indeed not work like capitalist ones.

In the empirical chapters that follow, I shall, therefore, not make any arguments which depend on assumptions about how economies work which assimilate them to those of the modern world, except the simplest ones, such as the relationship between supply, demand, and price—a relationship which was anyway demonstrably known about and acted on in our period, as the *geniza* amply shows.[39] But I will, in the last chapter of the book, use the data set out here as a springboard for considering, briefly, how better to understand the basic workings of the Mediterranean economy, and, more generally, the feudal economy as a whole.

A Note on Language

In the chapters that follow, I use a variety of translation and transliteration conventions, which are not exactly inconsistent, but which point in different directions.

I normally use the modern form for place names, not any medieval name, if any modern name exists. The exception is the chapter on Byzantium, where, to be consistent across many modern countries and their differing national languages, I privilege medieval place names (with modern ones in brackets) and then use them by preference in the text, except when discussing the archaeology; I also anglicize some well-known place names, such as Constantinople, Corinth, Nicaea, and Cappadocia. In Egypt, I anglicize only Cairo, Alexandria, Damietta, and Luxor. In Syria and Palestine, not discussed in detail in this book, I also anglicize an array of major towns, such as Jerusalem, Damascus, and Acre. In

[38] See for example Greif, *Institutions*, nominally based in our period in large part; for empirical problems with that book, see, pp. 128–9, 540, 543 below. For all this, see, already, Wickham, 'How did the feudal economy work?'; I use some sentences from the article in this paragraph.

[39] Goitein, *MS*, 1, pp. 217–29.

Tunisia, Algeria and Morocco, however, where a Francophone tradition is so strong, I use modern French spellings for place names, which are very generally used in the countries concerned, so Kairouan not Qayrawān, Sousse not Sūsa. In what is now Portugal, Spain, and Italy, I use the normal run of anglicizations of major cities like Lisbon, Seville, Milan, Genoa, and Rome.

In my chapters on Islamic lands, for both place names and personal names, my transliterations are all into the standard UK conventions for Classical Arabic, although modern Arabic dialects have some quite different pronunciations, which matter for place names—Jīza, a district capital across the Nile from Cairo, is generally called Giza today, for example. I do not use the short transliterations of Arabic words, so Abū'l-Khayr is always Abū al-Khayr here; I also do not assimilate the 'al-' before Arabic sun letters, so an-Naṣir is always al-Naṣir here; and I omit *hamza*s at the start of Arabic words. I use Arabic plurals very rarely, as they are often not easy for outsiders to relate to the singular; I usually add, as in this paragraph, a roman-typeface 's' to an italic Arabic singular. I leave out 'al-' at the start of place names (except al-Andalus, which is called this by everyone), but not at the start of *nisba*s or *laqab*s in personal names, such as al-Idrīsī. Outside the modern Arabic-speaking lands, I keep Arabic for personal names in al-Andalus, and for Muslims in Sicily, but in mainland Italy and Norman-period Sicily I use Italian forms for the names of everyone else except emperors, kings, and popes, plus Norman/French incomers.

For personal names of Greek-speakers in our period, I use English, not Greek, for first names when there is an English equivalent, and Greek for surnames; so John Komnenos, not Iōannēs Komnēnos (or John Comnenus: see below). In transliterations of Greek, kappa is k not c, upsilon is y not u except in diphthongs, and beta is b not v (except in modern place names in Greece); eta and omega are marked with macrons only in direct quotations from Greek. Latinisms, which seem to me weird, are systematically avoided except in book titles.

2
Egypt

2.1 Introduction

Egypt was where most people who were commercially active on the Mediterranean Sea in our period went to, sooner or later. It was far more central for maritime exchange than that exchange was for Egypt itself. That is one major reason why we have to start here; it was the determining region for Mediterranean trade. A second and, in fact, more important reason is that its internal economy had long been, and remained, more developed than that of any other region studied here, and is thus a point of reference for all the others. The different regions of the Mediterranean had different roles in the long eleventh century. As we will see in later chapters, Sicily and to an extent North Africa/Ifrīqiya were the hinges of Mediterranean exchange, linking most of the actors; al-Andalus and Byzantium, the major states in the northern Mediterranean, were economically strong but a bit more cut off from the main routes; later, the ports of north-central Italy were after *c.*1130 the new brash players, punching above their weight for a long time. But Egypt was the powerhouse. At least one of the other regions was necessary for an interregional Mediterranean economic network to develop—that is to say, without their participation, exchange would have been restricted to single regions, as proposed in Chapter 1—but the solidity of Egyptian production and demand were such that without Egypt there could hardly have been a Mediterranean-wide network of any type. Egypt had, then, not the most typical economy in the eleventh-century Mediterranean, but the most complex and the most stable one; and also, in most ways, the best-documented. The complexity of the Egyptian economy had been an abiding feature of Mediterranean history, already in the classical world and indeed well before; but in our period, and for some time later, it was even more important for the structuring of Mediterranean exchange than it had been in Roman times. As for best-documented, whereas in some regions our estimations of how economic structures worked are to an extent conjecture, here they are often fairly certain. And Egyptian documentation can be fascinating in itself, as we shall see.

There are, however, issues with the words 'complex' and 'stable', as also with 'best-documented'. They are adjectives which can apply to many periods of Egyptian history, and indeed, for the late Roman Empire and the centuries up to

The Donkey and the Boat. Chris Wickham, Oxford University Press. © Chris Wickham 2023.
DOI: 10.1093/oso/9780198856481.003.0002

800, I have used them and analogues before.[1] In the period we are looking at in this book, 950–1180, they have to be nuanced, and a few centuries later they would have to be nuanced further. The issue of complexity will recur throughout this chapter. Stability we will come to in a moment. But we need to look at the documentation first; for we cannot understand what can be done with Egyptian evidence until we understand its unusually complicated nature. As in earlier periods of Egyptian history, we have very large numbers of legal documents, accounts, and (above all) private letters surviving, largely by chance, in the dry air of the Nile valley. By now they are nearly always on paper (paper almost totally replaced papyrus in the early tenth century; see p. 75 below), which is, or can be, a cheap medium. That was convenient; and Egyptians of this period made intense use of the convenience, writing about everything they chose, and sometimes about very small-scale and temporary issues. Very often, such issues concerned the administration of local tax-raising, or patron–client relations, or else—and especially—details of buying and selling, at short or long distance. We can gain a genuinely large amount of information from them about daily economic transactions and their difficulties; and people wrote letters to each other (or paid to have them written) about such transactions all the time, as we can further tell from the frequent reference in those which survive to other letters that either have or have not arrived.

There are some 150,000 such texts for the whole Egyptian middle ages in Arabic and written in Arabic script, of which possibly a quarter come from our period. Under 9,000 of them have been published, however, and for the tenth to twelfth centuries the figure is around 1,300. This makes anything said on the basis of them provisional, even if it will take many decades, at the most optimistic assessment, to make obsolete the patterns set out here. In addition there are up to 40,000 similar texts, beginning in the late tenth century and largely coming from our period, in Hebrew script and a dialect of Arabic commonly called 'Judaeo-Arabic' (although, in fact, it is more or less the quotidian, sometimes colloquial, written Egyptian Arabic of the period, plus some Hebrew loanwords); of these, over 4,000, a more representative proportion, have been published, and the others have mostly at least been looked at.[2] The Hebrew-script letters and documents

[1] See Wickham, *Framing*, p. 23, as also later in that book. For 'complex', see also Chapter 1, n. 25 above. I am grateful to Alison Gascoigne and Stefanie Schmidt for critiques of some or all of this chapter, and to Lorenzo Bondioli, David Bramoullé, Alison Gascoigne, Roland-Pierre Gayraud, Jessica Goldberg, Eve Krakowski, Marie Legendre, Yossi Rapoport, Marina Rustow, and Gregory Williams for answering questions and sending as yet unpublished work; see further n. 199 below, for my thanks for help with the *geniza*. I also gained much from the expert audience participation in seminars on some of the material from this chapter which I gave virtually in Princeton in December 2020.

[2] For the overall figures, which are very rough for the Arabic-script materials in particular (since most of them have barely even been opened, so cannot be ascribed exact dates), see http://www.apd.gwi.uni-muenchen.de:8080/apd/project1c.jsp; Rustow, *The lost archive*, pp. 7, 453. For publications, see the lists in the Arabic Papyrology Database [henceforth APD] and the Princeton Geniza Project [henceforth PGP]; I shall, throughout, use the abbreviations for document citations which link directly

were found in Fusṭāṭ, the largest city and original capital of Islamic Egypt, which was eventually (after our period) eclipsed and absorbed by its newer neighbour, Qāhira (Cairo), founded as a new capital outside the older city for the first Fāṭimid caliph of Egypt in 969. The texts survived in the *geniza* of what is now called the Ben Ezra synagogue—that is to say, the attic where no longer useful written texts were thrown by pious Jews of the Palestinian community, one of Fusṭāṭ's three main Jewish communities, since writing, almost always mentioning God somewhere, was held to be sacred and could not be destroyed. (The letters and documents are, in fact, only a small proportion of the *geniza* collection, which also contains huge numbers of religious writings, but the latter are not our concern here.)

Of these, the *geniza* texts are by far the best-known, and also the best-studied. This major single collection of letters and documents has been called an anti-archive, for an archive is dedicated to the preservation of still relevant texts, which a *geniza* precisely is not; but it is an unusually coherent example of one. The same names crop up again and again, particularly in our period, and it is fairly clear that the papers of some of the most significant merchants of this community, particularly Yūsuf Ibn ʿAwkal (d. *c.*1040) and Nahray b. Nissīm (d. 1097/8), were thrown away as sets. Its importance became apparent in the 1880s, when the synagogue was scheduled for rebuilding; the story of how, after sectors of it were dispersed casually to a dozen collections, three-quarters of it were bought up by Cambridge University in the 1890s, has often been told.[3] That importance became visible to the world, as we saw in Chapter 1, above all thanks to the work of Shelomo Goitein (d. 1985), whose five-volume masterpiece, *A Mediterranean society*, began to be published in 1967. Building on that, Moshe Gil published most of the materials for the merchant community up to 1100, some 1,500 texts, with translations into modern Hebrew; and there are now three major online databases of transcriptions and/or high-quality digital photographs, associated with Princeton University, the Friedberg Jewish Manuscript Society of Toronto and Jerusalem, and Cambridge University Library itself.[4] Princeton is now the centre

to those databases—the editions for APD, the document numbers for PGP. In the latter case, the main editions of relevance to this book are by Moshe Gil, *Erets-Yishra'el* and *Be-malkhut Yishmaʿel* [henceforth Gil P and Gil K], with Hebrew translations; others will be cited in short title. A full list of editions of *geniza* documents published before 2019 can be found in *Jewish history*, 32 (2019), pp. 567–75. For the *geniza*, as many texts again have been catalogued in preliminary form and await full transcription—I thank Marina Rustow for access to the database. There are only a few texts in Hebrew, which was essentially a religious language in Egypt; it was used by Jewish immigrants, particularly from Europe, and in some very solemn writings. For Arabic and Judaeo-Arabic, see, e.g., Kaplony, 'Scribal traditions in documentary Arabic'; Wagner, 'Register and layout in epistolary Judeo-Arabic'.

[3] e.g. Goitein, *MS*, 1, pp. 1–6; Jefferson, 'The Cairo Genizah unearthed'; Goldberg, *Trade and institutions*, pp. 5–8; Reif, *A Jewish archive*. Note that a small 'new' *geniza* has also been found in Fusṭāṭ-Cairo, from one of the capital's other Jewish communities, but it is as yet inaccessible to scholars: for brief descriptions, see Cohen, 'Geniza for Islamicists', pp. 139–41; Zinger, 'Finding a fragment', p. 306.

[4] Respectively, PGP at https://genizalab.princeton.edu/pgp-database; the Friedberg Genizah Project at http://fjms.genizah.org/; and the Cambridge Digital Library at https://cudl.lib.cam.ac.uk/.

for documentary *geniza* scholarship—Goitein was actually at the Institute for Advanced Studies there, but the university has taken over the *geniza* focus, under Abraham Udovitch, Mark Cohen, and now Marina Rustow. Jessica Goldberg's 2012 *Trade and institutions in the medieval Mediterranean*, which joins Goitein's *A Mediterranean society* as the most significant two works as yet written on the whole topic of this book, although a Columbia thesis initially, was written under the strong influence of Udovitch and Cohen. The scholars associated with this tradition have been called the 'Princeton school' by Cohen, and although it is by no means a unitary group, it has made up a critical mass which ensures that the work of members of that loose community have worked to uniformly high standards.[5] It is fair to say, however, that the *geniza* texts which deal with the Mediterranean world are better studied for the eleventh century than for the twelfth; in the twelfth century, many of the major Fusṭāṭī merchants went into the spice trade connecting India to Egypt, and that has become the focus of research as a result, a focus again pioneered by Goitein. We do not have many systematic publications or analyses of *geniza* material for Egypt itself or the rest of the Mediterranean after 1100, except insofar as Mediterranean commerce was also carried out (as it often was) by India traders.[6] My conclusions for Egypt taken from this material will be more cautious for the twelfth century than the eleventh as a result.

The Arabic-script texts have had less study. They make up a less coherent group, as they were mostly bought in Cairo markets, across much the same period as the *geniza* texts, usually, however, from unknown locations—they were found buried in many places in the Nile valley (not the Delta, where the ground is wetter), and were largely found in rubbish heaps by diggers of fertilizer (*sibākh*), who discovered eventually that they could make more money selling papyrus and paper with writing on to academics than they could selling fertilizer to farmers. They are now scattered across more locations as a result (one of them, unlike for the Ben Ezra *geniza* texts, is Cairo itself), although Vienna has the largest collection by far. The reason for their lack of study—and lack of publication, particularly in the case of the Vienna collections—is essentially that they seemed less interesting to classically trained scholars than did the equivalent texts in Ancient Egyptian (including its latest form, Coptic) and Greek, the latter of which also had the advantage of being dominated by some very large single collections that were

[5] See the Bibliography for the authors cited in the text; there is also a strong tradition of sociocultural history based on the *geniza*, which I have not used here. The fundamental introduction to the study of the documentary *geniza* is now the special issue of *Jewish history*, 32, 2–4 (2019), ed. Goldberg and Krakowski. For the concept of the 'Princeton school', see, e.g., Cohen, 'Geniza for Islamicists', pp. 132–4, and, more critically, Ackerman-Lieberman, *The business of identity*, pp. 1–45; its coherence is doubted in Frenkel's review of the latter in *Journal of the American oriental society* 136 (2016), pp. 640–3. See Goldberg, 'On reading Goitein's *A Mediterranean Society*', for her own clear-eyed assessment of Goitein's work.

[6] See esp. Goitein and Friedman, *India traders* and *India book* IV/B; Margariti, *Aden*; Lambourn, *Abraham's luggage*. One exception is Frenkel, *Ha-Ohavim*, for Alexandria.

discovered and bought locally, such as Oxyrhynchos (modern Bahnasā) and Aphroditē or Aphroditō (modern Kōm Ishqāw).[7] There has been a tradition of important editors for the Arabic texts too, including, for our period, Adolf Grohmann, Geoffrey Khan, and Werner Diem, but there are few syntheses. Fortunately, the Arabic Papyrology Database (APD), run out of the University of Munich, matches the *geniza* databases in quality, and is becoming a transformative research tool as ever-higher proportions of the published material are imported into it.[8] Syntheses are indeed now possible, and I will attempt a partial one here. Whereas the *geniza* tells us most about Fusṭāṭ-Cairo and parts of the Delta, the Arabic-script texts—plus a very small handful of documents and letters in Coptic, which was losing ground fast after 900 as a secular written language[9]—tell us more about Middle Egypt, in particular the Nile valley between Cairo and Ashmūnayn, 280 kilometres south of the capital, and the Fayyūm oasis just west of the Nile, halfway along that stretch. The Arabic-script documentation, too, tells us less about the twelfth century than the eleventh or tenth. As yet, it is not clear whether this is really because of absence of survival or simply the result of a lack of scholarly interest among editors; but it may be that the millennia-long availability of documentation from the Nile valley sites, which starts as early as the fifteenth century BC, lessens rapidly at the end of the eleventh century AD and never fully revives after that. Either way, the absence of published texts again means that my conclusions for the period after 1100 will be more cautious.

One of the problems about this dual origin for Egyptian documentation in our period is that scholarship on the one very seldom deals with the material from the other. In many cases, documents with Arabic script on one side and Hebrew script on the other have even been published separately, and the same is sometimes true for Coptic and Arabic. The historiography based on the *geniza* often debates the degree to which the Jewish merchant community of Fusṭāṭ was representative of merchant communities of other religions (see pp. 119–22 below), but it very seldom cites the evidence in Arabic script to test this, except sometimes Khan's edition of documents in Arabic from the *geniza* itself; conversely, the historiography based on the Arabic-script evidence must, I conclude, take for granted the lack of relevance of the *geniza* material, as the latter is for the most part only cited in discussions of philology.[10] This is a mistake; the two must be treated in the same

[7] See esp. P.Oxy. I and XVI, and P.Lond. V with P.Cair.Masp., respectively. (For abbreviations of Greek documentary editions, see Oates and Willis, *Checklist*, https://papyri.info/docs/checklist.)

[8] Grohmann edited many series, of which the largest is P.Cair.Arab.; for Khan, esp. P.GenizahCambr.; for Diem, the most active recent editor, the largest series is P.Vind.Arab. Diem has published corrections of Grohmann's work, which was pioneering but also, for that reason, not always error-free, esp. in 'Philologisches zu arabischen Dokumenten'; critiques of his own work can also be found, by Yūsuf Rāġib, in *Bulletin critique des Annales islamologiques*, 14 (1998), pp. 171–9; 15 (1999), pp. 195–7; 16 (2000), pp. 185–6.

[9] Richter, *Rechtssemantik*, pp. 155–65, and Richter, 'Coptic papyri', pp. 417–19, give good guides.

[10] Exceptions include Almbladh, 'The letters'; Rustow, *The lost archive*; Bondioli, *Peasants, merchants, and caliphs*.

terms. There are clear differences in focus between the two—the *geniza* tells us far more about Fusṭāṭ-Cairo and about interregional trade (this, indeed, is well known), and conversely far less about the Nile valley, agriculture, and the land tax, than the Arabic-script texts do, but in my view this is a plus: it allows us to build up a complementary picture of a complex economy. We cannot do without both together if we want to understand Egypt as a whole.

The wealth of Egyptian evidence lies here, and it has limits. It is easy to say in a late Roman context that Egyptian material outweighs in quantity and breadth that of all other documentary evidence for the empire put together; that is not quite true of the Mediterranean in the long eleventh century. Italian legal documents (mostly published up to 1100 at least, and often later) are, in particular, well over ten times as numerous as those for Egypt, and do not, unlike Egyptian material, drop back after 1100 (indeed, they rapidly increase). They include almost no private letters before 1100[11]—Egypt remains unique here, except insofar as the *geniza* tells us about North Africa and Sicily as well, as we shall see in Chapter 3—and they are overwhelmingly land documents, not commercial texts, which are hardly visible in Italy, with the single exception of Venice, before the notarial registers of Genoa start in the 1150s. But this conversely means that one can say a lot more about estate management and landed wealth for Italy than for Egypt, which is important in an economy that was overwhelmingly agrarian, as all economies in our period were.[12] They are also dated—Egyptian letters rarely are—which adds to their exactness of reference. The Italian collections are, furthermore, all from archives, not the anti-archives which dominate in Egypt (given that the Arabic-script material seems have been largely thrown away, just as was that in Hebrew script); this brought weaknesses, as archive selectors had interests which are not ours, but it at least kept collections relatively coherent. It is true that Italy is effectively unparalleled in these respects anywhere in the Mediterranean before 1200; only Catalonia matches it in its surviving documentary density. All the same, it points up that there are things which we simply cannot say about Egypt. So does archaeology, which is relatively scanty for Egypt in our period, particularly for rural areas, so that the evidence which we would need to fully develop Mediterranean comparisons cannot mostly be deployed here as yet. I will, all the same, here, as in later chapters, use all the archaeology I can.

[11] Up to 1100, the eighteen originals (mostly formal appeals or part of ecclesiastical and aristocratic politics) are collected in Petrucci et al., *Lettere originali*, 1. I exclude papal letters, which are part of high politics, and the letter collections, by now normally ecclesiastical, which were compiled for publication. But Italy, it is worth adding, is less well provided with elite letter collections than is Byzantium, where there are many substantial sets. The latter were generally compiled for publication as well, and are competitive in their high-flown prose; they are equally far from the merchants' letters of Egypt. But they are sufficiently numerous that we can get more out of them for the purposes of this book: see Chapter 4 below.

[12] Cammarosano, *Italia medievale*, pp. 49–88. See Chapter 6 below.

The difficulties with these sets of evidence, and their lack of linkage, have one unwelcome spin-off. There is no study of the Egyptian economy in our period, nor, still less, any debates about it—except, as in all Islamic regions, one about when Egypt lost the head start over European regions which it had had in earlier centuries—a debate which is here even more implicit than usual, and so harder to grasp. (But as a pointer towards later sections of this chapter, I would myself propose that Egypt remained the most complex economy in the Mediterranean until the Black Death.) In all the other substantive chapters of this book, I shall set out the main historiographical framings for current understandings of the economy of each of my regions and how they developed, so as to make their arguments sufficiently clear in their own terms, and so as to allow the criticisms and nuances I seek to make to be put in a proper context. But for Egypt, apart from the high-quality studies of the economic world of the *geniza* merchants, we have no such equivalent. Eliyahu Ashtor devotes a few pages to a general survey of the economy of Fāṭimid Egypt, with his usual mix of suggestive detail and unconvincing generalization. For the rest, we have good accounts of Fusṭāṭ and Alexandria, thanks to the *geniza*; monographic studies of sugar and, to an extent, flax; plus several accounts of the tax system, some of them good, and of landed property, some of them problematic.[13] We cannot build up a coherent picture of Egypt's economy from these. There is no synthesis of what archaeology already tells us about internal production and exchange; nor about what the Arabic-script documents tell us. And in both cases, that is a substantial amount, even if the evidence from each will expand massively in the future. So, unlike in later chapters, much of what follows will consist of the creation of a synthesis for the first time, with all the strengths and weaknesses which this involves. It will, here, be for others to criticize and nuance.

Egypt has narrative sources which discuss our period too; these will be used much less in this chapter. This is above all because they are mostly very late (they tend to be from the Mamlūk period, 1250–1517) and because they focus almost exclusively on a Fusṭāṭ-centred politics. Historians tend to justify using them (particularly the voluminous works of al-Maqrīzī, d. 1442) because they claim in many cases to be based on earlier sources. How far this is really true can seldom be checked; and I am anyway much more cautious about believing such narratives than many historians of Egypt seem to be. But the issue is scarcely relevant to us, for the kinds of things this book is about are not mentioned more than fleetingly even by contemporary histories, when we have them—as in the cases of Yaḥyā al-Anṭakī and the surviving sections of al-Musabbiḥī, both written in the

[13] Ashtor, *A social and economic history*, pp. 191–208; see pp. 40–7, 39, below for Fusṭāṭ and Alexandria; pp. 73–6, 93–108, for sugar and flax. For taxation, two important recent discussions are Bramoullé, *Les Fatimides et la mer*, and Bondioli, *Peasants, merchants, and caliphs*, which has a much wider economic focus as well; for landed property, see my own critical discussion, 'The power of property'.

1020s–1030s.[14] (We might well have used the largely Egypt-based *Thousand and one nights*, which was available in some form in Fusṭāṭ by the twelfth century, as a *geniza* reference shows; but, sadly, all the versions we have, except for fragments, come from the Mamlūk period or even later.[15]) Rather more relevant are the Arab geographers, whose succinct accounts of individual Egyptian cities (as also, as we shall see, cities elsewhere in the Islamic world) tell us about agricultural and occasionally artisanal products; there were several of these writing in the tenth to twelfth centuries. They often copied each other, and some were written by people who never went to Egypt at all, but they do have useful material for an economic history. I would count in that number Ibn Bassām, whose description of his native city Tinnīs, written in the 1020s–1040s, although enthusiastically written up, gives us a sense of what a truly active town could look like.[16] But our documentary sources outweigh anything found in narratives of this kind. They are immediate, often urgent; they throw us into the middle of things; they may be hard to interpret (and doubtless often told lies, as any letter writer does), and they were certainly in most cases mediated by scribes and framed by flowery conventions,[17] but they take us as close as any text can to the real actors of history, the men and women of high, low, or (as usually in these texts) middling rank who made up the whole population of Egypt apart from the trivial percentage of political leaders.

* * *

Let us now come back to the word 'stable'. In what sense was Egypt stable, in its political system or its economy? The first point is that Egypt was politically solid in at least one crucial respect: for two centuries, between 969 and 1171, that is to say, for nearly our whole period, it was ruled by a single dynasty, the Fāṭimids, the longest-lasting Shīʿī rulers of any part of the medieval Islamic world, who contentiously claimed the title of caliph and kept it, first (from 909/10) in North Africa and then at Cairo, their new political capital, for a quarter of a millennium; Cairo was indeed, for the first century of its existence, at the centre of a political system stretching from North Africa and Sicily to southern Syria and into the Arabian

[14] We find relatively little about production and exchange even in al-Maqrīzī, *Khiṭaṭ*, trans. Bouriant and Casanova, and al-Maqrīzī, *Ighāthat*, trans. Allouche, which are not by any means only narratives (and the latter is very interested in famines and money). For Yaḥyā al-Anṭakī and al-Musabbiḥī, see *Tārīkh al-Anṭakī*, trans. Pirone, and *Akhbār Miṣr*, ed. Sayyid et al., respectively. Al-Maqrīzī's relatively exact use of Ibn al-Ma'mūn's history of his father's early career and wazirate in the early twelfth century is discussed by Bauden, 'Maqriziana XII', but this too was very much a court-centred text. So were the sources of Ibn al-Furāt's equally careful *Ta'rīkh al-duwal*, rehabilitated by Bora, *Writing history*.

[15] Irwin, *The Arabian nights*, pp. 48–62. *Geniza*: Goitein, 'The oldest documentary evidence'.

[16] The most useful geographers are al-Muqaddasī, *Aḥsan al-taqāsīm*, trans. Miquel (a preferable translation to the English trans. used in other chapters of this book, but restricted to the Egypt section of the text); Ibn Ḥawqal, *Kītāb ṣūrat al-arḍ*, trans. Kramers and Wiet; al-Idrīsī, *Nuzhat al-mushtāq*, trans. Jaubert and Nef; and the Persian traveller's account, *Nāṣer-e Khosraw's book of travels*, trans. Thackston. Others will be cited as relevant. Ibn Bassām: see n. 193 below.

[17] For some of the conventions, see Almbladh, 'The letters'; and for their syntactic structure, see Grob, *Documentary Arabic private and business letters*, pp. 23–83.

peninsula. This did not, however, prevent political crisis or civil war. The caliphate survived the eclipse of the power of the caliphs themselves after the unexplained disappearance of the controversial al-Ḥākim in 1021, and a succession of capable ruling *wāzir*s followed with little break to 1058, but then central government went into crisis. By 1067, rival claimants to power were in open war, and there followed at least five years of *al-shiddat al-ʿuẓmā*, 'the great calamity', in which blockades of the capital, made worse by low Nile floods and thus bad harvests, caused famine in Fusṭāṭ. The western provinces of the caliphate moved out of the Fāṭimid orbit in the mid-eleventh century too. Order was restored by two generations of military strongmen, Badr al-Jamālī (ruling 1074–94) and his son al-Afḍal (1094–1121), but after 1125 governmental stability was inconsistent at best, and (mostly military) leaders succeeded each other, usually by coup, for the final half-century of Fāṭimid rule. This culminated in invasion by the Frankish king of Jerusalem in 1168–9, the burning of part of Fusṭāṭ, and the takeover by Ṣalāḥ al-Dīn, that is, Saladin. Saladin was the caliphate's last *wāzir* and also its destroyer, for he replaced the dying caliph al-ʿĀḍid with his own direct rule in 1171, as the first member of the Ayyūbid dynasty, which ruled Egypt to 1250.[18]

This can be painted as a story of decline and worse. As stressed in Chapter 1, there is a whole historiographical tradition which has for long focussed on the theme of 'decline' in every Islamic region, as the later medieval centuries sadly fail, in the eyes of modern observers, to live up to the potential of the great days of the early ʿAbbāsid caliphs in ninth-century Baghdad. Ashtor, an influential commentator, although, as said earlier, unreliable in great part, certainly saw the second Fāṭimid century as the beginning of that 'decline' in Egypt.[19] But there were few—perhaps no—medieval polities outside China which maintained any form of stability for two-hundred-year stretches: perennial trouble was not just common but normal, everywhere. (Nor are there many today, for that matter; a rough count of countries in the world with continuous stable government and unbroken full autonomy since 1800 comes to just two, Sweden and Britain.) In Fāṭimid Egypt, in fact, only the years around 1070 and the 1160s were periods of more than short-lasting disturbance. The rest of the time, trouble was mostly played out inside the walls of the Fāṭimid palace in Cairo—plus outside the boundaries of Egypt itself, as the caliphate, which in the 990s stretched from the Algerian highlands to Damascus, had become by the end of the eleventh century restricted to the Nile valley, plus, at least nominally, Yemen. And each of the periods of crisis can be scaled down. Our evidence for both is focussed above all on Fusṭāṭ-Cairo itself,

[18] Brett, *The Fatimid empire*, is a good survey.

[19] Ashtor, *A social and economic history*, pp. 207–8, 238–9; Ashtor, 'Débat sur l'évolution', pp. 105–6. A recent version of this sort of argument is Ellenblum, *The collapse of the eastern Mediterranean*, which at least argues for climate change rather than institutional or moral failures, but which fails to show how climate crisis actually led to institutional or economic 'collapse' on any long-term basis: see the far more nuanced Preiser-Kapeller, 'A collapse of the eastern Mediterranean?'.

not on the rest of Egypt, where, in the late 1060s, the supposed moment of the 'great calamity', documents and letters show almost no visible trauma; that for the capital in the same period is anyway highly coloured to an extreme and mostly not believable. The so-called destruction of Fusṭāṭ in 1168 also has no back-up in our extensive *geniza* documentation for the city.[20]

It would be difficult even for the most optimistic person not to recognize that the Fāṭimid Caliphate was badly governed for long stretches, especially in the 1010s (under al-Ḥākim), the 1060s, and off and on after 1125. All the same, Egypt remained a single political unit, the only major Mediterranean region which did so across the long eleventh century, as we shall see in later chapters. And it also remained a tightly governed one, with an infrastructure for taxation which never let up, as we shall see in a moment. Injustice regularly prevailed in the localities, but that was a normal part of medieval (as also ancient, and indeed modern) stable government; it was anyway, so to speak, regular injustice, not chaos. And coinage was stable throughout our period, with a bimetallic currency, a gold dinar and a silver dirham/half-dirham; the gold, at least, remained of high quality throughout.[21]

There was a dialectic between the stability of the state and that of the economy: each reinforced the other. The economy remained prosperous throughout the Fāṭimid period—indeed, visibly expanding in many economic arenas, not least textiles. No political crisis seems to have affected this, and this fact in itself softened the problems associated with such crises. The danger of low Nile floods, a permanent potential threat to food production (and, above all, the supply to the capital), was certainly present, but can only occasionally be located in our documentary sources. The Nile anyway helped as well, for very few communities in Egypt were situated more than a day's donkey ride from it. The Nile held the country together, as it has for almost all of five millennia, simply because it was such an obvious route, for bulk goods and individual voyages alike. (The Nile was never easy to navigate; it required skill to spot and avoid the moving shoals, and both flood times and low water were dangerous.[22] But as long as you had experienced shipmen, it was always there.) The rest of this chapter will discuss how the economy worked in more detail; but Egypt can indeed be taken, in this period, as in earlier periods, as a case study for what a stable and complex economy could look like.

The iron chain connecting the stability of the economy with that of the state was the tax system. Egypt had always been taxed, and a land tax was standard

[20] For the argument that the chaos of the years around 1070 is exaggerated, see Wickham, 'The power of property', pp. 88–9. For 1168, see n. 43 below.

[21] Injustice: see, for example, P.Vind.Arab. III 23, or, earlier, CPR XVI 11 (9th century). For tight government (and its underpinning, regular archiving), see most recently Rustow, *The lost archive*, pp. 267–95, 321–77, and *passim*. For coinage, see n. 289 below.

[22] Goitein, *MS*, 1, pp. 296–9; Cooper, *The medieval Nile*, pp. 103–50.

from Pharaonic times. Under the Romans it was heavy; it was, however, run by local landowning elites, through city councils of relatively autonomous cities, and control over it was thus part of the elements which went towards the construction of not only imperial but also local power. This pattern continued in the early Arab period, well into the eighth century; unlike the Romans, the Umayyad government used the land tax—which remained high—and a poll tax to fund an Arab army based in their capital at Fusṭāṭ rather than sending resources abroad, but tax-raising remained locally controlled. Growing centralization, with centrally appointed financial administrators (*ʿāmil*s) replacing local elites, was matched by serious tax revolts in Egypt, particularly in and after the ʿAbbāsid Revolution of 749–50, first of Christians and then of Muslims as well, until Caliph al-Mamʾūn crushed the great uprising of the 810s–820s in 832.[23] For a generation after that, more tax went to Baghdad, partially bypassing Fusṭāṭ, but that was reversed when Aḥmad ibn Ṭūlūn, the new Turkish governor of Egypt in 868, was able to establish effective political and fiscal autonomy for his government, thanks to the ʿAbbāsid civil war of the 860s. His family, the Ṭūlūnids, ruled independently until 905, and were soon followed by a new sequence of autonomous governors, the Ikhshīdids, in 935–68; although some tax still went to the caliphs into the 960s, Egypt had been for the most part autonomous for a century by the time that the Fāṭimids took over in 969 and made Cairo their new capital and fiscal centre. The tax system, based above all on the land tax, *kharāj* (assessed in money, but payable either in cash—gold dinars and silver dirhams—or in kind), remained constant and very centrally controlled across these regime changes, all the same; the only major novelty was that, more and more, it was entrusted to tax farmers, *ḍāmin*s, who guaranteed the payment of fixed sums to district-based *ʿāmil*s and to the state in general, for the territory which they had leased as a tax concession (*ḍamān*), but could take what profits they could manage to get through the collection of taxation on the ground. From the 1070s, a higher level of tax farmer could also be army men, generally called *muqṭāʿ*s, taking taxation on their concession (here called *iqṭāʿ*) in lieu of pay, often again aided on the ground by local *ḍāmin*s; we find both civilian and military tax farmers from now on, through the twelfth century, although Saladin in the 1170s greatly extended a reliance on *iqṭāʿ*s as the basic form of military pay—and by now *muqṭāʿ*s tended to keep all the tax on their concessions.[24]

[23] See Wickham, *Framing*, pp. 62–72, 130–44 for general Roman and post-Roman bibliography up to 2005. After 640, Simonsen, *Studies in the genesis*; Morimoto, *The fiscal administration* (his pp. 145–72, notwithstanding problems, is still the best analysis of the tax revolts); Frantz-Murphy, *Arabic agricultural leases*; and esp. Sijpesteijn, *Shaping a Muslim state*, esp. pp. 85–111, 172–216. There were still some revolts in Egypt into the 860s: see Gordon, 'Ibn Ṭūlūn's pacification campaign', and see in general Gordon, *Ahmad ibn Tulun*, for the period 868–84.

[24] See Frantz-Murphy, *Arabic agricultural leases*, for lists and editions of tax-farming concessions; Frantz-Murphy, *The agrarian administration*, pp. 45–79, for continued state control; Sijpesteijn, 'Profit following responsibility'; Brett, 'The origins'; Wickham, 'The power of property', pp. 83, 90–2. Tax

That shift to military tax farmers, which continued throughout the rest of the middle ages, was labelled 'feudalism' in the 1930s by Abraham Poliak. The label has stuck in some historiography, even though the great analyst of *iqṭā*'s, Claude Cahen, always rejected the term as misleading in the Egyptian context—and so do I; it had nothing in common with western military feudalism, as Cahen made clear, and I myself will use the word in very different ways (see p. 673 below).[25] In reality, the experience of taxpaying by peasants probably did not change much across the shifts towards tax farming. It is interesting that, after tax farming came in, rural tax revolts ended for many centuries (we do not have significant record of them again until the thirteenth century);[26] a return to what was probably very often a local involvement in tax collection may have mediated the experience sufficiently to make it tolerable, for there is certainly no evidence, in any period, of taxation actually lessening significantly, unless for short periods in times of state crisis. (See pp. 66–8, below for the difficult issue of how heavy it actually was in our period.) Egyptian land taxation was, all the same, unusually controlling by now. It could in theory involve top-down decisions as to the choice of crops to be sown, as tax-farming contracts show, and as state officials could independently determine after the annual flood, at least by the late twelfth century—or so contemporary handbooks, particularly al-Makhzūmī's *Minhāj*, claim.[27] The possibility, however over-idealized, of exercising this level of state control—regardless of the potentially divergent interests of private landowners and tax farmers

receipts (there are substantial sets edited in CPR XXI and P.Steuerquittungen) commonly list quite small fractions of the dinar as having been paid; the complexity of Fāṭimid minting would have covered some of that, but some must also have represented kind payment or, possibly, credit notes. How often tax was collected in kind rather than money is, it has to be added, unclear. One could easily conclude from tax receipts that money was the norm; in the tax receipts surviving for the ninth to eleventh centuries, nearly all were in money, and I have only seen taxation in kind in P.Cair.Arab. 287, P.Philad.Arab. 25 (both ninth-century), and CPR XXI 85 (a. 967), plus, much later, an unpublished tax receipt in the *geniza*, ENA 3907.14 (a. 1140/1), a citation I owe to Lorenzo Bondioli. But it would have been pointless for tax-farming contracts and state officials also to specify types of crop to be sown, however over-optimistically (see n. 27 below), if all tax was in money; the percentage of payments in kind must have been more than trivial, even if we cannot give proportions, and even if it was generally calculated in money. See, for example, the references to both kinds of tax in al-Makhzūmī, *al-Muntaqā min kitāb al-minhāj* [henceforth *Minhāj*], the relevant sections ed. and trans. Frantz-Murphy, *The agrarian administration*, p. 35, 41–2; and also by Ibn Mammātī: see n. 123 below.

[25] Poliak, *Feudalism*, followed by Ashtor, *A social and economic history* (cf. the critical historiographical survey in Irwin, 'Under western eyes', pp. 34–7). Contrast Cahen, for example his 'L'évolution de l'*iqta*'', pp. 45–50.

[26] See Rapoport, 'Invisible peasants', pp. 14–22, for 1250 and following. Note Ibn Ḥawqal, *Kītāb ṣūrat al-arḍ*, trans. Kramers and Wiet, 1, pp. 161–2, who claims in the late tenth century that tax farming is much fairer than direct taxation; I would, however, not want to overstate this as a useful contribution to the argument.

[27] For examples of crops being specified in tax-farming contracts, see CPR XXI 16, 20, 29; al-Makhzūmī, *Minhāj*, trans. Frantz-Murphy, *The agrarian administration*, pp. 31–3. See also Wickham, 'The power of property', pp. 68n, 82, 93 for caution about taking al-Makhzūmī too seriously as an accurate account. The whole idea of officials determining (or even registering) the annual agricultural choices of every field in every village is in reality beyond the capacity of any state before the twentieth century, and most then too. Cf. below, p. 686.

alike—reinforces our sense of the importance of the land tax to the state, and of the success of the state in maintaining its intensity.

Under the Romans, the countryside was far more heavily burdened than were city dwellers. That changed under the Arabs. The state systematically exacted a poll tax on all non-Muslims (i.e. Christians and Jews), both urban and rural, called by our period *jizya*, which had some gradation by wealth (as the *geniza* shows us) but which was very burdensome for the poor, and worrisome even for the well-off. (Nahray b. Nissīm, our best-documented Jewish merchant in the eleventh century, was highly perturbed on a journey to Rashīd when he found that he had left his poll tax receipt in his other robe in Alexandria, thus risking a second exaction of the tax, and wrote at least twice to get someone to send it on.)[28] This tax was profitable, for Egypt was still for the most part Christian in 800, as is generally agreed, and, by my estimation, in 1100 too. Our documentary sources certainly show that Muslims were settled throughout the countryside to some extent, but above all the texts give us evidence of a predominant use of non-Muslim and, generally, actively Christian names, up until our rural sources drop sharply in number at the end of the eleventh century.[29] Only in the thirteenth century can we be sure that there was an overwhelming Muslim rural majority in at least one district, the Fayyūm.[30] In towns there were certainly more Muslims, but when and where these came to be a majority remains unclear, even in Fusṭāṭ, which was the major Muslim political centre for a long time, but also a vast artisanal and commercial centre where many actors in our period were visibly Christians and Jews. Some important towns are stated to be mostly Christian in eleventh-century (or later) sources, notably Tinnīs and Qūṣ.[31] The poll tax on non-Muslims is, therefore, up to 1100 at least, likely to have represented a level of taxation on urban centres which had by no means been seen in the Roman period. This was added to by an attention to customs dues on Egypt's very active commerce, which is rather more visible in the Fāṭimid period than previously, and which continued to be significant subsequently too.[32] The iron chain between

[28] See Goitein, *MS*, 2, pp. 380–93 on its burden, with Cohen, *Poverty and charity*, pp. 146–54, and Cohen, *The voice of the poor*, pp. 73–82; for Nahray's two letters, see ULC Or.1080J170, ENA 2805.14A (Gil K247–8).

[29] Contrary to Bulliet, *Conversion*, pp. 92–102, who argues for a late ninth-century cusp for Egyptian conversion to Islam; but he admits that the data for Egypt which he is using are poor (and indeed they are: they are late, few in number, and non-Egyptian in origin). For the substantially Christian environment in the eleventh century in many (not all) villages in the Fayyūm in the Jirja archive and other sources, see Mouton, 'La société villageoise', pp. 237–42 and below, p. 54; and see further pp. 49–50 below for the same in Ashmūnayn.

[30] See the analysis of al-Nābulusī's 1245 survey in Rapoport, *Rural economy*, esp. pp. 205–29; for the survey itself, see Rapoport and Shahar, *The villages of the Fayyum*.

[31] For Tinnīs, see n. 190 below; for Qūṣ, see Garcin, *Un centre musulman*, pp. 120–3. Aswān, however, was probably more Muslim by the eleventh century: see ibid., pp. 116–18, for al-Udfuwī's *'ulamā'* biographies, which begin then, and n. 243 below for Muslim religious figures in the early tenth century; cf. also Williams, *Syene VI*, pp. 127–8, who is more cautious.

[32] See esp. Bramoullé, *Les Fatimides et la mer*, pp. 588–647; Bondioli, *Peasants, merchants and caliphs*, pp. 218–65.

the state and the economy thus by now extended to cities and commerce, as much as it did to the countryside and agriculture, which was important in a region as commercialized as Egypt was in our period.

* * *

The foregoing offers a context inside which the discussions in the rest of the chapter should be seen. I shall begin with urban and rural hierarchies, to see what went on economically in settlements of different types, which will lead to an initial survey of Egypt's social strata; then move on to agriculture, the basic underpinning of wealth in all pre-industrial societies, even Egypt. That will then act as a basis for more detailed analyses of exactly how exchange worked, and what its networks were, which is a complex question in a land as complex as Egypt.

2.2 Urban and Rural Hierarchies

It is not straightforward to set out a hierarchy for Egypt's settlements. The twin cities of Fusṭāṭ-Cairo were obviously at the top, but how we assess the other urban centres of the Fāṭimid period in economic or demographic terms is much harder to be sure of. The administrative hierarchy of the state, with its fifty-odd *kūra*s—the descendants of late Roman city territories, amalgamated in the 1070s into half as many *aʿmāl*s and five main overarching provinces, three in the Delta and two in the Nile valley—is not much of a guide, as it is clear that the size of their central cities varied very considerably.[33] Nor is archaeology of enough help; excavations have been small-scale (as at Bahnasā and Akhmīm), or else at best only partially published (as at Fusṭāṭ, Alexandria, Aswān); indeed, only a handful of full publications of excavations or surveys for our period exist. It is also striking how few public buildings survive outside the capital for the Fāṭimid period: a handful of mosques and minarets, as, for example, at Qūṣ, which show little monumentality in themselves (far less than Christian churches had done in the past even in rural, never mind urban Egypt), almost complete the list.[34] And our documentary material hardly mentions public buildings at all, although it is clear that provincial centres all had a network of state officials in them to run justice, local taxation, and market regulations, who must have been based somewhere. Mosques

[33] Toussoun, *La géographie*, 1, pp. 38–57; cf., for the date and an overview, Brett, *The Fatimid empire*, pp. 209–12.

[34] The handful of full(ish) publications of substantial sites includes Kubiak and Scanlon, *Fustat expedition*, 2; Kiyohiko and Kawatoko, *Ejiputo Isurāmu toshi aru Fusutāto iseki*; Gascoigne, *The island city of Tinnīs*; Rousset et al., 'Tebtynis 1998'; Rousset and Marchand, 'Secteur nord de Tebtynis . . . 1999'; and Rousset et al., 'Secteur nord de Tebtynis . . . 2000'; and the set of high-quality interims for the monastic site of Dayr el-Naqlun in the Fayyūm, published in *Polish archaeology in the Mediterranean* since the 1990s. Aswān now has an overall survey: Williams, *Syene VI*. See n. 100 below for the mixture of local and central patronage at Qūṣ, and for the minarets.

and churches get casually mentioned when the boundaries of houses are described; that is all. Indeed, local urban elites are hardly visible either, a point we shall come back to.

All the same, from a network of indicators, a tentative picture can be set out, as a framework for further exploration (see Map 5). If we see Fusṭāṭ-Cairo as on its own at level 1 of a settlement hierarchy, another five levels can be postulated, including both towns and villages. Alexandria can certainly be located at the second level, as Egypt's main port, with (as the *geniza* in particular shows us, but also some narratives and archaeology) a thriving local society and economy, even if it did not match that of Fusṭāṭ in complexity and prosperity.[35] By the late eleventh century, Qūṣ, which was emerging as the capital of the far south, that is to say, Upper Egypt, probably goes here too;[36] so does Aswān, given the size of the populated area which is emerging from rescue excavations;[37] so does Madīnat al-Fayyūm, which, although not well documented in our period, was certainly a centre of importance, given its role as the permanent focus of the entire Fayyūm oasis (and it was visibly a significant economic centre in the ninth century at least, as a substantial cache of letters tells us[38]). We can add Tinnīs, one of the two great linen factory towns on the coast, which is well documented as a major economic centre in a variety of sources. At a third level, there were Maḥalla, Rashīd/Rosetta and Dimyāt/Damietta in the Delta (Damietta was the other great factory town, but is much less visible in our evidence, and seems to have been less important than Tinnīs until the end of the eleventh century), and in the Nile valley Ashmūnayn and probably Akhmīm.[39] There would then follow at level 4 the other, smaller

[35] There is now a good deal of work done on medieval Alexandria, linking narratives, *geniza* evidence, and archaeology, even if the last is largely unpublished. Significant contributions for our period include Udovitch, 'A tale of two cities'; articles in Décobert et al., *Alexandrie médiévale*, vols. 1–4; Frenkel, 'Medieval Alexandria' (the basic account of urban topography); Frenkel, *Ha-Ohavim*; François, *Céramiques médiévales*; the regular archaeological interims in *Polish archaeology in the Mediterranean*, usually in recent years by Grzegorz Majcherek; and the discussions in Goitein, *MS*, 1, *passim*. See also, for institutions, Müller-Wiener, *Eine Stadtgeschichte Alexandrias*. This work stresses the city's role as a major port and productive city (weaving and finishing cloth in particular: see, for one example from the eleventh century, T-S 13J15.19 [Gil K540], involving all of linen, cotton, and wool), relatively ambitious in its architecture, but otherwise as very much economically second to Fusṭāṭ, even though most imports came through it. (Rashīd and Tinnīs, and later Damietta, were also Mediterranean ports, but smaller.) It was, however, politically important enough to be the location for several revolts in the late eleventh century, the only provincial city of Egypt with this level of activism (see, e.g., Bramoullé, *Les Fatimides et la mer*, pp. 237–9).

[36] See Garcin, *Un centre musulman*, pp. 79–90, for Qūṣ. To follow general usage, the Nile valley between Aswān and, very roughly, Akhmīm will be called here Upper Egypt, with Middle Egypt being the valley stretching north from Akhmīm to Cairo (Lower Egypt being the Delta). In our period, the whole valley above Cairo was called the Ṣaʿīd, by both the state and letter writers; the Delta, very often, the Rīf.

[37] For Aswān, see n. 101 below.

[38] The documents are edited as P.Marchands; see pp. 94–5 below.

[39] Ashmūnayn: see pp. 47–53 below. Akhmīm was a significant way station on the Nile in the twelfth century (see n. 256 below), and occurs casually in letters, but we cannot assess its size so easily. Damietta appears much less often than Tinnīs in the *geniza*, in particular, and mostly as a port, unlike the latter town (see pp. 103–5 below). It is certainly true that it was treated systematically together with Tinnīs in our narratives and in official sources (one *diwān* covered both of them, for example).

administrative centres like Ahnās, Bahnasā, and Idfū in the valley, and lesser but active towns in the Delta like Ṭanṭa, Minyat Ziftā, and Samannūd. Level 5 would be big villages like (to take a well-documented example) Ṭuṭūn in the Fayyūm, and also Būṣīr just outside the oasis towards the Nile, a mushroom town in the eleventh century which did not maintain its centrality later. Level 6 would be the rest of the thousands of villages of the countryside; villages were generally highly nucleated settlements in Egypt (they needed to be spatially concentrated, on low mounds, to keep out of the way of the Nile flood), but were, of course, by no means all of them large, or generous in amenities.

I set this rough hierarchy out not to defend every element in it—one could query the exact status of several of the towns in it, Damietta or Akhmīm or Bahnasā—but to make clear that quite a complex set of levels for Egypt's settlements can indeed be constructed. That in itself has implications, as we shall see. First, however, I want to discuss three settlements as case studies, to show what economic role each of them actually can be said to have played. We will look, in turn, at Fusṭāṭ, obviously the dominant economic centre, Ashmūnayn, as the best-documented middle-level town, and, as a well-documented village, Ṭuṭūn. Tinnīs and Būṣīr will be discussed too, but later (see pp. 95–106), when we come to look at how flax and linen were produced and sold. Here, instead, I want to offer a sense of how urban and non-urban settlements worked in the round, which is itself a necessary underpinning if we want to understand how exchange worked.

* * *

Fusṭāṭ was founded in the 640s by the Arab conquerors around a relatively small fortified urban centre of the late Roman period called Babylon—hence, presumably, the fact that a common name for Fusṭāṭ-Cairo used in Italy at the end of our period was Babillonia. The Roman site still survives (rather better than the rest of Fusṭāṭ does); in our period, it was called Qaṣr al-Shamʿ, 'Castle of the candles', and was state property—it is very visible in the *geniza* texts, as it was largely populated by Jews (as also by Christians), and the Ben Ezra synagogue itself is situated there. By as early as 700, Fusṭāṭ had expanded substantially: north and east of Babylon there now stretched an enormous city (to the west the Nile flanked it), which began as an administrative centre but rapidly turned into a major commercial hub too (see Map 25). Just north of that were two later administrative suburbs, ʿAskar and Qaṭāʾiʿ, founded in the ninth century by the ʿAbbāsids and Ṭūlūnids respectively, but by the late tenth century either ruined or reincorporated into Fusṭāṭ. The Fāṭimids were thus not being novel when they founded Cairo, a

Indeed, al-Muqaddasī claims in his late tenth-century geography that Damietta was bigger than Tinnīs: *Aḥsan al-taqāsīm*, trans. Miquel, p. 122. All the same, my clear sense is that Tinnīs was the major one of the two until the late eleventh century. Bramoullé, *Les Fatimides et la mer*, pp. 97–8, shows that Damietta began to become more important in the 1070s, when it started to be used as a port for the Fāṭimid fleet by preference to Tinnīs; this also fits the fact that Venetian documents from the next century refer to Damietta exclusively, and not Tinnīs: see p. 144 below.

kilometre or so farther north still, as their own residence and as a military and ceremonial centre.[40] Cairo had rather more staying power, though. Not all state offices moved there at first, but they did in time, and some merchants and artisans had done so as well by the twelfth century, filling up the open land between it and Fusṭāṭ too. In the mid-thirteenth century there were maybe some 250,000 people in the twin cities, a figure which perhaps did not change much across the medieval period, until the Black Death (in 1000 it might have been 200,000).[41] By then, however, all the expansion was in and around Cairo, not Fusṭāṭ—the city complex as a whole, that is to say, was decidedly moving north. As noted earlier, it is certainly not the case that the burning of Fusṭāṭ in 1168 marked its final destruction, as historians and archaeologists used to assume (according to some but not all sources, it was ordered by the Fāṭimid *wazīr* himself, to stop the then unwalled city from becoming a base for an invading Frankish army).[42] When Saladin finally fortified the whole twin-city complex in the 1170s, he extended the walls to include most of the extent which Fusṭāṭ had once had, so clearly it was not a wasteland. The *geniza* documents do not refer to the fire, and continue, in all the parts of the city which they cover, without any significant break into the 1250s at the earliest. The Japanese-led excavations of the 1970s–1980s also found no break in their central area of the city until after the late thirteenth century. Narratives give little hint of a decline in Fusṭāṭ until the fourteenth century and later, in fact.[43] All the same, by 1250 or so some parts of the older city were beginning to turn into the refuse tip which they have remained ever since. Today, apart from two great mosques and a few smallish churches, the surviving standing remains of medieval Fusṭāṭ consist of a now illegible set of grand courtyard houses, excavated by ʿAlī Bahjat (publishing in French, more phonetically, given modern Egyptian pronunciation, as ʿAly Bahgat) in the 1910s, flanked by the largest modern mountains of rubbish I have ever seen.[44]

The geographers enthuse over Fusṭāṭ. It surpasses Baghdad (al-Muqaddasī) or else is a third of the size of the latter (Ibn Ḥawqal); it has apartment buildings around a courtyard going to four or five storeys (al-Muqaddasī), or five to seven (Ibn Ḥawqal), or eight (al-Iṣṭakhrī), or seven to fourteen (Nāṣer-e Khosraw); it is full of bazaars and large mosques; bread is cheap there (al-Muqaddasī); fruits and

[40] For Qaṣr al-Shamʿ (and elsewhere in Fusṭāṭ), in the leases and other texts of the Ben Ezra (Palestinian) synagogue, see Gil, *Documents* (pp. 485–520 lists all the documented houses). For urban topography as a whole, see esp. Sayyid, *La capitale*. For the early history of Fusṭāṭ, see Bruning, *The rise of a capital*. For Babillonia, see pp. 562–3 below.

[41] The most recent and careful (even if still speculative) estimates are those of Garcin in Behrens-Abouseif et al., 'Le Caire', pp. 179–80, 205–13. See also n. 197 below.

[42] See, for example, Sayyid, *La capitale*, pp. 625–34, although he recognizes later continuities.

[43] Goitein, *MS*, 4, p. 12; Kubiak, 'The burning of Miṣr al-Fusṭāṭ in 1168' (which I do not follow in its discussion of the 1060s); Behrens-Abouseif et al., 'Le Caire', pp. 182–3, 186–7, 211; and Garcin, 'Habitat médiéval', pp. 161–2, using Arabic narrative sources; and the texts in Gil, *Documents*, nn. 72–100 (up to a. 1200). For the Japanese-led site, see the indications in Kawatoko, 'Multi-disciplinary approaches', pp. 846–8.

[44] Bahgat and Gabriel, *Fouilles d'al Fouṣṭâṭ*.

vegetables are abundant, coming from everywhere from Syria to Tunisia; very high-quality ceramics and glass are made there (Nāṣer-e Khosraw).[45] Both *geniza* documents and archaeology fully confirm the existence of apartment buildings around a central courtyard, although *geniza* descriptions of houses do not mention buildings of more than four storeys, and none of the excavations has been of buildings which could support more than two further floors.[46]

There have, in fact, so far been four separate major excavations in Fusṭāṭ. They were those of Bahgat (who published the buildings but none of the finds), George Scanlon in the 1960s–1970s (who mostly only published interims, again with little systematic analysis of finds), Kawatoko Mutsuo in the 1970s–1980s (whose two-volume full publication came out in Japanese), and Roland-Pierre Gayraud in the 1980s–1990s (two of whose ten final volumes are so far published, plus interims). Other, scrappier excavations have not reached even the stage of publishing interims. As can be seen, there has been little full publication, and in some cases it is by now clear that there never will be.[47] The total area covered by all of them is also only a very small part of the land area of the city (the excavations could all easily have missed the high-rises, then), and the best-excavated, that of Gayraud on the hill of Isṭabl ʿAntar, was located at the far southern edge of the early Islamic city—Isṭabl ʿAntar had, in fact, become a cemetery at the edge of town by our period, as the city began steadily to move north, which was itself abandoned by the late eleventh century except for ragpickers and pottery kilns. But they do, nonetheless, taken together, present a quite coherent and solid picture. They have generally identified a major rebuilding phase in the Fāṭimid period—a rebuilding which included even the Isṭabl ʿAntar cemetery. Most of what has been excavated has also been reasonably prosperous quarters. They show dense housing with big courtyards, an aqueduct-based water supply, latrines and underground sewage disposal into cesspits (this is attested in the *geniza* too, which also shows some flow into the Nile[48]), and swept streets, decently surfaced. There was money in every house, and also glass, as well as pottery. One would, of course, expect pottery, but a striking feature of Fusṭāṭ, so far a nearly unique feature in the Mediterranean for this period, was the near-omnipresence of at least some Chinese ceramics.

[45] Al-Muqaddasī, *Aḥsan al-taqāsīm*, trans. Miquel, pp. 116–19; Ibn Ḥawqal, *Kītāb ṣūrat al-arḍ*, trans. Kramers and Wiet, 1, p. 144; al-Iṣṭakhrī, *al-Masālik wa-al-mamālik*, trans. Mordtmann, p. 29; *Nāṣer-e Khosraw's book of travels*, trans. Thackston, pp. 52, 54.

[46] See Goitein, *MS*, 4, pp. 70–3, 78–82; the document of *c.*1170 edited in Mouton et al., *Propriétés rurales*, n. 43, also describes a building with several storeys.

[47] Bahgat and Gabriel, *Fouilles d'al Fousṭâṭ*; for the list of Scanlon interims for Fustat-A and -B, see the Bibliography; Fustat-C was (more or less) fully published as Kubiak and Scanlon, *Fustat expedition*, 2; the Japanese site is published in Kiyohiko and Kawatoko, *Ejiputo Isurāmu toshi aru Fusutāto iseki*; for the Gayraud interims, see the Bibliography—here, the full publications so far are Rodziewicz, *Bone carvings* and Gayraud and Vallauri, *Fustat II* (covering ninth- and tenth-century ceramics), and the best brief overview is Gayraud, 'Fostat'. For other excavations, see the rather sad Foreword to Bacharach, *Fustat finds*, pp. vii–xi.

[48] T-S K21.98 (Gil, *Documents*, n. 8).

Indeed, Scanlon called his simplest building complex, Fustat-C, the only one with no courtyard, 'proletarian', because there were only a few sherds of Chinese pottery on the site.[49]

The *geniza* texts, which include numerous leases of rooms and floors of apartment buildings from the eleventh and twelfth centuries, often show a poorer Fusṭāṭ—for, of course, the majority of the inhabitants of any medieval city were poor. The eleventh century, in particular, may indeed have been one in which wages failed to keep up with price rises for wheat, which will have further harmed the lives of the poorest.[50] The Palestinian synagogue (in which the *geniza* was located) came to possess, largely thanks to pious gifts, a substantial amount of urban property, both around it (paying ground rent to the state, as it lay in Qaṣr al-Sham') and well to the north and east. It rented out its houses systematically, as sequential financial accounts show, often at low rents, earning a lot of money simply because the buildings were so numerous—although some of that was spent on rebuilding. Tenants (whether or not of the synagogue) could be men or women, Jewish or Christian or Muslim, and were often shopkeepers (bakers are among those whose wares are specified), or else artisans or traders.[51] Many of these were indeed poor. But, actually, the sense we take from these texts is that the tenants in them were of a widely varying range of prosperity, from water carriers to goldsmiths to merchants of relative wealth, with ranges of rents to match; outside

[49] Kubiak and Scanlon, *Fustat expedition*, 2, pp. 19, 47–9; Gayraud, 'Pauvreté et richesse', p. 176, however, thinks that this site was lived in by a 'classe moyenne' (even if doubtless not a prosperous one). Publications of Chinese wares include Mikami, 'Chinese ceramics' (the most synthetic); Kiyohiko and Kawatoko, *Ejiputo Isurāmu toshi*, 1, pp. 280–9, 2, pp. 440–519; and Gyllensvärd, 'Recent finds', which publishes Chinese materials from some of the Scanlon excavations (unfortunately without relating them to the excavated houses): they date from the late ninth to the early fifteenth century (and later too), with a high point in the twelfth and thirteenth. For the typologies of Chinese ceramics in the western Indian Ocean, see esp. Zhang, *An exploratory quantitative archaeological analysis*; Qin and Ho, 'Chinese ceramic exports' (with further bibliography). For a *geniza* citation, see Goitein, *MS*, 4, p. 146; see further Lambourn and Ackerman-Lieberman, 'Chinese porcelain'. The state bought Chinese pottery as well, in huge quantities, apparently for utilitarian purposes inside the palace: see *Book of gifts and rarities, Kitāb al-hadāyā wa al-tuḥaf*, trans. al-Ḥijjāwī al-Qaddūmī, ch. 385, for the year 1068–9. Outside the capital, Chinese pottery has been found on several Egyptian sites, and, more rarely, elsewhere in the Mediterranean; see n. 178 below. See also p. 114 below for a plausibly Chinese salt vendor somewhere in (probably) Middle Egypt; that he may not have been the only Chinese immigrant in Egypt is perhaps also shown by the 1971 find in the American-sponsored excavations in Fusṭāṭ of part of a Song dynasty portable wooden shrine, which would have been an unusual souvenir for any Egyptian merchant to bring back (Kubiak and Scanlon, 'Fusṭāṭ expedition: preliminary report, 1971: part II', pp. 78, 93, and plate XXI b).

[50] Ashtor, *Histoire des prix*, pp. 124–33, 454–8 (picked up, more schematically, in his *A social and economic history*, pp. 201–2); but his data are not good—they focus on periods of wheat shortage and are often rhetorical—and wage earners, even in the capital (the source of most of his data), were not necessarily a majority of the population. For the poorer urban strata, see further the unromanticized accounts in Cohen, *Poverty and charity*; Cohen, *The voice of the poor*.

[51] For synagogue leases for the eleventh century, see Gil, *Documents*, nn. 8, 11, 13–16, 22–7, 36, 38 (the trades included a baker, a shoemaker, a weaver, a linen dealer, etc.); cf. Goitein, *MS*, 4, pp. 92–7, 291–6; and, for two Christian merchants buying and selling a *dār*, a courtyard house, in Qaṣr al-Sham' in *c.*1170, see Mouton et al., *Propriétés rurales*, n. 43.

Qaṣr al-Shamʿ, house prices are similarly varied. And some of the descriptions of houses in the texts do, equally, show up a notable complexity in room design (in the richer ones, apartments of several rooms were common, with elaborate furnishings).[52] Given all this, it is highly likely that many of the houses concerned would have resembled at least Fustat-C, and in some cases the flashier houses excavated by Bahgat too.[53] The *geniza* thus matches the excavations fairly well, and gives at least partial support even to the enthusiastic reports of the geographers. Fāṭimid Fusṭāṭ, even though it was not the seat of political power now, was, with its sewage disposal and ubiquitous Chinese ceramics, a highly impressive city for the period.

And it was highly economically active too. Fusṭāṭ was both the home and the major economic focus for the Jewish merchants of the eleventh and twelfth centuries whose records survive in the *geniza*, of which Ibn ʿAwkal and Nahray b. Nissīm are only the best-documented out of dozens of others. The Arabic documentary sources have fewer concentrations of material, but some Muslim merchants, of whom the most clearly visible is the *amīr* Amīnaddīn at the end of the twelfth century (*amīr* is normally a military title here; other merchants of the same period included *qāḍīs*, i.e. judges), operated on at least as large a scale. Jewish merchants did not normally have similar official positions, but they could in some contexts; Ibrāhīm al-Tustarī (d. 1047) even became *wasiṭa* to the caliph's mother, a parallel office to that of the *wazīr*, a role which resulted in his death.[54] (In his case, his prominent wealth brought office; for *qāḍīs* it was probably the other way round.) Ibn ʿAwkal was very rich indeed (in one year, one of his agents sent 180 bales of flax across the Mediterranean, worth, at a minimum, nearly 5,000 dinars), and the Tustarī family (less well documented, for they were Qaraites and did not use the Palestinian synagogue and its *geniza*) seem to have operated at a similar level; but the others, like Nahray, prosperous but less wealthy, nonetheless regarded deals of 1,000–3,000 dinars as normal—6 dinars being ʿa reasonable [annual] rent for a decent middle-class home' in Fusṭāṭ, and 1–2 dinars a reasonable sum to pay for a wooden clothes chest.[55] They also transported goods on a

[52] See Goitein, *MS*, 4, pp. 82–97, 273–96 for rent and price ranges; cf. also Ashtor, *Histoire des prix*, pp. 183–9. For furnishings, see Goitein, *MS*, 4, pp. 105–50, 297–309; Frenkel and Lester, 'Evidence of material culture' (linking with archaeology, a welcome departure in *geniza* historiography), and Goitein, 'A mansion in Fustat' (a text of *c*.1190).

[53] Kubiak and Scanlon, *Fustat expedition*, 2, p. 11, surprisingly denied this for Fustat-C; I think they must have misread Goitein.

[54] For Amīnaddīn, see pp. 109–10 below; for Ibrāhīm al-Tustarī, see Gil, *Jews*, pp. 670–5; Rustow, *Heresy*, pp. 140–7, 177–8, 322 and *passim*.

[55] 180 bales: T-S 13J17.3 (Gil K181 [S47]); for the figure in dinars, see Stillman, 'The eleventh century merchant house', p. 29; but 35 dinars a bale would come out higher, at 6,300 dinars—for that figure, see, e.g., T-S 20.71 (Gil K367 [S81]), a one-off pricing but not apparently an exceptional one—and cf. Ashtor, *Histoire des prix*, p. 142 (which shows much variation) and Goldberg, *Trade and institutions*, p. 277n. See, more broadly, Goitein, *MS*, 1, pp. 215–17 for indications as to pricing and other examples of trading on a similar scale. For Nahray and his circle, see letters such as T-S K2.32, 16.339, 16.163 (I), Halper 389 (Gil K354, 348, 373, 751 [S106, 143, 150–1]), plus the accounts translated in

regular basis not just inside Egypt but to and from Palestine, Sicily, and Tunisia—and after 1090 or so India too. These transactions, and the social world of at least the Jewish merchants, have been very well studied by Goitein, Rustow, Goldberg, and others, and there is no need to discuss them in detail here (the main goods they transacted in and the routes they chose will anyway be discussed later); but I need to stress at least their scale. There were more goods passing through the hands of even second-level merchants like Nahray than of any documented dealers elsewhere in the Mediterranean in our period; in particular, the Genoese records, when they appear after 1150, are for smaller shipments, as we shall also see later.[56]

The great variety and specialization of Fusṭāṭ markets is visible in all our sources, from the *geniza* to political narratives (not least because of Caliph al-Ḥākim's habit of walking around them at night), much indeed as in modern Cairo. They, and the considerable number of government warehouses and commercial centres, *dārs*, charged with taking sales taxes and registering transactions in major products such as wheat and flax, were certainly all busy, pretty much all the time. (The great merchants rarely operated across the sea in the winter, as it was the close season for Mediterranean shipping, but they and others certainly did inside Egypt.) The government buildings and the markets seem to have often been situated around the Mosque of ʿAmr just north of the Roman fort (and close to the Nile and its quays), and, in general, in the western third of the city, leaving the higher land to the east as more residential.[57]

This was further matched by a wide array of types of artisan in our documentation. The building accounts for the *qōdesh* (the charitable foundation—the Hebrew equivalent of the Arabic word *waqf*) of the Palestinian synagogue show us a particularly striking division of labour in the construction trades: masons, sawyers/carpenters, gutter makers, cesspool-makers, lime-slakers, and plasterers; from Arabic-script texts we can add whitewashers and sawdusters.[58] This is matched in the food trades, with separate dealers in dates, fennel, sesame, and bananas—the range of food in the capital was always striking. Among niche markets, there were specialist dealers in combs, sponges, and ambergris.[59] And for cloth-making we find artisans or dealers in waist cloths, purple cloth, and horse

Goitein, 'Bankers accounts', pp. 38–62. Rent figure quote: Goitein, *MS*, 4, pp. 94–5; clothes chest: Ashtor, *Histoire des prix*, p. 177.

[56] See pp. 546–7 below for the Egypt–Genoa comparison.

[57] Sayyid, *La capitale*, pp. 594–5, 601–5; Goitein, *MS*, 1, pp. 193–5; for al-Ḥākim, see, e.g., *Tārīkh al-Anṭakī*, trans. Pirone, 12.38. For the *dārs*, see Bramoullé, *Les Fatimides et la mer*, pp. 591–601; Bondioli, *Peasants, merchants and caliphs*, pp. 224–36.

[58] Gil, *Documents*, nn. 8–30. For Arabic-script texts, see, e.g., P.GenizahCambr. 19, 23; P.Vind. Arab. I 68.

[59] Goitein, *MS*, 1, pp. 121, 155, 438, 4, p. 225, etc. For Arabic-script texts, see, e.g., P.GenizahCambr. 2, 11, 12, 15, 23. For the range of food, see Goitein, *MS*, 4, pp. 226–53; and Lewicka, *Food and foodways*, focussed on the Mamlūk period.

cloth; Fusṭāṭ was not actually a major cloth-weaving city, but its demographic size meant that workshops of any kind were always common, and, again, the scale of demand led to a clear-cut division of labour.[60] The capital seems to have been the main location for paper mills.[61] We hear from Nāṣer-e Khosraw that there were both glass-making and ceramics kilns in the city (documents show that Jews were particularly active in glass). Kilns for both, from different periods, have indeed been found in excavations (Scanlon's excavations of glass kilns show that they were often close, perhaps too close, to domestic buildings), and the archaeology shows that ceramics, in particular, were very elaborate and diversified—far more in this case than any written text says—as we shall see later (pp. 82–93).[62]

These characterizations are not complete. One could write a whole book about the economy of Fāṭimid Fusṭāṭ—and one would need a book-length study if one wanted to avoid simply repeating Goitein, whose account of the city (even if it predated most of the excavations and the relevant Arabic-script documentary publications) is particularly rich, and who laid strong emphasis on the division of labour in the *geniza* records over fifty years ago.[63] This is not feasible in a book with a much wider lens. But we need to get at least this much of a sense of Fusṭāṭ's wealth and complexity, for comparative purposes. It is, in fact, very likely that the city was the largest and most complex in the Mediterranean in the tenth to twelfth centuries; we will see this again in subsequent chapters when looking at its only possible rivals, Constantinople and Córdoba.

Such a statement is not controversial, in fact. But there is another important point to be made as well. Fusṭāṭ's overwhelming dominance over all other Egyptian cities might be seen as artificial.[64] It was the centre for the country's whole fiscal system; taxation and thus the greatest concentrations of wealth were almost exclusively focussed on Fusṭāṭ-Cairo, throughout the middle ages. In strong, tax-based states in the Islamic world and Byzantium, capitals were always the major cities for this reason, if for no other—not only Fusṭāṭ, but Kairouan, Palermo, Córdoba, Constantinople, and, of course, farther away, Baghdad. Fusṭāṭ's vitality was, however, more than that—as, indeed, was the case for all the capitals just mentioned, as we shall see in later chapters. It was the product of commercial relationships which were by no means only focussed on absorbing tax-based

[60] P.GenizahCambr. 9, 24, 38, 57; cf. Goitein, *MS*, 1, pp. 99–105. [61] See n. 149 below.

[62] *Nāṣer-e Khosraw's book of travels*, trans. Thackston, p. 54; for glass, see Goitein, *MS*, 1, pp. 109–10. For the archaeology, see esp. Scanlon, 'Preliminary report, 1965.II', pp. 73–9; and Scanlon, 'Preliminary report, 1972.I', pp. 59–61, where he thinks that some of the kilns date to around 1300; for pottery production, see Gayraud and Vallauri, *Fustat II*, pp. 19–21, 39–46.

[63] For the economy and society of Fusṭāṭ, see esp. *MS*, 1, pp. 75–116 and 4, pp. 1–150. Note that when discussing the division of labour (*MS*, 1, pp. 99–115), Goitein was concerned to draw a general picture of Mediterranean manufacturing as seen in the *geniza*, not specifically of that of Fusṭāṭ; although I am sure, for example, that there will indeed have been dyers in the city specializing in every colour (*MS*, 1, pp. 106–7, 420), his own citations are not tied specifically to a single location.

[64] For that dominance, see Goldberg, *Trade and institutions*, pp. 241–6, although she does not argue that it was artificial.

demand. It was an entrepôt for goods of all kinds, going both in and out, and also for large-scale productions of at least some goods (the clearest example, although certainly not the most important, is ceramics). The commercial patterns illuminated by the *geniza* records (which in this case are certainly representative of wider patterns, as we shall see) also made Fusṭāṭ an entrepôt for flax, a bulk good which was for the most part not destined for weaving in the city. The Jewish merchants whom we know so much about were in Fusṭāṭ because of its commercial centrality, and certainly not because they (or most of them) had close connections with state officeholding, a relationship which they knew was dangerous (even without Ibrāhīm al-Tustarī's fate, but that further underlined it).[65] That is to say, obviously, Fusṭāṭ was founded as a political and fiscal centre. Without such a choice on the part of the earliest Arab conquerors, Egypt's capital might have remained at Alexandria, as it had done for the previous millennium, oddly excentric to the region's heartlands though the latter was. But that choice resulted in a build-up of commercial activity which no longer depended on politics. Fusṭāṭ's economic importance came to depend, rather, on a highly complex set of economic relationships internal to the region, which marked Egypt out in our period, as before and after—and which is what the rest of this chapter will develop.

* * *

Outside Fusṭāṭ-Cairo, only three cities/towns have even halfway good documentation, Alexandria, Tinnīs and Ashmūnayn—the last being the only town in the Nile valley about which we can say anything significant in our period, up to 1070 at any rate (we have very little from after that). I choose it as a case study here mainly because it is documented above all in Arabic-script texts, so we do not have to worry about the representativeness of the *geniza*—and indeed, in part because a documentation which, in this city, focusses only on Christians and Muslims allows us to test, at least roughly, precisely that representativeness. It also has relatively little analysis for our period, so needs a bit of description.[66]

Ashmūnayn (or 'Ushmūnayn) is about 280 kilometres south of Cairo, some 3 kilometres from the Nile, between Minyā and Asyūṭ, which have now replaced it as district capitals (see the inset on Map 5). Its name means 'the two Ashmūns'—the name of the city in Coptic being Shmoun (in Greek, Hermopolis). How it was divided is not immediately clear, but an 'upper' and a 'lower' Ashmūn are documented in the earliest Islamic centuries.[67] Ashmūnayn is now a small, fairly compact urban centre lying south of an area in which classical ruins sit, including a

[65] They did, all the same, have connections to state officials, who were involved in trading on their own account; see n. 272 below.

[66] For up to 860, see Legendre, *La Moyenne-Égypte*, which is basic; Livingston, 'Life in the Egyptian valley', discusses much of the material from our period.

[67] *EI*^{2}, s.v. al-U<u>sh</u>mūnayn (A. F. Sayyid). For examples of 'upper' and 'lower' respectively, see, e.g., P.Cair.Arab. 174, CPR XXI 5, both eighth-century.

substantial Christian basilica. Three documents of 1050 refer to a house on the north side of town, on the hill above the 'little church' (*kunaysiyya*) of the Virgin (the house was next to other houses, but also to open land and a Muslim cemetery; note that the church of the Virgin, given its size, cannot be the basilica). North of it will have been the main area of ancient Hermopolis, the excavations of which have been published, and which show prosperity to *c.*850 and the slow end of identifiable material across the next century or so, with relatively little after around 950. The excavators of Hermopolis stressed that the uppermost levels of the site were disturbed by or lost to *sibākh* diggers; their periodization was, therefore, based on largely unstratified ceramics, of types which are not always perfectly datable. But only on one part of the site were there surface finds of one of the major post-950 (i.e. Fāṭimid-period) ceramic markers, lustreware. Given that the excavations are in a slightly lower-lying area, it is tempting to hypothesize that the area of the 'lower' town of previous centuries was precisely that of the classical city; if so, it would look as if 'lower' Ashmūnayn was slowly losing population to the 'upper' town in our period, and that the latter is that which survives.[68]

This would certainly explain why Fāṭimid documents show a town whose economic activity was considerable, which is quite at variance with the archaeology. It was in our period a town with a good deal of articulation, even if the upper-lower distinction had gone; at least four quarters or neighbourhoods (*khaṭṭ*s) are cited in Arabic texts as geographical markers. It had a 'greater *sūq*' (*sūq al-'a'zam*), a public fountain, and at least one *ḥammām*; it also had at least two mosques and at least two churches—or more, for a Coptic text from the later tenth century (or later still) lists twenty-three churches in its district, many of which were probably in the town itself. It had a bishop; one, Sāwīrus ibn al-Muqaffa' (d. *c.*989), was a significant intellectual, even if he did not compile the *History of the patriarchs of Alexandria* which was until recently ascribed to him.[69] It also had an active *majlis al-ḥukm*, a city tribunal, run by a *qāḍī*—it is visible in several documentary texts—as well as (at least in narratives) a military governor, *wālī al-ḥarb*, although we do not know where in the town they were based, as secular public buildings are not referred to as such in our documents.[70]

[68] Documents of 1050: P.Cair.Arab. 64–6, with 68 (a. 1067). For the archaeology, see esp. the data in Bailey, *Excavations at el-Ashmunein*, 5, pp. 9–58, 112–17. The lustreware was only found after the main publications were completed: Bailey, 'The pottery from the South Church', p. 84.

[69] For the urban topography, see esp. CPR XXVI 13, P.Heid.Arab. III 2, P.Cair.Arab. 64–6, 68–71, 138. For the network of earlier churches and topography, and the dating of the church list, see Legendre, *La Moyenne-Égypte*, pp. 86–90, 318–20. For a brief earlier discussion, see Grohmann, 'Contributions to the topography of al-Ushmûnain'. The main text now certainly ascribed to Sāwīrus is *Kitāb miṣbāḥ al-'aql*, ed. and trans. Ebied and Young; for the reascription of the *History*, see esp. den Heijer, *Mawhūb ibn Manṣūr*, pp. 8–10, 15–18, 81–116.

[70] *Majlis al-ḥukm*: P.GrohmannUrkunden 7, Chrest.Khoury I 78–9 (cf. also 81), II 31–3; see Tillier, 'Du pagarque au cadi', esp. pp. 31–4; Tillier, 'The qadis' justice', pp. 49–52; Livingston, 'Life in the Egyptian valley', pp. 442–5. *Wālī al-ḥarb*: see Legendre, *La Moyenne-Égypte*, p. 321.

It can already be seen that Ashmūnayn was a religiously mixed town, as indeed it still is. The countryside around it was principally Christian in the eleventh century, as names show; for, although people of any religion could call themselves Yūsuf or Ibrāhīm or Sara in our period, names of Christian saints like Jirja or Boqṭor (George or Victor) could not have been held by Muslims; and it is names such as these, plus a few more ancient names such as Ammūn, which dominate in the villages. In Nawāy, a little north of the city, a bishop (presumably of Ashmūnayn itself) and a deacon are recorded as landowners on an estate boundary in one tenth-century text. Indeed, an inhabitant of Dashlūṭ, one of the villages to the south of Ashmūnayn, by name Rafaēl son of Mina, kept the last known documentary archive to survive in Coptic, a language which by now had no legal force in the dominant Islamic courts, dating to 1022–62. Here, the formal documents in the archive are witnessed by Christians, which would also not have had any weight in such courts, but it was clearly enough for a wholly Christian community such as this.[71] There is a current debate as to how much, and up to when, Coptic was still a language in daily use, and even in Rafaēl's texts there is some Arabic—literate people, at least, were certainly bilingual, and so, by now, were plenty of (some would say most) others; but anyone who used Coptic at all was Christian, in effect by definition.[72] There were Muslims in the countryside too; Muslims had to be the witnesses in all legal documents in Arabic, and we regularly see them in that role—they were clearly normal neighbours of non-Muslims. But a Christian majority in the district of Ashmūnayn seems pretty clear. In the city, it is not quite so clear. The two mosques show this already; and the *qāḍī*s and military men whom we find in texts, plus the witnesses, and anyone called, for example, Muḥammad (there are several in the texts), were almost automatically Muslim. Arabic was here without doubt the dominant language too. But even in the city, Christian names are prominent in our texts; nor do we have any sign of the sort of wider community of *'ulama'* which any town the size of Ashmūnayn

[71] For Nawāy, see P.Prag.Arab. 9. The Dashlūṭ texts were originally edited in Green, 'A private archive', plus one (the only Arabic text) in Thung, 'An Arabic letter', and an extra one in Schenke, 'Übereignung'; most were re-edited in Richter, 'Spätkoptische Rechtsurkunden neu bearbeitet (II)', which is now the standard edition, referred to as P.Teshlot, from the Coptic name for the village. For Ammūn, see P.Vind.Arab. I 2. Note, however, that ancient Egyptian names were not automatically borne by Christians, even if they usually were; a sister of the Muslim Fayyūmī merchant Abū Hurayra in the late ninth century was—remarkably—called Anūbīs, presumably after the male Egyptian god (P.Marchands II 23); the name was common in Christian communities (as Anoup), but there it was certainly male.

[72] See Mikhail, *From Byzantine to Islamic Egypt*, pp. 99–105, and esp. Delattre et al., 'Écrire en arabe et en copte', which gives a bibliography of the debate. Whatever one concludes about bilingualism, to imagine an enclosed micro-community speaking only Coptic surviving into the eleventh century is effectively impossible; all the evidence for movement, discussed below, argues against it; and we have a letter about a tenth-century tax survey in Dashlūṭ in P.Heid.Arab. III 31 which reminds us, if we needed reminding, that Arabic was essential for dealing with the state. The point is developed in Weitz, 'Islamic law on the provincial margins', focussed on the use by Christians of Islamic legal institutions.

would have automatically had in Iraq or Iran. I would be cautious about any assertion that in 1050, say, Ashmūnayn itself had a Muslim majority as yet.[73]

Interestingly, we cannot say much about urban elites. Clearly, bishops, *qāḍīs*, governors, and other army leaders were among them, and so was the local *ʿāmil* or financial administrator, who appears in many texts; so, doubtless, was whoever owned the Nawāy estate. Some of the merchants discussed in the next paragraphs probably came into that category. But Egyptian cities after the eighth century did not have local governments with any corporate visibility, so we have to rely on casual citations in documents to identify urban leaders outside the defined offices just listed.[74] We do not find them here. I would not suppose that this means that Ashmūnayn's urban elites were restricted to a narrow set of officeholders, but this absence is significant, all the same. It fits the general lack of information we have about Egyptian elites in our period, and I will return to it later (pp. 57–60).

What Ashmūnayn did have, however, was an active economy. There are casual references in our documents to several dozen artisans and merchants. An eleventh-century list of receipts from an Ashmūnayn tax collector lists payments from two tailors, two silk merchants, a miller, a fuller, a joiner, two paper merchants, and a builder. There is not the extreme division of labour which is attested in Fusṭāṭ, but we do find some clear specialisms, as for example when a shield-maker owns land not far out of the city in the tenth century, or when a standard-maker owns a house in the Quarter of the Standard-makers (*bannādīn*). Sugar, too, was a specialized local production, with sugar factories, and a scale of operation going up to the very high figure of 10,000 dinars, at least in the rhetoric of one angry letter. In cloth-making, there were, beside the already cited tailors and fullers, tent-makers, dyers, bleachers, and weavers.[75] Ibn Ḥawqal too says that Ashmūnayn produced and exported linen cloth; and the raw material for linen, flax, is attested in rural Arabic documents and Dashlūṭ's Coptic texts.[76] There was, indeed, rural cloth-making too; in the Dashlūṭ texts there are transactions in

[73] For the mix of Muslims and Christians in the tenth century, see, e.g., Lev, 'Coptic rebellions', pp. 331–8; on the basis of Ibn Ḥawqal's comments, he argues that the Delta was becoming more Islamicized than the Nile valley. Muḥammad was not automatically a Muslim name in Christian-ruled twelfth-century Sicily (see Chapter 3, n. 164), but that was a very different situation, in which conversion to Christianity was increasingly common and Islamic culture as a whole was weakening. (Outside our regions, the same is true of the tenth-century Duero valley in northern Spain, recently taken over by Christian rulers, where the deacon Mahomet appears; see Zeller et al., *Neighbours and strangers*, p. 111.)

[74] For *ʿāmils* in Ashmūnayn, see, for the tenth to twelfth centuries, P.Berl.Arab. II 32, P.Vind.Arab. III 26, 32, CPR XXI 31–2; for the ninth century, CPR XXI has many more, and see the lists in Legendre, *La Moyenne-Égypte*, pp. 241–52. In CPR XXI 31–2 (a. 926), the *ʿāmil* Muzāḥim seems to be a local landowner: see Wickham, 'The power of property', pp. 84–5, clarified better in Bondioli, *Peasants, merchants and caliphs*, pp. 32–3.

[75] Tax list: P.Prag.Arab. 45. Other citations: P.Prag.Arab. 9, P.Cair.Arab. 69–70, 45, CPR XXVI 4, Chrest.Khoury II 24, P.Terminkauf 2, P.KarabacekPapiergeschichte, p. 164. For sugar, see pp. 73–4 below.

[76] Ibn Ḥawqal, *Kitāb ṣūrat al-arḍ*, trans. Kramers and Wiet, 1, p. 156; P.Heid.Arab. III 30, P.Prag.Arab. 42, 45, 46, 47; P.Teshlot 4, 7.

laaū, Coptic for a type of cloth, and in one eleventh-century text there are fiscal or landlordly accounts of people in the countryside with weaving looms (*nawl*s), twenty-eight in total, which must indicate weaving on some scale, for sale—for household weaving would not have interested a tax office or landlord. We know from the *geniza* that Jewish merchants bought both flax and cloth from the district across the eleventh century too.[77]

Finally, it is worth stressing the six examples of a silk merchant or silk worker (*qazzāz*). Two of these were father and son; a third, Abū al-ʿAlā, clearly their associate in some way—he buys a house from the younger of these, Qulta b. Kayl, and then sells it in the same year, 1050, to Qulta's son-in-law Isiṭūrūs—was the son of Mīnā the water carrier (*saqqā'i*), a clear case of social mobility.[78] Silk was not made in Egypt; it came in this period from Spain, Sicily, or perhaps Syria. It was a semi-luxury, an expensive product which Egyptians were keen to buy all the same, at least if they had a medium level of wealth. That Ashmūnayn, a long way from the sea, had enough demand for silk that we can find six dealers in it in the eleventh century is striking, then. Jessica Goldberg has remarked that silk was so common a good for Jewish merchants to carry on a small scale, both across the sea and inside Egypt (mostly in the Delta towns), that it was virtually an alternative currency to gold and silver; here in the Nile valley, that Jewish commerce was matched by one run by Christians (to judge from most of their names), and in some cases, as we shall see in a moment, Muslims too.[79]

Ashmūnayn's economy was active enough to encourage geographical as well as social mobility. People moved from the countryside to the town, as we would expect, but also in the opposite direction; and there was movement between villages too, as with Rafaēl of Dashlūṭ, who initially lived in nearby Bāwīṭ; and also ʿAbd Allāh, moving into the district from Būsh, which was a long way north, a flax village outside the Fayyūm (his case is a peculiar one, as he was reported by a village watchman to be beating the latter's own flax, presumably taking it by force, for he was defending himself with his sword).[80] Some of the incomers we see are attached to the army, which is less surprising, but a couple of examples of Maghribīs, that is, immigrants from North Africa, in the 990s do not seem to have military connections. (One of the soldiers, from a Black African regiment, has a wife who in 1069 demands a divorce from him because she 'hates his company',

[77] For *laaū*, see Green, 'A private archive', n. 9 (not in P.Teshlot); cf. also Delattre et al., 'Écrire en arabe et en copte', pp. 177–8, for an unprovenanced letter; for *nawls*, see P.Cair.Arab. 387, which has to be an Ashmūnayn text, because it mentions a village in the district (today a substantial town), Dayrūṭ. For Jewish merchants, see T-S 12.227, 12.2 (Gil K193 [trans. Stillman, *East-West relations*, pp. 365–70], 732); see also P.Vind.Arab. I 2 for Christians.

[78] P.Cair.Arab. 64–6, P.Prag.Arab. 42, 45, 46. The transactions of 1050 may cover a debt relationship, as Vorderstrasse, 'Reconstructing houses', pp. 286–92, argues.

[79] Goitein, *MS*, 1, pp. 222–4; Goldberg, *Trade and institutions*, p. 207. For silk vocabulary, see Gil, 'References to silk'.

[80] P.Teshlot 2, 6; P.Heid.Arab. III 30.

plus a considerable amount of goods which he owes her for maintenance.) Two Christian immigrants from Tinnīs on the coast nearly 500 kilometres away also stand out, for that was a major linen centre; we cannot say what they were doing in Ashmūnayn, but one of them, Isiṭūrūs, married into the above-mentioned silk merchant family, and may have brought some transferable expertise with him.[81] The city, anyway, evidently had long-distance attractions.

This is the economic context which gives structure to a number of interesting letters from the tenth and eleventh centuries which are specifically about exchange. A tenth-century letter to a Muslim politely notes that a silk garment has not come, and that the sender will pay for it only when it does; another to an associate in the town discusses sending weapons, including a shield, which seem to be expected from Kayl, a Christian; another refers to a grain seller who also sells papyrus (in a very late attestation of that writing material), rosewater, and saffron; another discusses the transport by Christian boatmen of flax and perhaps wheat, out of villages in the northern part of Ashmūnayn's district, on a very large scale (in one citation, 800 bales of flax). In the eleventh century, we find two letters to a Muslim in the city, Abū al-Qasīm Hishām: in one, he is accused of incorrect accounting when he sends lupins (lupin seeds are edible); in the other, he is asked to buy 200 *irdabb*s (*c.*18,000 litres) of cheap barley in Ismant, north of the city, and 100 dinars' worth of sugar—again a substantial amount—because Fusṭāṭī merchants are rumoured to be coming to Ashmūnayn and prices are about to go up. Another letter, from a village some way north of the city, reassures the sender's associates that he will not break his ties with them, even though Ashmūnaynī merchants came to him and offered more money. A legal document from 1028 with an Ashmūnayn provenance discusses the unblocking of holding charges for two eunuch slaves, and the payments to the different people who have been feeding them while the deal, which involved a cloth merchant's daughter, went through.[82] This reference to a slave trade in the area also gives some context to a frantic plea from the tenth century to a local judge by a man whose daughter has been abducted, sold into slavery, and found with an Ashmūnaynī; he has neighbours who can swear to her identity, and he evidently expects results.[83]

Most of these letters are one-offs; one cannot even imagine building a picture of any individual merchant from them, or of the relative importance of any type

[81] Non-military Maghribīs: Chrest.Khoury II 24, CPR XXI 88; cf. P.Cair.Arab. 383. Army: P.Cair. Arab. 68, Chrest.Khoury I 18 (the divorce); and Livingston, 'Life in the Egyptian valley', pp. 437–40. Tinnīs: Chrest.Khoury II 24, P.Cair.Arab. 66.

[82] Respectively, P.Cair.Arab. 307, P.Heid.Arab. II 62, P.KarabacekPapiergeschichte p. 80, P.Vind. Arab. I 2, 19 with 36, 20, Chrest.Khoury I 25.

[83] P.Heid.Arab. III 28 (both texts); but see P.Vind.Arab. II 21, 26, concerning another daughter sold off in the city. If, as is likely, these are earlier letters relating to the same case, they complicate it, for the daughter here has been taken by a woman whom the father had rejected in some way, and has apparently been married off.

of product in Ashmūnayn and its district. They provide, however, a further dimension, and a fascinating one at times, to the sense of activity which more mundane texts already convey. They show that commercial dealers in Ashmūnayn often dealt in many types of goods at once, even though they were often so specialized in their basic identities—cloth merchants dealing in slaves, grain sellers dealing in papyrus. They attest, as do documents from the whole of Egypt, to a capillary money economy, and to a widespread use of wage labour; in addition to those cited, one eleventh- (or twelfth-) century letter refers to wage labour used for winnowing grain on state land, and to the refusal of such labourers (*ajir*s) to work for an unpopular estate administrator, to his anger and embarrassment.[84] And—and this seems to me particularly significant—the commercial letters are strikingly similar to the sorts of ways *geniza* merchants wrote to each other. This is important for the long-standing debate about how typical the *geniza* was of commercial life in Egypt as a whole. I have already noted that Jewish merchants from Fusṭāṭ came to buy goods here; so, evidently, did those of other religions (this being the reason why I have stressed religious affiliation in the above descriptions, whenever I could be sure of it). And the mercantile environment they would have found matched that of the capital in many ways. Ashmūnayn's merchants were more integrated into the countryside than were those whose records survive in the *geniza* (and rural cloth-weaving also made the countryside less different from the city), but that is doubtless simply the result of the fact that their city was much smaller—the countryside was only half an hour away, even on foot. They also transacted in goods which, as is generally recognized, Jews did not, or not much: grain, slaves, and arms (see pp. 70, 115 below). But it is equally notable that flax and cloth, which Jews did specialize in, are prominent in this non-Jewish documentation too. At a provincial level, then, the evidence from Ashmūnayn reflects well the world of our Jewish sources, and this can give us greater confidence when we seek to integrate the evidence from documents in both Hebrew and Arabic script elsewhere too. We will come back to this issue later.

* * *

Finally, in this survey, let us look briefly at the village of Ṭuṭūn in the Fayyūm oasis (see Map 6). This was certainly a large settlement; it had been a city under the Romans (Tebtynis, Coptic Touton), although by now was called a *qurā* or *ḍay'a*, 'village', and was probably substantially reduced in size, even if it might well have been considered a small town in many parts of the Mediterranean. We have several documents for house sales from the village, in the ninth to eleventh centuries, and it is clear from these that the settlement was densely built up; the

[84] P.Vind.Arab. III 32. Compare Stillman, 'A case of labor problems', for similar resistance among wage labourers in Būṣīr in the 1030s, and cf. also p. 101 below for Būṣīr and p. 112 below for the Dākhla oasis; and Bondioli, *Peasants, merchants and caliphs*, pp. 73–5, for a winegrowers' strike in P.ReinfandtWeingutbesitzer recto.

boundaries of each house are routinely stated to be streets and other houses.[85] For once, we actually have archaeological back-up for this, in the form of a focussed French-led excavation of a mill, several presses for wine, sugar, or oil, and two attached houses of the ninth and tenth centuries, these built over an earlier house, in stone and brick. (Ṭuṭūn has moved site since, which makes excavation here easier than usual for an Egyptian village.) The ceramics from each were largely local, as one would expect, but included a substantial set of painted and glazed wares from Aswān, far up the Nile, and Fusṭāṭ, plus some LRA 7 amphorae from Middle Egypt, and even some apparently Iraqi lustreware. Ṭuṭūn, although the Fayyūm is geographically separate from the Nile valley, was fully part of region-wide trade circuits.[86]

Ṭuṭūn was a largely Christian village in our period, although Muslims lived there too (they appear, as elsewhere, as witnesses); it had a church, and most of its known inhabitants had Christian or probably Christian names into the mid-eleventh century, when its documentation stops. It was even a Christian intellectual centre, as is attested by the tenth-century Coptic religious manuscripts stated in the texts to have been copied there, apparently in clerical family enterprises.[87] One of its Christian inhabitants, Mīnā b. Jirja (*fl.* 983–1013), several of whose documents survive, was rich enough to buy three female slaves and a male child, Nubian Christians, for the substantial total of 53 dinars (one of them, somewhat disingenuously, was guaranteed not to have been previously acquired 'by pillage or theft, but through sale from one Muslim to another'); he is also recorded buying part of a mill. His family remained important until the very last document surviving from the village, in 1064, in which his grandsons bought land from a 'guardian' (*khafīr*); their father Danā'īl or Rabābīl b. Mīnā was in 1014 a local tax farmer, *ḍāmin*, and thus certainly a stable member of the village elite, but the *khafīr*, one of a new generation of local Muslim Bedouin bosses, marks the beginnings of a generalized Islamicization of the Fayyūm from then onwards.[88] We have some records of collective taxpaying from the village, organized in part by (probably local) Christians; they show a merchant, a land surveyer, and a fortune teller as taxpayers. We also have casual reference to a butcher, a fruit seller, an oil seller, a syrup seller, a builder, a tailor, and a silk merchant or silk weaver; Ṭuṭūn made

[85] *Qurā*, *ḍay'a*: CPR XXVI 10; Chrest.Khoury II 20; P.Vente 25. Housing: P.Frantz-MurphyComparison 1, 2; P.FahmiTaaqud 6, 9; P.Cair.Arab. 57–9; CPR XXVI 10.

[86] Rousset et al., 'Tebtynis 1998'; Rousset and Marchand, 'Secteur nord de Tebtynis . . . 1999'; Rousset et al., 'Secteur nord de Tebtynis . . . 2000'; see further pp. 84, 90 below.

[87] See for the manuscripts Mouton, 'La société villageoise', pp. 231–5. The village church (*kanīsa*) is documented in 879: P.FahmiTaaqud 3.

[88] Mīnā b. Jirja and family: P.Vente 9–11 (quotation from 9), 25, Appendix 1; Chrest.Khoury I 41, 57, II 20. (Other documents exist, according to Yūsuf Rāġib in the edition of P.Transmission, p. 2, but they remain unidentified and unpublished.) For *khafīr*s and the Islamicization of the Fayyūm, see Mouton, 'La société villageoise', pp. 251–9; Wickham, 'The power of property', pp. 94–8; Rapoport, *Rural economy*, pp. 171–248, esp. 231–48.

high-quality *ṭirāz*, embroidered cloth, in the tenth century too, for it survives with the village name on in the Louvre and other museums. Adding to the resources of the village was local natron, for glass production; and pigeon dung, a high-quality fertilizer (cf. p. 365 below), 13 *irdabb*s (some 1200 litres) of which was sold by a Christian to a Muslim for an unspecified sum in 953, which may fit with the ceramic parts of a pigeon cote found at the mill.[89]

We cannot get further inside the economy of Ṭuṭūn than this, but it is clear that the settlement was an active one, with several artisans and food vendors (some quite niche ones), and elites who were at least important locally. The manuscripts and the *ṭirāz*, although decidedly at the luxury end of production, point to an organizational ambition which has some urban aspects. What is equally important, however, is that Ṭuṭūn was surrounded by other documented villages in the southern Fayyūm with similar features: Buljusūq and Ṭalīt were under 4 kilometres away, Uqlūl and Aṭfīḥ, plus the monastery of Dayr Naqlūn, which is currently being excavated, were 15 kilometres away. Many of these show similar artisanal patterns, and Naqlūn's archaeology shows a similar connectedness to the exchange networks of the whole Nile valley. Aṭfīḥ had a silk merchant, Uqlūl two turban-makers; a tax receipt from a set of villages in and near the Fayyūm, including Buljusūq, Aṭfīḥ and the nearby small district capital of Ahnās, closer to the Nile, lists an oil presser, seven shopkeepers (one from each of Buljusūq and Aṭfīḥ), a washerman, a potter, a gardener, a miller, a tailor, a goldsmith, a brickmaker, a cheese seller, a joiner, two couriers and a camel driver. A cache of eleventh-century documents for the village of Damūya at the mouth of the Fayyūm lists two or three separate potters in the village, and two bakers.[90] This network of skills and expertise was dense, and partially specialized; Fayyūmī villagers, almost all peasants, of course, evidently often bought things which they could perfectly well have made at home. So we can see here that Egyptian peasants in the long eleventh century could be attached to at least local market production and exchange; we will see this again later in the chapter too, in some places even more clearly. Some of these villages may well also, earlier, have provided the rural weavers whose cloth was sold from the district capital of Madīnat al-Fayyūm to Fusṭāṭ, in a separate cache of ninth-century texts (see pp. 94–5 below); and the archaeology for our period shows exchange connections both with the capital and farther away still.

Ṭuṭūn thus stands for a network of villages and villagers with considerable access to the commercial economy, at least up to the mid-eleventh century. The

[89] Respectively, P.Prag.Arab. 48, 49, for the taxpayers; for others, P.Prag.Arab. 15, Chrest.Khoury I 41, CPR XXI 80, P.Cair.Arab. 119, P.FahmiTaaqud 9, Chrest.Khoury I 57, P.RagibTroisDocuments 3. For *ṭirāz*, see Mouton, 'La société villageoise', pp. 225–6, and esp. Durand and Rettig, 'Un atelier sous controle califal'; for natron, see P.RagibTroisDocuments 3; for pigeon dung, see P.RagibColombine; cf. Rousset et al., 'Tebtynis 1998', p. 199.

[90] In order, Chrest.Khoury II 2, 4, P.Prag.Arab. 37, and, for Damūya, P.Fay.Villages 6, 9, 11, 15, 16, 19, 20 for potters, 16 for bakers. See in general Mouton, 'La société villageoise', pp. 213–31; this article is basic for the Fayyūm as a whole.

evidence for the Fayyūm becomes much rarer after the 1060s, and runs out for a century after the 1130s; when the oasis comes into focus again in the year 1245, thanks to an exceptionally detailed land survey of the Fayyūm by the former court official al-Nābulusī, the picture is different. By then, almost all non-agricultural production (largely weaving) was apparently concentrated in Madīnat al-Fayyūm itself, as was a diversified market network; sugar and flax, by then the Fayyūm's main cash crops, were likewise concentrated in only a few villages. But we should not conclude that the peasantry of the villages was by now cut out of the exchange economy entirely; we will come back to the point later.[91]

* * *

The examples I have discussed here do not amount to a full history of Egyptian settlement, which cannot be written for this period: too few other towns and villages could be characterized even briefly. But some elements link not only a medium-sized provincial town like Ashmūnayn but even a large village like Ṭuṭūn to the very complex social and economic world of Fusṭāṭ. This is above all the case for the evidence for specialization. Ashmūnayn had a division of productive labour which was certainly rather less than Fusṭāṭ, but which was still conspicuous for a provincial town; both Ashmūnayn and the Fayyūm villages had specialized merchants and shopkeepers too, including sellers of semi-luxury goods. In our scrappier evidence for other places we find similar things: a village silk merchant in Rīfa near Asyūṭ in the eleventh century, or a sugar factory in the small Delta town of Minyat Ziftā in the twelfth.[92] In most of the rest of the Mediterranean in the eleventh century, this specialization was only a feature of large urban centres; and even in the twelfth, in (say) the steadily developing territory around Milan, it was only just beginning to be visible in medium-sized towns (below, pp. 604–8). This is an important part of the evidence, and of the underpinning, for the density of exchange in Egypt, as we shall see.

This specialization raises a wider economic question, however: who, exactly, was buying goods? We have seen that there are good empirical grounds to suppose a peasant market for artisanal goods in Egypt, but how wide did that market spread, socio-economically? The point is an important one for this book as a whole, and needs further discussion, both here and in the next section. Here we have to start with what we know about Egypt's different social strata. Any medieval documentation tells us little about the very poorest strata; and in Egypt, there was always a substantial part of the population which was not only illiterate, but also too poor to have access to scribes to write even the basic short letters which are such a substantial part of our evidence. ('You still owe me one dinar; when

[91] Rapoport, *Rural economy*, esp. pp. 53–141. The survey is edited and translated in Rapoport and Shahar, *The villages of the Fayyum*. Earlier, Madīnat al-Fayyūm had not only been a focus for cloth sales, as we have seen, but also glass-making, as a rare *geniza* text for the oasis tells us: T-S NS J131.

[92] P.Cair.Arab. 72 (a. 1068); see p. 73 below for the sugar factory.

are you going to pay it?' is a common refrain in our texts, and it is certainly small-scale by the standards of much of our commercial evidence; but a dinar could buy around 100 kg of wheat in 1000.[93]) As we saw earlier, Goitein showed that most Jews were poor in Fusṭāṭ, as a majority of its inhabitants of all religions will have been too; all the same, the really poor only directly appear for us in tax receipts, or else in petitions, again particularly in the capital.[94] But the question of how poor the poorest were is intricately related with how prosperous the less poor were, and how rich the rich were, thanks to the surplus the rich got from the peasantry and the urban working classes in tax and rent; and these issues we can say a little more about.

The first point which must be made—it has already been mentioned—is that, in Egypt as a whole, we know less about elites than we do for many other regions. The documentary evidence we have for Egypt in our period does not tell us much about urban elites; we have seen this for Ashmūnayn, and for other towns it is even less helpful. Nor can we say much about major landowners; it is clear that they existed, at least into the twelfth century, but our letter collections do not shed much light on them; they appear in the margins of our material, not in the centre.[95] Only in Fusṭāṭ-Cairo, and to a lesser extent in Alexandria,[96] do we get more than casual reference to rich and/or powerful people. We cannot easily guess at who they were in Ashmūnayn, never mind assess their wealth; and we can do so still less in less well-documented towns, even important ones. In Byzantium and Italy, the fact that texts survive in archives, and that surviving archives were kept by wealthy institutions (usually churches and monasteries in our period), means that rich and powerful laymen and -women regularly appear in them too, as donors and lessees of land, which is, furthermore, sufficiently clearly defined that we can often get a sense of what resources they each had (see pp. 344–5, 494–5 below). In Egypt we cannot. It is, instead, a middling level which most of our documentation, whether in Arabic-script or Hebrew-script texts, refers to. This very broad stratum extended, outside the capital, from peasant owner–cultivators up to lesser rural elites, rich peasants and small-scale rentiers like Mīnā b. Jirja in Ṭuṭūn and his younger contemporary Jirja b. Bifām in nearby Damūya, who called himself a peasant (*muzāriʿ*) in most of his documents (see pp. 64, 113 below); plus dealers in towns like the silk workers of Ashmūnayn, and middle-level tax officials (rather than their superiors): relatively prosperous but

[93] 'You owe me one dinar' (or less): P.Berl.Arab. II 71, P.Heid.Arab. III 8, 42 (here the return pledge is a turban), 43, Chrest.Khoury I 32, P.RichardsWrittenDocuments 4. For the buying power of a dinar, see Ashtor, *Histoire des prix*, p. 124; cf. p. 44 above.

[94] Tax receipts: esp. CPR XXI, and P.Steuerquittungen, often for under a dinar. You had to keep them with you: see p. 37 above. Petitions, etc: Cohen, *Poverty and charity*; for texts, see Cohen, *The voice of the poor*; these texts do indeed, unusually for the middle ages, give the poor a voice (but even then, it is less often the 'structural [i.e. long-term] poor'; cf. ibid., pp. 11–12, 15).

[95] See Wickham, 'The power of property', for what can be said about them.

[96] For Alexandria, see the indications in Frenkel, 'Medieval Alexandria', pp. 30–1.

not really rich. For most purposes I prefer the stress in the Egyptian evidence on the middling strata of society, for they were so much more numerous and socio-economically significant, and on their daily dealings and grievances, as these give a much denser sense of how local society and culture operated; conversely, it is certainly more convenient to use Byzantine and Italian evidence if one wants to discuss the rich and powerful.

One might treat this lack of evidence in a positivist way, and propose that there actually were few richer people in most Egyptian towns, apart from the state officials who do appear in our sources about taxation, plus local military leaders, who would have made up a pretty small and also a transient elite. As noted earlier, there are so few ambitious medieval buildings surviving for most Egyptian provincial towns—in fact, in most cases there are none—that one could well conclude that one level of elite spending was simply absent there. One could here contrast both eleventh-century Italy (where private tower houses for urban elites, in both stone and fired brick, survive in many cities[97]) and Roman imperial Egypt itself, where excavations show private spending on a considerable scale. Indeed, Egyptian documents for the sixth century, which survive as much by chance as do those for later centuries, tell us far more about elites, in a range of provincial towns, than those of the eleventh do, and we can sometimes be sure that these elites were wealthy—or at least locally powerful.[98] Even in villages, headmen are more prominent in earlier centuries (in Jēme across the Nile from Luxor, documents in the eighth century were even dated by their terms of office); village heads certainly existed in our period—we have explicit evidence from Damūya, for example—but are far less visible.[99]

All the same, we cannot use these contrasts, striking though they are, to show that Egyptian elites were generally poorer in the long eleventh century. As to the buildings, in southern towns we do at least have minarets, notably at Aswān, Isnā, and Luxor, which have been plausibly ascribed to local patronage, plus a rebuilding of the central mosque at Qūṣ; these are fairly low-key interventions, but they do show elite self-presentation, which is also shown in the more elaborate tombs in the extramural 'Fāṭimid' cemetery in Aswān, part of which is from our period. Otherwise, Egyptians in our period tended to build in mud brick, which does not last long enough in an ever-renewing urban context to be visible, except in the systematic urban excavations which we rarely have. Qūṣ, which was the most important town in Upper Egypt in the Mamlūk period, when a different sort

97 See the bibliography in Wickham, *Medieval Rome*, p. 160, and pp. 539, 568 below, for Italy.

98 For wealth, see Mazza, *L'archivio degli Apioni*, for the Apions of Oxyrhynchos (Bahnasā); for local power, see, e.g., Sarris, *Economy and society*, pp. 99–113. And this was so even though late Roman Egyptian city elites, taken as a whole, were probably modest by Mediterranean standards; see Wickham, *Framing*, p. 766.

99 For headmen in Jēme, see the lists in Till, *Datierung*, pp. 234–5; cf. Wickham, *Framing*, pp. 422–8. Damūya: Mouton, 'La société villageoise', pp. 183–4, and P.Fay.Villages 2, 8, 12, 30–3, 39.

of documentation also attests to a substantial stratum of local elites, has no surviving Mamlūk buildings either.[100] We can get a sense of what we are missing above all from Aswān. Here, although no standing building from our period except the minaret survives inside the medieval town, which underlies much of the modern one, the multiple rescue excavations of the Swiss Institute and the Egyptian Ministry of State for Antiquities in the last two decades in over a hundred small sites, although by no means fully published, show in the annual interims—besides the mud-brick shops, workshops, and houses from our period, as earlier and later in the middle ages, plus an organized sewerage system—sections of two or three substantial buildings in sandstone and fired or mud brick, which must have been either public or elite private buildings.[101] The use of stone reflects the fact that Aswān was close to sources of good-quality stone, as not all cities were; this can also be seen in the cemetery, and in a large Christian monastery, Dayr Anbā Hadrā on the other side of the Nile, also dating from our period; but the town's buildings still did not survive as standing monuments. Such capillary excavations are absent elsewhere, but they will almost certainly show something similar, if they happen in the future.[102]

As to elite invisibility, one thing which is clear is that urban elites in Egypt were less formally characterized in our period—and in the whole period after *c.*800—than they had been in, say, the fourth century. They were not any longer used systematically to run the tax system; by now, as in Ashmūnayn, this was focussed on a local financial administrator, an *ʿāmil*, nominated by and perhaps often sent

[100] Creswell, *The Muslim architecture of Egypt*, 1, pp. 146–60, argued that five minarets in Upper Egypt were put up by the de facto ruler Badr al-Jamālī in the 1070s–1080s, but Bloom, 'Five Fatimid minarets', argues convincingly that they were the result of private patronage. For Qūṣ, see Garcin, 'Remarques sur un plan'; Garcin, *Un centre musulman*, pp. 254–72 for the Mamlūks, pp. 273–85 for no surviving buildings. (The central mosque has a minbar which is more ambitious, but it was put up by a *wazīr* in the 1150s, not a local patron: ibid., 87n.) For the Aswān cemetery, see Creswell, *The Muslim architecture of Egypt*, 1, pp. 131–45; ʿAbd al-Tawab, *Stèles islamiques* (which, however, publishes only the pre-Fāṭimid gravestones).

[101] The interims can be found at http://swissinst.ch/html/forschung_neu.html; for substantial buildings, see esp. von Pilgrim et al., 'The town of Syene' (for the building in area 32); von Pilgrim and Müller, 'Report on the ninth season' (area 50); von Pilgrim et al., 'Report on the 16th season' (area 91); for the sewage system, see von Pilgrim et al., 'Report on the 19th season', pp. 13–14. For a focussed study of much of the Islamic-period ceramics, see Williams, *Syene VI*, which includes, pp. 15–34, 63–83, the best current summary of the rescue work as a whole for our period, and an overview of the city's ninth- and tenth-century society at pp. 110–30.

[102] For Dayr Anbā Hadrā (which is largely a tenth-century construction in its present form, with some earlier elements) see the DAI website, https://www.dainst.org/projekt/-/project-display/63443, and Dekker, 'The development of the church at Dayr Anba Hadra'. The monastery was presumably large because of gifts from Christian Aswānīs, some of whom were thus presumably themselves rich; no other towns are close. The other visibly large monasteries from the period—such as those of Wādī Naṭrūn, which still stand (see, e.g., Innemée, 'The monastery of St. Macarius'), or that of Naqlūn, which is being excavated (see the interims in *Polish Archaeology in the Mediterranean*)—are in rural areas, but are less far from Fusṭāṭ and Alexandria, and doubtless had a wider, not necessarily only rural patronage; indeed, St Macarius was a centre for the patriarchs of Alexandria. Note, however, that even though these are all large establishments, they are in themselves not particularly ambitious monumentally, at least by western medieval (or even Byzantine) standards, with the partial exception of the Aswān monastery.

from Fusṭāṭ.[103] Similarly, every town had a Muslim *qāḍī* to run justice of all kinds, who in contemporary cities in, for example, Khūrāsān in eastern Iran would have definitely been from the local educated/religious elite, the *'ulamā'*;[104] but we cannot be sure that *qāḍī*s were local in Egypt, and in fact, as again in Ashmūnayn, local *'ulamā'* are themselves little documented in our period. This may simply be because Egypt remained more Christian than were other Islamic regions, particularly Iraq and northern/eastern Iran, and that meant that even urban centres often had Christian, rather than Muslim elites which the rulers in Fusṭāṭ perhaps did not choose to recognize formally. But although elites remain hard to characterize, when we have any evidence, we find at least a few traces of them. However uncertainly, we did see this in Ashmūnayn. Tinnīs is another example; the *History of the patriarchs of the Egyptian church*, here a mid-eleventh-century text, relates that its Christian leaders in the 970s petitioned the recently arrived Fāṭimid caliph al-Mu'izz to rid the town of a violent youthful Muslim leading faction, and that the new Kutāma Berber *wālī* or military governor obliged by massacring them all at a banquet; the story is highly implausible in this form (although Tinnīs does seem to have been the focus of a tax revolt), but it certainly assumes the existence of potentially powerful informal elites, of two religions. The important Jewish community of Minyat Ziftā had identifiable leaders in the twelfth century, who cannot have been the only leaders, or perhaps even the most influential figures, in this average Delta town.[105] Every town must indeed have had its own substantial landowners, even if (in the absence of land documents) we can say little about them; and after the early tenth century each certainly had its own local *ḍāmin*s or tax farmers, who could be of any religion, and who visibly became, even if they were not at the outset, prosperous and locally powerful.[106] Given the wealth of the Egyptian countryside, it would be hard to argue that these figures were not, fairly frequently, rich.

The point is, then, that wealthy people did exist in towns, however indirect our evidence is for them. Here, we do not need to go further into why they were not more visible, or more corporately identifiable, or more important in local government; it is enough to show that they existed. They certainly had buying power. They will have been buying the provincial equivalents of the carpets, cushions, and hangings which we can see in accounts of houses in Fusṭāṭ, and also the silk

[103] See p. 50 above. The relatively decentralized system of the first Islamic century was already more top-down than it had been in the fourth century; see the overviews in Wickham, *Framing*, pp. 596–602 and (especially) Sijpesteijn, *Shaping a Muslim state*, pp. 64–81.

[104] e.g. Bulliet, *The patricians of Nishapur*. Egypt in this period has no surviving collective biographies of local *'ulamā'*, as in Nishapur; the first references to them I have seen are to al-Udfuwī's fourteenth-century compilations, which relate to Upper Egypt, and stress Aswān in particular; see n. 31 above and n. 243 below.

[105] *History of the patriarchs*, 2/ii, ed. and trans. 'Abd al-Masīḥ et al., pp. 131–3; for the tax revolt, see Brett, *The rise of the Fatimids*, pp. 307–8; for Minyat Ziftā, see Goitein, *MS*, 2, pp. 44–51.

[106] See Wickham, 'The power of property', for a survey; for *ḍāmins*, see esp. Sijpesteijn, 'Profit following responsibility', and the Jewish examples in Goitein, *MS*, 2, pp. 354–63, 606.

which is documented in Ashmūnayn and Uqlūl. (They, of course, bought more expensive luxuries on occasion too.) But, conversely, the bulk of our evidence shows that they were by no means the only people with buying power. There was also a very substantial stratum of reasonably prosperous urban figures, and also rural figures, as we saw in the Fayyūm, who could and did buy artisanal goods as well; Egyptian demand was by no means based exclusively, or even for the most part, on the rich. This is why the division of artisanal and commercial labour which I have been stressing, in both town and country, could be supported—because there were local buyers who extended well beyond elites. We will see this point made again when we look at the archaeology, which shows a wide availability of ceramic types on urban and rural sites alike, and also when we look at the production and sale of flax, which sometimes benefited peasants directly.

So there was a capillary economy in Egypt which by no means all looked to Fusṭāṭ, and which was not more than marginally driven by the tax system; it was based on demand for products at every social level except that of the destitute. It sustained the urbanism which we have looked at, but also crossed the country, large towns, small towns, villages alike. Egypt also had an urban waged sector, as all regions with substantial towns did, but not only that: it also had a much higher proportion of rural wage labourers than most of the rest of the Mediterranean (or indeed northern Europe) had in our period, even if they will have been greatly outnumbered by the peasantry. When wage labourers were paid in money, as was universally the case in urban environments—and in the countryside as well, in our rare references to what rural wage labourers were paid—the existence of a market from which non-elites could buy food and clothing must indeed be automatically assumed.[107] The economy was sufficiently elaborate that in some places it sustained artisans such as village bakers, whose buyers must mostly have been the peasantry.[108] Baking bread is not that hard, and peasants in most of Europe (even townspeople, sometimes), in much later periods than this, generally expected to make their own;[109] here, however, it was plausible for them to buy it from specialists. Artisans were not only supplying elites, but also, at least sometimes, a mass market.

[107] For urban wages (almost all from Fusṭāṭ), see Goitein, *MS*, 1, pp. 89–99, and, less usefully, Ashtor, *Histoire des prix*, pp. 223–5. Rural wage labour in money: P.Hamb.Arab. I 13 d, CPR XXVI 15; Richter and Schmelz, 'Der spätkoptische Arbeitsvertrag'; earlier, P.Cair.Arab. 96 (a. 842); and, from the Būṣīr flax area: T-S K15.53 (Gil K274), 12.27 with NS308.119 (Gil K191, 193; trans Stillman, 'A case of labor problems'), 12.31. There are plenty of other references to rural wage labourers (*ajirs*), but not to what they were paid. In the rest of the Mediterranean, wage labourers were rare in agriculture, and often paid in kind: see, e.g., p. 391 below.

[108] Citations of rural bakers (*farrāns*): P.Fay.Villages 16 (two at Damūya), P.Teshlot 6, plus the ex-rural baker in Ashmūnayn in P.Cair.Arab. 328—they are not so very numerous (cf. Mouton, 'La société villageoise', pp. 217–18), but they are enough to indicate their standard presence in the countryside.

[109] For Italian cities, one sign is archaeological finds of *testi di pane* for home baking (for Rome, see, e.g., Ricci, 'Ceramica acroma da fuoco', pp. 217–22), although urban bakers are certainly attested too; for bakers in Lombardy, see Chapter 6 below, esp. nn. 311, 336.

The existence of this market shows that whatever else we can say, peasant society and most levels of the urban poor were not so immiserated in Egypt that their demand could not sustain this capillary economy. Everyone paid taxes to the state, as we have seen, which paid for a large state official stratum, and peasant tenants paid rent to landowners as well; these obligations sustained the rich, but it should be clear from the foregoing that elite wealth, although for the most part based on surplus taken from peasants and urban and rural wage labourers, by no means meant that the latter themselves had no surplus at all beyond subsistence. We will come back to how that worked in the next section.

2.3 The Agricultural Economy

Famously, it hardly rains in Egypt. The country's agricultural economy thus depends entirely on the water of the Nile. Until the finishing of the Aswān High Dam in 1970, this always meant the annual flood, essentially in August and September, which ideally covered most of the agricultural land of the Ṣaʿīd (the Nile valley south of Fusṭāṭ) and the Delta, and allowed the irrigation of the rest through a series of carefully maintained canals (including the Fayyūm oasis, which was not flooded, but which was irrigated by a waterway, the Baḥr al-Yūsuf, running off the Nile higher up). If the annual flood was too low, and/or the canals badly maintained, crops failed, and famine and disease ensued; this was particularly the case for the twin cities of Fusṭāṭ-Cairo, which were large enough to have to be fed by supplies from a long way outside their immediate territory. No other city in Egypt needed supply networks of that complexity, except probably Alexandria and Tinnīs, important port and productive cities whose fertile hinterlands were very small. It follows that two aspects of the Nile's ecology had to be particularly carefully managed: the canal system and the supply of the capital. The latter was not the direct responsibility of the state, but the market system which brought grain to Fusṭāṭ-Cairo was watched over and managed by any government which cared about competence. So (later chronicles say) al-Yāzūrī, *wāzir* in 1055, dealt with the threat to the capital of one of the lowest Nile floods of the century by opening state granaries (which existed largely for this purpose) and fixing the prices of grain; earlier and more brutally, al-Ḥākim had supposedly dealt with the famine of 1008 by threatening to kill instantly anyone who was found to be hoarding even small quantities of grain, a plausible threat given that caliph's record.[110]

[110] See Bianquis, 'Une crise frumentaire'; Shoshan, 'Fatimid grain policy'; Elbendary, 'The worst of times', and Lev, *State and society*, pp. 162–78; they also discuss counter-instances, lowish Niles whose effects on the capital were made much worse by incompetence, esp. in 1023–5 and the late 1060s. For al-Yāzūrī and al-Ḥākim, see al-Maqrīzī, *Ighāthat*, trans. Allouche, pp. 32–3, 35–6. See pp. 280–2 below for Constantinople, which faced the same issues. Managed trade in both capitals had replaced the

As to canal maintenance, the state controlled the biggest canal dykes (for *ṣūltanīya* canals), but the rest (*baladīya* canals) were the responsibility of local communities. As al-Nābulusī put it in the 1240s in his detailed survey of the Fayyūm, this simply consisted of 'a large group of men from the villages of the Fayyūm, as well as engineers, [who] gather together'; in general, they did so under the leadership of local officials and community elders/headmen (*shaykh*s), who from the later twelfth century onwards included military tax farmers, *muqṭā*'s. The issue of such maintenance is less visible in Fāṭimid-period documentation than might be expected, even in texts written by or to officials; we mostly hear about it in the context of much later narratives lamenting (as chroniclers do everywhere) whatever was understood to be the ruin of their country in their particular period.[111] It is fairly clear that the century after the Black Death, the period of most of our narratives, was indeed a period of deteriorating canal maintenance, given that Egypt was then seriously underpopulated (see p. 126 below). Under the Fāṭimids, by contrast, the absence of discussion of the issue seems to me significant; it indicates that the business of repairing and managing canals and dykes was normally progressing without general problems, at least in the areas of Middle Egypt best illuminated by our texts. This is certainly confirmed by al-Nābulusī; even though he criticizes the ineptitude of locally run management, he testifies to its commitment. Administrative manuals from the decades around 1200, by Ibn Mammātī and, still more, al-Makhzūmī, which discuss at length (although schematically) the details of tax assessment after the flood, skip over the details of irrigation; it evidently did not seem problematic.[112] Essentially, it was in the interests of peasant communities to get their local irrigation right if they possibly could, in every century of Egyptian history, and they took it seriously. They might not have taken a wider social responsibility so seriously, but fortunately, as the Nile reached nearly everywhere, individual communities could not so easily channel it at the expense of others. The exception was the Fayyūm, for the water of the Baḥr al-Yūsuf could be drawn off for irrigation farther upstream in the districts of Bahnasā and Ashmūnayn—and indeed was, al-Nābulusī says—but even then to the detriment of only a minority of villages.[113]

annona of the Roman Empire, which provided free grain to the inhabitants of its capitals via the tax system—for which, see, among many, Durliat, *De la ville antique* (pp. 323–49 for Alexandria).

[111] Sijpesteijn, *Shaping a Muslim state*, pp. 17–24 gives a good brief survey, using both early and late medieval evidence. The best monographic account is Rapoport and Shahar, 'Irrigation', for the thirteenth-century Fayyūm (quotation at p. 9); see further Rapoport, *Rural economy*, pp. 61–8. For the division of responsibilities between the state and local communities, see Ibn Mammātī, *Qawānīn*, trans. Cooper, sect. 5 (pp. 60–77); at 5.11, Ibn Mammātī sees state dykes as like city walls, and local dykes as like urban housing, an interesting but not quite coherent image. For the thirteenth–fourteenth centuries, see also Sato, *State and rural society*, pp. 220–33; for the late middle ages and the sixteenth century, see esp. Michel, *L'Égypte des villages*, pp. 264–77.

[112] For al-Nābulusī, see Rapoport and Shahar, 'Irrigation', pp. 11–14. For al-Makhzūmī, see *Minhāj*, trans. Frantz-Murphy, p. 29, a bare reference. Ibn Mammātī (see n. 111 above) says more than al-Makhzūmī, but the detail is still not great there.

[113] Rapoport and Shahar, 'Irrigation', pp. 9–10.

Such local irrigation initiatives fit the fact that village names using the word *sāqiya*, bucketwheel (for lifting water in irrigation), were common, such as Sāqiyat Mūsā, north of Ashmūnayn, attested in the tenth century and still there today.[114]

The need to manage the Nile is often seen as contributing to the overwhelming dominance of the state in rural Egypt, which supposedly resulted in the state control of all rural property—extending even to the distribution of seed corn to peasants.[115] This was far from the case, in two separate respects. First, it seems as if the government intervened in canal maintenance in our period much less than under the Romans; it left much more to local initiative.[116] But secondly, conversely, under the Roman Empire private property-owning, by both the rich and the poor, was normal, and matched that of all the rest of the empire; there was state land, certainly, but it did not dominate in any part of Egypt which we have documents for. As I have argued elsewhere, this pattern continued well into our period. It is true that by 1300 (indeed, the 1240s, at least in al-Nābulusī's Fayyūm) the state did indeed claim ownership of most land, and the peasant majority simply paid tax—and not rent—to tax farmers and other officials. By contrast, however, in the tenth to twelfth centuries and perhaps sometimes later, private landed estates (worked by rent-paying tenants and by some wage labourers) and peasant proprietors owning land fragmented into sets of single fields are a standard part of our documentation, with state property making up perhaps a third of Egypt's cultivable land. As we saw earlier (p. 35), we have a large amount of evidence for tax-farming from 900 (and earlier) onwards, initially by private contractors, *ḍāmins*, who paid an agreed amount to the state and exacted, or sought to exact, a higher amount from the peasants in their assigned areas (*ḍamāns*), and then, after 1100 or so, also by soldiers, *muqṭā*'s, who similarly took tax from assigned areas (*iqṭā*'s) as military pay. These coexisted with private landowning, including that of peasants, as is shown by the land acquisitions of the rich peasant (*muzāri*ʿ) Jirja of Damūya, on the eastern edge of the Fayyūm, dating to the 1020s (for once, we are dealing with a real archive here; it was found by excavators in a ceramic pot); Jirja, like his contemporary Danāʾīl b. Mīnā in nearby Ṭuṭūn (see p. 54 above), was, in fact, both a landowner on a medium scale and a tax farmer for a nearby village. There was sometimes a visible tendency, in the twelfth century at least, for tax farmers to begin to consider their assigned land as, in effect, their property, or else to appropriate it into their own properties nearby, but this too only reinforces a basic pattern which had developed over the previous two centuries, that of a local

[114] Sāqiyat Mūsā: P.Prag.Arab. 89, P.Cair.Arab. 276, Chrest.Khoury II 25.

[115] For the problem of seed corn, see the citations in Wickham, 'The power of property', p. 78n. For total state control, see, e.g., Rabie, *The financial system*, pp. 68–72 (who does not stress the role of the Nile); criticism in Michel, 'Devoirs fiscaux', pp. 555–6, which is the best overall guide to the later medieval Egyptian peasantry.

[116] For the pre-Islamic period, see, e.g., Bonneau, *La crue du Nil*, pp. 53–5.

network of tax-farming coexisting with a local network of landowning, which, at least in the eleventh century, still extended to peasants.[117]

Exactly why this balance flipped over, doubtless at different speeds in different places, across the twelfth century and into the thirteenth, after which state land and military tax-farming apparently dominated, remains unclear. The moment of change unfortunately postdates the sharp drop in the number of published Arabic-script documents, and *geniza* texts say little about agriculture. I would tentatively associate it with the growing importance of *iqṭā*ʿs in the late Fāṭimid period, and the greater closeness of *iqṭā*ʿ-holders, given that they were essentially army men, to the state, which was particularly important in a country where the state never let go of the whole network of tax assessment and collection. The assumption that the lands so assigned were not only the state's to give out, but the state's to own, may well have developed for this reason; much Islamic law had also long made this assumption, at least in abstract terms, which will have given a theoretical backing to the process, but only once it had begun. When Saladin extended *iqṭā*ʿs to the whole of Egypt for his incoming army in the 1170s, this tendency probably speeded up, but it had already started before that. Local landowners, if they were influential (including, perhaps, the heirs of village leaders like Jirja), probably reshaped their local control into tax-farming rather than landowning, and sought to survive that way; elites across history have been the social group most prepared to change their whole identity and economic base in order to stay privileged. We have to deal in hypotheses here, as the evidence is thin for the twelfth century.[118] But either way, the idea that rural land in Egypt normally belonged to the state, although it was becoming more important in that century, was not immemorial, or Nile-related—far from it—and was an essentially contingent result of specific sociopolitical developments in the latest Fāṭimid decades and after. For most of our period in Egypt, it was not in evidence; instead, private landed property dominated.

This matters in a book about exchange, because it has important potential implications for how far trade goods got into local societies. Cultivators of the land were the great majority of the inhabitants of Egypt, as of every other region in the settled medieval world. Exactly how great a majority is unclear; we do not have the data for our period that Roger Bagnall and Bruce Frier had for the third and fourth centuries, when they calculated that roughly a third of Egypt's population lived in towns.[119] That was a very large percentage indeed by pre-industrial standards, and was never matched in medieval Europe until, perhaps, thirteenth-century Flanders and northern Italy. It is very possible that it continued in Egypt

[117] For all this, see Wickham, 'The power of property'. For Jirja, see P.Fay.Villages, which edits his archive: 5–6, 10–16, 19–27 for his land acquisitions, 28 for his tax-farming, here called *qabāla*. For state land, see Bondioli, *Peasants, merchants and caliphs*, pp. 2–102.

[118] Wickham, 'The power of property', pp. 88–103.

[119] Bagnall and Frier, *The demography*, pp. 53–6.

in the medieval centuries, however, for Egyptian agriculture was so productive; Fusṭāṭ-Cairo became bigger than the Roman capital at Alexandria had been; Aswān in our period had, as recent excavations show, a larger size than its predecessor, Roman Syene.[120] All the same, that would have left two thirds in villages, most of them working the land directly; and this is a minimum. The question is how far the latter were simply subsistence cultivators, growing the great bulk of what they lived on (including weaving linen and woollen clothing from their own flax and sheep), and how far they linked into wider markets. This would depend on how much surplus they had over and above seed corn, rent, and tax, and on how available markets and external goods were. The latter is at least easy to answer: markets were readily available in our period. We have already seen that artisans, including some niche ones, existed in villages, with presumably largely peasant buyers; some peasants even bought bread rather than making it themselves; and, as we shall see in the next section, many of them could indeed link into wider patterns of exchange, sometimes very large-scale ones, in fact, as, for example, when Nile valley peasants (*muzāriʿūn*) sold flax to Jewish merchants who sold it on as far away as Palermo (see pp. 100–3 below). The substantial presence of wage labourers on estates, paid in money, fits with a highly marketized economy too, as we have also seen (p. 61). There is a world of difference between an elite market based on a commercial economy which above all concerns wealthy landowners and state officials as buyers, and a mass market which involves the large peasant majority; we will explore the difference throughout this book. Egypt in our period had both, but, I conclude, was characterized by the latter still more than by the former.

Marketization is not the only issue, however; the amount of available surplus which peasants had to sell, in order to buy from outside, is at least as important, as it underpins all exchange. The core underlying point here is that wheat, Egypt's staple crop, had high yields there. Up to and over 12:1 can be argued for in the Roman period, and up to 20:1 (20 irdabbs of wheat per *faddān* of land) is claimed by the usually careful Ibn Mammātī, who wrote a manual for state administration at the end of the twelfth century—and there was less need for fallow in most places, thanks to the Nile flood (the Fayyūm was the main exception here). He says this is a maximum, so 12:1 would still work as an average, and it could have been more.[121] Wheat could thus sustain large numbers of non-agriculturalists,

[120] Williams, *Syene VI*, pp. 34, 142.

[121] Roman wheat yields: Bowman, 'Agricultural production in Egypt', p. 247, following Rowlandson, *Landowners and tenants*, pp. 247–52. Ibn Mammātī, *Qawānīn*, trans. Cooper, 6.3, p. 115; he makes it explicit that one *irdabb* (although sometimes only $^2/_3$ to $^5/_6$ of that) was a normal amount of wheat to sow per *faddān*. See Rapoport, *Rural economy*, pp. 81–2. The figure of 20:1 would be high, and indeed Ibn Mammātī says it could be between 2:1 and 20:1, 'depending on [the quality of] the soil'. But in Sicily, where dry farming dominated, we have good evidence for 10:1 yields (see p. 241 below), so it is reasonable to suppose that in always irrigated Egypt it was normally higher than that, as indeed Ibn Mammātī implies.

more than was the case in most other Mediterranean regions, living off both the rents and the taxes peasants paid. Unfortunately, providing figures for Egypt about exactly how heavy these were is very difficult, and frankly unreliable—more indeed than for some other regions, even though our evidence is otherwise so much better than it is elsewhere for so many aspects of the economy. Both rents and taxes are characteristically described as fixed sums of money in our documents, which are very hard to set against what resources peasants actually had. When we can attach rent levels to the size of tenures (which we can on a very few occasions, but only in the ninth and mid-tenth centuries), we find between just under 1 and 2.5 dinars taken in rent per *faddān* of land, in a period in which wheat prices seem to show a wide variation between 0.5 and 2.3 *irdabb*s per dinar, so a possible variation between ½ and 5 *irdabb*s: between 4 and 40 per cent of crop, to take the yield average suggested above. Our data here are too unfocussed and too early for this to be more than very indicative, but most of the rents are below 1.5 dinars, so 20–25 per cent of the crop might be a possible median here.[122] Tax levels, when taken in money, were probably similar: Ibn Mammātī in the same discussion specified 3 *irdabb*s per *faddān*, 25 per cent, for the land tax (*kharāj*) on wheat (although earlier it was at least sometimes less), and he states that it was then cut to 2½ *irdabb*s from 1176/7 onwards. We might, speaking very roughly, be looking at up to half the crop going to landowners and the state, when we are dealing with tenants, and up to a quarter or so when we are dealing with peasant owners. Christian peasants, still the great majority, paid the *jizya* poll tax on top of that, at a fixed rate of up to a dinar; this might push the figure to nearly 60 per cent of crop for Christian tenants. If all these figures can be relied on (a big if), this was a high and challenging figure, although considerably lower for landowning peasants.[123] Rent and taxation in money, even if money did not constitute the whole of the fiscal burden, forced peasants onto the market, simply to be able to supply the coins to tax officials and tax farmers. And what caused particular difficulties for peasants was that taxation was taken in tranches, at several points in the year. This very often meant that they had to find extra money at unfavourable times. Lorenzo Bondioli has shown how the practice of making advance wheat sales at low prices, which we have documentation for, was a logical

[122] P.Cair.Arab. 79 (early ninth century, 0.8 dinars per *faddān*), CPR XXI 15 (a. 867, 0.8 dinars per *faddān*), 20 (a. 881/2, 1.5 dinars per *faddān*), P.SijpesteijnTutun (a. 860, 2.5 dinars per *faddān*), P.Cair. Arab. 83 (a. 959/60, 1 dinar per *faddān*). For ninth- and tenth-century prices, see P.David-WeillLouvre 15, P.Prag.Arab. 71, P.Cair.Arab. 377, P.Vind.Arab. I 64; but we would expect prices to vary greatly, even in normal years, and, in fact, in the third of these we find nearly the whole range set out above, in a single document. Thanks to Lorenzo Bondioli for discussion and advice here.

[123] Ibn Mammātī, *Qawānīn*, trans. Cooper, 6.3, p. 115; for an earlier lower figure, see CPR XI 11 (a. 860, 1.3 dinars per *faddān*, around 20% of crop). For *jizya* of up to a dinar per taxpayer in the late tenth century and early eleventh, see P.Cair.Arab. 195, P.KarabacekPapier 2, 5, P.Steuerquittungen 27, 28. Tax was largely in money in our period, but there was certainly taxation in kind too, as Ibn Mammātī indeed makes explicit: see n. 24 above.

consequence of this; peasants lost out further by having to collect money in advance on bad terms, in order to pay the next tranche of taxation.[124]

It is not surprising that all our sources stress the burdensome nature of taxation, and rightly so. All the same, when yields were as high as they were in Egypt, even the levels of tax plus rent which might be hypothesized here would not reduce most peasants to penury, unless they had very small holdings, especially not peasant owners—and the documentation we have indicates that a substantial percentage of peasants did indeed own their own land into the eleventh century. It is also likely that the levels of overall exploitation eventually dropped. When the state took over all or most land, by the thirteenth century, al-Nābulusī's survey of the Fayyūm shows tax levels of 2.5–3 *irdabbs* per *faddān*, 20–25 per cent of the crop, matching Ibn Mammātī, with very little extra on top, as peasants here were by now overwhelmingly Muslim. Landowning peasants had by now in effect ceased to exist; but burdens seem not to have significantly worsened, for all that.[125] There was a margin for more than just survival here, and it is that margin which allowed for the clear evidence we have for peasant buying, throughout Egypt. Indeed, some peasants and rural wage labourers could be quite proactive: they could protest against wage rates; and they could engage in aggressive selling tactics in the flax villages south of Cairo, in an area where peasants were sufficiently far from simple subsistence strategies that they may have been cash-cropping flax, which was much more remunerative than wheat (see pp. 100–3 below). That flexibility was quite as much a marker of the Egyptian economy as heavy rent/tax levels were, and it is that which underpinned the economic complexity which we have seen thus far, and which we will see more of later.

* * *

We need now to look at what agriculture in Egypt actually did produce, for both subsistence and exchange. In the Roman Empire, most of our written evidence for what Egypt produced and exported concerns wheat. Its main artisanal productions for export seem to have been above all papyrus, the universal writing material of the period, which was grown and manufactured in the Nile Delta, and linen; but these are not as prominent in our sources. The wheat export, however, was above all in taxation; it was used to feed the city of Rome and later Constantinople, and also helped supply the imperial frontier armies. This focus on wheat had a strong colonial element; it reflected the needs of the empire, not of Egypt itself, and, of course, it was not paid for. Late Roman papyri otherwise give evidence for the production of wine, particularly in Middle Egypt, which was also the main area of production of the carrot-shaped amphora called by archaeologists LRA 7, used for wine above all; Egyptian wine was almost all consumed in the region, however, and was regarded by non-Egyptians as of poor

[124] Bondioli, *Peasants, merchants, and caliphs*, pp. 130–6.
[125] Rapoport, *Rural economy*, pp. 81–2.

quality.[126] After the Islamic conquest in 640–2, these patterns had to change, for the caliphal regime of the Umayyads did not transport wheat in the same way (they did use Egyptian wheat to supply the religious centres of Mecca and Madīna, a supply system which continued into our period, but these were only small towns). For the most part, as noted earlier, they used taxation from all their provinces to pay for occupying armies which lived in the region—which here meant the supply of Fusṭāṭ, for most of the Arabs in early Islamic Egypt lived there. It cannot be said that taxation lessened after the end of the great wheat exports of the Roman period, but Egyptian agricultural produce, however it was distributed, was for the most part consumed locally.[127] The early ʿAbbāsid Caliphate did aim to centralize taxation rather more, and once the tax revolts quietened down after 832, the middle third of the ninth century was the high point for external control of Egypt in the medieval period; this is also the only period in which we can find non-Egyptians—Iraqi high officials and ʿAbbāsid royals—holding substantial estates in the region.[128] After 868, however, when Ahmād ibn Ṭūlūn established effective autonomy for his own regime, Egypt did not pay tax to outsiders again on any scale (if we set aside the weaker ʿAbbāsid reoccupation of the period 905–35/44) until the Ottoman conquest in 1517. The colonial economy, which was at least part of the Egyptian experience under the Romans, was already far less in evidence when Ibn Ṭūlūn made himself autonomous, and it disappeared entirely after the 940s. The developments of the Ṭūlūnid period (which included, as we shall see, the expansion of textile manufacturing) made possible Fāṭimid economic patterns, although these developed in new ways as well.

Wheat remained the staple throughout Egypt in the Fāṭimid period. It is the most common food crop mentioned in documents; it far outweighs barley and rice, the main alternative grains—although rice is referred to in the *geniza* slightly more often than in the Arabic-script documents, which probably shows that it was grown in the Delta, and perhaps also that it was more important in the twelfth century than in the eleventh.[129] The trading of wheat was complex, as Arabic-script

[126] See, e.g., the survey in Wickham, *Framing*, pp. 761–4.

[127] See in general Kennedy, *The armies of the caliphs*, esp. pp. 74–6; for the Mecca transport, see, e.g., *EI*[2], s.v. al-Ḳulzum (E. Honigmann and R. Y. Ebied); and, extending into our period, Bramoullé, *Les Fatimides et la mer*, p. 57.

[128] Morimoto, 'Land tenure', pp. 130–4. Third-generation Egyptian Arabs also began to be landowners: Sijpesteijn, *Shaping a Muslim state*, p. 169; for examples of ninth-century Arab landowners, see P.Cair.Arab. 53, 240, 289; P.Khalili I 18.

[129] Barley appears for our period in P.Heid.Arab. II 34, III 4, P.Cair.Arab. 44, 291, 299, P.Prag.Arab. 73, P.HanafiTwoNewEditions 1, P.Steuerquittungen 30, P.GenizahCambr. 54 (the largest-scale), P.Vind.Arab. I 41, 64—a respectable group of texts. For rice before 1200, I have, however, only found P.Cair.Arab. 423 (9th century) and P.Hamb.Arab. I 13 d (*c.* 910). In the *geniza*, it appears in an account book from 1045/6 of Nahray b. Nissīm, T-S K15.53 (Gil K274), and then in up to twenty other texts of the eleventh and twelfth centuries; by 1120, there was a Dār al-Aruzz, a probably state-run rice warehouse, in Fusṭāṭ, which indicates a scale for rice exchange which we cannot see a century earlier (Goitein, *MS*, 1, p. 119). Ibn Ḥawqal in the later tenth century (*Kītāb ṣūrat al-arḍ*, trans. Kramers and Wiet, 1, pp. 135, 158), and, in the same period, al-Muqaddasī (*Aḥsan al-taqāsīm*, trans Miquel, pp. 121, 131) state that the Fayyūm is a major centre of rice production, but our extensive documentation

letters show us. We find imports into Fusṭāṭ, as we would expect, as the capital must have been dependent on massive wheat imports from many parts of the Nile valley (the examples in the texts are mostly from the Fayyūm), but we also find, in one letter, people coming into Fusṭāṭ to *buy* wheat, and in the same letter wheat from the district of Jīza, on the doorstep of the capital, is sold in Alexandria. In Upper Egypt, notwithstanding the relative rarity of letters for the far south, we find wheat being sent from Akhmīm upstream to Qūṣ, and separately to Aswān, and Isnā importing wheat too.[130] All these towns had prosperous agricultural hinterlands (except Aswān) and equal access to the Nile, and such imports must, therefore, be responses to possibly quite minor local price differences—this is certainly reflected in references to changing grain prices in these and several other letters. This was very possibly because some provincial towns were growing,[131] and perhaps also because of different competencies in grain storage. Some of the scale of this transport was very large: 500 *irdabb*s (*c.*45,000 litres) in the Qūṣ letter, and a similar scale for the planned acquisitions in Fusṭāṭ.[132]

The letters just mentioned are undated, and in these cases they could come from any part of the long eleventh century. We cannot attach them to dated low Niles—and anyone buying 400–600 *irdabb*s of wheat in Fusṭāṭ was certainly not doing it in a hard year for the city. They simply reflect that fact that wheat, even though it was available in every part of Egypt, was, nonetheless, bought and sold along a complex network of routes which by no means all focussed on the demand of the capital. It was probably not so often exported, in strong contrast to the Roman period; we cannot be quite sure of that, for our major source for exports, the *geniza*, tells us relatively little about wheat sales (Jews, as we saw earlier, did not often deal in wheat), but I have only seen references to export dating to the very end of our period. There is, by contrast, very occasional eleventh-century reference to small-scale private imports, particularly from Palestine; these must be ad hoc responses to low Niles and especially demand in Fusṭāṭ, for Egypt normally produced far more wheat than any other Mediterranean region. Palestine was governed by Egypt until the late eleventh century, so would be a logical source in times of low harvests on the Nile.[133]

for the oasis does not mention it; if they are right, it must have been in the north of the oasis, given that our texts focus on the south. This would fit our thirteenth-century evidence (in which, however, rice was a small proportion of local grain crops); see Rapoport, *Rural economy*, p. 77, and pers. comm. See in general also Müller-Wodarg, 'Die Landwirtschaft Ägyptens', 2, pp. 22–4, and Canard, 'Le riz', pp. 118–20. Müller-Wodarg provides the most systematic listings of medieval Egyptian agricultural products.

130 For even flour from the Fayyūm, see n. 229 below. See respectively P.Vind.Arab. I 45–6, P.GenizahCambr. 43, P.Vind.Arab. I 48, P.Cair.Arab. 300.

131 We only, however, have evidence here for specific cases, with specific explanations—the rise of Tinnīs after 900 (manufacturing) and that of Qūṣ after 1100 (a new political centre on the new route to the Red Sea) being examples: see pp. 39, 95–8. But Aswān had grown too: see p. 66.

132 P.GenizahCambr. 43, P.Vind.Arab. I 45–6.

133 Examples of Jewish wheat dealing are in T-S 10J14.26, 10J20.12, 12.388, 12.721, Moss. II,193 (Alt: L 195) (Gil K114, 491 [S101], 512, 566, 709) and 18J1.9 (a.1160), none of them visibly large-scale

Other staples are less often mentioned in our documents, although there is enough evidence from geographers, administrators' manuals, and private letters for us to be certain that virtually all crops then available were grown regularly in Egypt, notably beans (always an important Egyptian food), dates, a variety of different vegetables and fruits (not least bananas), ricin and sesame for oil, plus sheep and cattle for meat, milk, and cheese.[134] But it is worth looking at one other food crop, grapes, at least briefly, for its production and sale have wider implications.

Wine, of course, is forbidden to Muslims, at least if they are observant. In general, we can assume that many Muslims did indeed avoid wine, and that the substantial wine production which is attested for late Roman Egypt—with entire hills of sherds in major production centres of LRA 7 amphorae in Middle Egyptian towns like Anṣīna (classical Antinoopolis, modern Shaykh ʿIbāda)—might well have diminished by our period. Conversely, we have plenty of narrative accounts of the inconsistency with which the prohibition on wine was observed at the Fāṭimid court: al-Ḥākim not only banned the sale of wine, but even that of raisins, in case they were used to make alcohol; but that caliph had a (Christian) doctor who supposedly drowned while drunk in the palace in 1006/7.[135] And, of course, as we have seen, most of Egypt was probably still Christian, and Anṣīna, just across the Nile from Ashmūnayn (where the basilica area was another amphora production centre), was certainly in a Christian-majority area. Apart from under al-Ḥākim—whose decrees were abandoned after he disappeared in 1021—there were no religious prohibitions on Christians or Jews drinking wine, and there is every sign that they did. The geographers mention wine production in a few places in Egypt into the twelfth century; the *History of the Patriarchs* has bishops involved in the wine harvest in 1103. The Anṣīna kilns went on until the tenth century, and LRA 7 amphorae (from here or elsewhere in the valley) are found in the Fayyūm into the tenth century too; Egypt's other main wine amphora, LRA 5/6, mostly made just south of Alexandria, can be traced into the twelfth, in Sinai

except K709: see in general Goitein, *MS*, 1, p. 211 and Golb et al., 'Legal documents', p. 24. For wheat exports, see P.Vind.Arab. I 46 (dated to *c.*1200) and, in particular, the citations in al-Makhzūmī, *Minhāj* in n. 303 below. For imports, see T-S 13J17.11 (Gil K194 [S53]), from Sicily; and ULC Or 1080 J17, T-S 8J19.27 (Gil P506, 507 [Goitein, *Letters*, n. 5]), from Palestine, cited in Bramoullé, *Les Fatimides et la mer*, p. 500n. Larger-scale was the provision of food by the *amīr* ʿAlī b. Mujāhid of Denia in Spain at the time of the serious 1055 Fusṭāṭ famine (see p. 62 above), and so would have been the wheat shipment of the same year from the Byzantine emperor, which was in the end aborted (Bramoullé, *Les Fatimides et la mer*, p. 149)—both are reported in later narratives—but here we are dealing with high politics, not normal commerce. Similarly, the huge Rūmī shipment of grain in ENA 2805.18 B (Gil K656 [S154]), which was claimed to be worth 100,000 dinars, far beyond any documented trading scale, must have had a political context, although here we cannot date the text accurately.

[134] See Müller-Wodarg, 'Die Landwirtschaft Ägyptens' (§2 for plants, §3 for animals) for a range of citations; and for consumption in Fusṭāṭ-Cairo (mostly using later medieval sources), see Lewicka, *Food and foodways*, esp. pp. 133–246; for the range of produce in the thirteenth-century Fayyūm, see Rapoport, *Rural economy*, pp. 77–141.

[135] For the Anṣīna sherd hills, see Ballet and Guidotti, 'Identificazione e analisi'. For the court, see, among others, *Tārīkh al-Anṭakī*, trans. Pirone, 12.45, 88–90, 150, 152, 162–3.

and in the Fayyūm again.[136] There was clearly an overlapping of exchange routes here.

This is paralleled in our Arabic-script documents, where wine (including its less religiously marked variants, grape juice and vinegar, which might sometimes be euphemisms for wine) appears fairly regularly as a commodity to be produced or sold, sometimes contained in amphorae (*jarras*).[137] In the *geniza* too, wine (but not vinegar) was frequently mentioned, and could be the subject of investment; Goitein cites a wine-making partnership from 1136 in which four Jewish partners (including a glassmaker) collectively invested the large sum of 1,500 dinars, probably in vineyards not far from the capital.[138] It is my sense that these citations are fewer than they might be, all the same—the documents mentioning wine are rather fewer than those for the sixth century, for example, and most of those I have seen predate 1000—and that the archaeology too might indeed be telling us that the scale of production was lessening after the tenth century. It is striking, for example, that there are very few amphorae in the French-led excavations at Iṣṭabl ʿAntar in southern Fusṭāṭ already by 900, even if other sites in the capital show amphorae with later dates.[139] (Although wine might have been transported in skins instead of amphorae, we do not have significant references to them, even if they were certainly regularly used for oil;[140] barrels, which eventually replaced amphorae in, for example, Italy, are very unlikely in a wood-poor region like Egypt.) This may well be a marker of the slow Islamicization of Egypt. But, for now, wine was still a large-scale production, and—as the archaeology tells us more than the documents do—circulated across the country in complex ways. Anyway,

[136] Dixneuf, *Amphores égyptiennes*, pp. 143–53, 157–63, 172–3; and Ballet and Guidotti, 'Identificazione e analisi', pp. 170, 183, 187–8, 190, for the latest signs of production at Anṣīna. For the post-1021 period, see *Tārīkh al-Anṭakī*, trans. Pirone, 15.17; for 1103, see *History of the patriarchs*, 3, ed. and trans. ʿAbd al-Masīḥ et al., p. 1. For the geographers, see Ibn Ḥawqal, *Kītāb ṣūrat al-arḍ*, trans. Kramers and Wiet, 1, pp. 138–9; al-Muqaddasī, *Aḥsan al-taqāsīm*, trans. Miquel, p. 121; al-Idrīsī, *Nuzhat al-mushtāq*, trans. Jaubert and Nef, pp. 117, 228, 239; in general Müller-Wodarg, 'Die Landwirtschaft Ägyptens', 2, pp. 48–52, who argues, plausibly in my view, that there was no retreat in wine cultivation before the late tenth century. Note that written sources imply that Anṣīna was in serious decline by the ninth century, for different reasons: see Legendre, *La Moyenne-Égypte*, pp. 119–20, 272–5. Aswān amphorae were never as common, but continued longer; see n. 139 below.

[137] See, e.g., P.Heid.Arab. III 18, 19, 20, P.RagibEdfou 3 a, P.Cair.Arab. 302, 330–1, 376 (a wine harvest in the Idfū area), CPR XXXII 4, 10, 11, P.Vind.Arab. I 16, III 47. See, for an earlier period, Vorderstrasse, 'Terms for vessels', pp. 208–15.

[138] See in general Goitein, *MS*, 1, esp. pp. 122–4, 364; the 1136 agreement, T-S 10J9.30, is edited in Weiss, *Legal documents*, n. 141.

[139] Gayraud and Vallauri, *Fustat II*, pp. 351–2. The few amphorae published in the Japanese-led excavations seem all to be LRA 7, which, as we have seen, do not obviously go past 1000; see Kiyohiko and Kawatoko, *Ejiputo Isurāmo toshi*, 1, pp. 206, 231; but see Gascoigne, 'Amphorae from Old Cairo', p. 167, for some from Aswān from the tenth or eleventh centuries. Amphorae resembling the tenth/eleventh-century Byzantine Günsenin 1 type have been found in the French-led excavations just outside the northern walls of Cairo in eleventh-century levels; see Monchamp, 'Céramiques fatimides', p. 152; she says that a similar one was indeed found on the Japanese site.

[140] Goitein, *MS*, 1, p. 334 and 485n; he says that wine went in skins too, but without citations. In the texts for wine, I have only seen amphorae cited. Conversely, oil did sometimes still travel in amphorae too: see p. 139 above.

it never has vanished in an Egypt where 10 per cent of the population is still Christian.

If we find that complexity even for staples, we would certainly expect to find it for cash crops, and we do. Sugar is one important example. Its production in Egypt is first attested in the early eighth century, but it expanded considerably in the ninth, and onwards from there; it was grown all along the Nile valley in our period. Ninth-century accounts show regular production and delivery to a sugar refinery in Ashmūnayn; and a list of personnel in another (unlocated) ninth-century text shows a remarkable division of labour into thirteen sets of people, from cane cutters to those responsible for packing sugarloaves, making it clear also that cultivation and refining were closely related processes—as would make sense, since sugar cane is close to unusable without refining.[141] We find refineries fairly frequently in our sources, in fact. At the end of the twelfth century, Ibn Mammātī mentions sugar production at Ṣafṭ, just to the west of Fusṭāṭ, specifically for the state; sugar was also produced on a large scale on state land in the Fayyūm in the 1240s. But most of our evidence is for private production: there were several refineries in the capital itself, and one in the Delta town of Minyat Ziftā in 1140 and 1163/4—the source for these being the *geniza*, which makes it clear that Jews were active in sugar-working. And they were certainly not the only ones: an angry letter in Arabic script from the eleventh century makes the point, as well as making its potentially huge scale clear. To summarize: 'The bucketwheels for irrigation on our lord Ibn Milḥ's land have been out of order for three days; it's your responsibility and you're not doing anything; find people to fix them at once; I have warned the financial administrator (*'āmil*) in the city [Ashmūnayn]; 10,000 dinars' worth of sugar is at risk.' Another refinery added honey to its products, as we see from an account of 1102; and we saw, again for Ashmūnayn, that on another eleventh-century occasion 100 dinars were to be spent on *qand*, raw sugar, in expectation of prices rising when sales to Fusṭāṭ were made.[142] As with wheat and wine, sugar was produced and refined in many places, but sales criss-crossed the country all the same. This time, production was often for export, for Egypt was far

[141] Ouerfelli, *Le sucre*, pp. 67–81, is the best synthesis. Sato, *Sugar*, pp. 25–8, relies too heavily on the geographers, and his account of the expansion of sugar production dates it too late as a result; but the geographers do at least attest to plenty of sugar in every period (al-Idrīsī in the twelfth century has a relatively long list of producer areas; see *Nuzhat al-mushtāq*, trans. Jaubert and Nef, pp. 117, 119, 124, 228, 230, 237). For the cited texts, see P.Cair.Arab. 399–400 and 214 respectively; the latter was re-edited, and radically retranslated, in P.SauvagetPapyrus (Grohmann did not realize that sugar was involved at all; see Sauvaget, 'Sur un papyrus arabe', for the argument).

[142] Respectively: Ibn Mammātī, *Qawānīn*, trans. Cooper, 9.13.3, p. 284; Rapoport, *Rural economy*, pp. 105–18; Goitein, *MS*, 1, pp. 81, 125–6; 4, p. 15; for the Minyat Ziftā texts, T-S 8.4, translated in *Discarded history*, a Cambridge University library exhibition guide, p. 23, and T-S 24.25; cf. Goitein, MS, 1, pp. 126, 429n (it is my assumption that they relate to the same refinery, not two separate ones); another twelfth-century sugar refinery appears in the *geniza* in T-S 12.554 (ed. Weiss, *Legal documents*, n. 50); P.Berl.Arab. II 34 (Ibn Milḥ; the city is unnamed, but Mallawī, close to Ashmūnayn, is cited in the text), P.GenizahCambr. 134, P.Vind.Arab. I 19. See also CPR XXVI 15, P.Vind.Arab. I 5.

and away the major producer of sugar in the Mediterranean until the Black Death; but internal consumption and distribution were complex as well.

When we are looking at cash crops, however, even if sugar was important, flax was above all the major Egyptian product. It turns up everywhere, in records of both flax cultivation and exchange—whether as raw flax (usually converted on or near the fields into spinnable fibre), cloth lengths, or finished linen clothing. It was Egypt's main export up to 1100 or so; the Mediterranean trade routes of the *geniza* merchants would have been far weaker without it. Internally, it circulated in diverse ways, which are also much better documented than those of other primary products. We will, therefore, look at them in detail in the next section, for they, together with ceramics, are our best guides to the internal structuring of the Egyptian economy as a system. Here, however, we at least need to see where flax was principally grown. The answer, as with other crops, is almost everywhere (although probably little in Upper Egypt), but there were some particular foci (see Map 7). The geographers name some Delta towns (Manūf and Sakhā, for instance), plus the Fayyūm (al-Muqaddasī claims flax was mediocre there; he also mentions Būṣīr just outside the Fayyūm, the only reference anywhere in non-*geniza* sources to the production of this important flax-selling town); in the 1240s, flax-growing here was focussed on the mouth of the Fayyūm, between the Būṣīr area and Dumūshiyya, just inside the oasis. Farther south up the valley, Ashmūnayn, Bahnasā, and Akhmīm are cited by Ibn Ḥawqal.[143] The *geniza* helps further, for flax is listed there in dozens of types (twenty-six according to Goitein in 1983, up from twenty-two in his first volume fifteen years earlier), some of them with geographical ascriptions, and we can see there that Būṣīrī flax was particularly prized—it came from villages all around the mouth of the Fayyūm, and many of them had their own names on flax types too—and, after that, Fayyūmī flax from the oasis itself (which proves al-Muqaddasī wrong on quality), with Ashmūnayn also highly rated, and other localities in Middle Egypt are also mentioned.[144] This fits the Arabic-script letters too, which mention the Fayyūm, Ashmūnayn, and Bahnasā.[145] In our documents the Delta towns are less prominent, although they may be the source for widely sold flax types such as *malāl*, which is not a geographical name.

Maurice Lombard identified four major flax production areas in the Delta, around Manūf in the south, Maḥalla and Samannūd in the centre, Damanhūr in the west, and the villages closest to the two great weaving factory towns, Tinnīs and Damietta, in the north-east. His sources are rather too vague to give us

[143] Ibn Ḥawqal, *Kītāb ṣūrat al-arḍ*, trans. Kramers and Wiet, 1, pp. 137, 139, 156–7; al-Muqaddasī, *Aḥsan al-taqāsīm*, trans. Miquel, pp. 121, 123; for the Fayyūm, see Rapoport, *Rural economy*, pp. 119–21.

[144] Goitein, *MS*, 1, pp. 224–8, 455–7; 4, p. 167.

[145] For Ashmūnayn, see p. 50 above; for the others, see P.Fay.Villages 43, P.Vind.Arab. I 7, 21, and P.HanafiTwoNewEditions 1, for the substantial percentage of flax cultivation in an estate survey of 993 for Drinja near Ahnās, just south of the Fayyūm mouth.

certainty here, but this does seem roughly right—and the demand from the last-mentioned towns would certainly have encouraged flax cultivation nearby.[146] On the basis of the documents, we should then add to these four the Fayyūm and the villages between it and the Nile, and the stretch of the middle valley between Bahnasā and Ashmūnayn, as the two other major flax areas. In the most intense areas of production, for example between the Fayyūm and the Nile, cash cropping might have been so intensive that peasants had to buy some of their own food (cf. p. 103 below). That is speculation, for we do not have the sort of evidence which would allow us to be sure of it, but it is certainly a strong possibility, and it is the only part of the Mediterranean in our period where it is even conceivable.

Egyptian linen had always been a significant product of the country, from Pharaonic times, as also under the Roman Empire, as noted earlier. But there is not much doubt that production boomed in our period, probably starting under the Ṭūlūnids in the last third of the ninth century, when the first references to cloth from the factory towns appear (see pp. 95–9 below). One immediate result was the eclipse of papyrus production. Papyrus had for millennia been an Egyptian speciality, sold all over western Eurasia as writing material, and never successfully implanted anywhere else (in the ninth century, its cultivation was tried in Sāmarrāʿ in Iraq, and in the tenth in Sicily, but neither lasted). But it vanished almost overnight. Of published documents and letters from Egypt, the first dated paper text is from 879, the last papyrus is from 971—but that is the only one known after 946. The main changeover period was only a generation long, *c.*900–30.[147] After 970, the only place in the world which certainly used papyrus documents was the papal chancery in Rome, for which the last surviving papyrus original is from 1017 (with a later fragment from 1052, and indications in copies up to 1057 that papyrus was still occasionally used); whether this means that a niche Egyptian or, less plausibly, Sicilian elite production still existed for traditionalist foreigners, or whether the papacy was simply using up an old store of material, is unclear, although the latter seems most likely to me.[148] Paper was

[146] Lombard, *Les textiles*, pp. 165–6 and map II. Ibn Mammātī, *Qawānīn*, trans. Cooper, 9.13, pp. 283–5, also stresses the cultivation of flax on state land in the eastern Delta—i.e. closest to the weaving towns; see further Benjamin of Tudela, *The itinerary*, trans. Adler, p. 77, on flax cultivation near Damietta.

[147] Grob, *Documentary Arabic private and business letters*, pp. 11–14 gives a convenient survey of the changeover. The last dated papyrus so far published is P.Cair.Arab. 283. For Egyptian papyrus production in the ninth century (and a convincing argument that it was not all organized by the state), see Malczycki, 'The papyrus industry'. See ibid., pp. 195–6 for Iraq, and Ibn Ḥawqal, *Kītāb ṣūrat al-arḍ*, trans. Kramers and Wiet, 1, p. 121 for Sicily.

[148] The last complete original is Zimmermann, *Papsturkunden*, 2, n. 507, a. 1017; the 1052 fragment is registered at https://rcf.fr/articles/actualite/2-papyrus-du-moyenage-conserves-au-puyenvelay-bientot-restaures, a reference I owe to Dario Internullo, who first located it; the 1057 text is edited in Marini, *I papiri*, n. 50 (it is a copy from 1236 in Auvray, *Les registres de pape Grégoire IX*, nn. 3554–5, where it states that the document was on papyrus). Some copies of documents from Naples may possibly have been from papyrus originals of the early eleventh century too, but the dating is uncertain. See in general Carbonetti Vendittelli, 'I supporti scrittorii' and '"Sicut inveni in thomo carticineo"'.

above all a cloth by-product, usually made from rags, up to the nineteenth century (when wood pulp began to be used). For it to have become so cheap so quickly that it could oust such a long-standing production as papyrus must be a sign of a dramatically increasing scale of linen production in Egypt.[149] But what happened to the areas in the Delta which had previously produced papyrus? Interestingly, they were, as far as we can see, often in or close to areas which became flax producers—one town, Būrā, beside Damietta, is indeed said by the geographer al-Yaʿqūbī in the 870s to have produced both papyrus and cloth.[150] It is likely that as papyrus ceased to be in demand, many of the areas which specialized in it simply switched to flax. In those areas, long-standing commercial infrastructures must have existed too, which flax sales would have been able to exploit afterwards.

In Egypt in our period, sugar cultivation was important, and had emerged from nothing in 700; flax cultivation was even more important, and although it had long existed, linen production expanded massively in the decades around 900. These products were sold for profit, internally and abroad, not extracted from the region in tax; the colonial wheat economy of the Roman period had decisively gone. Were there downsides to this? Philip Mayerson argued twenty years ago in a brief but influential article that there were: there were serious famines in Egypt in the tenth century and onwards, caused by low Nile floods,

[149] Paper is first known outside China in Central Asia in the eighth century, then Baghdad, and then Damascus in the ninth (for general overviews, see Bloom, *Paper before print*, pp. 42–61, 74–9; Rustow, *The lost archive*, pp. 116–37; cf. Shatzmiller, 'The adoption of paper'). The technology of its production most plausibly came to Egypt from Syria. Did paper itself also come from Syria? There is, in fact, occasional reference to the import of paper from Damascus in the *geniza* in the early eleventh century (the main texts are T-S 13J15.5, CUL Or. 1080 J42 [Gil P514, 517; trans. Goitein, *Letters*, nn. 15, 16] and T-S 13J14.17 [Gil P516]; see Goitein, *MS*, 1, pp. 81, 410; Goldberg, *Trade and institutions*, pp. 226–8; Bramoullé, *Les Fatimides et la mer*, pp. 502–3), and also in one twelfth-century Arabic-script letter (P.Heid.Arab. II 23); but it is occasional, and seems to be expensive paper, very unlike the day-to-day letters which mostly survive in Egypt. The same is true for Spanish paper, which was particularly prized: see p. 435 below. For Egyptian production, al-Maqrīzī quotes Ibn Saʿīd, a thirteenth-century Maghribī observer, who is supposed to have seen paper mills in Fusṭāṭ (*Khiṭaṭ*, trans. Casanova, 4, p. 57); I am inclined to accept this as reliable, and anyway the capital is far more likely as a source for paper in the region.

A recent scientific study of some paper letters from Palestine in the *geniza* showed that their cloth basis was usually cotton, which fits the fact that Syria-Palestine was a major cotton producer; see Amar et al., 'The paper and textile industry', pp. 34–9. Conversely, an early microscopic study of Fayyūm paper, Wiesner, 'Mikroskopische Untersuchung' and Wiesner, 'Die Faijûmer und Uschmûneiner Papiere', pp. 235–9, showed above all linen, with occasional cotton and a little wool, evidently deriving from rags getting mixed together; this is indeed what one would expect for Egyptian paper. There is more to be done here, but more, fortunately, is beginning to be done, as with Cohen, *Composition analysis of writing materials*, a new scientific analysis of ink types on *geniza* documents.

[150] Al-Yaʿqūbī, *Kitāb al-buldān*, trans. Gordon et al., p. 175. The evidence for where exactly in the Delta papyrus came from in the Islamic period is not good; al-Yaʿqūbī is one of the few geographers to be writing early enough for papyrus to be worth describing. See Müller-Wodarg, 'Die Landwirtschaft Ägyptens', 2, pp. 56–8. Another location, however, Afraḥūn, near Sakhā, identifiable in protocols at the top of texts (Malczycki, 'The papyrus industry', pp. 195–6), was again beside or part of another later flax-producing area, around Damanhūr.

whereas in the Roman period, when wheat was more dominant, there were not.[151] I am less convinced here than others have been. The article is very succinct in its argument: there was more flax; there were more famines. It does not seem to me as simple as this, however. For a start, as we have seen, our evidence for famines tells us above all about Fusṭāṭ, which was very large and, inland as it was, reliant on the stability of internal exchange for its supply; Roman Alexandria, by contrast, far and away Egypt's biggest city at the time, could much more easily be supplied by sea if local supplies were inadequate. Secondly, we have almost no narratives from Roman Egypt; most of our information is external and essentially anecdotal.[152] Post-900 Egyptian narratives are, however, numerous, and disproportionately focus on the problems of the capital, using what one could call a rhetoric of famine as an image to imply problems of government. The existence of that rhetoric is, of course, significant—and, as we saw earlier (p. 62), it was partially accurate, in that good rulers could indeed avert famine more effectively than inept or malign ones—but it does not of itself show that famines were commoner. I would myself prefer to re-emphasize that wheat production under the Romans was to a substantial extent for compulsory and unremunerated export; it would hardly be surprising that once that was no longer necessary, wheatfields might be converted to more profitable uses. For flax was profitable, and, as we shall see later, both landlords and peasants—and also merchants—could profit from it. If there were occasional subsistence risks attached, which there might have been, it was probably worth it; it was part of the development of a complex internal exchange economy. Which leads us into the next section.

2.4 Internal Exchange

The Vienna collections of Arabic-script paper texts preserve two letters written by Safrā, an abandoned wife, to her husband Khiḍr—the editor, Werner Diem, plausibly thinks some time in the twelfth century.[153] They are letters written in able, even if fast hands—there is for the most part unusually good pointing in the script of the first, the more careful of the two. Safrā dictated them, as the second letter makes clear, but evidently to skilled scribes. I have seldom seen such human writing in fifty years of medieval research, so I want simply to set them out, to give

151 Mayerson, 'The role of flax'.

152 But there are famines associated with low Nile floods in one of the few we have, the *Life* of John the Almsgiver, ed. Festugière and Rydén as *Vie de Jean de Chypre*, chs 11, 30.

153 P.Vind.Arab. II 9, 10. I have worked from Diem's own translation, and my English text was kindly looked over by Marina Rustow, Lucie Ryzova and a Princeton seminar in December 2020, the latter of which agreed with a twelfth-century dating. Diem (ibid., p. 52) transliterates the husband's name as Khiḍr, although the text has a ẓ; Khiḍr is a Qur'ānic name, sometimes used in our period, and the text uses ẓ for ḍ on several other occasions.

Safrā respect. Their relevance to the argument will become clearer later. I begin here by presenting an English translation of them:

n. 9. In the name of God, the merciful and benevolent! This letter, from Safrā, goes to his excellency Khiḍr.

What I would like to tell you is that I believed that you were a man from a good family, and that I believed in human decency. But now, you already know in what distinguished circumstances I lived; I was not needy, and I was not a servant girl. You know what my situation was, and I do not need to tell you what situation you were in on your side. But God bestows and grants, and [even] king's daughters must endure the reversals of fate [literally, 'time descends on them']. May God bestow a good end!

What now the talk about you means is that I never knew you. Indeed, between me and you there is no friendship [*ṣaḥba*], although between me and you both there is no enmity either—you can assure her that you both have maintained your arrangement fully with me. For it has reached me that you have transported everything secretly to your pretty girl [*bint al-jamāl*, literally, 'daughter of beauty'], and that you said to her: 'By God, I take no pleasure in her appearance'; yes, you even told her things that God had made a secret, which concern only us two. Are these the noble qualities of people from a good family and of honourable conduct? And we said, are you not afraid that you will come to an evil end? Are you not afraid that ill luck will afflict you, concerning something which still lies hidden, so that you will bring yourself and others into disgrace? I suffer greatly about the things I have been told in the talk about you. If I were not a [good] Muslim, I would lift my face and curse you day and night, secretly and publicly; for there is no good reason for this unpleasant, evil, news.

God has permitted both marriage and divorce. So when someone is hated by their marriage partner, then they do not behave like you [i.e. they can divorce]. Supposing you were to say that someone had done so, then ask yourself about it; there is no one, who has become untrue to their marriage partner, who has talked like you did. I did nothing to you which could merit this news, for I honoured you despite your roaming around. That I had so much patience with you was because of your mother, as she is a distinguished woman; God, the powerful and sublime, is pleased with her. But you did not honour me and—given the news that we hear about you—you have not honoured yourself.

When you left, you took with you the box and the scales. The people have accused me of taking them, and said to me: 'We will bring you both before the prefect of police (*wālī*) of Miṣr [Fusṭāṭ].'

Often, I went away from you to the countryside (*al-balad*) and sought tranquillity. I said [to myself]: 'Let me be satisfied with what God, the powerful and sublime, has given,' and I gained distance from all these things. I left [the outstanding part of my dowry] with you as a loan, without asking you for it. I have committed three years [of marriage] with you, without asking from you clothing, maintenance and [money for] the rent, and without bothering you. In the end, you said to me: 'I do not want her, she brings me shame. I have given her up for your sake.' In the end, you worked on me and said: 'Come, move to Cairo!' So I came to Cairo, since you pestered me, whereupon you began to go down into inns (*fanādiq*[154]) whenever you felt like it, and seemed like a ghost to me. You appeared with the last evening prayers and left at dawn, so that people already suspected that you were not really my husband. And with all this I waited patiently and had my hands full of yarn [i.e. spinning, like a proper wife]. My property was squandered, and I was left behind on the empty ground [i.e. without goods]. I have never known such hatred and heartlessness from you. But I have received conclusive proof from a certain woman. I swore that only your pretty girl has sown discord between us. Now your liaison with her has already lasted two years, and she has divorced her husband for you and has promised you that she will give you something, as you really are an avaricious man. That is why you have done all this to me; when[ever] you got away from me for a little, you bought, while you sacrificed us, something for your pretty girl. So you are [now] dependent on various people, as you no longer have your father. If that really was your intention, then you should never be lucky before God!

I am pregnant, while you both laughed and said 'She is not pregnant at all,' and you played a treacherous game with me and laughed at me. But pay attention: I have put my case on record before the high judge (*qāḍi al-quḍāt*), as the first person to take this step against you, and he has notified you. Then, by God, I will not give up all my rights, only to offer them to my adversary, your pretty girl!

In closing, greetings to your mother! Men have become wicked! God alone be praised; he blesses our lord Muḥammad, his family, and his companions; and give them salvation!

[This letter] must be forwarded by the hand of a camel driver to Khiḍr, living in Qiman [near Bahnasā], to be handed to him personally in the market hall as entrusted property to be delivered.

* * *

n. 10 [evidently written a few months later]. In the name of God, the merciful and benevolent! Safrā complains about her ill luck, namely that the way in which you deal with me is not the behaviour of decent people. So I swear to you by God: turn back to God and give up the behaviour of the Devil! My situation is that my pregnancy is now visible. But no one could write a letter for me, while

[154] *Fundūq*s were lodging houses, often substantial buildings, for merchants and other travellers, as well as commercial centres for the same merchants: see esp. Constable, *Housing the stranger*, the basic survey. Often, wine and sex were also sold (ibid., pp. 100–3), which Khiḍr would presumably have been at least as interested in.

I was in such a very unlucky situation. So I swore to you by God: send for me, if God wills, and I will look around for something, something which is more advantageous than your [present] position. For even now it will come out [better] for me—that will depend on you! I have cried out loudly because of my ill luck, and different people have taken care of me.

Do not force me into opposition and a lawsuit, for it is not pleasant to show a face twisted with anger continuously before the people. I was satisfied that you would be punished, and the people were satisfied too, as these are decent people. Only the streetcleaners were not satisfied that you would be punished, by God; your good standing is certainly lost. Always behave to me as the law allows! Do not force me to a lawsuit or so that I send for you with bailiffs. Even if you were in Shām [Palestine or Syria], people would give me news of you. Don't take this too lightly, for what they did to your pretty girl for this reason is surely enough [to make the point].

They wanted to bring me before the prefect of police of Miṣr, since you have taken away the brass scales. If that were to happen, I would let you be pursued by them.

There is some formulaic language in these two letters. A rude letter from the same period to an errant colleague for example says 'Until now I believed that you were a reputable man,' which parallels Safrā's opening. But most of it is well outside the very elaborate Arabic letter-writing tradition of the period, and is, in fact, a deliberate subversion of it, so as to allow Safrā to be very personal and very hard-hitting.[155] We can only sympathize with Safrā here; of course, there is always another side to this kind of story, but if she is accurate at all, Khiḍr has behaved with a kind of heartlessness which we always tend to condemn when we see it today. (We can, of course, only speculate about why Khiḍr wanted to keep the letters at all.) But Safrā is not only a victim. She has the social capital to call in the law—and indeed to write letters of this kind at all, which few women did; one thing she seems not to fear, perhaps because of her status, is that Khiḍr will simply take his mistress as a second wife; and she eventually has 'the people' with her, who have already, as the end of the second letter shows, meted out some sort of unpleasant punishment to Khiḍr's mistress, even if not, with gendered predictability, to Khiḍr himself.

Safrā's story is so dense in its incidental detail, and so bound by time and place, that one could spend many pages teasing it out, using human ill luck to illuminate

[155] See n. 17 above for formulaic elaboration. See Diem and Edzard, 'Ein unhöflicher Brief', for the contemporary letter, which, although it was found in the *geniza* and was clearly written by a Jew, is mostly in Arabic script. More subversion in Safrā's letters includes 'greetings to your mother! Men have become wicked!'—the first phrase is a stock formula (although Safrā clearly does respect her mother-in-law), as is the invocation to the Prophet and his family which follows; the second, brutal phrase is unique.

a society, as historians generally do.[156] We can get out of these letters Safrā's own strong sense of her status and personal resources, such that she has never claimed her full dowry, though she could have done and still can (it is evidently an exaggeration on her part to say that she has been left 'on the empty ground'[157]); her sense that she is not good-looking, but that whether she is or not should be a private matter between herself and her husband; her implication that Khiḍr's inconsistent and lying behaviour to her is all of a piece with his ill luck in business, especially after his father died—he may indeed now not be well off at all, if he has, as she implies, stolen a set of scales—but Safrā is even now prepared to take him back and thinks she could help his career (she could have divorced him too, but has not); her shame in being thought by her neighbours in Cairo to be a mistress, even though she is herself behaving properly, but also her ability to persuade them that she is, in fact, in the right, sufficiently well that they have taken direct action on her behalf—and so on. In a book on the economy, this list of insights is as far as we can in practice go. But Safrā's letters are relevant here above all because of the commercial geography that they casually assume. Khiḍr—clearly, from his name, a Muslim, as his wife is—must be a merchant, for Safrā says twice that he has taken the set of scales, for weighing goods out, and his frequenting of *fundūq*s may not only have been for pleasure. He is currently accessible in a market hall near Bahnasā, a centre for the flax and linen trade and also that in woollen cloth; it is possibly his family home if his mother is there, but until recently he has been in both Cairo, which was by now slowly becoming more of a mercantile centre, and Fusṭāṭ. Safrā herself is not from Cairo, for she has to be coaxed to come there, she clearly has no family there to give her support, and she has often fled temporarily to the countryside. We do not know where in the countryside, but most of the letters from the Vienna corpus edited by Diem which had provenances came from Ashmūnayn, and that is certainly a possibility. For two families of—we can deduce—medium prosperity (her more than him), that is quite a lot of movement. And Safrā envisions, admittedly in a rhetorical passage, that Khiḍr might even go to Shām, the standard Arabic word for the Levant, that is, Syria and Palestine; we have other evidence that the Egypt–Levant trade route stayed open despite the Crusader conquest (see pp. 109, 143, 513 below), but whether he ever really planned to go there or not, it is a significant image. Khiḍr's circuit was at a minimum 200 kilometres, and it may have been four times that.

[156] With the proviso that it is unique so far in Arabic-script letters; nor are there examples as detailed in the *geniza*, despite frequent references to marital dispute and divorce there; see Goitein, *MS*, 3, pp. 160–223; Cohen, *The voice of the poor*, pp. 89–94; Kraemer, 'Women speak for themselves'; Zinger, *Women, gender and law*, esp. pp. 80–96. Levine Melammed, 'He said, she said', which translates and discusses the most comparable case, takes it from Maimonides's *Responsa*; I owe the reference to Eve Krakowski.

[157] It is a common rhetorical style; cf. the sister of the merchant Abū Hurayra in the Fayyūm of the 870s, who, she says, does not just need new clothes, but is 'entirely naked': P.Marchands II 23; and there are other examples of the latter phrase in the *geniza*: T-S 13J18.8 (Gil K334 [S79]); Zinger, *Women, gender and law*, pp. 88–9.

That circuit has wider implications. We have already seen that Christian, Muslim, and Jewish merchants are documented engaging in internal trade across quite long distances in our period, but, except for some of the merchants in the *geniza*, we have not seen quite such casual moving about as these letters assume. Egypt's economy did, however, allow even medium-level families to work regularly from several places. In doing so, they followed the goods; and to understand that economy, so must we. We will look here in detail at two artisanal products, ceramics and linen (both the raw flax and the cloth which was made from it); then more briefly at other types of product which our sources tell us (or do not tell us) about. That will then give us the basis for understanding how the Egyptian economy worked, in its overlapping and competitive networks of internal routes. (For what follows, see Map 7.)

2.4.1 Ceramics

Our evidence for ceramic production and exchange is almost all archaeological, everywhere. Written sources say little about it in most periods, and Fāṭimid Egypt is no exception: occasional throwaway (or indeed unreliable) remarks in a geographer's narrative, a couple of references to sales, and the occasional use of the words *qarmūsī* or *qaddār*, potter (the former in Arabic-script texts, the latter in Hebrew script) in receipts and documents listing artisans or house neighbours are the sum total of our non-material evidence. They show that there were potters in Fusṭāṭ, which the archaeology anyway makes clear, and also, significantly, that there were at least two potters in the smallish Fayyūm village of Damūya, as we saw earlier and which we will come back to. There are a few more specific terms: in the Arabic texts, *jīrarī* for an amphora-maker, in the *geniza*, *fakhkhārī* for a pipe-maker (a word which generically meant 'potter' elsewhere in the Mediterranean in our period, and by the later middle ages in Egypt too), and *kūzī* for a water jug-maker, showing a division of labour which we have come to expect in our period; but this too is made obvious by even a cursory look at the archaeological evidence. Ceramic archaeology will be what this section focusses on above all from now on, then.[158]

[158] For the *geniza* citations, see Goitein, *MS*, 1, pp. 110–11—the other terms he cites are not found in Egypt. Ibn al-Qaddār, a non-Jew, owns a ship in T-S 13J17.3 (Gil K181 [S47]), and has evidently come up in the world. For *qarmūsī*, see P.Prag.Arab. 37 (tenth century); P.Fay.Villages 6, 9, 11, 15, 16, 19, 20 (all for Damūya; five of these are for the same man; see Mouton, 'La société villageoise', pp. 219–22). *Qarmūsī* is from Greek *kerameus*; why the *geniza* texts do not use the word (it does not appear in a word search) is not clear—was it simply not used in a more linguistically Arabized Fusṭāṭ? For *jīrarī*, see P.Berl.Arab. II 66 (tenth century)—it is my assumption that this is a specific type of potter, as *jarra* is an amphora in other texts. Unreliable narratives: see *Nāṣer-e Khosraw's book of travels*, trans. Thackston, p. 54, on ceramics so fine that you can see through them. But he at least states clearly that fine pottery-making was a feature of Fusṭāṭ; the archaeology, as we shall see, amply supports and

Egypt had two major ceramic production centres, Aswān and Fusṭāṭ. The first of these had been making pottery on a large scale since the Roman Empire and before, the second since at least the early ninth century but not demonstrably earlier,[159] so we will look at them in that order, and then at other production sites. Aswān was long a major political centre. It was and is on the border between Egypt and Nubia (roughly the northern half of modern Sudan), at the southern end of Pharaonic, Roman, and caliphal power alike, so it stayed politically relevant, and was almost certainly the main city in the whole of Upper Egypt until the rise of Qūṣ around 1100. As a pottery producer, one of its USPs was a hard kaolinitic fabric, which was capable of making strong, thin walls for different types of pot, and which is also easy to recognize by any archaeologist interested in fabric analysis. This fabric, particular to Aswān and a small region around it, can be found in the ceramics on sites all along the Nile valley, northwards right up to the coastal ports, and a long way into Nubia southwards, from Roman times up to after the end of our period, a distance of well over 1,000 kilometres. In the Roman Empire, the finest Aswān ware was one of the Red Slip types which made up a *koinē* of empire-wide top-end taste from the first century to the seventh. Egypt was the only region where it continued to be produced after that, and by the eleventh century (at the latest) Aswān was the sole known producer, although by now it had lost its traditional fineness.[160] But the kilns, which evidently produced en masse for over a millennium, had long since diversified. A white-slipped version of its basic fine ware began in the fourth century; Aswān White ware, with painted decoration, began in the ninth, and continued past the twelfth. Common wares of a large number of different types, including amphorae and good-quality cooking wares, were also large-scale productions, and continued to be so up to 1500.[161] Red Slip, White ware, and many common wares are extensively documented on Islamic-period Egyptian sites. They are seen in Fusṭāṭ until at least the eleventh century: at Isṭabl ʿAntar kaolinitic fabrics begin to fade out after 900, but they are found for later periods on the Japanese-led sites in the city, and apparently on the

develops this. *Geniza* sales: T-S 13J17.1, DK 230.1 (Gil K537, 561 [S109])—the former includes lustreware; the latter is exported to Sicily (or will be, once it is finally loaded on the ship). For late medieval terminology, see esp. Milwright, 'Pottery in the written sources', a reference I owe to Alison Gascoigne, to whom I am very grateful for a thorough critique of this section.

159 For the latter, see Gayraud and Vallauri, *Fustat II*, pp. 19, 39–41.

160 See in general Adams, *Ceramic industries*, pp. 55–7, 527–60; Williams, *Syene VI*, pp. 49, 51: Rodziewicz, *La céramique romaine tardive*, pp. 54–68. Egyptian Red Slip was also made on a large scale in Middle Egypt under the Romans and for some time later (see esp. Bailey, *Excavations at el-Ashmunein*, 5, pp. 38–58). The report of the excavations in the 1980s at Bahnasā, published in 2006, seems to argue for a production going into the eleventh century, much later than has been proposed elsewhere (Fehérvári, *The Kuwait excavations*, pp. 88–92); to judge by the photographs, however, only a minority of these finds would normally be classified as Red Slip; and the certain kilns are early Islamic, not later (ibid., pp. 56–60).

161 Adams, *Ceramic industries*, pp. 527–60 still has the best set of (complicated) typologies, updated for the period to 1000 in Williams, *Syene VI*, pp. 48–62; see also Adams, 'Medieval ceramics from Aswan'.

US-sponsored sites too; tenth/eleventh-century Aswān amphorae have also been found in the Babylon fort in the west of the city.[162] Elsewhere, they are found until the tenth at Ashmūnayn (after which archaeological evidence there ceases), and probably at least into the eleventh at Tinnīs on the coast; until the eleventh at Ṭuṭūn and Naqlūn in the Fayyūm, and Akhmīm and Dandara in northern Upper Egypt; into the thirteenth at Ṭūd, near Luxor, the closest to Aswān of these sites, and at Quṣayr on the Red Sea coast. These patterns show that it is likely that the distribution of Aswān pottery slipped in the long eleventh century, and that after that it was restricted to Upper Egypt and Nubia, and also, most probably, the capital.[163] But until then it extended everywhere which has usable excavation publications; commercial routes with Aswān wares in them, that is to say, threaded across the whole of Egypt.

There was not a strong tradition of producing glazed wares in Aswān. These, however, became the new top-end ceramic type very quickly after their initial introduction into Egypt around 800—as indeed in the whole Islamic Mediterranean world between 750 and 900, and later, as we shall see, in the Christian world too.[164] This has in itself produced an alternative vision of the distribution of kaolinitic ceramics in Egypt, which needs comment. Actually, there are some lead-glazed wares, generally bowls, in kaolinitic fabrics, from the first century of Egyptian glazes—they are often, unhelpfully, called 'Coptic Glaze', but 'Aswan Glazed ware' is gaining traction as a name. The French directors of the Isṭabl 'Antar site, who are influential because this is such an important and well-excavated site, have long argued that these show that what was exported from Aswān was not the wares just described, but the clay they were made from, because Aswān itself produced no glaze, and because Aswān clay was indeed brought to the still active kilns in the former city of Fusṭāṭ in the twentieth

[162] Gayraud and Vallauri, *Fustat II*, pp. 345–7; Kiyohiko and Kawatoko, *Ejiputo Isurāmo toshi*, 1, pp. 179–230; Adams, *Ceramic industries*, p. 558, who states that Aswān White ware from the 1000–1250 period was found in Fusṭāṭ, presumably on the US-sponsored sites of the 1960s–1970s, whose ceramics have never been published; Gascoigne, 'Amphorae from Old Cairo', p. 167.

[163] Bailey, *Excavations at el-Ashmunein*, 5, pp. 9–38; Pyke, 'The ceramic material from Tinnīs', p. 183; Rousset et al., 'Tebtynis 1998', pp. 251–7; Żurek, 'Two pottery deposits', p. 165n [Naqlūn]; McNally and Schrunk, *Excavations at Akhmīm*, pp. 77–9, 91–2 (without much dating however); Marchand and Laisney, 'Le survey de Dendara', pp. 273–4; Pierrat, 'Essai de classification', pp. 175–93 [Ṭūd] (cf. Gascoigne, 'Dislocation and continuity', p. 187, for Idfū, closer still to Aswān, where surface finds continue at least until the eleventh century and perhaps later); Burke, *Archaeological texts*, pp. 81–6 [Quṣayr]. For a casual literary reference to Aswān pottery in the thirteenth century, see Milwright, 'Pottery in the written sources', p. 506. See now the systematic discussion in Williams, *Syene VI*, pp. 96–109, although that survey does not go past 1000, so does not track the later lessening of Aswān exports into the rest of Egypt.

[164] For the date, see, as the most recent statement, Gayraud and Vallauri, *Fustat II*, pp. 5, 368, with Gayraud, 'La réapparition'. By now, the main proponents of an earlier, eighth-century date for the appearance of glaze in Egypt are the German excavators of Abū Mīnā just south of Alexandria—see most recently Engemann, *Abū Mīnā VI*, pp. 125–34—but that site is said by the excavators to have ended in the mid-ninth century, so there is (just about) time for (most of) the glazed types found there to have appeared after 800.

century, as ethnography from around 1900 already shows.[165] The ethnography may not be a good guide; by 1900 transport was considerably easier in Egypt than it was a thousand years earlier, and the Aswān kilns were by then not in operation. Exactly what the production and distribution mechanism for the Aswān clay wares might have been if they were not produced in Aswān itself has also not been explored by anyone. (Was all production concentrated in Fusṭāṭ, including that of common wares, or was the clay distributed more widely? Either is problematic.) But what is most important is that the recent Aswān excavations have indeed shown us early lead-glazed wares with local fabrics inside the town; hence the new name for the type.[166] It seems to me beyond the bounds of the plausible that Aswān clay was sent over 800 kilometres to Fusṭāṭ in the ninth century so that Aswān-fabric glazed wares could be re-exported to the town of their origin, where unglazed versions of the same wares were being made contemporaneously. What must be the case is that Aswān—and maybe a variety of other centres—were experimenting with this early type of glaze, and that in Aswān's case its production was not persisted with, perhaps because it already had a wide range of productions; by now, other centres were producing glaze, and local taste in the south may anyway have been different. I thus conclude that we can, indeed, regard the distribution of kaolinitic fabrics as a marker of the distribution of Aswān-made ceramics. But even if we did not, the wide distribution of those fabrics still attests to far-reaching commercial connections.

Fusṭāṭ for its part did, beyond doubt, produce glazed fine wares throughout our period and for long after. It also produced common wares, although the scale of this is as yet unclear. We cannot easily track the distribution of the common wares, as their fabrics are not sufficiently specific—the capital made pots with both a limestone (calcareous) fabric and an alluvial Nile-silt fabric (the former more often for table wares, the latter more often for common and cooking wares, although with a substantial cross-over, and some fabric mixing), but both are found very widely in Egypt's geology, especially the latter. It is also the case that little work outside Fusṭāṭ has been done on identifying common ware types at all, even though they are always overwhelmingly dominant in numbers on sites; Ṭuṭūn and Tinnīs stand out here for their published work, but they are isolated examples.[167]

[165] See, e.g., Gayraud, 'La réapparition', pp. 106–8; Gayraud et al., 'Assemblages de céramiques égyptiennes', pp. 172, 190; Vogt, 'Les céramiques ommeyyades et abbassides', pp. 244–5. Aswān clay was still being brought to Cairo at the end of the twentieth century (Alison Gascoigne, pers. comm.). Mixed-fabric wares, which would prove some Fusṭāṭ production from Aswān clay in our period, are, however, now seen not to be documented here (Gayraud and Vallauri, *Fustat II*, p. 23); known Fusṭāṭ kilns are also not associated with kaolinitic fabrics (ibid., p. 21).

[166] See now esp. Williams, *Syene VI*, pp. 53–4; I am grateful to Gregory Williams and Alison Gascoigne for discussion. See also Pierrat, 'Essai de classification', p. 198, for Ṭūd.

[167] Gayraud and Vallauri, *Fustat II* is basic here. For common-ware typologies in Fusṭāṭ, see also Monchamp, 'Céramiques fatimides' (for Cairo), and, for one subtype, filters, see Scanlon, *Fusṭāṭ*

Fusṭāṭ glaze, by contrast, can be identified more easily. As always, we have to be careful here. Glazed wares come in a variety of different types of glaze and of decoration, quite apart from their fabric (in our period, this was most commonly, but not always, calcareous). A common rough typology of Egyptian glazes from the Fāṭimid period distinguishes monochrome glaze (either a lead glaze or, from the tenth century, a tin-opacified glaze) from polychrome glaze (by now, normally also a tin glaze), and then some particularly common types. Excavation reports generally distinguish three in particular: 'Fayyumi ware' (*c*.850–1150, with a tenth- and eleventh-century peak: see Fig. 1)—with bouncy and often clumsy uses of blobs of colour ('splash ware') and black-glaze lines, sometimes radiating out from the centre; 'Fusṭāṭ Fāṭimid Sgraffiato/Sgraffito' (*c*.1000 onwards; it is often, as here, abbreviated FFS: see Fig. 2), which is a high-quality type with under-glaze incised decoration; and 'lustreware', with a characteristic metallic sheen (see Fig. 3), which, when it came in around 975, was the most elaborate of

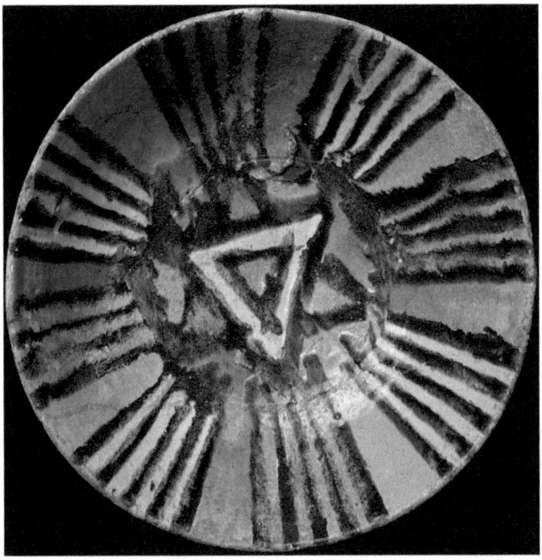

Fig. 1 'Fayyumi ware'

expedition final report, 1 (it focusses on design and says nothing exact about fabrics). Literary references to late medieval pottery-making in the capital are set out in Milwright, 'Pottery in the written sources'. For common-ware typologies outside the capital, see Bonnéric and Schmitt, 'Tinnîs' (p. 98: on their site, under 5% was fineware); Pyke, 'The ceramic material from Tinnīs', pp. 202–25; Rousset et al., 'Tebtynis 1998', pp. 217–45; and for the thirteenth century at Quṣayr, see Burke, *Archaeological texts*, pp. 86–156 (here, the types are classified by fabric, and include glazes). Owing to its late date, I have not fully used the Quṣayr material, but Burke's work stands out for its comprehensiveness and its use of the textual material found on the site. The fullest coarse-ware typologies are those of Nubia, thanks to the classic work by Adams, *Ceramic industries*; much of what he described and categorized was from Aswān, but not by any means all.

Fig. 2 Fusṭāṭ Fāṭimid Sgraffiato

Fig. 3 Egyptian lustreware

these productions, and was often (as was FFS) made of artificially mixed fabrics, often with glass frit and/or quartz to lighten them.[168]

There is a long debate about where these types came from, and indeed where the taste for glaze came from. Different types of monochrome glaze existed in the Roman Empire and in the Sasanian world. Did Egypt have a separate development to Syria and Iraq from these earlier traditions, or did it take skills directly from Iraq, around 800, the rough date of the first Egyptian glazes? Similarly, 'Fayyumi' and other glaze types clearly imitate certain Chinese productions, but again, did the Egyptians imitate Chinese types directly, or did they imitate Iraqi imitations of them, given that both can be found in Egypt?[169] It seems fairly clear to me that FFS, in particular, imitates Chinese ceramics directly; but it is probable that Egypt took many technical innovations from Iraq, particularly in the case of lustreware, which is so complex to make—and early Egyptian versions of it are so close to Iraqi ones—that the proposition that Egypt actually imported Iraqi potters to make lustreware, at the beginning of the Fāṭimid period, seems to me entirely likely.[170] I however record these debates only because they have occupied scholars so much (polychrome glazed types being seen by many as 'art objects', rather than as part of a wider material culture with a strong economic element); for my purposes here, they are fairly marginal. It is enough to make clear that glazed ceramics were often complex to make, which in such cases means that they were probably made in specialized centres; and that they had an international dimension, given that they were responses to ceramic imports (and were themselves exported), a point we will come back to.

Actually, however, when ceramologists offer fuller glaze typologies, one finds many more types than these mentioned here. And much criticism has been levelled in particular at the catch-all category of 'Fayyumi ware', which is very hard to define, has often been misused as a term, and was not, as far as we currently know, made in the Fayyūm.[171] Recent archaeological reports often do not use most of these typologies at all, but simply describe the decorations the excavators see. As Roland-Pierre Gayraud and Lucy Vallauri say in *Fustat II*, the final ceramic report

[168] In general, Gayraud, 'Les céramiques égyptiennes à glaçure'; Gayraud et al., 'Assemblages de céramiques égyptiennes' (although Gayraud and Vallauri, already cautious in this last article, have become even less keen on these typologies: see n. 172 below). 'Fayyumi ware': Scanlon, 'Fayyumi pottery'; Williams, *'Fayyumi' ware*, with a full bibliography in the latter. FFS: Scanlon, 'Fustat Fatimid Sgraffiato'. Lustreware: Philon, *Early Islamic ceramics*, pp. 63–262; Björnesjö, 'Approche archéologique'; Mason, 'Medieval Egyptian lustre-painted and associated wares', pp. 211–24; Salinas et al., 'From tin- to antimony-based yellow opacifiers'.

[169] Good contributions to this debate are Northedge, 'Les origines'; Gayraud, 'Les céramiques égyptiennes à glaçure', p. 266; Watson, 'Fritware'; Tite et al., 'Revisiting the beginnings'.

[170] See esp. Mason and Tite, 'The beginnings of tin-opacification'; Mason and Tite, 'The beginnings of Islamic stonepaste technology'.

[171] Fuller typologies: e.g. Mason, 'Medieval Egyptian lustre-painted and associated wares'; Mason, *Shine like the sun*, ch. 4. Williams, *'Fayyumi' ware*, although critical of inexact usages, makes a good case for a careful use of the term; he would prefer (p. 132) to restrict it to ceramics with a radial decoration.

for the ninth and tenth centuries for the Isṭabl 'Antar site (i.e. the period from the earliest glazes to the beginnings of Fāṭimid rule; their eleventh-century volume is not yet published), 'we have been struck by the extreme variety of these ceramics, which appears limitless.... one is never sure that one can group the products by workshop.... The absence of a notion of series appears specific to this period.... It announces the proliferation of forms, coatings, and decorations which characterize Fāṭimid and Mamlūk types.'[172] They are certainly right; unlike the slipped fine wares which the Romans preferred, glaze lent itself to very wide variety. Even when products were indeed turned out in series, all glaze except the simplest monochrome had to be applied individually to each pot, and was never exactly the same on each; potters could use the variability this allowed with gusto. I will use the typologies I have just listed, simply because they are used in so many excavation reports, but with great care (and 'Fayyumi ware', the least defensible, always in inverted commas). What matters here, anyway, is their origin and distribution. In our period, every type of glaze was indeed made in Fusṭāṭ; that is shown by wasters, and kiln bars with glaze on them.[173] But how many of them were also made somewhere else? Monochromes were certainly locally as well as centrally made. The same is probably true of 'Fayyumi ware'. All the same, scholars tend to assume that FFS was all made in Fusṭāṭ, as also lustreware, as, to repeat, they were complex to make. This cannot be proven, it has to be said, and caution is necessary before many more kilns have been excavated. But I will in what follows work on the assumption that both are likely to have been predominantly made in Fusṭāṭ.[174]

Like Aswān ceramics, probably-Fusṭāṭ glazes from the Fāṭimid period are found throughout Egypt. The whole set so far described is found regularly in Fāṭimid levels in Alexandria, on the huge Kōm el-Dikka site, 'the usual range of artefacts', as the ceramics expert for the site, Gregor Majcherek, calls it (the same is true for the major glazed types of every other century from the ninth to the fifteenth). So are they in the other main coastal city, Tinnīs, and also at Ashkelon, the closest Palestinian port to Egypt and in many ways an extension of the region.[175] In the

[172] Gayraud and Vallauri, *Fustat II*, p. 367 (my trans.).

[173] Williams, *'Fayyumi' ware*, p. 16; Scanlon, 'Fustat Fatimid Sgraffiato', p. 265; Scanlon, 'Excavations at Fustat, 1964', pp. 18–20; in general, Gayraud and Vallauri, *Fustat II*, pp. 19–21. For *geniza* references to ceramics made in Fusṭāṭ, see Goitein, *MS*, 4, p. 146—they are presumably glazed wares.

[174] Roland-Pierre Gayraud (pers. comm.; I am grateful for his help here) is himself cautious about the Fusṭāṭ origin of all FFS and lustre; future work is essential here. Note that lustreware was sufficiently high-status that artisans sometimes actually signed pieces: notably S'ad, and Muslim b. al-Dahhān ('the painter'), both in the eleventh century; for the potters' names, see Bahgat and Massoul, *La céramique musulmane de l'Égypte*, pp. 50–67.

[175] See François, *Céramiques médiévales à Alexandrie*, pp. 22–3, and, among the many interims for Alexandria, mostly in *Polish archaeology in the Mediterranean*, esp. Kubiak, 'Alexandria. Kom el-Dikka'; Majcherek, 'Alexandria...2006/2007', p. 42 (quote); cf. for later periods esp. Redlak, 'Syro-Palestinian underglaze painted ceramics'. For Tinnīs, see Bonnéric and Schmitt, 'Tinnîs', pp. 104–7; Pyke, 'The ceramic material from Tinnīs', pp. 190–7; for Ashkelon, see Hoffman, *Ashkelon 8*, pp. 358–79 (thanks to Hagit Nol for obtaining this hard-to-find report for me).

Fayyūm, at Ṭuṭūn (a substantial village, as we saw earlier, but not on the main Nile routes), we find them all as well, and so also at the nearby Naqlūn monastic site, except for lustre. We find 'Fayyumi ware' at Bahnasā, and also lustre; 'Fayyumi ware', FFS, and lustre at Ashmūnayn.[176] Strikingly, we find a wide range of Fāṭimid glazed wares, including FFS and lustre, in Ṭūd in Upper Egypt, even though it is a smallish village, in limited quantities admittedly; and there are 'Fayyumi ware' and FFS in nearby Luxor and also in the thirteenth-century levels at Quṣayr. Farther up, there is FFS in Idfū, lustre and other non-local glazed wares (including FFS, but mostly from the post-Fāṭimid period) in Aswān, and 'Fayyumi ware' and small quantities of lustre even in Nubia.[177] So, as with Aswān ceramics, in effect every site in Egypt from our period with a pottery report has glazes which probably come from the capital; for even if we do not assume that all 'Fayyumi ware' and certainly not all monochromes were from Fusṭāṭ, every site has FFS and/or lustre as well. Lustre, a high-status ware, might be expected to have been harder to find and buy hundreds of kilometres away from its main production sites, but it still reached villages.

Imported wares fill out this picture, and further emphasize it. Presumably along the same routes as glazes, Chinese ceramics reached Alexandria, Tinnīs, Bahnasā, and even Ṭūd, not in large quantities, but again marking an interest in relative luxuries in quite small places, and (also relevantly for us) merchants able to supply them.[178] But for me at least as interesting, among the imports found in Egypt,

[176] Rousset et al., 'Tebtynis 1998', pp. 256–7, with Gayraud, 'Tebtynis', p. 38; Łyżwa, 'Naqlun 2001', and Danys-Lasek, 'Pottery from Deir el-Naqlun', who, pp. 603, 606, implies a very early date for FFS and artificial fabrics found under a burned layer with a *terminus post quem* of 937, thanks to a coin hoard. But too close a date to 937 seems too early to me, given the dates in the Fusṭāṭ sites themselves, where such fabrics do not predate the last years of the tenth century, and the hoard could, of course, have been deposited later. For Bahnasā, see Fehérvári, *The Kuwait excavations*, pp. 65–79, 173 (there are several other glaze types identified here too, especially monochromes); for Ashmūnayn, see Bailey, *Excavations at el-Ashmunein*, 5, pp. 113–6, with Bailey, 'The pottery from the South Church', p. 84.

[177] Pierrat, 'Essai de classification', pp. 194–8 and Joel, 'Céramique glaçurée' [Ṭūd]; Masson, 'Overview of the ceramic productions', pp. 131–3 [Luxor]; Burke, *Archaeological texts*, pp. 110–11, 177n [Quṣayr]; Gascoigne, 'Dislocation and continuity', pp. 166, 183 [Idfū]; for Aswān, ibid., pp. 101–2, Gregory Williams, pers. comm., and see also Arnold, *Elephantine XXX*, p. 24; for Nubia, see Adams, *Ceramic industries*, pp. 586, 591–2.

[178] François, *Céramiques médiévales à Alexandrie*, pp. 143–53 (increasing from the twelfth century); Kubiak, 'Alexandria. Kom el-Dikka', pp. 38–9; Pyke, 'The ceramic material from Tinnīs', pp.185–8 (with, ibid., 188–90, some probable Iranian wares in the twelfth century too), and Bonnéric and Schmitt, 'Tinnîs', pp. 110–11; Fehérvári, *The Kuwait excavations*, p. 70 [Bahnasā]; Joel, 'Céramique glaçurée' [Ṭūd]. It cannot be said with certainty that Chinese ceramics came to the last two via the capital, as the main trade routes from the Indian Ocean were down the Nile, and over the desert from the ports in the middle of the Red Sea (see Mikami, 'Chinese ceramics', pp. 13–15, for Chinese wares in the port of Aydhāb, and, after 1200, Burke, *Archaeological texts*, pp. 156–69). But Chinese ceramics also came up the Red Sea to the very top, to 'Aqaba in modern Jordan, in the tenth and eleventh centuries, so could also have gone directly to at least Fusṭāṭ and the north coast; see Whitcomb, 'Excavations in the site of medieval 'Aqaba', p. 128. Those found in Ashkelon could have come either through 'Aqaba or down the Nile: Hoffman, *Ashkelon 8*, pp. 508–20 (T. Vorderstrasse). For Chinese pottery elsewhere in the Mediterranean, almost inevitably coming through Egypt, see Chapter 3, nn. 61, 74, 191; Chapter 5, n. 208 below.

is one quite ordinary common ware: a Palestinian amphora or storage container of roughly the tenth century, which has been identified in Tinnīs, the Wadi Naṭrūn, Fusṭāṭ, the Middle Egyptian monastic site of Suhāj (better known to historians as Sohag), and Aswān, and which seems from descriptions also to be identical to the amphora called by the excavators Naqlun 10, found in that monastery. Here, the contents were, of course, more important than the ceramic container, but all the same, a cheap imported product (quite probably olive oil; see p. 138 below) could be commercialized far into the Egyptian interior.[179]

Below the Egypt-wide range of the great Aswān and Fusṭāṭ productions, smaller-scale operations existed too. 'Ballas ware', including jugs and amphorae, doubtless did not come from Ballāṣ, on the left bank of the Nile opposite Quṣ in northern Upper Egypt, which in recent times has been a major producer of amphorae for water; but although unhelpfully named, this ware probably came from near there, given its clay, and it is well documented in Upper Egypt and to an extent outside. Its types have been found in Nubia throughout our period, but particularly in the twelfth century; Gascoigne has identified them in Ṭūd and Luxor, and they are visible in Aswān itself, increasing in number in our period; the production centre is perhaps also the source for the thin-walled bottles from Upper Egypt found at Naqlūn in the Fayyūm.[180] The substantial amphora sites in and around Anṣīna/Shaykh 'Ibāda (up to the tenth century) and Abū Mīnā (into the twelfth) had, as we have seen (p. 71), similar ranges. The Bahnasā kilns may not have produced a version of Red Slip ware into the eleventh century, or 'Fayyumi ware', but the very sketchy evidence here, taken as a whole, argues for a genuine production centre for other types. At the next level down, most site reports, when they are detailed enough (as at Tinnīs, Naqlūn, Ṭūd, Luxor, and also, for a slightly earlier period, Ashmūnayn) have monochrome glaze and common wares which seem to the excavators not to have close parallels elsewhere, and which they see as local.[181] And, finally, the existence of village-level potters in our documents, including

[179] Gascoigne and Pyke, 'Nebi Samwil-type jars'; Danys-Lasek, 'Pottery from Deir el-Naqlun', pp. 607, 627n; Pyke, 'The ceramic material from Tinnīs', p. 221; Williams, 'Medieval ceramics from Aswan', p. 300; Williams, *Syene VI*, pp. 61, 68, 71, 76, 81–2.

[180] Adams, *Ceramic industries*, pp. 571–6; Gascoigne, *The impact of the Arab conquest*, p. 108; Danys-Lasek, 'Pottery from Deir el-Naqlun', p. 607; Williams, 'Medieval ceramics from Aswan', p. 301; Williams, *Syene VI*, p. 58, for Aswān and for the lack of exact connection to Ballāṣ itself (for the modern ethnography of which, see Nicholson and Patterson, 'Pottery making in upper Egypt', and Gayraud and Vallauri, *Fustat II*, p. 32). In the thirteenth century, they are found in Quṣayr too; see Burke, *Archaeological texts*, pp. 114–15.

[181] Fehérvári, *The Kuwait excavations*, pp. 43, 56–60, 67, 88–92, 173 (see n. 160 above for caution about the Red Slip evidence; Williams, *'Fayyumi' ware*, pp. 42–4, is cautious about the evidence for that ware here too); Bonnéric and Schmitt, 'Tinnîs', p. 112; Pyke, 'The ceramic material from Tinnīs', pp. 197–200; Danys-Lasek, 'Pottery from Deir el-Naqlun'; Lecuyer and Pierrat, 'À propos des lieux de production' [Ṭūd]; Masson, 'Overview of the ceramic productions', pp. 131–3 [Luxor]; Bailey, *Excavations at el-Ashmunein*, 5, p. 113. See also Gayraud and Vallauri, *Fustat II*, p. 19. Rousset et al., 'Tebtynis 1998', p. 217, make clear that they do not have the comparators to be able to say how local their typologies are; this site was excavated and published earlier than most.

those for the small village of Damūya in the Fayyūm, testifies to the existence of very small-scale and doubtless relatively simple productions everywhere. Generalizing very widely, I would hypothesize that there were four levels of ceramic production here: first, the two great Egypt-wide productions; then substantial productions like 'Ballas ware' and Abū Mīnā, often of well-made common wares, including amphorae, but maybe occasionally also of products like 'Fayyumi' glaze, which reached widish areas but not the whole valley; then more local but still good-quality productions, which might well have also produced monochrome glaze (which was, among other things, used to seal cooking pots); then the village level of Damūya, which was doubtless an example of village productions of the simplest and cheapest products.

There are two main points which follow from this summary presentation of the ceramic evidence for Egypt in the Fāṭimid period, but, actually, for both before and after our period as well. First, and most obviously, that it was normal to buy and sell products along the whole length of the Nile valley. Aswān and Fusṭāṭ are at opposite ends of the valley, but they both did this, overlapping consistently; they both reached almost every known site, and were thus available at village level; and wares from the one are found in the other. There was not one direction for goods to go; the two major centres evidently specialized in different sorts of products, and so the trade could go in two opposite directions at once. And so could smaller-scale centres, partly competing, but also offering goods of a different quality and—doubtless—price. It was, anyway, normal to carry not very expensive products from one end of Egypt to the other, in any direction, and stopping everywhere. This firms up the picture I set out of wheat earlier, for it is more complete and more systematic. Ceramics are usually the easiest guide to how commercial systems work as a whole in the centuries before serial records, and here they show that these systems were in Egypt both very dense and multidirectional.

The other point is a related one: it is that the productive hierarchy which I have just sketched out did not entirely depend on the capital. Fusṭāṭ was obviously by far the biggest city in Egypt, and it may be that its ceramic productions were the largest-scale too (although this might not be the case if its major exports were only glazed wares, for these were too small a minority of total ceramics; the sorts of wares coming out of Aswān, by contrast, were certainly mass products). But they were not the only ones, and overall it cannot seriously be doubted that the network of ceramic commercialization, if we take all its levels at once, did not have Fusṭāṭ products as its principal focus. This productive hierarchy was firmly based, that is to say, on a network of local supply and demand. Local buyers of different types made their own choices as to what ceramics they wanted, and they could get them from a variety of places when they chose. I wondered earlier (p. 46) whether Fusṭāṭ, as the political centre and the recipient of the bulk of Egypt's taxation, might have had an artificial centrality, held up only by the economy of the state itself. The answer was in the negative; but for me the evidence of ceramic distributions clinches that negative. Egypt's economic system, taken as a whole, was based on a much wider and more solid structure of demand, which also outlasted the period we are looking at in this book.

It is normal to say that ceramics are a proxy for the most important artisanal commodity of all, cloth. Usually this is simply presented as an assumption, at least for the period before 1000, for there is not enough evidence for cloth to prove it one way or another, given that textile products so seldom appear in the archaeology, and so unsystematically in written sources too. In Fāṭimid Egypt, however, this is not the case for the written sources; as a result, we can, here, say a very large amount about linen and its many-levelled trade. Here also, the wealth of information in Egypt's documents and letters means that we can get a sense, in some cases, of merchant strategies and constraints, and even personalities, something which the archaeology of ceramics cannot provide. That is the task of the next section. But it is important to have started with ceramics, because it gives us the basic structure inside which the accounts of the sales of flax and linen make most sense. If it was possible to get the same ceramics from one end of the country to the other and everywhere between, we can ask whether it was the same for cloth, even when we do not have the direct evidence; and what are, in our written sources, only signs of wider commercial densities can be generalized more easily if we bear the evidence of ceramics in mind. It from this position that we should approach the data which we will look at in the next section.

2.4.2 Flax and linen

Most cloth produced and sold in Egypt in our period was linen.[182] Our most substantial evidence for the commercialization of linen cloth, and its raw material,

[182] Examples of woollen and cotton cloth have been found in excavations from our period; see, e.g., Mackie, 'Textiles'; Gayraud, 'Isṭabl 'Antar (Fostat) 1992', pp. 11–13. Both were probably more important than we know, but far less important than linen, particularly after linen production really took off around 900. Concerning wool: Bahnasā is called a major wool-weaving centre in Ibn Ḥawqal, *Kītāb ṣūrat al-arḍ*, trans. Kramers and Wiet, 1, p. 157, and al-Idrīsī, *Nuzhat al-mushtāq*, trans. Jaubert and Nef, p. 123; and other parts of the Nile valley are said by them to have produced wool too (see the references in Lombard, *Les textiles*, pp. 35–8; cf. Goitein, *MS*, 1, p. 419, n. 37 for imports and exports); but wool is mentioned in few Arabic letters, all probably predating 900: P.GrohmannWirtsch. 14, P.KarabacekKuenstler p. 67, P.MuslimState 28, P.Prag.Arab. 67, P.Cair.Arab. 394, P.David-WeillMusee, P.FahmiTaaqud 5. Some of the cloth mentioned in texts which do not specify linen might be from wool, but there was also linen in Bahnasā according to Ibn Ḥawqal, so we cannot assume that cloth even from there was necessarily woollen. By the twelfth century, woollens could be imported too: see n. 312 below.

Cotton has about as many citations, largely from the ninth century, several of them from the Fayyūm (the others are unprovenanced): P.Bodl.Arab. 1, 2 (a reference to cotton fields, so it was grown on at least a small scale), P.Marchands II 9, III 36, P.GrohmannWirtsch. 19, P.DiemWien p. 86, P.Cair. Arab. 311, P.FahmiTaaqud 5, P.Vind.Arab. I 23, and in some *geniza* letters too, e.g. Bodl. MS Heb. c 28/34, T-S 13J15.19 (Gil K458 [Goitein, *Letters*, n. 26], 540). The Fayyūm remained a cotton focus into the thirteenth century; see Rapoport, *Rural economy*, pp. 117, 120–1, 135–6. Cotton cloth was more

flax, comes from the *geniza*, but it is not by any means our only evidence; letters in Arabic script tell us plenty about it as well. We have already seen how in the Ashmūnayn district there was extensive weaving of local flax into linen (see pp. 50–1 above); some of that was for local consumption, of course, but Ashmūnayn exported both raw flax and linen, and via both Christian and Jewish merchants. This sort of capillary production and exchange probably matches the second level of ceramic production/exchange, for Ashmūnayn, as we have also seen, was in a relatively intense flax cultivation area. And it was not by any means new in our period. A cache of ninth-century papyri found in the regional centre of Madīnat al-Fayyūm shows the establishment of a formal partnership in 864 between two merchants of the city and one from Fusṭāṭ to buy Fayyūmī linen cloth for sale in the capital, and then the development of that partnership, above all through the eyes (and pen—he was a scribe too) of one of the two local merchants, Jaʿfar Abū Hurayra, whose archive this was. Several dated texts from the late 860s and 870s show Abū Hurayra buying advance sales of cloth, implicitly from local weavers (in one case explicitly so, from Jabr 'the weaver', *al-khayyāsh*)—it is often called 'cloth of Qūṣ', which here must be a type of cloth, not an import from Upper Egypt (other cloth types were 'Tinnīsī' and 'Fusṭāṭī').[183]

Most of this archive is undated letters from the same period. Some are from Abū Hurayra to his father and other family members or their letters back, about small-scale sales in cloth, grain, and other food, and occasional jewellery—here the sales are for both commercial and family needs, and in one case display family tensions, for Abū Hurayra thinks his father's second wife Sayyida is an unbeliever, presumably but not certainly a Christian (it is worth noting that here, for once, almost all the letters are between Muslims).[184] Many others, however, are from Abū Hurayra's partners in Fusṭāṭ; these show that he was sending variable quantities of cloth to the capital on a weekly basis, on donkey trains, to merchants who would do their best to sell at good prices (and sometimes did not sell if prices were too low), returning the money in purses of 8 to 16 dinars at a time,

often made in the Levant (and also Nubia, plus, traditionally, the Egyptian oases) and was certainly imported into Egypt; see, e.g., CUL Or.1080J17, T-S 8J19.27, 13J19.27 (Gil P506, 507 [Goitein, *Letters*, n. 5], K240 [S63]). Egyptian cotton did not get into other exchange networks on a large enough scale for it to be more visible, but it does occasionally figure in the twelfth century as an export to Italy (see n. 309 below; see also n. 219 below for Alexandrian cotton mixes), so cotton cultivation and production here did have some wider market. See also Lombard, *Les textiles*, pp. 70–1; for cotton in the period immediately preceding ours, see esp. Kelley, *Commodity, commerce and economy*, chs 4–6.

[183] P.Marchands collects the letters, two thirds of which have been published. See Rāġib, *Marchands d'étoffes*, 1, p. ix for uncertainties about the find spot. The only substantive analysis of these letters and texts is Younes, 'Textile trade'; Bondioli, *Peasants, merchants, and caliphs*, pp. 169–78 makes further important points; see also Ragheb, 'Marchands d'Égypte'. For 864, see P.Marchands I 1; for the cloth advance sales, see I 2–9 (6, a. 870, for Jabr). Qūṣ cloth: I 3, 4 (probably), 8, 10, II 14; Tinnīs cloth: III 33; Fusṭāṭ cloth: III 38. Abū Hurayra is a scribe in several texts, e.g. I 10. On advanced sales, see Diem, *Arabischer Terminkauf*, and esp., for the often exploitative nature of such sales, Bondioli, *Peasants, merchants, and caliphs*, pp. 105–58; see further n. 206 below.

[184] For the family letters, see P.Marchands II; II 3 for Sayyida (and her birth family) as unbelievers.

medium-scale sums, to Abū Hurayra and his associates (the largest sum mentioned is 44 dinars, to another merchant), and who would also take commissions from him for personal acquisitions. Abū Hurayra and his family and associates, some of whom lived in the Quarter of the Cloth Merchants (*bazzāzūn*) by the great mosque of Madīnat al-Fayyūm, were thus middlemen for the systematic sale of linen cloth made in the Fayyūm by local weavers to the capital—only once did any of them travel farther on, in that case to Alexandria.[185] It seems to have been largely in Fusṭāṭ that the cloth was finished and turned into garments, for much of the transport is generic cloth. But the scale of these sales was substantial, and we must be looking at a considerable degree of specialized weaving in the villages around Madīnat al-Fayyūm in the third quarter of the ninth century, as well as a large number of merchants committed to selling the cloth. Similar merchants appear in other parts of Egypt too in this period, as with the anecdotal narratives of traders in cloth and perfumes meeting brigands outside Ahnās and elsewhere in the Nile valley recounted in Ibn al-Dāya's late ninth-century *adab* stories.[186]

This was the economic context for the development of the great factory weaving towns of Tinnīs and Damietta, and an array of small towns or large villages near them, of which the best-known was Dabīq, the home of the finest-quality Dabīqī cloth, a much-cited type of expensive white linen (by no means all of which, however, can have been from this one village). Damietta was and is at the mouth of a branch of the Nile, whereas Tinnīs was on an island in a coastal lagoon (the island is now just outside Port Saʿīd); they were both ports too. Their high point was the tenth to twelfth centuries—the early twelfth for Tinnīs; and in fact the latter was deliberately abandoned as a functioning city in 1192/3, because it was too exposed to naval attack by Christians. (Damietta, which survived, was, however, similarly exposed; it was the only city taken in the Fifth Crusade in 1219–21.)[187] They were already active before the ninth century, but Ibn Ṭūlūn invested in them in the 870s–880s according to near-contemporary sources, and so did some of his officials; the earliest surviving dated *ṭirāz* (as we have seen, embroidered fabric, often including a date, place, and mention of the ruler) from Tinnīs is from as early as 776, but the references take off in the 890s.[188] It was also

[185] For letters to and from merchants in the capital, see P.Marchands III and V,1. Money purses with specific sums: V,1 2, 3, 5, 7 (44 dinars), 8, 11. Quarter of the Cloth Merchants: e.g. V,1 4. Alexandria: III 33.

[186] Ibn al-Dāya, *Kitāb al-mukāfaʾa*, trans. Panetta, pp. 59–60, 143–4.

[187] See in general Lombard, *Les textiles*, pp. 151–74 (wide-ranging but not always accurate); Frantz-Murphy, 'A new interpretation'; Lev, 'Tinnīs'; and now, as the essential guide, Gascoigne, *The island city of Tinnīs*, pp. 7–19 (A. L. Gascoigne). See Powell, *Anatomy of a crusade*, esp. pp. 157–91, for the Fifth Crusade.

[188] For Ibn Ṭūlūn and his officials, see esp. Frantz-Murphy, 'A new interpretation', pp. 281–90; for *ṭirāz*, see the summary lists in Kühnel and Bellinger, *Catalogue of dated tiraz fabrics* (p. 124 for Tinnīs); for one set of *ṭirāz* textiles, from Dumbarton Oaks in Washington, two of which are certainly from

from this period that, as we have seen (pp. 75–6), paper rapidly took over from papyrus, showing a very great expansion of linen production in the Delta in the decades around and after 900. By the Fāṭimid period, workshops were highly developed in these towns and villages, particularly at Tinnīs; they were both state workshops, supplying the Cairo court and army directly, and private workshops for the open market. Their cloth was mentioned as a luxury item in Iraqi narratives from the tenth century, so was clearly exported there, as it also was to Ifrīqiya; Dabīqī cloth also regularly appears (among other types of fine cloth) in trousseaux in the *geniza*, so was a luxury sold inside the country too; but they also and above all made cloth for a mass market.[189]

Our Arabic-script documents do not tell us much about these towns, which were situated too far into the Delta for our standard documentary find spots to be close to them (but see pp. 103–5 below for Tinnīs in the *geniza*). Conversely, all the geographers discuss and praise them, with varying degrees of plausibility; they universally stress the scale of production and the expense of the best cloth from the factories. They also tend to stress the fact that most of the inhabitants of the towns were Christian; this has confirmation for Tinnīs in near-contemporary Christian sources from both Syria and Egypt, and even Italy, but there is no doubt that there were plenty of Muslims there, and a small Jewish community too.[190] The workforce of Tinnīs was, several sources say, impoverished, and Bondioli has shown that this was in part due to a combination of heavy taxes and debt dependency on merchants; but production levels remained high all the same. Tinnīs and Damietta were sufficiently important to the state that their revenues had their

Tinnīs, see Glidden and Thompson, '*Ṭirāz* fabrics'. *Ṭirāz* cloth from the Delta towns is found in a wide range of modern museums.

[189] For a set of references to Dabīqī and other Delta cloth in Iraq, see Serjeant, 'Material for a history of Islamic textiles', pp. 91–3; for export to Mahdia in Ifrīqiya, see T-S 20.69 (Gil K380 [S69]); for trousseaux, see Olszowy-Schlanger, *Karaite marriage documents*, nn. 2, 23, 27, 29, 32, 36, 37, 44, 56; and see in general Goitein, *MS*, 4, pp. 165–6. References in Arabic-script texts include P.Vind.Arab. II 5, P.Cair.Arab. 308; the latter shows that *ṭirāz* was available for sale privately in Egypt, as also do excavations when these fabrics are found (e.g. for Fusṭāṭ, Mackie, 'Textiles'; for Naqlūn, Helmecke, 'Textiles'—and, in fact, it is only Nāṣer-e Khosraw, who did visit the Delta towns but was from Iran and not always well-informed, who says that it was not for private use; see *Nāṣer-e Khosraw's book of travels*, trans. Thackston, pp. 38–40). See also ibid., p. 40, for the only clear reference in a source to the making in Tinnīs of an artisanal product which was not cloth-related, in this case iron tools, and an iron workshop has indeed been excavated on the island; see Gascoigne, *The island city of Tinnīs*, pp. 103–4 (A. L. Gascoigne et al.). So have a glass kiln and a textile workshop; see ibid., and pp. 152–4 ('A. al-Shinnāwī et al.); T-S 13J26.18 (Gil P356) and 8J9.23 may possibly refer to pottery made there too. (Note that Bahnasā also had a state weaving industry according to Ibn Ḥawqal, *Kītāb ṣūrat al-arḍ*, trans. Kramers and Wiet, 1, p. 157, and al-Idrīsī, *Nuzhat al-mushtāq*, trans. Jaubert and Nef, p. 123.)

[190] See Lombard, *Les textiles*, pp. 151–74, and Lev, 'Tinnīs' for the references (here the most useful geographers are Ibn Ḥawqal, *Kītāb ṣūrat al-arḍ*, trans. Kramers and Wiet, 1, pp. 150–1; *Nāṣer-e Khosraw's book of travels*, trans. Thackston, pp. 38–40; al-Idrīsī, *Nuzhat al-mushtāq*, trans. Jaubert and Nef, p. 236). For Christians in Tinnīs *c.*826, see *Chronique de Michel le Syrien*, ed. Chabot, 3, pp. 62–4, here apparently reporting a contemporary source, Dionysius of Tel Maḥrē; *Das 'Itinerarium Bernardi monachi'*, ed. Ackermann, ch. 8 for an Italian visitor *c.*870; see p. 60 above for the Egyptian Christian source, a mid-eleventh-century account of events in the 970s. For the Jewish community, see n. 211 below.

own government office, the *dīwān Tinnīs wa Dimyāṭ*. Tinnīs, at least, was heavily built up, as Alison Gascoigne's field survey of the island makes clear, and Ibn Bassām's contemporary account makes the point as well, as we shall see in a moment.[191]

The luxury end of textile production in Tinnīs and Damietta is not our concern; it was impressive, but will have been a small minority of what was actually produced here. The scale of production as a whole is more important for our needs, and here we run into the problem of the essential unreliability of medieval figures. Did Ibn Killīs (d. 991), *wazīr* for the Fāṭimid caliph al-ʿAzīz, really leave 500,000 dinars' worth of cloth at his death, which he was evidently buying and selling, by implication from the factory towns, as a biographer stated a century and a half later? Did the Fāṭimids really seek to fine the inhabitants of Tinnīs 200,000 dinars for their role in a revolt in 972–3, as the late source al-Maqrīzī claims? Did the tax office for Tinnīs really collect 1,000 dinars a day in the 980s, as the contemporary geographer al-Muqaddasī states? And were there really 50,000 inhabitants in the island city in 1047–8, when the Persian traveller Nāṣer-e Khosraw visited it?[192]

We cannot trust any such figures, but one set at least is provided by a real expert. This was Ibn Bassām, a market supervisor (*muḥtasib*) in Tinnīs, who wrote an account of his city, the *Anīs al-jalīs fī akhbār Tinnīs*, between 1015 and (at the latest) 1050.[193] He (here, like other geographers) explains that the island had access to fresh water only during the Nile flood, when the lagoon in which Tinnīs was situated briefly became sweet. This water was kept in large cisterns, both public and privately owned, for the rest of the year; many of these cisterns have been investigated by Alison Gascoigne's archaeological team. Ibn Bassām adds that the town had two harbours, which are also visible in survey. That is to say, the archaeology, here and elsewhere, shows that he was not a fantasist.[194] He further stresses

[191] For the *dīwān* or *majlīs*, see, e.g., P.Fatimid 3 (a. 1130); cf. Lev, 'Tinnīs', p. 85. (I do not directly discuss Damietta here, as we know so much less about it; see p. 144 below for its greater importance by the mid-twelfth century.) For the density of settlement on the island, see esp. the plans in Gascoigne, *The island city of Tinnīs*, pp. 317–26. For impoverishment and debt dependency, see Bondioli, *Peasants, merchants and caliphs*, pp. 179–211.

[192] Ibn al-Ṣayrafī, *al-Ishāra ilā man nāl al-wizāra*, pp. 90–4; al-Maqrīzī, *Ittiʿāẓ*, trans. Jiwa, pp. 97–100, 112 (the fine was, however, supposedly substantially cut in the end); al-Muqaddasī, *Aḥsan al-taqāsīm*, trans. Miquel, p. 138; *Nāṣer-e Khosraw's book of travels*, trans. Thackston, pp. 38–9 (he also repeats al-Muqaddasī's tax figure); cf. Lev, 'Tinnīs', pp. 85–6 for more tax figures in later sources.

[193] For what follows, see Ibn Bassām, *Anīs al-jalīs fī akhbār Tinnīs*, trans. Gascoigne, *The island city of Tinnīs*, pp. 57–70 (A. L. Gascoigne and J. P. Cooper). The latest event mentioned in the text is for 1015; the *terminus ante quem* is provided by the fact that the text is quoted in the *Book of curiosities*, an annotated set of maps dating in its present form to 1020–50, which include a map of Tinnīs—see, for the Tinnīs section, Rapoport, 'Reflections of Fatimid power', pp. 199–202. See also Lev, 'Tinnīs', pp. 90–4. For the role of a *muḥtasib* in Egypt, see Shoshan, 'Fāṭimid grain policy'; Labib, *Handelsgeschichte Ägyptens*, pp. 179–83.

[194] For current topography and cisterns, see Gascoigne, *The island city of Tinnīs*, pp. 85–140, 165–77 (A. L. Gascoigne et al., N. J. Warner). For an overview of the city, see Bondioli, *Peasants, merchants and caliphs*, pp. 179–216.

the large number of mosques in the city—160—and that there had been 72 churches until al-Ḥākim had them destroyed (historians are, however, rightly in my view, cautious about concluding that the city was substantially Muslimized thereafter—Ibn Bassām was not writing much later, and the churches might not have been rebuilt or converted back from mosques yet). There were 56 *fundūqs*, 2,500 *ḥāns* for storing and selling goods, plus another 150 shops selling cloth, 160 flour mills, some of them substantial in size (the town's inhabitants did not grind their own grain), and 5,000 linen workshops with 10,000 cloth workers in them of both sexes, not including finishers and embroiderers. The town had to import all its food; it needed 200,000 *irdabbs* (*c.*18 million litres) of grain annually, which Ibn Bassām used as the basis for an estimation of a total population of 50,000—which is quite plausible, given standard nutrition calculations for medieval Latin Europe.[195]

So these figures roughly match up, and as a *muḥtasib* Ibn Bassām may well have known how much grain passed through the market system; the figure of 50,000 inhabitants also matches Nāṣer-e Khosraw's figure, which was probably independently obtained. I am inclined to accept it, at least as a ballpark. The figure of 50,000 is higher than the most optimistic calculations for any eleventh-century city in mainland Italy, even Rome (for which up to 30,000 is plausible for this period[196]) and Milan; perhaps more surprisingly, it might be a quarter of the contemporary size of Fusṭāṭ itself.[197] But even if the figure was arbitrarily halved, with all the other figures brought down too, we would still be dealing with a dramatically specialized weaving town by medieval standards, densely populated, given the size of the island, with thousands of workers in its workshops; and the town had to subsist entirely through market exchange, with boats bringing all necessities of life from outside (except fish, which were plentiful in the lagoon), including the flax which almost the whole city lived off. Supplying Tinnīs with food and

[195] For Latin Europe, see, e.g., Maire Vigueur, 'Les "casali"', p. 123, Dyer, *Standards of living*, p. 114. The figures for Italy and England in these two could make Tinnīs workers relatively poorly nourished, living as they would have done off *c.*600 litres of grain a year per person (500 was needed in Europe for a good diet). Goitein, *MS*, 4, pp. 235–6 however argues that a 'middle-class' family in Fusṭāṭ could live off *c.*1,100 litres a year, which would make the Tinnīs figures slightly more generous; anyway, if we scaled them down a bit, Ibn Bassām's grain figures would imply an even higher population. According to Dionysus in the early ninth century, Tinnīs workers were already daily wage labourers (*Chronique de Michel le Syrien*, ed. Chabot, 3, p. 63–4); outside observers do not necessarily get such things right, but it stands to reason that they should have been salaried. Grain or no grain, they were in general very poor, Dionysus claims; see n. 191 above. Thanks to Greer Phillips for help here.

[196] Meneghini and Santangeli Valenzani, *Roma nell'altomedioevo*, pp. 21–4.

[197] Here we are really dealing in guesstimates; but Garcin accepts around 200,000 inhabitants for the twin cities in the early Fāṭimid period, with slow growth from then up to 250,000 by the thirteenth century (see n. 41 above). Bianquis, 'Une crise frumentaire', p. 96, calculates 250,000 for the capital in 1055/6, using al-Maqrīzī's fifteenth-century data for grain consumption for that year. The bases for his calculation are, however, not rigorous, not least because al-Maqrīzī's data themselves amount to 44 million litres, remarkably close to Ibn Bassām's figure for Tinnīs. I am reluctant to use these late figures—that the two cities had a similar population in the eleventh century is wholly unrealistic—but if they were even partly accurate, Tinnīs would be less far behind Fusṭāṭ in size than I am supposing.

raw materials, and then selling the cloth the town produced, all also required a very complex infrastructure, which must have stretched a long way into the Delta. It is hardly necessary to say that large one-industry towns were unknown in Europe in the eleventh century, or anywhere else in the Mediterranean, or indeed, as far as I know, in the rest of the world apart from China. Nor could they have been possible in Egypt, whether or not they had state backing, if the other elements of the exchange infrastructure were not already present—and these were, as we have seen, normal throughout Egypt.

The other major focus for the flax trade was just outside the Fayyūm. We have seen that in the ninth century Fayyūmī linen was woven in the oasis and sold in the capital. By the eleventh, we do not have a similar document set to that of Abū Hurayra; but there was now a major market for raw flax at Būṣīr, a village just outside the entry into the Fayyūm from the Nile valley (see Map 6). We know of it above all from the *geniza*, which discusses it a great deal; it is hardly referred to as a centre in any other source—in particular, in only one (at most) of our Arabic-script documents—except, as already noted, by the geographer al-Muqaddasī in the 980s, who simply says that good flax comes from here, some of which is sold to weavers in Bahnasā.[198] By the eleventh century, however, the village's role was quite different. Jewish merchants of Fusṭāṭ regularly state in their correspondence that Būṣīrī flax is of the best quality and commands the highest prices, and all our well-documented merchants were involved in buying from there. They sometimes bought flax from Ashmūnayn and Bahnasā too, but above all, far more than all other places, they bought it from Būṣīr.[199] They went there a great deal, particularly in the second half of the year (August onwards), after the first two stages in flax processing were complete; sometimes the merchants bought flax which had only gone through the first process, retting (soaking), but often they were happy to buy flax fully prepared for weaving, sometimes through brokers, at a higher price. Jewish participation in the Būṣīr markets has been well studied, particularly by Abraham Udovitch and Jessica Goldberg.[200] They show the huge scale

[198] P.Vind.Arab. I 54 (note that this is a very casual reference, and that there were other villages in Egypt with the same name); al-Muqaddasī, *Aḥsan al-taqāsīm*, trans. Miquel, p. 123.

[199] For Ashmūnayn, see n. 77 above. For Bahnasā, see T-S 12.248, Moss. II,193 (Gil K580, 709). Jessica Goldberg points out to me that Būṣīr's prominence in the texts we have may in part be because it was the particular stamping ground of Nahray b. Nissīm, by far our best-documented flax dealer; but it was, nonetheless, clearly a major centre in this period, and the high value placed on flax from here shows that it was widely prized. From this point onwards I will be using substantial numbers of *geniza* texts which do not have published translations into western European languages; I am very grateful indeed to Marina Rustow and Jessica Goldberg for sending me MS translations made by Abraham Udovitch, to Lorenzo Bondioli for checking questions on the originals, and to Maayan Ravid, Netta Cohen, and Lorenzo Bondioli for translating and guiding me through the Hebrew translations made by Moshe Gil in his editions, Gil K and Gil P. (The other abbreviation here, S104, etc., marks, as it already has in this chapter, translations from Gil's Hebrew in Simonsohn, *The Jews in Sicily*, vol. 1.)

[200] Udovitch, 'International trade'; Goldberg, *Trade and institutions*, pp. 101–4. Gil, 'The flax trade', esp. pp. 85–7, is also useful; see further ibid., pp. 82–3 for the pacing of flax preparation across the year; but he wrongly sees (p. 85) the flax sold at Būṣīr as coming from the Delta.

of flax buying from the region, funnelling many thousands of dinars a year to the local population; from there, the flax was shipped (in this case, not put on donkeys) to Fusṭāṭ and from there to the port of Alexandria for the international markets of Mahdia and Palermo. Not surprisingly, the Būṣīr markets became complex and many-levelled; the merchants sold there, as well as buying: they dealt in hides, linen itself, and especially silk. One document (but only one that I have seen) refers to cloth-weaving, and even a *ṭirāz* worker.[201] I referred earlier to Būṣīr as a mushroom town; it was probably only a major economic centre for half the year, and there is no sign in any text of any kind of administrative or fiscal infrastructure. In addition, the evidence for intense activity there is only really from the mid- to late eleventh century. There is less from the 1020s and 1030s, although the Ibn ʿAwkal letters do show that the markets were already active by then; and by 1100 our evidence ends.[202] The major *geniza* merchants were getting into the Indian spice trade in the twelfth century, and it may well be that their retreat from Būṣīr caused the decline of its markets. The absence of a substantial artisanal network in the village may have added to its exposure to fashions in commerce, for no documented merchant who was involved in flax processing did it any other way than by hiring his own workers, apparently from an agricultural labour force. But in its high decades, selling in Būṣīr must have massively added to the prosperity of this part of the Nile valley.

Who was dealing with the Fusṭāṭī merchants? Sometimes brokers, as just noted; these could be trusted locals like Abū Muḥammad Qāsim, who people wanted to keep on the right side of (while also keeping an eye on him to make sure he bought the right quality of flax); sometimes, though, there were rather larger-scale 'great houses' (*al-buyūt al-akhbār*), like the Ṭansāwīs (evidently originally from Ṭansā, a village near Būṣīr), who were a tougher proposition—a letter to the young Nahray b. Nissīm from his uncle in 1048 advises him to avoid buying from them, as he does not have 'the strength' to deal with them, but instead to buy from 'beggars' (*ṣaʿālik*), presumably smaller dealers, who have less traction.[203] Very often, however, the Jewish merchants bought directly from peasants (*muzāriʿūn*). These were primary producers selling their own flax. They were seen as canny and untrustworthy; in another letter of advice, the young and keen Faraḥ b. Ismaʿīl is

[201] Pepper: AIU V.A.70 (Gil K789 [S104]); hides: T-S 12.793 (Gil K640); linen cloth: T-S Misc. 25.19 (Gil K245); silk: T-S Misc. 25.19, Bodl. MS Heb. d 74/46, Bodl. MS Heb. c 28/33, T-S AS 145.81+13J23.18, 12.793 (Gil K245, 257, 258, 372 [S149], 640); cloth-working: K15.114 (Gil K837). Boats to Alexandria (and Rashīd): T-S K15.53, Ar. 51.87, 10J29.10, 8J25.11 (Gil K274, 299, 330, 375).

[202] For the 1020s–1030s, see esp. T-S NS 308.119 and 12.227 (Gil K191, 193, both trans. Stillman, 'A case of labor problems'). For the post-1100 period, I have not found references in word searches.

[203] Qāsim: T-S Misc. 25.19, 13J13.11 (especially), 12.793, 13J27.18 (Gil K245, 479 [S102], 640, 643). A better edition and translation of T-S 13J13.11 is in Goldberg, 'Mercantile letters', pp. 406–10. 'Great houses': T-S 20.180 (Gil K379, trans. Goitein, *Letters*, n. 30); cf. also AIU VII.E.18, T-S 13J27.18 (Gil K483, 643), and Bodl. MS Heb. d 74/46, T-S K15.53, 8J16.31 (Gil K257, 274, 370) for a Ṭansāwī-owned boat.

told not to buy in advance from villagers (*ahl al-ḍiyāʿ*), because he risks being palmed off with poor-quality flax. They sold more cheaply, all the same, if the merchant was a good bargainer, as the middleman was cut out. Nahray in later years was very much in demand in this respect, as he was regarded by his peers as experienced in flax dealing.[204] In addition, if a merchant bought in the villages and was a skilled dealer, he could get flax at an earlier stage of preparation—and, again, more cheaply—and hire workmen (*ajīr*s or *ṣanāʾiʿīs*) to do the next stages in processing, scutching (beating) and hatcheling (combing). Not that hiring workers was easy; in one letter they may leave because they have not been paid; in another, Christian producers simply refuse to beat flax unless they are paid more. Indeed, many peasants in this area were as exigent as the merchants were. In one long letter from the 1050s, Salāma b. Nissīm complains to Nahray that he does not have dinars of good enough fineness to be accepted by peasants, *muzāriʿūn*, or by 'lords of great estates' (*aṣḥāb wusiya kabīra*), but only by *ṣaʿālik* and *ṣanāʾiʿī*. In this context, the former word can probably best be translated 'small fry'; the latter are presumably again wage labourers.[205]

We can conclude from this that direct producers of any local heft could demand more from merchants from the capital. But it is important that among the more exigent were primary peasant producers. This was doubtless because primary producers in this area were, mostly, indeed independent owners; the 'great estates' only appear in this one text, and state land does not appear at all. We have to be careful here: the advantage was by no means always with the peasants. Advance sales—particularly in wheat—are a marker of debt pressure on peasants because of the need to pay tax across the year, as we have seen (p. 67), and although we are dealing with flax here, not wheat, it is at least the case that Nahray once appears to be a taxpaying intermediary for peasants in one of the nearby villages, for sure not as an act of benevolence. Bondioli has stressed the role these merchants often had in coercive credit tax-related relationships.[206] All the same,

[204] For advice letters to Faraḥ, see T-S 10J20.12 (quotation), 13J16.19, 10J15.15, ENA 1822a.67 (Gil K491, 493, 495, 515 [S101, 112, 114, 107]), and cf. T-S 8.255 (Gil K505) for him assuring Nahray that he has not bought on credit. For Nahray as experienced, see, e.g., T-S 12.793 (Gil K640); see Goldberg, *Trade and institutions*, p. 103. For buying from peasants (*muzāriʿūn* and similar words), see T-S 10J12.26, 8J22.10, Moss. II,188.1, ENA 4020.20 ('the Christians'), T-S 13J13.11, 10J20.12, 13J16.19, ENA 4020.43, T-S 8.255, ENA 1822a.67, T-S 12.793, 13J27.18, 8J7.21 (Gil K253 [S135], 255 [S80], 256, 468, 479 [S102], 491 [S101], 493 [S112], 504, 505, 515 [S107], 640, 643, 728), plus, for the Delta, Bodl. MS Heb. d 65/17 (Gil K113 [S34]); cf. Goldberg, *Trade and institutions*, pp. 286–7.

[205] Hiring and hiring problems: T-S 12.227, NS 308.119, ENA 4020.20 (Gil K193, 191, 468); see Stillman, 'A case of labor problems' (and cf. n. 84 above for similar problems in other texts). Salāma: T-S 12.793 (Gil K640); peasants, *muzāriʿūn*, also raise prices in T-S 8J7.21 (Gil K728). For *ṣaʿālik* and *ṣanāʾiʿī*, see also ENA 4020.43, T-S 8.255, 13J27.18 (Gil K504, 505, 643).

[206] T-S 10J12.26 (Gil K253 [S135]); see Bondioli, *Peasants, merchants, and caliphs*, pp. 138–40, for the best reading of this document, and in general ibid., pp. 131–44 for advanced sales and tax indebtedness. See also for similar texts T-S 13J16.19, 8.255 (Gil K493 [S112], 505), although T-S 8J16.22 (Gil K401) seems to show peasants *preferring* advanced sales, because they expect, the writer thinks and hopes wrongly, that the Maghribīs will soon arrive (I am grateful to Jessica Goldberg for this text and to Lorenzo Bondioli for discussion). For the governmental *dār al-kattān* in the capital, see Bodl. MS

even if peasants were frequently under pressure, they could control the negotiations with merchants, sometimes with some force, at least as often. It is anyway clear that, around Būṣīr itself, it was the peasantry who participated most in the sale of flax—plus some middlemen—more than landlords, whether local or absentee. One of the documents in Jirja of Damūya's archive, from the 1020s, backs this up, in that in it a peasant (*muzāri'*), perhaps Jirja himself, is selling flax in advance—ten bales, a substantial amount—to a plausibly Jewish merchant. This is the only Arabic-script correlate to the Būṣīr *geniza* letters, and the village is not mentioned in it, but it conveys the same message: Būṣīr was only 10 kilometres from Damūya, after all.[207]

Nahray in the 1050s says in a much-cited letter to Faraḥ, who was clearly regarded as naive by his older peers, 'If you spend too much of your time in the villages (*ḍiyā'*), you will wear yourself out.... Your staying in Būṣīr will better your life and lessen your toil.' It is indeed likely that Būṣīr was a pleasant place to stay in, sometimes for weeks on end (no letter writer complains about being there) and that it was indeed convenient just to buy flax from its markets and not trail around the countryside, although it is true that Nahray himself in other contexts did precisely this, presumably because he was indeed more skilled than others.[208] The geography which casual references to villages shows is, however, interesting: it above all shows us a set of settlements immediately to the south of Būṣīr, Ṭansā, Maymūn, Bahbashīn, Būsh, Dalāṣ, and Dandīl. The distances here are small, under 15 kilometres; this must have been the countryside which Nahray and Faraḥ worked. By contrast, other nearby villages, like Lāhūn and Damūya at the mouth of the Fayyūm, do not appear at all, except by implication in the Arabic-script letter just cited. It is particularly significant how seldom the Fayyūm itself appears in the Būṣīr letters: as a location for warehouses; as the place of origin of visitors to the Būṣīr market who might change dinars into dirhams; but not as the place of origin of peasants selling flax, or indeed an area where Jewish merchants went much. Fayyūmī raw flax was doubtless still in part being turned into cloth locally; but, given its reputation for quality in *geniza* letters, it must also have been being

Heb. d 74/46, Bodl. MS Heb. c 28/33 (Gil K257, 258). For one other possible example of elite sales, see Bodl. MS Heb. d 65/17 (Gil K113 [S34]): 'buy the best flax from well-known people', *ma'rūfin*; but this is probably better glossed as 'well known to you/us'.

[207] P.Fay.Villages 43; the merchant's name is Sulaymān b. Dawūd, which does not have to be Jewish (Bondioli, *Peasants, merchants, and caliphs*, p. 110 doubts it; see further ibid., pp. 136–7 for the advance sale aspect), but the combination of names makes it quite possible all the same. The sale document is on the back of a tax-farming document for Jirja, so it came to him somehow; the only lacuna in the sale text is for the name of the *muzāri'*.

[208] Nahray to Faraḥ: T-S 8J22.10 (Gil K255 [S80]); see also, for similar advice to him, T-S 10J20.12 (Gil K491 [S101]), although it is less often remarked that in another letter Nahray does the opposite, advising him to buy in villages, Moss. II,188.1 (Gil K256). I use Goldberg's translation for T-S 8J22.10 (*Trade and institutions*, p. 103), slightly adapted; Udovitch, 'International trade', p. 277 has another translation. For Nahray himself buying in the villages, see, e.g., T-S Ar. 51.87 (Gil K299); an account of another merchant, Salāma b. Nissīm, may indicate that he was doing the same: Moss. Va, 9 (Gil K642).

sold directly to Fusṭāṭ via the donkey routes, not via Būṣīr and the Nile.[209] By contrast, it looks as if Būṣīr was the focus of a very small set of villages specializing very greatly in flax cultivation, which they could sell on a huge scale to Nahray and his associates. Given the small area we are dealing with here as the source of all that flax, if ever there was a dependence on cash cropping by medieval peasants anywhere west of China—that is, peasants who could sell so much flax that they could (and had to) buy their food in the market with the money they earned—it would be here. As with Tinnīs, this was a very focussed network; but it was, again, also a network which implied a much larger-scale commercial network elsewhere—of villages selling food to the peasants of the Būṣīr area, as well as, of course, the wider markets which the Jewish merchants were themselves selling to.

Tinnīs and Būṣīr are thus telling us versions of the same story: that flax and linen production were so developed in eleventh-century Egypt that entire specialized populations could rely on the market for their subsistence, and risk not producing wheat and other necessities themselves. This might be less surprising for a city like the former—cities routinely need a marketized supply if they are of any size—although, of course, Tinnīs's island location made supply that much harder; but the latter was a set of villages, whose crop specialization was notably striking. That is to say, they both again show, in different ways, how complex the Egyptian productive economy could be. But in another respect they are telling us quite opposite stories; for if there is one place to which the *geniza* merchants were not selling flax on any scale, it was Tinnīs.

Tinnīs does, it is true, appear reasonably often in the *geniza* (much more often, as noted earlier, than Damietta does). It was a port; merchants on their way to Palestine often stopped there. They bought rosewater and sold small quantities of lac (a red dye), silk, and other clothing; they both bought and sold flax too, but only in four or five texts (the largest quantity I have seen is an account of Nahray b. Nissīm, in which he sold nine bales of flax between Tinnīs and Ashkelon).[210] When Dabīqī cloth appears in trousseau texts, it shows at least that some Delta

[209] Ṭansā: T-S 16.339, 13J27.18, Freer F 1908.44V [formerly Gottheil-Worrell 22] (Gil K248 [S143], 643, 806); Maymūn: T-S Ar. 18(1).101, K15.53 (Gil K217, 274); Bahbashīn: T-S Ar. 51.87 (Gil K299); Būsh: T-S 13J14.9 (Gil K513); Dalāṣ: T-S Ar. 51.87, T-S 13J14.9, T-S 13J14.9 (Gil K299, 378, 513 [S111]); Dandīl: T-S 16.339, 10J12.26, 12.281, ENA NS 18.24, 8.255, 8.26 (Gil K248 [S143], 253 [S135], 254, 344 [S97], 505, 514). Fayyūm: T-S 13J13.11, 10J20.12 (Gil K479, 491 [S102, 101]). Fayyūmī flax was important (see, e.g., Goitein, *MS*, 1, p. 456), but it simply appears on the open market in Alexandria and Fusṭāṭ, and did not visibly come through Būṣīr. A Fayyūmī flax plantation is mentioned in P.Vind.Arab. I 7 (11th century). In the thirteenth century, Fayyūmī flax cultivation was concentrated around Lāhūn (Rapoport, *Rural economy*, pp. 119–21), so it is even more remarkable, if that was true two centuries earlier, that there was such a separation between there and Būṣīr.

[210] Excluding the Nissīm texts, for which, see nn 211–14 below, see BL Or. 5566A.3, Bodl. MS Heb. d 66/41, T-S 10J15.14, 13J23.6, AIU VIII.E.63 (Gil K110, 262, 264 [S70], 680, 718), 13J19.11 (clothing sent to Tinnīs); for flax, see T-S NS 228.6, T S 12.241, Moss. Ia,12.2, T-S K15.114 (Gil K452, 660, 721, 837 [Nahray's account]).

linen was getting into the Jewish world, even if not necessarily through direct sales to Jews on the spot. Conversely, it must be added, there were indeed some Jews there. There is evidence for a Qaraite community there in the eleventh century; in the mid-twelfth, Benjamin of Tudela says that there were forty Jews (and their families?) there. And one of Nahray's regular correspondants, Nissīm b. Khalafūn, lived there for much of the time in the third quarter of the eleventh century: we have nearly thirty letters to and from him.[211] As usual with Nahray's correspondants, he was a merchant, and he is our best guide to what an operator embedded in the city might be doing.

What Nissīm was buying, more than anything else, was cloth, which is just what one would expect, given the town. Over half the letters concerning him refer to it. But the interesting thing is the scale he was doing it on; for what Nissīm was above all doing was buying clothes to order, for individuals in Fusṭāṭ. Some of them were elaborate or relatively expensive; and he was evidently in part involved early in the production process, in that sometimes he ordered clothing and then waited for the order to be filled. He was living in a major factory town, but he was not buying cloth in bulk.[212] And conversely, he was also not selling flax in bulk—in fact, there are only a couple of vague references to him selling flax at all. More commonly, he sold silk and dyes, lac and indigo (for which, however, sadly, Alexandrians were flooding the market), sometimes sugar, and also traded in a variety of other goods with occasional citations, such as nuts, carnelian, lead, and soap. He is also recorded buying wheat and raisins for his own needs, but the wheat he usually got direct from the capital, and it is likely enough that he only mentions it when it was running short in Tinnīs.[213] Typical letters run like this (summarized): 'I've been buying scarves for you, but it's hard work; I have them in five colours, for between 1 and 2½ dinars each. I've waited two months for two other scarves from 'Alī b. Murābiṭ, who now says he has a rather attractive turquoise one—do you want it? If not, there are plenty of other buyers, from the Maghreb, Shām or Iraq. I have the lead and soap ready for you. I'm going to Damsīs now.' Or: 'You asked about the garments. I had two ready to send to Ramla

[211] The largest set is conveniently available in Gil K582–604. For Nissīm, see in general Goldberg, *Trade and institutions*, pp. 269, 288–90. For Qaraites, see Rustow, *Heresy*, pp. 188, 244n, 254n, 327—the last is a citation of a Qaraite merchants' representative (*wakīl*) in Tinnīs in the mid-eleventh century dealing in silk, T-S 13J26.2 (Gil P345). Another instance of a Jewish inhabitant is ENA 2727.29. For the twelfth century, see Benjamin of Tudela, *The itinerary*, trans. Adler, p. 78.

[212] T-S 10J10.29, Moss. IV,37.1, T-S 10J20.16, BL Or. 5566B.20, T-S Misc. 25.68, 12.246, 8J39.12, ENA 2805.6, T-S 8J18.33, BL Or. 5566C.19 and 20, Bodl. MS Heb. e 98/74, T-S 10J6.2, 12.368, 10J10.30 (Gil K584, 586–8, 590, 592–3, 596–7, 600–2, 604, P489); DK XVI.

[213] Selling: T-S 13J25.14, 10J10.29, BL Or. 5566B.20, T-S NS J13, CUL Or. 1080 J166, ENA 2805.6, T-S 8J18.33, 8J19.11, BL Or. 5566C.19 and 20, Bodl. MS Heb. e 98/74, T-S 10J6.2, ENA NS 22.15 (Gil K583–4, 588, 591, 595–7, 599–602, 784 [the Alexandrians]); and for flax, see T-S 8.18, 12.243, CUL Or. 1080 J166 (Gil K582, 594–5), all uncertain references. In T-S 10J10.30 (Gil P489), Nissīm is selling flax at scale, but in Tyre in Palestine, not Tinnīs. BL Or. 5566C.19 and 20 (Gil K600) has a particularly long list of goods transacted. Buying wheat and raisins: T-S 13J25.14, 10J10.29, 12.243, CUL Or. 1080 J166 (Gil K583–4, 594–5).

[in Palestine] but I'll send to you instead—they [the Palestinians] can wait. I've sent two others to Abu ʿImrān. Ask him if they have come; also ask Barhūn if the two turbans have arrived; the white headscarf is now ready, and I'll send or bring it. Tell Abū Zikri that the sugar hasn't arrived, but I don't need any more. What are the flax prices in Būṣīr?'[214] (That last query is a common refrain in eleventh-century *geniza* letters.) Nissīm was, that is to say, a good example of a small-scale merchant who was making the best use of his presence in a major cloth-producing town; but he was in no way contributing to the wider economic infrastructure of the town: he was only buying on individual commission. Contrast that with the dozens of bales of flax regularly referred to in Nahray's own letters and those of his associates in Būṣīr, bought and later sold on the open market; the level of trade was wholly different.

If one sets our Arabic-script letters against the *geniza* letters, and our evidence for Būṣīr against that for Tinnīs, there are thus two things which are strange about our overall picture, when seen against the other patterns we have looked at so far. First, Būṣīr is almost never mentioned in any Arabic-script letter or document from our period, even though the networks which supplied it must have been very similar to those described in our Arabic-script texts, some of which (particularly the Damūya archive) came from only a few kilometres away. This is probably simply a gap in our evidence, but it certainly shows that there were two or more different, competing exchange systems for cloth even in and around the Fayyūm. Secondly, and most importantly, the Jewish merchant community of the Ben Ezra synagogue was exporting raw flax, to be woven 1,500 kilometres away in Sicily and Tunisia—half the Mediterranean—when the biggest weaving factory towns outside China, Tinnīs and Damietta, were just down another branch of the Nile.[215] Why? Perhaps simply because the Fusṭāṭ Jewish merchants were so often Maghribīs of Tunisian origin, so they set up their routes initially to deal with relatives and friends, and the routes remained fixed thereafter; Tinnīs, by contrast, was a Christian town in large part, and had fewer Jews to act as intermediaries (although there were certainly some, as we have seen). Possibly a town so closely connected to the state also had specified brokers to sell its products inside Egypt,[216] which did not include this community of Jews (but then again, Nissīm was part of that community, was clearly a dealer in the city, but was not involved in either the supply of flax to the Delta towns or the bulk sale of their products). Probably, too, profits were higher if flax was transported overseas. But this choice seems to make the Jewish merchant routes we know about less typical of standard Egyptian practices (we will come back to this), as well as showing once again the density and complexity of the choices which merchants had about where to focus their activities. For there must have been *other* groups of merchants in Fusṭāṭ,

[214] T-S 8J18.33, Bodl. MS Heb. e 98/74 (Gil K597, 601).

[215] Goldberg, *Trade and institutions*, p. 104 stresses this too.

[216] Cf. Lev, 'Tinnīs', pp. 89–90.

maybe of all three religions, who we do not have documentation for, who were indeed acting as intermediaries to get flax and food in large quantities to Tinnīs and the other weaving towns.[217]

The evidence we have for the other flax networks in Egypt is more fragmentary. We could well assume that the Delta flax-producing areas were above all focussed on the factory towns, so we would see them less in our evidence collections, focussed, as they are, on the capital, the Fayyūm, and Middle Egypt. All the same, Jewish merchants did occasionally buy flax from the Delta, from Fīsha near Damanhūr on the Nile route to Rashīd and Alexandria, and even from Damsīs in the major flax zone serving Damietta and Tinnīs. To the south of the capital, both Jewish and Muslim merchants also bought from the Bahnasā/Ashmūnayn zone of flax production, as we have seen—in a couple of the Ashmūnayn references, on a very large scale.[218] There was, indeed, weaving not just in the major Delta towns (and abroad), but also—on a smaller but still substantial scale—in Ashmūnayn, Bahnasā, Fusṭāṭ itself, and Alexandria.[219] The examples of buying and selling cloth in the Arabic-script letters do on a few occasions make it clear, or likely, that cloth is being bought from the Delta towns; but also (often) from Fusṭāṭ, from Ashmūnayn, and even in the far south, from a village, Ṭārif, on the Nile opposite Luxor. Conversely, we find semi-luxury Sūsī cloth (from Sousse; it was generally reckoned to be the best-quality in Tunisia) sold in Qūṣ, again well inside Upper Egypt, if the reference is not simply to a type of cloth.[220]

These were, however, also almost all small-scale sales, of single or a few garments, like those of Nissīm b. Khalafūn. They were part of a generalized market economy which, of course, had clothing as one of its main artisanal exchange products. They do not tell us how cloth got from its main producers onto that market. We know it did, but the exact economic patterns escape us. Did networks of cloth dealers go to Tinnīs and the other textile towns to buy in bulk, and take it back to local markets? Or was it funnelled through Fusṭāṭ? (Both of these patterns

[217] One certain Muslim example is Manṣūr b. Abī al-ʿAlāʾ al-Tinnīsī, d. 1024, whose death is recorded in al-Musabbiḥī, *Akhbār Miṣr*, ed. Sayyid et al., 1, p. 103: see Bondioli, *Peasants, merchants, and caliphs*, pp. 192–3.

[218] For Fīsha and Damsīs, see Bodl. MS Heb. d 65/17, ENA 2727.41 (Gil K113 [S34], 214); plus, for Minyat Ziftā, see T-S 13J23.16 (Gil K682). For Ashmūnayn and Bahnasā, see nn. 77, 199 above, plus P.Vind.Arab. I 2.

[219] See p. 51 above for Ashmūnayn, pp. 45–6 for Fusṭāṭ, and p. 93 for Bahnasā, where woollens were also woven. For Alexandria, see Marzouk, *History of textile industry*, pp. 54–82 (with predominantly Mamlūk-period evidence, but, ibid., p. 80, some fabrics dated to the years around 900); for texts, see esp. Bodl. MS Heb. c.28/34, T-S 13J15.19 (Gil K458 [Goitein, *Letters*, n. 26], 540); in both cases they are weaving a linen-cotton mix, which would in Italy a century later be called *fustagnum* (fustian), a word arguably derived from Fusṭāṭ. (Mazzaoui, *The Italian cotton industry*, p. 199, doubts this, on the grounds that Egypt produced little cotton (which is not wholly true; see n. 182 above); but it is anyway the linen part of the mix which would have seemed Egyptian.) For fustian in Italy, see pp. 549–53, 600–4 below.

[220] Delta: P.Berl.Arab. II 66, P.Cair.Arab. 308; Fusṭāṭ: CPR XXXII 10, P.Vind.Arab. I 23, 44–6; Ashmūnayn: P.Cair.Arab. 307, 387, and see n. 77 above, for *laaū*; Ṭārif: P.Vind.Arab. I 14; Qūṣ: P.Vind. Arab. I 62.

are paralleled by the *geniza*'s references to Fusṭāṭ merchants going to Alexandria to meet the ships bringing cloth from Sicily and Ifrīqiya.) Or were cloth sales above all ad hoc and small-scale, as with Nissīm b. Khalafūn's dealings? The evidence might hint at the last of these, as that is the scale best attested in the Arabic-script and Hebrew-script texts alike, but it seems unlikely that this was the dominant way cloth was made available, given the relative centralization we have seen for other aspects of its production. Probably the answer is all three, but we will not easily ever know for certain.

That recognition of the limits of our knowledge does not, however, really matter. What the evidence we have for flax buying and linen production across a long eleventh century does show us is not only a highly complex set of networks of large-scale flax cultivation and linen weaving, but also both being practised on a smaller scale. Flax was sold to the central Mediterranean, to the specialized weaving towns in the Delta, to medium-scale centres such as Madīnat al-Fayyūm and Ashmūnayn (as we saw, p. 50, there was a considerable division of labour in the latter: weavers, fullers, dyers, tailors, tent-makers), and to villages. Cloth was produced on four levels: the major factory towns, several Delta and Middle Egyptian towns, and also specialist villages (even in areas where flax was not widely grown, such as Luxor[221]), before one reached the part-time weaver in the local neighbourhood, almost certainly always female, who will have existed everywhere—although female weavers operated at all these levels in our period.[222] There were areas of dramatic specialization in both flax-selling and cloth-making/selling, particularly Būṣīr for the former and Tinnīs for the latter, and then several overlapping levels of production and commercialization, including part-time and local. The picture which emerges is thus very close to that for ceramics, with large-scale and smaller-scale exchange networks again crossing the entire country. We can track the overlapping levels of production and networks of exchange better for ceramics, whereas for cloth, beyond doubt the more important of the two, we can show better the intensity of centralization and specialization at the

221 Apart from the Ṭārif (Luxor) citation in n. 220 above, see p. 51 for organized cloth-making in villages in Ashmūnayn. In the Fayyūm villages, by contrast, we find references to tailors, *khayyāṭs*, in P.Prag.Arab. 37, Chrest.Khoury I 46—and II 4, a turban-maker—i.e. workers in made cloth. But village production did not necessarily mean production of localized importance; as we have seen (n. 89 above), Ṭuṭūn in the Fayyūm made its own *ṭirāz* in the years around and after 900.

222 That cloth-weaving is in general gendered female is well known (e.g. for Europe, see Herlihy, *Opera muliebria*, pp. 75–102; for China, see Li, *Agricultural development in Jiangnan*, p. 143). Even in a factory town like Tinnīs, a more public space where one might expect more of the cloth work to be done by men, Ibn Bassām specifies women as embroiderers (*Anīs al-jalīs fī akhbār Tinnīs*, trans. Gascoigne and Cooper, p. 58). Earlier, in *Chronique de Michel le Syrien*, ed. Chabot, 3, p. 63, the women of Tinnīs supposedly spun and the men wove; this aims to represent a situation of the 820s, when the town was less developed; but Ibn Bassām is a less rhetorical and better-informed source. Anyway, even earlier, in the Roman period, women were regularly linen weavers in Egypt; see Kelley, 'Searching for professional women'. In the Mamlūk period, salaried female cloth workers were typical in Cairo and Syro-Palestinian cities; see Rapoport, *Marriage*, pp. 31–8, 45–50; here, they were mostly spinning, with only some weaving. See p. 437 below for female silk-working in Spain, and pp. 601–2 below for female cotton- and wool-weaving in Italy.

largest-scale end of the market (indeed, it is very unlikely that any ceramic centre, even Aswān, was as dependent on one industry as was Tinnīs). But both of them integrated the country both geographically and socially, involving every level of the economically active population—and certainly including the large peasant majority.

2.4.3 Wider patterns of trading

When we move away from flax and linen in the written sources, the scale of our evidence drops, but the complexity which we have already seen for both ceramics and linen continues. We would expect this, by now. But the evidence, taken more widely, gives us more of a sense of complexities in less obvious places; it also shows us situations in which the evidence from the *geniza* ceases to be uncharacteristic of the way the Arabic-script sources depict trading. That is to say, many of the same patterns appear in texts written in both scripts; the major difference is that, here, the *geniza* certainly tells us most about the Delta; the Arabic-script letters, by contrast, most about Middle Egypt. This, as noted earlier, makes the two sets of evidence complementary, and I shall treat both in the same way. But the reader must be warned that the evidence is also here more anecdotal. It builds up, but it is an accumulation of many different bits—some unusual but interesting in themselves, many much more ordinary, but almost all derived from often quite separate sources. I will begin with two sources, both atypical, to give an idea of the range of material we have for all kinds of exchange; then look at the *geniza*, which is, for the late eleventh century at least, less anecdotal than the Arabic-script letters; then offer an impression of the range of the latter material. We will end up with discussions of what is missing, and, in a conclusion, we will look at how the whole network fits in with the types of goods which we have just looked at in more detail.

Sebastian Richter published in 2016 a unique text, an account-book in Coptic, dating to the early 1060s, one of the very latest non-religious Coptic texts to survive. It is of a Christian merchant (necessarily so, given the language), probably from the southern part of Middle Egypt, buying and selling a striking range of commodities: in the order of the text, resin, clothing, a sieve, brimstone, veils, caraway, pots, saddlecloth, myrrh, mastic, blankets, salt, perfume, nails, sesame oil, 'real' [olive] oil, wax, figs, chains, a knife, copper, and soap.[223] He was not a major dealer, who would have, to judge from our letter collections, been selling at least sometimes on a very large scale, focussing on one or two commodities at a time plus silk, but, rather, a middling-level shopkeeper or merchant: his individual

[223] Richter, 'Ein fatimidenzeitliches koptisches Rechnungsheft'.

transactions were largely in silver dirhams and did not go over five gold dinars each (although it mounted up, reaching over 100 dinars in total). Such middling dealers often had a recognized specialism—hence the references to cloth merchants and silk dealers in Arabic-script letters, even if, as we saw for Ashmūnayn, many of them sold other things as well; but some were doubtless always generalists. Certainly the merchant of the 1060s accounts was a generalist on a very wide scale.

A century and a half later, around 1200, three original letters to the *amīr* Amīnaddīn are similarly atypical, and similarly illuminating. Amīnaddīn was a large-scale Muslim merchant operating between Fusṭāṭ-Cairo and Damascus (and currently located in the latter city); the letters show another wide range, although here by no means all carried in one shipment or by a single merchant, but in a far bigger operation. To summarize the first letter: 'We sold each of your necklaces for 10 dinars, even though (as Abū 'Abdallāh the jurist told us) the market price is not good; the transporter has the proceeds for the sack of ginger; the wooden trays have almost all been sold, for a low price, because the buyers were poor; I will change the silver money into dinars in the port and send it on to you; cloth is stagnating in Cairo but is dear in Alexandria; Yūsuf has asked the son of the judge to buy him 600 *irdabbs* [*c.*54,000 litres] of Fayyūmī wheat, I hope that's OK; Abū 'Abdallāh bought 10 pots of my oil in the port for 22 dinars, but then ships from Acre came in and the price dropped to 21, which is a problem as I have another 400 pots.' The other two letters, from Yūsuf himself (one certainly, one probably), are in the same vein, particularly concerning the same shipment of wheat, but adding pepper, silk, and hazelnuts; the pepper cannot be weighed because the senior official is out of town and we must wait for his return ('in his absence the officials, out of hatred for his honourable position, weigh only state pepper'). These letters are unusual among our Arabic-script texts because they go north of Fusṭāṭ, and show a mixture of internal and international trade, with the 'port' or 'border town' (unnamed, but it must be either Alexandria or Damietta) as a hub; it is also clear that Amīnaddīn is at the head of a major commercial enterprise, with senior subordinates acting semi-autonomously on the ground, of a type seldom seen in our other Arabic-script sources. But it is also striking that this trade is a mixture, not only of many products—apparently often chosen by chance, on the basis of whatever seems likely to bring a profit at the moment—but also of large and small, from tens of thousands of litres of wheat, or 800-plus dinars' worth of oil, to wooden trays sold individually. Even the biggest dealers could operate at all the different levels of Egyptian commerce at once.[224]

[224] P.Vind.Arab. I 44–6. The date of the letters is as usual unclear; Diem inclines to the very early thirteenth century for these three. They would repay closer analysis, but they are too late for such an analysis to fit into this book. The other 'big merchant letters' in Diem's edition, I 41–3, 47–8, are similar in the social standing of the merchants involved, although the scale is smaller; Diem gives a good commentary in the introduction to each in the printed volume, *Arabische Geschäftsbriefe*. P.Vind.

Amīnaddīn was, however, rather less atypical if we see him in the context of the *geniza* letters of the eleventh century. His operations recall those of Ibn ʿAwkal in their complexity; the difference is only that they are less focussed on flax and cloth, although Ibn ʿAwkal is actually also documented as being involved in the commerce of eighty-three different commodities, and, conversely, the range of the interests of the *amīr*'s agents could perfectly well have made a big flax shipment the following week plausible as their next choice.[225] Certainly, anyway, we see most of the best-attested *geniza* merchants mix large- and small-scale, and deal with a wide range of products, just as Amīnaddīn did. They are best documented doing this in their overseas activities, which will be looked at the end of this chapter, but they also did it inside Egypt.

It is easy, when looking at published *geniza* texts, to get the impression that the Jewish merchants of the Palestinian synagogue were not interested in local sales in Egypt, because so much of their energy was spent on Mediterranean trade and its relationship with the capital; and this impression is justified in some cases. But they can certainly be found in the localities too, especially in the Delta towns and villages, which they generically called the Rīf, with no reference to urban and rural hierarchies. Goldberg shows that this is more a feature of the Nahray generation of merchants (particularly the younger members of it) than that of Ibn ʿAwkal; our evidence is thus above all from the last half of the eleventh century, and into the twelfth as well. But it is clear, all the same. Yeshūʿā b. Ismaʿīl, an active merchant (though a very annoying man, as Goldberg documents), was in the Rīf a lot—too much for some of the people he dealt with; we find him, for example, in Malīj in the south-central Delta (see Map 5), where he is collecting debts and (unsuccessfully) selling clothes—the debts will have been for previous sales, for it was common practice, except for agricultural products, to pay for goods well after the actual sale. He was also in nearby Ṭaṭāy; and once, unusually for a Jewish merchant, he was even in a village well into Middle Egypt, Dalijā, between Ashmūnayn and Asyūṭ (Nahray writes to him there, mentioning Asyūṭī flax, so he is doubtless buying that).[226] Nissīm b. Khalafūn, based in Tinnīs much of the time, as we have seen, would have been regarded by many merchants from the capital as in the Rīf already, and he too can be found travelling there often, for weeks at a time. When he is in Damsīs on the Damietta branch of the Nile, he asks Nahray to sell a cloak

Arab. I 47 concerns trade to Damascus, as with the Amīnaddīn set; see also P.Heid.Arab. II 23 for Syrian trade; both are dated to the twelfth century.

[225] For Ibn ʿAwkal, Stillman, 'The eleventh-century merchant house of Ibn ʿAwkal' still gives the best introduction.

[226] See Goldberg, *Trade and institutions*, pp. 260–1, 322, 330; for Yeshūʿā, see ibid., pp. 120–3. For Yeshūʿā's letters from and about the Rīf, see Bodl. MS Heb. a 3/13, T-S 13J19.27, 13J19.20, 8J22.1, 10J15.25 (Gil K581 [S91], 240 [S63], 312 [S147], 316, 249 [the Dalijā letter]). For paying late as a norm, see Goitein, *MS*, 1, pp. 197–200; Goldberg, *Trade and institutions*, pp. 113–15. For the twelfth century, see Goitein, *MS*, 1, p. 175, and CUL Or.1081 J36 (a. 1116/17).

and to be prepared to sell other clothing, as well as sending money, probably to pay off debts; he writes from Samannūd, a little farther north, to say that he is selling lac in weaving villages, planning to sell silk, and trying to buy wheat to take back to Tinnīs; in Taṭāy, he tries to collect debts, sells silk and asks Nahray to send lac.[227]

This small-scale dealing was for Nissīm the kind of thing he was doing in Tinnīs anyway, so the difference was mostly geographical. In Yeshūʿā's case, however—and also for Nahray, clearly to an extent Nissīm's business associate—it was matched by as much or more attention to bulk international trade. These two were thus both prefiguring the later Amīnaddīn in getting involved with many levels of trade at once, and more concerned with engaging with the rural world than the latter may have been. This is in part because the rural was, in the Delta, by no means necessarily synonymous with the small-scale. Even leaving aside the flax sent from the eastern Delta in huge quantities to the weaving centres, we find consistent evidence of specialization for sale in the smaller Delta towns. In Minyat Ziftā, for example, a minor urban centre some 10 kilometres south of Damsīs, Jewish merchants from Fusṭāṭ bought flax across the eleventh and twelfth centuries, but also indigo and sesame; there was organized sugar production, tanning, and also some weaving of 'Rīf' cloth and dyeing; and locals in return bought silk. The indigo was itself for dyeing, and there were also dyers in Malīj and (in the twelfth century) Damsīs.[228] Silk was commonly sold elsewhere in the Delta towns too; as we saw earlier (p. 51), pretty much every merchant evidently found it useful to have some with him, whatever else he was travelling with. We have here, in this Delta evidence, a network of small towns and villages, all with a close connection to the commercial world for at least some of their activities, and merchants, even from the capital, who were happy to deal with them at least sometimes.

These patterns are then matched in Arabic-script letters; these show the same sorts of interlocking networks, and—with the exception of the handful of letters relating to people like Amīnaddīn—show merchants even more engaged with the local. A minority concern food for the capital: Fusṭāṭ and Cairo were buying from wide areas of Egypt. We would expect that; their inhabitants had to be fed, systematically, and we would not need any documentation to allow us to assume substantial specializations in foodstuffs for sale to the capital in many parts of Egypt; it simply has to have been the case. But we find it anyway: sugar from

[227] Nissīm in the Rīf: T-S 8.18, DK 238.5, T-S Misc. 25.68, NS J13, 8J39.12, 12.243, 8J18.33, 8J19.11, Bodl. MS Heb. e 98/74 (Gil K582, 589–91, 593–4, 597, 599, 601). Parallels in other texts: T-S 13J20.19, 12.794, AIU V.A.70 (Gil K349, 365, 789 [S116, 119, 104]); and T-S 8J32.3 (Ackerman-Lieberman, *The business of identity*, n. 7), for the mid-twelfth century.

[228] See Goitein, *MS*, 2, pp. 44–50 for Minyat Ziftā, esp. T-S 13J23.16 (Gil K682); for sugar, see n. 142 above. For Malīj and Damsīs, see T-S 13J1.3, 13J3.5, both discussed in Goitein, *MS*, 1, pp. 362–4 (in the latter, the dyeing partnership is based in Upper Egypt before its dissolution in 1143, another example of a wide economic range), T-S Misc. 8.66 (a. 1150).

Ashmūnayn, honey from Bilbays in the Delta, bananas from Maḥalla, and so on; and particularly significant is flour (*daqīq*) sent from the Fayyūm to the capital in the early twelfth century, for flour does not last nearly as long as grain—one normally mills it just before making bread—and this demonstrates an unexpected specialization and direction in food supply.[229]

In addition, however, these letters again show that there were also Egyptian networks which were less focussed on Fusṭāṭ. South of the capital, Madīnat al-Fayyūm, Bahnasā, Ashmūnayn, Akhmīm, Qūṣ, Aswān, and others which do not get into our documentation as much were real centres, with their own productions and their own interconnections. We have already seen this for Ashmūnayn, the best-documented of the set, but it is equally true for the others. The information here is once more anecdotal, but builds up. One letter is from an entrepreneur in Cairo (unusually, not Fusṭāṭ) who is in charge of a gang of wage labourers who cut fodder to supply, not Cairo, but Bahnasā; he writes to a contact in the Fayyūm to see whether he can get more workers.[230] Another, from Qūṣ, describes the arrival in neighbouring Luxor of a consignment of timber, apparently bound for Akhmīm a little farther north. A contract from 1140, slightly later, shows wheat being carried from Akhmīm back to Qūṣ (this was a very large consignment of 500 *irdabb*s, *c.*45,000 litres, as we have already seen, p. 70; it was apparently being organized by the state, but paying a Christian shipman, Abū al-Faraj b. Shanūda, 'leader of the sailors of the weavers', to carry it); Aswān buys wheat from Akhmīm in the twelfth century too.[231]

A further instance is a very long and interesting late tenth- or early eleventh-century letter from a local agent or junior partner to his landowning employer/senior partner, Khalīfa b. ʿUqba. It shows the former, Nihrīr b. Numayr al-Fadlī, castigating the latter quite roughly for not understanding when one should buy and sell wheat; in the same letter Nihrīr equally crossly describes how he had to travel to the Dākhla oasis, in the desert, 300 kilometres west of the Nile in southern Egypt, to try to look after Khalīfa's madder plantation, where he was caught between, on the one hand, the violent claims of the peasants (*muzāriʿūn*) over how big a share of the harvest they should have in return for irrigating the land and, on the other, the absence of any letters of instruction from Khalīfa; he only got out of it by lying to them about how large the harvest was.[232] A specialized madder plantation (for red dye) in such a remote place must have had a substantial outlet somewhere where cloth is made; Fusṭāṭ or the major weaving towns are not mentioned in this letter (only Aswān is, one of the nearer towns, but not a major cloth centre as far as we know), so it is likely that there was simply an open

[229] See P.Vind.Arab. I 19, III 27, I 41 (the Fayyūm reference); Ibn Ḥawqal, *Kītāb ṣūrat al-arḍ*, trans. Kramers and Wiet, 1, p. 141, for bananas. For the range of foodstuffs available in Fusṭāṭ-Cairo, see n. 59 above.

[230] P.Phil.Arab. 78.

[231] P.Cair.Arab. 306, P.GenizahCambr. 43; P.Vind.Arab. I 48.

[232] P.Cair.Arab. 291, re-ed. P.DiemVulgarismus.

market which could be reached by even very out-of-the-way producers. The way this built up is also visible in the documents of Jirja of Damūya in the 1020s: two letters survive to him from a Muslim merchant, perhaps based in Madīnat al-Fayyūm, in which Jirja—a rich peasant, not a professional merchant—is asked to buy and sell cloth, rope, rapeseed oil, and sponges; he is dealing in straw and wheat in two other letters, and probably (as we have seen) a seller of flax to a Jewish merchant in another.[233] In all these examples, that is to say, we again have a large, complex, and overlapping set of networks of exchange, which were exploited and developed in often quite ad hoc and opportunist ways, but also, when possible, on a large scale.

The sense of continual movement we get from these texts and also the sense of a capillary money economy, with silver dirhams and even gold dinars accessible to really quite minor players—not only shopkeepers, but also many peasants, even outside major commercial areas like Ashmūnayn or Būṣīr—fit also with a heterogeneous set of around 150 published commercial letters from the period 900–1200, which show rather more small-scale transactions. These often have no geographical markers at all, so we cannot pin them down, although most, even though not all, are almost certainly from Middle Egypt; theirs was a local and regional circuit, focussed frequently enough on Fusṭāṭ (even if very often at second hand), but not so often beyond. These are merchants who interrelated closely with the peasants whose rents and taxes and house sales also appear in Arabic-script texts. Here is a sample of such letters, again summarized. From the tenth century: 'Please reply to my letter; I have clothing for several named people; ask him to send the turbans if he has bought them, or else to get them by boat from Damietta; I'm going to Mecca; send me the money there.' In a letter from Idfū in the far south: 'I'm sorry your slave girl is ill, but I sold her to you healthy, and you still owe me the price; I've sent you perfumes worth 3 dinars; please sell them for me; please send me the sycamore wood you promised, and buy for me the acacia firewood and ricin oil for the lamp, 2 dinars' worth of each.' From Isnā, also in the far south: 'Your letter came with the ricin and the wheat; don't delay with sowing the millet and beans.' In another: 'The delay with the flax means that it has been nibbled by mice, so we couldn't leave it—it will go to Jīza by boat; I will be away, without leaving the barley for the children; get me the small dye cask, the large shawl, the provisions bags, and the small garment.' In another: 'I send a big packet with chickpeas, beans, dates, and fruits, plus all my pieces of clothing; let me know they have arrived.' In another, a very tense text: 'I keep asking you about the profit for the seeds and plants, and about our accounts, but you don't reply; we need to send the dyes to our patron; send me the inkpot, serving plate, nets, mats, and scales; get oil and sell it for me.'[234] From the eleventh century: 'I sold the pillows;

[233] P.Fay.Villages 36–7, 42–5; cf. Mouton, 'La société villageoise', pp. 211–13.
[234] P.Berl.Arab. II 66, P.RagibEdfou 1, P.Cair.Arab. 300, P.Vind.Arab. I 12, 15, 26.

please buy cloth.' In another, a rare female merchant writes to say that she has been told the veils have not come. In another: 'My partner has sent you 300 jugs of vinegar.' In another: 'It isn't true that I left your brother sleepless before my door—there's a doorkeeper; anyway, he bought the grain before it was winnowed, against my instructions, and he has run off with the 100 dinars.' In another: 'I haven't sent you the flax [or linen], as you know Abū Sahl has a grudge against you; but he is here in the Bahnasā district now, so I could try to get it from him and send it to you.' In another: 'Have you bought a dinar's worth of salt from the Chinese man (*al-Ṣīnī*)? If not, do so and send it.' In another, to a merchant from Ashmūnayn currently in Fusṭāṭ: 'Abū Bakr still has not settled my commission for the shawls; when I sent you the cotton, I forgot one bag—Jamāl will bring it—get it dyed; I also sent two chests plus locks; sell them and give the outstanding money to the plasterer's wife.'[235] From the twelfth century, when we have, as usual, fewer texts: 'Please send me two pieces of linen cloth, rough-weave, Persian-style, and one good linen coat, and give the cutter a deadline.' In another: 'Take the 35 dirhams which the shipman brings and buy me tamarind and pepper.'[236]

I have simply set out these letter summaries, end on end, to offer an impression—which is a very strong one as one reads them—of the range and density of activity they involve. Although they are often very small in scale, they are no less intense, at times, for that. Once again, they resemble *geniza* letters very greatly—in this context, particularly in their concern for detail, their mixing of all kinds of information together, their constant expectation that others can be trusted to do things for them (even when their immediate relationship is a difficult one), and the sense they give of a world in movement. However decontextualized, as a group they show us a world in which everything is or can be sold, on the large, medium, or small scale—or over long and short distances—or all at once. This does not change across the three centuries I have looked at in detail; the network of active daily transactions characterized Egypt throughout.

That network underpinned all the major specializations we have looked at so far, and indeed made them possible. It also shows at least some patterns. When we look at the number of references we find to different types of commodity, wheat and cloth are easily the most frequently mentioned; next come slaves, then timber and other wood (some imported, some acacia and therefore Egyptian). Also common, although with rather fewer citations, are barley, raw flax, wine, olive oil (always imported), sheep and cows, ceramics, and dyestuffs. There are not many references to silk, a semi-luxury, but there are at least some, which fits the notable concentration of silk merchants in Ashmūnayn (see p. 51 above). More surprisingly,

[235] P.Heid.Arab. II 36, P.Berl.Arab. II 69, P.Vind.Arab. I 16, 18, 21, 22, 23. (*Al-Ṣīnī* might denote any south or east Asian—we could not expect ethnic exactness here—but China features more often than other Asian regions in our evidence; see n. 49 above.)

[236] P.Heid.Arab. II 39, P.Vind.Arab. I 60.

there are only a couple of references each to paper, cheese, and pepper (though the scale is substantial in each case); the same number to ironwork, and no references at all to leather or wool.[237] This does partly distinguish these letters from those in the *geniza*, where flax and linen, dyes, silk, hides/leather, olive oil, pepper, and cheese stand out; Jews did not regularly deal in wheat, iron, timber, or slaves, although they were not excluded from these trades, for all appear sometimes.[238] Muslims and Christians (the Arabic-script letters include both) evidently did indeed deal in wheat, timber, and slaves; conversely, they seem to have left leather, cheese, pepper, and some silk to Jews; but no one can be shown to have dealt all that much in two major commodities, iron and wool.

How can that absence be explained? Not by arguing that Egypt did not have these items in large quantities. Wool, which was produced locally, has plenty of incidental references, even if it was certainly secondary to linen production in scale—as in Byzantium and Sicily (see pp. 249, 327–8 below), it was probably a largely household production, and this may explain why it is rarely cited in trade texts.[239] Iron was hardly ever mined in Egypt; it was an import from both Muslim and (increasingly) Christian lands. It was made into tools at least in Tinnīs, according to Nāṣer-e Khosraw, and in Dalāṣ near Būṣīr, according to al-Idrīsī. It was regularly worked in Fusṭāṭ, given the references to different types of artisan (and to the *sūq* of the sword-makers there), and to the metal objects which are standard in *geniza* lists of household objects and in excavations; several of the commodities in the Coptic account book of the 1060s are ironwork too, bringing out the normality of its daily use elsewhere. We will come back to iron later (pp. 146–7, 562), for in the twelfth century its import was controversial to some European Christian eyes—as with timber, it was used for warfare—but its near-absence from our letters does not derive from that, given its evident availability on the ground.[240] It is also worth stressing that it is surprising that leather is so

[237] I do not provide figures here, as they would give a spurious accuracy to what is a very heterogeneous group of texts, but wheat and cloth each appear in about a sixth of the commercial letters. The references to iron trading are P.Heid.Arab. I 62 for Ashmūnayn, and the Coptic account book cited in n. 223 above. In the *geniza*, see also, e.g., T-S 13J14.2, 18J3.13 (Gil K241 [trans. Udovitch, 'A tale of two cities', pp. 151–3], 395), both Nahray letters, which mention iron trading, although contrast, for its general absence in merchants' letters, Goitein, *MS*, I, p. 60. For timber, see pp. 147–9 below. Jews did deal in wheat sometimes: see n. 133 above.

[238] Goitein, *MS*, I, pp. 209–11 and *passim*; Goldberg, *Trade and institutions*, pp. 95–9; for slaves, see the overview in Perry, *The daily life of slaves*, pp. 28–54. Jews did not deal wholesale in slaves, but certainly bought and sold them; but they were anyway a semi-luxury, not a large-scale commercial item; see n. 284 below.

[239] For wool, see n. 182 above and cf. p. 619 below.

[240] See n. 189 above for Tinnīs; for Dalāṣ, see al-Idrīsī, *Nuzhat al-mushtāq*, trans. Jaubert and Nef, p. 124; for Fusṭāṭ, see Goitein, *MS*, 4, p. 143 and Lombard, *Les métaux*, p. 164; for the account book, see Richter, 'Ein fatimidenzeitliches koptisches Rechnungsheft'; for excavations, see esp. Kiyohiko and Kawatoko, *Ejiputo Isurāmu toshi*, 2, pp. 618–21 (though this does not show a huge quantity on the site). Iron (*ḥadīd*) does not, however, appear very often in the Arabic-script letters even outside the trading environment; for one casual citation of iron goods see P.AbbottMarriageContracts 2 (a. 989); for one in Coptic, see P.Teshlot 7 (a. 1062).

rarely cited in Arabic-script letters dealing with commerce, even though it was traded in Egypt by *geniza* merchants and was, obviously, a by-product of all stock-rearing (and was also stressed by some geographers; Yaʿqūbī, for example, writing in the ninth century, says that it was important in Akhmīm); indeed, it must have been a significant commodity always. We find saddlers and shoemakers among our casual references to artisans, as we would expect, but not to the materials they were using.[241] The absence of ironwork and leather goods, in particular, in our letters about internal exchange must undermine the full representativeness of our texts. But the other patterns we have seen are much more consistent, and can stand, at least until many more texts are edited.

We saw, when we looked at ceramics, that the major Egyptian productions of Aswān and Fusṭāṭ were available, even in villages, all along the Nile valley from the coast up to Nubia. Pottery is, indeed, attested in the Arabic-script letters a handful of times, which fits with that.[242] But more important than that is that the letters we have here show the wide availability of many more types of commodity, including at the very local level; they were doubtless using the same routes as did archaeologically attested ceramics (not just the Nile: much went by donkey even when the Nile was an alternative, and, of course, as soon as one left the riverbank, donkey transport was inevitable). And, above all, the letters show the sorts of people who were buying and selling, and how they did it. Medium-scale and small-scale professional merchants were operating in groups of varying levels of formalization; they operated very largely on credit and through trusted (even if not always trustworthy) counterparts elsewhere; the people they bought from and sold to were also very often people whom they knew—although that did not stop traders from travelling extensively, which necessarily required a wider range of contacts. This is true for merchants of all three religions, indeed. Of the people they knew, some—perhaps very many—were primary producers, on the spot, like Jirja of Damūya, who could be asked to deal in goods as if he was himself a regular trader. Rich peasants like Jirja were thus key intermediaries; and it is also clear that at Būṣīr a substantial stratum of peasants was capable of bargaining quite actively, even with influential merchants from the capital. We saw, in the context of both ceramics and flax/linen, that commerce operated at several different levels at once; in this set of letters, we have the local level above all. But what that shows is that there was hardly a product of any kind in existence in the Mediterranean in our period which was not available in every part of Egypt, as long as one had

[241] Leather-working: CPR XXXII 1; P.GenizahCambr. 25–6; P.Vind.Arab. I 68; al-Yaʿqūbī, *Kitāb al-buldān*, trans. Gordon et al., p. 169; al-Maqrīzī, *Khiṭaṭ*, trans. Casanova, 4, p. 57; and cf. the ninth-century wooden shop lintel found in Cairo which states that half the shop belongs to Muʿādh Abū Ṭālib the shoemaker: van Berchem, *Matériaux*, 1.i, n. 19—interestingly, most of these citations come from the capital. *Geniza* references to trading in leather include Bodl. MS Heb. d 74/46, T-S 13J19.20, 8J19.4, BL Or. 5566C.19 and 20, T-S 13J17.7 (Gil K257, 312 [S147], 502, 600, 808).

[242] CPR XXXII 9, 11; P.Vind.Arab. I 26—largely relating to plates, which might be metal in some cases; later, P.QuseirArab. I 22; and see n. 158 above for the *geniza*.

the money to buy it. What else it shows we will look at, more summarily, in the next section.

2.4.4 Internal exchange: concluding comments

We have now looked at ceramics, flax, and linen; earlier on, wheat, wine, and sugar; and a wider but more heterogeneous set of documents for Egyptian internal exchange in general. They are all telling us similar things; let us start here by summarizing what we have seen so far. First, we have seen different levels of merchant, from the major and complex enterprises of Ibn ʿAwkal or Amīnaddīn to large-scale but more individual buying and selling such as Nahray in Būṣīr and elsewhere to smaller-scale but still multicentred commerce, and then town- and village-level sales. The greatest merchants could, nonetheless, deal with smaller-scale enterprise too, and did so without a qualm: dealers operated at several levels at once. We have also seen goods being traded the length of Egypt or nearly, whether it is Aswān pottery on the Mediterranean coast and Fusṭāṭ pottery and even Palestinian amphorae in Aswān, or Sousse cloth in Qūṣ and Asyūṭī flax (and, of course, even more flax from farther north) sold across the Mediterranean; and shorter but still substantial distances for wheat, cloth, wine, sugar, dyestuffs, and timber. We have seen, that is to say, interconnections crossing the whole country, and often visibly extending to quite small villages (as with the ceramics from the major centres, found in all the village excavations that have been published). And we have seen the same commodities being sold in very different directions, presumably following information about prices and demand, or else competing routes for similar products, as with Fayyūmī flax, which was probably not going through Būṣīr, and Būṣīrī flax, which was certainly not going to Tinnīs. Egyptian exchange in our period did not run along tramlines, and varied substantially depending on market conditions; merchants were light on their feet, inside the country as also outside. It also did not all depend on Fusṭāṭ, which was merely (by far) the largest of a network of centres with their own interconnections. Perhaps the quickest additional demonstration of this is the remarkable range of trades attested on tombstones in the 'Fāṭimid' cemetery at Aswān; its early tenth-century gravestones alone (the latest to be published) document the activity in that far-southern city (or at least the death there) of two butchers, a carpenter, a money changer (*ṣarraf*), a mason, a fisherman, a dyer, a camel driver, a vegetable seller, a goldsmith (*ṣaʾīgh*), a smith, a carrier (*ḥajjār*), and a silk merchant.[243]

On the other side, we have also seen different levels of production. I identified four for ceramics, where one can be quite concrete about production, and also

[243] ʿAbd al-Tawab, *Stèles islamiques*, 3, nn. 310, 320, 349–50, 368, 382, 387, 402, 411, 422, 438, 449. There are also Christian and Muslim religious officeholders, and an *adab*-teacher (*muʾaddib*, n. 371).

can, sometimes, identify the place of origin of wares. For the making of other commodities, and in particular the weaving of flax into linen, we saw that a similar productive hierarchy could be recognized, in the same way as the complexities of the geographical patterns of sale of the two commodities visibly match. This is important in itself: as remarked earlier, archaeologists state often enough, hopefully, that ceramics are a proxy for cloth, but here, unusually, one can actually show it, for the parallelisms are so close. The only place where they do not fully match is in the arena of interregional trade, for Egypt imported plenty of things, including cloth, but not, until the end of the twelfth century, ceramics in any quantity (see p. 138 below). This is probably simply because Egypt's own pottery production was so strong; Egyptian lustreware, in particular, was exported into most of the rest of the Mediterranean in the eleventh and twelfth centuries, at least as a semi-luxury.[244] The productive hierarchy seen here is matched by a similar hierarchy for urbanism, with cities and towns of very varied sizes and levels of specialization in artisanal work. Every town which we have any information about at all was, indeed, visibly a major artisanal centre. (This does not, however, mean that these two hierarchies matched in any schematic way, with large-scale production only going on in the largest cities—Aswān, so important in ceramic production, and Tinnīs, where linen was made on a scale unmatched anywhere else, were rather smaller than Fusṭāṭ; conversely, in that city every type of product was probably made, but not always on any scale at all.) Linked to this is the remarkable range of trades which are attested in letters and documents for rural Egypt, in not only towns but also villages. The frequency of wage labourers, even in agriculture, who were paid in money makes the point too, for, as we have seen (p. 61), such wage labourers were dependent on the market for their subsistence, and indeed could not have existed at all if the market was not reliable enough to supply food and clothing on a regular basis.

These hierarchies and intercutting connections were important for the stability and vitality of Egypt's economy. If a total economy is to grow, it cannot depend on a single dominant centre, with everything else feeding into it and dependent on it; there need to be more complex networks.[245] We will see this again when we come, for example, to see how Milan grew to be the largest city in Italy: it could do so precisely because not everything depended on it, for the large and small urban centres around it were not only linked tightly to Milan but had their own interconnections too (see pp. 604–8 below). Cities which did not have that network did not develop as effectively. Egypt faced one minor difficulty here, the simple fact that the Nile for most of its length ran along a more or less straight line

244 For the export of Egyptian ceramics to Sicily, see Chapter 3, n. 193 below; to Ifrīqiya, Chapter 3, n. 61 below; to Byzantium, Chapter 4, n. 240 below; to north-central Italy, Chapter 6, nn. 135, 142, 210, 245 below.

245 And/or vice versa, as an economy grows, an urban hierarchy tends to develop: see, e.g., generalizing from the nineteenth-century USA, Fujita et al., 'On the evolution of hierarchical urban systems'.

through desert, with no alternative routes to allow, say, Ashmūnayn to connect to Qūṣ without going past Akhmīm, or to Alexandria without going past Fusṭāṭ; but it still managed to sustain a complex of intercutting and competitive directions for individual products, even in the Nile valley, and certainly in the Delta. (See Map 7. This was doubtless helped by the fact that although the Nile went through or close to nearly every major city, it was usually possible to sail on and not stop—even if it is unlikely that boats did not stop in Fusṭāṭ as they went by, if only because customs officers would have sought to tax them.[246]) Jessica Goldberg has stressed how much actually did pass through Fusṭāṭ; it was, indeed, the economic focus not only for Egypt, but in many respects for southern Palestine too.[247] All the same, although Fusṭāṭ(-Cairo) was, of course, overwhelmingly the largest city, and there were no significant rivals to its role as the only serious political centre—which was reinforced, in economic terms, by the fact that much of the taxation of Egypt was funnelled to it—not everything depended on it. Fusṭāṭ structured the patterns of Egyptian exchange, but did not constrain them.

Three further points are important to conclude this survey of Egypt's internal exchange economy during our period: the question of the validity of using *geniza* material for Egypt as a whole; the nature of regional demand; and the problem of the chronological pacing of exchange patterns in Egypt. First, the *geniza*. At several points in this chapter I have raised the issue of the typicality of the *geniza* documentation with respect to the other evidence for the Egyptian economy. This has, indeed, been a recurrent theme in *geniza* historiography itself. Goitein assumed it, in part on the basis of his ethnographic experiences in Yemen, in part because he saw signs of the overall conformity—even though not full identity—of Jewish commercial practice with that of the legal assumptions of the Islamic world around the Fusṭāṭ community; so did Udovitch, who developed the parallelisms between Jewish commercial practice and Muslim—particularly Ḥanafī—commercial law. Phillip Ackerman-Lieberman has nuanced this considerably, arguing that Jewish partnerships mostly ran by Jewish, not Islamic law; the argument is convincing, although the differences are not huge. Ackerman-Lieberman, and Goldberg even more strongly, also argue that Jewish commercial relationships were more formalized, and reliant on more precise institutional sanctions, than Goitein and Udovitch had thought; here I am fully in agreement with them.[248] I would only note here that we still lack a systematic study of what actually went on in courts of different kinds in the Fāṭimid period; we do not have as

[246] Bramoullé, *Les Fatimides et la mer*, p. 627.

[247] Goldberg, *Trade and institutions*, pp. 211–46 for Palestine; ibid., pp. 246–76 for the geography of travel; esp. ibid., p. 257 for Fusṭāṭ as the centre of spokes of travel.

[248] Ackerman-Lieberman, *The business of identity*, *passim* (see further p. 649 below); pp. 1–42 surveys the historiography—in particular Goitein, *MS*, 1, pp. 164–86, and Udovitch, *Partnership and profit*. See further, for institutions, Goldberg, *Trade and institutions*, pp. 120–64. On partnerships, see also the rather descriptive Gil, 'The Jewish merchants'.

many documents for this as we do for trade, but there are easily enough for indicative conclusions. But this debate is really one about Jewish identity in Fāṭimid Egypt, not about whether Jews actually behaved differently from Muslims in their commercial operations. Here, as I remarked at the start of this chapter, little use has been made of the Arabic-script sources; and, above all, some more practical similarities and differences have not been focussed on in the literature, notably on what scale Jews or Muslims/Christians bought and sold, and which commodities—that is to say, the important issues for the argument of this book.

In one sense, I would go further here than even the above-mentioned authors do. In legal terms, there are interesting indications that Muslim (and Christian) merchants in Egypt may actually have been less formal in their organization than were Jews. We have very few written Arabic-script partnership agreements of the kinds that Ackerman-Lieberman edited and translated in his book. Arabic words for partnership of different types, *shirka*/*khulṭa* (formal partnership), *qirāḍ* (capital investment in another's labour/trading), or *ṣuḥba* (formal but unwritten one-to-one association), fairly common in the *geniza*, are also very rarely used in our published Arabic-script documents; and words for partners, the related *ṣāḥib* or the less common *qarīn*, are used far more often in texts in their non-specific meanings of friend, spouse, holder, boss, or colleague. These are not chance absences. But they certainly do not imply that Muslim trading was by its nature more informal than Jewish trading; Ifrīqiyan jurists from the ninth to twelfth centuries regularly refer to *qirāḍ* and *shirka* in their *fatwās*.[249] Rather, they are markers of scale. The *geniza* dealers were major figures in

[249] For the *geniza*, see esp. Goldberg, *Trade and institutions*, pp. 123–34; Goldberg, 'Choosing and enforcing business relationships'; and Cohen, *Maimonides and the merchants*, esp. pp. 70–104. *Ṣāḥib*/*aṣḥāb* and *qarīn* seem to be used for business partners in our period in Arabic-script texts in only P.SijpesteijnProfit (a. 901); P.Khalili I 8; CPR XVI 16; P.Heid.Arab. II 14, III 46; P.Cair.Arab. 392; P.Berl.Arab. II 33; P.Vind.Arab. I 7, 16, 35, 45–6. P.Heid.Arab. III 46 (which also contains the only citation in Arabic-script texts from our period of the word *ṣuḥba*), in fact, concerns Jewish dealers in large part. So does P.GenizahCambr. 77, which, similarly, contains the only Arabic-script citation from our period of the word *qirāḍ*, even though this word is widely cited in general Islamic legal and theoretical sources such as al-Dimashqī (see esp. Udovitch, *Partnership and profit*, pp, 170–248), as also jurists from Ifrīqiya (see p. 187 below), and it has attracted interest among commercial historians because it matched the western *commenda* (see pp. 648–9 below). *Muqāraḍa*, a related word also meaning *commenda*, likewise appears only once, in a ninth-century letter, P.Berl.Arab. II 38. Another *ṣuḥba*-related word, *aṣḥābuna*, the frequent word for a community of [Jewish] merchants in the *geniza* (Goldberg, *Trade and institutions*, pp. 38–9, 139–43 and *passim*), never appears; and *ibḍā'* or *biḍā'a*, canvassed by Udovitch and Cohen as Muslim alternatives to *ṣuḥba* (see most recently Cohen, *Maimonides and the merchants*, pp. 72–3) only appear (as *biḍā'a*) meaning 'merchandise'. *Mu'āmala*, an unwritten contract in the *geniza* (Goldberg, *Trade and institutions*, pp. 155–7), usually simply means 'relationship' in these texts, although P.Marchands II 40, P.Hamb.Arab. II 45 and Chrest. Khoury I 41 (the least generic) refer at least to a commercial relationship.

For texts in Hebrew script for partnership agreements, see Ackerman-Lieberman, *The business of identity*, pp. 229–324. The only one in Arabic script known to me is early, P.Marchands I 1 (a. 864), for Abū Hurayra; there, the word *shirka* is indeed used (cf. Goitein, *MS*, 1, p. 170; *EI*[2], s.v. sharika (M. Y. Izzi Dien)), together with *sharīk*, 'partner', a word otherwise used more to mean 'co-owner' in the Arabic-script corpus. *Shirka*, however, only appears again with the plausible meaning of 'commercial partnership' in two other texts, P.Cair.Arab. 291 and CPR XVI 22; its synonym, *khulṭa*, does not appear with this meaning at all. I discuss this issue at greater length in 'Informal and formal

Mediterranean-wide trading, operating with thousands of dinars on occasion; the merchants documented in our Arabic-script texts were usually far smaller operators. They did not need an elaborate apparatus of partnership. The Abū Hurayra letters from the ninth-century Fayyūm were for slightly larger-scale dealers—and indeed they, almost uniquely in the Arabic-script texts we have, were linked by a formal *shirka* partnership; but in the rest of this correspondance, we are witnessing simpler deals, and not much by way of problems of third-party agency, which are so much a feature of the *geniza* letters—members of Abū Hurayra's family indeed lived at both ends of his fairly straightforward trade route, from the Fayyūm to Fusṭāṭ, so did not need agents so much. The range of formalized structures which is very clear in the *geniza* was simply not necessary in this sort of environment; and it was still less necessary for most of the individual merchants operating up and down the Nile in Middle Egypt.

Similar points recur when we look at other aspects of merchant practice. There were, as has been long recognized and as we have already seen, differences in the goods which Jews (at least of the Fusṭāṭ Palestinian synagogue) carried from those which other merchants did; wheat, in particular, is prominent as soon as we look at the documentation in Arabic script. And there really was a structural difference between our Arabic-script letters and those of at least the eleventh-century *geniza*, in that the latter show, as a nearly permanent preoccupation, the management of the network of Mediterranean trade, whereas the former very rarely do. Furthermore, Fusṭāṭ Palestinian Jews, unlike others, did not sell flax in Tinnīs on any scale, which seems to me a particularly important distinction; they also seldom went south of Fusṭāṭ (or at any rate Būṣīr), leaving that to others—at least until the India trade opened up (see p. 125 below). But what we saw with the three letters to Amīnaddīn is that as soon as we find documentary evidence for Muslim merchants operating on a large enough scale, a Mediterranean dimension appears. In this respect too, it is crucial that our Arabic-script documents for the most part privilege a different level of merchant activity, that of Middle Egypt, in which local sales were dominant. Again, this is not a religious difference; rather, it is that the merchants in smaller towns were more integrated than those in the capital into a set of rural communities, with whom they bought and sold (even if there were certainly exceptions among the Fusṭāṭ merchants, like Nissīm b. Khalafūn dealing in the Rīf, or Nahray b. Nissīm dealing in the villages around Būṣīr). Overall, traders of all three religions operated in similar ways, when we take into account the balance between larger-scale and longer-distance trade and the small-scale and the local. And above all, they dealt with each other in very similar ways. The obsession with detail ('You've paid me 180 dinars, but you still owe

trading associations in Egypt and Ifrīqiya, 850–1150', using some text from this chapter and Chapter 7 below.

me 1/16 dinar,' 'I sent the boatload of wheat, but I forgot the wooden bowl,' etc.), the apparently partly chance nature of at least subsidiary commodities (subsidiary to flax for Jews, to wheat but also sometimes flax for Muslims), and the trust in partners/agents (even if often somewhat bad-tempered and sometimes even suspicious) were all pretty similar.

Jessica Goldberg has written on trust in particularly valuable ways. She has been able to do so because the *geniza* contains so many letters between the same dealers and about other related dealers that she can build up a Geertzian thick description of how trust worked and failed to work.[250] The Arabic-script material is too heterogeneous to be able to add to that; but what it can at least allow us to say is that the same concerns are visible in the non-Jewish merchant community. Whatever the laws each religion invoked, the daily commercial environment of each was effectively the same. This means that Goitein was right to see the merchant network visible in the *geniza* as typical of the merchant networks of Egypt in general, or as typical as can be expected, given that different commercial communities among all religions had different scales of activity.[251] Notwithstanding all the ifs and buts about the particular directions of Jewish interest, we can firmly conclude that. And this also means that we can see international trade as a potential activity for all Egyptian merchants with sufficient capital, which anyway fits the casual references to non-Jews on the sea lanes in the *geniza*. It was not Jewish contacts with the Maghreb which were the main cause of that; it was—and indeed had to be—the internal structures of Egyptian (and also Ifrīqiyan and Sicilian) production and exchange, without which all the contacts in the world would not have produced enough commodities to sell. We will return to this point.

My second concluding point, which can be put more briefly for the moment but which is even more important (we will come back to it often in later chapters), is the nature of demand. In general, in the early middle ages, the discriminator for the density of trading systems was the wealth of elites, both landowning and state (tax-based) elites, for it was they who profited most from the selling of raw materials and did most of the buying of artisanal products.[252] Broadly, the richer elites were (and thus the more buying power they had), the more exploitation there was in the countryside; a growth in commerce thus did not by any means denote a growth in wealth overall and, in general, correlated with oppression. Subsistence peasants were less involved in buying, not only because of that exploitation, but above all because they lived off the land directly (and they could produce, if

[250] Goldberg, *Trade and institutions*, pp. 140–50, 180–4, and *passim*, together with Goldberg, 'Choosing and enforcing business relationships'.

[251] Goitein, *MS*, 1, pp. 70–4, and *passim*, supported and nuanced by Goldberg, *Trade and institutions*, pp. 24–9, 357, and *passim*, who is now the best guide. Cohen, *Maimonides and the merchants*, pp. 80–2, also stresses the importance of *geniza*-style reciprocity in Arabic-script letters. See also pp. 52–3 above.

[252] See pp. 666–8 below for a discussion of this.

needed, their own cloth; for the most part, they only needed to buy iron from outside); and subsistence peasants were the large majority of the population in Egypt, even if less of an overwhelming majority than in most parts of Eurasia. All this remained true, to an extent, in our period as well. The excitement which it is easy to express when showing the scale of the Egyptian productive and commercial economy must, therefore, be moderated; by no means all Egyptians were dealers, or indeed bought or sold on any scale, except to acquire the coins which they needed to pay taxes and rents. We do not know so much about this sector of society, for it was also, by and large, outside the world of writing, except for tax receipts, but it certainly existed. Virtually the whole range of products was available to anyone if they had the money to buy them, as we have seen, but burdened with tax and often rent as they were, far from everyone did have that money; overall, we have to assume (there are no firm data here, of course) that a non-trivial proportion of sales was to elites, whether in the capital, in provincial towns or in villages, or indeed to the state itself, which had its own voracious needs.

But that is not the whole story. Egyptian elites are not actually all that visible in our local evidence (cf. pp. 50, 57–60 above), and even under the Roman Empire they had not been as rich as they were in some other regions of the Mediterranean.[253] The complexity of the economy did not necessarily, here at least, depend exclusively on them. And by contrast, what marks Egypt out in our period is the frequency with which peasants are indeed visible buying and selling. *Muzāriʿūn*, the basic word for 'peasants', are regularly attested selling flax on a major scale at Būṣīr, to the extent that I hypothesized that they may even sometimes have been cash-cropping and thus reliant on the market for food, just as agricultural labourers were; whether or not they were, they will certainly have been making enough money to buy substantial amounts of artisanal goods. Jirja of Damūya, certainly, was a rich peasant who found himself trading, regularly enough to get particular requests from more permanent merchants. This peasant market was what allowed the rural specialisms and the village artisans which are well attested in Egypt to exist too. Here, that is to say, the density of commerce was clearly not only a sign of rural exploitation. There was here enough mass demand to make possible a commercial economy which extended into villages, linking them together with provincial towns, making a solid and complex system which further aided economic development, a substantial division of labour in many cases (particularly in towns, as we saw for Fusṭāṭ and even Ashmūnayn, but also in sugar factories), and thus a potential for technological change, as we can see most clearly with innovations in ceramics (we do not know enough about the changing technical details of the production of cloth). In seventeenth-century England, one would call the development of such an economy Smithian growth.[254] Egypt is a

[253] Wickham, *Framing*, pp. 242–55.
[254] For a classic example, see Wrigley, *Continuity, chance and change*.

particularly clear example of that in our period, although not, as we shall see, by any means the only one.

The final issue for us when looking at internal exchange in Egypt is its pacing across time. I have argued that, up to the seventh century, Egypt had a colonial relationship with the rest of the Roman Empire (p. 68), with a resultant emphasis on wheat production; but there is, equally, extensive documentation, both archaeological and documentary, of artisanal production and exchange, and the Egyptian internal economy was evidently already highly active and complex, with overlapping distribution networks and peasant demand, as we have seen for the tenth to twelfth centuries too. The colonial relationship was never as strong under the caliphate, because the tax owed to the centre was differently structured (it was by now essentially in money), but Egypt was still paying substantial amounts to Baghdad until the governorship of Ibn Ṭulūn from 868 onwards, after which any colonial relationship began to disappear. In other respects, anyway, although the evidence is less good for the eighth century and early ninth than for before the Arab conquest, we can see strong continuities in the economic infrastructure of the region.[255]

That was the basis for further development, which becomes visible above all under the newly autonomous Ṭulūnids in the later ninth century, who invested in Tinnīs. This was also the time of the Abū Hurayra letters from the Fayyūm, which show the regularity of some internal cloth trade. It is in particular in flax and linen, and also sugar, that we can see a real increase in scale in the tenth and eleventh centuries (ceramic production shows both increases and decreases, with Aswān and the Middle Egyptian amphora productions weakening but Fusṭāṭ coming up), but from now on we have steadily better evidence for the density of exchange at all levels. We do not have quantitative data which can allow us to be in any way sure about the exact degree to which Egypt's economy became more (or less) complex in any period, but there is a case for arguing for a very high base for internal exchange, on both the large scale and the small, which never really lessened (at most, perhaps to an extent in the century of internal uprisings between the 720s and 830s), but which was then built on in the Ṭulūnid period, and then continued to become more complex under the Fāṭimids. I in fact conclude, having at different times looked in detail at each, that the density of internal exchange in the eleventh century was rather greater than even under the Roman Empire. This was, I would propose, the long-term result of the end of a colonial relationship for the region. The growth in economic complexity in Egypt in the tenth and eleventh centuries was not, as it seems, as fast as that in other regions, as we shall see in later chapters, so it perhaps needs no more explanation than this;

[255] Wickham, *Framing*, pp. 759–69—a survey of the late Roman and early Islamic period which is now two decades old but which I would stand by (although I do not now accept the over-optimistic figures for Bahnasā as a Roman cloth town, ibid, p. 764 and n).

but the high baseline the region started from is at least enough to explain why it was not faster.

After 1100, there is less evidence of expansion, simply because there is less evidence. Fusṭāṭ's Jewish merchants traded less (but still some) in the central and even western Mediterranean, although, by contrast, they were a mainstay of the spice trade in the Indian Ocean (a relatively luxury trade, profitable but less economically central—see the next section); Amīnaddīn's letters conversely show, even if anecdotally, that Muslim sea merchants were active on a substantial scale, at least in the eastern Mediterranean, around 1200. So, overall, as we shall see in more detail in the next section, there is some evidence for Egyptian traders operating from the western to the eastern end of the sea across the twelfth century. More important here, however, is that what evidence we have indicates that internal exchange continued without significant shifts in structure. Much of the (largely still unpublished) *geniza* source material presented by Goitein for local merchandising and artisanal production, in Fusṭāṭ and the Delta, is in fact twelfth-century. Thanks to the fact that the favoured Indian Ocean port in this period was Aydhāb, placed implausibly far to the south, at the end of a dangerous desert route from Qūṣ (or sometimes Aswān) in Upper Egypt, we even have some evidence for Jewish merchants trading farther up the Nile valley, which we did not have before.[256] The published Arabic-script letters do not change in type at all either, even if they are less numerous. And the fiscal texts we have for the end of the century, al-Makhzūmī and Ibn Mammātī, show no signs of crisis in their descriptions of the internal affairs of Egypt.

After our period, in the thirteenth century, which I have not studied more than summarily, much the same seems true. Although by now Tinnīs had been abandoned and Damietta reduced in activity owing to Christian attacks, cloth production simply switched to Alexandria. And we have other solid signs of continued prosperity in that century, such as the specialisms in sugar and flax recorded by al-Nābulusī for the Fayyūm in the 1240s, even if there were changes too, as we saw earlier; for his text also shows that the cloth, leather, and ceramic production of the oasis, and an array of markets, which had been a feature of eleventh-century

256 See in general Goitein, *MS*, 1, pp. 99–116. Apart from the India trading texts and some synagogue documents (in Gil, *Documents*), over 250 *geniza* legal documents for the first half of the twelfth century are published, esp. in Weiss, *Legal documents*; most concern the capital, but see ibid., nn. 44, 254 (T-S 12.503, CUL Or.1081 J36) for the Delta. For Qūṣ and the desert route, see Garcin, *Un centre musulman*, pp. 100–2, 223–30. For texts for Upper Egypt, especially Akhmīm and Qūṣ (Akhmīm was apparently the main stopping point on the way: see T-S NS 321.1, which tells us that the Nile boat to Qūṣ stops for five days there), see Firkovitch II NS 1700 12AII, T-S 10J14.16 (Ackerman-Lieberman, *The business of identity*, nn. 9, 14a), T-S 12.18, 10J4.17 (Weiss, *Legal documents*, nn. 34, 135), Bodl. MS Heb. d.66/64–5 (Goitein and Friedman, *India traders*, n. I, 6–7, p. 189), T-S 10J16.15 (partial translation, ibid., n. II, 58), 13J33.1 (Goitein and Friedman, *India book* IV/B, n. 15), NS 329.999, 13J22.24, AIU XII.83, DK 353, ENA 2730.7, plus several others for Qūṣ, not all related to trade. Ibn Jubayr in the 1170s stresses Qūṣ as a market centre, and simply says that Akhmīm had a remarkable Pharaonic temple: *Riḥla*, trans. Broadhurst, pp. 53–5, 57–8.

villages, had by now largely become centralized in Madīnat al-Fayyūm. (Conversely, the town's cloth, criticized by al-Nābulusī for its poor quality, doubtless, precisely for that reason, had a largely peasant clientele.) The thirteenth-century business papers which have been published from the excavations at Quṣayr on the coast north of Aydhāb—it was a much more accessible port, in fact—show an intense trade in bulk agricultural goods (especially wheat) and flax/linen, thus further attesting to elements of the density of activity which we have seen for many places in Egypt in the eleventh century.[257] It is clear that Egypt produced cloth, and also sugar, on a large scale up to the mid-fourteenth century, and exported them; and the early fourteenth also saw substantial state-backed irrigation works in the countryside.[258] These data thus support an argument for the early Mamlūk economy, in the century after 1250, being as complex as that of the Fāṭimids. All of which makes wider sense, if we consider that Egypt in the eleventh century had been only marginally dependent on external commerce for its exchange complexity; internal demand would have been sufficient to keep the economy active well after that period as well, as it had before.

This is where we have to be cautious. The large-scale documentary sets currently at our disposal in both Hebrew and Arabic script run out soon after 1100, and we are back to the same sort of partial evidence that we had for (for example) the later eighth century. For the Mamlūk period, the historiography for Egyptian internal exchange is also very weak and often untrustworthy.[259] We thus cannot be sure of our picture of that period at all, and without fuller primary research, it would be unhelpful to discuss it in any further detail here. What we can see all the same, from our sketchy evidence, indicates the maintenance of a high-level equilibrium in the Egyptian economy which continued until the Black Death of 1347–9. That, however, was the real secular catastrophe for Egypt. The plague hit the Nile valley as badly as it hit anywhere, but its effects there were longer-lasting than elsewhere, owing to a breakdown in irrigation, which needed extensive manpower to be maintained, and the depopulation by the plague made that impossible. Other parts of both the Mediterranean and northern Europe could preserve

[257] For cloth in late medieval Alexandria, see Marzouk, cited in n. 209 above; Müller-Wiener, *Eine Stadtgeschichte Alexandrias*, pp. 235–9; further references to cloth production are given in Christ, 'Ein Stadt wandert aus', p. 155. For al-Nābulusī, see Rapoport, *Rural economy*, pp. 105–21, 133–7, 140; only one village was recorded as having a significant market. For Quṣayr, see P.QuseirArab., esp. I 1, 2, 4, 6, 10–12, 16, 21, 23–4, 27–8, 31, 34, 38, 42, 44, 47, 49, 60, 67, 69, II 2, 4–6, 8; Thayer, 'In testimony to a market economy'; and especially Guo, *Commerce*, pp. 35–69, 90–8; Burke, *Archaeological texts*.

[258] Ouerfelli, *Le sucre*, pp. 77–95; for irrigation, see Sato, *State and rural society*, pp. 227–33.

[259] For overviews, we still have only Eliyahu Ashtor's economic survey, *A social and economic history*, which is virtually unusable (cf. p. 19 above), and Subhi Labib's discussion of commerce, *Handelsgeschichte Ägyptens*, which, although certainly rather better, is highly descriptive and institutional, and focussed largely on long-distance trade; ibid., pp. 300–26, on internal markets and production, mixes sources of the tenth and the fifteenth centuries without comment. I have not seen the equally venerable Semenova, *Salakh ad Din i Mamlyuki v Egipte*, but see the critical review by Ashtor (with help from Claude Cahen), 'Débat sur l'évolution'. Abu Lughod, *Before European hegemony*, pp. 212–47, is much better in approach, but is also above all focussed on long-distance trade.

the basic structures of their economic systems with fewer people, but Egypt could not; half the land was simply abandoned, as irrigation failed.[260] All the evidence we have for the weakening of the Egyptian internal economy postdates 1350, and it had by no means recovered as late as the better-documented sixteenth century, as Nicolas Michel makes clear.[261] All the same, until the Black Death we can, again with due caution, see an equilibrium persisting. And that, to repeat, was an equilibrium of economic complexity at a very high level, higher than elsewhere in the Mediterranean, as we shall see across the rest of this book.

2.5 Interregional Exchange

When we look at Egyptian merchants and the Mediterranean, the evidence from the *geniza* dominates, up to 1100 at least—justifiably, given its scale—and the historiography concerning it is very strong. Since the publication of the first volume of Goitein's *A Mediterranean society* fifty-plus years ago, a steady stream of books and articles has appeared focussing on the routes of the Jewish merchants and the organization of their trading in the eleventh century, about which we can indeed say a great deal. The most important of these is undoubtedly, as we have seen, Jessica Goldberg's *Trade and institutions*, but almost all of them, and certainly all those cited in the footnote to this sentence, have useful material to contribute.[262]

[260] See in general Dols, *The Black Death*. For the effect on irrigation, the clearest guide is Borsch, *The Black Death*, pp. 34–54, plus Borsch, 'Environment and population'; Borsch, 'Plague depopulation and irrigation decay', a reference I owe to Tom McCaskie. In the book (but not so much in the articles) Borsch attributes failure here largely to the *iqṭāʿ* system in itself, which is less convincing to me. See too the survey in Christ, *A king of the two seas?*, which argues that post-1350 Mamlūk fiscal policy switched to a greater interest in international trade as a result.

[261] See esp. Michel, *L'Égypte des villages*, pp. 341–414, esp. 388–99; see also ibid., 264–77, 305–8, 365–73 for how dyke maintenance for irrigation worked by now. This book is now the essential guide to rural society at the end of the middle ages in Egypt, together with Michel, 'Devoirs fiscaux'. For sugar production, in which Egypt's Mediterranean dominance was also sharply reduced after 1350, see Ouerfelli, *Le sucre*, pp. 95–100, 662–3. Conversely, the area around Banī Swayf, which in the eleventh century had been the flax territory around Būṣīr, still specialized in linen in the sixteenth century according to Leo Africanus, which was sold throughout Egypt and also to Tunis; see Jean-Léon l'Africain, *Description de l'Afrique*, trans. Épaulard, 2, p. 530.

[262] See Goitein, *MS*, 1, obviously (that volume includes the text of several earlier articles too). Of later work, see, in particular, Stillman, 'The eleventh-century merchant house of Ibn ʿAwkal' (this article includes everything important in his unpublished thesis, *East-West relations*, except the valuable translations of Ibn ʿAwkal's letters at the end of the latter); Udovitch, *Partnership and profit*; Udovitch, 'Formalism and informalism'; Udovitch, 'Time, sea and society'; Udovitch, 'Alexandria'; Gil, 'The Jewish merchants' (based on his huge editions of texts); Greif, *Institutions*; Goldberg, *Trade and institutions*; Ackerman-Lieberman, *The business of identity*; Bramoullé, *Les Fatimides et la mer* (the book is focussed on the Fāṭimid navy, but has an important section on commerce, pp. 471–693). Heyd, *La commerce*, from the 1870s in its original version and so predating the discovery of the *geniza*, was of remarkable quality for its period, and remains useful for its systematic attention to items traded and to the history, above all, of the Italian commercial relationship with Egypt (see esp. 1, pp. 378–404, and 2, pp. 563–711—I cite the relevant pages only for the period to 1200); see also Schaube, *Handelsgeschichte*, pp. 145–90, equally pioneering but rather more intent on the Italian perspective. I need to say again that the cultural history of the *geniza* merchants is not the topic of this book, so the recent works of

We can say less about the twelfth century through the *geniza*, but there has been some work on that too, as a spin-off of the serious analysis of the India trade which has by now been done;[263] and by then Italian records start too, which need and have received a different sort of analysis. It might, therefore, given this range of material, seem paradoxical that this section is relatively short. There are two reasons for this. First, because it is a basic premiss of this book that we cannot understand interregional exchange properly until we have looked at the internal economies of *each* region; so far, we can only understand it from the Egypt end, and we have to look as well at the other ends of the routes, particularly in Chapters 3 and 6, before we can get a clearer picture of the commercial dynamics of the Mediterranean as a whole, which will be developed further in Chapter 7. Secondly, because much of the work on the economic history of the *geniza*, in particular, has been focussed on the organization and institutions of trade: the structure and the level of formality of partnerships, legal resources in the case of dispute, and financing—that is to say, investment, accounting, banking, and so on. These are topics which are for the most part less germane to the arguments of this book, which has different aims: to determine who bought and sold primary or manufactured products, which routes they went on, and which products were most important, as guides to the economic logic of the whole system.

It is, of course, not surprising that *geniza* economic historians have often focussed on these issues, for the letters say a great deal about them. They have also done so to subvert the long-standing grand narrative of Mediterranean trade which used to (and sometimes still does) focus exclusively on the Italian cities and their prominent role in Mediterranean trade in the twelfth century and later, and the financial institutions which derived from that. As we saw in Chapter 1, this tended to be a triumphal narrative of Italian dynamism and urban liberty, clearly superior to those of orientalized and subservient Islamic cities. The discovery and publication of the evidence of the *geniza* made this argument impossible, as Goitein showed from the start; he indeed suggested, among other things, that both the *qirāḍ* partnership and the patterns of banking in these letters were models for those of Italy a century or two later.[264] The triumphal narrative has been reworked more subtly by Avner Greif in his argument that *geniza* merchants

Rustow, Cohen, Krakowski, Wagner, and others (see the Bibliography for references), and indeed Goitein, *MS*, 2–3 and 5, have not been systematically used here.

[263] India trade: see esp. Goitein and Friedman, *India traders* and Goitein and Friedman, *India book* IV/B; Margariti, *Aden*; Margariti, 'Mercantile networks'; Margariti, '*Aṣḥābunā l-tujjār*'; Guo, *Commerce*; Lambourn, *Abraham's luggage*. The first of these discusses the twelfth-century Mediterranean too; for this, see also Zeldes and Frenkel, 'The Sicilian trade'; and pp. 195–8 below.

[264] Goitein, *MS*, 1, pp. 171–9, 229–50. He suggested the influence of the *qirāḍ* on the Italian *commenda*, tentatively, at 171. At 230, he denied that he was proposing Egyptian (or a more general Islamic) influence on Italian banking ('Such conclusions lie outside the scope of this book.'), but here too the suggestion remains. Udovitch had already been slightly more explicit about the former in 'At the origins of the western *commenda*', and was again in Udovitch, *Partnership and profit*, p. 170. See pp. 648–9 below for the *qirāḍ*/*commenda* debate.

relied on informal measures of agreement enforcement rather than the court-based enforcement which was normal for the more 'individualistic' merchants in Italian cities, specifically Genoa; in New Institutional Economic terms, this implies that the patterns of trade documented in the *geniza* could not expand outside the network of merchants who knew and relied on each other, so had limits which Italian trading did not. Goldberg has in my view disposed of this argument most effectively; she shows both that Jewish agreement enforcement was more formalized than Greif proposed, and that Italian commercial relationships were less court-reliant and more socially constrained than Greif assumed. (That latter point is reinforced by other more recent work on Genoa.)[265] Certainly, Italian merchant shipping did in the end largely dominate the Mediterranean; but the explanations for this are far more complex, as we shall see at several points in the chapters that follow.

This also lessens the need to analyse organization here. Partnership structures and banking in eleventh-century Egypt are important and interesting in themselves, but they do not, in my view, contribute to structural explanations for Egyptian commercial vitality in overseas trading in our period (or indeed to its eventual lessening); they are its products, not its causes. I would instead locate that vitality above all in the intensity of internal Egyptian exchange, of all types, and I argued precisely this in the previous section. So, not how people invested, but who invested and on what scale seem to me the issue of greatest significance for the arguments here.

Here, as usual, the answers can only be suggestive, but there are some indications. If we were starting with Europe here, we would start with land. Werner Sombart, indeed, regarded that as axiomatic for all pre-industrial investment.[266] Twelfth-century Italian investment, for example, was very largely (even if by no means entirely) based on wealth derived from landed property, which lay at the back of early merchant prosperity and mercantile investment in Venice, Genoa, and Pisa. It must, therefore, have started small, as these cities had few large landowners in that century. The same can be said for Florence a century later; the great banking and moneylending families of the decades around 1300 had had small-scale beginnings, and had steadily built up their wealth with smaller and

[265] Greif, *Institutions*, pp. 58–89, 309–49; Goldberg, *Trade and institutions*, pp. 41–2, 134, 148–9, 150–64, 178, 294–5, 357–8—and for the whole system of partnership and law, 120–79; see also Goldberg, 'Choosing and enforcing business relationships'; Ackerman-Lieberman, *The business of identity*, pp. 156–93. Earlier, Edwards and Ogilvie made some very effective critical points too ('Contract enforcement'; see also Greif's reply in 'The Maghribi traders'). For Genoa, see Van Doosselaere, *Commercial agreements*, pp. 5–8 and *passim*; and see further p. 540 below. Greif was, of course, relying in large part on arguments about informality made by earlier *geniza* scholars themselves (e.g. Goitein, *MS*, 1, pp. 164–9; Udovitch, 'Formalism and informalism'), and backed by a strand of more traditional Islamic historiography on the lack of institutions in Middle Eastern cities (e.g. Lapidus, *Muslim cities*, pp. 101, 107, 113–15; Stern, 'The constitution of the Islamic city').

[266] See in general Sombart, *Der moderne Kapitalismus*, 2nd edn, 1, esp. chs 9–12.

then larger transactions. (For more on this, see Chapter 6.) In Egypt, however, the situation was different. We know far less about how large landowners operated in the eleventh century; our evidence concentrates on rather more modest figures, particularly rich peasants like Jirja of Damūya—who can indeed be seen, rather more easily than can Italians of the same social stratum, to have made the first steps towards a trading profile in our period, but only the first steps. It is likely that larger owners did the same on a larger scale, but that is speculation. But there were two other significant groups of mercantile investors, who are better documented, Jews and state officials.

Jews, whose investment is, of course, very visible indeed, did not come from an Egyptian landowning background (there is almost no information about landowning in the *geniza* at all[267]). Two major early families, those of Yūsuf Ibn ʿAwkal (d. *c.*1040) and the Tustarīs (active into the 1050s at least), emerge in our documentation as acting on a very large scale; the former came from Ifrīqiya, but his family almost certainly came from Iraq; the latter certainly came directly from Iraq. The Tustarīs were already prosperous and influential in Iraq, and simply developed economically from there. In the case of Ibn ʿAwkal we have no background information, so we cannot say how he and his father built up their wealth initially, but the size of his operations (the largest recorded in the *geniza* in absolute) show that his capital must have been substantial, perhaps from trading in previous generations, already in the early eleventh century; if his family were also once Iraqi, its wealth may, as with the Tustarīs, have begun there.[268] Later emigrants from Ifrīqiya, notably Nahray b. Nissīm and most of his associates, were very prosperous for sure, but operated on a smaller scale. Their trading demonstrably began back in the Maghreb, for they kept links with family members there who were also merchants (Nahray's aunt's family, to which he was particularly close, was the Tāhirtīs, named from a town located well into what is now Algeria).[269] We might suppose that Iraq was a more favourable region in which to build up wealth than Ifrīqiya, which certainly fits the relative wealth of the two regions. But Jews (as also dealers in the capital from other religions[270]) also did not need to build up wealth elsewhere. There was so much buying and selling going on in Fusṭāṭ by the early eleventh century that we could not assume that it was impossible to start small and end up rich in that city, if one was both clever and lucky, and some contemporaries of Nahray are likely to have done just that (of course, we are talking about a small minority—most people never find that city streets are really paved with gold). That is to say, the internal commercial

[267] Goitein, *MS*, 1, pp. 116–18; in fact, there was perhaps less even than implied there: see Wickham, 'The power of property', p. 91n.

[268] For both families, see Rustow, *Heresy*, pp. 137–47; Gil, *Jews*, pp. 663–76, 679–87.

[269] For the Tāhirtīs, see p. 189 below.

[270] See, e.g., a Christian merchant who bought land in Fusṭāṭ in a document dating to shortly before 1173: Mouton et al., *Propriétés rurales*, n. 43.

complexity of Egypt made the build-up of resources from a non-landowning, petty trading base more conceivable and potentially faster than in many or most other regions, at least before 1200. As we shall see in Chapter 6, this included Italy as well, where such building up of resources was not as yet so very fast in our period.

State officials are, by contrast, not so well documented in the *geniza*; but they were doubtless even more important. The Tustarīs were the only major Jewish merchant family to fit that category for part of their careers, and they were also the family out of those just mentioned whose own papers did not end up in the attic of the Ben Ezra synagogue (they were, as noted earlier, Qaraites, from a different branch of Judaism). In our Arabic-script texts however, by 1200 or so at least, we find the *amīr* Amīnaddīn and also judicial figures who are clearly operating on an equally large scale (see p. 109 above); money from the state could easily have provided the basic capital to do that. Earlier, an *adab* text by an official of the Ṭūlūnids, Ibn al-Dāya, shows him and his family already investing in cloth manufacturing in Tinnīs in the later ninth century; and Ibn Killīs, the Jewish convert who was *wazīr* of Caliph al-ʿAzīz in the 980s–990s, supposedly died with half a million dinars invested in cloth, as we have seen. By *geniza* standards, this is anecdotal, but it is consistent. It fits also with the evidence, which we do find in the eleventh-century *geniza*, for high officials as shipowners, the *amīr* of Alexandria, the *qāḍī* of Tyre Ibn Abī ʿUqayl, and perhaps the caliph himself (and certainly the independent rulers of Denia in al-Andalus; see p. 407 below). Indeed, there was so much money floating around in all state offices (not least the central and local tax offices) that it would have been easy to accumulate a great deal of wealth from officeholding, whether legally or illegally, and there is any amount of evidence from the Islamic world in these centuries that such accumulations were common.[271] This would have been a far faster way to gain wealth sufficient to invest in trade than either land or the informal commercial apprenticeships which we can imagine for some Jews, and it is very likely that most of the biggest investors in a major commercial city like Fusṭāṭ were such officials and/or their families. Since they were generally Muslims, they would not often register in the *geniza*, except as shipowners, or, sometimes, as commercial (and perhaps also political) patrons. Senior state-paid officials indeed had considerable clout as patrons of merchants, getting them lower customs dues, or getting them out of trouble, as well, of course, as being themselves almost certainly, given the relative lack of prominence of

[271] Ibn al-Dāya, *Kitāb al-mukāfaʾa*, trans. Panetta, pp. 51–2; cf. 143–4; for Ibn Killīs, see p. 97 above; for shipowners, see Bramoullé, *Les Fatimides et la mer*, pp. 669–81; Goitein, *MS*, 1, pp. 309–13. In general, for legal and illegal wealth derived directly from officeholding, see, e.g., the stories in al-Tanūkhī's *Nishwār al-muḥāḍara*, trans. Margoliouth, written in Iraq in the 970s–980s: cf. Wickham, 'Administrators' time', pp. 430–40. It was often confiscated after a term of office, but, if one did not have powerful enemies, one could end up with major sums.

local landed elites, the richest private buyers.[272] Officials did not have to invest their money in commerce (land was, in almost every medieval society, the most typical, safest, and most status-bearing investment[273]), but the active internal economy of Egypt was such that it was easy to choose to do so. In particular, the potential for profit in Fusṭāṭ and the Delta ports—both in seaborne trade and food supply for the capital—was so great that it is not surprising to find examples of official figures, including major political figures, who did just that. After all, if they had been concerned above all with safety, they would not have been in government, which was a risky career path even under rulers less violent than al-Ḥākim.

The existence of this category of already rich commercial dealers once again points up the fundamental importance of the fact that Egypt had a strong state. Goitein argued that the Fāṭimids did not try to control maritime commerce, which in a narrow sense is true, but—as David Bramoullé and Lorenzo Bondioli in particular have argued—it intervened directly in it all the same, via a series of state warehouse complexes, *dārs*, in Alexandria and other ports through which imported goods had to come, and an extremely elaborate system of heavy customs tolls, varying in complex ways from commodity to commodity and even port to port on Egypt's north coast. These are described and listed in al-Makhzūmī's *Minhāj*, which we have already encountered discussing the land tax; it was written at the end of the twelfth century, but certainly reflected at least late Fāṭimid norms, and its complexity is probably a guide to the pre-1100 period too. Such tolls (called in general *khums*, a fifth) varied in reality from 10 per cent to 30 per cent for the foreign merchants which the *Minhāj* particularly discusses, unless (as we learn from other sources) their parent states or cities had cut trade deals. But local merchants often paid considerably less than foreign merchants; *geniza* letters, in particular, imply that they usually paid under 10 per cent (the typical figure for customs tolls across the rest of the Mediterranean), and often much less; and, as the Fāṭimids controlled North Africa, Sicily, and much of the Levant until the late eleventh century, all that area, if not exactly a free trade zone, was at least an area with relatively stable transaction costs. Fāṭimid power did not create the trade routes, which could not have existed without strong local productions, but all this in itself made the state a serious force in the maritime economy.[274] And

[272] For the specific example of Nahray's commercial relationship with the *amīr* of Alexandria, see Udovitch, 'Merchants and *amīrs*', pp. 57–65, citing T-S J2.66, 13J8.18, Bodl. MS Heb. c 28/33, CUL Or. 1080 J13 (Gil K271, 242, 258, 509 [S133]); see further Goldberg, *Trade and institutions*, pp. 166–7, 170–4.

[273] As noted earlier (n. 118 above), by 1200, and indeed sometimes 1100, land would in Egypt have mostly been controlled through tax-farming, so investment would have largely been in tax farms.

[274] Al-Makhzūmī, *Minhāj*, trans. Cahen, 'Douanes', pp. 282–312; for commentary on it, see the rest of Cahen's article, and Bramoullé, *Les Fatimides et la mer*, esp. pp. 494, 611–26. The text is incomplete, particularly for the main port, Alexandria, but Ibn Mammātī, *Qawānīn*, trans. Cooper, 9.6.1, pp. 276–7, backs al-Makhzūmī up: here, the 'fifth' at Alexandria can vary from under 20% to nearly 35%. For the

the state in Egypt was a major buyer, of all types of good. Government officials regularly reset market prices, as a guide to buying and selling; these did not constrain merchants in normal dealing, but if the state itself wanted to buy, it did so compulsorily and at the price it had set. Silk, linen, olive oil (in Tunisia), and lead were all forcibly bought at different times. Jewish merchants were often happy to sell to the state, if demand and therefore real prices were lower than the government rate (less happy if they were higher, of course); but more important is that they treated forced sales to the government as an entirely normal event.[275]

State demand was great, not just for luxuries which were regularly displayed in caliphal processions,[276] but for the more ordinary goods which lesser dependants needed, who were very numerous in a public sector as large as Egypt's. And we, of course, need to add here the army, which needed iron, necessarily an import in Egypt's case; and the navy as well, which in addition needed timber and pitch, both of which also mostly came from outside Egypt. In the tenth century, the Fāṭimid navy was highly active; in that period, it was equipped from the iron and timber resources of Ifrīqiya, Sicily, and (soon) the Levant highlands, which were under direct Fāṭimid rule. In the late eleventh century the power of the Fāṭimids effectively ended in all three, although that was a period in which the navy, at least, was far smaller. Supply problems became more of an issue in the twelfth century, when the navy had to be revived to face the Crusaders, but the traditional sources of timber and iron were no longer under caliphal control; but these problems were dealt with then too, as we shall see shortly.[277] State involvement extended to the ownership of linen factories in Tinnīs, and the government's interest in the registration of the sale of flax. So there were substantial sectors of the economy in which the state was involved as a regular—and very wealthy—player. As we shall see in later chapters, the Egyptian state was more prominent than that of Byzantium here, probably more so than other Muslim powers, and far more prominent than any public power in Italy. It was

geniza, see Goitein, *MS*, 1, pp. 266–72, 341–6; Goldberg, *Trade and institutions*, pp. 164–77 (esp. for merchant negotiation with the branches of the state); Bramoullé, *Les Fatimides et la mer*, pp. 603–8. For *dārs*, see ibid., 591–601; Bondioli, *Peasants, merchants, and caliphs*, pp. 224–36, and cf. in general ibid., 218–65 for the system as a whole. (*Dār* just meant 'court' or 'courtyard house', but had a precise meaning when it denoted the Court of Flax or of Silk.) See further p. 62 above for the need to ensure food for Fusṭāṭ-Cairo, which was, again, not directed by the state, but certainly managed with strong fiscal involvement. The Fāṭimid state also regulated many of the terms of trade in all periods—marketplace safety, regulations (usually over-optimistic) against price gouging, etc.—but this did not distinguish Egypt from other regions; not just other Islamic states, but also Byzantium and the Italian cities, standardly did this too.

275 Goitein, *MS*, 1, pp. 267–9, Goldberg, *Trade and institutions*, pp. 169–70.

276 Sanders, *Ritual, politics, passim*, but esp. pp. 29–30, 49, 64, 103, 151; for the extraordinary scale of Fāṭimid luxuries, see also the long lists in the *Book of gifts and rarities, Kitāb al-hadāyā wa al-tuḥaf*, trans. al-Ḥijjāwī al-Qaddūmī, chs 372–414, of the objects in the treasury which troops looted and sold off in 1068–9. However exaggerated these lists are, they are at least roughly contemporary and give an idea of the ambition and expense of political display.

277 For the basic sequences of Fāṭimid naval history, see Bramoullé, *Les Fatimides et la mer*, pp. 102–95.

a major element in internal and external demand alike, even if—as we have amply seen—not the only one. All of this fuelled the international trade network, at least as far as incoming goods were concerned.

We have seen who the *geniza* merchants bought from inside Egypt (that is to say, pretty much every social group, certainly including peasants); we will look in more detail in Chapter 3 at who they bought from and sold to abroad. As we shall see, they tended to deal exclusively in the open market, usually at ports—as also they did in Alexandria and Fusṭāṭ on their return, if they did not have specific commissions, or if they were not among the merchants who sold in the Rīf towns. For now, what is important to remind ourselves of is simply that the whole process was very complex and risky. Egyptian merchants in Ifrīqiya or Sicily could choose the wrong port, where prices were too low; their agents could fail to sell high, or fail to send the proceeds; whole markets could be 'paralysed' or 'shut', even Alexandria; ships could sink, war or piracy could intervene and wipe out a shipment, and so on.[278] Here, there can be no doubt that the practices of Jewish merchants fitted those of other religions, with and alongside whom the *geniza* merchants were trading; we could otherwise expect some comment in letters if their trading styles were different—as indeed we get with respect to Rūmī (i.e. Italian or Byzantine) merchants, who are criticized as being obsessed with pepper and weirdly/naively uninterested in bargaining.[279] One needed to be skilled to cope with risk—and, of course, with valuing quality, bargaining, and assessing the relative favourability and unfavourability of the prices of many commodities at once. But for the skilled and, as usual, the fortunate, profits were considerable: margins of 25–50 per cent in successful overseas trading seem here to have been normal, and this evidently more than balanced the risk.[280]

Which were the interregionally exchanged goods which mattered most for Egyptians? Can we put the goods which Jews did carry, and which merchants of other religions can be more dimly discerned as carrying, in any order of importance? Some of the historiography is unhelpful here: it often mistakes any reference to the import and export of goods, however casual or one-off, as a sign of interregional dependence—in my discussion below I shall ignore such isolated citations. It also often does not sufficiently distinguish between luxuries and bulk goods. That is a distinction which it is always essential to make from the start; for only bulk goods are really significant to any economy, as I stressed in Chapter 1. We can forget about jewels, pearls, coral, saffron, and the like, which have

[278] For moving ports, see Chapter 3, n. 2 below. For Alexandria as 'paralysed', see, e.g., ENA NS 2.13 (Gil K749 [S145]).

[279] Goldberg, *Trade and institutions*, pp. 334–5; for pepper and the Rūm, see, e.g., Bodl. MS Heb. a 3/13, ENA NS 18.24 (Gil K581, 344 [S91, 97]); for non-bargaining and not distinguishing between good and bad goods, see BL Or. 5542.27 (Gil K305, trans. Udovitch, 'A tale of two cities', pp. 155–8).

[280] Goitein, *MS*, 1, pp. 202–3. The evidence for Egypt is anecdotal, but the 25–50% level matches interest rates for sea loans in twelfth-century Genoa and Venice—see, e.g., Borsari, *Venezia e Bisanzio*, pp. 72–4—so it is plausible for Egypt too.

captivated so many writers on this topic. All the same, having said that, we have also to recognize a grey area between the two. Bulk goods moved interregionally above all on the Mediterranean, which was, therefore, by far the main arena for economically important maritime trade.[281] Indian Ocean trade to Egypt was in general less structurally important, for it was a trade which was largely in luxuries: expensive and high-profit goods, notably spices and dyes, which could make a lot of money for an individual merchant, but the quantities of which were generally small.[282] Only such goods, indeed, could easily be transported from such a strangely sited Red Sea port as Aydhāb. But trade from and via India could operate on a larger scale as well. Chinese ceramics were, as we have seen, so widely available in Egypt that we cannot really call them a luxury at all, even if the desert route was hardly adapted to them; the scale of Indian trade was evidently sufficiently great to allow a bulk element to develop as well. And indeed, some of the spices, notably pepper from south-western India,[283] were quite readily available, and there was substantial demand for them across the whole of the Mediterranean, and (as we have just seen) Europe beyond; we need to put them into the flexible category of semi-luxuries—relatively expensive goods which, however, greater numbers of people wanted and could afford. Some dyestuffs from Asia fit that category as well, such as lac and brazilwood—and indigo, although that was also grown in Egypt—simply because the Mediterranean clothing industries were large enough to need substantial quantities of them, however expensive. (Madder, which was an Egyptian-grown dye, is less often referred to in *geniza* letters; probably it went above all to the Delta weaving towns.) Coming the other way, mostly from Spain and Sicily, was a similar semi-luxury, silk, which was widely sold in small towns in Egypt, as we have seen, without ever being either cheap or an essential. Glass was the other main semi-luxury, this time made in Egypt (apparently largely by Jewish artisans), although also in most Mediterranean regions;

[281] Or on the caravan route by land from Ifrīqiya to Egypt and back, which was not only a luxury route (see, e.g., T-S 20.69 [Gil K380, S69]); but it was still far more expensive than the sea, and often interrupted by war—see Goitein, *MS*, 1, pp. 276–9; Goldberg, *Trade and institutions*, pp. 303–4. The Sahara routes were also the main sources of gold for the Fāṭimids, and not only them. But this was also the opposite of a bulk item, however essential it was for the stability of the Fāṭimid dinar (and it was indeed essential; see, e.g., Ashtor, *Histoire des prix*, pp. 119–21 for its stability, nuanced however by the citations in Nicol, *A corpus*, p. xii; cf., for the African end, Devisse, 'Trade and trade routes', pp. 383–403).

[282] See the lists of goods going through Aden in Margariti, *Aden*, pp. 127–31; these do, however, also include some iron and cloth. Lombard, *Espaces et réseaux*, p. 133, says that the Egyptians also imported teak for shipbuilding from India; this seems to be based on a one-line generic phrase of al-Masʿūdī, which cannot be taken as a reliable witness—and see Bramoullé, *Les Fatimides et la mer*, p. 661, for the insignificance of timber imports from the East. But teak for shipbuilding did reach Aden (Margariti, *Aden*, pp. 162, 285), and teak had reached Berenike on the Egyptian Red Sea coast in the Roman period, although not, as it currently seems, the Nile valley (Bouchaud et al., 'Fuelwood and fuel supplies', esp. p. 436), so its use cannot be excluded, at least for ships built on the Red Sea. For the growing Fāṭimid interest in the Red Sea and its trade networks, see esp. Bramoullé, *Les Fatimides et la mer*, pp. 529–87.

[283] For which see, for an overview based on the period before 800, Darley, 'Who ate all the pepper?'.

but given that it was common to melt it down and reuse it, so its origin is not as easy to determine archaeologically as is that of ceramics, we can be less sure about its interregional commercialization.[284] Silk, Chinese pottery, glass, pepper, and dyes were, then, relevant to the economy of Egypt and its neighbours. All the same, they were so on a rather smaller scale than the major bulk goods, which I will focus on here.

What Egyptians visibly exported overseas in the eleventh century was above all flax, sugar, dyes (including alum, a fixer for dyeing), and pepper, in that order; Goldberg indeed shows that flax was by an order of magnitude more significant in value than any other export. The first two, plus alum, were Egyptian products; pepper and most dyes were, as we have just seen, Indian Ocean imports. The evidence for this is mostly from the *geniza*, supplemented by some later Italian contracts. Alum, mined in the Egyptian desert (in this period, near Asyūṭ and southwards from there), occurs rarely in Egyptian sources, although this does not mean that it was only used for interregional trading.[285] We should also assume

[284] See Goitein, *MS*, 1, pp. 109–10 and 421, for glass in Fusṭāṭ. For the development of Egyptian glassmaking, see Schibille et al., 'Chronology of early Islamic glass compositions from Egypt', with, now, Schibille, *Islamic glass in the making*, pp. 62–75, which shows that the plant ash base of much Egyptian glass in our period was imported from the Levant. Levantine plant ash was quite widely used in the Mediterranean in our period, and so was Levantine glass itself; one archaeological marker is the Serçe Limanı shipwreck of *c.*1025, off the Turkish (i.e. Byzantine) coast, a ship coming from Beirut or a similar Fāṭimid-ruled Syrian port to the Aegean, and full of probably Syrian glass cullet (broken glass for reworking); see Bass and Allen, *Serçe Limanı*, 2, and p. 360 below; another is the glass from several sites in Sicily, some of which seems to have had a Levantine/Egyptian (and also Tunisian) origin (see Colangeli and Schibille, 'Glass from Islamic Sicily'; Molinari and Meo, *Mazara/Māzar*, pp. 484–6, 494–503 [F. Colangeli, N. Schibille and F. Colangeli]). Underpinning the Levant link here, T-S 13J33.5 (Gil P268), cited by Goitein, shows a large quantity of glass coming to Alexandria from Tyre in 1011. The study of glass in the Mediterranean for our period is currently taking off, but it is as yet hard to tell what the directions and scale of glass distribution networks were across the Mediterranean as a whole; this will be for future work.

Slaves, coming above all from sub-Saharan Africa and mostly female, were another semi-luxury in Egypt—they were above all for domestic and sexual exploitation; see Perry, *The daily life of slaves*, pp. 28–54 and *passim*, and, for the ninth century, Bruning, 'Slave trade dynamics'. They were not at all restricted to the highest elites but were, all the same, not cheap, and thus presumably not so very widely sold in Egypt. Prices attested for slaves in Arabic-script texts are from 13 to 110 dinars; in the *geniza*, where there was less variation, 20 dinars per slave was typical by 1100; see, e.g., P.Vente 1–11 (cf. also P.RichardsDay-book, a fragmentary sales register from 950–1050, which also has a few males, including one Rūm, i.e. Byzantine or Italian), and for the *geniza*, see Ashtor, *Histoire des prix*, pp. 208–11; 20 dinars equalled around a year's rent for a rich merchant's house in the capital and four to five years' for a less elite residence, ibid., pp. 190–1. The slave trade, being more of a luxury rather than a bulk trade (and also in this period decreasingly a trans-Mediterranean trade), will not figure much in this book as a result. For current views of slavery and the slave trade in the medieval period, see Perry et al., *The Cambridge world history of slavery*, 2, an unusually effective collective work.

[285] The first Venetian (and Italian) legal document concerning trade with Egypt, from 1072, is, in fact, for alum: *DCV*, n. 11; see also *CDVE*, 8, n. 2013 (a. 1148), doubtless alum from Egypt but being taken from Constantinople to Venice (see Chapter 6, n. 79 below, for *CDVE*). For alum as a whole, see esp. Cahen, 'L'alun avant Phocée'; for locations of the mineral, see Ibn Mammātī, *Qawānīn*, trans. Cooper, 9.8.2, p. 278. Pisa, for which we do not have significant numbers of trade documents, also imported alum from Egypt on a large scale; see Amari, *I diplomi arabi*, 2ª serie, nn. 7–8. For sugar, see in general Ouerfelli, *Le sucre*, pp. 71–8; in *geniza* texts, the scale of export is unclear, but references to it are regular, and Goitein, at least, saw it as substantial: *MS*, 1, pp. 125–6.

that the cloth towns on the coast were doing their own exporting of linen, given the scale of their production, documented by texts which do not survive, although we cannot say where to. But flax was anyway overwhelmingly the most important of these. Ibn ʿAwkal sent at least 180 bales in one year, around 40 tons, at up to 35 dinars a bale; merchants later in the century such as Nahray b. Nissīm operated at a scale of at most half of that, but that is still a very substantial amount, and there were at least 400 Jewish merchants active in sea traffic in the second half of the eleventh century (with, of course, many other merchants as well).[286]

Imports are not quite so easily characterized, but there are some clear patterns. Strictly, Egypt was not dependent on the Mediterranean for its economy to function—just like any other region around the sea, there had been plenty of times in its history when maritime commerce was not significant, but a complex economy survived without difficulty. Only two imports were crucial, iron and timber, neither of them, as we have seen, well documented in the *geniza* (and iron not in Arabic-script letters either); we will come back to them in a moment. The other major imports which Egypt can be seen to have bought, this time extensively documented in *geniza* letters, were, in rough order of importance, olive oil (including its by-product, soap), cloth (linen in particular, but also silk and cotton), hides, wax, and then silver; and, on a smaller scale, lead, tin, copper, honey, and cheese.[287] Cheese, the main meat protein for the poor, was also widely available in Egypt itself, given the cattle and sheep which were numerous there; but we do have some evidence for its import, from Sicily in the eleventh and twelfth centuries and Crete in the twelfth.[288] Linen is not as dominant as an import as is flax as an export in our eleventh-century evidence; it is likely that the weaving and finishing which took place inside Egypt, notably but not only in the Delta factory towns, satisfied much of the Egyptian cloth market, without so much recourse to the products of Tunisian and Sicilian factories, which anyway had their own regional markets. But it is, nonetheless, equally clear that cloth imports were substantial. They added to the mix of exchange alternatives inside Egypt; Tunisian and Sicilian cloth was valued for its own sake (and not just expensive varieties like Sūsī cloth, from Sousse, either)—its use shows the complexity which we have seen for internal exchange, extending to products from outside the country as well. As for silver, the Egyptians relied very much on silver dirhams and especially

[286] See esp. Goldberg, *Trade and institutions*, pp. 276–80, with ibid., p. 39 for the numbers of merchants in Nahray's circle; for the Ibn ʿAwkal reference, see T-S 13J17.3 (Gil K181 [S47]). One bale, *ʿidl*, was worth some 5 *qinṭār*s, of 100 *raṭl*s (roughly equivalent to UK pounds) each. For 35 dinars per bale (and also Nahray's trading scale), see n. 55 above; as is noted there, the dinar calculations by Stillman, 'The eleventh-century merchant house', p. 29, are slightly lower.

[287] For an undifferentiated list, see Goitein, MS, 1, pp. 153–4, with some wider comments on 209–29. The best general commentary is Goldberg, *Trade and institutions*, pp. 95–9, 276–8.

[288] From Sicily, T-S 13J17.11 (Gil K194 [S53]), 20.80 (ed. Goitein and Friedman, *India book* IVB, n. 68); from Crete, CUL Or.2116.10 (ed. Frenkel, *Ha-Ohavim*, n. 5); see discussion in Goitein, *MS*, 1, pp. 46, 124, 4, pp. 251–2; Jacoby, 'Byzantine Crete', p. 529; Bramoullé, *Les Fatimides et la mer*, pp. 508–9.

half-dirhams as a practical low-value coin for daily exchange, but although they were minted in Egypt (with a lessening silver content across the eleventh century), they were also brought in from outside, as was the silver itself, and can, in effect, be added to the list of semi-luxury commodities. They had a variable exchange rate with gold dinars, which *geniza* merchants priced in the same way as they did other goods.[289]

One relative absence needs signalling, ceramics, visible not in texts but in the archaeology. I remarked earlier that Egypt made sufficiently good pottery that it did not need imports from other Mediterranean regions; the only ones so far found for most of our period are Palestinian amphorae, i.e. containers for foodstuffs, with the exception, in the main Alexandria excavations, of a small number of Tunisian and Sicilian glazed wares. This situation changed after 1150, when we begin to find many more Tunisian wares, even a handful of Spanish ones, and, by the end of the century, Byzantine types; ceramic fine-ware imports reached their height in the thirteenth century. But even then they are so far only found in Alexandria and, after 1250, one of the Cairo sites; the Fusṭāṭ excavations show no published examples, except a few from Spain. As it currently seems, an Egyptian interest in foreign ceramics (apart from Chinese and sometimes Iraqi wares, which came by different routes), was skin-deep. Conversely, as noted earlier, eleventh- and twelfth-century Egyptian ceramics are found quite widely in the Mediterranean in small numbers, not least lustre types; this does not show scale in trade in itself, but it at least shows the reach of Egyptian products.[290]

Olive oil is in some ways the most interesting of these imports. Egypt has its own oil-bearing plants of differing palatability, used for eating and lighting: flax (linseed), sesame, radishes, even melons—as well as ricin or castor oil, the most horrible to western tastes, but doubtless essentially used for lighting. Olive oil was, simply, better than them, and known to Egyptians as such. In the Roman period, it was mostly imported from the north-eastern Mediterranean in LRA 1 amphorae, which are found widely in Lower and Middle Egypt. In the ninth century, Arabic papyri sometimes refer to oil from Palestine, which must be olive oil, and it is likely that the Palestinian amphorae which can be found in small numbers throughout Egypt in our period carried it.[291] Arabic-script paper documents after 900 have more sporadic references to it, without discussing its provenance—there it is called *ṭayyib* (good) oil, which recalls the 'real' oil of the eleventh-century

[289] See Nicol, *A corpus*, for lists; earlier, Balog, 'History of the dirhem', pp. 113–23. For the dirham trade, see Goitein, *MS*, 1, pp. 368–92 for documents.

[290] See esp. François, *Céramiques médiévales à Alexandrie*, pp. 71–132, 156–71 for Alexandria; Pradines et al., 'Excavations of the archaeological triangle', p. 195 for Cairo (a site outside the eastern walls). For Spanish wares, see Chapter 5, n. 210 below. For ceramic exports, see n. 244 above.

[291] For 'Palestinian' oil, see P.Berl.Arab. II 40, P.Cair.Arab. 311, 430, P.SijpesteijnPrivate; see also P.David-WeillMusee, explicitly olive oil. For other types, see, e.g., P.GrohmannWirtsch. 22 (linseed and radish oil), P.Cair.Arab. 427 (melon seed oil). All these texts are ninth-century. For the amphorae, see p. 91 above.

Coptic account book published by Richter. But from the *geniza* it is clear that it was imported on a large scale, and that by far the major region from which it was imported was southern Tunisia, which had already been the great oil-exporting area of the Roman Empire, with Palestine by now secondary to that.[292] (From Tunisia it was mostly by now carried in skins, as our letters show, but a few *mu'assala*s, ceramic containers of some kind, are documented for oil here, and large transport amphorae from our period have been found on sites along the oil-producing coast of Tunisia, so we may be able to confirm their presence in Egypt archaeologically in the future.[293]) In the late Roman Empire, Tunisian oil did not go to Egypt much, but Fāṭimid political links by now facilitated the trade, on a scale not attested in any of our earlier Islamic-period evidence. The key point is, however, that this was a relatively cheap import— that is to say, not at all a luxury, even if certainly more expensive than radish oil—visibly important in the eleventh century, which Egyptians did not strictly need, but simply liked; and enough of them could afford it to make the scale of trade considerable—there were specialist olive oil sellers (*zayyāt*s) in Fusṭāṭ.[294]

Goldberg generalizes all this, at least insofar as it related to the Fusṭāṭī Jewish merchants, in what she calls 'a *geniza* business model'. This was based on a reliance on exporting bulk goods, usually primary products, on a large scale, either from or to Egypt; outside Egypt, these were bought and sold wholesale in the main entrepôts, to aid a timely return on investments, which was crucial for investors, and necessary also for the merchants' own use of profits for other trading. Importantly, this meant that the merchants concerned did not significantly engage with the internal economies of any of the regions they dealt with. Only when goods were bought or sold inside Egypt was there much more buying directly from flax producers and some small-scale selling in the Rīf towns. Such staples did not vary in price so much as to be high-risk, so they were always the core of the activity of these traders, with high-value goods (i.e. luxuries) only there as extras, for their pricing and saleability were so unpredictable.[295] This was a business model we can associate with Italian merchants too, in the next century; it was a fundamental financial pattern for both the eleventh- and the twelfth-century Mediterranean, and we will return to it in later chapters.

[292] *Ṭayyib*: P.Vind.Arab. I 59 (11th century); P.MoutonSadr 1 (13th century); cf. Richter, 'Ein fatimidenzeitliches koptisches Rechnungsheft', p. 396. For the *geniza*, see, e.g., Goitein, *MS*, 1, pp. 154, 212, and the lists in Gil, 'Supplies of oil'. A classic letter about (among other things) oil from the Sfax area, maybe but not certainly from 1064, is Halper 389 (Gil K751 [S151]). By *c.*1200, P.Vind.Arab. I 44 shows one example of large-scale importing from Palestine again.

[293] For *mu'assala* and other ceramic terms, see Bramoullé et al., 'Le mobilier céramique', pp. 213–16; examples of *geniza* citations of oil in amphorae are T-S 13J28.2 (Gil K524 [S160]) for export to Egypt; and for export to Sicily, see Moss. VII,101, T-S 12.372, IOM D 55.14 (Gil P193, K513, 745 [S60, 111, 127]); for the amphorae themselves, see Chapter 3, n. 50 below.

[294] Goitein, *MS*, 1, p. 120, 4, pp. 252–3.

[295] Goldberg, *Trade and institutions*, pp. 276–88.

The routes which these products went on in the eleventh century are well known by now, thanks to the *geniza* historians as a group. The triangular trade between Alexandria, Mahdia, and Palermo (less often Mazara in Sicily and other Ifrīqiyan ports, although these become more significant after *c.*1050) overwhelmingly dominated, for this was the flax and linen route. The sea route to the Palestinian ports was there too, but was less important, and Goldberg shows well how Palestine was, in effect, simply a subordinate region of Egypt in the eleventh century.[296] These were the spine routes for the whole of the southern Mediterranean in this period. Those connecting to al-Andalus existed as well, but were certainly subordinate to the triangular spine as far as Egyptian merchants were concerned—and merchants in the central Mediterranean too, given that many of our letters are from traders based in Ifrīqiya itself (we will come back to them in Chapters 3 and 5). By contrast, as Goldberg shows effectively, the links northwards to the Christian world were as yet weak. There are Rūmī merchants in the *geniza*, but not many before 1100; even the geographers did not know much about either Byzantium or Italy; and for the *geniza* merchants themselves, these regions were, in effect, off the map.[297] We would not expect the more northerly east-west route connecting the Byzantine and ex-Byzantine lands together, which had existed throughout the early middle ages, or the slowly developing routes around al-Andalus, to appear in Egyptian sources (and they do not), but all the signs are that the former, at least, was less active than was the triangular spine; we will come back to this in later chapters. The *geniza* is probably otherwise a good guide to the relative importance of the eleventh-century Mediterranean routes. The only region linked to Egypt which may well be misrepresented by the *geniza* is northern Shām, what is now Syria; Egyptian exchange with the great ports of the north and the great inland cities, Damascus and Aleppo, was almost certainly greater than we know. Indeed, that exchange went back to the Roman Empire, with a smaller-scale continuity in trading between the main ports of Egypt, the Levant, and Cyprus which had never wholly ended; it became more visible again after 1100 too, as we shall see in a moment. But even if this route was more important, and connected to more places independently, than our documentary data allow us to see, there is no doubt that Egypt was at the centre of, the focus of, the main sea routes of the eleventh century.[298]

[296] Ibid., pp. 211–46.

[297] Ibid., pp. 19–21, 306–9. Bramoullé, *Les Fatimides et la mer*, pp. 486–9, 511–16, writes them up rather more, with a few extra examples; but his best evidence is post-1100. Note the sketchy treatment of mainland Italy in Ibn Ḥawqal, *Kītāb ṣūrat al-arḍ*, trans. Kramers and Wiet, 1, p. 197; this well-travelled tenth-century geographer did not see the northern European mainland as worth much discussion (or as possible to discuss in any informed way) at all.

[298] Goldberg, *Trade and institutions*, pp. 227–9. Cotton, in particular, would very often have come from Syria, even if Egypt had some of its own (see n. 182 above and n. 309 below); so did some glass (see n. 284 above). For the continuities in south-east Mediterranean trade, see p. 636 below; for links with the Byzantine lands, see pp. 354–7 below.

After 1100 at the latest, these patterns changed quite substantially. The *geniza* merchants moved to the Indian Ocean above all, so the density of information for the trading world of Nahray b. Nissīm ceases; and the best evidence for trade between Egypt and other Mediterranean regions begins to be Italian contracts, which slowly begin for Venice in the eleventh century and become more numerous from the 1130s, while for Genoa, even though there is little before 1130, there are so many for the years around 1160 that they can be, and have been, treated serially. This change in evidence type has been taken very literally by most historians, who have, of course, also been influenced by the simple fact that the former Fāṭimid political control of North Africa, Sicily, and the Levant was by 1100 replaced by political insecurity in North Africa and hostile Christian powers in Sicily (the Normans) and Syria-Palestine (the Crusaders); hence or otherwise, this is usually seen as when the Italians took over Mediterranean trade, establishing a dominance which would last for the rest of the middle ages.[299] Indeed, for many, that dominance had already begun by 1100, for the Venetians and Genoese are indeed occasionally documented in Alexandria well before then. We have seen, and will see again in Chapter 6, that 1100 is too early. Our early citations do not reflect more than a small-scale set of connections; indeed, any documentable upturn in Italian trade with Egypt does not really begin before the 1130s at the earliest. But it is clear that by the 1150s it was much more active.

Why this happened has got mixed up, again for many, with the grand narrative of western European economic superiority which goes back to Lopez and well before. If we ignore that, as experts on Egypt itself unsurprisingly tend to do, then the most common argument is that the Fāṭimids either could not or would not compete militarily with the Italians in their violent takeover of the sea routes. For Goldberg, Egyptian trading ships did not usually have military protection against enemies (whether navies or pirates), unlike many Italian convoys later. For Bramoullé, Fāṭimid naval protection existed but was at best intermittent, and after 1100 focussed on the Red Sea (which was the start of the India routes and also the link to Mecca and to Yemen, all of these being important for the Fāṭimids) and the routes up the Levant coast. The latter, thanks to the Crusader threat, were understandably the main concern of the revived navy of the twelfth century; in the Levant trade, merchant ships followed the navy, rather than vice versa.[300] These two authors are not wrong in their statements about Fāṭimid maritime politics; the problem is that there is no evidence in our period that Italian trading ships

[299] Emblematic here is perhaps Claude Cahen, who downplayed very substantially the economic importance of the Crusader states, and certainly did not believe in western economic superiority, but accepted the broad lines of the standard narrative nonetheless: *Orient et Occident*, e.g. pp. 108, 133–9, 210. For Venice and Egypt, from 800 onwards, see pp. 506–8, 514–16 below.

[300] See Goldberg, *Trade and institutions*, pp. 109–10, 174–5, 187, 358–9; Bramoullé, *Les Fatimides et la mer*, pp. 156–95, 529–87. Bramoullé, ibid., pp. 638–43, nuances the view that the state never protected merchant ships, but makes it clear that such protection was only occasional.

were any more regularly protected by war galleys than Egyptian ships were. Although it may well be that Italian cities were more violent than their Muslim counterparts and competitors, as is certainly shown by their attacks on Islamic ports, which began, in the case of the Pisans, as early as the mid-eleventh century (see p. 559 below), and on merchant ships in the early twelfth century, before treaties were established—and maybe also provided a higher proportion of pirates—this does not seem to me to be a full explanation in itself. Indeed, although there are fewer accounts of Egyptian merchants in the twelfth-century Mediterranean, problems of safety are not much more prominent in them than they were before 1100.[301] To me, then, the explanations we need lie elsewhere.

First, the dominance of our evidence by Italian trading ships, by 1150 at the latest, does not have to reflect much more than the simple fact that our most systematic documentation is by now overwhelmingly Italian. For Egyptian traders, our evidence becomes more anecdotal, but there is really quite a lot of evidence to deal with, which is worth listing. The *geniza* attests to normal trading with Sicily in the 1130s to 1150s, and with al-Andalus around 1140, and this at least is not anecdotal, even though far fewer letters concern it by now; a twelfth-century *fatwā* from Ifrīqiya cites Egyptians in Tunis, and so does an Arabic-script document of 1157; a letter of the Fāṭimid caliph al-Ḥāfiẓ to Roger II of Sicily in 1137 thanks him for protecting the caliph's ship, which was evidently trading in Sicily; Maimonides refers to ships going from Egypt to Seville too (for all this, see pp. 194–6, 450–4 below). Al-Idrīsī's geography, written around 1150, has Alexandrian merchants in Almería in Spain, and Muslim merchants from many places, presumably including Egypt, in Messina. Farther north, Egyptian merchants appear in Pisa in an Icelandic pilgrim account of the 1150s, and in Barcelona in Benjamin of Tudela's account from the 1160s; by 1229, city statutes show them in Marseille too; they would probably have reached none of these places before 1100.[302] Some of these texts mention Egyptians as part of excited accounts of ships from many lands in active ports, which, therefore, could well be simply rhetorical, but the rhetoric is still significant—it would not have had much

[301] Italian merchants did often travel in groups, in this period generally called *taxegia* and similar; their sailors were also armed (e.g. *Annali genovesi*, 1, ed. Belgrano, p. 39); but I have seen no systematic armed protection in twelfth-century texts. Rather, protection of merchant ships by war galleys appears to have been ad hoc, and located in particular in moments of formal war between Pisa and Genoa (*Annali genovesi*, 1, ed. Belgrano, pp. 21, 61, 69). For problems of safety for Egyptian merchants after 1100, see Bodl. MS Heb. c 28/60, b 11/15 (ed. Zeldes and Frenkel, 'Trade with Sicily', nn. 1, 2, trans. S171, S182 and Goitein and Friedman, *India Traders*, n. III, 48), but these are only two out of over forty *geniza* letters for the twelfth-century central and western Mediterranean. For Italian attacks on Arab merchant ships, see also *Annali genovesi*, 1, ed. Belgrano, pp. 28, 29. Conversely, by no means all pirates were Italian; see, e.g., Canard, 'Une lettre', pp. 129–31, for Jerba pirates in the 1130s. Pirates are, anyway, a guide to the density of trading, not to its failure, or else there would be no one to prey on; see, e.g., Horden and Purcell, *The corrupting sea*, pp. 156–8.

[302] Al-Idrīsī, *Nuzhat al-mushtāq*, trans. Jaubert and Nef, pp. 282, 312; Nikulás Bergsson, *Leiðarvísir*, ed. and trans. Simek, pp. 481, 486; Benjamin of Tudela, *The itinerary*, trans. Adler, p. 2; for Marseille, see Schaube, *Handelsgeschichte*, p. 186.

resonance if there was no one in these ports except Italians—and anyway many of the citations are rather more specific than that.

Furthermore, by the twelfth century there seems to have been a much more extensive Egyptian traffic with Syria, via the Crusader ports of (in particular) Acre and Tyre, than we can say for certain existed in the eleventh. Arabic-script letters survive which attest to it, especially those sent to Amīnaddīn, which show considerable scale, but others as well (see pp. 109–10 above). The *geniza* has Damascus trading documents for the twelfth century too, as many as for the eleventh, so in proportionately higher numbers. Egyptian and other Muslim traders turn up in several narrative sources for the Levant as well; and in the Caesarea excavations of the late tenth to late twelfth centuries, Egyptian ceramics were particularly prominent, although we cannot be sure, of course, who brought them.[303] Clearly, the existence and hostility of the Crusader states had only a relative effect on the Egypt–Levant trade, which, indeed, arguably increased, rather than decreased. This would have a later history too; the major enterprises of the Egyptian Kārimī merchants, who begin to be attested in Indian Ocean trading in the twelfth century and expanded from there, had a Syrian element as well in the late thirteenth and fourteenth century, at their height.[304]

This, as a collection of data, is quite substantial, going well beyond the anecdotal by now, and hardly supports the argument that the Egyptians were driven off the sea by the Italians; indeed, they seem to have extended their geographical reach. It does not, however, mean that Egyptians were as active in Mediterranean trade in the twelfth century as they had been before 1100. The core bulk element in the Egyptian trading of the eleventh century was, of course, flax; it was this trade that established the merchants we have documentation for as really large-scale dealers. As we shall see in Chapter 3, the flax trade lessened dramatically as the eleventh century turned into the twelfth, perhaps the result of a far less organic link between Muslim-ruled Egypt and now Christian-ruled Sicily, which had

[303] For the twelfth-century *geniza*, see T-S 8.196, 16.247, 8J5.4 (ed. Weiss, *Legal documents*, nn. 20, 85, 109), Halper 344 (ed. Goitein and Friedman, *India book* IV/B, n. 89), DK 237.1, DK 353, T-S 10J12.27, 13J26.22, 18J4.20 (Gil K90). For narratives, see, e.g., Usāma b. Munqidh, *Kitāb al-iʿtibār*, trans. Cobb, pp. 94–5 (Muslim pilgrims from the Maghreb, captured by Christians off the Palestinian coast); Ibn al-Qalānisī, *al-Maʿrūf bi-Dhayl tārīkh Dimashq*, trans. Le Tourneau, p. 101 (Damascus merchants in Egypt in 1110–11); Ibn Jubayr, *Riḥla*, trans. Broadhurst, pp. 301, 313, 324 (trade between Egypt and Damascus unaffected by war); and cf. Strehlke, *Tabulae ordinis theutonici*, n. 3 (Egyptian caravans going to Baghdad across the territory of the kingdom of Jerusalem in 1161). For ceramics, see Arnon, *Caesarea maritima*, pp. 42–8, 54; cf., more generically, Avissar and Stern, *Pottery*, pp. 34–5, 37 (however, in general in the kingdom of Jerusalem, there is less Egyptian pottery in the twelfth than the eleventh century). See also al-Makhzūmī, *Minhāj*, trans. Cahen, 'Douanes', p. 287 for the Egypt–Syria link in the later twelfth century; that text also mentions grain exports from Egypt, which in one case, dated to 1185/6, are on boats which arrived in Damietta empty (ibid., p. 292; cf. also 287, 289–90, 310), which implies to me a cabotage network which is most plausibly with the Levant ports. Many of the sea-going merchants' names in that text are also clearly Muslim; see ibid., esp. pp. 303–8.

[304] See, e.g., Labib, *Handelsgeschichte Ägyptens*, pp. 112–21, 204, 229–31, 402–4; Ashtor, 'The Kārimī merchants'; Abulafia, 'Asia, Africa', pp. 437–43; for their beginnings, see Bramoullé, *Les Fatimides et la mer*, pp. 571–3, 582–4.

needed to be particularly tight for flax to be sent to be turned into linen so far across the sea, as well as of a partial breakdown of the economic coherence of Ifrīqiya, flax's other central Mediterranean destination. Egypt's major export virtually stopped in the space of a generation; and Egypt's own Mediterranean trading is likely to have decreased simply because of this.

This would in itself help to explain why Italians are so much better documented in Egyptian trading from here on. They had not driven Egyptian merchants away, but they were interested in different trade goods, and also had different ones to offer to the inhabitants of the Nile valley. Italians are, indeed, henceforth better documented not simply in their own commercial record, but in narratives as well. Benjamin of Tudela's evocations of merchants from many lands extended to Alexandria as well, and this time were even more fulsome, as well as definitely stressing Italians; William of Tyre in the 1170s said much the same, describing the *Orientalium et Occidentalium... concursus populorum*, and mentioning the spice trade as he did so. The Genoese and Pisans also made trade treaties with the Egyptians, which could well have been the case for the Venetians too, who were probably the largest group in Egypt.[305] They went above all to Alexandria, and more occasionally Fusṭāṭ-Cairo, with, for the Venetians, Damietta as well (by now, significantly, not Tinnīs, which was losing ground rapidly in the twelfth century).[306] And, particularly concretely, two *geniza* letters themselves show that Italians were by now sufficiently prominent in trading with Alexandria and even Fusṭāṭ that their absence could create problems. In the first, the ruler of Egypt imprisons Genoese merchants, very probably in the context of Genoese help to the Crusaders in the early twelfth century, and business comes 'to a halt', apparently because business uncertainty extended to everyone; in the second, in 1133, business was in the previous year again at 'a standstill, because no one came in from the Maghreb, and only a few Rūm arrived', which implies a by now greater role for non-Egyptian merchants.[307] We will look at all this in more detail in Chapter 6, when we look at the way each of the three Italian port cities managed their twelfth-century projection into the Mediterranean. Here, though, we need to look, at least in summary terms, at what they wanted from Egypt, and what the Egyptians wanted from them.

[305] Benjamin of Tudela, *The itinerary*, ed. and trans. Adler, p. 75; William of Tyre, *Chronicon*, ed. Huygens, 19.27 (2, pp. 902–3). For the treaties, see Chapter 6, nn. 174, 224 below, and cf. p. 516 for Venice; Constable, *Housing the stranger*, pp. 113–26. See further pp. 353–6 below for Byzantine traders.

[306] Venetians in Damietta: *DCV*, nn. 41, 74, 77, 179, N23, 265, 301 (see Chapter 6, n. 92 below, for these abbreviations), and Lanfranchi, *Famiglia Zusto*, n. 6. Genoese in Fusṭāṭ-Cairo: *Giovanni Scriba*, n. 111, 661, to which can be added al-Makhzūmī, *Minhāj*, trans. Cahen, 'Douanes', p. 297. For Tinnīs, cf. p. 95 above; but the *Minhāj*, pp. 293–7, 311–12, discusses customs dues and customs organization in Tinnīs alongside those of Alexandria and Damietta. Even though by now it was seen as the least important port of the three, it was clearly still active into the late twelfth century.

[307] See Bodl. MS Heb. b 3/26 (Gil K794), T-S 13J33.1; both are quoted by Goitein, *MS*, 1, p. 45.

We have nearly sixty contracts for Venetian trade with Egypt up to 1180, well over half from the 1160s and the 1170s, which marked its height in this century; for Genoa, we have ninety from the first of the city's notarial registers, that of Giovanni Scriba, for the years 1154–64. Only a minority make any explicit reference to goods at all, nine for Venice, twenty-one for Genoa; the others only mention money. (The latter figures, I should add, are hardly changed if we were to add in the documents for the last two decades of the century; Italian trading dropped dramatically during and after the Third Crusade of 1189–92 anyway, as Saladin put a trade embargo on Italian shipping.)[308] How we should understand the dominance of money in Italian contracts we will look at later, but it has to be said at the start that it means that these references to goods are themselves anecdotal, even if the contracts are numerous. All the same, the texts are at least consistent in one respect: the goods mentioned as coming from Egypt, in sixteen contracts, were almost exclusively spices, dyestuffs, and alum.[309] This fits with the obsession with pepper which had struck the *geniza* observers of eleventh-century Rūmī trading, and not in a positive way (see p. 134 above). But if that is all the Italians wanted from Egypt, even in the twelfth century, then they were almost exclusively dealing in luxuries and materials for dyeing cloth; and although dyestuffs are closer to being bulk goods, we would not really need to spend much space here on them at all.

We cannot conclude this, all the same. Luxuries do not take up enough space in ships—or, if they do, then not many ships are needed to carry them (for if more were needed, they would be bulk goods, not luxuries); anyway, as Goldberg has stressed, luxury goods had pricings which were too volatile to be a secure basis for more than speculative or occasional trading.[310] As with the eleventh century, linen from the cloth towns would be a very likely addition (we have some sign of it for Venice; see p. 519 below), and it is hardly conceivable that sugar, not a luxury in Egypt (although much more so in Latin Europe) would not have continued to be as much in demand in the twelfth century as the eleventh. At least a few ceramics came too, at least to Venice and Pisa (pp. 527, 571). And, indeed, we have direct proof of most of this in al-Makhzūmī's *Minhāj*, which mentions the export of (among many other commodities) linen and sugar, plus leather and alum (but,

[308] The Venetian contracts are all in *DCV* (including *Nuovi documenti*), plus *CDVE*, 11, n. 2420 (see Chapter 6, n. 79 below), and Lanfranchi, *Famiglia Zusto*, nn. 6, 16, 19; and for Genoa, see *Giovanni Scriba*. For the trade embargo, see, e.g., Cahen, *Orient et Occident*, p. 151.

[309] *DCV*, nn. 11, 261–2, 266; *Giovanni Scriba*, nn. 1, 111, 113–14, 238, 243, 252, 425–7, 435, 661; cf. also Amari, *I diplomi arabi*, 2ª serie, nn. 8, 9 for alum. The single exception is a reference to cotton in *Giovanni Scriba*, n. 1; cf. the cotton sent from Alexandria to Genoa cited in a toll list from the 1130s (see Chapter 6, n. 172 below); this matches with the cotton export references in al-Makhzūmī, *Minhāj*, trans. Cahen, 'Douanes', pp. 287, 295. But its scale is very unclear; in Genoa, in fact, most cotton came from Sicily; see pp. 257–9, 547–9 below .

[310] Goldberg, *Trade and institutions*, p. 278.

here, not pepper), and, overall, discusses bulk goods rather more than spices.[311] So it is most likely that the rare references to Egyptian exports in Italian texts are only there to stress particular requests for luxury goods from particular investors, rather than to provide a guide for us as to what was normally transported, to make up most of the cargo of a trading ship.

What the Italians exported to Egypt in Venetian and Genoese contracts was even more heterogeneous. Coral appears twice in Genoese texts, saffron twice as well; these, and the silk and gold mentioned once each, were again luxuries, and also luxuries which the Genoese were simply intermediaries for: the coral and gold came from their North African trading, the silk probably from Spain, the saffron perhaps from either Spain or Tuscany. The few known Venetian trading goods, although this time not luxuries, were also mostly ones they were intermediaries for, this time from the Byzantine lands which made up the main part of their trading interests: cloth and horsehair from Constantinople and olive oil from Sparta; plus timber from Verona, which we will return to in a moment.[312] We cannot construct from these few citations any sense of what the Egyptians might have thought they wanted from Italy. But here, at least, other evidence gives us more of an idea of what Egyptian needs really were: it came down to two basic and this time definitely bulk commodities, timber and iron, both of which, as we have already seen, the Nile valley largely lacked, and which Italy had plenty of. These certainly need some discussion here.

Egypt was particularly poor in iron—it had some, but far too little to supply its active ironworking. The full range of where it got iron from in our period is impossible to see in the absence of good evidence (there are many alternatives, and probably many were used), but iron is prominent in al-Makhzūmī's *Minhāj*, which makes it clear, if we had doubted it, that it was indeed shipped to the Mediterranean ports, presumably on a regular basis.[313] Italian sources certainly show that it was imported from there in the twelfth century, probably particularly from Pisa's iron industry, but perhaps also from Venice, which also had ironworking. Its exact scale is hidden from us, for papal prohibitions insisted on its

[311] Al-Makhzūmī, *Minhāj*, trans. Cahen, 'Douanes', pp. 282–97; cf. ibid., 230–4. The text does not specify where the exports were going to, but the foreign merchants most systematically mentioned in it are Rūm, i.e. Italians or Byzantines, with Venetians and Genoese sometimes referred to explicitly (ibid., pp. 304–5, 308).

[312] *Giovanni Scriba*, nn. 105, 117, 435, 882 (silk to be sold for alum), 894, 12A; *DCV*, nn. 65, 149, 159, 248; Lanfranchi, *Famiglia Zusto*, n. 6. This can be set against the *Minhāj*, trans. Cahen, 'Douanes', pp. 293–4, which envisages the import into Egypt of (among bulk goods) ceramics, millstones, woollens, and even linen, here again showing the complexities of exchange, for the same text stresses linen exports too; but the letters to Amīnaddīn (see p. 109 above) are anyway probably the best source to show the very wide range of goods which could go by sea around 1200.

[313] Al-Makhzūmī, *Minhāj*, trans. Cahen, 'Douanes', pp. 282, 293, 297, with, for discussion, 258–9; Bramoullé, *Les Fatimides et la mer*, pp. 659–60. See ibid, pp. 653–4, 656, 661–2 for other evidence of iron imports, and esp. Jacoby, 'The supply of war materials to Egypt'. For iron sources as effectively absent in Egypt, see, e.g., Lombard, *Les métaux*, pp. 162–5.

illegality by 1179 at the latest, so regular citations of it might not appear in contracts; but we know for certain that the Pisans did bring it to Egypt, for their 1154 and 1173 trade treaties make this explicit. A source of nearly a century later indeed claims that in 1174 Saladin wrote to the caliph of Baghdad, remarking that the Venetians, Pisans, and Genoese, who were attacking Alexandria with the king of Sicily, had themselves supplied the weapons the Egyptians defended themselves with.[314] This is a good story, rather than documentary proof, but it certainly illustrates the degree to which the Egyptians were seen to be relaxed about their iron sourcing. And if, as is evident, this sourcing was very often in Italian ships, then this provides us with one clear example of the bulk goods which went from Italy to Egypt.

As to timber, Middle and Upper Egypt had acacia wood, which could be used for boats, including warships (it is also well adapted to furniture and other indoor uses), and in the Fāṭimid and Ayyūbid period acacia forests were controlled by the state for the supply of the fleet, as Ibn Mammātī tells us.[315] But for any major naval activity, larger timbers were also desirable, and they had to be imported. North-eastern Sicily and Lebanon could provide timber from inside the Fāṭimid state, and we have evidence (see p. 188 below) that at least Sicily did so. When the Fāṭimids lost control of these regions in the later eleventh century, Egypt was pushed onto the open market, which also included both Italy and the wooded areas of southern Anatolia (the first always, and the second often, transported by Italian ships). Venetian timber exports seem to have been continuous, given that a duke of Venice already in 971, on Byzantine instructions, sought to prohibit the export of timber; but they were probably small-scale before 1100, given both easier alternative supplies up to the mid-eleventh century and the fact that the eleventh century was the low point for Fāṭimid naval activity, with a rapid revival only after that. The Pisans and the Genoese followed in the twelfth century, despite, here too, church prohibitions. In the Pisan case, the Egyptian treaties and the 1156 Jerusalem treaty again make this explicit. One Arabic-script document for the early twelfth century makes timber export to Egypt clear for Genoa (and Amalfi)

[314] For prohibitions, see esp. Third Lateran Council, ch. 24 (a. 1179, ed. Tanner, *Decrees*, 1, p. 223). For the Pisan treaties, Amari, *I diplomi arabi*, 2ª serie, nn. 2, 7; the export of iron and arms (and timber and pitch) to Egypt is reinforced, earlier, by a clause in a Jerusalem trade treaty of 1156, which gives Pisans free passage in the kingdom unless they are found bringing these four items to sell in *terra Egypti*; see Caroti, *Le pergamene*, n. 65 (= Müller, *Documenti*, n. 5); cf. Jacoby, 'The supply of war materials to Egypt', pp. 106–7. For Saladin, Abū Shāma (d. 1268), *Kitāb al-rawḍatayn*, partial ed. and trans. Barbier de Meynard, p. 178. For Pisan and Venetian ironworking, see pp. 524, 566–74 below.

[315] See Lombard, *Espaces et réseaux*, pp. 128–40, which, however, exaggerates the absence of timber in Egypt. For acacia, see esp. Bahgat, 'Les forêts en Égypte', and his major source, Ibn Mammātī, *Qawānīn*, trans. Cooper, 9.22, pp. 288–9. See also Müller-Wodarg, 'Das Landwirtschaft Ägyptens', 2, p. 69. Although Ibn Mammātī states that acacia (and other wood for shipbuilding) can be found in Middle Egypt, it is very rare in APD, where I have only found it once, in CPR XXI 26 (ninth/tenth century). For an archaeological find in Qusayr on the Red Sea coast, probably dating to the eleventh to thirteenth centuries, of acacia wood which is apparently reused ship timber, see van der Veen, *Consumption, trade*, pp. 210–11, 224; here the ships must have been seagoing.

too, and a Genoese text from 1147 shows that the archbishop of Genoa was routinely taking a cut from ships sold in Alexandria.[316] So do an interesting set of contracts for Genoese merchants going to Alexandria in Giovanni Scriba's register which refer to what happens if the ship is sold rather than returning to Italy; this is generally expressed in formulaic terms, and is by no means stressed in the texts, but it is fairly clear that in the years around 1160 such sales continued to be routine. Selling a ship was for all parties a quicker and easier way to export wood than was transporting it in (or floating behind) a ship; but we do have a single contract for Venice for 1173 which shows one merchant apparently planning to do that, and on a considerable scale—1400 timber logs from Verona and 600 planks of fir—even if, for unspecified reasons, the contract was cancelled three months later.[317] From 1100 onwards, anyway, it is likely that these imports increased considerably, and will have been one of the impulses for the further development of north–south links across the twelfth century.

David Bramoullé shows very clearly in his book on the Fāṭimid navy how important iron and timber imports were to the state. As often in Egypt, with this importance went public institutional elaboration: in Alexandria and elsewhere, there was an institution, the Matjar, dedicated to buying materials for shipbuilding in Egypt's arsenal at Fusṭāṭ, plus other goods necessary to the state, very often from the Italians. Bramoullé, however, seems to me to exaggerate the degree to which the twelfth-century Egyptian state was in a weak position here. He sees the developing Fāṭimid interest in the Red Sea as a product of desperation: spices were all the Egyptians had to exchange for iron and timber, so the Indian Ocean trade—plus customs tolls to pay for shipbuilding—was by now vital for Fāṭimid survival.[318] But the wealth of the Egyptian state was always based on the land tax, far more than on customs dues; and I have already strongly doubted that spices and dyestuffs were the only export elements in Egypt-Italy trade. And, although shipbuilding was not cheap, I find it hard to see how it was so expensive that a permanent fleet in the twelfth century of eighty to ninety ships could have been such an existential commitment for the Fāṭimids, if a single middle-level merchant

[316] For 971, see Cessi, *Documenti*, 2, n. 49. See, e.g., Jacoby, 'Byzantine trade with Egypt', esp. pp. 35–6, 46–61, with some caution; for Venice, see also pp. 503, 508 below. For timber imports, see once again al-Makhzūmī, *Minhāj*, trans. Cahen, 'Douanes', pp. 282, 284, 293, 302, with commentary at pp. 258–60 and esp. Bramoullé, *Les Fatimides et la mer*, pp. 649–62, a general survey of Fāṭimid timber commerce. For Genoa and Amalfi, see P.SternItalianMerchants; for 1147, see Belgrano, 'Il registro della curia arcivescovile', p. 404.

[317] For selling ships, see *Giovanni Scriba*, nn. 104, 578 (the least formulaic), 610, 699, 708, 876; cf. also al-Makhzūmī, *Minhāj*, trans. Cahen, 'Douanes', p. 284. The Venetians sold ships abroad too, although we do not have examples of them doing so in Egypt; see Borsari, *Venezia e Bisanzio*, pp. 125–7. For Venice in 1173, see *DCV*, n. 248; later, two Venetian ships with timber were said to have arrived in Alexandria around 1200, as a *geniza* letter attests: T-S 10J31.13 (ed. Zeldes and Frenkel, 'Trade with Sicily', n. 4, trans. S205).

[318] Bramoullé, *Les Fatimides et la mer*, pp. 662–9 for the Matjar, 685–90, 698–700 for the general model of Fāṭimid weakness (he does not discuss the land tax here).

in Venice, Romano Mairano, could buy his own ship several times,[319] and if the Pisans could build forty-seven war galleys in one go, in or soon after 1166 (see p. 561 below). Even though the Pisans had had to take out a large loan to do so, and even though wood was local and, therefore, cheaper, they were still a single city, with resources immeasurably inferior to those of the whole Egyptian economy. Al-Makhzūmī's *Minhāj* is anyway rather more matter-of-fact: it simply envisages that alum was traded directly for timber.[320] I would instead see these two imports as the only ones the Egyptians really wanted from Italy, to set against not only spices and alum but also cloth and sugar, and leather, and doubtless many other finished goods which the Egyptians could provide, not only to Italy but also to other Mediterranean regions—the finished goods which we have seen being exchanged in every town and village in Egypt, many of which were by no means being made as systematically anywhere else around the inland sea as yet. And we should also remember that Egypt's shortage of both commodities was very twelfth-century-specific; Saladin's conquests in the late 1180s will have made it far easier to get timber from the mountains of Lebanon again, and quite possibly iron from the much more substantial deposits in Anatolia, now largely under Selcuk control (we have evidence for the latter for the 1260s–1270s, at least[321]); and Saladin could also block Italian trading during and after the Third Crusade without a qualm. What did not change, either before 1100 or after, or indeed after 1200, was the fact that Egypt was in economic terms the strongest region of the Mediterranean.[322] On the Italian side, as we shall see at length, Venetians were most interested in Byzantium, Genoese most interested in Sicily; but everyone wanted to go to Egypt too, as the one inescapable focus of trading, taken as a whole.

So Egypt dominated Mediterranean trade in the eleventh century, and, even if it was by now less systematically carried in Egyptian ships, it did so in the twelfth century as well. But it is important to repeat that that same Mediterranean trade was not vital for Egypt itself, except, again, for iron and at least some timber. It was convenient for Egypt to be able to buy olive oil rather than local oils, and Indian Ocean dyes to extend the range of locally made ones (which, however, continued to be produced); it was also highly convenient that in the eleventh century Ifrīqiya

[319] Borsari, *Venezia e Bisanzio*, pp. 121–9.

[320] Al-Makhzūmī, *Minhāj*, trans. Cahen, 'Douanes', p. 302; cf. 260; Ibn Mammātī, *Qawānīn*, trans. Cooper, 9.7, p. 277, says much the same (here alum is used to pay for two-thirds of all Matjar purchases over and above customs dues, and gold for the other third)—cf. 9.8, pp. 278–9, for alum in general, seen as a state monopoly.

[321] Anatolian iron (and timber) in the 1260s–1270s, exported via Cilician Armenia; see Jacoby, 'The supply of war materials to Egypt', pp. 119–26.

[322] Later chapters will make this still clearer. For one region unstudied here, the Levant, see Heyd, *Histoire du commerce du Levant*, I, pp. 378–400, Schaube, *Handelsgeschichte*, pp. 145–69, 178–90 (he is explicit at 145), and more recently Cahen, *Orient and Occident*, pp. 131–42; all argue effectively for the greater trading importance of Egypt by comparison with the Levant in our period.

and Sicily were very keen to buy Egyptian flax and thus pump money into the Egyptian countryside and the merchant houses of Fusṭāṭ. But it was not essential. It was more essential for Ifrīqiya and Sicily, which needed imports of flax—much as, later, the north Italian cloth industry could not have expanded as far as it did without imports of raw cotton and, after 1200, wool, from Sicily, North Africa, Syria, and eventually Castile and England. But Egypt itself would have carried on with little change without any of the Mediterranean trade discussed in this section; it would simply have developed its flax and probably sugar production less intensively, and gone back to eating inferior oil, and building ships from acacia. It might have become more involved with the interregional system in later centuries, but never as much as Italy, in particular, did. The whole commercial spine of the eleventh-century Mediterranean, and to a large extent in the twelfth as well, was, rather, an epiphenomenon of Egypt's internal commercial activity, a spin-off of all that complex hierarchy of buying and selling along the Nile. By the late twelfth century, as we shall see, there were more foci around the sea, but Egypt was still the central one. That is to say, the vitality of the Egyptian exchange sector encouraged an openness to the Mediterranean world, but only as an add-on to the internal exchange which continued to be the most important element of the Egyptian economy. For that Mediterranean world to open up in return, however, depended on the internal development of the economic structures of its neighbours. For it takes two regions to make an interregional commercial system; and it takes two regions with a complex internal economy to make a complex interregional system. How that happened we shall see in all the following chapters.

3

North Africa and Sicily

One often has the sense that the *geniza* merchants of Egypt saw Sicily and the central section of North Africa—Ifrīqiya in medieval Arabic—as, in effect, the same place.[1] A large shipment of fifty-four bales of flax, sent out from Alexandria by the Tustarī family in the 1020s, was destined for Sicily, but the local agent heard that the Zīrid *amīr* of Ifrīqiya, al-Muʿizz b. Bādis, had won a major battle; so he instead moved most of the shipment to Kairouan, the main inland Ifrīqiyan political centre, presumably via the major port on the Tunisian coast, Mahdia. Around 1030, an agent of Fusṭāṭ's other great Jewish merchant of the same period, Ibn ʿAwkal, related that in the middle of selling flax in Mahdia, he heard that prices were higher in Sicily, so immediately took the remaining flax across the channel to *al-Jazīra*, 'the island', even if then, sadly, he met a storm and lost much of the merchandise, and after that found that Palermo prices were not better after all.[2] The sea, as ever, presented its own risks, but in the minds of many merchants the 400 kilometres of water from Mahdia to Palermo were no real barrier. Until the mid-eleventh century the two regions had the same rulers, the Aghlabids in the ninth century, who conquered most of Sicily from their North African base, and then after 909 the Fāṭimids, the latter initially ruling directly, and then (after

[1] See also Udovitch, 'New materials', pp. 188–90. Ifrīqiya had a malleable boundary, and could include quite a lot of the North African coastline north of the Sahara; but I shall mean by it here what is now Tunisia, plus eastern Algeria from Béjaïa eastwards, and the Libyan coast as far as Tripoli and Leptis Magna, a usage which more or less reflects the commonest medieval one. Twentieth-century historiography in French often calls the region 'la Berbérie orientale', a phrase I shall avoid. Tunisia was the core of this region, and I will sometimes call it 'Tunisia' for simplicity and variation. When I use the term 'Maghreb', it will denote North Africa west of Tripoli in general; the word in Arabic just means 'the land of the west'. The term 'Maghribīs' in the *geniza* and (in particular) in *geniza* historiography (see Goldberg, *Trade and institutions*, pp. 43–5 for the distinction), however, refers to merchants in Fusṭāṭ whose families came from Ifrīqiya.

As noted in Chapter 1, in this chapter I shall use the modern French spellings of place names in North Africa, as used in the countries concerned, not the classical Arabic (so Kairouan not Qayrawān), except for settlements now abandoned. For Sicily I shall use modern Italian names throughout, including Enna for the medieval and early modern Castrogiovanni—the 'Giovanni' is, anyway, itself derived from classical 'Enna', as is shown by, e.g., a *geniza* letter, Moss. II,128 (Gil K460 [S158]), citing Qaṣr Īnī, and twelfth-century Arabic documents, Cusa, *I diplomi*, nn. 23, 169 (pp. 402–3, 496–8), for Qaṣr Yāna; cf. Malaterra, *De rebus gestis*, ed. Pontieri, 2.16, 17, 32, 46, etc., for Castrum Iohannis). I am very grateful to Lisa Fentress, Caroline Goodson, and Annliese Nef for reading the Africa sections, Lucia Arcifa, Alessandra Molinari, and Annliese Nef for reading those on Sicily, and to David Bramoullé, Jeremy Johns, and Viva Sacco for advice and unpublished texts.

[2] Bodl. MS Heb. d 66/15, T-S Ar. 5.1 (Gil K158, 176 [S43, 48]). Note that Kairouan was seldom in our period actually a capital in the sense of the seat of government, for it had smaller palace cities around it which usually fulfilled that role (see, e.g., Goodson, 'Topographies of power'); but it was Ifrīqiya's major centre until the 1050s, and I shall sometimes call it a capital for convenience.

The Donkey and the Boat. Chris Wickham, Oxford University Press. © Chris Wickham 2023.
DOI: 10.1093/oso/9780198856481.003.0003

948 in Sicily, 972 in Ifrīqiya) through families of Kalbid and Zīrid *amīrs* who at least formally looked to the Fāṭimids. People moved their bases from Africa to Sicily because of famine in the 1000s or war in the 1050s, and then others moved from Sicily back to Africa, again because of war, in the 1060s.[3] It was indeed common to have bases in both.[4]

That is the main reason for treating these two regions together. A second reason is that the evidence for both of them (especially Ifrīqiya) is far less extensive than for Egypt, so treatment of each has to be less detailed, and sometimes more speculative. The first, however, is the more important. Despite the sea channel between Africa and Sicily, and despite the political breakdown which followed the mid-eleventh century—with the fragmentation of Ifrīqiyan political power and the Norman conquest of Sicily—they really did, to a large extent, make up a single economic region, the most active in the central Mediterranean until the late twelfth century at the earliest. Looking at them in close parallel is thus not only defensible but necessary. So I shall discuss each in turn, North Africa and then Sicily, but will also analyse them together, when discussing the *geniza* in the middle of the chapter—which will act as a bridge between the North African and the Sicilian sections—and when generalizing at the end. The two regions need to be looked at in that order, for the evidence for Ifrīqiya, both documentary and archaeological, is much stronger for the period before 1080 or so; by contrast, although the archaeology takes us all the way through for Sicily, its non-*geniza* documentary and narrative sources privilege above all the second half of our period, from the 1060s onwards.

3.1 North Africa as a Historical Problem

The provinces of 'Africa' were among the richest in the Roman Empire. They exported major quantities of grain from the rich farmlands of the Medjerda river valley, running down to the sea some 20 kilometres north of Tunis (senators regularly had estates there), and from other parts of northern Tunisia and the coast to the west; the largest source of olive oil in the empire was the huge olive

[3] T-S 12.372, Moss. II,128 (L 130) (Gil K513, 460 [S111, 158]); Ibn 'Idhārī, *al-Bayān al-mughrib*, trans. Fagnan, 1, p. 380.

[4] Bases in both: e.g. Halper 389 (Gil K751 [S151]) for Salāma b. Mūsā; see Goldberg, *Trade and institutions*, pp. 296–300, 331–2, for Salāma and the way his *jāh*, his local prestige, worked in both regions of the central Mediterranean (but only there). For signs of landowning in both regions, see n. 54 below for the *Life* of Jawdhar, an important tenth-century Fāṭimid minister, and pp. 187–8 below for what more can be said thanks to this important near-contemporary text. For the possible Sicilian landowning of Jawdhar's contemporary and near-homonym the Fāṭimid general Jawhar, see also Amari, *Le epigrafi arabiche di Sicilia*, 1, n. 1 (pp. 11–17), for a Jaw[...] in an inscription who had buildings built in the 950s in Termini Imerese on the north coast; Amari is far from certain it is the general, and indeed it could be Jawdhar for that matter, but the names are not so common.

forests around Sfax and other cities in the Tunisian coastal south; and fine Red Slip ceramic productions from both areas were dominant in the tableware market of the whole Mediterranean into the seventh century.[5] But they are not treated like this in the historiography of our own period. Ifrīqiya, if anything, is seen as an economic failure, either because it faced crisis in the early eleventh century or because its economy was destroyed by invasions of nomads from the south-east in the 1050s—these were the Banū Hilāl, who were said to have been sent by the rulers of Egypt to undermine the power of the Zīrids, after the latter had in 1048/9 formally rejected Fāṭimid legitimate authority and recognized the ʿAbbāsid caliph instead. Both of these arguments are problematic; the second is better based in the sources, but all the same has substantial difficulties, which we need to look at carefully.

Ifrīqiya gained effective independence under the Aghlabids, who ruled it, without paying more than lip service to the ʿAbbāsid caliphs, from 800 to 909. They were then overthrown by the first great general of the Fāṭimid armies, Abū ʿAbd Allāh, who had united the Kutāma Berber tribes of the eastern Algerian highlands and who eventually conquered Kairouan, together with Raqqāda, its palace city just outside, before he called in the first Fāṭimid *imam*, al-Mahdī, to rule the newly established state, in 909. This was a Shīʿa victory, as we saw in Chapter 2, and al-Mahdī called himself caliph in 910, the only legitimate caliph in the Islamic lands in his eyes and in those of his followers. Al-Mahdī established a stable government under his own authority (Abū ʿAbd Allāh himself, his only possible rival, was executed in 911); he based himself in Kairouan and Raqqāda, but then moved to his own palace city and new capital on the coast at Mahdia in 921. The third Fāṭimid, al-Manṣūr, defeated another Berber religious uprising in 946–7, and immediately built a further palace city, once more very close to Kairouan, at Ṣabra, called from then on al-Manṣūriya; the caliphs shifted from here to Mahdia and back for the rest of their time in Ifrīqiya, before another general, Jawhar, took Egypt for them in 969 and they moved to Cairo in 972–3.[6] From then on, the Zīrid *amīr*s ruled in Ifrīqiya, both before and after their rejection of Fāṭimid authority, up to their own fall in the 1140s. They were based first in Ṣabra al-Manṣūriya, and then, after the invasion of the Banū Hilāl in the 1050s, back in Mahdia.

To understand the political systems of our period a little better, we need to see this geographically (see Map 8). Roman Africa had been ruled from the rich agricultural north, with a capital at Carthage, on the sea just to the east of modern Tunis. But the conquering Arabs in the seventh century replaced Carthage as a

[5] For a survey, see Wickham, *Framing*, esp. pp. 17–22, 163, 720–8; more recently, Bonifay, 'Africa'; Hobson, *The North African boom*; Dossey, *Peasant and empire*, pp. 62–97.

[6] See in general Dachraoui, *Le califat fatimide*; Halm, *The empire of the Mahdi*; Brett, *The rise of the Fatimids*.

capital with Kairouan, on the edge of the dry southern Tunisian steppe of the inland Sahel, often the home of pastoralists; this terrain, in fact, gets steadily less suitable for agriculture (unless it is irrigated) as one moves south, gradually, into the desert of the Sahara, and at different times in history it has been more agricultural or more pastoral. Carthage was virtually abandoned, and was replaced by Tunis as the main city of the north. Tunis was not, however, very politically active as a centre before the late eleventh century, nor (ever) was Béja, the other main northern town, located on a hill overlooking the Medjerda valley, even though these two controlled the major grain-growing areas of the region. The politics of Ifrīqiya revolved around Kairouan and its satellite cities, and the principal ports of the capital, Sousse and later Mahdia. So one does not actually hear very much in the narrative sources of our period about the grain areas or, indeed, about the great olive-groves on the coast south of Mahdia, around Sfax, at least until the governor of the latter pushed for his own independence in the 1060s–1090s.[7]

West of the lowlands of Tunisia, the land rises to the plateau of the Tell, which extends westwards far into Algeria, divided from the desert in the south by chains of mountains, the Aurès or the Hodna, which gradually turn into the Atlas. It is often good agricultural but also good pastoral land; like the inland Sahel, indeed, it can focus on either, and which focus is dominant at any given time has been crucial for the wider structures of the economy of the Maghreb. The Tell was always less urbanized, and more of a Berber-speaking area (Tunisia was mostly Latin- and later Arabic-speaking). Except for its main cities such as Timgad and Tébessa, it had been relatively marginal to Roman power; it had, it is true, some quite strong military defences, against Sahara nomads and internal unrest, but these by no means compared with the armies along the northern and eastern borders of the empire. Under Islamic rule, however—and indeed earlier, from the fifth century onwards—the Berber tribes who lived there became more active as political protagonists. Fāṭimid victory in 909 was, as already mentioned, the work of the Kutāma Berbers, recently turned Shʿīa, who lived in the Tell between Sétif and Constantine; the near-destruction of Fāṭimid power at the hands of another sectarian group, the Khārijites, in 944–7 (their leader, Abū Yazīd, took Kairouan itself in 944 and nearly took Mahdia, before al-Manṣūr fought them off) was the work of Berbers from the Aurès.[8]

This was the world later described by Ibn Khaldūn (d. 1406), the great political philosopher and historian. For him, the whole of the history of the Maghreb was one in which tribal groups, fortified by strong group loyalty or *ʿaṣabiyya*,

[7] For Sfax in this period, see the references in Idris, *La Berbérie orientale*, pp. 231–2, 249–51, 255–6, 285, 292–302.

[8] For Abū Yazīd, see Halm, *The empire of the Mahdi*, pp. 298–325; Brett, *The rise of the Fatimids*, pp. 165–75. See in general for the history of the Berbers Brett and Fentress, *The Berbers*; for the retribalization of the Tell, much of which was ancient Numidia, at the end of the Roman Empire, see Modéran, *Les Maures*, pp. 501–10, 541–61.

conquered the settled lands and established new dynasties, until they became more urbanized, more 'civilized' one might say, and thus weaker militarily, and were replaced by the next tribal group. Ibn Khaldūn actually thought this was a feature of the whole of Islamic history, which is not accurate—if the theory has any validity, it only fits state systems which are bounded by highlands and steppe, less accessible to state power, but also capable of sustaining fairly substantial populations, as the Maghreb surely is.[9] But it was also only a feature of polities which did not succeed in dominating these less accessible lands directly. The Romans had managed it; but tribal identities, including those in fully agricultural and settled areas, were by now rather stronger. The earliest account of the victories of Abū 'Abd Allāh and the Kutāma, by the early Fāṭimid theologian and jurist al-Qāḍī al-Nuʿmān, which, very unusually for Arabic-language narratives in the Maghreb, is nearly contemporary—it was finished in 957—puts the point quite clearly: the Kutāma, a settled community, are said to tell Abū 'Abd Allāh, when he first meets them, that they owe no allegiance to the cities around their lands, such as Sétif and Mila, and that the focus for the numerous tribes which make up their confederacy is simply the assembly (*jamāʿa*) of tribal chiefs.[10] This is a heavily idealized picture, but its imagery is still relevant. It was not thought to be easy to control the highlands by the tenth century, and one had to take their internal politics more seriously than the Romans had. It may, therefore, not be so surprising that the Zīrids, Berber themselves (from the Ṣanhāja tribal confederacy) but without the religious clout of the Fāṭimid caliphs, soon divided, and from 1016 a cadet branch, the Ḥammādids, established themselves as autonomous in the Tell, governing from a newly founded centre, today still called the Kalâa (or Qalʿa) des Béni Hammad; it was easier to rule the Tell from inside, rather than outside.[11] But all this also means that the Tell, like the inland Sahel, gets more attention in our narrative accounts than do the areas of Ifrīqiya which had the richest agrarian base.

The Ḥammādids were already publicly uncommitted to the Shʿīa caliphate, and, as we have seen, the Zīrid *amīr* al-Muʿizz (1016–62) joined them around 1049. Shīʿīs were demographically and politically marginal in Ifrīqiya after the Kutāma army had gone with the Fāṭimids to Egypt, although this was probably not the main reason for the break, and in fact al-Muʿizz accepted Fāṭimid hegemony again by 1057/8 at the latest. The break with Egypt might indeed not have been the main cause of the Hilālian invasion either: the Banū Hilāl, a confederacy of

[9] Ibn Khaldūn, *Kitab al-ʿIbar, Introduction*, trans. Rosenthal, esp. 1, pp. 282–99. For modern favourable comment, see—out of many—Gellner, *Muslim society*; and for a sharp critique, focussing on the rise of the Almohads, see Van Staëvel, 'La foi peut-elle soulever les montagnes?', a reference I owe to Annliese Nef.

[10] al-Qāḍī al-Nuʿmān, *Iftitāḥ al-daʿwa*, trans. Haji, ch. 5.

[11] See Idris, *La Berbérie orientale*, pp. 106–19 for the autonomy of Ḥammād b. Buluqqīn, the first of the family; for the Kalâa, see n. 39 below.

nomadic tribes living just outside the settled lands of the Nile, were, even before that date, moving west into what is now the Libyan semi-desert, and may not have been sent by the Egyptians at all.[12] Ibn Khaldūn, over three centuries later, called them a 'cloud of locusts', but there cannot have been all that many of them—large numbers cannot live in the Egyptian desert, or even in the backlands of Libya—and it was later seen as wholly unexpected that they should win their first major battle against the Zīrids, at Ḥaydarān in 1052.[13] They were not the conquerors that the Kutāma had been and, in fact, captured relatively few towns by force; they did not take Kairouan. But they did occupy the dry inland south of Tunisia, and, in particular, the lands around the capital, making it impossible to govern from there. Al-Mu'izz abandoned Ṣabra and Kairouan for Mahdia in 1057, leaving them to the Banū Hilāl to pillage. Kairouan was thereafter largely depopulated; as one of the *geniza* merchants in Mahdia sadly wrote, 'Only the poorest people are left there.' Furthermore, Gafsa and Sousse revolted in 1053/4, Sfax in 1059; the Banū Hilāl took Béja in 1054/5 and Gabès in 1062/3; the Ḥammādids controlled Tunis at least nominally from 1058/9 too—these being the largest provincial cities in the the Zīrid state.[14]

Our evidence for revolts here is mostly taken from late narratives, which it is always unwise to follow too trustingly; whatever the details, however, the Zīrid polity effectively broke up. The Ḥammādids too, who had taken advantage of the initial crisis, lost ground when the Hilālians also occupied part of the Tell and defeated them in battle, putting the Kalâa at strategic risk; in 1067/8 the Ḥammādid ruler al-Nāṣir moved his capital to Béjaïa, on the north coast of what is now eastern Algeria. The wider central Mediterranean geopolitical situation was furthermore by now unhelpful for the Zīrids, with Sicily by 1091 entirely in the hands of the Normans; in 1087 the Pisans and Genoese attacked Mahdia from the sea, sacking both the commercial suburb of Zawila and the capital itself, apart

[12] For a critique of the traditional account of the Egyptians sending the Banū Hilāl, see Brett, 'Fatimid historiography'; Brett, 'The flood of the dam'. His arguments are effective, but not conclusive; Schuster, *Die Beduinen*, pp. 60–9, is cautious about them too. The traditional story is recounted as well as anywhere else in Idris, *La Berbérie orientale*, pp. 206–18.

[13] Ibn Khaldūn, *Kitāb al-'Ibar*, trans. de Slane and Casanova, 1, p. 34. The claim in Sénac and Cressier, *Histoire du Maghreb médiéval*, pp. 109–10, that there were 'several hundreds of thousands' of Hilālians (even when modified, on the next page, to 'probably not over 200,000') is impossible, given the difficulty of maintaining large numbers of people in desert conditions, plus all contemporary military logistics. Kennedy, *The armies of the caliphs*, pp. 97–9, sees armies at the height of the 'Abbāsid Caliphate as being large if they were in the tens of thousands, with an estimated total of 100,000 paid soldiers for the entire caliphate; Schuster, *Die Beduinen*, p. 69, estimates around 3,000 Hilālians at Ḥaydarān on the basis of late sources.

[14] See Idris, *La Berbérie orientale*, pp. 222–31, 263–6, for the dates (Tunis gained its own autonomous rulers under a Ḥammādid hegemony); a more recent political history of the same period is Schuster, *Die Beduinen*. For the quotation, see T-S 16.179 (Gil K617 [S122]); the near-contemporary Spanish geographer al-Bakrī, *al-Masālik wa al-mamālik*, trans. de Slane, p. 61, said much the same—he never came to Africa, so his information may have been from the same sort of merchant informants as wrote T-S 16.179. The depopulation of Kairouan has back-up from the tombstones of the eleventh century too; see n. 72 below.

from the palace. That may have been the low point, however. By 1100, the Zīrid *amīr* Tamīm b. al-Mu'izz had retaken the coast from Tunis to Sfax, with occasional control farther south too, in Gabès and even Tripoli. Elsewhere, the north was largely under Ḥammādid hegemony; and the various groups of Hilālians mostly only held the inland steppes, with frontiers and allegiances which varied considerably, with the important addition of Béja and the upper Medjerda, which stayed in their hands.[15] But although this marks a measure of stability, internal war was the norm from the 1050s onwards, with cities constantly taken and retaken. Zīrid power was still considerable, but the *amīr*s depended on networks of ever-changing alliances, including by now the Normans in Sicily, alternately friends and enemies. In the end, they were not in a good position to resist the Normans, who conquered Mahdia and the rest of the east coast as far as Tripoli, putting a final end to the Zīrid state, in 1148. Sicilian rule did not last long either, however; by the end of the 1150s, the cities were in revolt. And, separately, the Almohads, another army based on a salvationist theology and Berber tribal loyalties, who had already rapidly conquered Morocco and most of al-Andalus in the 1140s, steadily moved across the Tell in the 1150s and took the east coast in 1159, uniting the whole of the Maghreb for the first time since the third century. The Almohads ended the instability which had marked the region for a century, but their peace left the Ifrīqiyans in a subject provincial situation such as they had not experienced since 800. This lasted beyond our period, until the long-lasting Ḥafṣid dynasty, based in Tunis, re-established effective independence in 1229 and for three hundred years on from that.[16]

For those who value strong state power, or even (less controversially) peace, the political history of the period 1050–1160 in North Africa is a depressing one. It is, nonetheless, not dissimilar to that experienced by al-Andalus in the eighty years after 1010, and also by northern Italy in the century after 1080, both of which also faced endless internal wars between newly autonomous cities and invasions by foreign armies; but these two are dealt with radically differently by the historiography—far less negatively—as we shall see in later chapters. Why, anyway, the Banū Hilāl (who were themselves defeated by the Almohads, along with every other North African power so far mentioned) should be seen as the cause of a crisis which marked the definitive end of Ifrīqiyan economic prosperity—and even agriculture, which was supposedly from now on replaced in many places by nomadic and semi-nomadic pastoralism—is not immediately clear. The direct causes of such an interpretation are threefold: first, a tendency by

[15] See in general Idris, *La Berbérie orientale*, pp. 249–302.

[16] King, 'Reframing the fall of the Zirid dynasty', describes early twelfth-century Zīrid power in more upbeat terms than do his predecessors. For the Normans in Africa, see Abulafia, 'The Norman kingdom of Africa'; Brett, 'Muslim justice'; De Simone, 'Ruggero II e l'Africa islamica'; Valérian, 'Conquêtes normandes'. For the Ḥafṣids, who need more study, see Brunschvig, *La Berbérie orientale*; Rouighi, *The making of a Mediterranean emirate*.

very many historians to accept the exact and highly coloured words of late sources (including Ibn Khaldūn, helped, of course, by his huge reputation, which far exceeds even that of al-Maqrīzī in Egypt, his younger contemporary); second, the false assumption by much traditional scholarship that there is a permanent, structural opposition between agriculturalists and pastoralists; and third, the felt need by too many historians to find a moment of crisis which would explain the apparent failure of North Africa in the modern era to match the wealth of the African provinces under Rome. We have seen in Chapters 1 and 2 that the first and third of these are common features of the historiography of our period, and I have argued against them already; in Ifrīqiya, the arguments are, if anything, more simplistic and more extreme. But counterarguments which have been offered are in many cases not much better. Let us look briefly at the debate, and then look at what local written sources we can actually use to get a sense of what changed in the underlying economic structures of North Africa in and after the 1050s. This will then act as a context which will allow us to make sense of our two best types of evidence for the exchange economy of the region, the archaeology and the *geniza*, which will be the focus of the following two sections.

The history of the medieval dynasties of Ifrīqiya has been dominated by substantial works in French, usually written in French or ex-French North Africa, one per dynasty. Mohamed Talbi on the Aghlabids restricts itself to political history, although Talbi wrote on agrarian society separately as well, as we shall see; Robert Brunschvig on the Ḥafṣids has the highest reputation, even though it was the earliest to be written, in the 1930s–1940s.[17] Hady Roger Idris on the Zīrids, published in 1962, is the most relevant for us, and also the most complete and the best-sourced. It does, however, stick very tightly to the narrative accounts at his disposal, all of them post-1200 (indeed, usually post-1300) compilations of lost contemporary histories whose accuracy cannot be tested; and Idris's judgement on the devastation of the Banū Hilāl is thus extreme—'crise', 'catastrophe', 'tourmente', 'anarchie' appear frequently in his pages.[18] This was sharply criticized by Jean Poncet in 1967, who did not hesitate to refer to the Hilālian 'myth' in the title of his article; for him, the crisis began half a century earlier, with the secession of the Ḥammādids, religious conflict, and serious fiscal problems, with the

[17] Talbi, *L'émirat aghlabide*; Brunschvig, *La Berbérie orientale*. For the politics and material culture of the Aghlabid period, see also the new directions in Anderson et al., *The Aghlabids*, and the thoughtful commentary on the image of Ifrīqiya in Arab sources in Nef, *L'état imperial islamique*, pp. 182–257.

[18] Idris, *La Berbérie orientale*. The earliest of the source compilations is by the Iraqi Ibn al-Athīr (d. 1233), *Kāmil fī al-tārīkh*, translated for its North African sections in Fagnan, *Annales du Maghreb*; the best, perhaps, is by the Moroccan Ibn ʿIdhārī (d. after 1313), *al-Bayān al-mughrib*, trans. Fagnan, 1; the longest is by Ibn Khaldūn (d. 1401), *Kitāb al-ʿIbar*, trans. de Slane and Casanova, 1–2. I add to the dynastic monographs, only to exclude it, Golvin, *Le Magrib Central à l'époque des Zirides*, a 1957 counterpart to Idris but focussed on Algeria; its racist romanticism leads to strangely contradictory arguments.

Banū Hilāl, although weak, acting as a 'revolutionary crisis', simply pushing over a tottering edifice; there was no economic collapse as a result (much of the damage to the economy was the work of the Zīrids themselves), and the outcome was simply the establishment of 'bourgeois republics' in the cities of the region. Poncet, despite his Marxisant rhetoric, set up a pretty vague (and also unfootnoted) argument, and Idris could defend his positions well enough the following year. Talbi did not do better in 1982, when he ascribed the early eleventh-century crisis not only to political conflict, but to the collapse of the slave mode of production itself, which somehow caused consistent famines in the early eleventh century and thus precipitated the Hilālian crisis; we will come to this highly unconvincing theory later (p. 173). Jacques Thiry accepted Talbi in 1995, although he also stressed the small numbers of Hilālians and the (indeed demonstrable) anti-nomad prejudice of the sources. Nor is Pierre Guichard more persuasive, arguing in the other direction in 2012; for him the supposedly total Hilālian takeover of the Tell simply represented the triumph of pastoralism. In a similar vein, for Philippe Sénac and Patrice Cressier in their short textbook published in the same year, cultivated estates returned to steppe and commerce declined.[19] None of these writers got much beyond presupposition in their arguments, and none is to be preferred to Idris, who, even if his arguments are, to me, greatly overstated, at least stuck to the sources.

There are more helpful analyses than these. Jacques Berque in 1972 restricted his focus to a critique of Ibn Khaldūn (and also of the very considerable oral epic literature which is still current, concerning the heroic deeds of the Banū Hilāl) but concluded in the end that the main effect of the Hilālian invasion was the beginning of the Arabization of the Berber tribes who existed in the region already. Allaoua Amara, in a review of the debate in 2003 which discusses all of those cited above which had appeared up to then and many other contributions too, with a focus on the lands of the Ḥammādids, came down on the side of those who regard the Banū Hilāl as of relatively restricted importance; he recognizes their relevance, but sees drought in the eleventh and twelfth centuries as much more of a problem. Gerald Schuster, in the most substantial recent discussion, sees them as far weaker than the historiography claims, and fairly similar to the less sedentary Berber tribes in their modus operandi.[20] Michael Brett too, in articles focussed on other matters, has argued that the Banū Hilāl were small-scale operators who controlled the countryside only. And Dominique Valérian in

[19] Poncet, 'Le mythe de la "catastrophe hilalienne"'; Idris, 'De la réalité de la catastrophe hilâlienne'; Thiry, *Le Sahara libyen*, pp. 223–33; Guichard, 'Sur quelques sites "castraux" du Haut Tell'; Sénac and Cressier, *Histoire du Maghreb médiéval*, p. 111.

[20] Berque, 'Du nouveau sur les Banî Hilâl?'; Amara, 'Retour à la problématique'; Schuster, *Die Beduinen*, pp. 50–69, 202–4. The droughts are certainly there in the late narratives; see n. 77 below. For the epic of the Banū Hilāl, see among others Brett, 'The way of the nomad'; Nacib, *Une geste en fragments*; Pantůček, *Das Epos*.

his major 2006 study of Béjaïa, the Ḥammādid capital after 1068, lays stress on the practical cooperation between the 'Arabs' (as the sources generally call the Banū Hilāl) and their settled neighbours, after an initial period of war, although with the caveat that this cooperation was punctuated by violence, and insecurity on the roads. He further stresses that the Algerian coastal ranges and the Tell had always been at least partly pastoral (which, indeed, simple ecological observation makes unsurprising), and that although pastoralism certainly increased from then on, this was not necessarily at the expense of an agricultural base, but was largely because of specialization, due to greater demand for African wool by the Italian cities after 1200 or so.[21] My own views are closest to those of Valérian and Amara. They both focus on what is now Algeria; we lack a systematic recent study of what really went on in what is now Tunisia. But what we can say about the latter fits the direction of their arguments.

As already noted, our narratives are late; it might be that we can trust them for dates of events, but the least likely element to be reliable is wider observations on social or economic trends. We can, however, add to them three other types of source. First, some remarks in the *fatwās* of contemporary jurists; these, too, only survive in late collections (notably that of al-Wansharīsī, d. 1508), which often decontextualize the pronouncements, but these collections are less likely than are the historical compilations to have altered content.[22] Whatever the problems legal rulings always have, these are the closest texts we have to the daily affairs of most people, as we have no legal documents of any kind from inside Ifrīqiya in our period, apart from a tiny handful of court hearings surviving in the *geniza*. The works of geographers, the second source type, are also contemporary, and some are by people who visited North Africa; if we set Ibn Ḥawqāl in the mid- to late tenth century against al-Idrīsī, who travelled in Ifrīqiya before he completed his work *c.*1154, we can get a rough sense of what changed, and also did not change, across two centuries. We also, finally, have the original and often first-hand accounts of Jewish merchants caught up in the events, which survive in the *geniza*. These give a partial view, as letter writers seldom gave their addressees the whole context, which, indeed, they may have been unaware of; they are often highly coloured as well, as writings by people caught up in violence often are, but they are at least unmediated by subsequent events. These are in most respects our best source of all; but unfortunately few such letters are actually dated. Their editor, Moshe Gil, dated the others according to his view of their relation to the events attested in the narratives, which is often unconvincing (he assumed, for example,

[21] Brett, e.g. 'The armies of Ifriqiya', pp. 115–17; Valérian, *Bougie*, pp. 197–205.

[22] Al-Wansharīsī's *al-Mi'yār* was edited in twelve volumes in Fès in 1898, and again in Rabat in 1981. I have used the convenient partial translation and summary in Lagardère, *Histoire et société*, which follows Idris's prior work; he cites the two modern editions of the text. Some of the most relevant *fatwās* for sea trade are translated or summarized in Idris, 'Commerce maritime et ḳirāḍ'. More recent discussions include Hopley, 'Aspects of trade'.

that the sequence stopped with the Norman conquest of northen Sicily, and provided relatively few dates after the 1060s), and anyway adds an element of circularity to their role as independent accounts. Work is being done on redatings, but it is not complete.[23] It is best at present to see the letters, mostly from the circle of Nahray b. Nissīm, who died, as we have seen, in 1097–8, as sources from a generic late eleventh century, without specific years, or, sometimes, even decades.

The *geniza* letters clearly show that the attacks of the Banū Hilāl, as also the Zīrid internal wars, could be serious and terrifying. The merchant communities lost substantially as a result of the fall of Kairouan. In one letter, already cited for its account of Kairouan being almost abandoned, the author, Labrāṭ b. Mūsā b. Sighmār, writing from Mahdia to his brother Yahūda in Fusṭāṭ, is unwilling to fight with him over 20 dinars, saying, 'It does not compare with the losses we suffered in Kairouan. They say here as a proverb, "If you only have one morsel (*ka'ba*) left, throw it in the sea."' Ismaīl b. Faraḥ wrote to Nahray with news from Ismaīl's brother Sulaymān, who had fled Kairouan for Sicily (he went as far as that because Sousse rose against the *amīr*, and much of the city was plundered; this fact, at least on this occasion, perhaps dates the letter to 1053/4); his brother had related that the 'Arabs' killed people on the way out of Kairouan and slit their stomachs looking for swallowed gold. We might be more struck by this ghoulish detail if it was not also recounted in Ibn al-Athīr's early thirteenth-century history, this time about people fleeing Mahdia from Abū Yazīd's siege in 945, and ascribed to Berber attackers; evidently it was a local oral motif which attached itself to frightening events.[24] But the events were not the less frightening for that, and they got in the way even when they were less extreme. There is a well-known account by the prosperous merchant Salāma b. Mūsā, in the *geniza*'s longest letter, to the same Yahūda b. Mūsā b. Sighmār, of his troubles in one particularly bad year. Much of them derived from his own tricksy dealings which had gone wrong, but before he left Mahdia in a hurry for Palermo and then Mazara, in all of which things went very badly, he was in Sfax, his home town; there he agreed with the local governor, who was in revolt against the *amīr* in Mahdia, to collect the taxes for one of the olive oil villages. This turned into a major opportunity to use his tax-raising authority to buy up the oil harvest, in association with an interregional group of Jewish and Muslim merchants from Mahdia, Tripoli, Palermo, and Egypt; but the *amīr* attacked Sfax, conquered the area whose oil Salāma had bought up after paying local Bedouin (*badwīn*), and prohibited anyone there from giving any oil to Sfax, so Salāma lost his money.[25] This is the sort of problem which war of all

[23] Gil, *Be-malkhut Yishma'el* (cited in this book as Gil K); contrast Jessica Goldberg, 'Writing history from the Geniza', pp. 512–14, and pers. comm.

[24] T-S 16.179, BL Or. 5542.9 (Gil K617, 488 [S122, 99]); cf. for others, e.g., T-S 10J20.12 (Gil K491 [S101]); Ibn al-Athīr, *Kāmil fī al-tārīkh*, trans. Fagnan, p. 333.

[25] Halper 389 and 414 (Gil K751–2 [S151–2]); I follow the reconstruction of Salama's very complex dealings in Goldberg, *Trade and institutions*, pp. 296–9. Gil dates the letter to 1064, followed by

kinds posed for merchants going about their business, just as much as the insecurity of the roads and sea routes. It is hardly surprising that their letter-writing could reveal how upset they got.

All the same, it does have to be said that the merchants survived. They were, rightly or wrongly, also hopeful: 'The disaster only affects Kairouan', after all; 'Mahdia is stable'—which it would be unnecessary to remark on if there was not potential danger, but the phrase recurs. Labrāṭ b. Mūsā's twice-cited letter also states how amazing it is that wheat prices—probably the best indicator of all of a steady economic situation—have been stable in Mahdia for eight years.[26] Even the most harrowing letters also include entirely normal instructions about what to sell and information about what prices are. And Mahdia and Sfax remained foci for trade for the whole period covered by letters of the Nahray circle.[27] It may indeed be the case that the major trouble only affected the interior, and that the ports had enough of a hinterland to allow them each to prosper. Sometimes one could not get from Ifrīqiya to Egypt directly, and had to go via Sicily;[28] but conversely, and strikingly, Salāma could move from Sfax to Mahdia even during a war between them. The letters from the next generation, from the 1090s onwards, although they are much less numerous, show us the same patterns, and with fewer citations of war by now; we will come back to these, and to the long-term effects of political instability, later (pp. 194–8).

This fits the geographers' accounts too. We have seen in the Egyptian context the degree to which they are full of commonplaces, but here they are not only more necessary, given the weakness of other written documentation, but also in many cases more helpful—North African towns were perhaps less unvaried in their eyes than those of Egypt. From south to north along the coast, Gabès was rich in oil, wool, silk production, and hides to Ibn Hawqāl around 950; in oil and

Goldberg in her account; but the *amīr* of Mahdia attacked Sfax on various occasions, and—as Jessica Goldberg has subsequently stressed (pers. comm.)—we cannot be certain when this attack was. The 'Bedouin' might have been olive workers, or field guards, or else the local Banū Hilāl taking a cut in protection money. Certainly the latter were capable of threatening the olive groves; a *fatwā* of the Mahdian jurist al-Māzarī (d. 1141), in al-Wansharīsī, *al-Mi'yār*, trans. Lagardère, *Histoire et société*, 3.70, deals with a situation in which 'Arabs' menaced the olive groves, so that harvesting had to be done too early or too fast or with extra wage labourers. The use in Halper 389 of the very rare Judaeo-Arabic word '*badwīn*', which does not reappear in a word search of the *geniza* published in PGP, might indeed indicate that too. But another *fatwā* of al-Māzarī, ibid., 3.71, discusses lending grain before the harvest to 'Bedouin' who do not have the coins to pay the value back later; in that case the community is one of poor agriculturalists; and the synonym *badū* appears in T-S 16.44, referring to them being oppressed, from as early as *c.*1016 (thanks to Lorenzo Bondioli for this reference), which shows that poorer 'Bedouin' communities were present in Ifrīqiya well before the Hilālians arrived. See also p. 173 below.

26 T-S 12.372, INA D55.13, ENA NS 2.13, T-S 13J23.18+AS 145.81 (Gil K513, 616, 749, 372 [S111, 141, 145, 149]). For Labrāt, see T-S 16.179 (Gil K617 [S122]).

27 Goldberg, *Trade and institutions*, pp. 319–21. Harrowing letters with sales, prices, etc.: ENA NS 18.24, BL Or. 5542.9, ENA 2727.38, T-S 10J20.12, 12.372, Halper 389 (Gil K344, 488, 489, 491, 513, 751 [S97, 99–101, 111, 151]).

28 For Ifrīqiya–Sicily–Egypt, see, e.g., T-S 13J26.10 (Gil K830 [S138]), a letter from after the 1070s, as it refers to Almorávid dinars; Goitein, *Letters*, p. 323, dated it to *c.*1140, but it must be earlier than that for the same reason.

leather (silk has moved to a subsidiary town) to al-Idrīsī around 1150—he stresses 'Arab' devastation to the east of the town, but, interestingly, Ibn Hawqāl had put an emphasis on the danger of nomad attack here too, 100 years before the Banū Hilāl. Sfax was above all an oil (and also fishing) entrepôt for both writers, although al-Idrīsī remarks that it has suffered as a result of the Norman conquest in 1148. Mahdia, fairly new when Ibn Hawqāl was there, was already a commercial and agricultural centre, although less active after Ṣabra al-Manṣūriya was founded; for al-Idrīsī, it was a major port for both Spain and Rūm (Italy and/or Byzantium), with large-scale commerce (if slightly less at present, again presumably because of the Normans), fine cloth production, and a rich agricultural hinterland. Tunis had cotton and ceramics, plus good agriculture, for Ibn Hawqāl; wheat, hemp, madder, and again cotton for al-Idrīsī. Inland, Béja was a major wheat centre for Ibn Hawqāl, and also for al-Idrīsī. In the north, Béjaïa, unmentioned by Ibn Hawqāl, was in al-Idrīsī a great port and arsenal, with rich cereal agriculture and iron mines as well, benefiting from the decline of the Kalâa (which, however, was also, he says, still prosperous). The only real contrast is unsurprisingly Kairouan, the major commercial centre of Ifrīqiya for Ibn Hawqāl (and still more for his younger contemporary al-Muqaddasī, who says little about the other towns), but now ruined, with few and poor inhabitants, and miserable commerce and artisanal production, for al-Idrīsī (though he adds that astrologers say it will revive). There are, therefore, some changes, as one could hardly doubt across two centuries, but, again apart from Kairouan, no devastating downward trends—and it can be added that this is true for lesser towns as well, even on the Tell.[29]

What is, nonetheless, new in al-Idrīsī is, precisely, the recurrent presence of 'Arabs' (*A'rāb*) in the countryside; as I have already implied, we can assume that they are connected directly or indirectly with the Banū Hilāl. Along the road between Béjaïa and the Kalâa, Arabs are around; they have a treaty with the inhabitants, but it is a tense one, sometimes broken. At Bādīs, west of the Aurès, and Mila, on the Tell, the Arabs are 'masters of its surroundings'. At Dār Mallūl, like Bādīs on the edge of the semi-desert, a former commercial and still an agricultural centre, one can stand on the ramparts and watch the Arabs. At Constantine, the treaty with the Arabs allows mutual cooperation over harvests. Around Majjāna, north of Tébessa, the Arabs dominate, and store provisions. To the east, in what is now Tunisia, there are fewer references to them, but in Tunis the inhabitants buy their wheat and barley direct from the Arabs, who also bring honey and butter for Tunis's famous pastries. Tabarka in the far north is much troubled by Arabs who do not keep agreements. The Arabs are again 'masters of

[29] Ibn Ḥawqal, *Kitāb ṣūrat al-arḍ*, trans. Kramers and Wiet, 1, pp. 66–71, 94–5; al-Muqaddasī, *Aḥsan al-Taqāsīm*, trans. Collins, pp. 202–3; al-Idrīsī, *Nuzhat al-mushtāq*, trans. Jaubert and Nef, pp. 165–7, 182–8, 192, 198 (Sétif on the Tell is also 'well populated': p. 174). Brunschvig remarked that the astrologers were not wrong, for Kairouan did revive under the Ḥafṣids: *La Berbérie orientale*, 1, pp. 359–60. For the geographers, see in general Vanacker, 'Géographie économique de l'Afrique du Nord'.

the countryside' and of its rich cereal produce around Béja. West of Kairouan, despite the drier land, there are grain fields and gardens; Arabs have, however, devastated the (largely semi-desert) lands east of Gabès.[30]

There are not so many citations of the 'Arabs' in al-Idrīsī—this is over half of them—but the picture is clear. The Arabs are independent, and one has to make formal treaties with them, but these exist, and some of them work. Furthermore, Arabs are not actually connected explicitly to pastoral activity, and several times, mostly in lowland Tunisia but even on the Tell, as around Constantine, simply control—or perhaps practise—agriculture. It is notable that Tunis and Béja are both closely associated with Arab agricultural interest, for Béja, in particular, lay at the heart of grain agriculture in Ifrīqiya in every period. And it is also significant that the way the Arabs are depicted in al-Idrīsī is very similar to the way the Kutāma Berbers living near Mila and Constantine were depicted in the tenth-century account of al-Qāḍī al-Nu'mān (see p. 155 above); in effect, the Arabs have simply replaced them in some of the same territories. It is implausible to see this as a process of direct population replacement—to repeat, there will never have been enough incoming Hilālians to achieve that; rather, it must represent the absorption into Arab tribal identities, and thus at a sociocultural level the Arabization, of a previous and continuing population, presumably in the context of local hegemonies of one or other of the Banū Hilāl tribes. But either way, the economy does not seem to have changed much, either in terms of an agricultural-pastoral balance or in terms of the levels of prosperity in different localities. It was, after all, as Valérian has also commented, not at all in the interests of the Arabs to destroy agriculture, for they benefited greatly from exploiting it, and, one can add, they too needed its products.[31] This is not altered by an equally likely conclusion, that the inhabitants of the countryside, even though they were not easily controlled already in 900, at least on the Tell, had become more threatening to neighbouring cities than they had been two centuries earlier, and that this meant a greater general level of insecurity, which would not help overall economic activity. That was, indeed, a medium-term result of the Hilālian invasions, but, conversely, also one which Almohad conquest, only a decade after al-Idrīsī wrote, would substantially lessen.

[30] Al-Idrīsī, *Nuzhat al-mushtāq*, trans. Jaubert and Nef, pp. 168–70 (quotation at p. 170), 187, 192, 195, 197–8. Amara, 'Retour à la problématique', pp. 13–14, has a convenient list of citations, nearly complete.

[31] For Arabization, compare the Islamicization/Arabization process which took place in the Egyptian Fayyūm between 1050 and 1240, discussed by Rapoport, *Rural economy*, pp. 231–48, and Wickham, 'The power of property', pp. 94–8; one of the 'Arab' tribes here, which absorbed and Islamicized a substantial population with a previously explicit Christian identity, was even the same as a Banū Hilāl tribe, the Banū Rabī'a. Arabization really is only a sociocultural process in this context, not an economic one: there was no abandonment of sedentary agriculture in the Fayyūm, just as we cannot say that there always was in Ifrīqiya either. See Valérian, *Bougie*, p. 202.

Fast-forward to the observations of Leo Africanus in the sixteenth century, and one still finds an only partially changed picture. Although around Tunis the land is by now hardly cultivated with grain (even if olive oil from here is exported to Egypt), Béja is still the centre of rich wheat fields, partly directly cultivated by 'Arabs'; so is the prosperous north coast around Annaba (Bône), from where wheat is exported to Genoa, and the Tell is agricultural in most of the areas which had been cultivated in the tenth century, even if many of its towns are largely depopulated. Olive forests appear down the Sahel coast (although no longer at Sfax) and east to Jerba as well. There does, indeed, seem to be more pastoral activity than before—Kairouan is by now in an uncultivated plain, for example, and 'Arabs' threaten the land around some coastal towns; wool is mentioned more often too; but it is also quite difficult to find much other hard evidence for it across the later medieval centuries.[32] In archaeological contexts, which admittedly do not usually in this region provide good enough data for claims like this, I have only seen a clear argument for an increase in pastoralism in one area, the hinterland of Leptis Magna, a relatively marginal area ecologically, dated to the twelfth century and onwards.[33] But anyway, it needs to be stressed that pastoralism is not in itself necessarily a bad thing for an economy, taken as a whole. Again, it seems best simply to follow Valérian, and see much of this pastoral increase as developing—as it also was in late medieval central Spain and the mountains of central and southern Italy—in the context of specialization for the export of wool and leather, in eastern Algeria through Béjaïa, in Tunisia through Mahdia and, by now, Tunis.[34]

What, then, apart from the Arabization of some rural populations, did the invasions of the Banū Hilāl actually change? There were certainly wars; but here we need to stand back a little. There were a lot of medieval wars. They killed people, in town and countryside; they destroyed city walls and, when towns and villages were plundered, goods, workshops, and tools. They were horrible to experience, as wars all are. But although Mahdia was wrecked by the Khārijite siege in 945, with artisans and merchants fleeing the town, and then the new foundation of Ṣabra al-Manṣūriya attracting them or others away later, the city was active again by the 960s at the latest, according to the nearly contemporary *Life* of Jawdhar. Mahdia was also fairly comprehensively sacked by the Pisans and Genoese in 1087, which gave rise to numerous lawsuits by creditors of artisans and merchants according to a *fatwā* of al-Mazārī (he favoured accepting the

[32] Jean-Léon l'Africain, *Description de l'Afrique*, trans. Épaulard, 2, pp. 360–401 (this modern French translation can stand in the place of the sixteenth-century Italian text, which is hard to find). See also Brunschvig, *La Berbérie orientale*, 2, pp. 217–24; Valérian, *Bougie*, pp. 205–12.

[33] Munzi et al., 'La Tripolitania rurale', pp. 228–9. More palynological work, which gives accurate guides to plant types in different periods, is greatly needed in this region; but see n. 77 below.

[34] Valérian, *Bougie*, pp. 204–5, 213–19, 379–95. For Italy and Spain, see, e.g., Martin, *La Pouille*, pp. 377–84 (for the development of pastoralism at the very end of our period in southern Italy) and the classic Klein, *The Mesta*.

testimony of artisans as to which goods had been taken), but was prosperous again pretty soon after.[35] Given the relatively restricted technological complexity of the period, as long as the basic agricultural or pastoral ecosystem and the route networks survived, economic activity could be re-established fairly soon after peace came. Northern Italy's wars in the twelfth century were at least as bad, and possibly worse, without the general upward direction of its exchange system being affected; Milan, which was systematically destroyed and then abandoned for five years in the 1160s, was not prevented from rebuilding itself as the largest artisanal focus and population centre in the peninsula by the 1180s (see pp. 600–8 below). It is true that perhaps even the ecosystem could sometimes be under threat: it is claimed in the narratives that the *amīr* Tamīm destroyed Sfax's olive forests during a war against its rebel governor, which fortified the views of historians like Poncet who were arguing against the importance of the Banū Hilāl. But it must be noted that it is exceptionally difficult to destroy an olive forest, especially if the trees are old and thick, as they will have been around such a long-standing olive centre as Sfax; armies tend to prefer less hard and unremunerative work; and olive trees grow back as well. Al-Idrīsī, anyway, said that oil production was important half a century later, which makes the claims in the narratives, themselves vaguely expressed, difficult to accept.[36] And I have already argued that the ecosystemic change most frequently ascribed to the invasions, the pastoralization of the agrarian economy, has relatively little documentary support for our period, even though it certainly increased in later centuries. We have also seen that the *geniza* merchants were not entirely prevented from carrying on their activity by these wars. So the simple fact that the last decades of the eleventh century were violent and unstable does not tell us much about what the economy of Ifrīqiya would be like even a generation later.

What we are left with, then, is simply the taking out of Kairouan. It was not total; archaeological work has shown late eleventh- and twelfth-century occupation there; but it was no longer a major political centre. This was no small thing; it had been the nerve centre of the Ifrīqiyan state and of the economy up to 1050. (On the Tell, the rise and decline of the Kalâa had less economic effect, for it was never so important, and it also survived.) It led to the shift of the whole political structure to the coast: its '*littoralisation*', as French-language historiography terms it.[37] The ports of Gabès, Sfax, Mahdia, Tunis, and Béjaïa were the new foci of politics, until the Almohads conquered the whole region (see Map 9). (After that,

[35] Al-Manṣūr, *Sīrat al-Ustādh Jawdhar*, trans. Canard, and (separately) Haji, 2.2, 4, 40, 45, 52; al-Wansharīsī, *al-Mi'yār*, trans. Lagardère, *Histoire et société*, 5.104.

[36] See the references in Idris, *La Berbérie orientale*, pp. 301–2, and, for the earliest narrative, Ibn al-Athīr, *Kāmil fī al-tārīkh*, trans. Fagnan, p. 512; cf. Poncet, 'Le mythe de la "catastrophe hilalienne"', p. 1117. For *c.*1150, see al-Idrīsī, *Nuzhat al-mushtāq*, trans. Jaubert and Nef, p. 183.

[37] See, e.g., Amara, 'Bône et la littoralisation du pays Kutāma'; Valérian, *Bougie*, pp. 2–5. For Kairouan in the twelfth century, see Khéchine and Gragueb Chatti, 'Contribution à l'histoire de la ville de Kairouan'; for the archaeology and the related issue of resettlement, see nn. 72, 83 below.

Tunis was the main political centre east of Béjaïa; there was no more fragmentation, but the capital was, nonetheless, still on the coast, as well as back in the agrarian north, as under the Romans.) In economic terms, we see the same shift; for these were the main economic foci too, even more than they had been before, as the geographers already make clear. But how the economy really worked, and how important this shift to the coast was, we cannot tell from the data we have so far looked at. The archaeology and the *geniza*, which we will now look at in turn, are the only things that can give us a real sense of that, before Italian contracts begin in the 1150s (for which, see pp. 264–8 below). Neither is perfect for our needs, but they are what we have. When they are set against the discussions I have already set out, we can at least get a sense of how the economy actually functioned and changed. This is why I have spent some time on the Banū Hilāl: because the debate about change in and after 1050 does give us a context in which our better economic data can make more sense. But that we will see later.

3.2 North African Archaeology and the North African Internal Economy

The best evidence for the internal structures of Ifrīqiya's economy is archaeological, so this section will concentrate mostly on archaeological data, with the addition of some brief comments on land tenure taken largely from the *fatwās* (see Map 8). But we also have to recognize that the overall quality of North African (in particular, for the purposes of this book, Tunisian) archaeology is not that high for our period; it is weaker than that of any other region discussed here, even Egypt. There is very little rural archaeology. Only two really good field surveys have provided effective evidence for the period, both well to the east of the core Ifrīqiyan lands; villages have hardly been excavated either, except some of those identified above the ancient city of Carthage—those which the excavators did not destroy in their haste to reach Roman levels, a general feature of Mediterranean archaeology until the 1970s, of course.[38] Even urban archaeology is not so very illuminating. There is scrappy material from plenty of sites, which I will use in my discussions of ceramic patterns; but the best substantial published site of the tenth and eleventh centuries remains Sétif in Algeria, excavated in the 1980s. An excavation at Uchi Maius (modern Henchir Douames) of a tenth-century reoccupation in the acropolis is well published but small. Of older sites (if we leave aside the pre-scientific work on the Kalâa des Béni Hammad), Mahdia

[38] For the field surveys, see Munzi, 'La Tripolitania rurale', and Holod and Kahlaoui, 'Jerba of the ninth century'; this, with Holod and Cirelli, 'Islamic pottery from Jerba', serves as an interim for the not yet published Holod et al., *Jerba studies*, 2. See also n. 59 below. For the villages, see the survey in Stevens, 'Carthage in transition', updating the still essential Vitelli, *Islamic Carthage*.

and Raqqāda have never been properly published.[39] The potentially most important site so far excavated, Ṣabra al-Manṣūriya in the mid-2000s, has not been published either, although its publication is believed to be imminent; it is apparent from citations of articles in press that some of the reports for the final publication have long been complete. At least there are numerous interims for that site, however; it is evident, among other things, that Ṣabra was by no means only a palace city, and had a substantial urban population, including artisanal productions of different types.[40] This confirms some of our narratives, which mention artisans or shopkeepers moving from Kairouan to Ṣabra in the mid-tenth century, and also being forcibly moved from Kairouan to Ṣabra in 1014.[41] The site was, we are consistently told in written sources, founded in 946–8, and such sources also say it was abandoned in 1057—it potentially acts in this respect as a one-period site. But actually, it is fairly clear from the archaeology both that it was occupied earlier—a carbon-14 date for mud brickwork gives us 695–899—and that there was ceramic production later there than any written source says, possibly into the early twelfth century.[42]

I will come to this in a moment, but the point can be generalized. Much of the dating of Tunisian sites depends on an assumption that site abandonments can be attached to the third quarter of the eleventh century solely because of the presumed effect of the Banū Hilāl. As we have just seen, no such assumption can be made; and to use the archaeology to support such a date, if the archaeology itself is dated by the written sources, is anyway a circular argument. I will seek in what follows to ignore such arguments, but to do so is not straightforward, for it is also the case that not many sites have been excavated which are securely of twelfth-century date. All the same, useful things can be said, above all from the patterns of ceramics.

First, some back history. The North African economy in the later Roman Empire was beyond doubt prosperous, to judge by its excavated cities and field surveys, but on one level was even more of a colonial economy than was that of Egypt, for it was structured, as perhaps no other region was, by exports, many of them—the wheat and much of the olive oil—going as taxation. Until the Vandal conquest in 439, much landowning was external too, imperial or senatorial, so

[39] Mohamedi, Fentress, et al., *Fouilles de Sétif*; Gelichi and Milanese, '*Uchi Maius*'; for the Kalâa, see Golvin, *Recherches archéologiques*, and Aissani and Amara, 'Qalʿa des Bani Ḥammād'; for Mahdia, see nn. 64, 83 below; for Raqqada, see the comments in the ceramic analysis of Gragueb Chatti, 'La céramique aghlabide de Raqqada'.

[40] Ṣabra interims: Cressier and Rammah, 'Ṣabra al-Manṣūriya'; Cressier and Rammah, 'Sabra al-Mansûriya'; Cressier and Rammah, 'Sabra al-Mansūriyya'; Cressier, 'Ville médiévale au Maghreb', pp. 128–31.

[41] For Kairouan to Ṣabra, see al-Muqaddasī, *Aḥsan al-Taqāsīm*, trans. Collins, pp. 202–3; al-Bakrī, *al-Masālik wa al-mamālik*, trans. de Slane, p. 58; Ibn ʿIdhārī, *al-Bayān al-mughrib*, trans. Fagnan, 1, p. 387.

[42] See Cressier and Rammah, 'Ṣabra al-Manṣūriya', p. 622, for the early date; and see p. 184 below for later.

even commercial profit from large-scale agrarian production largely went abroad. We cannot say who benefited from owning the major centres of African Red Slip (ARS) fine-pottery production, but we can see from the archaeology that the directions for its distribution substantially went, from its different kilns, to the east coast. There was relatively little internal distribution of the main ceramic types, except in the immediate hinterlands of kilns, and between them and the sea (ARS C, with a wider internal range, is the main exception); only the coastal cities were well connected. It is true that the rural economy was, conversely, evidently very successful in its own terms as well, with Red Slip from smaller kilns found on every site, even minor ones, and coins and metalwork too. However the rural economy was arranged, it did not take all surpluses from the peasantry, at least in the late empire—far from it; small farms were doing unusually well, and we can assume a level of successful peasant entrepreneurship, at least for the luckiest. But the main lines of wider exchange still went to the coast, not from inland city to inland city. Export, even if it was not the sole basis of African rural prosperity, thus nonetheless structured its directions to an unusual degree.[43]

There then followed the chaos of the Arab conquests in the period 647–98, which were rather slower and more disruptive than those elsewhere in the caliphate. Add to that the effective end of the Roman interregional exchange system in its traditional forms in almost all the western Mediterranean, which meant that anyone still wishing to export would have faced considerable difficulties; this will have on its own caused crisis in as export-orientated a region as this. It is not surprising that the eighth century is archaeologically hard to track here, after the last productions in a Red Slip tradition (in white fabrics by now, and no longer exported to any significant degree) ended around 730.[44] There are still a handful of examples of Tunisian amphorae, markers of (probably) oil export, which have been found in Italy (Rome) and Mediterranean France (Marseille), into the eighth century; conversely, Arab-ruled Ifrīqiya hardly took part in the smaller-scale but still dense exchange system, marked in the archaeological record by globular amphorae, which united the Byzantine provinces in the eighth and ninth centuries, not least neighbouring Sicily (see pp. 304–5, 636–7 below). A handful of such amphorae have been found in post-conquest levels in Tunisia, but that is all that is currently known, and a small version of the type made in both Jerba and Leptis Magna seems only to have had a local distribution.[45] The region may not even have had much of a functioning fiscal system before the Aghlabids, as we may be able to deduce from references in later sources (starting in the ninth century) to

[43] See n. 5 above and Chapter 8, nn. 4–5 below.

[44] Bonifay, *Études*, pp. 73, 210; Bonifay, 'Marqueurs céramiques', p. 297.

[45] Reynolds, 'From Vandal Africa to Arab Ifrīqiya', p. 147; Bonifay, *Études*, pp. 151–3; Holod and Cirelli, 'Islamic pottery from Jerba', pp. 174–5; Cirelli, 'Leptis magna', pp. 430–1; cf. Munzi et al., 'La Tripolitania rurale', p. 229.

Arab elite families owning land here; for this was as yet rare in the central caliphal provinces, where such elites were mostly paid out of taxation.[46]

What we can say from the sketchy archaeology is that the different sectors of Ifrīqiya had rather different histories in the eighth and ninth centuries. Kairouan was, of course, the major site, spreading out from its great mosque, rebuilt on a large scale by the third Aghlabid, Ziyādat Allāh I (d. 838), and structured by planned market streets and reservoirs, and even a privately built monumental mosque, the Mosque of the Three Doors.[47] The Medjerda valley was still economically coherent, thanks to its grain and some oil production, but its Roman hyper-urbanization, with a city every few kilometres in some places, had ended; some sites with post-Roman excavated levels, such as Bulla Regia and Belalis Maior (modern Henchir al-Faouar) remained visibly active, but others became substantially smaller (Uchi Maius, Chemtou) and some were abandoned altogether. That is to say, a site hierarchy remained, but became much simpler.[48] One major town, Béja, survived to provide a strong and lasting focus for the area, although, precisely because it has lasted until the present day, it has not been excavated, so how its prosperity and coherence changed (if they did) cannot be tested. Tunis too was probably emerging as Ifrīqiya's second city, although how it worked economically is close to invisible until after 1100. Along the Sahel coast, around what would later be Mahdia, where in many cases surviving Roman centuriated (squared) field systems show effectively unbroken agrarian continuity up to the present day, some of the cities formerly made prosperous by olive oil export, such as Leptiminus (Lamta), failed as well, turning into villages; all the same, others, like Sousse, with its late eighth-century *ribāṭ* and mid-ninth-century great mosque, and Sfax, with its partially surviving Roman square plan and another Aghlabid mosque, certainly continued to be significant centres. In the inland Sahel, excavation shows that Sbeïtla was occupied, with some artisanal activity, into the ninth century.[49] The continuing links between the port of Sousse and Kairouan will have helped the former; Sbeïtla was known for its olives long past the end of systematic export, as it is the location for a well-known anecdote by the mid-ninth century historian Ibn ʿAbd al-Ḥakam which shows that olive cultivation was still—or again—regarded as the symbol of Ifrīqiyan wealth; so Sfax too may well

[46] Talbi, 'Law and economy', pp. 210–13.

[47] Mahfoudh, *Architecture et urbanisme*, esp. pp. 49–82; Mahfoudh, 'La Grande Mosquée'; Goodson, 'Topographies of power', Khéchine and Gragueb Chatti, 'Contribution à l'histoire de la ville de Kairouan'.

[48] See in general Fenwick, 'From Africa to Ifrīqiya'; Fenwick, 'The fate of the classical cities'; Fenwick, *Early Islamic North Africa*, pp. 53–80; for Bulla, see Broise and Thébert, *Recherches archéologiques*, 2.i, pp. 394–7. See n. 68 below for Belalis, Uchi, and Chemtou.

[49] For Lamta and Sousse, see Stevens, 'Not just a tale of two cities'. For Sbeïtla, see Duval, 'L'urbanisme de Sufetula'; Bejaoui, 'Une nouvelle église'. For Sousse and Sbeïtla, see further Fenwick, *Early Islamic North Africa*, pp. 65–8, 70–1.

have continued to prosper thanks to its great olive forest.[50] This means that these cities must by now have benefited from elements of an internal exchange network, with Kairouan and other inland centres happy to buy their oil. Farther away, the main cities of the Tripolitanian coast survived as well, and here, interestingly, the hinterland of Leptis Magna shifted its rural economy from a pastoral to an agricultural focus in the ninth century, before changing back again in the twelfth–thirteenth.[51] We are not yet in a position to generalize very widely from these isolated examples, and signs of prosperity in some of the towns must be set against the fairly unambitious and localized (but generally well-made) commonware ceramic productions of the period up to the late ninth century, which provides a hint that internal exchange was not very developed;[52] but there was enough here to be built on later.

Before we look more closely at the evidence for exchange in our period, we need to ask who in Ifrīqiya might be the agrarian producers of exchanged goods, and also the buyers of both agrarian and artisanal products. This means that we need to look briefly at land tenure. Our evidence for it is very poor indeed, far poorer than for Egypt, for, as noted earlier, we have no documents; much of what we can say has to be highly hypothetical. It is, however, at least clear that both substantial state lands and private property continued in the region side by side, as they had done in the Roman Empire. As just noted, early Arab elite families were landowners; Mohamed Talbi set out the evidence for them in an important article on the ninth- and tenth-century Ifrīqiyan agrarian economy. The families are not attested later, and perhaps, as Michael Brett has supposed, were undermined by both the Aghlabids (although they survived until a major aristocratic revolt in the 890s) and the Fāṭimids, but landowning in itself continued thereafter.[53] Jawdhar (d. 972), a senior minister to the Fāṭimids in Ifrīqiya, had an estate (*ḍayʿa*) in either Sicily or Cap Bon, the peninsula north of Sousse, which was given him by the caliph al-Mahdī, and also several others (called both *ḍiyāʿ* and *manāzil*, which elsewhere means 'hamlets' or 'houses'—perhaps, here, 'smaller estates'); the letters preserved in his *Life* refer to this, and to other landowning. The Zīrid *amīr* Bādis (d. 1016) is also claimed by Ibn ʿIdhārī in the fourteenth century to have given to his kinsman and favourite Yūsuf b. Abī Ḥabūs numerous estates (*ḍiyāʿ*)

[50] The anecdote purports to date to the seventh century; in it, an inhabitant of Sbeïtla explains to a conquering Arab general the origin of the city's wealth in gold by producing an olive stone. See Ibn ʿAbd al-Ḥakam, *Futūḥ Miṣr*, trans. Gateau, pp. 46–9. A ninth-century amphora kiln has been found beside an olive press at Bourjine near Sousse, showing renewed (or continued) production for sale; see Fenwick, *Early Islamic North Africa*, p. 122. Continuities in the regional sale of oil are also indicated by Bahri and Touihiri, 'Des jarres des IVe–V^{e} s /X^{e}–XIe siècles de Qasr al-Āliya (Mahdiyya)'; a small number of these have been found in Sicily too (Viva Sacco, pers. comm.).

[51] Munzi at al., 'La Tripolitania rurale', pp. 226–9.

[52] Reynolds, 'From Vandal Africa to Arab Ifrīqiya', pp. 147–58, is the best synthesis, although he emphasizes that a synthesis is not currently possible. Cooking wares were often handmade, but seem still to have been professionally produced.

[53] Talbi, 'Law and economy', pp. 210–13; Brett, *The rise of the Fatimids*, p. 258.

and other properties across the whole of Ifrīqiya. Nothing in the texts requires us to think that these lands were held other than in full property, and the *Life* of Jawdhar is explicit about this on one occasion.[54] *Iqṭa'* concessions were rare here until the late middle ages; they were then usually of the direct possession of land, not tax rights—this is probably linked to the fact that tax farming was also not a feature of our period in Ifrīqiya. The *fatwā* collections refer, in eleventh-century pronouncements, to *milk*, private landed property, in casual contexts—that is to say, contexts which were assumed to be normal. We also have eleventh-century citations of smaller property owners, and it is quite possible that some of the more tribalized microsocieties, such as the Kutāma on the Tell (see p. 155 above), had fewer large owners. *Milk* was, anyway, standard into the Ḥafṣid period, even if perhaps by 1400 no longer the majority of land.[55]

The land of larger owners was, it seems, generally cultivated by tenants who owed a share of the crop; this is documented in *fatwās* from the ninth century onwards. Occasionally, wage labour is referred to too, but in our period fixed rent is not, unlike in Egypt (which had little or no sharecropping). The shares were, if we follow the *fatwās*, very unfavourable indeed to the cultivator. The texts are elliptic, but tenth-century/early eleventh-century citations seem to refer to rents of 25 per cent or 50 per cent if the tenant provides part of the seed, and 80 per cent (or even 90 per cent, on irrigated land) if the proprietor provides all of it. It is difficult to understand how an 80 per cent rent could have been a stable long-term arrangement, for one would think that cultivators could hardly live on this; but the *khimāsa* or fifth portion (for the cultivator) not only survived into the Ḥafṣid period, to the unease of jurists, but was still a common agrarian contract in the Maghreb in the early twentieth century. That is to say, it must, indeed, have been possible to live on it; but it was, nonetheless, the most oppressive agrarian lease

[54] Al-Manṣūr, *Sīrat al-Ustādh Jawdhar*, trans. Canard and Haji, 2.13 (for full property), 18, 30, 57–8, 64. In 2.18, Jawdhar gets an estate from the caliph in al-Jazīra; both Canard and Haji gloss this as Cap Bon, but the word is also regularly used for Sicily, at least in the *geniza*, as it means 'island'. See Talbi, 'Law and economy', p. 211 and Nef, *Conquérir et gouverner*, pp. 404–9 for *manzil* meaning 'hamlet' in Ifrīqiya and Sicily (cf. also n. 200 below); and (among many) P.Fay.Villages 3, 4, 6–8, 17, 19, 20; cf. Mouton, 'La société villageoise', pp. 196–7, for it meaning 'house' in Egypt, with al-Manṣūr, *Sīrat*, 2.12 for the same meaning even in Tunis, in an urban context. For Bādis, see Ibn 'Idhārī, *al-Bayān al-mughrib*, trans. Fagnan, 1, p. 389; cf. Idris, *La Berbérie orientale*, p. 110, who, ibid., p. 604, sees *ḍiyā'* as by definition estates held in sharecropping contracts; this is not accurate (for Egypt, see Wickham, 'The power of property', pp. 74–7), but in Ifrīqiya sharecropping was indeed dominant, as we shall see in a moment.

[55] For *iqṭa'*, see Idris, *La Berbérie orientale*, p. 604 (very few citations; cf. 543–8, 609–11 for a tax-raising regime which remained very centralized); later, Brunschvig, *La Berbérie orientale*, 2, pp. 184–9; Rouighi, *The making of a Mediterranean emirate*, pp. 62–5. Ibn Ḥawqal, *Kitāb ṣūrat al-arḍ*, trans. Kramers and Wiet, 1, p. 95 states flatly for the late tenth century that there is no tax farming in the Maghreb, except in Barqa, closer to Egypt. For *milk*, see al-Wansharīsī, *al-Mi'yār*, trans. Lagardère, *Histoire et société*, 3.34, 39. For small owners, see Talbi, 'Law and economy', pp. 213–14; Amara, 'L'organisation foncière', p. 58. For *milk* under the Ḥafṣids, see Brunschvig, *La Berbérie orientale*, 2, pp. 180–3, and Rouighi, *The making of a Mediterranean emirate*, p. 69.

known to me in our period and thereafter, anywhere in the Mediterranean.[56] As to wage labourers, they also included field guards (*ḥāris*); this is worth noting because some guards of this type were from the Riyāḥ tribe, who were part of the Banū Hilāl themselves. In the Fayyūm, in Egypt, we have attestations of such tribal guards who across the eleventh century made themselves into local lords, and eventually turned all their settled neighbours into members of the same tribe—and, as noted earlier, one of the tribes concerned, the Banū Rabīʿa, is itself attested as a member of the Hilālian confederacy; this could perfectly well have happened in Ifrīqiya too. All the same, some of the Riyāḥ were still paid field guards, near Kairouan, around 1400; they are an illustration that not all Hilālians were major players.[57]

The dominance of these references to rent-paying and small-scale wage labour is not disturbed by the half-dozen citations of rural slaves set out by Talbi in the least persuasive parts of his otherwise fundamental article. These show that dependent cultivators could indeed sometimes be referred to as *ʿabīd*, 'slaves', which may well fit the heavy rents we have just seen documented. But none of them shows the dominance, or even existence, of the sort of plantation slavery which Talbi invokes in his article. According to him, this slavery operated on such a scale that the loss of control over the seas by Muslims after 961 (itself no longer accepted—far from it) meant the end of the slave trade (this too cannot be sustained), and therefore such a serious loss of manpower in Ifrīqiya that famines became abruptly more serious after 1000 (these are indeed more often attested after that date; cf. p. 181 below; but it is very hard to see how this causal chain could have worked). That is to say, none of these arguments has support.[58] We are left with estates characterized, as far as the weak evidence takes us, by oppressive sharecropping contracts.

[56] Al-Wansharīsī, *al-Miʿyār*, trans. Lagardère, *Histoire et société*, 4.14, 5.9, 31, 41–2, 72; Idris, *La Berbérie orientale*, pp. 622–4; Amara, 'L'organisation foncière', p. 59; Brunschvig, *La Berbérie orientale*, 2, pp. 199–201; Voguet, *Le monde rural du Maghreb central*, pp. 340–3; Rouighi, *The making of a Mediterranean emirate*, pp. 68–71; Müller, 'Us, coutumes', pp. 38–43. For the early twentieth century, see, e.g., Milliot, *L'association agricole*, pp. 81–94, a detailed legal-style account without a hint of the problems involved; there are a few figures and a more critical commentary in Nouschi, *Enquête sur le niveau de vie*, pp. 80–1, 147–50, which also shows that in the mid-nineteenth century, in documented areas of Algeria, *khimāsa* tenants (*khammās*; in French, *khammès*) were between a fifth and a quarter of the population. Ḥafṣid jurists disagreed about whether the *khimāsa* was a wage, rather than a partiary rent; this sort of debate went back a long way in Islamic law, in fact, and is a reflection of legal and theological distinctions rather than of realities on the ground, but the extreme features of the documented contract do fit Jairus Banaji's discussions (now in *Theory as history*, pp. 145–50, 245–7) of the ways sharecropping can be seen as a form of coerced wage labour (Banaji, in fact, cites the *khimāsa* as one of his examples). See also pp. 392–3 below for the parallel evidence for al-Andalus, where it was certainly seen as a wage.

[57] For wage labour and field guards, see Idris, *La Berbérie orientale*, pp. 623–4; see n. 31 above for the Fayyūm; for the Riyāḥ, see al-Wansharīsī, *al-Miʿyār*, trans. Lagardère, *Histoire et société*, 5.112; Brunschvig, *La Berbérie orientale*, 2, p. 202.

[58] Talbi, 'Law and economy', pp. 214–19, 224–6, 235.

This evidence, if we took it as a real guide, would have real consequences for our assessment of the Ifrīqiyan economy in our period. The sort of peasant protagonism and demand which we saw in some Egyptian flax areas and will see again in Middle Byzantine Greece and al-Andalus—and which was probably a feature of late Roman North Africa itself, as we have just seen—would have been unlikely to have been strong in the parts of Fāṭimid and post-Fāṭimid Ifrīqiya with large landowning, if the rent figures cited above were really characteristic of the region as a whole; for there would have been too little surplus for any tenant to use except for the barest subsistence. So the oppressive nature of the contracts we do see referred to might possibly fit the fact that 'Islamic' (i.e. glazed) pottery, although not absent, has never been found on any scale in field surveys in the Ifrīqiyan heartland, north and central Tunisia, for this contrasts considerably with the situation in Sicily, Greece, and Islamic Spain.[59] It might, that is to say, indeed be the case that the major local buyers of any goods produced for markets inside the region in our period would mostly have to be landowning and official elites, plus town dwellers. But I resist this conclusion, all the same. We cannot, on the basis of *fatwā*s alone, make any sensible comments about the frequency of sharecropping—as contrasted with, in particular, simple taxpaying by owner-cultivators—across Ifrīqiya, or about the frequency of 80 per cent rather than, say, 50 per cent rent demands on the part of landowners; and it may well be that the focus on the *khimāsa* in juristic texts is only a product of its ambiguous standing in Islamic law, rather than of its real frequency. We will see this more clearly in Chapter 5, for the more elaborate evidence for al-Andalus certainly points in that direction; indeed, it is regarded as axiomatic by some scholars of Islamic Spain that the fact that immigrants there came from the Maghreb meant that autonomous village communities, without any landlords at all, were henceforth normative in the peninsula (see p. 380 below). I think we have, regrettably, to recognize that apart from the simple fact that some peasants in North Africa in our period paid rents and all paid taxes, we cannot be certain on the basis of any source we have, documentary or material, how much available surplus there was in the countryside. We have signs here, not statistics. All we can say is that we have some

[59] The caution is derived from the fact that none of these surveys had any post-Roman period as a research focus; the Islamic material is only referred to, not discussed or, mostly, even published. Conversely, glaze is easy to see in survey, and will have perhaps been recorded more systematically than any post-Roman common ware. See Dietz et al., *Africa proconsularis*, 2, p. 472, for Segermes, south of Tunis; Hitchner, 'The Kasserine archaeological survey 1982–1985', p. 180, Hitchner, 'The Kasserine archaeological survey 1987', p. 259; de Vos, *Rus africum*, pp. 66, 76, for the central Medjerda valley. Outside these central lands, the empirical situation is similar, but the ecology is harsher, and possible explanations are more complex, as with Fentress et al., 'Prospections dans le Belezma', p. 112, for the southern Tell. Glaze was also rare in the best surveys along the Tripolitanian coast, which certainly did record common wares; see Holod and Kahlaoui, 'Jerba of the ninth century', p. 454; Munzi, 'La Tripolitania rurale', p. 229; Cirelli et al., 'Insediamenti fortificati nel territorio di Leptis Magna', pp. 772–3; but this could equally be explained by problems of distribution to more peripheral areas. For Sicily, Greece, and Spain, see pp. 221–4, 300–2, 426–9 below.

signs that tenants could be forced to pay very high rents in some circumstances, and that there are some signs that other peasants were simply taxpayers. Our sources do not take us any further here.

* * *

However uncertain the foregoing is, it is the wider context for the first real archaeological sign that something was changing in the Ifrīqiyan economy. This is the appearance in Raqqāda of a local production of glazed pottery, which was previously unknown in the region, picking up on Egyptian and/or Middle Eastern styles and technologies, which can only have been the result of immigrating artisans, with the skills to make it and to train others (see Fig. 4). Raqqāda was said to be founded in 876. Of course, such a production might have pre-existed it in nearby and hardly excavated Kairouan; but a late ninth-century date for its beginning at least fits the fact that the first glazed ceramics in al-Andalus are attested in roughly the same period, at Pechina on the south-east coast, even if the styles and techniques there are unrelated to those in Tunisia. Cups and bowls with a very recognizable yellow (or sometimes white) glazed decoration appear from now on, some of which are of remarkably high quality. They were transparently made in the context of the Aghlabid court, and, like tenth-century Córdoba wares (see p. 398 below), often have a painted inscription on them, *al-mulk*, 'power', 'sovereignty', or 'kingdom'—although *al-mulku lillāh*, 'sovereignty to God', an alternative inscription, has a rather less secular ring. If this had remained only a court production, it would not tell us much in itself, but very soon afterwards, around

Fig. 4 Raqqāda ware

the end of the ninth century, similar productions are visible in Palermo, which shows that production at Raqqāda was by now sufficiently solid that the style could move outwards to by-now almost fully conquered Sicily; it would have a significant history on the island from then on.[60] When Ṣabra al-Manṣūriya was founded as a new capital around 948, ceramics moved there too; kilns have been excavated for both pottery and glass, and wasters found. The ceramic types found here were very similar to Raqqāda ware, although diversifying; there were also storage containers, common wares, and in the eleventh century, at the other end of the range, some signs of lustre production, which is rare west of Egypt. Production processes were slightly different (one fewer firing, some frit fabrics), but it is also much clearer from 950 onwards that this pottery was mass-produced. For the next century at least, it can be found all over North Africa.[61]

How can we be sure that glazed pottery in Ṣabra styles or, more widely, those of Kairouan and its palace cities, were actually made in or near the capital? Usually, we cannot; the excavations concerned were too early, or have been too sketchily published, for any kind of fabric or (still less) petrological analysis to have been carried out. But sometimes we have indications. Bir Ftouha, one of the Carthage sites, from the tenth century (extending perhaps into the early eleventh), well studied by Paul Reynolds, is emblematic; most or all of the polychrome glazed pottery here has Raqqāda and then Ṣabra styles of decoration, and the fabrics are central Tunisian. Ksar Lemsa or Limisa, a surviving Byzantine fortification closer to Kairouan (some 50 kilometres to the north-west), but already some way up in the mountains leading to the Tell, equally well studied by Soundes Gragueb, similarly had Ṣabra styles and fabrics in its glazed wares. The petrological work done at Dougga in the Medjerda valley points to Ṣabra as the origin for its glazed pottery from this period too; slightly farther up the valley, Ṣabra fabrics are found at Chemtou. Ṣabra is also indicated, even more strikingly, as the origin for much

[60] There are good surveys of the ware as a whole (including unglazed forms), and of the white ware and the inscriptions, in, respectively, Gragueb Chatti, 'La céramique aghlabide de Raqqada', and Gragueb Chatti, 'La céramique vert et brun à fond blanc de Raqqāda'; the yellow wares are also well illustrated in several publications (e.g. *Couleurs de Tunisie*, pp. 118–28). See p. 220 below for Palermo, pp. 418–19 below for Pechina.

[61] Cressier and Rammah, 'Sabra al-Mansûriya', pp. 471–5; Cressier and Rammah, 'Sabra al-Mansūriyya', pp. 294–8; Gragueb Chatti, 'Le vert et le brun'; Gragueb Chatti et al., 'Jarres et amphores' (for the storage containers); Gragueb Chatti and Tréglia, 'Un ensemble de céramiques'; for firings, Ben Amara et al., 'Distinction de céramiques glaçurées aghlabides ou fatimides'. For an overview, see the almost unfindable Louhichi, *Céramique islamique de Tunisie*, pp. 34–84; I am very grateful to Caroline Goodson for the loan of her copy. There were Chinese imports to Ṣabra; see Cressier and Rammah, 'Sabra al-Mansūriyya', p. 288; and also Egyptian lustre imports, beside local lustre; see Capelli et al., 'Il contributo', which gives a petrological analysis. See further Khéchine and Gragueb Chatti, 'Contribution à l'histoire de la ville de Kairouan', which discusses the ceramics of the most significant excavation there. Eleventh-century Tunisian glazed pottery also reached Sicily on a considerable scale, notwithstanding high production levels in the island itself; see, e.g., Sacco et al., 'Islamic ceramics and rural economy', pp. 49–51, 68–9, for Pizzo Monaco, a small coastal site west of Palermo.

of the glazed ware found at Tegdaoust, ancient Awdaghust in the south-western Sahara, a point we will come back to.[62] Conversely, over the whole of North Africa, the only other place where a clearly attested glazed kiln site has been found before 1100 is the Kalâa des Béni Hammad; it produced polychrome too, and even lustrewares, particularly for tiles. Elsewhere, the tenth- and eleventh-century geographers say that Tunis produced polychrome and thin-walled ceramics, although the glazes found in nearby Carthage from the same period, and Utica a little farther north, are generally from central Tunisia, which includes Kairouan/Ṣabra.[63] As for Mahdia, the *Life* of Jawdhar claims that ceramics were imported from Mahdia to Ṣabra itself around 950, close to the beginning of the main activity of the latter site; the caliph was very angry when they were stolen. He must have valued them, which implies that they were glazed. That Mahdia had its own kilns is not surprising in itself, given its importance, and Adnan Louhichi argues that some polychrome types found in tenth/eleventh-century excavations there are not from Ṣabra/Kairouan, so are arguably local in manufacture; all the same, kilns have not been found there with dates before the twelfth century.[64]

There was beyond doubt a ceramic production hierarchy in North Africa after 900/950, with Ṣabra/Kairouan at the top, followed by the Kalâa, presumably Mahdia, and perhaps Tunis. Given the economic fragmentation of the previous two centuries, however, we could hardly expect there not to be local productions too, and we indeed find them. At the next level, the island of Jerba had its own unglazed wares, with some glaze by the eleventh century; to the east, Leptis Magna was a producer of common wares; the handmade cooking wares found at Carthage in the tenth century, which have a late Roman background, were perhaps made in north-west Tunisia, and thus distributed fairly widely, notwithstanding their simplicity; on the Tell plateau, Sétif also had local glazed and unglazed ceramics, dissimilar to those of the Kalâa, as well as imports from there and perhaps farther afield.[65] Common wares and monochrome glaze must indeed have been produced in a variety of localities, and some smaller kilns almost

[62] Bir Ftouha: Reynolds, 'The pottery', esp. pp. 250–6, 264–6, and 259, 263–4 for common wares and lamps in Ṣabra fabrics (this article replaces the ceramic report in Stevens et al., *Bir Ftouha*, pp. 498–528), with Salinas et al., 'Polychrome glazed ware production in Tunisia'. Ksar Lemsa: Gragueb Chatti, 'La céramique islamique de la citadelle byzantine de Ksar Lemsa'. Dougga: Colomban et al., 'Identification par microscopie Raman'. Chemtou: von Rummel and Möller, 'Chimtou médiévale', p. 208. Tegdaoust: Louhichi and Picon, 'Importation'.

[63] Kalâa: Golvin, *Recherches archéologiques*, pp. 185–232; Golvin, 'Les céramiques émaillées'; Jenkins, 'Medieval Maghribi luster-painted pottery'; see also the cautious remarks in Heidenreich, *Islamische Importkeramik*, pp. 120–3. Tunis: see Ibn Ḥawqal, *Kitāb ṣūrat al-arḍ*, trans. Kramers and Wiet, 1, p. 70; al-Bakrī, *al-Masālik wa al-mamālik*, trans. de Slane, p. 85. For the ceramics, see Vitelli, *Islamic Carthage*, pp. 61–9; Reynolds, 'The pottery', pp. 264–6; for Utica, Paul Reynolds, pers. comm.

[64] Al-Manṣūr, *Sīrat al-Ustādh Jawdhar*, trans. Canard and Haji, 1.27. Louhichi, 'La céramique fatimide et ziride de Mahdia'; Louhichi and Touhiri, 'La céramique de Mahdiya'; see n. 83 below.

[65] Holod and Cirelli, 'Islamic pottery from Jerba', with Louhichi, *Céramique islamique de Tunisie*, p. 36 for glaze; Cirelli, 'Leptis magna', pp.430–1; Reynolds, 'The pottery', pp. 263–6, for the handmade cooking wares; Mohamedi, Fentress, et al., *Fouilles de Sétif*, pp. 206–9.

certainly also imitated Ṣabra styles. The hierarchy of production had a space for very localized handmade wares too, at the lowest level, as it still does. But pottery looking to Ṣabra/Kairouan is found on nearly every excavated site, in larger or smaller quantities. Ṣabra styles extended all through the Medjerda valley sites, along the Sahel coast, to some notably inland sites such as Haïdra (where some of the glazes are close to Kairouan types, although others may be more local), and down to the semi-desert oasis of Négrine (even if, here too, the variety of ceramics found looked more provincial to the 1951 excavator).[66] Broadly, we can accept the dominance of Ṣabra/Kairouan ceramics over tenth- and eleventh-century fine-ware production across what is now Tunisia, with the Algerian Tell perhaps looking more to the Kalâa. And it was exported: Kairouan-area polychromes have been found in Sicily, as we have seen, where they lay at the origin of the island's own polychrome productions—indeed, Tunisian exports to Sicily continued for a long time, on larger or smaller scales, well past our period (see pp. 185, 229 below); and Ṣabra types also appear, even if not in large quantities, in al-Andalus (Córdoba, Valencia, Málaga, and other sites), up the western Italian coast, and, as we have seen, across the Sahara to Awdaghust.[67]

This density of productive activity has one clear consequence: Ṣabra/Kairouan and Kalâa glazes are a convenient type fossil which allows us to date urban activity in Ifrīqiya in the tenth and eleventh centuries. Sétif has an excavated set of close-packed residential courtyard buildings, divided by streets with water/sewer drainage. The courtyard buildings have plenty of parallels in this period, at Chemtou and Uchi Maius, as well as at Belalis Maior, where they surrounded a fortified or at least heavily walled residence. Stone and fired brick for buildings are commoner in this context than mud brick,[68] as they also are at Ṣabra

[66] Haïdra: Louhichi, 'La céramique islamique d'*Ammaedara*', esp. 215 and 223 (image); Pianel, 'La céramique de Négrine'. Pianel might well be describing Ṣabra wares, all the same; his drawings are, however, too poor to allow one to tell. Surprisingly, five sherds of the find still survived in 2011 in Algiers; but Djellid, 'La céramique islamique', pp. 152–4, who records this, inexplicably does not analyse them. Tozeur, not so far away, was inside the range of twelfth-century Mahdia merchants, who in one *fatwā* sold purple dye and olive oil there; see al-Wansharīsī, *al-Mi'yār*, trans. Lagardère, *Histoire et société*, 5.95; so the Négrine ceramics could in principle have come from the capital. Other sites with probably Ṣabra wares include Sousse (Louhichi, 'La céramique d'Ifriqiya') and Bulla (see photo in Daouatli, 'La céramique médiévale', p. 196). Gragueb Chatti, 'La céramique aghlabide de Raqqada', p. 350, has a list of sites with Raqqāda ware.

[67] For exports, see for surveys Azuar, 'Cerámicas en "verde y manganeso"', pp. 66–8, 74–6 (Ṣabra, but not Raqqāda, wares reached Spain); Heidenreich, *Islamische Importkeramik*, pp. 240–3, 253–5, 264–70, 468 (some of these exports to al-Andalus, to Almería and elsewhere, seem to be from the Kalâa des Béni Hammad; see further pp. 406, 455 below); Gragueb Chatti, 'La céramique islamique de la citadelle byzantine de Ksar Lemsa', pp. 284–91; and see pp. 555–6, 571–2 below. The tenth/eleventh-century glazed ceramics found at Ghirza, in the Libyan semi-desert, which the excavators ascribed to the Kalâa (Brogan and Smith, *Ghirza*, pp. 274–6) might perhaps now, forty years later, be reascribed to Ṣabra.

[68] Mohamedi, Fentress, et al., *Fouilles de Sétif*, pp. 149–58; von Rummel and Möller, 'Chimtou médiévale', pp. 191–5; Gelichi and Milanese, '*Uchi Maius*', pp. 55–71; for Belalis, see Mahjoubi, *Recherches d'histoire et d'archéologie*, pp. 384–7, 451–2. See in general the updated synthesis of housing types in Fentress, 'Reconsidering Islamic houses'.

al-Manṣūriya itself, which was a regular town, with careful water management, squared streets inside an elliptical mud-brick city wall, and the palace at one end in a forecourt, rebuilt at least once, in and around which four kilns were found.[69] The scale and quality of residential buildings in these sites, and other scrappier ones, is unequalled since the sixth century. They had developed to match the large-scale public buildings which are associated with the Aghlabids a century earlier in many cities, as we have seen. It cannot be said that North African cities as a whole have been properly studied for this period, but the picture of Fāṭimid-Zīrid urbanism which results is a consistent one, and one which appears to have easily matched the urban commitment of the tenth and eleventh centuries in most places in the Mediterranean.

This also fits the geographers, who, as I have noted, were happy to praise the African cities, before and after 1050. They were struck that Gabès had no latrines (according to al-Bakrī, people defecated in the street, women veiling their heads for anonymity, and then the faeces were taken to the fields around for fertilizer), but this implies that such latrines were normal elsewhere—one has been found at Sétif.[70] Their lists of artisanal activities, although certainly fairly random, at least add to the ceramic patterns just discussed. Cloth, in particular, recurs regularly; wool and silk in Gabès (it was Ifrīqiya's only significant silk town), linen in Kairouan/Ṣabra, more generalized fine cloth in Mahdia and especially Sousse, the fulling of cloth in Sfax, cotton in Gafsa and Tunis. We might well have expected more linen than this, as we shall see in the next section; but the image is clear all the same.[71] The numerous tombstones of Kairouan reinforce this with more solid data; nearly 500 of them date to between the mid-ninth century and 1055 (over 350 of these postdate 1000), and over 100 ascribe a trade to the deceased. They too show a high proportion of cloth workers and merchants, some 40 per cent of those with trades excluding food sellers, although wool is stressed most of all there, and linen is not mentioned explicitly.[72] There was a large amount

[69] See n. 40 above.

[70] Al-Bakrī, *al-Masālik wa al-mamālik*, trans. de Slane, pp. 42–3; Mohamedi, Fentress, et al., *Fouilles de Sétif*, pp. 156–8.

[71] Ibn Ḥawqal, *Kitāb ṣūrat al-arḍ*, trans. Kramers and Wiet, 1, pp. 66, 70 (Gabès, Tunis); al-Muqaddasī, *Aḥsan al-Taqāsīm*, trans. Collins, p. 202 (Kairouan); al-Bakrī, *al-Masālik wa al-mamālik*, trans. de Slane, pp. 41, 46–7, 78 (Gabès, Sfax, Sousse); al-Idrīsī, *Nuzhat al-mushtāq*, trans. Jaubert and Nef, pp. 180, 182, 184, 188 (Gafsa, Gabès, Mahdia, Tunis); *Kitāb al-Istibṣār*, partial trans. Fagnan, pp. 7, 16–17 (Gabès, Sousse). Ibn ʿIdhārī is also explicit that linen shops were to be found in Kairouan, and then Ṣabra: *al-Bayān al-mughrib*, trans. Fagnan, 1, p. 387. For Mahdia, see also n. 81 below.

[72] See Roy and Poinssot, *Inscriptions arabes de Kairouan*, nn. 50–521. Other artisanal media included wood and leather; there were few metalworkers. In 1055, even before the formal evacuation of Kairouan in 1057, the tombstones suddenly stop; there are only three dated stones for 1055–1100, a drop from the first half of the century of 99%. There then follow thirty-five for the twelfth, including a few citations of trades from 1158 onwards, although no cloth workers; this might show resettlement after a gap, but there is some archaeology for the late eleventh century (see n. 83 below), plus the reference in a *geniza* letter to poor people remaining here (see n. 14 above), so abandonment was probably incomplete.

of activity in these solid and well-laid-out cities. And they were connected, as the ceramic distributions tells us. As we shall see, the *geniza* backs this up, and substantially extends it.

Ifrīqiya was also linked to other regions for the exchange of goods other than ceramics. Again, for Mediterranean routes we will need to look to the *geniza*, but something here should be said about the Sahara trade. This was for gold and slaves above all, both luxuries for the most part. The slaves are not actually so very well attested, apart from references to black slave or ex-slave soldiers at various times in North African history; we do not have the frequency of citations that Egypt has (they were exploited above all there, and doubtless here, inside households; see p. 136 above). The gold is mentioned by the geographers, although their comments are often clearly overexcited. More helpfully, however, recent archaeological work has made quite clear not only that gold did come from sub-Saharan west Africa to Ifrīqiya (which no one had really doubted), but also some of the routes it took: the dinars minted in Kairouan or Mahdia (as also Palermo), which have a very high gold content (97–8 per cent), have silver and copper trace elements which exactly match gold found in crucibles in the south Saharan trading town of Essouk-Tadmekka in the semi-desert of northern Mali—the gold itself may have come from near Gao on the middle Niger, a little farther south. Awdaghust, by contrast, well to the west, was the southern Saharan link for Morocco, via the north-west Saharan trading city of Sijilmāsa; later eleventh-century Almorávid dinars were made with gold which came, using this route, from modern Senegal.[73] That Awdaghust, nonetheless, bought Ṣabra ceramics is a significant crossover, a sign of the importance of this ceramic type and doubtless its luxury status in west Africa, although not necessarily a marker of other wider trading connections that can be seen. This underlines one key point, however: everything brought across such a difficult route as any path across the Sahara was a luxury by the time it got to the other side. What the Ifrīqiyans were trading in return is not fully clear, although glass is well attested archaeologically, and cloth is likely enough; these may not seem to match gold in value, but by the time they made the crossing they perhaps indeed did.[74] The reason why this particular luxury trade matters to us is simply that it enabled the rulers of Ifrīqiya to maintain a very stable and reliable gold coinage, which in its turn facilitated internal and Mediterranean bulk trade. The *geniza* merchants certainly valued it, and regretted its loss when Kairouan went down, and when, after the 1060s, for a

[73] The geographers' statements are conveniently collected in translation in Levtzion and Hopkins, *Corpus*, pp. 12–161. For the archaeology, see Nixon, *Essouk-Tadmekka*, pp. 174–87. I am grateful to Andrew Small for guidance here.

[74] For glass, see Nixon, *Essouk-Tadmekka*, pp. 152–73. He also discusses (ibid., pp. 217–20) two cloth fragments, one of silk, which doubtless came from north of the Sahara; the geographers' accounts would support that. The few fragments of glazed pottery (pp. 119–25) certainly seem to be from Ifrīqiya, and the single sherd of Chinese porcelain (pp. 120–3) doubtless came that way too; but their small number here is less indicative of a larger trade.

while at least, Mahdia and other centres did not mint new coins—for one thing we can at least expect the Banū Hilāl to have been capable of doing, masters of the semi-desert as they were, was to disrupt any Sahara trade routes, at least for a time.[75] After the cities started to mint again, Mahdia dinars were worth rather less than Almorávid or Egyptian ones, as *geniza* letters tell us. A *fatwā* of al-Māzarī similarly lists the poor-quality coins of Sfax, Sousse, and the Lawāta Berbers, and notes that they were by no means comparable to Almorávid dinars.[76] As usual, merchants coped with the absence of a stable coinage, but the steadiness of the Fāṭimid-Zīrid economy had certainly been helped by its presence.

One counterexample to this picture of an active internal economy is, however, the marketing of grain. The narratives describe a substantial number of famines across our period in Ifrīqiya, with high points for drought around 1020, around 1040, in the 1090s, and the 1140s; and a low point, with few citations, between 1043 and 1089. Interestingly, the dates with few famines cover the main period of Hilālian instability.[77] We can never be sure how far an insistence on famines in any given period is the result of rhetorical strategies by authors (not least because we are dealing with late compilations here), and we certainly can never say how far famines were generalized (it is in most cases fairly unlikely that they were very widely felt, given the ecological variety of North Africa). But we might, with considerable caution, accept that there might sometimes be a real factual basis behind chroniclers choosing one date rather than another; and we could perhaps also accept that this is a lot of famines, perhaps with a regular occurrence in some areas. This was the background to a significant feature of some Ifrīqiyan sources:

[75] For the changing patterns of coinage, see Idris, *La Berbérie orientale*, pp. 538–43. For money problems, see, e.g., ENA NS 18.24 (Gil K344 [S97]). Caravan routes to Egypt were disrupted too; these were less difficult than those across the Sahara, as they ran along land routes where there was water, forage, and food, but were still relatively expensive; see Goitein, *MS*, 1, pp. 275–81; Goldberg, *Trade and institutions*, pp. 108, 303–4.

[76] DK14, T-S Ar. 54.15b (Gil K388), cited in Goitein, *MS*, 1, pp. 235–6; for al-Māzarī, see al-Wansharīsī, *al-Miʿyār*, trans. Lagardère, *Histoire et société*, 3.64. Gold coins under the Normans, Almohads, and Ḥafṣids became stable again; for rapid summaries, see Idris, *La Berbérie orientale*, p. 542; Brunschvig, *La Berbérie orientale*, 2, p. 74.

[77] There is a useful list, taken from a variety of sources, in Amara, 'Retour à la problématique', pp. 8–11. The trend to famine rhetoric from the late tenth century onwards might seem to be linked to the beginning of the Medieval Warm Period in climate, which was (to put it exceptionally crudely) good news for northern Europe, bad news for semi-deserts; but the local incidence of this still needs to be pinned down better, and most data points for it are outside our region. Still, we do have a few regional guides, which considerably nuance that crude image: Faust et al, 'High-resolution fluvial record', focussed on Tunisia itself (the central Medjerda valley); this is developed by the more historically minded Fenech, *Human-induced changes*, p. 112, using data from Malta, 300 kilometres off the coast of Sousse and Mahdia. They argue that the Warm Period, here dated after *c.*1100, was slightly wetter than the cooler/drier period around 1000, the latter of which fits some of (but not all of) the famines. (Fenech also shows, ibid., pp. 108, 112, interestingly, given our other data for the Egypt–Sicily–Tunisia exchange triangle, that our rough period is a high point for flax pollen on Malta.) Conversely, dendrochronological analysis argues for a severe drought in the 1140s, which does fit the famine then (as well as another in Libya just before the invasion of the Banū Hilāl); see King, 'The sword and the sun', pp. 228–9, 232–4. But for us the point is less the climatic trend in itself than the way people dealt with it.

references to buying grain from Sicily. They appear in the *fatwās* of al-Qābisī, active in Kairouan (d. 1012), where the activity seems entirely normal (the grain is exchanged for gold; Sicily needed to buy gold coming through Ifrīqiya in order to supply its own mints), and of al-Māzarī, writing in Mahdia in the decades around and after 1100, after the Norman conquest of Sicily—his view was that it was wrong to buy from the Normans, as they were infidels and would use the money to attack Ifrīqiya; and that they would also restrike Muslim coins with Christian crosses.[78] We can add to this one *geniza* letter from Mahdia lamenting the Norman attack on Sicily, 'because this [land] is dependent on it for food'; and also the narrative accounts of the conquest of Mahdia by the Normans in 1148, which was, it was said, hard to resist effectively because Mahdia was dependent on Sicilian grain.[79]

Some of the modern historiography concludes from all this that Ifrīqiya was structurally dependent on Sicily for grain. This is doubly impossible. First, because no major agricultural region could survive, before industrial-age mass transport (and, indeed, often after as well), if it did not produce locally what it needed to subsist in normal conditions; secondly, because North Africa was, as we have amply seen, one of the Mediterranean's major grain producers, at least in non-famine years. Indeed, we have examples of Ifrīqiya sending grain elsewhere too, including once to Sicily, even if only for military supply, as well as to al-Andalus on several occasions.[80] But it does at least show that one feature of the internal exchange system of this region was that grain, usually wheat, from the Medjerda valley did not always so easily get to Kairouan and Mahdia—or at least no more easily than did grain from Sicily. The later citations come from a period in which all internal supply routes were likely to be weaker, given the political fragmentation of the region after the nomad attacks; Béja had different rulers from Mahdia, who were not necessarily friendly. It is easy to conclude that the *geniza* letter could refer to such a difficulty; the 1140s grain imports, furthermore, took place during the period in which perhaps the worst Ifrīqiyan famine of our whole period is documented. But the al-Qābisī *fatwās* point to a different situation: a relatively stable period in which, all the same, grain imports from Sicily to Mahdia/Kairouan were quite common. It is here that it is important to

[78] Al-Wansharīsī, *al-Mi'yār*, trans. Lagardère, *Histoire et société*, 6.23, 3.68.

[79] INA D55.13 (Gil K616 [S141]); for the Normans, see Abulafia, 'The Norman kingdom of Africa', pp. 27–34, which sets out the sources. He stresses this grain trade in the early twelfth century; but, before the 1140s, the only clear evidence from the Norman side dates to 1134 (Pirri, *Sicilia sacra*, 2, pp. 974–6), a text in which Roger II gives permission to a Messina monastery to exchange 200 *salmae* (*c.*35,000 litres) of grain for African oil and other *necessaria*—the scale is large, but the oil here appears to be more important than the grain.

[80] Al-Manṣūr, *Sīrat al-Ustādh Jawdhar*, trans. Canard and Haji, 2.1; cf. ibid., 2.28, for military supply; Ibn 'Idhārī, *al-Bayān al-mughrib*, trans. Fagnan, 1, pp. 471–2 (the governor of Tunis exports wheat even during the 1148 famine, and has to flee rioters). For Spain, see Constable, *Trade and traders*, pp. 162–4, and cf. p. 414 below.

note that we also have substantial archaeological evidence of wine amphorae from Sicily in several sites in Tunisia, not least in Ṣabra, where, indeed, Sicilian amphorae dominate over all others; timber too was a significant Sicilian export to eastern Ifrīqiya, as we shall see in a moment. Conversely, there is clear evidence that the Tunisians exported in return not only gold but also olive oil to Sicily, plus ceramics, as we have seen, to match the wine, timber, and grain.[81] So it looks as if the close commercial links between the two regions, including after the Norman conquest of Sicily, extended to an easy exchange of foodstuffs in any year in which there were deficiencies in the receiving region; we will come back to the point again later. But the evidence of grain does also indicate one important respect in which the internal market of the region was not complete.

Notwithstanding this, the overall coherence of Ifrīqiya's internal economy in the tenth and early eleventh centuries is made quite clear by the archaeology (see Map 9). Kairouan and the palace cities were its hub, exporting ceramics but also other goods across a wide area; but Mahdia, the Kalâa, and other centres were by no means dependent on it for everything, and goods will have been sent out in more than one direction from Mahdia, itself a serious producer (the *Life* of Jawdhar casually mentions swords, clothing, *ṭirāz* fabrics and prayer mats made there, plus shipbuilding; we have seen the cloth already). We have also already seen how the coastal cities of the Sahel were linked together independently of a Kairouan focus. The Tunis area had its own interconnections too, if Carthage could get not only fine wares from Kairouan but cooking wares from the north-west—and we can add here as well wine amphorae from Sicily.[82] That is to say, there was a complex network of internal exchange. This was the opposite of the colonial economy of the Roman period, when so much just went to the coast. I would guess—although we simply do not have the documentation which would allow us to know for sure—that this internal coherence was the long-term result of a fiscal recentralization on the part of the Aghlabids; certainly, all the signs are that Tunisia, at least, was very centralized in administrative and fiscal terms in the period *c*.850–1050. But whatever its underlining causes, all this gave the region a real internal economic structuring; and this was necessary for it to play a full part in the interregional exchange which the *geniza* and other sources clearly document for this period in the central and eastern Mediterranean, as we shall see in the next section.

But with the invasions and wars of the second half of the eleventh century, how much of this survived? Insofar as Ifrīqiya was held together economically by Kairouan, it is evident that there would have at once been potentially serious

[81] Oil to Sicily: Moss. VII,101, T-S 12.372, Halper 389 (Gil P193, K513, 751 [S60, 111, 151]); see also n. 79 above and n. 90 below. For Sicilian amphorae in Africa, see n. 189 below.

[82] Reynolds, 'The pottery'; for Mahdia, see al-Manṣūr, *Sīrat al-Ustādh Jawdhar*, trans. Canard and Haji, 1.4, 17, 37, 2.2, 52.

problems in the region's economic coherence after the city ceased to be a hub. But how serious? How easily could the non-Kairouan trade connections, which, as we have seen, were substantial, develop to cover it? That is to say, how effectively, could the cities of Tunisia, in particular (the Tell was more autonomous economically), deal with such a hole in the exchange system?

It is not easy to answer this from the archaeology, as twelfth-century sites are so rare. Some of this is, doubtless, as noted earlier, simply the result of excavators assuming that production and exchange abruptly ended with the Hilālian attacks. At Ṣabra itself, we can perhaps get past that. Archaeomagnetism gives a *terminus ante quem* of 1083 as a date of abandonment for the main glazed-pottery kiln, and of 1114 for the frit kiln. Although the excavators argue that each could well be dated earlier, and that, therefore, maybe both of them really failed in 1057 after all, we could well here see a continuity of production for another generation or two; and subsequent work on the ceramics shows that archaeological levels could indeed date to the early twelfth-century. This fits a recent small-scale excavation in Kairouan itself, which has clear late eleventh- and twelfth-century levels, and some good-quality ceramics in them.[83] Elsewhere, however, we only have evidence so far from Mahdia and Tunis/Carthage, none of it well published. In Mahdia, where we know that artisans were still active after the Pisan/Genoese attack of 1087 (see pp. 165–6 above), what we know of the Qasr al-Qaïm excavations in the city's former palace shows a continued production of ceramics, both glazed and unglazed, up at least to the late twelfth/early thirteenth century, the date of a kiln for glazed pottery found there, with glass production too.[84] In Carthage, the results of the unpublished Byrsa excavations for the late eleventh and twelfth centuries were summarized forty years ago by Giovanna Vitelli in her important survey of the city area in the Islamic period; they consisted of a set of domestic structures in which were found some local Tunis wares, but also wares from central Tunisia, Sicily, and mainland Italy. With due caution, Reynolds has more recently concluded that central Tunisian—that is, by now probably largely Mahdia—productions were still prominent in the Carthage area, and thus perhaps in nearby Tunis too, until the late twelfth century.[85] That would give us one set of tentative evidence for the connectivity between the coastal cities along the Tunisian coast in the twelfth. Only then and thereafter did Tunis's own fine-ware production, even though it already existed, really take off in what would soon

[83] Cressier and Rammah, 'Sabra al-Mansūriyya', pp. 294–8; for later ceramic datings, see Gragueb Chatti, 'Note sur un matériel céramique rare en Ifrīqiya', pp. 90–1; for Kairouan, see Khéchine and Gragueb Chatti, 'Contribution à l'histoire de la ville de Kairouan'. One potter (*qallāl*) is attested among the later twelfth-century tombstones from Kairouan; see Roy and Poinssot, *Inscriptions arabes de Kairouan*, n. 563 (a. 1158).

[84] See n. 64 above, with Louhichi, 'Un mode de cuisson', for the kiln.

[85] Vitelli, *Islamic Carthage*, pp. 45–6, 61–6; Reynolds, 'The pottery', pp. 265–6. At Oudhna, a little south of Tunis, eleventh- and twelfth-century glazed wares might have come from central Tunisia too, as they are similar to Carthage finds; see Gragueb Chatti, 'L'apport d'Oudhna'.

become the regional capital, a production characterized by high-quality blue and white tin-glazed decoration, called 'cobalt and manganese' in the literature (see Fig. 5), which would be the dominant late medieval fine ware in Ifrīqiya, and which was in the late twelfth century and onwards once again exported into Sicily, and up the Italian coast as far as Provence and Barcelona, on a much larger scale than previously.[86]

Given this evidence, however slight, and given also what al-Idrīsī says about urban activity around 1150 (see p. 163 above), I would argue that the Tunisian coastal cities continued to prosper in the twelfth century, and continued to have links both with each other and with the outside world. The same would certainly be true of Béjaïa too. How this really compared with the period before 1050 is as yet hard to assess, particularly on the basis of the material record. The onus of proof would be on anyone who wished to argue that the twelfth-century prosperity of these cities actually matched that of the earlier period, and indeed I do not know anyone who does argue this. North Africa may not have been destroyed by the Banū Hilāl, but the fragmentation and war which followed their arrival ensured that this region, unlike most of the others we are looking at, did not become more economically complex in the last part of our period, and almost

Fig. 5 Tunis cobalt and manganese ware

[86] See for a survey Louhichi, *Céramique islamique de Tunisie*, pp. 117–23. For Sicily, see p. 229 below; for Pisa, see Berti and Giorgio, *Ceramiche con coperture vetrificate*, p. 39; Baldassarri and Giorgio, 'La ceramica di produzione mediterranea'; Fatighenti, 'I corredi ceramici' (for the dominance of cobalt and manganese on the ex-laboratori Gentili site in Pisa in the early thirteenth century); and for the western Mediterranean coastal sites, see in general, Chapter 5, n. 215 below.

certainly lost some ground. The twelfth century, nonetheless, offered its own opportunities. Béjaïa, in particular, was a major port for the Genoese, as Valérian's model study shows, with a substantial Pisan presence as well.[87] Tunis was coming up too, in both Genoese and Pisan records. By contrast, to judge by the notarial register of Giovanni Scriba, from the mid-century, the Genoese did not visibly go to Mahdia at all, although they did sometimes go to both Gabès and Tripoli. That is to say, exchange both continued and was also perhaps rebalancing itself, even if, as we shall see, it would be wrong to conclude that this automatically meant that Mahdia was dropping behind Tunis or (still less) Gabès in its internal activity.[88]

We will need to look more closely at what Genoese and Pisan records do tell us about exchange on the North African coast in the twelfth century; but we are getting ahead of ourselves. We cannot get a proper sense of what that evidence means until we have looked both at what was going on a century earlier, in the *geniza* letters, and at how to balance what we know of internal exchange in Ifrīqiya against our evidence for the Mediterranean commercial network. This we can best do after looking at the evidence for Sicily, which is much richer than that for Ifrīqiya. Let us, therefore, first look at the *geniza*, and at some of our other more exact and immediate written documentation, to see what this adds to what we have seen so far, both before 1050 and after; we will come back to the twelfth century in North Africa in the conclusion to the chapter.

3.3 The *geniza* and Central Mediterranean Exchange

Historians often begin their accounts of the eleventh-century trade triangle linking Egypt, Ifrīqiya, and Sicily with the beginning of the *geniza* at the very end of the tenth century. We can be sure it started earlier, however, in some form at least. There are *fatwā*s and other rulings from jurists from as early as the mid-ninth century referring to it. An early example, by Ibn Abdūs (d. 874), discussed whether a merchant from Alexandria who was taking goods to Tripoli, when the wind blew the ship farther, taking it to Sousse, would have to pay the extra fare (answer: no), or, conversely, had the right to demand passage back to Tripoli (answer: yes, as long as he does not find out about market prices at Sousse before he does). Yaḥya b. ʿUmar (d. 901), discussed what would happen if people rented places in a ship but the wind pushed it back to the departure point. Did they have to pay the fare? The answer here was that they did not if the contract said the ship would *cross* the sea, for example to Sicily or al-Andalus; but if it was to run along the coast to Egypt, a fare was due for the distance the ship had gone. Sousse was as yet the

[87] Valérian, *Bougie*.

[88] For Gabès and Tripoli, see *Giovanni Scriba*, nn. 187, 412, 770, 823–4, 1238. For Pisa and Mahdia, see p. 265 below.

main port on the Tunisian coast, but even after Mahdia's foundation in 921 both appear; ships came to one or the other most often from Sicily in these legal opinions, but also, as we have just seen, from Alexandria, the Libyan coast, that is, Barqa and Tripoli, and al-Andalus. (Tunis appears in the texts as well, but only in the context of it being the wrong place to disembark, because of storms. Who pays for the transit to Sousse in that case? Or who benefits or is liable, if prices turn out to be higher or lower, when the merchandise has to be sold off in Tunis?) Merchants frequently, as early as in *fatwās* of the famous jurist Saḥnūn (d. 854), used *qirāḍ* contracts, in which a land-based capitalist invested in trade carried on by a seagoing merchant; we saw (p. 120) that contracts of this type are commoner in Egypt in Jewish than in Muslim documentary evidence, but in these *fatwās* merchants already regard them as normal.[89] The questions asked here about obligations coming from trading which did not go quite right are so close to those visible in the *geniza*, indeed, that it is as clear as in Egypt that merchants from both religions operated in effect according to the same rules and values. In the early tenth century, jurisprudence about maritime commercial law, with some parallels to the *Rhodian Sea Law* in Byzantium, was collected more systematically in the *Kitāb akriyat al-sufun*, a compilation of the rulings of Yahya b. 'Umar's brother, Muḥammad b. 'Umar al-Kinānī (d. 923), an Andalusī who had moved to Alexandria. It is evident that there was by now need for it.[90]

It is likely, all the same, that these routes still operated on a fairly small scale for a long time. The localization of Tunisian ceramic productions and distributions before *c.*880, and the weak links between them and the Byzantine amphora networks, do not indicate that the economic infrastructure of Ifrīqiya was sufficiently complex that a large-scale interregional exchange system could as yet operate effectively. Things changed at the end of the ninth century, when Raqqāda ware developed and was swiftly imitated in Sicily. It may well be that the stabilization of Aghlabid power in Sicily was indeed the catalyst for such a change, and it certainly was for the routinization of the Sousse/Mahdia to Palermo passage.

This was the context for the activities of Jawdhar, a senior minister to the Fāṭimids in Ifrīqiya, as we have seen. His *Life*, written in the 980s or 990s by his secretary Manṣūr, is invaluable not only because it is by an eyewitness, at least to the minister's later life, but also because it includes many apparently verbatim letters written to Jawdhar by the caliphs. Jawdhar got estates from the caliphs, as

[89] See al-Wansharīsī, *al-Mi'yār*, trans. Lagardère, *Histoire et société*, 5.8, 11, 16, and 40 (Tunis), and see also 50, 103; for the first reference to *qirāḍ*, see ibid., 5.2, and see in general Idris, 'Commerce maritime et ḳirāḍ' for a set of citations, and Bosanquet, 'Maritime trade', for a good recent commentary. Most of the legal opinions referred to here already appear in the tenth-century text cited in n. 90 below, so are certainly early.

[90] Muḥammad b. 'Umar al-Kinānī, *Kitāb akriyat al-sufun*, analysed in Khalilieh, *Admiralty and maritime laws*; see ibid., pp. 273–330 for a translation, pp. 288–93 for the legal opinions just cited. See further p. 648 below. Note also a claim in a mid-tenth-century Byzantine text that (probably) Ifrīqiyan olive oil ships went to Sicily as early as 880: *Chronographiae, Vita Basilii*, ed. Ševčenko, ch. 64.

we have seen; but the *Life* stresses that these were less important for him than his commercial activities. That he was 'content' with commerce, rather than landowning, was to Manṣūr a sign of abstinence; but abstinence or no, he made enough money from it that he could, Manṣūr says, give a gift to the caliph al-Mu'izz (953–75) for the conquest of Egypt in 969 of over 100,000 dinars. This commerce, by himself and others, was above all with Sicily. Among other things, Jawdhar imported timber from north-eastern Sicily on such a scale that he could also offer some of this to the caliph for shipbuilding, offers al-Mu'izz is said to have first turned down but later accepted.[91] Once, one of Jawdhar's boats sank, and he successfully asked the caliph whether he could replace it with one of the boats the latter had recently bought from the Rūm, Italians again or Byzantines. This sort of underwriting is something one might expect for a powerful official, and, indeed, on a smaller scale, it seems to have been routine for him; on another occasion, when he sent a ship to Sicily, he asked the governor to check whether there was anything lacking in the cargo, and paid the 100 dinars for the missing goods from the state treasury, an action then ratified by the caliph.[92] On the other hand, Jawdhar's huge gifts to the caliph can be seen, not just as a sign of the great wealth trading could produce in this period, but also as an integral part of an ongoing exchange of gifts and favours between them, of which underwriting ships and shipping was simply a small element.

The Tunisia–Sicily side of the trade triangle was, then, clearly strong before the Fāṭimid conquest of Egypt, as these instances show. And as we have also seen, it already extended in some form both east to Egypt and west to al-Andalus, with occasional links north to Christian lands too. But there is little doubt that the eastern route, in particular, was massively developed after all three regions began to be ruled by the same Fāṭimid regime. Egypt from now on figures more prominently than either of the other two in the context of the organization of maritime commerce. This is partially but not only because the *geniza* was found in Fusṭāṭ; it is, all the same, where the *geniza* comes into its own.[93]

* * *

As we saw for Egypt, the two great caches of Mediterranean mercantile documents found in the Ben Ezra synagogue were associated with Ibn 'Awkal (d. *c.*1040), a

[91] Al-Manṣūr, *Sīrat al-Ustādh Jawdhar*, trans. Canard and Haji, 2.7, 18, 28, 49 (in which the north-east of Sicily is explicit), 52, 56, 75. Cf. Bramoullé, 'La Sicile', p. 30. Sicily would be for another century the main source for timber for the Fāṭimid lands, but Ifrīqiya also imported from Venice; when the Byzantines demanded that Venice stop exporting timber and arms to *Saracenorum terras* in 971, the Venetians at once complied, except for three ships which were already laden; two were due to go to Mahdia and one to Tripoli (Cessi, *Documenti*, n. 49). This unique reference, however, tells us little about the scale of Venetian bulk export; see p. 508 below. It might, on the other hand, fit the reference to Rūmī ships in Mahdia harbour in an apparently 960s version of Ibn Ḥawqal, not transmitted by the Kramers edition and Kramers and Wiet translation; see Bramoullé, *Les Fatimides et la mer*, pp. 486–7.

[92] Al-Manṣūr, *Sīrat al-Ustādh Jawdhar*, trans. Canard and Haji, 2.67 (cf. 77), 75.

[93] For a rapid picture of these developments, see Picard, *La mer des califes*, pp. 324–32.

very rich merchant of the early eleventh century, and then, for fifty years (*c.*1045–97) with Nahray b. Nissīm, not quite so rich but with a very wide circle of associates. There are others, and also later ones, as we shall see, but the scale of these two sets, particularly the second, outmatches that of all other groups. Ibn ʿAwkal was from the Maghreb, although his family seem to have been Iraqi; Nahray came from Ifrīqiya for sure, and we have plenty of letters from his relatives by marriage, still based in Mahdia and Kairouan. Those relatives, the Tāhirtīs, show no links to Tāhirt (modern Tiaret in western Algeria) by the time their own letters, as preserved in the Nahray collection, begin around 1008, but they had certainly been in the Maghreb for a long time, and many of them stayed in Ifrīqiya. The Egypt–Ifrīqiya link shown in these texts was thus organic, built up from personal knowledge, long-standing friendship networks, and blood relationships.[94] It extended to Sicily from the start, and Sicilian Jews were part of the network from early on too; one of the best-known *geniza* letters, from Samḥun b. Dāʾūd b. al-Siqillī to Ibn ʿAwkal, accusing him of unreasonable demands, the non-payment of bills, and slander, dates to *c.*1000, and shows a man of Sicilian origin (al-Siqillī) operating for the Fusṭāṭ merchant in Kairouan, and on a large scale (420 pounds of silk, among several other commodities). In Sicily, the Egyptians had close business associates, rather than the density of kin links that could be found in Mahdia and Kairouan. All the same, the business associates we do see, for example in the middle decades of the century Ḥayyim b. ʿAmmar al-Madīnī, from a Palermo family (Palermo was commonly simply called the *Madīna*, 'the city'), are fronted in our texts in just the same way as Nahray's relatives in Mahdia, or the Ibn Sighmār family, whom we have already met in the context of the Ifrīqiyan troubles of the 1050s (see p. 161 above). It would be very hard to say that Sicily/Palermo was less economically important than Ifrīqiya/Mahdia to the Egyptian merchant entrepreneurs, and, as stressed at the start of this chapter, the two were seen very much as a continuum.[95]

Notwithstanding the organic family link between Egypt and Ifrīqiya, however, one of the most striking things about the *geniza* letters for the latter region is how little they tell us about anywhere but a handful of places. Kairouan (before its fall) and Mahdia, its port and successor as a capital, entirely dominate in our texts. Sfax is sometimes named as a destination, so are Sousse, Tunis, and, farther east,

[94] For Ibn ʿAwkal, see p. 130 above. For Nahray and the Tāhirtīs, see Gil, *Jews*, pp. 693–721; Goldberg, *Trade and institutions*, pp. 33–7. Goldberg, following Udovitch, sees Nahray's mother's sister as the marriage link to the Tāhirtīs, not Nahray's own mother, as Gil states; I have followed the former, but the difference is not significant—the two families were very close.

[95] For Samḥun, see DK 13 and 327 (Gil K221, trans. Goitein, *Letters*, n. 1). For Ḥayyim and his family, see Gil, *Jews*, pp. 587–8, with citations, and Goldberg, *Trade and institutions*, pp. 1–2 (Ḥayyim himself appears in over twenty letters in the *geniza*). For Sicily, see in general Gil, *Jews*, pp. 563–93 (with some inaccuracies), and the commentaries on the Sicilian parts of the *geniza* in Goitein, 'Sicily and southern Italy', Udovitch, 'New materials', and especially Nef, 'La Sicile dans la documentation de la Geniza cairote', with Goldberg, as in n. 96 below.

Tripoli; but other coastal cities hardly appear until the twelfth century, and inland, apart from Kairouan, nowhere at all is mentioned.[96] The same is true of Sicily: no inland town is referred to as a destination there either, and, among the ports, the merchants dealt almost exclusively with Palermo, plus, later in the eleventh century, Mazara del Vallo, one of the best harbours on the way to Palermo from either Egypt or Tunisia (but seldom Agrigento, Sciacca, and Trapani, or Syracuse in the east, which are most of the others). Only in the mid-twelfth century does the fast-rising port of Messina in the north-east appear.[97] Indeed, the eleventh-century *geniza* merchants did not, as it seems, even go through the Strait of Messina; Demenna (modern San Marco), on the north coast of Sicily near the strait, a source of silk, as we shall see later, was reached via Palermo, not via Messina. But others did go through the strait, as ceramic distributions imply, and the sea route southwards from Messina was operative too, for Jawdhar must have used it to get timber to Ifrīqiya from the mountains of the north-east.[98]

So, far more than inside Egypt, the *geniza* relationship with the two central Mediterranean regions was restricted to the main trunk routes. Goldberg's '*geniza* business model' (see p. 139 above) meant that even in a region which the merchants knew as well as Ifrīqiya, the task of most incoming merchants was to unload, sell as high as possible in the same port, buy as low as possible, and then return as soon as the leisurely practices of selling, getting the money, and hiring space for newly bought goods in another boat permitted. Cabotage and inland trade were evidently the work of others, that is to say, locals, who were probably also non-Jews—which almost certainly meant Muslims, for, unlike in Egypt, Christian merchants are undocumented in these regions before the Italians in the twelfth century. And so was production; in Egypt, Jews could sometimes invest in, for example, sugar refineries, and others were themselves artisans in the capital (see pp. 45, 73 above), but almost nothing similar is ever mentioned for the central Mediterranean—the *Life* of Jawdhar casually tells us more about artisans in Ifrīqiya than does the whole *geniza* collection.[99] (If Sicily had its own Jewish artisans, which is entirely likely, they did not transact directly with the Egyptians.)

Nor were the *geniza* merchants particularly connected to government in the central Mediterranean—even less than they were in Egypt (cf. p. 44 above). There are a handful of direct merchant links with Sicilian or Maghribī governmental

[96] Goldberg, *Trade and institutions*, pp. 319–28, discusses the loosening of the Mahdia (as also Palermo) focus in the later eleventh century.

[97] For occasional references, for Agrigento, see T-S 12.372 (Gil K513 [S111]); for Sciacca, see Halper 389 (Gil K751 [S151]); for Trapani, see ENA NS 18.24 (Gil K344 [S97]); the first reference to Messina I have seen is from the 1150s: ENA 2557.151 (ed. Gil and Simonsohn, 'More on the history of the Jews in Sicily', n. 2, trans. Goitein and Friedman, *India traders*, III, 43).

[98] The route to Demenna: T-S 20.4, 20.9 (Gil K821–2 [S67–8]); for Jawdhar, see n. 90 above.

[99] A couple of *geniza* references to artisans are cited in Goitein, *MS*, 1, p. 100 (Jerba wickerwork, *c.*1046); Goitein, *Letters*, n. 1, p. 30 (translated from DK 13, Gil K221: a casual reference to a dyer family in Kairouan, *c.*1000).

figures mentioned in the letters, but they seem to be chance pieces of opportunism. Examples are Salāma's tax-farming concession near Sfax in perhaps the 1060s, or a reference to one of the Tāhirtīs tax-collecting in Ifrīqiya in 1016, or the pleasure Yahūda Abū Zikri expressed around 1020 because the *sayyida* ('the lady', that is to say, probably Umm Mallāl, the aunt-regent of the young *amīr* of Ifrīqiya al-Mu'izz) had given him robes and a mule, or the appointment in probably 1069 of Zakkār, brother of Ḥayyim b. 'Ammar al-Madīnī, as head of supplies and of the local Jewish community for the new ruler of Palermo Ibn al-Ba'bā', himself a Muslim merchant with whom *geniza* merchants had dealt earlier. Each of these examples was of a figure of local, not Egyptian origin, which is not surprising in itself, but these links never match the tight association that Jawdhar, as a merchant, had with the tenth-century caliphs.[100] In the eleventh too, closer governmental connections doubtless remained the field of action of Muslims, although we have less sign than in Egypt that the public power intervened in trade to any significant extent, either positively or negatively.[101] All this underlines the basic point that the *geniza* view of Ifrīqiya and Sicily, however dense, was essentially an external one.

On the other hand, it was indeed dense as well, enough to get far beyond the anecdotal. The remarkable activity and bustle of Mahdia and Palermo, and the complexities of economic interactions in each, appear over and over in our letters.[102] I characterized this from the standpoint of Fusṭāṭ and Alexandria in Chapter 2 (pp. 127–40), but the trade patterns between the regions were, of course, triangular. We have seen that trade was underpinned by exports of Egyptian raw flax on a huge scale; these went to both Ifrīqiya and Sicily, along with those dyes which Egypt (or the Indian Ocean) alone could supply. Local buyers showed considerable discrimination over the many types of flax which the Egyptians sold.[103] Sugar and pepper were secondary to this, but again went to both of the central Mediterranean regions in substantial quantities. In return, Sicily sent back cloth—not just linen of different types (including turbans), but also, regularly, silk, both high-quality silk and *lāsīn*, which seems to have been a cheaper silk (it is conceivable, although wholly undocumented, that it was a silk–linen mix), and

[100] Respectively, Halper 389 and 414 (Gil K751–2 [S151–2]); T-S 16.64 (Gil K145, trans. Stillman, *East-west relations*, pp. 229–33); T-S 12.224 (Gil K155, trans. Goitein, *Letters*, n. 12); Bodl. MS Heb. d 76/59 (Gil K519 [S163]); see also T-S 13J36.1 (Gil K146, trans. Stillman, *East-west relations*, pp. 201–2) for the Jewish leader in Kairouan, Ibrahīm b. 'Aṭā', as close to the *amīr* Bādis. See n. 137 below for Ibn al-Ba'bā'.

[101] Two examples are T-S 16.163 (Gil K373 [S150]), in which, after a bankruptcy in Mahdia, the ruler required foreigners' debts to be paid first, to the sorrow of local merchants; and the imposition in Palermo of *'ushr*, tithe, on non-Sicilian merchant transactions (which was got around illegally, and rescinded not long after). For the latter, see esp. DK 230.1, Bodl. MS Heb. a 3/9, T-S 10J12.26 (Gil K561, P396, K253 [S109, 124, 135]); and Bondioli, 'The Sicilian tithe business', for a targeted analysis.

[102] Goldberg, *Trade and institutions*, and Goitein, *MS*, 1, both illustrate this throughout.

[103] For discrimination, see, e.g., T-S 13J17.11, 16.7, 12.366 (Gil K194, 574, 251 [S53, 84, 137]). For this whole paragraph, see the data in Goitein, *MS*, 1, pp. 209–29.

sometimes cheese.[104] Ifrīqiya sent olive oil (and its by-product, soap), and again linen, in a wide variety of different types. Both Sicily and Ifrīqiya also sent some hides, and some metals, lead, tin, copper, and (in the case of Ifrīqiya) silver coin, but these are less prominent in the letters; probably they sent iron too, although not via Jewish merchants.[105] As for the Sicily–Ifrīqiya trade, we have seen that Ifrīqiya exported oil, gold, and ceramics, and imported wheat, timber, and wine; the *geniza* merchants mostly dealt with oil out of this set, and again non-Jewish merchants, from both Sicily and Ifrīqiya, must have been the main carriers of the others. This is less likely to be a consequence of religious restrictions (Muslim merchants would otherwise be surprising wine purveyors), and more likely to be the consequence of the fact that the *geniza* merchants were most focussed on the routes to and from Egypt; the specific trade from Ifrīqiya to Sicily and back was less their concern. So although they certainly engaged in it substantially, it was dealt by them more opportunistically, except for oil, which they were used to trading in on a regular basis anyway.[106]

As has just been stressed, the *geniza* letters tell us nothing directly about production in the central Mediterranean. All the same, some things can be deduced from the balance of the letters as we have them. First, it is obvious that by early in the eleventh century, both Ifrīqiya and Sicily had the infrastructural capacity to weave flax into linen cloth on a large scale. It must have begun slowly, for central Mediterranean weavers cannot have known quickly that they could count on substantial levels of Egyptian flax imports, nor could Egyptian peasants know in advance that they had a ready outlet in Palermo and Mahdia if they switched to flax cultivation—the merchants must have told them, but it would have taken some time before trust would have built up enough for peasants to risk it. But across the decades around 1000 it evidently built up year on year. We saw in Chapter 2 that the choice by Egyptian merchants to sell flax to the central Mediterranean, a long way away, rather than to the great linen towns of the Nile delta, is remarkable; but

[104] Everyone assumes that *lāsīn* is a type of cheap silk (Goitein's latest statement was 'Two Arabic textiles', pp. 221–2), but there is no explicit contemporary statement to that effect anywhere that I have seen. It is a highly plausible assumption, for sure; but *lāsīn* is so steadily differentiated from *ḥarīr*, *qazz*, and *dibāj*, more normal silk words, that it could perhaps be a slightly different cloth type, hence the linen mix I suggest here. This might perhaps be supported by the fact that in the Norman period at least, flax was cultivated near the major silk centre of Demenna (see n. 117 below). A silk–linen mix was called *zenday* and variants in contemporary Puglia; see Ditchfield, *La culture matérielle*, p. 379 (it is the same word as the *sendada* of thirteenth-century Lucca, mentioned on p. 583 below, by then, as later in Europe, meaning silk; but in the Puglia texts it is a mix). For cheese, see, Chapter 2, n. 288 above.

[105] For Sicilian exports carried by Jews, see references in Gil, *Jews*, pp. 567–8, with Nef, 'La Sicile dans la documentation de la Geniza cairote', p. 290, for statistics. Iron was mined near Palermo and Messina (see n. 241 below), Béjaïa (see p. 163 above), and also on the Tunisian Tell near El Kef (Touati, 'Mines et peuplement', esp. pp. 132–5); this was for local use first, of course, but it is likely that the Fāṭimids took advantage of it too.

[106] Oil from Africa to Sicily: e.g. Moss. VII,101, T-S 12.372, 20.127, Halper 389 (Gil P193, K513, 573, 751 [S60, 111, 51, 151]). Wheat was transported in a few texts: T-S K2.32, 16.12, Bodl. MS Heb. d 76/59 (Gil K354, 654, 519 [S106, 162–3]).

so is the capacity of the regions which bought this flax, for they evidently had artisanal economies complex enough to depend on the external provisioning of basic raw materials, and to be able to transform these materials at a level which, given the scale of flax imports, must have matched that of the major cloth towns of Flanders from the twelfth century onwards, and of northern Italy a little later. We can show, as we shall see through the evidence of Sicilian archaeology, that the island indeed had a complex enough economy in the eleventh century to be able to cope with this; and the less extensive Ifrīqiyan archaeology is at least not in conflict with such a conclusion. The central Mediterranean cloth centres may not have been as hyperactive as Tinnīs in Egypt, and will certainly not have been as single-product-focussed as that city was, but they belong in the same continuum. Indeed, Ibn Ḥawqal, who disliked Sicilians very considerably (see p. 207 below), went out of his way to praise the quality of Sicilian linen already in the 970s, which was also, he claimed, a quarter of the price of equivalent cloth from Egypt. Given that flax brought from afar was a more expensive raw material, this speaks well, if true, for the efficiency of the island's linen workshops, and may also point to their scale.[107]

It is less easy, however, to be sure exactly where in each region the cloth industry was based. In Ifrīqiya, the most prestigious linen cloth came above all from Sousse; Sūsī linen was regularly sought after and priced at a higher rate.[108] This implies that it was not the only Tunisian cloth centre, and it is likely enough that Mahdia was another, as it would be a century later according to al-Idrīsī; Kairouan and its satellites were certainly others, for flax and linen are mentioned in that context by the geographers, and flax sales are sometimes directed there in the *geniza* letters; as noted earlier, cloth workers are also commonly mentioned on its tombstones, even though not specifically linen workers. Sfax, for its part, had fullers, for wool, which hints at a more complex spatial division of labour.[109] In Ifrīqiya, we can otherwise only be precise about silk, which, the geographers said, only came from Gabès; and indeed Qābisī (Gabès) silk was sometimes bought by the Egyptian merchants, a rare example of the claims of geographers

[107] Ibn Ḥawqal, *Kitāb ṣūrat al-arḍ*, trans. Kramers and Wiet, 1, p. 130. The association between linen and Sicily went up to the very end of Islamic rule; Amato of Montecassino, *Storia de' Normanni*, 5.24, has the ruler of Palermo sending a large array of luxuries to Robert Guiscard, which included linen cloth. Note that Neapolitan flax and linen, although praised and even priced by Ibn Ḥawqal (*Kitāb ṣūrat al-arḍ*, trans. Kramers and Wiet, 1, p. 197; cf. the 'Naples of linen' in al-Idrīsī, *Nuzhat al-mushtāq*, trans. Jaubert and Nef, p. 378), were not a significant part of this Sicilian economic world. Only T-S 20.127 (Gil K573 [S51]) may mention Neapolitan (*nāflī*) flax—thanks to Lorenzo Bondioli for checking the original for me.

[108] Sūsī cloth: e.g. T-S 20.69, 13J16.19, K2.32, Misc. 28.225, CUL Add. 3418 (Gil K380, 493, 354 [S69, 112, 106]; Gil P458; Goitein and Friedman, *India traders*, I,1).

[109] For flax sales directed to Kairouan, see AIU VII,E.18 (Gil K483: the best flax was to go to Kairouan and Sousse, lower-quality to Mahdia); see nn. 71–2 above for the geographers and the tombstones. For fullers in Sfax, see n. 71 above. Roy and Poinssot, *Inscriptions arabes de Kairouan*, n. 131 (a. 944) is the tomb of a fuller, so there was fulling in the capital too.

having direct documentary support.[110] We should, anyway, not assume that only towns had substantial artisanal capacity; in the Egyptian countryside, cloth-weaving on a considerable scale was certainly common (see pp. 51, 94 above), and we will find that the same would be true of twelfth-century Sicily. In Islamic Sicily, we can be even less sure of locations, except for Demenna silk—and unlike for Gabès, we have no grounds to conclude that only that town, or that area, produced it on the island (see pp. 243–6 below for the plateau south of Palermo in the twelfth century). All the same, the very extensive production of silk cocoons in the mid-eleventh century just across the Strait of Messina, in the hinterland of Reggio Calabria, hints that there may have been a steady supply of Calabrese cocoons to north-east Sicilian silk-weaving workshops, perhaps from Demenna along the coast eastwards to Messina. The geographers do not help us further here, for they hardly mention Sicily outside Palermo until the somewhat different situation described by al-Idrīsī in the mid-twelfth century (see p. 247 below). But the fact that flax was sold so regularly in Palermo and Mazara is at least a sign that linen-weaving is very likely to have been a major industry in or fairly near them; and Mazara had a specialist *sūq al-kattānīn*, a flax or linen market.[111] Both—especially Palermo—were significant centres for artisanal production of other kinds, which is likely to have made it easier for a substantial linen industry to take off there. We will come back to the issue when we look at Palermo in more detail later.

The great days of the Egypt–Sicily–Ifrīqiya trade lasted a full century, from the late tenth to the late eleventh, but then they ran into trouble. Moshe Gil's editions of *geniza* letters, as noted earlier, assume that the Norman conquest of Sicily marked the end of the eleventh-century correspondence concerning the triangular trade route between the three regions. There is no good reason to accept this, without much more extensive further work. All the same, after the death of Nahray b. Nissīm in 1097–8, and the end of the tranche of letters to and from his circle, the *geniza* records for the trade routes to the central Mediterranean, although continuing into the later twelfth century, become much reduced in number.[112] We

[110] Qābisī silk: T-S 16.339, ENA NS 18.24, 2.13 (Gil K348, 344, 749 [S 143, 97, 145]); see p. 179 above for the geographers. Roy and Poinssot, *Inscriptions arabes de Kairouan*, n. 318 (a. 1036), however, cites a *sūq* of the silk workers in the capital, which shows that Gabès was not the only centre, even if probably the main one.

[111] Flax market in Mazara: Bodl. MS Heb. c 28/61 (Gil K576 [S156]). It is worth adding that there was a (Latin) epitaph for a linen worker from Egypt, *linatarius Alexandrinus*, in Palermo back in 602; see Prigent, 'Palermo in the eastern Roman Empire', pp. 33–5. Reggio: see Guillou, *Le brébion*, an edition of and commentary on the Reggio *brebion* of *c.*1050, which lists nearly 8,000 mulberry trees (ibid., p. 154). Sicily was far more likely an outlet for Calabrese raw silk than was the Aegean heartland of Byzantium, which was so much farther away, and had its own supplies of silk (see p. 324 below); and the Reggio *brebion* also does its accounting in Sicilian *tarì* coins. For silk in the Islamic period, see further Jacoby, 'Seta e tessuti', pp. 133–5, although he doubts, on grounds unconvincing to me, that Sicilian raw silk came from Calabria.

[112] For the beginning of the century, see three hugely long court cases concerning Yūsuf al-Lebdī (the family was originally from Leptis in Ifrīqiya) in 1097–1101 (one had an Ibn Sighmār family

do not have a large-scale edition of twelfth-century letters, unlike Gil's for the eleventh, and it is likely enough that some have been missed. But Goitein, who published several, and looked at a high proportion of unpublished texts as well, saw the scale of letters for the Mediterranean routes as dropping substantially; merchants connected to the Fusṭāṭ *geniza* after 1100 were much more interested in Indian Ocean trade, or else in more local economic activities in and around Fusṭāṭ-Cairo. Miriam Frenkel, too, who published a further set of twelfth-century Sicilian letters and who worked on Alexandria in the same period, identified very few more; and the Princeton Geniza Project database, which registers unpublished as well as published texts, allows the identification of at most a handful of others.[113] Known twelfth-century letters relating to the central Mediterranean are well under a tenth of those surviving from the eleventh century; and I conclude that this is not simply the result of accidents of editing.

Does this drop in quantity matter? The later letters show the same sort of commercial structures as do those for the eleventh century, and they show that Jews still regularly made the journey from Egypt to the central Mediterranean; this is clear. The routes, and the ways merchants engaged with them, remained; and the fact that most *geniza* merchants seem henceforth to have looked by preference to the Indian Ocean tells us nothing about their Muslim counterparts. But there are signs that the scale of eleventh-century exchange had gone. Many of these letters relate to the India trader Abraham Ben Yijū, active between the 1130s and the 1150s, who was an Ifrīqiyan by origin, from Mahdia, and many of his family lived in Sicily, sometimes in Messina, sometimes in Mazara; these are close to eleventh-century patterns. But Ben Yijū himself did not do much trading into the central Mediterranean, and his brothers and nephews were not themselves for the most part merchants. Nor do these letters refer to other merchants in the casual way that those from a century earlier regularly did. The texts concerning exchange which we do have tend only to refer to single types of goods, not wide ranges; and although they still include spices and dyes, and the export of cloth

member as plaintiff; see pp. 161, 189 above) involving trade stretching from Ifrīqiya to India, in CUL Add. 3418, 3421, 3420, 3414, 3416, T-S 10J27.4, 28.22, 13J6.32, Bodl. MS Heb. d 66/64–7 and c 28/37, Moss. V, 374 1, ENA 2594.8 (trans. Goitein and Friedman, *India traders*, I,1–18, 20–2, with commentary, pp. 27–36, 167–230). Even these have a tangential link to Nahray.

[113] The next sets are Zeldes and Frenkel, 'Trade with Sicily', and Gil and Simonsohn, 'More on the history of the Jews in Sicily'; both are small sets published in Hebrew-only articles, although the first is partially translated in Zeldes and Frenkel, 'The Sicilian trade', and Simonsohn translated all twelve letters for the twelfth century in S171–94 (the numbering includes some non-*geniza* sources). These partially overlap with the Ben Yijū set in Goitein and Friedman, *India traders*, for which, see n.114 below. The other main references to Egypt–central Mediterranean connections I have seen in the twelfth-century *geniza* are DK 11, T-S 10J16.15 (trans. Goitein and Friedman, *India traders*, n. II, 58), 20.80 (ed. Goitein and Friedman, *India book* IV/B, n. 68), 8.9, 16.344, Misc. 28.33, 8J20.11, 13J26.10, 13J22.30, 13J21.26 (the last three trans. Goitein, *Letters*, nn. 53–4, 74); again, these are not so many. See Goitein, *MS*, 1, pp. 148–9, for the drop. Udovitch, 'New materials', p. 187, expresses confidence that many more post-1100 documents will appear for this trade; twenty-five years later, I think this may have been over-optimism.

from Sicily, they significantly do not refer to flax.[114] The intermittent evidence for Sicily–Egypt trading in other twelfth-century documentary sources, such as a letter of the Fāṭimid caliph to Roger II of Sicily in 1137 thanking him for protecting the caliph's ship and giving privileges to Sicilian ships in return, plus casual references in Maimonides' *Responsa*, although they certainly show us that it was normal, tell us hardly more about the actual goods transported. We have one clear example for Ifrīqiya, an early twelfth-century *fatwā* of al-Mazārī referring to a *qirāḍ* for flax and dyestuffs coming from Egypt to Tunis and Bizerte, new destinations but fully part of Ifrīqiya as a region, in return for silk and coral, but this too, although much more precise than others—it shows us a substantial shipment of flax and indigo, in fact—is not enough to allow us to say anything more about the overall size of the trade by now.[115] Yet the flax trade lay at the core of the huge scale which is clearly documented for eleventh-century *geniza* trading. Without more evidence, we could in no way argue that that of the twelfth century matched it.

That in itself had consequences. It is far from certain how much flax was ever cultivated in either of our two central Mediterranean regions. In Ifrīqiya, some parts of what is now eastern Algeria are mentioned as growing it by the geographers. These sources of flax never appear in our texts for the Tunisian cities, but geographers and historians continue to mention cloth-making in them, and Sousse cloth, presumably linen, was in demand as far east as Aden in Yemen in the 1130s; Tunis made linen cloth in the fourteenth century too. This, then, probably implies local supply, but its scale is still hard to assess.[116] As for Sicily, al-Idrīsī in his detailed survey of around 1150 only mentions flax cultivation once, in Galati in the north-east, just above San Marco (formerly Demenna; it was still a silk centre), with linen production also mentioned once, at Milazzo, on the coast not far away from San Marco; flax-retting appears near Mazara in 1126; there is also some reference around 1180 to flax production on the plateau south of Palermo, as we shall see (p. 245).[117] But these are not enough grounds for any proposal that

[114] For Ben Yijū and his family, see in general Goitein and Friedman, *India traders*, pp. 52–89, 551–799; the Mediterranean-orientated letters are T-S 10J10.15, 16.288, 8J36.3, 13J6.15, ENA NS 16.27, 2557.151, Bodl. MS Heb. d 66/139, b 11/15 (trans. Goitein and Friedman, *India traders*, III, 29–30a, 43, 45, 48–9, 57). Bodl. MS Heb. b 11/15 (trans. ibid., III, 48 and S182) mentions bales on their way to Messina, that is to say, bulk goods, but does not say they are flax.

[115] Canard, 'Une lettre', pp. 133–6 (the Egyptian caliph's ship in 1137); Maimonides, *Responsa*, 1, nn. 87, 93, trans. conveniently in S201–2 (the judgements refer to dyestuffs and medicines); al-Wansharīsī, *al-Mi'yār*, in Idris, 'Commerce maritime et ḳirāḍ', pp. 231–2. An Egyptian boat bringing food to Tunis is also referred to in a diplomatic document from 1157, ed. Amari, *I diplomi arabi*, 1ª serie, n. 1.

[116] For the cultivation of flax in Annaba/Bône and some areas of what is now the eastern Algerian semi-desert, see Idris, *La Berbérie orientale*, pp. 484, 489, 634. For Aden, see L-G Misc. 9 (trans. Goitein and Friedman, *India traders*, II, 44). Around 1150, al-Idrīsī, *Nuzhat al-mushtāq*, trans. Jaubert and Nef, p. 203, still saw Sousse as a cloth town, including for the making of turbans; Tunis and Sousse exported cloth—explicitly linen in the case of Tunis—in the later middle ages (Brunschvig, *La Berbérie orientale*, pp. 231–2, 265).

[117] Al-Idrīsī, *Nuzhat al-mushtāq*, trans. Jaubert and Nef, pp. 311–12, 337; Grégoire, 'Diplômes de Mazara (Sicile)', pp. 96–8, a reference I owe to Jeremy Johns. Another twelfth-century reference to

Sicilians or Ifrīqiyans could have replaced Egyptian flax with their own on any major scale, either as a cause or as a consequence of the Egyptians ceasing to provide it. This lack of replacement seems to have been even more serious for Sicily than for Ifrīqiya. Sicily's only surviving document on paper before the late middle ages, dating to 1109, is linen-based, but after that the developing Norman chancery abandoned paper for parchment.[118] It is as if that moment was the one in which the end of Egyptian supply forced the island to change tack dramatically, in its state record-keeping, but also, more importantly, in the fate, that is to say, almost certainly, in the rapid eclipse of most of Sicily's linen industry. In the Norman Kingdom of Sicily, which extended after 1127–40 into nearly half of the Italian mainland peninsula, linen was produced in Campania and, to a lesser extent, Puglia, more than in Sicily itself.[119] Sicily produced cotton in our twelfth-century texts, far more than linen, as we shall also see below (pp. 243–9).

Exactly what happened to Egyptian Mediterranean merchant activity in the decades around 1100, whether Jewish or Muslim, is an issue which was already broached in Chapter 2, and it will reappear later as well, in Chapter 7. It was in part related to the expansion of northern Italian shipping, which did not replicate its predecessor on every route (the flax trade evidently being one example), even if, as we also saw and will see, it is too simple just to say that Italian ships pushed Muslim-owned ships out of the sea lanes by force, and anyway their real protagonism had hardly started by 1100. Indeed, Ifrīqiya–Sicily links themselves remained tight, with oil and gold, exchanged for wheat, remaining a substantial element of twelfth-century commerce, and ceramic exports to Sicily again expanding later in the century, as we shall see. But the links to Egypt were clearly less tight by now. It is likely that more important than Italian naval attacks, here, was the reduced interest the new Norman rulers of Sicily had in maintaining the flax/linen trade; they looked north rather than east. It may not, indeed, have needed much for the organic link to break, given how long-distance the supply

linen, a more casual one, is Amico, *I diplomi*, n. 18 (a. 1176), for the hinterland of Messina, again in the north-east; there is also archaeobotanical evidence for flax in Malta (see n. 77 above) and Mazara (Primavera, 'Introduzione di nuove piante', p. 443), the latter of which is geographically closer to the evidence for the plateau south of Palermo.

[118] Cusa, *I diplomi*, n. 23 (pp. 402–3), with commentary by Johns, 'Paper versus parchment'. I see no reason why this linen paper could not have been made in Sicily (absence of reference to it in the Islamic period is not a counterargument, given how little we know about that period on the island); the technology for it was by 1100 no longer new. It is, however, striking that there are also, as Johns states, four references in early twelfth-century texts to pre-existing lost documents from the years 1097–1105 on cotton (*bambakinon* or *cuctunea*) paper in Sicily. That is to say, cotton was already appearing before 1100 as a significant cloth in Sicily, even if *geniza* merchants did not carry it; there are a couple of other eleventh-century references to it too (see p. 248 below), so cotton waste could perfectly well have produced paper, as it did in Syria (see Chapter 2, n. 149 above). Possibly cotton production was not yet sufficiently developed for the administration to pick it up on any long-term basis; but this moves us too far into speculation.

[119] Martin, *La Pouille*, p. 354; Ditchfield, *La culture matérielle*, pp. 373–81; for Campanian cloth, see esp. Feniello, *Napoli*, pp. 197–202, who discusses the earlier linen production of the tenth–eleventh century.

chains were. But this, in turn, had internal effects on Sicily. One consequence of the weakening of the Egyptian leg of the triangular trade does, indeed, appear to have been the end of a major linen industry in Sicily, and its probable substantial decrease in Ifrīqiya. But this does not mean either that the dense trade documented in the *geniza* was the direct cause of the prosperity of the regional economies of Ifrīqiya or Sicily (still less of Egypt), or that its weakening undermined that prosperity. In fact, it was the other way round. What the *geniza* shows is simply the possibilities which those regional economies, and their internal articulations, allowed across the Mediterranean as a whole, when conditions permitted. We have already seen that if Ifrīqiya faced problems in the twelfth century, it was for internal reasons, a point which I will come back to in the conclusion to this chapter, when we have looked at Sicily. And as for Sicily, what we know of its twelfth-century economy from documents, and above all now from archaeology, shows that it remained highly complex and articulated. That is what we must turn to now.

3.4 Sicily as a Historical Problem

The way medieval Sicilian economic development has been treated by historians is an interesting variant on the usual metanarrative of Mediterranean 'failure'. We have seen that, one way or another, this was generally seen as the 'fault' of the Arabs, who could not maintain the shimmering civilization of the 'Abbāsid or, sometimes, Fāṭimid period and instead sank back into the standard Orientalist tropes of pointless regime change, with economic opportunities missed or actively undermined. In Sicily, however, even before the *geniza* showed its eleventh-century centrality and long before archaeology did the same, the Islamic period was seen as the island's medieval height, with its eventual decline and economic marginalization becoming the 'fault' of the Normans, ruling from 1072/1091 to 1194, or else, even more, their Staufen and Angevin successors in the thirteenth. This image was partly the achievement of Michele Amari, Sicily's great nineteenth-century Arabist, who edited and translated almost all the medieval Arabic chronicles and poetry concerning the island, and who constructed a detailed historical narrative out of them; he was enormously influential at the time (he was even Minister of Education in the fledgling unified Italian state in the 1860s), and the quality of his work makes him still relevant now.[120] It was partly also because the Norman and Angevin kingdom was the ancestor of the Kingdom of the Two Sicilies, which was the chief internal enemy (along with the pope) of nineteenth-century Italian unity, and had also been a state strong enough to keep full control

[120] Amari, *Biblioteca arabo-sicula*, and ibid., *versione italiana*; Amari, *Storia dei Musulmani*, ed. Nallino. For a recent sympathetic critique of Amari, see Nef, 'Michele Amari ou l'histoire inventée'.

of the cities of the kingdom, with the result that major centres like Palermo, Naples, Salerno, and Bari did not become the independent city states that nineteenth- and twentieth-century Italian historians and theorists (and many still now) regarded as the pinnacle of medieval civilization.[121] This all meant that the 'questione del Mezzogiorno', the long-chewed-over debate about why it was that the post-unification Italian south was hard to govern and did not match the north in its economic take-off, seemed easily traceable back to the Angevins, and to an extent to the Normans, but could leave Sicily's Islamic rulers in effect untouched. Indeed, Amari claimed that the Islamic period was the only time in the island's history in which it was not dominated by great estates, the notorious *latifondi* of his own age, which were allegedly one of the main causes of the south's underdevelopment—an image best encapsulated nowadays by Giuseppe Tomasi di Lampedusa's 1958 novel *Il gattopardo* (*The leopard*), which is such an intense evocation of the compromises and degradations of nineteenth-century Sicilian life that people regularly forget that it is fiction, feeding off all the negative images of the 'Southern question' itself, rather than independent reportage.[122]

The most important book on the Norman-period exchange economy of Sicily remains that of David Abulafia, *The two Italies*, published in 1977. Given the relative weakness of internal Sicilian documentary material, he relied above all on the rich notarial registers of Genoa, which begin to survive as serial records in 1154. In doing so, he followed a venerable Italian and French tradition, although he avoided most of the commercial romanticism of that tradition, which I criticized in Chapter 1. Only rather tentatively, at the end of the book, did he advance (or, rather, accept and nuance, given that it was a normal position to hold at the time) the view that the interest the twelfth-century Genoese showed in Sicilian wheat and cotton might, 'in the very long term', have damaged the Sicilian economy by pushing the island into the role of a provider of raw materials for the more active economies of the north of Italy—unlike, we can add, the *geniza* merchants, who were providing flax for Sicilian, not Egyptian workshops. He has reiterated this position in later work, while at the same time stressing that this did not by any means imply that Sicily could not, or did not, develop complex patterns of artisanal activity in later centuries. He is certainly right there; all the same, the Genoa's-eye view in his first book made it hard to get further into the Sicilian internal economy than the Genoese did themselves, which was—in this respect much like the *geniza* merchants—not very far.[123]

[121] For an extreme recent US version of this, see Puttnam, *Making democracy work*, ch. 5.

[122] Amari, *Storia*, ed. Nallino, 2, pp. 41–2 ('così il conquisto musulmano guarì la piaga dei latifondi'); Tomasi di Lampedusa, *Il gattopardo*. Adolf Schaube in 1906 saw pre-1250 southern Italy and Sicily as 'die kommerziell passiven Gebiete Italiens': *Handelsgeschichte*, p. 456.

[123] Abulafia, *The two Italies*; p. 284 for the quotation; he looked at the internal economy more in 'The crown and the economy'. For his later position, see, e.g., Abulafia, 'Southern Italy, Sicily', pp. 1–8; 'Il contesto mediterraneo e il primo disegno delle due Italie'. Abulafia's work complements, but is also better than Pistarino, 'Commercio e vie marittime'; Pistarino, 'Commercio e comunicazioni'. Bresc, 'Le

I begin with Abulafia because he wrote about the period covered in this book; but the main recent medieval historian of Sicily arguing for a 'two Italies', often called a 'dualist' approach, that is to say, an approach which stresses the underdevelopment of Sicily by comparison with the Italian north, is Henri Bresc, in his huge French *thèse* of 1986, focussed on the fourteenth and fifteenth centuries. The Norman period is, however, here hardly discussed. The main culprits for Sicilian economic failure are, instead, seen as Frederick II, who finally destroyed the Muslim population of Sicily in the 1220s–1240s; the Sicilian Vespers, the uprising which re-established the independence of the island from the Naples-based Angevin kings in 1282, but thereby cut it off from a more organic mainland trade and exposed it to long-term war; and then the Black Death, which finished off Sicily's economic vitality and blocked its development, reducing it to a 'colonial' (one would now say 'neocolonial') position marked by unequal exchange, essentially as a supplier of wheat, with respect to northern Italy, Catalonia, and the rest of western Europe.[124] Bresc's book will stand as the most definitive account of Sicily's own medieval notarial registers likely to be written; but he had the ill luck to publish at the very end of the period in which a dualist thesis was something which could be accepted without question. Less than a decade later, Stephan Epstein published a substantial and sharp-edged rebuttal, stressing the considerable activity of late medieval Sicilian artisanal production and exchange (which, in a deliberate challenge to conventional historiography, he argued to have been more sophisticated in its infrastructure than that of Florence), and rejecting dualist models altogether.[125]

With some nuances—notably expressed in two important articles by Giuseppe Petralia[126]—this revaluation of Sicilian economic potential has become the new common ground. I accept it myself. It has flaws—notably, for our purposes, the lumping together of Bresc with the much more careful Abulafia, who has become tarred with the same brush. But the main problem for this book is that it has also pushed the debate far later in time (the cusp for major change is, indeed, now ascribed to the understudied seventeenth century, not the medieval period at all); the period which concerns us here, Islamic and Norman Sicily, has hardly been

marchand, le marché et le palais', which also discusses the pre-1200 Sicilian economy, is more problematic. Earlier work is unnecessary to cite. For how far into Sicily the Genoese actually got, see n. 254 below.

[124] Bresc, *Un monde méditerranéen*, e.g. pp. 7–21, 523–78, 917–22; for 'colonial', see, e.g., 522, 921; for 'blocked', see, e.g., 650. See n. 260 below for limitations in the number of major external markets for Sicilian wheat, even after 1250. A useful historiographical account of the arguments of Bresc and his contemporary Maurice Aymard, plus their predecessors and opponents, is Sakellariou, *Southern Italy in the late middle ages*, pp. 19–40, 58–62 (to be exact, Bresc and Aymard espoused a centre–periphery model, not a strictly dualist one, but I will use 'dualist' for convenience).

[125] Epstein, *An island for itself*; for the Florence comparison, see Epstein, 'Cities, regions'. See also the parallel argument of Sakellariou, *Southern Italy in the late middle ages*, for mainland Italy.

[126] Petralia, 'Economia e società'; Petralia, 'La nuova Sicilia tardomedievale'. Note that Backman, *The decline and fall of medieval Sicily*, is not focussed on the economy.

discussed by economic historians since Abulafia. In a way, this also means that the metanarrative of post-Islamic 'decline' has gone underground, because it has not been fully confronted and tested for the Norman period. The best recent historical work on Norman Sicily has been the work of a new generation of Arabists, the first major figures since Amari and his younger contemporary, the document editor Salvatore Cusa; they have focussed on the largely Arabic-language government of Roger II (1105–54) and his successors. Their arguments about the exact and changing status of the Arabic-speaking population under Norman rule often have an elegiac element, however, as we move closer to the pogroms of the later twelfth century, and then the Muslim revolts after 1190 and their defeat by Frederick II.[127] It is as if the fate of that sector of the population was a metonym for the wider fate of the cosmopolitan and economically sophisticated island, with Mediterranean connections in all directions, which the Islamic and perhaps also the early Norman period, up to 1154, apparently shows. Well, maybe; but maybe not, as well.

It has to be stressed, and not for this last time in this book, that the real answers to this debate, and the ways out of it, lie in the archaeological record, which has recently become so strong for Sicily. After a rapid framing of the island's geography and political history, plus an account of what the written sources tell us about the island's capital, Palermo, we will, therefore, come to the archaeology in the next section. Then, in the following section, we will look at the twelfth-century documents for the island, to balance the *geniza* for the eleventh century, already discussed, and to give a further context to the archaeological record. These documents are not generous with economic data, with the exception of the external records of the Genoese, as Abulafia knew already; but they do clarify some issues, and exclude others. And they are both better than those for Ifrīqiya in any period and show significantly different social and economic structures. If nothing else, they give us clues to why it was that the two central Mediterranean regions moved apart economically in the twelfth century, while remaining connected, an issue we will come back to at the end of the chapter. But they tell us other things in their own right too.

* * *

[127] Johns, *Arabic administration*; Nef, *Conquérir et gouverner*; Metcalfe, *The Muslims*; see also Davis-Secord, *Where three worlds meet*. For documents, see Cusa, *I diplomi*: this edition is still (2022), despite flaws, the best for most Greek and Arabic documents (of which relatively few have been found and edited since too). Latin documents are more scattered, although the largest sets were published (not very well) by Carlo Alberto Garufi in the decades around 1900; see Garufi in the Bibliography. The more recent attempts to re-edit at least royal documents have also stalled, but see Becker, Brühl and Enzensberger in the Bibliography. Guides to editions can best be found in the books by Johns and Nef, and Johns, 'Arabic sources for Sicily'. An ERC project for 2017–23, DocuMult, led by Jeremy Johns and Beatrice Pasciuta, aims to edit or re-edit all the documents for the island up to 1266 in their entirety; their website (currently http://krc.orient.ox.ac.uk/documult-it) will in the future contain all the Sicilian documentary sources used in this chapter, including much better texts.

Sicily has, all around it, a rich coastal plain, narrow in much of the island, but widening around Palermo and some other centres, and in particular in the more extensive lowlands behind Mazara in the west and Catania in the east (see Map 10). In some periods, which certainly included the long eleventh century, these plains were and are home to a very variegated agriculture, with many varieties of tree crops and a rich array of fruits and legumes. But the island is also large enough to have a substantial interior, an open plateau with hills in the centre of the island that is lower in the west, and in the east rises to a line of wooded and more pastoral mountains along the north-east coast, overlooked by the cone of Etna. This plateau is, and as far as we can tell has been for two millennia and more, a great wheat-growing region. Together with northern Tunisia, it was under the Roman Empire one of the main suppliers of the city of Rome and the imperial armies, and it still sent some wheat to Constantinople into the ninth century. The earliest medieval papacy had extensive estates there, amounting to maybe 5 per cent of the whole island, as the letters of Pope Gregory the Great (590–604) tell us in often surprising detail; these estates were for a long time, until their eighth-century confiscation by the Byzantine emperors, one of the major sources of papal wealth.[128] We have seen that Sicily also supplied wheat, at least occasionally, to Ifrīqiya itself in the eleventh and twelfth centuries; and it certainly did thereafter to some later medieval north Italian cities, as also to their successors up to the present day. One of the key questions in each period has to be what *else* the plateau produced, which is an issue we will come back to, for it is important if we want to assess the complexity of the insular economy. But it has also to be understood that this simple geographical configuration meant that there was always an irreducible minimum of internal exchange in the island; for the wheat, if it is consumed outside its production zones at all (and it never was not, even in the early middle ages), has to get down to the coast, and was, in the medieval period, in large part carried by donkey. The next key question then becomes whether the producers of that wheat gave it up in tax or rent, that is, without any recompense, or whether they sold at least some of it and were paid for it; that too has implications for the island's complexity. But we can take the regular movement of goods down to the coast, whether or not goods moved back up to the plateau in return, as a constant when we assess the Sicilian economy.

The other important aspect of the geographical contrast between the coast and the interior of Sicily is the fact that the island's major urban centres are, and have always been across recorded history, overwhelmingly on the coast, to a far greater extent than for any other region discussed in this book. Syracuse was the main city in the Byzantine period, with Palermo probably second; Palermo replaced Syracuse after the Islamic conquest and has been the island capital ever since, only

[128] See in general Recchia, *Gregorio Magno e la società agricola*; Prigent, *La Sicile byzantine*, is the basic starting point now (see pp. 393–400 for the figure of 5%). For the confiscation, see Prigent, 'Les empereurs isauriens'.

sometimes challenged by Messina, which came up rapidly after 1100. Syracuse was by then a second-rank town; it was matched by Mazara and Agrigento under the Arabs, with Trapani, Cefalù, and Catania developing under the Normans and Mazara slipping in importance. A third level, going anticlockwise, included Marsala, Sciacca, Taormina, Patti, Demenna/San Marco, and Termini Imerese. These are all coastal towns too (Demenna was 6 kilometres above the sea but closely connected to it). Inland, only Enna has been durably important across the centuries, but in our period it was not a major urban centre, even if it was the interior's most prominent fortified settlement, the strategic key to the island, which both Arab and Norman conquerors knew they had to take in order to get the upper hand.[129] The weakness of urbanism in the wheat-producing interior has led it to be seen as economically subservient to the coast, in much the same way as Sicily as a whole has been seen as economically subservient to northern Italy, from 1150 or so onwards. This image is as incorrect for the internal plateau as it is for the island as a whole. What in our period characterized the interior above all was a network of concentrated, although mostly not fortified, settlements. The minority of fortified centres were called *ḥuṣun* in Arabic, *castra* in Latin. These settlements were agro-towns in some cases—that is to say, large agricultural villages with artisanal activity as well, sometimes with some urban characteristics. They were sometimes the ancestors of modern inland centres, in the same places or close by—centres such as (roughly from west to east and then south) Partinico, Corleone, Castronovo, Petralia, Troina, Randazzo, Paternò, Piazza Armerina, Butera, and Ragusa[130]—even if archaeology, as we shall see, complicates this simple picture considerably. Their activity and interplay gave the interior a considerable vitality; many of them will recur in what follows.

* * *

Between 604 and the last years of the eleventh century, there is a half-millennium near-void in Sicily's written documentation. The period of Byzantine rule, up to the long and messy Arab conquest between 827 and 902 (extending to 965 for some far north-eastern settlements, which had revolted again, with Byzantine support, in the tenth century) has effectively nothing except coins and seals and occasional half-plausible citations in largely Aegean-focussed sources, plus one anguished account of the travails of the survivors of the fall of Syracuse in 878, the work of the *grammatikos* Theodosios.[131] But actually the Islamic period does

[129] For Enna, Prigent, *La Sicile byzantine*, pp. 1380–6; Metcalfe, *The Muslims*, pp. 12, 14, 25; Malaterra, *De rebus gestis*, ed. Pontieri, 3.7. For the archaeology of Enna, see Giannitrapani et al., 'Nuovi dati'; Bonanno et al., 'Da Henna a Qasryannah' (both are in Arcifa and Sgarlata, *From polis to madina*, the best archaeological guide to the cities of Sicily up to the Islamic conquest); Randazzo, 'La transizione bizantino-islamica'.

[130] See in general Maurici, *Castelli medievali*.

[131] See in general Prigent, *La Sicile byzantine*, esp. pp. 316–23, 590–874, 1076–370; for Theodosios, the best recent guide to this complex text (surviving partly in Greek, partly in Latin) is Rognoni, 'Au pied de la lettre?'.

not offer us much more: a short contemporary narrative, the so-called *Cambridge chronicle*, up to the late tenth century; a detailed but hostile account by Ibn Ḥawqal of his visit to Palermo in 973, the only pre-Norman Arab geographer actually to go there; one circumstantial but odd account of the affairs of Agrigento, the work of the jurist al-Dāwudī (d. 1011); a land sale, recently published, for the city of Palermo *c.*1000, plus two slightly later marriage and divorce texts; and, of course, the *geniza*, whose weaknesses as a guide to the internal history of Sicily we have already explored. Otherwise, as usual, we are in the dubious hands of late narratives, particularly, again, the thirteenth-century Iraqi historian Ibn al-Athīr, which, even if they were taken as accurate, regard Sicily as so marginal an adjunct to Ifrīqiya that long tracts of time are left out of the story.[132] It could all be read, at least summarily, in two days. It is hardly surprising that modern scholars get attached (too attached) to details in very late texts,[133] or else focus on either the Norman sources or the archaeology.

It is not part of my remit to offer my own reconstruction of the history of Islamic Sicily; it is, anyway, effectively offered elsewhere, particularly, recently, by Alex Metcalfe and Annliese Nef.[134] But I need once again to give the briefest chronology, and then comment on some elements that it seems to me we can trust, which have relevance to a strictly economic history. The Aghlabids were the main architects of the slow conquest of Sicily, and had nearly concluded it when they were overthrown by the Fāṭimids. It was an incoherent affair for some time; the Ifrīqiyan jurist Saḥnūn is said by al-Dāwudī to have remarked that no aspect of the conquest had any legitimacy in Islamic law—a remark which (if he made it) must, given Saḥnūn's death in 854, have dated to not long after the takeover of Palermo in 831, soon the new capital of the island. Also according to al-Dāwudī, Agrigento had three waves of Arab colonists in the ninth century alone, who all fought each other, although the 'central power', the *sulṭān*, forcibly removed at least some of them. The Aghlabids did, however, manage to establish some sort of fiscal system, presumably (although this is guesswork) using Byzantine elements

[132] Most of these, including the late texts, are extracted in Amari, *Biblioteca arabo-sicula*. For Ibn Ḥawqal, see *Kitāb ṣūrat al-arḍ*, trans. Kramers and Wiet, 1, pp. 117–30; for al-Dāwudī, *Kitāb al-amwāl*, see Abdul Wahab and Dachraoui, 'Le régime foncier'; for the land sale, see Mouton et al., *Propriétés rurales*, n. 7; for the other texts, see n. 143 below.

[133] One example, often cited, is an instruction of the Fāṭimid caliph al-Muʿizz, dating to 967, which supposedly required the setting up in each district of the island of a fortified town (*madīna ḥuṣīna*) with a mosque, in which local inhabitants were required to settle. This is only attested in two lines of al-Nuwayrī, a fourteenth-century narrative (for a convenient edition, see Amari, *Biblioteca arabo-sicula*, 1, p. 441, versione italiana, 1, pp. 134–5); and even if the tradition was actually reliable, which I would personally doubt, the track record in history for instructions of this kind having much effect is not a strong one. The only medieval mosque yet found on the island is twelfth-century; see Molinari, *Segesta II*, pp. 95–9; for the role of fortified settlements after the mid-tenth century see pp. 214–15 below.

[134] Metcalfe, *The Muslims*; Nef, 'Reinterpreting', with citations of earlier work; Nef, 'La fiscalité en Sicile'; Nef, *L'état imperial islamique*, pp. 258–314. See also Chiarelli, *A history of Muslim Sicily*, which is detailed but sometimes speculative.

as well as those they were used to in Africa.[135] The Fāṭimids built on this; by the time the Normans conquered, a tax regime seems to have been generalized across the island, even if it was apparently rather less complex than that of Egypt (see p. 239 below). But it is clear from the *Cambridge Chronicle* that revolts were normal, not least in reaction to a Fāṭimid rule which was new and therefore unpopular. Consistently, Agrigento, as a serial rebel city, was set against Palermo, although the latter too was not always loyal to the Ifrīqiyan regimes.[136] Parts of the Greek north-east resisted the Arabs for a long time too (non-Arab Sicilians were, as far as we can see, entirely Greek-speaking by now). Only after the Fāṭimids entrusted the island to a family of Kalbid governors, in 948, did a level of calm begin to appear.

Much later sources state that this calm began to break down again in the 1010s. However that may be, the Kalbids had certainly lost power by the 1040s, for, when the Normans began to be interested in the island shortly afterwards, it was divided between four or five warlords based in different cities. Palermo itself was in the 1040s, according to a comment by Ḥayyim b. ʿAmmar surviving in the *geniza*, governed by a council (*shūrā*) of the local elite, and then, as we have seen, in 1069–72, actually ruled by a merchant, Ibn al-Baʿbāʿ, who presumably was part of that elite.[137] It is perhaps less surprising, given this renewed confusion, that once the Normans invaded the north-east from their newly conquered lands in mainland southern Italy, in 1061, they managed to take over the island rather faster than the Aghlabids had before them. Although Norman interest in conquering here was intermittent, Palermo fell in 1072, most of the north-eastern and western parts of the island were in Norman hands more or less stably after that, and the rest of the conquest, until 1091, was essentially a matter of mopping-up operations. All this is recounted by a contemporary Norman chronicler, Geoffrey Malaterra; his view of what he saw is sometimes quite problematic—and if this is true even for a contemporary source, we should once again be even more suspicious of non-contemporary sources—but he could at least be expected to get the chronology roughly right.[138]

It would not be hard to make a case, given all this, that Muslim-ruled Sicily was dramatically unstable for all of the 250 years of its existence, except probably for

[135] Abdul Wahab and Dachraoui, 'Le régime foncier', pp. 430, 436–8.

[136] For the Fāṭimid period, see Amari, *Biblioteca arabo-sicula*, 1, pp. 168–73, versione italiana, 1, pp. 289–9.

[137] *Shūrā*: T-S NS J566 (Gil K648 [S61]); for Ibn al-Baʿbāʿ, see Gil, *Jews*, pp. 558–62; Metcalfe, *The Muslims*, pp. 97–9.

[138] Malaterra, *De rebus gestis*, ed. Pontieri, esp. books 2 and 3. For discussion of the conquest, see, e.g., Nef, *Conquérir et gouverner*, pp. 27–60. One example of the distortions of the text is Malaterra's view of the Pisans as incompetent fighters because they were really only merchants (for a critique of this sort of counterposition, still to be found in the historiography, see Petralia, 'Le "navi" e i "cavalli"'); in 2.34 this leads Malaterra to claim that they did not sack Palermo in 1064, even though in actual fact they began building their cathedral with the booty they gained (see p. 559 below).

the first fifty to seventy years of Kalbid rule from the mid-tenth century to the early eleventh—far more than Egypt was, and, indeed, more than Ifrīqiya was before the 1050s. Such a case would have to be hedged around with caveats—for example, that we know effectively nothing about the south-eastern third of the island after the Arab conquest, and little enough about the far west—but it still has some plausibility. This instability did not affect the overall power of state structures in Sicily, as far as can be seen; and it certainly did not have any significant negative impact on the prosperity of the island, as we have seen and shall see again. But beyond this, what these sources can tell us directly is for our purposes restricted. I will here single out two major aspects only, which, at least, are clear.

The first concerns the collective protagonism of Sicilian settlements, both on the coast and in the interior, throughout the Islamic period. Agrigento was clearly a violent and riven city in the ninth century and early tenth, but it is not described in any of our sources as having a leader (only *shaykh*s, unnamed elders); the citizens did it themselves. Palermo clearly developed a probably informal elite collective rulership, at least in the period of serious division in the island in the 1040s; this might also, possibly, fit with the late description by Ibn al-Athīr of the 'notables of the community' (*a'yān al-jamā'a*) whom the first Kalbid governor, al-Ḥasan al-Kalbī, has to win over in the capital when he arrives in 948.[139] In Malaterra, above all, both large towns and smaller ones (*castra*) act collectively. The Normans fight the *Messanenses* as a body; Petralia's and Palermo's inhabitants negotiate collective surrender; those of Troina and Jato revolt; those of Antillo kill one of the island's main Muslim warlords, Ibn Thumna; Castronovo has a local boss, but he mistreats a local miller, and the latter with his allies hands the *castrum* to the Normans. Interestingly, this protagonism was not restricted to elites, as the last example shows; nor was it restricted to Arabs. Al-Dāwudī described, rightly or wrongly, Agrigento as deserted when the Arabs came, and all the rival groups as incoming settlers; but at least in the east of the island, the actions of Petralia and Troina are both explicitly said by Malaterra to be the work of *Sarraceni* and *Christiani* or *Graeci* together.[140]

It would be a mistake to be too literal about all this, and to see the towns as actually leaderless, but the imagery of community action was clearly strong here.

[139] Amari, *Biblioteca arabo-sicula*, 1, p. 300, versione italiana, 1, p. 416. Nef, 'Islamic Palermo', pp. 49–51, stresses the informality of this form of elite dominance.

[140] Malaterra, *De rebus gestis*, ed. Pontieri, 2.5–6, 20, 22, 29, 45, 3.12, 20 (see Corretti et al., 'Tra Arabi, Berberi e Normanni', pp. 179–81 for *Antilium* being Antillo near Messina, rather than the commonly accepted Entella); Abdul Wahab and Dachraoui, 'Le régime foncier', p. 436. But we should, anyway, not be too trusting of al-Dāwudī; whatever was the case in the city, Colmitella, a large and partially excavated village some 10 kilometres to its north-east, shows effectively complete continuity of occupation from the seventh to the twelfth centuries (see Rizzo et al., 'L'insediamento rurale'). For al-Dāwudī, see also Granara, *Narrating Muslim Sicily*, pp. 82–98. For later community activism in 1175 on the western interior plateau, see Johns, *Arabic administration*, pp. 170–1.

Palermo was an obvious example of a major city with an active urban elite; that is not a problem to explain, and we could assume it even without evidence. But it would be harder, I think, for more rural communities like Petralia and Jato, agro-towns (Malaterra says Jato was large) but not major political centres, to be as active agents as this, even in a period of extreme political division, if they were mostly peasant tenants on large estates, as they very often had been in Gregory the Great's time. Given this, it is quite likely that Amari was right to argue for the substantial weakening of such estates during the Islamic period; we shall see later that this is backed up by what we know from Norman documents about land tenure (pp. 231–42). They point to a more balanced hierarchy, with local (relatively) rich and medium landowners, and people with urban-style occupations, all claiming some political role, alongside a not so dependent peasantry. We shall see this balance implied in the archaeology too. (We see it in most of our other regions too, for that matter, as other chapters show.) The confusion of the Arab conquest on its own may help to explain this shift, although how this worked in detail would be too speculative (and too early in time) for us to need to discuss it here. We will look at its implications later, but two have to be kept in mind at once: as in Egypt, there is no evidence of an aristocratic elite so all-powerful that its demand might have dominated the development of the whole economy; and, conversely, the possibility of relatively autonomous peasant strata also requires us to consider peasant demand as well.

The second aspect is the attention Ibn Ḥawqal gave to Palermo in 973. Geographers routinely stressed both the good and the bad sides of places they gave attention to, but Ibn Ḥawqal went a long way to be negative about the inhabitants of the city, and, by extension, the island as a whole (which he claims to have toured but does not describe). They were complete idiots, mostly because they were given to eating raw onions, which, as is well known, is bad for any reasoning capacity: 'One cannot find in this town any person who is intelligent, or capable, or really competent in any realm of knowledge, or animated by noble or religious sentiments.' Notwithstanding this constant negative undercurrent, Palermo is one of the cities in Ibn Ḥawqal's whole geography which most comes to life, with its five urban quarters (not systematically named, but they can be identified, between and on each side of the two rivers which ran down parallel to each other to meet in the city's port; see Map 25), its twenty-three specialized markets, with each specialization named, and several other trades mentioned separately, plus the great market down the main street (the Simāt—it is still today a major commercial artery) in the city's central quarter between the rivers, the old Roman-Byzantine city, called in other sources Balarm or al-Qaṣr, together with the city's 300-plus mosques (this, of course, is a more suspect figure). Ibn Ḥawqal adds the wealth of the irrigated gardens around the city, with their sugar, vegetables, papyrus (the only papyrus outside Egypt, used, strangely, not just for official documents but also to make cables for ships' anchors), vineyards, and, of course, onions. Outside the city and its suburbs, he stresses the island's production for export of wheat, wool, hides, wine, sugar, and (as we have seen, p. 193) linen; even if he talks down their quantity, and claims that the Sicilians hate merchants, he states that they need the latter.[141] The great street market is documented in the Norman period too; the wine, the irrigation, and the sugar have archaeological back-up; the linen, of course, plus the hides, has ample support in the *geniza*, so probably the hyper-complexity of the rest of Palermo's commercial life—and even the onions—is authentic as well. The activity of at least Palermo's linen market, as attested in the *geniza*, and the prosperity of the city's merchants whose letters survive in it, fill out this picture. And Palermo's expansion and artisanal activity, as we shall see, are abundantly attested in the archaeology, which shows that it started as much as a century earlier; indeed, the *grammatikos* Theodosios, who was brought as a prisoner to Palermo, describes it as very large already in 878.[142] By 973, even before the *geniza* gets going, it was evidently doing really well. Palermo's own agricultural surroundings, although very rich, are not large enough to sustain as much complexity as this; its links to a wider hinterland—which will have been new in the ninth century, as Palermo was not the capital before that—must have been extensive by now. The single pre-Norman land document we have for the city, although it, of course, cannot say much on its own, at least testifies to a close build-up of housing in part of the south of the city around 1000, which fits everything else just referred to;[143] but the archaeology, as we shall see later, tells us more than the written record does here.

* * *

Many things changed when the Normans came in, but not Palermo, so let us begin with the capital. I preface it with another brief political narrative, but the main political events of the Norman century in Sicily largely took place in Palermo as well.

Palermo surrendered to the Normans by treaty in 1072, with a formal agreement to keep its current rights and customs. Although certainly remaining Sicily's major city by far, it was no longer the sole capital, thanks to the island's mid-century divisions; and Roger I, the 'Great Count', who was the main leader of the Norman conquest of Sicily and who ended up in full control of most of it, died in 1101 without establishing a real political centre. His son Roger II, who succeeded as a child in 1105, however soon focussed his court on Palermo; and by 1130, when Roger claimed and was granted the title of king by Pope Anacletus II, it had

[141] Ibn Ḥawqal, *Kitāb ṣūrat al-arḍ*, trans. Kramers and Wiet, 1, pp. 117–23, 129–30 (123 for quotation).

[142] Rognoni, 'Au pied de la lettre?', pp. 220–1. For Palermo, see in general Nef, *A companion to medieval Palermo*; ibid., pp. 39–88 cover the Islamic period.

[143] Mouton et al., *Propriétés rurales*, n. 7. Jamil and Johns, 'Four Sicilian documents', show that this text, found in Damascus, has (at least) two pre-Norman analogues, one of which also refers casually to Palermitan urban property.

certainly become the single capital of the whole kingdom, including the newly conquered mainland, and remained so for over a century. Norman government was highly articulated, and its administrative departments, which were becoming influenced by Fāṭimid Egypt's practices, were numerous; they were all based from now on in Palermo, mostly in the huge and architecturally ambitious palace Roger had built at the top of al-Qaṣr (now Latinized as the Cassaro), at its western end, where it still stands, to replace the Fāṭimid/Kalbid governmental centre of al-Khāliṣa, closer to the port; the king too, as time went on, was more and more stably based in the capital. The government was mostly conducted by professional administrators operating in Greek and Arabic, led in turn by two able *amīr*s of Greek origin (the Egyptians would have called them, and probably did call them, *wazīr*s), Christodoulos and George of Antioch. The complex relationship between these administrators and the resentful Latin-speaking aristocracy, many of them from the mainland, who made up the rest of the royal court, was kept in check under Roger.[144]

When Roger died, however, his son William I (1154–66) found the balance harder to maintain. A third *amīr*, Maione of Bari, ironically the first of Latin origin, was murdered by disaffected aristocrats in 1160; they attempted a coup and took over the palace and the person of the king, until the coup failed in 1161 and most of the plotters were killed or blinded. We know about this mostly thanks to a detailed classicizing Latin narrative by an unknown but very well-informed courtier, randomly named 'Hugo Falcandus' in a sixteenth-century printed edition (I shall call him 'Falcandus' with inverted commas for convenience), which tells us a good deal about palace politics in the 1160s, from a position very hostile to the king and his non-Latin ministers.[145] William died early, and his son William II (1166–89), another minor at first, was less unpopular with his Latin barons, even if he remained firmly based in the palace. His court was very Arab-influenced, but the administration was becoming more Latinized. That would be a trend which continued after his death without a direct heir, and through succession conflicts in the 1190s culminating in the conquest of southern Italy and Sicily in 1194 by the western emperor Henry VI, acting for his wife Constance I (1194–8), who was Roger II's posthumous daughter; the Staufen period of

[144] For the basic political history, see Chalandon, *Histoire de la domination normande*, an old and extremely traditional account; a neat and rapid survey is in Nef, *Conquérir et gouverner*, pp. 585–625. For the administration, see Takayama, *The administration* (partially updated in articles in Takayama, *Sicily and the Mediterranean*), Johns, *Arabic administration*, and Nef, *Conquérir et gouverner*, pp. 237–356, which replace everything earlier. Johns establishes Fāṭimid influence in 'I re normanni' and in *Arabic administration*, pp. 257–83; see also Barone, 'Tra al-Qāhira e Palermo'. In fifteenth-century Egypt, both al-Maqrīzī and al-Qalqashandī characterize the Sicilian *amīrs* as *wazīrs*, on both occasions plausibly quoting earlier sources; see Johns, *Arabic administration*, pp. 81–2 and Canard, 'Une lettre', p. 134.

[145] Ugo Falcando, *Liber de regno*, ed. Siragusa; the best commentary is in the translation by Loud and Wiedemann, *The history of the tyrants*.

Sicilian history begins here. She and her son Frederick II (1198–1250), an even younger child at his succession, take us out of the period of this book, however; my main arguments will not go beyond William II.

However much or little we believe 'Falcandus''s stories of mutual treachery and malevolence, the picture he paints of a highly complex and competitive, by now trilingual administration fits what else we know about the Norman century. It also, and in particular, fits what else we know about Palermo. The wealth from royal lands and taxation flowed into it, probably on an even larger scale than under the Kalbids, since the kingdom now extended far into the mainland. Several texts attest to a very Islamic style of wealthy display, with rich Muslim figures acting as literary patrons, and Christians who dressed in Arab fashions.[146] The city itself was trilingual, thanks to Greek and Latin immigrants; 'Falcandus', writing a later eulogy of the city in 1190, now regards this cosmopolitanism as a plus not a minus. That eulogy interestingly complements Ibn Ḥawqal's characterization two centuries earlier. It says less about markets, but the 'market of the Arabs' is still prominent here. (Al-Idrīsī in his briefer account of the city stresses markets more, together with the shops of major merchants; the pilgrim account of Ibn Jubayr also stresses the dominance of Muslims in Palermo's markets in 1185.) But 'Falcandus' discusses at length the great palace silk workshop, the cloth sales of the Amalfitans by the harbour (silk and French fabrics), and, once again, the amazing wealth of the immediate surroundings of the city, with irrigation, citrus fruits, other fruit, and sugar. The city has the same size and structure as it had in 973, although the five city quarters are now three, each walled.[147]

For more solid information, we also have some land sales and analogous documents: eight texts in Arabic for the twelfth-century city and its immediate surroundings, which show the complexity of Muslim society, and a larger number in Greek. The city remains dense in these texts too, with Muslim elite figures (*qā'id*s), elders (*shaykh*s), government clerks (*kātib*s), and artisans (tanners, spice sellers) prominent, plus a *fundūq* (*phoundax*) and workshops (*ergastēria*) in the Greek documents; it was large enough that it was dependent on grain from outside its rich hinterland, and was blockaded in 1161.[148] The Palermitans as a community

[146] See, e.g., the poetry of Ibn Qalāqis for Muslim patrons in the late 1160s, edited and analysed in De Simone, *Splendori e misteri* and De Simone, '*Al-zahr al-bāsim* di Ibn Qalāqis'; and the discussions of Palermitan fashions in Ibn Jubayr, *Riḥla*, trans. Broadhurst, pp. 349–50.

[147] 'Falcandus', *Epistola*, in Ugo Falcando, *Liber de regno*, ed. Siragusa, pp. 177–86; al-Idrīsī, *Nuzhat al-mushtāq*, trans. Jaubert and Nef, pp. 307–9; Ibn Jubayr, *Riḥla*, trans. Broadhurst, p. 348.

[148] The land documents are edited in Cusa, *I diplomi*, nn. 14, 31, 43, 54, 56, 100–2, 105, 109, 111, 117, 123, 134–5, 141, 144, 153, 160–1, 163, 171–2 (pp. 6–12, 39–43, 44–6, 47–50, 61–7, 76–7, 85–6, 87–8, 101–6, 107–8, 109–10, 491–3, 494, 499–501, 505–6, 610–13, 622–3, 661–2, 663–4, 665–6, 667–8); von Falkenhausen, 'I documenti greci', nn. 1–4; plus one Latin text, Garufi, *Catalogo illustrato*, n. 11. Most of these are listed in Johns, *Arabic administration*, pp. 315–25. See the comments in Constable, 'Cross-cultural contracts' (with some misinterpretations; *dār*, for example, means 'house' here, not 'estate'; cf. also Nef, *Conquérir et gouverner*, p. 570n). Pezzini, 'Palermo in the twelfth century', is the best account for the Norman period. For the blockade, see Ugo Falcando, *Liber de regno*, ed. Siragusa, ch. 20.

were also active protagonists in the troubles of 1161, sometimes Muslims and Christians together; 'Falcandus', who has little sympathy for the people as a whole, still sees them as serious players. There were also, however, pogroms against the Muslims in 1161 (both in Palermo and in parts of the countryside) and 1189, the work of Latin knights in 1161 according to 'Falcandus'; by the end of the century there was a greater separation between religious communities, with more Muslims living in Seralcadi, the northern quarter, and the mixed mercantile community of the Cassaro becoming weaker. In the thirteenth century, the dominant language became Latin, and the descendants of the single most prominent Muslim of the second half of the twelfth century, Abū al-Qāsim, who appears in several different sources as a major political figure (including as a merchant; see p. 257 below), were by then Christian.[149]

The picture of Palermo that we get from twelfth-century written sources is thus not very dissimilar to that which we get in the tenth and eleventh, even if the linen industry had gone. It was a highly active city with a strong commercial and artisanal element; it is clear that the capital of the island maintained its earlier economic centrality. That is at least one result which we can take from the documentary record. For what else we can say we have to turn to the archaeology, which will be our central focus in the next section; it is essential as a guide to the economy, before we turn back to the written sources in the section after. We will see that there are differences between the types of exchange the *geniza* tells us about for the tenth/eleventh century and those which Norman documents tell us about for the twelfth, with the archaeology, which covers both periods, different again; how the three can be reconciled will be discussed later.

3.5 The Archaeology of Sicily in the Long Eleventh Century

Medieval archaeology in Sicily contrasts dramatically in quality with that in North Africa or, indeed, Egypt. Indeed, it has moved so fast on the island in the last decade or so that it is hardly necessary to pay much attention to syntheses earlier than the 2010s, and publications from before 2000 are mostly only useful because they publish raw data.[150] It is hard to remember that before that time

[149] Ugo Falcando, *Liber de regno*, ed. Siragusa, chs 6, 13, 14, 16, 19, 55 for Palermo's protagonism; 14 for the 1161 pogrom. For Abū al-Qāsim, see the discussions, with references, in Johns, *Arabic administration*, pp. 234–42 (242 for his Christian descendants); Metcalfe, *The Muslims*, pp. 215–22 (221 for his Christian descendants). This fascinating figure is, however, in himself a sign of problems for the Muslims; it is not just that he appears as a rich community leader, a patron of poetry, a dealer in Genoese commerce, and a figure in the government of William II (twice, with a treason accusation in between), but also that no one else in the Muslim community was anything like as visible in our sources in the later twelfth century—they were running out of major frontmen.

[150] Pioneering work before 2005 includes Molinari, 'La produzione e la circolazione', from 1995, and the whole of *Mélanges de l'École française de Rome. Moyen-Âge*, 116.1 (2004).

Sicilian medieval archaeology was close to being a black hole, with isolated figures trying to make sense of isolated sites. A generation of remarkable archaeologists have reversed that situation definitively. Not every site is published (far from it), but the syntheses which regularly come out are based on a close knowledge of what has been actually found in excavation. The result is that although new finds keep appearing, to nuance what has been discovered and generalized about already, we have by now a fairly clear picture of many aspects of the Sicilian material record in our period; what follows will be rendered out of date soon enough, but not, I think, unrecognizable. The archaeology has given most attention to rural settlement patterns and to ceramic distributions, and so shall I, for these match my foci in other chapters of this book. The major gap, apart from the late middle ages (a recurrent gap in Mediterranean archaeology, but not directly relevant here), is in urban excavations, outside the numerous sites in Palermo. Mazara, Agrigento, Syracuse, Catania, and Messina all have sites with medieval finds, which are valuable and will mostly recur below, but no real sense of the urban development of any of them appears from the archaeological evidence; that is a future task. But we have a substantial amount all the same. I will here first offer an overview of settlement and then discuss ceramic networks.

The evidence we have comes, as in the rest of the Mediterranean, from large and small (often rescue) sites and field surveys; more than a dozen field surveys have been carried out in recent years. These cover most parts of the island; only the far north-east is relatively little studied (see Map 10). Most of the Palermo sites are relatively small, but that is made up for by their number, for there are well over twenty. Larger-scale sites are not, in fact, all that many, but they include Segesta and Calathamet, neighbouring hilltop settlements in the west, and Villa del Casale, the tenth- to twelfth-century village placed above and beside the ruins of the famous Roman villa some 5 kilometres south-west of Piazza Armerina in the east-central interior. We can also add a smaller but impeccably published site inside the city walls of Mazara.[151] Wider context is often also available because the field surveys have been backed up by, or structured around, targeted excavation, as, for example, around Segesta and Calathamet, or Entella, an important hilltop site in the territory of the modern *comune* of Contessa Entellina on the plateau south of Palermo, or Castronovo di Sicilia farther to the east, halfway between Palermo and Agrigento, or Sofiana, another huge open site 7 kilometres south of Villa del Casale.[152] But it also has to be said that it is quite striking how successful

[151] Molinari, *Segesta II*; Lesnes and Poisson, *Calathamet*. For Villa del Casale, see Pensabene and Bonanno, *L'insediamento medievale*; Pensabene, *Piazza Armerina*; Pensabene and Sfameni, *La villa restaurata*; Pensabene and Barresi, *Piazza Armerina, Villa del Casale*—the last of which is the first to include an analysis of all the unpublished finds from earlier excavations of the central villa areas. For Mazara, see Molinari and Meo, *Mazara/Māzar*.

[152] For Segesta, see Molinari and Neri, 'Dall'età tardoimperiale al XIII secolo', pp. 122–7; for Entella, see Corretti et al., 'Tra Arabi, Berberi e Normanni', Corretti et al., 'Frammenti di medioevo siciliano', Corretti et al., 'Contessa Entellina (PA)'; for Castronovo, pers. comm. members of the SicTransit ERC

recent excavators have been in pinpointing significant sites. The excavators have evidently been skilled; but there is also a fair amount under the Sicilian ground surface to find, and the ceramic distributions match up particularly well.

One essential element in the rural settlement structure of Sicily in our period has been the identification of a substantial set of large open settlements, usually both undefended and on flatland sites, with a long continuity of life; it was not uncommon for them to start in the late Roman period and to continue into the twelfth century, as with Colmitella near Agrigento in the south-west, Casale S. Pietro near Castronovo in the centre, and Curcuraggi north of Syracuse in the east.[153] In much of western Sicily the eighth and ninth centuries are as yet hardly visible archaeologically, but there is a sufficiently clear similarity between the patterns of the seventh century and those of the tenth that we can assume—and sometimes show—such continuities; in the east it is easier, for there is a good quantity of Byzantine material up to 850 and often later, and the same continuities are more visible. Not by any means all such settlements lasted so long; Sofiana, for example, so large that it was semi-urban under the later Roman Empire, and an active artisanal centre in the eighth and ninth centuries, contracted substantially after 850 (it then continued on a small scale into the thirteenth century), although, here, it was in effect substituted as a central place for the area by nearby Villa del Casale, whose village rapidly expanded around 950.[154] Other similar sites across the island also ended or began in the middle centuries of the long period 600–1150. But there is enough evidence for this type of large village (some of

project; for Sofiana, see Vaccaro, 'Sicily', pp. 44–6, 54–7; Vaccaro, 'Re-evaluating a forgotten town'. A comparative study of three other recent surveys is Alfano, 'I paesaggi medievali'; see further, for one of them, for the upper Jato and Belìce Destro valleys, around the older Monte Jato site, Alfano and Sacco, 'Tra alto e basso medioevo' (Jeremy Johns's nearby Monreale survey is also, pers. comm., nearing publication). For Jato itself, see Nicole Mölk's doctoral thesis, *Giato/Jāṭū*, which summarizes decades of excavation by Hans Peter Isler and his successors. Another significant survey is of the Megarese north of Syracuse—see Malfitana and Cacciaguerra, *Priolo romana*, 1; Cacciaguerra, 'L'area megarese'. The most fully published recent survey, that for the land behind Gela, is Bergemann, *Der Gela-Survey* (pp. 82–3, 177–8, 207 for the middle ages), but it is sadly useless for our purposes. Although this area is well attested in texts as important in the late Islamic and Norman periods, and although Islamic/Norman glaze is hardly difficult to see, the archaeologists identified, or at least published, no ceramics for the 350+ years between the mid-ninth century and the early thirteenth—and did not problematize the gap at all. (They relied on an out-of-date dating for *ceramica decorata a stuoia*, which they used as a diagnostic for the Islamic period, although it is now clearly identified as Byzantine—see n. 173 below—as Bergemann recognized in 'Funde der islamischen Phase'; but they still had a gap of 300 years.)

[153] For Colmitella, see Rizzo and Romano, 'Le butte', with Rizzo et al., 'Il villaggio di Colmitella', and Rizzo et al., 'L'insediamento rurale', pp. 354–63. For Casale S. Pietro, only recently concluded as an excavation, I have used Molinari and Carver. 'Sicily in transition', pp. 7–10; Molinari, 'Sicily from Late Antiquity'; plus the contributions to the SicTransit Second Plenary Seminar in July 2019, and Alessandra Molinari, pers. comm. For Curcuraggi, see Cacciaguerra, 'L'area megarese', p. 382. As can be seen, full publications for these sites are for the future. For general analyses and other examples, see Molinari, 'Paesaggi rurali'; Molinari, '"Islamisation" and the rural world'; Vaccaro, 'Sicily', pp. 41–4; Arcifa, '"Insularità" siciliana'.

[154] Vaccaro, 'Re-evaluating a forgotten town', with Vaccaro and La Torre, 'La produzione di ceramica'; for Villa del Casale, see n. 151 above.

them, as clearly with Sofiana, could be called agro-towns) to allow archaeologists to argue convincingly that such villages were for the whole of that long period the dominant settlement structure in the countryside, acting as a focus for changing patterns of dispersed settlement around them, that is to say, hamlets and isolated farms.

Archaeologists tend to contrast these open sites with more defensible, and often defended, hilltop villages which only begin around 950, such as Jato and Entella, or indeed later, as with Calathamet.[155] This may sometimes be a problem of the evidence; in the east, where the dating evidence is better for the previous two centuries, some hilltop sites are known from earlier (Curcuraggi is one; Rocchicella, inland from Catania, a hill-slope village of the sixth–seventh century with later and well-studied short-lived reoccupations in the decades around 800 and again in the eleventh century, is another; although the hilltop site of Paternò, also inland from Catania, seems to have only started around 950).[156] It is also worth noting that some of the active rural *castra* mentioned by Malaterra, such as Petralia and Troina, have not been excavated, as they have occupied the same sites ever since, and we cannot assume that they were new a century earlier; the most important of all, Enna, certainly had a long back history. Sometimes we can posit that a hilltop site directly replaced a valley site, as Calathamet probably replaced Aquae Segestanae beneath it. But sometimes there was a more complex dialectic, such as that between Casale S. Pietro and two later and more defensible settlement sites above it, one Islamic (Castronovo itself) and the other Norman, plus a Byzantine-period walled site, Monte Kassar, on the mountain above the latter, which seems only to have been a military settlement; Casale S. Pietro coexisted with all of them as a prosperous route centre site until it was abandoned in the early thirteenth century.[157]

For me, the contrast between hilltop and valley or flatland sites has been overplayed. It has got mixed up with arguments about administrative structures under the Arabs and then Normans which do not map well onto settlement patterns, plus the influence of the *incastellamento* debates, which are more a part of the history of mainland Italy. I would rather see the whole of our period as one which was, in rural settlement terms, dominated by large villages, no matter where they were situated and how long they lasted, with a hierarchy of smaller and single-farm sites around them which were, as dispersed settlement tends to be, rather less stable. In one site, Colmitella, a specific area for grain storage has been found

[155] Ritter-Lutz, *Monte Iato*, p. 17; Corretti et al., 'Frammenti di medioevo siciliano', pp. 148–54; Lesnes and Poisson, *Calathamet*, pp. 347–50.

[156] For Rocchicella, see Arcifa and Longo, 'Processi di diversificazione'; for Paternò, see Arcifa and Messina, 'La frontiera arabo-bizantina'; Messina et al., 'Islamic pottery production'.

[157] Molinari and Neri, 'Dall'età tardoimperiale al XIII secolo', p. 123; for Casale S. Pietro and Castronovo, see n. 153 above. Monte Kassar belonged to a set of military defences set up by the Byzantines at strategic internal points around 800, well before the Arab invasion; see Arcifa, '"Insularità" siciliana', pp. 137–43.

in the Byzantine phase (some eighty small ditches, a common type of food store), which has been plausibly interpreted as showing a collective organization for the maintenance of family grain supplies. Following on from that, as we move into our period, one of the most important features of such villages is that it is quite difficult, in most of the sites which have been studied archaeologically, to see any major internal social differentiations, for houses all tend to be similar—only Calathamet has a separated-off, doubtless higher-status section. That is to say, the archaeology points to substantial and coherent communities without so very much social hierarchy. This was a good basis for the sharing of agricultural prosperity in one of the richest regions of the Mediterranean, and thus also for exchange.[158] It also fits well with the collective political protagonism of rural and even urban centres discussed in Islamic and Norman written sources (see p. 206 above).

This pattern continued into the early Norman period, but after *c.*1150 there was a change. Every survey points to a sharp reduction in dispersed sites, and the flatland villages themselves began to be abandoned. This is certainly when the big hilltop villages, which have been a key feature of Sicilian rural settlement ever since, became dominant, and some of them were new then as well, for example (out of the excavated sites) Segesta, which was first occupied in the mid-twelfth century—it was clearly initially a Muslim site, for, as has already been noted, it has Sicily's only known medieval mosque.[159] This settlement shift has tended to be associated with the beginning of urban and rural violence against Muslims, which at its height resulted in the Muslim revolts of the early thirteenth century; the impact of this violence on the material record therefore needs some discussion here, as a parenthesis.

'Falcandus' tells us that there was a movement of Muslims out of Christian-dominated rural areas of the island as a result of the pogroms of 1161. This is backed up by documentary evidence for immigration from northern and eastern Sicily into the territories of Jato, Entella, and nearby Corleone around or after the middle of the twelfth century; we know this from *nisba*s, indicating places of origin, for their mostly Arabic-named populations, who are very well documented in texts because they were all given to William II's new cathedral foundation of Monreale in 1176–83, as we shall see later.[160] The revolts after 1189, which had

[158] Lesnes and Poisson, *Calathamet*, pp. 107, 130–1, 144–53. For Colmitella, see Rizzo and Romano, 'Le butte'; for a complete list of storage silos across the middle ages in Sicily, see Alfano and D'Amico, 'La conservazione dei cereali a lungo termine'; see in general Molinari, '"Islamisation" and the rural world', pp. 205–9. The absence of internal hierarchies does not entirely fit our documents (see pp. 234–5 below), but it relativizes the hierarchies found there. On the problems of using the imagery of *incastellamento*, or of linking fortifications with private lordship, before the very end of our period, see Arcifa and Maurici, 'Castelli e incastellamento in Sicilia', pp. 447–63; the central-eastern area controlled by the Aleramici family in the twelfth century may be an exception (ibid., p. 462).

[159] Molinari, *Segesta II*, pp. 57–62, 95–8. For Norman-period hilltop fortifications, see Maurici, *Castelli medievali*, esp. pp. 131–95.

[160] Ugo Falcando, *Liber de regno*, ed. Siragusa, ch. 21; for the *nisba*s, see Nef, *Conquérir et gouverner*, pp. 735–6.

Jato and Entella as foci, furthermore coincide with a brief high point in archaeologically attested settlement in both, just as the abandonment of both hilltop sites in the mid-thirteenth century coincides with the moment when Frederick II finally defeated the revolts and in the years up to 1246 forcibly removed the surviving Muslim population to Lucera in Puglia. In the case of these two surveys, the archaeology (which also includes coin finds in Jato of the late-1210s Muslim leader, Muḥammad b. ʿAbbād, and a siege castle for Frederick II's troops) can thus be seen in effect as the archaeology of war.[161]

Elsewhere, however, it is less certain. We know that there was north Italian, 'Lombard' settlement in Sicily by the mid-twelfth century, which seems to have initially focussed on a north–south band in the centre of the island, from Cefalù and Patti through Piazza (Armerina) to Butera; and we gather from 'Falcandus' that it was the *Lombardi* of these towns who massacred many of their Muslim neighbours in 1161, which led to the population shifts just mentioned. This might fit with the fact that the settlement at Villa del Casale, near the modern town of Piazza, was mostly abandoned in the mid-twelfth century, and only partially occupied later in the century. But it also might not. Piazza was itself destroyed a year later by a royal army.[162] We do not know where 'Piazza' actually was in this period. Was it at the villa site, or in its present position a few kilometres away, or both? Even if the abandonment of the former villa was, indeed, the result of violence in the 1160s, which is quite possible, we do not know who perpetrated it, or who the victims were. (To assume that the inhabitants were, or were still, Muslims just because they had courtyard houses, which they did at Villa del Casale, would be an assumption too far.)[163] That is to say, it is best in most cases to abstain from attributing too much specific relationship between the archaeology and what we know from the written sources, whether about interethnic rivalry or about anything else, unless we have particularly good reason, as at Entella and Jato.

This point needs to be generalized further. I argued at the start of this book (p. 10) that it is methodologically essential to set up our archaeological knowledge with as little input from the documentary sources as possible, and to do the same in reverse with the documents, to avoid circular arguments. Who did what to whom around Piazza is a case in point. But we also need to be careful about

[161] For Entella and Jato, see the references in n. 152 above; Jato was not quite abandoned, but post-1246 settlement was poor-quality: Mölk, *Giato/Jāṭū*, pp. 63–5, 278–85. For the coins, see D'Angelo, 'La monetazione', and Isler, 'Monte Iato', pp. 127, 136–7; for the siege castle, see Alfano and Sacco, 'Tra alto e basso medioevo', p. 136; Maurici et al., 'Il "Castellazzo" di Monte Iato'.

[162] Ugo Falcando, *Liber de regno*, ed. Siragusa, chs 21–2; cf. the somewhat vague discussions in Peri, 'La questione delle colonie "lombarde"'. For the Villa, see Molinari, 'La Sicilia tra XII e XIII secolo', p. 350; Pensabene, 'Villa del Casale', pp. 17–20. See further Pensabene, 'Il contributo degli scavi', pp. 751–2, for the most recent discussion of the latest settlement, 'di carattere limitata', up to just after 1200, and a rejection of any precise link between the settlement phases and the revolt of the *Lombardi*.

[163] 'Both' is quite likely, given the distinction between *Placea* and *Placea veterem* in a document of 1148; see Garufi, 'Gli Aleramici', n. 8. Courtyards: Barresi, 'I risultati delle campagne di scavo 2004–2005'; Pensabene, 'Villa del Casale'.

attributing too much to ethnic or religious identity and practices more generally. Sicily went through more substantial cultural changes than any other of our regions in and shortly after the period discussed in this book, for it was both 'Islamicized' and 'de-Islamicized': half the island, or more, had become Muslim between the Arab and the Norman conquests, and few Muslims were left there by 1250.[164] What that means in material terms needs, however, to be treated very cautiously. There were not enough North Africans to Islamicize the island by immigration (just as, later, there were not enough 'Lombards', even though they also included urban traders and peasants, to Latinize everywhere by immigration either), and in the 1240s, it is, of course, impossible that the rural population of the whole of the western half of the island could have been fitted inside the walls of Lucera. It is clear that some sizable sectors of western Sicily were abandoned, but others equally were not: Calatafimi, near Segesta and Calathamet, is one example, Castronovo is another, and surviving population figures from 1283 for the Val di Mazara, the western half of the island, show there were many others. I would assume as a working hypothesis that the ancestors of most of the Italian/Sicilian-speaking Christian population of western Sicily in 1300 had ancestors who had been both Arabic-speaking and Muslim, just as those ancestors were themselves mostly descended from Greek- and Latin-speaking Christians in 800. It is worth remembering that the Greek east of the island was largely Latinized, in language and rite, in the thirteenth and early fourteenth centuries as well, without much recorded conflict—Annick Peters-Custot has called a similar shift in Calabria an '*acculturation en douceur*', and, whether or not it really was 'soft', it did not involve the violence suffered at Entella and Jato.[165] Much of the Muslim-to-Christian shift, even if doubtless more coercive, would probably have been similar.

There is a broader archaeological point to be made here too: this Latinization does not need to have involved any major shift in material culture, beyond that from mosques to churches. Alessandra Molinari has expressed considerable unease about the concept of 'Islamicization' in the archaeological record; for

[164] 'Islamicized' has, here as elsewhere, to be distinguished from 'Arabized', which in itself refers to two distinct concepts, Arabic language and Arab cultural identity. At least religious Islamicization and linguistic Arabization took place in Sicily, and the Venn diagram for all three overlapped considerably, but they were not identical; and when analysing individuals or groups, if we have evidence for only one, we cannot assume that this implies the others as well. Anyway, for most individuals who might fit into these categories, we only have their names, which might denote any of the three; I will often use the term 'Arabic-named' to describe them. See Metcalfe, *Muslims and Christians*, for an exploration of the issues (including, p. 94, two examples of Christians called Muḥammad—in Cusa, *I diplomi*, n. 132 (pp. 134–79), at p. 145—which is an exceptionally rare finding for the middle ages; cf. also Chapter 2, n. 73 above).

[165] Calatafimi: see, e.g., Giunta, *Acta Siculo-Aragonensia*, 1.1, n. 183 for its inhabitants in the 1290s (and cf. Molinari, *Segesta II*, pp. 35, 43); for Castronovo, where study of the excavations is, as of 2022, ongoing, pers. comm. Alessandra Molinari and other members of the SicTransit ERC programme; see n. 153 above. For the 1283 figures, see Epstein. *An island for itself*, pp. 42–3, 51. For Calabrese Greeks, see Peters-Custot, *Les Grecs*; for Greeks in Sicily, see Bresc, *Un monde méditerranéen*, pp. 587–94.

example, the homogeneity of ceramic use across the island around 1000 easily crossed the divide between an increasingly Arab and Muslim west and a Greek Christian east.[166] The same is true for its reversal in the thirteenth century. We shall see that there was by then, indeed, a partial divergence in material culture between the west and the east again. But outside the parts of the west devastated by war, this is hard to attach to either Muslim suppression or Latin immigration (which happened in the east too). The decrease in ceramic production in Palermo itself (see p. 225 below) may well be related to the departure of Muslim experts there, but there is no need to assume that the shift from Muslim to Christian religion has to have had a major impact on the wider patterns of production and exchange, and I shall not make that assumption in what follows. And this is equally true for settlement patterns. The thirteenth century does, indeed, show far less open and undefended settlement than the centuries before 1150, and also, perhaps most importantly, greater hierarchy inside settlements,[167] but—to close the parenthesis—we do not need to attach this too tightly to ethnic/religious difficulties or changes.

These were the spatial patterns of the rural societies which bought and sold agricultural and artisanal products. As usual, most of the archaeological evidence we have for production and commerce is ceramics; and so, as elsewhere in this book, I shall construct a narrative of the shifts in exchange patterns on the basis of that evidence, which is in this region a narrative easy to set out.

* * *

The whole of Sicily bought tablewares from North Africa up to the very end of the seventh century. More than was the case for any other region of the Mediterranean, it is now clear that the latest African Red Slip ware was available not only around all the coasts of the island but also on most sites in the interior which have been studied.[168] After that, however, for as yet unclear reasons (but also reasons which are not in the remit of this book), Sicily was more divided economically between east and west. It remained partially divided beyond our period, too, with the key exception of the mid-tenth to late twelfth centuries. But there were shifts in the balance between the two: in turn, first the east and then the west, and then, from the very end of our period, the east again, dominated the exchange of the island.

In the Byzantine period, lasting up to 831 for Palermo and 878 for the capital at Syracuse, the driving force was in the east. In the west, Palermo and one or two

[166] Molinari, 'La ceramica siciliana di età islamica', pp. 197–200, 217–19; Molinari, '"Islamisation" and the rural world', pp. 187–93.

[167] As with Brucato in the centre-north, for the most part a late thirteenth- and fourteenth-century site, which had a castle overlooking the village; see Pesez, *Brucato*, pp. 102–3 and *passim*. That is to say, Sicily belatedly started to look more like other parts of Latin Europe in its settlement structures.

[168] See now esp. Malfitana and Bonifay, *La ceramica africana nella Sicilia romana*, with the distribution map at p. 431. For what follows, Sacco, *Dalla ceramica alla storia economica*, ch. 8, is the most recent comprehensive survey.

other coastal sites were integrated into a Tyrrhenian exchange network, with glazed Forum ware (*ceramica a vetrina pesante*), perhaps from Rome, and Neapolitan wine amphorae coming in, in return for (we assume) Sicilian wheat from the papal and other estates in the interior, as well as a set of oil lamp types. The western interior is almost devoid of as yet identifiable finds, and much of it probably had little connection with exchange systems other than the very local, although there may possibly have been a wider availability of a cooking ware type, perhaps from the Cefalù area, called Calcitic ware in recent studies. In this period, the wheat in the west must just have gone to the coast as rent or tax, with little coming back in return, and with any commercial exchange restricted to the ports.[169] In the east, however, it was quite different. For a start, coins, which can be found on most Byzantine rural sites, were far more common in the east than in the west.[170] Secondly, east-coast sites, and some into the eastern interior too, were all closely associated with the network represented by eighth- and ninth-century Byzantine globular amphorae, probably mostly for wine, coming largely from the Aegean. This network, which is generally seen as in some way state-related, tightly connected the eastern half of the island—and also Malta, where finds of globular amphorae have been particularly rich—with the heartlands of Byzantium. Its scale of exchange in no way matched that of the sixth and seventh centuries, but by early medieval standards the network was very active, as we shall see in more detail later (pp. 304–5, 636–7).[171] Internally to eastern Sicily, there was active exchange as well. Similar forms of globular amphorae (demonstrably for wine) and a range of other ceramic types were produced in an artisan quarter at Sofiana, although it is not clear how far their distribution networks reached.[172] And, in particular, a type of handmade or slow-wheel cooking ware, mostly open casserole dishes, called *ceramica con decorazione a stuoia* because it has incisions along its sides imitating wickerwork, was available, despite its simplicity, in nearly two-thirds of the island, as far as Agrigento, plus Malta; it was made in numerous places in the east, and is best documented in the eastern Sicilian village of Rocchicella. This was not, strictly, a fully articulated exchange network, as it had so many local production centres, but it shows a cultural connectivity across a wide area (see Map 11). Lucia Arcifa, who first characterized it, dates the ware

[169] Ardizzone, 'Rapporti commerciali'; Ardizzone, 'Nuove ipotesi', pp. 58–60; Alfano and Sacco, 'I paesaggi medievali', pp. 9–11 for Calcitic ware (wares of this type would have a long future history, up to 1100: Sacco, 'Le produzioni da fuoco', p. 252).

[170] For the coins, see n. 244 below, with Vivien Prigent, pers. comm.; he hypothesizes, tentatively but convincingly, that estate structures were more fragmented in the east, which led to more rural taxpayers paying directly, not through landlords, which aided coin circulation.

[171] The basic current survey for Sicily is Arcifa, 'Contenitori da trasporto', developed for Syracuse by Cacciaguerra, 'Commerci e sistemi di scambio'. Eastern Sicily also saw non-Sicilian *ceramica a vetrina pesante*; it did not necessarily come from the Rome region, although exactly what its origins were is unclear; see Cacciaguerra, 'La ceramica a vetrina pesante'.

[172] See Vaccaro and La Torre, 'La produzione di ceramica'; pp. 79–80 for wine residues.

quite tightly to the very late eighth century and early ninth because of coin associations at Rocchicella. The extent of its availability perhaps argues for a longer period, up to the Islamic conquest perhaps, at least from other production centres; but it was, anyway, Byzantine in date, and shows the material cultural network of that period as clearly as any evidence does.[173]

The Islamic conquest shifted the balance of the island; from now on for three centuries, and throughout our period, the driving force was in the west, above all in Palermo. The numerous excavations in the city show a rapid urban expansion to the north by the end of the ninth century and to the south-east in the early tenth, and a filling out of all the urban space described by Ibn Ḥawqal in 973, covering three times the probable size of the Roman and Byzantine city. The geographer listed all kinds of goods sold there, as we have seen (p. 207); in terms of the archaeology of production, what is most visible is, of course, ceramics, and several kilns have been identified.[174] Every kind of pottery was made in Palermo, cooking wares, common wares, amphorae, glazed tablewares, plus vessels for irrigation wheels and making sugar loaves, with, probably, specialized kilns for different categories of pot. The glazed pottery is one of the most fully studied of these, even if, as we can see from the large samples available from sites such as the church of S. Maria alla Gancia, it made up under 2 per cent of ceramics available. It appears in the late ninth century, clearly as a direct result of Ifrīqiyan influence and doubtless, at the start, with Ifrīqiyan artisans—one of the early glaze types, the 'giallo di Palermo', is a skilled copy of the high-quality Raqqāda yellow glaze of the last decades of the ninth century (see p. 175 above)—but soon diverged in its decoration, developing its own polychrome styles, drawing as it did so on some eastern models as well (see Fig. 6). In part linked to this, a local production of glass vessels has been identified too, from the decades around 900 onwards.[175] The

[173] See Arcifa, 'Indicatori archeologici e dinamiche insediative', her most detailed account, with an up-to-date distribution map in Arcifa, 'La Sicilia bizantina', p. 144. For the ware lasting longer into the ninth century, perhaps from different production centres, see Alfano, 'I paesaggi medievali', pp. 337–8. The wide distribution of as simple a ceramic type as this recalls the wide success of the slow-wheel Pantellerian cooking ware under the late Roman Empire (see, e.g., Santoro, 'Pantellerian ware'); but that went by sea.

[174] For the range of Palermo excavations, see the articles in Nef and Ardizzone, *Les dynamiques*, pp. 165–269, concentrating on the period before 950; for later, see those in Arcifa and Sgarlata, *From polis to madina*, pp. 313–79. See further the lists and syntheses in Spatafora, *Da Panormos a Balarm*; Bagnera, 'From a small town to a capital'; Ardizzone et al., 'The role of Palermo'; D'Angelo, 'Le produzioni di ceramiche invetriate'; Spatafora et al., 'Ceramica da mensa'; Aleo Nero, 'Attività produttive a Palermo', with a list of kilns and other workshops known to 2016; Arcifa and Bagnera, 'Ceramica islamica a Palermo'; and now the wide survey of Palermitan ceramic production and its implications in Sacco, *Dalla ceramica alla storia economica*. For Palermo plausibly described as the most economically complex city in the whole of eleventh-century Italy, see Molinari, 'Riflessioni'.

[175] La Gancia percentages: Ardizzone et al., 'Lo scavo della chiesa di S. Maria degli Angeli alla Gancia', p. 199. The best general survey of Palermo glaze in the Arab period is currently Sacco, 'Le ceramiche invetriate', updated in Sacco, *Dalla ceramica alla storia economica*, ch. 4.2. Note that earlier publications put the date of the start of Palermo glaze production around 950; this has been decisively put back to the late ninth century in recent years, following the important revision in Arcifa et al., 'Archeologia della Sicilia islamica', pp. 245–56; see also Ardizzone et al., 'Aghlabid Palermo', and Arcifa

Fig. 6 Palermo yellow glaze

amphorae are the other category which is particularly well studied, and several typologies are currently available, the fullest of which is now the work of Viva Sacco; Palermo amphorae are easy to recognize, with their red fabric made from clays from at least two places not far from the city, frequent red-painted decoration, and deep grooves from the wheel-turning process (see Fig. 7).[176]

These two types of Palermo production expanded rapidly throughout the island (see Map 11). After 950, there is hardly a site, either on the coast or in the interior, which does not show one or the other, and almost always both, and sometimes other Palermo products as well. On the coast of eastern Sicily, amphorae from the Byzantine Empire are still attested in the tenth century, notably Otranto 1 and occasionally Günsenin 1; this is the case for Taormina, which was, anyway, not taken by the Muslims until 902 and which kept strong Byzantine links thereafter, but they are also found in Syracuse, which the Muslims by now

and Bagnera, 'Palermo in the ninth and early tenth century'. For the initial similarity and then partial divergence of Ifrīqiyan and Palermitan pottery of all types, see Gragueb Chatti et al., 'Le mobilier céramique en Ifriqiya et Sicile'. For glass, see Colangeli, *Il riflesso di vetri e metalli*, pp. 320–3.

[176] Sacco, 'Produzione e circolazione', building on Ardizzone Lo Bue, *Anfore in Sicilia*, as well as on her own doctoral thesis, Sacco, *Une fenêtre sur Palerme*, pp. 390–407, published in revised form as *Dalla ceramica alla storia economica*, ch. 4.3.

Fig. 7 Palermo amphora, Sacco 11

had firmly in their hands, and even on the Villa del Casale site, well inland (both are found in Palermo too, but only in tiny numbers); Constantinople's Glazed White ware (GWW) 2, from the same period or later, was found in the theatre of Catania, as well. Syracuse in the early tenth century also had its own semi-fine ware, a highly polished type which might show that artisans here were imitating the sheen of a glazed pottery which they did not yet have the technology to make.[177] But by the later tenth century Palermo amphorae and glaze had reached the east coast, and is on nearly every site even there; its amphorae were set against

[177] See pp. 304–14 for the Byzantine ceramic types. For a map of Palermo distributions across forty sites, see Sacco, 'Produzione e circolazione', fig. 9. For general surveys, see most recently Molinari, 'La ceramica siciliana del X e XI secolo'; Mangiaracina, 'La ceramica invetriata', which usefully explains some key elements of Italian-language ceramic terminology; Mangiaracina, 'La Sicilia islamica'. For Byzantine amphorae in the east, see Arcifa, 'Contenitori di trasporto', pp. 132–7; Cacciaguerra, 'Anfore altomedievali'; Cacciaguerra, 'Città e mercati'; Cacciaguerra, 'Siracusa', pp. 63–6, 82–3; in the west, Sacco, 'Produzione e circolazione delle anfore palermitane', p. 188; Ardizzone Lo Bue, *Anfore in Sicilia*, pp. 50, 162; Ardizzone et al., 'Il complesso monumentale', p. 416. For Villa del Casale, see Federico, 'Il saggio nord-ovest'; for the GWW 2, unpublished, pers. comm. Pamela Armstrong. For the polished ware, see Cacciaguerra, 'Cultura materiale', p. 370. For Syracuse compared with Palermo, see Cacciaguerra and Sacco, 'Due "capitali", due storie?'. Günsenin 1 has also been found in western Sicily, at Mazara (Molinari and Meo, *Mazara/Māzar*, pp. 251–3 (A. Meo)); for Otranto 1 at Palermo, see Sacco, *Dalla ceramica alla storia economica*, ch. 5.9.

local types, some already copying Palermo productions, but there are eastern excavations—such as Paternò near Catania, which even had its own kilns—where in the period 950–1000 85 per cent of the glaze was from the capital. This does not mean that all local tablewares were Palermitan (in Paternò, a local semi-fine *schiarito* (lightened) ware was twice as common) but it does show that the top of the market was entirely dominated by Palermo glaze, even in the east.[178] On sites and surveys in the west, in effect all diagnostic wares are from the capital.

How do we interpret this? The first point is that this dominance is extremely unusual. We did not see it in Egypt or Ifrīqiya, where, even though the capital in each case sat at the top of a productive hierarchy, its ceramics were matched by high-quality local productions too; we shall see that this was very much so in Spain as well, and, in Byzantium, the period when Constantinople produced the only classy fine ware, GWW 1, was also a period in which its distribution across the empire only occurred on a tiny scale (see p. 305 below). We could see the rapid expansion of the availability of Palermo glaze as a marker of the fact that it was a novel and attractive ceramic type, more expensive than common wares but never a luxury, which was only easily available from one place. But this in itself shows that knowledge about its availability and a conviction of its desirability had spread; and, of course, most importantly, there had already to be established exchange routes for the ware to reach so far, and so far into the interior. Such routes may well have been old, going back into the later empire, given the distributions of African Red Slip then.

Similar patterns are even more striking in the case of amphorae. As I said, it is easy to identify Palermo amphorae. Some certainly carried wine (Sacco 11, which often went to North Africa, is the main type that we can be sure of[179]); it is harder to say about the other types, and other liquid contents (such as fish sauce, and compotes of vegetables or fruit, cooked and/or salted to preserve them) are possible, but they certainly took food into the Sicilian interior. This must have been types of food which the coasts, and above all Palermo's own rich hinterland, produced more readily than did the interior—and given the scale of this exchange, their productions must have been even more organized for mass sale than the long lists of vegetables and fruits in the geographers might have made one expect. Conversely, all this also marked an ability of buyers to look outside a local area for food, which was not automatic in the middle ages anywhere, especially away from towns and coasts. In short, both glazed pottery and amphorae mark buying power for the interior, and established medium-distance distribution networks,

[178] Arcifa and Messina, 'La frontiera arabo-bizantina', esp. p. 380.

[179] Sacco, 'Produzione e circolazione', esp. pp. 182–4, and pers. comm. Sacco 7, the most common type of all, which was found at Ṣabra in Tunisia along with Sacco 11, may well have carried wine too; the proofs are not yet clear, however. See also Bramoullé et al., 'Le mobilier céramique', pp. 200–2; and Drieu et al., 'Chemical evidence', for proofs of wine in Sicilian amphorae, without, however, citing the amphora types.

necessarily using donkeys or mules, for the interior had no water-based communication. Local figures had the resources to buy from Palermo, and this must mean also that they were producing goods which they could sell, directly or indirectly, to Palermo. And if villages like Colmitella are guides to wider patterns in Sicily, these were not just local elite figures; peasants had this buying power too— that is to say, they were certainly not in this period handing over all their surplus in rent and/or tax, if they had access to products like these. There was an exchange network here, which covered the entire island (even, doubtless, the little-excavated north-east, given easy sea links along the north coast); we can only see the Palermo products, but it has to have been reciprocal. We are dealing with a 'crescita formidabile dell'economia siciliana', in Molinari's words.[180]

After 1000, Palermo's hyper-dominance slipped. Not so much in amphora distributions, but, from now on, the city's glaze productions, although still as widely distributed, competed with local fine wares, in effect in a process of import substitution. In Paternò, that 85 per cent dominance slipped to 45 per cent—still high, but showing the clear rise of local, doubtless cheaper alternatives. Syracuse kilns began to produce their own glaze, and in Villa del Casale, a large-scale ceramic production area developed by the early eleventh century, producing glazed and unglazed wares, beside those imported from Palermo.[181] There will, of course, have been other local wares too. The complexities of this are well shown by the case of Mazara. This town, around 1000 or a little before, began to produce its own ceramics, with the same wide range that already characterized Palermo—not surprisingly, given that it was probably by now the second port of the island after the capital. Inside eleventh-century Mazara, dumps from the kiln area show very little except Mazara products. But, interestingly, an eleventh-century village 10 kilometres inland, Casale Nuovo, still bought overwhelmingly from Palermo—glaze and amphorae (with their contents) and even cooking wares, with Mazara wares only a minority.[182] So the routes for products did not just run through the ports, or the main towns; there must have been a direct inland network for Palermo products which was competitive with that from the local urban centre.

[180] Molinari, 'La Sicilia e le trasformazioni delle reti di scambio mediterranee', p. 367. This also fits the identification of metalworking areas, near Entella and at Villa del Casale; we cannot tell with metal how widespread its distribution was, but it is significant that we are in both cases well into the interior; see Corretti et al., 'Entella', p. 602; Corretti and Chiarantini, 'Contessa Entellina'; for Villa del Casale, see Alfano et al., 'I nuovi scavi', p. 589; Carloni and Ventura, 'Il *calidarium*'.

[181] Paternò: see n. 178 above. Syracuse: Fiorilla, 'Primi dati'. Villa del Casale: Alfano et al., 'I nuovi scavi'; Alfano et al., 'Produzione e circolazione'; Alaimo et al., 'Produzione ceramica'; Alfano, 'La ceramica medievale', the fullest publication; and, earlier, Ampolo, 'Lo scarico di fornace'. Alfano, 'La ceramica medievale', p. 609, notes that Palermo imports were mostly found in the centre of the former villa, probably an elite focus, not in the artisanal area on the former Southern Baths complex.

[182] Molinari, 'La ceramica siciliana di età islamica', pp. 208–17. For Mazara itself, see Molinari and Meo, *Mazara/Māzar*, pp. 159–336 (A. Meo); the minority of non-local ceramics came from Palermo, (pp. 237–44, 256, 283–93), Ifrīqiya (244–50, 293–9), and Spain, a very small set of Spanish *cuerda seca* pottery (199).

These examples of internal competition are not, however, signs of the weakening of the coherence of the island's economy—quite the reverse; rather, they now show a more polycentric pattern of productions, which, however, as in Egypt, was still one linked together by the products of the capital.

This trend continued, as more products appeared at the end of the eleventh century (see Map 12). We see it not least in Agrigento, whose kilns developed a twelfth-century fashion for monochrome green glaze (often with furrowed (*solcata*) decoration under the glaze), and which extended its products to its own network of subsidiary sites (Colmitella was one) that were less independent from Agrigento than Casale Nuovo was from Mazara. Castronovo, halfway between Agrigento and Palermo, got products from both in the twelfth century, although its amphorae still came mostly from the capital, and its cooking wares too. Entella too may have produced its own unglazed pottery, although its distribution is likely to have been quite local.[183] So Palermo was less prominent in the twelfth century, but was still the largest production centre, with extensive distributions inside and well beyond its immediate hinterland, and, by now, a greater standardization of types.[184] The network was still more polycentric, but no site had fallen out of it, even quite small settlements; it is simply that there was more choice of productions, from Palermo or from provincial towns and large villages, as well as local wares. The complexity of finds on some rural sites on the island has indeed been compared to that on urban sites in mainland Italy.[185] What else was carried in these networks (at least in the twelfth century, when documents begin to be available) we shall see in the next section.

The late twelfth century is less easy to see in the archaeology, and the thirteenth is not much better; but by the latter century the structure of production had shifted substantially. Although this takes us some way beyond the end of our period, it is worth looking at it briefly, to get a sense of where Sicily would go next. Palermo seems by now to have imported more ceramics than it produced, including from outside the region, although its wares are still prominent on the Castronovo sites in the thirteenth century. The western coastal towns, reaching inland again to Castronovo, also used glazed wares imported from abroad—I will come to these imports in a moment. But most importantly, the driving force of regional ceramic production had shifted back to the east, to Messina and to the southern half of the Val di Noto in the south-east, neither of which until then had

[183] Fiorilla, 'Ceramiche medievali', pp. 205–10; a second set of kilns is published in Bonacasa Carra and Ardizzone, *Agrigento*, esp. pp. 247–63 for glaze (N. Cavallaro)—these kilns produced amphorae above all; see also the synthesis in Ardizzone, 'Le produzioni medievali di Agrigento'; for Colmitella, see Rizzo et al., 'Il villaggio di Colmitella'; for Castronovo, Antonino Meo and Paola Orecchioni in the SicTransit Second Plenary Seminar in July 2019. For Entella, see Corretti et al., 'Contessa Entellina', pp. 348–9.

[184] Sacco, 'Le ceramiche invetriate', p. 362; for one site, Cefalà, where the twelfth century is fairly well represented, see Pezzini et al., 'La ceramica', pp. 374–92.

[185] See, e.g., Molinari, 'La ceramica altomedievale', p. 281.

been major players. A well-made type of *pentola* (cooking pot) with internal glaze, which came above all from Messina, is found all over the island, again in the interior as much as on the coasts, and was exported as well, on a small scale.[186] And from about the 1220s, a tin-glazed *protomaiolica* often called Gela ware (see Fig. 8), one of the first types of maiolica, the dominant Italian glazed ware of the later middle ages and beyond, began to be produced in Gela itself (a new town of that decade) and a wider set of centres in the south-east. It too is found across most of the island, including in inland sites, although in smaller numbers in the west (see Map 12). The east–west divide, so visible under the Byzantines, but effectively cancelled across most of the Islamic and Norman periods, was slowly beginning to appear again—although it is countered by evidence of quite dense interrelationships focussed on some sites, such as the western port of Mazara, which visibly flourished in the thirteenth century as a communications hub, with

Fig. 8 Gela ware

[186] For Messina *pentole*, see Bacci and Tigano, *Da Zancle a Messina*, pp. 110–18, 147–9, 150–66 (articles by S. Fiorilla, G. Tigano and L. Sannino)—in earlier literature they are sometimes called 'Marsala ware', as they were first identified there. They reached Milazzo, close by (Italiano, 'I reperti ceramici'), which is not surprising, but that coastal site is also worth citing for its wide thirteenth-century ceramic repertoire, coming from western Sicily, south-eastern Sicily, and Campania. They are generally visible in the west, including, as noted, Marsala (Kennet et al., 'Uno scavo urbano', pp. 626–7) and Mazara (Molinari and Cassai, 'La Sicilia e il Mediterraneo nel XIII secolo', pp. 91–2, 97; Molinari and Meo, *Mazara/Māzar*, pp. 348, 352–6, 382–3, 415–16, 422–5 (P. Orecchioni)); in the interior, they are visible in the main sites studied for the period, Castronovo, along with Palermo wares (see n. 183 above), Jato (Alfano and Sacco, 'Tra alto e basso medioevo', p. 14), Entella (Corretti et al., 'Frammenti di medioevo siciliano', p. 163), and Brucato (Maccari Poisson, 'La céramique médiévale', pp. 290–2).

imports from inside and outside the island which the inhabitants must have had exports to pay for with.[187]

It is hard to tell what had happened here to make such a sharp set of changes. That Messina should become prominent is not in itself surprising, given its wider commercial activity in the twelfth century and later (see p. 252 below), but the origins of this novel style of production cannot yet be seen. That tin glaze (*smalto* in Italian) should appear in the island is also not surprising, given its frequency in Egypt and North Africa, as also, as we shall see, Spain—although why it should come in precisely now, and not earlier, is not yet fully clear.[188] What happened in Palermo is the hardest change to explain. It may, indeed, be the case, here at least, that Muslims had dominated pottery production in the capital, as is widely stated, and that enough of them had abruptly left to undermine the handing down of artisanal skills in this sector; but its productions nonetheless continued on a smaller scale. All the same, however these shifts are explained, one thing had not changed: the internal commercial networks which had brought Palermo amphorae and glaze to the whole island, and now brought Messina *pentole* to the whole island as well. At most, as just noted, there was a slowly growing trend for the network in the east to be more distinct from that of the west. We must conclude that the internal routes had persisted (even if the roads will by now have passed through hilltop sites more than flatland sites), but also that overall buying power, rural and urban, had not decreased. As I argued before, cultural shifts such as Latinization and Christianization are irrelevant to a consideration of how exchange worked; what matters is demand, and the effect this had on production, specialization, and distribution. Both production and distribution evidently continued; the only shift, yet to be analysed properly, might have been a greater restriction of this demand in some places, where local hierarchies had developed rather more, to aristocratic and village-level elites—as perhaps in the case of Gela ware. And this set of networks can be tracked in the later middle ages too, this time in the written record. We will come back to that later (pp. 260–2).

[187] The basic publication of Gela ware is Fiorilla, *Gela*, with an analysis at pp. 38–99, and a distribution map up to 1996 at 310–11. All the sites or surveys mentioned in n. 186 above except Jato showed Gela ware, although in differing percentages; see Fiorilla's map and the above-mentioned publications. Lucia Arcifa further points out to me that Gela ware has a socially skewed distribution; it is found more in urban than rural centres. For *protomaiolica*, see in general Patitucci Uggeri, 'Protomaiolica: un bilancio'; see further pp. 556, 569 below. For Mazara, see Molinari and Meo, *Mazara/Māzar*, esp. pp. 378, 390–2, 423–5, 604–8, 621 (P. Orecchioni, V. Aniceti et al., A. Molinari).

[188] D'Angelo, 'La protomaiolica di Sicilia' argues that Gela ware was influenced by Ligurian *protomaiolica*, but it is far from certain that the latter actually predated the former; see, e.g., Lunardon, 'Protomaioliche savonesi'. Note that there was some tin in Islamic-period Palermo glazed pottery (Claudio Capelli, pers. comm.; Molinari and Meo, *Mazara/Māzar*, p. 448 (C. Capelli et al.)); it was a small-scale production there, but it shows the availability of the metal; tin exports from Sicily are also cited in a few *geniza* letters, such as T-S 20.76, 12.389 (Gil K575, 317 [S83, 94]). For tin glaze in North Africa, which started in the eleventh century, see Salinas et al., 'Polychrome glazed ware production in Tunisia'.

Palermo products were also exported. We have already seen that wine amphorae were sent to Ifrīqiya, where they are prominent in the finds from Ṣabra al-Manṣūriya; they can be found more generally in Tunisia too, both on the coast (at Sousse and Carthage) and some way inland, at Ksar Lemsa.[189] But the real novelty was that both amphorae and glaze were also exported northwards, from 950 onwards. They are found all the way up the Italian west coast, with particular concentrations around Salerno and Naples, and along the coast from Pisa (the main northern Italian importer of Sicilian ceramics) to the Ligurian cities; the finds of amphorae extend farther still, into Provence and across to northern Sardinia, and also up the Adriatic to Ravenna and Comacchio. This is also the first moment in which outside observers begin to complain about Muslim merchants making Pisa too cosmopolitan; if this has any basis in fact, many of them must have come from Sicily. We do not know what else ships from Palermo carried in this period, or what the amphorae held apart from wine; but even without that knowledge we can say that this wine export (the amphorae being here rather more important than the fine wares) is, in absolute, the first known large-scale trade between the Muslim and the Christian worlds. That is a point we will come back to in Chapter 7.[190] It certainly did not match in scale Sicilian trade with Ifrīqiya, which was so close and capillary at all times, as we have seen and will see; the only Sicilian product the North Africans did not buy was glazed pottery, which they made so much of themselves. The Egypt trade in flax in return for linen, silk, and hides, at least before 1100, will have been much more substantial as well. But all of this marks the fact that Sicily had put itself back into its long-standing role as a hub for Mediterranean trade in all directions, after a break of nearly three centuries; it would not relinquish this role thereafter either. In the twelfth century, its glaze exports northwards dropped off substantially, and to a lesser extent those carried in amphorae decreased too,[191] but by now we have documents to show that it exported other goods to (most visibly) Genoa, as we shall see in the next section.

[189] Gragueb et al., 'Jarres et amphores', pp. 205–18; Gragueb Chatti, 'La céramique islamique de la citadelle byzantine de Ksar Lemsa', p. 275; plus the map in Sacco, 'Produzione e circolazione', fig. 9.

[190] For the distribution of pottery, see the map cited in n. 189 above. For Pisa, see Chapter 6, n. 226. My flat statement that this trade was the first large-scale north–south trade since the seventh century sets aside the long-standing intermediary role of the Amalfitans on almost every coast, and also the early Venetian links with Egypt; but these were, precisely, not large-scale. See pp. 506–8, 640–3 below.

[191] For the fall-off after *c.*1125 in glazed bowls from Sicily used as *bacini* to decorate churches in Pisa, see most recently Berti and Giorgio, *Ceramiche con coperture vetrificate*, pp. 32–4, 54–7, although there are some green-glazed Sicilian *bacini* from the end of the twelfth century. Amphorae were less exported after 1100; see Sacco, 'Produzione e circolazione', p. 188; but they have been found in some secure twelfth-century levels in Pisa and other Tyrrhenian sites; see Meo, 'Anfore, uomini e reti di scambio', pp. 229–32. Wine was, however, still being exported on a substantial scale from Palermo in 1177, at least to somewhere, in barrels (*barrilia*); see Enzensberger, *Willelmi II regis Siciliae diplomata*, n. 95, in which a Palermo monastery is granted twenty barrels a month from the port dues (*dohana*) in the capital.

Conversely, there is little archaeological evidence of imports for a long time. This is not true for Ifrīqiya: there was a regular availability of Tunisian glaze in very many Sicilian sites, across the whole island, for example Villa del Casale in the centre; traders were obviously using both the well-defined sea routes and the internal networks we have already looked at. This continued and grew into the thirteenth century, by which time cobalt and manganese glazes from Tunis arrived inland to Entella and Jato before their abandonment—that is, in the middle of (mostly low-level) warfare—and the Castronovo sites, plus, on or near the coast, Messina, Mazara, Marsala, Segesta, and Palermo, among others.[192] We might use this glazed pottery as a proxy for the distribution of olive oil too, which we know the Sicilians imported from the Tunisian coastal olive forests, given that this went by now in skins, far more than in amphorae (see p. 139 above), so we cannot track it. But in the tenth to twelfth centuries there are only scattered attestations of imports from anywhere else. Just a handful of Egyptian 'Fayyumi ware' and lustre sherds have been seen in Palermo, plus two Chinese sherds which will have come via Egypt, although, interestingly, there are some Egyptian ceramics at the rural centres of Calathamet and Jato too.[193] In the capital a handful of Byzantine amphorae have also been found, as we have seen, and a few Spanish sherds; there were hardly more on the east coast, even if its links to Byzantium continued; and even fewer elsewhere in the island. In particular, whatever was coming back from the exports to mainland Italy is not visible in the archaeology. Imports only begin to be prominent in the thirteenth century in western Sicily, by which time a majority of the fine-ware needs of Mazara, Marsala, Segesta, and, to an extent, even Palermo were supplied from abroad—not just Tunisian glazes (by now the cobalt and manganese associated with Tunis itself), but also Spiral ware from Campania, which is indeed found in numerous locations on the island, including again the interior, as well as smaller-scale imports from Spain and elsewhere in mainland Italy.[194] In the east, Messina, although it may well have made its own

[192] For Villa del Casale, see Alfano et al., 'Produzione e circolazione', p. 221. Imports of glaze in Islamic Palermo, which made up between 2 and 18% of the total glaze depending on the site and period, were mostly North African; see Sacco, 'Le ceramiche invetriate', pp. 341, 357. For after 1200, see Molinari and Cassai, 'La Sicilia e il Mediterraneo nel XIII secolo', pp. 97–8; for Messina, see D'Amico, 'Circolazione di ceramiche a Messina', p. 31; for Mazara, see Molinari and Meo, *Mazara/Māzar*, pp. 402–9, 420–3 (P. Orecchioni); for Castronovo, see n. 183 above.

[193] Sacco, 'Le ceramiche invetriate', pp. 357–8; Sacco, 'Ceramica con decorazione a *splash*' (which shows that in Palermo splashed/'Fayyumi' ware was soon copied in the late tenth century); Lesnes and Poisson, *Calathamet*, p. 224 (E. Lesnes), with some Spanish *cuerda seca* glaze—for which see also n. 182 above, for Mazara; for Jato, see n. 194 below.

[194] See esp. the 2006 survey in Molinari and Cassai, 'La Sicilia e il Mediterraneo nel XIII secolo', and the 2021 survey for Mazara in Molinari and Meo, *Mazara/Māzar*, pp. 396–425 (P. Orecchioni). Still useful is Fiorilla, 'Considerazioni sulle ceramiche medievali', from 1991 (p. 134 for Spiral ware). Every site mentioned in n. 186 above had Spiral ware. Byzantine glazed pottery is not so common in Sicily (Randazzo, 'The evidence of Byzantine *sgraffito wares*', updated in Randazzo, 'Middle Byzantine glazed wares'), but examples are more frequent by the end of the century, as excavations at Messina show (ibid., p. 692; D'Amico, 'Circolazione di ceramiche a Messina', p. 31; Scibona, 'Messina XI–XII secc.'), and Zeuxippus ware was found, perhaps surprisingly, in the very latest levels of Villa del Casale,

glazed tablewares, and certainly exported its *pentole*, by now imported substantially too, from a different balance of regions: *protomaiolica* not just from Gela but also from Brindisi, the other major early southern production centre (this, indeed, reached Castronovo in the centre of the island too), Ligurian, African, and Byzantine glazes, and some east Mediterranean wares.[195] So this is by now a period in which, while archaeologically attested Sicilian products were less available outside the island, external products visibly came in, and spread internally through the land routes; here, we cannot tell from the archaeology what Sicily exported in return—the reverse of the eleventh-century situation. We shall see later what written evidence can tell us, however.

Archaeologists sometimes see evidence of exports as a marker of strength, and evidence of imports as one of weakness. This is not the case; commercial exports must always have been balanced by archaeologically undocumented imports and vice versa in eras like this, when unbalanced trade was effectively an economic impossibility. (Indeed, Pisa's archaeology shows a similar dominance of imports among its fine wares up to the early thirteenth century, without archaeologists concluding that Pisa's economic dynamism was limited; see pp. 569–72 below.) What both imports and exports show is the existence of interregional networks, and when the visible goods exchanged were bulk goods, as in these cases, the existence of networks of bulk exchange. That is significant in itself. But it also must be remembered that interregional trade was, nearly everywhere, far less important than commercial (and also non-commercial) exchange *inside* regions. It is the organization of that internal exchange which will, in most cases, underpin both the creation of something to export, and the buying power for imports. This is a point which has been made before in this book, and it will be repeated later as well, for it is a key to understanding medieval economies. And we have now seen from the archaeology that in Sicily, internal exchange was indeed highly elaborate, from well before our period to well after. The very great complexity of the Sicilian economy which the material record shows, from 950 at the latest and often before, continuing throughout the thirteenth century, and the buying power of what looks to have been a high proportion of the island's inhabitants, including peasants, extending far inland, are, indeed, the key points which I wish to make in this section. They make sense of the evidence of large-scale linen production which the *geniza* showed for the eleventh century, which itself cannot only (or perhaps mostly) have been for export; and it will also make sense of, and extend, what we can say of Norman-period patterns of demand and production on the basis of the documentary evidence, which we must turn to now.

around 1200, and also at Jato; see Pensabene, 'Villa del Casale', p. 18; Ritter-Lutz, *Monte Iato*, pp. 99–101 (which also documents Egyptian lustre).

[195] Bacci and Tigano, *Da Zancle a Messina*, pp. 112–13, 155–8 (articles by S. Fiorilla and L. Sannino); D'Amico, 'Circolazione di ceramiche a Messina'. For Castronovo, see n. 183 above.

3.6 Norman Sicily: Rural Society and the Web of Production

Norman-period documents for Sicily, beginning around 1090, are richer than anything else in the written record for our two central Mediterranean regions, apart, of course, from the *geniza*. They are not so rich that they can displace the picture of the Sicilian economy which can be derived from the archaeology, which we have just looked at, and, anyway, they do not significantly contradict that picture. But they do point up other aspects of Sicilian socio-economic development as well, and they point us in some extra directions which the archaeological record does not document. We will first look at the peasant majority of the island, and then at commerce, moving from the inside outwards: the exchange of the interior, then that around the coasts, and finally that outwards into the Mediterranean—the last being a network above all documented, and to an extent dominated, by the Genoese, the heirs of the Egyptian merchants and shipmen whom we have already looked at for the preceding period. So let us begin with the countryside, and what we can say about the agricultural economy. This necessarily brings us first to a subject much discussed recently: the fiscal registers of the Norman kings.

* * *

Sicily and Calabria share a type of source which is rare outside the region: lists of people, mostly but not always men, known as *jarāʾid* (sing. *jarīda*) in Arabic and *plateiai* in Greek.[196] Their linguistic form is complex: some are bilingual in Arabic and Greek; some later ones are also bilingual in Arabic and Latin; for some, we only have later Latin translations. They appear when kings gave areas of land to churches and monasteries, and also to lay aristocrats—these survive more rarely, but we do have some of them, including gifts to the (perhaps originally less-aristocratic) wet nurse of one of Roger II's children. In Sicily, surviving texts are particularly a feature of the 1090s, when Roger I was re-establishing an episcopal structure in Sicily and giving donations to cathedrals; the 1140s, when Roger II recalled and renewed all such cessions; and the years 1176–83, when William II founded the monastery-cum-cathedral of Monreale above Palermo and endowed it with an enormous area of land to its south, the last cession of this type in the Norman period; but there are others in between as well.[197] They sometimes go

[196] Johns, *Arabic administration*, *passim*; Nef, *Conquérir et gouverner*, pp. 481–583. Johns, *Arabic administration*, p. 43, draws parallels in the Crusader states with the *jarāʾid*; by contrast, Egypt and the central lands of Byzantium did not regularly have documents like these. Tax registers there had a far more complex articulation, reflecting the different sizes and types of landholding, and the different resources, of taxpayers; see, e.g., Svoronos, 'Recherches sur le cadastre byzantin'; P.Prag.Arab. 36–49; and the theoretical discussions in al-Makhzūmī, edited in Frantz-Murphy, *The agrarian administration*, pp. 20–42.

[197] Johns, *Arabic administration*, gives us the best chronological articulation. For Adelina the wet nurse, see ibid., pp. 101–2, 304, with the editions in Cusa, *I diplomi*, n. 50 (pp. 115–16); Garufi, *I documenti inediti*, nn. 12, 21.

together, in the same document or separately, with an inquest to establish the boundary of the lands given, the *ḥadd* in Arabic, the *periorismos* in Greek, the *divisio* or *divisa* in Latin (the words seem to refer both to the boundary itself and to the process of establishing it and writing it down), which could be very detailed, and which very often shows, through its use of geographical markers rather than references to named landholders on the boundary, that the land in question was substantial in size—often, indeed, such lands explicitly included whole settlements, some of which were themselves large.[198]

The great complexities of such texts are well discussed in two relatively recent books, by Jeremy Johns and Annliese Nef; here I have given only the briefest summary. But one simple thing is clear, above all from the Arabic-language *jarā'id*: in their original form they reflect fiscal registers. In two of the three earliest ones (gifts of Aci Castello and Catania itself to the bishop of Catania, both from 1095), and several later too, the listed people are divided into categories: widows, slaves, Jews, and blind people are separated off in the Catania *jarīda*; widows again in that of Aci. Some other texts also separate off newly married men. These are separations which fit most clearly into the context of Islamic rules for the poll tax, the *jizya*, imposed on non-Muslims in Islamic states. Indeed, the word *jizya* is itself occasionally used in later Sicilian texts, notably one of 1177/9 in which three men from Mezzoiuso near Palermo, who had fled the land, agree to return and to pay both the *jizya* and the *qānūn*, a word for land tax, to S. Giovanni degli Eremiti in Palermo, a monastery which had evidently benefited from a royal cession of tax rights. A converging set of sources, in fact, makes it clear that one of the major results of the conquest was that Muslims would henceforth have to pay the same tax that non-Muslims had paid to the state before 1061,[199] which means that *jarā'id* are, as a set, concessions to churches and aristocrats not of landed estates, but of fiscal rights over specified territories. And this, in turn, means that the lists of people are not lists of dependent tenants, but simply of heads of household, and that many of them could perfectly well be—and sometimes demonstrably were—landowners themselves. This also helps to explain why the land blocks which the boundaries include could be so large. We do not have here to worry about how to accommodate the standard patterns of medieval

[198] Johns, *Arabic administration*, esp. pp. 172–86. *Divisa* came to mean the territory inside the boundaries as well.

[199] See Johns, *Arabic administration*, pp. 31–9 for the *jizya* and its exaction from Muslims; see ibid., pp. 46–58 for the different categories of people. At pp. 57–8 he also stresses that the registers of Muslim taxpayers, which are very likely to be based on pre-conquest lists, cannot originally have been for the *jizya*, for Muslims did not pay it before the conquest. For me, this is also a sign that the main lines of Islamic-period taxation in Sicily must have been very simple by the standards of other Islamic states (cf. Nef, *Conquérir et gouverner*, p. 497, Nef, 'La fiscalité en Sicile', and n. 196 above). The best edition of and commentary on the Mezzoiuso text is Johns, 'The boys from Mezzoiuso'. Note that Jews paid a poll tax both before and after the Norman conquest; for 1187/8, see Wansborough, 'A Judaeo-Arabic document from Sicily' (here the tax is called *rūs*).

fragmented landowning; we are dealing, rather, with the taxpaying of whole communities. These communities could be big or small; fortified centres (*ḥuṣun*, *castra*) were listed beside open settlements (*raḥā'il*, *manāzil*, *casalia*, *chōria*), some of them with only a few families, across the island.[200]

This much is not a problem, then; but other problems remain. One is the exact status of such taxpayers; a second is the issue of the Greek-speaking Christian community, by now presumably freed from paying the *jizya*; a third is what and how much tax or rent actually was paid. We need to look at these before we can assess how local communities actually functioned economically, above all insofar as this related to exchange.

One of the problems of the historiography has been in dealing with the terminology used for these taxpayers. In Arabic, they are the *ahl* or *rijāl al-jarā'id*, the 'people' or 'men of the registers'; but in Greek they are often *bellanoi*, from Latin *villani*, a word itself also used as more Latin appears in the texts. This was thought by earlier scholars to show that they were or had become unfree or semi-free dependent tenants, 'villeins' or 'serfs'; this seemed to be confirmed by the fact that they were, in general, tied to the land they lived on—for many *jarā'id* and indeed other texts refer to the obligations of concessionaries to give back people who belong on the registers of others, and the Mezzoiuso document, already referred to, points the same way.[201] Such *bellanoi*/*villani* were not, however, defined as tenants here; the tying to the land must simply reflect a coercive approach to the control of taxpaying, which was common enough in premodern tax systems—it was also used in the late Roman Empire and early Islamic Egypt. But the words 'villein' and even (less comprehensibly) 'serf' do still get used by historians, apparently on the grounds that they are simply representations of the word *villanus*; I will not follow them, for *villanus* has too many different meanings in medieval sources, and most of them convey no sense of unfreedom or semi-freedom at all, unlike 'villein' in English technical terminology.[202] A second problem comes from

[200] See esp. the analysis and survey in Nef, *Conquérir et gouverner*, pp. 392–428; I am more inclined than she is to see *raḥal* and *casale* as synonyms under most (even though not all) circumstances. Exactly how the *raḥā'il* or *casalia* in these texts match up with the often very large villages plus smaller and dispersed settlements of the archaeology (see p. 213–15 above) remains an open question; more excavation and fieldwork are needed before we get it clear. But the first steps are being made in the best area for such comparisons, the great Monreale concession; see Alfano and Sacco, 'Tra alto e basso medioevo'; Corretti et al., 'Frammenti di medioevo siciliano'.

[201] The classic point of reference here, well grounded in the sources too, is Peri, *Villani e cavalieri*, pp. 5–121, esp. 5–68; the first effective criticism of it was Petralia, 'La "signoria"'. A court case of 1158 for Scicli in the far south-east concerns the registration of two Arabic-named *villani* in rival *plateae* (the Latinization of *plateiai*); see Ménager, *Les actes latins*, n. 7.

[202] Niermeyer, *Mediae Latinitatis lexicon minus*, pp. 1103–4, lists nine meanings, of which only one refers to unfreedom. This is not to deny that some *bellanoi* in the Greek east of the island were much more visibly personally dependent; see most recently Rognoni, 'Disposer des hommes dans la Sicile du XIIe siècle', pp. 148–9, with commentary at 133–40, where 'my household *bellanos*' in Milazzo is given by a layman to a monastery. This fits the plurality of forms of dependence, including some very personalized ones, discussed for the Mezzogiorno as a whole by Carocci, *Lordships*, pp. 325–38, but

the fact that some *jarā'id*, notably those for Monreale, distinguish between *rijāl al-jarā'id* and other Arab inhabitants, *muls* and *rijāl al-maḥallāt*; who are the last two groups? The *rijāl al-maḥallāt*, who are cited least often, may perhaps be tenants of the lands of others; the *muls*, whatever their tenurial status, seem to be incomers—they are often given *nisbas* in the lists which show that they come from elsewhere, in Sicily or, indeed, not seldom, North Africa. There has been debate about these points, which we do not need to rehearse here; but we can at least take away the conclusions that there may be some—even if vague, and inconsistent from text to text—references to tenants in the registers, and also that some taxpayers did, indeed, legally or illegally, move from place to place.[203]

Conversely, there are also signs of differences in status and resources between the taxpayers. Status first: we find *qā'ids* (pl. *quwwād*) and *shaykhs* (pl. *shuyūkh*) in the texts, quite regularly. *Shaykh* means 'elder', both literally, on grounds of age (the Greek word *gerōn*, 'old man', also appears), and figuratively, as a community leader. When land boundaries were established, local *shaykhs*, plus *boni homines* and *kaloi anthrōpoi*, 'good men', the long-used Latin term for local males of public standing and its exact Greek equivalent/translation, typically witnessed to what they should be; *shaykhs* were evidently the same sort of people as *boni homines*, or, when they were actually all Arabic-speaking, exactly the same people.[204] *Qā'ids* could also be *boni homines*, but the word means a member of a more clearly defined elite. Elsewhere in the Islamic world, *qā'id* meant 'military leader' or even 'governor'; but in Sicily its use was far wider. It is a title used for senior administrators in Palermo, but it is also a status marker for other members of the Palermitan elite, and, in villages, one or two men are regularly given the same title as well, so it must apply to the most status-filled individuals in each community, no matter what its size—a handful of them even had Greek names and may have been Christians. It is, actually, quite curious that Sicilian Arabic made do with just one word for people of such widely different political and social positions, but it certainly did, and indeed the word is simply Latinized and Graecized, as *gaitus* (Latin) and similar, in other sources.[205]

As to resources, rural *qā'ids* could be landowners. The bishop of Agrigento, for example, bought land from several *gaiti* in the later twelfth century, and *qā'ids* and other Muslims sell land on the plateau south of the capital in other twelfth-century

not the *jarā'id*. For a quick survey of the situation in the Roman Empire and Islamic Egypt, see Wickham, *Framing*, pp. 136–7, 142–3, 520–6.

[203] For debate, see Johns, *Arabic administration*, pp. 145–51; Nef, *Conquérir et gouverner*, pp. 492–507; Metcalfe, *The Muslims*, pp. 268–72; De Simone, 'Ancora sui "villani" di Sicilia'; Takayama, 'Classification of villeins'.

[204] Some examples: von Falkenhausen et al., 'The twelfth-century documents of St. George's of Tròccoli', n. 5; Cusa, *I diplomi*, nn. 8, 63, 94 (pp. 302–6, 317–21, 367–8).

[205] *Qā'ids* are very common indeed in the Arabic sources, which are listed in Johns, *Arabic administration*, pp. 301–25; for full lists of citations in non-Arabic sources, see Nef, *Conquérir et gouverner*, pp. 465–9; see in general ibid., pp. 463–73.

documents, close to the areas later given to Monreale. Elsewhere, they appear in documents on land boundaries, and they turn up in some of the sale documents for land around Palermo, already cited (p. 210).[206] There are also signs in the Monreale documents that some *qā'id*s and other Muslims were, or had been, holders of tax concessions of whole small villages, of the kind that churches obtained in the documents which survive. And some Arabs could be larger-scale owners, like the Roger Aḥmad who gave estates to the archbishop of Palermo in 1141; he got them from Roger I, that is, before 1101, although he, at least, will not have been a *jizya*-payer, for his name and seal, plus the rhetoric of the donation, show conversion to Christianity.[207] All the same, taxpaying Arabs could evidently be smaller or larger landowners or holders of substantial fiscal cessions; they could also have a local status as elders and *qā'id*s; they could also be tenants of others, including other Arabs, although also of churches and monasteries. There could, therefore, be complicated hierarchies in the Muslim countryside, even if, as we have seen, many settlements did not have huge material differences in wealth between the top and the bottom (see p. 215 above). All this is relevant to the issue of buying power; we shall come back to the implications of it later.

The historiography, in recent years at least, has concentrated on the areas of Sicily where Muslim populations were dominant. There were Muslims in the east (for example in Aci and Catania in 1095), as there were Greeks in the west (for example, landowners near Agrigento in 1112 and 1155);[208] but Muslims and Arabic-speakers are most visible in the western half of the island, the Val di Mazara, the location of many of the major *jarā'id*, particularly those of Monreale, which overwhelmingly list Arab names. Less attention has been paid to the north-east, the Val Demone, where most of the population was Greek-speaking; but this sector of Sicily actually has the most documents. (The third historic *vallo* (administrative division) of the island, the Val di Noto in the south and south-east, has relatively few in this period.)[209] The documentation for the Val Demone includes

[206] For Agrigento, Collura, *Le più antiche carte*, nn. 17, 25 (note though that in the latter document the *gaitus* 'Abdisalemo' holds *ius sub dominio eius existens*, which in mainland Italy, at least, would imply that he did not hold it in full property (see Wickham, '*Iuris cui existens*'); this may be a tax concession); for the plateau, see Bresc, 'La propriété foncière', pp. 89–97, and the whole article for wider discussion. See also Cusa, *I diplomi*, n. 38 (pp. 471–2), in which an Arabic-named family is attested as having bought a mill outside Ciminna, south-east of Palermo, directly or indirectly from a Latin dependant of Roger I; the land sale was presented to a court in 1123 in the context of a dispute between family members.

[207] For tax concessions, see Nef, *Conquérir et gouverner*, pp. 416, 421, and n. 206 above; for Roger Aḥmad, see Cusa, *I diplomi*, n. 59 (pp. 16–19); for the seal, see Johns, *Arabic administration*, p. 238n.

[208] Becker, *Documenti latini e greci del conte Ruggero I*, n. 50; Cusa, *I diplomi*, n. 77 (pp. 563–85); Collura, *Le più antiche carte*, nn. 10, 16.

[209] For early references to the *valli*, see, e.g., Bresc, 'Limites internes de la Sicile médiévale', p. 323, with sensible comments in Nef, *Conquérir et gouverner*, p. 373n; they came into general use in the Norman period, but were not yet as crucial as points of reference as they would be later. That they are pre-Norman in origin is likely enough, as the three *valli* are all named after places which were more significant before 1100 than after. There is one pre-Norman reference to the Val Demone (named after Demenna) in the *geniza*, T-S Ar. 54.88 (Gil K325 [S73]); it is worth noting that in the unvocalized text

royal cessions with lists of Greek names, as well as others with Greek and Arab names both included; but we ought to be assuming that the Greeks here were no longer *jizya*-payers, since most of the people with Greek names will have been Christians. Are they paying some other kind of tax, which everyone paid, of whatever religion? If so, there is no sign of it. Conversely, the documentation also refers to cessions by rulers, or to sales between private parties, of *chōraphia*, a word which in mainland Italy and the Byzantine Empire just meant 'landed properties', often small ones, on which there are at least sometimes *paroikoi* (tenants), plus not a few *ampelōna* or *ampelia* (vineyards). That is to say, these documents seem to be focussed for the most part on landowning, not fiscal rights.[210]

These lands often enough explicitly came from the fisc. Roger I, in particular, set up a network of cathedrals and monasteries from scratch, and handed over lands to them, which seem to have included both regular estates and (as with Aci and Catania) tax rights.[211] In 1145, however, a monastery in the north-east, S. Angelo di Lisico (later di Brolo), asked Roger II to confirm an earlier confirmation of Roger I in 1084 of all the lands it had held under Arab rule. This survives only in a late Latin translation, so we cannot assess the authenticity of the monastery's claim; but similarly, in 1109, the monastery of S. Barbaro, near Demenna/San Marco, sought confirmation from Roger II, then a child, of land that it too had, it claimed, owned before the Norman conquest. In this case, authenticity is even harder to assess, for S. Barbaro had no documents for it (they had, the monastery asserted, been lost in the wars). But again, even if the claim was untrue, it is a significant one to make. Indeed, the idea that Greek monasteries in Sicily survived the Islamic period with their own lands is a far from implausible one (it was routine in Egypt)—the surprise about Sicily is, rather, that the diocesan network had failed, for it survived elsewhere under Islam without trouble, and Sicilian Christians had remained numerous in the east.[212] Anyway,

this is *Fā'l Dmnsh*, which excludes the common suggestion of Arabic *wilāya* (administrative territory) as an etymological origin for *vallo* (it is almost as if *Fā'l* is a loanword from Latin, although this would be hard to explain for the mid-eleventh century, the date of the text).

[210] Examples of ruling family cessions in the north-east: Becker, *Documenti latini e greci del conte Ruggero I*, nn. 16, 26, 45, 59, 66; Guillou, *Les actes grecs*, n. 3; Cusa, *I diplomi*, nn. 17, 28, 30, 79 (pp. 394–5, 407–8, 409–10, 472–80); Garufi, *I documenti inediti*, n. 15. Examples of lay sales: Cusa, *I diplomi*, nn. 88, 107, 127 (pp. 330–1, 347–8, 420–1); Guillou, *Les actes grecs*, n. 5; plus the gifts to churches of a single *chōraphion* of 1 *zeugarion* (measured as 16 *modia*) plus a *kampos* (field) of 7 *modia* in 1168, and in 1148 of all the possessions of a Greek family, *chōraphia* and *ampelia*, in Cusa, *I diplomi*, nn. 87, 108 (pp. 481–2, 484–6). This, however, needs more work. What one does, for example, with cessions of Greek-named and Arabic-named peasants in the same text, as with Cusa, *I diplomi*, n. 79, is in itself a problem. Is that a mixing together of fiscal and tenurial rights? Such a mixture has been analysed for Calabria (see n. 215 below), but less for the Val Demone.

[211] See in general Nef, *Conquérir et gouverner*, pp. 447–63; Loud, *The Latin church*, pp. 313–14, 324; the cessions are edited in Becker, *Documenti latini e greci del conte Ruggero I*.

[212] See Pirri, *Sicilia sacra*, 2, pp. 1225–6 (cf. Johns, *Arabic administration*, p. 42); Cusa, *I diplomi*, n. 24 (pp. 403–5). Probable pre-Norman lay landowning is also implied in Cusa, *I diplomi*, n. 8 (pp. 367–8). For the failure of the diocesan network under Islamic rule, see Prigent, 'L'évolution du réseau épiscopal sicilien', pp. 99–102. For Egyptian monasteries, see P.Fatimid 1; Abū Ṣāliḥ, *The churches &*

either through comital/royal gift or through earlier property rights, a network of large and small estates held in full property is visible in the Sicilian north-east from early in the twelfth century onwards, with, in some cases, quite fragmented landowning.[213] These existed alongside big blocks with boundary inquests which match those of the west, and, indeed, some villages in which there were local proprietors, but as in the west, rights of some kind could be given over their heads to churches.[214] Renders on documented estates could, as we shall see, include labour services, not just payments in money or kind; it would be hard to see agricultural labour dues as anything other than part of standard land rents. But comital/royal concessions of *plateiai* listing *bellanoi/villani* survive too; it is just that here they could well be tenants as often as autonomous taxpayers, and the latter might also, given the dominance of landed estates in the east, turn into the former. This is quite like the situation found in neighbouring Calabria, where local independent taxpayers were ceded to churches and monasteries by the Normans alongside tenants on fiscal or private land, with no real distinction; they all slowly became tenants as a result.[215]

It is well known that the Normans on the Italian mainland ceded tax rights to their aristocrats and to newly founded Latin churches, and that these were steadily privatized. This privatization could be tenurial or it could be signorial—for territorial *signorie*, private lordships with judicial and other quasi-fiscal rights, a common feature of the Latin world from the eleventh century, including the Norman-ruled mainland South, often contained within them land owned by others as well.[216] *Signorie* are not yet documented in Sicily in our period, so that aspect of mainland local power does not have to be dealt with here; all the same, the Calabrese parallel to the situation in the Val Demone certainly points up the ease by which what started out as cessions of tax-collecting rights could turn into rights of ownership quite quickly in a world in which the major recipients were all part of an incoming, conquering, ruling class. But this also gives a different perspective to the *jarā'id* in the Val di Mazara, where ecclesiastical and aristocratic landowning was much less extensive, and where kings and their fiscal rights over

monasteries of Egypt, trans. Evetts, pp. 1–2, 15, 183–4, 195, 197–8, 203, 206, 248, 250, 281; monastic lands were substantial and recognized by rulers, until confiscations by Saladin.

[213] Fragmented landowning: e.g. Pirri, *Sicilia sacra*, 2, pp. 1042–4; Garufi, *I documenti inediti*, n. 42; Guillou, 'Les archives de S. Maria di Bordonaro' (a text of 1189).

[214] The *kaloi anthrōpoi* of the *chōra* (village) of Alcara, inland from San Marco on the north-east coast, appear as at least recent proprietors in a court case of 1125; see Cusa, *I diplomi*, n. 39 (pp. 416–17); but according to a confirmation of Roger II in 1143, much or all of the village territory had already been given to the bishop of Messina by Roger I (Brühl, *Rogerii II. regis diplomata latina*, n. 57).

[215] Peters-Custot, '*Plateae* et *anthrôpoi*'; Peters-Custot, *Les Grecs*, p. 325 for a specific example from 1130. Cf. also Carocci, 'Le libertà dei servi', pp. 64–7.

[216] Martin, *La Pouille*, pp. 301–17 (306: 'le fondement de la seigneurie apulienne consiste en droits banaux plus qu'en redevances foncières'); for the slow development of signorial powers in Sicily, see Petralia, 'La "signoria"', esp. pp. 252–61; Mineo, *Nobiltà di stato*, pp. 2–29; and see in general the basic study in Carocci, *Lordships*. For *signorie* in north-central Italy, see, pp. 496–501 below.

Muslims dominated the extraction of surplus. Norman kings could think of a *jarīda* as a temporary cession of tax rights; they were clearly sure that such rights were not permanent, as the forced confirmations of the 1140s show, and they took cessions away from aristocrats on occasion too. But the same cession could well seem to a Latin lord or churchman to be a simple gift of land with tenants on it. This assumption, indeed, could well have been at the back of the use of the imported word *villanus*/*bellanos* in the first place. There is an interesting story in 'Falcandus' in which a Frenchman, who takes over the *terra* of one of the 1161 conspirators, demands half of the movables of its inhabitants, 'claiming it to be the custom of his own land'; the inhabitants, evidently Latin immigrants, retort that they do not have to pay any *redditus* or *exactiones*, and that only Arab and Greek *villani* owe annual rents (*redditibus annuisque pensionibus*).[217] The assumed equivalence, as rent payers, of all indigenous peasants is striking here, given what has just been argued; but equally striking is the assumption by a recently arrived aristocrat that his French customs might allow him to make new claims over surplus. So, in particular, the vast lands given by William II to Monreale around 1180—which were, beyond doubt, given the content of the very detailed texts which describe the gift, cessions of tax rights over large sets of autonomous Arabic-speaking local societies—may very well have seemed to Monreale to be, de facto at the very least, something significantly different: the gift of a huge tract of land with its tenants, whether rich or poor. It cannot be chance that it was exactly this land which was the epicentre of the great Muslim revolts, starting only a decade later, in 1190, and reaching their height between the 1200s and 1220s.[218]

These arguments have not, I think, been made as explicitly before, although, conversely, they only differ in nuance from those made by recent writers on the topic. The major nuance concerns the lack of fit between what aristocrats and churches may have sometimes thought their rights were and those which were assumed by the people on the ground (and also by the kings and their administrators). The more ignorant of the Latin aristocracy might even have thought that *villani* actually were 'serfs', although that view of the peasantry did not win out in Sicily; but the view that they were at least tenants, conversely, eventually did. But I would like also to invert the issue. For our purposes here, it does not matter so very greatly whether we are dealing here with concessions of taxpaying or rent-paying, or how far one slid into the other. In order for us to understand the prosperity of the inhabitants of the countryside, what matters most is how much they actually had to pay.

[217] Ugo Falcando, *Liber de regno*, ed. Siragusa, ch. 55 (pp. 144–5); cf. Petralia, 'La "signoria"', pp. 259–61. For a concession to an aristocrat taken away (it is here a *feudum*, conditional almost by definition, but it is of tax rights), see Falletta, *Liber privilegiorum*, n. I.22.

[218] For Monreale, the basic documents are edited in Falletta, *Liber privilegiorum*, nn. I.1, 4, III. 6, 8, for texts in Latin; Cusa, *I diplomi*, nn. 132, 137, 143 (pp. 134–79, 179–244, 245–86), for the *jarāʾid*. For the history of the revolts, see Metcalfe, *The Muslims*, pp. 275–87; Nef, 'La déportation'.

In the *jarā'id*, there is only one reference to what people paid: in 1095, in Corleone and neighbouring settlements, on the plateau some 30 kilometres south of Palermo. Here, seventy-five Arabic-named household heads, assessed collectively, paid annually—henceforth to the cathedral of Palermo—1,500 *tarì* (quarter-dinars) and 150 *modia* of each of wheat and barley. This comes out at 20 *tarì* and 4 *modia* of grain per household; the neatness of the division makes it indeed likely to be a genuine poll tax, paid equally, and collectively, by all.[219] The fact that no other fiscal document refers to any sum paid makes it probable that the tax was regarded as standard and well known, as well as the same for everybody; there was, therefore, no need to assess land values, for example, as was normal in Egypt and Byzantium, and this also explains the fact that what the documents usually give us is simple lists of taxpayers. The tax owed was, nonetheless, not a tiny sum. Even if we set aside the grain, just over 4 dinars (around 17 *tarì*, less than the 1095 figure) was the highest of the three bands of *jizya* payable in Egypt by Jews in the eleventh and twelfth century, and we know from the *geniza* that even the lower bands (just over 1 and 2 dinars respectively) were there regarded as oppressive by the poor majority.[220] Related figures recur in the 1177/9 Mezzoiuso document (which makes clear that the grain was seen as a land tax, not technically as *jizya*, although this too is never attested except as a tax paid by Muslims, and, at Corleone at least, it too was probably paid equally). Here the figure for money is only 10 *tarì* per head, plus 10 *mudd*s of grain, although, if the three brothers who accepted this figure were still a single household, we might have interpreted this as 30 *tarì* for the household, which would then be rather higher a figure than in Corleone a century earlier.[221] There are too many random uncertainties in these two texts for us to be able to be more precise, and two texts

[219] Cusa, *I diplomi*, n. 6 (pp. 1–3); the word *modion* is used rather than the Arabic *mudd* because the first section of the text is in Greek. See Johns, *Arabic administration*, pp. 46–51, 146; Nef, *Conquérir et gouverner*, pp. 493–6. How much a *modion*/*mudd* was as a measurement of volume is always a delicate matter to establish, for it was so variable, but in a document of 1149 (ed. Johns and Metcalfe, 'The mystery at Chùrchuro', pp. 242–7, line 4; cf. 248–52, line 3), four landless peasants are assigned to land sown with 120 *mudd*s of grain, which makes 30 per peasant; following that figure, the 4 *modia* of 1095 would be some 13% of the grain needed to sow a peasant holding, which would not be a high obligation if yields were at 10:1 (see n. 225 below). (The figures for the land sown by *mudd*s given ibid., p. 230, therefore, seem to me too high; cf. Wickham, *Medieval Rome*, p. 151n., for some of the huge variation, over two orders of magnitude, in the *modius* (the Latin form of *modion*/*mudd*) in Europe between the classical period and the fourteenth century.) I refer to the Sicilian *ṭarī* or *rubāʿī* quarter-dinar coin by the later Italian form of the word, *tarì*.

[220] Goitein, *MS*, 2, p. 387; cf. ibid., pp. 380–94 for its overall oppressiveness; we have complaints about the weight of Sicilian *jizya* too (for the references, see Johns, *Arabic Administration*, pp. 35–6), although these seem to me rather more rhetorical. Note that the Norman *tarì* had only a 69% gold content, only just over two-thirds that of the Egyptian, so technically around six, not four, of them could be seen as equivalent to an Egyptian dinar; see Travaini, *La monetazione*, pp. 101–4, 144–5. If we were to assume smooth currency transactions (a big if, but between Ifrīqiya and Egypt the *geniza* merchants did them), 5 Sicilian dinars (=20 *tarì*) would have been worth only 3.5 in Egypt; but the overall comparison made here would still be valid.

[221] See in general Johns, 'The boys from Mezzoiuso'. He sees the three brothers as substantial landowners, which is likely.

are also not enough to generalize much from, but we can at least take it that the tax paid by Muslims was by no means a nominal one; we will come back to how heavy it really was in a moment.

Contrast this with the almost equally rare figures for eastern Sicily, where we are apparently dealing, rather, with rents. Cefalù first, some 60 kilometres east of Palermo on the north coast, seems to have had a social structure more similar to the Greek lands farther east, although the peasants here almost all have Arabic names. A list, now in Latin, of 83 *villani exteri* with mostly Arabic names (they are possibly the equivalent of *muls* in Arabic *jarā'id*, although they are not obviously recent incomers) probably dates to late in Roger II's reign; they all owed dues in money, almost all either 6 or 8 *tarì*, although there is a variance between 4 and 16 (a *rā'is* or local leader paid 12), and the first name on the list, evidently another leader, ʿAbd al-Raḥmān al-Ḥanash, owed 40 *tarì*.[222] This list has been discussed because it also requires labour service, corvée, unlike any other document for Arabic-named payers, of twenty-four days (*dietas*) a year—what sort of labour is not specified, but the figure is not high. This implies that the dues are rents, not tax, as also does the variability in the money. Many of these men were artisans, a point we will come back to. Less stressed in the historiography is that the numbers of *tarì* here are actually in almost every case rather low too, and far lower than in the 1095 Corleone text—even if *jizya* was perhaps demanded on top of the rents, given the parallelisms in names with the 1145 *jarīda* for Cefalù.

Labour service could be rather higher than this in the Greek lands. A text in Greek from 1117, certainly for agricultural corvée labour, from the monastery of S.Bartolomeo in Patti (part of the mother monastery on the island of Lipari), concedes to the Greek community (*laos*) of Librizzi, just inland from Patti, the henceforth lighter *enkaria* (from Latin *angaria*, corvées) of as much as one week in four, plus another forty-four days, mostly for sowing. That was, nonetheless, matched by lower levels of rent; an undated Latin list from the second quarter of the twelfth century, surviving in the Patti cartularies, gives the money rent for the seventy *villani* of Librizzi as 256 *tarì*, averaging at 3.7 each, slightly less than at Cefalù; similarly low rents in money and grain are due from three other villages in the same text; and here they certainly will not have had any *jizya* added on top.[223] The rent is also low for Calabrese settlers near Paternò in 1196,

[222] Mirto, *Rollus Rubeus*, pp. 39–41, re-edited by Metcalfe, 'Historiography in the making', pp. 50–6, who dates the list to not long after 1145, given the presence of several of the *villani*, including ʿAbd al-Raḥmān, or their sons, in the Cefalù *jarīda* of that year (Cusa, *I diplomi*, n. 79, pp. 472–80); see also n. 250 below. I do not follow Metcalfe in his assumption that these dues are tax, given the differences from explicit *jizya* documents and the greater similarity to Greek texts from eastern Sicily—and the tax would be low if so—but my main arguments do not depend on that. Nef, *Conquérir et gouverner*, p. 500n, dates the text to the thirteenth century, not convincingly, given Metcalfe's arguments.

[223] Cusa, *I diplomi*, n. 35 (pp. 512–13), set against Garufi, 'Censimento e Catasto', n. 3, pp. 92–6, re-edited by Catalioto, *Il vescovato di Lipari-Patti*, appendix A, n. 52 (here, the names of the *villani* are all Greek; the text says fifty-nine *villani*, but there are seventy names). Nef, *Conquérir et gouverner*,

10 kilometres inland from Catania: a mere tenth of grain and oil, plus half the wine and other tree crops, although here corvées were again high, at a day a week, plus extra at high seasons. Conversely, ten peasants (*bellanoi*) with Greek names given to the cathedral of Troina *c.*1157 owe 20 *tarì* each and 4½ *modia* of grain, but no *anchōra* (labour); we are here back to the levels and patterns of the Corleone *jizya* of 1095.[224]

This is unsatisfactory evidence; the fact is that in eastern Sicily there are not enough documents (even if we set aside their bitty and generally poor-quality editing) really to establish trends. But these patterns, taken broadly, fit Sandro Carocci's calculations for the total range of dues owed respectively to the bishop of Patti and the fisc in 1249 from two villages, Santa Lucia and Sinagra, one 30 kilometres east of Patti, one 10 kilometres to the south-west. These are documented in an amazingly detailed and exact survey, made when the bishop and Frederick II exchanged the villages. Rents in wheat and wine in each village seem to have been set at 10 per cent of crop, equivalent to the lowest figure we have so far seen. Peasants in both also owed labour service, at different levels depending on their category (here, interestingly, the *villani* were the most prosperous stratum, followed by *burgenses* and then *angararii*); but the levels of corvée were low by now, at around a week a year in Sinagra, and less in Santa Lucia. As a result, the demesnes in each village (whose revenues are calculated in the text—as also is, as far as I know uniquely, even the financial value of a day's corvée labour) were fairly small too: in Santa Lucia, they produced under 20 per cent of total revenues. By now, each lord had rights of local justice, which we can call signorial in the case of the bishop's village, but these rights also brought less than 10 per cent of revenues. All in all, adding in several other sorts of dues, and using the figure of 10 to 1 for grain yields, which is also clearly documented elsewhere in late medieval Sicily (some figures are even higher), Carocci calculated that barely more than a sixth, 17.5 per cent, of total peasant production was taken by the two lords. This represented an average of 13–14 *tarì* required from each household in Santa Lucia, and just over 9 *tarì* from each in Sinagra, according to the precise money valuations of dues in kind and labour made by the surveyors in 1249.[225]

pp. 510–11, argues plausibly that the corvées were new; hence the resistance to them; she is less convinced about the early date of the second text, and also proposes that the corvées could simply have been bought out at a later date—which, however, seems to me unlikely, given the low money rents in the second text.

224 Garufi, 'Un contratto agrario'; Cusa, *I diplomi*, n. 98 (pp. 315–16). A parallel to the tenth at Mesepe near Paternò in 1196 is the tenth owed in 1095 to S. Bartolomeo by peasants who are prepared to stay on lands in Lipari; see Garufi, '"Memoratoria"', p. 119; both are in partial land clearance contexts.

225 Carocci, *Lordships*, pp. 413–21; p. 419n for yields of 10:1 (which is a secure figure for Santa Lucia); Johns, 'The boys from Mezzoiuso', p. 246, has the same figure for wheat. For wheat yields of around 10:1 in (in particular) the 1370s, with some lows and also some remarkable highs, see further Bresc, *Un monde méditerranéen*, pp. 120–5. Compare 12:1 for Egypt, as at p. 66 above; and the references in n. 226 below.

This is only one text, but it is a crucial one, as for once it gives us comprehensive data. It not only shows us that in the mid-thirteenth century peasants were at least in this area really not paying all that much to lords by medieval European or Mediterranean standards, but it also gives us a context for our twelfth-century texts. Even with much heavier levels of labour service, peasants in eastern Sicily under the Normans were probably not paying significantly higher percentages of total revenue than this. And now we can see that the *jizya* paid in western Sicily too, although high by the standards of Islamic poll taxes, and a more burdensome levy than the rents paid by most Christians in the east, all the same could be handled without so much difficulty as well. The 1095 Corleone figure, 20 *tarì* plus some grain, would be less than double the Santa Lucia figures; we do not reach a third of the grain crop, on an island where yields were very high by medieval standards, and the figure could well be less, particularly when non-agricultural activities are added in as well. A third of the grain crop was a common rent in northern Italy, where yields were far lower; and combined tax and rent, when peasants paid both, were also rather higher in Egypt, where yields paralleled those of Sicily.[226] Only those Muslim peasants in the west who were also paying rent, who seem to have been in a minority, at least on the lands the king had kept control of, would be handing over more than that to others. Muslim taxpayers were, on the face of it, more heavily burdened than Greek (and, later, Latin) Christian rent payers on the island. All the same, I conclude that, whether taxpayers or rent payers, only the poorest peasants in twelfth-century Sicily did not have access to disposable surplus, which could sometimes, probably, be substantial. The enormous wealth of the Norman kings, and also of their senior churchmen and aristocrats, was due to the very large scale of the lands they controlled, not to the extreme nature of their surplus extraction.[227] And as we saw in the last section, and as is now backed up by the documents, it is very likely that peasant demand played a considerable role in the overall commercial network of the island. There is more rural hierarchy visible in the documents than there was in the archaeology, given the prominence of *qā'id*s and others, but all the same not so much. As Amari thought, although for different reasons, large estates and very subject peasants, and thus a dominance of aristocratic demand, hardly seem to have been a feature of Sicily in our period.

In the previous section, we saw that the archaeological record showed that there was considerable internal exchange inside Sicily, and that the links between the interior and Palermo were dense and long-standing. What has been argued here

[226] For north Italian yields of 3–5:1, see Chapter 6, nn. 45–6 below; for rents, see Chapter 6, n. 59 below. For Egypt, see p. 67 above.

[227] Cf. Carocci, *Lordships*, for the whole of the Italian South; in Norman Sicily, perhaps outside parts of the north-east, lordship was also not very pervasive, a key indicator for Carocci (ibid., pp. 24–5, 483–6).

about the ability of Sicily's peasant strata to hang onto substantial proportions of their surplus fits very well with that archaeological picture. From what we have just seen, we would expect that peasants and other inhabitants of the central Sicilian plateau, and of the interior in general, would have the resources to buy goods from the coast, above all but not only Palermo; and the archaeology demonstrates that indeed they did. The networks which resulted were strong and complex. They had developed substantially in the Islamic period, for, as we have seen, at least in western Sicily the material evidence for exchange under the Byzantines is much weaker. This, then, also fits with the end of the great estates in the west and centre of the island of the Roman and Byzantine periods: peasants by the early tenth century, no longer paying rent, were newly able to buy goods, using the exchange routes which had always existed to take rents and taxes down to the coast. The roots of Molinari's 'crescita formidabile' (cf. p. 224 above) in the tenth century lay here, and the evidence for rents just laid out shows that the situation had not greatly changed in the twelfth. But for what else Sicilians did with their resources in the Norman century, we have to look more specifically at our written evidence for artisanal production and artisanal/agricultural exchange on the island—which is far from generous, but which complements what we can say from the archaeology in some significant ways. As noted earlier, we will look first at internal production and exchange, then coastal traffic and the ports, and come to international exchange at the end.

* * *

Our main set of documentary evidence in order to understand Sicilian artisanal production under the Normans is once again the *jarā'id* and *plateiai*. What these texts show, beyond what has already been discussed, is a dense network of rural craftsmen. The first big set is actually urban, the list of men and widows of Catania given to the bishop there in 1095 (we know it from its renewal in 1145); there were nearly 700 of them, and the proportion of names of trades was not huge, but fourteen were silk workers (*ḥarīrī*—I here use singulars throughout), five cotton workers (*qaṭṭān*), four tailors (*khayyāt*), and thirteen smiths (*ḥaddād*), and there followed workers in construction, tar, stonework, sugar, and ceramics; a *ṣāḥib al-sūq* is also listed, a market supervisor.[228] This sounds right for a city; and we shall see active textile workers in 1145–57 in another town as well, Cefalù, later. But on the other hand, in the Troccoli *jarīda* from 1141, for a very rural area on the edge of the plateau above the south coast near modern Caltabellotta, we also find a sawyer, a druggist (*'aqqār*), two silk workers, and a hatmaker (*qalānisī*). Furthermore, four silk workers and two builders (*bannā*) plus a merchant (*tājir*) are attested at Aci near Catania in 1095, a weaver near Piazza in the centre in (supposedly) 1122, one or more tailors near Patti in 1132, a dyer at Collesano near Cefalù on the

[228] Cusa, *I diplomi*, n. 77 (pp. 563–85); see n. 231 below for modern analyses.

north coast in 1181—that is to say, the balance is here very similar to that of Catania, and these are all rural locations.[229]

This is above all the case for the Monreale *jarā'id* of 1178 and 1183, bilingual in Arabic and Greek, which cover the areas of Jato, Corleone, and Calatrasi on the plateau south of Palermo (see Map 10). In these two very long texts, listing nearly two thousand people, we find thirty-seven silk workers, fourteen cotton workers, seventeen tailors, and, staying with textiles, a dyer, an embroiderer (*ṭarrāz*, i.e. a maker of *ṭirāz*) and a wool carder (*naffāsh*); then, in non-textile trades, thirteen smiths, nine carpenters/sawyers (*najjār*/*nashshār*), seven mat weavers (*ḥaṣṣār*), six potters of different types (most often *qalālā*), five leatherworkers, a glazier, two merchants, and others again, including even a caulker (*qalfāt*), even though we are here by no means on the sea. To these we can add not only a number of common agricultural specializations, such as shepherds and garden/orchard workers (*jannān*), but also specialist shopkeepers such as four bakers (*farrān*) and three butchers (*jazzāz*) and at least one druggist, which are not automatic specializations in villages, however large, as we saw earlier (p. 61); and another market supervisor, this time a *mutaqabbil al-sūq*.[230] Nearly a tenth of the total are explicitly non-agricultural workers. These are minima too, in the sense that not by any means every artisan will necessarily have been identified as such—indeed, many trades are only located through the names of fathers, in the format 'ibn al-ḥaddād' and the like, which fits common Arabic naming rhythms, but adds to the level of chance as to whether the trade is mentioned or not.

These lists of trades have been looked at and set out by several scholars, but have not been studied systematically for their wider economic implications; only Nef has remarked that the Monreale textile workers fit into the commercial network linking Palermo to the countryside—which is certainly the case, for the capital is only 35 kilometres from Corleone as the crow flies and half that from Jato, even if over mountains.[231] But there is more here for our purposes, especially

[229] For Troccoli, see von Falkenhausen et al., 'The twelfth-century documents of St. George's of Tròccoli', n. 4, pp. 49–61; the notes to this text are especially valuable, but all the same, *pace* ibid., p. 55n, I continue to translate *ḥarīrī* as 'silk worker', its normal meaning, not as a more generic 'weaver', as it is listed together with cotton workers too often. For the others, see, respectively, Becker, *Documenti latini e greci del conte Ruggero I*, n. 50; Garufi, 'Le donazioni', pp. 223–4, 227–8 (forged texts, but the list of Arabic-named people is obviously taken from a real source; for Piazza, see Nef, *Conquérir et gouverner*, p. 527); Cusa, *I diplomi*, n. 44 (pp. 513–14); Garufi, *I documenti inediti*, n. 72.

[230] Cusa, *I diplomi*, nn. 132, 143 (pp. 134–79, 245–86). See n. 231 below for the useful lists of professions made by others, which I have drawn from as well as checked; the *qalfāt*, not mentioned by others, is in Cusa, p. 161.

[231] See Bercher et al., 'Une abbaye latine' (a fundamental article, but descriptive rather than analytical); Nef, *Conquérir et gouverner*, pp. 524–37, 554–7, 730–3 (555–6 for the link to the capital); Metcalfe, *Muslims and Christians*, pp. 226–31; Messina, 'Uomini e mestieri', which is a complete set of lists of artisans in both Arabic and Greek/Latin documents. The fullest analysis of the *jarā'id* from this perspective is in a doctoral thesis, Smit, *Commerce and coexistence*, pp.116–56; it veers in its discussions between seeing these artisans as simply being signs of self-sufficiency (132–8, an unconvincing position) and seeing them as signs of a 'vibrant' economy (155). These works disagree slightly with

in the Monreale lists, which I shall focus on. The fact is that these are strikingly large sets of rural artisans. There are no equivalents anywhere else in the Mediterranean in our period, except in Egypt, and the raw numbers are greater than any single set even there. In mainland Italy in our period, even cities do not surpass them, except for Genoa, thanks to the unparalleled evidence in its notarial registers (see pp. 550, 552 below). In Rome, eleventh- and twelfth-century documents cite three times as many across two centuries; but this is very different from a single snapshot, and anyway Rome, along with Palermo, was the largest city in what is now Italy up to 1100 or so.[232] (Palermo has left too few documents to allow a comparison, although there can be no doubt, as we have seen, that artisans, and the range of trades, were very great in number there.) If we had the Monreale lists for Milan, we would be making use of them with some enthusiasm (37 silk workers!) as part of an account of its economic development. Instead, we are in the countryside. Corleone and Jato certainly had urban features, but they are best seen as large villages with urban elements, of which these artisans are, indeed, an example; and anyway, many of the artisans lived in smaller settlements, *casalia*/*raḥā'il*. This was, as we have seen, wheat country, and the detailed boundary descriptions of the *casalia*, which we have in a separate bilingual Arabic and Latin text from 1182,[233] show both the wheat and the fact that there was space for plenty of sheep on its uncultivated higher fringes, which fits the references to shepherds; but the artisans do not particularly reflect that—indeed, wool workers figure relatively little. In and around the larger settlements, there was, however, a dense network of, in particular, weaving, in silk and cotton, and the finishing of cloth, as the tailors show—and specializations too, as, for example, with the embroiderer.

It is not obvious where these textile workers got their raw materials. The 1182 text describes landscape features; these include a couple of references to flax cultivation (including a retting ditch, in the Latin *menaka, ubi mollificatur linum*) and also hemp, although no linen or hemp workers are mentioned in the other texts. There are no certain references to mulberry trees for silk, or to cotton. This may well be because the text, although highly detailed, just lists boundaries, which are often streams and mountains; but it mentions agricultural activities often enough (there are also references to vineyards, mills, cattle, pigs, sugar, and

each other and with me as to numbers, but it is easy to miss trades in these very complex texts; indeed, further refinement is likely to change the totals further, but not by very much.

[232] See Wickham, *Medieval Rome*, pp. 137–54; Wickham, 'Gli artigiani'; cf. Molinari, 'Riflessioni', for Rome set against Palermo. As we shall see in Chapter 6, other cities had more references to artisans as well, especially if urban and rural workers are combined, but, as with Rome, these are collections of casual references across two centuries.

[233] Cusa, *I diplomi*, n. 137 (pp. 179–244). The most convenient text for searching is the fourteenth-century Latin copy edited electronically in Falletta, *Liber privilegiorum*, n. I.4, but it does not have pagination, so for that I cite Cusa.

irrigation).[234] I conclude that these upland textile workers got much, maybe all, of their raw material from elsewhere: in the case of cotton, either from Partinico, on the coast just to the north-west of this area, which al-Idrīsī *c.*1150 explicitly says grew cotton,[235] or, conceivably, from Palermo itself in a putting-out arrangement. A putting-out arrangement would be a quasi-industrial relationship, which is perhaps too much to expect here; Partinico (and the coastal plain it is in) is more likely, being only 10 kilometres from Jato, 30 from Corleone. But this would still imply that the upland cloth workers were getting, probably buying, their raw materials autonomously from outside their own immediate territories, which is in itself a significant conclusion. It needs to be added that all this excludes the alternative interpretation of all these textile terms, which is that the silk and cotton workers were simply cultivators of the raw materials for export, to Palermo or to Genoa (as we shall see shortly), for making into cloth elsewhere; since there is no evidence of the two textile types actually being grown in these settlements, this is the least likely explanation of the whole set. But even if raw cotton and silk cocoons were produced locally, that explanation would anyway be effectively eliminated by the citations of weavers, tailors, and the embroiderer—and also by the citations of all the other artisans, for it is evident that they too are markers of considerable local activity in the transformation of raw materials into made goods.

We have to conclude that these artisans were making goods for a market, as the local merchants also imply. The silk is an obvious example; as we have seen and will see again, this is a semi-luxury cloth, not worn by peasants and seldom worn in the countryside. But a market orientation will have been true for the cotton, and probably the leather, for we are looking at production here beyond local needs; and even if the ceramics and glass were for local consumption, which is likely, this shows (particularly in the latter case) local prosperity. The market must have included Palermo; it might also have included centres on the west coast such as Mazara and Trapani, not so far away; but it anyway shows a network of artisanal production in the interior of considerable complexity. The donkey drivers

[234] See Cusa, *I diplomi*, p. 182 for the *menaka*. The *murra*, ibid., p. 200 might conceivably be a mulberry tree; it transliterates *al-mra* in the unvocalized Arabic, ibid., p. 240, but the meanings of the latter (e.g. 'once') do not obviously work on a boundary, so *murra* <*morea*/*murus*, 'mulberry tree' in Greek and Latin respectively, is a plausible (though still hypothetical) interpretation. For the sugar and the irrigation, see Bercher et al., 'Une abbaye latine', pp. 528, 530. The sugar is striking, up on the plateau. It is closely associated with irrigated land around Palermo, and here, too, it is a clear sign that agriculture around (in this case) Calatrasi could be elaborate. The excavators at Calathamet (Lesnes and Poisson, *Calathamet*, pp. 223–4), 25 kilometres west of the Monreale estates, also found noria pots, which imply irrigation, around that castle. Castronovo in the centre of the island had irrigated cultivation too, again immediately around the site (Alessandra Molinari, pers. comm.); and we find irrigation casually cited for the coast near Catania in documents of 1143–4; see von Falkenhausen, 'I mulini della discordia', nn. 1–2 (pp. 233–5). I do not doubt that further research will find other examples. But Islamic/Norman Sicily never, as far as we can tell (and we would be able to tell from the landscape), adopted irrigation agriculture on any real scale outside the Palermo hinterland, in strong contrast to Islamic Spain (see pp. 447–8 below).

[235] Al-Idrīsī, *Nuzhat al-mushtāq*, trans. Jaubert and Nef, p. 320. See n. 240 below for the wider evidence for cotton.

(*ḥammār*), also cited in the Monreale and other *jarāʾid*, will have been vital intermediaries here.[236] The other *jarāʾid* do not really add to this picture, for the information in them is so much slighter, but they at least support it, and extend it to areas with Arabic-named inhabitants in the centre-south (Troccoli) and parts of the north and east. So, there was a lot going on in the commercial exchange of the interior of Sicily, and also, at Patti or Aci, in non-urban centres on the coast too. This will also have fitted the network of markets which are a feature of what al-Idrīsī describes for the island; in the interior, Naro, Enna, Piazza, Adrano, Petralia, Maniace, Randazzo, and Castiglione have them. These are all in or beside the Val Demone, except Naro and Piazza, and al-Idrīsī does not mention markets for Corleone or Jato, but we do not need to worry about absences when dealing with citations as chancy as those of the geographers; rather, what this picture implies is that the Val Demone in the north-east was similarly active to the Val di Mazara in the west, in the centre of which the Monreale estates lay.[237] And all this fits well with the picture I have already drawn, of a peasantry not too overburdened with the paying of tax and rent. That lack of overburdening, plus the high wheat yields of the island, freed up a substantial minority of its rural inhabitants to become non-agricultural workers, supplying their neighbours in exchange for food, but in particular selling to the coast, in potentially complex networks, as their peasant neighbours were presumably also doing with the rest of their wheat surpluses. Such complexity is explicit in one case, a Muslim merchant from Corleone in the mid-twelfth century who can be seen moving goods along the north coast from Cefalù to Messina—neither of them obvious sea outlets for Corleone—as we shall see shortly.[238]

Which brings us back to the archaeology. I have sought to set up the evidence from the documents entirely separately from that from the material record; all the same, the picture I have set out here fits the archaeology well. It does so in detail; the Monreale potters and smiths fit with the local ceramic production and iron-working identified by Alessandro Corretti's team around Entella—Entella is not mentioned in the documents except in a boundary clause in the 1182 text, but that boundary runs straight across the settlement, presumably deliberately, and the Entella survey area was partly included in the Monreale estates.[239] But, more importantly, the overall ceramic picture is very similar in its complexity to that which we have just seen for cloth, with Palermo productions and distributions balanced, particularly after 1100, against local productive hierarchies. Were the capillary productions on the Monreale estates a marker that textiles were more

[236] See most conveniently Smit, *Commerce and coexistence*, pp. 144–5, for Catania, Troccoli, and the Monreale estates.

[237] Al-Idrīsī, *Nuzhat al-mushtāq*, trans. Jaubert and Nef, pp. 327–37.

[238] Johns, 'Arabic contracts of sea-exchange', pp. 68–9, 72–3.

[239] For the unglazed ceramics (probably) and iron (certainly), see Corretti et al., 'Contessa Entellina', pp. 348–9; Corretti and Chiarantini, 'Contessa Entellina'. For the boundary, see Corretti et al., 'Frammenti di medioevo siciliano', pp. 155–7.

structurally decentralized than ceramic production, or was this simply a specifically twelfth-century picture everywhere? I would propose the latter; it is significant that the likely centralization of eleventh-century linen production in a few large centres, which best fits the trading patterns in the *geniza* (see p. 194 above), matches the still substantial productive dominance of Palermitan ceramics in the same period, and that the production of rural cloth in the twelfth century fits the growing decentralization of ceramics. But the fact that the flax for linen production was mostly imported and that twelfth-century cotton was locally grown—which in itself favours local cloth productions—must have played a part as well. The cloth of Corleone and Jato around 1180 was partly destined *for* the capital, unlike the situation with ceramics, which still came *from* the capital to compete with local productions; indeed, the two may well have been exchanged for each other, just as inland wheat was exchanged for Palermo wine and other foodstuffs. All the same, the production and distribution systems involved are likely to have been parallel in scale.

* * *

We now have enough material to put together the patterns of Sicilian production and internal exchange across our entire period. To summarize, starting with ceramics, here, we can see at the start of our period a dominance of Palermo over, in effect, the whole island, in both fine wares and amphorae—that is, the distribution of wine and other, largely liquid foods—and in the west, at least, many cheaper ceramic goods too. After 1000 this dominance changed into a more complex hierarchy of productions and distributions, and that more complex hierarchy continued to the end of our period and beyond, by which time Palermo's prominence was rather less, and eastern Sicilian productions were now rather more important—but the overlapping networks still covered the island. This changing set of patterns of production and distribution can now be seen to have matched up well with those of cloth. Sicily produced linen on a large scale in the tenth-eleventh centuries, in, probably, Palermo and Mazara, and possibly other centres, as the *geniza* shows. The scale of that textile production dropped sharply around the end of the eleventh century, but was replaced by cotton, which was more widely grown on the island. Cotton is referred to casually by Ibn Ḥawqal in the tenth century, is stressed as a feature of Sicilian agriculture by the well-informed Andalusī agronomists Ibn Baṣṣāl in the 1070s and Abū al-Khayr, his younger contemporary, and then is cited in 1095 in Catania. Archaeobotany shows the presence of cotton in eleventh-century Mazara as well, although its great years there were after 1200. It was, however, much in demand for the Genoese by the 1130s at the latest, as we shall see.[240] Cotton cloth production was probably more

[240] Ibn Ḥawqal, *Kitāb ṣūrat al-arḍ*, trans. Kramers and Wiet, 1, p. 118; Ibn Baṣṣāl, *Kitāb al-qaṣd wa al-bayān*, trans. Millás Vallicrosa and Aziman, pp. 151–3, with Abū al-Khayr, *Kitāb al-filāḥa*, ed. and

decentralized and rural-based than linen had been, but the Monreale evidence shows that it was extensive in the second half of the twelfth century. Silk cloth was also produced all through our period, at least in the north-east, and by the twelfth century on the plateau south of Palermo, and, on a substantial scale, in the capital itself. The Sicilian uplands, good sheep areas, must have produced wool as well, but we have no signs of major woollen cloth centres in the Arabic texts—in western Sicily, as elsewhere in the southern and eastern Mediterranean, it was probably above all a local family-based production—but fullers and some wool workers are visible in Greek and Latin texts.[241] Our scarce Norman-period sources thus indicate the commercialization of cloth production; cloth, indeed, was probably distributed inside the island much as Palermo ceramics are known to have been, along the land-based donkey routes. We can add to this iron, which was available in only a few places in Sicily—the geographers mention the surroundings of Palermo and Messina, late medieval sources confirm the latter, and both are locations for ironworkers in the documents—but which was evidently distributed widely by the same routes, if it was also being worked in inland Entella; and also, well ahead of other trades, leather.[242]

The internal routes were doubtless old, even if they will have changed in detail as settlement foci shifted—Sofiana, for example, had been a major route centre since Roman times, but that route must have later moved slightly north, first going through Villa del Casale, and then through Piazza. We can assume that their basic patterns had been laid down long since by the carriers who brought

trans. Carabaza, p. 323 (it should be noted that these authors refer to named places very rarely, so their stress on Sicily here is significant); for Mazara, see Primavera, 'Introduzione di nuove piante', pp. 441–3, and Primavera in Molinari and Meo, *Mazara/Māzar*, pp. 586–8 (aubergines were identified too, which, alongside Ibn Baṣṣāl, *Kitāb al-qaṣd wa al-bayān*, trans. Millás Vallicrosa and Aziman, pp. 173–7, is their earliest appearance in Europe, plus many other legumes). For a pre-Norman reference to cotton cloth in (probably) Palermo, see Jamil and Johns, 'Four Sicilian documents', commenting on P.MariageSeparation 4 (whose translation is, they show, faulty), although this might be an import. Cotton cultivation does not appear in Sicilian texts for the twelfth century, apart from the Partinico reference cited in n. 235 above. This is not in itself a problem, given the wide areas for which we have no documentation at all, but it does mean that we cannot say more about this element of the economy. Cotton might not have needed to have been grown so widely just to export to Genoa, but it is clear from the above that it was also being woven, doubtless on a far larger scale, by and for the Sicilians themselves, and its cultivation had certainly expanded by 1200, as the Mazara excavations show.

[241] For the continuity of silk production under the Normans, see Jacoby, 'Seta e tessuti', pp. 135–8, the basic survey article, which stresses the complication of production by now, with continuing private silk weaving in both towns and the countryside set against the palace workshop in Palermo (cf. n. 147 above). I would not put stress on the forced removal by the Normans of weavers from Thebes to Sicily in 1147, as Jacoby does; as we shall see later (pp. 325–7), most of these seem to have worked in linen, even if their descendants in Sicily apparently did come to weave silk too—it is not clear whether or not this was in the palace workshops. For wool production, see the lists in Messina, 'Uomini e mestieri', pp. 22–3, 37–8.

[242] Ibn Ḥawqal, *Kitāb ṣūrat al-arḍ*, trans. Kramers and Wiet, 1, p. 122 for Palermo; al-Idrīsī, *Nuzhat al-mushtāq*, trans. Jaubert and Nef, p. 312, for Messina. For late medieval Messina, see Epstein, *An island for itself*, pp. 227–30. For iron, leather, and smaller-scale trades in the twelfth century, see Messina, 'Uomini e mestieri'.

wheat down to every coast, for provisioning the port towns and for export abroad. The evidence we have for tax and rent levels in our period, furthermore, does not indicate such high and oppressive levels of surplus extraction that it would have been impossible for peasants to sell at least some of their grain surplus; Islamic elites in Palermo before 1072, and after that the small minority of incoming Norman aristocrats and clerics, plus above all the kings, certainly became very rich indeed, but the rents and taxes they took were low per person. We have seen that there were local inequalities; there was a hierarchy of *qā'id*s and *shaykh*s. But it was not always a very pronounced one, as the relatively socially undifferentiated patterns indicated by the archaeology show; that is to say, hierarchies were not so elaborate locally for it to be unlikely that the peasantry would have participated in this network of exchange. The example of Cefalù may be a guide here: the mid-twelfth-century list of differentiated rents paid by Muslims clusters around the modal average, with a few slightly higher and only one substantially higher (see p. 240 above), even though this was an at least partly urban community, including artisans and religious/social leaders (see p. 253 below). It is highly likely, as Carocci has argued, that active village-level exchange itself furthered economic inequalities; *qā'id*s were much more likely to benefit from it than their poorer neighbours.[243] But in Sicily, up to the end of our period at least, such inequalities do not seem to have extended very far, to judge by the archaeology.

In early medieval western European contexts, prosperous peasantries had tended to go together with relatively low levels of production and exchange, for peasant demand on its own was not great enough to allow the complex networks of the Roman Empire to survive. But in Sicily taxation, plus a level of elite wealth and thus demand, never lessened, and the wheat routes certainly always remained open, even in the early middle ages; when, for example, the Byzantine Empire's money economy broke down in its Aegean and Anatolian heartland (at least outside the capital) in the late seventh to mid-ninth centuries, Sicily was the only imperial province where we regularly find coins on sites, including inland ones, at least in the east.[244] That is to say, still more than in the Byzantine heartland, Sicily's internal networks never failed; and the fact that great estates do not seem to have survived the Islamic conquest allowed more surplus to be kept in the hands of peasants, which they could henceforth use to buy goods. As a result, after 950 at the latest, these networks became among the most developed in the whole Mediterranean. And finally, it was this complexity of internal communications, and the hierarchy of local specializations, which allowed Sicily's products to be exported widely after 950: in schematic terms, timber, leather and cloth to Egypt

[243] Carocci, *Lordships*, pp. 505–6, 514–15.

[244] Morrisson, 'La Sicile byzantine'; Prigent, 'Monnaie et circulation monétaire', and see n. 171 above; for inland sites, see, e.g., Arcifa, 'Indicatori archeologici', p. 70. For the structural point, see Wickham, *Framing*, pp. 706–7. I will discuss this issue in more detail in Chapter 4, where we look at Byzantium, and in Chapter 8.

in return for flax and dyes, wheat and wine to Ifrīqiya in return for oil and gold, glazed tablewares and wine to Tyrrhenian Italy and Provence in return for less obvious products (in the twelfth century, as we shall see, they would perhaps include silver). These were always less important than the internal network, but they are striking all the same. Which brings us back to empirical discussion, for we need, finally, also to see what happened to these sea-based networks in the Norman century.

* * *

I have been focussing here on what happened in Sicily's interior in the Norman period, but it is certain that there was a good deal of traffic around the coasts, for this is also where Sicily's main towns were always located, all of them ports. The network appears in plenty of twelfth-century texts. Al-Idrīsī mentions twenty-four ports in his geography. The 1186 version of the Pisan law code lists the standard interest due on sea loans if the contract does not specify it in a range of Mediterranean ports, including, in Sicily, Messina, Syracuse, Licata, Agrigento, Sciacca, Mazara, and Palermo. They were all interconnected; in an Arabic-language sea loan in Cefalù from probably the 1150s, made by *ser* Guglielmo, probably a Genoese, to a set of Muslim merchants (*tujjār*) from Cefalù itself and Corleone, other Arabic-named merchants from Termini Imerese, Trapani, plus Sciacca on the other side of the island, all appear as witnesses.[245] The kings kept strict control over a variety of port dues, plus tuna-fishing rights and a salt monopoly, as we can tell from the ten or so surviving royal cessions of immunities from tolls to monasteries and other churches, immunities restricted for the most part to ships bearing necessities for the monks or nuns, and/or to a single boat for each house, much as Byzantine emperors did for the monasteries of Athos (see p. 321 below). That restriction is an interesting one, for it implies (as the Athos ones also do) that monasteries did expect to trade—the cession to Cefalù in 1132, renewed in 1180, indeed allows a port immunity for monastic ships going to Calabria, the principality of Salerno, and Amalfi, which is quite far if one wanted simply to gather necessities.[246] These dues (generically called *kommerkion*, the

[245] See the lists in al-Idrīsī, *Nuzhat al-mushtāq*, trans. Jaubert and Nef, pp. 305–40; *Constitutum Usus*, ch. 25 (in Vignoli, *I Costituti*, pp. 230–1; for the date, see pp. lxxvi–lxxix); Johns, 'Arabic contracts of sea-exchange'. Johns dates the sea loan text to 1130–60, because coinage of the first Almohad caliph is mentioned. I think we can narrow this down a bit: to me it is most likely that it dates to after the Almohads took Béjaïa in 1152 and became Mediterranean players, and, as Johns implies, before 1162, when the Genoese lost their privileged position in Sicily for a decade—hence, roughly, 'the 1150s' here.

[246] For Cefalù, see Cusa, *I diplomi*, n. 136 (pp. 489–90); I accept Johns's argument (*Arabic administration*, pp. 92–4, 303) that the 1132 text surviving in a later Latin translation (Spata, *Le pergamene greche*, Cefalù, n. 4) is inauthentic in this form. An example of a single boat is Garufi, *I documenti inediti*, n. 10, for a Marsala monastery *c.*1131. The best account of these immunities is Abulafia, 'The crown and the economy', pp. 5–9, although I cannot follow him when he says (pp. 7–8), 'There did not exist in Norman Sicily an extensive textile industry or leather industry. There is some evidence for the export from Sicily of modest cloths and leather goods in the documents of the Cairo Genizah, many of which date from the eleventh century.' This in my view misconstrues the evidence considerably.

Byzantine term) were by contrast standardized and customary for lay merchants, whether Arabic-speaking *tujjār*, as in a royal cession to the bishop-abbot of Lipari-Patti in 1134, or the Genoese city consul Ogerio Capra, who got a trading deal in Messina from Roger II as early as 1116 in which he and his brother were granted a building plot by the sea in Messina, plus freedom from the customary *komerkion* for commercial transactions (*pragmatiōn*), but only up to 60 *tarì* per year. Customs dues probably amounted to 10 per cent, to judge by a late cession in 1198 by Constance I to the bishop of Agrigento of the *decimae* of the ports of Agrigento, Licata, and Sciacca; this was a standard figure in the Mediterranean, as we shall see throughout this book.[247]

Apart from Palermo, the major port was by now Messina. Every twelfth-century account which mentions it says so. It had an arsenal, and ships from both Christian and Muslim lands, according to al-Idrīsī around 1150; it was enormously active, but dirty and without many Muslims, to Ibn Jubayr in the 1180s; it was also dirty, with non-observant Jews, to a relative of the Egyptian Jewish merchant Ben Yijū in the 1150s; it was simply full of crooks (and Latin ships going to the Levant) to 'Falcandus' around 1170—as well as being sufficiently protagonistic that the citizens, Greek and Latin together, lynched an overbearing governor in 1168. We sometimes find Messinesi in non-Sicilian contexts; Pagano of Messina was in Genoa in 1158, acting as a witness, and reappears as a shipman for a south Italian boat in the Aegean in 1169; other men from the city appear in later Genoese records, in the 1190s and into the next century. Documents show the city with shops (*apothecae*) around the port and on the main street (*maistera rhōga, ruga magistra*).[248] Historians tend to say that Messina was important because of Mediterranean trade in general, as opposed to Palermo, which was important for specifically Sicilian trade; this is probably largely true—Messina is partially cut off from the rest of Sicily by mountains, relying on Milazzo to the west and Catania to the south for its grain. But it did have road routes to the interior via Taormina to its south, and the town was connected enough to sell cooking pots to most of the island by and after 1200, as we have seen (p. 226). It was, anyway, closely linked to the other Sicilian ports; this is where *ser* Guglielmo's ship

[247] Cusa, *I diplomi*, nn. 47, 33 (pp. 517–19, 359–60); Kölzer, *Constantiae imperatricis et reginae Siciliae diplomata*, n. 62. For Ogerio, see Abulafia, *The two Italies*, pp. 62–4. For 10%, see n. 270 below.

[248] Al-Idrīsī, *Nuzhat al-mushtāq*, trans. Jaubert and Nef, p. 312; Ibn Jubayr, *Riḥla*, trans. Broadhurst, pp. 338–9; ENA 2557.151, ed. Gil and Simonsohn, 'More on the history of the Jews in Sicily', n. 2, trans. Goitein and Friedman, *India traders*, pp. 736–41; Ugo Falcando, *Liber de regno*, ed. Siragusa, chs 32, 53, 55. For the Messinesi abroad up to 1300, see Penet, 'Les communautés marchandes de Messine', pp. 234–41 (Pagano appears in *Giovanni Scriba*, 2, p. 315; *DCV*, n. 217); see also Abulafia, *The two Italies*, pp. 278–9. For shops, see Amico, *I diplomi*, n. 13; Guillou, *Les actes grecs*, n. 12; Garufi, *I documenti inediti*, n. 76 (= Enzensberger, *Willelmi II regis Siciliae diplomata*, n. 126). See also the general account in Pispisa, 'Messina, Catania', pp. 147–82. The only other major port with anything approaching a monographic study is Agrigento, in Peri, 'Per la storia della vita cittadina'.

was going from Cefalù in the mid-century, and there was regular traffic to and from Palermo.[249]

Cefalù is the other town we can say a little more about. To judge by standing buildings still visible in the modern town, it was quite substantial in size by the end of our period. It had a citizen community, *cives* or *burgenses*, who gained a judicial immunity from Roger II in 1132, and a set of rights and agreed customs from the local bishop-abbot in 1157, setting out butchers' dues to the bishop, the fees millers and bakers could claim, and rights to have citizens' vineyards protected from the incursions of rabbit hunters. This text also makes clear that the weavers, *tesitores*, of the town are sufficiently important that flour for them has been gratis (although henceforth will not be); it also bans any price increases for cloth except on grounds of the thickness of thread (*pro grossitudine et subtilitate filorum)*. Many of these *burgenses* were Latin immigrants; one such rented an *apoteca* by the port from the bishop *c.*1164 for the large sum of 60 *tarì* per year.[250] But not all were Latins; the *jarīda* to the bishop in 1145 lists Arabic-named dependents who include a carpenter, two barbers, a hatmaker, a dyer, and two sons of a merchant, as well as local leaders, *shaykh*s, *qā'id*s, and *qāḍi*s. As we have seen for Monreale, artisans and indeed *qā'id*s could be country dwellers, but here they contributed to the commercial and artisanal activity of the town and its hinterland. Anyway, the Cefalù merchants who dealt with *ser* Guglielmo were certainly Muslim town dwellers, *āhl Jaflūdī*. So, if we draw together all the evidence for it that we have seen, this was a multilingual weaving town and an active port, with links to Messina and to other Sicilian ports, as far as Sciacca, and also to the south Italian mainland coast—with ships from everywhere, as al-Idrīsī said when describing it. It would be hard to assume that this was exceptional. We certainly know Mazara was like that a century earlier, and Trapani was coming up in a similar way by now. The links northwards are to be expected for a port on the north coast; on the west and south coasts, links were with Africa, at Scicli, Sciacca, and Marsala, according to al-Idrīsī, with Trapani added by Ibn Jubayr.[251] But the ports will have sent ships around the island much more than they sent them overseas. They were transporting all the goods we have looked at so far, that is to say, those of them which were produced or sold to buyers close enough to the coast for it to be easier to get to the sea and go by ship than to take the donkey routes across the interior.

[249] Mediterranean trade: see, e.g., Pistarino, 'Commercio e vie marittime', p. 252. For Catania, see Ugo Falcando, *Liber de regno*, ed. Siragusa, ch. 55 (p. 154); for Cefalù, see Johns, 'Arabic contracts of sea-exchange'. For Palermo, see, e.g., the back-to-back cessions to the cathedral of Messina of a house in Palermo and vice versa in 1158–9: Enzensberger, *Guillelmi I. regis diplomata*, nn. 25, 27.

[250] Brühl, *Rogerii II regis diplomata latina*, n. 19; Garufi, *I documenti inediti*, nn. 32, 38.

[251] For Cefalù, Cusa, *I diplomi*, n. 79 (pp. 472–80); see also n. 222 above; Johns, 'Arabic contracts of sea-exchange'. For Cefalù and the other ports, see Al-Idrīsī, *Nuzhat al-mushtāq*, trans. Jaubert and Nef, pp. 310, 316, 318–19; Ibn Jubayr, *Riḥla*, trans. Broadhurst, p. 351.

These were all connections between Sicilians, above all; but we have already seen examples of the involvement of the Genoese. The *ser* Guglielmo text is unusual among sea loans I have seen, in that Guglielmo, who had hired the ship, planned himself to travel to Messina with the nine Muslim merchants involved, and they would provision him in Cefalù and then Messina until the debt was paid. The interest rates for the merchants (they are each calculated separately in the text) were also in one or two cases exceptionally high, which indicates that some were not in a strong position. But conversely, the rules for lending were seen in the text as standardized, the way 'the *tujjār* lend amongst themselves', and the merchants as a whole were investing largish sums—over £100 Genoese in total for the ship, well above the average for most years around 1160 for Genoese ships bound for Sicily, as Giovanni Scriba's notarial register for 1154–64 shows.[252] Anyway, however we interpret this, it is evident that the Genoese by this point, probably the 1150s as noted earlier, were inserting themselves into the network of trade around the island. They had houses in Messina, as we have seen for Ogerio Capra in 1116; in 1183 another Genoese, Bubonoso, received a similar house on the main street from King William II; the colony was sufficiently well established that in 1162–3 Ogerio Vento, from one of Genoa's leading families, asked in his will to be buried in a Messina church. Ibn Jubayr in 1184–5 travelled on Genoese ships both to Messina and from Trapani back to his native Spain, even though not between the two; when he mentioned the tight African connections with Trapani, he referred to the ships of the Rūm, which by now will have been either Genoese or Pisan; indeed, already some fifty years earlier, it had been considered normal that a 'Christian' ship should take Jewish merchants from Mahdia to Sicily (but less normal that the Christians, doubtless Italians, then despoiled the merchants, who, indeed, planned to complain to the *qāḍī*). When in 1168 Étienne du Perche, the recently expelled chancellor for the infant William II and his queen-regent mother, Margaret of Navarre, left Palermo for Jerusalem, his ship ran into trouble at Licata; but a Genoese ship just happened to be there, and he bought it to travel onwards.[253]

None of these sources, except for Giovanni Scriba, is from Genoa itself; but the Genoese still crop up everywhere. As I have already commented, they were much like the Egyptians of a century earlier, and they were almost as separate from the island's internal network as the Egyptians had been—there are some references to

[252] Johns, 'Arabic contracts of sea-exchange'; for Giovanni Scriba, compare the tables in Abulafia, The two Italies, pp. 105, 111, 113, 119. For a Venetian parallel to lenders travelling, see Chapter 6, n. 102 below.

[253] Cusa, *I diplomi*, n. 33 (pp. 359–60); Garufi, *I documenti inediti*, n. 76 (= Enzensberger, *Willelmi II regis Siciliae diplomata*, n. 126); *Giovanni Scriba*, nn. 1006, 1047; Ibn Jubayr, *Riḥla*, trans. Broadhurst, pp. 27, 351, 353; Bodl. MS Heb. c 28/60, ed. Zeldes and Frenkel, 'Trade with Sicily', n. 1 (S171); Ugo Falcando, *Liber de regno*, ed. Siragusa, ch. 55 (p. 161).

the Genoese going into the interior, but they are few and casual.[254] But once one got to the sea, they were regularly there, together with the Sicilians (of all languages and religions) who also sailed the coasts. And when one went from Sicily to elsewhere, or at least beyond the Norman kingdom of Sicily and southern Italy, they were far more present.

There were certainly Sicilian merchants who continued to go long distances by sea, not least to Egypt. A diploma of Roger II from 1137, for example, refers casually to the rights of Sicilian merchants in Alexandria (henceforth, those of Salerno were to have the same rights); Benjamin of Tudela stated that Sicilian ships were in Alexandria in the 1160s (he said the same of Barcelona); al-Makhzūmī at the end of the twelfth century also refers to Sicilian merchants (*tujjār*), of unspecified religion, coming to Egypt. Northwards, Nikulás Bergsson, an Icelandic pilgrim, also claimed that Sicilian ships came up to Pisa in the 1150s. It might be thought, anyway, that a state capable of producing a navy which attacked both Byzantium (especially) and Egypt on a fairly regular basis across the twelfth century could manage merchant ships as well, as the Italian port cities themselves did. But we cannot go beyond the anecdotal here, even if the anecdotal is an important correction to the assumptions one can too easily make on the basis of Genoese sources alone. Conversely, the Genoese were more prominent by now for sure, even if we do not have the data to say whether or not they were fully dominant. As a Sicilian poet, Abū al-ʿArab al-Zubayrī, is reputed to have said in 1072, 'The sea is of the Rūm.' We need not fixate on that date, as the source which contains this is from the later thirteenth century; but in the twelfth century, around Sicily, the statement was getting truer. And we certainly can say far more about the Genoese than about any other merchant groups from the mid-twelfth century onwards.[255]

The patterns of twelfth-century traffic in Italian boats, from Sicily across the sea to the ports of the north, have been well studied, in particular by David Abulafia; they will recur in Chapter 6 as well, so I will only summarize them here. The Venetians had only occasional links to the island—a handful of sea loans

[254] There are, in fact, four. Ogerio Capra's commerce in the 1116 document, cited in n. 253 above, was stated to be with the *chōrai* (villages) of Sicily; in the 1156 treaty between William I and the Genoese (see n. 258 below), the Genoese were envisaged as sometimes bringing cotton to Palermo *a casalibus* (from smaller settlements). As to landholding, a Genoese will of 1162 (*Giovanni Scriba*, n. 950) refers to a *vinea et terra* in Sicily—the phraseology does not indicate a large holding; and there is a reference in the Monreale boundary document of 1182 to the land boundary of the *cultura* (Arabic: *burub*ʿ, literally 'quarter') of a *Ianuensis*, a single Genoese who evidently had received a tax concession from the king—but the boundary given there is quite small-scale, so this was not a large area (Cusa, *I diplomi*, n. 137 (pp. 179–244, at 184–5, 210–11); *pace* Abulafia, *The two Italies*, p. 281, who saw it as being bigger, and the land of the Genoese as a community). This is not much, even if it is more than the *geniza* gives us for any Egyptian involvement in the economy of Sicily outside the ports.

[255] Brühl, *Rogerii II. regis diplomata latina*, n. 46; *The itinerary of Benjamin of Tudela*, trans. Adler, p. 76 (cf. also 2); al-Makhzūmī, *Minhāj*, trans. Cahen, 'Douanes', p. 283; see also n. 115 above. For Pisa, see Nikulás Bergsson, *Leiðarvísir*, ed. and trans. Simek, pp. 481, 486. For al-Zubayrī, see Amari, *Biblioteca arabo-sicula*, 2, p. 629, versione italiana, 2, p. 520.

(largely for voyages to Messina), dwarfed in scale by those they made for Byzantium or Egypt, plus a church in Palermo for their presumably quite small colony.[256] Genoese interest in Sicily, however, was far greater. It evidently began quite early in the Norman period, to judge by the 1116 text—and Ogerio Capra was, as already noted, actually a ruling consul of the city, even if here clearly acting in a private capacity. Pisan interest may date to earlier still, if Malaterra is right to say that the Pisan sack of Palermo in 1064 was the result of *mercatores* receiving 'injuries' from the Palermitans (although this may just be an invention on Malaterra's part). We know much less about Pisan trade with Sicily, for we do not have the city's notarial registers or a *Liber iurium* collecting city documents; but it was probably less important in this period, given the fact that it is almost exclusively the Genoese who appear in casual references. The trade of the Pisans certainly extended all around the island, however, given the port list mentioned earlier (p. 251), and they had a colony in Messina just as the Genoese did (they fought each other in 1129); it is likely that what can be said about the Genoese is valid for the Pisans too.[257] But I shall focus only on the Genoese from now on.

After 1116, Genoese trade with Sicily steadily grew for nearly half a century, with a sharper upturn in the 1150s. Casual references to trade with and voyages to Sicily steadily increase in our documents (most of the relevant ones survive in the Genoese city cartularies of the thirteenth century, the *Libri iurium*; see p. 541 below). In 1156, this culminated in a comprehensive treaty with William I, which set out the standard dues owed by Genoese traders and the privileges they enjoyed, which included specific customs dues for each commodity traded in each city. The notarial register of Giovanni Scriba, which includes contracts from 1154 to 1164—mostly for our purposes sea loans and the establishment of temporary trading consortia, *societates*—backs up the general picture in the 1156 treaty, and shows that commerce was by now extensive. Genoa, however, was forced by Emperor Frederick Barbarossa in 1162 to agree to help his planned invasion of the Norman kingdom—Frederick promised them in return a street in every port, plus the whole of the city of Syracuse, which sounds like a lot, but was less than the Pisans were promised (the Pisans were keener on the war, in part presumably because their Genoese rivals were currently doing better in trade here). Frederick never did invade, and the only result of this was a rapid decrease in the intensity of Genoese trade; in Giovanni Scriba's register, contracts for Sicily

[256] *DCV*, nn. 40, 50, 141, 278, 279, 299; for the church, see Garufi, *I documenti inediti*, n. 18. See in general Abulafia, *The two Italies*, pp. 76–80, 141–9; Venetian interest in the Norman kingdom was largely focussed on its mainland Adriatic coast.

[257] Malaterra, *De rebus gestis*, ed. Pontieri, 2.34; *Annali genovesi*, 1, ed. Belgrano, p. 24 for 1129; for other documents concerning Pisa, Abulafia, 'Pisan commercial colonies', is basic. Savona could be added here, for it apparently established an early treaty with Sicily, in 1127/8—see Brühl, *Rogeri II. regis diplomata latina*, n. 10—but even if we set aside the oddness of the text, this was brokered by the Genoese, and it is a marker of the early interest of Genoa in the south as much as that of its Ligurian neighbour; see the sceptical account in Abulafia, *The two Italies*, pp. 64–70.

dropped from an average of 15 per year before 1162 to an annual average of one for the last three years of the text. Indeed, the only loan from the year after the 1162 treaty with Frederick was the only one in the entire register clearly to a Sicilian, none other than Abū al-Qāsim, the community leader of Sicily's Muslims. As Abulafia comments, King William seems to have temporarily restricted access to the Genoa route to traders from his own kingdom. After this embargo, trade seems not to have picked up again until William II agreed a renewal of his father's treaty in 1174, although from then on it continued without a break, and by the end of the 1180s, as later registers show, was very substantial indeed. After 1191, renewed German designs on Sicily, and renewed treaties between the port cities and Frederick's son Henry VI, led to a further collapse of trading, until Henry's successful conquest in 1194 and indeed for some time after; but that is outside our period, and was, anyway, again only a temporary blip. Notarial registers do not survive between 1164 and 1179, and are not substantial again until 1182; I shall not consider the post-1180 registers here, although I survey them briefly when Genoa is discussed later (see pp. 551–5 below).[258]

What the Genoese wanted from Sicily was above all wheat and cotton—not cotton cloth, which, as we have seen, was made in the normal way on the island, but simply the raw material, to supply weavers in northern Italy, who we will look at in more detail in Chapter 6. This is evident from early on; a document of 1142 refers to wheat as a standard product coming from Sicily, and the treaty of 1156 stresses it too. Cotton appears already in the 1130s as an export commodity. Then, it is called *bombacium*, a Greek loanword; in 1156, however, it is *cuttone*, from the Arabic *quṭn*, which presumably indicates a growing familiarity with Sicilian vendors (all the same, *bombax* is normal in the notarial records later). If we follow the treaty of 1156, it seems that the Genoese expected to export grain and [salted] pork from Messina, grain, cotton, and raw wool from Palermo; and grain, cotton, and leather from Agrigento and Mazara. (These last two ports are not, however, mentioned in the register of Giovanni Scriba, which specifies only Palermo, Messina, a generic 'Sicily', and, once, Trapani.) No imports to the island are mentioned except woollen cloth to Palermo. These products we have already seen, except for the pork (exported from a Christian area) and the wool. The latter is interesting, for it fills a gap in our internal Sicilian records, but all the same wheat and cotton are the products most stressed.[259] Genoa did not have much of

[258] Abulafia, *The two Italies*, sets all these developments out; for the treaty of 1156, see *LI*, 2, n. 289 (*CDGE*, 1, n. 279). For the supply problems which the 1162–74 period caused Genoa, see p. 536 below. For Abū al-Qāsim, see *Giovanni Scriba*, nn. 970, 972; cf. Abulafia, *The two Italies*, pp. 131, 247–9. Pistarino, 'Commercio e vie marittime' is relatively weak on Roger II; Pistarino, 'Commercio e comunicazioni' is stronger on the two Williams.

[259] 1142: *LI*, 1, n. 5 (*CDGE*, 1, n. 119); 1130s: *LI*, I, n. 6; 1156: *LI*, 2, n. 289 (*CDGE*, 1, n. 279—here, I accept the emendation to the text by Pistarino, 'Commercio e comunicazioni', p. 240n); for *bombax* later, see the nearly complete lists in *Giovanni Scriba*, 2, p. 333, here wrongly glossed 'silk', followed inexplicably by Jehel, *Les Génois*, p. 348. For the terminology, see also Ditchfield, *La culture matérielle*,

an agricultural hinterland, and it was expanding fast, so needed grain supplies (see p. 536 below); Sicily, as ever, was the most attractive supplier. (It should be noted that it is unlikely that other northern Italian cities were as yet buying Sicilian wheat through Genoa; there is no evidence of it in twelfth-century or early thirteenth-century sources.[260]) It has to be said, however, that the 1156 treaty gives us no clue as to scale; these were evidently the main products the Genoese wanted, but how important they were, to anyone except in a single, even if thriving Italian town, is unclear.

Giovanni Scriba gives us a greater sense of scale, and complicates the picture. For a start, the loans and *societates* concerning Sicily (and indeed other destinations) were overwhelmingly in money, and, as we saw for Egypt, most—here, all but 17 out of over 100 contracts—mention no goods at all; they were straightforward capitalist transactions, with typical annual interest rates of 25 per cent for the loans. The sums could be substantial, although only a quarter were for more than £100 (cf. pp. 546–7 below). Cotton exports from the island, doubtless raw cotton, are mentioned two or three times (but much more often when referring to goods inside Genoa itself), plus silk (which must be cloth, not raw silk), skins, and, once, iron and tin; and of goods imported into Sicily, cloth is the commonest, either fustian (a cotton and linen mix) from Lombardy or woollens, although steel appears once, and so does timber, possibly from a different wood from that grown in Sicily. One can see why fustian, a north Italian speciality, might have been attractive on the island, where linen was by now not much produced; wool-weaving was also more highly professionalized a trade in the north than in the southern Mediterranean lands; but there is as yet not much record of either. Some of the wider complexity of this exchange system appears in an agreement of 1157 in which a shipper contracts to take to Palermo copper, Arabic books (*libros sarracenicos*), a barrel of mixed spices, another of sal ammoniac,

pp. 370–2. Wool was also exported to Ravenna in an Amalfitan ship in 1105 (see Chapter 7, n. 32 below), so there may have been more of a commercially orientated sheep economy than we know, but it is otherwise obscure.

[260] For the thirteenth century in the north, see in general Peyer, *Zur Getreidepolitik*, with caution. A good case study for Bologna (a large town, even if not as large as Milan or Venice), whose grain in the thirteenth century, outside its own contado, was above all supplied from the Romagna and Ferrara, is Pucci Donati, 'Ravitaillement en céréales', pp. 16–18, a reference I owe to Alexis Wilkin. Even Milan, however, seems also to have relied mostly on the grain of the Po plain; see Chapter 6, n. 309 below. Tuscany (i.e. normally Florence, but other cities too) did buy Sicilian grain in the later thirteenth century; see Epstein, *An island for itself*, pp. 271–2; Day, *The early development of the Florentine economy*, pp. 325, 330–3; Dameron, 'Feeding the medieval Italian city-state'. Florence, at around 100,000 inhabitants by 1300, certainly had outgrown the grain production of its hinterland by then, and probably a few decades earlier (not in the first half of the century, though; it was still small in 1200), although Sicily was not its only grain source—for more discussion, see Chapter 6, n. 293 below. Genoa and Florence were thus probably the major Italian markets for Sicilian grain in 1300 (Venice, the other large city, looked to Puglia first). Bresc, *Un monde méditerranéen*, pp. 523–57, gives the data for grain exports after 1250 from the Sicilian side; Pisa (here acting largely as the port for Florence), Genoa, Barcelona, and North Africa were the main directions of export. Of course, the Black Death then greatly reduced urban demand, for at least a century after 1350.

mantles, and caps; all these except the mantles were items which one would expect to have exported *from* Sicily, not the other way round, and it would seem, as Abulafia has proposed, that these were indeed Sicilian (or, less likely, Ifrīqiyan) goods warehoused in Genoa for resale.[261] That certainly shows the degree to which the sea route was already routinized. But it must also be stressed that the lists of goods are sometimes stated to be in *addition* to money, which was, as just noted, the normal way the Genoese calculated contracts. It is thus conceivable, as Abulafia argues, that the mid-century Genoese often took silver coin to Sicily, not goods, to exchange for cotton and wheat (maybe after using that silver to make other transactions around the island's coasts, in the context of internal Sicilian trading)—conceivable, although, in fact, far from certain; I will come back to the point later. But it was not until the 1180s and onwards, when northern Italian cloth production began to take off, that the Genoese really started to send cloth (from both Italy and northern Europe) to Sicily on a large scale.[262]

We shall come back to the wider framework of Genoese trading, and of north Italian cloth, in Chapter 6. That the last quarter of the twelfth century marked the beginning of the economic take-off of the central Po plain (for which Genoa was an intermediary) and most of Tuscany, not any earlier, is an argument I will make there. That will be in opposition to an older historiography, although some scholars have certainly argued it (Abulafia being one of them). But up to that date, the conclusion I reach, on the basis of the evidence presented here, is this: by 1150 or so the Genoese—with the Pisans—were the most prominent traders along the sea routes in the Tyrrhenian Sea, between Sicily and the Italian and Provençal coast, and indeed some of those eastwards to the Levant and Egypt as well. This was a new development which was in part the result of successful violence, plus, at any rate sometimes, the encouragement of a new Norman ruling class which found it easier to look north than south or east. But this did not mean that the north Italians dominated Sicilian trade. Most of the sea trade around the island was Sicilian, although the Genoese, in particular, were evidently active in it as well; and this more local traffic was much more extensive than the longer-distance sea traffic to the north. Trade internal to the island was more important still, and that was entirely the work of Sicilians. What the north Italians did most of all, in the years 1115–80, particularly after 1150, was to carry away Sicilian surpluses in wheat and cotton, and bring back unspecified goods (maybe including silver) in return. The impact of the Genoese was part of the slow Latinization of the island, not a shift in its basic economic orientation, which continued to look in all

[261] Exports from Sicily: *Giovanni Scriba*, nn. 280, 285?, 857, 909; cf. 1212; imports: nn. 68, 287, 383 (steel), 385, 404 (timber), 415, 641, 678, 937. Of these, nn. 415, 641 mention, uniquely among exports in this period, cloth from northern France. For the 1157 text, n. 287, see Abulafia, *The two Italies*, pp. 220–1; and pp. 217–54 for the Giovanni Scriba evidence as a whole.

[262] Abulafia, *The two Italies*, pp. 219, 225–6, 255, 264, 273. See, pp. 548–50 below for further discussion of silver.

directions: there were still some Egyptian merchants in Messina and other ports (see p. 252 above), and links with Ifrīqiya, in particular, remained strong. The gold content of Sicilian *tarìs*—which hardly varied into the thirteenth century, except for a roughly 10 per cent drop in weight in, probably, William II's reign[263]—further underlines the continuing strength of Ifrīqiyan links, since that gold had consistently African origins.

Once we get to 1180, however, we might begin, if we wanted, to see the start of the grand narrative of Sicilian economic 'failure' which I criticized earlier (pp. 198–200). So, although the issues involved in that postdate our period, we do need to look at them briefly. It is true, from then on, that finished cloth more visibly came into Sicily on Genoese ships, and that raw materials, again and consistently wheat and cotton (plus, later, cheese), went northwards. But this does not mean that Sicily, finally, did become dependent on the large-scale productions of northern Italy, in particular in cloth—far from it. The late medieval picture, as demonstrated most clearly by Stefan Epstein, was, in fact, wholly different from this; after 1300 and into the sixteenth century, the period he studied, cloth imports were a very small minority of the total cloth used in the island, and probably were essentially (semi-) luxury goods. Cotton, linen, fustian, and woollen cloth were instead very much Sicilian products, made above all in the eastern part of the island, especially the Val di Noto, where cotton and flax were also grown (raw wool came more from the Val di Mazara)—and so also, on the luxury end, was silk, which was still produced in the Val Demone and exported on some scale. Rural production was strong, much as it was in the twelfth century south of Palermo. Flax cultivation had evidently expanded since the time frame of this book, although we have to recognize that the Val di Noto is the least documented part of the island in both the Islamic and Norman periods, so it might have always been practised there. Sugar cultivation was also expanding, in part to fill the gap left by the decline of Egyptian sugar after the Black Death, and was exported, as was iron from Messina.[264] If there was a 'dualist' economy here, it could be said to be between eastern and western Sicily, not between Sicily and northern Italy, for the west was the focus of the great grain estates by now; the transfer of the driving force of the Sicilian economy from the west to the east around 1200, which I have described on the basis of the archaeology, evidently continued and indeed strengthened thereafter. But as Epstein also argued, that 'dualism' would be an exaggeration here too; among other things, wheat cultivation and commercialization could itself be innovative, and it was in the west that sugar manufacturing began to develop too—or, perhaps better, to be documented again, since this is

263 Travaini, *La monetazione*, pp. 101–4, 133–7, 144–6.

264 Epstein, *An island for itself*, pp. 182–239, 300–3 (210–22 for sugar, 227–30 for iron; note that raw cotton was less important as an export than it had been in the twelfth century, even if it continued: 185–6, 301–2); see further Epstein, 'The textile industry', for more on cloth. For sugar, see also Ouerfelli, *Le sucre*, pp. 149–67 (less reliable on the period before 1350, however).

where it had been strong before 1200. It is certainly true that late medieval Sicily did not, apart from silk, develop an export market for the island's cloth—a point which Epstein's most effective critic, Giuseppe Petralia, has underlined. But the internal coherence of the island was still the key, for eastern cloth must have gone westwards, just as western grain went eastwards; and internal exchange far outweighed any external commerce, of either import or export. On Epstein's figures, wheat exports after 1300, excluding some short-term peaks, averaged between 5 and 15 per cent of local production (the higher figures are all after 1450); cloth imports were around 5 per cent of total consumption. The internal market made up all the rest.[265]

We are here very far from the late medieval period being the age of a blocked and colonial economy for Sicily, dominated by the monoculture of wheat, as Henri Bresc saw it. Indeed, it was, in the eyes of both Epstein and Petralia, the twelfth century, not the fourteenth or fifteenth, which was the period of a 'weak development of markets'.[266] This in my view is a misunderstanding as well; the historiography Epstein drew on here is outdated, and they both wrote before the archaeology became strong. But I would not wish at all to contest the argument that the later medieval Sicilian economy was more complex—still more complex—than that of the eleventh and twelfth. Much had changed by then in the macro-economy of Europe and the Mediterranean, after all, which it is not my task to confront: banking and credit were vastly more complicated; there were many more large-scale productions, of cloth and metals; state and market infrastructures were more elaborate nearly everywhere. These two scholars agreed that they were making assumptions about an unstudied twelfth and thirteenth century which needed to be looked at more closely; all the same, other things being equal, what I have set out for the twelfth century, as also for the eleventh, shows the period to be more similar to their late medieval world than they then knew. The thirteenth century is the least understood period by now, but what we already know about ceramic patterns implies both continuities with the twelfth, and indications that some of the specificities of the later medieval economy were already beginning to appear then: the distribution of Messina *pentole* would certainly point strongly to

[265] Petralia, 'La nuova Sicilia tardomedievale', pp. 158–9 (the rest of his far from negative critique concerns specifically late medieval issues such as the use of foreign credit which are not relevant here); Epstein, 'A reply'; Epstein, *An island for itself*, esp. pp. 162–239, 270–91, 296–300; for the grain percentage, 168, 275; for the cloth percentage, 296–7, 300, and Epstein, 'The textile industry', pp. 143, 146. Cf. also n. 260 above for the limitations in the demand for Sicilian grain, even at the high point of medieval urbanism around 1300. Actually, 5% is to me (as also to Epstein) a very high figure indeed for the middle ages, not a low one, as has been thought by some; see p. 13 above and Chapter 7 below. The details of the internal exchange network of late medieval Sicily are not, in fact, at all well documented, and it was certainly by no means complete; see Epstein, *An island for itself*, pp. 117–18. Ceramic evidence would be useful here, but is not yet available.

[266] Petralia, 'La nuova Sicilia tardomedievale', p. 160; Epstein, 'A reply', p. 166. Epstein was also at times inaccurate about details of the Norman period, not, of course, at all his research focus, in *An island for itself*, as, e.g., on pp. 186, 201, 210, 243.

an island-wide exchange network, which would then be modified by the growing east–west division implied by the distribution of Gela ware.

So Sicily continued to have the strong internal market which enabled it to be a major hub of Mediterranean-wide exchange, as that developed and shifted. I have already stressed and will continue to stress that import and export could not dominate the economy of any medieval region larger than a single city; what happened to Sicily after the Genoese took over external trade does not at all contradict this, and indeed late medieval data, far greater in quantity as they are, clearly demonstrate it. So, external networks characterized the Sicilian economy all through, but that economy was never dependent on them. Blips in external trade, like the end of the *geniza* traffic around 1100 or the sharp drops in Genoese trade in the 1160s and 1190s, and even political crises—as with the early tenth century, the mid-eleventh, the late twelfth, and the late thirteenth—had no effect on the internal economic complexity of the island. That internal structure was itself far from static, as Palermo developed at the expense of Syracuse after 900, or Messina developed partially at the expense of Palermo after 1150; but it did not go away. And it was more significant, in the final analysis, than who controlled the seas and what they did with it.

3.7 The Central Mediterranean Regions into the Twelfth Century

From 950 or so onwards, Sicily and North Africa were the hinge of Mediterranean exchange. They did not match in scale the economic powerhouse of Egypt, which was so much larger both in its demography and in the complexity of its internal economy—its division of labour in agricultural and artisanal work, its cash cropping, the intricacy of its fiscal system. But they were in the middle of the great inland sea, and their links went far, westwards to Spain, at least to a limited extent (see pp. 449–56 below), and northwards to mainland Italy and Provence, as well as to Egypt, of course, and, again to a lesser extent, to Byzantium. As I have argued, the links after 950 between Sicily and the Tyrrhenian coast of Italy and Provence represented the first large-scale commercial relationship between the Christian north and the Muslim south since the seventh century. When Christophe Picard anticipates Lopez's 'commercial revolution' and relocates it in the Fāṭimid period, it is this network he means, and it has become well known, thanks to the force of *geniza* studies—and in the distinct arena of medieval archaeology, thanks to recent work on ceramics.[267]

Picard is not alone in ascribing this to the Fāṭimids themselves, who unified Ifrīqiya, Sicily, and Egypt, and who, therefore, made possible an ever larger scale

[267] Picard, *La mer des califes*, pp. 324–34.

of maritime exchange.[268] This in turn lessened transaction costs, although the frequent complaints in the *geniza* letters about surprising or arbitrary customs duties show that such costs had by no means ended. I have argued here that the real driving forces which underpinned this Mediterranean activity were, rather, interior to each of the two central regions: the internal economic coherence that Ifrīqiya had, centred on Kairouan and its satellite capitals, and that Sicily had, centred by now on Palermo, plus, naturally, that of Egypt itself, which we looked at in detail in Chapter 2. This was reinforced by the close economic links between the two central regions, which are visible, not least but not only in the archaeology, at every point from before our period starts to after it ends. The Fāṭimids certainly facilitated the extension of that close relationship eastwards to Egypt. But the build-up of large-scale linen production in both central Mediterranean regions, fuelled by Egyptian flax, would have been impossible without a considerable pre-existing exchange infrastructure in both—otherwise, there would not have been enough demand for that linen in both regions, or a sufficiently developed network of exchange to make the satisfaction of that demand possible. We have seen in detail how that internal network of exchange worked too, thanks to ceramic distributions, which are very well studied by now in Sicily; they are much less well studied in North Africa, but, even there, we know enough to be able to see an economic coherence stretching across at least the Tunisian lowlands, and extending to an extent into the Tell, up to the mid-eleventh century at least. The *geniza* merchants were not concerned with that internal network, and say nothing about it, but we can hardly doubt that they knew very well that it was there, and that their buying and selling depended on it. It should be added that there is absolutely nothing, in either the archaeology or the *geniza*, which indicates that this network grew weaker in the early eleventh century; the crisis in Ifrīqiya before 1050 canvassed by some historians (see p. 158 above) is imaginary.

The political chaos provoked by the Hilālian invasions and the political fragmentation which followed them caused rather more of a crisis in that region, however. I have argued here against the view that war and political breakdown in themselves necessarily ruined economic infrastructures; I shall come back to the point in Chapters 5 and 6, when I discuss al-Andalus and north-central Italy, which experienced serious political breakdown at different points in the eleventh century without any significant involution of economic structures—often, indeed, the reverse. We have, anyway, seen here too that Islamic Sicily had usually been politically unstable, with two later conquests of the island before 1200, without this having much effect on its strong economic coherence; and it is important to remember that the political fragmentation of Ifrīqiya, too, was reversed by the

268 See some of the articles in Cressier and Nef, 'Les Fatimides et la Méditerranée centrale'; and Bramoullé, *Les Fatimides et la mer*, esp. pp. 483–91, who, however, stresses the solidity of earlier commercial links too.

Almohads in the 1150s, at the end of our period. But the failure of Kairouan and Ṣabra, which was not reversed, seems to have had more effect than that. More and more, the most intense economic activity in Ifrīqiya seems to have been restricted to its coastal cities. These, of course, had hinterlands, but it is harder to be sure how far, or whether, these hinterlands were at all connected internally. From this point on, there was a potentially sharp contrast in the developments of North Africa and Sicily, even though they stayed so closely linked. But how much effect did this have on the wider economic role of the two central Mediterranean regions, as the eleventh century moved into the twelfth, and can their wider role shed any light on that internal contrast? To help to answer that, we need to look briefly at a final empirical issue: the international links Ifrīqiya did have after the end of the main evidence from the *geniza*, that is to say, in the twelfth century; and that means looking again at the evidence from the Italian maritime cities, as we have just done for Sicily.

Half of the Ifrīqiyan coast was in the hands of the Norman kings of Sicily in the 1150s; however unhappy that occupation was—and since it ended in uprisings in most of the major Tunisian ports, we can suppose that it was indeed unhappy—it certainly helped to maintain the links between the two regions. The Almohads then conquered Béjaïa and the Ḥammādid state in 1152, and then, after a failed attack on Tunis in 1157, the whole of Ifrīqiya in 1159.[269] It is in this period that our documentation begins for commercial links with Genoa and Pisa. This slightly predates the Almohad conquest: the Genoese were trading in Tunis and Béjaïa as early as 1143, and in 1157 the independent ruler of Tunis ʿAbd Allāh, having fought off the Almohads, agreed that Pisan ships could trade without paying customs tolls, and could also export all Tunis's alum. But the newly victorious Almohads were already in 1161 prepared to grant trading rights to the Genoese in North Africa, against a reduced customs toll of 8 per cent (but in Béjaïa they paid the standard toll, which was 10 per cent, as in Sicily and Byzantium, and also as in Islamic law as it developed[270]), and the Pisans—who may have been on peaceful terms with the Almohads even before 1159—had similar rights before 1181, confirmed in a surviving treaty of 1186, though they by now had to pay the standard toll. This is interesting, for the Almohads were rather more hostile to Christians than were most other Islamic powers; they were the only ones in the period of this book to match Latin Christian hostility to Muslims. They also had a

[269] Idris, *La Berbérie orientale*, pp. 367–70, 387–400. For the Normans, see n. 16 above.

[270] For Sicily and Byzantium, see p. 252 above and p. 332 below. For Muslim jurists, see, e.g., Lagardère, 'Structures étatiques et communautés rurales: les impositions légales et illégales en al-Andalus et au Maghreb', pp. 65–7; theoretically, the 10% tax was to be imposed on foreign Christians, with Muslims paying 2.5% and Jews and local Christians paying 5%, but this was not often a rule used in practice. The situation in Egypt was, by contrast, far more complicated, with wildly varying levels of customs, as we have also seen (p. 132 above), even if 10% was recognized in some cases. The variation in practice may have been a feature of other less fully documented political systems too, although all we tend to see is the lightening of the 10% tax for favoured merchant groups.

strong fleet, potentially matching those of the Italian ports; and they certainly negotiated from a position of strength, in that in the 1186 treaty they limited Pisan (and thus probably by extension Genoese) trading to Tunis and Béjaïa, plus Ceuta and Oran in Morocco, outside the region we are looking at. The effectiveness of this restriction is confirmed by the fact that the Genoese commercial contracts for North African trading in Giovanni Scriba's register, that is to say, from the years around 1160, are limited almost entirely to Tunis and Béjaïa (plus again Ceuta), with no parallels to the generic trading around Sicily which contracts for the island routinely show. Port-to-port cabotage was clearly excluded, and by implication restricted to North African boats; and major ports like Mahdia almost drop out of our Latin evidence too, although this by no means shows that they ceased to trade.[271]

We do not know the extent of Pisan commerce with Ifrīqiya. Here, unlike in Sicily, it plausibly matched that of Genoa, but the only concrete sign of size is the fact that the city needed to have in the *duana*, the customs house, of Béjaïa in the later twelfth century a *publicus scriba* for Pisan *mercatores*, in which capacity Leonardo Fibonacci's father was employed; it was here that Leonardo himself learned Arabic/Indian numbers, with considerable effects on the future of European mathematics. The Genoese, however, were already in the years around 1160 operating in Béjaïa on a considerable scale, with over forty contracts surviving for the years of Giovanni Scriba's register (Tunis and Ceuta each had around half as many contracts as Béjaïa), and the North Africa trade in general in these years, even though restricted to so few outlets, almost matched that of Sicily in the number of

[271] For Pisan treaties, see Amari, *I diplomi arabi*, 1ª serie, nn. 1 (a. 1157), 2–3 (a. 1181), 5 (a. 1186), 2ª serie, nn. 13, 14 (a. 1181). In 2 and 13 the Pisans complain to the Almohad ruler that a ship taking grain from Sicily and Tripoli has been unjustly confiscated; but Tripoli is not on the Almohad lists, and this may well have been because the trade was illegal. In 3 and 14, indeed, their trade is temporarily restricted even in Béjaïa. In 1166, they added a *fondacum* (*fundūq*) in Mahdia, that is to say, in its suburb of Zawila (Maragone, *Annales pisani*, ed. Lupo Gentile, p. 40), but this concession may have been time-limited. For some comments, see Banti, *Scritti di storia*, pp. 305–50. For the Pisan 'peace' with the Almohads in 1159, see *Vita S. Raynerii*, ed. Zaccagnini, ch. 77, in which Pisan merchants in Tunis are not killed during the Almohad conquest of the city for that reason. For the Genoese treaty, see the brief reference in *Annali genovesi*, 1, ed. Belgrano, p. 62; for 1143, see Belgrano, 'Il registro della curia arcivescovile', p. 9, a list of (some of?) the places across the sea from which the archbishop of Genoa expected tolls from Genoese merchants entering harbour. For Genoese contracts, see *Giovanni Scriba*, s.v. *Buçea* and Tunis in the index. There are, all the same, a handful of Genoese contracts for Gabès and Tripoli (see n. 88 above), and the list of ports Pisans expected to trade in, as listed in their 1186 law code (see n. 245 above), included Tripoli, *Capsa* (Gabès? Inland Gafsa is implausible), and *Soaxi* (Sfax?), as well as Tunis, Béjaïa, and Ceuta; it may be that, out here in the far east of the Almohad state, control was more intermittent than elsewhere. For the Almohad fleet, see Picard, *La mer des califes*, pp. 334–40. For a Tunisian-owned boat in 1184, taken over violently by a Pisan, see D'Amia, *Diritto e sentenze*, n. 23; the Pisan consuls fined the pirate, and the goods were returned. See also Hopley, 'Aspects of trade', pp. 24–35; Schaube, *Handelsgeschichte*, pp. 275–99, is still useful too. Note finally that Roman aristocrats seem to have been interested in trade with Béjaïa as early as 1076; see *Gregorii VII Registrum*, ed. Caspar, 3.21 (cf. Wickham, *Medieval Rome*, p. 165); but this had no follow-up that we know of.

related documents and the size of total financial investments.[272] What Genoa got from Ifrīqiya is impossible to tell in this period, as the contracts never specify it, except two for alum; it is only in the 1180s that we get the first citation of North African wool, which would be the basic export in the thirteenth century from Béjaïa, and also references to leather. What Genoa sent is also ill-documented, but the few references to it, mostly concerning Béjaïa, are above all to cloth—silk, probably from Sicily via Genoa, possibly hempen cloth, fustian by the 1190s, and *tela Yspanie* (cloth of Spain)—plus pepper, and also apparently the raw materials for weaving, flax and raw cotton, the last again presumably originally from Sicily.[273] It is at least clear that Béjaïa, notwithstanding these references to cloth imports, itself had a large enough cloth production for it to be prepared to import raw materials which it had too little of (we might, however, imagine that the basic cloth made there was woollen, for the regional market), just as Sousse on the east coast of Tunisia still had, this time for linen (see p. 196 above), with its own eastern-orientated export trade.

We cannot reconstruct an entire economic system out of under a dozen references to goods, of course. But all the same, the great interest the Genoese and Pisans showed in Béjaïa and Tunis, even if we just take this very early period in their dealings with North Africa, shows that one could make money out of trading here; this in itself shows that some twelfth-century Ifrīqiyan cities did, indeed, have an elaborate enough economy to support such trading—including, doubtless, the cities which were not included in the Almohad trading agreements, which could have funnelled their Italian commerce, using African-owned ships initially, through the two external-facing ports. The ability of Tunis, in particular, to export its glazed ceramics to Sicily, Pisa, and elsewhere from the end of the twelfth century (see p. 185 above) is another sign of this. And some elements of these urban economies depended on a wider hinterland which could supply raw materials; even if wool was not yet produced on a large scale in the mountains and plateaux behind Béjaïa, it soon would be, which resulted, as Valérian argued, in the pastoral specializations which are increasingly attested there for the later middle ages.[274]

[272] See Abulafia, *The two Italies*, p. 99, for overall comparative figures for Genoa. For Fibonacci, see Leonardo [Fibonacci] Pisano, *Liber abbaci*, ed. Boncompagni, *Scritti di Leonardo Pisano*, 1, p. 1. Venetian commerce was also occasional at best: before 1180, only a single voyage appears in Venetian commercial documents, going to Ceuta or Béjaïa in 1177; see p. 515 below.

[273] See *Giovanni Scriba*, 812, 1132, 1222, 1230 (cloth and pepper out), 509, 511, 609, 849 (raw cotton and flax out: this could conceivably be cloth, but it is assessed in sacks or by weight), 812, 1132 (silk, and, unusually, paper out), 1227 (alum back—plus, in 812, wax, and if neither, then gold); a stray document from 1184, appendix X, n. 6, is an early reference to wool from Béjaïa. For comments, see Valérian, *Bougie*, esp. pp. 334–400, 571–9, 596–606 (the most acute study by far, with post-1180 citations of types of goods; 348–50 shows that he too thinks that the exports to Béjaïa around 1160 included flax and raw cotton); and Pistarino, 'Genova e il Maghreb', a detailed analysis. See also Krueger, 'Genoese trade with northwest Africa'; Mansouri, 'Produits agricoles et commerce maritime'; and for a later period, see Rouighi, *The making of a Mediterranean emirate*, pp. 76–94.

[274] Valérian, *Bougie*, pp. 204–5.

Is this, however, enough for us to be able to argue that Ifrīqiya had, in the twelfth century, as coherent an internal economy as it had had in the eleventh, and as Sicily had in each century, and both before and after? The answer here has to be no. As already noted, what has just been presented is not good enough evidence for us to say either way; and the rest of what we know of the region's economic context argues against it too. The fact that the region's major cities were by now all on the coast is not in itself a problem—it was true for Sicily too, and had long been—but the fact that in the twelfth century the interior was not visibly integrated with the port cities, apart from some specific areas, notably Béjaïa's developing wool supplies, and doubtless also the wheat-rich backlands of Tunis, is more of a difficulty. The recurring need for Sicilian wheat in the cities on the coast, mentioned earlier, also shows that internal connections with the Tunisian wheat lands were sometimes imperfect. Ifrīqiya's most active economic elements were stretched thin, all along the coastline. The fact that much of the interior was more ecologically challenging, on the edge of the Sahara as it was and is, than was that of other regions in this book, would not have helped here. Kairouan was a really good choice for a capital, it turned out, for in its heyday it linked the coast with the interior better than Ifrīqiya otherwise managed for the rest of its premodern history. Africa was, of course, rich under the Romans, as we have seen, but that was in large part as a specialized export-focussed economy, in the only period in human history when the Mediterranean was ruled by a single state, which itself had considerable need for African products, especially grain and oil. So we should see the situation in our period not as a comedown, but, rather, as normal for the region, with the Roman period as atypical.

The other reason why the development of Italian trade with Béjaïa and Tunis, although it was clearly substantial in scale from quite early, is no guide to the wider region has already been shown by our late medieval Sicilian evidence; after the end of Roman state demand, external trade, even in bulk goods, which is what we are discussing here, was a very small proportion of the regional economy. In Sicily, this was underpinned by considerable levels of internal demand, not least because the peasantry of the island very often had access to a substantial amount of disposable surplus. We cannot be sure of the same for Ifrīqiya, where documented rent levels—even given that the evidence is wholly inadequate—seem to have been unusually high, even if not all peasants were tenants (pp. 172–5); peasant buying power may have been patchy as a result. Furthermore, in the case of Ifrīqiya after 1100, what traders were dealing with was a set of economically complex micro-regions, not linked tightly together. Béjaïa was one, Tunis another; Mahdia, given its active past history (as well as some sketchy archaeology; see p. 184 above) was probably a third; and the olive region down the eastern Tunisian coast to Sfax was doubtless a fourth, since, for centuries to come, it remained the largest-scale source of quality oil in the Mediterranean, an obvious source for anyone who needed it. This is hypothesis; only a proper, excavation-based study of ceramics in Tunisia and eastern Algeria for the period after 1100 would allow it properly to be tested. But it seems to me to best fit the evidence we have. And what it means is that as a more fragmented regional economy, Ifrīqiya was by now, as it was not earlier, the junior partner to Sicily, even though the two economies remained tightly linked.

So in the tenth and eleventh centuries, the first two-thirds of the period of this book, Sicily and North Africa together were central to Mediterranean exchange, thanks largely to Egyptian shipping, and thanks above all to their internal economic strength. In the twelfth, thanks by now largely to northern Italian shipping, Sicily remained central, with its southern neighbour becoming less central, if still, certainly, active. Sicily's resilience owed much to the long-term agricultural prosperity of its interior, which we have been able to look at in detail, including in its developments and changes in focus, thanks to the archaeological and (to a smaller extent) the documentary record; the lesser resilience of Ifrīqiya owed much to the absence of anything similar. As a result, far from facing economic marginalization, as used to be argued, Sicily was one of the success stories of the Mediterranean, not just in our period but for long after. It remained the hinge of Mediterranean exchange. As such, it will be a point of reference for the regional discussions that follow.

4
Byzantium

4.1 Introduction

The Byzantines were fascinated by the sea. They sailed on it, they ate its products, and they used it, over and over again, in literary imagery. John, the founder of the monastery of Phoberos a little to the north of Constantinople, in a rule for his monastery dating to after 1113, remarks that 'If a helmsman were to flee from the sea because a storm occurred once or twice or often, we would not sail the sea and life would become useless, everything would be utterly ruined, and the earth uninhabited.' Instead, a shipwrecked trader would relaunch and face off uncertainty, as, presumably, a monastery would do too. Alexander Kazhdan held that 'The Byzantines were afraid of... the sea,' apparently because shipwrecks were a major feature of literature; that is certainly true, as we find with some repetition in verse romances, but John of Phoberos helps us to see that this was simply a recognition that the sea—essential to human existence—should be treated with respect.[1]

The sea was, indeed, seen as an inescapable part of normal life. The politics of officeholding, as John Mauropous remarked in the mid-eleventh century, was, after all, itself like sailing in storms.[2] People who could afford it routinely travelled by ship rather than by land, as when monks from Mount Latros, a major monastic focus halfway down the western Turkish coast, did when they had to go to Constantinople for a court case, or when monks from Mount Athos, a peninsula with straightforward access to land, went out for quite ordinary monastic business. Monasteries, if near the sea, as these and many others were, were regularly fitted out with boats which they used to sell their products, some of them on a large scale; this was particularly the case for the Athos monasteries, but not only them. Luke of Steiris (d. 953), a saint who spent much of his life on or near the north coast of the Gulf of Corinth, regularly encountered sailors, both as friends and enemies, and did miracles for some of them, according to his saint's life. The

[1] The text is edited in Papadopoulos-Kerameus, *Noctes Petropolitanae*, ch. 18 (pp. 31–2); the translation is taken from *BMFD*, 3, p. 903; for the romances, see Jeffreys, *Four Byzantine novels*. For comment, see Kazhdan and Constable, *People and power*, p. 42; contrast Browning, 'The city and the sea.' I am very grateful to Pamela Armstrong, Leslie Brubaker, and John Haldon for critical readings of this chapter.

[2] Mauropous, *Poems*, ed. Bernard and Livanos, n. 92. Cf. Psellus, *Epistulae*, ed. Papaioannou, n. 383 (Psellos, *Epistolai*, ed. Sathas, n. 150), refusing the abbacy of a monastery; he is in retirement, so is like an old sailor, of no use in a shipwreck; see also Psellus, *Chronographia*, ed. Reinsch, 7.55: Constantine IX took over the state as if it was a ship loaded to the waterline; he overloaded it, and it sank (cf. McCartney, 'The use of metaphor', pp. 87–9, for this text's sea imagery).

The Donkey and the Boat. Chris Wickham, Oxford University Press. © Chris Wickham 2023.
DOI: 10.1093/oso/9780198856481.003.0004

Life of Cyril Phileotes (d. *c*.1110) recounts how he became the assistant to a ship's captain (*kybernētēs*) as part of his ascesis, and here too compares a boat to a monastery and the captain to the abbot. Untrained priests from trading backgrounds, according to Christopher of Mytilene in the mid-eleventh century, supposedly said 'Let us set sail' rather than 'Let us worship' in the liturgy.[3] Bishops and other letter writers from the literary elite routinely sent fish to each other as gifts, generally preserved in salt—and, indeed, we know far more about fish-eating from a wide range of Byzantine sources than is the case for any other part of the Mediterranean in our period.[4] Inland towns were wretched if one could not get fish there, as John Mauropous complained about Euchaita (modern Avkat or Beyözü) in north-central Anatolia, where he had become bishop in around 1050; sea views were, Michael Psellos said, a plus for houses.[5]

The centrality of the sea in texts like these was, of course, closely linked to the fact that the Byzantine Empire of the long eleventh century itself centred on the Aegean Sea—and its offshoot, the Sea of Marmara. It was a land empire too, certainly, but its very structure depended on a maritime involvement, and writers like these reflected that in their values. Constantinople, its capital, was surrounded by sea on three sides; it was the only capital of any of the major states discussed in this book to be on the sea at all, apart from Palermo. The Byzantines, even those who were not merchants, were more involved with the sea than most of the inhabitants of the other regions analysed here, except the Venetians, Pisans, and Genoese in Italy—and the Venetians, at least, counted as Byzantine citizens in part. And certainly, its trading and exchange activity very often went by sea and was greatly facilitated by it. Paradoxically, this did not result in a greater openness to the wider Mediterranean than we find in other regions—almost the opposite, in fact, as we shall see at the end of this chapter. But it certainly meant that the Aegean was an active internal trading zone; at its height, in the twelfth century, it was arguably the most densely trafficked sector of the whole Mediterranean. It will feature very substantially in what follows.

Byzantine exchange—and the Byzantine economy in general—is currently well studied. In fact, for the subject matter of this book, Byzantium is (together with

[3] *Life of Paul the younger*, ed. Sirmond, ch. 34; *Life of Athanasios of Athos, version B*, ed. Greenfield and Talbot, ch. 77, which features boats elsewhere too: chs 33, 35, 69, 72; *The life and miracles of Saint Luke of Steiris*, ed. Connor and Connor, chs 31, 49, 52, 54; *La vie de saint Cyrille*, ed. Sargologos, 5.1–2; Christopher of Mytilene, *Poems*, ed. Bernard and Livanos, n. 63. See p. 321 below for Athonite shipping, which was often substantial, and that of the monastery of Patmos.

[4] See, e.g., *Theophylacti Achridensis epistulae*, ed. Gautier, nn. 13, 73; Psellus, *Epistulae*, ed. Papaioannou, nn. 83, 444 (Psellos, *Epistolai*, ed. Sathas, n. 104, and *Epistole*, ed. Maltese, n. 9); Michel Italikos, *Lettres*, ed. Gautier, n. 19; cf. Karpozelos, 'Realia', esp. pp. 23–5. For fish-eating, the satire in *Poèmes prodromiques*, ed. Hesseling and Pernot, poem 3, ll. 93–6, 144–63, 174–85, 203–6, 275–80, on monastic diets is classic (note that I use this edition of Ptochoprodromos rather than the more recent one by Eideneier, following W. J. Aerts's review of the latter, 'Ptochoprodromos'). See in general Ragia, 'The circulation, distribution and consumption of marine products', with earlier bibliography.

[5] Mauropous, *Letters*, ed. Karpozilos, n. 64; Psellus, *Epistulae*, ed. Papaioannou, n. 258 (Psellos, *Epistulae*, ed. Kurtz and Drexl, n. 125).

Sicily) the best-synthesized of all the regions covered here. I shall be using the findings of a wider set of scholars, especially recent ones, as a result, and make fewer claims here for novelty of interpretation. This is the case both for its documentary history and for its archaeology. Byzantine archaeology is currently active, which helps here, of course. Although it does not have the densest archaeology in the Mediterranean in the long eleventh century—that is certainly Italy (including Sicily), with the Iberian peninsula next—it does, nonetheless, have a number of archaeologists who wish to develop wider syntheses for our period. This is important. Documentary historians of the Byzantine economy do use the archaeological record, but not very systematically for the most part, as is true for documentary historians elsewhere. But field surveys tell us a great deal about the growth in rural settlement; and the distribution of ceramics, a particularly successful part of recent archaeological work on the Byzantine lands, is a direct indicator of the intensity of exchange, as we have seen for Sicily. The material record, when it is clear enough, as here, can be used to build up a more immediate picture of economic structures and change than most written evidence can provide. It is not perfect—it is, in particular, rather better for what is now Greece than for the parts of the empire now in other countries—but it has reached enough critical mass, not only for Greece but for some other places as well. I will privilege it here as a result; after introducing the regions of the Byzantine Empire, I shall discuss the archaeological evidence for exchange first and on its own, before looking at what written sources have to say. As we have already seen, it is essential, where possible, to develop arguments based on each of these two data sets separately, before attempting to synthesize them. The two data sets for Byzantium do not fully match each other at first sight, but they largely do, and they are, anyway, the necessary building blocks for a wider synthesis.[6]

A stress on the archaeology is also necessary because the written evidence for Byzantium in our period, although extensive (it is far more extensive than the evidence for Ifrīqiya and Sicily, which we looked at in Chapter 3), does not by any means tell us as much about the economy as we would like. Contemporary chronicles and other narratives are much more numerous here than in most other parts of the Mediterranean, but, as elsewhere, contain little about exchange or other aspects of economic life—just single nuggets, which are used over and over again by recent historians, but which remain isolated. Poetry, unusually, is sometimes more generous with such nuggets, but they remain casual references, and, as with other sources, can only be understood inside their rhetorical context. Letter collections are similar, for, although there are many of them, they are, as in Latin Europe, worked-up collections from members of the literary elite, and are very different from the original letters from members of less elevated social groups which survive more casually from Egypt. At most, here, the more extensive of

[6] See n. 103 below for some particularly good archaeological syntheses.

them—particularly those of Michael Psellos, from the middle decades of the eleventh century—show networks of interrelationships which we can use to see how, and how far, different provinces were connected.[7] Legislation, another Byzantine strength, does contain some quite detailed discussions of the economic oppressions of the powerful, and attempts to stop them; these are important, although they suffer from the problem which law always has, namely that it tells us more about the minds and fears of legislators than about what actually happened on the ground.[8]

And what Byzantium lacks is large-scale sets of legal documents. The most numerous by far, from the Athos monasteries, make up under 200 texts before 1200. There are others (including some very long and informative foundation texts for monasteries, and some equally long imperial diplomas or chrysobulls), but they hardly, taken as a whole, amount to as much as another hundred, excluding those for Byzantine Italy, which is not discussed here, as southern mainland Italy is not one of the regions covered in this book.[9] Egypt in our period has as many similar texts (backed up by far more private letters), north-central Italy more than a hundred times more. That absence is not the fault of the Byzantines, who were as text-obsessed as the Egyptians (and far more than the Italians), but rather the result of centuries of later foreign conquests by ruling elites, Latin or Turkish, who did not speak Greek and did not value Greek documentation. But it results in the same problem for historians—that our documentary data rarely reach critical mass—and the largest set, those of the Athonite monasteries, are in part an atypical group. They are filled out by Venetian and Genoese commercial documents concerning the empire in the twelfth century, which actually in number nearly match all the pre-1200 documents in Greek put together, but these are equally atypical, although for different reasons.[10] I will be using both a good deal, but their particularity will inevitably limit how much we will be able to generalize from them. On the other hand, when seen in the light of the archaeology, some generalizations can indeed be made, as we shall see as well.

* * *

[7] Psellos' letters have recently been edited in full by Stratis Papaioannou, as Michael Psellus, *Epistulae*. I cite in brackets previous editions, as these have been used by other authors up to now. I have also derived great benefit from the discussion and summary of the whole set in Jeffreys, 'Summaries'. See pp. 281, 290, 295 below.

[8] The laws are all collected in Zepos and Zepos, *Jus graecoromanum*; later editions of parts of the legislation will be cited as relevant. The *Peira* of Eustathios Rhomaios (in Zepos and Zepos, 4, pp. 11–260) is important because it shows some of the laws actually in operation. See p. 341 below.

[9] The Athos texts are edited in the Archives de l'Athos series, by now almost complete; the largest sets for our period are *Actes de Lavra*, 1, and *Actes d'Iviron*, 1–2 (I cite the varying editors of this series only in the Bibliography, so as not to weigh the notes down). For a high percentage of the other documents, see Miklosich and Müller, *Acta*, 4–6, and the set of *typika* conveniently assembled and translated in *BMFD*; later editions of documents will be cited as relevant.

[10] Most of the Venetian commercial documents are edited in *DCV* and *Nuovi documenti* (for texts missed by these, see Chapter 6, n. 94 below); for Genoa, see esp. for our period *Giovanni Scriba*, with a few extra texts in *I libri iurium* [*LI*], a re-edition of most of the still convenient *CDGE*. See pp. 332–9 below.

What historians and archaeologists call the Middle Byzantine period is generally reckoned to stretch from 843, the final end of the disputes over Iconoclasm, to the Fourth Crusade, which captured Constantinople and destroyed the coherence of the Byzantine Empire forever in 1204. The long eleventh century, here as elsewhere 950–1180, sits neatly inside this. The period as a whole was a switchback of success and failure for Byzantine emperors and for the imperial state, although, as we shall see, the economy remained on a more stable—and rising—curve, to an extent even past the fall of the capital. At the beginning of our period, the Byzantine Empire, then called Romania in both Greek and Latin (Rūm in Arabic), consisted essentially of the Aegean and most of its coastline, extending into nearly half of modern Turkey, and also, in the west, to southern Greece and most of the southern Italian mainland. It was a coherent political unit, based on tax-raising powers which it had never given up, even at its low point in the later seventh century, reeling, as it had then been, from the Islamic conquests of over half its territory. The 950s–960s then saw the beginning of a period of Byzantine territorial expansion, profiting from the weakness of the 'Abbāsid Caliphate, which included the capture of Crete, thus securing the Aegean Sea, and which soon saw the extension of imperial power into eastern Anatolia as far as Armenia—whose major kingdoms were taken over one by one, the last of them in 1045, when Byzantine rule briefly extended farther east than had that of the Roman Empire before it—and south-east to Antioch in Syria. From the 970s, this was accompanied by the conquest of the Bulgarian empire, completed in 1018, which had occupied most of the Balkans between the Danube and what is now Greece. The Byzantine state roughly doubled in size as a result, and this has been seen as its apogee by historians who think in politico-military terms. The family ruling at the time was the long-lasting Macedonian dynasty (867–1056), but this gives the wrong impression taken on its own; in the years 919–44 and 963–76 military strongmen took over, with Macedonians as child co-emperors, and then after 1028 two surviving daughters of the family mostly acted as legitimators for male rulers, who succeeded each other with some speed, only one of them, Constantine IX (1042–55), lasting more than a handful of years. The major conquests were the work of two of the strongmen, Nikephoros II Phokas and John I Tzimiskes, in the 960s–970s, and then the long-lived Macedonian, Basil II (963–1025, but ruling in his own name only after John's death in 976).[11]

Historians still argue as to how badly the empire was run after Basil's death; there are certainly cases to be made for the competence of several of the rulers of the next half-century, but there was little continuity of political or military strategy. Byzantium had, anyway, reached what was in effect its maximum plausible extension in terms of the military logistics of the age, and soon had to

[11] See Whittow, *The making of Orthodox Byzantium*, for a convenient survey to 1025; see Kaldellis, *Streams of gold*, for 955–1081 politics.

go onto the defensive in the face of new threats. In the 1050s it lost southern Italy to bands of Norman mercenaries, with such speed that it is hard to see that much attempt was made to prevent it; this was in part because by then it also faced nomadic attacks in the Balkans, as well as the most dangerous military power in the east since the early ninth-century 'Abbāsids, the Selcuk or Saljūq Turks, who defeated and captured Emperor Romanos IV in 1071. The Selcuks did not conquer Anatolia directly (they were more interested in Syria and Iraq), but Byzantine control over it broke down, Turks increasingly settled there, and elsewhere in the empire the faction-fighting which had marked imperial politics since the 1050s turned to civil war. By 1081, when Alexios I Komnenos (1081–1118) emerged as the final winner—he was, indeed, to become the longest-ruling emperor since Basil II—the Balkans and Anatolia were half lost.

In the 1080s Alexios regained the Balkans, which were by now also under Norman threat, but Anatolia slipped further out of his control, and Turkish warlords held some of the eastern Aegean towns. Alexios asked for western help, and it came in 1096 in the largely unwelcome form of the First Crusade. The Crusaders at least helped Alexios to regain the eastern Aegean, however, and by his death the Byzantines had retaken the Anatolian coasts, north and south, and the more fertile parts of the western interior. There the frontier stabilized, under Alexios's son and grandson, John II and Manuel I, who ruled until 1180. So, after the period of military disaster of the 1070s–1080s, the empire righted itself, a sign of its long-term institutional solidity, which had taken it through serious crises before. The three main Komnenoi, in fact, ran the empire firmly for a hundred years, the longest period of government uninterrupted by coup since the sixth century. The empire fell apart after Manuel's death (and after our period), with no able ruler between 1180 and the Latin conquest of 1203–4, and with, by the latter date, a set of provincial revolts which were unmatched in earlier ages, when uprisings had generally been to obtain the imperial title. As always, this has led historians to look for the seeds of collapse well beforehand. But by and large it has recently come to be accepted that the Komnenian century was a period of considerable success and coherence for the Byzantine state. It was a period of considerable economic activity too, as we shall see. We have seen that institutional solidity was by no means vital for economic complexity in our period; but in the twelfth century in Byzantium the two did at least go together chronologically. Alexios I reformed the coinage in the early 1090s, after a period of serious instability, creating a new monetary system based on gold *hyperpera* and copper alloy coins which lasted until 1204; this will certainly have helped.[12]

This rapid political overview illustrates one essential point: the geographical mutability of the Byzantine state in the long eleventh century. (See Map 13.) In

[12] There is no general recent history of the Komnenian period. Magdalino, *The empire of Manuel I*, only covers one reign, but his insights work for all of them. For the stabilization of the coinage and the twelfth century, see Hendy, *Studies*, pp. 513–19; Hendy, 'Byzantium, 1081–1204: the economy revisited', pp. 36–41; Laiou and Morrisson, *The Byzantine economy*, pp. 151–5; Baker, *Coinage and money*, pp. 8–18.

950, the core of the empire was the Aegean/Marmara and Anatolia, with inland Greece and southern Italy as, in effect, appendages of that heartland. Only for the brief period *c.*1020–50 did the empire remain at its farthest extent; and after the troubles of the late eleventh century, it emerged with a very different territory. In 1150, the core still included the Aegean/Marmara, but by now it was joined to the Balkans (including Greece), and it was western Anatolia which was an appendage. The Aegean and its islands and coasts, plus, of course, the lands around the capital, were thus the only area which stayed imperial all through our period, as a stable and safe territory—safe after the conquest of Crete in 960–1 at least (though there was certainly Aegean exchange before that), with the single and brief exception of the 1090s, when part of the Anatolian coast was occupied by Turks. That is to say, for all that there were plenty of hinterlands in every period, only the Aegean remained central—which is another reason why the sea was so important for the Byzantines. It also means that it is hard to deal with the empire as a single block; it consisted of half a dozen smaller regions, which had quite different histories, were also very different ecologically and socio-economically, and therefore need to be dealt with separately. We will come to them after this introduction. But first, let us look at how the economic history of Byzantium has, overall, been treated by the historiography hitherto.

* * *

Until the 1980s, the Middle Byzantine economy was largely seen as unchanging, if not stagnant. This paradigm for the period had three main strands. First, the state was seen as increasingly dominated by what the Russian/Yugoslav historian George Ostrogorsky in 1940 called *Feudalmächte* or (in the English translation) 'feudal magnates'. They were supposedly part of the faction-fighting around emperors, representing a military wing opposed to civilian bureaucrats (see p. 316 below), and they increased their landed wealth and power systematically from the ninth century onwards, despite imperial legislation in the tenth against the 'powerful' (*dynatoi*). The taxpaying peasant base of the empire was undermined, and so was commercial enterprise in towns. This reached its height when the aristocracy fully took over the state under the Komnenoi, and began to 'feudalize' even the army, through the farming out of local tax rights in *pronoia* to members of the military elite. This picture fully matches a similar interpretative imagery for the Islamic world, that of the negative effects of military tax-farming grants of *iqṭā*ʿ, which historians have also called 'feudal' (see p. 36 above); in both contexts, this form of feudalism apparently stifled economic growth, more completely than did its supposed role in the West. Even a strong opponent of the terminology of feudalism, Paul Lemerle, did not disagree with this last point; he could in 1977 regard the twelfth-century economy as 'cassée' ('broken').[13] Secondly, the commerce of the

[13] Ostrogorsky, *History of the Byzantine state*, 2nd edn, pp. 239–44 for feudal magnates, and 327–33 for Komnenian feudalization, *pronoia*, etc. For the general assumptions of the 1970s, see, e.g., Svoronos,

empire was steadily taken over by the Italians, above all by the Venetians, who had trading privileges by 992, made even more extensive, with almost total customs immunities, by Alexios I in 1092 after the Venetians helped him against the Norman invasions of the Balkans. This meant that any commercial profit that there was accrued only to outsiders, who slowly gained an ever-increasing role in the empire; this was made that much worse because the Venetians in the end were the architects of the Fourth Crusade's taking of Constantinople in 1203–4—they were, so to speak, fifth columnists in the heart of the Byzantine polity.[14]

The Venetian argument is implausible in this form, although variants of it survive, as we shall see. The aristocratic argument, however, has developed a different inflection, in the third strand of the paradigm. It certainly was the case, as we shall also see, that aristocratic—including ecclesiastical—landowning steadily increased across our period (although the *pronoia*, even if perhaps expanding under Manuel I, remained marginal until after 1204,[15] and the 'feudalization' of the state under the Komnenoi is a mirage). What effect that had on the economy is by now, however, much more a matter of debate. Michel Kaplan in 1992, in his major work on the agrarian economy, stated that the problem of great estates for the economy was that the rents they took were too low, thus not allowing for investment and commercial demand. This argument turns the argument of Ostrogorsky and others on its head; the economy was 'cassée' because of aristocratic weakness and thus insufficient buying power, not aristocratic strength; but it was still in trouble. Kaplan has more recently changed his views, in the face of new interpretations and evidence.[16] But the idea that the Byzantine economy was not going anywhere much was widely accepted until quite recently.

Things suddenly changed in the late 1980s. Michael Hendy had actually made an entirely opposite argument as early as 1970, proposing that the Byzantine economy was 'expanding rapidly' in the eleventh and twelfth centuries; this was a minority view then, but it was reinforced by Alan Harvey's 1989 book, explicitly influenced by Hendy, which was called, flatly, *Economic expansion in the Byzantine Empire, 900–1200*. Neither stressed commerce very much—Harvey, in particular, paid more attention to agrarian growth—but Alexander Kazhdan and Ann Wharton Epstein had made a similar argument about the urban economy slightly earlier (in Kazhdan's case earlier still, in Russian). David Jacoby's 1990s articles

'Remarques'. For Lemerle, see *Cinq études*, p. 309; the specific context for the phrase is the monetary devaluation of the eleventh century, which Lemerle saw (wrongly) as a permanent disaster, but pp. 309–12 take us quickly to the *pronoia* as well.

[14] See, e.g., (out of many) Mango, *Byzantium*, p. 58, on the Venetian privileges. I accept the redating of the chrysobull of Alexios from 1082 to 1092 by Frankopan, 'Byzantine trade privileges to Venice'.

[15] See most recently Bartusis, *Land and privilege*, esp. pp. 160–70.

[16] Kaplan, *Les hommes*, esp. pp. 535–40 (some modest agrarian expansion in the eleventh century, all to the profit of aristocrats), 569–73 (but, on the other hand, aristocratic underinvestment); his later views are more visible in Kaplan, *Byzance: villes et campagnes*, pp. 282–314, Kaplan, 'Monks and trade', and Estangüi Gómez and Kaplan, 'La société rurale'.

on, among other things, Byzantium's active silk production emphasized commerce more, which brought it into focus too.[17] These views from then on rapidly gained support, and by 2002 the huge international *Economic history of Byzantium*, masterminded by the Harvard scholar Angeliki Laiou, took (with only a few outliers) this new position for granted. Laiou and the French numismatist Cécile Morrisson then generalized it in a short but very dense volume on the Byzantine economy as a whole in 2007: 'there is no question that the Byzantine economy experienced secular growth' from the late eighth century onwards, and 'accelerated' from the tenth; the urban economy 'reached its heights' in the twelfth. In this context, the driving force was now the positive effect of greater aristocratic wealth and demand, and thus a wider market which peasants, even if more exploited, could participate in, which was not limited until well after 1204.[18]

Laiou and Morrisson's book, in effect, represents the currently dominant interpretation.[19] Indeed, I fully agree with its main thrust, and it uses archaeology too; its insights will reappear throughout this chapter. But it is interesting that it had been possible to overturn the views of half a century and more of scholars without changing the evidence base very much at all. Hendy initially used the early Corinth and Athens excavations as bases for his arguments, it is true, and so did Kazhdan. Later, however, Harvey, Jacoby, and even most of the *Economic history*, did not use archaeology much (it is true that in the 1980s–1990s there was less to use); they relied on reinterpretations of already substantially studied documentary sources, plus, in the case of Hendy and Morrisson, a dense understanding of the numismatics of the period. That it was possible to do this is a further sign of the weakness of the Byzantine written record in itself, at least concerning the economy; it does not lend itself to a single interpretation without question. This is a further reason why I will pay more attention to the archaeological evidence. Written texts give depth to the archaeology, and—as is normal when comparing the two sets of evidence—a far clearer understanding of agency; but in the

[17] Hendy, 'Byzantium, 1081–1204' (quotation at p. 52); Harvey, *Economic expansion*, developed in Harvey, 'The middle Byzantine economy'; Kazhdan and Wharton Epstein, *Change*, pp. 25–48. See the Bibliography for Jacoby's many articles on this topic; Jacoby, *Trade, commodities* collects the articles of the 1990s; 'Byzantine trade with Egypt', from 2000, and 'Byzantine maritime trade', from 2017, one of his last articles, are also important. Cf. also, from the 1990s, Patlagean, 'Byzance et les marchés du grand commerce'. Surprisingly, Hendy, *Studies*, his major book on the monetary economy, hardly discussed economic growth at all; it was focussed on the relation of money to the state's fiscal needs, and downplayed commerce. But Hendy, 'Byzantium, 1081–1204: the economy revisited', written in the light of Harvey's book, is a much stronger statement of the development of commerce in the empire, and reinterprets some of his 1985 material with more commercially focussed explanations (e.g. the distribution of smaller coinage in twelfth-century Greece, p. 25; cf. Hendy, *Studies*, pp. 601–2).

[18] See in general Laiou, *The economic history of Byzantium*; Laiou and Morrisson, *The Byzantine economy*, pp. 90–1 (quotations), and, more generally, 90–165; of Laiou's other works, I would single out her 'Exchange and trade' and 'The Byzantine city: parasitic or productive?'. Morrisson, 'Revisiter le XIe siècle', pp. 614–18, is a parallel historiographical survey to this.

[19] As shown in three significant article collections on trade: Mundell Mango, *Byzantine trade*; Morrisson, *Trade and markets*; and Magdalino and Necipoğlu, *Trade in Byzantium*; and also the journal, *Travaux et mémoires*, 21/2 (2017), pp. 419–807, a set of articles on the eleventh century.

specific context of Byzantine evidence, they are much better understood if the framework is derived from archaeology.

4.2 Byzantine Internal Economic Differences

As already noted, the Byzantine Empire was not a single economic unit; it was, indeed, more varied in its economy and even ecology than any of the other regions discussed in this book. Broadly, at least five separate economic areas, or subregions, can be distinguished in the empire in the long eleventh century. They need to be kept distinct in what follows in this chapter, for lumping them together would mean that we were not comparing like with like. In turn, they are: the capital and the lands around the Sea of Marmara; the Aegean Sea and its coastal areas; the Anatolian plateau; the northern Balkans, that is to say, what is now Bulgaria and some of the states of the former Yugoslavia; and the southern Adriatic and Ionian Seas, that is to say, the western Greek/Albanian seaboard and the far south of mainland Italy. These are rough divisions, but I think that they can be distinguished with reasonable clarity, on the basis of both archaeology and written sources. Let us look at them briefly in turn, although with most emphasis on the first three (for all of them, see Maps 13 and 14).[20]

4.2.1 Constantinople and the Marmara

Constantinople sits on the Sea of Marmara, and on the Bosporos strait looking north to the Black Sea. It had been since the fourth century—as Istanbul still is today—the focus for the provinces (*themata*, 'themes') immediately south and north of the Marmara, Bithynia (from the seventh century the theme of Opsikion, although it was later subdivided), and Thrace, which supplied the capital, and in which many leading figures owned estates; they, therefore, belong in this section too. Constantinople, like the Islamic capitals we have been looking at in Chapters 2 and 3, was the centre of a strong and centralized tax-raising state, and most of its principal landowning and salaried official elites lived there; it thus drew in a substantial

[20] Cherson is missed out: the Byzantine Crimea was physically separate from other imperial provinces, and was part of a Black Sea network which this book does not discuss. See most recently Rabinowitz et al., 'Daily life in a provincial late Byzantine city'. It had a complex economy in the late eleventh to early thirteenth century, and was probably the focus for twelfth-century export penetrations into what is now Ukraine and Russia (see, e.g., Vroom, 'Shifting Byzantine networks', plus Günsenin, 'La typologie des amphores Günsenin', p. 97 for the tenth and early eleventh centuries). Byzantine southern Italy will not be treated directly either, as noted in the Introduction; but it was linked sufficiently into Mediterranean networks that it cannot be entirely cut out, as we shall see. For a general historical geography of the whole empire, focussed on the twelfth century, see Lilie, *Handel und Politik*, pp. 117–242; it is incomplete, but it is a useful starting point.

part of the surplus of the whole empire, and both its size and its demand were considerable. In the long eleventh century Constantinople grew rapidly, from a low point around 700, and was, by 1150 or so, at least the second-largest city in the Mediterranean as a whole, after Fusṭāṭ-Cairo.

How large was that, though? We saw (pp. 41, 98) that it is very hard to guess at the size of the Egyptian capital, but that 200,000 in 1000 and 250,000 in the thirteenth century are quite possible figures. It is even harder to guess at Constantinople's size at its twelfth-century height. Hendy estimated it at around 200,000, Jacoby at 250,000. But Geoffroy de Villehardouin, a contemporary French chronicler, put its population at 400,000 inhabitants in 1204; he did so in a highly rhetorical context, but Paul Magdalino is inclined to accept this figure as a ballpark estimate for the end of our period, for it roughly fits other figures (the 54,000 clerics in *c.*1200 claimed by a Russian traveller, for example). Gilbert Dagron, Laiou and Morrisson, and Kaplan are happy to follow him.[21] That would almost certainly make it the largest city in the Mediterranean. But the land area of Saladin's walls around Fusṭāṭ-Cairo is much the same size as the walled area of Constantinople, and the population of the latter by no means extended to the whole territory inside its walls (see Map 25); the Egyptian city also had high apartment blocks of a type never described for the Byzantine capital (see p. 41 above), where houses with just an upper storey, and occasionally an extra floor, are the most that is recorded.[22] Even allowing for a high density for Constantinople's housing, one would be hard put to argue that medieval figures given by external visitors, which are generally greatly inflated, are enough to push the population past that which is now coming to be accepted for Fusṭāṭ-Cairo. So I would myself propose that for Constantinople we might be looking at 150,000 inhabitants or a bit more in the twelfth century, after a period of substantial demographic growth. All the same, I, like Jacoby and Magdalino, am engaging in guesstimates which do not much differ in their weak empirical base from those of Villehardouin, and all these figures really just mean 'a lot'. What is more important is simply that this figure, whatever it ends up as being accepted to be, was very high by medieval standards, and that it was as

[21] Hendy, 'Byzantium, 1081–1204: the economy revisited', p. 19; Jacoby, 'La population', p. 109; Magdalino, *Constantinople médiévale*, pp. 55–9; Dagron, 'The urban economy', pp. 394–5; Laiou and Morrison, *The Byzantine economy*, p. 131; Kaplan, *Byzance: villes et campagnes*, p. 270. Cf. Villehardouin, *La conquête*, ed. Faral, 2, ch. 251; strongly doubted by Jacoby, 'The Greeks of Constantinople', p. 54, and Jacoby, 'Byzantine maritime trade', p. 629. Magdalino's book remains the best introduction to the city's topography in our period.

[22] City housing frequently consisted of courtyard houses (*aulai*) with shops, in both Constantinople and Thessaloniki—in this respect with some parallels in Fusṭāṭ. Examples for Thessaloniki: *Actes de Docheiariou*, n. 4, *Actes de Xénophon*, n. 1, *Actes de Lavra*, 1, n. 59; for Constantinople: Gautier, 'La diataxis de Michel Attaliate', p. 43. See in general Sigalos, 'Housing people', pp. 198–210; Sigalos, *Housing*, pp. 73–9; Dark, 'Houses, streets and shops'. Three floors: Tzetzes, *Epistulae*, ed. Leone, n. 18 (p. 33); *Der Epitaphios des Nikolaos Mesarites*, ed. Heisenberg, p. 46; both are references in rhetorical contexts. I am grateful to Francisco Lopez-Santos Kornberger for helping me with Tzetzes's prose, here and in nn. 135, 143 below.

politically vital as it was for Fusṭāṭ to get the city fed properly. This need dominated imperial administration, almost as much as did military defence.

It has to be said immediately that the Byzantine state seems to have been pretty successful in supplying its capital with food. Famines are reported, but they do not reach the scale of those claimed for the Egyptian capital.[23] Military blockades by enemies or usurpers sometimes aimed at starving the capital of food—it was a logical thing to attempt to do, and Egyptian rebels did the same—but they never succeeded here, in large part because Constantinople was above all supplied by sea, and it was hard to block all directions at once, into Thrace/Bithynia on each side of the Marmara, north up the Bosporos to the Black Sea, and west through the Dardanelles to the Aegean. But the worry was always there. Eparchs (city governors) and other administrators who did not oversee a satisfactory food supply were reviled, as with Nikephoros II's brother Leo in the 960s.[24] The Middle Byzantine government did not feed the city with state grain or other foodstuffs; everything was brought in by private enterprise. But the *Book of the Eparch*, a set of rules made by the city authorities for Constantinople's traders, artisans, and food sellers dating to around 900, shows how controlled the supply of food was—or was supposed to be. Hoarding was prohibited. Bakers (*artopoioi*) had to buy in state warehouses and at prices fixed by the eparch, and could only make 4 per cent profit, after paying their workmen; 17 per cent was the permitted profit for grocers (*saldamarioi*), who sold other basic foods. Cattle and sheep butchers (*makellarioi*) had to buy their animals far out of the city, on the edge of the Anatolian plateau, where we know from other sources there was extensive stock-raising, and only shepherds themselves (i.e. small-scale figures) could bring their own sheep into the capital to sell; pork butchers (*choiremporoi*), by contrast, could only buy in the capital, and not outside; fishmongers (*ichthyopratai*) could not buy up catches at sea, but only on the shore. Such contradictory rulings were evidently to keep prices down and to prevent the corralling of markets. This sort of control recalls that of Fusṭāṭ quite closely (see p. 62 above), and, as there, we can hardly imagine that such tight regulation worked all or even much of the time; but it was there for use if needed, and its ambition was striking. Laiou has argued strongly that this was a free market, unlike that of the Roman Empire, and in strict terms she is correct, but it was a market whose full freedom was too risky, and the state did not take risks.[25]

[23] e.g. *Theophanes Continuatus*, ed. Bekker, p. 479, for the famine of 961, dealt with by the state bringing in merchant ships with grain from 'east and west'; for the 1037 famine, grain was similarly bought from central and southern Greece; see Skylitzes, *Synopsis historiarum*, ed. Thurn, Michael IV, ch. 10 (p. 400).

[24] Leo the Deacon, *Historiai*, ed. Hase, 4.6; Skylitzes, *Synopsis historiarum*, ed. Thurn, Nikephoros II, ch. 20 (pp. 277–8): Leo (and Nikephoros) supposedly sold state grain at excessive prices.

[25] For the text, see Koder, *Das Eparchenbuch*, who argues (pp. 31–2) for the date of *c.*912. Good recent commentaries with full bibliography are Dagron, 'The urban economy', pp. 405–14, 438–61; Howard-Johnston, 'Le commerce à Byzance', pp. 316–35. The over-complex rules for buying meat are

Grain came in from Macedonia and Thessaly and the Black Sea coast, wine from the Aegean coasts and islands.[26] But Thrace and Bithynia were the closest provinces, and there is no doubt that the core food supply for the capital depended on them first. Bithynia had long been a preferred location for the estates of the elites of Constantinople (including emperors) and thus for produce destined for the city in rent, and it was very much inside the mental horizon of their members. Out of Psellos' more than a hundred letters to provincial governors from the middle decades of the eleventh century, to friends, patrons, and clients alike, well over a third were to the themes of Bithynia alone (he owned estates there too).[27] As to Thrace, it is not chance that the dominant amphora type in tenth- and eleventh-century Byzantium, Günsenin 1, a wine amphora, was largely made at Ganos (modern Gaziköy), a major production centre some 160 kilometres west of the capital on the Marmara coast, and has been found in very large numbers in the wrecks excavated from the Port of Theodosios (Yenikapı) in Istanbul. As we shall see, Ganos amphorae travelled in many directions, but their scale was underwritten by the needs of the capital.[28] Just 30 kilometres closer in, at Rhaidestos (Tekirdağ), there was a large grain market in the eleventh century focussed on the needs of Constantinopolitan buyers, which had small-scale as well as large-scale dealers—peasants, not just landlords. In the 1070s, in a much-quoted passage of the chronicler Michael Attaleiates, a senior imperial official for Michael VII centralized that market in a state warehouse or *phoundax* (from Arabic *fundūq*), which both sellers and buyers henceforth had to deal through and (not least) pay the commercial tax, *kommerkion*, to—such a system would, indeed, have made

perhaps undermined by Leo of Synada's casual early eleventh-century reference to all kinds of animals being imported into the capital from the port of Pylai, just across the Marmara: *Letters*, ed. Vinson, n. 54. For the free market, see Laiou, 'Exchange and trade', pp. 718–21, 741–6; this stresses government action as well, as does Laiou, 'Byzantium and the commercial revolution', pp. 249–51. Laiou sees the market as getting steadily freer after the mid-eleventh century; but the state could not have taken provisioning risks in 1150 either. For relatively late references to a direct imperial intervention in grain transport, see, e.g., Psellus, *Epistulae*, ed. Papaioannou, n. 372 (Psellos, *Epistolai*, ed. Sathas, n. 31), for state grain inspection and pricing; John Oxites, ed. Gautier, 'Diatribes', p. 31, for imperial grain merchants in 1091; and see n. 24 above for famines. The state-organized commissariat for Crusaders coming through from 1096 onwards was particularly elaborate, even if for the most part the emperor sold, rather than gave, food to the armies; see, e.g., Anna Komnene, *Alexias*, ed. Reinsch et al., 13.7.2, on Bohemond's army, and, in general, Laiou, 'Byzantine trade with Christians and Muslims', pp. 161–8.

[26] See, e.g., Michael Choniates, *Epistulae*, ed. Kolovou, n. 50. *Poèmes prodromiques*, ed. Hesseling and Pernot, poem 3, gives numerous references to wine from Chios and other islands. Fish and vegetables could—and had to—be obtained locally; see Koder, 'Fresh vegetables'; Dagron, 'Poissons, pêcheurs'. For the supply of the capital in general, see also Gerolymatou, *Agores, emporioi*, pp. 74–89; Jacoby, 'Mediterranean food and wine for Constantinople', a helpful overview, although focussed on the period after 1204.

[27] Estates: Cheynet, 'L'époque byzantine', pp. 320–3; Andriollo and Métivier, 'Quel rôle pour les provinces', p. 515; Jeffreys, 'Michael Psellos and the monastery', pp. 53–5. Figures for letters are from Jeffreys, 'Summaries'.

[28] Günsenin, *Les amphores*, pp. 47–56, updated in 2018 in Günsenin, 'La typologie des amphores Günsenin', pp. 92–7; *Stories from the hidden harbor*, pp. 9, 211–15. A little later, there was glazed-ware production on the site too; see Armstrong and Günsenin, 'Glazed pottery production at Ganos'.

the tax much harder to evade. Attaleiates, who had estates in Rhaidestos and was evidently one of the dealers, was outraged, claiming that the price of grain shot up. Whether or not this is true—in terms of simple economics it is certainly plausible—the next emperor, Nikephoros III (1078–81), abandoned the *phoundax*, after the rebel Nikephoros Bryennios in 1080 took Rhaidestos and it was destroyed.[29] But the whole sequence underlines the importance of Thrace as a food supplier to the capital, and the importance of the capital to the Thracian economy, especially, but doubtless not only, on the coast.

So this part of the empire was structurally tied into the capital at all times, and made considerable amounts of money out of it. We know less about the major cities of the Marmara region, Adrianople (Edirne), Prousa (Bursa), Nicaea (İznik), and Nikomedeia (İzmit), but they appear sufficiently often as active centres in our texts for us to be able to argue that they also benefited from the economy of Constantinople's food supply.[30] That in itself justifies separating the region off from its neighbours, particularly the otherwise similar Aegean Sea coasts, at the other end of the Dardanelles straits. Those coasts regularly supplied Constantinople too, and with all kinds of products—in addition to grain and wine, Spartan oil, or Cretan and Thessalian cheese[31]—but it is less easy to argue that their economies depended on it. (It can be added that one thing they could not easily avoid was the *kommerkion*, for anyone coming to the Marmara by sea had to stop at Abydos, close to modern Çanakkale, the great harbour and state depot on the Dardanelles.[32]) How those economies themselves worked we will come to shortly.

Constantinople did not only consume. Urban archaeology in Istanbul is weaker than for Fusṭāṭ-Cairo and Palermo, or (as we shall see in Chapter 5) Córdoba, and in this period hardly tells us about more than churches, plus the ceramics found in their levels and in the Yenikapı port;[33] we also do not have anything which can remotely match the wealth of the *geniza* evidence for Fusṭāṭ's commercial life. All the same, our normative and literary source material, even though it seldom discusses economic topics except glancingly, shows that almost every type of production can be attached to the city. The *Book of the Eparch* focusses on silk

[29] Attaleiates, *Historia*, ed. Pérez Martín, pp. 366–72, 444–54; cf. Gautier, 'La diataxis de Michel Attaliate', pp. 23, 25, 29, 39, 43, 49, 99 for his land in and near the town, turned into a monastery in 1077. Commentary on the *phoundax*: among many others, Magdalino, 'The grain supply', pp. 39–45; Harvey, *Economic expansion*, pp. 236–8; Gerolymatou, *Agores, emporioi*, pp. 198–201; Laiou and Morrison, *The Byzantine economy*, pp. 135–6.

[30] Adrianople: see, e.g., Magdalino, *The empire of Manuel I*, pp. 152–3. For Prousa, Nicaea, and Nikomedeia, see Bondoux, 'Les villes', pp. 384–6, 396–402. Nicaea is written up by al-Idrīsī, *Nuzhat al-mushtaq*, trans. Jaubert and Nef, pp. 414–15.

[31] Cretan cheese: see, e.g., *Poèmes prodromiques*, ed. Hesseling and Pernot, poem 3, l. 98.

[32] See Oikonomides, 'Le kommerkion d'Abydos', pp. 241–4. For commercial taxes in general, see Gerolymatou, *Agores, emporioi*, pp. 204–21. Not surprisingly, excavation in the Dardanelles area shows up almost every ceramic type from both the Marmara and the Aegean: see, e.g., Türker, 'A Byzantine settlement', for Kepez just outside Çanakkale.

[33] The classic site is Saraçhane, for which see esp. Hayes, *Excavations at Saraçhane*, 2; for a rapid survey of the ceramics of the city as a whole, see Dark, 'Pottery production'.

weavers/dyers, as well as three types of silk merchant; this concentration of interest is because the Byzantine state—far more than other states—was very involved in silk production and sale, which it controlled in order to maintain supplies of fabrics and not least dyes (including purple, from murex shells) as status markers for the emperor and his officials. But it also has a section on linen merchants (*othōniopratai*), who could deal in goods made of cotton (*bambakinōn*) too. It is not clear from this text whether their linen was woven in the city from raw flax by professional weavers, or finished on the basis of cloth woven elsewhere, or just sold; but other sources make it clear that all three occurred. Tailors and dyers, both part of the finishing process, are cited in literary texts; and a mid-eleventh-century work by Psellos discusses professional female linen carders and weavers. Outside the professional world, raw flax was also, unsurprisingly, woven inside urban households by people—again women—who could not afford made clothing.[34] We also have written references to a variety of other professional artisans, goldsmiths, bronze workers, shoemakers, tanners, plus a wealth of food sellers of different types—a random list, dependent on the whims of writers, but a wide enough range.[35]

These artisans, like other artisans and shopkeepers in the Byzantine Empire, worked out of *ergastēria*, workshops and/or shops, which were situated both on the main streets (which were wide in the city, much wider than in the Islamic world, to allow for the capital's heavily developed processional activity) and on alleys farther away. We have records of sales of five such workshops in the 950s, attached largely to silk and linen dealers, and rented, as were other shops, from officials and aristocrats; Attaleiates owned two as well, a bakery and a perfumery, plus a doctor's office.[36] And we have archaeological evidence for glassmaking and above all ceramics. Constantinople's potters made wares with a white fabric, in both unglazed and green- or yellow-glazed types, called White ware in the literature. It is now certain that this was made inside the city (and the clay for it equally certainly came from the Bosporos). Glazed White ware (GWW) 2, in particular, the late ninth- to twelfth-century form, had an exceptionally wide distribution; it

[34] Koder, *Das Eparchenbuch*, chs 4–8 for silk, 9 for linen; *Accounts of medieval Constantinople: the Patria*, ed. Berger, 3.118, for purple (i.e. probably silk) dyers; for carders and weavers, see Laiou, 'The festival of "Agathe"'; for a woman spinning and weaving for herself, see *Poèmes prodromiques*, ed. Hesseling and Pernot, poem 1, ll. 95–8; for an emblematic tailor and dyer, see ibid., poem 4, ll. 90–6, 114–20.

[35] See, e.g., Hendy, *Studies*, pp. 588–90 for a list of the trades in Ptochoprodromos, although cf. pp. 319–20 below for the problems of too literal a reading of this text; for before 1100, see Kaplan, *Byzance: villes et campagnes*, pp. 297–307. A Jewish pancake maker in the city is recorded in a *geniza* letter of 1137: T-S 13J21.17, ed. and trans. Goitein. 'A letter from Seleucia', p. 300.

[36] For the 950s sales, see Oikonomides, 'Quelques boutiques de Constantinople'; for locations, see also Koder, *Das Eparchenbuch*, chs 2.11, 5.2, 10.1, 11.1, 13.1; for Attaleiates, see Gautier, 'La diataxis de Michel Attaliate', pp. 43, 45; for processions, see Brubaker and Wickham, 'Processions, power and community identity'. There were *ergasteria* in the Venetian concession on the Golden Horn, the capital's north shore too: see, e.g., Lanfranchi, *S. Giorgio maggiore*, n. 69 (a. 1090).

has been found all across the coasts of the empire with few exceptions, and sometimes inland too.[37]

We will come back to these glazed wares. But it is important to stress them here, because they are one of the few pieces of evidence that shows that Constantinople produced for more than just its inhabitants.[38] We are much less able to say than we could for Fusṭāṭ, and indeed Kairouan and Palermo, that Constantinople started as a focus for taxation and the spending power that came from taxation, but developed into a productive and commercial centre in its own right, with buyers elsewhere in the empire. We might not expect all that much other evidence, for our written sources are above all for the capital, and tell us little about what other towns imported from it, but the absence may be a hint that the Byzantine capital was, indeed, less active as an exporter than some of its comparators. In particular, as we shall see later, if Constantinople dominated the commerce of the empire in, say, 1000, which is likely, this was considerably less the case in the twelfth century, when other exporting centres were active in the Aegean. All the same, Glazed White ware at least helps us see that Constantinople's productions could indeed be commercially important for a wider hinterland; it can be seen as a proxy for a wider economic role for at least some of the city's other manufactures.

4.2.2 The Aegean Sea

Constantinople was, of course, the centre of the empire; but the Aegean and its coasts were the core provincial subregion, and the most important for an understanding of a wider exchange economy. The Aegean will dominate my later discussions of the evidence for commerce itself, as a result; here, let us look at its major structural elements as a framing for that. It is surrounded by some quite sharp mountain ranges, but also numerous agriculturally prosperous hill areas, as in Boeotia and Attica in central Greece—and in Anatolia these could extend quite a long way inland, up the Maiander and Hermos (today Menderes and Gediz)

[37] For GWW 2, see Hayes, *Excavations at Saraçhane*, 2, pp. 18–29, and François, *La vaisselle de terre*, pp. 54–6; see ibid., p. 52, with, now, esp. Waksman, 'Byzantine pottery production in Constantinople/Istanbul', for the Vezniceler kiln site, which can be linked to GWW 2. See Sanders, 'Byzantine Polychrome pottery' and White, *An investigation*, p. 141 for clay from Arnavutköy on the Bosporos, which is one of the certain clay sites; White argues convincingly that different white fabrics for GWW imply several workshops. François, *La vaisselle de terre*, pp. 119–21 has recent distribution maps; see also pp. 307, 311 below. For glass, see Henderson and Mundell Mango, 'Glass at medieval Constantinople', which is somewhat inconclusive; but it is plausible that the glass cullet in the Serçe Limanı wreck from the 1020s was destined for the capital; see in general Bass and Allen, *Serçe Limanı*, 2.

[38] The other evidence is money, for that from the capital's mint is overwhelmingly the main coinage found, in ever greater numbers as we move from the tenth century to the twelfth, on the archaeological sites of the empire, until the Thessaloniki mint was opened for a longer period at the end of the eleventh century and through the twelfth—although these distributions will have reflected the tightness of the tax system as much as commercial networks. See Hendy, *Studies*, pp. 434–9.

rivers—and some classic grain-growing plains, the largest of which is in Thessaly and northwards around Thessaloniki. It is one of the most obvious trading seas in the world, given its wealth of safe ports, and its dense scatter of islands to provide geographical markers and fresh water (although also rocky coasts to shipwreck off). Only two things stand in the way: pirates (a common danger until the Arabs lost control of Crete, and also in the later twelfth century, when Italian ships preyed on each other and on others as well);[39] and the fact that the Aegean tends to produce similar agricultural produce all around its coastline—for if there is ever a place where the 'Mediterranean triad' of grain, wine, and olive oil is a standard feature of a wide area, it is here. For dense exchange, specializations need to be built up, as does urban demand. We will look at specializations, and the countryside, later; here, let us look at the towns.

There are several ways to look at the urban centres of the Aegean empirically in our period. First, the provincial capitals: these varied, as themes were divided and amalgamated, but the three major ones were Thessaloniki for Thrace and Macedonia, Thebes (Thiva) for the theme of Hellas (that is to say, central Greece) and the Peloponnesos, and Smyrna (İzmir) as the main political focus on the eastern Aegean coast. We know very little about Smyrna—oddly, it has few even casual references in sources, and its archaeology is very small-scale.[40] But Thessaloniki and Thebes were certainly major centres—the latter even though it was not actually on the sea, which is 25 kilometres away. Narrative sources and archaeology, a second point of reference, again show both Thessaloniki and Thebes as key foci, and add Corinth and Ephesos to them, plus Euripos (Chalkis), Athens, Argos, and Sparta. Venetian documents stress a marginally different set, as we shall see (p. 334 below): Corinth, Sparta and Thebes, Halmyros in Thessaly, which was a rising port for Thessalian grain, and Kitros, just south of Thessaloniki, plus Rhaidestos on the Marmara. They rather neglected the eastern side of the Aegean. But there is enough overlap here, from different types of source, to give us some confirmation of basic patterns. We might propose an urban hierarchy here, with Thessaloniki at the top, Thebes and probably Smyrna next, then Corinth and probably Ephesos, then Athens and Euripos/Chalkis (which may well have been of greater importance than this, but its first role was as Thebes' port), and then the rest. Other towns were of more local importance, as ecclesiastical or military or local market centres.

[39] For the later period, see Michael Choniates, *Epistulae*, ed. Kolovou, nn. 14, 20, 27, 42, 44, 46, 50, 60, 65; Niketas Choniates, *Historia*, ed. van Dieten, p. 55; and see n. 132 below. Cf. Magdalino, *The empire of Manuel I*, pp. 137–40.

[40] Doğer, 'Byzantine ceramics', presents a small amount of twelfth-century ceramic material from the *agora*. Smyrna was presumably an agricultural centre, given the *horreiarioi* which are documented on seals from the city, an office which in Anatolia is otherwise only attested in Bithynia; see Nesbitt and Oikonomides, *A catalogue of Byzantine seals*, 3, p. 50; cf. p. 201. For a survey of all the towns around the Aegean, see Gerolymatou, *Agores, emporioi*, pp. 122–71.

Thessaloniki had a long tradition as a major city, including a mint by the end of our period. John Kaminiates, writing to lament the Arab sack of 904, lists its merchants coming in by land and sea, and its makers of woollen and silk cloth, metalwork in six metals, and glass.[41] Rescue archaeology shows that there was candle-making in the precinct of the important Hagios Demetrios church, glass in the centre and south of the city, generic kilns on the waterfront and on the east side of town outside the walls, a pottery kiln in the centre (although not glazed ceramics, until an organized production began in the later twelfth century), dyeing in the north-east, and metalwork in several places. In the 1160s the city's Jews were involved in silk-weaving, according to Benjamin of Tudela.[42] The city was a major buyer for wine from the Athos monasteries. A much-commented document of 1117 lists seven *ergastēria* in the centre of town, around a courtyard with a second floor and arcading, abutting on several others, which had recently passed through the hands of at least three laymen, two of them local officials (a pattern we have seen in the capital), before coming to the Docheiariou monastery on Athos. Another *ergastērion* on the marketplace (*phoros*) was valuable enough to be left undivided by two brothers who shared out their property in 1110; an earlier example from 952, by the sea, was a *kerameion* or *ergastērion pros keramōn*, which is translated as brick or tile workshop by modern authors, but which could equally be a ceramics workshop.[43] This is all anecdotal, or else based on hardly published rescue sites, but it is rather greater than most towns have as a source base. It is also worth noting that the examples cover at least half of the Roman city, which was large, and extended beyond the walls. The city had an annual extramural fair as well, praised in the *Timarion*, a comic mid-twelfth-century text about a descent into Hell; this was said to have sold cloth imported by ship to the city from central Greece and goods from a wide array of foreign countries. I would be more cautious than others about taking very seriously the details of places of origin here, which are clearly listed for rhetorical effect, but the image of the fair is a striking one.[44]

[41] Kaminiates, *De expugnatione Thessalonicae*, ed. Böhlig, 9.4–9. Kazhdan, 'Some questions', argued on several grounds (some less convincing than others) that this texts is fifteenth-century; Frendo, 'The *Miracles of St. Demetrius* and the capture of Thessaloniki', best argues the majority view, that it is contemporary. Regardless of this debate, the archaeology shows an array of trades in the city which does not depend on this text.

[42] For the rescue archaeology, the main synthesis is Antonaras, 'Artisan production'; see also Bakirtzis, 'Imports, exports'; Konstantinidou and Raptis, 'Archaeological evidence of an eleventh-century kiln'; Raptis, 'Seeking the marketplaces of Byzantine Thessalonike'; Zavagno, *The Byzantine city*, pp. 110–16; Vasileiadou, 'Glazed tableware from the Middle Byzantine workshops of Thessaloniki'. For Benjamin, see *The itinerary of Benjamin of Tudela*, trans. Adler, p. 11. See also Magdalino, *The empire of Manuel I*, pp. 149–50, 158–9, for Thessaloniki's activity in the 1180s.

[43] *Actes de Docheiariou*, n. 4; *Actes de Lavra*, 1, n. 59, 4; for other *kerameia*, cf. *Actes d'Iviron*, 1, nn. 4 and perhaps 23. For wine coming to the city, see e.g. *Actes du Prôtaton*, n. 7.

[44] *Timarione*, ed. Romano, chs 5–6.

Thebes, too, is largely attested through rescue excavations and interim publications. Here the walled town was much smaller, but all the same, archaeologists have found, for our period, dense housing in its centre, housing outside the walls, a water supply system, over thirty small churches, and extramural ceramic and dyeing workshops. The city is, however, well known to historians for its extensive twelfth-century silk industry, casually referred to in too many texts for it to be anecdotal, and it had linen-working too. It is not now seen as the main ceramics producer in Boeotia, for the major production centre of both glazed wares and amphorae was at its port of Chalkis, possibly the most important such centre after Constantinople, which provided pots for the city and a wide hinterland. But the two together were a considerable powerhouse, and we will discuss them further in the next sections.[45]

Corinth, for its part, is the best-studied site of all, from the 1920s–1930s onwards, when a far-seeing US team actually excavated the Byzantine housing on the classical agora, rather than removing it without record. It has been the type site ever since for Middle Byzantine archaeology, and we will come back to it too. Corinth was a major commercial centre, situated as it was above both the Aegean Sea and the Gulf of Corinth stretching westwards towards the Ionian Sea—the historian Niketas Choniates, writing after 1200, said it had two ports, one for each sea—as well as being another cloth-making centre, although the evidence for that is less full. It was also very important for ceramics, and most of the glazed-ware typology we have for Byzantium after 1080 or so depends on the Corinth publications; substantial metalworking and some glassmaking were identified by the archaeologists too. Corinth was large; the agora site was by now residential and small-scale industrial, with the city's political and monumental centre, and also what Choniates calls its marketplace, *emporion*, by now located elsewhere—exactly where is uncertain. But paralleling Thessaloniki, its pottery kilns are found across much of the wide area of the ancient city; this may show fairly substantial settlement across that area, which extended down to the port on the Gulf coast, 2.5 kilometres away.[46]

Ephesos, after Smyrna the most weakly documented of this main set, had contracted considerably from its huge classical size, in particular to the northern

[45] See Armstrong, 'Byzantine Thebes' (the best publication but small); Louvi-Kizi, 'Thebes', summarizes twentieth-century rescue work; for the post-2000 period, see Koilakou, 'Byzantine Thebes'; Kontogiannis, 'A tale of two cities', pp. 216–25 (which also includes a comparison with Chalkis); and the brief survey in Symeonoglou, *The topography of Thebes*, pp. 162–9, which focusses on churches. For cloth, see pp. 323–8 below; for ceramics, see pp. 311–13 below.

[46] See pp. 308–11 below; Morgan, *Corinth XI*, Scranton, *Corinth XVI*, Sanders, 'Corinth', and Sanders, 'Recent developments' give the basic archaeological data for the city and its Gulf port. An up-to-date introduction is Athanasoulis, 'Corinth', with White, *An investigation*, pp. 46–51 for ceramic kilns; see also Zavagno, *The Byzantine city*, pp. 116–19. The Aegean port, Kenchreai, less close to the city, has been partially excavated too: see esp. Adamsheck, *Kenchreai*, 4, pp. 100–4, 109, 116–17, for a sketchy account of the Middle Byzantine pottery—the publication is too early to be reliable about dates, but many of the basic Morgan types are there, so the harbour was clearly in use in our period.

area around the cathedral church of St Mary, plus a new and expanding site farther north still, Ayasoluk, around the extramural pilgrimage church of St John. Its harbour had largely silted up, and it may well be that Smyrna had taken over much of its earlier leading role as an Anatolian port. But it remained an important centre. It turns up in too many texts for us to be able to write it off, for example the late eleventh-century *Life* of Lazaros of Galesion, where it is a major point of reference for Galesion's monks, who regularly travel there on business. It had a set of workshops in Ayasoluk, including its own local glazed-pottery production, plus a Middle Byzantine amphora type, which has been recently identified, and plenty of imported wares have been found there.[47]

We will come back to the next rung of towns in the next section, for most of them do not show us more significant patterns, as specifically urban centres, than those we have seen so far. But two further comments are worthwhile. The first is about Athens. Athens seems on the surface to have been less active than Corinth. It too had a dense settlement on the classical agora, excavated in the 1930s, although it is far less well published than Corinth; but even if it certainly had numerous workshops, including several for glazed and unglazed ceramics, it is explicitly not associated with silk. It did have local murex for purple dye, and vats for dyeing, bleaching, or tanning have been found; it doubtless made cloth of some kind, perhaps for a local market. (It is often assumed that the murex was for Theban silk; there is no direct evidence for that, but it is certainly true that purple dye was usually for silk.) It had at least two major workshop areas, but also a geographical spread of artisanal activities, and several pottery kilns. Perhaps its most striking feature, however, is its more than forty Middle Byzantine churches, which are still standing. It may not have matched Corinth or Thebes, but forty churches are by no means a small number, and show urban elite wealth. Athens had had enough political protagonism as a community to kill an unpopular governor in *c.*916 too, and in the eleventh century landowners from the city owned as far away as Thebes; Michael Choniates, Niketas's brother and another of Constantinople's intellectual elite, who was made bishop here in 1182, attacked the local leadership for usurping the lands of others (not least his own church), so they were certainly active a century later too. We may downplay Athens simply because Choniates hated it, writing graphic letters about what a poor and wretched place it was; but metropolitan intellectuals always did that in Byzantium—nowhere could ever match up to the capital. One of the recipients of his letters, who had been governor of

[47] For brief discussions, see Foss, *Ephesus*, pp. 120–37; Daim and Ladstätter, *Ephesos in byzantinischer Zeit*, pp. 25–6; and esp. Ladstätter, *Die Türbe im Artemision*; and the *Life of Lazaros of Galesion*, ed. Deleheye, chs 75, 107, 154, 249 (there are plenty of citations of its lay and ecclesiastical officials too). This text says nothing about a commercial role for Ephesos, but the city is prominent in it all the same. For ceramics, see Parman, 'The pottery from St John's basilica'; Böhlendorf-Arslan, *Glasierte byzantinische Keramik*, 1, pp. 240–4; Waksman. 'Medieval ceramics from the Türbe'; Vroom, 'On the trail of the enigma amphora'.

southern Greece, had indeed praised it as a seaport; Choniates indignantly denied this. It is at least true that Venetians are never documented here in this century, but the ex-governor may well have had a clearer view of it, all the same. At any rate, if this was a third-rank town, it reflects interestingly on that ranking.[48]

The second comment concerns the Anatolian Turkish coast. Smyrna has almost no documentary information, Ephesos little enough. It might be that we underplay the eastern side of the Aegean in this period simply because of this, and because its archaeology is less well developed too. But there are some well-excavated ex-classical sites besides Ephesos, and they do not show much more. Miletos was almost deserted in this period, until a fortification was built above the theatre at the end of the eleventh century. Pergamon (Bergama) was much the same, with a probable late eleventh-century reoccupation; although after 1150 it was a thematic capital, and it had a good range of ceramic imports, the excavator calls the site a 'small rural settlement'. Hierapolis (Pamukkale), farther inland, had more settlement continuity, and a few early ceramic imports such as GWW and Günsenin amphorae; all the same, such imports are not common before the twelfth century (and at least one Middle Byzantine site in the city had almost none at all), and its locally produced pottery had a range more or less restricted to the upper Maiander valley. Nearby, Aphrodisias (Geyre) was not large, although it certainly had settlement continuity, with ceramic imports in every period up to the thirteenth century, and substantial coin use except under the Komnenoi. In Sardis (Sart), perhaps the most substantial of the five, the seventh-century castle above the classical town remained occupied, expanding in the eleventh; from the later twelfth century (not, it seems, earlier) a substantial variety of ceramics were found. Below, in an abandoned Roman bath complex, there is evidence of iron, glass, and again pottery production, probably with a localized distribution.[49]

[48] See esp. Bouras, *Byzantine Athens*, for standing buildings and surveys of unpublished excavations (pp. 117–24 for evidence of production), and Kondyli, 'The view from Byzantine archaeology' (pp. 53–6 for workshop areas). See Svoronos, 'Recherches sur le cadastre byzantin', pp. 13, 14, 17, for Athenians in the Thebes cadaster; Michael Choniates, *Epistulae*, ed. Kolovou, nn. 60 (poor port, no silk), 44 (usurpations), 10, 19, 20, 24, 26, 46, 62, 65 (generic awfulness); and for local landowning/official *archontes*, see Herrin, 'Realities of Byzantine provincial government', esp. pp. 270–6. For the death of the governor at the hands of Athenian *oikētores* (inhabitants), see *Theophanes Continuatus*, ed. Bekker, p. 388. One substantial estate in Attica is described in a *praktikon* or fiscal survey, which lacks a date or the name of the owner, but which is certainly from our period and probably for an Athens monastery; see Granstrem et al., 'Fragment d'un praktikon'.

[49] Miletos: Niewöhner, 'Neue spät- und nachantike Monumente von Milet'; Böhlendorf-Arslan, *Glasierte byzantinische Keramik*, 1, pp. 252–8. Pergamon: Rheidt, *Die byzantinische Wohnstadt*, pp. 197–8, 237–9, 246–8, with Rheidt, 'The urban economy of Pergamon' (p. 625 for the quotation; but Rheidt then goes on to say that the town could have held 2,400 inhabitants, which is not tiny, and the book makes clear that the settlement increased in size substantially after 1200); Böhlendorf-Arslan, *Glasierte byzantinische Keramik*, 1, pp. 191–209; Spieser, *Die byzantinische Keramik*, pp. 1–8, 45–8. Hierapolis: Arthur, *Byzantine and Turkish Hierapolis*, pp. 74–83; compare Cottica, 'Micaceous White Painted Ware from insula 104 at Hierapolis/Pamukkale, Turkey'; Böhlendorf-Arslan, *Glasierte byzantinische Keramik*, 1, pp. 258–60, also summarizes unpublished work. Aphrodisias is most effectively surveyed in Jeffery, *The archaeology of Middle Byzantine Aphrodisias*. Sardis: Foss, *Byzantine and Turkish Sardis*, pp. 66–76 (synthesizing the never fully published US excavations), updated in Foss and

It might be that newly prominent sites, like Adramyttion (Edremit), 'well populated' until Turkish attack according to Anna Komnene, could tell us more about Middle Byzantine urbanism on the Anatolian west coast. But without evidence for more sites like Sardis, it looks as if the ruralization process which is well attested in a large number of Byzantine cities from the seventh century onwards had not fully reversed itself here. Ephesos, after all, had been an exception to that process even in the eighth century.[50] Rural sites in well-studied parts of the Anatolian coast, like the area around Miletos and the Troad, show a decent level of prosperity; the *praktikon* (fiscal survey) of Andronikos Doukas of 1073 lists a dense set of villages in the lower Maiander valley.[51] This was not a poor coastline. And it was certainly not politically marginal; its theme, Thrakesion, was prominent in Psellos' letters to governors, second only to Opsikion in Bithynia.[52] But it did not have as many major centres as Greece in this period, and as a result had a less developed urban hierarchy too. This puts even more analytical pressure on the main absence, Smyrna, which might indeed have been a centre as important as Thessaloniki, although casual references to it are rarer than they are to Athens. For the foreseeable future, we cannot know where it really sat in the hierarchy. But all this does mean that our best evidence for economic activity in the Aegean, at all levels, is for Greece, and that must affect how we see the subregion as a whole. We will see that contrast amply confirmed in the evidence for ceramic and cloth production, discussed in the next sections.[53]

The Aegean and its coastal margins were, as a whole, a sufficiently coherent subregion to have an urban hierarchy, as sketched out earlier. That will have helped the organization of exchange. So will the fact that urban elites, often called *archontes* (*arcontes* in Latin texts), seem to have been prosperous and active, as well as, of course, locally oppressive; we have seen that Athens's elites were aggressive across our period, and we find this also in Sparta in the eleventh-century *Life* of Nikon (a local notable is here trying to seize land from a monastery), and Larisa, a fourth-rank town in the middle of the Thessalian plain,

Scott, 'Sardis', and Böhlendorf-Arslan, *Glasierte byzantinische Keramik*, 1, pp. 225–32, with Waldbaum, *Metalwork from Sardis*, p. 9.

[50] For Adramyttion, see Anna Komnene, *Alexias*, ed. Reinsch et al., 14.1.4. Identified Byzantine ceramics in Edremit postdate 1200; see Böhlendorf-Arslan, *Glasierte byzantinische Keramik*, 1, pp. 209–11. For the great eighth-century fair (*panēgyrion*) in Ephesos, see Theophanes, *Chronographia*, ed. de Boor, 1, pp. 469–70.

[51] Thonemann, *The Maeander valley*, pp. 259–70 and Niewöhner, 'The Byzantine settlement history', pp. 274–80, for Miletos and its hinterland; Böhlendorf-Arslan, 'Surveying the Troad'; for 1073, see Branousē et al., *Byzantina eggrapha tēs monēs Patmou*, 2, n. 50; cf. 1, n. 1.

[52] Relative prominences again calculated from the total set of letters summarized in Jeffreys, 'Summaries'.

[53] It should be added that there were fewer small-denomination coins available in twelfth-century western Anatolia than in Greece; see Hendy, *Studies*, p. 437. He then assumed that this was simply a by-product of the state's fiscal policies (which it certainly was in part), although he later wondered, as do I, whether it reflected differences in commercial activity; see n. 18 above.

whose leaders (*archēgoi*) staged an uprising in 1066. Closer to the capital, the archons of Adrianople also supported Nikephoros Bryennios' revolt in 1077. The rural church-building which can be widely seen from the eleventh century onwards also generally attests to elite conspicuous spending.[54] Such elites were, above all, of subregional importance; they did not constitute the aristocracy of the empire, Constantinople-dwelling in large part, who turn up in so many of the main political narratives. But they had buying power, and the towns developed to fit that. The leading towns had overlapping productions, but they were also complementary, and we can show that they traded with each other—both inside Greece and with the Anatolian coast. That trade is our key guide to how the Byzantine economy worked, and we will come back to it shortly.

4.2.3 The Anatolian plateau

The land rises up from the sea quite rapidly in Anatolian Turkey, except on its western side in the river valleys, and at the top of the Maiander valley it rises up definitively there too. The centre of Anatolia is a high plateau, mostly un-Mediterranean in its relative lack of vines and almost total lack of oil; often treeless too, it is grain and stock-raising territory.[55] Many or most of the animals sold in Constantinople came from here, as we have seen. It would be wrong to see it as above all ranching country, all the same. Recent palynological studies on pollen from the Middle Byzantine period indicate that in a range of study areas, cereals began to expand considerably from a series of different dates between 800 and 1100 (very roughly speaking, 800 in the south-west, 850 in the north, 950 in Cappadocia to the east, as late as 1100 in the north-east), alongside plants which are characteristic of pastureland.[56] This partly reflects the fact that the central plateau was no longer a frontier after Byzantine military expansion began around

[54] See in turn *The life of Saint Nikon*, ed. Sullivan, chs 60–1; Kekaumenos, *Consilia et Narrationes*, ed. Roueché, pp. 66–74; Bryennios, *Histoire*, ed. Gautier, 3.10. See Angold, 'Archons and dynasts', pp. 236–43, for the protagonism of local elites elsewhere. Neville, *Authority in Byzantine provincial society*, is a further guide to the local societies which *archontes* dominated. She, however, in my view overestimates the lack of involvement in such societies of the public power; the court cases in the Athos documents, for instance, show considerable activity of state officials on the ground, both in their concern for detail and the extent of their local information, regardless of whether that activity was disinterested or corrupt (see, e.g., Morris, 'Dispute settlement'; good examples are *Actes d'Iviron*, 1, nn. 2, 4; 2, n. 52), and so do Psellos's letters. See now Nilsson, *Aristocracy, politics and power*, arguing for a closer relation between state and elite provincial society. For rural church-building, see, e.g., the survey evidence found near Sparta: Armstrong. 'The survey area', pp. 362–3, 366–7.

[55] See Hendy, *Studies*, pp. 90–145, for a historical geography, with Koder, 'Regional networks'. Cf. Leo of Synada, *Letters*, ed. Vinson, n. 43, for there being no wine, oil, wheat (only barley), or firewood in his new bishopric; Synada was not so remote, though, and this may be another metropolitan intellectual exaggerating. Perhaps more interesting is that he says that he could get supplies from Thrakesion and Attaleia (Antalya); this at least reflects the lack of remoteness of the town.

[56] Izdebski et al., 'Exploring Byzantine and Ottoman history'; Eastwood et al., 'Integrating palaeoecological and archaeo-historical records'.

950. Indeed, it became the focus of the landholdings of most of the empire's major aristocratic families, who were at their height in the following century. When emperors inveighed about 'the powerful' usurping the lands of the poor, the plateau was certainly one of the main areas they meant, given the scale which aristocratic estates seem to have had in these regions, as Hendy and Jean-Claude Cheynet have shown in detail—the Phokades in Cappadocia, the Argyroi in Charsianon, and so on.[57]

One can envisage pockets of considerable local landowner wealth here as a result, plus, of course, poverty for their tenants as well. And we have the material proof of this in at least one aristocrat-dominated area, that of the tenth- and eleventh-century rock-cut settlements of Cappadocia, many of them recently convincingly reinterpreted by Robert Ousterhout as elite residences and villages, not monasteries. All the same, emperors—particularly Basil II—were determined that the plateau should not become an alternative centre of power to the capital, which it was all the more likely to do because of the importance of the armies here. He and his successors required, with varying degrees of insistence, such aristocrats to live in Constantinople, as with Eustathios Maleinos, who supposedly entertained Basil lavishly in Cappadocia in the 990s, and was transferred to the capital forthwith for his pains.[58] This, it must be added, has a further consequence, namely that Anatolian aristocrats who spent most of their time in the capital were sources of elite demand in Constantinople, rather than on the plateau. So, notwithstanding our Cappadocian evidence, the largest source of inland demand was probably the army.

Anatolian aristocrats were, however, of little danger to the state in themselves. Part of the reason for this is structural; it was army leaders who could overthrow emperors, not any private landowner sitting on an estate. Only the very richest landowners could, anyway, match the wealth of state officials. At most they could suborn the tax system, as elites do in every period, although the fiscal system of the Middle Byzantine period remained tightly centralized. (Many aristocrats were, indeed, army leaders, and dangerous for that reason, but the fit was never exact; as many were civilian ministers, and some generals were by no means aristocratic.)[59] The other part is the simple fact that when the crisis of the 1070s

[57] Hendy, *Studies*, pp. 100–7; Cheynet, *Pouvoir et contestations*, pp. 213–29. See further the tables in Andriollo and Métivier, 'Quel rôle pour les provinces', pp. 510–17.

[58] Ousterhout, *Visualising community*, pp. 275–368, developing the architectural work on his main site, Çanlı Kilise, discussed in *A Byzantine settlement*, 2nd edn, esp. pp. 170–85. Unfortunately, Cappadocia has had almost no excavation, so these dramatic settlements have few small finds; Ousterhout, however, found almost no glazed wares at Çanlı Kilise (where settlement seems to have begun in the tenth century) before the end of the twelfth, a century after the Selcuk takeover: *A Byzantine settlement*, 2nd edn, pp. 228–31, 239. For the Basil story, see Skylitzes, *Synopsis historiarum*, ed. Thurn, Basil II, ch. 21 (p. 340).

[59] See esp. Holmes, *Basil II*, pp. 461–8. For taxation, see pp. 342–50 below. For comparisons between the wealth of landowners and of officials, see Frankopan, 'Land and power', pp. 148–53.

hit Byzantium, it was precisely the plateau which was lost to the Turks permanently, and not the lowlands of the Aegean. The old great families lost force, except the Komnenoi themselves (exiles from Paphlagonia in the north) and their near relatives the Doukai (also exiles from Paphlagonia, but owning land closer to the capital too).[60] These became the paid ceremonial officials of the Komnenian government. Far from the state being in the hands of landed aristocrats, it took time for aristocratic landed power to build up again, this time largely in the Balkans.

The Anatolian plateau was not a major area of urbanism. There were nodal urban centres, certainly, like Ankyra (Ankara), Ikonion (Konya), and Kaisareia (Kayseri), and probably in particular Doryleion (Eskişehir) on the edge of the plateau looking towards the capital, a major centre for exchange and army movements. They were quite far apart, however, and it is unclear how large most of them were.[61] Ankyra has substantial and long Middle Byzantine walls and had a prosperous urban elite, but there has been no serious excavation there for our period. Euchaita (Avkat/Beyözü), a bishopric and pilgrimage centre on the edge of the plateau in the north-east, reduced today to a village, has a good field survey which shows settlement in both the upper and lower town, but predominantly local pottery. Its annual fair (*panēgyris*), talked up by John Mauropous when he was not complaining about his exile, was probably important above all because the more pastoral economy of the plateau could there meet the more agricultural economy of the north coast—much as the annual *panēgyris* of the town of Chonai (Honaz) at the very top of the Maiander valley, praised by Michael Choniates in the later twelfth century (he came from there), must have done for the economic relationship between the plateau economy, by now Turkish-ruled, and that of the lower Maiander.[62] Amorion, today abandoned, is the only major town which has a

[60] Cheynet, *Pouvoir et contestations*, pp. 216–19, 237–41. For the Doukai, see Polemis, *The Doukai*, pp. 8–11, for the meagre information about their landowning. The family also came to own land at the mouth of the Maiander valley, which was not lost to the Turks; a chrysobull and *praktikon* of 1073 (Branousē et al., *Byzantina eggrapha tēs monēs Patmou*, 1, n. 1; 2, n. 50) show Andronikos Doukas registering a very large gift from his cousin, Emperor Michael VII, here. This area was, however, also not otherwise an aristocratic focus—Thrakesion had the smallest number of known aristocrats out of the major Anatolian themes, and it was not on the plateau. See Hendy, *Studies*, pp. 101–3; however, Cheynet, *Pouvoir et contestations*, pp. 235–6, and Andriollo and Métivier, 'Quel rôle pour les provinces', pp. 514–15, show that Hendy exaggerated the absence of aristocratic land in Thrakesion.

[61] See Vryonis, *The decline*, pp. 10–30 for the literary evidence for towns on the plateau. His is a maximum view, now not shared by anyone in the field; he takes a very literal approach to the write-ups in the sources (including obviously inflated figures), and develops them into hypotheses about high urban populations which are way beyond plausible. But as a collection of sources, his book retains its value. For Doryleion see esp. Kinnamos, *Epitome rerum*, ed. Meineke, 7.2, pp. 294–5; and the collection of references, almost all to military action, in Belke and Mersich, *Phrygien und Pisidien*, pp. 238–40. Cheynet, 'La société urbaine', p. 458, also makes a case for the importance of Melitene (Malatya) in the far east of the plateau.

[62] For Ankyra, see Foss, 'Late antique and Byzantine Ankara', pp. 79–84; Peschlow, 'Ancyra', pp. 353–60, with Bryennios, *Histoire*, ed. Gautier, 2.8, for the elite. For Euchaita, see Haldon et al., 'Euchaïta'; Haldon et al., *Archaeology and urban settlement*; with *Iohannis Euchaitorum Metropolitae quae in codice Vaticano graeco 676 supersunt*, ed. Bollig and de Lagarde, n. 180 (pp. 130–7). For Chonai, see Michael Choniates, *Ta sōzomena*, ed. Lampros, 1, p. 56; here, the inhabitants of Konya, farther into the

good-quality excavation; that shows a repopulation of the classical lower town and the refurbishment of churches there after an Arab sack in 838. But we are not looking at Corinth or Ephesos here; for the striking thing about Amorion's material culture is again how local it is. It has signs of wealth in its churches and associated tombs, including silk cloth which was certainly imported, and coin finds. It was a metalworking centre too. But its ceramics, although high-quality and including glazed wares, are overwhelmingly local; only a few fragments of GWW from the capital have been found. Amorion is likely to have been a central place for its immediate region, but it was not seriously linked into any wider trade networks.[63]

And this is the conclusion which other recent archaeologists have almost universally reached. The Avkat survey shows the same pattern of a handful at most of GWW 2 and Günsenin 1 amphora sherds, and the rest local wares. Indeed, this is also what was found even on the north coast, in a field survey around Cide on the Black Sea only some 200 kilometres east of the Bosporos. The large-scale Balboura survey in the south-west found two pieces of GWW 2 only, plus two Aegean amphorae. In village excavations there is even less, as with Çadır Höyük in the province of Yozgat, 60 kilometres from Avkat, and Boğazköy not far away in the old Hittite capital of Hattusas, 150 kilometres east of Ankara, in neither of which any extra-local material has been found, apart from coins (Boğazköy had active metalworking, however). It therefore makes sense that Aşvan Kale, an eleventh-century site far to the east on the upper Euphrates, should have no imports either, except a single coin of the 1060s, although it, like Amorion, had a local glazed-ware production of good quality.[64]

There is only one major exception, Sagalassos (Ağlasun). This, formerly a major late Roman city, is now seen to have remained populated after the seventh century, and on a hill above the old town a twelfth-century settlement was found which had the full range of Aegean glazed pottery, from both Corinth and Chalkis.

plateau, are by now simply *barbaroi*; for the history of the fair, which existed already in the ninth century, see Thonemann, *The Maeander valley*, pp. 125–9.

[63] For a recent interim, see Lightfoot, 'Amorium'; for ceramics, see Böhlendorf-Arslan, 'Die mittelbyzantinische Keramik aus Amorium'; for an earlier period, cf. Böhlendorf-Arslan, 'Pottery from the destruction contexts'.

[64] See, respectively, Haldon et al., 'Euchaïta'; Haldon et al., *Archaeology and urban settlement*, pp. 139–48 (J. Vroom); Cassis, 'The Cide-Senpazar region', pp. 305–9; Coulton, *The Balboura survey*, 2, pp. 65–6 (two cooking pots also had Aegean parallels, and two pieces of glazed red ware could not be identified); Cassis, 'Çadır Höyük'; Böhlendorf-Arslan, 'Das bewegliche Inventar'; Böhlendorf-Arslan, 'Boğazköy'; Mitchell, 'Aşvan Kale'. Böhlendorf-Arslan, *Glasierte byzantinische Keramik*, which aims to be a complete listing of Byzantine glazed wares found in Turkey up to 1999 or shortly after, only cites one plateau site, Amorion (1, pp. 220–5), and nothing on the north coast. There is a little more on the south coast; see ibid., 260–6. She omits Attaleia (Antalya), for which there is good evidence in the written record; see Foss, 'The cities of Pamphylia', pp. 7–123; Hellenkemper and Hild, *Lykien und Pamphylien*, pp. 297–341—it was a major naval and commercial centre (see nn. 160, 223 below). It had connections with the interior (see n. 56 above), and was on the main Byzantium–Syria sea route in all periods.

There was some attention to the long-term preservation of these ceramics, for many of the sherds show repair holes; it was not available every day, probably. But this settlement, 100 kilometres east of the top of the Maiander valley and 100 kilometres from the south coast, was also not as far into the plateau as the others. Its excavators propose that it was a military outpost, which by implication had non-commercial or else advantaged commercial supplies. It was, after all, a fortified site, and was situated on the edge of Byzantine rule under the Komnenoi. That explanation is quite possible; anyway, this late date for a Byzantine plateau site makes it unlikely to be a model for any settlement farther away from the sea a century earlier. But unless and until parallels for Sagalassos appear in the material record, the isolation of the plateau as a whole from the Aegean and Marmara seems pretty clear.[65] It was militarily central, and of major economic importance for anyone whose lands were here, but marginal in other respects. Psellos, so active in his personal networks around the seas, hardly wrote to the plateau governors at all; one of the few such communications, to the governor of Charsianon north-east of Cappadocia, regrets that few letter bearers went that way.[66]

The only other point which needs to be made here is that we should not be very surprised by this. The Anatolian plateau had long had very weak economic links with the Mediterranean. In the late Roman Empire, almost no Mediterranean Red Slip fine wares or amphora types came farther into Anatolia than the Maiander valley. The only Red Slip which was available there on any scale was made well inland—by coincidence, at Sagalassos itself—and we do not know much about the extent of its distribution. Its societies were connected to those of Constantinople and elsewhere by army and fiscal movements, not by organic exchange relationships; the state funding of the public post in the sixth century was said at the time to be the only way money got onto the plateau.[67] And later, after 650, its crucial importance to the Byzantine state was as a military bulwark and a source of army manpower—paid locally, and in kind, for many centuries. Money returned to the internal organization of the Byzantine army in the tenth century, and indeed has been found on sites here, as we have seen, up until the crisis of the 1070s.[68] We have also seen that its stock-raising fed the capital; and that there were fairs on the

[65] Vionis et al., 'Ceramic continuity'; Vionis et al., 'A Middle-late Byzantine pottery assemblage'; Kaptijn and Waelkens, 'Before and after'. Balboura, closer to the coast, may be a parallel; the tiny amount of Middle Byzantine pottery there has been interpreted as denoting armies passing through a largely empty landscape: Coulton, *The Balboura survey*, 1, pp. 175–81, 2, pp. 79–80. So, perhaps, is Karacahisar, another military centre above Doryleion (Eskişehir; see Turnator, *Turning the economic tables*, pp. 219–21), but this is on the edge of the plateau. These do not, taken as a whole, disturb the picture.

[66] Psellus, *Epistulae*, ed. Papaioannou, n. 366 (Psellos, *Epistolai*, ed. Sathas, n. 121).

[67] Prokopios, *Anekdota*, ed. Haury and Wirth, 30.11; John Lydos, *On powers*, ed. Bandy, 3.61; Poblome, *Sagalassos Red Slip ware*, pp. 288, 314–18.

[68] For army pay, Haldon, *Warfare*, pp. 120–8, conveniently synthesizes his numerous studies of the topic; in general for money in Anatolia, which reached a peak of availability in the eleventh century, see the tables in Morrisson, 'Coins', pp. 77–80.

edges of the plateau, even after central Anatolia was taken over by the Turks, which certainly show economic interconnections. But these patterns, although by no means negligible, did not make the Anatolian plateau an integral part of the exchange network of the empire as a whole, in any period. It was, essentially, separate from the subject matter of this book, in both our period and well before. Its loss at the end of the eleventh century marked a political and strategic crisis for the Komnenian emperors (although not, as it turned out, a major military danger, after the frontier stabilized), but it had surprisingly little effect on the wider economy.

4.2.4 The northern Balkans

Bulgaria was conquered in bloody wars in the generation up to 1018. It then remained fully part of the Byzantine Empire until 1186; more intermittently, so did the lands west of it which are now Serbia and its smaller neighbours. Periodic nomadic attacks kept the northern Bulgarian lands and some other areas unstable for the rest of our period. A large-scale revolt in Bulgaria in 1040 was seen by one Byzantine chronicler as being against its inhabitants having to pay taxes in money rather than kind. That was certainly a new enactment of the 1030s, although recent work questions whether it actually caused the revolt; but the events at least show that the integration of the subregion into the imperial monetary regime was not immediate.[69] We have archaeological evidence for frontier fortifications along or near the Danube, going upstream as far as Belgrade, for both the eleventh century and the twelfth, which show that the sites sometimes had access to wine and glazed ceramics from the Aegean—doubtless as part of military supply—besides local productions. At the mouth of the Danube, denser sets of imports, including GWW 2 and Günsenin amphorae, and a wide availability of coins, indicate commercial links with the Black Sea at border entrepôts.[70] But local productions predominated in most other places, whether of relatively high-quality glazed wares (and also glass, and metal- and stonework), in the town of Veliko Tărnovo in north-central Bulgaria—inheriting the expertise of artisans working for the independent Bulgarian rulers of previous centuries in their capital of Preslav farther east—or of simpler but well-made slipped wares, called 'golden engobe' (*zlatista angoba*) in the literature, as in the eleventh- and twelfth-century village

[69] For general overviews, see Curta, *Southeastern Europe*, pp. 248–365; Stephenson, *Byzantium's Balkan frontier* (pp. 135–6 for doubt cast on the relationship between the money tax and the revolt). The situation changed soon: coins are found across most Bulgarian sites, at least in the east of the country, after 1050 and especially 1100; see Borisov, 'Settlements of northeast Thrace', pp. 83–5.

[70] See, e.g., Bjelalac, 'Byzantine amphorae'; Popović and Ivanišević, 'Grad Braničevo', pp. 147–8. For sites at the mouth of the Danube, see Stephenson, *Byzantium's Balkan frontier*, pp. 84–9, 97–9, 105–6; Barnéa, 'La céramique byzantine'; Todorova, 'Policy and trade'.

of Dyadovo in the south-east. Twelfth-century Aegean ceramics are quite common on the Black Sea coast, but only a few came westwards to central and southern Bulgaria (Dyadovo is an example here again; it must have been a prosperous village), or up the rivers from Thessaloniki into what is now North Macedonia and southern Serbia.[71]

All this shows that the Balkans cannot all be seen as the Wild North of the empire. Furthermore, the eastern Bulgarian lowlands are good cereal farming land; doubtless they, like other lowlands, supplied Constantinople.[72] Byzantine aristocrats were building up their land here after the mid-eleventh century, as shown in the large gifts of land, some ex-imperial, to Petritziotissa (Bačkovo) monastery by its founder Gregory Pakourianos, an Armenian general who had recently moved to the area, in 1083. If Tărnovo was making its own fine wares, Philippoupolis farther south (Plovdiv, close to Bačkovo) has even turned up a piece of Egyptian lustreware from the late twelfth century, one of the very few examples found anywhere in the empire.[73] In the western Balkans, Bishop Theophylact of Ochrida (Ochrid) at the end of the eleventh century was sending the same whiny letters about exile as John Mauropous in Euchaita and Michael Choniates in Athens, but was equally connected to the doings of the capital. Ochrida, which was near the main land road from the capital to the Adriatic at Dyrrachion (Durrës), was, indeed, according to al-Idrīsī, a local entrepôt in itself.[74] All the same, Balkan connections with the wider exchange networks of the empire were relatively minor, hardly greater than those of the Anatolian plateau.

4.2.5 The southern Adriatic and Ionian Seas

I shall spend as little space on this part of the Byzantine Empire, but not because, as with the Anatolian plateau and the northern Balkans, it was distant from the

[71] A general survey of imports is Manolova-Voykova, 'Import of Middle Byzantine pottery'; see further Koleva, 'Byzantine sgraffito pottery'. For Veliko Tărnovo, see Dochev, 'Tŭrnovo', and Georgieva, 'Keramikata ot dvoretsa na Tsarevets', pp. 58–61; for Preslav, see, e.g., Curta, *Southeastern Europe*, pp. 218–21 and Kostova, 'Polychrome ceramics'. For Dyadovo, see Borisov, *Djadovo*, 1, pp. 215–20 for golden engobe, pp. 193–4, 231–44 for imports. Dyadovo's prosperity is further underlined by its large number of iron tools and weapons; see ibid., pp. 79–131. A brief general account of golden engobe is Manolova, 'Medieval ceramics', drawing on Bulgarian-language publications. For other imports, see, e.g., Popović, 'Importation et production locale', for Ras; see also Miholjek et al., 'The Byzantine shipwreck of Cape Stoba' and Todorova, '"Dark Age" amphorae from present-day Bulgaria' for amphora imports, largely on the coast or the Danube. See also Kazhdan and Wharton Epstein, *Change*, pp. 32–3; for Thessaloniki's links up the rivers to the north, see Laiou, 'Regional networks', pp. 135–7.

[72] One of the study areas reported on in Izdebski et al., 'Exploring Byzantine and Ottoman history', is in eastern Bulgaria, where cereals and vine palynology show growth after 1000.

[73] Gautier, 'Le typikon du sébaste Grégoire Pakourianos', pp. 35–43; cf. Lemerle, *Cinq études*, pp. 115–91; for lustre, see Archaeology, https://www.archaeology.org/news/6549-180417-bulgaria-medieval-murals/, accessed 21 September 2022.

[74] For the context of the letters, see Mullett, *Theophylact*; for the entrepôt, see al-Idrīsī, *Nuzhat al-mushtaq*, trans. Jaubert and Nef, p. 403.

Mediterranean exchange systems of our period. Rather, it is because the evidence for the west coast of what is now Greece and Albania is relatively restricted in quantity (the Byzantines had little foothold farther north in the Adriatic after Venice slipped away from its authority); and mainland Italy—in this case the Byzantine themes of Laggobardia (modern Puglia) and Kalabria—is not part of the sectors of the Mediterranean I have selected for analysis. In fact, the subregion was not cut off at all. The western Balkan coast was tied both to the exchange of the Aegean and to that of Italy, and had been since the eighth and ninth centuries, when the Ionian Sea was the focus of the west Byzantine networks marked by amphorae which linked the Aegean to the Adriatic, Sicily, and the Tyrrhenian Sea.[75] In our period, Bouthroton (Butrint), the best-excavated site, at the southern tip of Albania opposite Corfu, was an active town, with settlement spreading out of the old urban core to suburban villas. It was so closely connected to Italy that half of the ceramics found there, dating to between 900 and 1050, were from Puglia (the rest were mostly local); Pugliese Otranto 2 amphorae were important into the twelfth century too.[76] That is a significant sign of the unity of the two sides of the Adriatic, for by 1060 the Normans had conquered the Byzantine provinces of Italy, and spent much of the next century, on and off, attacking the west Balkan coastline as well.

And on a smaller scale, there were also Aegean connections. Günsenin 1 amphorae were found in Butrint, as also in fairly piecemeal field surveys in Epiros to its south, plus in Arta, in the centre of Epiros, which was newly important after 1100. Both Butrint and Arta had Aegean fine wares in the twelfth century, and so did Durrës, farther up the coast from Butrint, where Corinth wares are found with a few GWW, Otranto 1 and 2 amphorae, and some Günsenin 3. Otranto had Corinth wares as well, for that matter, for all that it or its hinterland was a major ceramic centre on its own account.[77] The main port of Corinth looks westwards in geographical terms, down the Gulf of Corinth, even though its own closest links were with the Aegean; Corinth, indeed, made amphorae closely resembling Otranto 2.[78] This makes Corinth glaze less surprising as a find around the Ionian Sea, but Günsenin amphorae and GWW had to have come from farther away. This is emphasized still more by the finds from wrecks. On the tenth- or eleventh-century

[75] See in general the collection of articles on amphorae in *Archeologia medievale*, 45 (2018), and pp. 304–5, 636–8 below.

[76] Hodges, 'Excavating away the "poison"', p. 14; Reynolds, 'The medieval amphorae'. For this site as a whole, see the publication volumes, Hodges et al., *Byzantine Butrint*, and Hansen et al., *Butrint 4*.

[77] Vroom, 'The medieval and post-medieval finewares'; Veikou, *Byzantine Epirus*, pp. 220, 222–5. For Otranto, see esp. Patterson and Whitehouse, 'The medieval domestic pottery', and Arthur, 'Amphorae for bulk transport', updated in Leo Imperiale, 'Anfore e reti commerciali'. Where in Puglia 'Otranto' amphora types were actually made is not yet clear, and a few seem also to be products of the Aegean; see n. 78 below. For Durrës, see Tartari, 'Amforat e muzeut arkeologjik të Durrësit', esp. pp. 265–6, 276–7; Metalla, 'La céramique médiévale en Albanie'; Metalla, 'Les données céramiques', pp. 600–4.

[78] Leo Imperiale, 'Anfore e reti commerciali', pp. 54–6.

Mljet wreck found near Ragusa (Dubrovnik) in the south-central Adriatic, most of the numerous amphorae were apparently of Aegean and even Black Sea types (here there were only a handful of Günsenin amphorae, which perhaps hints at a tenth-century date rather than later); another probable wreck off Brindisi shows Otranto amphorae together with Günsenin types.[79] Although the internal exchange of the southern Adriatic and Ionian Seas was, as usual, the most important relationship for the urban centres on its coast and for their hinterlands, it was open to traffic from much farther afield too.

One of these links for longer-distance traffic was Venice; and when Venetian trade began to expand beyond luxury items in the eleventh century and above all in the twelfth, the southern Adriatic, which was on its route to everywhere, was inevitably linked into it as well.[80] That we will look at, however, in more detail in Chapters 6 and 7.

* * *

This survey of Byzantine subregions can serve as an introduction to the empire as a whole, and to its urban hierarchies, which we will need as we move on in this chapter. But it is above all set out so as to make it clear that the empire cannot be considered to be a single economic and geographical unit. Its economic history is sometimes discussed as if it was one, with examples chosen from Butrint to Ankara; that is a mistake. For different reasons, the large inland areas of the Anatolian plateau and Balkans do not usefully fit together with the economy of the Aegean. Egypt can be seen as an ecological whole; Sicily and Tunisia are both small enough for us to be able to treat them as one. But the Byzantine Empire is different, for it is a region defined politically, not geographically or ecologically. Technically, it is a category error to set it beside the others. It is a convenient category error, and it does at least reflect the fact that its subregions were linked together by a highly active and pervasive state, although less than the Roman Empire had managed (and even it found Anatolia hard to incorporate economically). But it has meant here that I have had to spend some time explaining which subregions of the empire will not be further discussed in this book, and why. The rest of this chapter, accordingly, will focus on the exchange networks of the Aegean and Marmara Seas and their immediate hinterlands.

4.3 The Archaeology of Byzantine Exchange

Archaeological field survey has left no doubt that the Middle Byzantine period, particularly in central and southern Greece, was one of agrarian expansion, and

[79] Miholjek et al., 'The Byzantine shipwreck of Cape Stoba'; for Brindisi, see Leo Imperiale, 'Anfore e reti commerciali', p. 58 (it is not certain that these amphorae came from a wreck, but it seems likely to me). Aegean amphorae also reached Ravenna in this period; see Cirelli, 'Anfore medievali'.

[80] See esp. Dorin, 'Adriatic trade networks'.

of a growth in prosperity for at least some sections of the rural population. The palynology for central Greece, from several sites, shows a pick-up for cereals around 900, with vines perhaps earlier.[81] In the Lakonia survey, of 75 square kilometres of land just outside Sparta to the north-east, there were three main sites visible in the tenth century, later to be the main villages of the area, all with some utilitarian Constantinopolitan ceramics, including an amphora type, Saraçhane 35, and one GWW 2 sherd; in the eleventh, there were twelve new sites; in the twelfth there were as many as sixty-seven inhabited sites in all. By then there was a settlement hierarchy, in which ceramic finds were backed up by phosphate analysis, with what the archaeologist responsible, Pamela Armstrong, calls villages, hamlets, estates, and single houses, that is to say, numerous examples of dispersed settlement set alongside more concentrated villages. At the top end of the hierarchy, one of the former village sites was beginning to develop urban features and its own dependent settlements. There were also sites with no signs of habitation, but still with amphorae, perhaps to hold water for agricultural workers. In general, smaller sites were identified only by amphorae, of a variety of local types, plus a number of rather commoner wars with local fabrics. Sites of varying sizes had glazed wares from Greece by the twelfth century, and one even had a glazed bowl from Iran. The twelfth century was here a high point; the evidence was much less extensive after 1200. And all this matches the scrappier evidence from small-scale excavation in Sparta's city centre, which shows dense eleventh- and twelfth-century housing in the few sites which have been studied, and a substantial area of brick kilns.[82]

Lakonia has had the good luck to have both a large-scale survey and a systematic publication; but the patterns it shows are repeated elsewhere (see Map 14). In the Peloponnesos, we find it in smaller surveys for the eleventh and twelfth centuries around Nichoria in the south-west, in the Argolid in the north-east, and around both Limnes and Nemea between Argos and Corinth. Farther north, the island of Kea, off the coast of Attica, had a twelfth-century high point, with some sites marked by Greek glazed wares from the early and late twelfth century, and many more by Günsenin 3 wine amphorae from Chalkis, which was a major production by the mid-twelfth century (here the amphorae were being reused, but they had to get to Kea in the first place).[83] Boeotia (it was called Hellas or Katodika in our period), around Thebes, has had the most intense surveys, which unfortunately have only been partially published. Here, all the same, in surveys

[81] See Izdebski et al., 'Exploring Byzantine and Ottoman history'.

[82] Armstrong, 'The survey area', pp. 353–68 and Armstrong, 'The Byzantine and Ottoman pottery', updated in Armstrong, 'Greece in the eleventh century' (which also discusses the town).

[83] McDonald et al., *Excavations at Nichoria*, 3, pp. 354–424 (a survey and an excavation; p. 379 for Constantinople and Corinth glaze in the latter); Koukoulis, 'Medieval Methana'; Jameson et al., *A Greek countryside*, pp. 405–9; Hahn, 'The Berbati-Limnes project', pp. 347, 432–3; Athanassopoulos, 'Landscape archaeology', pp. 88–94; Cherry et al., *Landscape archaeology*, pp. 353–7, for Kea. Most of these smaller surveys are very sketchily published for this period.

north-west, west, east, and south of Thebes, it is clear that the eleventh and particularly the twelfth century showed a sharp increase in identifiable sites, and the early twelfth to early thirteenth showed glazed wares, and again Günsenin 3, all largely from nearby Chalkis, on many village sites. Indeed, in western Boeotia, the latter amphora type, plus late twelfth-century Fine and/or Incised Sgraffito ware, were found on almost every Middle Byzantine site, alongside the plain glazed wares which are the most common fine wares everywhere. This must indicate that the area exported wine, for amphorae made in Chalkis, Boeotia's main port, could not easily indicate imports to the province (anyway, wine imports on that scale, to land which could for the most part produce its own, are implausible); but that export must have been fairly systematic for amphorae to be brought in from the coast to carry it.[84]

Let us look at demographic change first, and then the growth in exchange. Surveys show the availability of recognizable pottery most directly, not the rise or fall of settlement in itself. Periods where the pottery is unrecognizable do not show up in survey (this is a classic problem for the eighth and ninth centuries). Nor do sites where the inhabitants do not have access to recognizable pottery, either because trade routes do not reach them or because their inhabitants cannot afford them. As to access, very little of Greece is more than 50 kilometres from the sea, which helped availability in this part of the Byzantine world at least. (The same is true for the Marmara region, and only the upper Maiander is farther away in Aegean-facing western Turkey; but surveys for this period are anyway less good in Turkey than in Greece.) I would be unsurprised to find few recognizable Middle Byzantine types in Greece's mountain interior, but fewer people have ever lived there. As to the problem of affordability, one of the best-surveyed western Boeotia sites fits such a picture very well: a hamlet site just outside modern Thespies, some 10 kilometres west of Thebes, named THS14 in the survey, had tenth- to twelfth-century wares, but only one of them was glazed, and few of the amphorae definitely came from elsewhere. This was clearly a site with people too poor to buy much glazed pottery, given that it was widely available in sites not so far away, although even they had some access to imported goods. A less intensive survey might not have identified it at all; and we cannot on the evidence say that it was unoccupied before 900 either.[85]

So the great increase in the number of pottery-dated sites after 1000 and especially 1100 does not in itself automatically show demographic growth. The

[84] Armstrong, 'Some Byzantine and later settlements' (this is technically Phokis not Boeotia, but is part of the same geographical area); Vroom, *After Antiquity*, pp. 133, 152–64, 192–3; Vroom, 'Shifting Byzantine networks'; Vionis, 'Current archaeological research'; Vionis, 'The Byzantine to early modern pottery from Thespiai', pp. 354–68; Vionis, 'Understanding settlements', esp. pp. 160–9; Liard and Kondyli, 'Pottery traditions "beyond" Byzantium'. Cf. the more scattered twelfth-century rural activity in Thessaly and the Peloponnesos listed in Gerousi, 'Rural Greece'.

[85] Bintliff et al., *Testing the hinterland*, pp. 75–7, 179, 285–92; Vroom, *After Antiquity*, pp. 123–4.

Corinth expert Guy Sanders has even argued that pottery is not particularly cheap. But his own evidence, late medieval and late modern pottery prices set against wages, also shows that it was still inside the pockets of even agricultural wage labourers; and excavations and surveys of apparently poor sites, such as THS14 or fourteenth-century Panakton between Thebes and Athens, simply show less pottery and (especially) less glazed pottery than elsewhere, rather than by any means none at all. Anyway, the availability of non-local eleventh- and twelfth-century glazed wares and amphorae on very many sites in an area shows beyond doubt that people on very many sites could afford to buy them, usually for the first time in this period. Indeed, local wares, generally more utilitarian types but in this period mostly well made, will almost always have been bought too. Whether buyers of glazed wares were only village elites or whether they represented a wider range of peasants cannot easily be known, but they certainly show greater buying power on the part of someone; and effectively everyone bought utilitarian wares in larger or smaller quantities. Véronique François has recently commented that 'Glazed pottery, in whichever period, and by contrast with what one can still too often read, was not a luxury ware,' even if, as she too assumes, the very poor did not buy it; this is my view too. Furthermore, a critical reading of the Lakonia survey report in my view clearly supports Armstrong's argument that there really were more—and larger—sites there as well, after 1100 in particular, which means that population growth increased at the same time as buying power per site.[86]

Here we need also to factor in the written evidence for demography, for it points in the same direction, and adds Macedonia to this central and southern Greek set. (There is no useful written evidence for other areas before 1200.) The documentation of the Athonite monasteries of Iviron and the Lavra shows a steady growth in the number of their tenants in what is now northern Greece, even at times when monastic land was not increasing—growth which is first identifiable in the eleventh century, and continued into the early fourteenth. Iviron data for a set of nine villages in and around the Chalkidiki peninsula indeed show an increase in tenant families of 82 per cent between the early twelfth and the early fourteenth centuries.[87] This is matched by some explicit evidence in

[86] Sanders, *Recent finds*; Papanikola-Bakirtzi, 'Byzantine glazed ceramics on the market', p. 215, calls glazed wares of this period 'semiluxury goods' until after 1200, which matches Sanders's view. Conversely, see François, *La vaisselle de terre*, p. 153 (quotation). For Panakton, see Gerstel et al., 'A late medieval settlement at Panakton', esp. pp. 218–23. Boeotia as well as Lakonia has been argued, convincingly, to show glazed wares which were widely available to peasant strata in our period; see Vroom, *After Antiquity*, p. 364; Vionis, 'The Byzantine to early modern pottery from Thespiai', p. 368; Vionis, 'Understanding settlements', pp. 160, 168. In late medieval Valencia in eastern Spain, where we also have documents with prices, glazed pottery was certainly relatively inexpensive, which supports François's argument; see Almenar Fernández, 'Why did villagers buy earthenware?'.

[87] Lefort, *Société rurale*, pp. 238–40, with the figure of 82% in Lefort, 'The rural economy', p. 270; Harvey, *Economic expansion*, pp. 47–61. The island of Patmos is sometimes added to the evidence for Macedonia, but the data set is too tiny there, and I doubt very much the rhetoric of prior

our written sources for land clearance: the early tenth-century *Fiscal treatise* (see p. 343 below) discusses the foundation of new settlements outside villages and the improvement of land; and several landowners in wills and other sources congratulate themselves on having built housing, cleared land, or paid for irrigation in Thrace, Bithynia, and even eastern Anatolia—which, however true the claims are, at least shows us that such clearance was seen as a positive act. (Irrigation does not actually appear so very often in the sources, nonetheless; Kaplan saw its incidence as relatively modest, and it seems to have been used above all for gardens, sometimes under the control of village communities.) But the evidence from the Athos documents is more solid than this. It also shows the appearance, and sometimes foundation, of new villages, and the bringing of 'klasmatic' (abandoned and therefore untaxed) land into cultivation; for example, the village of Dobrobikeia on the eastern Macedonian coast was uninhabited in the late tenth century, was acquired as klasmatic land by Iviron before 1041, had twenty-four tenant families later in the eleventh century, and twenty-eight by 1104. The Thebes cadaster (the surviving section of a local tax record from the late eleventh century) also hints at cleared klasmatic land, matching the rather better evidence from the archaeology there.[88] Indeed, even for Macedonia the written sources do not seem to me stronger than the archaeological data we have for farther south. But the two support each other; and the written evidence also explicitly introduces another side to demographic growth, which is the increase in land cultivated, and the intensification of production on that land. Without that, such growth would, anyway, lead to impoverishment, and not to the expansion of production and exchange.

This is because, overall, what is clear, above all from the archaeology, is that agrarian production and exchange did increase across our period. The long eleventh century was a period in which estates were growing in size, which means a greater proportion of rent-paying tenants than in previous centuries (see pp. 340–9 below), but this did not weaken the capillary commercial networks which the archaeological distributions clearly show—quite the opposite. People could buy fine tablewares, and in some areas sell wine for export, far into the countryside. So there is no doubt that this picture of the eleventh and twelfth centuries is one

abandonment of the island used by the monastery's founder (e.g. Miklosich and Müller, *Acta*, 6, n. 19, p. 64)—it is a topos in foundation texts.

[88] See Harvey, *Economic expansion*, pp. 57–66 (for Dobrobikeia, pp. 61–2, and *Actes d'Iviron*, 1, n. 30; 2, nn. 32, 52; see also Lefort, *Société rurale*, p. 75); Kaplan, *Les hommes*, pp. 533–40; Lefort, 'The rural economy', pp. 271–5; they all give good general overviews. For other texts, see, in turn, Dölger, *Beiträge*, pp. 115–16; Gautier, 'Le typikon du sébaste Grégoire Pakourianos', pp. 37, 127; Psellus, *Epistulae*, ed. Papaioannou, n. 91 (Psellos, *Epistolai*, ed. Sathas, n. 29); Lemerle, *Cinq études*, pp. 21–2, for Eustathios Boilas. The last two of these praise their own patronage of irrigation, for which see Harvey, *Economic expansion*, pp. 134–5; Kaplan, *Les hommes*, pp. 67–8, 193–4, 307, 566; Lefort, 'The rural economy', pp. 253, 280. For Thebes, see Svoronos, *Recherches sur le cadastre byzantin*, cf. Harvey, 'Economic expansion in central Greece', pp. 24–7.

of growth in buying power and exchange networks, which in the countryside means agrarian growth regardless of demography; but there is equally no doubt that there was demographic growth too.

* * *

This picture of an expanding agrarian economy is a good backdrop for what we can say directly about exchange, in both artisanal and agricultural goods, on the basis of the archaeological record. I here offer a narrative of its development, taken from the patterns of ceramic types. I argued in Chapters 2 and 3 that ceramic distributions—which, as we have seen, are generally taken as a proxy for other bulk artisanal goods, especially cloth (and also a direct guide to one major food item, wine, which was carried in amphorae)—could in Egypt and Sicily be shown actually to match the patterns shown by the documentation for flax/linen and cotton. This is the case for Byzantium too, given our written evidence for silk, as we shall see in the next section of the chapter. But silk is not a good marker for bulk trade; ceramics is a better guide. So let us start with that archaeological narrative, before we ask questions of it.

In the eighth and ninth centuries, most Byzantine ceramic exchange was local. It is not straightforward to establish typologies for pottery in this period, and, when we do, the identifiable types are usually not found outside relatively small areas. There are two particularly significant exceptions to this: Glazed White ware (GWW) 1 from the capital, and amphorae. There has been a large amount of recent work on post-Roman amphorae in the Mediterranean, summed up in a major conference publication in 2018. In rapid synthesis, Byzantine amphorae from that period appear in only a small number of forms, above all a globular form which resembles the pre-seventh-century LRA 2 type sufficiently that they are often called 'post-LRA 2' (alternatively, LRA 13 or Saraçhane 29, 32–42), and in fairly standard sizes; they were mostly for wine, but probably with some olive oil (see Fig. 9). But fabric analysis makes it clear that they were made in a variety of different places: some in Italy, notably Naples and Otranto; some perhaps in the Black Sea; and much in the Aegean, where some of the seventh- and eighth-century island kilns, on Crete, Kos, Paros, and Leipsoi near Miletos, produced either post-LRA 2 or late versions of LRA 1 amphorae or both. These productions overlapped quite substantially, at least in that Aegean globular amphorae have been identified in a variety of locations in Italy together with Italian types—for Aegean types are found nearly everywhere, whereas the Italian productions had more local or regional distributions. They connected the Tyrrhenian Sea, the Adriatic, and the Aegean, with the Ionian Sea in the centre, even though they came from different places; the Aegean, closest to imperial power, was the most important production and distribution focus. They operated as an east–west exchange network, in fact the most active in the Mediterranean in the ninth century, as we shall see in Chapter 7, but they were almost exclusively restricted

Fig. 9 Byzantine globular amphora

to regions under Byzantine rule. Their quantities are low by the standards of both before and after, but not trivially low, and, in some fortunate find-spots such as Malta, high; this pattern is steady across two centuries, with finds across all the Byzantine lands, overwhelmingly on or near coasts. Their relatively regular size leads one to conclude that they may well have had a fiscal context. It is less likely that this was a tax in wine (or oil), for even though this is a period when taxation was taken in kind more often than money, one would expect there to be more Italian amphorae in the Aegean and fewer Aegean amphorae in Italy in that case; but they could have been related to army supply.[89]

For GWW 1, a direct fiscal connection is less likely, but the fact that fine ceramics from the capital, again available (in much smaller quantities than the amphorae) everywhere along the coasts of the empire, were the only non-local

[89] Wickham, *Framing*, pp. 785–93 summarizes knowledge to 2003; see Haldon, 'Commerce and exchange', of 2012, for a more up-to-date picture of the economy as a whole up to the early ninth century. For the importance of local productions after the early eighth century, set against some more widely available products, see most recently Vionis, 'Bridging the early medieval "ceramic gap"', with some new typologies; Poulou, 'Sailing in the dark'; Vroom, 'A gentle transition?'. For amphorae, see esp. the collection of articles in *Archeologia medievale* 45 (2018). For the Aegean, see also Poulou, 'Transport amphorae and trade' (p. 205 for wine and oil), and Poulou-Papadimitriou and Nodarou, 'Transport vessels'; for Malta, see Bruno and Cutajar, 'Imported amphorae'; for Sicily, see Chapter 3, n. 172 above. For some of the Aegean sites, see further Papavassiliou et al., 'A ceramic workshop'; Didioumi, 'Local pottery production'. Note that Egypt (probably the western Sinai coast) also produced globular amphorae in the eighth century, which is the best example of the wide cultural diffusion of this amphora type; Egyptian versions have been found in Fusṭāṭ and Beirut, but have not been identified in the Byzantine lands themselves. See Gayraud and Treglia, 'Amphores, céramiques culinaires et céramiques communes omeyyades', pp. 366–7; thanks to Joanita Vroom for alerting me to this.

Fig. 10 Glazed White Ware 2

Fig. 11 Günsenin 1 amphora

tablewares in these centuries, emphasizes the centrality of the capital in an otherwise very localized period, and that reflects the political and fiscal role of Constantinople quite closely. GWW probably always followed the old main Aegean sea routes, from the Dardanelles west to Thessaloniki and then down the west coast, or else due south down the east coast, the basic routes out from the capital.[90]

The tenth and eleventh centuries show similar patterns to this, but by now they are more complex (see Map 14). GWW 2, the tenth- and eleventh-century form

[90] For a recent distribution map of GWW 1, see François, *La vaisselle de terre*, p. 119.

of Glazed White ware (see Fig. 10), has a much denser distribution than its predecessor, particularly in the Aegean, but outside it too.[91] A finer type of it, Polychrome ware—finer because it used a range of colours—is also attested very widely, although on a very small scale, across the same centuries, probably starting in the mid-ninth; a version of Polychrome ware was also made, presumably influenced by Byzantine craftsmen, for a short period from the late ninth in Preslav, the capital of then independent Bulgaria.[92] These were the dominant fine wares we have record of so far; Corinth produced glazed pottery too by now, a plain brown-glazed type apparently imitating GWW (and plenty of unglazed), but this is above all attested locally.[93]

As to amphorae, Ganos/Günsenin 1 amphorae (see Fig. 11) were very widely available in the tenth and eleventh centuries, as we saw earlier. Otranto amphorae (a misleading technical term; as we saw earlier, they were not necessarily made in Otranto itself, and some were made outside Puglia, including at Corinth) were widespread too, particularly in the Adriatic and Ionian Seas, alongside a range of other amphorae, as seen, for example, in the Mljet wreck. One amphora type from that wreck, sometimes called Saraçhane 55–59, again with a distribution stretching from the Adriatic to the Black Sea, was made, given its fabric, in the Ephesos area; the eleventh- and twelfth-century Günsenin 2 was made, as recent kiln finds and petrological analysis show, in large part in Chalkis. These amphorae, and others which are less often seen (John Hayes identified twenty-four different types from the tenth to late twelfth centuries in Saraçhane, although other scholars amalgamate several of them), were no longer regular in size or shape.[94] Ganos wine, as we have seen, fed the capital; and the variety and intermingling of these types in general indicate not a fiscal purpose, but, rather, commerce, just as GWW and Polychrome ware does.

Commerce in what, though? My comments on the post-900 period so far tend to assume wine, which was certainly the major production at Ganos. Recent analyses of contents both nuance this and confirm it. Amphorae in our period could, in principle, as noted earlier, in addition to wine, carry olive oil, vegetables, fish and fish sauce, and, occasionally, dry goods too. The fact that they were generally

[91] Hayes, *Excavations at Saraçhane*, 2, pp. 18–29, with, for other sites, Böhlendorf-Arslan, *Glasierte byzantinische Keramik*, 1, pp. 155–69; and François, *La vaisselle de terre*, pp. 119–22.

[92] For Polychrome ware, see Hayes, *Excavations at Saraçhane*, 2, pp. 35–7, with a proposed later redating by Sanders, 'Byzantine Polychrome pottery'; but the Preslav finds, even though production there was on a very small scale (Kostova, 'Polychrome ceramics in Preslav'), seem to show that the ware started earlier than Sanders says (cf. Dark, 'Pottery production', pp. 119–21).

[93] Sanders, 'Recent developments', p. 391; White, *An investigation*, pp. 69–70. But see n. 103 below for Brown glaze in Aphrodisias; it may have been exported more often than is yet thought.

[94] For Günsenin types, see Günsenin, *Les amphores byzantines*, updated in Günsenin, 'La typologie des amphores Günsenin'; for Otranto types see esp. now Leo Imperiale, 'Anfore e reti commerciali' for a new Otranto typology. See also Garver, *Byzantine amphoras*, Miholjek at al., 'The Byzantine shipwreck of Cape Stoba', and Hayes, *Excavations at Saraçhane*, 2, pp. 73–7, for overviews of these and other types, with competing typologies. See Waksman et al., 'Investigating the origins', for Günsenin 2 being mostly made in Chalkis; Vroom, 'On the trail of the enigma amphora', for Ephesos; White, *An investigation*, pp. 45–53, for Corinth amphora (and also glazed-ware) kilns.

resinated or pitched inside did not by any means restrict them to carrying wine; and they were regularly reused for different purposes. All the same, contents analysis so far tends to imply that they were, in fact, *mostly* wine amphorae, as at Ganos.[95] It can be added that the only area of the empire where we have really good evidence for oil production, at least in the twelfth century, is Lakonia, around Sparta; but the local amphorae found there in detailed survey were not exported outside the area. Olive oil, which was along with wine the most important content by far for amphorae under the Roman Empire, was largely carried in skins in the Fāṭimid world, as we have seen (see p. 139 above); it is likely that the same was true of Byzantium by now, and one casual reference to skins in the letters of Michael Choniates backs this up.[96] With due caution, then, we can indeed see amphora distributions as above all a guide to wine sales. Their overlapping interconnection might be a marker of different wine types—Ganos, for instance, seems to have been, at least sometimes, sweet wine.[97] I will come back to this; but the key point is that from 900, and still more from 1000, there are clear archaeological signs of a commercial distribution of wine in the Aegean and Marmara and outwards from there, at least on the coasts, plus a steadily wider availability of fine wares from the capital.

This was then built on, from the last decade or so of the eleventh century onwards (see Map 15). A major new amphora by the mid-twelfth century is Günsenin 3, made in Chalkis above all, which is found not only on virtually every archaeological excavation around the Aegean, but also on some quite small sites in surveys, as we have seen; it is the best-attested amphora out of all those from our period (see Fig. 12).[98] But it is in glazed pottery that a particularly clear step change took place. As we saw earlier, Byzantine archaeology is fortunate in having, from before the Second World War, an early type site at Corinth, which was also very well excavated by the standards of the period. In 1942, Charles Morgan published the medieval glazed ceramics from those excavations, establishing a typology which has lasted until the present day, with only minor refinements—the only major change is in its chronology, which Guy Sanders redated in the

[95] Pecci, 'Analisi dei residui organici e anfore medievali' gives a sensible overview of the issues; Pecci et al., 'Residue analysis of medieval amphorae', indicates wine contents for Günsenin 3 and 4; this is also supported, more tentatively, by Koutsouflakis, 'The transportation of amphorae'.

[96] For Sparta oil in Venetian documents, see n. 155 below. Armstrong. 'Greece in the eleventh century', notes the absence of oil amphorae. (In Armstrong, 'The Byzantine and Ottoman pottery', pp. 133–8, she identified locally made types, but these do not have a wider distribution, and she now sees them as being for water, not for transport.) She favours barrels as an alternative container, which is certainly possible as well (see also McCormick, 'Movements and markets', p. 93), as it was not in wood-poor Egypt; but see Michael Choniates, *Epistulae*, ed. Kolovou, n. 84.3, citing an *askos* (skin) of oil.

[97] Sweet Ganos wine: *Poèmes prodromiques*, ed. Hesseling and Pernot, poem 3, l. 285.

[98] See recently in general for Günsenin 3, Armstrong, 'Greece in the eleventh century'; for Chalkis, see Waksman et al., '*Investigating the origins*', Vroom, 'Shifting Byzantine networks'. Some other surveys: for Tanagra, see Vionis, 'Current archaeological research'; for Kythera, see Vroom, 'The medieval pottery', p. 56. Koutsouflakis, 'The transportation of amphorae' shows the wide distribution of wrecks containing Günsenin 3, and argues for a late twelfth-century height for Byzantine wrecks. One such wreck, found in Rhodes harbour, also contained cheese inside a goatskin.

Fig. 12 Günsenin 3 amphora

1990s.[99] (This contrasts very notably with Egyptian typologies for glazed pottery, which have been disputed for decades, and have had, as mentioned earlier, p. 89, recent well-argued criticisms of the legitimacy of typology at all, at least for glazed decorative schemes.) The white wares from the capital we have already seen; by now, as well as GWW 2 still, we are moving into the period of GWW 4, which had a similarly wide distribution.[100] But from here on they are matched in Corinth and other Greek sites by red-fabric glazed wares, with slipped, painted, and above all sgraffito (incised) decoration, under the glaze: in rough chronological order from *c*.1090 to *c*.1190, Slip-Painted (or Light on Dark Slip-Painted) ware, Green and Brown Painted ware (both of these two were made across the whole century), the rare Spatter Painted ware, Measles ware (a name which has survived more po-faced variants: it has neat spots of red between incised decorations; see Fig. 13), Painted Sgraffito ware, Fine Sgraffito ware (see Fig. 14), and then from 1150 or so, going on into the thirteenth century, Incised Sgraffito ware and Champlevé ware. All these types, however, overlap in time very substantially. At the very end of the twelfth century and above all in the thirteenth we also find Zeuxippus ware, the only one which Morgan did not name; this is too late for us as a type, but I will occasionally refer to it all the same. All these sat beside plain glazed wares, which were the majority of glazed ceramics produced throughout

[99] Morgan, *Corinth XI*; Sanders, *Byzantine glazed pottery*, ch. 5, set out most clearly in Sanders , 'Recent developments', which is the fundamental article for ceramic dating in Corinth, and is developed systematically by White, *An investigation*, pp. 64–82.

[100] See Hayes, *Excavations at Saraçhane*, 2, pp. 18–40. GWW 3 and 5 do not have much of a distribution outside the capital; GWW 4 is the major successor to 2. Some of both have painted decoration.

Fig. 13 Measles ware

Fig. 14 Fine Sgraffito ware

the period, but which generally had more local distributions. This complex set is, in fact, even more complex in expert hands, with several subtypes proposed by Morgan and Sanders and more recently Harriet White, but this is enough for now.[101] Few

[101] See n. 99 above for the Corinth-based typologies. For all Middle Byzantine types, Vroom, *Byzantine to modern pottery in the Aegean*, pp. 67–106, is also an excellent and convenient starting

of these types had more than two colours, and are in this respect unlike many top-of-the-line Islamic wares; but it is incised decoration which, even if originally an Islamic innovation, is the real hallmark of a Byzantine ceramic aesthetic from now on. These red-fabric glazes had a different chemical composition from Constantinopolitan glaze, with lead rather than lead alkali as the basic chemical constituent; this marked technological innovation for sure, and so did a steadily increasing fineness of fabric across the twelfth century. Conversely, Byzantine potters of our period never adopted much tin glaze technology or frit fabrics, let alone lustre, from the Islamic world.[102]

These types were all identified in Corinth, but they did not all come from there. Some were certainly local, given the work done on several kilns in the city, and petrological analysis of types found outside them; glazed wares of several different types began to be made around 1090 there. But Chalkis has recently emerged as a major alternative production site for glazed ware too, given petrological analysis again, and the excavation of a kiln area; it seems to have begun about the same time as Corinth, or slightly later. Both of these towns had a back history of more utilitarian productions or simple glazes before the late eleventh century, as we have seen, including amphorae, and this will of course have helped to give potters in each the requisite expertise, plus in the case of amphorae an already established set of export routes. But from now on they took over the Aegean market for fine wares, partly displacing GWW, which in its twelfth-century forms (themselves more decorated than before) was less dominant; wares from Constantinople remained by far the most important in the capital itself and the Marmara coasts, and competed with red-fabric glazed wares in western Turkey, but in Greece the latter are far more visible. Aphrodisias in western Turkey is as good an example as any of the way these patterns developed: eleventh-century imports there tended to be from the Marmara (GWW 2 and Günsenin 1), but in the twelfth Greek red wares are much commoner, particularly Fine Sgraffito ware.[103]

point. Waksman and François, 'Vers une redéfinition typologique et analytique', establish a typology for Zeuxippus ware. The percentage of glazed wares among total pottery finds went up as well in the twelfth century, from—using Corinth percentages—0.7% before 1100 to 6% by 1150 (and 20% by 1250); see Sanders, 'Recent developments', p. 394; at Chalkis the percentage of glaze was even higher (Vroom, 'Shifting Byzantine networks'). Note that English-language Byzantine archaeology universally uses the spelling Sgraffito, and not Sgraffiato, which is commoner in Egyptian work. Both are Italian words, but Italians studying our period often regard the former as an English technical term for *graffito* decoration (see, e.g., Gelichi, 'La ceramica bizantina in Italia', p. 25).

[102] See White, *An investigation*, pp. 133–9, for the lead analyses (they are more complex than my rapid summary); for the absence of Islamic influence, see François, *La vaisselle de terre*, pp. 51, 97–9; there was some tin-glazing, but it was relatively rare. It is worth adding that this was not the result of metal availability; although tin resources are almost absent in the Byzantine lands, this is even more true of the Islamic eastern and southern Mediterranean, where tin glaze was significant—the closest deposits are in Italy (in Sardinia and Tuscany) and Spain. See W. Sheppard Baird's maps, 'The distribution of tin (casseritite)', https://www.minoanatlantis.com/Tin_Distribution.php, accessed 10 January 2022.

[103] For good surveys of the complexity of twelfth-century production and exchange, see François, *La vaisselle de terre*; Vroom, *After Antiquity*; Vroom, 'Byzantine sea trade'; Dimopoulos, 'Trade of

Which of Corinth and Chalkis was the major producer is as yet unclear, and probably not really important. More significant is that both sat at the top of a hierarchy of other producers. These included Sparta, Argos, and Athens, plus, on the Turkish coast, Ephesos with its amphora production, the only major Anatolian ceramic site known before the thirteenth century; and then, on a smaller scale, central Crete, with its imitations of mainland glazes and Günsenin 3, and also the smaller Boeotian centres, with local glaze production. It is also noteworthy that the main Greek sites produced fairly similar wares. There is some specialization: Measles ware seems to have been made in Corinth and Argos; Fine Sgraffito ware was more a Chalkis product. But these specializations are only relative, and it is clear that potters imitated each other. The only major ware which neither Corinth nor Chalkis produced was Zeuxippus ware from the end of the twelfth century onwards; this was a type with a centralized production, given its standardized fabrics, but the site for it has not yet been identified, although some of its many imitations have been localized (one was at Pergamon).[104]

The routes each of these ware types took were intricate and overlapping. Surveys routinely find both Corinth and Chalkis wares together with GWW, when analysis is recent enough to be specific. We find Chalkis and Sparta pottery in Corinth, and, conversely, Corinth pottery in Boeotia, inland from Chalkis.[105] At the atypical inland Anatolian site of Sagalassos, there was no GWW, even though

Byzantine red wares'; White, *An investigation*; Papanikola-Bakirtzi, 'Byzantine glazed ceramics on the market'; Papanikola-Bakirtzi, 'Ergastēria ephyalōmenēs keramikēs'; Vassiliou, 'Early Green and Brown Painted ware'; Armstrong, 'Greece in the eleventh century'; Turnator, *Turning the economic tables*, pp. 154–341, which takes the story on into the thirteenth century. See n. 101 above for Zeuxippus ware. For Chalkis, see Skartsē and Baxebanēs, 'Ē Chalkida kata tous Mesobyzantinous chronous'; Waksman, 'Defining the main "Middle Byzantine Production" (MBP)'; Vroom, 'Shifting Byzantine networks'. In Constantinople, GWW dominated the Saraçhane site, with only some Fine Sgraffito otherwise significant (Hayes, *Excavations at Saraçhane*, 2, pp. 44–7), but the latter is much more visible in the Hippodrome, and is found on other sites too (Böhlendorf-Arslan, *Glasierte byzantinische Keramik*, 1, pp. 169–71). For Aphrodisias, see Öztaşkin, 'Byzantine and Turkish glazed pottery finds' (p. 168 for some eleventh-century Brown glaze from Corinth too); Jeffery, *The archaeology of Middle Byzantine Aphrodisias*, pp. 97–106. Ephesos was similar; see Vroom, 'Bright finds, big city'.

104 Apart from the general works in n. 103 above, for Argos, see Yangaki, 'Céramique glaçurée'; Basileiou, *Byzantinē ephualōmenē keramikē apo to Argos*, 1, which sets Corinth and Chalkis imports against local imitations of most types; Vassiliou, 'Measles ware'. For Sparta, see Vassi, 'An unglazed ware pottery workshop'; Sanders, 'Medieval pottery', pp. 264, 267; Bakourou et al., 'Argos and Sparta'; Katzara, 'Byzantine glazed pottery from Sparta'. For Crete, see Poulou-Papadimitriou, 'Middle Byzantine pottery from Eleutherna'; for smaller Boeotian centres, see Vionis, 'The Byzantine to early modern pottery from Thespiai', pp. 360–2. For Pergamon, see Waksman, *Les céramiques byzantines des fouilles de Pergame*, e.g. pp. 178–9.

105 Among others, White, *An investigation*, pp. 147–8, 155–9 for Corinth; Vionis, 'Current archaeological research', for Boeotia; Sanders, 'Medieval pottery', for Sparta; see the maps in François, *La vaisselle de terre*, pp. 120–9 for overlapping networks. Surveys and smaller excavations: for Turkey, see the full and varied lists in Böhlendorf-Arslan, *Glasierte byzantinische Keramik*, 1; glazed wares from both Constantinople and Corinth/Chalkis, plus, later, Zeuxippus ware, were also found in the only ceramic publication I have seen for Smyrna: Doğer, 'Byzantine ceramics', pp. 103–4. For Greece, see, e.g., Vroom, 'The medieval pottery' (Kythera); Cherry et al., *Landscape archaeology*, pp. 354–7 (Keos); Tsanana, 'The glazed pottery of Byzantine Vrya'; Yangaki, 'Observations on the glazed pottery' (Nauplion).

access to it will have been via coasts where that ware was easily found, but Corinth and especially Chalkis wares were both present. On Naxos, Corinth and Chalkis wares showed similar percentages (and, here too, substantially outweighed imports from the capital). Only Measles ware had a visibly different distribution, above all in the Peloponnesos and in western Greece and Albania, plus some sites in Italy. The other distributions match those of Günsenin 3 amphorae, which similarly spread across the Aegean from Chalkis in all directions, including directly to eastern Aegean sites.[106]

We are dealing here with a far more complex set of interrelations than the old main routes out from the capital and down the coasts. But this overlapping pattern does not mean that the trade in these wares was a casual process, simply the by-product of cabotage. A wreck from the mid-twelfth century off the island of Alonnesos in the Sporades group—it is generally called the Pelagonnesos-Alonnesos wreck in the literature—had a large cargo of some 1,400 Fine Sgraffito bowls and plates, and no other fine wares, although plenty of Günsenin 3 amphorae. It was not going on the old main route up the west coast when it sank, but, rather, on a direct route across the sea towards the Marmara—as were the striking number of other wrecks with Günsenin 3 amphorae found off the Sporades islands.[107] Commentators on this wreck almost universally call it a ship which was above all carrying fine wares; this seems unlikely to me, for 1,400 items hardly compare with, say, the 55,000 Chinese Changsha bowls found in the ninth-century Belitung wreck off Sumatra, in, apparently, a smaller vessel.[108] The ship, which was doubtless coming from Chalkis, but which would also have passed the Thessaly ports before it sank, could perfectly well have had cloth and/or grain as a main cargo, plus the wine which was probably in the amphorae; cargoes were, in fact, regularly very variegated, as a document of 1182 shows us for this region

[106] Sagalassos: Vionis et al., 'A Middle-late Byzantine pottery assemblage', pp. 444–50. Naxos: see the pie chart in Vionis, 'Island responses', p. 67, although it is my assumption that his database is Naxiot above all, and that his 'central Greece' means Chalkis. Measles ware: François, *La vaisselle de terre*, pp. 122–3; Dimopoulos, 'Trade of Byzantine red wares', p. 186; Vassiliou, 'Measles ware'. For Günsenin 3, see n. 98 above.

[107] Kritzas, 'To byzantinon nauagion Pelagonnēsou-Alonnēsou'; Ioannidaki-Dostoglou, 'Les vases de l'épave'; Dellaporta, 'The Byzantine shipwreck'; Dimopoulos, 'Trade of Byzantine red wares', pp. 181–2; Papanikola-Bakirtzi, 'Byzantine glazed ceramics on the market', pp. 200–1. For the amphorae, not recognized by earlier discussions, see Koutsouflakis, 'The transportation of amphorae'; he also discusses the other wrecks in the area, and also a wreck found in open sea, halfway between the Sporades and the island of Limnos, even more clearly on the direct route to the Marmara, which also contained Fine Sgraffito and Günsenin 3.

[108] For the Belitung wreck, see Krahl et al., *Shipwrecked*, and esp. Flecker, 'A ninth-century Arab shipwreck in Indonesia'; see ibid., pp. 102–7 for the size of the ship, which had an estimated total length of 18 metres. The Pelagonnesos wreck's length seems to have been 25 metres (Throckmorton, 'Exploration of a Byzantine wreck'), long for a Byzantine transport ship: compare the range of lengths, from 8 to 14.5 metres, for three tenth-century round ships (plus 30 metres for two galleys, sometimes but less often used for trading) excavated in the Istanbul harbour; see Pulak et al., 'Eight Byzantine shipwrecks', p. 43; and the 15.7 metres for the Serçe Limanı ship of *c*.1025, see Steffy, 'Construction and analysis of the vessel', p. 167.

(see p. 334 below). But fine wares were at least a significant payload on the ship, and it was a single type of fine ware as well, which indicates differentiated routes for ceramic types, perhaps depending on different workshop or buyer choices. This pattern has parallels on other wrecks from the same period or later, and it is a striking one.[109] Clearly, workshops could deliberately produce for regional-level export. Here, as in the Roman Empire but unlike sometimes in the Islamic world, ceramics could be a substantial-scale bulk good in themselves. And they continued to be; the success of Zeuxippus ware and later Corinth and Chalkis glazes, plus new types from Thessaloniki and Serres, among others, shows these patterns to have continued well beyond 1204.[110]

The picture which we have for the twelfth century in Byzantium, in the last part of our period, is, therefore, a much more complex one than that for the centuries before 1090. Boeotia produced wine for export, Lakonia oil. Chalkis and Corinth, and smaller centres too, produced fine ceramics to rival Constantinople. The scale of the major productions must have been considerable; White has convincingly proposed that the Corinth workshops were 'nucleated workshops' according to David Peacock's classic typology of types of ceramic production, which almost certainly goes for the other two major production centres as well; few, if any, Mediterranean ceramic producers in our period are likely to have been operating on a more organized scale. François has pointed out that there must have been a division of labour inside fine pottery workshops too, for potters and painters have different rhythms.[111] There was clearly also a hierarchy of production, with at least three levels: the three or so major centres at the top, then more localized glazed-ware and amphora producers, and then small coarse-ware producers, that is to say, the workers in the smaller kilns excavated in towns and the village potters who occasionally turn up among lists of peasants in Athos documents, whose products have not yet been separated out by archaeologists.[112] The overlapping distributions of the major amphora types, plus the glazed wares, show that the

[109] For parallels, see François, *La vaisselle de terre*, pp. 115–16.

[110] Papanikola-Bakirtzi, *Byzantine glazed ceramics*; François, *La vaisselle de terre*, pp. 72–85; Waksman and François, 'Vers une redéfinition typologique et analytique', esp. pp. 635–6; Turnator, *Turning the economic tables*, pp. 248–341 (who argues that after 1204, the Asia Minor/Anatolia coast became more prosperous than Greece—a contrast with the previous period, and doubtless a direct reflection of its being the centre of the surviving Byzantine Empire of Nicaea).

[111] White, *An investigation*, p. 172; cf. Papanikola-Bakirtzi, 'Byzantine glazed ceramics on the market', p. 214: 'a professional structure and organization' for workshops; see also François, *La vaisselle de terre*, pp. 96–7. For the workshop typology, see Peacock, *Pottery in the Roman world*, pp. 6–51. The next level up for Peacock was the manufactory; I hypothesized in Wickham, *Framing*, pp. 761–2, that the Middle Egyptian wine amphora productions might have been a manufactory in the sixth century, but as we have seen (p. 71) they were less active by now. Aswān, Fusṭāṭ, and Palermo seem to have had substantial sets of linked workshops; some may well have been larger-scale than the three major Byzantine ones, but they were most probably similarly structured. The giant scale of Córdoba ceramic production in the ninth and tenth centuries, however, may well have had manufactory elements; see p. 398 below.

[112] Bouras, 'Aspects of the Byzantine city', pp. 516–17, gives a useful list of urban kiln sites found before *c.*2000. For rural potters (*tzykalai*), see, e.g., *Actes d'Iviron*, 2, nn. 51, l. 69, 52, l. 236; cf. François,

inhabitants of most or all of the Aegean coast could choose where to buy from, if they wanted—and had the resources—to buy these goods.

Given the ease of sea travel in the Aegean, with land never out of sight, one could postulate a dozen trade routes for the twelfth century, supplementing and bypassing the old main routes down the west and east coasts. It is, anyway, clear that sailing straight across from central-southern Greece past the islands to Smyrna and Ephesos, again by several routes—the ones used to get to the islands themselves—was by now normal (see Map 15). In 1102, the English pilgrim Saewulf took ship from Chalkis to Athens, then across the sea to Naxos, and then to Samos, before going south to Rhodes and along the south Turkish coast; coming back, he picked up a fast *minorem navim* at Rhodes, but left it at Chios in order to proceed to Constantinople—the ship itself was evidently planning to go westwards across the sea on a slightly more northerly route, back to Chalkis again, or maybe Halmyros. All these boats stopped at islands on the way as well, to buy 'necessaries for sustenance, as in all islands', to quote the Saewulf text, and doubtless to sell goods too. Later on in the century, al-Idrīsī lists such a range of distances from island to island that his text here resembles a Greek ferry timetable. These routes had always, of course, existed, but they were now being more and more used for bulk goods.[113] Buying power must have been substantial to make all this network possible; and, to return to the archaeology, it unquestionably, given rural ceramic distributions, extended beyond urban elites.

Amphorae by now largely transported wine, as we have seen, and are a direct guide to that commerce. The way they moved about the sea is plausibly a proxy for olive oil transport too, which is no longer in this period visible archaeologically. They are not a proxy for grain, however; Ganos amphorae may match Rhaidestos (i.e. Thracian) grain, it is true, but the other obvious grain areas, such as Bithynia, Thessaly, and Macedonia, were not major ceramic producers in our period. Grain, anyway, is grown more or less everywhere, and, apart from windfall opportunities in the case of localized famines, its export will have been above all to the capital, the only Byzantine city which could not sustain itself from its immediate surroundings. That is in general true for wine in the Aegean as well, of course, but here there must have been differences in type, and some greater specializations, for amphora traffic to have worked as it did; this is much less plausible for grain. Fine wares, for their part, seem to have been traded on their own account on some

La vaisselle de terre, pp. 100–2. François, 'Cuisine et pots de terre à Byzance', offers a typology of kitchenwares, but not of their origins, which would require large-scale petrological analysis.

[113] For Saewulf and al-Idrīsī, see *Peregrinationes tres*, ed. Huygens and Pryor, pp. 75–7; al-Idrīsī, *Nuzhat al-mushtaq*, trans. Jaubert and Nef, pp. 349–51. Saewulf's route out is not straightforward to unpick, as the text lists a range of islands which he could not have visited on any sensible itinerary. See also the *Life of Lazaros of Galesion*, ed. Deleheye, ch. 228, for a direct route from Phygela (Kuşadası), near Ephesos, to Crete. For the network of routes in general, see Pryor, *Geography, technology*, pp. 97–9; Avramea, 'Land and sea communications', pp. 83–6; Malamut, *Les îles de l'Empire byzantin*, pp. 546–61; Kislinger, 'Verkehrsrouten zur See im byzantinischen Raum'.

scale, not just as casual extras on ships; so it is worth considering how far the patterns of their distribution acted as a proxy for cloth, an issue I raised earlier in this section. We will come back to this when we look at the documentary evidence.

This is as far as ceramic analysis on its own can currently take us, but it is a long way, as the last three paragraphs show. The Byzantine Empire in the long eleventh century, particularly its maritime core, had undergone a visible process of agrarian expansion, which led to greater buying power for many people in the countryside, and as a result urban expansion too. And this set of developments further allowed the entrenchment of an intricate exchange system. Trade by now did not just follow the old main routes; nor did it focus on Constantinople, except in that the capital remained by far the largest city in the empire and itself an active producer as well as consumer. In the twelfth century (starting in the later eleventh), the Aegean and Marmara Seas, and the coasts around them, developed the sort of dense internal market which we saw in Egypt and Sicily. It probably operated on a smaller scale than in Egypt, but on the other hand, given the fact that Egypt only really had one internal route except in the Delta, it was geographically more complex. The archaeology gives us, in fact, the skeleton of a whole exchange network. It allows us to make sense of the rather sketchier written sources, which we will come on to in the next section.

4.4 Byzantine Exchange in the Written Record

As noted earlier, Byzantine historical narratives in this period are both contemporary and rich. Indeed, some—notably those of Psellos, Attaleiates, Anna Komnene, and Niketas Choniates—were written by serious political players; they are the mark of the often extensive cultural hinterland of politicians across our period, as before and (in the case of the main part of Choniates' career) after. It is easy to adopt their perspectives as a result, and only recently have some focussed and critical accounts of the narrative strategies of each historian allowed us to get past these perspectives, at least to an extent.[114] One of the longest-lasting results of this is the belief of many modern historians that the mid-eleventh century—the period between Basil II and Alexios I, 1025–81—saw a conflict, perhaps even a systematic one, between a civilian/bureaucratic and a military faction in politics. This derives from a reading of Psellos in particular, who, indeed, had little sympathy for most military figures in the constant swirl of politics in this period. It is an overstated reading, for so many major players held both civilian and military roles at different points in their careers—for example, Nikephoros Ouranos, who was Keeper of the Imperial Inkstand, a letter writer, a general and author of a

[114] e.g. Krallis, *Michael Attaleiates*; Kaldellis, *The argument of Psellos' Chronographia*; Neville, *Anna Komnene*; Simpson, *Niketas Choniates*.

military manual, and military *doux* of Antioch under Basil II.[115] But it has also had results which are relevant to the way the Byzantine commercial world has been understood by modern historiography. 'Civilian' figures in the minds of many analysts were less separate from major commercial figures—the shadowy leaders of Constantinople's most powerful guilds, for example—than were army men; and it is clear that Attaleiates, at least, was active in the grain market for the supply of the capital, as we have seen. The mid-eleventh century has, partially as a result, also been seen as the main period in Byzantine history in which the leaders of the commercial world had some role in politics.

Major steps in this argument are undoubted facts. Michael IV (1034–41) and his nephew Michael V (1041–2) came from a non-aristocratic background: Michael IV, and his brother and patron John the *orphanotrophios*, are claimed to have been part of a family of money changers by two chroniclers, although, as usual, who knows how exact this is; Michael V's father is said to have been a ship caulker.[116] Furthermore, in the faction-fighting of the period the urban crowd sometimes played an active role (including in the fall of Michael V himself); Constantine IX, who succeeded him, allowed guild leaders to be senators in 1042; and Alexios I, certainly a military figure, weakened that right in 1090. Alexios I has, indeed, been seen as marking the end of this period, and has often been depicted in a partially negative way for that precise reason; his weakening of senatorial rights is an element in the older picture of the 'feudalization' of Byzantine politics under the Komnenoi, or at least that of the final victory of the military faction, which still persists in the literature. To Kazhdan in 1985, this was part of the sad fact that 'Economic growth... was not accompanied by political liberation. Subjugated to the state, to the episcopate, and to the landed magnates, the urban populations did not become an independent, antifeudal political and cultural force.' To Laiou and Morrisson in 2007, in the best account, 'It seemed for a moment that the wealthier merchants might acquire formal political power... This was stopped when the landholding aristocracy secured the throne for a hundred years and more, with the accession of Alexios I, in 1081. The "aristocratic" view of society... became part of imperial ideology in the court of the Komnenian emperors.'[117] There are plenty of equivalent quotations from others.

[115] For a critique of the traditional reading, see especially Cheynet, *Pouvoir et contestations*, pp. 191–8; for a rapid survey, see Kaldellis, *Streams of gold*, pp. 224–8. For Ouranos, see Holmes, *Basil II*, pp. 349–52, 384–5, 409–11, 523–4.

[116] For John and Michael IV, see Skylitzes, *Synopsis historiarum*, ed. Thurn, Romanos III, ch.17 (p. 390) and Kedrenos, *Synopsis istoriōn*, ed. Bekker, 2, p. 504. Both add that the family adulterated coins; this, certainly, does not have to mean anything more than standard commercial activity, given the prejudices of writers. For Michael V called a caulker or *kalaphatēs*, see, e.g., Psellos, *Chronographia*, ed. Reinsch, 4.26; Skylitzes, *Synopsis historiarum*, ed. Thurn, Michael V (pp. 416–21).

[117] Kazhdan and Wharton Epstein, *Change*, p. 56; Laiou and Morrisson, *The Byzantine economy*, p. 141.

This seems to me an unhelpful way of looking at the period, and at the long eleventh century as a whole. It is a lament for an opportunity lost, but the opportunity was never there in the first place. It is true that Byzantine politics did not have to be dynastic, and that some emperors could have very 'humble' origins—the classic example of that was Basil I in 867, said to be a former peasant, whose rapid and unscrupulous rise did him no harm at all in his imperial career.[118] All the same, every emperor in the unusually non-dynastic period 1028–81 was an aristocrat except for the two Michaels, and their family had been influential in court politics for a generation. As to the senate, it is true that Psellos says that Constantine IX opened it to commercial figures—it is part of a long-standing line of complaints, going back to the fourth century, about official titles going to new men—and that Alexios seems to have downgraded them, but the senate had no political power at all; it was entirely a ceremonial body with a formalized status attached to its members. It is also striking that Alexios' act is only documented in a judicial decision of 1090, turned into law; it was never mentioned by any contemporary historian, whether favourably or unfavourably—that is to say, it had less significance at the time than has been assumed by some recent writers.[119] As to the Constantinopolitan crowd, its role in politics is undoubted; the fall of Michael V is only the most spectacular example in our period, and popular protest and, perhaps even more important, the fear of it, had a visible role in political decision-making at other times too. All the same, this had always been the case in the city, back to the sixth century at least, including at the low point for the demography of the capital in the late seventh. It tells us nothing about new opportunities for commercial strata, whether rich or poor, in our period.[120] And not

[118] See Dagron, *Emperor and priest*, esp. pp. 13–24, on the non-dynastic nature of power. See Tobias, *Basil I*, 19–93, for the accounts of Basil's origins, which were as usual reworked by contemporary writers, often substantially (he was of humble, presumably peasant origins to Symeon the Logothete, but a descendant fallen on hard times of Armenian royalty to his son Leo VI, and even a descendant of Constantine to his grandson Constantine VII), but which seem certainly to have been from the poorer strata of society.

[119] Psellos, *Chronographia*, ed. Reinsch, 6.29; Zepos and Zepos, *Jus graecoromanum*, 1, pp. 645–6, following the dating in Burgmann, 'Lawyers and legislators', p. 190. For the legal decision, see, e.g., Lemerle, *Cinq études*, pp. 291–3, 309–10; Hendy, *Studies*, pp. 583–5; Dagron, 'The urban economy', p. 416 (who convincingly minimizes its implications—for, indeed, Alexios did not cut guild members (*systēmatikoi*) out of the senate, as is often claimed, but simply cancelled one of their legal privileges). Cheynet, 'La société urbaine', pp. 476–82, also downplays the senate narrative. It can be added that guild organization seems to have been strong for some trades in Byzantium—or at least Constantinople—unlike in the Islamic world in general or even, as yet, Italy; see, e.g., Vryonis, 'Byzantine *dēmokratia* and the guilds', with a large bibliography; Laiou, 'The festival of "Agathe"', for the likelihood of female guild members; Dagron, 'The urban economy', pp. 405–18, commenting on the extensive evidence for them in the *Book of the eparch*; Maniatis, 'The domain of private guilds'. Guilds have an ambiguous role in economic historical metanarratives as a whole, now positive, now negative. I do not discuss them here, however, as they seem to me marginal to the way exchange developed in our period. See p. 660 below.

[120] Garland, 'Political power and the populace'; developed and generalized to other periods by Kaldellis, *The Byzantine republic*, esp. pp. 118–64.

even one figure in the long eleventh century (or before or after) rose to political prominence directly because of commercial wealth rather than landed wealth, or than a salaried career in the bureaucracy and/or army. Nor was there any chance of it: aristocrats, bureaucrats, and generals had far more money and power. One might get into the bureaucracy in the first place because of money gained by other means—as probably with John the *orphanotrophios*—but that had always been the case as well, and would continue to be, for office-holding always brought more wealth than commerce.

The idea of the opportunity lost seems to me, in the end, to derive not from actual Byzantine data, but, rather, from an implicit comparison with the west, in the still strong metanarrative of Byzantine failure. Twelfth-century Italian cities could be seen to be ruled by a commercial class, and they flourished in this period and after, whereas Byzantine urban centres supposedly did not. But this is a misapprehension. It is broadly true of Venice, but the future *Serenissima* was strikingly unlike other Italian cities; it is already less true of Genoa, and when we reach Milan, we find a city whose elites, mostly rich through landowning, were attached to fighting more than trade, as was indeed the case for the ruling urban militias of north-central Italian cities in general, as we shall see in Chapter 6. Even when, later, the regimes of the later thirteenth-century *popolo* were undoubtedly more commercial, they were also highly atypical of the west as a whole. Successful and prosperous western states such as France, England, or Castile were just like Byzantium in this respect. So, for that matter, was Fāṭimid Egypt, or any other major Islamic power. The influence of commercial elites could be considerable in each, but was in every case informal. We need to remember that this was the medieval and indeed post-medieval norm; anything else was a trend of the seventeenth or even nineteenth centuries.

What is certainly true, on the other hand, is that Byzantine writers, whether directly involved in politics or just part of the substantial intellectual stratum of our period, frequently did not respect the commercial strata, and did not in the least identify with them, even if they had economic links to them. This means, as implied earlier, that they did not say much about them, and we are short of legal documents to fill out our knowledge by other means. A well-known example of what we do have is supplied by Theodore Prodromos (d. *c.*1170), an active writer of the Komnenian period. In a poem to Anna Komnene he lists the artisan (*banausidos*) trades which would make him more prosperous than does his chosen one as a scholar, including those of bronze worker and weaver. He, or a contemporary author pretending to be him, the so-called Ptochoprodromos, develops this with some panache in a deliberately less elevated style, listing the delicious foods that various artisans in the leather and cloth trades, plus food sellers, and odder traders like pepper mill merchants and sieve makers, can eat, while he is starving. The satire is too obvious: these are lesser beings, often with comic occupations, therefore unfairly better off.[121] John Tzetzes, a similar figure from the same period, made similar complaints, and so had Christopher of Mytilene a century before. In general, the word *banausos*, artisan, is often a pejorative one in our authors (as, indeed, it had been in classical Greece). Even market-selling was 'shamelessness' (*anaischynton*) according to the *Patria* in the late tenth century.[122] It has to be said that saints' day market fairs, *panēgyreis*, were otherwise normally seen by writers as a positive feature of the capital and other towns, and the rights of merchants to relocate them was regarded as valid by Basil II, as a law makes explicit. Furthermore, as Laiou has stressed, profit (*kerdos*) was in itself good in the theology of Symeon the New Theologian (d. 1022).[123] But *being* someone who might actually make a profit, from his or her own labour, was clearly less good in the eyes of other writers.

But all this does not mean that the Byzantine intellectual (or landowning, or official) elites rejected commerce, which is another claim of an older historiography.[124] What they did was invest in the work of others. In part this was simply by owning land where trade was carried out. As noted earlier (pp. 283, 286), officials are said to have owned shops and workshops in documents for both Constantinople and Thessaloniki. Attaleiates too, as his *typikon* for his own monastery shows, owned similar properties in the capital, as well as in Selymbria (Silivri) and Rhaidestos, both on the Marmara coast. Similarly, a certain Chrysobasileios (Gold Basil) controlled the *scala* (dock) of St Marcian on the northern shore of the capital, until it was given to the Venetians in 1148. Indeed, Attaleiates claims in his *History* that the *skalai* of the city were mostly owned by hospices and monasteries, and the Jewish traveller Benjamin of Tudela in the 1160s claims that Manuel I gained 20,000 gold *hyperpera* per year from both

[121] Prodromos, *Historische Gedichte*, ed. Hörandner, n. 38; *Poèmes prodromiques*, ed. Hesseling and Pernot, poem 4. For the literary and satirical aims of this poem, which are well known, see the major contribution of Alexiou et al., 'The poverty of écriture'. Alexiou cannot see a reason not to attach these vernacular poems to the pen of Theodore Prodromos, even though no final proof is possible; more recently, Janssen and Lauxtermann, 'Authorship revisited: language and metre in the *Ptochoprodromika*', who take a rather different approach, are equally uncertain as to authorship.

[122] Tzetzes, 'Iambi', ed. Leone, pp. 135–44; Christopher of Mytilene, *Poems*, ed. Bernard and Livanos, n. 63; *Accounts of medieval Constantinople: the Patria*, ed. Berger, 2.103.

[123] See n. 62 above for literary accounts of fairs. See in general Vryonis, 'The panēgyris of the Byzantine saint'; Laiou, 'Exchange and trade', pp. 754–6; Ritter, 'Panegyric markets'. Fairs were also frequently elements in monastic foundations; see most conveniently *BMFD*, 2, pp. 535, 556, 769, 828–9, for Bačkovo, the Pantokrator and Kosmosoteira. For Basil II, see *Les novelles*, ed. Svoronos, 14.7.1. For Symeon, see Laiou, 'Economic thought', p. 1130.

[124] There has been too much emphasis on Kekaumenos, a retired army man who in the 1070s advocated to his sons self-sufficiency and the avoidance of credit–debt relationships, standard views among older conservative commentators in every period (*Consilia et Narrationes*, ed. Roueché). Even he, though, recognized that *archontes* and other people like himself indeed lent money at interest, or with a promise of commercial profit, and he did not see trade as bad in itself, as Magdalino, *Empire of Manuel I*, p. 156, notes. See in general for an argument similar to my own in this section Laiou, 'Exchange and trade', pp. 736–59 and Laiou and Morrisson, *The Byzantine economy*, pp. 90–165; cf. also Gerolymatou, 'L'aristocratie et le commerce'.

commercial taxes and the rents from shops in the capital.[125] The word 'mostly' in the first and the sum of money in the second might well not be reliable, as usual, but the point is clear, nevertheless: all sectors of the ruling class could invest in commercial rent. The fact that *archontes* (elites) are attested in the *Book of the Eparch* as involved in silk production fits with this concern for ground rents, and in this case it seems to have extended to capital investment in the production process too.[126] Added to this was the sale of produce by landowners, very often to the capital (we saw it once again for Attaleiates, p. 282), but also, in the Athos documents, to Thessaloniki. The Athonite monasteries indeed had numerous boats for selling wine and other goods, certainly to Thessaloniki, and Ainos farther east, but if possible to Constantinople as well, which they maintained even though emperors tried to restrict their number and geographical range on the grounds that trading was unbecoming to monks. Several of their boats had imperial immunities from the trade tax, the *kommerkion*, attached to them, and other dues, which seem to have been in some cases even more total than the ones the Venetians enjoyed after 1092.[127] In one interesting early text, from 984, the monastery of the Lavra actually gave the imperial immunity for a large boat to the new monastery of Iviron; such cessions were evidently transferable. (Iviron was a Georgian monastery; the 1040s *Life* of its founders defends the taking on of Greek as well as Georgian monks by explaining that Georgians have no experience in seafaring.)[128]

A third form of dealing was direct investment in trading. Here our evidence is even scantier, but we do have one clear instance, Kalopetros Xanthos, a silk merchant (*vestioprata* in the Latin of the text—it was *bestiopratēs* in the *Book of the Eparch*) and also, importantly, *imperialis vestarcha*, so a senior official to the supposedly anti-commercial Alexios I, who in 1111 loaned 125 *hyperpera* at 20 per cent interest to a middle-level Venetian merchant, Enrico Zusto, for a voyage to Damietta in Egypt to sell cloth.[129] Venetians usually borrowed money for

[125] Attaleiates, *Historia*, ed. Pérez Martín, p. 506; *The itinerary of Benjamin of Tudela*, trans. Adler, p. 13. For Chrysobasileios, see Pozza and Ravegnani, *I trattati con Bisanzio*, n. 5. The Constantinople Great Church was said to have owned as many as 1100 *ergasteria* in the city in 537 (*Corpus iuris civilis*, 3, ed. Schoell and Kroll, Novel 43); the figure was repeated, whether accurately or not, by Leo VI around 900: *Les Novelles de Léon VI*, ed. Noailles and Dain, n. 12.

[126] Koder, *Das Eparchenbuch*, ch. 8.2.

[127] For good discussions, see Kaplan, 'Monks and trade' and Morris, 'The "life aquatic"', with, for the *kommerkion* in general, Smyrlis, 'Trade regulation' (pp. 76–80 for exemptions). Significant references include *Actes du Pantocrator*, n. 1, *Actes du Prôtaton*, n. 7, 8, *Actes de Lavra*, 1, n. 55, *Actes d'Iviron*, 1, nn. 6, 25, *Actes de Saint-Pantéléèmôn*, nn. 4, 7. See also, for Patmos, Branousē et al., *Byzantina eggrapha tēs monēs Patmou*, 1, n. 11 (a. 1197), a later exemption, with Karlin-Hayter, 'Notes sur les archives de Patmos', pp. 210–15, and Malamut, *Les îles de l'Empire byzantin*, pp. 448–53; for other monastic boats, see *BMFD*, 2, pp. 678, 829.

[128] *Actes d'Iviron*, 1, n. 6; *Life of John and Euthymios*, trans. Grdzelidze, *Georgian monks*, ch. 7.

[129] Lanfranchi, *Famiglia Zusto*, n. 6. Jacoby, 'Silk crosses the Mediterranean', p. 496n, notes the downgrading of the office of *bestarchēs* by 1100 or so, following *ODB*, s.v. *vestarches* (which does not cite this text), but it had been very high-status indeed earlier, so even a downgrading would not necessarily mean that the office became unimportant. The only other Greek who loaned to a Venetian in

trading from other Venetians, so the numerous loan documents we have for them mostly tell us little about the commercial interests of the 'Greeks' (as Italians called them), but this document sheds a shaft of light on what was doubtless a rather more common activity. (Venetians, one should add, regarded 20 per cent interest—it was called 'six for five'—as normal; it was a higher figure than 16.67 per cent, the maximum for Byzantine maritime loans, but not dramatically so.[130]) All these examples, and especially Kalopetros Xanthos, point up one crucial element in this official and landowning interest in trade: capital. As in contemporary Egypt (see pp. 109, 131 above), elite investment meant that the scale of exchange could become considerably greater, whenever demand made it profitable, which by the twelfth century in the Aegean it did.

Merchants themselves are frequently mentioned in our sources, but usually it is impossible to get a sense of their scale—casual references do not tell us whether they were local pedlars, small-scale shipmen, or major operators. We can assume that both John the *orphanotrophios* and Kalopetros Xanthos were successful enough at financing to get into the official hierarchy, but how successful that needed to be cannot be said. This is why modern writers so frequently cite the example of Kalomodios, a money changer or banker (*kollybistēs*) of great wealth, based in the *agora* of the capital, who often travelled for trading (*kat' emporian*); in 1200 or 1201, according to Niketas Choniates, he was imprisoned by imperial financial officials who wanted his wealth, but was freed when the urban crowd (*agoraioi*) threatened the patriarch in Hagia Sophia. Choniates, true to form, despised all three of Kalomodios, the crowd, and the officials, and wrote it all up in very highflown terms; we cannot tell anything about the rights and wrongs of the incident, and as the event is late for us, they hardly matter here; but it is at least clear that this writer assumed that travelling merchants could get very rich.[131] This is supported by a concrete set of figures, the amount seized in 1192 by Genoese and Pisan pirates from a group of Constantinopolitan merchants coming from Alexandria (on a Venetian ship), which was nearly 40,000 *hyperpera*, a very large sum—the figure is more reliable than most, for we know it from diplomatic documents of Emperor Isaac II, who tried and failed to get it back by confiscating Genoese and Pisan property in the capital and using this as a threat

surviving documents for that city is Michael Anaxioti in 1167–8 (*DCV*, n. 203), whose status cannot be pinned down; a list of documents from 1086 in ASV, SZ, b. 12, n. 3 (see Chapter 6, n. 79 below for the abbreviation), which mentions two *cartulae* concerning the dealings of Constantinus Voris *grecus* of Constantinople with Giovanni Gratiadei and his sons, probably shows us a third. Borsari, *Venezia e Bisanzio*, pp. 105–6 and Jacoby, 'Byzantine trade with Egypt', p. 72, discuss the first two.

[130] Laiou, 'Byzantium and the commercial revolution', p. 245.

[131] Choniates, *Historia*, ed. van Dieten, pp. 523–4. The wealth of merchants is also assumed by Bryennios, *Histoire*, ed. Gautier, 2.26, who relates how a certain Maurex, a very rich non-elite maritime dealer (the author does not say of what kind), is the host of the future emperor Alexios Komnenos *c.*1076 at his house in Herakleia (Ereğli) on the Black Sea coast.

against the two cities.[132] This is on a vastly larger scale than the affairs of Kalopetros Xanthos eighty years earlier, which, even if it was evidently spread between many merchants, may tell us something about the development of commerce across the same period.

When we look for written information as to what Byzantine merchants actually traded in, our information gets slightly better. The food supply of the capital and other major towns certainly figured highly, and we have seen this with both the Rhaidestos *phoundax* and the Athonite documents, which, together with Venetian loans (which I will come onto), are our most explicit written evidence for the intensity of such traffic. But our direct information about artisanal goods is highly partial, because it focusses on one product, silk. At least the data about this are clear. The capital produced silk in substantial enough quantities in the early tenth century to have a considerable division of labour in its production and sale, as we have seen in the *Book of the Eparch* (see pp. 282–3 above).[133] Two centuries further on, however, it was by no means the only production centre in the empire. Benjamin of Tudela in his Jewish-focussed travel account from the 1160s records Jewish silk workers (and also rich merchants) in Pera, just across the Golden Horn from the capital. These were perhaps ancillary to the older silk traders in the city (although the *Book of the eparch* mentions Jews in its silk sections as well), and it is clear in his text that there is some hostility between them and neighbouring Christians. By now, however, he also records silk weavers in Thessaloniki too, and above all in Thebes, where a very large community of some 2,000 Jews were second only to Constantinople in their number, and said to be highly skilled in silk and purple garment-making.[134] Thebes then recurs often in other more casual references, such as letters of Tzetzes in the mid-twelfth century (who praises female weavers there—although not explicitly silk weavers; weavers were, as we have seen, p. 283, often in large part female in Byzantium, even in substantial workshops), and of Michael Choniates a few decades later (the latter complains that Athens has no silk workers, unlike Thebes). Niketas Choniates says that

[132] Bertolotto and Sanguineti, 'Nuova serie di documenti', nn. 12 and 13 (pp. 448–64; cf. *CDGE*, 3 nn. 25, 35 for an improved Latin text but without the Greek) for Genoa; Müller, *Documenti sulle relazioni*, n. 1.41 for Pisa. See Laiou, 'Byzantine trade with Christians and Muslims', pp. 157–60. For trade with Egypt, see pp. 354–9 below.

[133] By 1050 Byzantine Calabria, outside our regions, was a silk producer, too (Guillou, *Le brébion*); that is to say, the scale of raw silk production here from mulberry trees was high here, although where it was to be woven into cloth remains unclear: as noted in Chapter 3 (p. 194), it was probably Islamic Sicily, given its closeness to Sicilian silk-weaving areas, and the fact that the money of account in the text is the Sicilian quarter-dinar (*tarì*).

[134] *The itinerary of Benjamin of Tudela,* trans. Adler, pp. 10–11, 14; cf. Koder, *Das Eparchenbuch*, 6.16; see Jacoby, 'Jews and the silk industry of Constantinople', and, for outside the capital, 'Silk', his key article on the subject, which is an invaluable source for data, as well as a paradoxical mixture of careful source criticism and over-interpretation. The substantial other bibliography for silk in general includes, in an incomplete list, Lopez, 'Silk industry', the first systematic study of the subject; Jacoby, 'Silk crosses the Mediterranean'; and most recently, two theses, Turnator, *Turning the economic tables*, pp. 353–75, and Galliker, *Middle Byzantine silk in context.*

Alexios III was asked to give Theban silk in gift to the sultan of Konya in 1195; and one Venetian document from our period, from 1171, refers to silk-dealing there (41 *hyperpera* for two pieces of silk clothing). In 1169, the Genoese unsuccessfully asked Manuel I for rights to trade in silk cloth from Thebes 'as the Venetians were accustomed to do'. It might be that Michael Choniates is also referring to silk when he says that the capital receives cloth from both Thebes and Corinth.[135] Corinth, anyway, is mentioned side by side with Thebes on several occasions as a cloth producer, although not explicitly as a silk centre. Both also had dyers; we have seen that for Thebes, and Corinth has a Middle Byzantine epitaph for a Jewish dyer. Al-Idrīsī also calls the Gulf of Corinth (which runs not only up to Corinth but also along the southern shore of Boeotia, where Thebes is) the *Fam al-ṣabbāghīn*, or 'Dyers' Gulf'.[136] Dyers by no means had to be dealing with silk, but, as noted earlier, purple dye is most clearly related to that cloth in a Byzantine context, for it was the protected imperial colour; the Gulf of Corinth has murex shells for purple dye—as does Athens—and Archibald Dunn has made a persuasive argument for murex dyeing in one of Boeotia's minor towns, Kastorion (Thisvi), between Thebes and the Gulf coast.[137]

There was clearly a network here of silk towns, and of dyeing specialists who could be in the town but also could be on the coasts or in smaller towns, perhaps supplying more than one place at a time. There was silk elsewhere too—on the island of Andros in particular[138]—but the Thebes and perhaps Corinth sector of Greece dominates our texts, and probably dominated non-Constantinopolitan silk production as a whole, at least by the twelfth century, the date of the majority of these references. The networks spread more widely too. The Peloponnesos had mulberry trees for silkworms, as its medieval name, Morea, probably implies; that at least fits Corinth, and Thebes is not so far away. And mulberry trees are in 1163 also recorded at Stagoi (Kalambaka), quite a long way inland in Thessaly; raw silk

[135] Tzetzes, *Epistulae*, ed. Leone, n. 71; Michael Choniates, *Epistulae*, ed. Kolovou, nn. 50, 60; Niketas Choniates, *Historia*, ed. van Dieten, p. 461; *DCV*, n. 243. For Genoa, see *CDGE*, 2, note to pp. 114–16, the instructions to the Genoese ambassador about what to ask for which did not end up in the agreement with the emperor itself (ibid., n. 50, = *LI*, 2, n. 352, a better but partial edition). Jacoby, 'Silk', p. 466n, dates this to 1171, after the Venetian dispossession of that year; cf. p. 332 below; his only reason seems to be that the Venetian rights are referred to in the past tense—which is highly problematic as an argument, given that the attested date of the agreement itself is actually two years earlier, in 1169.

[136] Notwithstanding Jacoby, 'Silk', p. 468, we do not have direct evidence for silk-weaving at Corinth; all the references to Thebes and Corinth together are vaguer citations. Silk there must remain only a possibility, even if, in my view, a quite likely one. For the Gulf of Corinth, see al-Idrīsī, *Nuzhat al-mushtaq*, trans. Jaubert and Nef, p. 347. For the dyer, see Starr, 'The epitaph' (cf. Jacoby, 'Silk', p. 455, for doubts about dating, but it has to come from this broad period); the text does not say what cloth he dyed. Cf. also the Jewish finisher for cloth in Sparta in the mid-eleventh-century in *The life of Saint Nikon*, ed. Sullivan, ch. 35 (Jacoby, 'Silk', p. 455 has a good commentary); here too we cannot say of what sort of cloth.

[137] Thisvi: Dunn, 'The rise and fall of towns'. Athens: Bouras, *Byzantine Athens*, p. 120; Granstrem et al., 'Fragment d'un praktikon', pp. 27–8, 35.

[138] See Jacoby, 'Silk', pp. 460–2 for references.

from here could have gone to Thebes, or possibly Thessaloniki, but these are each over 100 kilometres away.[139] This network was by no means upset when Roger II's Norman navy sacked both Thebes and Corinth in 1147; the Normans took female and male weavers captive from both cities according to a much-quoted (and misquoted) passage from Niketas Choniates, and even after a treaty was made in 1159, an exception allowed them to be kept in Sicily; Choniates says they were still there when he was writing two generations later.[140] But given the rest of our data, these captives were clearly only a minority of the weavers of the towns.

The network of production just described is a striking one. It is for this reason that silk features so heavily in recent accounts of the upswing in the Byzantine economy, particularly after 1100 or so, following Jacoby's influential articles. But there are problems about it. The main one, of course, is that silk is not the most important cloth in any society. It is very prominent in these texts because it was imperial and otherwise high-status, and costly enough to come into the field of vision of our writers. It was a prized element in diplomatic gifts to the Latin west, where it was a very expensive luxury, and the export outside Byzantium of the highest-quality types was carefully controlled as a result, as the western historian and diplomat Liutprand of Cremona found out to his cost in 968 when his contraband silk was confiscated. Commerce westwards became easier later, but silk remained expensive there.[141] Conversely, it was sufficiently common in Byzantium that it was only a semi-luxury, as in Egypt (see p. 51 above); people of medium means could sometimes buy it. So the angry wife of the feckless husband in the first Ptochoprodromos poem can complain that he has not bought her anything made of silk for twelve years; clearly, they cannot afford it, although, equally clearly, they might be able to if they were somewhat better off, and indeed she has a garment in a silk and cotton mix.[142] But all the same, one could not sensibly build an economy on silk production—it would be a tiny proportion of what cloth was worn, or used for decoration. The overwhelming focus on silk in the recent historiography is, therefore, it seems to me, an error. And then it is worthwhile looking more closely at what Choniates actually said about the 1147 raid; for (contrary to what is often claimed) he does not actually say anything about silk at all. Rather, when he describes the kidnapping of people from Thebes and Corinth initially, he focusses on the fact that they are women with deep cleavages, clearly captured for the purpose of rape; only when he discusses Thebes

[139] For Stagoi, see Astruc, 'Un document inédit'. Mulberry trees are not that common in our texts, but there were some in the theme of Opsikion (Psellus, *Epistulae*, ed. Papaioannou, n. 347 (Psellos, *Epistulae*, ed. Kurtz and Drexl, n. 107)), which may well have supplied the capital; see also n. 133 above, for the Reggio *brebion*. Jacoby's collection of Athonite citations, 'Silk', p. 471n, all postdate 1204.

[140] Choniates, *Historia*, ed. van Dieten, pp. 74–6, 98.

[141] Liudprand of Cremona, *Relatio*, ed. Chiesa, chs 54–5; see in general Jacoby, 'Silk crosses the Mediterranean'.

[142] *Poèmes prodromiques*, ed. Hesseling and Pernot, poem 1, ll. 50, 59; Jacoby, 'Silk', p. 475 and n, is helpful here on the terms used.

does he say casually that some of them are expert weavers too. The gold-threaded pieces of cloth that the Normans also seized from Thebes are not silk but *othonai* (linen); so also is the cloth woven by the weavers kept in Sicily in 1159. Silk only appears when Choniates describes what their descendants weave now, which might not be surprising, given that Sicily had been a major focus of silk production from at least the tenth century (see pp. 194, 210, 244–9 above)—the Normans did not need silk-weaving expertise, as the island already had it. Some of the weavers doubtless did have a proficiency in this fabric; Latin chronicles, less close to the scene but closer to Sicily and also to the date of the raid, do at least mention silk. But Choniates is thinking above all of linen, and this really is a cloth which anyone might wear.[143] It seems most useful to follow him here. Thebes was doubtless justifiably famous for silk, but we have already seen that what was produced at Corinth is not so clearly characterized. It is arguable that a—or the—key cloth production which actually came from both towns was linen.

We know much less about Byzantine linen than about silk—or, of course, than about Egyptian linen, discussed at length in Chapter 2. But there is some evidence. The *Book of the eparch* may have stressed silk, but it regulated *othōniopratai* or *mithaneis* (linen merchants) too. The flax they used was from the Black Sea coast and the Strymon valley east of Thessaloniki, plus Bulgaria.[144] In fact, both raw flax and linen cloth came into the capital. Ptochoprodromos refers to clothing in a linen–cotton mix (it would have been called fustian in Italy); but linen was, anyway, a normal cloth in the city—Skylitzes assumes, in a story related to the reign of Michael VI (1056–7), that head coverings were routinely of linen. Linen and wool were normal fabrics for army clothing, according to Leo VI's *Taktika* from *c.* 900. Linen (*kattān* in the Arabic source) was exported to Syria by the 960s. Linen merchants remained important in the capital for a long time: Choniates thought it dreadful that such people, *pratai tōn othonōn*, could gain the title of *sebastos*, as they could under Alexios III at the end of the twelfth century.[145] Outside the capital, Kaminiates says that there was high-quality linen cloth (*linon*) in Thessaloniki in 904, which fits the Strymon flax. And we find casual reference to flax cultivation in other sources: an early document for the Patmos monastery at the end of the

[143] See n. 140 above for Choniates; cf. Otto of Freising and Rahewin, *Gesta Friderici I.*, 1.34 and *Chronicon Romualdi Salernitani*, ed. Garufi, p. 227. Jacoby, 'Silk', p. 462–5, is unhelpful here (at 462n, he excludes the linen references because Thebes is a silk town, which looks like circular reasoning to me), although he does recognize, as other historians often do not, that Sicily had its own silk. (Bon, *Le Péloponnèse byzantin*, p. 130 is more measured.) Given all this, the Tzetzes citation, already mentioned (n. 135), becomes interesting in a different way: he does not say what cloth his Theban weavers wove, but he prefaces it with a Homeric quotation citing weavers of *othonē*, which, whatever it meant in Homer's time, was a linen word by this period.

[144] Koder, *Das Eparchenbuch*, ch. 9.

[145] *Poèmes prodromiques*, ed. Hesseling and Pernot, poem 1, ll. 95–8; Skylitzes, *Synopsis historiarum*, ed. Thurn, Michael VI, ch. 2 (pp. 482–3); *The Taktika of Leo VI*, ed. Dennis, 6.12; Farag, *The truce of Safar A.H. 359*, ch. 20 (thanks to Catherine Holmes for reminding me of this); Choniates, *Historia*, ed. van Dieten, p. 484. See Georgacas, 'Greek terms for "flax", "linen"', pp. 255–6 for some other references.

eleventh century, the 1073 cession in the Maiander valley to Andronikos Doukas (these two add the central east coast of the Aegean to the north coast, as loci for flax-growing), and occasional Athonite documents all through our period. Linen cloth turns up as constituting a loan between two Venetians at Corinth in 1136, one of the very few times in which Venetian loans are not in money.[146] These geographically spaced references give some context to the famous account in the mid-tenth-century *Life* of Basil I of the fabulously rich widow Danelis of Patras, west of Corinth, an early patron of the future emperor, who is supposedly feted by Basil after he gains the throne in 867; she comes with gifts to the emperor of 500 household servants and 100 *skiastriai*, a unique word which most plausibly means female cloth workers of some kind (*skias* means a canopy); and also cloth itself, both variegated *sendais* (silks) and *linamalōtaria* and *amalia lina*, other rare words which, however, have to mean linen cloth of some type (*linamalōtaria* was probably a linen–wool mix). Modern commentators have focussed on the silk (and have sometimes assumed without clear grounds that the *skiastriai* were silk workers).[147] I think the linen is easily as important; and from an early date—that is to say, the mid-tenth century, the date of the account, and regardless of whether the event actually happened—its production was said to be located not far from Corinth.

These references are not huge in number, but they are significant. On one level, it is entirely unsurprising that the Byzantines should have worn a lot of linen; it was a standard Mediterranean fabric, and flax could be grown in the Aegean as easily as on the Nile. For that matter they must have worn wool too, and they are likely to have worn cotton, or at least mixes—in fact, to back up Ptochoprodromos, we have seen that the *Book of the eparch* allows linen merchants to sell cotton (*bambakinōn*) too; and at least once (in a rare document from Crete, from 1118) *bambakēra* is referred to as being grown by independent peasants. We do not know where cotton was woven, apart from, probably, the capital; we know from one Venetian document that cotton (*bambaci*; we do not know whether raw cotton or cloth) was exported from there to Corinth in 1168. Wool is the easiest to prepare, and was doubtless, here as in the rest of the northern Mediterranean, the standard peasant-woven cloth everywhere where there

[146] Kaminiates, *De expugnatione Thessalonicae*, ed. Böhlig, 58.7; Branousē et al., *Byzantina eggrapha tēs monēs Patmou*, 1, n. 6, l. 55; 2, n. 50, ll. 118–21 (a. 1073); for the Patmos economy see Karlin-Hayter, 'Notes sur les archives de Patmos', although she did not stress flax; for Athos, see, e.g., *Actes de Lavra*, 1, n. 48, l. 41 (the formula is, however, the same here as in the first Patmos document); for Venetians, see *DCV*, n. 68.

[147] *Chronographiae, Vita Basilii*, ed. Ševčenko, ch. 74; cf. chs 11, 73, 75. There are too many modern references to this passage to cite. *Skiastriai* as silk workers: see, e.g., Prinzing, 'Sklaven oder freie Diener', p. 162; Jacoby, 'Silk', p. 458, just calls them 'female weavers', but in the context of a general discussion of silk. For *linamalōtaria*, see also Haldon, *Three treatises*, pp. 108, 214, who concludes that the word by now just means a type of linen, and Ditchfield, *La culture matérielle*, p. 380, who doubts this.

were sheep. In the capital, at least, it was dyed and carded—and, therefore, presumably, woven—professionally.[148] Neither of the two fabrics is stressed significantly in our sources (even though Greece has long been sheep country), so we cannot say more. But linen is better-evidenced, and as we saw for Egypt (pp. 99, 101), requires several different production processes in sequence before it is spun; it is likely often to have involved some element of productive specialization, and the data presented here support that. These data also point to at least Constantinople, Thessaloniki, Thebes, and the Peloponnesos as foci for production. These were actually the main foci for silk production too; and I would propose that silk developed on the back of the far larger-scale bulk production which linen represented, not just in Thebes and Corinth but across the empire. That has to remain a hypothesis, but it helps to make more sense of the balance of our evidence.

* * *

What we have here is only a partial picture. The evidence available for linen is anecdotal. It is certainly usefully backed up by that for silk; but since silk is not a bulk product, although it may be a helpful context for larger-scale commercial patterns, it cannot provide the evidence for them on its own. Our evidence for cloth also tells us more about production than distribution. It is clear that part of the demand for Theban and Peloponnesian silk was located in Constantinople; it is highly unlikely that it all was, since the capital had its own silk-weaving, but it is hard to tell where else it went, except insofar as Venetian involvement doubtless means that some was for export westwards. Scattered data, for example the *Timarion* in the mid-twelfth century, at least hint that Thessaloniki was another focus of demand for cloth in general (including, supposedly, from central-southern Greece), and/or an entrepôt for the demand of unspecified other places. The *Taktika* citation reminds us that army supply, again from unspecified sources, will have been an important source of demand for non-luxury cloth and metal in all periods too.[149] But that is all we can say. Nor do we have any other useful written evidence about bulk trade, except for the food supply of the capital; we have

[148] For cotton, see Koder, *Das Eparchenbuch*, ch. 9.1; Miklosich and Müller, *Acta*, 6, n. 23; *DCV*, n. 192 (Laiou, 'Regional networks', p. 139, wrongly says this is cotton sent from Corinth to Constantinople); also Constantin VII Porphyrogénète, *Le livre des cérémonies*, ed. Dagron and Flusin, 2.45 (3, p. 339), a reference I owe to Anna Kelley. For wool-working, see Laiou, 'The festival of "Agathe"', pp. 112, 116. Kaminiates, *De expugnatione Thessalonicae*, ed. Böhlig, 9.8, 58.9, implies that it was the standard cloth. References to wool are anecdotal, but also include *La vie de saint Cyrille*, ed. Sargologos, 23.4, 25.1, in which the saint, in a hermitage in his brother's monastery a little west of the capital, makes and sells woollen garments.

[149] See p. 286 above for the *Timarion*. In general on army supply, see Haldon, *Warfare*, pp. 131–4, 140–8, which implies imperial ranches for horses on the Anatolian plateau, state arms production for more specialized armour, and both state storehouses and local levies in lieu of taxation for other metalwork and general supplies—evidence is, however, lacking as to exactly where from in our period, although sourcing was apparently distributed across much of the empire. For the commercial upswing in general see also the effective account in Jacoby, 'Byzantine maritime trade', pp. 627–38, and for the Greek peninsula in particular, Laiou, 'Regional networks', pp. 137–46.

evidence for village ironworking in some documents (and also, often, in the archaeology), which tells us that this form of production was generalized, but this is an indicator of local prosperity, not wider exchange.[150] So this is where the ceramic archaeology is of crucial importance, for this is much less anecdotal. Here it is clear that the archaeology gives us almost exactly the same main production foci, at least for the twelfth century: the centres for glazed pottery production were Corinth from *c.*1090, Chalkis, the port of Thebes, from shortly after, and Constantinople all through, with Thessaloniki added by the end of the twelfth century. This certainly helps us to be surer about the picture of a concentration of active production for cloth in twelfth-century central-southern Greece. And here, unlike in the written sources, we have extensive evidence for distribution from the Thebes–Corinth area: which was, as we saw earlier, actually less to the capital than to every site on the Aegean coast, and some farther inland, using a complex network of routes. Since the centres of production of glazed ceramics and cloth match so well, it is likely that the same is true for their distribution; that is to say, it is plausible that central-southern Greek cloth—particularly, as I have argued, linen—was bought by anyone in the Aegean who lived reasonably near to the coast and could afford it.

This interwoven map, then, can be added to what we know of primary food specializations. Grain from Thessaly and Macedonia certainly mostly went to the capital along the old main western route, as we have seen; and the only other city which was likely to have been a major consumer of grain was Thessaloniki, which, situated beside a large agricultural plain as it is, probably did not buy from long-distance trade. The olive oil specialization around Sparta may well have fed the capital too, but, precisely because it was a specialization, we could suppose that it had buyers elsewhere along the trade routes as well. This might well also be so for the most easily portable protein, cheese; Crete was a major production centre for it, and it could well have been available as a competitor to local cheeses elsewhere.[151] Wine is more illuminating, however. Here, whereas in the tenth and eleventh centuries the commonest wine amphora came from Ganos on the Marmara, close to the capital, in the twelfth century wine in amphorae from Chalkis (and sometimes other places, such as Corinth) came to dominate the sites

[150] See, e.g., Meyer, *Die Haupturkunden*, p. 139 (for the Lavra); Borisov, *Djadovo*, 1, pp. 79–131; Böhlendorf-Arslan, 'Das bewegliche Inventar' for Boğazköy; and, generalizing, Pitarakis, 'Témoignage des objets métalliques'; Lefort, 'The rural economy', p. 235. Commercial exchange was not necessarily part of the requisitioning of ironwork for the army; see, e.g., *Actes de Lavra*, 1, n. 55.

[151] Cretan cheese: see al-Idrīsī, *Nuzhat al-mushtaq*, trans. Jaubert and Nef, p. 349, and n. 31 above; see Jacoby, 'Byzantine Crete', the basic study, which also argues for the island's relative marginality to the major Italian routes before 1200, except for the cheese trade. The Venetians, who sometimes went to Crete (see ibid. and p. 333 below), were regarded as standard cheese sellers in Constantinople by Ptochoprodromos: *Poèmes prodromiques*, ed. Hesseling and Pernot, poem 3, l. 109; cf. also *DCV*, n. 2, as early as 1022. For salt (from Marmara and Halmyros among other places), see Koder, 'Salt'; for wood, see Morrisson, 'Trading in wood'—these two articles are important for reminding us about other essentials, but the data for each are thin.

we know about in the Aegean, as well as being prominent in Constantinople. The capital got its wine from many places; but what it looks like is that the twelfth-century distribution networks of artisanal goods out of Chalkis or Corinth had become sufficiently developed that local wines too could be more easily, and widely, commercialized from here. And that had its reflection back in the countryside as well, with the glazed ceramics and amphorae available so generally on rural sites in central and southern Greece. We might, indeed, have expected this; urban demand for food was increasing; linen and silk production depended on buying flax, and raw silk from mulberry trees, elsewhere; and wine and oil were being exported on their own account. Someone in the countryside will have been getting prosperous as a result. But the ceramic distributions show it for sure, and indicate that this prosperity was quite widespread—and extending to peasants or, at least, richer peasants.

The complexity of exchange in central and southern Greece, and, from there, in the Aegean as a whole, was clearly above all a twelfth-century development. (On the Marmara it had always been there, as also perhaps around Thessaloniki.) Jacoby, who was concentrating only on silk, puts its start a little earlier, in the mid-eleventh century;[152] that is quite possible, but the ceramic evidence currently argues for a later date, from 1090 or so onwards, for the scale of exchange to have properly begun to increase. Renewed archaeological research might well change that date by a few decades—putting it slightly earlier, if so; I would not be surprised, then, if future work ended up agreeing with Jacoby. But a dating to the 1090s might help to explain why such a rapid development does not seem to have had much of a counterpart on the coast of Anatolia, around Smyrna and Ephesos, or inland from there, for the 1090s were a difficult time for the eastern Aegean in terms of military security—although it remains striking and indeed surprising that things did not pick up there later (as we have seen, in ceramic terms it was not until the thirteenth century that we see the first visibly active period for fine-ware production in the east). The Anatolian coast and the Maiander valley towns certainly bought things from the west, in exchange for supplying, among other commodities, raw materials to the Greek towns, such as, probably, flax (see p. 327 above), plus the wine which doubtless went in Ephesos amphorae. For the eastern Aegean to import as much Greek ceramics as it did, indeed shows that it had products to sell. But it is hard to avoid the sense that it had a less complex economy than the west in this period, and indeed we shall see in a moment that the Venetians went there much less as well.

Why did production and commerce develop in Greece, and why then? One factor we can fairly certainly exclude was direct state intervention. State workshops existed in the capital, but rarely elsewhere except for army supply, and, anyway, the evidence for them is better before our period begins—even the *Book*

[152] Jacoby, 'Silk', p. 481.

of the eparch does not stress them.[153] Private capital investment is more likely, particularly as exchange picked up and profits were more visible. David Jacoby, in particular, stresses the investment of local *archontes* as an initial driver for the production of silk. We saw investment by officials in cloth workshops in Egypt (p. 131), although in Byzantium there is no evidence for this outside the capital; the detailed analysis Jacoby offers is hypothetical, even if quite plausible—particularly if one adds in a partially distinct set of elites, merchants, who had a direct interest in developing production. It is, however, also based on the less plausible presupposition that workshops need to be large, with an 'industrial infrastructure'.[154] They could be in Egypt, but in Byzantium that scale is improbable even for silk, and still less for the other goods commercialized from central-southern Greece. The networks of nucleated workshops, in Peacock's terms (see p. 314 above), which artisanal production most probably involved in Thebes, Corinth, Chalkis, and other localities, could have had very small beginnings. Those beginnings could, certainly, have been helped along by investment by local landowners and merchants, and their small size may be the reason why we cannot see the process in our texts. All the same, where the involvement of *archontes* is particularly probable from the start is in the sale of agricultural produce, including, we could suppose, flax and silk fibre. We know this from the inside in the case of the Athos monasteries, which are our best-documented large-scale landowners; and we have one Venetian document which makes clear that Spartan *arcontes* sold oil to Venetians to sell in Constantinople in 1150–1 (unfortunately for them, the first ship with the oil was lost, because it was taken by the Norman navy in one of their attacks).[155] We could also expect investment in boats and trading expeditions, as we have already seen for Kalopetros Xanthos. That capacity for investment probably lay behind much of the steady expansion of production in these twelfth-century Greek towns and their hinterlands. But it still does not explain the take-off, for one does not invest in production or transport unless there is some expectation of sales. Where the impetus for this must have come from is increasing urban and indeed rural demand—fuelled first, as always in pre-industrial societies, by state and landowning elites, but extending to peasants and urban craftsmen as well. We will come back to the point in the next section, for the argument, although crucial for us here, cannot be seen outside the specific context of changes in agriculture and rural property-owning, which will need a different discussion.

* * *

[153] Jacoby, 'Silk', pp. 488–92, proposes state interventions of different kinds in the case of Theban silk; most of these seem to me to go beyond the evidence.

[154] Jacoby, 'Silk', pp. 476–80 (quotation from 479). Laiou and Morrisson, *The Byzantine economy*, p. 129, also call it 'conjecture'. The best evidence he cites is a member of a Theban elite confraternity *c.*1100 called Blatas, from *blattion*, silk cloth, but the prosperity this implies could have come from trading or production itself, not the investment.

[155] *DCV*, n. N11; cf. N9 (see n. 158 below for the abbreviation); cited by Borsari, *Venezia e Bisanzio*, p. 105; Jacoby, 'Silk', p. 479; Armstrong, 'Merchants of Venice at Sparta'.

The other players in this trading network were, of course, the Venetians (the Amalfitans, Pisans, and Genoese were much less important[156]). They had long been closely associated with the Aegean world, as they were originally Byzantine subjects; well into the eleventh century, Venetian documents date by Byzantine emperors. They had formalized trading rights from 992, but certainly long before as well. Any imagery of subjection to the Byzantine emperor was gone by the later eleventh century, but the Venetians were all the same very familiar with the trading networks of the empire for ever after. In 1092, as noted earlier, Alexios I exempted them from paying the *kommerkion*, which gave them a 10 per cent advantage over other traders in the empire except some major monasteries; in 1126 this exemption was extended to anyone trading with them too. They could trade in a long list of ports, which was extended in 1147 and greatly extended in 1198. In the meantime, all the same, Manuel I had taken against them, and he imprisoned all the Venetians he could get his hands on, confiscating their property, in March 1171—they did not get their position back until the mid-1180s—and although the Pisans and Genoese picked up some of their trade in the 1170s, they themselves faced expropriation and massacre by the army and the inhabitants of the capital in 1182. In the last years of the century, the Italian cities were more active than ever, but relations between the Italians and the Greeks were increasingly poisoned thereafter, and the Fourth Crusade was not far over the horizon. It is not surprising that they were painted in dark terms by an older Byzantine historiography; and even now, when it is more normal to see their trading activity in (in particular) the twelfth century as a spin-off of internal Byzantine economic expansion, historians can still see their trading privileges as in the end undermining the position of native merchants and their conditions of trade.[157]

This seems to me an exaggeration; we need to look at why. There are a large number of Venetian commercial agreements surviving from our period: only 35 before 1100, but then another 390, up to 1180. This is a large enough set to allow us to establish some at least tentatively reliable data. Over half of these texts concern Byzantium, which shows the importance of Aegean trade to Venice

[156] For them, see most conveniently Balard, 'Amalfi et Byzance', Skinner, *Medieval Amalfi*; Jacoby, 'Commercio e navigazione degli amalfitani'; Balard, *La Romanie génoise*, pp. 18–33; Borsari, 'Pisani a Bisanzio nel XII secolo'; see in general also Banti, *Amalfi, Genova, Pisa e Venezia*. The Pisans did, all the same, have a trade treaty with the Byzantines from 1111, renewed in 1192; see Müller, *Documenti sulle relazioni*, n. 34. It conveyed fewer rights than the Venetian agreements, but did cut the *kommerkion* from 10% to 4%. The Genoese were here substantially less prominent than the Pisans until after 1204.

[157] See Laiou and Morrisson, *The Byzantine economy*, pp. 145–7, for the most recent synthesis and the cautiously negative conclusion. The historiography here is huge; the best accounts of the specific Venetian involvement in Byzantium up to 1204 are, however, Lilie, *Handel und Politik*, which supplies the basic narrative for all the cities at pp. 325–595, and especially Borsari, *Venezia e Bisanzio*, which develops Borsari, 'Il commercio veneziano' and Borsari, 'Per la storia del commercio veneziano'. Thiriet, *La Romanie vénitienne*, pp. 29–62, has aged. For the treaties, see Pozza and Ravegnani, *I trattati con Bisanzio*, esp. nn. 1, 2, 3, 4, 11. For Venetian trade in the Italian and wider Mediterranean context, see Chapter 6 below.

even in the era of commercial networks stretching across much more of the Mediterranean. It can be added that 1171 certainly hit the Venetians hard; many of the documents for the 1170s concern the postponement or the writing-off of bad debts as a result, although activity quickly picked up again after 1185 or so.[158] We will look at the detail of these texts and at the merchants in them again in Chapter 6, for they are strictly parallel to the commercial agreements in both the *geniza* and the notarial registers for Genoa, although, oddly, they do not figure as much in current discussions of the way Mediterranean-wide commerce worked in this period. But what they were concretely doing in the Byzantine world does need attention here.

First of all, it is clear that Venetians behaved in Constantinople just as they did in Rialto, the city's principal island. In both places, they stood loans to each other and financed sea voyages, and in most cases, got their money, plus interest or profit, back with reasonable ease (many of the documents are sign-offs for repaid loans). The *embolos* or Venetian quarter of the Byzantine capital was, in a sense, their second city. Mostly, they dealt in money (and also, mostly, in Byzantine coins); they were proper capitalists, in the specific sense that they started with money and ended with (ideally) more money—generally, as noted earlier, 20 per cent extra, but sometimes higher figures (or, less often, lower ones), or else a specified share in the profit of the whole of the planned expedition. What the taker of the loan, the man actually acting as a merchant, did to buy and sell goods was not usually the creditor's concern, so it was less often part of the agreement. Very often the document specified that the merchant had to travel in a flotilla (*taxegium*) to a given town in the empire, and also come back on the next return flotilla, although documents could also sometimes say that the merchant could go wherever he wished in Romania, that is to say, the empire as a whole, for a given period.[159] (This is also the case for the rather fewer relevant documents in the first Genoese register, from 1156–64; the twenty-six texts mentioning voyages to Byzantium only mention goods once, and destinations outside Constantinople and a generalized Romania four times.[160])

[158] Most are in *DCV* and Lombardo and Morozzo della Rocca, *Nuovi documenti* (both here are referred to as *DCV*, but the latter is numbered as, e.g., 'N12'), plus texts in Lanfranchi, *Famiglia Zusto*. This was catalogued after *DCV* was edited, so it is not surprising it was missed by the editors, but they missed several other texts too; see Chapter 6, n. 94 below. For the 1170s, see *DCV*, nn. 241–319.

[159] The classic article on the structure of Venetian contracts is Luzzatto, 'Capitale e lavoro', in Luzzatto, *Studi*, pp. 89–116.

[160] See *Giovanni Scriba*, n. 899, in which Milanese cloth is to be sent to Constantinople; nn. 126–7, 224, 752 for references to Attaleia, Halmyros, and Crete. The greater attention to 'Romania' as a whole in the Byzantine citations in this register, the only one which survives before 1180, is probably because the Genoese did not yet have a stable base in the capital. See Balard, *La Romanie génoise*, pp. 105–12, for its slow and chequered development, plus the documents in *CDGE*, 1, n. 271 (*LI*, 2, n. 181), 309 (= *Annali genovesi*, 1, ed. Belgrano, s.a. 1162), 2, nn. 50 (*LI*, 2, n. 352), 52, 95–6, and the lists of losses cited in the notes to n. 96, pp. 207–21, which are better presented in the older Bertolotto and Sanguineti, 'Nuova serie di documenti', pp. 373–405. In the last of these texts, dating to 1174, the scale of overall Genoese investment is shown by the precise accounting of losses at the hands of attacks by

Where the Venetians went in the Aegean in itself fits the basic picture that we have been looking at, both in the archaeology and from Byzantine written sources (see Map 15). Outside the capital, they are recorded in Corinth and in the Thessalian port of Halmyros over twenty times; some fifteen times in each of Thebes (presumably via Chalkis) and Sparta (which they called Lakedemonia as the Byzantines did, or, dropping what they saw as the definite article, Kedemonia). They were in Thessaloniki rather less often, for they preferred Kitros just on the edge of the bay leading into that city, but references to the two of them together come to fifteen as well. They did not go to the islands (except sometimes to Crete and once to Rhodes), and hardly at all to the east coast (to Smyrna a handful of times, Adramyttion twice).[161] That is to say, it is obvious that they were reacting to exactly the same commercial opportunities discussed earlier in this chapter, or, on the eastern side of the sea, to their absence. They had colonies in several of these places too, particularly Halmyros, Corinth, Thebes, and Sparta, and, less often referred to, Rhaidestos.[162] And on the occasions when they mention the goods they were carrying (under a tenth of the set), it is the type of goods which have been discussed here as well: cloth (including all of linen, cotton, silk, and horsehair), cheese, copper, and, in particular, oil from Corinth and Sparta, plus, once, wood or timber, which was a long-standing Venetian export (see p. 147 above and p. 508 below)—all of them bulk goods except the two references to silk. A slightly later text, from 1182, lists much of this set and more, on a single boat loaded in Nauplion, diverted from Constantinople because of violence against the Italians and sent to Alexandria instead: oil in particular, linen, copper, armour, wax, soap, almonds, raisins, and four lobsters (this text shows, better than any other, how very varied normal shiploads were). Ceramics and wine are missing from our Venetian texts, and grain is rare, but we do not know what most merchants actually did carry, and Halmyros was a major port for grain-rich Thessaly. Sometimes this was supplies for the capital, but oil once went to Egypt, the cotton went from Constantinople to Corinth, and the horsehair was sent from Constantinople to Crete and Egypt; the Genoese are also recorded as transporting grain once, from Constantinople to Genoa itself.[163]

Byzantines, Venetians, and Pisans, plus imperial gifts unpaid, which are said to amount to around 85,000 *hyperpera*; see Hendy, *Studies*, pp. 595–7. Some of these losses were again at Halmyros, in this case at the hands of the Venetians, in the war after the coup against the latter of 1171; see *CDGE*, 2, p. 215 and n (= Bertolotto and Sanguineti, 'Nuova serie di documenti', pp. 388–9).

[161] Here I mostly follow the *DCV* index, which I find to be accurate. The Genoese also went to Attaleia (Antalya) on the sea road to the Levant; see n. 160 above.

[162] Halmyros: *DCV*, nn. 35, 54, N10, 107–8, 115, 133, 151, 172, 202, 212, 214–17, 219, 221–3, 238, N29, 313. Corinth: 54, 65, 67–9, 72, 80, 88, 146, 192, 314. Thebes: 137, 166, 233–5, 239, 243, 273, 308 (all after 1150). Sparta: N9, 135, 205–6, 233, 311, 315–16. Rhaidestos; N8, N12; see also Lanfranchi, *S. Giorgio maggiore*, n. 276 (a. 1157), which mentions the *ruga Fracigenorum* there, the street of the Franks, outside the city walls. Rhodes: see Chiaudano, 'Una pergamena'.

[163] See *DCV*, nn. 2, 46 for cheese, 7 for generic cloth, 68 for linen, 149 and 159 for horsehair, 192 for cotton, 208, 243 for silk, 329, 401 for copper, 65, 67, N8, N9, N11, 316, 338, 358, 360–1, 365 for oil

So this Venetian trade, in its very ordinariness, does precisely fit what we have been discussing; but if one looks closer, it also does not. The first point is that this set of locations is not a very large one. It in no way reflects the long lists of ports and markets in the Byzantine imperial privileges to Venice, which themselves do not include Halmyros before 1198—historians have paid too much attention to these lists, which are most probably simply a list of significant commercial centres in the empire. The Venetians focussed on the most important ones only, and as the case of Halmyros shows, independently of the theoretical rules. (Halmyros was probably missed off in 1092 because it was only recently important—Alexios' cession instead mentions the older Thessalian port of Demetrias a couple of kilometres farther north, which Halmyros replaced, evidently rapidly: by the 1160s, Benjamin of Tudela stresses, uniquely in his discussions of the empire, the presence in the latter of Venetians, Genoese, Pisans, and 'all the [presumably Greek-speaking] merchants'.[164]) Furthermore, a high percentage of the commercial contracts which are to specific towns also, as just noted, specify that merchants were to come back with the next *taxegium*; they were not to stop on the way, except for necessary halts for water and food. In the case of the Smyrna *taxegia*, all from Constantinople in the years 1156–8, the voyage there and back was to be complete in one or two months, a strikingly short period, which certainly did not allow for dawdling.[165] Lenders wanted their money back sooner rather than later; and that cut out the sort of flexibility, with both targeted voyages and cabotage, which was necessary to get goods across all the routes which ceramics show were used in the twelfth-century Aegean. That is to say, most Venetians were going on the old main routes in and out of the capital, not on the newer and more complex network. None of the contracts shows the crossing of the Aegean from the western ports to the east at all, in fact. The basic Venetian route still ran through Corinth (sometimes clearly coming there around the Peloponnesos, given Venetian interest in Sparta, but sometimes plausibly coming directly along the Gulf of Corinth and over the isthmus between the city's two ports), up the west coast, and then along the north to the entry to the Sea of Marmara, sometimes stopping off at Kitros/Thessaloniki and sometimes maybe cutting off the corner and skipping them. The east coast route then began in Constantinople, and was

(almost all from Sparta, although once from Corinth and once Rhaidestos), 118 for wood, 314 for pepper; for the 1182 text, 331. For linen cloth, transported from Rhodes to the capital already in 1087, see Chiaudano, 'Una pergamena'. In 1180, a Genoese merchant brought a ship full of grain to Genoa; see *Annali genovesi*, 2, ed. Belgrano and Imperiale di Sant'Angelo, p. 15. See also n. 160 above for a Genoese reference to cloth, and n. 151 above for Venetians selling cheese in the capital. For all this, Lilie, *Handel und Politik*, pp. 264–84, is a helpful summary; metalwork is documented at the end of the century too.

[164] Pozzo and Ravegnani, *I trattati*, n. 2; *The itinerary of Benjamin of Tudela*, trans. Adler, p. 11; cf. al-Idrīsī, *Nuzhat al-mushtaq*, trans. Jaubert and Nef, p. 409. For examples of too much attention given to the treaties, the bibliography is too great to list, but good-quality overinterpretations include Lilie, *Handel und Politik*, pp. 1–68; Borsari, *Venezia e Bisanzio*, pp. 1–29; Jacoby, 'Italian privileges'.

[165] *DCV*, nn. 122, 127–8, 130–2.

most often used to go farther, to Acre and the Levant or to Alexandria and Damietta in Egypt.[166]

All this recalls the activity of the *geniza* merchants in North Africa and Sicily, described in the previous chapters, in what, as we have seen, Jessica Goldberg calls the '*geniza* business model': the need rapidly to repay loans and primary producers favoured selling bulk goods in entrepôts and coming back as soon as practicable, rather than getting involved in local traffic. The *geniza* merchants wrote about the details of bales of flax and the like, not loans in money, because we above all have letters about the specifics of shipping rather than contracts, but the concerns were similar. As we saw for North Africa and, in more detail, Egypt, this meant that this activity was only part of the network of exchange, and other merchants were expected to do the rest. The same was true for the Venetians who took sea loans like these in Byzantium; the 'Venetian business model' was only one element of the total network.[167]

It is certainly true that some Venetians also made up some of those other merchants. That was true of the *geniza* merchants as well, as with the case of Nissīm b. Khalafūn, who toured the Delta towns from his home in Tinnīs (see pp. 110–11 above). In the Aegean, those who were actually living in Corinth or Halmyros were doubtless much more likely to engage in smaller-scale or more opportunistic trading around where they lived, as when in 1129 two Venetians in Constantinople wound up a partnership (*compagnia*) with a third, a shipowner living in Halmyros, which had traded 'through other parts of Romania and Syria'. The small number of loans for generalized trading in Romania were presumably similar.[168] And so were the half-dozen contracts for something quite surprising to anyone who has absorbed the maritime obsessions of the Venetians, trading by land; so, when a priest of the church of St Nicholas in Thebes made a *collegancia* with another Venetian in 1159—the priest putting in two-thirds of the partnership of 150 *hyperpera*, and the merchant who was actually travelling putting in the other third, as was normal for partnerships of this type—the agreement was that the merchant would travel 'by land throughout Catodica [as we have seen, Katodika was another name for the theme of Hellas around Thebes] and the Peloponnesos, and from Thebes to Thessaloniki'. This was certainly the kind of local trading that would get cloth and whatever other goods around the towns and villages. In two contracts this was extended to the sea as well, in the set phrase *per terram et per culfos et per passaios*, 'by land and by sea [literally, by gulfs] and

[166] For a general overview of the main routes, see Lilie, *Handel und Politik*, pp. 243–63; see further Pryor, *Geography, technology*, pp. 97–9. For the Gulf of Corinth, see *The life and miracles of Saint Luke of Steiris*, ed. Connor and Connor, ch. 52, for a ship from Italy on the Gulf in the mid-tenth century, the date of the text.

[167] Goldberg, *Trade and institutions*, pp. 276–86. Jacoby makes a similar point about the Aegean in 'Byzantine trade with Egypt', p. 67; Jacoby, 'Byzantine maritime trade', pp. 646–8.

[168] *DCV*, nn. 54 (quotation), 62, 106, 308.

by [shorter] sea passages'.[169] And Venetians who did this presumably included the six documented twelfth-century cases of citizens who refused to return to Venice when its duke required them to, generally in times of war, and lost some or all their possessions in the city as a penalty; staying in Romania meant more to them, at least at that moment. (Two of these men got others to pay the fine of an equivalent amount, and later repaid at standard interest rates to get the property back; two others also paid fines; another, Enrico Zusto, whom we have already met, p. 321, died in Greece and his property was later reconstituted by his family.)[170]

Interestingly, this move towards being far more part of the local commercial environment did not make Venetians who made such a choice more popular in the empire itself. Niketas Choniates remarks, concerning Manuel's confiscations in 1171, that the trouble with the Venetians was that you could not tell them apart from real Byzantines: 'They dispersed throughout the Roman Empire, keeping only their family name (*genous onoma*) and, looked upon as native and full Romans (*symphyloi kai pany Rhōmaioi*), increased and became common.' Kinnamos, when discussing the same events, put more stress on the commercial advantages that the Venetians had, but he too added that they had begun to take Roman wives; again, their integration was a threat.[171] Modern historians tend to stress unfair trading advantages more than this menacing integration, but Italians had been treated cautiously from well before the privileges of 1092; in the *Life* of Nikon, a mid-eleventh-century hagiography, one of two *Latinoi* brothers from *Akouilia* (Aquileia or possibly Equilo (now Jesolo), both in the Venetian hinterland), in Sparta for trade (*emporia*), falls insane, but cannot easily go to the saint's tomb to be cured, as, the two are *xenoi* (foreigners), so unable to leave their lodgings for any time without arousing suspicion—in the end, the sane brother has to pray, successfully, for long-distance help by the saint. The Venetians appear here more than anything as like the Armenians in the Ottoman Empire in the early twentieth century, an essential part of the landscape of local trading but not regarded as fully integrated, and very much at risk if political power turned against them. These, then, were indeed the competitors to what the *Life* of Nikon calls *autochthosontes* (natives) in the complex exchange networks we have looked at. But what is equally important is that they were few in number. The great bulk of the evidence we have for the Venetians is not for this; it is for the old main routes of commerce only. It may well be that they were resented for their trade advantages there too; but precisely because they were mostly restricted to a few routes, it cannot be said that they would have undermined the position of most

[169] *DCV*, nn. 110, 137 (quotation, a. 1159), 209, 235 (*per culfos*), 239, 308 (*per culfos*). We can add 129 and 150, which deal with Venetians travelling on the via Egnatia from Dyrrachion on the Adriatic to the capital.

[170] *DCV*, nn. 143, 163 (the well-documented Romano Mairano), 226; Pozza, *Gli atti originali*, nn. 11–13; Lanfranchi, *Famiglia Zusto*, n. 8; cf. nn. 10, 11, 17, 20, 21.

[171] Choniates, *Historia*, ed. van Dieten, p. 171; Kinnamos, *Epitome rerum*, ed. Meineke, 6.10.

Greek-speaking merchants or their conditions of trade. Those Venetians who were directly competing were not numerous enough (it needs to be remembered that, anyway, we are only dealing with the mercantile strata of a single city here), and the others were operating at a different level from that of most Byzantines.[172] Indeed, the 1192 account mentioned earlier (p. 322) of the loss of 40,000 *hyperpera* by Byzantine merchants on a single ship from Egypt (even if a Venetian one) does at least imply that Italian trading had not undermined that of the Greeks even at the level of the great international routes.

Michael Hendy calculated in a neat piece of extrapolation from reliable figures (that is to say, Italian reparations demands in the 1180s, agreed by the Byzantines, after the attacks on them) that the losses of the Venetians in 1171 amounted to some 345,000 *hyperpera*, that the total investment of the Italian cities in Byzantium was at most a million *hyperpera* at any given time and perhaps less, and that the *kommerkion* immunity may have been worth some 37,000 *hyperpera* a year to the Venetians—one could quibble over the details, but the scale is sound. This is when a mule cost around 15 *hyperpera* and a pair of oxen 7 *hyperpera*, so the *kommerkion* figure might be worth around 2,500 mules.[173] This was in itself a very small part of the imperial budget, and Italian trade as a whole was, anyway, a tiny element in any hypothetical Byzantine GDP, which was, of course, as were all pre-industrial systems, predominantly based on agriculture.[174] Hendy himself then compared these figures with much higher ones for imperial expenditures which are based on narrative sources, so are rather less reliable; this may be why his calculations have not had so much impact on more recent historiography. But at least the just cited 1192 figure shows that the scale of Venetian trading, taken as a whole, was very unlikely to have been higher than that of the Byzantines themselves.

Indeed, the Venetian loan and partnership documents we have for the period to 1180 also show sums that were not enormous. Of those in Byzantine money, which number around a hundred, most were for less than 100 *hyperpera*, and only ten were for over 300, the highest being 830 *hyperpera*. These seldom match the ranges in Genoese transactions in the later twelfth century, and Genoese

[172] *The life of Saint Nikon*, ed. Sullivan, ch. 74. For the comparatively small numbers of Venetians in the empire, see Schreiner, 'Untersuchungen zu den Niederlassungen westlicher Kaufleute', notwithstanding the claims of the Venetians themselves—see Chapter 6, n. 124 below. Another hint at Venetian–Greek tensions is the reference to the potential danger of *violentia populi* in Halmyros in a document of 1150; see *DCV*, n. N10 (= Lanfranchi, *S. Giorgio Maggiore*, n. 231).

[173] Hendy, *Studies*, pp. 590–602, taken up again and slightly modified in Hendy, 'Byzantium, 1081–1204: the economy revisited', pp. 25–7 (the *kommerkion* figure is from the latter). For the mules and oxen, see Morrisson and Cheynet, 'Prices and wages', pp. 839–40; the prices are anecdotal, but the scale for the twelfth century is consistent with other figures in the same article.

[174] For a hypothetical model of the structure (although not size) of the twelfth-century Byzantine GDP, see Laiou, 'The Byzantine economy: an overview', pp. 1154–6.

ranges were themselves lower than those considered normal in the *geniza*.[175] It is true that merchants could borrow from many different people at once; the clearest evidence we have for that is of Romano Mairano, our best-documented merchant, borrowing from eight separate people (including one Greek) to take a ship from Constantinople to Alexandria in 1167, which totalled nearly 800 *hyperpera* by the end, and another eight in 1170 to go from Venice to Constantinople, for, probably, as much as 1,500 *hyperpera*.[176] All the same, these too are far less than the 1192 figure, which was for the same route as the 1167 voyage. So it is likely that even when shipping between major ports, the Venetians were not by any means operating at a level which could overwhelm Byzantine merchant activity; and, as we have seen, they hardly participated at all in the wider network of routes. They were simply an important adjunct to a regional trading system which was already highly active on its own account, and indeed stayed active, even after the disaster of 1204. Nor can their steadily greater prominence on the scene from the 1070s onwards (that being the decade in which the numbers of documents for them begin slowly to rise) have had any causal effect on the sharp rise in commercial activity which can be seen more widely in the next decades, for this activity was focussed on the development of an exchange network which the Venetians hardly participated in. To repeat, for that we have to look more closely at demand, which will be the focus of the next section. But what the Venetian evidence does show, clearly, is how the old main commercial routes along the east and west coasts of the Aegean, stopping at four or five major centres only, actually worked. This both adds essential detail to what we know from other sources and puts into relief just how many active routes were missed out by that older set.

[175] For sums above 300 *hyperpera*, see *DCV*, nn. N10, 117, 135, 224, 252, 267, N30, 303, 308, 314–15. Half of them concern post-1171 repayments of (mostly) pre-1171 debts. (See also Chapter 6, n. 117 below for Venetian contracts in £ Veronese, the most typical currency used in Venice itself before 1180, which were slightly, but not much, higher.) As to making parallels with Genoese transactions, Spufford et al., *Handbook of medieval exchange*, pp. 286–8, registers the *hyperperon* as equivalent to 4–7 Genoese *solidi*, so 100 *hyperpera* would be £20–35 Genoese, and 830 would be £166–290 Genoese. Of these, however, the 100 *hyperpera* to £35 Genoese figure is in my view the correct one for our period, for the Genoese notarial register for the years around 1160, *Giovanni Scriba*, nn. 666, 674, 676, 689, all from 1160, gives 3.75 *hyperpera* to £1 Genoese, which, given the 25% interest regarded as normal in Genoa, would give a 3:1 exchange rate (for the record, though, nn. 219, 746, and 1256 give lower rates, and n. 84 a higher one). Furthermore, the *hyperperon* was also worth about the same as £1 Veronese, and on Spufford's figures (Spufford et al., *Handbook of medieval exchange*, p. 107) £3 Veronese was worth £1 Genoese, which fits. On the basis of these calculations, 100 *hyperpera*, the normal maximum for Venice, matches only the lower end of the figures recorded for Genoa; see Chapter 6, p. 546 with n. 185, below, for the Genoese figures, and also the comparison with those in dinars in the *geniza*.

[176] For the first set, which include doublets, because the repaid creditors in Alexandria also needed to return loan documents located in Constantinople, see Borsari, *Venezia e Bisanzio*, pp. 120–1. They were very variable in the interest agreed to, but some were for up to 50%. For the second, for which we mostly only have the charters of repayment, see ibid., pp. 122–33; Romano owed at the end 2,225 *hyperpera*, which Borsari calculates to have reflected 1,500 of initial investment. See p. 513 below for more on Romano's career.

4.5 The Logic of Byzantine Economic Expansion

So far in this chapter, we have been looking at the detail of exchange, without considering the underpinning of the Byzantine economy as a whole, which was, as in every pre-capitalist society, agriculture. We have at least seen that the evidence from field surveys in Greece in particular, plus the Athos documents, points clearly towards demographic expansion, and also that the archaeology shows the expansion of rural demand—the former beginning in the eleventh century, possibly the tenth, and the latter best-attested in the twelfth. These underpinned the development of the complexity of Byzantine bulk exchange, for sure. But how did they work, and what caused them? That cannot so very easily be answered with the written documentation we have, but it is at least the case that historians, particularly in France, have tried to discuss the issue in recent years, with interesting—and largely consistent—results.

The interest of historians in agrarian change in Byzantium has been helped, beyond doubt, by a notable feature of its evidence, unique in our period: a substantial set of new laws, 'novels', of tenth-century emperors, aimed at combating the local aggrandisement of a social group called here the 'powerful' (*dynatoi*) at the expense of the 'weak' or 'poor' (*penētai, ptōchoi*).[177] These laws, which were attached to a synopsis of the great late ninth-century translation and rewriting of Justinianic law known as the *Basilika*, are most of the new law which survives for the century after the death of Leo VI in 912, and are important for any debate about rural society in our period. They were explicitly aimed at ensuring that *dynatoi* did not buy up peasant land and impose themselves on villages (*chōria*) and village communities or communes (called *koinōtai* and similar words). The first important novel is that of Romanos I in 928, after a serious famine, in which peasants fled the land and sold up to lords to survive; they continue up to that of Basil II in 996, with every tenth-century emperor adding to them in between, except John Tzimiskes. Romanos, echoed here by all his successors, enacted that inhabitants of the same commune had rights of pre-emption of land sales to outsiders, and that no *dynatos* could buy land in a village where he had no land already. It became clear to subsequent emperors that *dynatoi* had continued to do so nevertheless; Constantine VII in 947 allowed sellers, including communities, to take such land back, and prohibited peasants with military obligations from

[177] The basic edition, which puts them in the context of other novels, is in Zepos and Zepos, *Ius graecoromanum*, 1; but the best edition is now *Les novelles*, ed. Svoronos; a good translation and framing is McGeer, *The land legislation*. The main current commentaries on these texts remain Lemerle, *The agrarian history*, pp. 85–156; Morris, 'The powerful and the poor'; Kaplan, *Les hommes*, pp. 360–2, 414–44. Very little lawmaking survives from anywhere else in Europe in the middle ages aiming specifically to protect the rights of peasants (the Islamic world did not have formal legislation in this period); only a handful of laws protecting *liberi homines* in the legislation of the high Carolingian period—rather less effectively than the Byzantine set—offer any real parallels (see, e.g., Müller-Mertens, *Karl der Grosse*).

buying land from anyone poorer; Nikephoros Phokas in 964 brought expanding monastic land into the equation, and in 966 enacted, in very late Roman phrasing, that *dynatoi* should only sell to *dynatoi*, soldiers and the 'poor' (*penētai*) to people of the same status. Basil II rounded all this off in 996 in the longest of the laws, reiterating and reinforcing the main messages of the others; he also picked up on something not really developed since Romanos I in 934, that village collectivities were also under threat by peasants rising socio-economically in their own community, and he cited a certain Philokales, who had gained an official position and bought up his entire village—Basil voided his acquisitions, and reduced the by now unlucky man to the level of his neighbours again.[178]

These laws were not repeated or revised after 996; but they were not for show. Although it is fairly obvious from the texts themselves that the legislation had failed to stop the increasing landowning of *dynatoi*, they were not abandoned; several of them are cited in the *Peira*, a mid-eleventh-century legal handbook which summarizes and comments on the judgments of a senior imperial judge named Eustathios Rhomaios, probably largely dating to the 1020s—Eustathios had apparently, indeed, used the laws to reverse land seizures by both lay elites (including members of the major aristocratic Skleros family) and monasteries.[179] Even in the twelfth century they were referred to, by Manuel I in 1166, as legislation which was still current. But conversely, we have documents from the Athonite monasteries which precisely show the monastic buying up of village land, in ways which look like clear infractions of the novels; much went on, on the ground, which was difficult for any judge to influence.[180]

I summarize a set of complex enactments in a few lines here; they have been amply discussed elsewhere. But they raise questions of direct relevance to this chapter. First, who were the *dynatoi*? Emperors often left this vague, but Romanos I said that they were anyone who was 'capable of intimidating sellers', and later glossed this as including all civil and military officials, and senior ecclesiastics, including abbots of monasteries.[181] In a world where aristocratic status was not legally defined, this was as wide-ranging a definition of the imperial elite as we find anywhere, although one would have to add regional and local lay landowners, who could certainly also intimidate. For their part, the 'weak' or 'poor' were generally characterized as villagers; villagers were clearly not all necessarily poor in economic terms, and could buy up the land of weaker neighbours, but that could be permissible as long as they did not go as far as Philokales, whose actions

[178] *Les novelles*, ed. Svoronos, 2.1, 2.2.1, 4.2.1, 4.3.1, 5.2.3, 8, 11.1.1, 14 prologue, ch. 4 (cf. 3.3.1)—but there is much repetition of individual enactments.

[179] *Peira*, in Zepos and Zepos, *Jus graecoromanum*, 4, 42.18–19, 69.5 for the Skleroi, 23.3 for a monastery; see n. 200 below for commentaries.

[180] For 1166, see Macrides, 'Justice under Manuel I', pp. 130–2, 177–8; for Athos, see *Actes de Lavra*, 1, n. 14, *Actes d'Iviron*, 1, n. 13.

[181] *Les novelles*, ed. Svoronos, 2.2.2 (quotation, following McGeer's translation, *The land legislation*, pp. 46–7), 3.7.1.

potentially undermined the coherence of the village commune. It seems to me, as to Lemerle and Kaplan, that these laws (particularly those of Romanos I and Basil II) really were, as the texts claim, aimed to protect such communes, as communities of taxpayers ('The contribution of taxes and the fulfilment of military obligations... will be completely lost should the common people disappear,' as Romanos said in 934), rather than being either laws to safeguard peasant-based thematic armies (Byzantium was no longer dependent on such armies for its security) or laws simply targeted at dangerous office holders and landed aristocracies who might undermine imperial power in the provinces. Conversely, it does also have to be recognized that it is striking how negative the novels are about imperial elites, whose bad behaviour they constantly stress; and they would certainly have helped any emperor concerned about excessive aristocratic power.[182]

Why, however, did village communes matter to emperors? Emperors, of course, knew that taxation was harder to collect from the powerful than from the weak, which underpinned some of the rhetorical urgency of their legislation. But there was more than that: this was an issue about the coherence of tax-raising. Village communities in our period were probably more organized in Byzantium than in most parts of the Mediterranean. Fāṭimid Egypt had village headmen, as we have seen, and villages there had clear economic roles in the maintenance of irrigation (see pp. 63–4 above), but they are not visible as collectivities with any political protagonism or much of a tax-raising role—less, indeed, than under either the Romans or the Mamlūks. In Italy, village communities rarely gained any collective organization until after 1100, when rural communes slowly began to appear; only in the Iberian Peninsula, in both its Christian- and its Muslim-ruled sectors, are structured village collectivities sometimes as visible as in Byzantium.[183] Byzantine settlement was also largely concentrated, with villages more visible in both the archaeology and the documents than hamlets or isolated farms, which undoubtedly helped social cohesion.[184] It is true that Byzantine communes, however active (and, doubtless, themselves socially coercive), did not dominate local economies. There is little sign that they were important in the organization of agriculture: villages had some communal land, and do seem sometimes to have planned irrigation collectively, when land was irrigated (see p. 303 above), but farming in the northern Mediterranean was generally individually organized. For peasants themselves, the *chōrion*, village (and its *koinotēs*, commune) was

[182] *Les novelles*, ed. Svoronos, 3.1.2 (quotation, following McGeer's translation, *The land legislation*, p. 55). See Lemerle, *The agrarian history*, pp. 85–108; Kaplan, *Les hommes*, pp. 421–39. To protect armies: Ostrogorsky, *History of the Byzantine state*, 2nd edn, pp. 241–4; anti-aristocratic: Morris, 'The powerful and the poor' (whom I do not follow here, although this article remains, as already noted, one of the best analyses of the laws).

[183] See in general Wickham, *Community and clientele*, pp. 192–241; Wickham, 'La cristalización de la aldea'; see further pp. 387–8 below for al-Andalus.

[184] Here the bibliography is immense, and unnecessary to rehearse in detail here, but a good point of departure is Lefort et al., *Les villages dans l'empire byzantin*.

probably most important as an expression of local solidarity against outsiders, and it was certainly that; for we find, for example, villagers acting collectively in court cases against monasteries in the Athonite documents, a point we will come back to. But for tax-raising the *chōrion* had come to be central, and that was at the heart of imperial concerns.[185]

The importance of village communes to the state is particularly visible in the (probably) early tenth-century *Fiscal* (or *Marcian*) *Treatise*. This describes in detail how tax is assessed at the village level, and how tax-raising interfaces with different levels of landowning and land abandonment; and we have clear signs of an element of collective liability for taxpaying. That is to say, although tax was taken from individual families, it was regularly structured by the villages they lived in and to which they also had mutual obligations.[186] It is significant that one word for 'villagers' in disputes which pit Athonite monasteries against rural communities is *syntelestai*, 'co-taxpayers'.[187] It might be—Ostrogorsky certainly thought so in the mid-twentieth century—that if emperors failed to protect peasants here, the entire fiscal and military basis of the state was under threat, and that indeed, when they did fail, it changed dramatically, becoming, in his terminology, 'feudal'.[188] This was, however, never really plausible, and as we saw earlier (pp. 275–6), is no longer accepted. On one level, indeed, the fears of the tenth-century emperors, who may have romanticized free taxpaying communities as much as Ostrogorsky did, turned out to be excessive. Basil II himself had no trouble in accumulating financial reserves on a legendary scale, despite half a century of constant and expensive war.[189] But this did not mean that the importance of village communes to the whole fiscal structure of the empire was overstated—only that the aggression of the *dynatoi* did not lessen it. Tax-raising continued to be structured by villages, whether they were communities of peasant landowners or else, by now, part of the estates (*proasteia*) of larger landowners—or, very commonly, both. References to taxation structured by estates exist after 1100, but are not common.[190] It is not the case that either the eleventh- or the twelfth-century state was weak, or structurally different from before, even if there was more lay

[185] See in most detail Kaplan, *Les hommes*, pp. 186–218, with Lefort, 'The rural economy', pp. 279–83, and, more generally, Krallis, 'Popular political agency'. For taxation in general, see Oikonomidès, *Fiscalité*.

[186] The *Fiscal Treatise* is edited in Dölger, *Beiträge*, pp. 113–23, followed by an extensive commentary. See in general Kaplan, *Les hommes*, pp. 205–15; to put it very simply, tax obligations were individual, but the community was collectively liable for non-payments.

[187] *Actes de Lavra*, 1, n. 37, *Actes d'Iviron*, 1, n. 9. See Estangüi Gómez and Kaplan, 'La société rurale', pp. 538–9.

[188] Ostrogorsky, *History of the Byzantine state*, 2nd edn, pp. 241–3, 248–50, 271–2, 329–30.

[189] Psellos, *Chronographia*, ed. Reinsch, 1.31, although the underground tunnels, in which Basil supposedly hid his surplus, are most probably a folktale motif; another example is al-Ṭabarī, *Tārīkh al-rusul wa al-mulūk*, trans. D. Waines, *The revolt of the Zanj*, pp. 9–10, for the mother of the 'Abbāsid caliph al-Mut'azz in 869.

[190] *Actes d'Iviron*, 1, n. 30, 2, n. 52, is one example; but the settlement, a village subsumed into an estate, had here actually been founded by the monastery of Iviron. See Lefort, *Société rurale*, pp. 72–6, who

and ecclesiastical landowning; great landowners are, after all, generally oppressive and committed to tax evasion everywhere, without states having to be undermined by them, as the late Roman Empire had shown well before this.[191]

If the (at least partial) failure of the laws did not entail the failure of the state, however, what did it mean? This depends on how much land lay aristocrats, officials, monasteries, and other *dynatoi* actually did gain, which is more of a problem. It is common in the historiography to find the confident statement that whereas before 900 or so peasants often owned their land, by 1100, after the 'powerful' had moved in on the 'weak', most peasants had become tenants, *paroikoi*, of large landowners, on estates which had replaced villages as a dominant element in the landscape;[192] the only question that then arises is how subjected such *paroikoi* were. Such historians are generally influenced not only by the land laws—and the well-chronicled and clearly well-financed political activities of some of the great aristocratic families[193]—but also by the documents of the Athonite monasteries, which certainly show by 1100 some substantial arrays of estates, and, often, part of the process of expansion; some historians add in the cadaster of Thebes (see p. 303 above), a section of a local tax record from the late eleventh century, which does not obviously show many owner-cultivators, although there are certainly some.[194] The problems are that laws are, as usual, not direct records of activity, but only of the preoccupations of lawgivers—and that narratives and archival documents always privilege the politically visible, and the actions of people prosperous enough to make documents and then archive them. Only the Thebes cadaster is a real support for the argument that peasant owners had become few, as it covers a whole (even if small) territory. Peasants who are not dependants of a landlord fly under the radar in most medieval documentary environments; in many cases, indeed, the more independent peasants there are, the less documentation there is at all.[195]

I would not argue that precise point here. All the same, the evidence which we do have, although it certainly shows that many large landowners were gaining more land, tells us little about how large a land area they actually occupied. But we can say that by the standards of (say) north-central Italy, let alone France or England, the best-documented larger owners (notably the Athonite monasteries)

regards it as more typical than I would; cf. also Estangüi Gómez and Kaplan, 'La société rurale', pp. 551–7.

[191] See, e.g., Wickham, *Framing*, pp. 71–2, 161, 255, 527–9.

[192] e.g. Lefort, 'The rural economy', pp. 236–8, 283–90; Kaplan, *Les hommes*, p. 264 ('la très grande majorité'), and more generally on *paroikoi*, 264–72; Laiou and Morrisson, *The Byzantine economy*, p. 101; see also Smyrlis, 'Social change', a good synthesis. Magdalino, *The empire of Manuel I*, pp. 160–1, and Estangüi Gómez and Kaplan, 'La société rurale', pp. 543–57, are more sceptical as to the evidence.

[193] See esp. Cheynet, *Pouvoir et contestations*.

[194] Svoronos, 'Recherches sur le cadastre byzantin', p. 142; the numbers are minimized by Harvey. 'Economic expansion in central Greece', pp. 22–4, but there were still a few.

[195] Wickham, *Framing*, p. 535.

do not seem particularly dominant. In the eleventh century, 100 square kilometres (80,000 *modioi*) is a rough calculation for the lands of Iviron, some 65 square kilometres (a little over 50,000 *modioi*) for the Lavra, which were easily the richest two monasteries on Athos as far as we can tell, and quite possibly in the empire; these are large but not huge figures.[196] Of the few lay owners whose lands we can calculate because they wrote surviving wills, all of them of reasonably high status, Gregory Pakourianos in 1083, who left some thirty-six estates variously defined, certainly owned more—he may well be a guide to the scale of the doubtless still richer and more powerful families on the Anatolian plateau, whose lands are only referred to casually in the sources—but the other will makers had substantially less. And the really powerful Anatolia-based families, who would have overmatched Gregory, numbered barely more than a dozen.[197] One would, however, need some two hundred other—undocumented—owners as rich as Iviron to make up half of the cultivated land area (thus making tenants half the cultivators) even of Greece, let alone the whole empire.[198] I would not wish to exclude that out of hand; imperial land, in particular, was very substantial;[199] and there were, of course, countless smaller landowners too, who had at least some tenants, as the Thebes cadaster makes clear. But it cannot be said that we have the proof for it, or anything approaching it.

[196] See Lefort, 'The rural economy', pp. 287, 290, summarizing his own calculations in *Actes de Lavra*, 1, p. 74 and *Actes d'Iviron*, 1, pp. 25–32; see also Smyrlis, *La fortune des grands monastères*, pp. 47–8, 52–4. (Iviron had gained a little more by 1100, but much of the total was then confiscated; see *Actes d'Iviron*, 2, pp. 29–32.) For the main texts, see *Actes de Lavra*, 1, nn. 50, 52, 58, *Actes d'Iviron*, 1, n. 29, 2, n. 52. For other monasteries, see Morris, *Monks and laymen*, pp. 212–40; the figures cited there are all rather lower, except, we can assume, for Bačkovo, founded by Gregory Pakourianos; see n. 197 below.

[197] Gautier, 'Le typikon du sébaste Grégoire Pakourianos'; cf. Lemerle, *Cinq études*, pp. 135–8, 175–81, and Kaplan, *Les hommes*, pp. 337–8; in the other four surviving wills—*Actes d'Iviron*, 2, nn. 44, 47; Lemerle, *Cinq études*, pp. 20–9; and Gautier, 'La diataxis de Michel Attaliate'—we find at most half a dozen estates each. See again Lemerle, *Cinq études*, pp. 58–63, 105–12, 188–91, and Cheynet, 'Fortune et puissance', pp. 200–2. For the plateau, see Cheynet, *Pouvoir et contestations*, pp. 213–20; Cheynet, 'Fortune et puissance', p. 204 (he sees the plateau families as richer than Gregory Pakourianos). The supposed huge wealth of the ninth-century Danelis of Patras (*Chronographiae, Vita Basilii*, ed. Ševčenko, chs 11, 74–5) is a literary construction. The well-known large estate of Andronikos Doukas in 1073, with five villages (see n. 51 above), made up only a little over 7.5 square kilometres; see Thonemann, *The Maeander valley*, p. 262. Note also the small scale of landowning in Byzantine Puglia, where peasant owners are well attested: Martin, *La Pouille*, pp. 299–301.

[198] Greece's total land area is now some 129,000 square kilometres. In 2008, before the financial crash, the cultivated part of this was estimated at 83,000 square kilometres (Trading Economics, https://tradingeconomics.com/greece/agricultural-land-sq-km-wb-data.html); I have for the purposes of this rough argument cut that to 40,000, to reflect medieval conditions at least hypothetically. For north-central Italy, see, e.g., the brief survey of aristocratic wealth in Wickham, *Medieval Rome*, pp. 206–8, 252–6, plus pp. 494–5 below. Iviron and the Lavra would have counted among medium-scale aristocratic families there, Gregory Pakourianos perhaps among the larger-scale ones, but not the largest.

[199] Kaplan, *Les hommes*, pp. 317–26; Lefort, 'The rural economy', pp. 287–9; the evidence for imperial lands is, however, not that good. Note that Kazhdan thought, perplexingly, that all the land of the empire belonged to the state; see Kazhdan and Ronchey, *L'aristocrazia bizantina*, pp. 177–85; this is not a viewpoint which has convinced others, and certainly not me.

Set against this, what is equally striking, to someone who knows western Europe best, is the protagonism of the villages we do have evidence for, particularly in the eleventh century—that is to say, after the land legislation had ended (we know less about rural relations in the twelfth; there are fewer Athos documents, in particular). Villages did not just fight Athos monasteries, but sometimes—unlike in Latin Europe—won, or at least forced their opponents to a draw. Eustathios Rhomaios' judgments contain several similar cases.[200] And Michael Psellos' letters, from the mid-century, contain several examples of outright village aggression, as seen from his elite standpoint at least. The late Theodore Alopos, formerly of Rhodes and recently living in the capital, has his island estates stolen by nearby villagers; an impoverished estate owner in the Optimaton theme (in Bithynia, Psellos' own rural base) has villagers doing the 'customary things' (clearly bad ones) to him; two other villages there are fighting each other over land; in eastern Thrace the peasants of Mamytze are diverting monastic water to their own mill.[201] We might not expect Bithynia and Thrace, so close to the capital and thus full of urban-owned estates, to have such active peasant communities as this, if most of the land of the empire was held by tenants. Farther from the capital and later in time, Theophylact of Ochrida around 1100 had trouble with independent-minded peasants too; in Crete in 1118, in another court case, the peasants of the *chōrion* of Menikos prevented a certain Achillios Limenites from taking their water rights; in 1133 a villager encroached on monastic land near Smyrna. In Italy of this period, only some upland pastoral communities, with a greater collective cohesion based on common land, were acting like this with any regularity; very few of these Byzantine instances are likely to fit that model—they are above all lowland examples—but even so, such cohesion was very visible here.[202]

It can be seen that I am unconvinced that the majority of peasants in the Byzantine Empire were tenants by 1100, even if there were certainly very many. One could suppose anyway that only a minority of villages were single estates of landlords; the Thebes cadaster shows very fragmented tenure, so do many documents from Athos, and the solid estates which are also found in the latter are often visibly, as are the estates of Gregory Pakourianos and Andronikos Doukas,

[200] *Actes de Lavra*, 1, nn. 14, 37, *Actes d'Iviron*, 1, nn. 1, 4, 9, 2 n. 40, 51, *Actes du Prôtaton*, nn. 4–6. For the *Peira*, in Zepos and Zepos, *Jus graecoromanum*, 4, see, e.g., 15.8, 23.3, 40.12, 42.18, 19. (Some of these are for Hierissos, the town closest to Athos, which held off most monastic encroachment in our period; it had a large peasant population (cf. Kaplan, *Les hommes*, pp. 226–7), even if we cannot be sure that it was its peasants who achieved that on their own.) For discussion, see Kaplan, *Les hommes*, pp. 193–4; Morris, *Monks and laymen*, pp. 247–56; Morris, 'Dispute settlement', pp. 132–5; Harvey, *Economic expansion*, pp. 42–4; Nilsson, *Aristocracy, politics and power*, pp. 229–40.

[201] Psellus, *Epistulae*, ed. Papaioannou, nn. 232, 235, 340–1 (Psellos, *Epistulae*, ed. Kurtz and Drexl, nn. 251, 50–2). See also the *Life of Lazaros of Galesion*, ed. Deleheye, ch. 109, for a monk of Galesion, near Ephesos, who fears the aggression of the nearby village against his monastery.

[202] *Theophylacti Achridensis epistulae*, ed. Gautier, nn. 96, 98; Miklosich and Müller, *Acta*, 6, n. 23, 4, n. 18. Community protagonism would continue; see Kondyli, *Rural communities in Late Byzantium*, for the thirteenth to fifteenth centuries, with previous bibliography.

ex-imperial land.[203] Fragmented tenure makes landlordly control harder, and allows for more autonomous collective action between peasant owners and their tenant neighbours; that would certainly be the norm in Italy when villages developed communes in the twelfth century.[204] It is likely, in fact, that many villages in Byzantium had a complex mixture of tenure, with some inhabitants rich enough to have their own tenants (these would certainly also have been the *oikodespotai* or *prōteuontes*, village leaders, mentioned in some texts, plus local priests), some owner-cultivators, some part-owners and part-tenants, and some tenants of local or external owners.[205] That was certainly typical elsewhere in the Mediterranean. It ensured that peasant internal hierarchies were marked, and might be on occasion as oppressive as those of great landowners, but it did not in itself undermine village cohesion, and it often strengthened it. And it gave space for peasants to organize their own economic life autonomously.

Where I am more in agreement with the historiography is over the conditions of tenants (*paroikoi*) themselves, which do not seem to have been as onerous as in some Latin European societies. Tenants were generally free in Byzantium (unfree agricultural workers are little documented[206]), and had full access to courts; nor was there a trace in this period of any version of the seigneurial subjection which was developing in the eleventh-century west. They had security of tenure. Furthermore, they do not seem to have paid extortionate rents: perhaps a sixth of the grain crop in the case of rents in kind according to Kaplan's figures, with tax as half that—this making up in total, for tenants of all kinds, between a fifth and a quarter, and much less for peasant landowners. Lefort offers higher figures, up to a third for rent and tax for tenants (as against under a quarter in tax for landowning peasants), but he sees them as maxima, with real figures probably rather lower.[207] We are here in the same arena as the figures for twelfth-century Sicily discussed in Chapter 3 (pp. 239–42), in which Muslims seem to have paid under a third of their grain yield in tax, and Christian Greeks in the east of the island paid perhaps

[203] Svoronos, 'Recherches sur le cadastre byzantin' for Thebes; Gautier, 'Le typikon du sébaste Grégoire Pakourianos', pp. 127–31 for his imperial chrysobulls; Branousē et al., *Byzantina eggrapha tēs monēs Patmou*, 2, n. 50.

[204] See in general Wickham, *Community and clientele*.

[205] Kaplan, *Les hommes*, pp. 200–2, 226–31; Kaplan, 'Les élites rurales byzantines'; Estangüi Gómez, 'Richesses et propriété paysannes', pp. 171–5, 205–9; Estangüi Gómez and Kaplan, 'La société rurale', pp. 536–40, 557–60.

[206] For references to the unfree, see Lefort. 'The rural economy', pp. 241–2; Oikonomides, 'Oi byzantinoi douloparoikoi'; Kaplan, *Les hommes*, pp. 276–7. They are vague for the most part, and seem to me to be above all to unfree tenants—as the *douloparoikoi* were, beyond doubt.

[207] Kaplan, *Les hommes*, pp. 501–3; cf. 505–15, 572; Lefort, 'The rural economy', pp. 301–4. I simplify here some very complex calculations on the part of each writer. Security of tenure: e.g. *Peira*, in Zepos and Zepos, *Jus graecoromanum*, 4, 15.2–3 (cf. Oikonomides, 'Ē Peira peri paroikōn'). We need to set these figures against the parallel figures for yields, which have been estimated as between 4:1 and 5:1, on a sketchy evidence base (Lefort, 'The rural economy', pp. 301; Oikonomides, 'The role of the Byzantine state', p. 1002)—not so high by Mediterranean standards, but slightly higher than those of northern Italy (see p. 488 below).

only a sixth in rent; and in Byzantium, as in Sicily, this created space for peasants to keep agricultural surplus, and potentially sell it for their own gain. This fits the wide distribution of glazed tablewares in twelfth-century Greek villages (see pp. 300–2 above), which peasants were evidently able to buy.

Sometimes, historians of Byzantium say that the condition of *paroikoi* was not necessarily always worse than that of peasant owners, given that the former often benefited from the protection of their landlords against agrarian crisis, and also from tax exemptions, particularly on monastic land. I would not put as much faith in landlordly charity as that, and it is plausible that the attested immigration of peasants onto Athonite lands may have, rather, often been to enjoy favourable rents in land clearance areas.[208] Kaplan and Lefort's calculations as to the possibilities of peasant surplus in the eleventh century, even if they are open about their speculative nature, anyway imply that there was probably almost no normal circumstance in which any *paroikos* was likely to be better off than an owner, even if they held the same amount of land—and owners could well hold more.[209] If we believe Athonite rhetoric about the potential effects of devolving tax-collecting on some of the lands of the Lavra to Alexios I's brother at the end of the eleventh century (we will become *paroikoi*, the monks claimed), the status was one to be avoided.[210] All the same, we can find at least some *paroikoi* who were not so ground down by the conditions of their tenure that they had no access to enough surplus to buy things, or to invest in improving the land. And that was still more the case for Byzantine peasant owners, even in periods of high levels of taxation; Estangüi Gómez and Kaplan indeed see, convincingly, peasant elites as among the main actors in, and beneficiaries of, the economic expansion of the eleventh and twelfth centuries.[211]

Eleventh- and twelfth-century Byzantium thus offers us a picture in which relatively few landlords, apart from the state, owned so very widely; uncalculated but substantial numbers of landowning (and independent-minded) peasants survived; and rents were not uncontrollably high. The concentration of landed wealth in general here was by no means as great as the traditional models of the great estates of Latin Europe have proposed, although those models do not, in

[208] Oikonomidès, *Fiscalité*, pp. 211–18; Lefort, 'The rural economy', pp. 237–9; Kaplan, *Les hommes*, pp. 268–9. For peasants moving to Athonite estates, see, e.g., *Actes de Lavra*, 1, n. 6, *Actes d'Iviron*, 1, nn. 2, 10, and probably 30. Estangüi Gómez and Kaplan, 'La société rurale', pp. 551–7, downplay the significance of this.

[209] Kaplan, *Les hommes*, pp. 500–22; Lefort, 'The rural economy', pp. 299–308.

[210] *Actes de Lavra*, 1, n. 46; cf. *Actes du Prôtaton*, n. 2, here a dispute between two monasteries.

[211] For *paroikoi*, see Lefort, 'The rural economy', pp. 307–8, and Laiou and Morrisson, *The Byzantine economy*, pp. 106–8 (note also that the yield figures cited in n. 207 above do not include vines and tree crops, which were much more likely to be remunerative); for rich peasants, see Estangüi Gómez and Kaplan, 'La société rurale', pp. 557–60. Estangüi Gómez, 'Richesses et propriété paysannes', further stresses the benefits to tenants of economic expansion in the twelfth to fourteenth centuries, citing among others *Actes d'Iviron*, 3, n. 56 (a. 1152), which shows previously poor *paroikoi* who became able to acquire plough oxen.

fact, fit even the Latin parts of the Mediterranean, as we shall see later when discussing northern Italy (pp. 494–6 below). It was substantially added to by paid office, especially in the capital and the army, and indeed the financial advantages of office-holding were that much greater because not all officials had extensive private estates. The land tax paid to the state was in large part directly spent on state employees, after all, so tax-taking, as well as rent, added to elite wealth. There was, all the same, a balance here, between a relative but not extreme elite prosperity and a good possibility of an economic breathing space for peasants, particularly, but not only, for richer peasants.

Kaplan argued in 1992 that the consequence of this balance was a blocked, largely autarkic economy, with peasants, and even most landlords, aiming first at self-subsistence, and without the scope for much investment in the land, or in artisanal goods; landlords were not rich enough to push hard for enough agrarian improvement, which was the only way the empire could develop economically, and peasants could not take enough risks to do it for them.[212] But this interpretation does not work for Byzantium in our period, where, as we have amply seen, from both the archaeology and, more anecdotally, the written documentation, exchange was growing in intensity in the later eleventh and, above all, the twelfth century. We have to look again at what the logic of the economy could have been to produce this result.

I would see the development of the Middle Byzantine economy as going roughly like this. The demographic rise in our period (see pp. 302–3 above), plus the clearing of land, may or may not have increased the amount of resources per capita in the countryside; but what it did do was create more space in the system, and certainly a growing gross total of surplus, however it was to be used. In some provinces of the empire there was increasing peace too, especially—for the Anatolian plateau—with the moving of the frontier well eastwards in the 960s, plus—for Macedonia—the ending of the Bulgarian wars in 1018. Peace allowed for the accumulation of wealth, in some areas for the first time, which made these processes easier.[213] In many western European socio-economic systems in the early middle ages, a growing surplus would have most likely been used, at least by peasants who did not have to surrender too much to others, to consume more on the spot; it was too difficult to sell surplus elsewhere, for the routes, and the merchants on them, were not active enough (see pp. 666–8 below for further discussion of the point). But Byzantium had a network of routes for the movement

[212] Kaplan, *Les hommes*, pp. 562–73. It is necessary to stress again that Kaplan has changed his views: see for this esp. Estangüi Gómez and Kaplan, 'La société rurale'.

[213] It should be added that the most active twelfth-century subregion, central-southern Greece, had not been exposed to war since the ninth century; conversely, the dramatic loss of most of Anatolia at the end of the eleventh, although inevitably disruptive to so many aspects of the Byzantine system, did not affect the commercial uplift of the twelfth in the Aegean, except for parts of the western Anatolian coast, as we have seen (p. 330).

of goods which had survived since the late Roman Empire, especially for the lands around the Aegean and Marmara, close to the sea or not far inland. The tax system underpinned these routes, for that had never failed. Tax went to local armies, but also to the capital. Increasingly in the ninth century, and onwards from there, it was collected in money, which enforced the selling of goods by the peasantry. In particular, the old main maritime exchange routes along the Aegean coasts were active throughout the early middle ages as a result, as the movement of eighth/ninth-century globular amphorae above all demonstrates (see, p. 304 above). They were much less active as routes than they had been under the Roman Empire, but their maintenance made surviving interconnections possible.

Initially, this integrated very localized societies; Byzantium in the eighth century had, as archaeology shows, highly local (and often simple) productions which were linked by small quantities of goods from the capital and by army supply. But the routes remained there, and were ready for the moment in which local surpluses increased because of demographic growth and land clearance, from the tenth century onwards. When that happened, as we saw in Sections 4.3 and 4.4 of this chapter, first, the traffic on the same routes became denser, as the distribution of Ganos wine amphorae and the more intense circulation of GWW 2 ceramics from Constantinople show. Then, in the late eleventh century and the twelfth, there were two developments: many more types of goods can be identified in both archaeological and written sources, ceramics and cloth being the ones we can say most about; and the networks of exchange became substantially more complex. New foci for artisanal production emerged, particularly in central-southern Greece and Thessaloniki, and they sold directly to places which were not the capital, linking new sections of the Aegean together. Urban demand increased as a result too, as towns expanded.

What was happening here was a steady build-up of possibilities for both peasants (particularly richer ones) and landlords to do something different with their surpluses, thanks to the interconnections which already existed. And one thing which they could do, which was particularly useful for peasants—risk-averse as they do indeed tend to be[214]—was develop productions which were not only helpful for subsistence but more saleable, notably wine, animal products such as leather and cheese, and olive oil. It is not chance that the first sign of the large-scale selling of rural goods is Ganos wine amphorae, given the demand from the capital, not so far away. Land improvement certainly went in the direction of the establishment of vineyards and tree crops, elsewhere as well. *Paroikoi* of Iviron can be seen owning their own vineyards in a detailed land register of 1104.[215] That in turn will have helped them move into productions which were not for subsistence, such as flax, and mulberry trees for silk. We might suppose that

[214] See for Byzantium, very generally, Harvey, 'Risk aversion'.

[215] *Actes d'Iviron*, 2, n. 53, l. 394, discussed in Laiou and Morrisson, *The Byzantine economy*, p. 109n.

landlords would be the first people to do that, but once the possibilities of sale were there, peasants could follow them too.

In many other societies, this sort of growing exchange intensity followed increased aristocratic wealth and demand, above all.[216] But the pre-existing Aegean routes, kept active by the fiscal system of the Byzantine Empire, had a different effect here. Precisely because substantial landowners were not so overwhelmingly dominant, not only landlords but peasants as well had access to the possibilities of the sale of goods, and then, later, the production of goods for sale, using those sea routes, and the acquisition of the products of others with the money thus obtained. Landowners may have sold oil in Lakonia in the twelfth century (p. 331), and the Athos monasteries, whether or not they were getting high rents, definitely had enough to sell, entrepreneurially, to make them very concerned with the preservation of their boats and customs privileges (p. 321); but we also saw that peasants, not just landowners, sold grain at Rhaidestos (p. 281), and that peasant owners were growing cotton in Crete (p. 327). Peasants could here, then, benefit from the possibilities of exchange, to consume differently—that is to say, consume products from outside, such as artisanal goods. This, then, as just noted, gives a structural context to the ceramics, by now close to being mass-produced, found on so many twelfth-century rural sites in field surveys; it must be that peasants—except, probably, the poorest—could now produce for sale sufficiently actively that they could buy them. Exchange in this society reached wider sections of the population than it did as yet in most of the Latin west, including north-central Italy. We are, rather, looking at an economy with strong similarities to those of both Egypt and Sicily, as discussed in Chapters 2 and 3. Egypt was like this all along; the internal exchange system of the Nile valley, a route well oiled by the moving of fiscal goods, never failed. Sicily showed similar stabilities too, especially in the east—and, even in the west of the island, exchange links were clearly visible from the tenth century onwards. In the heartland of Byzantium, by contrast, where the seventh-century crisis really hit, it became highly attenuated for two or three centuries. But when the demographic upturn started, the fiscal network was still there, and a dense exchange network could begin slowly to develop again. The possibilities of an upturn of this kind will be looked at again when we come to al-Andalus in Chapter 5, where a parallel, but even sharper development occurred.

That network then fed on itself because of investment—in artisanal production in Constantinople and possibly elsewhere, in the renting out of docks and shops there and in other cities, and in direct investment in shipping ventures by the end

[216] If we had enough evidence, we might conceivably have seen this on the Anatolian plateau, the main area for aristocratic estates in Byzantium in the two centuries before the 1070s; but we do not, and the fragmentary evidence we do have for it gives us little obvious sign of it (see p. 292 above), unless the good-quality ceramics made in Amorion (see p. 294 above) turn out to reflect a wider internal distribution area.

of the eleventh century (see pp. 321–2 above), as well as in land improvements (see p. 303 above). But it doubtless in particular fed on itself because of increasing production for the market. This was all the stronger a pattern because not only landed elites, but peasants too, were doing it. It was sufficiently stable that it could even survive the next set of disasters, in 1204 and the years following; for although that period is too late in time for us to explore it here, recent work stresses more and more that the thirteenth century was by no means always economically simpler than the twelfth in the Byzantine and ex-Byzantine lands, and sometimes the reverse. Laiou and Morrisson, in, as we have seen, easily the best overall characterization of these structural patterns, argue for the increased wealth of peasants even though levels of exploitation rose. They ascribe it simply to the enlargement of the market, its role as a 'structuring mechanism of the agricultural economy', indeed its 'beneficial role'.[217] I think they neglect a key element, namely the fiscal underpinning of the exchange routes, which allowed this complex network to grow in the first place; 'the market' appears in their book simply as an external positive force, as in too much other economic history. But they are right about the paradox of the possibility of greater prosperity set against increased exploitation. It is a classic medieval paradox, and we find it elsewhere. We will come back to it, and to the issues which Laiou and Morrisson present, in later chapters.

The only thing to add is that inside this economic logic, there were also limits to growth. Kaplan was by no means wrong in 1992 to stress the importance of autarky, or self-subsistence, for peasants first, before any opening to the market. That was a permanent limit to the degree to which exchange could dominate their lives. We do not have the data which would be able to tell us how much they ever bought, of course, but the theoretical point is hard to avoid. Only the development of rural wage labour might have changed that situation; there is some sign of waged workers in the countryside (including Athos monks themselves), but overall, their role was marginal, often restricted to certain sorts of specialism such as shepherding.[218] And the limitations on elite wealth—plus, of course, the limited percentage of elites themselves—also made difficult an endless cycle of exchange development. We have to expect that; it was true for all our societies, and I will come back to it in Chapter 8. But here it may have set limits earlier than in some other places. Byzantine towns, apart from Constantinople and probably Thessaloniki, although expanding, remained small—smaller than north Italian

[217] Laiou and Morrisson, *The Byzantine economy*, pp. 104–15; 112, 115 for quotations. For the thirteenth century as at least as economically complex as the twelfth, see, e.g., Estangüi Gómez, 'Richesses et propriété paysannes'; Baker, *Coinage and money*, pp. 245–66, 287–97, 320–6; François, *La vaisselle de terre*, pp. 99–110 (on ceramic hierarchies).

[218] Kaplan, *Les hommes*, pp. 274–5, 350; Harvey, 'Risk aversion', p. 80. For some examples, see Dölger, *Beiträge*, p. 115; Gautier, 'Le typikon du sébaste Grégoire Pakourianos', p. 99 (both of these call them *misthioi*, the standard ancient term); *Actes du Prôtaton*, n. 7, l. 118 (a monk as a wage labourer). Sarris, 'Large estates and the peasantry', pp. 444–5, seems to me to overstate wage labour in the Middle Byzantine period.

towns were beginning to be by 1180, and than those of al-Andalus already were a century or more earlier, as we shall see in Chapters 5 and 6. This must have restricted the scale of specialized artisanal activity. The empire may have resembled Egypt in its infrastructure, but it has to be said that exchange seems to have remained less dense in the Aegean than along the Nile. Byzantium, as far as we can tell, did not move towards cash cropping, unlike the situation proposed earlier (p. 103) for the flax cultivation of at least some areas of Egypt; we do not have the data to be sure of this, but nothing even hints at it. Egypt certainly used wage labour rather more (see p. 61 above). But the Byzantine economy had, all the same, moved remarkably fast in the two centuries from 950 to 1180, especially in the last half of the period, when it outmatched the steady growth visible in Egypt. Only al-Andalus, out of the regions discussed here, showed a greater growth in economic complexity in our period, as we shall see in Chapter 5.

4.6 Byzantium and the Mediterranean

There was never a moment in our period, or indeed earlier, in which some connectivity across all parts of the eastern Mediterranean cannot be identified, and that is certainly true for the Byzantines. There were always Byzantine trading ships, as the later eighth-century *Rhodian Sea Law* shows, and in saints' lives and the like they conveniently appear to take pilgrims along the Anatolian south coast, past Cyprus, to Palestine; the early east–west trade route network stretching across all the Byzantine lands is attested materially by globular amphorae, as we have seen (pp. 304–5). That east–west route linked to a less well-documented south-east Mediterranean commercial network between Egypt and the Levant, with continuity from the Roman Empire, which again included Cyprus—whose inhabitants traded with both the Byzantine and the Muslim world, as Yaḥyā al-Anṭakī, from nearby Antioch, remarks when he recounts the Byzantine conquest of the island in 965; we will look again at the south-eastern network, and also at the east–west Byzantine route, in Chapter 7.[219] The Byzantines imported silk from Syria, at least around 900, to the extent that there is an entire section on it in the *Book of the eparch*. Interestingly, a treaty with Aleppo in 969 shows that they exported it to Syria too, which shows exchange complexity; Byzantine silk in this period is, indeed, hardly distinguishable technologically from Islamic silk, and there must have been close links between artisans here.[220] Letters from the Byzantine lands in the *geniza* may not be so very common, even in the better-studied

[219] *The Rhodian Sea Law*, ed. W. Ashburner (dated in Humphreys, *Law, power*, pp. 179–92); McCormick, *Origins of the European economy*, p. 544; *Tārīkh al-Anṭakī*, trans. Pirone, 7.72. For the south-eastern commercial network, see Chapter 7, n. 22 below.

[220] Koder, *Das Eparchenbuch*, ch. 5; Farag, *The truce of Safar A.H. 359*, ch. 20; for technical similarities, see, e.g., Desrosiers, *Soieries*, pp. 20–1; Turnator, *Turning the economic tables*, pp. 380, 385.

eleventh century, but also, as it appears from chancier publication, in the twelfth, but they certainly assume the possibility of regular communication. Jewish merchants with Egyptian connections lived in Attaleia (Antalya) on the Anatolian coast in the eleventh century—they were captured by pirates and ransomed by the Egyptian community on more than one occasion from the 1020s on. Up to twenty known texts in the *geniza*, mostly from the eleventh century but some from the twelfth, in fact refer to Jews who moved from Egypt or Syria/Palestine to Byzantium, or in the opposite direction. The Crusader conquests in the Levant by no means undermined this; one letter from 1137, from an Egyptian doctor who had—possibly—once worked in the Fāṭimid navy, but has now married a Byzantine and is living in prosperity in—probably—Seleukia (Silivke) in Byzantine Cilicia, casually mentions him being in Constantinople, Chios, Rhodes, and Jaffa in Palestine, as well as writing often to family back in Fusṭāṭ.[221]

This connectivity in our period is also backed up by numerous citations, at least anecdotally, of direct trading connections between the Byzantine and Islamic worlds. There was a 'market of the Greeks' in Fusṭāṭ in 959; there were eventually two mosques for Muslims in Constantinople. The Persian traveller Nāṣer-e Khosraw in the 1030s bothered to say how long it took to sail from Tinnīs to Constantinople.[222] Attaleia (Antalya) and Ṭarābulūs (Tripoli, in what is now Lebanon) are both cited as entrepôts where merchants from, respectively, the Islamic and Byzantine world came, which in the former case (according to Ibn Ḥawqal in the 960s) supposedly resulted in the Byzantine state taking 30,000 dinars a year in trade taxes. The Byzantines had, after all, expanded their territory as far as Antioch in 969, not so far from Tripoli, and a substantial cache of Günsenin 1 amphorae was found there in Byzantine levels; Byzantine trading would not have had to extend much farther to reach Tripoli.[223] We usually do not know whether the Rūmī merchants coming

[221] See de Lange, 'Byzantium in the Cairo Genizah', for lists of letters; for the 1137 letter, see T-S 13J21.17, ed. and trans. Goitein, 'A letter from Seleucia' (see also some revisions in the Princeton *geniza* database, at https://geniza.princeton.edu/pgpsearch/?a=object&id=1025, accessed 8 October 2021). In it, Seleukia is not named, but a probable nearby town is—there are some problems about the geography, but it remains the most likely place; the sender had been at Jaffa in 'the army camp', from which, however, it is a bit more of a stretch for us to conclude that he was part of the Egyptian naval attack on the town in 1124, as Goitein proposes (ibid., p. 302). See in general for all these examples Jacoby, 'What do we learn about Byzantine Asia Minor'; for the Antalya Jews, see pp. 87–8, 91.

[222] Goitein, *MS*, 1, p. 44; Magdalino, *Constantinople médiévale*, p. 88; *Nāṣer-e Khosraw's book of travels*, trans. Thackston, p. 40.

[223] For Attaleia, see n. 64 above, with Ibn Ḥawqal, *Kītāb ṣūrat al-arḍ*, trans. Kramers and Wiet, 1, pp. 192–3. For Tripoli, see *Nāṣer-e Khosraw's book of travels*, trans. Thackston, pp. 12–13 (who says ships from both Rūm and Firank, the Frankish lands [Italy?], came there); Goldberg, *Trade and institutions*, pp. 227–8. Jacoby, 'Byzantine trade with Egypt', p. 39, cites a Jewish merchant taking linen to Tripoli (T-S 12.241 (Gil K660, partial trans. Goitein, *MS*, 1, p. 321)); we cannot say, *contra* Jacoby, that this merchant, Ya'qūb b. Salmān al-Ḥarīrī, was from the Byzantine lands, and, indeed, in one of the several other letters concerning him he turns out to have parents in Kairouan, in Ifrīqiya (Moss. IIIa,11 (Gil K661)). Here and in the pages following I often follow Jacoby's very detailed article, but restrict myself to data which I consider certain, omitting his more hypothetical examples of Byzantine trading relationships. See also, for similar arguments, Bramoullé, *Les Fatimides et la mer*, pp. 516–21. For Antioch, see De Giorgi and Eger, *Antioch*, pp. 318–19.

to Alexandria in *geniza* letters were Italians or Byzantines, but sometimes we can pin it down: men from Constantinople, Crete, and Genoa focussed on pepper in a letter of the 1060s; *al-Rūm* would not buy indigo in another letter, from the 1090s, because it was selling badly in Constantinople; in another, from the same decade, they waited to buy pepper until other ships from the Byzantine capital came; in the same decade or shortly after, a merchant of Constantinople appears in another letter.[224] The fine Rūmī cloth in Egyptian Jewish trousseau lists from the eleventh century must have been Byzantine as well, as we do not hear of the export (or indeed, of much production) of luxury cloth from Latin Europe in this period. A story in Orderic Vitalis's *Ecclesiastical history*, from the 1130s, claims that Byzantine merchants were in Cairo *c.*1101 with *multimodis mercimoniis*. And in 1154, when the Pisans established a trade treaty with the Fāṭimids, the text specified that (much like the Venetians in Byzantium) the tolls they would henceforth pay would be lower than those owed by either Muslims or 'Greeks'.[225]

Having listed all that, however, we need to confront the problems which go with too enthusiastic a picture of this exchange. First of all, we must ask again what this trade was actually in, outside the empire itself. The documented commodities bought by known Byzantines from Egypt in the eleventh-century *geniza* texts were essentially spices and dyestuffs, and those sold to Egypt were above all luxury cloth and medicaments (Chios mastic, for example[226]). Indeed, even if we include all references to the Rūm, much the same is true. As we saw earlier (p. 134), *geniza* letter writers, on the rare occasions they mentioned the Rūm (in barely a dozen commercial letters before 1100), often treated them with some scorn, as being bad at bargaining; that is to say, in the eleventh century at least, they were not integrated into normal Egyptian exchange. As Jessica Goldberg remarks, notwithstanding the movement of Jews from Byzantium to the Islamic world and back, and the existence of letters between them, one of Nahray b. Nissīm's correspondents in the 1050s fell off the commercial map when he moved to Constantinople, and ceased to do business with his former associates for a decade.[227] This was not, for the most part, an organic bulk trade relationship. Once in the later eleventh century, the Rūm buy palm fibre, for ropemaking and the like, and once they are said to be interested in flax, but these are the only such citations I have seen.[228] Even if we add in the Venetian and Genoese documents for Byzantine trade in the

[224] ENA NS 2.13 (Gil K749 [S145]); Bodl. MS Heb. d 66/79 (Gil K431, trans. Udovitch, 'Time, the sea', p. 528); T-S 12.693 (ed. Frenkel, *Ha-Ohavim*, n. 25); ENA NS 2.6 (ed. Frenkel, *Ha-Ohavim*, n. 14). These may not be the tip of an iceberg; the small number of references to Rūm in commercial documents is stressed by Goldberg, *Trade and institutions*, pp. 19–21.

[225] For trousseaux, see Olszowy-Schlanger, *Karaite marriage documents*, nn. 2, 23, 27, 29, 32, 36, 37, 44, 56; Orderic Vitalis, *The ecclesiastical history*, ed. Chibnall, 10.23 (5, pp. 350–2); for 1154, see Amari, *I diplomi arabi*, p. 247.

[226] Jacoby, 'What do we learn about Byzantine Asia Minor', p. 92.

[227] Goldberg, *Trade and institutions*, pp. 306–7.

[228] T-S 10J16.2 (Gil K679; see Jacoby, 'Byzantine trade with Egypt', p. 45); BL Or. 5542.27 (Gil K305, trans. Udovitch, 'A tale of two cities', pp. 155–8).

twelfth century, we do not find much more, although we have to recognize again how seldom any commodities are mentioned in them, rather than just money. The Venetians did, as we saw earlier, ship some bulk Byzantine goods to Egypt, namely cloth, horsehair, and olive oil, and took alum back to Venice with stopovers in Byzantine ports. There are also a few references to cheese sold to Egypt from Crete.[229] These do show some larger-scale exchange by now, but the references remain casual. Timber, which Egypt certainly needed (see pp. 147–9 above), might have come from the Byzantine Empire in our period, given the forests of southern Anatolia, but all our evidence concerning it for the twelfth century concerns export from Italy; timber exports from Byzantium to Egypt are not, in fact, directly documented until the thirteenth.[230]

All of this means that it is only with great difficulty that we can get from the extensive evidence for a generic eastern Mediterranean connectivity to any real sense of a north–south trade in bulk goods, between the Fāṭimid lands and Byzantium. Attempts to bridge this gap have not been successful. For me, the strongest evidence is that for Antalya and Tripoli, the two ports of the north-east Mediterranean most visible in our written sources—which, if they interconnected substantially, as they probably did (almost inevitably via Cyprus, which is between them), did not necessarily depend on or contribute to wider networks in the Mediterranean—a point we will come back to.

After 1100, there were certainly changes. Above all, boats from Italian cities become more visible in eastern Mediterranean trade. We have already seen what their role was in the Aegean, where I have argued that Italian trading was only an overlay onto a rather more complex set of routes which the Venetians and the others hardly participated in. When, however, we get to the wider networks which linked the Byzantine lands with Egypt and the Latin principalities in the Levant, the Italian cities are by now rather more prominent. This is above all because the documentation for commercial shipping in the eastern Mediterranean is from this point onwards overwhelmingly from either Venice or Genoa, which, of course, leads historians to talk about them rather more, and about Byzantine, Egyptian, or Sicilian ships rather less—we have seen this already when we looked at both Egypt and Sicily. Occasionally, Byzantine traders do appear, as with the reference to Greeks in the 1154 Pisan treaty, just mentioned; and they were dominant in the Aegean, as we have seen, so the Byzantines were not short of boats, as, indeed, the establishment of an imperial navy in the twelfth century itself shows. But it is actually rather hard to find any accounts of Byzantine-owned commercial shipping beyond the coasts of the empire in this century; there are some, but apart from the Syria route, they are anecdotal.[231] Conversely, we do have references in

[229] See Chapter 2, n. 288 above. [230] See Jacoby, 'The supply of war materials', pp. 104–13.

[231] Jacoby, 'Byzantine trade with Egypt', pp. 62–9 has a list of examples of Byzantine traders, some speculative; the article also documents the growing Italian presence on the routes. See further Pryor,

the twelfth century to Byzantine or Egyptian envoys travelling on Italian ships, one of which, from 1192, shows Byzantine merchants themselves doing the same (see p. 322 above); [232] and we have just seen that Venetians were indeed transporting at least some Byzantine bulk goods to Egypt. As with Egyptian shipping after 1100, although there is more evidence in that case (see pp. 141–4 above), this does not mean that Byzantine Mediterranean traders did not exist, and they were, indeed, probably active, hidden from us by the shipwreck of Byzantine documentation in the centuries after 1204; we shall see an archaeological example of this shortly. But it is likely, all the same, that by the middle decades of the twelfth century, Italian ships were more prominent as figures along the long-distance eastern Mediterranean routes. They also, as we cannot see anyone else doing, connected all three of the Byzantine Empire, the Crusader principalities, and Egypt in a single trading network; strategically, they therefore dominated the system, even if other players were also active. We will come back to the point in Chapter 7.

But once again, we have to ask about what this means for exchange as a whole. On the one hand, we have seen signs that the Byzantines invested in Venetian commercial ventures; and the Byzantines certainly sold goods to other Venetians to take elsewhere. Since Byzantine ships had not themselves been very active in the Islamic sectors of the Mediterranean before 1100, it is, in fact, quite likely that the expansion of Italian shipping across the twelfth century directly benefited the wider availability of goods from the empire. But on the other hand, it is also important—a point made in every chapter of this book—not to overstress the importance of this wider east Mediterranean trade. We have already seen that it did not involve so very many bulk goods. References to them increase in the twelfth century, but our best evidence remains for spices and silk, not the foodstuffs, ceramics, and linen which were the core elements in Aegean internal trade. They therefore played much less of a part in exchange systems, taken as a whole.

This discussion has not started with archaeology, unlike my presentation of the Aegean evidence; I wanted here to begin with connectivity and its limits, and to look at a range of goods, which only written sources can tell us about. But these sources do not, on the other hand, tell us about quantities. Archaeology does, and, taken as a whole, gives us better evidence for bulk transport; so let us turn to that now. Once again, when we are faced with the issue of the material evidence for

Geography, technology, pp. 149–51, and nn. 223–4 above. *The itinerary of Benjamin of Tudela*, trans. Adler, pp. 2, 76, has Byzantine merchants in Barcelona and Alexandria, as also those from Sicily and Egypt (cf. Chapter 2, n. 302, Chapter 3, n. 255 above). The thirteen imperial galleys (*galeae*) which arrived in Venice in 1151 (Lanfranchi, *S. Giorgio maggiore*, n. 240), seem too many to be part of an official Byzantine embassy, so some of them could have been commercial. Prinzing, 'Zur Intensität der byzantinischen Fern-Handelsschiffahrt', lists more examples, but only to argue that most are not real proofs of any Byzantine sea trade at all; many of the points he makes are fair, although the conclusions seem too negative, and he does not use the archaeology.

[232] Jacoby, 'Byzantine trade with Egypt', pp. 71–2; see further Jacoby, 'Diplomacy, trade, shipping and espionage'.

the transport of bulk goods, our best evidence is tablewares and amphorae. I will look at them together, as guides to different forms of export and (to a lesser extent) import.

Byzantine ceramics are found to the west, with very various distributions. In Italy, where most work has been done, several Otranto sites show a pattern of ceramic finds which would not look out of place in the Aegean, both before and after the Norman conquest of Byzantine Puglia in the 1050s; other sites in Puglia are similar. Some Campanian sites, in the south but outside direct Byzantine rule, also have a range of Aegean glazed wares, into the twelfth century. In Arab Sicily too, a few Otranto 1 and Günsenin 1 amphorae from around 900 have been found along the east coast, on several Palermo sites, and at Mazara in the west. In the twelfth century, after the Norman conquest, glazed red wares have been found in very small quantities at Messina, the island's rising eastern port; isolated pieces of GWW 2 and GWW 4 have been identified too.[233] Farther north on the mainland, the only real foci for finds are Genoa, Pisa, and (above all) Venice, with very few finds on inland sites; the exceptions are *bacini*, decorated glazed bowls on church facades and campanili, in Pavia and some other cities, which were obviously put there as luxury objects.[234] The pottery is, above all, twelfth-century glaze, particularly Fine Sgraffito ware, from Corinth or Chalkis (less often Constantinople), but there are Günsenin amphorae too, as well as Otranto types. This thin veneer of finds, rather lower in quantity than those of Sicilian wares on the Tyrrhenian coast (see p. 228 above), extends into Provence, where a couple of Günsenin amphorae have been found, doubtless brought by Italian intermediaries. The main period of imports is everywhere the twelfth century, which fits what we know of Aegean productions; the Norman conquests do not seem to have affected these patterns in the south. Venetian and Genoese/Pisan involvement in twelfth-century internal Aegean trade evidently had one material spin-off, the import of Aegean glazed wares from that period to these cities, but they were not sold on, to any significant extent, anywhere else in northern Italy; I will develop this point in more detail in Chapter 6, for it has importance for our understanding of how Italian internal exchange itself worked. The early thirteenth century showed Byzantine types such as Zeuxippus ware in western Sicily and mainland Italy, but fewer as the century wore on; this may well be linked to the appearance of the production of Italian glazed maiolicas in the second quarter of the thirteenth century and onwards from there, which reduced demand for similar eastern products.[235]

233 For the mainland south, see Arthur, 'Byzantine and Turkish glazed ceramics' for Puglia, and in general see D'Amico, *Byzantine finewares in Italy*. For Sicily, see Chapter 3, nn. 177, 194 above.

234 For Byzantine *bacini*, see Chapter 6, n. 142 below; for Byzantine amphorae and glaze at Ferrara and Nonantola, the main inland Italian sites where they have been found, see Chapter 6, nn. 139, 140 below.

235 D'Amico, *Byzantine finewares in Italy*, is the main recent survey of glazed ware discoveries, up to around 2010, and I follow her findings. (She calls Fine Sgraffito 'Sgraffito I' and 'II', but the illustrations make it clear which Morgan type this is.) For glaze, see also the articles in Gelichi, *La ceramica nel*

Southwards, into Egypt, the distribution of Byzantine types is even less dense. In Alexandria, Aegean glazed wares are very rare until the final years of the twelfth century and onwards, and in Fusṭāṭ-Cairo they have not been recognized at all; only a couple of Günsenin 1 amphorae have been found, on two sites in the capital. If we put the two cities together, Chinese pottery sherds far outnumber Byzantine finds.[236] Eastwards, into the coastal sites of Israel and Lebanon, we find only a little more. Günsenin 3 is the only Byzantine amphora found in any quantities for our period, at Acre and one or two other Israeli sites and to a smaller extent at Beirut, plus a rarer earlier Byzantine amphora, Hayes 57–9, in eleventh-century levels at Caesarea. Of glazed wares, Fine Sgraffito is again by far the commonest, but is still not so very common; local glazes dominated overwhelmingly, as in Egypt. There is, thus, little significant export here before the later twelfth century (although rather more in the thirteenth).[237]

I discussed earlier the question of whether the distribution of medieval glazed wares is really as reliable a proxy for that of other artisanal products as was that of the mass-produced red slipped wares of the Roman Empire. We have seen that it both is and is not. It fits very well with what we know of the production and commercialization of cloth inside regions, as we saw in Egypt in Chapter 2, as we could conclude without much difficulty in Sicily in Chapter 3, and as we have now seen for the Aegean in the twelfth century in this chapter. It also fits well with the considerable extent of the trade between Sicily and Ifrīqiya across our whole period. Conversely, over the longer distances of interregional trade, the undramatic numbers of Tunisian glazes in eleventh-century Egypt and Egyptian glazes in Palermo do not by any means match the extensive trade in flax and linen which we know to have occurred along those routes. So, for Byzantium, it might well be that the thin distribution of Aegean glazes outside the Aegean and its hinterland before 1200 is not an adequate guide to how Byzantine goods were

mondo bizantino, including, for *bacini*, Berti and Gelichi, 'La ceramica bizantina', and for Genoa, Gardini, 'La ceramica bizantina in Liguria', with Chapter 6, n. 140 below for inland northern Italy. For amphorae, see most recently Negrelli, 'Modelli di scambio', p. 21 and Leo Imperiale, 'Anfore e reti commerciali' for the Adriatic, and Meo, 'Anfore, uomini e reti di scambio', pp. 229–32 for the Tyrrhenian, with Chapter 6, n. 139 below. For Provence, see Vallauri and Demians d'Archimbaud, 'La circulation des céramiques byzantines', pp. 139–40. For Zeuxippus ware, see also Chapter 3, n. 194 above. For maiolicas, a convenient starting point is *La protomaiolica e la maiolica arcaica*; the earliest are discussed briefly on p. 226 above and pp. 556, 569 below. Note, finally, that one non-Mediterranean area where Byzantine ceramics, esp. amphorae, are found outside the empire is Ukraine and Russia (see n. 20 above); we can best see this as the hinterland of the Crimea, itself, of course, a Byzantine territory.

236 François, *Céramiques médiévales à Alexandrie*, pp. 99–132; for China, see ibid., pp. 143–53, and Chapter 2, n. 48 above; for the amphorae, see Monchamp, 'Céramiques fatimides', p. 152.

237 Avissar and Stern, *Pottery*, esp. pp. 40–4, 105; Stern et al., *'Akko 1*, pp. 65–9, 70–1, 136; Getzov et al., *Ḥorbat 'Uẓa*, 2, pp. 153–7; Arnon, *Caesarea Maritima*, pp. 47, 53, 55; Mesqui and Martineau, *Césarée Maritime*, p. 300; Reynolds, 'Amphorae in Beirut', p. 106. In Ashkelon, Byzantine glazed wares only appear after the Crusader conquest in 1153, and no Byzantine amphorae; see Hoffman, *Ashkelon 8*, pp. 405–20. I have not seen references to Byzantine imports in excavation reports for cities of the Syrian interior, even those not so far inland, such as Apamea; see Vezzoli, *La céramique islamique*.

exchanged elsewhere. But the fact that Aegean amphorae are equally seldom found supports a minimalist position. Although it is never obvious that imports of wine would be necessary on any scale around the Mediterranean, all of whose regions could and did produce it, the fact is that in the Roman Empire, and in the eleventh-century in the regions north and south of Sicily, such imports were indeed welcome and normal, as they also were around the Aegean coasts in the eleventh and twelfth. Byzantium's wine exports beyond its frontiers, however, by no means matched those of Sicily. That for me is a sign of the absence of a real bulk trade between the empire and its neighbours, which fits the meagre written evidence for such trade. Westwards, the only organic link we have so far seen is with Puglia in south-eastern Italy, even after the Norman conquest: Pugliese amphorae are regularly found in Greece in our period, and Aegean amphorae in Puglia (cf. p. 298 above). We must, of course, add the ever-strengthening link to Venice as well, but, as with Puglia, that route was established when Venice was still Byzantine. Genoa and Pisa are the only real additions to the old east-west routes which had existed as early as the ninth century. The clarity of that pattern does reinforce its absence in other parts of well-excavated Italy, and probably elsewhere too.

So far, in fact, there have been only two archaeological finds which could easily support the proposition that there was at least some bulk exchange elsewhere in the Mediterranean outside the imperial frontiers; both are wrecks. One is the well-known Serçe Limanı wreck off Rhodes, dated to *c.*1025, in which substantial quantities of glass cullet from the Fāṭimid world were found, plus reused Günsenin 1 amphorae—which point to a Byzantine crew and probably ownership for the boat—and also a small set of tablewares, which have been recently recognized as having come from (Fāṭimid-controlled) Beirut. This, therefore, is a clear sign that the Byzantines were importing glass from Syria on a considerable scale, possibly, as suggested earlier, for workshops in the capital.[238] The second is less often cited, probably because the report on the excavation is so hard to find; it is a wreck off the Syrian coast near Ṭarṭūs, not far north of Tripoli (and indeed Beirut) in which some 5,000 Günsenin 3 amphorae were found, from the later twelfth century. Ṭarṭūs and Tripoli (Beirut a little less) are at the end of one of the easiest routes from the Mediterranean coast to the great cities of the Syrian hinterland.[239] The substantial scale of this cargo gives us another clue that Byzantine trade with Syria was perhaps rather more significant than we might have supposed from the relatively few Byzantine finds in Beirut city excavations. And this fits the more

[238] Bass and Allen, *Serçe Limanı* (esp. vol. 2); Waksman, 'Ceramics of the "Serçe Limanı" type'; for Levantine glass in general, which is better known than is glass elsewhere in the Mediterranean and may have been more important too, see Schibille, *Islamic glass in the making*, pp. 105–23. For the capital as a possible outlet for the glass, see n. 37 above.

[239] Tanabe et al., *Excavation of a sunken ship*, pp. 36–8. I am very grateful to Caroline Goodson for sending me photocopies from this barely available book.

casual written evidence we have for Tripoli too, as also that for Syrian silk in the capital, and that for Byzantine linen and silk exported to Syria (see pp. 326, 353–4 above). Until excavation becomes possible again in Syria itself, this is as much as we can say here; but I think it is likely that the one non-Byzantine region to the east and south which was regularly associated with the empire in economic terms was Syria, doubtless using the Antalya-Tripoli sea route already discussed. But if so, it did not extend to other regions, as far as we can see.

Finally, a minimalist picture fits what we know of ceramic imports to Byzantium. Here, we would not expect any from Italy in our period, for too few wares of any ambition and exportability were as yet produced there. But we might well expect Islamic glazed types, given their fineness and high reputation; they were certainly available in Italy. And we do indeed find them. There were around 160 fragments of probably Selcuk ceramics from Iran or eastern Anatolia in twelfth-century levels at Saraçhane in Istanbul, and some Syrian Raqqa ware elsewhere in the city; other Iranian pieces in Sardis and once even on a field survey, in Lakonia; Syrian sherds at Pergamon, Aphrodisias, and the coast south of Ephesos; some from both Iran and Egypt at Corinth; and Egyptian ceramics, including lustreware, in Athens, Corinth, and Plovdiv. Others will doubtless be found. But even more than for Byzantine glaze abroad, these appear in tiny quantities (the larger numbers for Saraçhane must be set against the many thousands of sherds from the same period which were locally made). And as Véronique François has stressed, the Byzantines did not fully adopt the new Islamic ceramic technologies which are most associated with this period, such as frit fabrics and lustre (see p. 311 above); unlike in the case of silk, they simply copied Islamic pottery styles, such as sgraffito, using the ceramic traditions they already had. This too does not support any claim that the Byzantine world was closely integrated economically with most of its neighbours, for all its internal vitality.[240]

* * *

What I draw from all of this is two main conclusions. One is that that the east–west Byzantine exchange routes of long standing, connecting its often far-flung

[240] François, 'Céramiques importées à Byzance', pp. 388–92, has the fullest lists as they stood in 1997, updated two decades later in François, *La vaisselle de terre*, pp. 138–40. Some specific sites: Hayes, *Excavations at Saraçhane*, 2, pp. 43–4; Armstrong, 'The Byzantine and Ottoman pottery', p. 130; Sanders, *Byzantine glazed pottery*, p. 291; Joanita Vroom, pers. comm. for Athens and Corinth; for Plovdiv, see n. 73 above. Even in Cyprus, Islamic pottery was not necessarily that common; for a twelfth-century example from Nicosia, see von Wartburg and Violaris, 'Pottery of a 12th-century pit'. For the relative figures in Saraçhane, see *Excavations at Saraçhane*, 2, pp. 138–42, for one of the key closed deposits, from a cistern, dating to *c.*1150–75: it contained some 3,500 sherds of amphorae and unglazed wares, and of glazed wares, excluding small fragments, 175 GWW, 9 Fine Sgraffito or similar, and 4 Islamic. Waksman, 'Byzantine pottery production in Constantinople/Istanbul', pp. 72–7, argues convincingly for at least some Islamic influence on Byzantine ceramic techniques, particularly bar kilns and the colours used in Polychrome ware.

provinces, and certainly involving bulk goods, notably wine, did not develop into a major role in Mediterranean-wide trade. Byzantine commerce, although very active indeed inside the boundaries of the empire—above all, in and around the Aegean—and increasingly active as the eleventh century turned into the twelfth, did not extend on any scale to other regions of the Mediterranean, with the exception of parts of southern mainland Italy and Syria, the former of which had been in the Byzantine exchange sphere since the eighth century, and above all, of course, Venice itself, also formerly Byzantine. It did not match the interregional economic connections of Sicily. All the same, as a second conclusion, in the light of this and also Chapters 2 and 3, we are also beginning to see some clearer patterns in the other long-distance, Mediterranean-wide sets of networks. Let us look at these in a preliminary way, to end the chapter.

The south-eastern corner of the Mediterranean, extending up to Cyprus, had been the most active interregional network outside Byzantium in the eighth and ninth centuries. This still existed (Palestine was part of the Fāṭimid economic as well as political world, and links here continued after the Latin conquests), but it was by now matched by a north-eastern trade network too, from the Byzantine south coast of Anatolia to Syria, which also doubtless involved newly Byzantine Cyprus. Although the control of the Levant coast by different Crusader states in the twelfth century does not in itself seem to have unified these two systems, the Italian shipping which was so important in the Latin principalities came increasingly to do so—the Italians were more interested in the Italy–Levant–Egypt triangular trade, but they came along the older Byzantine trade routes to get there, and the Venetians, at least, often operated directly from their Constantinople base.[241] I will not develop this here, for Syria and Palestine are not one of our case studies; but the point will, anyway, recur in later chapters.

We have also seen in Chapters 2 and 3 how important the triangular trade between Egypt, Ifrīqiya, and Sicily was in the eleventh century; that really was a large-scale bulk commercial network, involving flax/linen and a range of other commercial goods, including foodstuffs. This matched, and indeed surpassed in scale, the Byzantine east–west routes. The two were connected at the western end by a Sicily-focussed network, which exported wine and sometimes grain not only

[241] For a rapid survey of Levantine exchange, see Balard, *Les Latins en Orient*, pp. 127–40. For the triangular trade, see, e.g., Schaube, *Handelsgeschichte*, pp. 165–7, with the critique in Bach, *La cité de Gênes*, pp. 52–7. We will look further at the evidence for this in Chapters 6 and 7, but it was far from being the only way the Italians traded; most trading contracts were between Venice/Genoa and a single port or region, and even the Venetian commerce between Acre (and other Levant ports) and the Byzantine Empire, cited in a dozen documents from the period 1120–80, mostly went directly from and to Constantinople. Almost none of these documents give any indication what goods were bought and sold (except *DCV*, n. 63, from Tyre to Constantinople, which involved cinnamon).

southwards to Ifrīqiya, but also northwards to Tyrrhenian Italy; that was the main north–south exchange network in the Mediterranean in the century and more after 950, and was the first north–south route which was really important after the end of the Roman Empire.

In the twelfth century, the major change was that most of these networks were by now linked together. This was the work of Italian merchants, who further extended their privileged roles in the external exchange of Sicily and the Levant, newly conquered by Christian powers, and a developing but not dominant role in the internal exchange of the Byzantine Empire, to one which connected all these regions at once, and Egypt and parts of Ifrīqiya as well, adding themselves to older routes which non-Italians still traded on. But did this new development actually extend and strengthen the main networks of the previous century? Here I would be less certain. The major triangular flax-based network was by now weaker. Egypt's internal economy expanded across our period, but not rapidly; that of Ifrīqiya perhaps did not face as many problems in the twelfth century as is often stated, but the region was certainly less of a protagonist than it had been in 1050; Sicily, by now less closely connected to Egypt, waited until after 1150 before it began to capitalize economically on its new political connections with the Italian mainland. Northern Italy was by no means developing in its internal economy as rapidly as its port cities were coming to be prominent in long-distance exchange. The two parts of the Mediterranean whose internal economy was developing fastest in the early to mid-twelfth century, the Byzantine heartland and, as we shall shortly see, al-Andalus, had external links which were no stronger than they had been before. And we will find later (esp. pp. 546–7) that the scale of Italian contracts, even with all the port cities taken together, was probably also not larger than that of Egypt a century earlier. I will come back to all of this in Chapter 7, where I will argue that on balance, twelfth-century commerce was indeed, taken as a whole, slightly larger-scale than that of the eleventh, as well as, certainly, more complex. But it was less of a step change upwards than most historians have thought.

This set of statements is rather different from those assumed by the grand narratives of the 'commercial revolution', discussed in Chapter 1. I set them out here so as to make clear where the argument of this book is heading, but they will need further development in order to be fully established, and I will seek to do precisely that in the next chapters. For now, I will simply end with an evocation of the internal force of the Byzantine economy, which we have amply seen across the rest of the chapter, in the eleventh century and in particular the twelfth: a series of active productions of artisanal goods developed, especially in Greece but elsewhere too; a network of routes criss-crossed the Aegean, carrying cloth and foodstuffs, and ceramics, from Greece to the Anatolian west coast, and to and from both Constantinople and Thessaloniki, as well as a network of smaller towns;

sailors and maritime imagery turn up in all sorts of texts; officials invested in shipping and workshops; the population increased, markets were developed, and land was improved; peasants in many places gained access to a range of commercial goods; mulberry trees for silk turn up in relatively remote locations; and a figure said to have had a background in commerce, Michael IV, made it to emperor. These are striking patterns, even if there were limits to growth as well, as we saw in the previous section. That too will be developed later.

5

Islamic Spain and Portugal

In the ninth century, al-Andalus—the word writers in Arabic used for the Muslim-ruled parts of the Iberian peninsula, today Spain and Portugal[1]—was regarded even by its leaders as provincial. Its *amīr* ʿAbd al-Raḥmān II in the 820s paid the Iraqi musician and poet Ziryāb remarkable sums to come to his capital at Córdoba and be a cultural icon there instead.[2] By 950, when we start: not any more. Written texts by then are numerous, and increase steadily in number from here on. For every Muslim-ruled region we have looked at so far, our main narrative sources have been late and usually pretty unreliable; those of al-Andalus, however, whether accurate or not, were largely written in our period, often close to the events. Andalusī texts also cover a wide range of genres. We have contemporary examples of history, geography, poetry, law and theology, medical and scientific texts, biographical dictionaries, market regulations, and agricultural manuals; and some of these are of high quality and/or strikingly detailed. If you want to know about how best to graft a tree, or about the different kinds of manure (that from doves is the best, as the Romans knew already), or when to plant aubergines, look no further.[3] Overall, there are far more contemporary and near-contemporary literary sources—although not, regrettably, documents and letters—than for any other Islamic region discussed in this book. It is true that al-Andalus was not entirely central to the economic history of the Mediterranean in our period. Andalusī ships were a common sight in Alexandria in the eleventh century, and the region was greatly valued as a source of silk and metals; conversely, however, not so many boats made the long east–west voyage there from other regions, either in the relatively Egyptian eleventh-century Mediterranean or the relatively Pisan and Genoese twelfth. Why this may have been we will see at the end of the chapter. But it was a highly commercially active region in its own internal

[1] Arabic geographers distinguished between al-Andalus and Ishbāniya (from Latin Hispania), the latter meaning the whole of the Iberian peninsula, although they were not always precise about it; see, for examples, al-Bakrī, *al-Masālik wa al-mamālik*, trans. Vidal Beltrán, p. 15; al-Idrīsī, *Nuzhat al-mushtaq*, trans. Jaubert and Nef, p. 255 (cf. 1, p. 197, of Jaubert's original trans.). In this chapter, I have changed the Spanish transliterations of Arabic into English ones, except in book titles. I am grateful to Wendy Davies, Eduardo Manzano, Robert Portass, and Elena Salinas for reading and critiquing the text, and to many people for bibliographical help and advice; see esp. nn. 123, 214–16 below.

[2] Ibn Ḥayyān, *Muqtabis II.1*, trans. Makki and Corriente, p. 199; cf. Manzano Moreno, *Conquistadores, emires*, pp. 307–8. Ziryāb supposedly received 2,400 dinars a year, plus lands worth 40,000 dinars, plus extra for musical compositions.

[3] See, e.g., Ibn Baṣṣāl, *Kitāb al-qaṣd wa al-bayān*, trans. Millás Vallicrosa and Aziman, pp. 55–60, 123–34, 173–7; *Le calendrier de Cordoue*, ed. Dozy, trans. Pellat, pp. 62–3, 76–7.

The Donkey and the Boat. Chris Wickham, Oxford University Press. © Chris Wickham 2023.
DOI: 10.1093/oso/9780198856481.003.0005

economy; if that economy was less connected to the outside world than some others, this does not make it so very different from that of Byzantium, which we looked at in detail in Chapter 4. And anyway, it is too interesting in itself to leave out.

That range of texts also parallels Islamic Spain and Portugal with Byzantium in our period. But even Byzantium could not always match the seamless interplay between literature and politics that we see in the Islamic west. In the last quarter of the eleventh century, for example, when al-Andalus was politically fragmented, two of the main local rulers, al-Mutʿamid of Seville and ʿAbd Allāh b. Buluqqīn of Granada, on and off allies and rivals, were serious literary figures, in poetry and history respectively. Once overthrown by the Almorávid *amīrs* of Morocco, in 1090–1, they were both confined to Aghmāt, the former Almorávid capital outside Marrakech, and wrote, respectively, poems and an autobiography in philosophically minded self-justification.[4] One would have to go back to before the start of our period, to Leo VI and Constantine VII, to find anything parallel in Byzantium, or to a couple of unusual twelfth-century city consuls, Caffaro di Caschifellone in Genoa and Oberto dall'Orto in Milan, to find anything parallel in Italy. And none of their works rival ʿAbd Allāh's *Tibyān* as a piece of ironic and dense analysis; indeed, vanishingly few other rulers have ever written about total political failure before the twentieth century.[5]

Al-Mutʿamid's and ʿAbd Allāh's works lie at the back of my mind as I write this, for they mark out the fascination of al-Andalus very clearly; all the same, it has to be said at once that they are not directly concerned with the economy. Others are, rather more so. But as with Byzantium, we have to piece together, cautiously and often suspiciously—more cautiously and more suspiciously than some modern historians have—chance references from our literary narratives. Furthermore, unlike for other regions, we here have less help from the *geniza* or from Genoese documents, which only glancingly deal with Spain (and Venetian texts do not at all). Nor, as just noted, do we have many internal Andalusī documentary sources to flesh economic practice out. Once again, the most solid evidence we have is archaeological; here, however, although there are more and more sites, more, in fact, by now than anywhere else in the Mediterranean except for Italy, we have fewer of the wide syntheses which make dealing with Sicily or the Aegean straightforward. There remain uncertainties here. But the parallels and contrasts with other regions are significant and interesting all the same. After a brief

[4] Al-Mutʿamid, *Dīwān*, these poems translated in Nykl, *Hispano-Arabic poetry*, pp. 136, 147–54; ʿAbd Allāh b. Buluqqīn, *al-Tibyān*, trans. Tibi. Their *wāzirs* could be poets too: Ibn ʿAmmār for al-Mutʿamid, Shemūʾel or Ismāʿīl Ibn Naghrīla (who wrote in Hebrew) for ʿAbd Allāh's grandfather and predecessor Bādis; but high officials as literary figures have more Byzantine parallels.

[5] I can only think of one: John VI Kantakouzenos (d. 1383), a failed Byzantine emperor, whose *Historiai*, ed. Schopen, confront and defend his reign and his fall. For a stimulating literary-historical analysis of the *Tibyān* and some of its author's rhetorical strategies, see Martínez-Gros, *L'idéologie omeyyade*, pp. 253–310.

account of the quite complex political-institutional history of al-Andalus in our period, and of the often sharp debates about its socio-economic development, we will look in turn at urban economies and at evidence for exchange at local and regional, and then Mediterranean-wide, levels. In each of these sections, as I have done elsewhere, we will look separately at the written sources and at the archaeology, to see how they work internally, before coming to a synthesis of what is known at the moment.

5.1 Framings: Politics, Geography, and Sources

Muslim armies, of Berbers first and Arabs later, never conquered the whole of the Iberian peninsula. A narrow strip along the north coast and Pyrenees remained in the hands of two or three separate Christian kingdoms after the conquest in the 710s, mostly poor land except for Galicia in the far north-west (Jillīqīya was, as a result, the name which Arabic-speakers tended to give to the whole of the Christian north). To that was added northern Catalonia, conquered by the Franks under Charlemagne, and then—during the first great civil war or *fitna* of al-Andalus, dating to *c.*880–930—much of the Duero valley, north of the central mountain range going from west to east across the middle of Spain. The Muslim-Christian frontiers stayed there without much change for nearly two centuries. They shifted south over the mountains in 1085, when Alfonso VI of Castile took over the *ṭāʾifa* (factional) kingdom of Toledo; Christian rule from then on included the upper Tajo valley, and from then on steadily spread down the northern side of the river to its mouth at Lisbon, taken in 1147; the Ebro valley was taken by the kings of Aragón, a hitherto tiny kingdom in the Pyrenees, across the same period. By the end of our period, around 1180, Muslim rule covered a little under half of the peninsula, rather than the three-quarters which it had had in 950; but the casual border wars and encroachments of the twelfth century did not extend to a full-blown conquest on the part of the Christian kings until the 1230s–1240s. The Christian kingdoms will, however, not be discussed in this chapter; they were almost entirely unconnected to the Mediterranean world—apart from Catalonia, for long ruled by the Franks—until the union of Catalonia and Aragón in 1137; a history of a Christian Iberian Mediterranean presence essentially postdates our period.

For 250 years, al-Andalus was ruled by the Umayyad family, the heirs of the first caliphal dynasty of the eastern Mediterranean; the first of them was ʿAbd al-Raḥmān I in 756–88, the last was the short-lasting Hishām III in 1027–31. They ruled as *amīr*s for most of that time (hence the phrase 'emiral period', the standard term for the eighth and ninth centuries), but when ʿAbd al-Raḥmān III (912–61) ended the first *fitna* by defeating a string of separatist leaders, he called himself caliph from 929 onwards—in rivalry with the ʿAbbāsids, of course, but above all with the Fāṭimids, whose caliphate had, as we have seen, begun in 910. 'Abd al-Raḥmān III and his son al-Ḥakam II (961–76) were the significant caliphs; then, under al-Ḥakam's son Hishām II, real power was exercised—although very effectively—by a strongman, the *ḥājib* (chamberlain) al-Manṣūr (981–1002) and successively by his two sons, up to 1009.[6] But after that the system broke up, quite suddenly, in a second *fitna*, far more serious than the first. Rival armies set up new caliphs and new strongmen every few years from 1009 to 1031, and the capital, Córdoba, was severely sacked in 1013. Córdoba lost its longstanding centrality; and warlords, governors, and city judges across the whole of al-Andalus were already, with varied levels of enthusiasm and resignation, setting themselves up as de facto local rulers, well before the elites of Córdoba itself decided to abolish the Umayyad Caliphate, a century after its foundation, in 1031.[7]

These local rulers were the *mulūk al-ṭawā'if*, the 'factional kings' (although they used various titles) of the *ṭāi'fa* kingdoms of the next sixty or so years. There were some thirty at the start, but after several rounds of conquests they were reduced to nine by the time of the Almorávid takeover in 1090 and the years following (the last *ṭāi'fa* king, of Mallorca, lasted until 1115). The most significant were Seville in the west, which steadily absorbed most of southern Portugal and the rich Guadalquivir valley (including Córdoba) across the eleventh century, Granada in the south (which came to control Málaga too), the southern port of Almería (politically weak but economically strong), Badajoz in central-southern Portugal and up the Tajo valley, Toledo on the Meseta plateau, Zaragoza in the Ebro valley, and Valencia and Denia on the east coast, the Sharq [east] al-Andalus (see Map 16).[8] When the Almorávid *amīr* of Morocco and the western Sahara, the Ṣanhāja Berber Yūsuf b. Tāshfin (d. 1106), was invited in to help defend the Andalusī kingdoms against Alfonso VI in 1086 after the fall of Toledo, he quickly saw that they were far too disunited to establish a common front, and, half-reluctantly, he decided that it was best to take them over and rule directly. He managed this with little difficulty except for the rulers of the north-east, who had been relatively autonomous from Córdoba earlier as well. As al-Mut'amid of Seville supposedly said, it was preferable to pasture camels [with Saharan Berbers] rather than herd

[6] For a good recent guide, see Manzano Moreno, *Conquistadores, emires*; Manzano Moreno, *La corte del califa*, is fundamental for the reign of al-Ḥakam II.

[7] The fullest account of the *fitna* is Scales, *The fall of the caliphate of Córdoba*. After 1031, however, the Ḥammūdids in Málaga claimed the caliphal title until 1056, and the 'Abbādids in Seville recognized a fake Umayyad caliph between *c.*1035 and 1060: see in general for these and other searches for legitimacy Wasserstein, *The caliphate in the west*.

[8] The *mulūk al-ṭawā'if* were so named because they were seen to resemble the successors to Alexander the Great, who were already called this in Arabic historics; see, e.g., Ibn al-Athīr, *Kāmil fī al-tārīkh*, trans. Fagnan, p. 437; cf. Ohlhoff, *Von der Eintracht zur Zwietracht?*, pp. 102–4. For the *ṭāi'fa* period in general, which has had some detailed work recently, see Wasserstein, *The rise and fall of the party-kings*; Viguera Molins, *Los reinos de taifas*; Viguera Molins, *Historia de España*, VIII.1; Guichard and Soravia, *Les royaumes de taifas*; Clément, *Pouvoir et légitimité*; Sarr, *Ṭawā'if*.

pigs [with Castilian Christians].[9] The *ṭāʾifa* kings were famous for their lives of luxury, a reputation sometimes deserved; Yūsuf came from a rather more ascetic Sunni tradition, and he may indeed have seen this conquest as a moral necessity too. It was also popular: the Almorávids were (at least initially) determined only to exact taxes which were approved by Islamic law, which the *ṭāʾifa* kings, who each needed an army, and many of whom by now paid tribute to Christian powers in the north, systematically exceeded. ʿAbd Allāh of Granada, the first king to be removed in 1090, regarded the desire for lighter taxes as one of the major reasons why his own people deserted him. (But what do you expect, he wrote; 'money is of no value to a king unless it comes in vast amounts'.)[10]

The Almorávids only lasted sixty years; they were replaced in Morocco by another army of tribally based Berber ascetics, the decidedly heterodox Almohads, who took Marrakech in 1147, Ifrīqiya (as we saw in Chapter 3) in the 1150s, and most of al-Andalus in the years after 1147 as well (Seville, by now the dominant city in the peninsula, fell in 1148). In the 1140s, however, a new set of *ṭāʾifa* rulers had also appeared, in revolt against the Almorávids, and these took some time to remove; Ibn Mardanīsh was a powerful opponent in Valencia and Murcia from 1147 until 1172. From then on, the Almohads re-established a unitary state in al-Andalus, based in Seville; but it too only survived another half-century, until 1228, when they in effect retreated to Morocco and the Christians steadily moved in, taking Seville two decades later.[11] The Almohads have a mixed reputation: as Muslim extremists (many Andalusī Jews fled to Christian Toledo), but also as rich patrons of a new cultural efflorescence, with literary experts of all kinds, such as the philosopher and polymath Ibn Rushd (Averroes), benefiting from their patronage. Neither of the Berber dynasties, however, despite their initial military sweeps into Islamic Spain, apparently had the capacity to push the Christians back. It is not clear why; they were highly successful on the African continent, after all. It may well be that they were never fully committed to a Spanish-centred politics; and they did not reverse the tendency of Andalusīs to think and act locally.[12] But they kept, for all that, the frontiers of most of al-Andalus fairly stable for well over a century after the fall of Toledo, and the economy of the region did not falter during the period we are looking at—far from it, in fact, as we shall see.

* * *

[9] See (among several citations of the phrase) *Al-Ḥulal al mawshīyya*, trans. Huici Miranda, p. 59.

[10] ʿAbd Allāh, *al-Tibyān*, trans. Tibi, pp. 128, 136–7, 152–3, 191 (quotation).

[11] A recent survey of the Almorávid and Almohad period in al-Andalus is Viguera Molins, *Historia de España*, VIII.2.

[12] Kennedy, *Muslim Spain and Portugal*, p. 307, speculates that it is because they were not good at besieging towns; but they had no trouble with this in North Africa. The lack of a full sense of the unity of al-Andalus even under the North African dynasties is illustrated by a later anecdote in Ibn ʿIdhārī, *al-Bayān, Nuevos fragmentos*, trans. Huici Miranda, p. 305: the new Almohad governor of Seville has drums beaten for the victory in battle of the governor of Córdoba in 1155, and is criticized for celebrating the victory of a non-Sevillano by local *shaykhs*.

If we want to see the meaning of these political events for the arguments of this book, we must again situate them in the landscape. The geography of al-Andalus, even if less ecologically varied than that of Byzantium, was nonetheless complex. Schematically, we can distinguish five main subregions on geographical grounds, which in some cases had some form of institutional significance too (see Map 16). The core was always the rich Guadalquivir valley in the south, with Córdoba and Seville as its main centres; the network of interrelationships along and around the river extended into valleys closer to the mountains to the south and east, to Granada and Jaén, and over mostly lower hills to Málaga on the Mediterranean coast. Málaga was a significant port as a result; but when 'Abd al-Raḥmān III developed Almería as a walled city and arsenal in 954/5, the latter became the main port of the caliphate, even though it was separated by rather more difficult roads from the Guadalquivir valley.[13] Córdoba in its boom years, under the caliphs in the tenth century, expanded dramatically, well beyond the capacity of its smallish agricultural hinterland to supply it, as we shall see. The second *fitna* substantially reduced its footprint again, although it remained an important city. Slowly, across the eleventh century, not only political but also demographic primacy shifted to Seville, which prospered greatly from then on up to the Christian conquest in 1248 (and after as well). The rise of Seville, whose hinterland was particularly fertile (every geographical account, plus other texts, lyricizes over the olive trees and figs of the Aljarafe, a tract of rich land just over the river from Seville[14]), pushed the centre of gravity of this subregion westwards; for Seville also looked towards the Gharb [west] al-Andalus, the lands between the Guadalquivir and the Atlantic coast of Portugal, the southern edge of which is still called the Algarve today.

There is no real natural boundary between the Guadalquivir valley and southern Portugal, but the landscape slowly changes. North of the Algarve, in particular, the dry rolling hills of the Alentejo and then the again very rich agricultural land around Santarem in the lower Tajo (in Portuguese 'Tejo') valley and down to Lisbon need to count as a second subregion as a result. It was often called the Lower March, the frontier region which eventually became the core of the *ṭāʾifa* of Badajoz, as well as being, more generically, part of the Gharb—which has now

[13] See among others al-'Udhrī, *Tarṣī' al-akhbār*, trans. Sánchez Martínez, 'La cora de *Ilbīra*', pp. 45–7; all the same, Almería was a naval port and arsenal already in the 930s; see n. 98 below.

[14] It is worth listing some of the accounts of the Aljarafe, to give a sense of the unanimity of authors here, not all copying each other by any means: in rough chronological order, *Crónica del moro Rasis*, ed. Catalán and de Andres, pp. 92–3; al-'Udhrī, *Tarṣī' al-akhbār*, trans. Valencia, pp. 115–16; al-Bakrī, *al-Masālik wa al-mamālik*, trans. Vidal Beltrán, pp. 31–3; al-Idrīsī, *Nuzhat al-mushtaq*, trans. Jaubert and Nef, p. 260; Ibn Ghālib, *Farḥat al-anfus*, trans. Vallvé Bermejo, p. 381; Ibn al-'Awwām, *Kitāb al-filāḥa*, trans. Clément-Mullet, 1, pp. 197, 216, 304, 576, 2, p. 57; al-Shaqundī, *Risāla fi faḍl al-Andalus*, trans. García Gómez, p. 121. See very generically El Faiz, 'L'Aljarafe de Séville', and (rather better) Valor Piechotta et al., 'Espacio rural y territorio en el Aljarafe de Sevilla'. For some recent archaeological work there, see Valor Piechotta and Lafuente Ibañez, 'La arqueología medieval en el Aljarafe sevillano'.

become a common term for Islamic Portugal, extending across the Spanish border to Badajoz and Huelva, as, indeed, it was in our sources. These more distant lands do not get mentioned in many texts, and were fairly politically marginal until the *ṭāʾifa* period, when Badajoz was successful for a time.[15] This economically separate subregion does not really include the Algarve and its immediate hinterland (stretching up to the small but important river port of Mértola), which were closer to Seville economically, but modern Portuguese writers understandably tend to see their country as a whole, and I shall not always separate the Algarve from the Alentejo as a result.

The centre of Spain is a flattish and mostly fairly arid plateau, called the Meseta (literally, 'tableland'), between 600 and 750 metres above sea level. The Umayyads never controlled the northern Meseta in any depth, and it was Christian-ruled by 950, as we have seen; but the southern Meseta, looking above all to Toledo as a political centre, was fully part of Islamic Spain until Alfonso VI took the city. This was and is substantially pastoral land, except along the Tajo and Guadiana rivers. It was regarded by the Córdoba elites as rather separate: as the most important military frontier (the Near or Middle March, *al-thagr al-adnā* or *al-awsaṭ*), but resistant to southern control in any period except during the caliphate; in some areas relatively Christian in its population, although also quite Berberized in the eastern highlands, where the Banū Dhī al-Nūn family ruled, first in rural Santaver from the ninth century, and then as *ṭāʾifa* kings in Toledo itself in the eleventh; and as both economically and culturally distinct as a largely pastoral region. It was the equivalent of the Anatolian plateau for the Byzantines, although the distances are far smaller (that between Toledo and Córdoba is only 200 kilometres as the crow flies).[16]

The Middle March is hardly separable from the Lower March in south-central Portugal, for the Meseta slopes very gently down to the west, but in most other directions it was bounded, and thus defined, by mountains. In particular, it was hard to get from here to the Upper March, the Ebro valley in north-east Spain, centred on Zaragoza, my fourth subregion. This was fertile agricultural land in large part, and thus quite distinct from the Middle March economically. It was, however, also the most politically separate region in al-Andalus, ruled as it was by autonomous local rulers in every period: from the ninth century at the latest by the Banū Qasī family, then, from *c.*920, the Tujībīs, who became *ṭāʾifa* kings a

[15] For the *ṭāʾifa* of Badajoz, see Zozaya Stabel-Hansen and Kurtz Schaefer, *Bataliús III*; for Portugal in the written sources, see Picard, *Le Portugal musulman*, esp. pp. 303–18; for the archaeology, see nn. 137–8, 146, 153 below. The wealth of Santarem is stressed by the geographers, e.g. *Crónica del moro Rasis*, ed. Catalán and de Andres, pp. 83–4; al-Idrīsī, *Nuzhat al-mushtaq*, trans. Jaubert and Nef, p. 269; it is also praised in a narrative of the Almorávids, al-Marrākushī, *Kitāb al-muʿjib*, trans. Huici Miranda, p. 123, supposedly in a letter sent to Yūsuf b. Tāshfin in 1091.

[16] Manzano Moreno, *La frontera de al-Andalus*, gives a context for all the Marches up to the eleventh century; see pp. 54–7, 233–310 for the Middle March.

century later, until they were replaced in their turn in 1038–9 by the Banū Hūd.[17] Here, then, as also to an extent in Toledo, there was a pattern of local rule which does not map neatly onto the standard emiral–caliphal–*ṭāi'fa* chronological divisions of the southern heartland. It is important to note that it was Toledo and then, in the 1110s, Zaragoza, in many ways the territories least integral to al-Andalus as a political system, which were also the main territories conquered by the Christians before the 1230s. Toledo, unlike the Ebro valley, was a strategic danger to al-Andalus, but their separation from the polities based in the Guadalquivir valley was in each case not new.

The fifth subregion was the east, the Sharq al-Andalus along the Mediterranean coast. Except for the Ebro, the Iberian peninsula's longest rivers all run into the Atlantic, and the hinterland of the Mediterranean coast is, as a result, mostly not very deep, except around Valencia, where a rich coastal plain rises up fast into dry mountains. Urban continuity from the Roman period was here less strong than in most other parts of al-Andalus, and indeed several of the major cities of the Sharq in, say, 1050 were new developments, Murcia in the ninth century, Almería in the tenth (nearby Pechina had been of some importance before, but again only from the ninth). Denia and Valencia at least had Roman roots, but they were not major urban centres again before the late tenth or eleventh century. Like the Gharb, the Sharq is seldom mentioned in narratives until the *ṭāi'fa* period, although the port of Almería, in the far south and closest to the cities of the Guadalquivir, is the exception to that.[18] Much of it, particularly in the north, was settled by Berbers in the conquest period, and the subregion has as a result been a focus of some active debates, as we shall see shortly. Separately from that, however, the Sharq is of considerable interest for this book, for it was the main gateway to the Mediterranean. It is not that it was only through here that the Andalusīs could reach regions farther east; Málaga was a good alternative port to Almería, and so was Seville, not so very far along the Atlantic coast. All the same, how closely it was linked to the Guadalquivir at different times and how well its cities prospered are proxies for how closely connected Islamic Spain was to the Mediterranean as a whole.

We will come back to geographical constraints later; but before we leave them here, it is important to stress that internal communications in the Iberian peninsula were in many ways more arduous than they were for most of our regions, taken as a whole. It is true that both the Byzantine Empire and Ifrīqiya had a substantial plateau area, matching the Meseta here, and that river communications were not good in North Africa or Sicily, less good, indeed, than in Islamic Spain, although here too only the largest rivers, particularly the Guadalquivir, are

[17] See Manzano Moreno, *La frontera de al-Andalus*, pp. 71–136; Lorenzo Jiménez, *La dawla de los Banū Qasī*; Sénac, *La frontière et les hommes*.

[18] Guichard, *Al-Andalus frente a la conquista*, Gutiérrez Lloret, *La cora de Tudmīr*, and Azuar Ruiz, *Las taifas del Sharq al-Andalus* are three important ways into a large historiography.

navigable for more than short stretches. All these, then, were regions which, in their internal routes, privileged the donkey rather than the boat. But al-Andalus is more sharply mountainous than many; until railways and motorways, it was genuinely difficult to move between some of the subregions just discussed, particularly between the west and the east. As a result, it would be less surprising if society and the economy were sometimes more localized than elsewhere. Nonetheless, they were not by any means always so, in particular in the tenth century and under the Almorávids/Almohads. Why this was we will consider later.

In this chapter, we will look at the caliphal period and onwards, until well into the Almohad period. My principal focus will be the Guadalquivir valley, always the core of al-Andalus, as we have seen, plus the lowlands westwards into the Gharb al-Andalus and eastwards along the coast of the Sharq up to Valencia—it is almost exactly the territory ruled by the Almohads, in fact, although that is not the main reason for my choice. As already stated, we will not be looking at the Christian North or at Catalonia. I will also, however, say little about the Ebro valley, which was so separate politically, and more closely integrated with a northern economic environment. (It was also not particularly linked to the Mediterranean; although the Ebro is navigable, from Zaragoza one has to go through semi-desert and then a mountain gorge to get to the sea.) The southern Meseta around Toledo might be excluded for the same reason, as an inland subregion always standing a little apart; but I will discuss it when relevant. It did have some organic economic links with the lands to its south, as we shall see, more than the Ebro valley did, and also, from the 1080s (although mostly after the Christian conquest), has the largest set of documents in Arabic surviving from the peninsula before the fourteenth century.[19] These show how Toledo and its hinterland were steadily, under Christian rule, separating from the Andalusī world, but they give us helpful guides to the patterns of local property-owning, which we will need in order to draw a rounded picture of the economy of Islamic Spain. My reasons here parallel those set out in Chapter 4 for concentrating on the Aegean and Marmara seas when discussing Byzantium. It is not that either the Aegean or the Sharq al-Andalus actually was, across the whole time period of this book, closely linked to the rest of the Mediterranean; but when each of Byzantium and al-Andalus did have organic links to other Mediterranean regions, it was these areas which were the most interconnected. The Guadalquivir valley and, increasingly after 1000 or so, the Sharq were also the sectors of the Iberian peninsula which had the most complex economy, whether or not that economy was connected to elsewhere—which, as usual, is a major concern for the arguments of this book as a whole.

* * *

[19] They are edited, not well, in González Palencia, *Los Mozárabes de Toledo*, and the documents will be cited as P.Mozarab.

I have already praised the variety of sources we have for al-Andalus in our period; we need now to be more specific, about what they can tell us and what they cannot. The first point is that up to the middle decades of our period, by far the most central narrative historian is Ibn Ḥayyān, who wrote accounts of the history of al-Andalus from the conquest up to nearly his own death in 1076. But he is central in two distinct ways. We do not have his complete history, which was supposedly in sixty volumes—far from it. For the period before his own lifetime, we have four separate blocks of his *Muqtabis*; but each of these copies and, doubtless, adapts the work of previous writers, notably Aḥmad al-Rāzī (d. 955)—parts of his work also survive separately in a Castilian translation of a lost Portuguese translation—and his son ʿĪsā ibn al-Rāzī (d. 989). The latter writer, whom Ibn Ḥayyān follows in the so-called *Muqtabis VII*, surviving for the years 971–5, has a particularly specific style, in that he wrote, evidently at the request of the caliph or his administrators, a virtually day-by-day account of formal comings and goings in the Umayyad palace city of Madīnat al-Zahrā', not far from Córdoba—it resembles more than anything a Chinese Veritable Record, the official chronicle of the imperial court.[20] By contrast, for the eleventh century, which Ibn Ḥayyān himself lived through, his *Matīn* does not survive, but was itself copied and, doubtless, adapted by later writers, in particular Ibn Baṣṣām (d. 1148) in his *Dhākhira* and Ibn ʿIdhārī (d. after 1313), whose *Bayān* I have already cautiously used for Ifrīqiya. In this case, however, these two authors generally more or less match up when they cite Ibn Ḥayyān, which gives us more confidence that we may be seeing many of his actual words.[21]

Understandably, Ibn Ḥayyān has greatly interested scholars, and there are arguments about when he wrote his different works (separately or simultaneously?), as well as whether the two main sections of his narratives were really distinct. But there is no argument that he was a determined and bitter Umayyad legitimist, for whom the great *fitna* was the worst experience of his life (he indeed says so explicitly); none of the *ṭāʾifa* kingdoms could ever have been for him a proper successor to the caliphate, and he denigrated most of the rulers of his lifetime.[22]

[20] The surviving parts of the *Muqtabis* relevant for us are *Muqtabis V*, trans. Viguera and Corriente, and *Muqtabis VII*, trans. García Gómez. The latter has an extensive recent analysis by Manzano Moreno, *La corte del califa*. The Romance translation of al-Rāzī is *Crónica del moro Rasis*, ed. Catalán and de Andres; although it contains no narrative for our period, it has an important geographical section, which is the earliest surviving for al-Andalus. For China, see the classic surveys in Beasley and Pulleyblank, *Historians of China and Japan*.

[21] Ibn ʿIdhārī's *Bayān* for this period is translated in Maíllo Salgado, *La caída del califato de Córdoba*. For Ibn Baṣṣām, *al-Dhakhīra*, ed. ʿAbbās, which has no full translation, I have consulted the substantial sections on the *ṭāʾifa* of Seville edited and translated into Latin in the nineteenth century in Dozy, *Scriptorum arabum loci de Abbadidis*, 1, pp. 189–379, 3, pp. 34–174. For an excellent survey of *ṭāʾifa* historiography, see Maíllo Salgado, 'Fuentes árabes'.

[22] For Ibn Ḥayyān as a historian of the eleventh century, see Soravia, 'Ibn Ḥayyān' (pp. 113–15 translates Ibn Ḥayyān's own account of his historical intent), and esp. Ohlhoff, *Von der Eintracht zur Zwietracht?*.

He is no neutral source; nor does he tell us much about the economy, as usual with narrative histories. But precisely because he (and before 1000, his sources) was not very interested in the economy, it is possible to use at least some of what he says about it. The same is true for his successors' writings, of which I have found most useful ʿAbd Allāh b. Buluqqīn's *Tibyān*, already mentioned, and the late twelfth-century history of Ibn Ṣāḥib al-Salā, precisely because they are again both detailed and exactly contemporary for much of their work (the *Bayān*, it is worth adding, is fragmentary for the second half of our period, and much less clearly based on contemporary accounts).[23] We will meet several other less detailed histories as we go on as well, for one of the joys of studying al-Andalus in this period is precisely the fact that we have overlapping sources, and we can triangulate our own reactions to them as a result. But those already mentioned are for me the core texts.

Five other literary genres are of more direct relevance to us. (I set aside the extensive surviving poetry, for this tells us even less about the economy than did its equivalent in Byzantium, plus biographical dictionaries, and scientific and theological treatises, of which there are again many. Major cultural and intellectual figures, like Ibn Ḥazm in the eleventh century and Averroes (Ibn Rushd) in the later twelfth, will thus seldom reappear here.) The first is the geographers, here as elsewhere in the Islamic world; to the by now recognizable pair of particularly detailed accounts, of Ibn Ḥawqal in the mid-tenth century and al-Idrīsī in the mid-twelfth, we can here add home-grown observers too: among other works, the careful but succinct listings of al-Rāzī in the mid-tenth century, and the more clichéd accounts of al-Bakrī in the mid-eleventh and Ibn Ghālib in the late twelfth, plus an enthusiastic text praising the glories of al-Andalus, in contrast to Berber North Africa, by al-Shaqundī in the early thirteenth.[24] The second is the collections of *fatwā*s we have already seen for Ifrīqiya, which involve al-Andalus quite as much as the Maghreb, to which we can here add collections of formulae for documents—real and ideal—by a number of writers, from Ibn al-ʿAṭṭār around 1000 onwards. These often illuminate the preoccupations of jurists rather than the problems of everyday life, but we certainly come to know a great deal about these preoccupations.[25] Documents themselves, the third set, are

[23] ʿAbd Allāh, *al-Tibyān*, trans. Tibi; Ibn Ṣāḥib al-Salā, *al-Mann bi al-imāma*, trans. Huici Miranda. For the *Bayān* after 1090, see Ibn ʿIdhārī, *al-Bayān*, trans. Huici Miranda, and *al-Bayān*, *Nuevos fragmentos*, trans. Huici Miranda; the second is the more relevant here.

[24] See the citations of geographers in n. 14 above, plus Ibn Ḥawqal, *Kitāb ṣūrat al-arḍ*, trans. Kramers and Wiet. For the difficulties of using Ibn Ḥawqal (and also al-Idrīsī) for al-Andalus, see Christys, 'Did all roads lead to Córdoba under the Umayyads?'; I have sought not to be reliant only on them here, but they do sometimes offer significant and useful details which are not out of line with other sources.

[25] See esp. al-Wansharīsī, *al-Miʿyār*, trans. Lagardère, *Histoire et société*; Ibn al-ʿAṭṭār, *Kitāb al-wathāʾiq wa al-sijillāt*, trans. Chalmeta and Marugán. A good guide to formulary collections is Aguirre Sádaba, 'Notas acerca de la proyección de los "kutub al-waṯāʾiq"'. A Hebrew-language formulary collection from the 1020s, less often cited by scholars, is *Jüdische Urkundenformulare*, trans. Mutius.

rare outside the formularies, but we do have some for Toledo, as just noted; a handful of others will recur as relevant.[26] We again have, of course, both the *geniza* and a few Genoese commercial contracts as well; they tell us much less about Spain than they do about the central Mediterranean, but they do help our understanding of the peninsula's wider context, and we shall come back to them at the end of the chapter.

The other two genres are, if not quite unique to al-Andalus, at any rate unusually well represented there. We have three *ḥisba* manuals, accounts of how markets should be run, by Ibn 'Abd al-Ra'ūf for Córdoba in the mid-tenth century, Ibn 'Abdūn for Seville in the early twelfth century, and al-Saqaṭī for Málaga in, probably, the late twelfth; these texts are very moralistic indeed—this being considered fully appropriate for market supervisors in Islamic societies, who were responsible for public morality in general, not just the regulation of commercial transactions—but do, all the same, give us a sense of what commercial structures in twelfth-century towns were like.[27] We cannot take them too literally—as, indeed, we cannot take any of our written sources too literally—but they are guides to a strongly textured imagery of urban life. And finally, we have several manuals of agronomy, from the eleventh century onwards, some of them very detailed indeed; I have got most out of Ibn Baṣṣal in the late eleventh century and Ibn al-'Awwām in the late twelfth. They show that some Andalusīs were exceptionally experienced in up-to-date agricultural management. They, at least, can sometimes be taken fairly literally, for their findings are carefully explained, and are explicitly related, not just to extensive reading in their Greek, Latin, and Arabic predecessors, but also to their own experiences. They do not show an 'agricultural revolution', as Lucie Bolens put it in her pioneering work on the texts in 1978, for they are no guide to the practices of more day-to-day agriculture, but they certainly show us the quality of the best management available (on royal estates in large part) in our period, and they hardly have any parallels outside Spain in our period.[28]

[26] For Toledo, see n. 19 above; for others, see, e.g., n. 61 below for Guadix; it is also worth signalling Mubārak Esmail, 'Cinco cartas inéditas', an extract from her unpublished doctoral thesis on two unpublished Almorávid letter collections, *Cartas de la época almorávide*, which I have not seen.

[27] Ibn 'Abd al-Ra'ūf, *Risāla fī ādāb al-ḥisba wa al-muḥtasib*, trans. Arié; Ibn 'Abdūn, *Risāla fī al-qaḍā' wa al-ḥisba*, trans. Lévi-Provençal; al-Saqaṭī, *Kitāb fī ādāb al-ḥisba*, trans. Chalmeta Gendrón (I have not seen the—rare—revised translation, Chalmeta and Corriente, *Libro de buen gobierno del zoco*). Chalmeta, *El "señor del zoco"*, esp. 367–93, 415–49, discusses these and related texts.

[28] Ibn Baṣṣāl, *Kitāb al-qaṣd wa al-bayān*, trans. Millás Vallicrosa and Aziman; Ibn al-'Awwām, *Kitāb al-filāḥa*, trans. Clément-Mullet; see also Abū al-Khayr, *Kitāb al-filāḥa*, ed. and trans. Carabaza. All Arabic agricultural manuals are listed and discussed by the Filāḥa Texts Project at www.filaha.org (*filāḥa* means 'cultivation'). For commentary, see Bolens, *Agronomes andalous du Moyen Âge*; Bolens, *L'Andalousie du quotidien au sacré* (an article collection including her 1978 'La révolution agricole andalouse du XIe siècle'); García Sánchez, 'Los cultivos en al-Andalus'; García Sánchez, 'Agriculture in Muslim Spain'.

Each of these genres only sheds partial light on the economy of al-Andalus. But sometimes that light is a powerful one; and at every stage our written evidence can be, and will here be, set against what we know from the archaeology. I shall draw a less rigid separation between these two overarching source types in this chapter, for to discuss one as a whole and then the other as a whole, as I did for Sicily or Byzantium, would lead us into too much repetition; but they still need to be kept methodologically distinct, and I shall, as elsewhere in the book, do my best to do that, as we go through the various topics of the chapter in turn.

5.2 Debates

One debate which one might have expected to have seen in the historiography of Spain and Portugal would be about the negative effect of the disunity and infighting of the *ṭāʾifa* period on the economic coherence and prosperity of al-Andalus. As we have seen (pp. 158–60), this has been an important element of the historiography for Ifrīqiya, in particular, after 1050. And indeed, it used to be regarded as obvious that the *ṭāʾifa*s did not match the caliphate—which has always been seen, and is still seen, as the high point of Andalusī history and culture—in any way; the hostility of Ibn Ḥayyān and Ibn Ḥazm to the *ṭāʾifa* kings was taken for granted as reportage. In recent years, however, opinion has changed, and with relatively little difficulty. It was increasingly noticed that the fact that there were many centres of patronage in Islamic Spain after the 1010s, instead of only one, had its advantages as well as its disadvantages; the flowering of poetry, in particular, in the eleventh century was seen as a definite plus. *Ṭāʾifa* historiography has become quite upbeat as a result; the local kingdoms come to be seen, at least implicitly, as if they were like the late medieval Italian city states, vibrant, active, and sophisticated, even if both fractious and poor at defending themselves against external attack—a view of them with which I would not disagree.[29] Although there has still often been a tendency to see the austerity and initial lack of urbanity (and sometimes the foreignness) of the North African dynasties after 1090 as a negative, scholars concerned with culture now usually recognize that the patronage of poets, jurists, and scientists by no means lessened thereafter. And more relevantly for us, anyone who had an eye to archaeology and economic change could hardly help noticing that cities expanded in size, that archaeological finds became more complex, and that more geographers waxed lyrical about the wealth of al-Andalus from the late tenth century onwards (even if, in this case, that is simply because there were more geographers). The standard recent surveys of the economy of the *ṭāʾifa*s and, in particular, the Almorávids/Almohads, stress

[29] This view underpins the more recent works cited in n. 8 above, e.g. Sarr, *Ṭawāʾif*.

complexity rather than decline;[30] I would certainly agree with that, as we shall see later. So this issue has not been strongly debated. However, debates have indeed been in places very violent; it is just that they have been focussed elsewhere—on nothing less than the identity of Spain itself.

Al-Andalus is of much greater importance for Spanish national culture than are most of the other political systems discussed in this book for any twentieth- and twenty-first-century population—the only one which remotely compares is that of the north Italian city communes of the twelfth century. (The debates about it have had, it should be noted from the outset, much less resonance in Portugal.) The exact role played by Arabs and Islam in the formation of modern Spain has long been a fought-over political issue, with—among many variants—the fascist/falangist government of 1939–75 under Francisco Franco exalting the Christian Reconquest; with one extreme falangist, Ignacio Olagüe, a geologist by training, even denying that there had ever been an Arab invasion; with Franco's exiled opponent Claudio Sánchez-Albornoz, a medieval historian of considerable importance (but still a very Catholic and conservative one), denying that there had been any continuity at all, even demographic, between the Arabs and their Christian successors; and with a more liberal post-1976 trend playing up the cultural sophistication (and often overplaying the inter-faith collaboration, *convivencia*) of Islamic Spain. Nearly fifty years on, the positive or negative role of medieval Islamic/Arab politics and culture can still be fiercely argued about in politics and journalism, in ways that would hardly make sense elsewhere in western Europe: three centuries of Habsburg rule in Milan or English rule in Bordeaux have virtually vanished from the relevant national past in their respective countries, but five of Arab rule in Seville and Córdoba remain visceral.

And that, in its turn, has had an effect on academic debates, consciously or unconsciously. Andalusī historiography was already before the Civil War separated off into Arabic studies departments, and there is little crossover with medieval history departments, which, in effect, only cover periods of Christian rule. The book reviews in *al-Qanṭara*, Spain's flagship Arabic studies journal, sometimes police the boundary with some care, with unenthusiastic or indeed hostile critiques of books on al-Andalus written by non-Arabists (or non-Iberian writers, or both).[31] The recent rise of medieval archaeology, which covers the whole peninsula, has only partially helped, for, with some notable exceptions (Barcelona is one), departments in the formerly Islamic south mostly excavate Islamic sites, and their counterparts in the north mostly do not. So there is less integration than one would hope for here; a mutual understanding has already been weakened. And inside the history and archaeology of al-Andalus, there are sometimes not only

[30] Of the two articles in the large *Historia de España* volumes, Benaboud, 'La economía' is too early (1994) for the author really to respond to newer views of the *ṭāʾifa*s, but Molina López, 'Economía, propiedad', stresses prosperity for al-Andalus under the North African dynasties.

[31] For the back history of this, see Manzano Moreno, '"Desde el Sinaí de su arábiga erudición"'.

violent but abusive arguments, including between academics who in political terms are on the same side, with accusations that the scientific work of different, serious scholars is—I quote, translating—a 'historical novel', worth 'nothing', 'a chapter with a juicy taste to fill out stupid CVs', 'absolutely barren', written by 'a disciple of Olagüe'. This in turn leads to problems when *real* disciples of Olagüe write books, as (given the fraught political climate in Spain and the still relevant role of al-Andalus in it) they still do, for the rhetorical arsenal of their critics has already been exhausted.[32] Every historical field has its hot spots, apparently ordinary debates which take on quite unordinary emotional importance for their practitioners—the exact details of the land settlement of the Germanic invaders of the Roman Empire, the strength of the late Anglo-Saxon state, the degree of urbanism of early medieval Italian towns—to take only early medieval examples, which I know well. In every case the intensity of the argument derives from the (often unrecognized) importance that the 'truth' has for national grand narratives of different kinds.[33] But it is as if almost the whole of al-Andalus is a hot spot for a substantial sector of Spanish historiography.

I raise this issue because I do not support it. (Who knows what some people will say about this chapter?) But there is another side to the coin, which I like much more—that, here to a large extent, people are debating real problems. It *matters* to people how Islamic economies and societies in al-Andalus really worked; how far the Berber (or Arab) settlement of Visigothic Hispania changed local societies/economies and culture; when local irrigation systems were developed; how long large-scale property-owning continued after the Islamic conquest; when and why ceramic forms began to show influences from elsewhere in the Islamic world; how strong Andalusī state power was, and what its constituent elements were. These questions matter to me too, and it is often not so much that they are discussed more peaceably elsewhere, but that they are actually not discussed at all. In Spain (and in Portugal as well, particularly in the field of archaeology), when the dust dies down, we get real results.

I do not want here to follow the course of these debates over the last four decades. This has been done, ably, by several recent commentators, of whom the most effective is for me Alejandro García Sanjuán.[34] Very briefly, though, it is to Pierre Guichard that we owe the argument, novel in the 1970s, that Arabs and,

[32] I deliberately do not cite sources here; this tendency is so frequent, including not just members of the personally angry fringes of the field, who exist in every country, but apparently generous and open-minded people, that I would be singling out individuals unfairly. I commented briefly on this twenty years ago (*Framing*, p. 41); coming back to the field, I am struck by it even more forcefully. But the vehemence of the debates has, it seems, lessened in the last decade or so: its high point, at least with regard to serious academic work, was the 1990s–2000s.

[33] I have argued this elsewhere too, for the period before 2003, in Wickham, 'The early middle ages and national identity'.

[34] García Sanjuán, 'El concepto tributario'; the article is from 2006, but is not currently (2022) outdated, as the direction of the debates was clear by then. I refer to this article's ample bibliography for other interventions; here I restrict myself to the main lines of the debates.

above all Berbers, substantially changed the society of the Iberian peninsula, as they brought in segmentary and tribal social systems from the Maghreb, which marked the history of al-Andalus for a long time; the hilltop fortifications of the Sharq al-Andalus that he studied with the archaeologist André Bazzana were also seen as for the most part community refuges and not at all as signs of private aristocratic power.[35] It is to Miquel Barceló that we owe the current historiographical importance of irrigation systems as a marker of the impact of those same settlers; Barceló saw all such systems as products of tribal and collective social action, very much bottom-up constructions, which in turn reinforced the survival of coherent village/tribal communities.[36] It is to Manuel Acién that we owe the common current conceptualization of the changes in material culture after 711, sometimes quite slow ones, as being a process of Islamicization which culminated, after the first *fitna*, in the defeat of post-Visigothic landowning elites, and a subsequent imposition of an 'Islamic social formation' by 'Abd al-Raḥmān III and his associates; through this process, a tax-raising state imposed itself forcefully on local communities, with strong state power continuing on a smaller geographical scale under the *ṭāi'fa*s, and more widely again under the North African dynasties after 1090.[37]

These three basic arguments are not at all in opposition, and were initially pursued not only in parallel but with some mutual support. This was not least because all three authors were influenced, to different extents, by Marxism, which, of course, reinforced the interests of each in the important topic of peasant protagonism—it led all three to archaeology too, although all of them started out as historians. But contradictions slowly began to appear. For Guichard, communities lost their initially tribal coherence from the eleventh century onwards with the slow growth of property-owning; for Acién it was just the opposite, with large landowning dismantled in the tenth; for Barceló, neither was possible, for communities were tribal throughout.[38] And there were, of course, also critical interventions by others—by people who doubted the stress on Berber settlement (and/or the resultant use of modern Maghribī ethnographic parallels) in the work of Guichard and Barceló, or people who doubted that either fortifications or irrigation were clearly, or always, a product of early communitarian intervention.[39]

[35] Among others, Guichard, *Structures sociales*; Guichard, *Al-Andalus frente a la conquista*; Bazzana et al., *Les châteaux ruraux d'al-Andalus*; Bazzana, *Maisons d'al-Andalus*.

[36] Among others, M. Barceló et al., *El agua que no duerme*; the irrigation argument is well generalized with wider bibliography to 1995 by Glick, *From Muslim fortress*, pp. 64–91.

[37] Among others, Acién Almansa, *Entre el feudalismo y el Islam*; Acién Almansa, 'El final de los elementos feudales'; Acién Almansa, 'Sobre el papel de la ideología'. Acién's position is broadly accepted by major scholars of the next generation such as Sonia Gutiérrez, Eduardo Manzano, and Alejandro García Sanjuán; their work will recur in other contexts in this chapter.

[38] We will come back to Guichard and Acién, in particular; cf. M. Barceló, *El sol que salió*, pp. 7–18; M. Barceló, *Los Banū Ru'ayn en al-Andalus*, pp. 115–47.

[39] On Berber settlement, see, e.g., C. Barceló, '¿Galgos o podencos?', although this article is in my view overcritical. For fortifications, crucial starting points are Bazzana et al., *Les châteaux ruraux*

I have my own views on all of this, which differ, to greater or lesser extents, from those of all of the main figures in the debate. Most of them will recur in the course of what follows. Of those that will not: I already, nearly twenty years ago, made it clear that I did not see sharp or immediate material changes with the Berber-Arab conquest of 711, and I have not changed my view—localized examples of such change do not seem to take hold for at least a century after.[40] Nor do I accept that there was a particularly large-scale settlement of Berbers in most cases (as Bazzana has convincingly remarked, 'It is quite evident that the majority of the population of al-Andalus was authochtonous')[41]—few writers have explicitly claimed this, but some of the postulated socio-economic changes in the peninsula would be hard to understand without it—and I, like others, am uneasy about ethnographic parallels, as these have tended to come from the remotest parts of the Maghreb, even though Berber communities occupied and occupy the most varied social and ecological environments there. As I argued in the context of Sicily (see pp. 216–18 above), it is, anyway, irrelevant to the basic themes of this book whether the Andalusīs of our period had ancestors in 700 who lived in Visigothic Hispania or Berber Mauretania, or—as was in many places doubtless typically the case—both. But that most incomers were indeed Berbers seems an inescapable proposition, as there were so few Arabs in the Maghreb in the eighth and ninth centuries, and there are only sporadic references in even the most optimistic source to any coming from farther east (the settlement of Syrian and Egyptian *jund* (provincial) armies in 741 being the clearest example, and politically important, but they can only have been a few thousand men at the outside).[42] And on the topic of water management, to claim, as has repeatedly been done, that there was no continuity between Islamic-period irrigation systems and their Roman predecessors in the great *hortas*/*huertas* around Roman cities like Valencia seems to me unproven and counter-intuitive; but that there was a rapid expansion in irrigation seems to me clear and important. That this mostly dated to the eighth century is again unproven, but there are some systems which seem to go back to the ninth; and over all, the ever greater reliance on irrigation in the peninsula, particularly from the tenth century onwards, will have had a major effect on productivity levels, as well as on the ranges of crops which could be produced as a

d'al-Andalus; M. Barceló and Toubert, "*L'incastellamento*". But I shall not discuss the huge bibliography on castles, *ḥuṣūn*. The issue is important for the structuring of rural political power in the countryside, but not for a book about exchange. I shall tend simply to call these 'fortified sites', and leave aside what kind of power they actually represented—except their buying power, of course.

[40] Wickham, *Framing*, esp. pp. 741–58. For later changes, see Section 5.4.

[41] Bazzana, *Maisons d'al-Andalus*, 1, p. 380.

[42] For the *junds*, see Manzano Moreno, 'El asentamiento y la organización'; the *junds*, nonetheless, remained a feature of the historical memory of the Andalusīs, as shown, for example, in their ceremonial roles as representing particular Spanish provinces where they are supposed to have settled, into the 970s; see *Muqtabis VII*, trans. García Gómez, p. 75.

result, including a variety of fruits and vegetables, and, not least, sugar.[43] Al-Andalus was never only irrigated land, of course—the emphasis in much rural archaeology on irrigation systems has resulted in the large areas of *secano* (unirrigated land) being neglected by scholars. But there was *more* irrigated land in Islamic Spain than, for example, in Islamic Sicily, where the great fertile grain plateaux were mostly dry-farmed, to say nothing of most Christian-ruled lands. In al-Andalus, indeed, even grain land was often irrigated, not just fruit and vegetable plantations, as around Palermo and in the occasional foci of Sicilian irrigation elsewhere, or the gardens close to rivers which seem to have been the focus of Byzantine water management.[44] Parts of Spain, indeed, resembled Egypt in this to an extent, rather than some of the closer Islamic lands, notwithstanding dramatic differences in geography and ecology. That fact needs always to be part of our analytical perspectives.

What is most important, however, for the arguments set out in this book is to establish what the parameters of property-owning in al-Andalus were in our period. As I set this out, other aspects of my position with respect to these authors and others will also emerge. Acién has shown more clearly than anyone else the degree to which major Muslim landowners continued to be powerful up to the first *fitna* around 900, and were a backbone of rebellion in it. Some (the *muwalladūn*, in Spanish *muladíes*, of the historiography) were indeed said to be of Visigothic ancestry, including the best-known three, the family of ʿUmar ibn Ḥafṣūn in the lands behind Málaga, the Banū Ḥajjāj, who made themselves rulers of Seville, and the Banū Qasī in Tudela in the north. How far that ancestry was actually accurate, or even claimed by the families concerned, is a matter of debate, and does not matter here; but the sort of wide rent-based local control that they seem to have had, over some parts of al-Andalus at least, is very plausibly something that had pre-Islamic structural roots.[45] What happened under the caliphate,

[43] For Valencia, the fundamental survey is now Esquilache Martí, *Els constructors de l'Horta de València*; but his explanation of the supposed lack of continuity with Roman irrigation (esp. pp. 21–3) is schematic. Glick, *From Muslim fortress*, pp. 65–6, 89, is brief but sensible. Martín Civantos, 'Working in landscape archaeology', among others, nicely stresses the productivity increases which irrigation allows. For the ninth century or possibly the late eighth for some irrigation systems, see Gutiérrez Lloret, 'The case of Tudmīr', for the Segura valley in the province of Alicante. Puy and Balbo, 'The genesis of irrigated terraces', date a very small section of one terrace in the same valley to the seventh or eighth centuries using carbon-14, which may be a guide to an earlier dating for some systems, but, interestingly, it could equally well predate the Berber-Arab conquest of 711. See further p. 447 below. For sugar, see Lagardère, *Campagnes et paysans*, pp. 359–67, 377–84.

[44] A good exception to the neglect of *secano* land is Jiménez Castillo and Simón García, 'El poblamiento andalusí en las tierras de secano'. For irrigation on Sicilian inland sites, see Chapter 3, n. 234 above; it is likely that others will be discovered, but these systems were very localized, and do not compare to those in al-Andalus. For Byzantium, see Chapter 4, n. 88 above; for northern Italy, see pp. 488–9 below.

[45] Acién Almansa, *Entre el feudalismo y el Islam*, pp. 56–70; for debate, see Fierro, 'Cuatro preguntas', with Acién's reply, Acién Almansa, *Entre el feudalismo y el Islam*, pp. xxiv–xxx; Wasserstein, 'Inventing tradition'; Fierro, 'El conde Casio'; Lorenzo Jiménez, *La dawla de los Banū Qasī*. As for the Banū Ḥajjāj, our only source is Ibn al-Qūṭīyya, *Taʾrīkh*, trans. James, p. 51, although it is at least

however? Acién was explicit on the last page of his influential book on ʿUmar ibn Ḥafṣūn: 'From this moment on, with the social Islamicization of the population, the appearance of rent-based lords [*señores de renta*] would be impossible in al-Andalus'; instead, what prevailed was tax-raising from subject, but generally autonomous rural populations. Sometimes he pushed this further, stating that feudal rent (also henceforth 'impossible') was defined as being in kind, and that this was incompatible with the taxes by now exacted, which were in money and thus presupposed market exchange; and indeed, as we shall see, references to rent in al-Andalus do overwhelmingly concern produce, although this did not stop in periods when market exchange had become very active. But his basic point remained: tax won out over rent, possibly with some minor exceptions. The second *fitna* was not at all like the first; whatever its causes, it was perpetuated by factions of paid armies, which presupposed state power from the start. The 'Islamic social formation' was, rather, marked out by the 'hegemony of the private over the public' and the 'pre-eminence of the urban world', both of them elements in the power and self-representation of a tax-raising state elite which did not need to own land to be dominant.[46]

Overall, Acién's models for the development of and changes in Andalusī history are those I find myself closest to. I too would see the tenth century as the first in which a strong and spatially coherent fiscal system was fully established in al-Andalus, even if (and Acién would not have disagreed) plenty of elements of it were in place, especially in the lands closest to Córdoba, earlier. We can take for granted, for the whole period of this book, that taxation was as systematic in al-Andalus as in any other Islamic region, and, indeed, as in Byzantium as well. But the 'impossibility' of rent-taking from the caliphate onwards is an empirical, not a theoretical, claim, and needs to be tested.

If we look for references to landowning on a scale which extended beyond the village community in the caliphal and post-caliphal periods, we can, in fact, easily find them. Some are well-known examples. Ibn Ḥawqal asserted that in Spain, which he visited in 948, there was more than one *ḍayʿa* (estate) with over a thousand Rūmī (in this context Christian) tenants. Ibn al-Qūṭīyya (d. 977), who wrote a surviving history of al-Andalus, openly claimed—and is the only writer to claim—Visigothic ancestry for himself, royal no less, via Sara, the granddaughter of King Witiza—the 'Gothic woman' (*qūṭīyya*) of his *nisba*; he was a firm Umayyad loyalist, but makes great play of the dealings of his female and male ancestors in the first generation of the conquest. Most of what he wrote here is an origin myth,

significant that he claims female-line Gothic descent for this family, whatever they themselves thought. Guichard and Barceló minimized these structural roots; the former was rather more open to Acién's arguments, however (see Acién Almansa, *Entre el feudalismo y el Islam*, pp. xxxix–xliii).

[46] *Señores de renta*: Acién Almansa, *Entre el feudalismo y el Islam*, p. 124. Rent in kind: Acién Almansa, 'Sobre el papel de la ideología', p. 945; this article is his fullest exposition of the 'Islamic social formation', and pays much attention to the role of ideology as well.

with folk-tale storylines; but it is important that, in the great years of the caliphate, he could claim for his ancestors landowning amounting to 3,000 estates (*ḍiyāʿ*), symbolically divided between three sons in the west, centre, and east of al-Andalus (which to Ibn al-Qūṭīyya meant Seville, Córdoba, and Toledo—the real east was evidently off his radar), much of which was then distributed to elite Arab clients. The whole imagery of this section of his *History* is one of land gifts; land-based myth-making, a generation after the first *fitna*, did not seem at all inappropriate.[47] And this imagery was not only seen as part of the past; according to Ibn Ḥayyān (via his epitomists), Abū al-Qāsim Ibn ʿAbbād, the first *ṭāʾifa* king of Seville (1023–42), owned before his rise to power, when he was a senior city judge (*qāḍī*), a third of the territory of Seville in landed estates (*ḍiyāʿ*). Ibn Ḥayyān elsewhere chronicled the development of such private estates (again *ḍiyāʿ*) around Valencia in the 1010s, claiming them to be the result of overtaxation on the part of the first *ṭāʾifa* rulers there, which forced smaller owners to abandon their land and become tenants.[48]

All these citations involve the standard rhetoric of narratives, and should not be taken literally, but again, it is significant that this rhetoric included the evocation of substantial private landowning. Anyway, we have more technical citations as well, including some isolated documents. The first formulary book to survive for Muslim Spain, that of Ibn al-ʿAṭṭār (d. 1009) preserves a land sale from the 990s, of urban and rural lands in and around Córdoba, worth the large sum of well over 1,000 dinars. Al-Wansharīsī's *al-Miʿyār*, the fifteenth-century collection of often early *fatwās* discussed already in Chapter 3, which preserves as many Andalusī as Maghribī rulings, cites Ibn Zarb (d. 991) on the division of an estate which included not only lands but whole villages (*qurā*), and Ibn Ward (d. 1146), who can envision that a man owns the entire village (*qarya*) he lives in. A *fatwā* of Ibn al-Ḥājj (d. 1134/5), which survives separately, contains a document of 1082/3 showing a private owner obtaining a third of a village, somewhere in the territory of Córdoba; another of Ibn Rushd (d. 1126), Averroes's grandfather with the same name, refers to a *ḍayʿa* worth 250 dinars.[49] The surviving original Arabic documents from Toledo have only one text from before the Christian conquest, from 1083, but in it a half-vineyard is sold by a Muslim to a Jew for the surprising figure

[47] Ibn Ḥawqal, *Kitāb ṣūrat al-arḍ*, trans. Kramers and Wiet, 1, p. 110 (he says the peasants were prone to revolt, which has led some commentators to backdate the datum to the period of the first *fitna*, but that is a circular argument); Ibn al-Qūṭīyya, *Taʾrīkh*, trans. James, pp. 49–51, 75–7. See Fierro, 'La obra histórica', for an important analysis of Ibn al-Qūṭīyya's text. For the mythic aspects, see esp. Christys, *Christians in al-Andalus*, pp. 172–83; Fierro, 'Les généalogies du pouvoir'.

[48] For Ibn ʿAbbād, see, e.g., Dozy, *Scriptorum arabum loci de Abbadidis*, 1, pp. 221 (Arabic), 228 (Latin); for Valencia, see the translation and commentary of de Prémare and Guichard. 'Croissance urbaine'.

[49] Ibn al-ʿAṭṭār, *Kitāb al-wathāʾiq wa al-sijillāt*, trans. Chalmeta and Marugán, n. 6; al-Wansharīsī, *al-Miʿyār*, trans. Lagardère, *Histoire et société*, 3.266, 5.233, 6.194; Benaboud and Bensbaa, 'Privatisation and inheritance', n. 4.

of 300 dinars—this must have been a very large vineyard indeed. (Later, after the conquest, sales were generally smaller, in the tens of dinars and sometimes less, but there remained Muslim landowners there owning in full property, called, according to a Mediterranean-wide Arabic formula, *māl* and *milk*, into the thirteenth century.)[50] Lands of rulers, and lands attached to the maintenance of mosques and other religious/charitable bodies, called *aḥbās* (sing. *ḥubs*) in western Islam, would only add to this list.[51]

Most of these examples were also collected by Vincent Lagardère in his book on Andalusī rural society, largely but not only based on *fatwās*. He indeed adds several others, in which the size of estates is less explicit, to make the frequency of substantial landowning even more visible, as well as giving an ample account of rent regimes, which we will come back to.[52] The word *ḍayʿa* could shift meaning in Arabic from 'estate' to 'village', as Egyptian examples show. Arabic in the Iberian Peninsula must have eventually experienced the same shift, given that *aldea* and *aldeia* mean 'village' in modern Spanish and Portuguese respectively. But the word is often, in the texts from our period, specifically contrasted with *qarya* (village); the eventual semantic shift simply reflects the fact that estates could absorb villages in some areas—indeed, the Latin word *villa* experienced a similar shift in meaning in Christian Europe, and for the same reasons.[53] Conversely, there is never a sign that *ḍayʿa* did not mean full property; when tax-farming over substantial tracts of land became commoner, in the late tenth century and later, Andalusī writers used for that *inzāl* (originally, a tax for lodging state officials) or, as farther east, *iqṭāʿ*.[54] Ibn ʿAbdūn in early twelfth-century Seville, although he was

[50] P.Mozarab 1 (the text is re-edited and commented on in Beale-Rivaya, 'Shared legal spaces'). For *māl* and *milk*, see, e.g., Wickham, 'The power of property', pp. 79–80, 96. Across the period to 1150 (P.Mozarab 40), the average price of land steadily drops in the Toledo texts, although an irrigated terrain can still go for 200 dinars in 1146 (P.Mozarab 33). The percentage of Christians also rises steadily, as is unsurprising in land now ruled by Castile, although Arabic-language documents continued into the thirteenth century. Note that the name 'Mozarab' (a Christian under Islamic rule, and/or a Christian who uses the Arabic language) is a misnomer for many of the people in these texts, as plenty of them are Jews and Muslims. See most recently Olstein, *La era mozárabe*, esp. pp. 73–80 for most people in these texts being Christian, but by no means all. All the same, the religion of the actors in the texts is less important here than the continuities of assumptions about land tenure, which lasted, even if weakening, well into the twelfth century, as Olstein shows.

[51] For *ḥubs* in al-Andalus, see García Sanjuán, *Till God inherits the earth*.

[52] Lagardère, *Campagnes et paysans*, pp. 58–64, 101–9 (this work is not at all problematized, however, or located in any debate, as García Sanjuán, 'El concepto tributario', p. 127, notes; it also mixes Maghribī and Andalusī evidence without comment). Picard, *Le Portugal musulman*, pp. 285–97, has some other examples for Seville and westwards from there. The chapters on the economy in the *Historia de España* volumes, by Lévi-Provençal, Benaboud, and Molina López respectively, are not helpful on this issue, although Molina, the most recent, at least cites Lagardère. See n. 30 above, plus Lévi-Provençal, *Histoire*, 3, pp. 204–8 (the French original of his *Historia de España* contribution).

[53] For the shift in meaning to 'village' in Egypt and in Latin, see Wickham, 'The power of property', p. 80n.

[54] For *inzāl* and *iqṭāʿ*, see Lagardère, *Campagnes et paysans*, pp. 27–50. ʿAbd Allāh of Granada refers regularly to *inzāls* when he discusses landed concessions to officials and soldiers: *al-Tibyān*, trans. Tibi, pp. 56, 75, 101, 127, 138, 140, 143.

concerned above all to write a guide to the governance of urban markets, thought it worth saying that it was essential for ministers and elites to hold their own lands, for they needed to understand how crucial the grain supply was.[55] It is not clear what sort of legal title these estates were supposed to have, but the moral imperative towards elite landholding in this very moralistic text is nonetheless evident.

Acién was, of course, aware of most of these texts; indeed, in a later article he discussed some of them, although without relating their data to the model he had already set out.[56] What he must have meant by the 'impossibility' of *señores de renta* was something much more generalized: the impossibility of establishing wide-ranging landed political power of a Latin European type (the French *seigneurie banale*, the Castilian *señorío*) on the basis of owning wide estates, after the first *fitna*. That is not an unconvincing position at all; but it remains the case that it is not what he wrote, and what he wrote can mislead. Here, the more nuanced position of Guichard—whose *thèse d'état* on Valencia covered, precisely, the eleventh to thirteenth centuries, and who was the first person to put stress on the account of Valencian *ḍiyāʿ* in the 1010s—is more helpful. Guichard has no problem seeing the existence of some clear examples of private estates (they were generally called *raḥal*s in the País Valencià, where they meant 'small estates', not 'small villages', unlike in Sicily; see p. 233 above); it is just that they made up a minority of land. Most land was, by contrast, in the hands of small and medium owners inside *qarya*s, villages. That is most visibly the case in the *Llibres del Repartiment* created by the kings of Aragón to survey and distribute the conquered lands in the 1230s–1240s, for, like *Domesday Book* in England, these sometimes pay attention to prior property rights; in them, *raḥal*s and other estates are relatively few, and small ownership clearly dominant.[57] So the argument becomes a different one: how typical were the large estates I have listed, and how typical, instead, were smaller village-level owners, across the whole of al-Andalus? Here, two others of the *Libros del Repartimiento* of the rest of the conquered lands in the thirteenth century—those, at least, which give us real information about the pre-conquest period, which not all do—give us a hint. That for Murcia, although it does not by any means show equality of ownership inside villages (that is the case for Valencia as well, and indeed Guichard used the Murcia text too), given that 15 per cent of the owners held 50 per cent of the land, all the same does not show large properties: the biggest are only around 6 hectares each. In contrast, the Seville equivalent, for the Aljarafe, shows large owners above all, with few references to peasant

[55] Ibn ʿAbdūn, *Risāla fī al-qaḍāʾ wa al-ḥisba*, trans. Lévi-Provençal, ch. 3. Ibn ʿAbdūn does not say what form such landholding should take; he simply refers to cultivation (*ḥarth*). Thanks to Lorenzo Bondioli for checking this for me.

[56] Acién Almansa, 'Poblamiento y sociedad en al-Andalus', pp. 154–7.

[57] Guichard, *Al-Andalus frente a la conquista*, pp. 308–17, 504–22.

proprietors.[58] We thus have a geographical opposition here, at least between small parts of the west and small parts of the east. This does not help the question of which was more typical, but it does at least show us that schematic answers are not the most helpful.

We have to recognize here that there is no final solution to this problem; we cannot know what the real balance of landowning was in al-Andalus, or where in the region different types of ownership were strongest. It is at least clear that it was a mixture, with substantial tracts in the hands of large owners, and substantial tracts where they were hardly present.[59] It is thus quite possible that, for example, the territories of Córdoba, Seville, and Toledo, core areas for caliphal power, had larger owners, as members of the state elite used their wealth, as pre-capitalist elites do almost everywhere, to buy land (all three have recurred in the examples set out above), whereas Valencia, marginal until the eleventh century, had unusually few; but this is speculation. It is also highly likely that, as elsewhere in the Mediterranean, even large estates were regularly fragmented, thanks to standard partible inheritance rules, and interspersed with those of other owners; estates and village territories thus intercut, doubtless regularly, as is shown in one *ḥubs* text in Ibn al-ʿAṭṭār's formulary, which lists lands in a given village but also in neighbouring villages. This would tend to help village coherence, because larger owners would have less power to undermine it, although such more powerful owners might very often try to evade paying the taxes which were collectively due from the village community. The occasional text shows how this could work, or fail to work. Ibn al-ʿAṭṭār records sample documents in which the tax immunities of a large landowner are recognized, but also others in which neighbouring villagers protest against this, because the tax would fall on the rest of the community. The jurist here envisages both that the villagers may lose in court and that they might be successful. Here, a parallel example is a *fatwā* of Ibn Rushd the elder, who discusses a case in which villagers (*ahl qarya*) have an irrigation canal with water shared out on fixed days; it crosses the *sulṭān*'s land, clearly a larger state property; but one of the villagers leases that land and builds, first a *ḥammām*, and then a mill, using the canal water, against the will of his relatives, who are other villagers. Can he do this? Only if the legitimate owners of the water agree.[60]

[58] See Manzano Martínez, 'Aproximación a la estructura', for Murcia; González Jiménez, 'Repartimientos andaluces', p. 111, and Picard, *Le Portugal musulman*, pp. 290–2, for Seville; some of the landowners in the thirteenth century were families already known in the ninth. (The difference between the *Llibres* and the *Libros* is that between Catalan and Spanish.)

[59] Garcin et al., *États, sociétés*, 2, pp. 89–95, a manual, but one written by experts, comes to a parallel conclusion; so does Picard, *Le Portugal musulman*, pp. 297–302. Note that it is also sometimes proposed (e.g. Lagardère, *Campagnes et paysans*, pp. 51–6) that large estates (here *munyas*) were often close to cities, and at least sometimes used as gardens and recreational areas for their owners. Some caliphal and other estates around Córdoba, in particular, clearly fit this; but the wider distribution of references to estates does not.

[60] Ibn al-ʿAṭṭār, *Kitāb al-wathāʾiq wa al-sijillāt*, trans. Chalmeta and Marugán, nn. 76–80 (*ḥubs* texts), 228–31, 233 (tax exemptions; in the last example the villagers win); for commentary, see García

We saw something similar on Byzantine Crete in the same period, with an individual trying to privatize water rights and being successfully prevented by a village community (see p. 346 above).

This shows how tensions between larger landholders and village communities did not have to lead to the victory of the former. It also shows that village communities could hold water rights collectively—and needed to, not least because canal systems could regularly involve several villages. Two documents for the territory of Guadix (prov. Granada), from 1139–41 and 1187 (surviving separately, by sheer chance, as usual), show this well: in the first, men from seven *qarya*s testify as to how they share water out between each village; in the second, two *qarya*s fight over springs and a canal system, but a collectivity (*jamā'a*) of experts gets them to divide the water channels up.[61] Conversely, however, collective land-*owning* was less common, at least in our documentary sources. When we see it, it was not unchangeable: some *fatwā*s deal with what happens when villagers wish to share out collectively owned lands. The clear impression one gets from formularies, *fatwā*s, and casual references in other sources is that most land, even inside coherent village communities with communal control over water supplies, was individually owned, and could be bought, sold, inherited, and leased, without regard for any other constraints except, perhaps, the legal rules for leasing.[62]

So what we have here is a pattern in which there were certainly large owners, but also numerous small/medium ones. The numerous small/medium owners were based in villages which, routinely, are shown as having a considerable collective coherence, not least in irrigated areas, but also, as far as we can tell, outside them. And over all this there was a strong tax-raising system, which took taxes from rich and poor alike, at least in theory. Taxation is regularly described as oppressive, particularly under the *ṭāi'fa* kings, but at other times as well—we will look critically at that in a moment. More importantly at this stage, it seems to have been based on the *qarya*s, with the tax determined village by village, and the villagers themselves responsible for internal tax divisions, and for the local tax obligations of the absent and the tax-immune.[63] This too will have reinforced the

Sanjuán, *Till God inherits the earth*, pp. 114–15; Manzano Moreno, '¿Existieron comunidades rurales autosuficientes en al-Andalus?'; for Ibn Rushd, see al-Wansharīsī, *al-Mi'yār*, trans. Lagardère, *Histoire et société*, 5.301.

[61] Molina López, 'El documento árabe de Guadix'; González Palencia, 'Documentos árabes de Cenete', pp. 321–8; for more on community activism, see the examples cited in Guichard, *Al-Andalus frente a la conquista*, pp. 294–6. All these are quite similar to contemporary examples of collective village protagonism in León-Castile, north-central Italy, and Byzantium: see further Wickham, *Community and clientele*, pp. 192–241.

[62] For the *fatwā*s, see, e.g., al-Wansharīsī, *al-Mi'yār*, trans. Lagardère, *Histoire et société*, 5.286, 303. Another text which shows a standard pattern of fragmented landowning, pledged, rented, and sold with no interventions by village communities, is *Jüdische Urkundenformulare*, trans. Mutius, for Lucena (prov. Córdoba) in the early 1020s.

[63] See Barceló, 'Un estudio', in *El sol que salió*, pp. 103–36, developed in Manzano, *Conquistadores, emires*, pp. 299–305, for village-based taxation in the ninth century, according to the detailed testimony of al-'Udhrī, and its continuities in the caliphal period.

collective coherence of each village. Conversely, the pattern of villages needs to be set against the generalized dominance of towns, strong urban centres from where government and taxation was organized. This was, we could say, the 'Islamic social formation' working out in practice for, in effect, the whole of our period—not quite as other historians have set it out, but not all that far from their proposals either.[64]

My only qualm is that this is almost exactly what we saw in Chapter 4 as characteristic of the Byzantine Empire in our period. The only real difference is that irrigation seems to have been less prominent (even if certainly present) there. For Byzantium, I had to argue (pp. 346–7) that village communities were stronger and more protagonistic than some of the literature claimed; here, I have had to argue that they were less wholly dominant than some of the literature has claimed. That is one reason why the similarity has not been remarked on before; the other is, not surprisingly (but still regrettably), that historians of the Islamic and the Byzantine worlds do not regularly read each other's work. Norman Sicily was much the same, although it may be that Islamic Sicily, before that, actually had fewer large owners than Islamic Spain did. So was Fāṭimid Egypt, although there, at the end of our period, state control over landowning seems to have begun slowly to develop, in a way that does not have any clear parallel in our other regions. (So, as we shall see in Chapter 6, was northern Italy, but in that case with the crucial distinction that there was as yet no significant land tax, which meant that basic economic patterns were differently structured. For Ifrīqiya there is too little evidence to say.) There were differences between our regions, then; but with respect to the balance of larger and smaller owners we are quite like the Red Queen: after considerable running, we find ourselves in much the same place. The 'Islamic social formation' was a real social structure, but was not particular to al-Andalus, or indeed to Islamic regions.

We have, however, also seen in other chapters that title to property is not the only issue. For our purposes, now that we have got this far, what matters most is what peasants, and peasant communities, actually had to pay, out of their surplus, to others; exactly who the others were, landowners or state elites paid out of taxation, is less crucial. Here, the evidence is less detailed than it was for Byzantium, but we can say some things at least. Pierre Guichard has confronted the problems here most usefully. He has set out, on the basis of the evidence for Valencia (including Aragonese fiscal calculations for the post-conquest period in the later thirteenth century), the proposal, well based in the Christian evidence, that global taxation never went over a sixth of total agrarian production (that is to say,

64 The major element absent from this picture is Acién's 'hegemony of the private over the public' (esp. in Acién Almansa, 'Sobre el papel de la ideología', pp. 936–44); I confess that I cannot really see how this worked, and I have the sense that others do not either (e.g. Manzano Moreno, 'Relaciones sociales en sociedades precapitalistas', pp. 900–3; García Sanjuán, 'El concepto tributario', pp. 131–7).

without pretension to overexactness, up to 17 per cent), and was more commonly an eighth. He has pointed out that the norm, in the eyes of writers of narratives of the Islamic period, was that Muslim cultivators should pay a tithe or tenth (*'ushr*) of their produce; even 'Abd Allāh of Granada, while defending his own exactions (which went well beyond that) as products of necessity, regarded exacting only the tithe as normal and praiseworthy. (Non-Muslim cultivators certainly paid more, but we do not know by how much in our period—as we also do not know, at all, how numerous they were by the tenth century and later.) Guichard is inclined to argue that the 'illegal' extra taxes (illegal in the eyes of juristic interpretations of Qur'ānic law, that is to say) which every regime, from the caliphs onward, resorted to sooner or later (the *ṭāi'fa* kings from the start; the Almorávids after legalistic beginnings) were not so dramatically high that they destroyed the whole basis of peasant production and property-owning. The fact that the later Christian taxes hit a sixth at the outside does, indeed, support his case. We might conclude, on the basis of this, that 'illegal' taxes, when they were exacted, never more than doubled the basic fiscal obligations of the peasantry, which might reach a fifth of the yield, but perhaps for the most part did not get as far as that figure. This is hypothesis, but we do not have the data to go further. It could put the standard realities for taxpaying higher than Guichard proposed, at least sometimes, but we do not have any empirical grounds for saying that they were significantly higher.[65]

[65] Guichard, *Al-Andalus frente a la conquista*, pp. 325–67; cf. 'Abd Allāh, *al-Tibyān*, trans. Tibi, p. 45. Guichard bases himself in part on Barceló, 'Un estudio', although the latter focusses above all on the emiral period. For the caliphal period, Manzano, *Conquistadores, emires*, pp. 461–9 is an excellent brief account. Al-Ḥakam II in 973 was, indeed, explicit that tax should be—in theory—even lighter: 10 per cent on irrigated land and 5 per cent on *secano*, dry-farmed land: *Muqtabis VII*, trans. García Gómez, p. 144, with the correction to the translation in García Sanjuán, *Till God inherits the earth*, p. 427. It is highly unlikely that any ruler took this seriously in practice. Other authors are vaguer about taxation, including the contributors to the *Historia de España*—except Molina López, 'Economía, propiedad', pp. 244–58, who is, however, explicit (p. 255) that under the North African dynasties there is no evidence about the scale of tax-raising. Lagardère, 'Structures étatiques et communautés rurales: les impositions légales et illégales en al-Andalus et au Maghreb', strangely, despite its title, concerns itself largely with taxes on commerce.

Note also that the written sources these authors and others cite almost universally assume that this taxation ended up in the hands of rulers in the form of money, even though it is generally calculated as a percentage of crop, and in several texts—al-'Udhrī, see Barceló, 'Un estudio', p. 72, in the ninth century; *Le calendrier de Cordoue*, ed. Dozy, trans. Pellat, pp. 102–3, in the tenth; Ibn 'Abdūn, *Risāla fī al-qaḍā' wa al-ḥisba*, trans. Lévi-Provençal, ch. 4, in the twelfth—is explicitly exacted in grain. Surviving grain-only taxes are referred to at times as well (e.g. *al-Tibyān*, trans. Tibi, p. 45, for the late tenth century), although they were sometimes being converted to money by the beginning of the eleventh century (Lévi-Provençal, *Histoire*, 3, pp. 37–8; Manzano, *Conquistadores, emires*, p. 465). There seems to have been a trend towards taxes in money; but it may well be that taxes taken in grain were, anyway, for the most part converted into money at once, through fiscal or forced peasant sales, on the urban grain market. We cannot, however, say more about how this worked. The less frequent references to direct exactions in kind of specific products such as silk (e.g. *Le calendrier de Cordoue*, pp. 90–1, 132–3, 144–5) or linen (Ibn Ḥazm, ed. and trans. Asín Palacios, 'Un códice inexplorado', p. 43) seem to have been a very small percentage of total tax.

We saw (pp. 241–2), in Sicily, that a sixth of the total yield was a plausible payment for tenants of thirteenth-century estates, although Muslim taxpayers in western Sicily had perhaps paid up to twice that a century earlier. Even that amount in Sicily, a fertile island, was by no means so high as to grind the peasantry uncontrollably down. But Sicilian agriculture was also not, for the most part, based on irrigation; in Valencia, whose irrigation system in its *horta* was enormous and famous, producing substantial yields, often more than once a year, these figures were not high at all, and nor would they have been in the other irrigated areas, the *regadío*, of the rest of al-Andalus. Indeed, our scanty and anecdotal information about yields offers extraordinary figures: 100:1 outside Santarem, 180:1 outside Lorca, 320:1 outside Murcia. We cannot believe these, but on irrigated land, we would have no grounds for thinking that yields were below the substantial 10–12:1 figure for Egypt and Sicily (see pp. 66, 241 above), and they were quite possibly higher. If we follow Guichard's reasoning, then, and if we can generalize from Valencia (which, in the matter of fiscality, a relatively homogeneous burden, it seems to me that we can, at least for irrigated areas), tax levels were by no means extreme—notwithstanding frequent tirades against them, and the corruptness of their collection, by our authors.[66] Even more than with the Norman kings of Sicily, given their universality, they provided wealth for rulers ('Abd al-Raḥmān III had accumulated 20 million dinars in 951 according to Ibn Ḥawqal—doubtless an exaggeration, but a contemporary one[67]) but not necessarily poverty for the ruled.

The situation was probably rather different for levels of rent. Here our sources are the *fatwā*s of the jurists and the formulary books, which were also written by jurists. One thing is clear from the start: almost every discussion of rent, and there are many, concerns sharecropping—rents of half the crop or more. Even wage labour (*ijāra*: the labourer himself is an *ajīr*, as elsewhere in the Islamic world) was in almost all cases described as remunerated in kind, and sometimes again in a percentage of the crop. The sharecropping tenant (a common word is *'āmil*, which was a very generic term; it meant a senior financial administrator elsewhere) could sometimes be an intermediary who did not cultivate himself, and who had his own wage labourers. The texts use overlapping terminology for both tenants and wage labourers, but the latter were, nonetheless, distinct; writers advocate that they be made to work separately, to stop them talking or

[66] For tirades, see, e. g., Ibn Ḥazm, ed. and trans. Asín Palacios, 'Un códice inexplorado', pp. 34–44; Ibn 'Abdūn, *Risāla fī al-qaḍā' wa al-ḥisba*, trans. Lévi-Provençal, chs 4–6. For yields, see for Santarem al-Idrīsī, *Nuzhat al-mushtaq*, trans. Jaubert and Nef, p. 269 (among others); for Lorca and Murcia, see al-Rushāṭī, *Iqtibās al-anwār*, in the selection edited and translated by Molina López, 'Noticias geográficas y biográficas sobre Tudmīr', pp. 1095–6.

[67] Ibn Ḥawqal, *Kitāb ṣūrat al-arḍ*, trans. Kramers and Wiet, 1, p. 111. For other tax figures, see Manzano Moreno, *La corte del califa*, pp. 62–7, who proposes an average annual income of 4 to 5 million dinars for the caliphate.

disputing.[68] It is wrong to translate *ḍayʿa* as 'sharecropped estate', as some historians do, but in practice one has to conclude that most estates in al-Andalus were, indeed, sharecropped—as also in Ifrīqiya, but in sharp contrast to Egypt, Byzantium, or most of Sicily.

The jurists thought that the most proper contract was a *muzāraʿa* or *munāṣafa*, which they generally saw, as in other parts of the Islamic world, to be a contract in which the landowner supplied half the seed and the tenant paid half the crop in rent—the exact equivalent of the late medieval Italian *mezzadria*. (The sharecropper was thus a *muzāriʿ*, as frequently in Islamic law; by contrast, as we have seen, p. 57, this word just meant 'peasant' in Egypt, where there was no sharecropping, and there it could also mean an owner-cultivator, not only a tenant.) They also thought that this contract could have its percentages changed, so that the tenant might supply only a third, quarter, fifth, or sixth, of the seed, and only keep the same proportion of the yield. They were edgy about all uncertainty (*gharar*) in contracts, as Islamic legal experts always were, and they were almost all Mālikī jurists, following the Arabian law school founder Mālik b. Anas (d. 795), who was particularly opposed to all uncertain contracts and only regarded a strict 50:50 *muzāraʿa* contract as legitimate, but they recognized that local custom was looser, and could be regarded as acceptable. They argued about whether it was best to see the *muzāraʿa* as a commercial association (*shirka*), with both parties sharing risk, rather than a lease; the formulary writer Ibn al-ʿAṭṭār was clearly uncertain here.[69] They also argued about whether some of these contracts could really be best seen as *ijāra*. This was particularly so for the *khimāsa*, in which the cultivator (*khammās*) has not supplied seed and gets a fifth of the crop, which was clearly regarded by Andalusī jurists as a wage labour contract. They did not like it, however, for wages should be fixed, not uncertain, and were prone to pick holes in its details. We get the sense that they saw it as a Maghribī issue imported into Islamic

[68] For wage labour, see, e.g., al-Wansharīsī, *al-Miʿyār*, trans. Lagardère, *Histoire et société*, 3.302, 5.204 (a percentage), 218–19, 276, 337. For *ʿāmil*, see, e.g., ibid., 3.212, 5.202–3, 259. For sharecropping in general, see ibid., 3.312, 5.202, 205–6, 218, 226–8; Ibn al-ʿAṭṭār, *Kitāb al-wathāʾiq wa al-sijillāt*, trans. Chalmeta and Marugán, nn. 18, 19, 20 (here the sharecropper is an intermediary), 21–3. For surveillance, see Ibn ʿAbdūn, *Risāla fī al-qaḍāʾ wa al-ḥisba*, trans. Lévi-Provençal, ch. 202; Ibn Wāfid, *Majmūʿ fī al-filāḥa*, the medieval Castilian translation of which is edited in Millás Vallicrosa, 'La traducción castellana', pp. 304–5. Manzano Moreno, *Conquistadores, emires*, pp. 396–9, discusses the ways landowners could add extra charges to these contracts. The fullest discussion of this material is Lagardère, *Campagnes et paysans*, pp. 125–74, but he does not question the overdetailed distinctions of the jurists, and, as elsewhere, does not separate out al-Andalus and the Maghreb. One significant exception to the overwhelming stress on percentage rents is, however, the Hebrew formulary book of the 1020s from Lucena, that is to say, free from the *idées fixes* of the Muslim juristic tradition (although fully part of another religious-based legal system, which also did not have all its roots in Spain, far from it), which has a sample contract for a fixed money rent, as well as a sharecropping agreement; see *Jüdische Urkundenformulare*, trans. Mutius, nn. C14–15.

[69] The classic *muzāraʿa* contract is set out in Ibn al-ʿAṭṭār, *Kitāb al-wathāʾiq wa al-sijillāt*, trans. Chalmeta and Marugán, nn. 18–23, with the percentages different from sample text to sample text. For Ibn al-ʿAṭṭār's uncertainty, see ibid., pp. 158–62, 166–9, discussed by the translators at 147–53.

lberia; it was, indeed, documented in the Maghreb, then and into the twentieth century, as we have seen (p. 172).[70]

What do we make of this? I was earlier very cautious about seeing any contractual type as typical of rents in Ifrīqiya, simply on the basis of *fatwās* (p. 174), and the evidence from al-Andalus seems to me still more clearly problematic. It is hard to believe, when reading these texts, that most jurists had any understanding of or interest in the actual social conditions of the countryside. Not even the apparently actual cases they are called to pronounce upon can be taken at face value. Ibn al-ʿAṭṭār gives us a set of formulae for *muzāraʿa* leases involving different percentages of crop simply because he is working through legal possibilities, rather than because these were either typical or atypical. The sample problems which the jurists pronounce on in their *fatwās* were, similarly, in large part simply set out to allow the jurist concerned to formulate law more explicitly: the *khammās* who cultivates land he has not ploughed and is asked to plough another field to make up (this is illicit); the cultivator duly given his seed corn who instead cultivates flax and cucumbers; the man who leases out an orchard for—in a rare instance—money, but realizes that this is illegal, as he has sold the figs or grapes from it in advance (this can be seen as acceptable if it is refigured as a sharecropping contract).[71] We cannot assume that situations such as these actually happened and came to courts.

It is obvious, then, that rural realities varied greatly, and went well beyond the rigid frames of reference of jurists. So what we can actually say about these realities can only be very generalized. It is certainly likely that the oppressive *khimāsa* contract did exist in al-Andalus, somewhere, and that landowners could add extra burdens to apparently simple 50:50 agreements. I do not, however, think that we can assume that the really heavy rents, of 66 per cent, 75 per cent, 80 per cent of crop were necessarily common, just because we have the formulae for them, even if a two-thirds rent would have been possible for the cultivator to live off on a long-term basis on (and only on) *regadío*. On the other hand, we would have no grounds at all to conclude that 50 per cent rents were uncommon; they recur too often for us to exclude them, and lower rents are never mentioned. If Italian peasants could manage to live off that in the late middle ages and later, Andalusī peasants could too, especially on irrigated land, where yields were far above those in Italian dry-farming. Anyway, these figures are, however we take them, very much higher than taxation seems to have demanded. Peasants who were tenants must have had much less available surplus than peasants who were

[70] Al-Wansharīsī, *al-Miʿyār*, trans. Lagardère, *Histoire et société*, 5.219, 222, 227, 244; cf. Lagardère, *Campagnes et paysans*, pp. 137–44, mostly using Maghribī evidence. Chalmeta and Marugan in their commentary on Ibn al-ʿAṭṭār, *Kitāb al-wathāʾiq wa al-sijillāt*, pp. 153–4, stress the unacceptability of this contract in al-Andalus, but are wrong to see it as dating only to the eleventh century or later; the *fatwās* cited in this note are all from the tenth.

[71] al-Wansharīsī, *al-Miʿyār*, trans. Lagardère, *Histoire et société*, 5.222, 225, 212.

landowning taxpayers; the contrast between the two was, it seems, much greater than in Sicily or the Byzantine Empire, and the rates of rent were substantially higher than in both as well. That is a very generic conclusion, but it seems to me sound. As I have already stressed, we cannot, at all, tell how many of each there were in relative terms. But the fact that we can find good-quality ceramics in quite small settlements across al-Andalus, as we shall see later, argues further, now we can see the extent of this contrast, against any complete dominance for heavy rent-paying, for peasant buying power was clearly not trivial in the peninsula.

5.3 The Andalusī Urban Economy

It cannot be said that cities in al-Andalus are poorly studied. Syntheses are few, and recent syntheses of the archaeology are almost absent, but there has been so much work, whether targeted excavations or (usually) rescue digs, that we can begin to build up quite a dense picture of urban activity, denser than for any region we have looked at so far.[72] This, by and large, is supported by what we know about urban commercial life from the geographers, the *ḥisba* manuals, and more casual comments in other sources. Given the lack of synthetic work here, it makes most sense to go city by city, and then generalize briefly. I will start with Córdoba and Seville, the two main successive capitals of Islamic Spain (Córdoba will be discussed at the greatest length, as there is more to say about it), then look at Málaga, Almería, and Denia; after that we will do a quicker run-through of other centres. All the major cities of al-Andalus, and several minor ones, have, in fact, at least some good archaeological work done on them, so we can indeed reach conclusions which are more complete than for several other regions about how the urban economy worked and changed.

Córdoba was famous in our period for its great mosque, the most remarkable in the Mediterranean lands (geographers wrote about it at length; they were as impressed as any visitor is today[73]). But for our purposes the city is important because of its size. In particular, it was in the tenth century the largest-scale boom town of the whole of Eurasia. It had already by the early ninth century expanded well beyond its Roman walls; one of the two main early suburbs, the artisanal and commercial focus of Shaqunda across the river Guadalquivir, was already

[72] Mazzoli-Guintard, *Villes d'al-Andalus*, is the best general account. Valor and Gutiérrez González, *The archaeology of medieval Spain*, pp. 46–55, is a useful, very rapid archaeology-based survey; the whole book contains accounts of Andalusī archaeology in general. So does Cressier and Gutiérrez Lloret, 'Al-Andalus', a problematized archaeological introduction, including urban sites. For conferences focussed on surveys of urban archaeology, see, e.g., Cara Barrionuevo, *Ciudad y territorio*; and *Al-Ándalus: país de ciudades*; the latter in particular offers overviews of smaller towns as well.

[73] See, e.g., al-Idrīsī, *Nuzhat al-mushtaq*, trans. Jaubert and Nef, pp. 294–8; Vallvé Bermejo, 'La descripción de Córdoba de Ibn Gālib', pp. 671–3; Castrillo Márquez, 'Descripción de al-Andalus', pp. 89–92.

sufficiently active to stage a revolt against the *amīr* al-Ḥakam I and was, therefore, destroyed in 818, never to be reoccupied (hence its well-preserved archaeology, excavated equally well in the last decade or so).[74] The other, al-Sharqiyya (the Eastern suburb), in modern Spanish the Axerquía, has remained to the present day, doubling the land area of the Roman city. But from the end of the first *fitna*, under the caliphate, maybe beginning slightly earlier, the city exploded in size (see Map 26). As with Fusṭāṭ and Cairo, a new palace and governmental city, Madīnat al-Zahrā', was built a little under 6 kilometres away to the west from the 940s on, and Córdoba expanded towards it, plus north and east as well.[75] Numerous recent excavations to the west of the city show planned suburbs as far as 3 kilometres from the walls; and the planning was systematic. Regular squared lots, with housing around courtyards or patios, were aligned with the roads out of town, and sewerage systems were built in from the start; this area, at least, was transparently a top-down development, with none of the randomness of boom towns today.[76] The total land area of the late tenth-century twin city, if one generalizes from the excavations which have been carried out, could easily have been one and a half times the size of the populated area of Constantinople, and possibly larger even than Fusṭāṭ-Cairo; and this expansion took place in under three generations, *c*.930–1010.[77] This in itself shows how remarkably effective, and fast, the political and fiscal recentralization under 'Abd al-Raḥmān III must have been. Suddenly, al-Andalus could be seen to match the great old-established states of the east Mediterranean, with a similar disproportionately large capital.

It is much harder to estimate how large the population of Córdoba actually was, however. Guesstimates vary hugely, as usual, between 50–100,000 (Manzano) and over 300,000 (Guichard and Soravia), to cite only recent authors.[78] We cannot, however, simply match the land area of the city with that of the eastern capitals and argue from that (so making Córdoba exceed the guesstimates of 150,000 for Constantinople and 200–250,000 for Fusṭāṭ-Cairo; see pp. 41, 279 above). It is,

[74] Casal García, 'Caracteristicas generales', Casal García, 'Contextos arqueológicos' (among many publications by the same author, the excavator), and Mayte Casal, pers. comm.

[75] For a full publication of the buildings, see Vallejo, *La ciudad califal de Madīnat al-Zahrā'*. Its building stone was for the most part local, but its marble came from as far away as the area of Estremoz in modern Portugal (ibid., pp. 103–17, 359–60). Ibn Ḥawqal, *Kitāb ṣūrat al-arḍ*, trans. Kramers and Wiet, 1, p. 111, claimed that houses connected the two cities without a break; if true, this was probably only a narrow line of housing. For the spatial patterning of the cities and the caliphal processions between them, see Manzano Moreno, *La corte del califa*, pp. 297–335; see also Mazzoli-Guintard, *Vivre à Cordoue*, esp. pp. 65–80.

[76] Among the very numerous publications here are Fuertes Santos, 'Aproximación al urbanismo'; Fuertes Santos, 'El Sector Nororiental'; Clapés Salmoral, 'Un baño privado'; Clapés Salmoral, 'La formación y evolución del paisaje suburbano'; Clapés Salmoral, 'La actividad comercial de Córdoba'; Camacho Cruz, 'Evolución del parcelario doméstico'; González Gutiérrez and Clapés Salmoral, 'La ciudad islámica'.

[77] For a recent map, see Camacho Cruz, 'Evolución del parcelario doméstico', p. 31.

[78] Manzano Moreno, *La corte del califa*, p. 301; Guichard and Soravia, *Les royaumes des taifas*, p. 159. Both cite earlier guesses.

for a start, generally recognized by the archaeologists that the density of housing varied greatly, with extensive tracts reserved for gardens and cemeteries; secondly, the great developments in the western suburbs, although dense and getting denser, seem to have been above all one-storey houses, unlike in the eastern capitals, and the palace city of al-Zahrā' was certainly less built-up.[79] On the basis of that alone, I might have been prepared to offer a guess of 150,000 for Córdoba at its height.

But there is another problem, hardly discussed in the historiography: food supply. We have seen how complex and important, and—at times of bad harvest and war—difficult and dangerous, the supply of Fusṭāṭ and Constantinople was. Córdoba ought to have found it still more difficult, for it is far from the sea, and it has only a small (even if fertile) hinterland, the Campiña de Córdoba, which might have been able to feed the city before and after the caliphal period, but certainly not at its demographic height. The narrative accounts of caliphal Córdoba never say a word about this, although Spain will have had as many bad harvests as anywhere else. Food must have come along the Guadalquivir, from the wider lands around Seville in particular, and also from Jaén and elsewhere; but, to judge from the experiences of other very large Mediterranean towns in the middle ages, this would not have been enough either. (Archaeology ought to help with respect to where food came from, as it does for other major cities in the Mediterranean, but so far does not; see pp. 431–3 below.) We have only the briefest hint of how this worked in our sources: most explicitly, a peace treaty in *c.*900 between two of the main rebels of the first *fitna*, Ibrāhīm b. Ḥajjāj of Seville and 'Umar b. Ḥafṣūn of Bobastro behind Málaga, which is said by Ibn al-Qūṭīyya in the 960s–970s to have reopened the Córdoba–Seville road, thus giving back the capital's access to granaries (this would have been before most of its great expansion, but Ibn al-Qūṭīyya may have been thinking of the situation of his own time).[80] But for there to be no reference to emergency measures for the capital, or even their potential governance—which must have become more and more necessary explicitly to organize as the city grew so fast, just as the planning of new suburbs did, and we know a fair amount about the city's administration—indicates that supply problems, despite Córdoba's inland position, were probably not as acute as they were for the great eastern capitals.

I conclude that 150,000 is too high a figure for the population of Córdoba, and that 100,000 would be a safer guess. But as with the other capitals, whatever the eventual figure, it was still high, and still challenging. It is generally thought that the siege and then violent sack of the city in 1010–13 was the cause of the rapid

[79] For single storeys, see, e.g., Clapés Salmoral, 'La actividad comercial de Córdoba', p. 230; for growing density, Aparicio Sánchez, 'Los primeros indicios de saturación'.

[80] Ibn al-Qūṭīyya, *Ta'rīkh*, trans. James, p. 122; note also his references to the ancestors of noted grain merchant families, presumably of his own day, at pp. 71, 90; that is to say, they were recognized as important.

decrease in the population again; the western suburbs and palaces were immediately abandoned, as it appears, often after damage by fire, and the city more or less returned to its Roman walls, plus the Axerquía.[81] But the larger a city, the less likely it is that a siege and sack can destroy everything. It is to me highly likely that after the temporary ravages of the siege, the immediate economic result of the division of al-Andalus into *ṭāʾifa*s was simply the end of any systematic food supply to Córdoba, which will have previously, almost certainly, been underpinned by the taxation of the provinces. This alone would necessarily have resulted in the steady emptying out of the remaining surplus population (doubtless mostly to the provinces they had fairly recently come from), or else their choice not to return. Henceforth, the city will have been supplied by the Campiña around it again.

Equally important for us is the scale of the economic activity generated in the city itself. Córdoba, again like Fusṭāṭ and Constantinople, was very far from being a city which simply lived off the revenues of others. It had active merchant elites, who provided, we are told, at least one of the city's chief *qāḍī*s in the early tenth century, and the *wazīr* of the last caliph of all, Hishām III, at the end of the 1020s.[82] The *sūq*s seem to have remained concentrated in the old Roman city (the western suburbs were largely residential, except for some specific artisanal areas, plus a handful of *fundūq*s[83]), but were big and expanding; the *Muqtabis* tells us that al-Ḥakam II in 971–2 extended the clothes *sūq* because of lack of space, widened the main street through the *sūq*s because shops had encroached on it, and rebuilt the great Roman bridge over the river to the city's south which led straight into the market area, temporarily displacing the city's huge number of floating mills.[84] We have a mid-century *ḥisba* treatise by Ibn ʿAbd al-Raʾūf which discusses which urban crafts needed to be under public surveillance to prevent usury and fraud and to promote cleanliness; this is the closest Córdoba got to the near-contemporary *Book of the Eparch* in Constantinople, although, significantly again, it does not specify issues of food supply. Nonetheless, it lists problems

[81] See Camacho Cruz, 'Evolución del parcelario doméstico', p. 46, for fire damage; she adds that coin hoards and covered wells indicate a hope by inhabitants that they would be able to return.

[82] Al-Khushanī, *Kitāb al-quḍā bi-Qurṭuba*, trans. Ribera, pp. 216–17; Hishām III's *wazīr* was Ḥakam b. Saʿīd al-Qazzāz, whom Ibn Ḥayyān calls a weaver, *ḥāʾik*, lowering the status of a man he loathed, but his father's name is that of a silk merchant. He was controversial, all the same, and was said to have been assassinated in 1031 for his oppression of other members of the merchant elite (*aʿyān al-tujjār*); the caliphate ended immediately after. See Ibn ʿIdhārī, *al-Bayān*, trans. Maíllo Salgado, pp. 128–30; and commentary in, e.g., Amabe, *Urban autonomy*, pp. 113–14; Soravia, 'A portrait of the *ʿālim* as a young man', pp. 39–42; Mazzoli-Guintard, 'Quand, dans le premier tiers du XI siècle, le peuple cordouan s'emparait de la rue . . .', p. 127.

[83] For *fundūq*s, Clapés Salmoral, 'La actividad comercial de Córdoba', pp. 246–50. There were also artisanal activities in the residential areas on occasion, as is well shown in Aparicio Sánchez, 'Una estructura de probable uso industrial'.

[84] *Muqtabis VII*, trans. García Gómez, pp. 77–8, 87, 93; cf. Manzano Moreno, *La corte del califa*, pp. 308–11 for the *sūq*s; for the huge numbers of mills, see *Crónica del moro Rasis*, ed. Catalán and de Andres, p. 21, and, four centuries later, al-Shaqundī, *Risāla fi faḍl al-Andalus*, trans. García Gómez, p. 129.

concerning a very wide variety of artisans and shopkeepers, covering the full range of, in particular, weavers and clothiers, leatherworkers (Córdoba was internationally famous for leather), and fifteen types of food sellers.[85]

Then, north of the city, was the biggest set of ceramic kilns ever found in medieval western Eurasia. We have seen that excavators in the Mediterranean have been delighted to find half a dozen kilns in major cities, as signs of economic vitality; in mainland Italy, the figures are even lower. The total number of kilns at present (2022) attested for Islamic Córdoba is roughly 177, of which 154 were located in the single area north of the city. Of these, 110 were actually from the emiral period or only a little later; the main caliphal kiln set has not even been found yet, and must have been substantially bigger.[86] Caliphal Córdoba is known for the wide production and distribution of a high-quality glazed ware, very often bowls (*ataifores* in Spanish) decorated in copper-green and manganese-black on a tin-opacified white background, frequently including the word *al-mulk*, 'power', in the design (see Fig. 15; these are called 'green and manganese' in the literature, and will be in this chapter too, when we return to them in Section 5.4). The

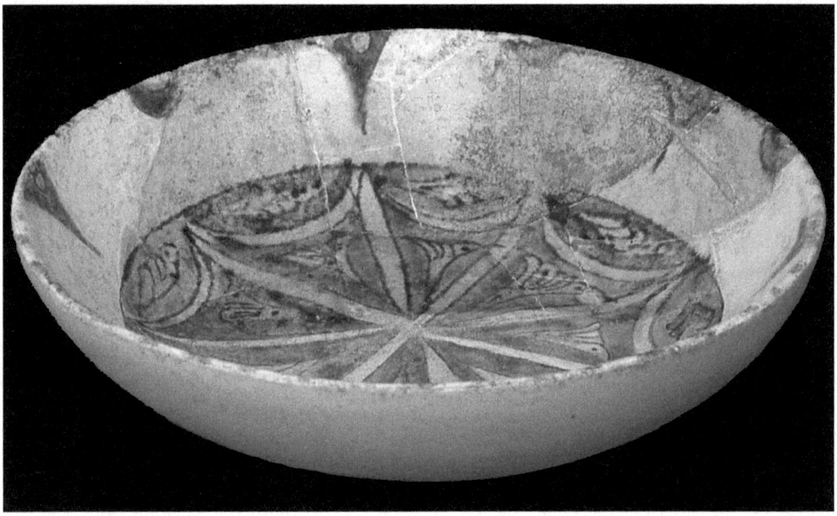

Fig. 15 Green and manganese ware

[85] Ibn 'Abd al-Ra'ūf, *Risāla fī ādāb al-ḥisba wa al-muḥtasib*, trans. Arié; one interesting absence is metalworkers. For a brief discussion, see Chalmeta, *El "señor del zoco"*, pp. 381–7. For Córdoba leather and the international (above all Latin European) market, see Constable, *Trade and traders*, pp. 192–4.

[86] For the figures, Elena Salinas, pers. comm. Of the 154, 10 kilns were caliphal (plus a few emiral ones still in use), 6 *ṭāi'fa*/Almorávid, and 28 Almohad. Publications of ceramics for the period up to 1000 include Salinas, 'Cerámica vidriada de época emiral'; Fuertes Santos, *La cerámica califal del yacimiento de Cercadilla*.

production of these, doubtless linked directly to the projection of caliphal power, has been associated with the palace area of al-Zahrā', although there is no evidence up to now for them being made there, and evidence is growing that the great extramural pottery area of Córdoba itself made this pottery type.[87] But the city was, anyway, making far more pottery than that; it was regularly producing literally tons of ceramics of all kinds, utilitarian and semi-luxury, associated with specialized kiln areas.

Tenth-century Córdoba was a city with a large artisan population, then. This was the context for a rare event in the period we are looking at, a popular revolt, which was, in fact, connected with the start of the second *fitna* in 1009. The *ḥājib* al-Manṣūr's second son, 'Abd al-Raḥmān Shanjūl (ruling 1008–9), was unpopular and inept, and sought the caliphal title for himself. He was brought down and killed by an Umayyad prince, Muḥammad II al-Mahdī, who sought and rapidly obtained the active support of the urban plebs, itself increasingly hostile to the regime and the Moroccan Berber army of al-Manṣūr's family (one of the first things they did was pillage al-Manṣūr's palace east of the city, carrying off—of course—untold wealth). This plebs is described in very contemptuous terms by our aristocratic chroniclers, in particular Ibn Ḥayyān. He found various synonyms for 'the lowest in society, the rabble of the markets' (*al-sifla wa-sā'ir ghawgha' al-aswāq*), and stressed the low status of most of the trades he mentioned—goatherds, abattoir workers, bloodletters, collectors of human sewage—even if also weavers and doctors; it seems in reality that almost all levels of the non-governmental urban population were involved. It was this artisanal and commercial collective which ended up defending the city during the three-year siege by the Berber army after Muḥammad's death in 1010. They were far from an incapable group, then, even if they failed, and bore the brunt of the subsequent sack of the city.[88]

It was not until the 1930s at the earliest that Córdoba again reached the scale of its tenth-century height. But it remained a prosperous and substantial city afterwards all the same, and indeed, from the 1160s, under the Almohads, expanded again. The new Almohad regime patronized rebuilding; abandoned parts of the Axerquía were reoccupied; the number of known kilns in the north increased again; a new extramural ceramic and metalworking area opened to the northwest and in other areas around the walled city; this in some places turned into

[87] Barceló, '*Al-Mulk*, el verde y el blanco', in *El sol que salió*, pp. 187–94; no evidence for palace production: Salinas and Pradell, 'Madīnat al-Zahrā' or Madīnat Qurtuba?'; links with Córdoba's kiln area: Salinas and Pradell, 'Primeras evidencias de producción de cerámica verde y manganeso califal en un alfar de Córdoba'.

[88] Ibn 'Idhārī, *al-Bayān*, trans. Maíllo Salgado, pp. 61–105, esp. 61, 64–6, 74–5, 84, 96, 100. These events have generated a good deal of commentary, including Scales, 'A proletarian revolution', who interpreted this plebs, unconvincingly, as really being an urban elite; Mazzoli-Guintard, 'Quand, dans le premier tiers du XI siècle, le peuple cordouan s'emparait de la rue . . .', the best analysis; and Amabe, *Urban autonomy*, pp. 94–106, with an alternative translation of the *Bayān*.

suburbs with well-built patio houses.[89] We shall see that this twelfth-century urban expansion was common in al-Andalus; and it is more clearly documented in this city than in many others thanks to the recent intensive archaeological activity—and publication—which marks Córdoba out. The fact that it does not match the great days of the tenth century must not cause us to undervalue it. In many ways, it is, in fact, more significant than that high point, for it is the product of a wider economic expansion, rather than simply of the power of a newly centralized and wealthy political regime, which is what underpins all the account of the preceding pages. But Córdoba's temporary massive expansion under the caliphate at least sets a marker down for the economic possibilities which centralized power could generate in al-Andalus. The interplay between political power—which remained strong thereafter across our period, whether it was centralized or localized—and wider patterns of expanding economic complexity will mark the rest of this chapter.

Seville, a major political centre under the *ṭāʾifa*s and Almorávids, and the Almohad capital after 1156/1163, is a case in point. It may already have been slightly larger in the caliphal period than it had been under the Romans, but it doubled in size in the *ṭāʾifa* period, when it was the capital of a kingdom which systematically increased its territory until the Almorávid takeover; and then again, aided by the Guadalquivir riverbed moving westwards, it doubled again under the Almohads. This was certainly in part a product of its new political and fiscal centrality. It was accompanied by some substantial investment in public buildings: the Alcázar palace to the south of the city was founded in the later eleventh century on top of an area of pottery kilns on the edge of town, and then was systematically rebuilt in every century until the fourteenth; the central mosque was rebuilt on a large scale by the Almohad caliph Yūsuf I (1163–84) in the 1170s, together with an aqueduct, and the great bridge over the new course of the Guadalquivir to connect the city with the Aljarafe; later, in the 1190s, the still standing mosque minaret, the Giralda, and a refurbished central market, were the work of Yūsuf's son al-Manṣūr.[90] The expanding city was not planned as Córdoba had been, however; it seems to have been as much a product of greater commercial exchange as of political and fiscally supported direction. Seville was a port for

[89] There has been a substantial amount of archaeological work on Almorávid and Almohad Córdoba, including León Muñoz and Blanco, 'La fitna y sus consecuencias'; Blanco Guzmán, 'Vivir en la Córdoba islámica'; Blanco Guzmán, 'Córdoba y el califato almohade'; Salinas Plegezuelo, *La cerámica islámica*; Salinas Plegezuelo, 'Producciones cerámicas de un alfar del siglo XII'. All this makes unbelievable the often cited claim by Ibn Ṣāḥib al-Salā, *al-Mann bi al-imāma*, trans. Huici Miranda, p. 49, that before the Almohads started to patronize the city in 1161 (when it was temporarily made their capital), it had only eighty-two inhabitants, even if he was an eyewitness.

[90] For Almorávid patronage, see Ibn Ṣāḥib al-Salā, *al-Mann bi al-imāma*, trans. Huici Miranda, pp. 65, 188–204. Bosch Vilá, *La Sevilla islámica*, is a basic account of the city's political history, although, written as it was before the archaeology really began, it is more generic on its economy. For the Alcázar, the location of a large amount of excavation, see Tabales Rodríguez, *El Alcázar de Sevilla*; Tabales Rodríguez, *Excavaciones arqueológicas*, two out of many publications on the palace sites.

the agricultural products of the Aljarafe, notably oil, which al-Idrīsī said was sold in the eastern Mediterranean (even if its export there is unlikely to have compared with that of Tunisian oil), and cotton; and already in the eleventh century, the city had its own high-end ceramic production, the first lustreware made in al-Andalus. Private housing in the caliphal period was still in reused Roman brick, but under the *ṭāʾifa*s there was new brick and stone as well, and this was regular by the time of the North African dynasties; most houses were rebuilt in the later twelfth century too.[91]

And the scale of production in Seville steadily increased. By the Almohad period, the major ceramic kiln site was across the river on what is now the island of La Cartuja, and as in Córdoba, it was highly active, including export to other cities in its vicinity, as we shall see later.[92] Seville too had a *ḥisba* manual, by Ibn ʿAbdūn, writing under the Almorávids. He stresses the river port area to the west, which is the vital focus of import and export—as a result, it must remain under state control. He confirms among other things that new bricks are by this time normal in urban building. Like Ibn ʿAbd al-Raʾūf in Córdoba, he regulates production and market sales by a variety of trades, here including metalworking, to try to eliminate uncleanliness and fraud, and also hoarding (Ibn ʿAbdūn was more aware, by now, of the issue of grain supply), as well as poor workmanship in general. Ibn ʿAbd al-Raʾūf had banned wine being bought by Muslims from Christians; over a century later, although he repeats that proscription, Ibn ʿAbdūn is as worried that Muslims might make it themselves, and prohibits both the sale of grapes in large quantities and the making of wine glasses. (This was certainly effort wasted; half a century later, the agronomist Ibn al-ʿAwwām was setting out the way vineyards were planted around Seville.)[93] In the early thirteenth century too, al-Shaqundī had no difficulty in fronting Seville's special qualities while praising al-Andalus in general. The gardens along the riverbank are lovelier than those of the Nile in Cairo or the Tigris in Baghdad. In most houses there are running water and citrus trees. 'If in Seville you wanted bird's milk, you would find it'.[94] From all this, the sense we have is of a commercially active and expanding city, benefiting from its political centrality but not dependent on it. And—unlike

[91] For Seville as a port, see the overview in Picard, *L'océan atlantique musulman*, pp. 380–2, 399–402, 484–93; cf. al-Idrīsī, *Nuzhat al-mushtaq*, trans. Jaubert and Nef, p. 260. For urban expansion, housing, and overviews of ceramics, see *Sevilla almohade*; Valor Piechotta, *Sevilla almohade* (the best overall synthesis, to 2008); Valor Piechotta, *El ultimo siglo de la Sevilla islámica*; Valor Piechotta and Lafuente Ibáñez, 'La Sevilla ʿabbādí'; Huarte Cambra and Lafuente Ibáñez, 'Los siglos X y XI en Isbilia'. For lustre, see Barceló and Heidenreich, 'Lusterware'.

[92] de Amores Corredano, 'Las alfarerías almohades de la Cartuja'; Vera Reina and López Torres, *La cerámica medieval sevillana*, pp. 35–8; and see esp. n. 140 below.

[93] Ibn ʿAbdūn, *Risāla fī al-qaḍāʾ wa al-ḥisba*, trans. Lévi-Provençal, esp. chs 60 (the port), 73 (bricks), 104, 183 (hoarding), 116, 129, 204 (wine), 218–20 (metalworking); cf. for wine Ibn ʿAbd al-Raʾūf, *Risāla fī ādāb al-ḥisba wa al-muḥtasib*, trans. Arié, p. 209; Ibn al-ʿAwwām, *Kitāb al-filāḥa*, trans. Clément-Mullet, 1, pp. 357–8. See also above, p. 386, for grain supply.

[94] Al-Shaqundī, *Risāla fī faḍl al-Andalus*, trans. García Gómez, pp. 119–24 (120 for the quotation).

many Andalusī cities—this is reinforced by the fact that it continued to be prosperous after the Christian conquest in the thirteenth century as well.

Málaga was the other city with a *ḥisba* manual, that of al-Saqaṭī (or, to be exact, of a pupil who wrote his pronouncements down), in the twelfth century or just after. It is the longest of the set, although it is similar in its sermonizing tone to the others, and includes micromanaging instructions about how to make bread, the ingredients and costs of different kinds of sweet and cheese pastries, and the number of nails needed for a shipbuilder to build a galley; al-Saqaṭī went so far as to spend the night in a mill to figure out how millers cheated. The list of artisans (and their frauds) is more extensive than in the others too, covering the whole normal range, and including niche trades like puppeteers, sieve makers (but cf. p. 319 above), and the makers of cork shoes—as well as potters, not at all niche but not so often cited. Al-Saqaṭī is also the only manual writer to discuss the slave trade, mostly in women (slave dealers were here rich, and often aristocratic). I would suppose that this is because Málaga was a port looking to Morocco; by now, with the end of easy supplies from northern Spain and the Slav lands, slaves probably came with gold, up from south of the Sahara. There is here a considerable division of labour in some trades, most explicitly baking (five types of employee of a master baker (*khabbāz*) are mentioned). Málaga was a significant port city, but not a political focus, except when it was the centre of a small *ṭāʾifa* kingdom; all the same, these lists show as wide a range of artisanal activity as the two capitals.[95]

Archaeologists have tracked urban expansion here too, in the eleventh century and then the twelfth–thirteenth. Below the castle in the east of the city, there was a higher-status urban quarter on the hill slope, and there developed in the west a substantial artisanal area on both sides of the river on the plain, with shipyards and *fundūq*s on the eastern side, plus leatherwork, dyeing, and weaving. One eleventh-century house in this central area lies on top of a ninth-century ceramic kiln site, which had probably then been on the edge of town; as in Seville, kilns moved farther out as the city expanded. The late ninth-century kilns produced, among other things, very early glazed wares, second only to Pechina near Almería and Córdoba itself. In the eleventh century the kilns, by now of considerable

[95] Al-Saqaṭī, *Kitāb fī ādāb al-ḥisba*, trans. Chalmeta Gendrón, chs 22 (bakers' employees), 48–52 (millers), 67, 86, 170 (pastries), 108–26 (slave dealers), 144 (cork shoes), 155 (potters), 159 (puppeteers), 163 (sieve makers), 169 (how to make bread), 176 (nails). For discussion, see Chalmeta, *El "señor del zoco"*, pp. 423–49, and for the bakers, see Latham, 'Some observations on the bread trade'. For slaves, Constable, *Trade and traders*, pp. 203–8, gives a brief overview; for the period before the second *fitna*, when the trade from the north was at its height and supplied a substantial portion of the army, see *EI*², s.v. al-Ṣaḳāliba (P. B. Golden et al.); Meouak, *Ṣaqāliba*; Manzano, 'Circulation des biens', pp. 162–8. More work needs to be done on the period after 1025 or so. In Spain in our period, as elsewhere in the Mediterranean, slaves were a semi-luxury—and still more so once slaves ceased to be recruited into armies, after the *fitna*; it is not chance that the slaves in al-Saqaṭī were mostly female, for domestic service and sexual exploitation. So, as we saw for Egypt (Chapter 2, n. 284 above), they are less relevant to the arguments of this book.

complexity, were moved both farther north and over the river to unwalled western suburbs, alongside what seems to have been a sugar factory.[96] The pattern here is, then, of a prosperous and expanding town with a large number of trades, some of them operating on a large scale; the archaeology and al-Saqaṭī support each other on this, and there is no need to interpret the one through the lens of the other.

When we reach Almería, we are looking at the port city par excellence, active as an entrepôt throughout our period, even though it lies in semi-desert, backed by mountains. But we know less about it. Neither Almería nor nearby Pechina, some 8 kilometres inland, was a Roman town. Pechina developed as an urban centre in the late ninth century, founded supposedly by a collectivity of sailors (*baḥriyyūn*).[97] Almería, initially its port, is said to have been a fortification already in the 840s, and then appears as a centre for shipbuilding and a caliphal war fleet in the 930s, for attacks on Christian ports in Catalonia and France, according to Ibn Ḥayyān and al-ʿUdhrī. It was walled and in some sense refounded by ʿAbd al-Raḥmān III in 954/5 after being itself sacked by a Fāṭimid fleet, and it took off from then as the main Mediterranean port and arsenal of al-Andalus for at least 200 years; it also supposedly absorbed the inhabitants of Pechina in 1011/12, according to al-ʿUdhrī, who lived in the city a couple of generations later.[98] It was known for its silk-working; al-Rāzī's geographical account, which must have predated its refoundation in the year of his death, already mentions it. (Ibn Ḥawqal, however, writing shortly after, still simply calls Almería the port of Pechina; he discusses linen exports from the latter, and not silk.) Al-Idrīsī in around 1150 stresses its huge wealth, claiming that up to 1147 it had 800 silk looms of different kinds, for export to the eastern Mediterranean—Spanish silk export from here is, indeed, amply confirmed by the *geniza*, as we shall see (p. 453–4 below)—plus iron- and copper-working, the port of course, and nearly a thousand *fundūq*s for passing merchants. Shipbuilding as well is stressed by an earlier contemporary,

[96] Íñiguez Sánchez and Mayorga Mayorga, 'Un alfar emiral en Málaga'; Íñiguez Sánchez, 'Arqueología de los Ḥammūdíes'; Espinar Cappa et al., 'La producción de cerámica verde y manganeso en Málaga'; López Chamizo et al., 'La industria de la alfarería en Málaga'; Salinas et al., 'The beginnings of glaze technology in Garb al-Andalus'.

[97] Lévi-Provençal, *Histoire*, 1, pp. 348–56, popularized the concept of the maritime 'republic' of Pechina; this seems to me too romantic an idea, undermined by the evident links of the town with the emirate in Córdoba in the 880s and even during the first *fitna*, which are stressed by the recent thesis book of López Martínez de Marigorta, *Mercaderes, artesanos y ulemas*, pp. 115–55, now the essential starting point. See also Picard, 'Pechina-Almeria aux IXe–Xe siècles'. The idea of the 'republic', anyway, does not fit easily with Pechina's innovative and widely distributed artisanal activity in the period, in particular, which is unlikely to have been the product of a small town autonomous from the rest of al-Andalus; see n. 104 below.

[98] *Muqtabis V*, trans. Viguera and Corriente, pp. 243, 275–6, 341–2; al-ʿUdhrī, *Tarṣīʿ al-akhbār*, trans. Sánchez Martínez, "La cora de *Ilbira*", pp. 30–5, 39, 45–7; for surveys, see Picard, *La mer des califes*, pp. 151–3; López Martínez de Marigorta, *Mercaderes, artesanos y ulemas*, pp. 231–75. A substantial set of medieval geographers' accounts of Almería is collected in Lirola Delgado, *Almería andalusí*.

al-Rushāṭī, who was writing there in 1133.[99] In the *geniza*, Almería was the dominant port mentioned for Egyptian merchants in the eleventh and especially the early twelfth century (in the eleventh, together with Denia); a group of merchant letters from after 1100 shows that it was also a significant port for trade with western North Africa, in particular Tlemcen and the inland city of Fès.[100] An extra source for the city is tombstones, of which there are many for the early twelfth century; among them are half a dozen merchants (*tājir*), including an Alexandrian and a man from Xàtiva, near Valencia, and a possible Syrian.[101] At least the range of types of evidence here goes a long way to counteract its lack of density, for our sources all reinforce each other.

All this, however, brought the most systematic Italian naval attack on al-Andalus in our period. This was the work of the Genoese navy, in concert with the count of Barcelona, and the land army of Alfonso VII of Castile. They took Almería in 1147, and the first two forces then moved on to Tortosa on the Ebro frontier of the county of Barcelona the following year, which they also captured. Tortosa stayed in the hands of the Catalans; but Almería was far too far south to hold on to, and a decade later, in 1157, the Almohads retook it for the Muslims. The Genoese treated these conquests as signs of their power and virtue, and the war was written up with verve by Genoa's chronicler Caffaro, but they were also expensive, and the Tortosa war, in particular, was ruinous for them—they had to sell off to individual Genoese aristocrats all their customs dues to pay the *maximum debitum* they had incurred. In the case of Almería, they only seem to have had to cede half; all the same, the enterprise and its eventual failure did no good to Genoa's wider trade in al-Andalus.[102] We will come back to this later (pp. 460–1).

What remains less clear, however, is what harm this did to Almería's own prosperity in an Andalusī context. The issue is not straightforward. Al-Idrīsī says the

[99] *Crónica del moro Rasis*, ed. Catalán and de Andres, p. 28; Ibn Ḥawqal, *Kitāb ṣūrat al-arḍ*, trans. Kramers and Wiet, 1, pp. 113, 115 (cf. the effectively contemporary chronicle of ʿĪsā ibn al-Rāzī, *Muqtabis VII*, trans. García Gómez, p. 111, who refers to Pechina as the port here in 972); al-Idrīsī, *Nuzhat al-mushtaq*, trans. Jaubert and Nef, pp. 281–3; al-Rushāṭī, *Iqtibās al-anwār*, trans. Lirola Delgado, *Almería andalusí*, p. 49. For all this, see the commentaries in Molina López, 'Economia, propiedad', pp. 283–4; Mazzoli-Guintard, 'Almería, ¿ciudad-mundo en los siglos XI y XII?'.

[100] *Geniza* letters for the eleventh century include T-S 13J16.19, 8J20.2 (Gil K493–4 [S112–13]); for the twelfth, see, e.g., T-S Ar.30.255, NS J197 (Goitein, *Letters*, nn. 48–9), 8J18.3 (Goitein and Friedman, *India book* IV/B, n. 33); for more on Almería, Fès, and the twelfth-century network in general, see pp. 451–6 below.

[101] Ocaña Jiménez, *Repertorio de inscripciones árabes de Almería*, nn. 37 (Alexandria), 51, 59, 63 (Xàtiva), 103, 106 (late twelfth-century), 116. Here, n. 59 is for an al-Sha'mī (not here explicitly a merchant); Syria and Palestine was Shām to the Arabs, as we have seen, but the Arabic spelling of the two words is almost identical. Al-Rushāṭī, *Iqtibās al-anwār*, trans. Lirola Delgado, p. 49, also mentions a merchant from Baghdad.

[102] See *Annali genovesi*, 1, ed. Belgrano, pp. 33–5, plus 79–89, Caffaro's separate account of the war, *Ystoria captionis Almarie et Turtuose*; for the relevant treaties and cessions, see *CDGE*, I, nn. 166–9, 182–3 (half the *introitus* of Almería), 190–1, 193 (the *maximum debitum* for Tortosa), 202–4, 214–16, 243–4 (most of these are re-edited in *LI*, 1, nn. 94–5, 113, 115–17, 122, 125, 2, nn. 294–5, 297, 6, nn. 932–4).

city was ruined after 1147, but he was writing immediately after the Christian conquest, and we cannot extrapolate from that to after 1157. Our written evidence lessens considerably in the later twelfth century; there are fewer tombstones, for example (though one is again for a merchant), and narratives are not good for this part of Spain. Late twelfth- and thirteenth-century geographers, Ibn Ghālib, Yāqūt, and al-Ḥimyarī, write the town up, but in terms which resemble al-Rāzī or al-Idrīsī too much for us to be sure this is contemporary reportage; only al-Shaqundī in the 1230s uses his own phraseology—he still stresses silk-working, and states that the ships which export goods from Almería are by now Christian, though their tolls accrue to the city. Conversely, French and English texts now help us here, for they refer to exported Almería cloth, again usually silk, in the late twelfth century and into the thirteenth; some of this is literary cliché, but Roger of Howden's detailed and near-contemporary account of a voyage around the Iberian peninsula to the Third Crusade in 1190, which twice mentions Almería's silk, is not one such.[103] I stress uncertainty here, to counteract the tendency, among both historians and archaeologists, to assume that Almería never recovered from the ten years of Christian rule. It is, I would argue, quite unlikely that a port with such a good infrastructure should not have recovered fairly fast, just as other sacked cities did, Palermo in 1064 or Mahdia in 1087; and the Genoese certainly intended to benefit from Almería's tolls. And it is striking that Almerían silk recurs later in the scattered texts which we do have; this production, at least, certainly carried on.

The archaeology for Almería is unfortunately as yet less detailed than for some Andalusī cities. Pechina is well studied, particularly its important ninth-century levels, for an artisanal quarter has been found there, including extensive evidence of ceramic-working. The town was the first known producer of glazed pottery in al-Andalus, in fact, in the third quarter of the ninth century, influenced directly by eastern Mediterranean styles, given that its techniques and aesthetic are quite different from early glazes in Ifrīqiya; later, there were workshops for glass and textiles too.[104] Almería itself, however, shows us less. We can certainly track its urban expansion across our period, for the walling of new areas has been analysed. So have some buildings in the centre of the city, including three tanneries, a

[103] Ibn Ghālib, *Farḥat al-anfus*, trans. Vallvé Bermejo, p. 373; Yāqūt, *al-Muʿjam al-buldān*, trans. ʿAbd al-Karīm, 'La España musulmana', p. 284; al-Ḥimyarī, *Kitāb al-rawḍ al-miʿṭār*, trans. Lévi-Provençal, p. 222–3 (following al-Idrīsī quite closely); al-Shaqundī, *Risāla fi faḍl al-Andalus*, trans. García Gómez, pp. 135–7. For the Latin and French texts, see Constable, *Trade and traders*, p. 179, and esp. *Chronica magistri Rogeri de Houedene*, ed. Stubbs, 3, pp. 48, 51.

[104] Acién Almansa et al., 'Excavación de un barrio artesanal'; Castillo Galdeano and Martínez Madrid, 'La vivienda hispanomusulmana'; Castillo Galdeano and Martínez Madrid, 'Producciones cerámicas en Baŷŷāna'; Salinas and Zozaya, 'Pechina'; Salinas, 'Revisando Pechina'; Salinas et al., 'Glaze production at an early Islamic workshop'; López Martínez de Marigorta, *Mercaderes, artesanos y ulemas*, pp. 163–91. Schibille, *Islamic glass in the making*, pp. 189–94, updates our knowledge of the scale of glass production in Pechina; see ibid., pp. 183–222 for an up-to-date survey of Andalusī glass in general, which makes it clear that its detailed production and distribution is not yet fully known.

copper workshop, a probable *fundūq* from the decades around 1100, and several ceramic kilns to the north (one, from *c.*1000, had a good range of glazed types); in the eleventh and twelfth centuries, it was certainly a major pottery-making centre. It was a focus for—among other types—the production of *cuerda seca total* glazed wares (see p. 417 below), which were widely available across twelfth-century Islamic Spain and Portugal, and outside al-Andalus as well. Eleventh-century ceramics have been found in the city from the Kalâa des Béni Hammad in upland Ifrīqiya, and from elsewhere in al-Andalus. So the general picture of a city open to a wide set of maritime and inland interconnections is clearly visible in the archaeology, independently of the written sources. Furthermore, for the post-1157 period, after the Christian parenthesis, the work of Isabel Flores on Almerían high-end lustrewares indicates a dating later in the twelfth century for much of their production; and many of the coins in a hoard found in the city were minted in Muslim-ruled Valencia and Murcia during the decade of Christian occupation. The latest coin in this hoard dates to 1156/7, so it was deposited then or not long after; but continuing links between Almería and other cities are clear here, whether the hoard dates to the final moment of Christian rule or to a slightly later period.[105] This and the Christian cloth references are clear signs that we cannot assume too drastic a weakening of the economy of Almería after *c.*1150. But more work is needed before we can track, as clearly as we could for the other centres we have so far looked at, the ongoing development of the city.

We have an easier time with Denia, the last of this set. Denia was a Roman city, but there is no evidence for its activity again until the tenth century, when al-Rāzī praises its port. One of the first *ṭāi'fa* rulers to declare himself independent, Mujāhid, did so in Denia as early as 1010—he had apparently been close to al-Manṣūr's sons, and this was just after their deaths. But he was no legitimist here; his initial aim seems to have been to take over the whole coast of the Sharq al-Andalus, up to Tortosa and Valencia and down to Almería, although he ended up with just Denia, still a very small town. He responded to this by extending himself seawards, taking Mallorca in 1014–15. From there, immediately afterwards, he did his best to conquer the much larger target of Sardinia in 1015–16, and although the Italian naval cities, Pisa and Genoa, prevented him, he then used his Balearic base to raid Barcelona, Narbonne, and Pisa across the next decade; such

[105] Cara Barrionuevo, 'Ciudades portuarias'; Cara Barrionuevo et al., 'Arqueología urbana e historia de la ciudad'; García Porras, 'La producción de cerámica en Almería'; Ortíz Soler et al., 'Ámbitos ocupacionales'; Cantero Sosa and Egea Gonzáles, 'Aportación al estudio de la producción local'; Muñoz Martín and Flores Escobosa, 'La cerámica medieval en los intercambios comerciales mediterráneos'; Flores Escobosa et al., 'Las producciones de un alfar islámico en Almería'; Flores Escobosa, 'La fabricación de cerámica islámica en Almería: la loza dorada'. For the hoard, see Ferrandis Torres, 'Tesorillo de dinares almorávides'. For imports and exports, see also Azuar Ruiz, *Las taifas del Sharq al-Andalus*, pp. 157–9, 163, 168–72, 194; see also in general Fábregas García, 'Almería en el sistema de comercio'.

raids continued later too, under Mujāhid's son 'Alī (1045–76).[106] As with Almería, early connections with the Christian areas of the Mediterranean were warlike, and wars here continued through the *ṭāʾifa* period. Denia was, in fact, of all the Andalusī cities, the one which resembled Pisa and Genoa most closely, as an initially small but self-propelling city with a restricted hinterland, and a pronounced tendency to attack other cities from the sea, although it would have at once to be said that Pisa and Genoa, although active militarily in the eleventh century, were not yet themselves in any way politically autonomous, and did not become so before Denia itself ceased to be independent, with its conquest by Zaragoza in 1076, or indeed for a generation later.

Mujāhid and 'Alī were also interested in commerce. They owned at least one ship, the *markab Mujāhid* or *Ibn Mujāhid*, which *geniza* letters refer to several times as one of the trading ships Jewish merchants encountered. 'Alī is said to have used this or another vessel at Egyptian request to sell food during the Egyptian famine of 1055 according to Ibn 'Idhārī, who bases himself here on a twelfth-century source. We have seen that rulers could have their own ships elsewhere in the Islamic Mediterranean (p. 196); this is the clearest example for al-Andalus. Denia's Jewish community had their own commercial links with at least Ifrīqiya too.[107] But we would be wrong if we saw Denia's (and Mallorca's) trade as only focussed on Islamic lands, leaving Christian lands to the house of war. Glazed green and manganese bowls from Mallorca and perhaps also Denia are found as decorative elements (*bacini*) in church facades in and around Pisa in the eleventh century. More significantly, both green and manganese and *cuerda seca* glaze, a particular Andalusī speciality, have been found on contemporary and later urban sites in that city, which indicates that Spanish glazed tablewares were not only isolated luxuries there; it is less likely here that the *cuerda seca* was made in Denia, for the kilns there do not show their production, but it is probable that they came to Pisa via Denia or Mallorca. Pisan imports from Spain continued throughout the twelfth century, as we shall see later.[108]

[106] *Crónica del moro Rasis*, ed. Catalán and de Andres, p. 36. For the basic political history of the *ṭāʾifa* of Denia, see among others Azuar Ruiz, *Las taifas del Sharq al-Andalus*, pp. 51–4 and *passim*; Bruce, 'Piracy as statecraft'; Bruce, 'The politics of violence and trade'; and especially Bruce, *La Taifa de Denia*, pp. 59–114, 207–47 for internal Andalusī politics, 145–91 for Denia's maritime projection. I would be more hesitant than is Bruce to call Mujāhid and 'Alī's attacks on Christian lands and ships 'piracy'; they seem like normal sea war to me, as does the parallel activity of the Pisans and Genoese. Bruce tends to restrict the word 'piracy' more to Muslim than to Christian violence.

[107] For the ship, see T-S 12.372, 13J16.19, 8J20.2, 13J19.20 (Gil K513, 493–4, 312 [S111–13, 147]), Bodl. MS Heb. e 98/64 (Gil K273; Goitein, *Letters*, n. 64). For Denia Jews, see T-S 12.570, 13J21.7 (Ashtor, 'Documentos españoles', nn. 8–9), 13J7.11 (with the commentary in Goitein, *MS*, 1, p. 407, n. 45). For the community, cf. Abraham ibn Daud, *The book of tradition*, trans. Cohen, pp. 82–4; Bruce, 'The taifa of Denia and the Jewish networks', pp. 12–15. For 1055, see Ibn 'Idhārī, *al-Bayān*, trans. Maíllo Salgado, p. 191.

[108] For the green and manganese, see n. 218 below. For *cuerda seca* in the city, see Alberti and Giorgio, 'Nuovi dati', pp. 29–30; Gattiglia, *Pisa medievale*, p. 191. For Denia and Pisa in general, see Bruce, 'The politics of violence and trade', and below, pp. 459–62.

This takes us to the archaeology, which has been extensive in this city. Denia started small, as already noted, but it expanded substantially across the eleventh and twelfth centuries, first widening the original settlement behind its castle, situated on a promontary, and then extending south-east along the coast to a walled suburb, El Fortí, and a shipyard area beyond. El Fortí had some very regular planned housing, dating to its foundation around 1100; it was an active area up to the Christian conquest in 1244. Excavations have also identified several *fundūqs*, mostly for the period after 1100; one may have become Genoese-controlled and another Pisan, after treaties in 1149.[109] Denia imported glazed ceramics in the eleventh century and early twelfth from the Kalâa des Béni Hammad in Algeria and Toledo on the Meseta, among other places, but it made its own on a large scale too. There were substantial pottery-making sites outside the older town. One was eleventh-century, and produced green and manganese wares of the type that ended up as *bacini* in Pisa; another, calle Teulada/avenida Montgó, had eleven kilns dating to the period after 1150, making a range of ceramic types from cooking wares to glazed tablewares (by then, largely monochrome green glaze, as tastes had changed). These productions, in fact, dominated the finds in the El Fortí area in that period, with by then few imports from elsewhere. We have very little information as to what Denia otherwise produced by way of artisanal goods—a casual reference to a rich leatherworker in an eleventh-century *fatwā* is a rare example, here with (unspecified) links as far as Toledo—but its ceramic productions must be a sign of substantial activity in other areas as well.[110]

Mediterranean links may have been less tight after 1100, for ships are documented going from Genoa to Denia only a couple of times in the mid-century—Valencia was more important for them. But they had by no means ended. We have a *geniza* letter from *c.*1155 recording the export from Denia to Alexandria of silk, mercury, and tin; Pisan ships intercepted four Denia galleys which had captured a Genoese merchantman in 1160; other Denia galleys captured a Pisan ship off Sardinia in the 1160s (one of its crew was saved by a miracle; one 'Saracen' ship in the subsequent battle was a merchantman); and later, a Genoese boat took Ibn Jubayr in 1185 from Trapani in Sicily back to Cartagena via Denia.[111] Anyway, even if such links loosened, this did not affect the overall prosperity of the town,

[109] See Azuar Ruiz, *Denia islámica*, pp. 25–63; Gisbert Santonja, *La cerámica de Daniya-Dénia*, pp. 23–66; for the *fundūqs*, I have not found a formal publication, but see Gisbert Santonja, 'La ciudad y la cocina', https://lamarinaplaza.com/2014/12/21/el-paraiso-culinario-de-daniya/. For the 1149 treaties, see *CDGE*, 1, n. 196 (= *LI*, 1, n. 118); Amari, *I diplomi arabi*, n. II.1.

[110] Gisbert Santonja et al., *La cerámica de Daniya-Dénia*, pp. 30–100; Gisbert Santonja, *Cerámica califal de Dénia*; Gisbert Santonja, 'Cerámicas del siglo XI'; Azuar Ruiz, *Denia islámica*, pp. 296–7, 332–3; Déléry, *Dynamiques économiques*, pp. 206–7. For the *fatwā*, see al-Wansharīsī, *al-Mi'yār*, trans. Lagardère, *Histoire et société*, 3.279.

[111] *Giovanni Scriba*, nn. 487 (a. 1158), 1096 (a. 1163); *Annali genovesi*, 1, ed. Belgrano, p. 61 (a. 1161); and see n. 109 above for 1149. The city does not appear in later twelfth-century Genoese registers. For the *geniza*, see T-S 10J14.16 (Goitein and Friedman, *India traders*, III, 47); for Pisa, see Maragone, *Annales pisani*, ed. Lupo Gentile, p. 20; cf. also ibid., p. 40, for Denia galleys operating near the

which carried on into the thirteenth century. The protagonism of the *ṭāiʾfa* period in Denia created the city, but the city was not subsequently dependent on that for its success. This is interesting in itself, for Denia does not dominate a particularly rich area in agricultural terms—its hinterland has nothing to match the great *huertas* of Valencia and Murcia to the north and south. But it managed to create a centrality for itself, nonetheless, as a trading and productive focus, which lasted as long as Muslim rule did.

These five cities were all different, as capitals or not, as port cities or not, as foci of rich hinterlands or not, but they had features in common. The main one for us is that whatever their other differences, they were expanding rapidly in size across our period, with steadily larger urbanized areas and steadily more complex artisanal productions. Obviously, this is not the case for Córdoba in the early eleventh century, but by the late twelfth the same developments can be found there too. In the archaeological record, we know most about ceramics, and ceramics are also our only real guide to the scale of urban production; but this is at least backed up by references to, in particular, textile production in the geographers, and a wide range of other trades in *ḥisba* manuals. There is no doubt that in these cities there was far more economic activity, taken as a whole, at the end of our period than was the case at its start, and the various regime changes do not seem to have affected that at all. We have seen a similar growth in economic complexity in most of our regions, with different (usually not as rapid) pacings, but it was by no means an automatic development, and as elsewhere, it needs its own explanations. We will come back to these later. First, however, we need to set these cities more briefly into a wider urban context; then, in the next section, we will look at what we can say about the history of production as a whole, across our period.

* * *

The other cities of al-Andalus, when we can say anything about them, reflect the patterns seen so far quite closely. Far more of them have usable evidence, especially archaeological material, than for any other of our regions except north-central Italy. We, therefore, do not have space to discuss them all in detail, but the highlights of eight of them are worth setting out rapidly. Lisbon, in the far west, was expanding westwards from the Roman and early Islamic settlement in the hill-slope Alfama area below its castle, where its mosque also was, up to the Christian conquest in 1147. In the lower town, the modern Baixa, several kilns have been found from the tenth to early twelfth centuries, largely producing common wares, but including the Gharb al-Andalus's characteristic white-painted pottery; sites in the city, mostly from the same period, also show imports of ceramics which

Italian coast in 1166; for the miracle, see *Vita S. Raynerii*, ed. Zaccagnini, ch. 85; for Ibn Jubayr, see Ibn Jubayr, *Riḥla*, trans. Broadhurst, p. 365.

plausibly came from all the cities discussed above, plus perhaps Toledo.[112] Mértola, just north of the Algarve, located close to the farthest point inland that the river Guadiana is navigable, was a major supply centre for the inland Alentejo towns; it was and is quite small, but it was very active in our period and has some very good archaeological studies. Here, a set of patio houses has been excavated on the edge of the castle hill, new at the end of the eleventh century and continuing to the thirteenth, including leather and silver workshops; the buildings were roughly orthogonal, roughly planned, with latrines in the houses. Farther up the hill, houses have been found from the tenth century onwards, with signs of ironworking. Outside the centre, on the slope down to the river port, there was glass production, and an Almohad-period pottery kiln has been found slightly farther north. Mértola's excavations show both a substantial amount of local pottery (including, surprisingly, lustreware, from the years around 1200), but also plenty of imports, as one would expect in a transit town. We will come back to their patterning later, as Mértola has been so well analysed that it is a major point of reference for the Gharb al-Andalus. For now, however, this was a small town which was growing steadily from the tenth century, with a high point in the twelfth.[113] Saltés, eastwards into Spain, abandoned at the Christian conquest and therefore straightforward to excavate, also had a largely orthogonal plan, and a functioning sewerage system. It is located on an island just outside Huelva, and the two together were briefly the centre of an early eleventh-century *ṭāʾifa*, before nearby Seville absorbed it. Here, there is good evidence of systematic metallurgy, mostly ironworking, from the tenth century onwards (al-Idrīsī mentions it too), although here too the Almohad period is the best documented and marked the town's high point—90 per cent of the ceramics excavated came from that period.[114]

Jaén, east of Córdoba, is another city with clear urban expansion. A suburb appeared outside the older walls in the tenth century; after its destruction in the *fitna*, three others appeared in the eleventh; the Almohads walled them at the end of the twelfth, but there was then more extramural settlement. The city, taken as a whole, was by 1200 three times the size of the ninth-century city.[115] Granada, to the south, is atypical in one crucial respect: the town was moved in the early eleventh century by its Zīrid *ṭāʾifa* kings from the ninth- and tenth-century

[112] For the city of Lisbon as a whole, see Fialho Silva, *Mutação urbana na Lisboa medieval*, a reference I owe to Catarina Tente; see ibid., pp. 251–60 for expansion to the west. For ceramics, see Bugalhão, 'The production and consumption'; Bugalhão et al., 'La production céramique islamique à Lisbonne'; Bugalhão and Gómez Martínez, 'Lisboa'; Filipe et al., 'Cerâmica de importação'.

[113] Macías, *Mértola islâmica*; Gómez Martínez, *Cerámica islámica de Mértola* (pp. 54–63 for excavations, 187–8, 198, 249–58 for lustre). See further pp. 420–4 below.

[114] Bazzana and Bedia García, *Excavaciones en la isla de Saltés* (pp. 199–211 for metalworking, 259–329 for ceramics); cf. al-Idrīsī, *Nuzhat al-mushtaq*, trans. Jaubert and Nef, p. 261.

[115] Castillo Armenteros, 'Los alcázares de Jaén'; Salvatierra Cuenca, *El Alto Guadalquivir*, pp. 124–9, 144, 153–4, 173–82; Salvatierra Cuenca, 'Crecimiento y transformación urbana'; Salvatierra Cuenca, 'Algunas cuestiones'; nuanced by Salvatierra Cuenca and Alcázar Hernández, 'A 12th-century urban project'.

political centre of Ilbīra (now the abandoned, but excavated hill of Cerro del Sombrerete) to Granada itself, a largely Jewish settlement before the Zīrids moved there, as also later, including after a major pogrom there in 1066. In its new location the city thrived; it rapidly spread from the hill-slope Albaicín area down to the plain, where a post-1050 kiln and eleventh-century housing have been found; Granada ceramics from here on dominate the irrigated *vega* to its west. The first major fortification of what became the Alhambra palace on a nearby hill followed in the later eleventh century, although its famous decorated halls are much later, the work of the independent Naṣrid state, after the Christian conquests of the rest of al-Andalus in the thirteenth century. Granada had a complex social structure by the time its inhabitants rejected ʿAbd Allāh in favour of the Almorávids in 1090; the fallen king distinguished between the army, the courier corps, the slaves, and the eunuchs and women among his own staff, each of which had a different reason for deserting him, and the merchants, artisans, and *raʿiyya* (common people) who wanted to avoid a siege and pay lower taxes.[116]

Murcia, an important city, has had less systematic urban excavation, but it is worth adding because of the notable set of kilns that have been excavated here, both in the centre and on the periphery of town, dating from the ninth century to the thirteenth. It was the place of production of some of the earliest glazed wares, from the years around 900, and made green and manganese of a Córdoba type earlier than anywhere else did in the late tenth; under the Almohads, as we shall see, it was the main centre of production of the *esgrafiado* wares which characterized south-eastern al-Andalus so clearly in that period. Murcia expanded into a large extramural suburb, the Arrixaca, and retained a productive centrality throughout the Islamic period.[117] Valencia, up the coast to the north of Denia, expanded as well; it is hard to trace a clear continuity from the Roman period (although the fact that it developed on exactly the same site, with the same central area, is a good sign of that), but from the ninth century into the eleventh the city steadily increased in size, by which time it was the centre of an active *ṭāʾifa*. In the twelfth century, the city pushed farther to the west, outside its Roman wall circuit. But by now Valencia, far from being on the margins of power, as it had been before the *ṭāʾifa* period, was a real regional capital, together with Murcia the

[116] Sarr, *La Granada zirí*; Malpica Cuello, *Granada*; López Martínez de Marigorta, *Mercaderes, artesanos y ulemas*, pp. 285–96; Carvajal López, *La cerámica de Madīnat Ilbīra*, pp. 253–93, 315–38; ʿAbd Allāh b. Buluqqīn, *al-Tibyān*, trans. Tibi, pp. 152–3. For early Jewish settlement, see, e.g., ibid., p. 56; *Crónica del moro Rasis*, ed. Catalán and de Andres, p. 26; Abraham ibn Daud, *The book of tradition*, trans. Cohen, pp. 76, 80–1. For ceramics in the *vega*, Granada's irrigated plain, see Carvajal López et al., "Combinación de análisis petrográfico y químico"; Molera et al., 'Vidriados, colorantes y decoraciones'.

[117] Navarro Palazón, 'Los materiales islámicos'; Navarro Palazón, *La cerámica esgrafiada andalusí de Murcia*; Jiménez Castillo and Pérez Asensio, 'Cerámicas emirales y califales de Murcia'; Molera et al., 'Lead frits'; cf. the early survey in Azuar Ruiz, 'Alfares y testares', pp. 63–4; for the Arrixaca, see Eiroa Rodríguez et al., 'Nuevas investigaciones arqueológicas'.

largest city in the Sharq al-Andalus, and agriculturally rich from the products of its *horta*; it produced a range of fine-ware pottery after 1000 at the latest; its coinage was important too, as we shall see.[118] Under Ibn Mardanīsh, its ruler in the 1150s–1160s, it developed links with Genoa and other Christian powers, and at the latest this was when it began to build itself up as a new focus of Andalusī eastward trade (see pp. 460–1 below). It was well placed to become one of the two principal cities of the expanded kingdom of Aragón, second only to Barcelona, after its conquest in 1238.

The smallest town of this set, indeed hardly more than a large village, is, nonetheless, finally, worth a paragraph of its own. This is Siyāsa, some 40 kilometres upriver from Murcia, dominating an irrigated valley bottom area below it, called by its Arabic name by archaeologists because it lies on the other side of the steep river valley from its Christian-period successor and namesake Cieza. The earliest surviving houses seem to have eleventh-century origins, to judge by the pottery found in one rubbish tip, but the settlement expanded rapidly in the twelfth century, and in the years around 1200 and into the early thirteenth it might have reached up to 800 houses, possibly up to 5,000 total inhabitants. The town was then moved to Cieza, so it counts as a not-failing site which can, nonetheless, be analysed in depth; nineteen houses from the early thirteenth century were excavated in the 1980s–2000s, marking—as the excavators say with justifiable pride—the best domestic assemblage from the period anywhere in the Islamic west. Siyāsa is worth noticing here simply because of its wealth. It had plenty of Murcian pottery, and seems to have had its own local glass production. Its houses were complex in spatial planning—many stood on hill slopes—but the patio layout which is regularly seen in towns was standard, so were latrines (they had mats of esparto grass associated with them), and kitchens and separate washrooms could be studied in detail. Even small, probably comparatively poor, houses were well built. And above all, because the walls of houses often stand, still today, up to 2 metres in height, it was possible to analyse second storeys, with galleries around the patios. Here, amazingly, enough plasterwork survived to allow whole sets of highly decorated windows and doorways to be reconstructed, including those of some of the smaller houses. This is the sort of decoration which one tends to admire in Islamic palaces, but here made for a tiny town on a not so very much smaller scale. Finally, several inscriptions were found in the settlement, stressing *al-yumn wa al-iqbāl* (happiness and prosperity), a slogan associated with (among many others) Ibn Mardanīsh, the local ruler in the mid-twelfth century.[119] This

[118] Martí and Pascual, 'El desarrollo urbano de Madīna Balansiya'; Pascual et al., 'València'; Soriano Sánchez and Pascual Pacheco, 'Aproximación al urbanismo de la Valencia medieval'; Soriano Sánchez and Pascual Pacheco, 'La evolución urbana de Valencia'. For ceramics, see Lerma, *La cerámica islámica*, 2. For coinage, see n. 184 below.

[119] Navarro Palazón and Jiménez Castillo, *Siyāsa*; Eiroa Rodríguez, 'Representations of power'. For the glass, see Navarro Palazón, 'Murcia como centro productor de loza dorada', p. 143. The Museo de

settlement is very late for us, but it makes one obvious point: if this is the sort of comfortable and, indeed, ambitious existence which characterized a settlement in broken hills above a narrow valley, either a large village or a very small town, in al-Andalus around the end of our period, what can it have been like in richer areas, or in major cities? Nothing like it still stands anywhere else in the Mediterranean, except in the most active cities in northern Italy—for we are by 1200 coming into the take-off period for the Italian north—but again, this is a smallish site in difficult countryside. Siyāsa is, that is to say, a marker for the prosperity of al-Andalus at all levels. It must stay at the back of the mind of the reader in what follows.

* * *

Historians and archaeologists sometimes write about 'the Islamic city' in al-Andalus. I do not believe there was any such thing. These were urban centres like the other urban centres in the Mediterranean which we have looked at and will look at. Their market (*sūq*) area was often around the central mosque, with a castle beside or above the town, but Christian towns were much the same, with the main church substituted for a mosque, in northern Spain, Italy, Byzantium, and indeed elsewhere. There is no special spatial configuration which marks them out—we have seen several square-planned urban sectors already; and anyone who thinks that narrow curving streets and surprising cul-de-sacs are somehow 'Islamic' has evidently not been to Venice. Many of them were centres for tax collection, but that was true for Byzantine towns as well, which, however, were not always as materially impressive or active artisanally as some Andalusī towns visibly were; being a fiscal centre helped prosperity, but it had to be leveraged into a wider productive capacity for it really to make a centre rich. As elsewhere, some of them were very large, others less so—there was a normal urban hierarchy. Only in the caliphal period was there one city, Córdoba, as super-dominant here as Palermo, Kairouan, Constantinople, and Fusṭāṭ-Cairo were for their respective polities and regions. But Seville was larger than other cities later, with Almería, a reduced Córdoba, and perhaps Murcia (plus Toledo and Zaragoza, not discussed here) on the next rung, Valencia rising onto it, and Málaga and Granada not far behind—and then steadily downwards, past Jaén, Denia, Lisbon, and plenty of other towns we have not looked at, to, at the lowest urban level, Mértola and Siyāsa. Nowhere in al-Andalus was without one or more significant urban centres, except the remote south-eastern Meseta; this was a society and economy dominated by towns, as was most of the rest of the Mediterranean, Muslim and Christian. This, as elsewhere, had important implications for the maintenance of a minimum of urban–rural exchange relations in every period.

Siyâsa in Cieza contains the window and doorway reconstructions, which are a marvellous experience to see.

But some things do mark out Andalusī cities as different. We can see this all the more clearly because the evidence is particularly good for this region. They were almost all expanding in size, very considerably, across our whole period, with no serious breaks. No generalized economic crisis can be identified at times of political difficulty, such as the years of the second *fitna* and the fall of the caliphate, or the years in the later eleventh century when the *ṭāi'fa* kingdoms paid heavy tributes to the Christian kings. It is worth adding that in the twelfth century, when the towns were reaching their height, we begin to get more—even if sporadic—references to wheat being imported into al-Andalus. This, as we have seen (p. 182), cannot mean a general dependence of the region on grain from elsewhere, but it may in this instance show that some towns were expanding beyond the capacity of their hinterlands to supply them, at least in bad years, as was the case for many capitals, or, at a level closer to these Andalusī towns, twelfth-century Genoa.[120] A high percentage of cities had extensive pottery production; Córdoba may be exceptional, but, to repeat, its largest known set of kilns dates to before the years of its huge expansion, and over all, Andalusī towns have revealed far more kilns than has any other region of the Mediterranean.[121] This is a marker, as we will find in the next section, of less centralized productive hierarchies here than elsewhere, but it is also a marker for the considerable productive activity of each town in other sectors as well. And there is good reason—if we generalize from Siyāsa in particular, but not only—to conclude that these cities were, as a group, unusually rich in material terms. These observations, however, provoke other questions; I will come back to them at the end of the next section of the chapter.

5.4 Andalusī Production and Exchange in the Archaeology and Written Sources

As with the cities of al-Andalus, we have by now a very substantial data set for the basic patterns of Andalusī production and exchange, but it does not have a recent overall synthesis. The important survey by Remie Constable dates back to 1994; that was before most of our archaeological excavations, however, and, in fact, she did not use more than a part of what material evidence then existed.[122] Other discussions are sketchy and incomplete. So although, as elsewhere in this book, the detail of what follows is certainly known to specialists, the patterns I want to

[120] See Constable, *Trade and traders*, pp. 9, 48–50, 83, for cautious but not quite consistent discussions of the impact of tribute (*paría*) payments; see ibid., 142, 162–4, for wheat from the Maghreb (and a few exports of Andalusī wheat too), to which we need to add al-Wansharīsī, *al-Mi'yār*, trans. Lagardère, *Histoire et société*, 5.273, for the mid-eleventh century. For Genoa, see pp. 536–7 below.

[121] For comparative comments, see Gutiérrez Lloret, 'La mirada del otro', citing at p. 586 the illuminating kiln map in Coll Conesa and García Porras, 'Tipología, cronología y producción', itself now more than a decade out of date.

[122] Constable, *Trade and traders*.

set out have not all been generalized about before. Constable used as a major guiding structure the *geniza* and then the Genoese records, which I have been happy to do as well in earlier chapters; but as we shall see, these are rather less important as sources for al-Andalus than they are for the central and south-eastern Mediterranean. The *geniza* is here above all useful for understanding some of the international trading patterns in cloth (especially, here, silk), which will be discussed in the last section of this chapter. But in al-Andalus as elsewhere, it is ceramics which can tell us much more about bulk trade, and, in fact, the complexity of what they can tell us about exchange in this region is quite striking. I shall begin with them, and then move on to cloth and metals, and finally money, in their internal (including coastal) distribution, although, in this region in particular, most of these do not tell us so much on their own as ceramics do.

5.4.1 Ceramics

I remarked earlier that the internal communications of Islamic Spain and Portugal were not so very easy. Al-Andalus was really a network of subregions; each of these was potentially self-sufficient, and that they should be closely linked is not automatic. Its history is, in fact, the history of the *creation* of a single economic region: first, very top-down, by the caliphate, united somewhat superficially under a strong central government, and then, starting with the *ṭāi'fa* kingdoms, through the development of sufficiently active and coherent subregional economies that they could grow together across the twelfth century, reaching another moment of relative economic and material-cultural unification, this time more bottom-up, under the Almohads. The history of ceramics allows us to tell this story with some density of detail; so I shall start out by setting out such a narrative.[123]

Andalusī ceramic typologies of forms were first set out scientifically by Guillermo Rosselló in 1978, in a tour de force of analysis; even though he based this on a geographically marginal area, Mallorca, and made no claims for generality (indeed, in later work, he denied it), it has remained as the basic patterning for ceramic work. Nothing has replaced it, and only minor modifications tend to be made to it. Less ambitious ceramic reports simply go through his forms one by one, *ollas* (large cooking pots), *cazuelas* (casseroles), *jarros* (one-handled liquid containers), *jarras* (two-handled containers), *tinajas* (the same, with a wide mouth), *jarritas* (jugs), *ataifores* (bowls), *candiles* (oil lamps), *arcaduces* (pots for *noria* waterwheels), and so on.[124] Many of these are not only recognizable now,

[123] I am for this entire section greatly indebted to the detailed guidance of Elena Salinas. I am also very grateful for the help given to me by Rafael Azuar, Rebecca Bridgman, Alberto García Porras, Sophie Gilotte, Sonia Gutiérrez, Catherine Richarté, and Catarina Tente.

[124] Rosselló Bordoy. *Ensayo de sistematización*. Gómez Martínez, *Cerámica islámica de Mértola*, for example, makes few changes in her model analysis, except for renaming *jarras* as *cántaros*; but

but were recognized as distinct in our period; two eleventh-century formulary books have a formula for the advance sale of different ceramic types, which are listed, and they fit the ones in Rosselló's typology in large part, as he made explicit—indeed, thanks to the influence of Arabic on Spanish, many (*jarra*, *qandīl*, [*al-*]*qādūs*) have the same names today.[125] In diachronic studies, we are offered genealogies of these forms, as they slowly changed over time. And they did change, with new types coming in as well; by 800, for example, we find *tannūr*s (portable ovens, often for bread; the Arabic word is related to 'tandoori') coming in from North Africa, as part of a steady shift from forms similar to those of the later Roman Empire to forms with parallels across the Islamic world.[126] This process is called 'Islamicization' in much of the literature; I resist that usage, as it seems to me, as to others, that the shift has no religious content. But it certainly did represent a trend towards the (at least partial) homogenization of Andalusī material culture with that of North Africa and the Islamic lands to the east.

This formal typology, plus studies of decoration, has not been matched so quickly by the development of more science-based techniques of analysis. Fabric analysis is often carried out, but it is usually done by eye; petrological work, which allows one to propose clearer provenances, is not so very common, even now. Given the remarkable number of kilns found in al-Andalus, one of the subtexts of much analysis seems to be that most ceramics, unless belonging to a set of well-known fine-ware types, can be assumed to be local. This was by no means always the case, but it is hard to be sure of the contrary in the absence of focussed study. Conversely, the glazed fine-ware types, which are much studied, are recognized as often being part of quite elaborate exchange networks.[127] Among the fine wares, I have already mentioned green and manganese (see Fig. 15); this was followed after the tenth century by other colour sets, often preferring *melado* (honey-coloured; I shall simply write 'honey') to green or white. Green, honey, white, and black or dark purple (*morado*) were the basic colour scheme of most Andalusī

I recommend this book to the non-expert reader as the publication which best explains all the ceramic forms, their decorations, and their functions. Gutiérrez Lloret, *La cora de Tudmīr*, the other fundamental guide, has a more elaborate typology, to reflect the important differences in productive processes between handmade, wheel-made, and glazed wares, but she relates it to Rosselló's types. Retuerce Velasco, *La cerámica andalusí de la Meseta*, has a typology which is for me too complex to be usable.

[125] The formulae are edited, translated, and commented on in Aguirre Sádaba, 'Notas acerca de la proyección de los "kutub al-waṯā'iq"'. These texts, plus a few similar later ones, are unique; I have not seen a more detailed textual characterization of ceramic types than this anywhere else in the late antique or medieval Mediterranean, up to 1200 at least.

[126] For *tannūr*s, see, e.g., Gutiérrez Lloret, *La cora de Tudmīr*, pp. 85–7, 140–5. One has now been found in Shaqunda, so dating to before 818: Casal et al., 'Aproximación al estudio de la cerámica emiral del arrabal de *Šaqunda*', p. 197.

[127] We will see later some good examples of petrological work now being done; but a significant step forward is the 2018 publication, edited by Grassi and Quirós Castillo, *Arqueometría de los materiales cerámicos de época medieval en España*. Note that glaze was also often used on the interior surfaces of cooking wares, to keep them watertight, as later in Messina; see, e.g., Gómez Martínez, *Cerámica islámica de Mértola*, p. 85.

glazed fine wares. From the late tenth century, and especially the eleventh onwards, the patches of these colours were sometimes separated out by thin unglazed lines, possibly to stop the colours from running into each other: this was *cuerda seca*, either partial (*parcial*), not covering the whole pot (the earliest type to appear), or *total* (see Fig. 16).[128] The other decorative type which is worth signalling at the start is *esgrafiado* (see Fig. 17). This had no relationship at all to the sgraffi(a)to wares of the eastern Mediterranean, for it was not normally glazed; it involved incising lines or sculpturing patterns, often in ambitiously elaborate ways, on pottery blackened with manganese oxide, on *jarras* and smaller *jarritas* (pitchers), plus other forms as well. *Esgrafiado* was a ceramic type which appeared after 1150, particularly in Murcia and the rest of south-east Spain, where it was prominent in some of our latest Islamic assemblages, as, for example, at Siyāsa.[129] This range of fine wares sometimes shows decorative overlaps with other regions of the Mediterranean, but, taken as a whole, it presents quite a distinct aesthetic from that elsewhere. It is not hard to distinguish Spanish pottery from that from regions farther east, in sites like Pisa which have varied collections of imports, even if one would need to remember that, in the twelfth century, developing Moroccan fine wares increasingly followed Andalusī typologies as well.

In what follows, I have often been quite schematic, as I stress some particular kinds of pottery at the expense of a wide range of others, and as I also try to avoid getting into the intense but often as yet unresolved debates as to the actual provenance of particular types; I have done my best to restrict myself to relative certainties. A ten-page survey can do no more than that, but the works

Fig. 16 *Cuerda seca*

[128] The essential work on *cuerda seca*, which includes petrological work, is the unpublished thesis of Claire Déléry, *Dynamiques économiques*; one useful published spin-off is Déléry et al., 'Contribution à l'étude de l'évolution technologique et du commerce des céramiques de *cuerda seca*'.

[129] See the survey in Crespo Pascual, 'Cerámica esgrafiada'; earlier, Navarro Palazón, *La cerámica esgrafiada andalusí de Murcia*.

Fig. 17 *Cerámica esgrafiada*

footnoted will make the issues clearer. Much of the detail presented here will be out of date in a decade; all the same, I think that most of the basic patterns and trends will remain valid for longer.

In the eighth and ninth centuries, Iberian ceramic productions were all very local indeed. In some areas, they were also very simple, with handmade pottery important, probably often indicating levels of demand which were too low for specialist potters to be supported; this was not universal by any means, but we can find no evidence at all of patterns of exchange between the different parts of al-Andalus (and still less the northern Christian fringe, as it then was, of Spain). Overall, these were simpler patterns than anywhere else in the Mediterranean in the same period—only southern France and Croatia offer parallels—and, as I have argued in earlier work, must indicate a weakness in elite wealth and buying power in at least some parts of the Iberian peninsula which was rather greater than elsewhere. This was reversed by our period, when good-quality wheel-turned wares were close to universal, and handmades themselves became a specialized pottery type, restricted to certain forms of cooking wares. But local productions were still dominant in 950 in al-Andalus; that is our starting point, and it is a more geographically limited one than we have seen in any other region so far.[130]

The first glazed wares appear in Córdoba and Pechina in the late ninth century, and Málaga shortly after. As noted earlier, the idea for them must have come directly from the eastern Mediterranean; but interestingly, the glaze techniques

[130] Wickham, *Framing*, pp. 743–6, 752–8. For the patterns of local development from the eighth to the tenth centuries, Gutiérrez Lloret, *La cora de Tudmīr*, is a classic study; see also Pérez Alvarado, *Las cerámicas omeyas*, for Jaén.

adopted here were largely autonomous, developing out of earlier glass production, probably in Córdoba.[131] With the caliphate, this developed further; we find Córdoba green and manganese glazed wares in small quantities on very many sites across al-Andalus. It is likely that the capital had a monopoly on the production of this ware for most of the caliphal period. With the second *fitna*, production of it suddenly appears in more than a dozen Andalusī cities; it is quite possible that some of them had already started production in the last years of the tenth century (in Murcia, in particular), but not, as it appears, earlier.[132] Anyway, in the tenth century the pattern of ceramic finds across the Islamic parts of the peninsula tends to be one of local common wares made with steadily more skilled productive techniques, with a thin veneer of Córdoban imports as well.[133] The pattern has some similarities to that of eighth- and ninth-century Byzantium (see pp. 304–6 above), and seems to have had a similar meaning: the fiscal unity of the state allowed a certain level of exchange with the capital to reach nearly all the provinces of the Umayyad Caliphate, probably partly in return for supplying the capital, but this was essentially an overlay onto much more localized productive systems which had their own dynamic. The only fine ware which seems to have been independent of this caliphal focus is *cuerda seca parcial*, which began in the second half of the tenth century and can be found widely across the caliphate, even if never in large quantities. Its principal production centres were coastal, particularly Pechina/Almería and Murcia, but production foci for it steadily spread out to include by the end of the caliphate centres as far apart as Lisbon and Zaragoza—plus, among others, Córdoba itself, although it was not actually very common there yet, and the version of it there is different from that of the coastal towns.[134]

In a sense, a local dynamic continued under the *ṭāʾifa*s too; but the patterns of production look very different indeed now. Every major centre, and many minor ones, developed its own glazed wares, both green and manganese (and its

[131] For Pechina and early glass production, see n. 104 above; for glass and glaze, see Salinas et al., 'From glass to glaze in al-Andalus'; see further Salinas and Pradell, 'The introduction of the glaze in al-Andalus'; Salinas, 'Ceramica vidriada de época emiral en Córdoba'; Íñiguez Sánchez and Mayorga Mayorga, 'Un alfar emiral en Málaga'. For the quite wide distribution of these early glazed wares along the coasts, see also Déléry, *Dynamiques économiques*, pp. 775–83; Salinas, 'Revisando Pechina'; Salinas et al., 'The beginnings of glaze technology in Garb al-Andalus'.

[132] For Córdoba, see Cano Piedra, *La cerámica verde manganeso de Madīnat al-Zahrā*; Fuertes Santos, *La cerámica califal del yacimiento de Cercadilla*, esp. pp. 168–83; see further n. 87 above. For Murcia, see Navarro Palazón, 'Los materiales islámicos', Jiménez Castillo and Pérez Asensio, 'Cerámicas emirales y califales de Murcia'. For some other eleventh-century productions, see Espinar Cappa et al., 'La producción de cerámica verde y manganeso en Málaga'; Bazzana, 'La céramique verde e morado califale à Valence'; Gisbert Santonja, *Cerámica califal de Dénia*, pp. 5–32; Valor Piechotta and Lafuente Ibáñez, 'La Sevilla 'abbādí', pp. 209–11.

[133] For an example of the wide but thin veneer of imports into Portugal, see Gómez et al., 'El verde y morado', pp. 22–4.

[134] Déléry, *Dynamiques économiques*, pp. 81–103, 784–839. For its relative absence in Córdoba, see ibid., pp. 100–3, 792–7, and Fuertes Santos, *La cerámica califal del yacimiento de Cercadilla*, pp. 181–2.

honey-coloured successors) and increasingly, particularly in the northern *ṭāʾifas*, *cuerda seca*, even if for the most part using quite similar forms. We could suppose that one of the results of the *fitna* and the rapid contraction of Córdoba was a diaspora of ceramic experts from the capital to supply new capitals, with their own smaller-scale fiscal centrality, focussed on new courts and new sets of elites around each *ṭāʾifa* king. But the result now made al-Andalus quite different from Byzantium. There, Constantinople's fine wares became more and more common across at least the Aegean from 950 or so onwards, and were eventually, by 1100, matched by provincial productions at Corinth and Chalkis which had as wide a distribution as did Constantinopolitan White wares. Here, the 'provincial' productions developed much more quickly, but they did not have as wide a range. We have already seen the example of Denia in this context, with its early western Mediterranean exchange relationships; it is, however, significant that these were rather more extensive than the inland spread of its eleventh-century fine wares, which are distinct from those found around Valencia and Murcia, respectively 80 and 140 kilometres away.[135]

Seville is another example of this. In the eleventh century, it was making green and manganese bowls with a honey glaze on the back, plus *cuerda seca*, both *parcial* and (by 1100) *total*, in a complex set of tablewares which extended beyond glaze to painted jugs with careful patterned decorations. This was in addition to what was everywhere the largest percentage of ceramic products, common and cooking wares, here in a wide range of good-quality types. In Seville, at the top end there was also lustreware production, the first known in Spain as we have seen, with inscriptions naming two of the three *ṭāʾifa* kings of Seville, al-Muʿtaḍid and al-Mutʿamid (1042–69, 1069–91); as with tenth-century Córdoba green and manganese bowls, this was a sign of power.[136] Seville was making plenty of ceramics in the eleventh century, then, which shows a substantial local market. But as yet these do not seem to have been widely exported. Some *cuerda seca* oil lamps, possibly from Seville, reached Portuguese sites, and some of the Seville lustre has been found there too, at Silves and Mértola in the south (both part of Seville's territory by the end of the *ṭāʾifa* period), and even in Coimbra, just after its Christian conquest in 1064, in the centre of modern Portugal. Seville pottery reached centres in the lower Guadalquivir too. But thanks in particular to the work recently done on a range of southern Portuguese sites, it seems clear that Seville was not producing most of the fine wares even of its own *ṭāʾifa* kingdom; there were many other centres producing good-quality ceramics too.[137]

[135] Gisbert Santonja, *Cerámica califal de Dénia*, p. 24. For the lack of range of each regional production of *cuerda seca* in the eleventh century, see Déléry, *Dynamiques économiques*, pp. 200–1, 862–3, 866–75.

[136] Valor Piechotta and Lafuente Ibáñez, 'La Sevilla 'abbādī', pp. 204–20; Barceló and Heidenreich, 'Lusterware', pp. 253–4, 258–72.

[137] See Gómez Martínez et al., 'A cidade e o seu território', pp. 39–40; Gómez Martínez, 'La cultura material del Garb al-Andalus', esp. pp. 165–6, 171–6, for the scarce information about imports to

In the twelfth century, these patterns continued, but some exchange relationships were by now wider (see Map 18). Although the origins of ceramics found on particular sites often remains uncertain, glazed wares resembling those known to have been produced in Málaga, Almería, and Murcia in particular (but also other centres) begin to appear in less and less obvious places. The best way to illustrate the way that local production patterns were slowly opening out is to look at some specific areas. So let us see how these patterns developed in the Gharb al-Andalus, in particular in Portugal; and then in the Guadalquivir valley and the south-east.

The Gharb, the west of al-Andalus, has been particularly well studied, and can serve to an extent as a model, even if it was a relatively conservative part of Islamic Spain and Portugal, and slightly less active economically (there are fewer coin finds here, for example). From the emiral period onwards, it had its own white-painted semi-fine wares, which marked the region out and are hardly found elsewhere; these were for long more common than glazed wares, and were still being made in the late twelfth century. It had particular *olla* types as well, which were not homogeneous even across the west. Broadly, in fact, the Gharb can be divided into two zones, reflecting the geographical subregions discussed earlier (p. 370), with the Tejo valley and the Alentejo distinct from the Algarve to the south, which had closer links to Seville and beyond. Along the Tejo/Tajo, three cities, Lisbon, Santarem, and Badajoz (the *ṭāi'fa* capital of the northern zone), had significant sets of kilns from at least the eleventh century. These produced, among fine wares, a distinctive type of *cuerda seca total* glaze, with a dark background; this aesthetic choice linked them to Toledo on the Meseta rather than to anywhere farther south, and it was not widely exported. But green (or honey) and manganese glazes linked the whole of the west to the central areas of the former caliphate throughout the eleventh century; these were largely locally produced, but had similar styles everywhere. The eleventh century showed greater diversity than the tenth; local economic complexity was certainly growing, and demand for professionally made ceramics was quite generalized. There was by now a hierarchy of productions, active mostly in towns (to the Tejo towns we must add Mértola in the south, plus Vilamoura on the Algarve coast, close to Faro, the centre of a short-lived *ṭāi'fa* kingdom, and doubtless others), each linked to a wider local environment; the northern group and the southern group were separate but had

southern Portugal in the eleventh century; she is also in the latter article very cautious about an ascription to Seville of the oil lamps, but it seems more plausible than other alternatives. Imports from elsewhere did arrive in the Algarve, all the same, as with a south-east Spanish version of green and manganese from the late eleventh or early twelfth century found across the western Mediterranean, including a substantial group at Silves; see Gonçalves, 'Objectos de troca no Mediterrâneo Antigo'; Gonçalves, 'Evidências do comércio'; she excludes that they could be locally made, but the issue of their origin has been disputed elsewhere, in Gómez Martínez, *Cerámica islámica de Mértola*, pp. 288–9; Azuar, 'Cerámicas en "verde y manganeso"', pp. 70–4; Azuar, *Las taifas del Sharq al-Andalus*, pp. 169–72; Gisbert Santonja, 'Cerámicas del siglo XI'. For Coimbra, see Barceló and Heidenreich, 'Lusterware', p. 272; the sherd found there contains part of an inscription of al-Mut'amid, who began to rule in 1069, although Coimbra had already been taken by the Christians.

exchange relationships too. And all were also linked to other parts of al-Andalus, probably often via the river port at Mértola, which was on the edge of both zones, as well as having good connections south-eastwards down the coast.[138]

In the twelfth century, the local productive hierarchy persisted in the Gharb, but these connections just described grew—not so much north of the Tejo, at least after Christian conquests took Santarem and Lisbon in 1147, but from there southwards. *Cuerda seca* glazed wares were by now numerous and, indeed, dominant among fine wares (green and manganese was declining in popularity), and many of them came in from outside, above all from Almería, plus, later, Seville and the other Mediterranean coastal cities. So did lustreware, from some of the same towns (although Mértola made it too). By the Almohad period in the second half of the century, productions, even for some cooking wares, were much more homogeneous across the Gharb as a whole, and indeed elsewhere in the new caliphate; so, for example, wares with stamped or moulded decorations, both glazed and not, spread rapidly across every sector of al-Andalus. The only major external ceramic type which was rarer in the west was Murcian *esgrafiado*. Mértola was far from being the largest town in the Gharb, but, apart from its importance as a route centre, it is a key site owing to the quality of its ceramic publications by Susana Gómez, which are also, as is less common, based on petrological analyses. Here in particular we can see the interplay between local productions—Mértola made the whole range, as can be seen from fabric analysis, except probably *cuerda seca*, although only a kiln for white-painted and common wares has been found—and imports from the Spanish coastal cities. The key point here must be that centres in the Gharb al-Andalus produced most ceramic types across the twelfth century, at a good level of quality, and they were available in urban and rural sites alike (although with a smaller range in rural sites, as we shall see), so towns produced enough for buyers in the countryside as well; but the west was all the same very open to imports from elsewhere in al-Andalus, particularly, but not only, of *cuerda seca*. Local and extra-local productions were balanced in what Gómez calls 'a dynamic and flexible market'.[139]

The work on the Gharb takes for granted that it was not at the vanguard of Andalusī production, probably rightly. No known ceramic types were exported from there to other parts of Islamic Spain, although, of course, the west must have exported commodities of some kind in exchange for its imports. When we get to what are seen as more central areas of al-Andalus, our evidence is unfortunately less fully synthesized; but we have some good indicators all the same. One

[138] For all this, see Fernandes et al., 'O comércio da corda seca'; Gómez Martínez et al., 'A cidade e o seu território'; Gómez Martínez, 'La cultura material del Garb al-Andalus'; Gómez Martínez et al., 'El verde y morado'; Gómez Martínez and Santos, 'Évora y Mértola'; Catarino et al., 'La céramique islamique'. For the scarcity of coin finds, see n. 183 below.

[139] See the articles in n. 138 above, plus Gómez Martínez, *Cerámica islámica de Mértola* (quotation at p. 294); Gómez Martínez, 'New perspectives'; and also for *cuerda seca* imports, see n. 143 below.

example of what can be done is Rebecca Bridgman's petrological work on the kilns of La Cartuja in Seville, dating to the Almohad period (here 1148–1248) and on some other towns in or near the Guadalquivir valley, plus again Mértola. She could show that Seville fabrics, in both fine and common wares, could be identified in Mértola, and particularly in Écija, a medium-sized town halfway between Seville and Córdoba. Conversely, out of the Seville pottery she studied, even though the city was producing large amounts of pottery—among the fine wares, *cuerda seca*, honey glaze, and stamped wares—and was in general self-sufficient in ceramic terms, up to 13 per cent of the identifiable wares were imports, including semi-fine glazed and stamped *tinajas* for water storage and small numbers of *esgrafiado*, but also some common-ware kitchen pots.[140] In Córdoba, by contrast, which was an active city again by now but was more inland, Elena Salinas's work on the same period, also using petrological analysis, argues for relatively few imports, fewer than in much of the Gharb al-Andalus—no more than, again, limited sets of *esgrafiado* jugs. Bridgman stresses that the great bulk of Seville's ceramics was produced and consumed locally too; the city was not in this respect a manufacturing centre specifically aimed at wider exchange. This, doubtless, remained true in most places in every period. All the same, it seems that Seville, given both its exports and imports, was more open to the regionwide, sea- and river-based, exchange network than was Córdoba; and it was also more interconnected than it had been a century earlier, in the *ṭāʾifa* period, when, as we have seen, its large-scale productions began.[141]

In the twelfth century, then, we can begin to speak of a complex exchange network which, although it remained less large-scale than the main structures of production and consumption, which remained above all local or subregional, was by now connecting all—or nearly all—parts of al-Andalus. This network was often bringing ceramics to places which made their own similar types, which shows the existence of buyers who were discriminating on the basis of price, quality, nuances in taste, or all three; it was also creating a set of interconnections which made ceramics across the whole region more and more similar in forms and technical qualities. A significant sign of this, just after the end of our period, is the case of Calatrava la Vieja in the generally unurbanized far south of the Meseta, which was taken from Castile by the Almohads in 1195 and held until the

[140] Bridgman, *Potting histories*, esp. pp. 177–8, 188–220, with 279–80 for the likelihood of some imported transport containers. This is her thesis, which I am indebted to her for letting me see; her published articles are Bridgman, 'Potting histories'; Bridgman, 'Re-examining Almohad economics'; Bridgman, 'Contextualising pottery production and distribution'. Cf. for elsewhere in the city Lafuente Ibáñez, 'La cerámica almohade en Sevilla'; Vera Reina and López Torres, *La cerámica medieval sevillana*.

[141] See Salinas Pleguezuelo, *La ceramica islámica*, esp. pp. 551–3, 703–53. For Seville, Bridgman stresses local production and consumption in her urban site analyses, *Potting histories*, pp. 222–99; cf. 301–6, even on the prestige Alcázar site (244–54, 288), which was, however, the one out of her four sample sites where imports were over 10%.

disastrous defeat of the latter in 1212 at Las Navas de Tolosa; in that brief window, Calatrava flowered as a centre for fine-ware ceramic production, largely a revived green and manganese, but also including lustreware.[142] That is to say, the Andalusī economic network was strong enough to create rapidly, doubtless for political reasons, a frontier productive centre in the most unpromising of landscapes.

In this general context of linked productions, as already noted, there is little doubt that the main twelfth-century export towns for fine-ware ceramics included, in particular, Málaga, Almería, and Murcia. Exactly which city produced the wares that have been found in other locations—largely, by now, *cuerda seca*, stamped wares, and *esgrafiado*, with some lustre—is not yet easy to say, and will need much more work. Almería is likely to have been a major centre for *cuerda seca* and lustre production and distribution, including into the Gharb, as we have seen, at least up to 1147 and probably later, although fabric analysis cannot demonstrate this for certain as yet, for its geology is quite like that of Málaga. After that, Málaga and Denia perhaps picked some of the production up, with Murcia continuing across both halves of the century.[143]

Here, Murcia may be a useful model for the sort of patterns we can suppose for the others too, because it was the main focus of the production of *esgrafiado* pottery after 1150. As Rafael Azuar has made clear, it was not the only producer in its rough orbit; Lorca, some 50 kilometres to the south-west, and Elche, the same distance to the north-east, did so too. Elche produced almost only for its local area. Murcia did so too, including Siyāsa, as we have seen, but also had a wide spread of export by sea, bypassing Elche but reaching Denia and Valencia, as well as major centres well to the west. Lorca was another localized centre, but it was closely linked to Murcia down a river valley, and from there was taken on the Murcian routes, doubtless together with Murcian ceramics. Outside the modern provinces of Murcia and Alicante, however, find-spots of *esgrafiado* wares tend to be restricted to urban centres; if this ceramic type was produced outside the Murcian area, which is certain for Denia and Palma de Mallorca, it must have had much more localized distributions.[144] So *esgrafiado* did not connect the whole of

[142] Retuerce Velasco et al., 'La cerámica islámica de Calatrava la Vieja'; Retuerce Velasco and de Juan García, 'La ceramica almohade' (with a petrological analysis which confirms local production); cf. Melero Serrano et al., 'La ceramica del siglo XIII', for production continuing after 1212—the quality of the Christian-period ceramics was, however, lower.

[143] For *cuerda seca*, see in general Déléry, *Dynamiques économiques*, pp. 903–1058; for the geological issue, see ibid., p. 532, although she and others are sure that the Almorávid finds in Mértola came from Almería (ibid., pp. 562–3, 667–9, 928–33); note also the interesting lack of Murcian *cuerda seca* productions in Almería and vice versa (ibid., pp. 943, 964). After 1150, the south-east exported less to the south-west, which developed its own productions (ibid., pp. 1003–5, 1065–6). For Murcian lustre, see Navarro Palazón and Jiménez Castillo, 'La producción cerámica medieval de Murcia', pp. 192–202.

[144] For *esgrafiado*, see Crespo Pascual, 'Cerámica esgrafiada'; Azuar Ruiz, 'Alfares y testares', esp. the map at p. 67; for Murcian production at least sometimes reaching Valencia, see Navarro Palazón, 'La cerámica con decoración esgrafiada', p. 132. For Denia, see ibid., map at p. 66, developed in Azuar

the Almohad Caliphate in the way that *cuerda seca* did. But what it shows us is the way that overlapping productions could link local and much wider exchange networks together. Again, this is the same type of exchange structure as we have seen for the Gharb al-Andalus, although in the south-east there was more production for export, and probably more commercial activity in general. This, indeed, was the pattern that marked out the Almohad period as a whole; it was the product, by 1180/1200, of two centuries of steady development.

One important way in which we can understand how far exchange extended in al-Andalus is by looking at rural sites. We have seen that in the Byzantine heartland and in Sicily, field surveys have turned up substantial numbers of sites from our period which show identifiable non-local wares (both glazed pottery and amphorae), and thus rural buying power. The Islamic-ruled parts of Spain and Portugal have relatively few systematic field surveys for our period; on the other hand, many rural sites in al-Andalus have had targeted excavations, large and small, and we can build up a picture of the availability of pottery from elsewhere, and thus the density of exchange, as a result (see Map 17).

The first point worth making on the basis of these rural studies is that one option in a local economic environment could be actually not to use ceramics. One striking find made in a cave just outside Liétor in the south-eastern Meseta, 115 kilometres inland by road from Murcia, was a hidden deposit of what appear to have been all the valuables of a single rich peasant family, around 1000. It included a large amount of metalwork, for ploughing, harvesting, woodcutting, and even mining, plus tools for weaving and working with esparto grass, a set of scales, a set of arms for a single mounted soldier, and some high-quality bronze oil lamps, obviously bought from a specialist, even though this is the least urbanized part of al-Andalus. Added to this, surviving thanks to a very dry atmosphere in the cave, were a substantial number of wooden plates, bowls, and larger containers. But there were no ceramics. It is hard to imagine why a presumably fleeing family should have hidden their woodwork but not their pottery, or that they should have taken their ceramics with them and not their resellable oil lamps (or, for sure, their sword); the most obvious conclusion is that, notwithstanding their prosperity and their links with other productive systems, they did not actually use pottery at all. The use of wood for tablewares would, in fact, continue in eastern Spain, alongside ceramics, for centuries, as late medieval probate inventories show for Valencia and its hinterland; to use one rather than the other was a genuine cultural choice there, for tablewares, including fine wares, were, by then at

Ruiz, 'Castillos y espacios marginales', pp. 104–5, for Denia's very localized distribution; see Gisbert Santonja et al., *La cerámica de Daniya*, pp. 76–8, for production. For Palma, see Rosselló Pons, *Les ceràmiques almohades*; for the multiple kilns in the town, see most recently Coll Conesa et al., 'La alfarería musulmana'.

least, not at all expensive. So, in Liétor, not to use ceramics at all could also have been a deliberate choice, and it is a significant one for us to bear in mind.[145]

All the same, if it was a choice, it was a minority one. One striking feature of the two dozen or so rural studies I have looked at—we will begin with survey work, and then move onto one-off excavations—is that nearly all of the sites analysed had some access to relatively fine wares. Only in one area were they effectively absent, a set of villages in a poor area of *secano* (dry-farming) in the south-eastern Alentejo, north of Mértola, found in rescue excavations before the Alqueva dam was filled up. The two identifiable sites from our period were very small and simple settlements, showing almost no glazed pottery and few pieces with any elaboration. Around Lisbon and Santarem too, here on rich land, glaze was not common throughout our period (particularly not around Santarem), but that was because white-painted wares were still standard locally; these were urban productions, available in the countryside, as glaze was elsewhere. So too, farther east on the Meseta, even though in a fairly remote area, a set of hilltop sites in the province of Cáceres showed sets of green and manganese bowls which must have been produced in an urban or quasi-urban centre, probably Badajoz or Toledo (they did not have *cuerda seca*, however, which may have been more expensive).[146] Similarly, now in irrigated areas, a survey of nearly twenty sites around the small town of Loja (prov. Granada) regularly showed glazed wares from our period. So did a study of a valley west of Málaga, at least from the eleventh century onwards, with a high point under the Almohads. A particularly systematic survey of a set of villages near Chinchilla (prov. Albacete) in the south-eastern Meseta, a *secano* area which appears only to have been settled in the eleventh to thirteenth centuries, with a fall-off already after 1100, showed green and manganese bowls from the eleventh century, and *cuerda seca* and stamped wares from the twelfth; locally made *ollas* outnumbered them by far, but it is clear that these villages had at least some access to urban-made goods. One targeted excavation of an eleventh-century house, at La Graja, fitted this too. The archaeologists speculated that this was a sign of pastoral expansion, and that these were specialist wool villages, given that al-Idrīsī said Chinchilla itself was a carpet-making centre; that

[145] Navarro Palazón and Robles Fernández, *Liétor*. Where did they buy the oil lamps from? Maybe not Murcia, as they would have had ample access to ceramics there (if they wanted them); perhaps from a travelling merchant, not a fixed urban centre. Obtaining wood would have been easy; wooded mountains are close, in the Sierra de Segura. For Valencia, see Almenar Fernández, 'Why did villagers buy earthenware?'.

[146] Marques et al., *Povoamento rural*, pp. 208–29; Gómez Martínez et al., 'A cidade e o seu território', pp. 23–30; Gilotte, *Aux marges d'al-Andalus*, 1, pp. 227–30, 301 (only one of her main sites showed little fine ware). The villages around the town of Albarracín (prov. Teruel), in the mountains between the Meseta and the Sharq al-Andalus, similarly showed green and manganese, and later honey glaze, from the eleventh and twelfth centuries, available to the peasants in what the excavator calls an 'efecto goteo', a trickle-down effect; see Ortega Ortega, 'Una gobernanza poscalifal' (quotation at p. 468).

is likely enough, in fact, given the apparent prosperity of an agriculturally marginal area.[147]

Targeted excavations show similar patterns, on both large and small sites, and across the whole of al-Andalus, east and west, coast and inland, and on the Meseta. Here, before developing the point, I will simply offer a list. On the Meseta, Albalat (prov. Cáceres), which in the eleventh and especially early twelfth century was a significant metalworking site with wide connections, had some glazed bowls with forms common in the Gharb al-Andalus to the west, but others which have closer parallels in Córdoba and as far as the south coast. In Vascos (prov. Toledo), not far away, a large village or small town, probably a caliphal foundation, which was occupied slightly earlier, between the 940s and the 1080s, most houses (although not all) had green and manganese pottery and *cuerda seca*, with no evidence of local production; here we might assume they were imported from Toledo. These two sites were elite centres, and the ceramics would doubtless have arrived more easily as a result. Conversely, Guarrazar, close to Toledo, a smaller site from the period *c.*950–1050 with fewer glaze finds, was less likely to have been an elite centre, but it, nonetheless, had green and manganese and green monochrome, and here the ceramics certainly match those from the Toledo kilns.[148]

In the Sharq al-Andalus, Uixó, a fortified site in the hills north of Valencia, had green and manganese from *c.*1000 and, later, some *esgrafiado* from *c.*1200. Torre la Sal, a late tenth- and eleventh-century artisanal and agricultural site on the coast north of Castelló, had green and manganese and variants, one type of which was identified as from Mallorca, and some *cuerda seca*. Benetússer, a late tenth- or eleventh-century site in the *horta* of Valencia, had both green and manganese and *cuerda seca*. Farther south, Guardamar (prov. Alicante), a small coastal fortification of the same period, showed the same wares on a small scale, plus monochrome glaze, here from kilns in both Elche and Murcia. That small scale fits Sonia Gutiérrez's wider work on rural sites in Tudmīr, roughly the provinces of Alicante and Murcia, plus Albacete on the plateau, which shows that in general, glaze was relatively rare on sites there into the late tenth century, unlike in the eleventh and twelfth.[149] And by the twelfth century, the ceramic repertoire in the east was, indeed, much more varied: at Bofilla (prov. Valencia) there was green

[147] See the lists in Jiménez Puertas, *El poblamiento del territorio de Loja*, pp. 257–313; for Málaga, see Ordóñez Frías, 'La formación de nuevas entidades poblacionales', pp. 401–3; for Chinchilla, see Jiménez Castillo and Simón García, 'El poblamiento andalusí en las tierras de secano', with Jiménez Castillo et al., 'El campesinado andalusí', for La Graja. Cf. al-Idrīsī, *Nuzhat al-mushtaq*, trans. Jaubert and Nef, p. 279. We find much the same in villages behind Valencia; see Bazzana, *Maisons d'al-Andalus*, p. 155.

[148] Gilotte et al., 'Un ajuar de época almorávide'; Gilotte and Cáceres Gutiérrez, *Al-Balât*, esp. pp. 80–115, with Sophie Gilotte, pers. comm.; Izquierdo Benito, *La ciudad hispanomusulmana de Vascos*, pp. 72–82, with Eduardo Manzano, pers. comm.; Eger, 'Guarrazar', esp. pp. 293–7.

[149] Bazzana et al., *Les châteaux ruraux d'al-Andalus*, pp. 247–50; Flors and Sanfeliu, 'Los materiales cerámicos', pp. 335–52; Escribà, *La ceràmica califal de Benetússer*, pp. 36–7, 67 (which argues for the late tenth century; that date seems to me a little too early for local copying of green and manganese);

and manganese and *cuerda seca*, and by now *esgrafiado* too, found in every house, even if greatly outnumbered by the some 98 per cent of common and cooking wares on the site. El Castillo del Rio (prov. Alicante), a late twelfth-century fortification in the hills just outside Elche, had monochrome glaze, stamped ware, *esgrafiado*, and even lustre, from both Elche and Denia.[150] Again, some of these sites had a significant elite presence, but not all—certainly not Torre la Sal, Benetússer, and Bofilla—and in the last the presence of glaze in every house is striking.

Farther west, in what is now Andalucía, buying glazed wares seems to have started earlier than in the Sharq. La Rijana (prov. Granada), a tenth- and eleventh-century coastal site, showed green and manganese, honey glaze, and *cuerda seca*. Inland, Montefrío (prov. Granada), a site in poorer hills, had monochrome glaze by the tenth century at the latest, with some green and manganese; so did Setefilla, halfway between Seville and Córdoba, this time probably in the eleventh, and now including *cuerda seca*. In this part of Spain, however, the site which for me is the most striking is the Cueva de la Dehesilla (prov. Cádiz), where in the later eleventh century there were green and manganese plates, and *cuerda seca* and green tin-glaze *jarros*, followed after a settlement break by honey glaze in the twelfth; the standard array of fine wares was here available in a mountain cave, as far from the sea or rivers as one can get in the southern tip of the peninsula.[151]

These, as said earlier, were large and small sites; some had elites whose demand will have helped the wider availability of goods, but not by any means all of them did (and that demand would not, anyway, explain the generalized availability of glaze on survey); and they were also in both irrigated and *secano* areas, including in the latter case some very poor land. But with very few exceptions—as one might find in any region or period—they all had access to glazed wares from the mid- to late tenth century to the late twelfth and onwards from then, which the inhabitants of each site, largely peasants, did not produce themselves and will, therefore, have had to buy. They evidently had the means to do so. Here, it does not matter so much if they bought from travelling merchants, or from the nearest town, or even, in some cases (presumably mediated by that town), from a long way away—and anyhow, we usually cannot tell, for the fabric analyses have not been done. I would assume that in most cases they bought wares made more or less locally, although when they bought from farther afield, as at Albalat, the fact is, of course, significant for wider relationships—probably, in that case, the sale of iron (see p. 440 below). I would also assume that with the exception of some of

Azuar Ruiz, *La rábita califal de las dunas de Guardamar*, pp. 134–5, with Menéndez Fueyo, 'La cerámica de la rábita califal', esp. pp. 127–9; Gutiérrez Lloret, *La cora de Tudmīr*, pp. 191–5, 198–9.

[150] López Elum, *La alquería islámica en Valencia*, pp. 292–5, 355–6; Azuar Ruiz, *El Castillo del Rio*, e.g. pp. 47–8, 70–4, 135–6, 145–50.

[151] Malpica Cuello and Gómez Becerra, *Una cala que llaman La Rijana*, pp. 65–78; Motos Guirao, *El poblado medieval de 'El Castellón'*, pp. 98–9; Kirchner, *Étude des céramiques islamiques*, pp. 20–3, 31–3; Taylor et al., 'La secuencia arqueológica andalusí'. For the peri-urban Marroquíes Bajos site outside Jaén, cf. also Pérez Alvarado, *Las cerámicas omeyas*, p. 121.

the larger and fortified sites, where not only peasants would be living, such as El Castillo del Rio, villagers would rarely be able to afford the real top-of-the-line wares, whichever they were in any given area. At Benetússer, for example, the green and manganese found there was of low quality; even at El Castillo del Rio that was sometimes the case, and there was some evidence there of riveting, that is to say, the repair of broken pots, which hints at the difficulty of replacement.[152] This is reinforced by a wider synthesis of the rural sites of the Gharb al-Andalus. Here, particularly in the southern Alentejo and Algarve, where imports were commoner than in the Tejo valley to the north, fortified sites had more glazed wares than smaller unfortified ones, and urban sites themselves show more such wares than either; and neither type of rural site had much access to the highest-quality glazed wares, *cuerda seca total*, lustre, and *esgrafiado*—the last being, as noted earlier, rather rarer in the west than in the east of al-Andalus. All the same, some glaze was available on all sites.[153]

So we can conclude that differences in wealth did indeed result in differences of access to the more expensive wares. Nonetheless, the exchange network which connected the towns of the west—and, indeed, the towns of every part of al-Andalus—extended into the countryside pretty much everywhere. Not only could peasants afford to buy ceramics almost everywhere, if they were rich enough (and some excavations show non-local ceramics in every house), but commercial linkages were sufficiently complex to reach them, both to sell them goods and to buy from them the agricultural products which they must have been selling in return. Interestingly, the exchange network in itself does not seem to have changed so much from the tenth century to the twelfth, given the substantial number of rural sites from the caliphal period which could already get at least a little green and manganese, which at that point was still made for the most part in Córdoba. But there is, equally, no doubt that the variety and quantity of urban fine wares which are seen on rural sites rapidly increased across our period, in line with the increasing scale of urban productions.

So what we can see across our period is a network of strong and active productions, at a high technical level, with (after the second *fitna* and the decline of Córdoba) none of them in any clear way dominant over the others. This, to repeat, is substantially unlike any other region we have so far looked at, although we will find in Chapter 6 that the lack of dominance of a single centre certainly describes northern Italy. But, as we shall see as well, Andalusī production and exchange, at least of ceramics, had also—from a low baseline in the eighth century—come to be far more complex than anything we can yet see in the material culture of northern Italy during our period. Furthermore, the different productive networks in Spain and Portugal overlapped continuously, more and more as we come into

[152] See n. 149 above, with Azuar Ruiz, *El Castillo del Rio*, pp. 136–41.
[153] Gómez Martínez et al., 'A cidade e o seu território', pp. 34–46.

the twelfth century, with Málaga or Seville buying from Almería or Murcia and vice versa, and the less prominent Portuguese towns buying from everyone; and, beneath the level of these urban centres, villages could buy ranges of goods which could sometimes include wares not produced by the nearest town. Here, however, al-Andalus was not so different from other regions we have so far looked at. Distribution networks overlapped in Egypt, Byzantium, and Sicily too. We have seen the signs of that in each of Chapters 2–4: for fine wares and cloth in Egypt, and for fine wares and wine in both Byzantium and Sicily. Urban and urban-mediated products reached peasant buyers in all our regions (except possibly Ifrīqiya) as well. The networks do not always look as complicated in these regions, but that is because there was, indeed, one dominant centre in each, unlike in Spain. And by the twelfth century, the rise of Corinth and Chalkis/Thebes as ceramic, wine, and textile centres in Byzantium meant that there was complication there too, even if it was in the framework of what seems—at least in the Aegean heartland—to have been a more unified market than in al-Andalus. So this western region had very many of the same characteristics as others did, although set in different configurations. It also shows clearer signs of a steady growth in economic complexity than do any of the others across our period except Byzantium, and in my view also shows more such growth than Byzantium did. Why this might have been is the crucial question, of course; we will come back to that at the end of the section.

Two other issues, however, pose themselves right here, and need to be confronted briefly before we go on. The first concerns the underpinnings of peasant buying power. We have seen (pp. 389–94) that taxation was not so very high in al-Andalus, and that rent was much higher, although probably, at least in irrigated areas, not so high that all surplus was taken away from cultivators. The generalization of non-local pottery across rural sites in this region must show that peasants had enough surplus to sell, in order to buy it. It might well be, indeed, given this, that a majority of peasants were small owners, not paying rent, as was argued for Byzantium (p. 346). But such a generalization of availability was *so* complete that in my view it is highly likely that many tenants could and did buy ceramics too, and presumably other goods as well. This means that we can move away from the sometimes sharp debate about whether Andalusī villages were tenurially independent autonomous communities or not: the issue here is one not of autonomy (anyway, no community, however internally homogeneous, is really autonomous if the state is strong[154]) but of prosperity and interconnectedness—which themselves imply peasant protagonism, quite as much as autonomy does. And we have clear signs of both prosperity and interconnectedness here. Sometimes, we have, indeed, very striking signs of them, as at Siyāsa (which was perhaps a

[154] Cf. Manzano Moreno, '¿Existieron comunidades rurales autosuficientes en al-Andalus?'.

small town, but which must have also had a substantial peasant population to cultivate the surrounding lands), or at Liétor, or in the Cueva de la Dehesilla above Cádiz; and we have very few signs of real poverty by medieval standards.

So peasants were, indeed, very widely across al-Andalus, selling their surplus in order to be able to buy. Towns, as we have seen, were themselves expanding substantially everywhere, so local urban buying power would have matched this. Some less perishable crops—wine, oil, wheat, flax, cotton, and silk—were also, as elsewhere, capable of being sold farther afield too. We do not have the unique Egyptian evidence to help us track down the detail of this, but we can at least use simple logic to help. Tenth-century Córdoba was too big and too far inland not to have been supplied at least in part with the help of the state, but after that it is likely that for the most part commercial structures were adequate for major cities, even Seville. All the same, it is obvious that the largest cities, Seville or Almería or Murcia, would have needed to develop a wider network of commercial connections with the countryside than a Mértola or an Elche did. Larger towns might well have competed with smaller ones on some occasions as a result; exchange networks would then have lengthened; and this competition, too, might well have helped peasant prosperity. This is as far as logic on its own will get us, but it is a start.

The second issue concerns the limits of what ceramic archaeology can tell us in al-Andalus. We must ask again what it is a proxy for, among productions which were doubtless, at the time, larger-scale and more important. We have seen that the general assumption that ceramics were at least a proxy for cloth works empirically in Egypt, Byzantium, and Sicily; we cannot show that for Islamic Spain and Portugal, but it is likely here as well; and given that al-Andalus was a metal-producing region, it was probably the case for metalwork as well, the other main artisanal product. We will come on to both very shortly. But we cannot assume the same for food production and distribution, which we have been able to say a good deal about for other regions on the basis of the ceramic record. The reader will have noticed that amphorae have not been brought into the equation in this chapter. This is because, surprisingly, they are almost unrecognized as a ceramic type in Spanish and Portuguese medieval archaeology. Rosselló did not identify them as a distinct category; and so no one else has. In 1978, when he wrote, it is fair to say that it was still quite widely thought that amphorae ended when the ancient world did, and Rosselló did remark that the *jarra* had the amphora as its predecessor; this remark has, however, not been picked up in the more recent literature, even though not a few archaeologists are by now perfectly well aware of the great similarity between many types of *jarra* (or *tinaja*, similar but with a wider neck, or sometimes *cántaro*) and the transport amphorae from our period which have been by now extensively discussed for every other part of the Mediterranean. Pots which would be called *tinajas* in Spain have even been found in London in thirteenth-century levels, presumably associated with wine or oil imports, and are, indeed, in that context described as amphorae; they seem from the petrology to have come from south-west Spain. *Tinajas* have also been found on wrecks of early tenth-century ships from al-Andalus found off the coast of France, and their function as transport containers for wine has been recognized there. Rosselló categorized these ceramic types as having been used for both storage and transport; this phrase is used often enough in the literature, but in practice storage has been seen as their major purpose.[155] The result of all this is that *jarras* and *tinajas* have not been analysed by specialists with the question in mind that they might have come from somewhere else.

Sometimes, of course, they did not. *Jarras* are common enough finds when kilns are excavated, which shows that they were, indeed, made where they were found; some fabric analysis shows local production too. Some are also so highly decorated, particularly in the twelfth century, that they count as fine wares, and would never have been used for transport. And we cannot, of course, simply assume, without evidence, that the Andalusīs used amphorae with the same normality as contemporary Sicilians or Byzantines did. We have seen (pp. 72, 308) that oil was routinely, even if not invariably, moved around in skins, along the main route from Tunisia to Egypt, and probably also from the olive productions of Sparta into the main Byzantine exchange arenas. This might well have been so in Islamic Spain too, for example from the productions of the Aljarafe outside Seville. But we do have at least one hint in a written source that wine, at any rate, was commercialized in ceramic containers in al-Andalus, as it also was in all the other regions we have so far looked at.[156] I would wonder at the very least whether, if we looked, we might find wine containers from Seville or Jeréz in tenth-century Córdoba, or, later, from the coastal cities which al-Idrīsī said were major wine producers, such as Almería, Murcia, and Denia, in other locations in the twelfth century—or, indeed, any examples of the set of twelfth-century *cántaros* found on one of the major Seville sites, on sites elsewhere in al-Andalus, given that they look remarkably like contemporary Byzantine amphorae in their overall aesthetic, but seem to be locally made. One important article by Rafael Azuar and Omar Inglese Carreras, appearing as this book goes to press, indeed begins to classify Andalusī amphorae, and argues, among other points, that an underwater find off Alicante is an amphora type from Seville from *c.*1000; this is a marker of what can be done in the future, for it now offers the possibility that we will soon be able to

[155] Rosselló Bordoy, *Ensayo de sistematización*, p. 31; Vince, 'Medieval and post-medieval Spanish pottery', pp. 138–40; for the wrecks, see Richarté-Manfredi, 'Navires et marchandises', and n. 216 below.

[156] For the Aljarafe, see n. 14 above. For wine in general, see, e.g., Martínez Salvador and Bellón Aguilera, 'Consideraciones sobre la simbologia', a brief discussion, with references to the geographers and agronomists, of how wine was a normal commodity in al-Andalus, notwithstanding the hostility to it shown in Islamic normative sources and by the occasional political figure. The source is a poetic reference to the destruction of ceramic containers for wine by Ibn Jahwar, the *ṭāʾifa* ruler of Córdoba in the second quarter of the eleventh century (Cour, *Un poète arabe d'Andalousie: Ibn Zaïdoün*, pp. 82–3).

say rather more about amphora types from the material record, when targeted research has been done.[157] That will remain for for the future. In the present, however, whatever we think of this absence, the data from fine wares nevertheless speak for themselves: the networks of exchange inside al-Andalus were highly complex, and were becoming more so across our period. On the basis of that, let us turn to the generally more restricted evidence we have for other major commodities, and for trading in general.

5.4.2 Cloth, metal and other interconnections

The urban *sūq*s of al-Andalus were full of artisans, and vendors of artisanal goods. We have seen this already in the *ḥisba* manuals for Córdoba, Seville, and Málaga, listing as they do dozens of different types of makers and sellers (including of ceramics, which, however, is eclipsed by the general areas of cloth, leather, and food); but casual references show their normality in other places too: a spice-merchant in Málaga or Granada, a prosperous leatherworker in Denia or Almería, as well as some fifteen separate trades in the Arabic land documents for immediately post-conquest Toledo.[158] More generalist merchants were omnipresent too, as Remie Constable showed in detail, whether sedentary, based in a single place, or themselves travelling. Judges and jurists, army leaders, and doctors could be merchants on the side as well, without attracting comment, as we have seen already for Egypt. This was the context for sample contracts for partnerships in the formulary books, as with Ibn al-ʿAṭṭār's tenth-century model *qirāḍ* contract in which the sedentary merchant agrees to hand over money to the travelling merchant, with a split of the final profits of ⅔ to ⅓, so that the latter can transact with cloth sellers, perfumists, money changers, or bakers in the *sūq* of Córdoba or elsewhere, either in one type of merchandise or many. Jurists' *fatwā*s also deal with problems in the world of commerce in the same way as they discuss agriculture: a vendor of goods should be paid, if he asks, in silver money used by ordinary people, not that which only merchants (*tujjār*) use [by implication gold]; the exchange of coins of different currencies in the *ṭāʾifa* or post-*ṭāʾifa* period must

[157] Al-Idrīsī, *Nuzhat al-mushtaq*, trans. Jaubert and Nef, pp. 276, 279, 285; he adds, pp. 282–3, that Almería's very numerous *fundūq*s paid a wine tax. For the site in Seville, see Vera Reina and López Torres, *La cerámica medieval sevillana*, pp. 114–25. See now Azuar and Inglese Carreras, 'Contenedores cerámicos de transporte marítimo de al-Andalus'.

[158] For ceramics in the *ḥisba* manuals, see Ibn ʿAbd al-Raʾūf, *Risāla fī ādāb al-ḥisba wa al-muḥtasib*, trans. Arié, pp. 357, 361; al-Saqaṭī, *Kitāb fī ādāb al-ḥisba*, trans. Chalmeta Gendrón, ch. 155. For spice merchants, see Abraham ibn Daud, *The book of tradition*, trans. Cohen, pp. 72, 80. For Denia, see al-Wansharīsī, *al-Miʿyār*, trans. Lagardère, *Histoire et société*, 3.279; for Almería, see Ocaña Jiménez, *Repertorio de inscripciones árabes de Almería*, n. 104; for Toledo, see the index in González Palencia, *Los Mozárabes de Toledo, Volumen preliminar*, pp. 234–41—they included in 1135 a Muslim 'trustee of the potters', *amīn al-fakhārin*, P.Mozarab 23.

reflect their differing metal content [this is to avoid fraud, but also potential usury]; one should not buy cloth before it is finished when more than one weaver is involved, as this involves illegal risk.[159] There is a tendency in the historiography to concentrate on overseas trading; but—as in previous chapters, and as the Córdoba *qirāḍ* indicates here too—internal exchange was at least as important, and indeed, as we shall see, much more so. A strict eye was kept on commerce by market supervisors, to avoid fraud and squalor (as we have seen in the *ḥisba* manuals), and to collect commercial taxes for the state. One *geniza* reference indicates that the basic customs due for ships coming into Almería was 10 per cent, which we have seen to be normal elsewhere in the Mediterranean. Ibn ʿAbdūn regards this rate as standard for goods coming into Seville from the countryside too. But there were plenty of extra charges as goods moved around, including inside cities, as he also says, legal and illegal.[160]

Our direct information about Andalusī merchants is restricted. All the same, what we know indicates that their patterns of activity were similar to those of the Jewish merchants in the *geniza* operating not only overseas but also inside Egypt, between Fusṭāṭ and Alexandria and the other Delta towns, set against the Muslim and sometimes Christian merchants operating similarly in larger and smaller centres, as we saw in Chapter 2. Many such merchants were Jews in al-Andalus too, in important Jewish centres such as Granada and Lucena—the latter, as we have seen, had an early eleventh-century formulary book of its own, in Hebrew, with draft credit and agricultural contracts, and one commercial agreement—but also in every other major city in the country, at least up to 1150. There is then a drop-off in references to them, which is sometimes associated with Almohad persecution, although it is unclear whether it really means a lessening in their activity.[161] Again as in Egypt, we cannot detect significant differences between the activity of Muslims and Jews—including in the doubling up of professions, for Jewish merchants could be Talmudic scholars, just as Muslim merchants could be jurists.

On the basis of the written sources, we know most about the production and commercialization of cloth, which was, as usual, the most important artisan-made commodity in the Andalusī economy. Here, it may not have been quite as dominant over iron or leather as in some other regions, as the Iberian peninsula produced quantities of both. But we cannot say much about leather (though see p. 398 above for Córdoba); iron we will come back to; cloth will be our starting point. Islamic Iberia produced every type of cloth. The agronomists are clear that flax

[159] Constable, *Trade and traders*, pp. 52–96. For contracts, see Ibn al-ʿAṭṭār, *Kitāb al-wathāʾiq wa al-sijillāt*, trans. Chalmeta and Marugán, n. 31; al-Wansharīsī, *al-Miʿyār*, trans. Lagardère, *Histoire et société*, 3.255, 258, 292, 294.

[160] T-S NS J197 (Goitein, *Letters*, n. 49); Ibn ʿAbdūn, *Risāla fī al-qaḍāʾ wa al-ḥisba*, trans. Lévi-Provençal, esp. ch. 65; cf. 61–6. For the Mediterranean as a whole, see Chapter 3, n. 270 above. For merchants and the state, see esp. Constable, *Trade and traders*, pp. 112–37.

[161] Constable, *Trade and traders*, pp. 85–96, gives a survey; see the next section for *geniza* data, including n. 196 below for post-1150 *geniza* references. For Lucena, see *Jüdische Urkundenformulare*, trans. Mutius; n. C30 for the commercial agreement.

and cotton were standard productions in the countryside, and mulberry trees were as well, for silk; and here we can say something about wool too.

Flax was grown in al-Andalus in many places. The geographers mention the territory of Granada, and by the twelfth century, Segorbe near Valencia. The agronomists state that even if *regadío* is better for flax, dry-farmed *secano* is appropriate too; and indeed, we gain the distinct impression from these writers that it was common everywhere, 'in all the terrains which are similar to the soil of Egypt' (Ibn al-'Awwām); Abū al-Khayr, indeed, reckoned that as a crop it was second only to wheat.[162] The Egyptian flax trade which is so much a part of the eleventh-century *geniza* did not have to go to Islamic Spain, as the peninsula produced so much of its own, and there is no sign that it did. It is thus to be expected that linen weavers would be a standard feature of Andalusī cities, and both the geographers and the *ḥisba* manuals indeed imply that this was the case.[163] There is no sign of a trade in raw flax between the cities, and perhaps there was little, as it was grown so widely; what was sold across the region and beyond was linen cloth. Again in the geographers, Valencia and its region appears here explicitly as a producer, and Granada by implication, plus Pechina, the predecessor of Almería. Ibn Ḥawqal already in the tenth century claimed that Pechina's linen coats were exported to Egypt from Spain, although linen exports are not confirmed by the *geniza*.[164] On the other hand, what was definitely exported was Spanish paper—perhaps above all from Xàtiva, on the edge of the plain running down to Valencia, which is praised for its production by the geographers, but doubtless from elsewhere too; Ibn 'Abdūn mentions papermaking for Seville. Paper, as we have seen, is a cloth by-product, and is thus as clear a sign of a wider cloth specialization as is the cloth itself. Spanish paper does appear in the *geniza*, even though Egypt made plenty of its own, probably because it was particularly good: Goitein comments on the remarkable quality of the paper of one Spanish letter, from 1130. This may mean that it was cotton-, not linen-based, as cotton-based paper is often of a higher quality; but Xàtiva, at least, was quite close to the flax productions around Valencia. That would in the future be possible to test scientifically, of course, given the known Spanish origin of some of the *geniza* texts.[165]

[162] *Crónica del moro Rasis*, ed. Catalán and de Andres, p. 30; the later al-Ḥimyarī, *Kitāb al-rawḍ al-mi'ṭār*, trans. Lévi-Provençal, p. 30–1, also locates flax in the *vega* of Granada; cf. also López Martínez de Marigorta, *Mercaderes, artesanos y ulemas*, pp. 322–3. For Segorbe, see Ibn Ghālib, *Farḥat al-anfus*, trans. Vallvé Bermejo, p. 375. Agronomists: Ibn al-'Awwām, *Kitāb al-filāḥa*, trans. Clément-Mullet, 2, p. 109; Abū al-Khayr, *Kitāb al-filāḥa*, ed. and trans. Carabaza, p. 322. Cf. García Sánchez, 'Las plantas textiles', pp. 427–30; Lagardère, *Campagnes et paysans*, pp. 413–39.

[163] *Ḥisba* manuals: Ibn 'Abd al-Ra'ūf, *Risāla fī ādāb al-ḥisba wa al-muḥtasib*, trans. Arié, pp. 37–8, 353; Ibn 'Abdūn, *Risāla fī al-qaḍā' wa al-ḥisba*, trans. Lévi-Provençal, chs 175, 199; al-Saqaṭī, *Kitāb fī ādāb al-ḥisba*, trans. Chalmeta Gendrón, chs 140–1.

[164] Al-Zuhrī, *Kitāb al-ja'rāfiyya*, trans. Bramón, p. 519 (Valencia); Ibn Ḥawqal, *Kitāb ṣūrat al-arḍ*, trans. Kramers and Wiet, 1, pp. 113–14 (Pechina).

[165] Xàtiva: e.g. al-Idrīsī, *Nuzhat al-mushtaq*, trans. Jaubert and Nef, p. 276; cf. Ibn 'Abdūn, *Risāla fī al-qaḍā' wa al-ḥisba*, trans. Lévi-Provençal, ch. 150, and Bloom, *Paper before print*, pp. 86–8. For the 1130 letter (CUL Add.3340), see Goitein, *MS*, 5, p. 288 with 587, n. 73; for Spanish paper export to

Cotton was grown in the Aljarafe of Seville, but also along the Spanish coast. Seville cotton was, according to al-Rāzī in the tenth century, sold throughout al-Andalus and abroad, and later geographers claim North Africa to be an importing region, which would make sense (Sicily, after all, produced its own by before 1100).[166] Cotton appears in an advanced sale and in a sharecropping contract in Ibn al-ʿAṭṭār's formulary book, together with wheat, barley, and beans, which implies that it was a standard crop; it is there in all three *ḥisba* manuals; and cotton cloth is casually referred to in other texts.[167] So it was common enough, and seems to have been grown and woven consistently throughout our period—there is no sign of shifts in production between flax/linen and cotton in al-Andalus of the sort that we have seen in Sicily. I have the sense that cotton was, all the same, less common than linen. This is hard to substantiate, as we are reliant on very chance references; but it is not stressed quite as much. Still, it is associated with different areas of the peninsula in our texts; the two must have been complementary.

As for wool, its production was, when located by writers, associated with the relatively pastoral Meseta, as with Chinchilla and Cuenca carpets, mentioned in al-Idrīsī. There was a good deal of plateau and mountain land in Islamic Spain, which might imply substantial wool production in our region—it is well attested in the Christian north already by 1000—even if it did not match the major specializations of the later middle ages.[168] And it was available more widely than just on the plateau. Wool-weaving and/or woollen cloth again appears in all the *ḥisba* manuals (in al-Saqaṭī in the form of felt, which is also, together with high-quality woollens and carpets, mentioned by Ibn Ḥawqal). Carmona, in the middle of the Guadalquivir plain near Seville, in as lowland an area as one can find in Spain, apparently had a woollen-cloth market in the twelfth century; the raw material in this case certainly came from elsewhere.[169] This is less evidence than we have for the other two fibres, but it is rather more than we have seen for most regions so far. Woollen-cloth production in our period was, probably, more often the work

Egypt, see Moss. IV,18 (Gil K429), ENA NS I.4 (Goitein and Friedman, *India book* IV/B, n. 37, trans. Goitein, *MS*, 5, p. 464). Spanish paper exports to Sicily and Genoa in the later twelfth century are also proposed by Bloom, *Paper before print*, pp. 209–11; I would be cautious about this before 1200 without more evidence.

[166] *Crónica del moro Rasis*, ed. Catalán and de Andres, p. 93; al-ʿUdhrī, *Tarṣīʿ al-akhbār*, trans. Valencia, p. 116; Ibn Ghālib, *Farḥat al-anfus*, trans. Vallvé Bermejo, p. 381; for the coast, see Ibn Baṣṣāl, *Kitāb al-qaṣd wa al-bayān*, trans. Millás Vallicrosa and Aziman, p. 152. Cf. García Sánchez, 'Las plantas textiles', pp. 421–5.

[167] Ibn al-ʿAṭṭār, *Kitāb al-wathāʾiq wa al-sijillāt*, trans. Chalmeta and Marugán, nn. 11, 19; cf. also n. 51; for the *ḥisba* manuals, see the references in n. 163 above; see also, e.g., al-Wansharīsī, *al-Miʿyār*, trans. Lagardère, *Histoire et société*, 3.305.

[168] Al-Idrīsī, *Nuzhat al-mushtaq*, trans. Jaubert and Nef, p. 279; for the north, see, e.g., Wickham, *Land and power*, pp. 142–51.

[169] Ibn ʿAbd al-Raʾūf, *Risāla fī ādāb al-ḥisba wa al-muḥtasib*, trans. Arié, p. 353; Ibn ʿAbdūn, *Risāla fī al-qaḍāʾ wa al-ḥisba*, trans. Lévi-Provençal, ch. 174; al-Saqaṭī, *Kitāb fī ādāb al-ḥisba*, trans. Chalmeta Gendrón, ch. 166; cf. Ibn Ḥawqal, *Kitāb ṣūrat al-arḍ*, trans. Kramers and Wiet, 1, p. 113. For Carmona, see al-Marrākushī, *Kitāb al-muʿjib*, trans. Huici Miranda, pp. 80–2.

of professionals in al-Andalus than in the eastern Mediterranean. Raw wool was even occasionally imported from Egypt and North Africa, perhaps wool of a different quality from that available locally; this would have been pointless had there not been a commitment to professional weaving in the peninsula. And this may be because it was seen as a necessary cloth; the tenth-century *Córdoba calendar* claims that in October, as it gets colder, people change 'white clothes' [linen? It is less white than cotton, but is harder to dye] for raw silk and wool clothing.[170] Southern Spain and Portugal do not get as cold as Greece and Turkey, where, in the Byzantine lands, wool production is not much stressed in our sources (see pp. 327–8 above); but it is hard not to agree that such a change in clothing would have been sensible, for anyone who could afford it, and also that wool was more likely to be inside most people's price ranges than silk.

All the same, silk was also produced on an unusually large scale in al-Andalus. As a producer region, it matched Sicily in its Mediterranean penetration, as we shall see in the next section; and as Islamic Spain and Portugal was a much bigger region, its silk manufacture was probably more substantial than that anywhere else, maybe excepting Byzantium. Silk cannot have been as important a production as any of the other Andalusī textiles, given its high cost and thus its (at least semi-) luxury status. All the same, the sorts of information we have about silk production match entirely what we have seen for other types of textile; the major difference is that the skilled task of caring for, collecting, and unfurling silk cocoons seems to have been a speciality of women.[171] Here the main areas of mulberry cultivation are said by the geographers (but also other sources) to be Granada and Jaén. There will certainly have been others too; a 1092 document from Toledo, far away from other places from which we have citations, refers to 'Alī b. al-Ḥarīr, 'son of the silk worker'.[172] The *ḥisba* manuals make it clear that silk cloth was woven and sold (sometimes also in mixes) in Córdoba and Málaga; Alicante, not then a major town, gets a namecheck in al-Rāzī for silk production as early as the tenth century; by the 1140s we can add Valencia to this list, for Ibn

[170] Imports: Constable, *Trade and traders*, p. 160. 'White clothes': *Le calendrier de Cordoue*, ed. Dozy, trans. Pellat, pp. 158–9.

[171] *Le calendrier de Cordoue*, ed. Dozy, trans. Pellat, pp. 48–9. There is, as elsewhere, some evidence for female participation at every stage of the spinning and weaving process in al-Andalus, and then in the sale of textiles, although *ḥisba* manuals are hostile to this; see Marín, *Mujeres en al-Ándalus*, pp. 253–6, 290–1, 307. This work is seldom referred to, but could be skilled, given that Ibn 'Abdūn refers to (and again, is hostile to) female *ṭirāz* embroiderers: *Risāla fī al-qaḍā' wa al-ḥisba*, trans. Lévi-Provençal, ch. 143.

[172] For Granada, see *Crónica del moro Rasis*, ed. Catalán and de Andres, p. 30; *Al-Ḥulal al mawshīyya*, trans. Huici Miranda, p. 109; and the references in López Martínez de Marigorta, *Mercaderes, artesanos y ulemas*, pp. 62–4, 188, 191. For Jaén, see al-Idrīsī, *Nuzhat al-mushtaq*, trans. Jaubert and Nef, pp. 287–8; al-Shaqundī, *Risāla fi faḍl al-Andalus*, trans. García Gómez, pp. 120–1. For Toledo, see P.Mozarab 2. See in general for silk the data in Lagardère, *Campagnes et paysans*, pp. 391–412.

Mardanīsh made a treaty with Genoa in 1149 promising a tribute from there which was partly in silk cloth.[173]

But everyone concurred that the main location for silk weaving and silk cloth production was Almería. We have seen that al-Idrīsī claimed that there were 800 silk workshops in the city; whatever we think of that figure, it is to Almería that foreign merchants consistently came to take silk back to sell in their own countries, as we have seen and will see again. Almería was not so very far from either Granada or Jaén (even if over mountain passes and through semi-desert), and it is likely enough that these were its sources of raw silk; but if so, this is a clear example of the large-scale artisanal production of a commodity being physically separate from the land it came from—which was also, in the *ṭāʾifa* period when our references take off, in a separate kingdom, and we know from the *Tibyān* that Granada (which usually also included Jaén) and Almería were often at war.[174] The expansion of silk production in Almería was, therefore, far from a given; it must have been because it was a port, both for the other towns of al-Andalus and for export abroad. This is a sign, in cloth as in ceramics, of a focussing of major productions on places with good communications.

Cloth production in al-Andalus was extensive and large-scale. It often used horizontal looms, not just the vertical looms which were typical of simpler household production; triangular plaques which are part of the equipment of such looms have been found by archaeologists both in medium-sized centres, Cerro del Sombrerete, Mértola, Albalat, and Vascos, and in smaller castle sites and villages such as Serpa (north of Mértola), Montefrío, and Liétor, starting in the tenth century at the latest.[175] If even some rural production was technologically more specialized, urban production will certainly have been. We can, anyway, presuppose a high level of activity in towns when it came to cloth, given the good evidence for urban wealth which we explored in the last section, and this is certain for all the larger urban centres. We could presume a productive hierarchy here too, with the greatest specialization in the major centres, then less as settlements got smaller, but in the case of cloth at least, a considerable space for household production too, which was more normal for basic cloth-weaving than for any other major artisanal activity.

[173] Ibn ʿAbd al-Raʾūf, *Risāla fī ādāb al-ḥisba wa al-muḥtasib*, trans. Arié, p. 353; al-Saqaṭī, *Kitāb fī ādāb al-ḥisba*, trans. Chalmeta Gendrón, chs 137–9; *Crónica del moro Rasis*, ed. Catalán and de Andres, pp. 35–6; *CDGE*, 1, n. 196 (*LI*, 1, n. 118).

[174] *Crónica del moro Rasis*, ed. Catalán and de Andres, p. 28; al-Idrīsī, *Nuzhat al-mushtaq*, trans. Jaubert and Nef, pp. 281–2; cf. Constable, *Trade and traders*, pp. 174–5; ʿAbd Allāh, *al-Tibyān*, trans. Tibi, pp. 58–9, 76–7, 102–3.

[175] Retuerce Velasco, 'El templén'; Motos Guirao, *El poblado medieval de 'El Castellón'*, pp. 130–2; Navarro Palazón and Robles Fernández, *Liétor*, pp. 72–3; Morena Narganes, 'Tejiendo en casa'. The last-mentioned article, discussing Mértola and Albalat, sees weaving there as being sufficiently *tecnificado* that it must have been for sale, not just household use. (But al-Ruṣāfī's love poem to a male weaver (see the convenient translation in Nykl, *Hispano-Arabic poetry*, p. 327) does not seem to me specific enough to be describing weaving on a horizontal loom, as Retuerce proposes, 'El templén', p. 73.) Most of these references are early for the rest of Europe, where the take-off of horizontal looms can best be put in the eleventh and especially the twelfth centuries; see Cardon, *La draperie*, pp. 400–12.

It has to be recognized that these presuppositions, taken on their own, do not take us all that far forward. That Andalusī towns were significant productive centres we already knew. That cloth was important in all the ones we know of is what we would expect; it would be far more unusual, and in need of explanation, if it was otherwise. But what we can at least say is that the export of Seville cotton across the peninsula, the wool market at Carmona, and the supply of Almería with substantial quantities of raw silk from between 160 and 220 kilometres away are signs of a network of internal interrelationships—all of them, doubtless, by donkey more often than by boat, and sometimes across difficult terrain—which was more complicated than any simple picture of each city making cloth and selling to its surrounding area. Possibly the fact that each of these basic types of textile, which were probably available everywhere, is said by the geographers to have had distinct areas of specialist agrarian production is also a sign of interconnectedness, but that would mean putting too much faith in the exactness, in both what they included and what they left out, of these writers. Essentially, what we can above all conclude is that the picture of cloth manufacture that our written sources supply us with does not in any way contradict that which we gathered, in far greater detail, including in its chronological development, from ceramics. There, we could see productive hierarchies which were local first and above all, but which also steadily gained in complexity and geographical range, and which were, therefore, both polycentric and overlapping. I would think it highly likely that cloth was just the same, as it was in most of the regions we have looked at, and that indeed it operated as the exchange underpinning for the better-evidenced patterns of ceramics. But in al-Andalus that must remain a hypothesis.

* * *

Metals in al-Andalus present slightly different issues. In particular, although Islamic Spain and Portugal was lucky in its range of locally mined metals—it had all it needed of every major metal except gold—exactly where they could be found was far less under the control of humans than was the case for agricultural products, and many were in relatively remote areas. To summarize from the collective comments of the geographers, who are clear about the importance of metals even when we can be suspicious of the details, silver was found in the territories of Tudmīr (i.e. Alicante and Murcia), Granada, and the Alentejo/Algarve, plus other places as well (an Islamic-period silver mine was identified in the 1920s near Villaviciosa, in the mountains above Córdoba), lead near Almería, mercury north of Córdoba (this at least is effectively certain; al-Idrīsī claimed after he had visited them that the mines here were huge, with over a thousand workers), zinc in Granada and Córdoba, and copper in Toledo and Almería.[176] Out of all these, the

176 *Crónica del moro Rasis*, ed. Catalán and de Andres, pp. 24, 33, 82; al-Bakrī, *al-Masālik wa al-mamālik*, trans. Vidal Beltrán, pp. 38–9; al-Idrīsī, *Nuzhat al-mushtaq*, trans. Jaubert and Nef, pp. 272,

major exports out of al-Andalus were copper and mercury, to judge from the *geniza*, as we shall see in the next section.

The commonest of all the metals was, however, iron. It is attached by the geographers to numerous places, which is indeed plausible, as iron remains widely available in the Iberian peninsula. It could be effectively smelted thanks to Spain's sufficient supplies of wood, as Matthias Dinnetz remarks in a good survey of Andalusī iron; and it was already being converted into steel, for Ibn ʿAbdūn refers to it in Almorávid Seville (he demands that scissors and knives be made using steel).[177] Metalworking is also far easier to identify archaeologically than is cloth-making, and when such sites have been located in Spain, it is iron, rather than other metals, which predominates there. The mountains above Guadix, at the pass between Granada and Almería, have several ironworking sites with eleventh- and early twelfth-century ceramics; Albalat (prov. Cáceres; see p. 427 above) has a set of ironworking workshops from the same period operating on a considerable scale; not far to the east, the substantial settlement of Vascos (prov. Toledo), from slightly earlier, also has an abundance of iron slag. And in the south-west, Huelva and its province have several sites from the eleventh and twelfth century, both in the mountains and down on the plain, which fits the fact that there are considerable iron resources here too. The town of Saltés on the coast (see p. 410 above) was a particularly important ironworking centre, using metal from more than one place in the province, starting in the tenth century and reaching a height under the Almohads, after 1150.[178]

What the archaeology shows us here is scale. Albalat was transparently not only producing for its own local area, but it is some 100 kilometres from the nearest large towns, Toledo and Mérida/Badajoz; and anyway, as we have seen, it could get ceramics from the south, so probably exported there too. Al-Idrīsī, who mentions the Saltés iron-manufacturing, remarks that it is often the case that ironworking occurs in ports, where great transport ships moor—so it was used for shipbuilding, doubtless, but also for easy export elsewhere.[179] The Andalusīs obviously had to deal with the fact that metal had to be transported from where it was mined to where it would be sold as a finished product, but what both Albalat

292–3, 300; Ibn Ghālib, *Farḥat al-anfus*, trans. Vallvé Bermejo, p. 374, 378; al-Marrākushī, *Kitāb al-muʿjib*, trans. Huici Miranda, p. 298. For the 1920s discovery, see Carbonell, 'La minería', pp. 205–7, persuasively dated by green-glazed ceramics, including oil lamps, even if we cannot pin it down to a century; cf. also Grañeda Miñón, 'La explotación andalusí de la plata en Córdoba'.

[177] Dinnetz, 'Iron and steel'; Ibn ʿAbdūn, *Risāla fī al-qaḍāʾ wa al-ḥisba*, trans. Lévi-Provençal, ch. 220. One surprising absence in our evidence is, however, much contemporary reference to the making of weapons.

[178] Bertrand and Sánchez Viciana, 'Production du fer' (Guadix); Izquierdo Benito, 'Vascos'; Pérez Macías, 'La producción metalúrgica' (Huelva province); Bazzana and Trauth, 'Minéralurgie et métallurgie à Saltés' (all these from an excellent collective volume edited by Canto García and Cressier, *Minas y metalurgía*); Gilotte and Cáceres Gutiérrez, *Al-Balât*, pp. 155–6, 159; Bazzana and Bedia García, *Excavaciones en la isla de Saltés*, pp. 199–211, esp. 204–6.

[179] Al-Idrīsī, *Nuzhat al-mushtaq*, trans. Jaubert and Nef, p. 261.

and Saltés show is that where it was worked into metal could be separate from either. These are chance finds, of course; but they are more substantial than the archaeological evidence of mining or metalworking anywhere else in the Mediterranean in our period, with the sole exception of the dense and well-studied set of sites in Pisa and on the coast to its south (see pp. 573–5 below). As with cloth, they fit into the picture which can be constructed from ceramics, of networks of exchange which go well beyond local areas—even if, as we have seen, local areas had their own internal exchange networks, and communications by land were often difficult. And it is also worth noting that the eleventh and twelfth centuries are more visible in these sites than is the tenth. The sample here is small, but it fits with the pattern of steadily growing economic complexity which the ceramics also show.

The final set of data we can use is money, for the mints named on coins are markers of origins which are even more secure than the petrology of ceramics. Al-Andalus in our period had a bimetallic system of gold and silver coins (the gold was introduced by ʿAbd al-Raḥmān III when he took the caliphal title in 929); the gold came from west Africa for sure, whereas the silver must have been local, given the mines in the peninsula which we know of. As was normal in the Islamic world, the gold dinar was the basic standard coin, heavily used for large-scale commerce and the storage of wealth, but silver of varying degrees of fineness is what most people bought and sold with, as far as we can tell. Both appear in hoards. Under the caliphate, the only mint was in Córdoba (after 947, Madīnat al-Zahrāʾ), so we cannot use mint names to track exchange relationships. By the time of the Almohads too, although they had many mints, these are not consistently named on their unusual square silver coins, so we can say much less about their origins.[180] But we do have a window of a century or so, from the first period of extensive minting by the *ṭāʾifa* kings around 1038 (previously, only the Ḥammūdids, minting especially in Ceuta, were coin producers on any scale) to the decline of the Almorávids, in which we have coin finds with a range of mint names.[181] In the *ṭāʾifa* period, in particular, coins found outside the kingdoms in which they were minted, unless they are found in major political centres, when they might derive from inter-kingdom tribute, must be markers of commercial exchange of some kind; we could not be so sure of that under the Almorávids, when fiscal movement is more possible, but it is likely enough in most cases that we are here seeing commercial movement too. It is worth adding that this is evidence which we can only use for al-Andalus and northern Italy, for in the

[180] For the basic account of Andalusī coinage, see Medina Gómez, *Monedas hispano-musulmanas*. For a guide to what we can say about Almohad evidence, see Ariza Armada, 'El tesorillo almohade', which surveys hoard sites. Named mints were most often North African, but this does not, in a state in large part ruled from Morocco, automatically show commerce.

[181] For the complex origins of *ṭāʾifa* minting, see López Martínez de Marigorta, 'Acuñaciones monetarias de al-Andalus'.

other states we have looked at minting remained largely centralized, so we cannot easily track movements outside minting areas. See pp. 614–15 below for Italy.

We have to be tentative when looking at money. Hoard finds are chancy by definition, and I have not seen any syntheses based on coins found on archaeological sites in al-Andalus apart from Carolina Doménech's work on the Valencia region; we can only make the broadest generalizations.[182] All the same, we can already say that finds seem to be rare in the Gharb al-Andalus, and comparatively rare on the plateau.[183] Coins were commonest on the coast, especially in the far south and in the Sharq, and also in the Guadalquivir valley; this in itself fits the patterns of ceramic trading we have already seen. In the *ṭāi'fa* period, however, it is significant that the mint most often seen on coins found outside its kingdom was Valencia, and the second was Toledo. The first could allow us to propose that the rise of that town as an exchange centre was already beginning in the mid- to later eleventh century; it is worth noting that Denia coins are rather scarcer. To find Valencian coins dominating a *ṭāi'fa* hoard at Vélez Blanco in the southern mountains, east of Murcia, or another at Cihuela, inland from Zaragoza, is, nonetheless, noteworthy; these are not close either to the mint or to major exchange routes.[184] Toledo is more surprising, given its plateau location; it must reflect the city's political projection in part (Toledo even controlled Valencia for a decade), but all the same, one would not have expected money from here to be as visible as it is at Alcañiz, down the Ebro from Zaragoza, or at Belalcázar in the hills north of Córdoba, even if the latter was closer to the Toledo border. These do, it seems to me, show beyond doubt that money—and thus commerce—was regularly moving across frontiers, and often on a considerable scale. Indeed, there is hardly a single hoard from the *ṭāi'fa* period which has coins from only one mint.[185]

In the Almorávid period, hoards almost never have coins from a single mint either. One exception is Alcaudete (prov. Jaén), where the identifiable coins are all from Córdoba, but that city is not so far away. So the coins from Murcia (especially), Valencia, Seville, and Granada are not surprising in the 1150s hoard from the major exchange centre of Almería (see p. 406 above), even if we might have expected more than one coin out of thirty-two to have come from the city's own mint. Conversely, it is significant that in a hoard from Jimena in the hills above Jaén, not a central area at all, we find coins from Seville, Murcia, Almería, Valencia,

[182] For what follows on hoards, I have relied on the lists in Canto García, 'La moneda'; Doménech-Belda, 'Fatimíes y taifas'; Doménech Belda, *Dinares, dirhams*, pp. 143–71, 204–8 (for the País Valencià); Retamero, *La contínua il·lusió del moviment perpetu*, pp. 144–52, 246–51 (for the *ṭāi'fas*); Retamero i Sarralvo, 'Sobre els ocultaments de peces almoràvits'.

[183] See, e.g., Gómez Martínez, 'La cultura material del Garb al-Andalus', p. 143; Gilotte, *Aux marges d'al-Andalus*, pp. 301–23; Canto García, 'Numismática taifa'.

[184] Doménech Belda, 'Fatimíes y taifas', pp. 206–7. See Map 17 for hoard sites.

[185] I have seen reference to only three for the *ṭāi'fa* period out of sixty-three on the mainland, in Bonete (prov. Albacete), Xaló (prov. Alicante), and near Zaragoza; see Retamero, *La contínua il·lusió del moviment perpetu*, pp. 246–9.

Granada, and even Badajoz.[186] Jimena was in the part of the hinterland of Jaén which then produced raw silk, and this may well explain the range here; but it is still a striking one. And whether or not it is silk-related, it implies that villagers, at least rich ones, were accumulating money from wide areas, on the basis of sales—as do, indeed, the other hoard sites mentioned here, almost all of them entirely rural, in areas without productive specializations that we know about.

So all these patterns, of cloth, metal, and coin hoards, point in the same direction, which is also that most clearly visible in the distribution of ceramic finds. We are dealing here with complex local productions and distributions. These were already interconnected in the caliphal period, through region-wide exchange linkages which stretched deeply into the countrysides of most of al-Andalus, although as yet they were relatively lightly travelled. In the *ṭāʾifa* period, local production and distribution networks developed considerably; and then, with the relative recentralizations of the Almorávids and the Almohads, both the local economies and the links between them became far stronger, which meant that the polycentricity of the economy did not change as the region-wide network developed further. The moving of *cuerda seca* pottery both to rural sites in Portugal and to other cities which also produced it, the moving of Granada raw silk to Almería, even though Granada was itself a substantial town, the moving of iron to Saltés to smelt it into artisanal products which were then sold elsewhere, or the moving of coins considerable distances from the inland and frontier city of Toledo are all signs of the increasing density and overlapping complexity of the links which held this web of local economies together, ever more tightly. And underpinning this was the growing size and productive capacity of towns in al-Andalus, as shown by, for example, their unrivalled numbers of ceramic kilns, and thus also their growing buying power, matched by the fact that peasants had enough surplus to sell. We can easily be impressed by this. But we also have to try to explain it; and the last part of this section will attempt to do that, at least in schematic terms.

5.4.3 The roots of growth

We have seen that all the other regions so far discussed in this book had periods in which local economic complexity increased, often substantially; and all except one, Ifrīqiya, was beyond doubt more economically complex in 1180 than it had been in 950. But there is no simple monocausal explanation which can be claimed to have affected all of them—far from it. Indeed, when discussing them, I gave quite different explanations for each, associated with the other structural changes

[186] Retamero i Sarralvo, 'Sobre els ocultaments de peces almoràvits', pp. 236–7; for the Almería hoard, see Ferrandis Torres, 'Tesorillo de dinares almorávides'.

that can be seen to have characterized them; furthermore, the shift upwards took place in different centuries, according to the region. To be brief, in Egypt, we can hypothesize that the steadily increasing density of production and commercial exchange in the tenth and eleventh centuries, in particular, was the long-term result of the end of a colonial relationship between the region and the Roman Empire, and to a lesser extent the 'Abbāsid Caliphate; but explanation was least necessary here, as the increase was from a very high initial baseline, and was also not as fast as elsewhere. In Ifrīqiya, the apparently sudden tenth-century rise could tentatively be linked to the fiscal recentralization of the Aghlabid rulers, built on by the Fāṭimids. In Sicily, where the power of the state seems always to have been strong, I was less tentative about arguing that the even clearer tenth-century take-off was related to the end of the great estates of the plateau and a resultant increase in peasant buying power. In Byzantium, the moment of upward economic movement was, rather, the late eleventh century and especially the twelfth; there, where the power of the state had not changed much since the late ninth century, at least in the Aegean heartland which was the main focus of discussion, and where peasant independence or dependence did not change dramatically either, notwithstanding the steady growth in influence of private landowners, it seemed most likely that the initial motor for change lay in a documented trend to demographic growth and land clearance, that is to say, an increase in total agricultural production. And in north-central Italy, as we shall see in Chapter 6, demographic growth and land clearance, a steady and related increase in the size of towns, plus the growth of elite landowning and lordship, lay at the base of a later but fast development of exchange at the very end of our period.[187]

These distinct explanations may in each case be incomplete. It is highly likely, for example, that a demographic rise was more generalized than we know in these regions; it is, so far, hard to see outside Byzantium and north-central Italy, but it is probable elsewhere, especially where we also have indications of urban expansion, as plausibly in Sicily. But in each case, they depend on the stability of other parameters. In Egypt, Sicily, and Byzantium, a tax-raising state had long been dominant, and thus a set of routes for the movement of surplus, in kind or money, to sometimes distant state elites continuously existed, which would have helped the further growth of commercial exchange when that became significant; but in Ifrīqiya state power was probably a more recent development, so it would have had a greater impact. In the first three, we can also see by our period, beside state-paid and landowning elites, a relatively autonomous peasantry with its own buying power; in Sicily, however, although the other elements remained the same, that peasant autonomy was a more recent development, so it is this which could have had a greater impact. In this array of difference, however, there were two

[187] See pp. 124–5, 183, 243, 250–1, 301–4, 349–52, 616–17 above, and 650–62 below for a general synthesis.

elements in common. First, a feature of all of them (except perhaps Ifrīqiya, where the evidence is too poor to say) was not just a coexistence but a long-term balance between the rich official and landed elite, whose demand in each case also allowed for networks of region-wide exchange, and—at least in many areas of each region—communities of peasants who were themselves prosperous enough to buy goods, sometimes from a long way away, using the exchange networks which the state had already established. Even in Italy, where the state was weakest, and public taxation was particularly weak until the very end of our period and after, the twelfth century saw the same sort of balance between rich elites and autonomous peasant buyers, which came to have the same effect on the growth there of a region-wide exchange system in the thirteenth century. This balance is important as a common feature, and we will look at its implications in Chapters 7 and 8.

The second element is that none of these explanations rested on any economic relationship which a given region had with any other. It is true that Sicily's linen industry in the eleventh century entirely depended on a tight and ongoing link with Egypt, which supplied it with flax, but when it ended, the island had plenty of other internal resources (and indeed switched production to cotton). Anyway, that industry was the concern of only a few towns; the rest of the island was never reliant on it economically, and may not have been affected at all by its collapse, except insofar as mass-produced linen presumably became less available locally too. That is to say, major economic change was always internally driven, a point stressed throughout this book. We will see that much the same parameters were a feature of northern and central Italy in our period as well. But how does al-Andalus fit in with this?

It seems to me that the growth in complexity of the Andalusī economy, taken as a whole, was greater than that in any of the other regions discussed in this book—including northern Italy, until after our period. It started from a uniquely low base before 900, with a set of disconnected and localized economic structures, some of them very simple, and by the end was more complex than Byzantium and perhaps even rivalled Egypt. So the challenge to explain it is that much greater. But the *sorts* of explanation we have seen for the economic expansion of the other regions in this book were fully applicable to al-Andalus as well; it is just that here we can find all of them, fiscal centralization, urban expansion, agrarian growth, and peasant buying power at once.

Full fiscal centralization in al-Andalus only came in the tenth century, with the defeat of the first *fitna*. It is not, of course, that the *amīr*s in Córdoba failed to tax; indeed, they did so from the start, often as heavily as later. The wealth of Córdoba as early as the late eighth century is clearly seen in the rich archaeology of the Shaqunda suburb, mentioned earlier (p. 394). But the state at best coexisted with some very powerful local aristocrats, and it is likely that central control over the fiscal system—and even perhaps the geographical range of taxation itself—was for long incomplete. The vision of the tenth century as being the first period in which the Umayyad *amīr*s, now caliphs, fully controlled al-Andalus, an interpretation associated in recent years with Manuel Acién and Eduardo Manzano among others, seems inescapable to me too, as noted earlier;[188] in material terms, it fits both the remarkable expansion of the capital in this period and the availability of green and manganese ceramics almost everywhere across the caliphate. It was then that the network of fiscal routes was first properly laid out, to bring food for the capital, and money or goods for state elites, the army, and the caliph's ever-active builders, which increased their buying power, at the same moment as it linked the subregions of Islamic Iberia together economically for the first time.

A development of this kind probably set off Ifrīqiya's productive growth, and certainly it did the same for al-Andalus. But it was not reversed when the region split up into *ṭāʾifa* kingdoms; in a time of political division, the latter region had a very different trajectory from the former. In al-Andalus, all that happened at the moment of that division was that the fiscal centralization which had been established by ʿAbd al-Raḥmān III was relocated to the provinces, to the new *ṭāʾifa* capitals, and could contribute to the prosperity of more cities than just Córdoba. Local elite buying power could thus develop; and it continued, with provincial centres continuing to be active and prosperous, when the state and the fiscal system were to an extent recentralized again under the North African dynasties. Urban expansion, well documented in the archaeology of two dozen towns, continued without a break in the eleventh and twelfth centuries—by the later twelfth century, including Córdoba again. And we have seen that this expansion and the productions which it involved were large-scale and geographically extended: overlapping networks of production and distribution developed across the region, extending to quite remote areas, such as Albalat on the northern plateau frontier, which was, nonetheless, a major metalworking centre with connections to the south. The linkages which facilitated all this were related to the networks established by the state—but, by now, not only the state.

Urban production added greatly to the complexity and scale of al-Andalus's overall economy, its GDP, to use an anachronism. But, as in all pre-capitalist societies, the basic production here was always agrarian. For a start, urban expansion, which is clearer here than in any other region so far discussed (only northern Italy matches it, although elsewhere we do not have good enough data), always means immigration from the countryside, and thus doubtless demographic growth there too. But, above all, towns could not have expanded as much as they did if they were only producing for themselves; what was needed was buyers, and, of course, food suppliers, who had an agrarian base. The buyers could be aristocratic elites, either rich from a taxation system which was above all based on land taxes, or

[188] For Acién, see n. 37 above; Manzano Moreno, *Conquistadores, emires*, esp. pp. 298, 358–9, 461–6.

landowners, rich from rents (or indeed both at once, as rulers themselves were). We have seen that landowners did not cease to exist with the second *fitna*, and that rents could be very remunerative. Their demand, as much as those of state-paid officials, structured productive systems everywhere. But in al-Andalus, as in our other regions, peasants had buying power as well, as we can see from the regular finds of fine wares, certainly not village-made, on almost every rural site, even many remote ones, all the way across the region, as well as a smaller set of largely rural coin hoards. This fits with the relatively contained levels of taxation attested here, not above 10–17 per cent, and may mean that rent payers were in a minority, even if, as we have seen, it may equally be that even 50 per cent rents did not always cut peasants out out of the market. Peasants, as well as elites, here as elsewhere, could make money by selling their surplus to satisfy urban needs, and use that money to buy artisanal goods.

Further underpinning this was agrarian growth in absolute terms. For what clearly marks Andalusī agriculture out from that of other regions is the wide development of its irrigation systems; they are best documented in the south and east of the region and on the Balearic islands, but they were common elsewhere as well. These are difficult to date, as we have already seen, and had both Roman roots in some cases and probable initial layouts in the emiral period in some others; but the tenth and eleventh centuries have been repeatedly canvassed as a major period of expansion for them. They are often associated with fortifications, structuring irrigated territories, which appear then; earlier dates have been proposed for some, for example in the lower Segura river (prov. Alicante), or parts of the Alpujarras (prov. Granada and Almería), but other such systems were later as well, and the tenth century remains the most likely period when irrigation systems really took off, and from then on expanded further.[189] Irrigation hugely increased agricultural surpluses everywhere it was practised. It is in this context above all that 10–17 per cent taxation and 50 per cent for rents did not undermine the ability of peasants to accumulate surplus; this surplus was evidently sufficient for them to buy the ceramics which archaeologists have found, plus metalwork (as, for example, the Liétor find showed; see p. 425 above; Liétor had and has a well-defined system of *regadío*[190]), and doubtless cloth. In this context it does not matter so much that villages were very unlikely to have been egalitarian;

[189] For brief framing syntheses, see Bazzana, *Maisons d'al-Andalus*, pp. 392–3; Cressier, 'Agua, fortificaciones'; Manzano, *Conquistadores, emires*, pp. 458–60. For specific case studies, see, e.g., Torró Abad, *La formació d'un espai feudal: Alcoi*, pp. 42–53; Eiroa Rodríguez, 'Arqueología de los espacios', pp. 109–11; and for early examples, see n. 43 above. Even the *horta* of Valencia, which certainly predates 900 in some form, expanded several times later; see Esquilache Martí, *Els constructors de l'Horta de València*, pp 299–303 and figs. 38–40. It should be noted that in the Balearic islands, where much important work has been done on irrigation systems (see, e.g., the work collected in Barceló et al., *Les aïgues cercades*, and Kirchner, *Por una arqueología agraria*), the Islamic systems must be tenth-century and later, as the islands were only conquered in 903.

[190] See Navarro, 'Los espacios irrigados rurales'.

at least richer peasants could buy, which was sufficient for the exchange system to work, and, anyway, acquisitions sometimes extended to wide proportions of the village population. It was this development which most singled al-Andalus out in our period; the spread of irrigation was rather less marked in Sicily or Byzantium or northern Italy, whereas in Egypt and (parts of) Ifrīqiya it was there already. It makes the considerable scale of urban expansion here less hard to explain, for the towns could count on a much wider market for their production.

Many of the roots of growth lie here, then: in the development of irrigation and the resultant considerable expansion of agricultural surplus, which in turn fuelled the expansion of towns, for more people could live off the surplus; generalized demographic expansion in al-Andalus is strongly implied by this too. But the networks which were created by the fiscal system in the tenth century were equally important, for without them it would have been much harder for the commercial routes to be established which brought goods to the countryside. On both sides of this equation, the starting point was the tenth century, and the development of both could run in parallel and reinforce each other, up to the very complex systems of the late twelfth. It would in some cases even outlast the crisis of the Christian conquests of the 1230s–1240s, which had very different results from place to place (Seville and Valencia did well out of it; many other areas certainly did not). But the effects of those conquests do not have to concern us here; unlike in Sicily, they took place some time after the latest dates for this book. We do not have to go beyond the high Almohad period, one of notable activity in all aspects of the Andalusī economy, in which both urban and rural production and exchange systems were doing remarkably well, and with rather less oppression of the peasant majority than is often found in buoyant economies too. I ended my survey of the towns of al-Andalus with Siyāsa in the years around 1200, and it is worth ending this section with it too—a small urban centre with mediocre communications, fed by a small but intensely cultivated irrigated valley, and full of good-quality housing, striking plaster decoration, and Murcian *esgrafiado* pottery. That can stand for the density of exchange as well as the prosperity of urban centres, and also, we can now see, its links with a hinterland of *regadío*.

The final point to be made here concerns routes. We have seen that al-Andalus had poor land communications, simply because of its geography; but this did not prevent economic relationships from developing. We cannot doubt that the substantial localization of the economies of the emiral period was reinforced by communications difficulties. After that, however, donkeys will have been regularly used, to get across not just the passes but pretty much from everywhere to everywhere else inland, given the relative paucity of navigable rivers—including to Siyāsa. But so must boats have been (see Map 18). As elsewhere in the Mediterranean, it is not chance that many—even if by no means all—of al-Andalus's major towns, Málaga, Almería, Denia, or Valencia, were on the coast, with Seville and Murcia very close, and they were certainly connected. As in other regions, we can also assume that coastal shipping from port to port was a normal feature of economic relationships—and, indeed, this was true along the Atlantic coast and up some rivers as much as in the Mediterranean, as we saw for Mértola—so small, so far west, so well connected. But it has to be said that we do not know much about it. Ibn Ḥazm says he went by boat when he travelled from near Seville to Valencia. Other poets expressed their fear of the sea, while travelling on it anyway.[191] But we do not have the range of sources we had for maritime interconnections in both Byzantium and Sicily; we simply have to assume it. On the other hand, we can assume it all the more because we also, of course, have evidence for Andalusīs travelling abroad, and incomers to the region as well; except for those from and to inland Christian Spain, all of them travelled by ship. This is where we must move onwards, from the internal exchange of al-Andalus to a reconstruction of what we know about its links to other regions, to conclude this chapter.

5.5 Islamic Spain and the Mediterranean, 950–1180

As for other regions, some maritime commerce between Mediterranean Spain and the rest of the Islamic world was routine throughout our period. We have little evidence for the period before 1000, although it is clear from some of the *fatwā*s quoted in Chapter 3 (pp. 186–7) that Ifrīqiyan jurists already saw at least some travel to al-Andalus as normal in the ninth century, and the refoundation of Almería in 954/5 probably had a commercial as well as a warlike intent. To get a sense of the projection of al-Andalus in the Mediterranean after that, however, we need to go back to the *geniza* again. As soon as it begins around 1000, we find evidence of Egyptian Jewish merchant enterprises going to the Spanish coast. This was particularly a feature of the early eleventh century; it dropped off in the second half of the eleventh, for reasons which are unclear. So Ibn ʿAwkal often sent goods and agents to Spain, but after 1050 or so Nahray b. Nissīm and his associates did so much more rarely; few of them went there themselves, and when a certain Abū al-Faḍl went there from Sicily, he organized the settling of his accounts with Nahray first, indicating that he was going outside his normal range. To Nahray and his associates, as Goldberg has argued, al-Andalus was like Byzantium, in being in effect off the map.[192]

[191] For the Atlantic, see Picard, *L'océan atlantique musulman*, esp. pp. 377–458; Ibn Ḥazm, *Tawq al-hamāma*, trans. García Gómez, pp. 245–6; Pérès, *Esplendor de al-Andalus*, pp. 217–18.

[192] For Ibn ʿAwkal, see, e.g., DK 327 (Gil K221, Goitein, *Letters*, n. 1), Bodl. MS Heb. d 65/9, T-S 12.218, 8.12 (Gil K148, 117, 166, Stillman, *East-west relations*, pp. 208–13, 281–4, 288–90); for other texts from the earlier period and for developments later, see Goldberg, *Trade and institutions*, pp. 256, 313–19; see also Goitein, *MS*, 1, pp. 21, 213–14; for Abū al-Faḍl, see Bodl. MS Heb. c 28/61 (Gil K 576 [S156]).

On the other hand, the Nahray letters contain many references to Andalusī ships coming into harbour in Alexandria. There was also an active merchant family there called al-Andalusī in the mid-century; even if there is no direct evidence that the family traded with Spain, it had obviously come from there, and Constable commented that it is entirely plausible that family members maintained commercial links westwards.[193] The Spain–Egypt connection, anyway, evidently continued; it is just that for a while it had less relationship with the Ben Ezra synagogue. Indeed, the Andalusī ships by no means have to have carried Jewish merchants; Mujāhid of Denia's ship (see p. 407 above) shows a Spanish political involvement in commerce which was, presumably, largely Muslim in orientation; a century later, so do the ships of the *sulṭān* (presumably the Almorávid state), and of the *qa'īd* Ibn Maymūn (who controlled the Almorávid fleet in Almería), which are attested in the years around 1140.[194] But we do have a number of texts from Spain itself surviving in the *geniza* from the later eleventh century; not all relate to trade, but some do, and the very fact that they ended up in Fusṭāṭ indicates some form of connectivity which still extended to the Jewish community of that city. Some of the letters also refer to independent Andalusī links with both Sicily and Ifrīqiya, in a western version of the triangular trade linking these two regions with Alexandria and Fusṭāṭ. This matches the interesting make-up of those eleventh-century hoards of coins in Spain (above all found along the east coast and around Córdoba) which include Fāṭimid money, for over two-thirds of this was minted in Sicily, and nearly all the rest in Ifrīqiya, with almost none from Egypt.[195] And after 1100, *geniza* references to Egyptian merchants going to al-Andalus pick up again, or at least the percentage of texts relating to the far west substantially increases, among the smaller number of Mediterranean trading letters which survive for the twelfth century. There is no equivalent to the drop in references that we find for Ifrīqiya and Sicily until the 1140s;[196] and indeed, the

[193] For Andalusī ships, see Goldberg, *Trade and institutions*, pp. 304, 315, 317; for the family, see Constable, *Trade and traders*, pp. 90–3.

[194] For the *sulṭān* and the *qa'īd*, see T-S 12.290 (Frenkel, *Ha-Ohavim*, n. 22), 13J14.21, 10J10.23, 13J15.16+13J15.20 (Goitein and Friedman, *India book* IV/B, nn. 34, 73, 74); for comment, see Goitein, *MS*, 1, p. 310; Constable, *Trade and traders*, pp. 123–4, with more citations; I am less sure than either of them that the *sulṭān* was the ruler of Béjaïa. Ibn Maymūn, shortly after this, in the mid-1140s, refused the independent rulership of Almería during the revolts against the Almorávids, according to al-Marrākushī, *Kitāb al-mu'jib*, trans. Huici Miranda, pp. 170–1, saying that he was only a sea captain, and would only be able to help the city in its sea defence; the sentiment, if authentic, was admirable, but the Genoese claimed in 1137 that they had chased away his fleet (*Annali genovesi*, 1, ed. Belgrano, p. 29), and if he was still active, he certainly failed to prevent the capture of the city in 1147.

[195] For the Spanish texts, see Ashtor, 'Documentos españoles'; of these, nn. 8–9 (T-S 12.570, 13J21.7) are for commerce in cinnabar to Mahdia. For other references to early triangular trade, see, e.g., T-S 20.71, Bodl. MS Heb. a 3/13, DK 230.1 (Gil K 367, 561, 581 [S81, 91, 109]), T-S 12.261, 13J29.1 (Gil K159, 228). For the coins, see Doménech-Belda, 'Fatimíes y taifas'; Doménech-Belda, 'The Fāṭimid coins'.

[196] After the early 1140s, references do drop off sharply, although they do not entirely end. The last *geniza* text I have seen for al-Andalus is from around 1155, T-S 10J14.16 (Goitein and Friedman, *India traders*, III, 47); but after that there is little *geniza* material for trading anywhere in the Mediterranean.

latest-documented Egyptian Jewish merchant with Spanish connections, Ḥalafūn b. Nathaniāl, best known to the historiography by the Hebrew version of his name, Ḥalfōn b. Nethanel, active in the 1120s–1140s, is the dealer with the closest personal links to al-Andalus out of any of those documented in the *geniza*. We will come back to him shortly.

This was quite a complex network, then, of triangular or quadrangular trading, carried out by both Muslims and Jews. We should not, however, conclude from these data that al-Andalus was a real far-western equivalent to Egypt in the route systems of commerce in the Islamic world. It is interesting how little we hear about how trading with Spain was actually carried out. Goldberg points out that in both the early and the late eleventh century, merchants simply go to an undifferentiated al-Andalus, or buy goods from merchants from there; they do not go to specific ports such as Denia or Almería, or compare prices between them, as they do in the central Mediterranean, and indeed there are hardly any references to ports at all in our eleventh-century letters, although on the occasions when they are, these two indeed figure, plus Seville. Nor can we get any real sense of which Andalusīs the Egyptians traded with, either on the Spanish coast or in Alexandria, for the whole of that century. Al-Andalus was the other end of a very long supply route. It is clear that many Andalusīs came directly to Egypt without stopping, but it was equally possible for Egyptians to let the ports of the central Mediterranean, such as Palermo or Mahdia, act as the effective entrepôts, and, in particular in the later eleventh century, they probably did.[197] Trade from the eastern end of the Mediterranean to the western end continued through the century, without breaks, but the lack of reference to the sort of personal connections which the *geniza* merchants prized elsewhere shows that it was rarely so very dense.

This was for one straightforward reason: Islamic Spain's major export was silk. As mentioned earlier, mercury (in the form of cinnabar, the mineral from which both mercury and vermilion dye is refined) and copper were also standard exports; so was paper, even if we cannot tell on what scale. The geographers also list as exports Seville's cotton and olive oil, and once linen, but the last two will have competed in Egypt with the nearer productions of Tunisia and Sicily, and the *geniza* does not refer to any of them. These were not luxury products, but silk, to a substantial extent, was, and we hear about it more often—including in the

The routes continued, all the same; Maimonides refers to regular boats to Seville at the end of the century; see Goitein, *MS*, 1, pp. 213, 452.

[197] Goldberg, *Trade and institutions*, p. 313. For Denia, see, e.g., T-S 12.570, 13J21.7 (Ashtor, 'Documentos españoles', nn. 8–9), 13J7.11 (cf. Goitein, *MS*, 1, p. 407), 8J20.2 (with Almería), 10J16.17 (Gil K494 [S113], 420, trans. Udovitch, 'A tale of two cities', n. 1). For Seville, see T-S 8J27.2, CUL Or.1080 J167 (Gil K447, 448). 'Directly without stopping' is a manner of speaking; texts imply it, so boats may not have stopped to trade, but they have to have taken on water. See Pryor, *Geography, technology*, pp. 75–86, for how hard it was for sea transport to carry enough water for more than two to three weeks, which might allow a boat to cover up to 1,800 kilometres at most; the Almería to Alexandria route was over 3,000 kilometres.

geniza, which pays considerable attention to bulk goods—than we do any other commodity. In return, Spain imported spices and dyestuffs above all, plus, occasionally, as we have also seen, wool.[198] But out of all these, silk, whether raw or woven, predominated. Andalusī silk was a more important commodity even than that from Sicily, to judge by the references to it. Silk cloth was made, it seems (see p. 403 above), on the largest scale in Almería itself, the perfect location for export. This is what the Egyptians were waiting for when Andalusī ships docked at Alexandria; when they arrived, silk prices went down.[199] But as we have seen for Byzantium, where the evidence for silk production is more generous (see pp. 323–6 above), building a large-scale trading system out of silk is impossible; even as a semi-luxury available to less privileged elites, it only reached a smallish minority of the population.

Ḥalfōn b. Nethanel, precisely because he is the well-documented exception here, illustrates these points quite well. A total of 103 texts survive concerning him, dating to 1120–46, but concentrating in the years 1130–41; Goitein and Friedman edited them with a Hebrew translation as part of their *India book* series. Ḥalfōn's presence in al-Andalus is best attested in 1138–9; for most of the 1130s he was in Aden and India, transacting in pearls, spices, and the other basic goods of the India trade, and then in the 1140s he was a sedentary merchant in Egypt before he went out on his last documented voyage, this time to Damascus.[200] That in itself is quite a range, the widest anywhere in the *geniza*, and the western Mediterranean is not at first sight so important in it; but in fact, a letter from 1130 makes it clear that he was already closely involved in al-Andalus. Indeed, by then he had family there, at least by a set of indirect marriage links, who were part of the intellectual elite in major Jewish centres such as Granada and Lucena: the Ibn Ezra family of Hebrew poets and religious writers (some of whose members were involved in trading with Ḥalfōn) and Yehūda ha-Levi, also a major theologian and poet. Ḥalfōn was himself a scholar (as were two of his brothers, both *yeshīva* judges in Fusṭāṭ); we have short theological and juristic tracts among his letters, and he was regarded by ha-Levi as a friend and equal. Together, when Ḥalfōn was

[198] Constable, *Trade and traders*, pp. 151–208, has full lists and citations; other exports were less important. For paper, see n. 165 above. Constable notes, pp. 229–30, that iron was not an export commodity, and indeed it is not mentioned as one, in either the geographers or the *geniza*. But it was a significant product in al-Andalus, and it was a commodity Egypt was short of; and we have little evidence for its import into Egypt from anywhere, until our scarce references to Italian trading in it in the twelfth century (cf. pp. 146–7 above). We might, then, regard it as a potentially significant export; but we cannot develop the point in the absence of evidence. If it really matched silk in its scale, it is hard to imagine that no one would ever mention it at all.

[199] For the importance of Spanish silk, see Constable, *Trade and traders*, pp. 173–6, and, briefly, Goitein, *MS*, 1. p. 102, with 4, pp. 168–9; Goldberg, *Trade and institutions*, p. 345. For silk prices going down, see T-S 13J22.30 (Goitein, *Letters*, n. 53), 13J25.14 (Gil K583).

[200] The letters and other texts, with an extensive commentary, are in Goitein and Friedman, *India book* IV/B; a loan contract from 1139, CUL Or.1080 1.88+T-S NS 99.55, is added in Friedman, 'An India trader's partnership', which also briefly discusses the Ḥalfōn set as a whole.

in the west in 1138, they collaborated to raise money to redeem Jewish captives in Toledo; and Ḥalfōn was the architect of ha-Levi's pilgrimage east in 1140–1 to the great religious sites in Palestine—during which he spent so much time being lionized in Alexandria and Fusṭāṭ that he only just made it to the Holy Land before his death in the summer of 1141.[201] So, given these Spanish links, it is not surprising that when we look at Ḥalfōn's commercial letters concerning al-Andalus, all from 1138–41, we find, on this occasion, some of the characteristic elements of *geniza* mercantile letter-writing a century earlier, such as obsessive (but necessary) lists of prices in different places, references to other boats and merchants arriving and leaving, and greetings sent to or from more merchants and state officials—the features which we missed in the mid-twelfth-century letters for Sicily (see p. 195 above). This trading, at least, was dense.

Ḥalfōn's trading to al-Andalus was—unlike his wider personal links—all to and in Almería, which again confirms the importance of that town in the years before the Genoese attack of 1147 (see pp. 403–6 above). He operated as much in the Maghreb, however, in Tlemcen in the far west of modern Algeria on the Moroccan border—the Maghribī city that was nearest to Almería, not on the sea but close to it—and in the major inland city of Fès; indeed, some of the letters we have for 1138 show him in the Maghreb and his business partners in Almería.[202] This was certainly a triangular trade pattern, this time linking Spain, Morocco, and Egypt. It is supported by some early twelfth-century *geniza* letters which do not involve Ḥalfōn, but which, similarly, deal with an Almería–Fès route as part of normal traffic. This was a trading world made easier by the Almorávid conquests on both sides of the Strait of Gibraltar, which both unified the two coasts and greatly developed the buying power of Morocco's main cities, but it preexisted them: one *fatwā* from Córdoba concerns a detailed court case of 1066 about a partnership (*mufāwada*) selling silk in Fès.[203] The Ḥalfōn letters discuss goods coming from Morocco, which were dyes, perfumes, and particularly alum, plus gold from south of the Sahara (and once also, surprisingly, given Spain's own production, copper, although copper was also exported from Almería to Tlemcen and Fès[204]); prices for pepper appear too, presumably brought by Ḥalfōn and

[201] For 1130, see Goitein and Friedman, *India book* IV/B, n. 3 (CUL Add.3340); for Ḥalfōn's own tracts, see ibid., nn. 93, 96, 102 (T-S 16.40, AS 172.68, NS 226.166); for Toledo, see ibid., nn. 35–6 (T-S 8J18.5, 10J15.1); the first and last two of these are translated in Goitein, *MS*, 5, pp. 288–9, 463–4; see ibid., pp. 448–68, for Ḥalfōn's relationship with ha-Levi and the latter's pilgrimage to the east, which is extensively documented across the last half of Goitein and Friedman, *India book* IV/B.

[202] Goitein and Friedman, *India book* IV/B, esp. nn. 27–8, 30–2, 34, 37–40, 100 (T-S 8J19.28+13J26.12, 12.274, Bodl. MS Heb. d 74/41, T-S 8J18.1, 12.285, 13J14.21, ENA NS I.4, T-S 10J11.27, CUL Or.1080 J94, 8J14.22+NS J431, CUL Or.1080 J94, T-S 13J21.12).

[203] Bodl. MS Heb. d 66/52, T-S 12.435 (Goitein, *Letters*, nn. 6, 7); al-Wansharīsī, *al-Mi'yār*, trans. Lagardère, *Histoire et société*, 5.279. See also Picard, *L'océan atlantique musulman*, for western routes.

[204] Copper: Goitein and Friedman, *India book* IV/B, nn. 30, 100, with T-S 12.435 (all translated in Goitein, *Letters*, nn. 7, 59–60; n. 100 has a revised translation in Bennison and Gallego, 'Jewish trading in Fes').

similar merchants from Egypt; but the main commodity in the letters was once again silk. This was the basic export which the mercantile community seems to have expected from al-Andalus, and it paid for all the rest. Indeed, when Ḥalfōn was back in Egypt in 1140–1, he was still trading in silk, presumably using the same web of western associates who are documented in 1138–9. In one of his letters to ha-Levi, he says that he would have stayed in al-Andalus had not one of his brothers died; all the same, his Spanish connections did not strictly require his physical presence, and silk continued to come to Egypt.[205]

This set of documents shows us, then, a continuous exchange relationship between al-Andalus and Egypt—between Almería and Alexandria—which was structured by one main product, silk, going eastwards. It seems also to have been that which went southwards, via Morocco, to buy the gold from west Africa necessary for the gold coinage of the Andalusī states; after 1100 or 1150, when the buying power and exchange systems of Latin Europe had become more developed, some of it went northwards too, as it had done earlier into Christian Spain;[206] but all the signs are that the route to Egypt remained the most important throughout our period. There was, as noted earlier, no set of sudden shifts in this exchange relationship, as there were for Ifrīqiya and Sicily, as we explored in Chapter 3. Indeed, when Sicily faced temporary difficulties in the later eleventh century, Spanish silk may well have been all the more needed in the east. But the scale of this trade was always restricted by the simple fact that silk was not a bulk good. It cannot ever have rivalled the scale of the trade in flax for linen between Alexandria, Mahdia, and Palermo in the eleventh century. Spanish silk and, secondarily, Spanish metals, were convenient ways of obtaining eastern products such as spices and some dyes, and even wheat on occasion (see p. 414 above), but it does also have to be said that al-Andalus produced everything it really needed itself. From that standpoint, it was even less dependent on the Mediterranean than was Egypt. This is the essential underpinning for the fact that we hear much less about this trade from the *geniza* in this region than we do for trading in the central Mediterranean. I will come back to the point.

What we can see from the archaeology confirms this pattern very broadly, but, for Mediterranean-wide trade, the data it provides are rather thinner than we have seen for the economy of al-Andalus itself. We are here reliant on the distributions of fine wares, and, through them, we certainly find the links we have just seen in the *geniza*. East Mediterranean lustre was imported to Madīnat al-Zahrā' in the late tenth century, and is then visible above all in Valencia in the eleventh; if it dropped off after that, it is largely because Seville and then Zaragoza and other

[205] Goitein and Friedman, *India book* IV/B, nn. 67–70, 73, 80–1, 85, 89 (T-S 8.60, 20.80, 10J9.27, NS J7, 10J10.23, 12.287, 13J14.1, Bodl. MS Heb. c 28/12, Halper 344), and 92 (T-S 24.47) to ha-Levi about his brother.

[206] For silk going into Latin Europe, see Constable, *Trade and traders*, pp. 177–80.

centres started to make it themselves, in a process of import substitution, but also, initially at least, to make political claims (see p. 420 above).[207] Chinese imports, which have to have come through Egypt, are above all eleventh-century as well, and have been found in particular in Valencia and Almería. We can add here a large cache of eleventh-century bronze candlesticks from the Fāṭimid lands (probably in this case Palestine, again presumably coming via Egypt) which were found in Denia.[208] As for Ifrīqiya, its ceramics begin to be found in al-Andalus in the late tenth century, from both Ṣabra al-Manṣūriya and, in the eleventh century, the Kalâa des Béni-Hammad; after 1000, these wares were found above all on the east coast.[209] The twelfth century is not a well-documented period for imports; the wave of cobalt and manganese glazed wares from Tunis and related centres, which can be found not only in Sicily but also on northern Mediterranean sites stretching from Pisa to Barcelona in the later twelfth century and onwards (see p. 185 above), does not seem to have reached Islamic Spain. Sicilian glazed wares were not visibly exported to the region in any period either, although we have just seen that Sicilian coins did come in, particularly in the Sharq al-Andalus, again in the eleventh century. But even if ceramic imports seem to show a dip in the twelfth century, exports do not; the detailed work done on Sicily shows some Spanish *cuerda seca* on an eleventh-century site at Mazara and on the predominantly twelfth-century site of Calathamet, and on other sites Spanish lustreware plus, once, *esgrafiado*, after 1150 or so. Twelfth-century Andalusī ceramics have also been found in Fusṭāṭ and Alexandria. So the routes did not cease to exist when our *geniza* evidence fades out in the mid-century, and something was necessarily exchanged for each of these imports and exports.[210]

These finds are almost all in very small numbers. As we saw for Byzantium (pp. 359–60 above), it is always hard to be sure how much weight one can put on a handful of sherds of a ware from another part of the Mediterranean on any given site. Is it the tip of an iceberg of much more intensive commerce in other goods? Or does it simply denote a casual connection, or the spin-off of a trade simply in luxury items, as with the glazed bowls used as *bacini* to decorate the facades and

[207] See Heidenreich, *Islamische Importkeramik*, esp. pp. 251–2, 257, 264–70; Heidenreich, 'La loza dorada temprana'. I would date any Egyptian lustre in Madīnat al-Zahrā' to the very end of the tenth century, given its current dating in Egypt itself—see p. 88 above; but in fact, chemical analysis shows that the lustre here was from Iraq; see Polvorinos del Río et al., 'Estudio arqueométrico de la loza dorada de Madinat al-Zahra, Córdoba'; Salinas and Pradell, 'The introduction of the glaze in al-Andalus', p. 95.

[208] Heidenreich, *Islamische Importkeramik*, pp. 255–6; Azuar Ruiz, *Las taifas del Sharq al-Andalus*, pp. 177–80; Ortega Ortega, 'Una gobernanza poscalifal', pp. 464–6 (Albarracín, extending perhaps into the twelfth century too); Gutiérrez et al., 'The earliest Chinese ceramics in Europe?'. For the candlesticks, see Azuar Ruiz, 'Bronces fatimíes de Denia', one of his many discussions of them.

[209] Azuar, 'Cerámicas en "verde y manganeso"', gives the fullest synthesis.

[210] See, e.g., Molinari and Meo, *Mazara/Māzar*, p. 299 (A. Meo); Lesnes and Poisson, *Calathamet*, pp. 224–5 (E. Lesnes); Molinari, *Segesta II*, pp. 148–9, for *esgrafiado*; Molinari and Cassai, 'La Sicilia e il Mediterraneo nel XIII secolo', p. 104, for lustre. For Egypt, see Rosser-Owen, '"From the mounds of Old Cairo"', pp. 168–72; Déléry, *Dynamiques économiques*, pp. 1015, 1049–50, 1054–5.

campanili of north Italian churches (see pp. 529–30 below), which were clearly regarded as special in some way? The finds discussed above at least denote more than the latter interpretation, as they come from, among other places, excavations of ordinary housing on rural and sometimes inland sites in Sicily. But it is hard to say that they show a really intense relationship. When we looked at Sicilian exports, it was amphorae, probably for wine, which marked the density of the trade from the island up the Italian and Provençal coasts (see p. 228 above); fine wares probably moved on the back of that. We do not have anything similar in our archaeological evidence for Andalusī trade with the Islamic Mediterranean. And it must also be added that when western Sicily began to import fine wares from other regions on a large scale, which was at the end of the twelfth century and onwards from there, it was Tunisian and south Italian pottery which dominated, and after them, for the first time, Byzantine wares; Spanish imports were very minor compared with these.[211] Equally, although I do not doubt that more work on sites in Islamic Spain and Portugal will show us more examples of ceramics coming from elsewhere—as we can see to an extent in Almería, which in the twelfth century was at its height as an entrepôt[212]—we already know enough about Andalusī ceramic patterns under the Almorávids and Almohads to be pretty sure that we are unlikely to find the degree of fine-ware import penetration that we see in western Sicily around 1200, on any major site in the future.

What I would instead take away from this ceramic material is two things. First, that it does, indeed, show a small-scale commitment to export, plus a similar small-scale receptivity to imported manufactures, across the whole of our period, as we saw in greater detail for the *geniza*. Second, however, imports not only arrived on the coast, which we would expect, but hardly extended beyond it—after the decline of Córdoba, at least—even though we have seen at length how complex internal exchange routes in al-Andalus were. This certainly points to a relative marginality for such imports in every period. And both these conclusions support the argument that Andalusī connections to the rest of the Islamic Mediterranean were, even if long-lasting, not very dense.

* * *

When we come to al-Andalus's relationship with the Christian world, the problems are slightly different. Although it is not part of the remit of this book, it should first be said that exchange by land between al-Andalus and the Christian north of the Iberian peninsula was not elaborate. Andalusī goods had long gone northwards. They are mentioned in Latin documents because some of these list

[211] Molinari and Cassai, 'La Sicilia e il Mediterraneo nel XIII secolo', pp. 103–5; Molinari and Meo, *Mazara/Māzar*, p. 377 (P. Orecchioni), although here, in a port, there was slightly more from the eleventh century; see ibid., pp. 251, 299, 314 (A. Meo).

[212] See, e.g., Muñoz Martín and Flores Escobosa, 'La cerámica medieval en los intercambios comerciales mediterráneos', pp. 75–7.

high-quality movables; they were also sometimes used in lieu of money in the Christian kingdoms, which did not mint coins until the late eleventh century. In exchange, the Christian lands were also mediators for, and (against their will, perhaps) suppliers of, the slave trade, which, however—apart from being a luxury trade—had reached its height already in the tenth century, and was of minor importance after the second *fitna*. Trade continued; a *fatwā* of Ibn Rushd in the early twelfth century allows Christian merchants from Toledo to be held under specified circumstances as hostages in Córdoba to exchange for Muslim captives, which at least shows that they had regarded it as normal to come. But most of the goods traded seem to have been luxury or semi-luxury. Silk is again an important example, but the north bought fine linen and cotton too, plus quality leather, luxuries to northerners—their quality must have been backed up by their rarity, and/or their availability only to elites.[213] By contrast, Andalusī glazed wares are very rare on archaeological excavations of this period, even if they are sometimes found on elite and urban sites. It might also be that some of the ironworking sites on the Islamic side of the border sold product northwards as well as southwards, but we do not have evidence to prove it.[214] The north was much less economically complex than the south throughout our period, which will not have helped the establishment of systematic commercial routes, at least outside the ex-Islamic and still economically active cities of Toledo and Zaragoza. In general, then, north-south land links were not so developed that they alter our picture of the wider connections of al-Andalus.

As to the Mediterranean Christian lands, stretching from Catalonia eastwards into Italy, written sources are scarce before Genoese records begin, around the middle of the twelfth century. That date also fits the first appearance of fine wares from Islamic Spain and North Africa in any numbers on sites in Barcelona,

[213] See in general Constable, *Trade and traders*, pp. 44–8, 180, 191–3; for slaves, see n. 95 above; for cloth, see the lists in Serrano-Piedecasas Fernández, 'Elementos para una historia de la manufactura textil andalusí'; see further the wider discussions in Davies, 'Notions of wealth'; Rodríguez, 'À propos des objets nécessaires'. For the *fatwā*, see al-Wansharīsī, *al-Miʿyār*, trans. Lagardère, *Histoire et société*, 6.196.

[214] For some of the still rare instances of glaze, see Sanz García et al., *Intervención arqueológica integral*, p. 220 for Zamora (very little glaze, but there are more unglazed Andalusī imports; note that Zamora also has one of the very few finds of Islamic money in the Kingdom of León, silver dirhams from the caliphal period; see Blázquez Cerrato and Martín Esquivel, 'Conjunto de *dírhams* califales hallado en Zamora'); Villanueva et al., 'Burgos en torno al año mil'; for Pancorbo (prov. Burgos), see Quirós Castillo, 'Castillo de Pancorbo y recinto de Santa Marta', and Juan Antonio Quirós, pers. comm., whom I thank for help and bibliography on this issue; for Senhora do Barrocal, a relatively high-status site in the central Portuguese mountains, where the glaze is early but the excavators doubt it arrived commercially, see de Souza et al, 'The Islamic pottery from Senhora do Barrocal', and Catarina Tente, pers. comm. For iron, see n. 178 above, for Vascos and Albalat. What did the northerners sell in return? Speaking very schematically, we could reply: slaves in the tenth; the money they had obtained from the Muslims themselves as *parías* (tribute) in the eleventh; by the twelfth there was more artisanal work in the north, and woollens are a possibility. We can also imagine that travelling traders could live well in the north by selling high, after they had bought low in the south. But we cannot really say with any certainty yet, and to develop the question would take us away from our main topic.

Provence, and Liguria, which are above all from the twelfth century, usually the second half, and onwards. When they appear, in fact, Tunisian glazed pottery predominates over that from Spain, so the restricted commitment to export by sea which we have just seen for the southern Mediterranean was apparently replicated in the north, once wider Andalusī links to the Mediterranean Christian world began slowly to get going, around 1150.[215] I will come back to the point, using the Genoese registers, in a moment. Before 1100, however, there are a small and diverse handful of examples of Muslim–Christian trading which are themselves interesting, particularly with the coast of Provence and with Pisa. Let us look at these in turn.

The first is a set of wrecks off the Provençal coast, which are a fairly homogeneous group, and seem to date to around 900—before the start of our period, but significant all the same, as signs of exchange possibilities. The wrecks, significantly, are dominated by transport containers (amphorae to the French and Italians, *tinajas* and *jarras* to the Spanish), with close parallels in Tudmīr and Pechina (the date is too early for there to be many glazed fine wares, although there are a few, probably again from Pechina); some of them had Arabic personal names written on them, presumably of merchants, and residue analysis shows that many of them contained wine. I cited them earlier, when commenting on the lack of interest Iberian archaeologists so far have had in amphorae. Here, however, it is clear that they show wine export from the Spanish south-east coast (which was a wine area, at least in the twelfth century, according to al-Idrīsī; see p. 432 above) to Provence—the only archaeologically attested example of bulk trade out of al-Andalus. To whom? The lack of chronological follow-up visible for these exports makes people think of the Arab military outpost at *Fraxinetum*, probably La Garde-Freinet above modern Saint-Tropez on the Provençal coast, which had an active life in the later ninth and most of the tenth century; two of the wrecks (the most important two, Agay and Batéguier) sank only 30–50 kilometres farther east, between there and Cannes. People here may be right, but it is also the case that the ships were not obviously going to Saint-Tropez itself; the ships look as commercial as any medieval wrecks yet found; and a few very early Andalusī glazed wares have been found on Provençal religious and castle sites.[216] They thus show

[215] Beltrán de Heredia Bercero, '*Barcino*, de colònia romana', p. 77; Beltrán de Heredia Bercero and Miró i Alaix, 'Los contactos comerciales en Barcelona', pp. 113–14 (thanks to Alexandra Chavarría for help here); Déléry, *Dynamiques économiques*, pp. 1017–21, 1039–42, 1050–6, with Déléry, 'Using *cuerda seca* ceramics as a historical source', pp. 43–7; Capelli et al., 'Caractérisation des céramiques glaçurées et importées en Provence', p. 944; de Vingo, 'La céramique d'importation islamique dans la Ligurie médiévale', pp. 289–91 for Spain (which here begins in the early twelfth century; Sicily and Tunisia had begun to export a century earlier, even if here, as elsewhere, Tunisian wares increase substantially in the late twelfth); for Liguria, see also García Porras, 'La ceramica smaltata'; Benente, 'Ceramica di importazione', pp. 61–5.

[216] See Richarté-Manfredi, 'Navires et marchandises'; Richarté-Manfredi, 'Céramiques glaçurées'; Richarté et al., 'Céramiques et marchandises'. For the inland sites, see, e.g., Bramoullé et al., 'Le mobilier céramique', p. 194; Déléry, 'Using *cuerda seca* ceramics as a historical source', pp. 35–7. I am

that the Arab outpost not only made war—as, indeed, would be unlikely, given its century-long longevity—but, rather, at least some of the time, facilitated international bulk exchange over its wider hinterland. Either way, however, neither the outpost nor the trade lasted; later amphorae in Provence are, so far at least, Sicilian.[217]

The Pisan connection is a more important one for us, for it continued longer. We have already seen (p. 407 above) that in Pisa glazed ceramics from Mallorca (then ruled by Denia) appear as *bacini* on churches, and also in urban excavations from the eleventh century onwards. Apart from the Provençal sites, this is the earliest evidence we have of Andalusī fine-ware exports. There is disagreement about their dating, with Graziella Berti arguing firmly for a dating around 1000 for the earliest of them, going above all by the date of the building of the church which contains them, and Rafael Azuar arguing for later in the eleventh century, on the basis of excavations in Spain. I am myself persuaded by the latter, and more recent Pisan archaeological work is starting to agree.[218] But, either way, the finds link Denia/Mallorca with Pisa, and this is a link which has other elements. When Mujāhid, the ruler of Denia and Mallorca, failed to take Sardinia in 1016, he lost his son 'Alī to captivity in Pisa and then Germany, but the Pisan Ildeberto Albizo supposedly ransomed him and sent him back to his father. Ildeberto and all his heirs were in return said to have been recognized as *fratres*, in some form of brotherhood, by Mujāhid, his family, and his successors in Mallorca. This did not, when 'Alī succeeded his father in 1045, prevent the two cities from continuing to fight; but when the Pisans and Catalans attacked Mallorca in 1113–15, a descendent of Ildeberto, Pietro Albizo, was the man responsible for establishing a treaty at the end of the war, because—as the Pisan poetic account of their victory, our source for this whole story, claimed—his family had maintained links with Mallorca's rulers thereafter.[219]

here grateful for discussions with both Catherine Richarté and Sonia Gutiérrez. On *Fraxinetum* itself, the bibliography is substantial, notwithstanding the very few written sources; convenient surveys are Versteegh, 'The Arab presence'; Sénac, 'Le califat de Cordoue et la Méditerranée occidentale'.

[217] For Sicily, see Tréglia et al., 'Importations d'amphores médiévales'; Sacco, 'Produzione e circolazione'. Another linkage with no follow-up was the arrival of Amalfitan merchants in Córdoba in 942, where, Ibn Ḥayyān (i.e. probably al-Rāzī) says, they established a merchant colony, bringing in luxury cloth and silver (*Muqtabis V*, trans. Viguera and Corriente, pp. 358–9, 365). Some of the cloth was purple, and thus probably Byzantine imperial silk, which is likely to have been a welcome import. But anyway, this, as is usual with references to Amalfitans, was clearly a small-scale luxury trade, and the colony is not attested again. See the very cautious account in Skinner, *Medieval Amalfi*, pp. 235–45, and for the Byzantine connection, see Manzano, 'Circulation de biens', pp. 175–80; see further pp. 640–3 below.

[218] Azuar Ruiz, 'Una necesaria revisión'; Berti and García Porras, 'A propósito de "Una necesaria revisión"'; Berti and Giorgio, *Ceramiche con coperture vetrificate* (the most up-to-date account of Pisan *bacini* as a whole, here pp. 42–7); and most recently and convincingly, Meo, 'L'ordinario e l'eccezione'.

[219] *Liber Maiorichinus*, ed. Scalia, 3, ll. 111–19, and (for the negotiations) 7, ll. 331–8, 432–56. Note that Arabic accounts of 'Alī's captivity do not mention any of the rest of the story; see, e.g., Ibn 'Idhārī, *al-Bayān*, trans. Maíllo Salgado, p. 136–7 (here he is ransomed by his father). But the Genoese in 1164 and 1166 claimed to have captured 'Musaitus' themselves and to have sent him to Germany; see *Annali genovesi*, 1, ed. Belgrano, pp. 161, 197–8; this would at least back up the German part of the story, and does not disprove the Pisan part. The poem simply calls the Pisan ransomer 'Albicio', but

There is an obvious legendary element to this. All the same, the Albizo family—later called the Casapieri after Pietro—was, of all the Pisan elite families, that most visibly associated with commerce in the twelfth century, and it is far from implausible that this commerce would have included the Andalusī east coast and the Balearics. Certainly, it did later in the twelfth century, when the Pisans established trade and non-aggression treaties with Ibn Maymūn in Almería in 1133, Ibn Mardanīsh of Valencia in 1149, and successive governors of Mallorca in 1161 (probably), 1173, and 1184.[220] Denia/Mallorca and Pisa were, after all, as noted earlier, quite similar as small but rising maritime polities; war and commerce went together regularly in this period too. We have seen in the context of the *geniza* how important personal links were for establishing trade networks; this link may well have been constructed in the same way. But whether the story explains the commercial contacts or vice versa, one result was not only that Spanish ceramics appear around half a century earlier than they do elsewhere in the Christian lands; it was also that they remained important. Andalusī green glaze, *cuerda seca*, and stamped wares were a high percentage of Pisa's substantial imports up to the moment in which it began to make its own glazed maiolicas around the 1220s. The ceramics may well have been a proxy for silk imports, given Spain's major export to the Islamic world; it is worth adding that the Casapieri also controlled the silk warehouse (*embolus*) in Pisa by the 1230s.[221]

Pisa's private documents give us no more than hints about the detail of its commercial activities in our period, however (see p. 564 below). For that, we need to turn to Genoa; but Genoa seems to have been rather less involved in trade with al-Andalus than was Pisa. Its *Annals* stress war until after the capture of Almería in 1147. Thereafter, although, as we have seen (p. 404), the Genoese gained rather

Ildeberto Albizo, the ancestor of the family, was the only one active in 1016; see Ticciati, 'Strategie familiari', the basic account of the Casapieri. Pietro's cousin Ardecasa was again chosen to negotiate with the governor of Mallorca in 1161; see Maragone, *Annales pisani*, ed. Lupo Gentile, p. 23. For discussion, see Bruce, 'The politics of violence and trade'; Bruce, *La taifa de Denia*, pp. 145–65.

[220] Ticciati, 'Strategie familiari'; Wickham, *Sleepwalking*, pp. 104–5. I was wrong to say there that the kings of Mallorca in the 1110s were descendants of Mujāhid; late accounts, which are our only sources, give divergent origins for the two Mallorca kings who fought the Pisans in the 1110s, but not that one (Viguera Molíns, 'Las Taifas', pp. 64–5). For the treaties, see Amari, *I diplomi arabi*, nn. I.4, 46, II.1, 16, 17; *Annales pisani*, ed. Lupo Gentile, pp. 9, 23, 59. In the 1180s, the Pisans considered the three Andalusī ports worth mentioning in their list of Mediterranean ports in their law code (Vignoli, *I Costituti*, pp. 230–1) to be Valencia, Denia, and Mallorca, which fits these patterns. Valencia wine was being sent to Pisa by the 1150s: see Chapter 6, n. 230 below. Constable, *Housing the stranger*, p. 127, thinks that the concession to Pisa in 1166 by the Almohad caliph (*Annales pisani*, p. 40) of a *fundacum* in 'Subilia' means Seville, not Zawila outside Mahdia, as successive editors have supposed; this seems to me less likely, given the known Pisan interest in the Tunisian coastal towns (see pp. 264–5 above); and indeed, Maragone, *Annales pisani*, p. 6, himself certainly calls Zawila 'Sibilia'. Picard, *L'océan atlantique musulman*, pp. 410–11, also talks up Italian trade with Seville, but the first explicit reference is well into the thirteenth century.

[221] For the ceramic figures, see esp. Baldassarri and Giorgio, 'La ceramica di produzione mediterranea'; see also Gattiglia, *Pisa medievale*, pp. 189–93. For the *embolus*, see Ticciati, 'Strategie familiari', pp. 86–8. A textile workshop from the early thirteenth century found by the church of S. Eufrasia in Pisa has tentatively been seen as for silk (Meo, 'Archeologia della produzione', pp. 38–42); it is not, however, clear to me that we can tell what sorts of textiles it made.

little profit from their ten years in Almería and their taking of Tortosa in 1148, they did in 1149 establish a trade treaty with Ibn Mardanīsh, on more favourable terms than the Pisans did, in that the king also paid them a tribute of gold and silk across a ten-year period—this, at least, must have been a consequence of the menace brought by their naval success in the previous two years.[222] But there is no real sign that they built on this. There are only some twenty citations of mainland al-Andalus (here *Yspania*) as a trading partner in Giovanni Scriba's register for the years around 1160, a very small number when compared with those for Sicily, or Béjaïa and Ceuta in the Maghreb, and most of them are very vague. Valencia was the main trading partner, but even it gets cited only four times; Denia only appears twice, and no other town at all. Cloth is sold in *Yspania* once and bought from there once; other goods are hardly mentioned. It may be that Castilian alum, mentioned a couple of times, reached the coast via Valencia, but even this is not certain. In the registers from the 1190s, which have many more contracts, references to trade with al-Andalus are actually fewer—by now, it is clearly Morocco (*Garbum*) which was the main focus of Genoa's western interests. The only exception to this absence is Mallorca, which turns up in as many contracts as the whole of the rest of Islamic Spain (the Genoese exported cloth twice to the island, linen and silk); it was clearly a point of reference for the Genoese as well as for the Pisans, even if the mainland was not.[223] The totals for sums invested in different regions, set out by David Abulafia in his work on Genoa and Sicily, show how low Spain featured in every year for which figures are available. This wholly fits the very small quantities of Spanish glazed pottery found in Genoa and the rest of Liguria, and west from there as far as Barcelona; Islamic Spain was simply not an important part of the networks which the Genoese were establishing with everywhere else. This would not change until well into the thirteenth century, after the Christian conquests.[224]

It seems to me, then, that of the major Christian trading cities, only Pisa was particularly involved in commerce with al-Andalus in the twelfth century, and we cannot tell on what scale it operated there. The archaeology supports the view

[222] For 1149, see *CDGE*, 1, n. 196 (*LI*, 1, n. 118). The Genoese already traded with Almería before its capture, however; see the lists of ports, ships from which paid tolls to the Genoese archbishop in 1143, in Belgrano, 'Il registro della curia arcivescovile', p. 9.

[223] *Giovanni Scriba*, nn. 69, 143, 290, 888 (Valencia), 487, 1096 (Denia), 626, 812 (cloth), 193, 1212 (alum), s.v. index for *Yspania*. For later in the century, see esp. *Guglielmo Cassinese*, s.vv. *Ispania*, *Garbum*; Granada cloth appears once, in *Oberto Scriba 1186*, n. 263. For Mallorca, see *Giovanni Scriba*, nn. 141 (linen), 487, 495, *Oberto Scriba 1190*, nn. 441, 414, 443 (silk), *Guglielmo Cassinese*, nn. 1287, 1525; and see Bach, *La cité de Gênes*, appendix, s.v. 1182 Majorque, for the substantial group from 1182. These fit the trading concessions from Mallorca to Genoa in the 1180s; see *CDGE*, 2, nn. 133, 177.

[224] Abulafia, *The two Italies*, pp. 105, 109, 111, 113, 119, 158, 161, 166, 174, 177, 182. Constable in *Trade and traders*, pp. 98–105, and her earlier article, 'Genoa and Spain', which is the most complete analysis I have seen, talks this trade up; I cannot follow her there. (Much of her evidence is, anyway, mid-thirteenth-century.) But she stands here for most of the historiography, which tends to stress individual examples of trading, not their small percentage in the documentation, even though the latter is something Constable explicitly recognizes.

that its activity was greater than Genoa's, but how much more the Tuscan port did by way of commerce can only be guessed at. We could not easily say, given the evidence we have, that Pisa's involvement here was sufficient to create or mediate a large-scale trade between Islamic Spain and its Christian neighbours on its own; it is hard not to conclude that even after it got going more widely in the mid-twelfth century, such trade was operating on an even smaller scale than Andalusī commerce with the rest of the Islamic world.

This lack of connection between Islamic Spain and the Christian lands in the twelfth century, a period in which Italian trading increased very greatly, cannot have been because of the lack of attraction to the Pisans and Genoese of Andalusī goods, given what we have seen in this chapter hitherto. It was probably at least to some degree because the Almohad Caliphate was unwilling to cede control of the south-western Mediterranean Sea to Christian maritime powers, and had a sufficiently strong fleet to prevent it; that is to say, the Almohads were in a good position to make the rules here. It is noteworthy that the Pisan commercial agreement with the Almohad caliph in 1186, which gave the city rights in a restricted number of ports on the North African coast (see p. 265 above), mentions no ports of trade in Spain. That this is not chance is shown by a clause which allows the Pisans to buy food and repair ships in Almería, but specifically prohibits trading there. Almerían trade was to be restricted, evidently, to al-Andalus itself and the Islamic lands. Nor would this restriction in itself have done much harm to Almería's economy, given what we have seen of the balance of economic activity in this part of the Mediterranean hitherto, in which trade with the rest of the Islamic world, limited though it was, was much greater than with that of the Christians.[225] But any Almohad restraint on exchange with the Christian world, although it does seem to have been a feature of the period, was certainly not consistently effective, as Spanish ceramics in Pisa and elsewhere, and Genoese trading with *Yspania*, however occasional, both show; it is not enough to explain the limitations in the evidence for all kinds of maritime shipping that we have seen in this section.[226] For that, to conclude, we have to look at al-Andalus's wider Mediterranean location.

* * *

[225] Amari, *I diplomi*, n. I.5. For the fleet, see Picard, *La mer des califes*, pp. 334–40. The most extensive Andalusī external trade in the Almohad period was with nearby Morocco, which was, of course, as already under the Almorávids, part of the same political system; see Picard, *L'océan atlantique musulman*, pp. 377–458 (note that he too stresses trade with the Italians as well, pp. 410–14, more than I would for this period); Déléry, *Dynamiques économiques*, pp. 1039–42, 1046–9 (in terms of *cuerda seca*, this trade only really develops after 1150).

[226] We have seen the Pisans unsuccessfully try to circumvent Almohad rules in Tripoli (Chapter 3, n. 271). But given the texts cited in n. 220 above, the Pisans evidently considered their traditional connections in the Sharq al-Andalus still to be operative, presumably in part protected by the separate Mallorca treaties. As for the Genoese, they could take a ship from Trapani in Sicily to Denia and then Cartagena in 1185 without recorded trouble; see Ibn Jubayr, *Riḥla*, trans. Broadhurst, p. 365. Prohibitions were relative, then; but they still had some weight, and Almería, although still an active port and silk producer, is conspicuous by its absence in the late twelfth-century Italian material.

It is important to remember that al-Andalus was very far west. Its immediate neighbours were not the long-lasting states of the eastern Mediterranean, or even the thriving commercially orientated systems of Sicily and Ifrīqiya, but, rather, Christian León, Castile, and Catalonia, and Islamic Morocco. Until the twelfth century, none of these, even Catalonia, the most developed, was so complex an economy that there would have been much for the Andalusīs to buy from it, apart from African gold coming through Morocco. Even in the twelfth century, out of these neighbours, only Morocco was really active in trading with al-Andalus, and it may well be that it had a more complex economy than the others, although exactly how the Moroccan economy worked in our period is not yet at all easy to discern. It may be added that what even the twelfth-century Italian trading cities, energetic though they were beginning to be, could have offered the Andalusīs is also unclear, unless they were already able to act as intermediaries with Sicily and elsewhere, which we have almost no documentation for;[227] this may well be another reason why their activity in this region was so limited. So al-Andalus was not close to regions which could match its own internal complexity, and which both had the resources to buy and the attractive products to sell that would allow a complex pattern of bulk exchange to develop. This was already the main reason why Egyptian evidence, above all from the *geniza*, treats the region rather sparsely, even though Egypt was certainly complex enough to trade with the far west; the links were there, but they required long voyages, and were only used for a restricted range of products.

We have amply seen, of course, that al-Andalus had an intensely active economy in our period. So, as a region, it certainly had goods which it could potentially have sold elsewhere. But here, I think, its internal economic history is of relevance. Islamic Spain and Portugal consisted of a network of subregions, each of which had developed its own productive hierarchy, particularly in the eleventh century. In the twelfth, these subregions had grown together, to create a regional economy, which was strong precisely because it was based on each of these active local realities. But it seems quite likely that the preoccupation of a Seville or a Granada or a Murcia was more likely to have been the maintenance and development of relationships with other Andalusī cities than it would have been to look outside the peninsula to regions elsewhere. This was all the more a concern because internal routes in al-Andalus were so often difficult, simply because of the geography of the peninsula. It was not possible to rely only on the network of coastal traffic, because many important towns were inland, and often also far from navigable waterways, unlike in most other regions we have looked at. This

[227] There are just two references in twelfth-century Genoese registers to the sale of Spanish goods to Sicily and Béjaïa; see *Giovanni Scriba*, nn. 287, 812. (The first of these is (presumably woollen) cloth from Huesca, now conquered by the Christians.) These would, in turn, have been matched by equivalent sales of Sicilian/Ifrīqiyan goods back to al-Andalus, but we have no evidence to say what, and the references are no more than casual.

will also have made the task of any Egyptian or Italian entrepreneur much harder too; there was no Aegean Sea at the heart of Spain and Portugal for them to be able to sail into and link with most of the region directly—the coastal ports, which is all we see any of them ever trading with during our period, were very active, but only contained some of the necessary buyers. Donkeys, rather than boats, were the key means of transport here. So al-Andalus was set up geographically and—given its tendency to break up into small units at moments of crisis—also politically to focus on its own internal relationships, and not to consider the world outside more than marginally. It was a more inward-looking region, in economic terms, than any we have looked at, more even than Byzantium, which, as we saw in Chapter 4, also had rather less Mediterranean presence than it could have established. Added to this is again the crucial fact that except for gold and some dyestuffs, al-Andalus produced everything it needed; there was no pressing reason to look elsewhere.

So, in the context of a book on the Mediterranean economy in a long eleventh century, Islamic Spain has less of a role than one might expect, and than some of its more enthusiastic analysts might wish for. It was not close to other complex economies except, by the end of our period, parts of Morocco; to unite its whole regional economy was already a major achievement, and its merchants were more interested in that than in the wider Mediterranean world. But we have to ask: why should they? Al-Andalus did, indeed, produce everything it needed. It may be surprising that it did not have a closer relationship with, in particular, Sicily, the closest really active region, and one which was certainly well connected to interregional routes; but Sicily itself, apart from its long-lasting relationship with Ifrīqiya, looked first eastwards and later northwards, and did not really need the west either.[228] Islamic Spain is thus the best model for one of the several alternative paths to economic growth in the history of the Mediterranean in the long eleventh century, one based not just *mostly* on internal developments—that was a feature common to every region discussed in this book—but *wholly* on them. It disproves, better than anywhere else, the most common misconception about the history of economic development in this period, that the principal measure for it is interregional, long-distance exchange. Al-Andalus was a world to itself, in economic terms at least, and that was enough for the time being.

[228] Though the Sicilian coins from the eleventh century found along the east coast of Spain may indicate some closer links in that period; see n. 195 above.

6
North-Central Italy

Of all the regions discussed in this book, north-central Italy is the hardest to approach. This is a serious paradox: it is generally reckoned to be the best-studied, by both historians and archaeologists, and this is basically accurate; it is certainly far and away the most fully studied. It has the most extensive evidence too; hence the length of this chapter. It is also the one that I, personally, know best. But the northern half of Italy, in its economic history as in every other area, tends to be studied piecemeal, city by city, with fewer overviews, unlike Byzantium and, indeed, in this period, Sicily. Furthermore, as in all our regions, our understanding of its economic development has been beset by grand narratives, not least of these being the 'commercial revolution' itself, which has been seen to have been based on the major Italian cities more than on any other players in the Mediterranean—it is not chance that Roberto Lopez, who did so much to popularize this term, was Genoese, and only forced to the USA by the Fascist racial laws—but also by the related metanarrative of Italian communal autonomy, with its civic dynamism and urban culture, the harbinger of the Renaissance. We will come back to the grand narratives; but I want to confront the problem by laying out a set of data which seem to me to illustrate it clearly.

In the twelfth century, the Lombard, then Carolingian, and then Ottonian kingdom of north-central Italy had collapsed as a political reality. This was essentially the result of the civil wars of the 1080s and 1090s, in the context of the first major political and military confrontation between the German emperor (who was also king of Italy) and the pope. This, in turn, had several consequences which are relevant for us, as we shall see, but one was continuing civil war, now between individual cities. As Otto, bishop of Freising in Bavaria, commented in his historical account of the 1140s:

> In these days, because of the absence of the king, the towns of Italy having fallen into insolence, the Venetians fought atrociously with the Ravennati, the Veronesi and Vicentini with the Padovani and the Trevigiani, the Pisans and Florentines with the Lucchesi and Senesi, mixing almost the whole of Italy with blood, booty, and arson.

Otto was no neutral observer, being the half-brother of the king concerned, Conrad III; but the observation was a truism in the period—it recurs, for example, in a north Italian letter collection created as a stylistic model in the 1130s, which

The Donkey and the Boat. Chris Wickham, Oxford University Press. © Chris Wickham 2023.
DOI: 10.1093/oso/9780198856481.003.0006

states, almost casually, that 'throughout *Longobardia* [the Po plain west of Verona and Bologna] and, indeed, throughout Italy, wars are very dangerous (*infestissima*).'[1] And anyway, it was perfectly true as well. The annals of every city recount these wars with repetitious enthusiasm; each city had one or more neighbouring cities as personal enemies (they very often remain the same enemies in the twenty-first century), which it attacked as often as possible. The 1150s–1160s are particularly well documented for what is now Lombardy in the central Po plain, because Conrad's nephew, Frederick I Barbarossa (1152–90), was then trying to re-establish the Kingdom of Italy under his own control, and chroniclers in the Lombard towns (plus again Otto of Freising) wrote about this at length; in this period, intercity wars carried on even in the presence of the king. This was in part because he was using the urban rivalries to bring down his major opponents, particularly Milan, which he destroyed in 1162 and forced the abandonment of for five years, but also in part because the cities were using him in return to prosecute their own enmities.

Armies were usually small, and cities themselves were seldom taken (except by the largest armies, of Milan and the emperor himself). But frontier castles on the edge of city territories were fought for, and both castles and villages laid waste; and in all our accounts, even though they, of course, cannot be taken at face value, grain crops were systematically trampled or burned, and vines and fruit trees were cut down or again burned—that is to say, larger and smaller sectors of the agrarian base of the economy were regularly targeted and destroyed, every few years, and sometimes annually.[2] This can hardly have helped either economic prosperity or commerce, and indeed, commerce seldom appears in these narratives, except, casually, as something which is, indeed, disrupted—or else something which is being improvised, for the needs of the armies themselves.[3] Nor does commerce appear significantly in the parchment documents for Lombardy, or for any other part of north-central Italy for that matter, with the sole exception of Venice, as we shall see later. So, as with the civil wars in Ifrīqiya and al-Andalus, one might well doubt that economic development could easily take place under these circumstances.

As we have seen, this is, indeed, what some historians of North Africa have concluded; and if historians of Islamic Spain and Portugal have not in recent years, it is for different reasons, not least the remarkable archaeology which has

[1] Otto of Freising, *Chronica*, 7.29; Beyer, *Die lombardische Briefsammlung*, n. 43. I thank Sandro Carocci, Patrizia Mainoni, Giovanna Bianchi, Sauro Gelichi, and Paolo Grillo for reading and critiquing this chapter, as a whole or in part.

[2] Otto of Freising, *Chronica*, 7.29; Otto of Freising and Rahewin, *Gesta Friderici I.*, 3.44, 4.38; *Gesta Federici I.*, p. 40; Otto and Acerbo Morena, *Historia Frederici I.*, pp. 45, 57, 135, 137–8, 146, 192.

[3] Disruption: Otto of Freising and Rahewin, *Gesta Friderici I.*, 4.39; *Carmen de gestis Frederici I.*, ll. 144–6; *Gesta Federici I.*, p. 42; Otto and Acerbo Morena, *Historia Frederici I.*, p. 149. Improvisation: *Liber Cumanus*, ed. Stampa, l. 1688; *Gesta Federici I.*, p. 19; Otto and Acerbo Morena, *Historia Frederici I.*, p. 26. For an analysis, see Bargigia, 'I Pavesi e la prassi bellica'.

been discovered on Andalusī sites, towns and villages alike. But the archaeology for the north Italian towns—here with the sole exception of Pisa—has not been similarly forthcoming. Workshops are few for our period; kilns are rare, rather than surviving in their dozens, as in Spain. And there are few fine wares in the ceramic record. In Liguria, Tuscany, and the eastern Po plain at the top of the Adriatic, there are some imported glazed types, and some local glazed semi-fine types too; but in the central Po plain, in Milan and the cities and countryside around, there are almost no fine wares known, until around a century after the period we are looking at ends. For Venice and its hinterland, and also Genoa and its hinterland, Pisa and its hinterland, we can track the sort of development that we have been looking at in other chapters, slower than in some Mediterranean regions, but steadily more visible; but the crucial area around Milan resists any easy version of a similar analysis, even though it was clearly, a century later, Italy's own economic powerhouse.

We shall, of course, look at all this in detail in this chapter. But for now it can be argued that neither the written evidence nor excavation gives us, at a preliminary overview, any clear sense of a region-wide economic expansion in north-central Italy in our period, unlike in any other region discussed in this book. As we shall see, many historians, mostly writing before the archaeology of medieval Italy became strong (a development of the 1980s and onwards), had a teleology of Italian economic and urban success in their minds, and thus found it easy to take isolated citations of merchants or artisans or markets, which begin as early as the eighth century, and to track a steady rise in commercial activity from there onwards, with an upswing in the tenth century, when we see more evidence of markets in Italy, and/or in the eleventh, when we first see the Pisans and the Genoese active in the Mediterranean, and a continuous upward trajectory from then onwards. But those citations are indeed isolated, outside the port cities themselves, and do not become much more common in the twelfth century either, in most places. Given that, and given the productive weakness implied by much of the archaeology, plus the pervasive evidence for capillary civil war across the century after 1080 (and indeed, off and on, for the following three centuries as well), we might perhaps better say that Italy's real economic take-off, far from being under way already in the eleventh century, would have to postdate the end of our period around 1180, possibly substantially.

This, in fact, has been the implicit conclusion of much current work. After all, it is in the thirteenth century that we move from isolated references to artisans to citations of their guilds (*arti* or *corporazioni* in Italian; each city had its own Latin terminology), which emerge into the documentary record, city by city, between (most often) the 1210s and 1250s, indicating a greater degree of organization and, therefore, scale; we also see then the related emergence of a new political force in cities, the *popolo*, which reflected—in part—some of those guilds; and we have many more references to cloth and to varieties of cloth.[4] So, more recently, some historians of the thirteenth century, when they discuss these developments, note that in the twelfth century the evidence for them is much weaker, and conclude that the date of the Italian take-off in production and exchange did not precede 1200 by so very much; now, often, the end of the twelfth century is seen as being the point of inflection, with real expansion particularly after 1200. Not least because this is also backed up by the archaeology, this is my view too. But it is based on assumptions. Historians who argue for a long period of growth at least have the problem of causation in the front of their mind; those who propose a shorter period discuss this issue more rarely. That is to say, what has seldom been done is to trace the moment of change and see what its roots are. This is what I will try to do here.[5]

The problem here is this. Although the point of inflection can, indeed, as we shall see, best be located in the late twelfth century, there is too much evidence for the productive and commercial activity of Italian towns in the thirteenth century, sometimes early in the century—and for cities documented in the Genoese notarial registers, already in the 1190s—for absolutely everything to have begun with a flash of a light in a generation, after the wars with Barbarossa mostly ended in 1177, even if (as I shall argue) much of it did.[6] Our sense of sudden new exchange activity, in fact, comes above all from these notarial registers, which, except for fragments, do not survive before the 1220s in any city outside Liguria—for these registers, generally written on paper, document all the contracts which a professionally qualified notary gave legal validity to, simply because of his handwriting and his personal *siglum* or logo on the text. When such registers survive, we suddenly get a complete list of every deal parties made in front of that particular

[4] For artisans and guilds, see in general Degrandi, *L'economia artigiana*; Greci, *Corporazioni*; Epstein, *Wage labour and guilds*; none says much about the twelfth century, although merchant corporations do, as they stress, appear by then in many cities, and in a few cities some artisan guilds can be tracked before 1200 (Greci, *Corporazioni*, pp. 100–20, sets out much of the evidence); for their appearance, see also Racine, 'Associations de marchands'. For the *popolo*, even brief surveys of the uncontrollable range of recent work would overload this footnote; a good critical account of current historiographical trends is Milani, 'Contro il comune dei *milites*', which says almost nothing about the economy, although Poloni, *Potere al popolo*, the best current manual, recognizes economic change as a key underpinning of its rise, pp. 4, 13–18. There are several critiques of the automatic association between the *popolo* and guilds; see, e.g., Artifoni, 'Corporazioni e società di "popolo"'.

[5] I argued this point already, briefly, in 'Prima della crescita'. Significant works arguing for a post-1150 date are Menant, *L'Italie des communes*, pp. 267–8, 276–7; Franceschi and Taddei, *Le città italiane*, esp. pp. 79–111; Franceschi, 'La crescita economica', pp. 5–18, which is more explicit; Mainoni, 'Le produzioni non agricole' (the last two do confront the issue of causation). Cammarosano, *Economia politica classica e storia economica*, esp. pp. 265, 306–16, also stresses the thirteenth century as the moment of the shift across Europe.

[6] Intra-city conflicts had dropped back as well, a decade earlier, as the dangers involved in a German victory—notably a fiscal system which imposed heavy taxes on the Italian cities for the first time—had become clearer, and urban alliances became more attractive; although such conflicts certainly eventually restarted, with some verve and violence, their scale dropped substantially until the 1190s. For the urban alliances, see most recently Raccagni, *The Lombard league*; for Barbarossa in Italy, see n. 13 below.

notary, however temporary, and not just the more permanent or momentous ones which they paid extra to have written out in full on (more expensive) parchment; and prominent among temporary deals were commercial transactions. The suddenness of the appearance of commercial activity in Italy is thus for the most part a product of a new type of source, and not, with any plausibility, an accurate description of the pacing of economic change.[7] It is only reinforced by the development of guilds, and by the political protagonism of the *popolo*. These will not be discussed here, for they appear too late for us; but exactly how they developed is just as unclear. So we have to look more carefully at what came before, to see what lies behind the opacity—and often genuinely negative evidence—of our texts and of the archaeology, which would fully emerge in the open only in the 1190s to 1220s, or sometimes 1250s, depending on the city.

As stated in Chapter 1, I have not pursued the surviving evidence systematically after 1180, for its scale after that in north-central Italy is out of control for a single project. But even before that there are signs that we can use—fewer than historians of previous generations claimed, but visible all the same, if one looks carefully. They are not only single citations of merchants and artisans, which, although important for the balance of trades in individual cities, tell us too little about scale, but also urban expansion, surviving urban buildings, the shift to stone building in the countryside, the glazed ceramic imports already mentioned (both in this chapter and in those preceding, but we will come back to them), the evidence for mining on the coast south of Pisa, the wide distributions of some coarse wares, the growing network of small towns around Milan. These were usually less grand than has sometimes been claimed in the past, even if exception here has to be made for surviving urban buildings, from 1050 onwards, which are, in the case of churches, far more numerous than are churches and mosques from our period in most other cities in the Mediterranean, and in the case of private houses (mostly tower houses, in stone and brick) unparalleled elsewhere. But it is not just hindsight that shows that something really was moving in north-central Italy in—in particular—the later twelfth century, with an uptick after 1100 in the port cities, around the mid-century in Milan and Piacenza (even if it was then delayed by the wars, not least in the period of Milan's forced depopulation), late in the century in several other cities, such as Lucca or Padua, although not until after 1200 in others, such as Florence. A fully articulated regional economy did not exist in north-central Italy before 1200, unlike in most of our other regions; but we can see, with care, how it was forming and would eventually form. That is the task of this chapter.

* * *

[7] For the same point, cf. Wickham, 'Gli artigiani nei documenti italiani', pp. 429–31. For the chronology of notarial registers, see the lists in Meyer, *Felix et inclitus notarius*, pp. 179–222; for notarial *fides publica*, see ibid., pp. 7–107, *passim*.

Before we move on, I need to specify more clearly how this chapter will approach the Italian evidence. The Kingdom of Italy of the seventh to eleventh centuries included the whole of northern Italy, that is to say, the plain of the river Po, and of its tributaries and smaller sister rivers, essentially a triangle of flat land between the Alps to the north and the rather lower Appennines to the south—with the exception of the coastline along the Adriatic, north-east of the mouth of the Po, which from the eighth century was ruled by the dukes of Venice. Its capital was Pavia, although Milan, some 30 kilometres to the north, was always the largest town. Beyond the Po plain, it included Liguria—the thin coastal strip each side of Genoa—and, more importantly, Tuscany, which from the ninth century was a powerful march, ruled from Lucca (see Map 19). The kingdom also extended into the central Appennines and down the west coast of the Adriatic, which was more marginal territory, both politically and economically, and which we will not look at here.[8]

The Po plain, the largest area of flat land around the Mediterranean apart from the Libyan desert, was agriculturally prosperous in large part. The lower plain, nearer the river, was, nonetheless, often waterlogged and in parts quite thickly forested, although always used for its silvo-pastoral resources, until land clearance resulted in a shift to agriculture in many places, from the tenth century onwards. The coastal deltas of the Po and the rivers to its north created a string of marshes and lagoons around the Adriatic from Rimini to Trieste too, much of which was, precisely, Venice's territory. Tuscany is more broken up; it consists of an interconnected set of small but fertile agricultural basins between tracts of lowish hill country, which were thickly settled in the north (the hills of Chianti, for example), although less so in the south. In our period, the Po plain and Tuscany were together structured by a network of some forty active cities, which we have already seen fighting each other in the early twelfth century. Almost all of them had Roman origins (the two main exceptions were Venice and Ferrara). Added to them was a set of smaller episcopal centres with less urban activity, and, from the eleventh century and especially the twelfth, some rising newer towns, *burgi* in Latin (*borghi* or *quasi-città* in the Italian historiography), with less institutional autonomy, such as Prato outside Florence and Monza outside Milan. This urban network has to be our focus, for the Kingdom of Italy was never strong by Mediterranean standards and, as already noted, vanished as a political reality during our period. But the need to study a network of some forty increasingly independent cities itself imposes the need to make choices, for we cannot look at them all in equal depth.

First, a general geographical restriction. We will look here above all at the central and eastern Po plain, and at Liguria and northern Tuscany. The north-west,

[8] For the Appennine regions of the kingdom, see Feller, *Les Abruzzes médiévales*; Fiore, *Signori e sudditi*.

modern Piemonte, had few large cities, and (apart from Asti and Vercelli) less exchange activity even in the thirteenth century; and both the far north-east, beyond Venice, and the south of Tuscany were similar, as well as being poorly documented. I will pay less attention to these parts of the former kingdom, except for the sectors of central-southern Tuscany between Siena and the sea, which have had exceptionally dense archaeological study. Inside this already limited area, however, I will also concentrate, as indicated earlier, on a smaller subset of cities: in turn, the three port cities of Venice, Genoa, and Pisa, which had the closest immediate connections to the other regions of the Mediterranean, with shorter surveys of the most immediate neighbours of the first and third, Padua and Lucca, and a look also at Florence; and then on Milan and the smaller towns around it, extending in that case to the river port of Cremona and a brief look at Piacenza—seven to nine major cities out of the forty.

This is even more necessary for logistical reasons. Italy has by now plenty of archaeology by the standards of the Mediterranean and, indeed, of most of Europe, which allows for quite complex accounts in the areas where it is strongest—in the context of this chapter, Tuscany and the eastern Po plain stand out. In addition, between 50 and 100,000 documents survive for north-central Italy from 950 to 1200. They are almost all fairly easily accessible in archives (far more easily than, say, the Arabic-script texts for Egypt), and are largely edited in one form or another (over 80 per cent up to 1100, around half for the twelfth century); but they have never even been counted, let alone read, by a single person. After 1150, in some cities they increase exponentially in quantity. Large books have been written on single cities which do not exhaust the potential of the documentation for even that town. In the whole of the rest of the Mediterranean, only Fusṭāṭ (thanks to the *geniza*) and Barcelona match the wealth of material for the cities I shall focus on here, or (among cities I shall say less about) Verona, Bologna, or Ravenna. Florence was still a small town by Mediterranean standards and as yet relatively quiet in economic terms, but we can say incomparably more about it and its hinterland than we can for great capitals like Kairouan or Córdoba, or economically vibrant centres like Tinnīs, Almería, or Corinth.

Conversely, most of these large document sets tell us very little about commerce. They are land documents: gifts, sales, and leases of land, court cases about landed property, or—at most—credit agreements with land as a pledge. These were, indeed, the documents for which people were prepared to pay money to have written on parchment, and then (perhaps in particular) to keep afterwards, as land was so important for prosperity, status, and the construction of political power. They were overwhelmingly also preserved by churches, not lay actors; and the churches kept them from our period right up to the confiscation of most ecclesiastical archives, and the establishment of an Archivio di Stato in each city, in the nineteenth century. Only Venetian and Genoese documents stand out for their interest in commercial contracts; and in the Genoese case, as we have seen, this is because of the survival from earlier than elsewhere of a different kind of source, the registers of individual notaries. Add to that a larger group of cities, including Genoa again, Bologna, and Piacenza, whose communal cartularies, established by the city government in the thirteenth century, contained and thus preserved documents of importance to the city as a secular collectivity; but only a minority of these documents too (a small minority except for Genoa) are about commercial arrangements.[9] So an added element to the practical impossibility of reading and analysing tens of thousands of texts here is the prior knowledge that most of them would not directly help the main arguments of this book. They would contextualize them, for sure; the landed politics and estate management of political actors were of basic importance for local economies in general, as we have so far most clearly seen for Byzantium, and have a fundamental role in any attempt to explain economic changes in general, including commercial ones, as we shall again see here. Thanks to such documents, we can also assess overall wealth for some well-documented landowners, as we cannot for anyone else in the regions of this book except a handful of monastic houses on Mount Athos (see pp. 344–5 above). But they would, if we looked at them in full detail, also unbalance the book; we would end up with a very thick sandwich and a very thin slice of cheese inside it.

The other reason why it is reasonable to sample in Italy, rather than look at absolutely everything, is that the Po plain in particular, but even Tuscany, was for many purposes quite homogeneous. Italian cities are famous for all being totally different from each other, and impossible to generalize about. This is entirely true; they had distinct political histories, and variant details in their social structures that produced quite different socio-economic results as urban history moved on across the centuries. In particular, here, otherwise similar cities entered into the commercial world at different speeds and with different intensities. Although they were neighbouring cities, with similarly good river connections, Piacenza developed much faster than Pavia. Milan and Venice were major economic players already in the ninth century, and never ceased to be; conversely, at the end of our period in 1180, no one could have predicted that Florence would, across the next century, eclipse Pisa both in its demography and in its urban production. But all the same, the basic resources of most city territories were fairly analogous. In the Po plain, nearly all of them contained three distinct ecological zones: a tract of mountains, whether Alpine or Appennine (the major exceptions were on or near the river: cities such as Cremona, Ferrara, and, of course, Venice), a high plain area which had the most continuous settlement, and a lower and wetter plain area, only partly cleared, and, although certainly exploited, more lightly

[9] For an overall survey, see Cammarosano, 'I *libri iurium* e la memoria storica'; for the cities mentioned here, see Puncuh et al., *I libri iurium* (vol. 1 is henceforth cited as *LI*); Trombetti Budriesi and Duranti, *I libri iurium del comune di Bologna. Regesti*, 1; Falconi and Peveri, *Il Registrum Magnum*.

settled. Tuscan cities had similar resources too, balanced between mountains/hills and plains; here, only Pisa had a territory which was mostly low-lying, and it expanded into hillier areas in the twelfth century. And although by no means all cities lay on a major river, they nearly all had good water-based connections, particularly in the Po plain, where the river network is extensive and navigable for long distances (Milan is the most striking exception, as it was set 30 kilometres from the nearest major rivers). There were also few serious geographical barriers between them, unlike (for example) in Islamic Spain; the Po plain presented few obstacles apart from river crossings, and the Appennines, set between it and Liguria and Tuscany, had plenty of practicable routes for donkeys and mules, particularly the low pass between Genoa and Milan. Agricultural resources and the ability to move goods around were thus fairly widely shared; and the types of crops and stock-raising available to each city were also fairly uniform. Tuscany and the southern fringes of the Alps had more olives; only Pisa and, in the north, Brescia, Bergamo, and Milan had easy access to iron; there was more rye and less wheat in the Po plain than in Tuscany; these were real differences, but not enough really to allow further distinctions to be made between their resource bases. So, although what I say about Padua would not be equally true for nearby Vicenza, and Cremona is a poor guide to Piacenza or Parma, its closest neighbours—and the four cities at the centre of my discussions are certainly atypical in a long list of ways—the same *sorts* of conclusions can be drawn for each. And I would rather proceed through case studies than present the whole set together, using isolated examples to illuminate a tapestry of (supposed) common development; this is not a helpful way of proceeding, even though it is quite frequent in the general accounts of the period. So the spotlight will be put on only parts of the whole in this chapter. But before we look at these case studies, I shall, nonetheless, set out quite a generalized survey of the north Italian rural economy; I will also try to bring them together at the end.

6.1 Modern Narratives

Our first task, to frame the rest of this chapter, is to look in turn at Italy's two great metanarratives for our period, concerning the origin of the city communes and the origins of the 'commercial revolution'. From the start of our period—to be exact, from 961—the Kingdom of Italy was ruled by the kings of Germany, who would in 962 take on the title of emperor, in succession to a Carolingian tradition for the kings of Italy which had continued up to 924. In the tenth century, the kings were in Italy often; in the eleventh, seldom. But the state, centred on Pavia, continued to be operative, whether kings were there or not. It was structured around regular public assemblies in each city, which had judicial and other public/political functions, run by local counts and marquises, and coordinated by legal experts; these legal experts had considerable local status, often across generations, but also looked to the judges in the capital.[10] It was the most tightly governed state in Latin Europe (apart from Rome, not part of the kingdom, where the papal bureaucracy was highly complex); its structure was, however, skeletal by the standards of Byzantium and the great Islamic polities of the Mediterranean.

Above all, Italy had no effective land-tax system before the mid-twelfth century. Kings took customs tolls, unless they granted immunities from them; these were numerous, although we do not know how much money was derived from them. But kings essentially relied for their wealth on their own land, just as Italian aristocrats and ecclesiastical institutions did, although on a far larger scale, for royal land was very extensive. It is becoming clear that some royal land was being developed economically—we shall see examples of this later (p. 613); furthermore, we have less evidence than we have for France that they ever granted large percentages of it away, or lost control over what they did not grant, at least before the late eleventh-century crisis.[11] That wealth was sufficient to keep the major aristocrats of the kingdom close to the royal power, which could give them, if not always land directly, at least office-holding which came with land. Bishops, wealthy and powerful in nearly every diocese, were also for the most part reliable royal servants, as well as looking to their own interests. German kings could, for a long time, come down into Italy knowing that they had a relatively secure power base there. If the absence of taxation meant that they had fewer resources than even quite small rulers in the Islamic world, they also had fewer outlays—above all, no standing army. But it remains the case that Italy was devoid of—could not have afforded—the large-scale state-backed building programmes which characterized Córdoba or Cairo. And there was no stratum of officials who derived high salaries directly from the state; no one was really rich unless they held land. The concentration of tax-based wealth in the capitals and major administrative centres of Byzantium and the Islamic states was simply absent here; indeed, as already stated, Pavia was far from being the largest city in the north.

Marc Bloch saw land-based states of this type as characterized by a 'fragmentation of powers', for kings had the same sorts of resources as their aristocracies, and risked both the undermining of their power if they conceded too much land and the related danger that aristocrats might set themselves up on their own in areas where they had concentrations of their own lands and thus local power.[12] How this might, and often did, occur across Latin Europe has been the focus of too much historical work even to begin to cite here. But in Italy we see little of this in the later tenth and eleventh centuries, until after *c.*1080; the kingdom was in

[10] Bougard, *La justice*, is the essential starting point for assemblies and justice.

[11] For royal land in the heartland of the kingdom, see Darmstädter, *Das Reichsgut in der Lombardei und Piemont*, well over a century old but not yet superseded, and, for a new approach, several articles in Bougard and Loré, *Biens publics, biens du roi*.

[12] Bloch, *Feudal society* (quotation at p. 446, with my own modified translation).

general stable, apart from one attempt by an Italian aristocrat, Arduino of Ivrea, to take the kingship in the early eleventh century, and temporary uprisings in some of the major cities, most notably Milan. The years between 1081 and the late 1090s were, however, marked by a civil war, between the king-emperor Henry IV and his supporters on one side and a succession of popes on the other, who had their own supporters, most notably the most powerful aristocrat of the age, Countess Matilda, the ruler of the March of Tuscany, who also had a dense network of lands and military dependants in the middle of the Po plain. By its end, the coherence of the kingdom and the authority of its ruler were seriously undermined, a trend which became even more marked in the next half-century, when the kings rarely returned to Italy. When in 1154 Frederick Barbarossa made his first entry into his Italian kingdom—the first of many, for he hoped to use his still surviving royal lands there, and his remaining public rights, which he by now interpreted as including the right to exact taxation, as a basis for real power—the political situation south of the Alps had radically changed.[13]

This was in two ways above all. The first was that aristocratic elites across the kingdom had by now, indeed, begun to use their local power to substitute themselves for the state, and to assert themselves as local political rulers over villages and wider territories. This was less of a problem for Barbarossa himself, as such lords were often very happy to be loyal to him when he appeared; but it marked a considerable change for local inhabitants, for the new lordly, 'signorial' powers could include substantial payments and other burdens (forced labour for castle-building, for example). I will come back to this issue in the next section, for it has implications for us.[14]

The second was that cities had had fifty years to establish themselves as local rulers on their own behalf. This was not necessarily in contradiction to the growing extension of signorial powers, for many aristocrats were themselves city dwellers, and saw their status and authority to be as much the result of being part of a collectivity of city leaders as deriving from their rural power bases, even if cities in many cases also had to subdue independent-minded rural lords by persuasion or force. Initially, urban leaders ran local affairs as a sort of rearguard action, substituting for a state which had, perhaps only temporarily, disappeared. But the dissolution of public authority was already considerable. Judicial assemblies had vanished in almost all parts of the kingdom. They were substituted by

[13] For recent discussions of the effects of the civil wars, see Wickham, *Sleepwalking*; Fiore, *The seigneurial transformation*. The most recent and wide-ranging of many collective books on Matilda is *Matilde di Canossa e il suo tempo*. For tax exactions by Barbarossa's representatives, see Güterbock, 'Alla vigilia della Lega Lombarda' for Piacenza; for more normal taxation, see n. 75 below. A good recent overview of the political history of Barbarossa's Italian rule from an Italian standpoint, with full bibliography, is Grillo, *Legnano 1176*; and for typically insightful comment, see earlier Tabacco, *The struggle for power*, pp. 208–22.

[14] See, e.g., Fiore, *The seigneurial transformation*, esp. pp. 50–74; for Tuscany, see Wickham, 'La signoria rurale in Toscana'.

much more informal, initially ad hoc, deliberative assemblies, which developed in each city, and were by the years around 1100 in many of them—particularly in Lombardy and Emilia, the core of the old kingdom—the basic local political body. Bishops were usually also influential as the last effective representatives of traditional public hierarchies, but increasingly they were flanked by, and in the end replaced by, city leaders who had been chosen by the citizen assemblies themselves, even if this meant, in reality, by urban elites, who also provided most of the leaders the assemblies chose. Such leaders were usually called consuls, a new title looking back to Republican Rome, and soon had rotating, usually annual offices; the urban communities they ruled, from the 1120s onwards in particular, came to call themselves 'communes'.[15]

These communes were violent: each one aimed to take over its former civil and diocesan territory (its *contado*), often by force, and in large part eventually did so. They also, as we have seen, fought each other with considerable commitment. Consuls themselves were not initially, in most cases, aware that they were creating a wholly new political structure; all the same, slowly, city by city, across the middle decades of the twelfth century, they came to realize its novelty, and came to value it. Those who had not done so yet, when Barbarossa tried to reassert a strong version of an older political system, became sharply more aware of it then. Surprisingly soon after the fall of Milan in 1162, from 1164 onwards, the cities reacted against the new taxes and the authoritarianism of local imperial governors, and in 1167 war began between the newly formed Lombard League and the emperor. In 1176 Barbarossa lost the crucial battle of Legnano; in 1177 peace was established, and formalized in 1183, with the emperor recognizing in effect every aspect of the autonomy of the north Italian cities and their consular rulers.[16] North-central Italy was by now to all intents and purposes no more than a collection of forty independent cities and a small handful of great rural lords, and, with modifications, it continued to be from then on until the nineteenth century.

I have discussed elsewhere the debates over the origins of city communes in Italy, and have given my own views on them; these are summarized only very briefly here. My main divergence from the standard narrative concerns the level of consciousness city leaders had concerning what they were doing in the early decades of the twelfth century, and the level of enthusiasm with which they embarked on an initially very uncertain journey. But—and more relevant here—the standard narrative is also very much more excited about the appearance of the communes than seems to me helpful; as I have noted elsewhere, for many writers, their crystallization marked the entry of Italians as actors into their

[15] This paragraph and the next summarize Wickham, *Sleepwalking*, which gives a fuller bibliography. For the terminology of 'communes', see most recently Faini, 'Il comune e il suo contrario'.

[16] See nn. 6 and 13 above. For the Peace of Constance in 1183, see *Friderici I. diplomata*, n. 848; as the textual citations there show, it survives in a notably wide range of communal archives and cartularies in Italy.

own history, a history of autonomous city communities which would generate the economic leap forward of the twelfth and thirteenth centuries, and the cultural leap forward which would lead to Dante, Petrarch, and then on into 'modernity'. Whether this is empirically right or wrong, the excitement has got in the way of understanding how Italy actually did change—in particular, for our purposes, in its economy. People take it for granted that it did, without discussing how; and the detailed historiography on how the economy of the crucial twelfth century really operated has been, apart from some important archaeological work, much less extensive in recent years than are discussions of communal society and politics.[17] That communes were ruled, for the most part, by a wide and stable stratum of militarized elites has become clear.[18] They were not at all merchant republics, as they are still sometimes described (to be fair, mostly by non-specialists[19]), with the partial exception of Venice. That was true even for Genoa, which was the only other city for which we can, before 1200 at the earliest, show for sure that the richest urban families were heavily involved in commerce (see pp. 512–13, 543–6 below). And it was even more true for inland cities; in most cases, elites were landowning first, commercial sometimes only a distant second, until rather later than our period. That there was in the end a commercial take-off is, of course, undeniable, and crucial. But I would see that as quite separate from the political development of communes; the two processes initially occurred side by side, with little mutual influence.

I would, in fact, go further. For the purposes of commercial development, the division of Italy into self-governing communes was, at least at the start, quite largely negative. It resulted in war and destruction, as I stressed at the start of this chapter. It also resulted in a set of toll barriers, and insecurity for merchants outside their own city territory; that is to say, transaction costs which had to be overcome by a cumbersome set of individual intercity agreements—such as those preserved in Piacenza's communal *Registrum magnum* between that city and Ferrara in 1181, Florence in the same year, and Cremona in 1183, over the safety of merchants travelling in the territory of the other city (in each case paying some tolls, however).[20] And it meant that when contemplating capital investment, each

[17] A new start is the 2015 Pistoia conference published as *La crescita economica*. Mainoni, *Economia e politica*, pp. 13–18, is an earlier survey of the little we know of cloth production, developed further in her article in the Pistoia volume.

[18] Maire Vigueur, *Cavaliers et citoyens*, is here the key text; see ibid., pp. 264–75 for the economic activities of such *milites*.

[19] Although I am sorry to say that here they included Lopez too, in *The commercial revolution*, p. 70 (but he had said it in earlier work as well): 'In the twelfth century the Italian communes were essentially governments of the merchants, by the merchants, for the merchants'—a seriously inaccurate and misleading claim.

[20] Falconi and Peveri, *Il Registrum Magnum*, 1, nn. 39, 45, 215. Such agreements were in particular facilitated by the Lombard League; see Raccagni, *The Lombard League*, pp. 119–22; for this and the decades following, see further Grillo, 'Vie di comunicazione'; for examples, see Manaresi, *Gli atti del Comune*, nn. 51–2, 54, 62, 65 (aa. 1167–8)—but these, which cancelled nearly all tolls, were evidently

city was initially dependent only on the accumulation of landed resources which was possible in its own city territory, for investing in another city was rare and risky (I have only seen signs of it in Genoa, and few there too; see pp. 545, 554 below). This investment was in many cases quite restricted, as we shall see, and less extensive than in the major states of the eastern and southern Mediterranean. Only Genoa and Pisa really as yet benefited economically from autonomy, in that they began in the twelfth century to make trade treaties across the whole Mediterranean (Venice was sovereign anyway, so the issue did not arise there). Elsewhere, autonomy helped the expansion of exchange only when cities took charge of infrastructure as collectivities, digging canals, widening and paving roads, draining marshes, and beginning to establish urban sewerage systems, which was in nearly every case a development of the thirteenth century.[21] By then, there is no doubt at all of urban economic protagonism; but it took until then for it to begin.

I have briefly characterized the other great metanarrative of central medieval Italian history, Lopez's image of the 'commercial revolution', in Chapter 1 of this book; but we now need to meet it head on. Here, Lopez himself is less crucial, for, given that he was much more interested in commerce than in urban production as the key marker of economic change, he tended to stress the projection of the port cities into the Mediterranean, rather than the internal development of north-central Italy. Instead, I will confront it by setting out and critiquing the views of two major historians of the generation before mine, Cinzio Violante and Philip Jones, one after the other—for Jones says most about the period after 1050, the date at which Violante stopped. I choose these two in part for their importance as historians, but also because they were strong proponents of the view that the Italian commercial take-off was old, which, as I have said, has been contested more recently, but less systematically. This will give the essential framing for the discussion of agricultural changes which will follow it, and then the case studies which make up the bulk of this chapter.

* * *

temporary. An extreme case of urban division undermining trading is the treatment of Lodi by Milan: well before the forced abandonment of Milan and the dispersion of its population into several rural *burgi* in 1162–7, Milan had done exactly the same to Lodi for the much longer period 1111–58; this culminated around 1150 (so Lodigiano plaintiffs complained to Frederick Barbarossa in 1153) in the forced move of the Lodi market, still a focus for merchants from the rest of Lombardy, to an open field well away from the *burgi*; see Otto and Acerbo Morena, *Historia Friderici I.*, pp. 3–5.

[21] For a neat short survey, see Menant, *L'Italie des communes*, pp. 169–74. For the earlier absence of sewage systems, see, e.g., Merati, 'La rappresentazione dell'esperienza', which edits a set of witness testimonies from Milan in 1207, but referring back to the 1160s. The witnesses discuss an open space just outside the Porta Vercellina to which people went to *ludere ad ossa et cagare et pixare* (play dice, defecate and urinate; for the latter, *mingere* is also used; see pp. 477, 480, 482, 485–6, 490). Two privies (*necessaria*) are also cited (pp. 473, 481–3, 487, 490), but the defecation and urination seem to have been on the open land as well. It is conceivable that there was a gender difference here.

Violante's 1953 publication, *La società milanese nell'età precomunale*, is a brilliant work, ultimately deriving (as was then not uncommon) from his undergraduate thesis. It was highly influential in its time, and is still the first point of reference for any economic study of the central Po plain in the eighth to eleventh centuries. Here I set out the main data the book used, across the more than three hundred years it covered, for we need to have it in front of us in what follows. It tracked the 'revival of commerce', as Violante's first chapter is called, right back to the pact which Liutprand, Lombard king of Italy, made in 715 (or 730) with the men (*milites*) of Comacchio in the Po delta, outside the Kingdom of Italy, concerning the dues owed by the Comacchiesi in a set of ports along the Po and its tributaries, as they brought salt (and also pepper) from the delta to the Lombard towns. By 840, Venice itself had become the major coastal centre, and from that date onwards a long line of treaties survives between the Venetians and the Carolingian—later German—kings of Italy, continuing into the twelfth century with hardly changed text, which from the start envisaged that the Venetians would come into the Kingdom of Italy to trade. The special position of the Venetians was stressed in the *Honorantie civitatis Papie*, a late tenth- or early eleventh-century description of the rights of Pavia as the capital; 'many rich merchants' from the Venetian region brought eastern spices and other luxuries to the city, and are given more attention in the text than other merchants who also came there, whether from the cities of Campania, Salerno, Gaeta, and Amalfi, or—more surprisingly—from England (the English paid a flat rate in silver and luxury gifts every three years, in return for commercial rights). The text otherwise specifies a toll of 10 per cent on the main Alpine passes, as we have seen a standard commercial tax, for any non-English merchants who brought in horses, slaves, woollen or linen or hempen cloth, tin, or swords. The Venetians paid 2.5 per cent (this was by now laid down in the treaties as well), plus another flat rate in silver and luxury gifts. These, for Violante, were real signs of generalized economic growth, starting particularly, he concluded, between 850 and 950.[22]

[22] Violante, *La società milanese*, pp. 7–70, 99–134, sets out the data in this paragraph and the next, including more individual citations than I can summarize here; see ibid., p. 40 for the 850–950 date. I cite from the first edition; the second has new pagination but unchanged text. For the late eighth century and earlier, important more recent books with an upbeat picture are McCormick, *Origins*, pp. 630–8, 778–98; Di Muro, *La terra, il mercante*, the latter now being fundamental for the Lombard kingdom. Notwithstanding the economic effervescence they set out, I share the caution expressed by Alessia Rovelli in 'Coins and trade in early medieval Italy', and elsewhere. Liutprand's pact is edited in Hartmann, *Zur Wirtschaftsgeschichte*, pp. 123–4, and most recently in *Privilegia episcopii Cremonensis*, ed. Leoni, n. 2; the Venetian treaties for our period are mostly edited in the relevant volumes of *MGH, Diplomata* (the first, in 840, is *MGH, Capitularia*, 2, n. 233, and nn. 234–41 contain later Carolingian agreements; that for Barbarossa in 1154, little altered, is in *Friderici I. diplomata*, n. 94); the *Honorantie* are most recently edited in Brühl and Violante, *Die 'Honorantie civitatis Papie'*. The 2.5% (one-fortieth) began with Berengar I: *MGH, Capitularia*, 2, n. 238, ch. 17 (= Schiaparelli, *I diplomi di Berengario I*, n. 3, p. 20).

Inhabitants of the kingdom could be merchants too. Already in 750 King Aistulf legislated about their military service obligations; by 852 the men of Cremona were taking over part of the salt trade along the Po. Merchants are steadily more often recorded in the documents of Milan and its hinterland from the ninth century onwards; in 861 an individual merchant, Gennaro, a protégé of the monastery of S. Giulia di Brescia, received an unusual personalized toll immunity from King Louis II; by the eleventh century, kings were granting commercial privileges, particularly toll immunities, to *negociatores* or *mercatores* from Asti, as also other cities, as we shall see. Markets are attested both in cities and in the countryside, increasing in numbers of citations from the ninth century on. Artisans are attested too; Pavia already had a version of a guild structure according to the *Honorantie*, the *ministeria* not only of merchants, but of moneyers, gold panners, fishermen, leatherworkers, and soap makers, which Violante saw as a new development, the result of a steadily strengthening commercial network across the Po plain. In the eleventh century in Milan, some merchants were getting rich enough to move into the urban elite; indeed, people of all kinds were by then moving into Milan, and land and urban house prices rose. These and parallel developments were for Violante 'all symptoms of the rising up of a new life', 'the new luxuriance (*rigoglio*) of economic and social life', by the second quarter of the eleventh century.[23]

We need to pause here, and look at this image of vitality. The evidence presented by Violante is important, and pretty complete, at least for his central focus, Lombardy; it has only been added to in detail. He did not discuss Tuscany here, but the evidence there is similar; Lucca, by far the best-documented Tuscan city, had artisans—among others, cauldron makers, builders, goldsmiths—as early as the eighth century, mostly attested as witnesses or dealers in rural land, even if evidence then drops back for them for 250 years as formulae for document-writing changed. But it does not, for me, convey as much 'luxuriance' as Violante proposed. The fact that his starting point was international trade was typical of the period he wrote in, and went back to Pirenne—and, of course, Heyd and Schaube, although Pirenne, who he disagreed with in detail, was particularly in his mind. That was, however, almost entirely a luxury trade, as far as the documents tell us (archaeology, which did not exist when he wrote, in effect confirms it, as we shall see); the cloth and tin brought over the Alps according to the *Honorantie* are, of course, bulk commodities, but they are also not attested again, although silver came from Germany from now on, for coinage, and copper later (p. 554). Almost the only bulk good which the Venetians are described as

[23] Quotations from Violante, *La società milanese*, pp. 134–5; he discusses the merchants of Milan at pp. 44–6, 66–8, 127–33; prices at 100–10. For Milanese merchants and markets in the early middle ages, see further Balzaretti, *The lands of Saint Ambrose*, pp. 240–5, 520–3; D'Acunto, 'Mercato, mercati e mercanti'. For 750, see *Leges langobardorum*, ed. Beyerle, *Ahistulfi leges*, ch. 3; for 852, see Manaresi, *I placiti*, 1, n. 56; for 861, see *Ludovici II. diplomata*, n. 32; for Asti, see *Ottonis III. diplomata*, n. 99, *Conradi II. diplomata*, n. 245.

bringing into the kingdom was salt from their own salt pans, which is the very minimum a trading system can include, since it is a necessity of life; the only exception here is that in 862 they are documented as bringing linen to Mantua as well.[24] We will look at this in more detail when we look at Venice, later on in this chapter; but, so far, luxuries plus salt dominate our evidence.

Violante, however, given that he was one of the most innovative European medievalists in the 1950s, also saw that at least as—and probably more—important was the growing network of markets inside Italy, both rural and urban. The former, doubtless, focussed on agricultural products, the latter, however, were potentially for the exchange of artisanal goods as well, made for example by the metalworkers and a handful of other trades which appear in Milanese land documents.[25] Indeed, recent work on the ninth-century manorial system of north-central Italy (the *sistema curtense* in Italian) shows clearly how manorial structures themselves gained much of their point from the possibility of producing from demesnes a marketable surplus, linked in some cases directly with rural and then urban markets.[26] As a result of this, several historians see the revival of markets and rural growth as being a phenomenon of the tenth century at the latest; and urban growth can by the end of the tenth century be identified as well, with, in some cities, formally defined suburbs beginning to appear outside their Roman-period walls. These writers sometimes, rather optimistically, use the word *rinascita*, 'rebirth', to describe this process, clearly looking forwards to the 'commercial revolution'. Whether or not one follows them, the fact that there was an active network of internal exchange by now, focussed on towns, and linked together (in northern Italy, at least) by the river network centred on the Po, seems clear. The rival narrative, always commoner among historians of France than of Italy, that there was limited commerce before 1050 or so, with a 'gift economy' prevailing until then, is, in particular, wholly unfounded.[27]

[24] *Calderarii* in Lucca: *Chartae latinae antiquiores*, 31, n. 921, 34, n. 996, 35, n. 1032, 36, n. 1041; *aurefices*: 31, n. 916A, 34, n. 1001, 36, n. 1041; *casarii*: 38, n. 1117, 74, nn. 18, 42. For the last, builders, see esp. Violante, 'I transpadani in Tuscia nei secoli VIII e IX'. For the linen in Mantua, see Castagnetti et al., *Inventari*, p. 138 (cf. also 159). For silver, see Benvenuti et al., 'Metals and coinage in medieval Tuscany', for Saxon silver in Italian coins in the period prior to the opening of Tuscany's own silver mines.

[25] For the artisans, see Violante, *La società milanese*, pp. 48–9; Balzaretti, *The lands of Saint Ambrose*, pp. 242–4.

[26] See n. 54 below for manors and markets, but the classic account for Italy is in Toubert, *Dalla terra ai castelli*, pp. 215–45.

[27] Suburbs: for Lucca, north-central Italy's best-documented city until the twelfth century, see Belli Barsali, 'La topografia di Lucca', pp. 505–6, with evidence starting in 998; but there was extramural settlement, less explicitly characterized, as early as the eighth century in several cities. For early medieval markets, see Settia, '"Per foros Italie"', the most systematic and balanced account; Bocchi, 'Città e mercati'; and see n. 23 above for Violante on Milan. For early medieval markets in general it is still necessary to mention Carli, *Il mercato nell'alto medioevo*, esp. pp. 245–75, 290–303, for its data, although not for its outdated interpretations (the same is true for his second volume, *Il mercato nell'età del Comune*, which is a mixture of very wide reading and careful data collection, esp. for our purposes at pp. 63–99, 165–202, and an interpretative frame which is no longer usable). For *rinascita*, see,

All the same, we get no idea from the evidence we have here about scale. We will come back to the issue of rural growth shortly, but most of the mercantile data are chance references, without context. Italy's network of active towns, in which local aristocracies lived, was close to unique in Latin Europe (even if far from unique in the Mediterranean), but this meant that they had buying power simply because they concentrated land rents and thus wealth into single centres, without needing to be major productive hubs. Furthermore, urban and rural markets, whether documented or not, are a normal part of all city–country relationships, and urban artisans (catering, not least, to these landed elites) are also entirely typical everywhere, including in relatively small towns—as eighth-century towns in Italy for sure were, even if they began slowly to expand from then onwards.[28] Merchants are a standard part of even relatively simple socio-economic systems too. Violante clearly had in his mind the impressive future of Milan's economy, and he also wanted, most immediately, to set up an economic explanation for the city's striking set of uprisings in the second and third quarters of the eleventh century. The large number of casual citations of merchants in Milan certainly helped him there, and so do—I would say, even more certainly—the price rises he discussed, but they are not matched in most other cities. Even in Milan references to merchants in documents dry up, for unclear reasons, after the 1050s; this was certainly not because commerce dropped, but it does not help our understanding of what happened next.[29]

I would, therefore, summarize the period up to the late eleventh century much more cautiously. There was certainly commercial movement visible in the eighth and ninth centuries, and more clearly from the later tenth century onwards. Across northern Italy in particular, we can be sure that the river network allowed for easy mercantile interconnections, and archaeology gives us some evidence for it, as we shall see (pp. 594–6). Cities, as they slowly expanded, must have grown as foci of buying power too. But this exchange expansion was as yet fairly gentle; it was restricted, one might say, to the patterns normal in the economically active regions of the *early* middle ages, not the central middle ages, in Europe. It was coming to be similar to those already visible in the river systems of Carolingian,

e.g., *La rinascita del mercato nel X secolo*; Toubert, *Dalla terra ai castelli*, p. 155 (with scare quotes). For the 'gift economy' narrative, see, e.g., Duby, *The early growth*, pp. 97–107, 177–81, 257–60; Little, *Religious poverty*, pp. 3–18.

[28] For small eighth-century towns, see Brogiolo and Gelichi, *La città nell'alto medioevo italiano*, from 1998 but still the most detailed archaeological overview; Wickham, *Framing the early middle ages*, pp. 644–56—the foci and tone of these two diverge, but they agree on this.

[29] The last urban *negotians* in Vittani et al., *Gli atti privati milanesi*, the standard edition of eleventh-century Milanese private documents, is attested selling land in 1050 (n. 339), although the son of a deceased *negotians* buys urban housing in 1057 (nn. 397–8), and the neighbouring small town of Vimercate had two merchant brothers in the 1050s too (see n. 335 below). But Milan had an *ordo negotiatorum* in 1067 (Mansi, *Sacrorum conciliorum nova et amplissima collectio*, 19, col. 948), which had some political role, even if an undefined one, in the conflicts of the period; although this too had no later history, merchants had unsurprisingly not gone away; see pp. 598–9 below.

ninth-century, northern Francia;[30] but that was two centuries before any real take-off in the production and commercialization of cloth in Flanders and its neighbours. It in no way matches the intense internal exchange activity that we have seen so clearly for eleventh-century Egypt and Sicily, and that we have also seen beginning to develop by now, quite fast, in Byzantium and al-Andalus as well. We do not as yet have a clear indication of any real density in these internal Italian interconnections, or any real growth in artisanal production, or, indeed, any real hint that this density and this growth were even about to appear on the horizon.

I pick up the narrative with Philip Jones, in his *The Italian city-state* of 1997, building on and partly repeating a long and influential article in Italian of 1974. Jones saw the early middle ages, to 1100, as economically precocious, with the 'un-Roman vocation of trade' already established by the eighth century, with Italian towns by 1000 'overtaking all but the greatest Byzantine and Islamic cities', including a range of eleventh-century export manufactures. As we have just seen, and as the previous chapters have shown, these claims are tenuously supported in the documentary record as yet—he was better grounded when he discussed land clearance, urban expansion, and the growth of smaller towns—although, as usual with Jones, they were all balanced by the apparently contrary recognition that early medieval trade was still 'circumscribed', 'modest', 'limited', and rather less important than agricultural wealth.[31] After 1100, however, there is no doubt of his view. He was content to call his large chapter on the twelfth and thirteenth centuries 'Commercial revolution'; here urban expansion is still clearer, from the twelfth century onwards. Towns settled into a complex economic network stretching across the whole northern half of the peninsula; commercialized and often specialized agriculture developed to feed the towns, which soon had to look farther afield for grain; Italian trading extended eastwards and westwards and northwards; banking developed, urban production developed massively, capital investment was great and increasing. 'Italy was the home of *mercatores*.' On the subject of production, Jones was oddly inconsistent: Italian cloth production lagged behind that of France and Flanders until the late thirteenth century, remaining 'generally passive', and imported much, but at the same time massively exported its own cottons, fustians, and woollens, not only into the Mediterranean but also to the north.[32] But the overall picture was wholly positive, and often convincing and effective.

[30] For Francia, see Verhulst, *The Carolingian economy*; Devroey, *Économie rurale*; Bruand, *Voyageurs et marchandises*. I discuss the significant differences between early medieval and central medieval economic structures in Chapter 8.

[31] See Jones, *The Italian city-state*, pp. 73–120; 78, 96, 101, 102–3 for citations. In its economic sections, the book is a more up-to-date version of his earlier article 'La storia economica', but it is in places less detailed, and, conversely, sometimes repeats the article word for word.

[32] Jones, *The Italian city-state*, pp. 152–231; 196 for the *mercatores* quotation; for the contradiction, 181–3, 191–2 (and already, in little-changed wording, 'La storia economica', pp. 1706–9). I think this contradiction derives from Jones's partial, but incomplete absorption of an older model of the relative

Jones then, once again, turned this picture around in a second, almost unrelated section of his book. In reality, Italian cities were not really bourgeois; noble values were dominant, and so were landowning families in most towns. In a separate article, also drawn from in the book, he discussed with vigour and conviction the 'legend of the bourgeoisie', so much so that he is sometimes thought of, in Italy, as having actually been an opponent of the idea that Italian cities had a commercial vocation and civic values, although he never, in reality, argued that: 'in Italy's hybrid urban world, feudal balanced bourgeois influence'.[33] For me, however, the problem with Jones's vision of these economic changes is different: it is a lack of causal exactness and temporal precision. Unlike Lopez, Jones put a great deal of stress on urban production in his overall picture, and I would entirely agree with him; but the twelfth century gets entirely subsumed into the far better-documented and more active thirteenth here. One is left with the clear sense that the main moment of change was already at the end of the eleventh century, with, as the quotations I have given show, a long back history, but there are no argued grounds, and the process of take-off is unexamined. Jones is no longer fully representative here; as noted earlier, recent overviews of economic change in Italy locate the most important economic upturn in or near the late twelfth century.[34] But Jones wrote at the greatest length, and started early enough in time to allow himself to be able to pose the questions of how or why. All the same, he did not; even though he was well aware that urban and rural production and urban growth went tightly together, he did not spend any space on asking what actually happened to allow this remarkable expansion to take place. Simply, it was obvious to him. Jones was a complex and subtle analyst, but that obviousness got in his way. And it seems to me, it has got in the way of plenty of others too, although they have not written at Jones's length, or with his sometimes alarmingly dense footnotes.

Let us stop here a moment, and look at one particular source, imperial grants to cities, which punctuate our period, especially between the early eleventh and

importance of luxury and bulk goods, in this case higher-quality and higher-priced French and Flemish woollens set against Italian simpler woollens and still cheaper fustian (see further n. 202 below); for many historians had assumed that high-quality goods were, in effect, more economically significant than cheaper and mass-produced bulk cloth—see, e.g., Hoshino, *L'arte della lana*, pp. 66–7; Racine, *Plaisance*, 1, p. 324 (but there are many others; the idea goes back at least to Pirenne's concern with luxuries as guides to the nature of the early medieval Mediterranean economy, *Mohammed and Charlemagne*, pp. 169–73). This view is, as the whole argument of this book proposes, radically mistaken; the opposite was true. I criticize Lopez enough in this book, but it is fair to recognize that he knew this; see, e.g., Lopez, *Studi sull'economia genovese*, pp. 77–9; so also did Sapori, 'I beni del commercio internazionale nel Medioevo', although this article, more than anything by Lopez, represents the history-writing of a lost world.

[33] Jones, *The Italian city-state*, p. 331 for the quotation; for the wider argument, see Jones, 'Economia e società nell'Italia medievale: la leggenda della borghesia'; for Jones seen simply as a critic of the dominance of Italian civic values see, e.g., Polica, 'Basso Medioevo e Rinascimento', pp. 289–306. Nobili, 'L'equazione città antica–città comunale', more balanced, puts Jones's arguments in a wider historiographical frame.

[34] See n. 5 above.

the mid-twelfth centuries. These may seem a very external source for urban economic activity, but they are important above all because they give us a direct clue to city aspirations, in a period in which emperors were still the source of legal rights, even when they were losing effective power. Cities presented wish lists to the emperor and his entourage, which were then turned into the formulae of imperial grant-giving. They may not always have got all they asked for, but there was almost no circumstance in which an emperor coming from Germany would have any preconceived idea as to what a city might want (sometimes, indeed, we know—there is a well-known case for Cremona in 996—that they were deceived as to what rights cities already had), so we can assume that what cities were granted largely reflected the texts they presented for imperial approval.[35] They often sought commercial privileges. Some cities were simply granted toll-free shipping along the Po and its tributaries: Ferrara in 1055, Cremona in 1115, Bologna in 1116, Lodi in 1158, or Pavia in 1164.[36] But often these requests were rather more localized. In 1014 (and again in 1116 and 1159), the men of Mantua were to be free of tolls taken *pro negocio* (for trade) up to Brescia and Lake Garda, not at all far away, as well as down the Po to Ferrara, Comacchio, and Ravenna, but not elsewhere. In 1081, in two separate diplomas, the men of Lucca and Pisa could go toll-free from Pavia right down to Rome, but the Lucchese text is most concerned to specify rights to buy and sell in the market of San Donnino (now Fidenza, prov. Parma) and with the men of Parma—and that the Florentines would not have that right. The Bolognesi in 1116 asked for rights along the Po network, but only Ferrara is actually specified; here too there were to be trade restrictions for others, the *negotiatores de Tuscia*, who could henceforth only cross Bolognese territory twice a year. In 1119, the men of Piacenza were simply freed of tolls at Firenzuola and at San Donnino again—both of them being along the road from there to the next city, Parma.[37]

These were not very ambitious requests. Historians have been struck by the fact that a casual reference in an eleventh-century Latin poem from southern Germany, *Ruodlieb*, mentions a man clad in leggings from *Lukka*; maybe this

[35] The argument that this was a standard way of getting an imperial cession is best made by Hartmann, 'Heinrich V. im Diskurs Bologneser Gelehrter', pp. 206–9, who shows that the Bologna diploma of 1116, edited most recently in *Die Urkunden Heinrichs V.*, n. 179, uses Bolognese, not imperial formulaic conventions, and thus argues that the text we have—preserved in Bologna's *Registro Grosso*—is the draft made for Henry V, not the final text, if, indeed, there was one. In 996, in *Ottonis III. diplomata*, n. 222, Otto withdrew a concession to the citizens of Cremona on the grounds that they had deceived him as to the commercial rights they already had, which were, in this case successfully, contested by the bishop (see further pp. 592–4 below).

[36] Respectively, *Heinrici III. diplomata*, n. 351; *Die Urkunden Heinrichs V.*, nn. 143 (by now, the citizens of Cremona had, in effect, got back the rights they sought in 996), 179; *Friderici I. diplomata*, nn. 246, 455.

[37] Mantua: *Heinrici II. diplomata*, n. 278, *Die Urkunden Heinrichs V.*, n. 174, *Friderici I. diplomata*, n. 263 (and cf. the similar rights in *Heinrici III. diplomata*, n. 356 and *Heinrici IV. diplomata*, n. 421). Lucca and Pisa: *Heinrici IV. diplomata*, nn. 334, 336. Bologna: *Die Urkunden Heinrichs V.*, n. 179. Piacenza: ibid., n. 217.

might show that the Lucchesi were already weaving luxury cloth for transalpine buyers;[38] but in 1081 the Lucchesi themselves were more concerned to get market rights in the first two towns on the Po plain that they would reach after crossing the Appennines. And although the Lucchesi, at least, became more ambitious by the 1150s, when some of them were going over the Alps to France (see pp. 542, 581 below), once the communes were established, the trade barriers along the Po and elsewhere came down again. We have seen that the Po and its tributaries could, indeed, be regarded as a whole, already in the eighth century, in fact. But in these grants, which continue into Barbarossa's time, we get a clear sense that cities were thinking above all of their nearest trade outlets, and also their nearest rivals: despite all the references to toll rights along the Po, there is no sense in them of a large-scale integrated commercial network as yet. But surely, for a 'commercial revolution' to deserve its name, such a network ought to be one of its basic elements?

I will come back to these issues later. But as an interim conclusion, it seems to me that the very success of the thirteenth-century north Italian cities—and, by now, smaller towns, *burgi*, as well—has impeded an understanding of where that success came from, and when. It is too easy to try to track it quite far, too far, back, in ways which are often too generic—or else not to track it at all, and simply begin with the thirteenth century, with what came before left implicit. As stated earlier, I would myself now put the major moment of change for most of north-central Italy in the late twelfth century, although I would not wish to be schematic about that date either: cities had begun to expand demographically well before that point, urban housing was becoming much more ambitious too, and the countryside was beginning to change in significant ways. In order to get a bit closer to possible explanations, it is best to begin with the countryside, which in Italy is certainly well studied, not least because of the land transactions which survive, in larger or smaller numbers, from nearly every city. So let us survey the main lines of the rural economy across our period, before we return to cities.

6.2 A Rural Italy

If we look at what Italian documentation does tell us, rather than what it does not, the floodgates open. Not only do we have tens of thousands of documents, but we also have to deal with the great bulk of recent economic history-writing on early and central medieval Italy. Whole schools of Italian scholars have written about developments in agriculture, land clearance, village societies, estate management,

[38] *Ruodlieb*, ed. Vollmann, p. 140; cautious commentary in Mainoni, 'La seta in Italia', p. 374; Del Punta, *Mercanti e banchieri lucchesi*, p. 42; Tomei, 'Il sale e la seta', pp. 29–32. For documented developments in Lucchese fine cloth-working, all much later than this, see pp. 581–4 below.

and the growth of signorial lordship.[39] The major French *thèses d'état* on north-central Italy in this period also either looked at cities above all in the context of the countryside around them (Arezzo, Padua) or focussed on the countryside only, and left the urban world largely alone (Lazio, eastern Lombardy)—the only exception is Pierre Racine's book on Piacenza, which, although traditional, remains one of the few relatively detailed accounts of an urban economy in our period.[40] Indeed, this was for a long time true of my own work on Italy, which focussed on the countryside, mostly in Tuscany, before, relatively recently, I attempted an urban monograph on Rome. There is, in fact, too much to present in detail, and there is no difficulty in relying on the weight of excellent scholarship here. I will therefore offer a bare synthesis, generalizing very greatly from the mass of local studies. Every statement in the next pages will have exceptions somewhere in north-central Italy; so much material is being summarized here that this is inevitable, and my citations are by no means exhaustive. But at least we can recognize that, however incomplete our evidence, we have fewer uncertainties than we had in most of the rest of the Mediterranean; and it is not necessary here to offer a synthesis of the whole of rural development in itself. Rather, we need to have enough of it set out to allow us to have clear two points by the end: first, the directions of agrarian growth and surplus extraction; and second, the degree to which peasants managed to keep enough of their surplus to be able to engage in wider exchange, these being the elements which I have stressed in earlier discussions of other regions of the Mediterranean.

North-central Italy had a standard Mediterranean dry-farming agriculture on its plains in most places and for most of our period. In the mountains, it did as well; real specializations in pastoral production were only beginning at the end of our period. Grain production predominated; in the Po plain rye was the principal crop, in Tuscany wheat, but both were accompanied by a wide range of other grains, barley, millet, panic, sorghum, and others, as well as beans, as leases and rent lists show us. Wine production was everywhere as well; in northern Italy flax cultivation was sometimes prominent too; and in several areas, as noted earlier, there were also olives. It is, indeed, interesting that olive cultivation was common around the lakes in the foothills of the Alps, as the Po plain in general is not really in the olive zone; it shows how it was valued culturally even where it was not a natural crop, for lighting and liturgical purposes as well as for food, and we can find it cited as early as the eighth century.[41] Vegetables are mentioned only very

[39] A bibliographical survey up to 2001, region by region, is Cortonesi and Montanari, *Medievistica italiana e storia agraria*; for a more synthetic general survey up to 2010, see Cortonesi and Passigli, *Agricoltura e allevamento*, pp. 3–27, with another extensive bibliography; for a good social-historical synthesis of research directions, see Provero, 'Forty years of rural history'.

[40] Delumeau, *Arezzo*; Rippe, *Padoue*; Toubert, *Les structures du Latium médiéval* (out of the area covered by this chapter but historiographically central); Menant, *Campagnes lombardes* (though Menant did discuss the cities of Bergamo and Cremona in more detail in later work); Racine, *Plaisance*.

[41] See Brugnoli, 'Dal Mediterraneo all'Europa', with ample bibliography.

casually, but they were certainly a feature of, for example, urban gardens, which were intensively cultivated.[42] Mixed farming was normal, and Massimo Montanari has shown in detail how, before 1000, Italians regularly turned to silvo-pastoral products to supplement their diet, as the cultivated lands were surrounded by, and interpenetrated with, zones of woodland.[43] But there was always exchange, except where resources were very homogeneous. Around Lucca, again as early as the eighth century but more clearly in the twelfth, rents from the plain were above all in grain and beans, whereas from the hills above they were rather more in wine and oil. Although rents in documents show landlordly needs more directly than they do the range of peasant activity (by the end of the twelfth century rents in wheat could be standard in areas where it was a minority crop—that is to say, it was only grown for rent-paying there, not for peasant consumption), the distinction around Lucca implies exchange, doubtless largely via the market in the city.[44]

The higher stretches of the Po plain and the Tuscan lowland basins, which were the core zones of agricultural production, had unbroken continuities of cultivation stretching back to the Roman Empire and before; extensive traces of Roman centuriated field systems survive nearly everywhere here. These lands are regularly described by historians as fertile and prosperous; for that matter, I have used these adjectives earlier here myself. It does have to be recognized, however, that yields were not high. The evidence for them is (as in all our regions) unsatisfactory, but some does exist, starting with early tenth-century polyptychs or estate records. It has amply been discussed by historians, and the current common ground, convincing to me, is that 3:1, sometimes rising to 4:1 but probably only rarely reaching 5:1, was a normal yield across north-central Italy, and was lower on poor land.[45] This is slightly lower than the similar tentative figures for Byzantium (see p. 347 above), and far lower than those for Egypt or Sicily or the irrigated areas of Spain (see pp. 66, 241, 391 above). There is little sign that it became higher at any point in our period or, indeed, later, at least up to the Black Death.

The exception may have been in the areas of, in particular, Lombardy where, in the higher plain around some cities (Bergamo has been well studied here), irrigation began to be developed. This was a feature of the twelfth century in particular, as we can see from more frequent references to canals on agricultural land. Some of this land was cultivated for grain and vines; all the same, as far as we can see, most of it was water meadows for pasture, or, closest to cities, gardens and

[42] Montanari. *L'alimentazione contadina*, pp. 308–28, 356–65; Goodson, *Cultivating the city*, esp. pp. 108–14, 148, 231–6.

[43] Montanari. *L'alimentazione contadina*, esp. pp. 222–53.

[44] Wickham, *Community and clientele*, pp. 18–19; for wheat grown only for rent, see, e.g., Menant, *Campagnes lombardes*, pp. 238–41.

[45] See esp. Montanari, 'Rese cerealicole'; Menant, *Campagnes lombardes*, pp. 341–3; Cortonesi and Piccinni, *Medioevo delle campagne*, p. 26; Pasquali, *Sistemi di produzione agraria*, p. 283; Jarrett, 'Outgrowing the Dark Ages'.

orchards.[46] We do not have the evidence to tell us how far this improved grain yields, although it must have done in a few places; but, anyway, it is only in the latest middle ages, with the development of the landed estates known as *cascine* on the lower Lombard plain, that landlords and peasants moved into irrigation-based grain agriculture on a large scale.[47] The huge canals (in many places called *navigli*), built with the support of city communes across the northern Po plain from the end of the twelfth century onwards, helped meadow irrigation too, and certainly milling, although they were above all dug to develop internal communications (and as defences), supplementing the river network.[48] We are here, in our period at least, at (at most) Byzantine levels of water management (see p. 303 above), and a long way from those of al-Andalus or Egypt.

Where agrarian growth lay was not, by and large, in the improvement of techniques (otherwise yields would have gone up), but in specialization, and above all the extension of agricultural land in woodland clearance. Specializations in local products are important for us, for they all show the existence of exchange networks which go beyond, sometimes well beyond, producer areas. The olive specializations on the edge of the Alps must show the existence of networks of exchange which extended widely from an early date, although we cannot easily tell how far, either geographically or socially—that is to say, beyond elite consumption, which we can assume was their main market.[49] But if we are looking for change, the clearest example is the development of transhumant pastoralism. When sheep are moved from summer pastures in the mountains to winter pastures on the plains, their numbers can and do increase substantially, and mountain areas can begin—and here did begin—to focus far more on stock-raising for sale, as a result, of

[46] For Bergamo, see Menant, *Campagnes lombardes*, pp. 182–200, cf. 344 (with map at 928); for Milan, see Rapetti, *Campagne milanesi*, pp. 99–103; for after 1200, see Grillo, *Milano*, pp. 97, 171–6; Chiappa Mauri, *Paesaggi rurali*, pp. 84–94. See in general Campopiano and Menant, 'Agricolture irrigue'. Contrast the elusive evidence for the period before 1000: Squatriti, *Water and society*, pp. 79–96. Panero, 'Rese cerealicole', a wide-ranging survey, by contrast argues for a near-continuous increase in grain yields in northern Italy 900–1500; on pp. 203–5, he discusses highish yields (by Italian standards) of 3.3 to 4.3:1 in the territory of Vercelli in the early thirteenth century. He sees these figures as part of that increase, and attributes it to irrigation, but it did not produce yields in any way comparable to those of irrigated lands elsewhere.

[47] For the late middle ages, see, among many studies, Chittolini, 'Alle origini delle "grandi aziende" della Bassa lombarda'; Chiappa Mauri, 'Riflessioni sulle campagne lombarde del Quattro-Cinquecento'; Chiappa Mauri, *Terra e uomini*, pp. 42–68.

[48] Menant, *Campagnes lombardes*, p. 175; Roveda, *Uomini, terre e acque*, pp. 260–77; and Biscaro, 'Gli antichi "Navigli" milanesi', for the first of all, Milan's Naviglio Grande, plausibly begun in 1179 and extended greatly after 1200. Bologna also had early commune-developed canals, starting in the 1170s; see Pini, 'Energia e industria'; but most cities, here too, began the process after 1200. We should add to this two earlier canals, dug for communications purposes: the disastrous deviation of the Brenta by the city of Padua in 1142 (see n. 128 below, as also for an unsuccessful Adige canal in 1191), and the fossa di San Romano, connecting the Po above Ferrara with one of the minor rivers running parallel to it, dug as early as the 1030s–1040s: see Castagnetti, *Il processo per Ostiglia*, pp. 85–110.

[49] Our evidence is above all for church estates, which had their own needs for lighting and diet, although there is occasional evidence for a concern for sending oil to cities too; see Brugnoli, 'Dal Mediterraneo all'Europa', pp. 145–6.

skins and above all wool for both rural and urban tanning and weaving. Indeed, transhumance is precisely a sign of the development of these productions, for the specialization would have little point otherwise. In eastern Lombardy, where it has been well studied, transhumance of sheep is visible already in the late eleventh century, and could be earlier sometimes, but it only really took off in the mid- to late twelfth. Poorer evidence matches the latter date in Tuscany for the route between the mountains above Lucca and the plains around Pisa.[50] This dating is obviously significant for urban production; I will come back to it later in that context, when discussing Lucca and then Milan.

As for woodland and marsh clearance, we have some accounts of it being developed quite systematically already in the tenth century, for example in the Canossa lands around S. Benedetto Po (prov. Mantua) and Brescello (prov. Reggio Emilia), both now just south of the Po.[51] The two types of clearance are quite different in the way they were practised—felling trees and the drainage of wetlands require different skills—but they both occurred above all in the same broad area, the lower Po plain, on each side of the river. In the eleventh and twelfth centuries, at its high point, clearance seems to have been mostly capillary, promoted by landlords on a relatively small scale, and probably at least as much at the initiative of peasants themselves, who wished or needed to extend agricultural land for grain at the expense of silvo-pastoral exploitation. Toponyms refer to newly cleared land across the whole of our period. Milan and Bergamo have been particularly well studied here, but other systematic work shows that the phenomenon was generalized across the Po plain, although it was probably less important in Tuscany, where there was less good land left to clear.[52] There was also, undoubtedly, demographic growth across our period in north-central Italy. In particular, towns expanded very considerably, as we shall see, which is an important sign in itself; there is less evidence for villages, but some, at least, can be pinned down; and, of course, as elsewhere in Latin Europe (and, as we have seen, Byzantium: p. 303), land clearance must be a proxy for demographic growth too.[53] The scale of land clearance, however, again as elsewhere in Latin Europe, was sufficiently great that it must have proceeded at a greater pace than did the rise in population,

[50] For eastern Lombardy, see Menant, *Campagnes lombardes*, pp. 255–87; for Tuscany, see Wickham, *The mountains and the city*, pp. 24–5, 136–41, 168–70.

[51] Fumagalli, *Le origini di una grande dinastia feudale*, pp. 4–9, 20–8, 78–80.

[52] Menant, *Campagnes lombardes*, pp. 203–30; Rapetti, *Campagne milanesi*, *passim*; for Padua, see Rippe, *Padoue*, pp. 505–17; for other parts of the Po valley, see, among many, Montanari, *L'alimentazione contadina*, pp. 469–76, who stresses the ambiguities of land clearance—not least, the fact that peasant diet became much less diversified. See Rao, *I paesaggi dell'Italia medievale*, pp. 85–102, 119–24, and Campopiano, 'The evolution of the landscape', pp. 320–5, for good overviews.

[53] For one useful study of village expansion based on written sources, see Menant, *Campagnes lombardes*, pp. 69–74. But archaeological work, which ought to be determinant, does not show so many clear examples of villages expanding demographically until around 1200, even in well-studied areas of Tuscany; I am very grateful here for discussion with Giovanna Bianchi, Federico Cantini, and Marco Valenti.

and thus average agricultural surplus per head above subsistence is likely to have become steadily greater. The issue then for us, of course, must be how that surplus was divided.

We know a good deal about the history of estate management in north-central Italy; we know less, although some, about the global weight of rent. Let us start with the former of these, to give a context for the latter; it was rather more locally variable than the agricultural trends just described. There were some highly organized manors in the ninth century in the north, and two of the largest-scale monastic estate networks, those of Bobbio in the Piacenza Appennines and S. Giulia di Brescia, are described in particular detail in the longest polyptychs surviving for Italy. Manors, characterized by a division between the lord's demesne and peasant holdings, with the demesne worked by corvée labour service owed by tenants as part of their rent, were a feature of the whole of north-central Italy. They went back on a small scale to the sixth century, but they expanded very greatly in the decades around the beginning of the ninth. They seem to have been commonest, and also most highly structured, in the central Po plain; and as noted earlier, a complex manorial organization was in general aimed at the creation of surplus for sale.[54] But not all manors were as complex as this. Closer to the coast, especially in Romagna south of the Po—up to 751, Byzantine- rather than Lombard-ruled territory; hence the name *Romania*—they appeared rather later in the ninth century and were considerably less tightly organized, with only a few days labour due per year from peasants, which means much smaller demesnes. In Tuscany, although here manors already appear in the eighth century, demesnes were often fragmented, and corvées often too high for the demesnes they were supposedly serving. Labour service here was more an instrument of peasant subjection than a structural element in economic development, as Bruno Andreolli remarked, in what remains the most complete analysis of ninth-century Tuscan manors.[55] Anyway, across the kingdom, tight manorial structures largely broke down in the first quarter of the tenth century. Corvées continued thereafter, almost everywhere, for some tenants, but were by now generally (even if not universally) on a small scale, and had turned into a sign of subjection above all.[56]

Developments from here on are harder to summarize, but, broadly, what replaced manors in most places was simple rent-paying by peasant tenants to

[54] There are far too many studies here to cite in full. Recent ones include Pasquali, *Sistemi di produzione agraria*, and Mancassola, *L'azienda curtense*; both have ample bibliographies; earlier, essential are Andreolli and Montanari, *L'azienda curtense in Italia*, and Toubert, *Dalla terra ai castelli*, pp. 115–250.

[55] Mancassola, *L'azienda curtense*, pp. 9–99; for Tuscany, see Andreolli, 'Contratti agrari'; Andreolli, 'L'evoluzione', pp. 36–40.

[56] See e.g., for Emilia and Romagna, Mancassola, *L'azienda curtense*, pp. 41–62, 125–54; more generally, see Pasquali, *Sistemi di produzione agraria*, pp. 230–42. In Tuscany, whereas around Lucca manors cease to be documented in the early tenth century, around Florence they are still visible, sometimes with meaningful labour services, into the twelfth: see Tabarrini, *Responding to change*, ch. 2.

landlords, both in money and, in particular, in produce; this is visible in places where we have runs of tenth-century leases to cultivators, for by now they much more rarely mention corvées.[57] But these leases to peasants tend to dry up before the end of the tenth century; instead, we have leases from churches and monasteries—as always, the keepers of our documents—to intermediaries, largely aristocratic, for (usually) low rents in money; indeed, sometimes these leases to non-cultivating tenants directly succeed our last references to manors. Political relationships had partially replaced direct economic advantage for churches, and it was now their aristocratic tenants who were taking much of the surplus from peasant cultivators, even if in most cases we cannot say with any clarity how much land churches and monasteries actually rented away to intermediaries. From now on, for a century and more, it seems that rent agreements with cultivators had increasingly become customary and oral, so do not survive. In most places, it is only with the twelfth century that we have evidence again of peasant obligations, sometimes in new types of leases, sometimes in lists of rents drawn up by ecclesiastical owners, both showing a renewed concern for closer management. They were by now above all rents in produce, presumably reflecting what most peasants had previously paid in customary rents.[58]

Both in ninth- and tenth-century leases to cultivators and in those from the twelfth, some of these rents were fixed quantities of produce; others were in percentages of crop. In the twelfth century, when we have percentages—which is more often in Lombardy and Emilia, much less often in Tuscany—they are almost always a quarter to a third of the grain, a quarter to a half of the wine, sometimes with some money on top. François Menant did some cautious ballpark calculations on the fixed rents for eastern Lombardy, and concluded that they were similar in their weight, or slightly heavier. These were high figures. The only important exception was again ex-Byzantine Romagna, where far lower grain rents, of a tenth to a seventh, were standard.[59] When we consider that yields were only 3–5:1, it becomes clear that peasants very often only had access to a third, or less, of the crop, after rent and seed were taken out. This was less than in any other region we

[57] For how these developments worked in Lombardy, see, e.g., Violante, *La società milanese*, pp. 76–84; Rapetti, *La terra degli uomini*, pp. 88–111; Chiappa Mauri, 'Tra consuetudine e rinnovamento'.

[58] See, e.g., Jones, 'An Italian estate', pp. 24–5; Panero, *Terre in concessione*, pp. 25–9 (who stresses the continuance of customary rents); and the discussions cited in n. 59 below.

[59] See, e.g., Panero, *Terre in concessione*, pp. 56–8; Menant, *Campagnes lombardes*, pp. 325–44 (including discussion of fixed rents at 341–3, explicitly hypothetical); Chiappa Mauri, 'Tra consuetudine e rinnovamento', pp. 65, 74; Fumagalli, 'L'evoluzione dell'economia agraria'. For the lower figures in Romagna, see Fumagalli, *Coloni e signori*, pp. 95–9, for the cultivator leases in the tenth-century *Codice Bavaro*; the levels are the same in the more recent editions of Ravenna originals, Benericetti, *Le carte ravennati dei secoli ottavo e nono*; Benericetti, *Le carte del decimo secolo*; Benericetti, *Le carte ravennati del secolo undicesimo* (though drifting slightly upwards in the last, e.g. vol. 1, n. 97, a. 1024). For the rarity of percentage rents in Tuscany, see most recently Tabarrini, *Responding to change*, chs 2–3; but in Arezzo, where they can sometimes be found, a third was again the norm; see Delumeau, *Arezzo*, p. 161; see also n. 239 below for Pisa.

have looked at, for similar or higher rent and tax levels were associated with much higher yields in Egypt, Sicily, and al-Andalus, and in Byzantium, where yields were only slightly higher, the totals of rent and tax were lower—only in the *khammās* tenures of North Africa and al-Andalus, involving really high partiary rents, was the situation clearly worse.[60] In Italy, tenant holdings would have to be very big for any real prosperity for such tenants to be possible, and we have no indication that this was the case, although most tenant holdings were very highly fragmented, with dozens of separate fields, so we cannot be sure how large they actually were. At and after the end of the twelfth century in much of Tuscany, fixed rents in kind were increased further, sometimes replacing surviving corvées, by landowners who saw new possibilities in urban markets. From then on, after our period, a renewal of tight land management began slowly to appear in inland Tuscany and then later in Emilia and Umbria in the form of the *mezzadria* contract, in which, in return for the landlord supplying half the seed, tenants owed half the crop in rent—a weight of obligation which partly cut peasants out of the market altogether, indeed for centuries, given that the last *mezzadria* contracts were only abolished in the 1980s.[61]

But, on the other hand, by no means all peasants were tenants. This is important. The percentages of owner-cultivators in Italy were high in our period, almost everywhere. We cannot give exact figures for any statement in this paragraph, but peasant landowning is well attested everywhere that the documents are dense enough to show it. Indeed, in some places peasant owners seem to have been in a majority—in mountain valleys, very often; in marsh or ex-marsh areas, like the Saccisica between Padua and Venice; but in some individual villages even in the dry plains.[62] They did not pay rent, and there was for a long time no taxation to add to that. Peasant owners certainly had the chance of prosperity. And given the fragmentation of holdings of all kinds, which could be extreme, not only did the lands of peasant owners intercut with those of tenants, but so did the two social groups. For a start, many richer peasants rented some of their own land out to their poorer neighbours. But also and, indeed, complementarily, as common as fully landowning cultivators were peasant owners who took some land in rent to fill out their own property; and in many areas most tenants owned at least some

[60] See pp. 66–8, 172–3, 238–43, 347–8, 389–94 above.

[61] Kotel'nikova, *Mondo contadino*, pp. 26–64; Tabarrini, *Responding to change*, ch. 2. As Tabarrini says, the *mezzadria* system was only just beginning in the 1220s, when his study ends; for its early years around Florence, see, e.g., Muzzi and Nenci, *Il contratto di mezzadria*, 2; Faini, *Firenze*, pp. 97–109; the bibliography on *mezzadria*, however, is endless and mostly long postdates our period.

[62] There are again too many discussions to list; I can only be indicative. For mountain areas, see, e.g., Wickham, *The mountains and the city*, pp. 135–47, 242–56; Menant, *Campagnes lombardes*, pp. 90–3. For the Saccisica, see, among others, Rippe, *Padoue*, pp. 166–84. For the dry plains, see, e.g., Bortolami, 'Monselice "oppidum opulentissimum"', pp. 106–7, 114–15, 140; Conti, *La formazione*, 1, pp. 155–6, 163–70; Wickham, *Community and clientele*, pp. 82–6, 110–27. See also n. 346 below for the territory of Milan; for an earlier period, see Mancassola, *Uomini senza storia*, pp. 171–218. For a rapid synthesis, see Fiore, *The seigneurial transformation*, pp. 90–4.

land as well. (This was in other respects a good thing too; in some places, the minority who did not do so found their practical freedom menaced.)[63] The complexities of village society could be considerable as a result, with an array of micro-strata marking social difference. When rural communes developed in the twelfth century, matching and partially copying those of cities, the richer peasant strata came to control them, in villages where we have enough documentation to tell.[64] But what is most important for us here is that, although there were certainly plenty of peasants who were fully subjected to seriously high rent regimes, there were also very many others whose independent landowning meant that overall rent obligations were less, often much less, and frequently absent. And peasants in the latter categories could, as easily as any landlord, take produce to a nearby market, very often in a nearby town, large or small, to sell. Towns were not simply collectivities of landowners who could feed themselves and support local artisans out of the rents which came to their urban residences; they had to pay for much, probably most, of their food, often to peasant sellers.[65] This will have had a considerable effect on one issue which has been stressed throughout this book—the ability of peasants to buy things.

Except in clearance areas, landownership was a zero-sum game: the more land peasants owned, the less aristocrats and other non-peasants did. This, of course, does not mean that we cannot find evidence of some very wealthy landowners in Italy. In the Carolingian period, counts and bishops headed the list, after kings; the counts were often from families coming in from over the Alps, and derived much of their initial wealth from fiscal land. Some monasteries, such as Bobbio and S. Giulia, were similarly rich, with dozens of estates, again originally in large part thanks to royal gifts, although also—as were episcopal churches as well—beneficiaries of a wave of lay pious gift-giving in the eighth and early ninth centuries. Bishops, cathedrals, and monasteries remained rich in land throughout our period. And so did many lay aristocrats. In the tenth and eleventh centuries, when local landed power began to be focussed on estates with castles, the major lay families of the Po plain and Tuscany could have very many of them. I list some examples: the Giselbertingi counts of Bergamo in the eleventh century had over

[63] Almost all the studies in n. 62 above discuss the mix of property and tenures for individual families. The classic discussion of fragmentation is Conti, *La formazione*, 1, pp. 133–43, 212–15. There were few legally unfree peasants in north-central Italy by 950, but in the twelfth century we find growing evidence of a stratum of non-landowning tenants, called variously *manentes* or *coloni*, who, although technically free, were highly subject to lords; in some areas, such as the territory of Florence, they were quite common. See Panero, *Terra in concessione*, pp. 207–76; Panero, *Schiavi, servi*, pp. 206–60; Wickham, '*Manentes* e diritti signorili'; Conte, *Servi medievali*, esp. pp. 91–120; Tabarrini, *Responding to change*, ch. 1.

[64] See in general Wickham, *Community and clientele*.

[65] Rome is the only exception here, for it had a unique landowning structure: the immediate hinterland of the city was dominated, overwhelmingly, by large urban (generally ecclesiastical) property-owning, and a stratum of (generally aristocratic) long-term tenants. See Wickham, 'La struttura'; Wickham, *Medieval Rome*, pp. 53–62, 78–88.

twenty castles and other estates; the counts of Padua and Vicenza had over fifteen; a son of the count of Piacenza around 1000 had eighteen; the da Soresina family in the territory of Cremona had a dozen or so in the early eleventh century; the Suavizi family of Florence had two dozen in the 1060s. The Aldobrandeschi counts who dominated largely rural southern Tuscany had as many as forty-five as early as the 970s; and other great Tuscan and Ligurian families, such as the Obertenghi and the Guidi, dominating different parts of the Appennines and extending into the plains, would soon have similar numbers. When Frederick Barbarossa listed the Obertenghi and Guidi estates in back-to-back privileges of 1164, the families by then had—or claimed—even more.[66] Many of these estates were held as part of comital office-holding, or else leased or held in fief from bishops, so total fiscal and church landowning was not necessarily in addition to this, but there is no doubt that these were extensive ranges of land; and as time went by, comital lands, leases, and fiefs turned into real property-ownership in many cases.

All the same, these families, however rich, were a small minority. Most prominent families, especially those living in cities, controlled far less than this. Even in the twelfth century, when the number of richer families seems to have been increasing, as we shall see in a moment, families of *capitanei*, the highest stratum of urban elites in the Po plain, generally only held one or two castle estates; only a few, such as the da Casalvolone in Vercelli, might have half a dozen.[67] And not many cities had more than a couple of urban families with even this level of wealth; indeed, there were some city territories, such as that of Pisa, in which even rural castle-based landowners hardly owned more.[68] Near to cities and often elsewhere as well, land was owned in very fragmented lots, tenant house by tenant house, field by field. Half a dozen estates or, indeed, just two are easily enough to live comfortably on, providing a serious market for artisan production, as well as to hire at least some armed men, and to be influential in city politics. But if this was the standard resource for major lay elites, apart from exceptions like the Giselbertingi and the Guidi, then there was, for sure, plenty of space for autonomous peasantries in city hinterlands.

Landed wealth in Italy was thus owned on a very even curve, stretching, gradation by gradation, from peasant owners up to kings. Inside villages it was much

[66] See, in turn, Menant, *Lombardia feudale*, pp. 80–7; Rippe, *Padoue*, pp. 129–30; Bougard, 'Entre Gandolfingi et Obertenghi', pp. 23–6, 42–8; Violante, 'Una famiglia feudale', pp. 673–83; Cortese, *Signori, castelli*, pp. 41–2. For the Aldobrandeschi, see Kurze, *Codex diplomaticus amiatinus*, 2, nn. 203, 206, with Collavini, *'Honorabilis domus'*, pp. 80–5; for the Obertenghi, see Ricci, *La marca della Liguria orientale*, pp. 129–42; for the Guidi, see Delumeau, *Arezzo*, pp. 384–410, with Collavini, 'Le basi materiali', and *Friderici I. diplomata*, nn. 462–3.

[67] Degrandi, 'Vassalli cittadini', pp. 22–5, 29. For *capitanei*, see in general Castagnetti, *La vassalità maggiore*.

[68] For Pisa see Cortese, *L'aristocrazia toscana*, pp. 230–9, 307–14, and Wickham, *Sleepwalking*, pp. 97–112, both summarizing a host of detailed studies of Pisan families; for the general patterns, see the brief overview, ibid., pp. 190–3.

the same, with *coqs de village* and maybe a bailiff for an absentee owner at the head, unless a rich lord happened to reside in a castle there; village territories where a single owner held all the land were few. This was the pattern from the Lombard-Carolingian period onwards (under the Lombards in the eighth century the stratum of really rich owners had, indeed, been still smaller[69]), and was still the basic pattern in the twelfth century. Cities, it is true, held enough landowners to allow for a concentration of demand which ensured that produce regularly entered the city in every century, and professional artisans were always there to service that demand as well; rural lords will have been buyers too. This was the resource base for the fairly modest exchange system of the ninth century, particularly along the Po and its tributaries, the one described (and talked up) by Violante and others. As discussed above, markets steadily developed from the ninth century onwards, to match increasing aristocratic and urban buying power, and, as we can now see, peasant buying power as well, into the eleventh century and beyond. But it is not obvious that there was as yet the basis for a real step change in regional demand sufficient to alter dramatically the productive and commercial structure of the Kingdom of Italy and its myriad of urban communal successors, so as to create such a different economic world in the centuries after 1200. We have, indeed, also seen that even after 1100, city privileges from emperors were not always particularly ambitious in scope. There was, of course, steady agrarian growth, thanks especially to a demographic rise, and achievements in land clearance which went well beyond that. When discussing Byzantium (pp. 344–53), which had a parallel tenurial structure, with not so many really rich owners and an often autonomous peasantry there too, I attributed most of the considerable exchange upturn of the twelfth century to patterns of agrarian growth very similar to those just described for Italy. But there, the region was unified by a long-lasting tax system, which not only established a set of routes for goods to flow along on a large scale, but also created important foci of tax-based wealth, in money and thus spending power, which quite surpassed those available to all but the very richest landowners. Italy did not have that in the eleventh century, so it is not at all clear that land clearance and high-aristocratic or episcopal wealth on their own would have had the same effect.

There were other changes in Italy, however. One was the growth in signorial power. As noted earlier, the collapse of the kingdom directly helped the generalization of patterns of local power which had previously been exercised only on a relatively small scale—those in which powerful local landowners took over public powers such as rights of justice (and the dues from judicial fines), and added to them a variety of other claims to money and labour, often at the time called *servitia*, and now called signorial rights by historians—dues from the use of pasture

[69] Wickham, 'Aristocratic power', modified by Gasparri, 'Mercanti o possessori?'; Di Muro, *La terra, il mercante*, pp. 13–18.

and woodland, castle-building and castle guard, tolls of different kinds, the hosting of the lord's officials or money in lieu of that, and sometimes direct, potentially arbitrary payments. Some of these (a form of justice over tenants, in particular) had long roots in landlordly power, but most were new, and, increasingly, they came to be exacted not just from the tenants of lords, but also from all those in a given territory, including peasant landowners, in what is currently called the *signoria territoriale*—in the twelfth century, a common term was *dominatus loci*.[70] Castle-building, which had begun in the early tenth century for the most part, and continued from then on for three centuries, did not in itself have to entail signorial dues, or most of them at least. Royal concessions of the rights to build a castle, which are a feature of the early tenth century in particular, often mention justice and tolls, but little else, and only a minority of castles had such cessions. Indeed, most early castles seem to have been fairly simple structures, often made from wood, not even stone, and building them would not have yet entailed a major commitment.[71] But when signorial rights became more generalized—slowly in the mid-eleventh century in some areas, especially in the central Po plain; more rapidly, from the 1090s onwards, more or less everywhere—they tended to become attached to castles. By the twelfth century, indeed, much of the former kingdom was divided up between signorial territories; the main exceptions were larger or smaller areas closest to cities, which also tended to have few or no castles, and which were regarded by cities as important arenas for the direct exercise of urban/communal power.

This new form of lordship marked an important change in the social relations of the countryside. At best, peasant landowners might possibly have felt that having to cope with this new form of power over them was preferable to having their lands expropriated, which tended not to be part of the process of signorialization in Italy. But from now on lordly interference in the lives of rural communities and their inhabitants—the pervasiveness of lordship, as Sandro Carocci has put it for southern Italy—even if variable, was generally much greater than it had ever been before; and certainly lordly exactions, and sometimes violence, were greater. They were often contested, and in some parts of Italy rural communes developed precisely to contest such *malae consuetudines* (evil customs), or at least to establish

[70] See most recently Fiore, *The seigneurial transformation* (and ibid., pp. 254–6 for the impact this had on the economy in areas of strong *signorie*; for Europe, cf. also Mainoni, 'Le produzioni non agricole', pp. 226–33). Earlier essential studies, again a small selection from very many, include Violante, 'La signoria rurale nel secolo X'; Keller, *Signori e vassalli*, pp. 118–36, for Lombardy (a classic account, which dates the process earlier than I would); Provero, *L'Italia dei poteri locali*; Dilcher and Violante, *Strutture e trasformazioni*; Menant, *Campagnes lombardes*, pp. 395–485.

[71] Settia, *Castelli e villaggi*, pp. 168–76, stresses the lack of fit between early castle-building (in the tenth century and even part of the eleventh) and signorial rights. For how castles developed as physical structures, the articles in Molinari, 'Mondi rurali d'Italia', from 2010, remain an essential point of reference. Only in the twelfth century did stone walls and towers become routine in castles, which marked a sharpening of both signorial exactions and rural investment, plus in some cases a greater commitment by lords actually to live in them. See pp. 574–7 below for how this occurred in Tuscany.

deals with lords to make signorial dues more stable and predictable.[72] All the same, from the standpoint of the argument here, what matters most is the economic weight of these new forms of lordship. It is impossible to know exactly what this was in any individual *signoria*, simply because the dues involved were so numerous, and almost never precisely quantified, although it is at least clear that the weight of lordship was again variable in the extreme, depending on how much lords could get away with. Direct prestations could in some weaker lordships amount to little more than annual recognitive gifts of a chicken and eggs, and a shoulder of pork, plus judicial rights of unknown scale. But we hear of more substantial dues too. On example was the collective rate of £10 required by the canons of Verona cathedral in lieu of rights of justice in the fortified village of Marzana (prov. Verona) in 1121, which was doubled if the king passed by and exacted his own taxes—to which was added the obligation to rebuild the walls and tower of the castle in stone. The basic royal tax, called *fodrum* (we will come to it shortly), would later in the century often be 26 *denarii* per hearth, not itself a huge sum, but the 1121 requirement is likely to have been a higher figure—unless there were as many as ninety-two families living in Marzana, a substantial number—and the signorial dues to the canons were clearly analogous. Other individual figures are similar; and as the twelfth century progressed, our evidence for heavy signorial dues increases—in eastern Lombardy, Menant argued that the signorial *fodrum* could sometimes multiply by a factor of ten between 1130 and 1200.[73]

We should not overstress these changes when looking for explanations of shifts in either elite or peasant demand in Italy, for two important reasons. One is that the development of signorial powers was far from uniform. As just noted, some *signorie* were far less oppressive than others; and as an extension of that, some city territories had *signorie* which were far weaker than others. Much of Pisa's territory had no territorial lordships, for example, and that of Milan had unusually few by the standards of northern Italy as a whole (see pp. 574, 609 below)—and these were two of the city territories whose economic development in the twelfth century is particularly well attested. The second reason is that even though they were at the heavier end of signorial dues for the twelfth century, the dues from Marzana and similar localities seem to have been less than most rents amounted to, and, elsewhere, often very much less. As usual, the figures are very approximate; but if

[72] For the south, see Carocci, *Lordships*, esp. pp. 24–5, 483–9, with Carocci, 'The pervasiveness of lordship', for the north as well. For the north, see Fiore, *The seigneurial transformation*, pp. 220–47, esp. for violence; cf. Wickham, *Community and clientele*, for communes resisting (or else not resisting).

[73] Marzana: Lanza, *Le carte... di Verona*, 1, n. 48, discussed in Fiore, *The seigneurial transformation*, pp. 55–6, with slightly different arguments. For Lombardy, see Menant, *Campagnes lombardes*, pp. 448–63 for the wide range of signorial obligations, 473–7 for the multiplication of the signorial *fodrum*. For a significant case study for the northern Appennines between Florence and Bologna, see Pederzoli, *I poteri signorili in un' area di confine*, esp. pp. 361–92; although this was an area of relatively strong signorial power, the bulk of the evidence for its exercise is from the thirteenth century. For the huge variability in the weight of *signorie* inside a single subregion, northern Tuscany, see Wickham, 'La signoria rurale in Toscana', pp. 376–90.

they are even roughly accurate, they mean that the rents due from landowning remained much more important than signorial levies in the twelfth century. But all the same, they were cumulative. Precisely because rents from peasant tenants were often very high, we must recognize that, when signorial dues were heavy at least, the extra burden on many tenants must have pushed them to the edge of subsistence. Conversely, the burden on peasant *owners* would not have been so great as to cut them out of the commercial world. I conclude that the importance of signorial dues is not so much the fact that they were too heavy to bear, but rather that they were fairly widely generalized. For the first time, peasant owners in many parts of Italy did have to pay something. Landowners, particularly major ones, from the years around 1100, and increasingly across the twelfth century, gained an extra dimension to their resources.

This needs to be set beside the fact that there was more pressure from non-cultivators, simply because there were more levels of non-cultivating elites. This may well have been more important, but is even more difficult to quantify. In western Europe as a whole, the shift to local power structures associated with the 'seigneurial revolution' brought many more families into what can be very generically called military status. In the Italian countryside, as aristocratic hierarchies became more clear-cut, particularly after the late eleventh century, we begin to find that smaller-scale figures, who might have been best seen as rich peasants in previous century, but who are now called *milites* in our sources, are often attached to castles in some way, and begin to figure as militarized rural elites; they did not always obtain signorial rights anywhere, but they seem often to have become landowners on a larger scale than previously, and were thus both greater burdens on their peasant neighbours and more consistent sources of demand.[74] Cities, for their part, were increasing in population, which meant that urban collective demand was increasing. From the standpoint of agricultural production, whether these new urban mouths to feed were artisans, notaries and other medium elites, or *capitanei* and rich churchmen, did not matter—they were all non-cultivators who consumed agricultural produce. Many were themselves landowners, so did not, strictly, need to buy food, but artisans were rarely significant owners, apart from suburban gardens and vineyards, and they relied on the market, which, indeed, richer urban buyers often will have done in practice as well. And some former villages were turning themselves into small towns with semi-urban elites (often again *milites*) and artisans, which pushed urban-style demand farther into

[74] For Europe as a whole see, as a fairly recent synthesis, West, *Reframing the feudal revolution*. Italian militarized elites have a considerable visibility in the historiography, but there are few assessments of their landed wealth. An important recent survey, with wider bibliography, is Cortese, 'Rural *milites* in central and northern Italy'; the article stresses the variety of means that rural elites could use to increase their resources. It may be added that some *milites* ended up dominating rural communes, but, conversely, that many such communes were instead dominated by local leaders who had failed, or not tried, to get into the military hierarchy. I have discussed this elsewhere (in Wickham, *Community and clientele*, pp. 209–41), but it has less bearing on the issue of commercial demand.

the countryside, as we shall see in particular for Milan (pp. 604–8). With respect both to the city and to the countryside, greater landowning pressure went together with greater demand and greater marketization. As we have seen for other regions, peasant owners and part-owners were better able to benefit from the possibilities of marketization, whereas many of their poorer neighbours will simply have been cut out of the market by the increased weight of rents and dues; but when peasants had greater access to selling, to expanding cities and small towns alike, their own demand increased too.

We can add that after the mid-twelfth century, a final change occurred: the development of direct public taxes, initially on hearths (in effect, poll taxes, per family), which added greatly to the longer tradition of commercial tolls going back to the Roman Empire. Kings had exacted variable amounts in *fodrum* before 1150, but only when they came into Italy, which was not very often. Frederick Barbarossa generalized it as a tax in the late 1150s; in his time 26 *denarii* per hearth was the norm, although sometimes raised substantially, or lowered, for local political purposes. Cities successfully resisted this, as we have seen, but by the end of the twelfth century they were exacting it themselves, to pay for wars, city walls, and, in the next century, urban and rural infrastructure. The first references to urban direct taxes in fact go back to the 1120s, but again, the second half of the twelfth century was the first time that this taxation became more regular. The scale of urban taxation varied considerably from city to city, but the same figure of 26 *denarii* per hearth is often found in Tuscany. This was, as already noted, not so very high, but it steadily increased from then onwards, into the thirteenth century and beyond. On the other hand, cities soon began to develop—already by the 1160s in Pisa, Genoa, and Piacenza; much later in other cities, such as Milan—tax structures varying according to *estimi* (estimates of personal landed and mobile wealth), as elsewhere in the Mediterranean, which were both more even in their incidence and harder to evaluate in terms of their global weight (although early percentage figures, when we have them, are again low).[75] This communal *fodrum* or *datium* or *collecta* was in competition with signorial dues too, and as a result communes, when they took over their *contadi*, tended eventually to abolish signorial *fodra*/*datia*, substituting them, again, with their own taxation. When signorial rights persisted into the thirteenth century, they increasingly became restricted to the smaller-scale *servitia* mentioned earlier, and increasingly also to rights over tenants, not independent owners. (The often strong and onerous

[75] For *fodrum*, see esp. Brühl, *Fodrum, gistum*, pp. 534–77, 659–751 (709–10, 724–32 for 26 *denarii*, including in cities); cf. Menant, *Campagnes lombardes*, pp. 463–7, 473. For early city taxes, see ibid., pp. 530–4; Fiore, *The seigneurial transformation*, pp. 121–3; and esp. Mainoni, 'A proposito della "rivoluzione fiscale"' and Mainoni, 'Sperimentazioni fiscali', which explore the very complex instances of urban taxation across the twelfth century, including indirect taxes, and the royal taxes which the cities reacted to. Some of the few figures we have for the weight of early *estimi* are 2.5% in Genoa in 1165–6, and 0.4/0.5% in Siena in 1208–9; see *Annali genovesi*, 1, ed. Belgrano, pp. 188, 200; Ascheri, *Antica legislazione*, pp. 51–64, chs 20, 39.

lordships of the later middle ages tended to be new developments, often belonging to impeccably urban families.)[76] But even in the thirteenth century communal direct taxation—by far the most potentially remunerative tax, here as elsewhere—seldom matched the weight of rents; nor was it, even then, always annual in incidence.

So many lords exacted taxes, which increased in weight across the twelfth century, and by the last decades of the century (but rather more after 1200) so did cities, as territorial rulers. That is to say, by the end of the twelfth century and later, Italy began to resemble far more than before—at least in this respect—the tax-raising states of the rest of the Mediterranean. These dues and taxes were substantially lower than in the longer-established tax-raising states we have looked at so far; it is quite likely that the increase in the numbers of non-landowning elites was more significant than either. But when all these were put together, they were enough to make lords, and then cities as collectivities, much richer, while all the same leaving substantial sectors of the rural population, those families which owned their own land or much of it, relatively prosperous—especially given the agricultural developments which we have seen occurring at the same time—and capable of engaging with the commercial world autonomously. It is this shift, in my view, which above all underpinned the step change for the economy of north-central Italy; it made it possible for urban production and exchange to grow on a much larger scale, for there was more wealth, and thus buying power, coming to elites, and also at least some wealth, and again buying power, staying in the villages. And it puts a date on the process. If this analysis is even partially accurate, it would have developed during the twelfth century—steadily, as military elites became more entrenched, and dues and taxes became higher, above all from the third quarter of the century onwards.

These developments, in the intensity of local exploitation and local commercial demand, help us to explain Italy's economic take-off, together with demographic growth and agricultural and urban expansion, city by city across the northern half of the peninsula. They had a direct material visibility in the urban tower houses which already began to be built from the mid-eleventh century onwards—many of which still stand in Pisa, Bologna, and other cities—as markers of the prestige and wealth of landowning elites old and new. Builders may indeed have been among the first non-luxury artisans to respond to this growing demand, based initially on agricultural surplus, but across the next century and a half many others would follow. This would have to be nuanced, for it certainly worked differently from city to city. The different levels of linkage each city, each *contado*, had with pre-existing and locally developing patterns of exchange would have been as important as the

[76] For early thirteenth-century *signorie*, see, e.g., Wickham, 'La signoria rurale in Toscana', pp. 401–8, for northern Tuscany. For the weight of lordship in the later middle ages, Gamberini and Pagnoni, *La signoria rurale*; Ginatempo, 'I prelievi non fondiari'.

weight of rents and dues. So, to develop it, we will have to look at smaller territories in much more detail; and this is where we move on to our case studies. Those for Pisa and the Tuscan hinterland behind it, and for Milan and Lombardy, will (among other arguments) pick up the issue of lordship and the growing density of local elites. But all four studies, including, of course, those of Venice and Genoa which I begin with, will show how the internal economy of north-central Italy interlinked—when it did—with that of other Mediterranean regions.

6.3 Venice and its Hinterland

I start with Venice not because it was typical of Italy as a city. In fact, in most ways relevant to this book, it was arguably the least typical city in the peninsula—as, indeed (although for partially different reasons), it still is. But it is the city which had, for a long time, including from before our period starts, easily the closest economic links with at least one of the large-scale states we have been looking at, Byzantium. It thus fits particularly well into the general patterns we have seen in the previous chapters, and contributed materially to them at the time. We saw in Chapter 4 (pp. 332–9) how the Venetians acted as bulk traders in the Aegean, with foci in Constantinople and along the longest-standing coastal routes, down both the east and west coasts of the Aegean Sea, above all in the twelfth century, though starting earlier. They did not dominate Aegean trade, as has sometimes been claimed, but they were certainly integral to it; and they were so, in large part, as figures internal to Byzantium's society and economy. They were both internal and external, for they were not Greek-speakers and did not, by the mid-eleventh century, any longer see themselves as part of the Byzantine Empire (although the Byzantines may have had a different view), and they ran into serious trouble in 1171, when Emperor Manuel I turned against them. All the same, it was perfectly possible to see them simply as an integral part of the Byzantine exchange system. In this chapter, however, we need to look at them from the standpoint of the Rialto island, not Constantinople. The picture of the Venetians will not be inconsistent with what we have already seen, but the perspective changes very considerably, as we shall see.

Venice was by no means a Roman city. It was a scatter of marshy islands in the early middle ages, and was only one of several political foci for the first dukes of *Venetia*—a word which itself included a good percentage of the northern Adriatic coast throughout our period, not necessarily only the islands of Rialto and its neighbours.[77] (Venetian urban documents in our period are registered as being written in *Rivoalto*, not *Venetia*.) *Venetia* was simply one of several Byzantine

[77] Gasparri, 'The formation of an early medieval community', pp. 47–50; the double meaning of *Venetia*, 'Venice' and the whole coast, is explicit in the late tenth-century *Translatio S. Marci*, ed. Colombi, '"Translatio Marci evangelistae Venetias"', 2.2–4, repeated in Giovanni Diacono, *Istoria Veneticorum*, ed. Berto, 1.1.

outposts in the northern and eastern Adriatic after the seventh century, and was politically marginal until the fall of the exarchate of Ravenna to the Lombard king Aistulf in 751. It already had dukes by then, however, and simply continued that tradition, in fact for another millennium, until 1797. (By then, Venice's rulers are universally called *dogi* (doges) in the literature; this is simply the Venetian word for 'duke'. For our period, Italian historians are not consistent in their usage, between *duca* and *doge*; I will stick to 'duke'.) Dukes were elected by an initially ill-defined *populus*, which was certainly controlled by local *nobiles*; the beginnings of a regularization of an electoral system—always restricted to elites—did not appear until 1172. They were not hereditary, although the office for long ran in families, the Particiaco and the Candiano in the ninth and tenth centuries, the Orseolo in the tenth and eleventh, the Falier and the Michiel in the eleventh and twelfth. But the last father-son succession was in 1008 (it was a controversial one, as the incoming duke, Ottone Orseolo, was only 15), and the range of ducal families steadily increased from then on. The appearance of communal institutions in the 1140s changed little, except for furthering a wider participation in and an institutionalization of politics.[78]

Venice was for long still part of the Byzantine Empire. Documents were dated by the reigning emperor until 1037, John I Tzimiskes could require the Venetians to stop selling timber to the Arabs in 971, and the privilege to the Venetians which Basil II issued in (probably) 992 certainly treats them as subjects—among other things, they are to ship his troops to the Byzantine provinces of southern Italy; and they, indeed, came to the aid of Byzantine Bari, to fight off an Arab naval attack in 1002/3.[79] But the Byzantines had little direct control over the northern Adriatic, and already in the ninth century the Venetian dukes were operating to an extent autonomously. The slow but steady expansion of Venetian effective power down much of the eastern Adriatic (Dalmatian) coast from the

[78] See in general the political history chapters in the *Storia di Venezia* volumes, Ortalli, 'Il ducato e la "civitas Rivoalti"'; Gasparri, 'Dagli Orseolo al comune'; Castagnetti, 'Il primo comune', with West-Harling, *Rome, Ravenna, and Venice*, esp. pp. 89–107, 235–74.

[79] The last extant document dated by a Byzantine emperor (Michael IV) is Lanfranchi, *Codice diplomatico veneziano*, 1, n. 80; from 1038, incarnation dating begins (nn. 83, 85), with only sporadic examples earlier. The *Codice diplomatico veneziano* (henceforth *CDVE*), also called the *Codice Lanfranchi*, is a typescript edition of all documents between 1000 and 1200 by Luigi Lanfranchi, available for consultation in PDF in the Archivio di Stato di Venezia. I cite it for all Venetian documents which do not have full publications (many of them by the same Lanfranchi, the doyen of Venetian palaeographers), except for the unpublished documents of the female monastery of San Zaccaria; see https://asve.arianna4.cloud/patrimonio/206f5e39-93ac-4549-ae59-12140168499c/001-serie-pergamene, accessed 23 September 2022—a rare example of original texts being of easier access than their edition. The full citation for the latter is Archivio di Stato di Venezia, Patrimonio, San Zaccaria, pergamene, starting with b. 1, pergg., n. 1; here, this will be abbreviated to ASV, SZ, b. 1, n. 1, and following. John I: Cessi, *Documenti*, 2, n. 49; Basil II: Pozza and Ravegnani, *I trattati con Bisanzio*, n. 1; Bari: Giovanni Diacono, *Istoria Veneticorum*, ed. Berto, 4.66–8, a near-contemporary account; cf. ibid., 4.71, for a marriage alliance between Duke Pietro Orseolo's son and a Byzantine princess, shortly after.

early tenth century onwards may well have been seen in Constantinople as a consolidation of Byzantine authority, in the face of Slavic expansion and state-building in the developing kingdom of Croatia in the middle of the Dalmatian coast, but Venetian documents and chronicles see it largely as an independent expression of ducal protagonism.[80] Increasingly, in the eleventh century, the empire and the duchy were clearly separate; all the same, it is by no means chance that Venetian commercial activity was for so long, including in our period, carried out above all inside the exchange networks of the Byzantine world. Inland in Italy, as we have seen, the Carolingian emperors and their successors were keen to establish and then reaffirm treaties with the Venetians. There were a couple of imperial attempts at gaining more control over the Venetian islands and coastline—in the 800s and 980s—but they did not come to much. Venetian coins were, however, minted according to Carolingian and post-Carolingian standards, and even iconography; Venetian judicial assemblies developed following Carolingian models. Venetian aristocrats and churches/monasteries owned land on the mainland, the *terraferma*, from as early as the ninth century too, and this gave the kings of Italy some traction over them. Indeed, the Candiano family, who lost power dramatically in Rialto in 976–9, ended up as counts of Padua and Vicenza in the Kingdom of Italy.[81] That is to say, Venice was located firmly in its Italian hinterland in sociopolitical terms as well. The Venetians sat between two empires and had organic links with each. Whatever else changed across our period, this did not.

The northern Adriatic coast was formed by the deltas of the great rivers coming off the Alps and Appennines, which themselves offered the easiest routes from the Po plain to the sea; there was always commerce there. To give a proper context to what Venice did with that, we need to begin quite early. In the fifth to seventh centuries, when it was the western imperial and then exarchal capital, Ravenna had been the major commercial centre of the coast; but from the seventh century onwards the foci of land–sea exchange diversified, and came to extend from Ravenna northwards, to Comacchio in the Po delta, to several places in Venice's large lagoon, and onwards from there. The early decades of the eighth century were the low point for Mediterranean exchange as a whole, but that is exactly when the 715 or 730 trade treaty between the Lombard kingdom and the men of Comacchio (see p. 479 above) was established. As we have seen, this treaty privileged salt, from the lagoons of the coast, but Comacchio was much more than that. Recent excavations there, under the eighth-century cathedral and in the former port, have shown that it was importing wine from the Aegean, thanks to the survival in large numbers of the characteristic globular amphorae of the eighth and ninth centuries—here, already in the seventh as well, along with a handful of

[80] See, e.g., Tafel and Thomas, *Urkunden*, 1, nn. 10, 15; Giovanni Diacono, *Istoria Veneticorum*, ed. Berto, 4.45–54.

[81] For an overview, see Ortenberg West-Harling, '"Venecie due sunt"'.

the latest late Roman amphora types.[82] We have seen (pp. 304–5) that globular amphorae rarely circulated outside the lands ruled by Byzantium, which included Comacchio initially, but some of them have turned up, even if in small numbers, in towns of the Kingdom of Italy—Verona, Brescia, and Milan, as also in the rich monastery of Nonantola (prov. Modena), where there has been recent excavation. These obviously came via the harbours of the Adriatic coast, certainly including Comacchio, maybe still Ravenna (though the evidence for that is weak), but also, already, some of the islands of the Venetian lagoon, where they have been found from the late seventh to early ninth centuries in recent excavations. From the early seventh century, glass was being made in Comacchio too, on a substantial scale, using raw materials from the eastern Mediterranean, matching that of the probably slightly later glass kiln found in the 1960s at Torcello in the lagoon. Comacchio was not a large centre (it gained a bishop in the eighth century, but it is regularly called a *castrum*), but it was clearly unusually productive, given its size and early chronology, and its salt remained important through the ninth century and (perhaps to a lesser extent) the tenth. The smaller-scale parallels from the Venetian lagoon sites (including one, beginning perhaps in the seventh century, on the Rialto island itself, Ca' Vendramin Calergi, which we will come back to), indicate that something similar was happening there as well.[83]

Venice ended up a political power centre, and Comacchio did not; this is a major reason why the latter did not last. Indeed, the Venetians sacked it *c.*932, and it was never important again.[84] From then onwards, exchange concentrated above all in a single place again, Rialto. Before that, both Comacchio and the lagoon sites benefited from the possibilities for traffic which the coast as a whole offered, as the only available point of contact between the cities of the Italian

[82] For Comacchio, see in general Gelichi, 'Comacchio e il suo territorio'; Gelichi and Hodges, *From one sea to another*; and the final report of the excavations, Gelichi et al., *Un emporio e la sua cattedrale* (see pp. 700–17 (S. Gelichi), for a cogent analysis of the economic implications of the site). For the globular amphorae and their links to the Aegean, see most recently ibid., pp. 212–20, 235, 246–66 (C. Negrelli; there were also some very early Otranto types from the latest phases, and a handful of possibly Sicilian amphorae too), 285–92 (C. Capelli et al.), 295–302 (A. Pecci, for the probability of wine in the Aegean globular amphorae); earlier, esp. Negrelli, 'Modelli di scambio'.

[83] For globular amphora distributions on the Italian mainland, see, e.g., Cantini, 'Produzioni ceramiche', pp. 356–8; Gelichi et al., 'Importare, produrre e consumare', pp. 82–8, gives a ceramic survey for the lagoon. For glass, see ibid., pp. 56–81, with a tentative redating of Torcello and a comparison with Comacchio; Gelichi et al., *Un emporio e la sua cattedrale*, pp. 51–63 (E. Grandi), 403–15 (M. Ferri); Ferri, 'Le strutture produttive di Comacchio'; and see in the same volume Neri, 'Produzione e circolazione del vetro', pp. 25–9, for an overview of the development of Italian glass production, which was, in Venice, tied to eastern imports of soda ash into the central middle ages. The most recent survey of the depressing range of hardly published and unpublished Venetian archaeological sites is Gelichi, 'Jumping on the dunes'; there is very little we can say for sure about the origins of the Rialto settlement(s) from archaeology at present. For Comacchio (and also Ravenna) salt up to 1000, see Cortese, 'Sui sentieri del sale'.

[84] Giovanni Diacono, *Istoria Veneticorum*, ed. Berto, 3.44, although (see n. 83 above) it still produced salt. The last reference I have seen to Comacchiesi outside the coast dates to as late as 1139, when a certain Ottone *de Commacio* appears in Piacenza (Falconi, *Le carte cremonesi*, n. 322), but it is an isolated citation.

interior and the Mediterranean, even at the quietest point for the history of Mediterranean exchange; but from here, it is Venetian commerce that expanded. In our ungenerous evidence for the ninth century, there is quite an amount of casual reference to it, particularly in the 820s. A famous document, the 829 will of Duke Giustiniano Particiaco, refers to, among other things, his '*laboratorii* (working) *solidi*, if they come back safe from seagoing'; this investment—as has often been said, the first reference in medieval history to capital investment—amounted to the surprisingly high figure of £1,200, which would be high even in the twelfth century, as we shall see. The 824/5 quasi-will of Fortunato, the patriarch of Grado along the coast to the east, a busy and controversial political figure of the period with independent links to the Byzantines and the Franks, lists a notable number of luxury goods, certainly not for the most part locally made, which he gave to Grado's churches. The 820s were also when the Venetians stole (or claimed they stole) the body of St Mark from its tomb in Alexandria, which at the very least shows that shipmen from there were already familiar with the Egypt route; the *Translatio S. Marci*, the text which celebrates this, is from the late tenth century, but Giustiniano referred to the body in his will, so the date is right.[85]

Michael McCormick sees this commercial activity as dominated by slave-trading, and suggests that it began in the late eighth century. This is very plausible; indeed, the Carolingian treaties with Venice specifically mentioned slaves, in that they banned the sale across the border of slaves who were Christian, and so nominally not subject to slave raids. That still left considerable scope for such trading, however, given that Venice was close to the eastern border of the Carolingian Empire; the Slav tribes of the north-east Adriatic were small-scale enough to be raided easily, and there were routes down to the coast from central Europe too. There were, indeed, still Slav slaves coming into Venice in the twelfth century (which we know because some of them were bought locally by prosperous families, and manumitted in wills), even though by then the Slav peoples were certainly Christian. Alice Rio's convincing critique of the idea that most of Latin Europe saw large-scale slave-trading in this period specifically excepts Venice, and a single town could get rich on it. But the trade in slaves was largely a luxury trade, as we have seen in earlier chapters; in our Egyptian documentation, they can be shown to have been expensive. There was no large-scale use of slaves in this period anywhere in the Mediterranean, and they were above all used in the household service of elites, plus, particularly in Spain before the fall of the

[85] The most recent edition of the will of Giustiniano is Lanfranchi and Strina, *SS. Ilario e Benedetto*, n. 2. For Fortunato, see most recently the text and analysis in Marano, *Le fortune di un patriarca*. The most recent edition of the *Translatio* is Colombi, '"Translatio Marci evangelistae Venetias"'; for the argument for its late tenth-century date, which I fully accept, see ibid., pp. 75–81. For the Egypt route, perhaps see Eberwin of Trier, *Vita Sancti Symeonis*, 2.11 (p. 91), for Venetians sailing the Nile from Cairo down to the coast in the 1020s (and being killed by pirates); this is a near-contemporary account, but it has too many implausible details to add usefully to our knowledge.

caliphate, army service.[86] Conversely, the wine amphorae, which do mark some form of bulk trade connecting the Byzantine lands with northern Italy, are actually less attested inland as we move later, into the ninth century. Our documentary evidence for commerce drops back for a century as well.

In the late tenth century, at the start of the period of this book, Venice was the only significant intermediary between the Italian kingdom in the Po plain and the richer and more productive states of the eastern Mediterranean. In this period, our evidence still stresses luxuries. The stern and detailed enactment from 960 of Duke Pietro III Candiano, apparently repeating an earlier one of the 870s, that the slave trade with the Byzantines must stop *right now*, simply tells us that the trade was thriving. In return, the Venetians, as we have seen, brought spices, plus high-end artisanal goods such as ebony combs and mirrors, to the king's court at Pavia, according to the *Honorantie* of the early eleventh century. This fits with a remark of Liudprand of Cremona, in his account of a failed embassy to Constantinople dating to 968, that the Venetians were accustomed to bring Byzantine silks to Italy, to sell in exchange for food. The *Honorantie* indeed state, in another famous quote, that the Venetians 'do not plough, nor sow, nor harvest grapes', and that the agreement with the Italian kingdom allows them to buy grain and wine 'in every [river] port'. Later in the century, in 1099, an agreement refers to grain, wine, and dried meat imports from Imola in Romagna, which can be seen as a concrete example of this.[87] We could see, then, the Venetians as taking slaves eastwards and bringing Byzantine silk and Egypt-bought spices back to mainland Italy, with food for themselves as a spin-off—important to Venice, but not in any sense the main item, for Venice was still small, and many of its inhabitants did, contrary to the *Honorantie*, own agricultural lands on the *terraferma*. The *Translatio* in the late tenth century says proudly that 'it is normal for the Venetians frequently to seek out places for buying and selling (*loca mercationis*)'; what they were doing in that intermediary role was to deal in luxuries for the most part, with the

[86] McCormick, *Origins*, esp. pp. 523–31, 731–77 (the latter section being a maximalist view of the slave trade which I only follow in part); cf. already Violante, *La società milanese*, pp. 33–4. For caution, see Rio, *Slavery after Rome*, pp. 19–41, and see now also the wider framing in Perry et al., *The Cambridge world history of slavery*, 2, which is also less maximalist than earlier surveys. For a twelfth-century example, see p. 513 below. For Carolingian treaties, see, e.g., *MGH*, *Capitularia*, 2, n. 233, ch. 3 (a. 840). For Egypt, see Chapter 2, n. 284 above (Egyptian slaves, anyway, usually came from Africa, not the Mediterranean); for Spain, where slaves did come from the north (although certainly not via Venice), see Chapter 5, n. 95 above. In fact, Venice was probably selling slaves to Byzantium, for the most part, doubtless, again, for household service.

[87] Cessi, *Documenti*, 2, n. 41 (a. 960); Brühl and Violante, *Die 'Honorantie civitatis Papie'*, ch. 3 (at p. 41, the link between the ploughing quotation and biblical citations seems to me less tight than the editors think); Liudprand of Cremona, *Relatio*, ed. Chiesa, ch. 55; cf. Thietmar of Merseburg, *Chronicon*, 7.76, recounting a shipwreck of four Venetian ships carrying spices (*pigmenta*) in 1017. For grain etc. in 1099, see Lenel, 'Ein Handelsvertrag'; 100 *anphorae* of wine were coming in annually from Istria already in 932; see Tafel and Thomas, *Urkunden*, 1, n. 10; cf. in general Rösch, *Venezia e l'impero*, pp. 225–50, which lists other food imports. For Venetian eastern trade in the whole period between 800 and 1100, see Jacoby, 'Venetian commercial expansion'; this is a genuinely good guide, even if too optimistic in its tone and in some of its hypotheses.

Byzantines above all, but also with the Islamic lands, particularly Egypt. There is only one clear reference to bulk trade by sea in these early texts: it is the already cited prohibition of John Tzimiskes in 971—again, doubtless, unsuccessful—against Venetian trade in timber and arms to the Islamic lands, which details at some length the possible ways wood was sold (it was, among other things, used to make tablewares such as bowls, *scutellae*). It is clear from this that there was a trade in wooden goods, including, as the text says, to Ifrīqiya. The main source for timber is likely in this early period to have been the woods of Istria, which was by now under Venetian control; that is to say, it does not as yet prove a timber trade across the northern Italian hinterland, although one would develop later, as we shall see shortly.[88]

But actually it is probable that the main commercial activity of the Venetians inside mainland Italy for most of our period was, indeed, a bulk trade, that is to say, in salt. As we saw earlier, in the eighth century it was the Comacchiesi who sold salt from the Po delta to northern Italy, and they still did in a Cremona court case of 851; they produced it into the tenth century, although by now its commercialization largely passed through Ravenna, which also had its own salt pans. But the Venetian takeover of the route between the sea and the Po plain shifted the main focus of production northwards. The first document for salt around Venice is as late as 958, but after the end of the tenth century evidence for Venetian production begins to spiral; salt export from here, in this instance to the Veneto town of Treviso, is first documented in 1000.[89] I would see these very much as *termini ante quem*. Salt production was strong in the northern lagoon, initially and throughout our period, but from the mid-eleventh century it focussed in particular on Chioggia at the lagoon's southern end. The evidence for salt pans (*salinae*) in these areas is huge by the standards of this period: Jean-Claude Hocquet, the main expert on the topic, counts 494 documents for salt up to 1200, some 12 per cent of all surviving Venetian charters, six times as many as the next best-documented salt pans in Italy, those of Rome at the mouth of the Tiber.[90] They were mostly, when we can tell, owned by Venetian aristocrats (including dukes) and monasteries, and this is not surprising: they were serious

[88] *Translatio S. Marci*, ed. Colombi, 8.3 (note, however, that the text says nothing useful about what goods were transported; that they included pork (ibid., 13.5, 14.1) is unlikely); Cessi, *Documenti*, 2, n. 49 (a. 971); cf. p. 188 above. The treaties between Venice and the Franks discuss the *capulandum* of trees by Venetians in the Kingdom of Italy, especially in the territory of Treviso and in Friuli; see, e.g., *MGH, Capitularia*, 2, n. 233, chs 24–5, 29 (but the text was regularly copied in later treaties). This would normally mean coppicing for firewood, not the cutting of timber; but either way, it is at least conceivable that bowls could be made out of some of that wood.

[89] Manaresi, *I placiti*, 1, n. 56; Cessi, *Documenti*, 2, nn. 40, 89. For Ravenna, see Cortese, 'Sui sentieri del sale'.

[90] Hocquet, 'Le saline' (note that his huge *thèse*, *Le sel et la fortune de Venise*, deals with a later period); see also Merores, 'Die venezianischen Salinen', a thoughtful and still important analysis, although only based on documents already edited in 1916. For Rome, see Toubert, *Les structures*, pp. 641–51, 681–3; Maggi Bei, 'Sulla produzione del sale'; Wickham, *Medieval Rome*, pp. 100–5.

investments. And they had buyers all across the north of Italy, which meant profit as well. These were the most profitable local resource the Venetians had, by far; they were also the most likely source of capital for more ambitious trading, when it began to appear. But one thing which must be stressed when considering Venetian salt is that this was by no means a maritime import. The Venetians could have prospered from the salt trade without ever going to sea. Clearly, they never failed to do this; but, throughout the eleventh century, salt was probably the most important way that the Venetians intersected with the main lines of the exchange economy of northern Italy, seen as a whole. The only addition to this which we can perhaps discern in this early period is cloth, for we have a fragment of a text of *c.*1020 in which Duke Ottone Orseolo specified that the *pallia que portabant per loca Italie* ('the cloth which they took through the places of Italy') could only be sold in Pavia and at the Ferrara fairs. This might well be the silk which we know they brought from Byzantium, and the restriction to two selling points might support this; it would not be a substantial addition to our knowledge if so. But we cannot exclude that it could be linen, which we know the Venetians sold in Mantua in the 870s. Probably if so, it, like salt, would have been local to the Veneto; flax was grown around Padua, and, indeed, we know that by 1005 men from the Saccisica in the territory of Padua gave an annual tribute of 200 pounds of flax to the duke of Venice in lieu of mercantile tolls, so it is very likely that linen was woven in Venice itself.[91]

I would, therefore, see Venice, up to the early eleventh century, as essentially a small, active, but luxury-focussed trading centre, with a further specialization in salt, produced on some scale, and possibly cloth by the end of that period. But by the middle decades of the eleventh century something was seriously changing. From here on, commercial documents begin to survive on an ever larger scale, and they show us aspects of the city which are quite unlike those of any other in Italy. As we saw earlier, parchment single-sheet documents in Italy overwhelmingly concern land, and tell us little or nothing about commercial relationships, which were more transient, and not worth the expense of setting down on parchment and/or archiving after the transaction was complete. (A certain number of credit documents survive in many cities, it is true, most usually after 1100 or so, but this is because the loans were backed by pledges in land, which usually means in these cases that the loan was never repaid and the land was kept by the creditor, often the church in whose archive it survived.) Before doing the work for this book, I had hardly read any Venetian documents, and I was frankly startled when

[91] *Cronache Veneziane antichissime*, ed. Monticolo, pp. 178–9; Gloria, *Codice diplomatico padovano dal secolo sesto*, n. 82 (a. 1005); see n. 24 above for Mantua. *CDVE*, 9, n. 2199 (a. 1154), shows that the men of Chioggia, always subject to Venice, still controlled the flax—and also grain—transport down the Brenta from the territory of Padua to the sea. We cannot exclude the import of linen from Byzantium as well—this was entirely plausible by the twelfth century as we shall see, and by then from Egypt too—but it would be gratuitous to suppose it for this early period.

I opened Morozzo della Rocca and Lombardo's *Documenti del commercio veneziano*, the basic collection of Venetian commercial texts. Already in the 1020s–1030s, when they begin, there are documents recording repaid loans, which refer to capital (*caput*) and, soon, standard interest, *prode*. Interest was set at an annual rate of *de quinque sex*, 'six for five', i.e. 20 per cent, a rate which remained the norm for 150 years and more (as documents sometimes put it, it was *secundum usum patrie nostre*), although in practice sea loans, which were riskier, were often at higher rates. One of the first documents refers to the sale of cheese; another concerns the lease of an anchor; the first dated text, for 1031, concerns a contract for the transport of cloth; by the 1070s, texts survive for trading in Thebes and Alexandria, in the latter case in alum, for fixing cloth dyes—that is to say, no longer exclusively luxuries. And we begin to find for the first time short-term loans, for one or two months, and also formal registrations of their repayment.[92]

The *Documenti* volumes are selections from a wide range of document collections, so, of course, they are not in themselves a guide to the prevalence of commercial transactions. But one of the largest collections of Venetian documents, that of S. Giorgio Maggiore, which is a standard set of charters from a monastery rich in land (and, especially in this case, salt pans), in fact has our earliest short-term loan of all, from 1026, and a string of others afterwards, some of them not picked up by the editors of the *Documenti*. A characteristic Venetian property formula, most often used when referring to inheritances, and first documented as early as 976, includes the phrase *omnes collegancias, rogadias, commendaciones, prestito, negociis, raciones*; the first two or three of these nouns refer to trading contracts, and *prestito*, 'loan', and *negotiis*, 'deals', speak for themselves.[93] Almost none of these texts has any serious parallels elsewhere in north-central Italy in the eleventh century, and they were only the start; the twelfth century saw substantial developments too.

The eleventh- and twelfth-century commercial documents for Venice (36 for the eleventh, 390 for the twelfth century up to 1180, picking up in number particularly from the 1130s[94]) are, in fact, in effect unique. They parallel, quite closely,

[92] For these citations, see *DCV*, nn. 1–14, N1 (here, as earlier, 'N' denotes the additional later collection by the same editors, *Nuovi documenti*). For higher rates for sea loans, see Luzzatto, *Studi*, pp. 99–102. For interest of 20% as Venetian *usus*, see, e.g., *DCV*, nn. 16, N6.

[93] Lanfranchi, *S. Giorgio maggiore*, n. 6 (a. 1026). For the *collegancias* formulary, I quote from *DCV*, n. 4; the earliest surviving is in Cessi, *Documenti*, 2, n. 54 (= Manaresi, *I placiti*, n. 181).

[94] The standard editions, *DCV* and *Nuovi documenti*, located a majority of commercial documents, 28 for the eleventh century and 326 for 1101–80. But they missed 18 now edited in Lanfranchi, *S. Giorgio maggiore* (and also several other documents, not explicitly commercial, written inside the Byzantine Empire). Lanfranchi, *Famiglia Zusto*, also edits a highly commercially focussed family archive, not known to *DCV*'s editors (it is a rare lay archive surviving as such in our period), which provides another 9 commercial contracts. Other *fondi*, edited in newer fully published editions and, above all, in *CDVE*, provide another 8 for the eleventh century and 37 for the twelfth; so in total *DCV* and *Nuovi documenti* missed, by my count, 71 texts in all. Most are simple credit documents or registrations of paid or defaulted loans. Missed documents attesting maritime commerce directly are Chiaudano, 'Una pergamena'; Lanfranchi, *S. Giorgio maggiore*, n. 136; Lanfranchi, *Famiglia Zusto*, 6, 10,

those for Genoa from the 1150s onwards, but the latter are notarial registers on paper, which survive, when they do, because the families of notaries put them into city archives as a public record; surviving Genoese single-sheet documents, by contrast, all as usual kept by churches, are as land-focussed as are those of any other city. This was not the case in Venice, as the S. Giorgio texts just cited already tell us. But in addition, one process which happened in Venice was quite particular. One of the main Venetian monasteries, S. Zaccaria, a female monastery very close to the ducal families (ducal daughters were often abbesses there), kept a substantial archive, which largely survives to this day. Alongside the daughters of the elite, S. Zaccaria was happy in our period to admit the daughters of a few merchants, if they could pay the dowry needed to enter; some of these were also from aristocratic families, but others, although rich or at least prosperous, were decidedly not. With some of these daughters came the commercial archives of their fathers, which, it turns out, in Venice at least, could perfectly well be on parchment. S. Zaccaria chose to keep these too, and, indeed, the great bulk of commercial texts for the city in our period, over two-thirds, survives as a result of the monastery's choices here.[95] We thus have large sets of the dealings of individual merchants from the 1030s onwards, notably Leone da Molin and then his heirs, who begin the surviving sequence of documents but continue into the twelfth century, Dobromiro Staniario and his son and grandsons, who are documented from 1125 and well into the thirteenth, and Romano Mairano and his brother Samuele, whose affairs cover the second half of the twelfth century, 1150–1201—the largest and most famous set, in fact, making up well over eighty documents in all. We have plenty of others too, mixed in, which often came from elite families, but by no means always did. It is important to stress that these merchant archives do not provide a snapshot of Venetian trading as a whole, as the Genoese registers do (although there are problems of typicality even there; see p. 543 below); we cannot say that they tell us about more than the choices of some individual merchants. All the same, we get reliable data about commercial dealings at all levels of society, and it is equally clear that all levels of society could engage in trade.

At the beginning of the last century, there was a small *querelle* between the historian Reinhard Heynen and the sociologist Werner Sombart. Heynen had read the Mairano documents and, very struck by them, argued, explicitly against Sombart, that Venetian commercial capital came above all from small trading beginnings, building up as time went on into much larger investments, including land. Sombart, who was more interested in overview than detail, rejected this;

14, 16, 19, 22; *CDVE*, 3, n. 273 (= ASV, SZ, b. 12, n. 3), 5, n. 522, 8, n. 2013, 10, nn. 2337, 2356, 11, n. 2420, 13, n. 2786, 16, n. 3139 (see n. 114 below), 17, n. 3232.

[95] See *DCV*, 1, pp. xv–xviii; Fees, *Le monache di San Zaccaria*, pp. 41–3, which discusses the few nuns with a demonstrable commercial background.

Romano Mairano was only a small fish; the richest merchants all had land to back them first, throughout pre-industrial Europe. Historians of the Venetian economy across the twentieth century lined up on one side of this argument or the other. More recently, it has become clearer that it is a false opposition.[96] There is no serious doubt that most of the highest elite families, when we find them trading—the Falier, the Michiel, the Contarini, the Badoer—had a landed backing already, including salt pans, and occasionally we can see the direct use of that landed backing, as with the Foscari, dealers in the eastern Mediterranean from the 1120s onwards, who in 1072 borrowed £80 against the pledge of a landed estate previously given them by Vitale Candiano, from one of the oldest families of all. Even dukes are regularly attested as lending money for trading; and the dukes of the half-century after 1172 are also documented as trading before their election, as are their sons.[97] Against the view that the great families were all Venice-based investors, leaving less prosperous merchants to do the actual trading abroad, is an account of the translation of part of the body of St Stephen from Constantinople to Venice in 1110; the text claims that on the ship, which was transporting luxury goods (*auri, arge<n>ti aliarumque preciosarum diviciarum affluentia*) to Venice, were members of most of the aristocratic families of the city, including three Falier and eight Michiel; so these were almost certainly active abroad. But land was, all the same, not essential for success. The Ziani, a rising family, not known before the 1070s, who became hugely rich in the later twelfth and early thirteenth century and provided two dukes between 1172 and 1229, are first documented in the credit market in 1110, were in Constantinople investing largish sums in the Aegean trade network by the 1140s (this was Sebastiano Ziani, the future duke in 1172–8), and only got into land, and salt pans, and, of course, supreme office, in the last half of the century.[98]

[96] Heynen, *Zur Entstehung des Kapitalismus*, pp. 1–6, 121–4, reacting against Sombart's first edition; Sombart, *Der moderne Kapitalismus*, 2nd edn, 1, pp. 150–2, 309 (a brusque one-line rejection); more with Heynen (which is still a useful survey) are Luzzatto, *Studi*, and Fees, *Reichtum und Macht*, esp. pp. 83–99; more with Sombart are Cracco, *Società e stato*, esp. pp. 11–46, and Rösch, *Der venezianische Adel*, esp. pp. 73–80, 108–11. But Fees and Rösch move easily beyond the divide (see also Rösch, 'Lo sviluppo mercantile'), as does Borsari, *Venezia e Bisanzio*, the other major study.

[97] Lists of largely aristocratic salt pan owners can be found in Merores, 'Die venezianischen Salinen', pp. 78–9, 90–1—the whole article stresses their importance as an economic backing for families; for the general point, see also Rösch, *Der venezianische Adel*, esp. pp. 75–6. For the Badoer, see Pozza, *I Badoer*; pp. 23–7 for their trading, extensive even if less well documented than some. For the Foscari, see Lanfranchi, *S. Giorgio Maggiore*, n. 29; cf., e.g., *DCV*, n. 54 (a. 1129). For dukes, future dukes and their sons, see, e.g., *DCV*, N7, 125, 174, 253, 257, 262, 266, 268, 289, N30. Only Orio Mastropiero (ruling 1178–92) does not appear as a trader.

[98] For St Stephen, see Borsari, *Venezia e Bisanzio*, pp. 65–8; Lanfranchi, *S. Giorgio Maggiore*, 3, appendix, n. 144. The text is redated to the later twelfth century in Cracco, 'Santità straniera', pp. 451–4; he also doubts (p. 458) that the Venetian aristocrats could have been travelling merchants, which is part of his argument against the reliability of the source; but for a source to claim that so many aristocrats were all located on a boat from Constantinople to Venice seems to me significant in itself. For the Ziani, see Fees, *Reichtum und Macht*, esp. pp. 47–102.

Particularly interesting are less prominent families, which certainly had no significant original landed base, for they show clearly how one could, indeed, prosper by trading, even if by no means on the scale of the Ziani. Romano Mairano, whom we met when looking at Byzantium (p. 339), easily the best-documented merchant in the Mediterranean in our period outside the *geniza*, has had so many accounts of his life and activities that we do not need to explore his career in detail. He was active in Byzantine trade throughout the 1150s and 1160s, until the Venetians were expropriated and expelled in March 1171 (a moment in which he gained respect and gratitude for picking up numerous Venetians in his ship and carrying them to safety in Acre in Palestine). By then he too was often based in Acre, and, both from the Aegean and from Acre or Tyre, he also traded in Alexandria, so he could easily switch to the east, particularly Egypt, after 1171; but he moved back to Byzantium when he could, in the 1180s. He was a travelling merchant for the first half of his career, more often a sedentary merchant thereafter (this shift, more a product of growing age than increasing wealth, was common in Venice). He sometimes accumulated loans from many different people at once to finance his voyages; he is not recorded as defaulting on any of them, even those for goods lost in 1171, although he took, as others did, until the 1180s to pay them all off. He was prosperous enough to buy ships, which were by no means cheap pieces of capital investment; he took in lease a concession of a substantial part of the Venetian port in Constantinople in 1169 (a moment of prestige, but not much profit, given Manuel I's confiscations less than two years later); by the end of his life he owned a set of houses in Rialto—we do not have his will, so we do not know how much money he had in addition—all of which were signs of respectability and relative affluence, even if not of high social status.[99] We could say, yes, scholars who say that Romano Mairano remained a small fish are right, for this is not so very much after fifty years of trading; at most he was part of the medium elite of the city. But we could also say this was an effective and probably attractive way of making a living, and Romano avoided the most serious consequences of all the many risks he faced, with considerable success.

Perhaps even more illuminating are examples of freed slaves who went into trade. The best-documented is Dobromiro Staniario, who was freed by the heirs of Pietro Staniario in 1125, presumably following the terms of Pietro's will. He kept the charter of manumission all his life, as did his heirs, for his is one of the family archives which went to S. Zaccaria. In that text he is called a Croat (*ex genere Hgroaticorum*); he called himself Dalmatinus in later documents to reflect

[99] For accounts of Romano Mairano's career, see Heynen, *Zur Entstehung des Kapitalismus*, pp. 86–120; Luzzatto, *Studi*, pp. 108–16; Rösch, 'Lo sviluppo mercantile', pp. 146–50; and Borsari, *Venezia e Bisanzio*, pp. 116–28, who, at 145–53, also edits documents for Romano which are not in *DCV*. The port concession is *DCV*, n. 245; Romano taking Venetian refugees to Acre is recorded in Pozza, *Gli atti originali*, n. 18. Cf., for a parallel, the Zusto family, documented in Lanfranchi, *Famiglia Zusto*, and discussed briefly on pp. 321, 337 above.

his Slavic origins, as well as, by 1135, Staniarius after Pietro. But he was not supported by Pietro's family; in 1130, indeed, Pietro's daughter Dorotea agreed a settlement with Dobromiro over a court case the family had brought against him. So Dobromiro was very much on his own after he gained freedom. He was, nonetheless, already borrowing £100 for a year, presumably for trade, as early as 1128; in 1134 he defaulted on a loan of £300, not a small sum, and had to give up a set of urban houses; but in 1135 he was back on track, selling oil from Corinth in Alexandria. In 1136, he finalized a linen deal in Corinth; and in (probably) 1148 he borrowed £100 to trade in Corinth again, which his son Pancrazio paid off in 1150. So he was sometimes doing well, sometimes doing badly; he was probably at the lowest level of traders in financial terms, but was surviving. Pancrazio Staniario was a trader for his lifetime too, often a sea captain. He was for the most part less prosperous than Romano Mairano. But he invested in land, not only in the city but in the countryside; his sons operated on a larger scale; and after the fall of Constantinople in 1204 one of them was a Venetian official in the former Byzantine capital. That is to say, they had fought their way up into the medium Venetian elite two generations after their freedman grandfather began with nothing, essentially on the basis of trading. And there was evidently not yet any structural opposition between the old landed families and very new families like the heirs of Dobramiro Staniario, or else the latter's documents would never have come to the highly aristocratic S. Zaccaria.[100]

The Venetians began their maritime commerce in the ninth and tenth centuries, above all trading with Byzantium, as we have seen. In the eleventh and twelfth, notwithstanding all the many changes in the island city's activity, this remained entirely true; there are almost as twice as many surviving seagoing contracts for the Byzantine lands as there are for everywhere else put together. Egypt came second—up to 1180, nearly sixty contracts mention Alexandria or Damietta (see pp. 144–5 above)—then the Levant, usually Acre or Tyre. Sicily (generally Messina, on the eastern side) and Puglia were a long way behind. Puglia, at least, may simply not have been often mentioned because when the Venetians put into ports there, at the very least to take in water (as they must have done on the eastern shore of the Adriatic too, full of good ports as it is), they were on their way to the regions farther east which were their main destination; we do have a few signs that this was common, in fact.[101] The western Mediterranean, by contrast, was

[100] For Dobromiro, see *DCV*, nn. 49, 51, 58, 65, 67–9, 72, 76, 80, 97; for him and his heirs, see esp. Borsari, *Venezia e Bisanzio*, pp. 109–16, and pp. 139–45 for documents not in *DCV*, to which should be added ASV, SZ, b. 7, nn. 16, 41, b. 20, n. 25. We do not know how the family archive came to S. Zaccaria; there are no documented nuns with the Staniario surname; see the lists in Fees, *Le monache di San Zaccaria*, pp. 45–70. Giacomo Venier, of 'Saracen' (i.e. Arab or Berber) origin, was another example of a freed slave who traded, this time for six years on behalf of the heirs of his former master, before continuing on his own: see Borsari, *Venezia e Bisanzio*, pp. 108–9.

[101] Italian mainland stopovers on the way out of the Adriatic are cited in *DCV*, nn. 40, 289, 291, 301, 306. For the Venetians and the Adriatic, see Dorin, 'Adriatic trade networks', and the long-term perspectives in Skoblar, *Byzantium, Venice and the medieval Adriatic*; for Sicily, see pp. 255–6 above.

not a normal trading goal. When Romano Mairano decided to send a ship to Béjaïa and Ceuta in 1177, he refers in his loan documents to a merchant flotilla (*taxegium*) going there, although this may just be a notarial formula; he certainly knew that North Africa used Almohad dinars (*massemutini* are the money cited in the contracts) and that he would have to pay customs dues (*doana*); he expected to be able to pay back Venetian creditors there too, who may have travelled with him. But he had to pledge his ship to them, a highly unusual commitment, and also sell it when he arrived to pay off his debts. It is not clear whether Romano made any money at all out of the venture, in fact, and we do not have any evidence that other twelfth-century merchants imitated him. If Sicily was not so common a region for Venetians to focus on trade with, the Maghreb was, in effect, off the map, and perhaps only someone as bold as Romano would have considered it.[102]

It is common in the historiography to say that the Venetians were slow to take advantage of, and to help, the crusading enterprise, and that Genoa and Pisa consolidated their position in the Levant first. This is quite true; but it is equally true that, even though there were Venetian colonies in both Acre and Tyre, and from the 1110s concessions in Jerusalem and Tripoli as well, the Crusader states remained of less interest to them. Not only did Byzantium remain far more important, but also, if they had to choose between the Levant and Egypt, usually they would choose Egypt, and did so particularly in the 1160s and 1170s, the decades with the largest numbers of Venetian contracts. Indeed, we have seen that bulk trade with Alexandria is visible as early as 1072, by which time export of alum from Egypt—throughout our period the dominant production centre for this crucial fixer for dyeing (see p. 136 above)—was evidently routine. Trade with the Levant is first attested not long after, in 1083, but it may be significant that the port in that case was Tripoli, not actually a common Venetian destination after the First Crusade, but, conversely, the Syrian port with the closest links to Byzantium.[103] The temporal exceptions to this relative Egyptian dominance were two: first in the 1120s, when Venetian fleets helped the Crusaders take Tyre, and tried to help them take Ashkelon, both from the Fāṭimids; there are no contracts to Fāṭimid Egypt in that decade. The same drop in contracts occurred during the Third Crusade, which used—and needed—ships from all three of the great Italian port cities; it is clear that Saladin closed off Egypt to them as a result, as also to the Genoese (see p. 145 above), and Venetian contracts to Alexandria only begin again in 1197. Conversely, when the Venetians were excluded from Byzantium in

[102] *DCV*, nn. 284–5, 287, 293–4, 296–7. For a creditor apparently travelling with the ship of the debtor (Romano Mairano again, in fact) from Venice to Alexandria in 1180, see *DCV*, nn. 322–3; cf. p. 254 above for Sicily.

[103] For the eleventh century, see *DCV*, nn. 11, 15 (see p. 354 above for Tripoli and Byzantium); for the treaties and similar public acts, see Tafel and Thomas, *Urkunden*, 1, nn. 36, 40 (referring to help at Ascalon), 41, 46, 55, 59, 63; for the colonies, see *DCV*, nn. 126, N17, 161, 171, 295.

1171, a heavy blow, it was above all to Alexandria that they went instead—we know in particular that Romano Mairano and Pancrazio Staniario went, but we have contracts for other merchants too. In the 1160s, when the seas were most open for the Venetians, Romano had been happy to trade to Alexandria or Acre from Constantinople, and to Alexandria from Acre as well, as we have seen. He knew them all, and had contacts in all, which was, as with the *geniza* merchants, normally essential in order to be successful. So it is significant that in the 1170s it was Alexandria which became his major focus.[104] The Venetians had a *fontica*, that is, a *fundūq*, there by 1173, just as they had colonies in Acre and Tyre. Both Benjamin of Tudela in the 1160s and William of Tyre in the 1170s stressed the wide range of merchants who congregated there (see p. 144 above). This simply reflects the centrality that trade with Egypt had and maintained across the Mediterranean, in our period and after as well, a recurrent argument in this book. The Venetians, however, may have been the largest group of all, and this dominance probably continued into the thirteenth century, after the effect of Saladin's embargoes, and then the negative impact of the Fifth Crusade of 1218–21 against Egypt itself, had lessened. So, even if Byzantium was the key focus for the Venetians at all times, they essentially looked to Egypt next.[105]

Standard Venetian contracts in our period included the *collegancia*, in effect the same contract as the Genoese *commenda*, in which (in the classic version, for there were plenty of variants) the sedentary merchant put in two-thirds, the travelling merchant one-third, and the profit was halved between them, if the ship the latter went on returned undamaged *a mare vel a gente*, from shipwreck or pirates. The other main contract was the sea loan; some of these were for a percentage of the profits, and some simply for an agreed interest rate, which, as already noted, could sometimes be above the 20 per cent which Venetians considered normal, particularly when the context seemed to involve more risk.[106] From around 1170, references to interest are markedly less common, and instead the travelling merchant simply took the *habere* (the money or goods) of the sedentary merchant abroad, and committed himself to paying a fixed sum at the end of the voyage, back in Venice (or Constantinople), or else to the creditor or his agent in a port

[104] For Romano in Egypt in the 1170s, see *DCV*, nn. 247–8, 256–62, 265–6, 293, 296, 306, 312, 318, 321, 323. For Romano not in Egypt in the same decade, excluding references to earlier contracts, see *DCV*, nn. 270–1, 309–10 for Acre, and see n. 102 above for the 1177 expedition to North Africa.

[105] *Fontica*: DCV, n. 247. Jacoby, 'Les Italiens en Égypte aux XIIe et XIIIe siècles', an account focussed on institutions, assumes, e.g. pp. 82, 86, that the Venetian presence in Egypt after 1200 was more substantial than that of Pisa or Genoa; this is implicitly backed up by Balard, 'Le commerce génois à Alexandrie', pp. 271–5, who downplays the importance of Genoa–Alexandria trade from the late twelfth century onwards. *CDVE*, 9, n. 2135 (a. 1152), mentions a niece of the aristocrat Ugerio Badoer called Cleopatra; this name, unique in Italy to my knowledge (it was almost unknown by now even in Egypt, though one possible example is P.Cair.Arab. 185), hints at the importance of Egyptian imagery in one Venetian family.

[106] For basic discussions, see Luzzatto, *Studi*, pp. 97–108 (100–2 on interest often being high); Borsari, *Venezia e Bisanzio*, pp. 68–82.

elsewhere. This new vagueness was probably to avoid increasingly vocal ecclesiastical prohibitions on lending at interest; so also, doubtless, were many of the agreements to repay a specified sum in a different currency.[107] It certainly did not indicate any lapse in the precision with which Venetians went about their business.

Earlier in the twelfth century, loans and *colleganciae* often stated that the travelling merchant could travel anywhere: 'wherever it seems good for me to travel', as a *collegancia* contract to Acre put it in 1138.[108] But increasingly, in particular from the mid-1160s, investors wanted the merchant to return on the first ship or flotilla (*taxegium* or *mudua*) back, or else required repayment so soon that any delay would have been impossible. I discussed this in the context of Venetian trading inside Byzantium (where, indeed, it started earlier), and called it the 'Venetian business model', along the lines of Jessica Goldberg's '*geniza* business model': it assumed rapid sales in major entrepôts to produce fast profits for investors, which meant that all the more extensive network of local and regional traffic was left to other, presumably non-Italian merchants.[109] And although Venetians certainly travelled on Acre–Alexandria routes or Constantinople–Crete–Egypt routes, these, even if outside Venice itself, were all interregional too. There is even less sign than there was in the Aegean that they engaged in any trade at all beyond the ports, inside Egypt or the Levant. That is to say, what we have is loans and collective commitments in money which aimed to produce—and which, as documents attesting repayments show, did very frequently produce—more money; they were pure merchant-capitalist agreements, generally focussed on single trans-Mediterranean destinations, with a minimum of stop-offs (probably largely for water) on the way there and back.

One result of this is that we can say very little, even less than we could for Venetian trade inside the Aegean, about what goods the merchants actually transported to and from Venice itself. It could conceivably be argued that when engaging in Byzantine trade, they took money to the Aegean, and traded there in bulk goods, foodstuffs and cloth in particular—which we do have information about there, on the basis of sales made to them in Corinth or Halmyros or another of their main centres (see pp. 334–6 above)—then selling up after a while and taking money (plus silk) back to Venice. But we cannot say so on the basis of any evidence, and it would, anyway, be highly unlikely. Indeed, once investors wanted merchants to return early, it would be close to impossible, for there would have

[107] Lending at interest was prohibited by the Second Lateran Council in 1139, ch. 13, and this was reiterated in the Third Council of 1179, ch. 25 (Tanner, *Decrees*, 1, pp. 200, 223); Pope Alexander III in the 1160s was hard-line on the subject in papal letters, although, curiously, he advocated the use of usury to pay off a debt in a letter to the canons of Pisa in 1161, Migne, *Patrologiae cursus completus, series latina*, 200, cols. 125–6, n. 52: church creditors were evidently different. See Parker, '*Papa et pecunia*'.

[108] e.g. *DCV*, nn. 71 (quotation), 54, 95, 109.

[109] For up to 1180, see *DCV*, nn. 90, 136, 182, 191, 265, 284, 298, 299, 302, 309, 321. See p. 336 above for Byzantium.

been too little time for the necessary trading. In a court record from 1072, a witness stated that a ship's captain initially refused to take a cargo of Egyptian alum back to Rialto from Methoni on the southern Greek coast because he was *caricatus* (fully loaded), presumably with bulk goods, which makes more sense, even if we cannot tell with what. I would suppose that one commodity would by now be the low-cost cloth which the Venetians were otherwise trading inside the Aegean, as it would be a particularly obvious Byzantine product to take back, plus, probably, the olive oil which was such an important export from Sparta and its region, another known Venetian trading commodity in the Byzantine context; we have a contract from 1180 referring to very large quantities of oil in Venice, even if where it came from is unspecified. We have some concrete proofs of the cloth, or at least the raw materials for it: the *bambax* (cotton) in a warehouse in Venice in 1125, which a widow dealt with after her husband's death (this must have come from Byzantium, given the weakness of Venice's links to Sicily, and the fact that its links to the Crusader states were only just beginning in the 1120s); and the 1132 will of Enrico Zusto, who died in Greece, listing large quantities of cotton, indigo, and yarn (*filado*). Into the twelfth century, they certainly also took back wine in Byzantine amphorae, plus glazed ceramics from Corinth and Chalkis, for these have been found in excavations in the Venetian lagoon, as we shall see later in this section; indeed, Duke Sebastiano Ziani, when fixing food prices in 1173, explicitly referred to *vinum de Romania*, which here almost certainly means Byzantium, not Romagna. Ceramics and cloth had similar patterns of trade in the Aegean, so it is possible that they did so on the way back to Venice as well. But what the Venetians were themselves exporting to Byzantium, apart from slaves, remains obscure; a rare concrete example is the large quantity of copper which Romano Mairano took from Venice to Constantinople in 1170.[110]

The Venetians equally certainly took goods when they came from and went to Egypt or the Levant in the twelfth century. A contract of 1139 refers to *mercimonia* which were to be taken from Acre to either Constantinople or Alexandria, before returning to Venice, where the merchant was to pay his creditor £100 Venetian; but although this tells us what we would expect to be hidden elsewhere under references to money, it again does not say what these *mercimonia* actually were. We only have a few indications, particularly of imports into Venice. A will made in Acre in 1128 asks the dying man's executors to spend some of his money on *ramisini*, perhaps one of the copper currencies of the early Crusader states, but also perhaps copper goods of some kind, to take to his mother back in Venice.[111] That is all the information we have for the Levant in surviving trade documents,

[110] See respectively *DCV*, nn. 11, 320, 47, *Famiglia Zusto*, n. 10; Pozza, *Gli atti originali*, n.17 (a. 1173); *DCV*, n. 329, for the copper; a later example of copper imported into Byzantium is n. 401.

[111] *DCV*, nn. 75, 52. For copper coins in the early Crusader states, particularly the northern ones, see Malloy et al., *Coins of the Crusader states*, pp. 9, 26–7, etc.

even if historians regularly assume the Venetians bought spices there. Romano Mairano, however, bought pepper on a substantial scale in Alexandria on several occasions in the 1170s and 1180s; he also bought alum, and we have seen that the Venetians were importing alum as early as the 1070s. We can certainly assume that other spices came with these, from Egypt's India trade, as, indeed, the *Honorantie* show that they had done since 1000 at the latest (and as they certainly did to Genoa; see p. 547 below). More indicative still is the 1188 will of a deceased Venetian in Alexandria, which shows that he owned, besides pepper, 28 *cantaria* (at least 840 kg) of linen, a commodity which we saw at length in Chapter 2 to be a major Egyptian bulk production.[112] As with Byzantine cotton and perhaps linen, that would certainly have profitably filled much of a ship going back to Rialto, and it is likely enough that the Venetians imported Egyptian linen on a reasonably regular basis.

This time, however, we do have a few clues about exports. It is doubtful that Venetians exported slaves to Egypt; as we have seen, documented slaves in Fusṭāṭ in our period were above all from Africa. But in 1162 Romano and Samuele Mairano agreed to export 50 *cantaria* of iron from Venice to the Templars in Acre; as for Egypt, Romano also planned to export wood on a large scale to Alexandria in 1173, partly coming from Verona (see p. 148 above). This is significant, given that exporting timber (for shipbuilding, plus iron, for arms) to Islamic lands was illegal, at least in theory; but whether voluntarily or not, Romano did it again when he sold his ship in Béjaïa in 1177. The Venetians were thus exporting both iron and timber to the East (although probably not to Byzantium, which had enough of each); the Levant needed less timber than Egypt did, thanks to the forests of Lebanon, but it is quite likely that a good proportion of the *mercimonia* and the *habere* of merchants going to Alexandria consisted of both. Historians have assumed it; but these anecdotal contracts give support to the assumption.[113] We can equally assume that other goods went with them, other Italian products or else goods picked up on the way. This is shown by the wide variety of goods (again *habere*), bought in Greece and destined for Constantinople, on a ship which was diverted to Alexandria in 1182 (see p. 334 above). It is also clear in an intriguing and unique document, the account of the goods of Graziano Gradenigo, from a Venetian elite family, who died on board a Pisan ship and whose goods were listed and then sold at auction in Pisa in 1176; it is hard to disentangle his sales goods from his substantial array of personal possessions

[112] See DCV, nn. 261–3, 266, 345, 359, with 368 for the 1188 will, and the pepper and alum in the 1148 will of Giovanni Badoer in Constantinople, Pozza, *I Badoer*, pp. 118–21—they must here have been imports from Egypt. See also *CDVE*, 8, n. 2013 (a. 1148), for alum, pepper, and cloth, probably again mostly from Egypt. For the weight of a *cantarium*, which could be very variable (this is the minimum), see Zupko, *Italian weights and measures*, pp. 70–2. *CDVE*, 10, n. 2324 (a. 1158) mentions a rent paid from one church to another which is partially in pepper; this shows that this commodity had some fungibility in Venice, although not as much as in Genoa (see p. 547 below).

[113] *DCV*, nn. 158, 248, 297. For iron export and prohibitions, see Chapter 2, n. 314 above.

(including his feather mattress and three pairs of boots, two sold off and the third, the ones he died in, given to the poor), but he was certainly trading in linen cloth, had some fifteen boxes (*bussuli*) and other containers, six combs and some coral, and brought with him tailor's equipment and account books.[114]

It is obvious that Venetian society was shot through with trading interest and commitment, and even some production, from the start; it had very fluid credit-based economic arrangements already in the 1020s, with hints at it even before, and these never ceased. The Rialto market, documented from 1097, will have been very active by then, and doubtless earlier.[115] But, conversely, the actual scale of trading was not as great as one might expect. As has been pointed out often enough, several of the earliest texts, in the eleventh century, concern the hiring out of anchors for sea voyages, including to the elite da Molin family; there are only two after 1100, so the level of basic capital had evidently increased, but it cannot have been so high as late as the 1090s if shipowners could sometimes not afford their own anchors.[116] What is still more important, however, is that even in the twelfth century investment in Venetian voyages did not match the scale documented for other major trading centres, Alexandria and even Genoa. I discussed in Chapter 4 the figures for investment in Byzantine gold *hyperpera*, the standard currency used in the Aegean, in Venetian commercial documents for the Byzantine lands, and already made that point there, but it needs to be made here too.

Coinage in north-central Italy was universally based on the silver *denarius* in our period, generally expressed in pounds of 20 *solidi* or 240 *denarii*. It was minted in several mints, including that of Venice itself; but money minted on the island is relatively rarely referred to before the 1180s, and Venetian coins for the period are also now rare. The coin most commonly used by the Venetians up to then, both in the city and overseas, was the Verona silver *denarius*. But for trading in the Aegean, the Venetians above all used the Byzantine *hyperperon*; this seems to have been worth around £1 Veronese in the period up to 1180 (there are several contracts for Byzantine trading which give evidence for exchange rates), so they

[114] *CDVE*, 16, n. 3139, edited with commentary in Buenger Robbert, 'L'inventario di Graziano Gradenigo' and Buenger Robbert, 'Twelfth-century Italian prices'; I am cautious about her deduction that he was murdered on board, although she is probably right that the goods had been partly looted before the ship landed, as (among other things) the boxes seem to have been empty. Where Graziano had been trading is, however, unclear; I doubt North Africa, Borsari's suggestion (*Venezia e Bisanzio*, p. 98), given the lack of interest the Venetians showed for the region, but the coral could have been African, and it is conceivable that the Pisan ship had come from there. Tafel and Thomas, *Urkunden*, 1, n. 53, also implies that the Venetians exported silk and linen to Antioch; it is not clear where these were from either, but Egypt is here again a strong possibility for the linen; see further Chapter 2, n. 311 above.

[115] Romanin, *Storia documentata di Venezia*, 1, pp. 396–7 (this is a gift by the Orio family to the Venetian people of part of the market and its *stationes* (stalls)—the Gradonico/Gradenigo family held other *stationes* next door).

[116] *DCV*, nn. 5, 8, 20, 21, 24, 26, and, after 1100, 41, 153. See, e.g., Luzzatto, *Studi*, p. 94.

were in effect equivalents.[117] In the Aegean, as we saw in Chapter 4, most investments were for less than 100 *hyperpera*. Figures for investments over 300 *hyperpera* were quite rare, with 830 the highest single figure, and *c.*1,500 the highest figure for a voyage of Romano Mairano, which he made with loans from eight separate people (see p. 339 above). For the smaller number of documents for maritime trading in Veronese money, mostly to Egypt, the scale was a little higher than for Byzantine trading: two-thirds of the sixteen contracts were over £100, and three reached £1,000. But even this latter figure, or Romano's most substantial collective borrowings, was far lower than the highest figures for Genoa, which were respectively nearly three times and twice as high. £100 Veronese/100 *hyperpera*, a maximum for most Venetian trading, was also at the bottom end of Genoese norms, and even lower than the norms in the *geniza*. I will come back to this point when we look at Genoa itself.[118]

Rich Venetians, of course, possessed more money than this. Wills show Pietro Enzio in 1123 to be worth £4,807, partly in cash and credit notes but largely in land (including salt pans), and Romano, a chaplain of S. Marco, in 1151 to be worth over £1,700; Duke Pietro Ziani in 1228 left the remarkable sum of £13,285. Short-term loans inside the city could be high too; another chaplain, Marino Roibulo, borrowed from his cousins £3,000 for a month in 1145 (a month being far too short a time for him to be trading overseas). And when the city began to ask for loans from major citizens, in one of the first moves towards a public debt for city government (along with those of Genoa and Pisa; see pp. 540, 561 below), the sums involved were even greater: in 1187 the commune raised as much as £56,000.[119] But that was what rich people could eventually accumulate from land

[117] Exchange rates: *DCV*, nn. 89, 91, 118, 129, 146–7. In the first four, the repayment for a loan in Veronese money is a higher sum in *hyperpera*, which in each case is around 20% higher, fitting standard Venetian 20% profit rates; the last is a repayment of 75 *hyperpera* for a loan of £75 Veronese, between family members, which implies that no interest needed to be calculated in. *DCV*, nn. 143 and 163 are for a lower figure, 12 Veronese *solidi* for 1 *hyperperon*, but each relates to a penal settlement, which may explain the difference. See also the lists in Bertelé, 'Moneta veneziana e moneta bizantina', pp. 32–4; these include some contracts in Venetian pounds, which were worth roughly £2 Venetian to £1 Veronese until the 1170s (*DCV*, n. N4, a. 1142; cf. Day et al., *Medieval European coinage*, 12, pp. 555–6), and were, as a result, also more or less £2 Venetian to the *hyperperon* (see also Borsari, *Venezia e Bisanzio*, p. 83). The figures match up, with some minor differences. It should be noted that things changed at the end of our period, when a new Venetian *denarius* was coined in the 1170s at the same weight as that of Verona, and then again in the 1180s, when the Veronesi issued a lighter *denarius*. For all this, see Day et al., *Medieval European coinage*, 12, pp. 63–5, 70–1, 555–7, 636–7, 655–6, with complexities based on analyses of the coins themselves which do not affect the arguments in the text here.

[118] *DCV*, nn. 71 (£1,000), 81, 123, 136, 247, 262 (£1,000), 265, 287, 297, 299, 301, 302, 306, 318 (£1,000), 321, 323; plus the £1,850 Venetian in *DCV*, n. N4, which was worth £925 Veronese. For Genoa's exchange rates with the *hyperperon*, see Chapter 4, n. 175 above; for Genoese trading figures and exchange rates with the Egyptian dinar, see pp. 546–7 with n. 185 below.

[119] Lanfranchi, *S. Giorgio Maggiore*, nn. 136 (Pietro Enzio), 215 (Marino Roibulo); *DCV*, n. 100; for Pietro Ziani, see Fees, *Reichtum und Macht*, pp. 60–75. Pietro Enzio was part of the Encio family, sometimes involved in eastern trading (*DCV*, nn. 80, 167). For the major loans to the commune, see, e.g., Luzzatto, *Studi*, pp. 128–9.

and trading; the trading itself consisted of rather smaller individual operations. Venice's early start in trading (much earlier than that of Genoa, which cannot have significantly got off the ground at all before the late eleventh century, as we shall see), the island city's privileged position in Byzantium (a position Genoa had to negotiate in every region), and even the fluidity of Venetian familiarity with formalized short-term credit from a very early date did not produce a greater scale in actual seagoing commerce. The reason why Venice's investments might have been smaller in scale in our period than those of Genoa may well have simply been its greater separation from the main trading routes of the Mediterranean, set right at the top of a narrow sea as it was. It was probably only the 1204 conquest of Constantinople, and the setting up of a colonial presence in the Aegean, which would really change that. But why neither matched Egypt is easier to explain: the landed backing of the richest families in Venice, as also (as we shall see) in Genoa, was not in any way as substantial in investment terms as that available to officials in a major tax-raising state such as Egypt, or, for that matter, to elites of all kinds in a city as large as Fusṭāṭ-Cairo. Land was not absolutely essential for large-scale profit, as the Ziani show, but they too made their way up with individual investments which were usually quite small.

These restrictions in capital and, in general, in commercial scale in themselves limited the effect Venice could have had on wider exchange systems. It is certainly true that as a city it prospered overall very greatly in our period. In political terms, it punched above its weight; for example, the early revolts in the Veneto in 1164 against Barbarossa's rule were at least in part because of Venetian financial support (or bribes).[120] The city's internal economy was becoming more complex too. A small number of artisans appear casually in twelfth-century Venetian documents; iron, leather, and cloth, in that order, are the main trades—we will come back to iron in a moment. When guilds begin to be documented, in the thirteenth century, the tailors were the first to have statutes, in 1219 (here, smiths had to wait until 1271).[121] And builders of different types were active: San Marco as a church, built in its present form in the late eleventh century, and covered in mosaics inside

[120] From opposite sides, *Historia ducum Venetorum*, ed. Berto, ch. 14–15; Otto and Acerbo Morena, *Historia Frederici I.*, p. 174. The Venetians were genuinely, not only instrumentally, opposed to Barbarossa's regime; see the reference to the *tyrannide Theotonicorum* in a document of 1164, ASV, SZ, b. 4, n. 2 = b. 5, n. 1.

[121] There are some three dozen citations of artisans in twelfth-century Venetian documents, usually in witness lists, which is not so very many; this small number is probably because most people in Venice had surnames, and did not need to use trade names—and, indeed, a few of the artisan names had visibly become surnames by now. Although the figures are too low to be certain guides, metalworkers make up roughly half the citations; leatherworkers come next. Only four cloth workers are recorded, dyers and tailors, but one of the dyers, Giovanni *tintor*, who appears a dozen times, was unusually rich and influential; he lent money, and was present in the ducal *curia*—see, e.g., *CDVE*, 11, n. 2651; *DCV*, n. 277 (= Lanfranchi, *S. Giorgio maggiore*, n. 377); ASV, SZ, b. 35, n. 230. Dyeing is also implied by the references to Venetians importing alum from Egypt. For references to early guild statutes, see Bonfiglio Dosio, 'Le arti cittadine', pp. 578–83; food, cloth, and building trades are the earliest attested, in the 1220s.

from then on through the twelfth, was a huge, highly innovative, and expensive marker of Venetian self-esteem and ambition.[122] Conversely, in terms of its urban material identity, the great days for the city in itself were well in the future. On the Rialto island, the systematic concern for marsh drainage, woodpile foundations and large-scale building (apart from churches) was only really a feature of the thirteenth century. Ca' Vendramin Calergi, an archaeological site beside Venice's casino, on the Grand Canal half a kilometre from the railway station, does show a substantial building which was already being built up in stone and brick, with a pebble courtyard, from the eleventh century onwards. But we also still have plenty of references to wooden buildings, open areas, and marsh; these were not eliminated until after our period ends. Stone buildings slowly become more common in the twelfth century (although, of course, tower houses, frequent in other cities, were not a feature of a city originally built on mud), but they too were not generalized until after 1200.[123] We cannot estimate a population for Venice in our period, and, anyway, 'Venetians' could come from a substantial number of islands, and parts of the nearer coast as well, as they still can; but Rialto itself would not as yet have been able to sustain so large a number of people.

In addition, the city was, as we have seen, overwhelmingly focussed, in international commercial terms, on its dealings with Byzantium. There were many Venetians who in effect lived there, in preference to commuting from Rialto; we saw earlier that some of them refused to come home even when recalled by dukes at times of crisis (p. 337 above).[124] Emperor Manuel's imprisonment of as many as he could find, plus the confiscation of their goods—amounting to 345,000 *hyperpera* (a credible figure; see p. 338 above), not a huge amount for the empire but enormous by the standards of Venice itself, six times the public debt of 1187—struck at the heart of the 'Venetian business model'. Trade with Alexandria and Acre could not make up for that in the fifteen years before peace was restored. Venice before 1204 was more fragile in its international relations than some of its historiography implies. We must not overestimate its economic force in the Mediterranean in our period.

* * *

[122] Demus, *The mosaics of San Marco*, 1, pp. 1–3, 21–30, 280–90.

[123] See in general Dorigo, *Venezia origini*, 2, pp. 516–23. For the archaeology, see Fozzati, *Ca' Vendramin Calergi*, pp. 47–50. In the twelfth century, references to wooden houses are approximately twice as common as those to stone houses, excluding the formulaic *case petrinee et lignee*, which is standard in documents. Sample texts with stone houses are *DCV*, nn. 144, 246; *CDVE*, 8, n. 1121, 12, n. 2642, 16, n. 3131. For wooden houses, see, e.g., Lanfranchi, *S. Giorgio Maggiore*, n. 377; Rosada, *S. Maria Formosa*, nn. 12, 21; *CDVE*, 9, n. 2176, 10, n. 2244, 11, n. 2505, 12, n. 2685; ASV, SZ, b. 7, nn. 11, 32–4, 103–4. Crouzet-Pavan, 'La conquista e l'organizzazione dello spazio urbano', tracks thirteenth-century building and marsh clearance.

[124] Note that the 20,000 Venetians going to the empire in 1171 claimed by a thirteenth-century chronicle, *Historia ducum Venetorum*, ed. Berto, ch. 18, an often cited figure, is a gross exaggeration (that would certainly have made up over half—perhaps nearly all—of the inhabitants of the city).

We need now to look in the other direction, at Venice's relationships with northern Italy as a whole. Venice was, of course, the major link to the sea for all of the Po plain, particularly before the rise of Genoa in the twelfth century—and for the eastern half of the plain, for long afterwards as well. The large-scale salt trade (plus, always, silk and spices, the luxury trade) continued throughout the north, in return, in part, for food for the islands of the lagoon. Our documents show that there were dealings in raw materials as well. I suggested earlier that in the 970s the wooden goods exported from Venice might have come from Istria, and this remained a likely source in the 1170s too, but Romano Mairano was by then, as we have seen, explicitly getting timber from Verona. That is to say, and importantly for the arguments of this chapter, Venice was by now importing at least some goods in bulk from the inland Po plain. Venetian iron, as with the sale to the Templars, implies the same; the alluvial Po plain does not have iron, and it has to have come from somewhere in the Alps—possibly the mountains of Friuli and westwards to the Trentino, where iron deposits are known to have been worked in the later middle ages, but more probably those of the valleys behind Brescia and Bergamo, which we know were active in our period.[125]

We actually know of Venice's own ironworking from as early as the 1030s, thanks to a court case text surviving, anomalously but significantly, in the manuscripts of the main early Venetian chronicle by Giovanni Diacono. In it, a certain Giovanni Sagornino *ferrarius* and his kin, who have been required by the ducal supervisor of ironsmiths (*gastaldus fabri ferrarii*) to work iron for too high a percentage of their time inside the ducal *curtis* and *palacium*, regain their older rights to work ducal iron in a putting-out process in their own workshops (*mansiones*)—that is to say, for profit (the text refers to *capita*, the capital of each smith), not any longer gratis. Ducal interest in iron is obvious here, and important in itself, but the considerable scale of Venetian ironworking is equally clear in the text (other *fabri* are referred to as well). Although we have few enough later documents mentioning artisans, as we have seen, ironsmiths are the most prominent trade in them; and a loan contract of 1131 confirms the sense of scale and family commitment that the Sagornino text gives us—here, a man owes his aunt 291 pounds of iron, made into ploughshares, and pledges as many as four salt pans against their repayment in a month's time. Although this is ploughshares, not swords, the Venetians could, doubtless, make both, and thus sell them on eastwards. All this again required at least some bulk trade from the inland Po plain, to get the iron to the Rialto island.[126] In the same way, we have some evidence that the Venetians made linen using flax from Padua by the early eleventh century (see p. 509 above),

[125] For the late middle ages, see Sprandel, 'Die oberitalienischen Eisenproduktion'; for Brescia and Bergamo in our period, see ibid., pp. 298–302; Menant, 'La métallurgie lombarde', pp. 128–30; Menant, 'Pour une histoire médiévale de l'entreprise minière en Lombardie'; and see p. 600 below.

[126] *Cronache Veneziane antichissime*, ed. Monticolo, pp. 175–6; *DCV*, n. 60.

as well as, very probably, importing cloth from the east. Not only imports from overseas but some of this local production could well have responded in return to a wider north Italian demand as well.

The first known trade treaty between two Italian cities was between Venice and Verona in 1107. Here, the exports from each city to the other included cloth and leather—bulk goods, as with the later reference to Verona's timber.[127] Later in the century, treaties with other cities appear too: Cremona in 1173, Ferrara in 1177 and 1191, Treviso in 1198, and many others after 1200. As for Padua, the closest city and thus a natural enemy, there was a war between the two in 1144, but then, to end it, another early treaty. But actually the Padovani were keen enough to trade with Venice that in 1142 they even deviated the river Brenta to facilitate a water route—with, unfortunately, dramatically disastrous results for local flooding and the silting up of the lagoon, including the annihilation of a whole village. (Similarly, a canal of 1191 linking the Adige and the Po, to improve Venetian communications to the Po itself, was never finished; but evidently the cities concerned, here Mantua and Verona, thought it worth trying.)[128] With the appearance of the communes, and the weakening of the force of the traditional toll concessions made by emperors, Venice thus re-established its relationships with other cities bit by bit, even if with frequent setbacks because of war, and steadily they extended. Ferrara, a particular danger because it was close to the Po route and could block it, was, indeed, in effect instructed by the Lombard League to make the 1177 agreements, in which all parties guaranteed the opening up of the Po to everyone, although one would imagine that the last thing which that city, so well placed commercially as it was, would really have wanted to do was block the Po for more than short periods, to make political points.[129] But, as usual, we cannot tell much from these texts about scale. Northern Italy only once appears in all the Venetian commercial contracts for our period: an agreement concerning £300-worth of goods taken to the Ferrara market in 1160.[130] This may not be a significant absence; it could well be that we simply do not have the documents for non-seagoing trade; but it encourages caution. Archaeology can help us here, however; so let us move onto the material record, to take the argument further.

The dominant ceramics in the whole of the Po plain, right across our period, were coarse wares, above all for cooking and storage. This contrasts very greatly with every other part of the Mediterranean we have looked at so far, both in the level of sophistication of productions themselves and in the absence of ceramic

[127] Castagnetti, *Mercanti, società e politica*, pp. 167–73, has the most recent edition; gold and silver are mentioned too.

[128] For 1142, see Rippe, *Padoue*, pp. 52–3, with earlier bibliography. For the agreements, see Rösch, *Venezia e l'impero*, pp. 170–89, and 67 for the Adige canal. See also n. 48 above.

[129] For 1177, see Manaresi, *Gli atti del Comune*, nn. 105–6, 109. For Ferrara's own economy, which was based on the Po trade, notably its two major fairs, plus fisheries/salt and agriculture, but not artisanal production except some leather, see Castagnetti, *La società ferrarese*, pp. 79–99.

[130] *DCV*, n. 255.

tablewares as part of them. The latter may be explained by different eating habits, or else by proposing that tablewares were not generally ceramic in this period—metal for the rich and wood for the poorer majority have been canvassed. The wood is supported by the 971 text cited earlier (p. 508), which mentions wooden bowls as a product for Venetian export; such bowls have not yet been identified in excavation, even in waterlogged sites such as those in Ferrara, where wooden buildings survive in good condition, but old ones will normally have been used for firewood.[131] More important for us, however, is the considerable simplicity of most of the ceramic productions, which certainly do not attest to elaborate economic processes. We will come back to them later when we look at Lombardy, for there are some signs at least of longer-distance commercialization of some of these coarse types, plus *pietra ollare*, soapstone from the Alps, which was also used to make cooking wares.

Venice and its immediate region participated fully in this basic material culture, including *pietra ollare*.[132] But in Venice there were two differences. First, there were always imports from overseas. We have seen that globular wine amphorae from the Byzantine Aegean were a feature of the eighth and ninth centuries. These were succeeded without a break by the next sets of Byzantine amphora types, above all Otranto 1 from the southern Adriatic and perhaps the Aegean, and, on a smaller scale, Günsenin 1 from the Aegean, plus other Adriatic types.[133] They were above all bringing wine, and show the existence of a continuous traffic with Byzantium in this commodity, to match the documentary evidence for grain and probably oil imports.

The second difference is that the Adriatic coast had its own more elaborate ceramic productions. In the ninth century, a very small-scale production of heavily glazed ceramics is attested, copying the Forum ware of Rome; it was conceivably made at Comacchio (no kilns have been found in this part of Italy at any point in our period, but the clays fit the alluvium of the coast), and was available both at Venice and around Ravenna in small quantities. In the tenth and eleventh centuries, this was succeeded by a Sparse Glaze ware, as again in Rome, above all of partially glazed pitchers; this is sometimes called Sant'Alberto ware, and sometimes simply (as in Rome) *ceramica a vetrina sparsa*. It was again made on the coast, at one or more locations. Its quantities were still not obviously very great, but the scale of production was rather larger, as was the range of its availability,

[131] See Guarnieri and Librenti, 'Ferrara, sequenza insediativa pluristratificata', parts 1 and 2; the same was true for the village site near S. Agata Bolognese, where wooden buildings were found but, explicitly, no wooden bowls: Sbarra, 'I materiali ceramici', p. 148.

[132] For a good synthesis of the general dominance of coarse wares, see Gelichi and Sbarra, 'La tavola di San Gerardo', pp. 120–3. For Venice itself, see, e.g., Fozzati, *Ca' Vendramin Calergi*, pp. 45–7, 95–7, 103–4; Moine et al., *Paesaggi artificiali a Venezia*, pp. 163–6; Maccadanza, *La diffusione della pietra ollare*, pp. 164–6.

[133] See esp. Gelichi et al., 'Importare, produrre, consumare', pp. 56–72; for some case studies, see Moine et al., *Paesaggi artificiali a Venezia*, pp. 159–61; Bortoletto et al., 'Laguna di Venezia', p. 223.

extending across the whole of Romagna plus Venice.[134] It shows a greater degree of productive specialization than was normal in northern Italy before 1100. It at least shows that the eastern Po plain had sufficient demand for a slightly more ambitious product to allow its development and continuous production for two centuries.

These two differences met, after 1050, with the beginnings of glazed imports from the eastern Mediterranean, largely of bowls which could be used for table service. The first so far found in excavations are Egyptian, from, probably, the second half of the eleventh century: a tiny group of 'Fayyumi' and FFS wares, doubtless from Fusṭāṭ, identified at Jesolo on the mainland beside Venice's northern lagoon, and at the monastery of Pomposa (prov. Ferrara), not far from the coast—plus an occasional availability of GWW from Constantinople.[135] In the twelfth century, however, these were far surpassed by a substantial set of Byzantine sgraffito wares from production sites in Greece such as Corinth and Chalkis, particularly the mid- and later twelfth-century types such as Fine Sgraffito, succeeded at the end of the twelfth century and beyond by Zeuxippus ware, plus Günsenin 3 amphorae (for all these typologies, see pp. 86–8, 308–11 above). These are regularly found on sites in and around the lagoon; they are still accompanied by south-east Mediterranean types, fritwares from either Egypt or Syria, but these appear on a much smaller scale.[136] This twelfth-century Byzantine import dominance, of course, fits closely with what we know from documents about the main directions of Venetian overseas trade, as, indeed, do all the other patterns of imported ceramics so far mentioned: they testify to continuous links with Egypt and Byzantium, with those with the latter in particular growing very markedly after 1100. (Sicily and the Maghreb, by contrast—again as we would expect from the documents—are almost unattested.) Clearly, men like Romano Mairano could very well have been carrying glazed pottery in their holds on their return from the eastern Mediterranean, as well as alum, cloth, and so on. The Byzantine types continued to be important in and around Venice until the Venetians themselves began to make glaze, initially imitating south Italian wares in the second quarter of the thirteenth century (Santa Croce ware), and then imitating Byzantine sgraffito in a set of mid-century types, of which the most important was *spirale-cerchio* ware.[137] Venice was in this respect, as we shall see, just like

[134] See esp. Sbarra, 'I materiali ceramici', pp. 173–6, esp. for the range of Sant'Alberto ware; Gelichi, 'Nuove invetriate', which discusses previous work, and abandons (p. 299) the term 'Sant'Alberto ware', coined earlier by the same author.

[135] For Egypt, see Gelichi, 'Islamic pottery' (pp. 121–2 for Pomposa); for GWW, see Moine et al., *Paesaggi artificiali a Venezia*, p. 163; Gelichi et al., *Nonantola 6*, p. 201, much farther from the coast; Fozzati, *Ca' Vendramin Calergi*, pp. 107–8, discusses it for the twelfth century, too. For our whole period, see in general Saccardo et al., 'Ceramiche importate a Venezia'.

[136] Fozzati, *Ca' Vendramin Calergi*, pp. 107–8, 117; Lazzarini and Canal, 'Ritrovamenti di ceramica graffita bizantina'; Lazzarini and Canal, 'Altra ceramica graffita bizantina'; Gelichi et al., 'Importare, produrre, consumare', pp. 95–6; d'Amico, *Byzantine finewares in Italy*, pp. 349, 423–34.

[137] Gelichi, 'Ceramiche "tipo Santa Croce"'; Saccardo, 'Contesti medievali nella laguna'; Saccardo, 'Contributo alla conoscenza'.

Pisa in the early thirteenth century, and Genoa's subordinate town Savona only a little earlier, in producing wares which imitated and partially replaced glazed imports.

The existence of these productions and imports in Venice and its immediate surroundings thus establishes the availability of good-quality ceramics in northern Italy, especially after 1100 but even before. This brings us back to the issue of the scale of the commerce between Venice and the north Italian hinterland (see Map 20). Sparse Glaze (Sant'Alberto) ware in the tenth and eleventh centuries was, as noted earlier, above all available in Romagna, even if not everywhere even there. It has been found on a village site near S. Agata Bolognese on Romagna's inland edge, but a little to the west, it is not seen at San Benedetto Po (prov. Mantua), a rich monastery on the river itself, or at the even richer monastic site of Nonantola (prov. Modena). North of the Po, a good set of Sparse Glaze sherds has been found at Nogara (prov. Verona), but not on other sites in the territory of Verona, even Verona itself. The farthest west it has so far been identified is at Poviglio (prov. Reggio Emilia).[138] Byzantine amphorae from our period are common at Nonantola (especially Otranto 1) and at the market focus of Ferrara, but are rare elsewhere, once the globular amphorae, which had a wider range, faded out in the ninth century.[139] Byzantine glaze from our period has been found at Ferrara again, Treviso north of Venice, Verona, and Modena, but not so far at any rural site apart from Nonantola, which, to repeat, was unusually rich—although many of the most fully excavated rural sites in the eastern Po plain, such as S. Agata and Nogara, stop before 1100, when Byzantine glaze begins to be common on the coast. In all these cases, such finds are normal near Venice and in Romagna, even if (as also elsewhere in the Mediterranean) never in very high percentages by comparison with coarse wares, but as one moves farther west, not all sites have them. Indeed, even when they did, the scale was often tiny: Verona's main published site, which in our period was a central public area including a church and the city's mint, beside the Roman forum, had only three sherds of glazed pottery, only one of them identifiably Byzantine. And west of a line running roughly between Verona and Modena they are almost unknown.[140]

[138] See n. 134 above for where Sparse Glaze has been found; for Nogara, see Buzzo, 'La ceramica invetriata'; for absences, see Gelichi et al., *Nonantola 6*, pp. 199–201; Lusuardi Siena and Giostra, 'Archeologia a San Benedetto Po', pp. 660–1; for Verona, see the absence of reference in Hudson, 'La ceramica medievale'.

[139] Gelichi et al., *Nonantola 6*, pp. 198, 201–3; Librenti and Negrelli, 'Le indagini archeologiche 1990–1991 a Ferrara', pp. 111–13; Guarnieri and Librenti, 'Ferrara, sequenza insediativa pluristratificata', 1, pp. 296–301 (a rich collection of imported and coastal-made ceramics of all kinds).

[140] For Ferrara, see n. 139 above; Gobbo, 'Treviso, ex Ospedale dei Battuti'; for Verona, see Hudson, 'La ceramica medievale', pp. 486–7, also referring to his own unpublished excavation of another Verona site which had a small number of Byzantine sherds; Benassi and Bosi, 'Modena, corso Duomo'; Gelichi et al., *Nonantola 6*, p. 205. Note also the single fragment of unidentified eastern glaze found in a twelfth-century workshop in Piazza Duomo, Milan; see Andrews, 'Lo scavo di piazza Duomo: età medioevale e moderna', p. 176.

Of course, this will be filled out by future excavations. And we always need to remember—as we shall see again—that Lombardy, arguably the north's most active economic subregion from the mid-twelfth century onwards, has so far been much less well excavated than the eastern plain. (I would be very surprised, in particular, if some of these wares did not turn up in the major river port of Cremona, from where I have not seen any published excavation for this period.) But all the same we get a clear sense, from quite an extensive set of sites along and around the north–south line from Verona to Modena, that coastal productions and imports were here only intermittently available, which supports the fact that they have hardly been identified at all farther west.[141] Following the logic seen in the rest of this book, in which we have seen ceramic distributions visibly matching the exchange patterns of other bulk goods, notably cloth—and amphora distributions matching the movement of other foodstuffs—we can conclude that the impact of Venice as a major importing centre, and a less important but not inactive production centre, did not extend on any scale at all into the Po plain beyond a hinterland of some 80–120 kilometres, much of it marshland, until after our period ended.

The Venetians, as already noted, were content with basic cooking wares throughout our period, and in this respect were culturally similar to other northern city and country dwellers. But they were evidently very happy to use Byzantine tablewares when they could get them, which was after 1100 in particular. If this was not the case in Lombardy, the absence seems to me significant. This is especially so because there was one particular use that Lombard elites (particularly ecclesiastical ones) did find for glazed bowls from the east—as *bacini*, bowls used to decorate the facades and campanili of major churches. This was an aesthetic statement which stressed their role, not as tableware, but as luxury goods. The monastery of Pomposa placed eleventh-century Egyptian wares very prominently on its campanile, but they were also identified there in excavation, so were used for other purposes as well. In Pavia, they were equally prominent on the eleventh-century Torre Civica beside the cathedral before it collapsed in 1989; here, no such wares have otherwise been found, except inside the tower itself. Similarly, in the twelfth century, Byzantine *bacini* are present in several buildings in the central Po plain, in areas where no Byzantine ceramics have been found in excavation.[142] That is to say, they were, indeed, available along the river routes; but west of

[141] For absences of these wares on or near that north–south line, from both castle and monastic sites, i.e. elite centres, see Saggioro and Varanini, *Il castello di Illasi*, pp. 165–75 (prov. Verona); Saggioro et al., 'Insediamento ed evoluzione di un castello', pp. 177–82 (Bovolone, prov. Verona); Mancassola, 'Le ceramiche da cucina dal castello di Terrossa' (prov. Verona); Maccadanza and Mancassola, 'La ceramica di cucina' (Leno, prov. Brescia); Brogiolo and Portulano, *La Rocca di Manerba*, pp. 151, 301–7 (prov. Brescia); for San Benedetto Po, see n. 138 above.

[142] For Pomposa and Pavia, see Gelichi, 'Islamic pottery', pp. 119–22; Blake, 'Ceramiche romane e medievali', pp. 147–52; Blake and Aguzzi, 'I bacini ceramici della Torre Civica'. For Byzantine *bacini*, see Gelichi and Berti, 'La ceramica bizantina nelle architetture', esp. pp. 128–34.

Modena and Verona they had *turned into* luxuries, and their use became quite distinct: as a decorative element on elite buildings. So Venice seems to have been a source for bulk goods in the eastern Po plain only; in the centre and the west, it was still a supplier above all of luxuries. At the end of our period, as at the beginning, its major bulk commodity, sent as far as the central plain, probably remained salt. When the inhabitants of Lombardy began to deal with the Mediterranean later in the twelfth century, they did so via Genoa, as we shall see later.

On the basis of all this, I would argue that the eastern Po plain was a rather more fully integrated subregion in economic terms than the Po plain was as a whole. How it actually worked economically is less easy to tell. The Verona–Venice treaty of 1107 is at least an initial guide; Verona was selling cloth and leather to Venice, and later timber; here, the cloth was most probably woollen, for in the thirteenth century Verona was a major woollen manufacturer. Verona merchants were politically influential in the twelfth century too, and there were certainly goods to sell, including cloth and copper, as an account of market tolls from 1173 makes explicit. The documentary traces of Verona's artisans in the twelfth century are not all that generous; cloth-making (weaving, dyeing, and tailoring) is slightly better documented than leather and iron, but the *fabri* who are also documented, here not directly identified with ironworking, could have been any of these. (Note that *faber* could mean a smith in Italy in our period, its standard dictionary meaning, as already in Venice, but could also mean any artisan; it depended on the usage of each city, and I shall make judgement calls in each case.) But anyway, it is at least clear that there was textile activity in the city before 1200; and as early as 985 a fulling mill, for cleaning and thickening wool, is cited in a Veronese document, one of the first such references in Italy. Venice was selling cloth and leather back as well; this cloth was most likely linens and cottons, by now probably imported from Egypt and Byzantium, and (in the case of linen) made locally too; by the 1220s, and plausibly earlier, they also exported olive oil to Verona, which they will have got from Greece, although perhaps they did not add many imported ceramics, for few have been found in Verona, as we have seen.[143]

[143] For Verona, see Castagnetti, *Mercanti, società e politica*, pp. 21–70, 143–7, 167–73 (55–6 for the oil, 61–2 for twelfth-century artisans); but I have taken my own calculations from the edition of the documents of the cathedral chapter, Lanza, *Le carte... di Verona*, 1 and 2, which are only a little more than 10% of the city's charters for the twelfth century but at least are enough, nearly 300, to be representative; ibid., 2, n. IX, is the 1173 document, pointed out to me by Patrizia Mainoni. See further Rossini and Fennell Mazzaoui, 'Società e tecnica nel medioevo'; for 985, see Rossini, 'La tecnica nell'alto medio evo', pp. 733–6. (The reference is not, in fact, the earliest in northern Italy, as Rossini thought. Parma has one from 973; see Malanima, *I piedi di legno*, p. 62; see in general ibid., pp. 45–69; and in fact, the earliest known fulling mills in Italy are in Abruzzo in the central Appennines, starting in the ninth century; see *Ludovici II. diplomata*, n. 86.) Verona was on the edge of Lombardy too, and exported copper, probably from Germany, through Genoa by the end of the twelfth century, a relationship which we do not see in the Venetian documents; see Castagnetti, *Mercanti, società e politica*, p. 55, and n. 205 below; cf. Schaube, *Handelsgeschichte*, pp. 443–50 for data on German dealings with Verona and Venice, which are documented in the later twelfth century (the 1173 market document cited above mentions them, for instance) but picked up markedly in the thirteenth. Castagnetti, *Mercanti a*

To the south, Bologna was expanding rapidly in the twelfth century, and was a plausible third point in a commercial triangle with Venice and Verona. Numerous leather- and metalworkers and some tailors are attested in its twelfth-century documents. As the tailors imply, it seems to have focussed on finishing already woven cloth, until it hired a large number of wool workers from Verona and other cities in 1230–1 to underpin a planned increase in the scale of cloth-making there.[144] That it was closely linked to the Veneto cities in economic terms cannot be said for certain in our period; but we have a single reference to a loan by a Venetian which was taken out in Bologna in 1188, the Venetian church of S. Giorgio Maggiore owned a surprising amount of land in the city's territory, Venice certainly imported grain from nearby Imola, and, to repeat, all this triangle of territory was linked together by the common availability of imported and coastal-made ceramics.[145] These cities may well have been further interconnected thanks to the two great fairs of Ferrara, which sits inside this triangle. And the availability of products was not restricted to cities and elites, for although the excavation at S. Agata Bolognese was quite probably of an ordinary village, its inhabitants could still in the tenth century buy Sant'Alberto ware from the coast—that is to say, there is some evidence here, even if it is not yet extensive, for peasant demand.

Much of this is, in effect, hypothesis; the hard evidence is restricted to the ceramic distributions and the 1107 treaty. It is included here to give a sense of what this subregional economic system, extending across the plain up to some 100 kilometres from the coast but no farther, *could* have looked like. But as we shall see later for Lombardy, the density of economic relations in the interior of northern Italy remained for a long time less great than those closer to the coast; and even the eastern network did not by any means match in density or size the networks of, say, Sicily or the Aegean, before 1200 at the very earliest. Some of the practical implications of this can best be seen by looking at one city in more detail, and here we can turn to Padua, located between Venice and Verona.

Padua was, like most northern Italian cities, an autonomous commune by the second quarter of the twelfth century; its first consuls are attested in 1138, already running court cases. It lay in flat and watery land close to the Brenta river, some 20 kilometres west of the Venetian lagoon. The land between it and the lagoon, the Saccisica, was a significant zone for the production of flax, as we have seen, going back to the ninth century, in fact; there are also by the end of our period increasing numbers of references to retting ditches for the initial preparation for

Verona nel secolo XII, is a recent prosopographical study of some of the merchants themselves; pp. 19–38 list all twelfth-century references to merchants in the city.

[144] For Bologna's twelfth-century urban expansion, associated directly with artisans, see, e.g., Wickham, 'Sulle origini del comune di Bologna', pp. 223–5 (but the topic has not had a focussed study); for 1230–1, see Fennell Mazzaoui, 'The emigration of Veronese textile artisans'.

[145] *DCV*, n. 367; Lanfranchi, *San Giorgio Maggiore*, *passim*; see n. 87 above for Imola.

making linen thread. Many Venetian monasteries and aristocratic families owned land in the Padovano and could exploit it, but so could the *Saccenses* themselves, who included a higher percentage of landowning peasants than in many other places.[146] Padua has little published archaeology for our period, but both standing buildings and documents show that elites, here as elsewhere on the Italian mainland, were investing in brick and stone tower houses by the twelfth century.[147] Historians argue that Padua as a manufacturing centre did not really take off until the thirteenth century, later than Verona, but already by 1219 linen workers (*linaroli*, mostly from the Saccisica) had a guild (*misterium*) and a recognized selling point in Verona, in 1216 cloth merchants appear in the city council, a guild list survives from the 1230s, and by the 1240s, perhaps the 1230s, there was also a wool-working area on the edge of town.[148] So Padua would end up, across the decades after 1200, a fairly typical participant in the production and exchange network which, by the mid-thirteenth century, characterized northern Italy almost everywhere.

In our period, Padua had an important market on the southern edge of town, now the Prato della Valle, a curiously compelling open space relaid out in the eighteenth century, and a series of water routes to neighbouring cities such as Vicenza and, of course, Venice; but references to merchants themselves are sparse.[149] It is largely for this reason that Padua is generally reckoned to have started relatively late as an economic focus. But, as noted earlier, even if Padua's closeness to Venice meant political friction, it also meant a potential trading relationship which the Padovani were keen to further. The city's economic structure certainly became more complex. After 1100, we find some short-term and/or usurious loans, resembling those we have seen for Venice, always against a pledge of land, some of these referring to the crops grown for the period of the loan as interest, *usuris*. In four cases there is an explicit reference to interest in money, here called *proficuum* (a typical word for profit in Genoa and sometimes Pisa) rather than the commonest word in Venice, *prode*. This shows that the Padovani were choosing their own legal formularies here, not just borrowing them from Venice, and also shows some fluidity in the city's commercial economy, even if the interest demanded in them varied so greatly, from 12.5 per cent to 33 per cent, that we could not say that Padua had a settled practice.[150] In addition, we find references,

[146] Rippe, *Padoue*, pp. 179–84 (Saccisica), 336–46 (consuls, with Gloria, *Codice diplomatico padovano dall'anno 1101*, n. 339, the first citation), 569–73 (flax).

[147] Chavarría Arnau, *Padova: architetture medievali*, pp. 23–33, 228–49. The major excavation I have seen, Chavarría Arnau, *Ricerche sul centro episcopale*, showed very little from our period.

[148] For the thirteenth century, see Rippe, *Padoue*, pp. 661–3, 757; Bortolami, *Urbs antiquissima et clara*, pp. 278–81; Castagnetti, *Mercanti, società e politica*, pp. 85–91.

[149] For the market, see Gloria, *Codice diplomatico padovano dal secolo sesto*, n. 237 (= Manaresi, *I placiti*, 3, n. 439), 2, nn. 432, 501, 1147, 1227; Gloria, *Codice diplomatico padovano dall'anno 1101*, n. 1182 (a. 1175), is the first reference to a *mercator*.

[150] Gloria, *Codice diplomatico padovano dall'anno 1101*, nn. 9–10 (part of a complex set of deals), 109, 125, 154, 265, 402, 452, 1284. Note, now that we have reached the more agricultural mainland,

beginning in the late eleventh century and becoming more frequent in the twelfth, to artisans, in the city, the countryside and the rising *burgus* of Monselice: in the century after 1080, some 90 separate figures in over 1,400 documents, a larger number than in many Italian towns (including Venice, in fact), even if smaller, given the numbers of artisans set against the number of documents, than Verona. The commonest are leather- and ironworkers, but tailors, and a few dyers and weavers, appear as well. There was also a potter, *ollarius*, in 1169, a maker of coarse storage or cooking jars. The leatherworkers were overwhelmingly urban, but the tailors and dyers appear most often in the Saccisica; evidently rural linen-making, including finishing, was developing there in the twelfth century already, as an alternative to sending raw flax to Venice, which fits the *linaroli* of 1219.[151] We can see here the first signs of the later thirteenth-century take-off for the city. These attestations, although casual ones as usual, are, in fact, not so very much out of line with those for Verona; they imply an earlier start for an active urban economy in Padua than has been implied by other writers, even if Verona was already ahead, and Veronese woollen cloth-making later, in the thirteenth century, became more important than the cloth of not only Padua, but also most other cities.

The point here is that Padua was, indeed, developing economically—not fast, but steadily. It obviously will have been helped in this by its nearness to its island neighbour. But the way Padua's isolated references to artisans in the twelfth century are fleshed out in the thirteenth by references to greater concentrations of them, and to their guilds, and to their greater political activity, is typical of a great number of Italian cities.[152] Conversely, this pattern of development diverges from anything we can see in Venice, except in the thirteenth-century date for early guilds. Venice was hyperactive economically, and visibly rich, as a maritime trading centre, already in the eleventh century and still more in the twelfth, as we have seen at length—and as historians take for granted. This fact is as intriguing to me as it has been to plenty of others. I have argued here that it had a smallish Italian hinterland for bulk trading as well, in which buyers could, indeed, be interested in imported goods, and perhaps Venetian-made goods as well, even if we know little about them, and even if the networks were probably not as yet very intense; that hinterland certainly included Padua. But what we see in the

that the appearance of credit documents does not mean the appearance of credit–debt relations in themselves; rural and urban credit exists in all complex societies—not least in early and central medieval Latin Europe, where low-value coins were mostly not minted—and such texts simply show that it has reached the documentary record. But regularized documentation for credit and references to interest are at least indicative of the greater formalization of such transactions, which is in itself a sign of a more fluid economy.

[151] Lists in Gloria, *Codice diplomatico padovano dall'anno 1101*, pp. lxiv-vi. The *ollarius* is n. 959; for Verona, cf. Lanza, *Le carte... di Verona*, 1, n. 114; 2, nn. 44, 113. For cloth-making in the Saccisica, see Gloria, *Codice diplomatico padovano dall'anno 1101*, nn. 85, 180, 412, 518, 683, 858. For Monselice, see Bortolami, 'Monselice "oppidum opulentissimum"', p. 115.

[152] See, e.g., Degrassi, *L'economia artigiana*; Greci, *Corporazioni*, pp. 93–128.

economic history of the nearest city to the lagoon is a type of development in productive intensity which seems to have owed very little to Venice at all. Venice was an important part of an eastern Po plain exchange network, but the rest of that network was far from being markedly influenced by Venice's special, Mediterranean-focussed economy. The opportunity for Padua, and, by extension, doubtless Verona and Bologna as well, to look to possible organic links with the seagoing trade which was going on so actively a day's journey away, by donkey or by boat, was already there in our period, but it was not being taken up very fully as yet. Visible exchange links between Venice and its neighbours existed and were easy, but, in fact, seem to have been less focussed than those of Genoa over the Appennine pass to Lombardy, when the latter finally took off, at the very end of the twelfth century. This seems to me significant, and we will return to it.

6.4 Genoa

We have so far looked at the Genoese as external figures, intervening in the maritime economy of the twelfth century in Egypt and especially Sicily. They were also active, to a rather lesser extent, in Byzantium and al-Andalus, and were developing their trading in North Africa and the Levant as well—a wider spread than even Venice. Now, as with Venice, we have to look at these processes, at least summarily, from the point of view of the city itself. This is particularly essential, because the development of the Genoese economy has been and has remained at the heart of the whole grand narrative of the 'commercial revolution'. And, it has to be said, not wrongly. When it comes to twelfth-century commerce, no part of Italy—or the Mediterranean as a whole—is as well documented as Genoa. It has the earliest surviving notarial register, that of Giovanni Scriba from the years 1154–64, over 1,300 documents in total, which largely focuses on trading transactions from the start. These are then followed, after our period ends, by those of Oberto Scriba de Mercato, from 1179 to 1214, and Guglielmo da Sori from 1191 to 1202, both more incomplete; the full register of Guglielmo Cassinese for sixteen months of 1190–2, including a massive set of 1,442 documents for 1191 alone; and then several others from the end of the 1190s onwards.[153] As noted earlier, no other city (except Savona, dependent on Genoa) has more than fragmentary equivalents before the 1220s. So, while we had hundreds of commercial documents to illuminate Venice, we have thousands for Genoa.

These are backed up by two other significant sources: the most detailed civic chronicle for twelfth-century Italy, beginning in 1099, which pays great attention

[153] See *Giovanni Scriba*, *Oberto Scriba 1186* and *1190*, *Guglielmo Cassinese*, plus the lists of other notaries in (among other places) *Cartolari notarili genovesi*; Meyer, *Felix et inclitus notarius*, pp. 188–90; Calleri, 'Un notaio genovese'.

to Genoa's Mediterranean projection; and one of the most substantial surviving sets of *Libri iurium*, the cartulary collections of the official documents of a city commune, dating initially to the mid-thirteenth century in the case of Genoa, which also contain very many texts concerning Genoa's Mediterranean relationships from 1098 onwards.[154] All of this is in addition to more ordinary document collections, both originals and archiepiscopal cartularies, which tell us less about commerce than those of Venice, but which all the same show how much the archbishop himself profited from it; and there is some urban archaeology, which, however, is here secondary to what we can learn from written texts.[155] If the notarial registers give us less direct information about what was actually traded, as we have already seen, and if they are also much less generous in their information about personal relationships than are the *geniza* letters, all the same they lend themselves to serial treatment in a way that no other sources from the twelfth century do, and an array of scholars have taken advantage of this. The fact that Giovanni Scriba, the *Libri iurium*, the archbishop's cartularies, and the annals were already all published in the nineteenth century, even if in editions of varying quality (most have now been replaced), means that Genoa figured large in the foundational texts for Mediterranean trade, particularly Adolf Schaube's monumental survey of the whole Mediterranean from 1906, and then, of course, the works of Roberto Lopez. The fact that the Genoese registers do not only start early but also continue, on an ever larger scale, across the thirteenth century and later, has also meant that if there is anywhere where the easy commonplaces of 'commercial revolution' historiography are actually valid, it is here; for it was on the basis of Genoese evidence that they were above all forged.[156]

But all the same, we have to go beyond this. Genoa, even more than Venice, was not a major producer city for the most part, until after our period ends. It was dependent on others not only for the consumption of the majority of the goods it traded, but also for their creation—the only artisanal products it seems to have made itself on any scale before the 1180s were metal and leather, as we shall see.

[154] *Annali genovesi*, 1–2, ed. Belgrano and Imperiale di Sant'Angelo, contain the twelfth-century sections of the annals. For the *Libri iurium*, I cite both scientific editions, the convenient chronological sequence in *CDGE*, and the most recent edition in *LI*, 1, which follows the sequence as set out in the *Libri* themselves. *CDGE* includes some other communal texts, and misses out a handful of texts from the *Libri*, so both are needed.

[155] The major editions of originals for our period are Calleri, *Le carte del monastero di San Siro*, 1, and Calleri, *Codice diplomatico del monastero di Santo Stefano*, 1. The archiepiscopal cartularies are edited in Belgrano, 'Il registro della curia arcivescovile' and Belgrano and Berretta, 'Il secondo registro'. For the archaeology, see nn. 210–11, 213 below.

[156] Schaube, *Handelsgeschichte*. Lopez was the main driver for later developments of this, especially in his *Studi sull'economia genovese*; but it is important also to signal the early interest of American scholars in the notarial registers, which resulted in the publication of several of them, as well as path-breaking early articles such as Byrne, 'Genoese trade with Syria', from 1920, Reynolds, 'The market for northern textiles in Genoa', from 1929, and Krueger, 'Genoese trade with northwest Africa', from 1933. Robert Reynolds's support in turn allowed Lopez to begin his new academic career in the USA after he left Italy in 1939; see Guglielmotti, 'Lopez, Roberto Sabatino'.

The extent of its commerce is, therefore, above all a guide to the economic activity and complexity of other regions. It also had still less of a hinterland than Venice. Venice, although politically independent, was a major player in the politics and economy of the eastern Po plain, as we have seen, which was always an economically active area; Pisa too, as we shall see, had a similar role in the steadily developing economy of western Tuscany. Genoa was, however, in the centre of Liguria, a narrow coastal strip rising sharply into the Appennine mountains. Not only did it not have direct river routes into a hinterland, as the other two cities did, but it was cut off from the Po plain by these mountains; the best one can say is that the pass separating Genoa from Lombardy is low and easy. Liguria is also one of the parts of Italy with the least prosperous agriculture. The Genoese took political control of the whole coastline from Ventimiglia in the west to Porto Venere in the east fairly quickly in the early twelfth century, which involved establishing hegemony over potentially rival cities such as Savona, but it is significant that this did not in itself bring a secure food supply for an expanding city. Already in the 1120s–1140s, communal regulations show that grain imports by sea were important, much more than they were for Venice: ships carrying grain from Sardinia, Corsica, Sicily, and elsewhere paid lower tolls than others, as did salt ships from Sardinia and Provence. Sicily was probably the main supplier, and the 1156 treaty with William I of Sicily regularized the traffic.[157]

That this was essential for Genoa is shown by what happened when the Sicilian king closed down trade with the north in 1162–74 (see pp. 256–7 above), for it had to look for alternative sources of food supply, which carried their own risks. One was the Po plain, as the events of 1171 showed, recorded in the city's contemporary *Annals*: when Genoa was required to choose between the Lombard League and Barbarossa, it chose the emperor, but the Lombards then stopped sending it wheat, and it faced famine for a time.[158] This is the only reference to Lombardy supplying Genoa with food, however. The famine of 1171 only makes any sense in the context of the temporary end of Sicilian wheat imports, and it is likely that this supply crisis was one of the reasons for the re-establishment of trade links

[157] For the takeover of the coast, the key sources are the *Annali genovesi* and *CDGE/LI*: all accounts base themselves on these. These include Polonio, 'Da provincia a signora del mare' and Epstein, *Genoa and the Genoese*, both of which stick closely to the sources. For twelfth-century Savona, which had its own commune and political life under Genoese hegemony, see Rao, 'Cavalieri, mercanti e consoli'. For grain and salt, see esp. *LI*, 1, nn. 3, 5; 2, n. 289, the 1156 treaty (*CDGE*, 1, nn. 51, 119, 279); Belgrano, 'Il registro della curia arcivescovile', pp. 9–10, 56–9 (in which tolls are called the *decima de mari*—they were not at all a literal tenth in these cases, but the phrase recalls the standard 10% toll accepted across the Mediterranean). The dues from grain and salt ships were generally calculated in *minae*, with the dues in *minae* owed to different powers in Genoa counted in single figures, but a *mina* was only just over 100 litres (Jehel, *Les Génois*, p. 462). The small scale of these dues is shown by a contract of 1160 (*Giovanni Scriba*, n. 722), in which a ship carried 1,500 *minae* of salt; cf. also ibid., n. 181, in which 2,600 *minae* were commercially warehoused in the city. In the thirteenth century, Provence matched Sicily as a grain supplier; see Jehel, *Les Génois*, pp. 339–40.

[158] *Annali genovesi*, 1, ed. Belgrano, p. 246.

three years later. The event thus illustrates the unusual degree to which Genoa depended on others even for a basic staple of life; we cannot track a similar grain trade, long-distance and between independent polities, on a regular basis anywhere else in our period, even for the really large cities of the Mediterranean, cities far larger than Genoa. The Ligurian city depended on others just as much for the artisanal products which made up most of the rest of its trade. The grand narrative of the 'commercial revolution' sets Genoa up as the tough guy, even more than its Italian competitors, starting from nowhere but imposing itself by force across the Mediterranean regions by the early twelfth century, and then developing trade links with verve from Flanders to Egypt, and into the Black Sea a century later—to repeat, the widest geographical stretch of any other Mediterranean port, ahead of Alexandria, Venice, and Pisa alike, at least in this respect. But although most of that is true (even if a city of some 20,000 inhabitants— we will come back to the figure—could not control the economy of millions), it needs to be remembered that it had no choice, if it was to get past being a smallish town in a poor hinterland—a problem neither Venice nor Pisa faced to anything like the same degree—and that it had to keep on pushing outwards, to stay in the same place.

To see how this worked, let us look at Genoa chronologically, up to and including the decade around 1160 covered by Giovanni Scriba's register. Then we will need to look forward, more summarily, to the years around 1190—after our period, but actually the first moment when we can see important changes in the economy of the city and of some of the places it traded with.

Genoese documentation before 1100 is more or less restricted to land transactions, as is normal in Italy, without the credit texts (Venice) and poetic narratives (Pisa) which shed light on the activity of the other major port cities, so exactly what the Ligurian city was up to commercially in the eleventh century remains relatively obscure.[159] But it is at least clear that the Genoese fought alongside the Pisans in Sardinia against Mujāhid of Denia in 1015–16, and again against Mahdia in the raid of 1087; they had active shipping already. There are occasional references to Genoese trading in Egypt in *geniza* letters of the mid-century too; and there was evidently a stable Genoese presence there in the first years of the twelfth century, because its members were imprisoned for a time by the Egyptian ruler.[160] This fits with the fact that the rights in Levantine cities which the victorious

[159] There are groups of eleventh-century texts in, in particular, Calleri, *Le carte del monastero di San Siro*, 1; Calleri, *Codice diplomatico del monastero di Santo Stefano*, 1; and Belgrano: 'Il registro della curia arcivescovile', esp. in the appendix; but fewer than a hundred in each.

[160] The wars only appear in Pisan sources; see Maragone, *Annales pisani*, ed. Lupo Gentile, pp. 4–5; Scalia, 'Il carme pisano', ll. 36, 41, 134, 197, 232; see further p. 559 below. For the Egyptian letters, see ENA NS 2.13 (Gil K749 [S145]), T-S 10J16.17, Bodl. MS Heb. b 3/26 (Gil K420, 794, partial trans. Goitein, *MS*, 1, pp. 318, 45); see p. 144 above. See Kedar, 'Mercanti genovesi in Alessandria', for some discussion. For a positive picture of Genoese maritime activity before 1100, see Musarra, 'Genova e il mare nell'Alto Medioevo'.

Crusaders granted the Genoese in 1098–1109 in return for their army supply and for their direct military engagement (which were, indeed, doubtless the cause of the Egyptian reprisals against them) so firmly focus on trading privileges. They included, among other things, a *fundūq* in Antioch, a whole third of (among others) the towns of Lādhiqīya, Tripoli, Caesarea, and Acre, and general freedom from port dues, not only for Genoa but for other Ligurian towns under its control, in particular Savona and Noli.[161]

These privileges have been seen as themselves the origin of Genoese future commerce; that is mistaken, given the pre-existing Egypt route. But we also have, as with the other port cities, no real sense of scale in this period; we have seen (pp. 134, 140) that the scale of all Rumī involvement in Egyptian trade before the twelfth century was relatively minor, and any build-up could not have occurred fast. All the same, to some degree or other the Genoese were already active as traders in the eastern Mediterranean, including being, by now, more visible in Egypt, and, as we saw in Chapter 3, they were in Sicily shortly afterwards as well. This fits with the fact that, in archaeological terms, small quantities of Islamic glazed wares are found on sites in both Genoa and Savona already in the eleventh century, even if these came from Sicily and Ifrīqiya, rather than from farther east.[162] Eleventh-century Sicilian amphorae have been found in Liguria too, probably for wine (see p. 228 above), although that trade dropped back in the twelfth century, and is not documented in written texts. A thin network of trading with Genoa already covered much of the Mediterranean at the end of the eleventh century, then, although (as with Venice) exactly what the Genoese were selling can only be guessed at.

This was the basis for much more certain evidence in the first half of the twelfth century, the period of the rapid crystallization of Genoa's city commune, and thus of communal documentation. Genoa had consuls by 1098, who were running court cases by 1105, and issuing legislation by 1130—rather earlier than in any other Italian city except Pisa.[163] More than one might expect of this legislation concerned urban infrastructure. In 1133–4, the consuls decreed that the colonnade in front of the houses along the sea should be in stone, not wood, and they set out norms for building above it; they also legislated on the width of new streets, and gave instructions to specific citizens as to how they should build their own sections of these colonnades. In 1138 they reordered the port as well.[164] The

[161] *LI*, 1, n. 61 (it also survives in an authenticated contemporary copy), 119 (*CDGE*, 1, nn. 15, 24), with *CDGE*, 1, nn. 7, 11. Some of these grants are repeated later across the century; see, e.g., *LI*, 2, nn. 337, 341 (*CDGE*, 1, n. 47; 2, n. 49). Van Doosselaere, *Commercial agreements*, pp. 33–4, comments sensibly on the implications of these texts.

[162] De Vingo, 'La céramique d'importation islamique dans la Ligurie médiévale', pp. 283–8, and see further n. 210 below.

[163] For the basic analyses, see Bordone, 'Le origini del comune di Genova'; Dartmann, *Politische Interaktion*, pp. 121–294. Cf. Wickham, *Sleepwalking*, pp. 162–6.

[164] *LI*, 1, n. 24, 2, nn. 567–8 (*CDGE*, 1, nn. 67–8, 93). Basic for the urban patterning of the city in this period is Grossi Bianchi and Poleggi, *Una città portuale del medioevo*, pp. 40–75.

city was expanding rapidly in the eleventh and early twelfth century too, which compounded the problems of ensuring food supply. The extra-urban church of S. Siro was already by 1034 *in burco novo*, and this *burgus* was larger than the old *civitas* in size by the late 1150s, when (as in Pisa) the consuls put considerable effort and money into building a new wall which included both (see Map 26). One recent historian has postulated a population of 20–40,000 people by the end of the twelfth century. The higher figure here seems to me unsustainable, but we might think of around 20,000 as a ballpark guesstimate for Genoa's population in the third quarter of the twelfth century.[165] This figure is lower than the more certain estimate possible for Pisa in the 1220s, of 24–27,000 (see p. 571 below; as noted earlier, we cannot offer a comparable one for Venice). That difference, however, seems fully defensible to me: the Pisan estimate is for a city with a walled area rather larger than Genoa's, even if we have to balance that fact against the indications that Genoa's population filled its own walls and was already fairly dense, whereas Pisa's walls enclosed some areas of relatively empty space. Genoa's exceptional documentation by twelfth-century standards has sometimes in the past underpinned an assumption that Pisa was always the also-ran in their economic projection and rivalry, but up to the end of our period and beyond that was far from clear, as we will see in the next section of this chapter.

As for urban density, tower houses appear, as they do in all mainland Italian cities, with regularity in texts from here on (the consuls enacted that they should not be more than 80 feet, some 24 metres, in height, a figure adhered to in at least one private document). So does a sewer in a sale of 1162, unusually early for Italy (when sewers are stressed in such texts, it means that buildings are close together), although, unlike in Islamic regions, it simply ran into the street.[166] Several urban excavations, notably those of the archbishop's two residences, show us the considerable scale of ambition that elite building interventions could reach already in the late eleventh century.[167] And particularly important is the fact that in the 1140s the consuls were having to make sure that open spaces were preserved, as with the *vacuum de Sarzano* on the southern edge of the *civitas*, which in 1145 was to remain devoid of building, because the city's *populus* (i.e. the urban assembly) met there. In the same year, the monastery of S. Siro was allowed to build on the Castelletto hill to the north of the town, located only just inside the future

[165] Calleri, *Le carte del monastero di San Siro*, 1, n. 33; cf. nn. 54–5, 68, etc.; for the wall, see ibid., nn. 120–1 (a. 1156), fitting the beginning of the wall-building in 1155 in *Annali genovesi*, 1, ed. Belgrano, pp. 41; cf. 48, 51, 54, 60. For 20–40,000 people, see Polonio, 'Da provincia a signora del mare', p. 160, an open guess. For the extent of the new walled city, 55 hectares, see Hubert, 'La construction de la ville', pp. 113–14.

[166] The 80-foot rule is set out in *CDGE*, 1, n. 128 (p. 165), the text of the consular oath; for it being obeyed, see *Giovanni Scriba*, n. 668 (a. 1160); the sewer is ibid., n. 1012 (cf. also n. 1054). Other towers are referenced ibid., nn. 54, 667, 731, 916, 1216. The twelfth-century Embriaci tower has been excavated; see Boato, 'La torre degli Embriaci'; for other tower houses, see Cagnana and Mussardo, 'Le torri di Genova'.

[167] Surveyed in Cagnana, 'Residenze vescovili fortificate'.

walls, as long as the overall space remained *vacuum*, so that 'the *populus* can see from there the city and the sea'. In 1186 the consuls also regularized the space of the city's three main markets, measuring them out in detail, in feet and inches, with respect to neighbouring houses.[168] The concern for planning shown by the colonnades and these open areas, which have as yet no parallels in other cities, clearly shows the degree to which the consuls of the Genoese commune saw the city's *urbanistica*, which was focussed on the port and its markets—and on the rebuilding of the cathedral, which was also being facilitated by the consuls later in the century[169]—as a collective good, just as they did the city's food supply.

That collectivity was not undermined by the more difficult political events of the second half of the century. Genoa mostly stayed out of the Barbarossa wars, but it faced plenty of other challenges. One was the heavy debts which the commune faced after the debacle of the conquest of Tortosa (see p. 404 above), which led to political stasis in the 1150s—the city's first annalist, Caffaro di Caschifellone, refers to the city in 1154 as 'sailing the sea without a helmsman', in a maritime image which recalls those used in Byzantium (see p. 269 above)—until the city paid off what seems to have been its main creditor, the commune of Piacenza, with £6,000 in money and commodities in 1154–5.[170] Another was, after 1160, over thirty years of on-and-off factional fighting between Genoa's leading families, who also, as in all Italian city communes in the twelfth century, controlled the government. The coherence of Genoa as a collective entity was, by contrast, sustained by the more serious (and expensive) turf war with Pisa, which was fought out at sea, in Constantinople, and above all in Sardinia, in particular in 1162–75, although already in 1118–33 too. The factional conflicts, which reached their height in the early 1190s before a comprehensive peace in 1194–5, rarely undermined that cohesion abroad. And they certainly did not undermine Genoa's economic activity, which, indeed, developed rapidly in the same years.[171]

We can get a proper sense of that activity for the first time, as it concerned Genoa itself, in the years around and after 1130. Two entries near the start of the

[168] *LI*, 1, n. 63 (*CDGE*, 1, n. 142); Calleri, *Le carte del monastero di San Siro*, 1, n. 107 (a. 1145; see also *LI*, 1, n. 53); for the market, see *LI*, 1, n. 272 (*CDGE*, 2, n. 151).

[169] *LI*, 1, n. 230 (*CDGE*, 2, n. 87).

[170] 'Without a helmsman', *sine gubernatore* (a phrase perhaps taken from Suetonius, *De vita caesarum*, 7.1), see *Annali genovesi*, 1, ed. Belgrano, p. 37; cf. a similar image for 1169, ibid., p. 220. The Piacenza money is documented in *LI*, 1, nn. 170–5, 178 (*CDGE*, 1, nn. 252–7, 260–1). It is possible that Genoa's regular direct taxation, documented from 1165, began as a result of the Tortosa fiscal crisis around 1154; see Felloni, 'Note sulla finanza pubblica', pp. 342–3, 351; Mainoni, 'Sperimentazioni fiscali', pp. 719–20; but the beginning of the war against Pisa in 1162, with all the expense of replacing war galleys, seems to me a more immediate explanation.

[171] The fullest survey of the faction fighting is Inguscio, *Reassessing civil conflicts in Genoa*; among other things he shows, through a network analysis based on the notarial registers, that the two main opposing factions had notably few commercial relations with each other. The structural analysis in Greif, *Institutions*, pp. 217–37, is based on too many errors of fact and false assumptions to need further consideration; see Inguscio, *Reassessing civil conflicts in Genoa*, pp. 175–6, 278–81, for one of several critiques. For the war with Pisa (one of the elements Greif ignores), see Polonio, 'Da provincia a signora del mare', pp. 161–7; and esp. Bernwieser, *Honor civitatis*, pp. 37–239.

Libri iurium record tolls for entry into the city in, respectively, 1128–30 and before 1139: men from a set of French and Italian ports pay specific sums of money per person; slave dealers from Barcelona pay more; men *de ultramontanis partibus* (i.e. northern France or the Low Countries) pay money for each bale of wool or hemp (probably in each case cloth, not thread); Lombards from the Po plain pay for bringing in cloth and arms; from Pisa, money is paid on iron; from Sicily, Alexandria, and Antioch, on cotton; from anywhere, it is paid on pepper, coral, cinnamon, tin, and copper, as well as on dyes (brazilwood and lac), and alum as a dye fixer. These texts do not tell us about scale either, but they at least delineate the goods which were coming into the city, in most cases to be then exchanged for others and re-exported; and they are the goods which, by and large, mark Genoa out for the next century and more. The tolls due on goods like these, plus grain and salt, and—by 1149—linen, oil, almonds, and pitch, were evidently in themselves financially important to the city.[172] They were also divided up, with a substantial portion going to the archbishop from 1117 onwards, who defended his rights in a dozen court cases surviving in his cartularies across the rest of the century, and others going to communal officials; furthermore, sections of them were at times sold off for specified periods to raise money to pay communal debts.[173]

This was the background for a set of trade treaties, again mostly surviving in the *Libri iurium*. They are with coastal towns in Liguria, Provence, and Languedoc, and, in the 1150s above all, Ibn Mardanīsh in Valencia, the Byzantine emperor, the king of Sicily, and (a text not surviving) the Almohad caliph—in effect, given Genoa's continuing visibility in the Levant as well, with every player in the Mediterranean. The Ligurian and French treaties were in part intended to restrict the rights of the towns concerned, which, in the case of Savona and even, more surprisingly, Montpellier, required ships from that city to start from Genoa when trading outside the north-west Mediterranean; the treaties with powers farther afield assumed that it would be Genoese ships which would be coming in and paying stable, reduced, or sometimes zero tolls. Successive treaties with Pisa were more between equals, and also more fraught; in 1149, one explicitly excluded Sardinia, which the two cities were fighting over, although the treaty of 1175, a longer-lasting one, simply split the island into spheres of influence.[174]

[172] *LI*, 1, nn. 3, 6, 123 (the first and last are *CDGE*, 1, nn. 51, 200). For this period, see Abulafia, *The two Italies*, pp. 70–6.

[173] For the archbishop, see Belgrano, 'Il registro della curia arcivescovile', pp. 56–9, 110, 117–18, 127–8, 269–70, 391, 396, 404, 460; Belgrano and Beretta, 'Il secondo registro', nn. 137, 150, 183 (these rights involved an unusual amount of contestation and evasion by others); for one communal official, see *LI*, 1, n. 5 (*CDGE*, n. 119); for the handing over of toll rights to private persons, see, e.g., *LI*, 1, nn. 113, 134, 150 (*CDGE*, 1, nn. 132, 193, 227); Belgrano and Beretta, 'Il secondo registro', nn. 22, 54.

[174] See in general, e.g., Jehel, *Les Génois*, pp. 19–22, 34–43. For restrictions on commerce, see *LI*, 1, n. 156 (Savona), 2, nn. 940–1 (Montpellier; *CDGE*, 1, nn. 236, 266–7), a selection from a much larger set; for treaties with more distant powers, see *LI*, 1, nn. 118 (Valencia), 181 (Byzantium), 2, n. 289 (Sicily; *CDGE*, 1, nn. 196, 271, 279), with *Annali genovesi*, 1, ed. Belgrano, p. 62 for the Almohads. For Pisa, see esp. *CDGE*, 1, nn. 64, 80, 195, 2, nn. 101–2. A treaty, or a treaty draft, also survives in

Few of these texts tell us much about goods sold; they were more concerned with stabilizing the Genoese commercial network on terms as favourable as possible to the Ligurian city. The main exceptions are the treaty with Ibn Mardanīsh, which specified a tribute to Genoa in silk, which was thus not going to be sent, strictly speaking, by trading; and the 1156 Sicily treaty, which, as we have seen (pp. 256–7), stressed sales of wheat and cotton above all. Two further documents, however, shed some light on this. One, from 1153, is a ten-year agreement with Lucca, which was Pisa's enemy and thus Genoa's ally, but the relation between the two was more organic than that; the Lucchesi were here to be allowed to use Genoa as a base for taking goods *ad ferias ultramontanas*, probably already the Champagne and perhaps also the Flanders fairs, and to bring back goods which are not *contrarie nostris mercibus*, 'contrary to our [Genoese] goods': these were white, blue, and grey-blue cloth, on which they would pay tolls at 5*s* per bale. In 1157, the text of the oath sworn by every member of the commune of Genoa also listed goods which were not *contraria* to Genoese commodities: here they are, strikingly, cloth, copper, tin, iron, and coral.[175] That as late as 1157 the Genoese could regard cloth and metal, the main artisanal products in any bulk commercial system in our period, as not seriously in competition with their own trading, tells us a good deal about their expectations in the first half of the century. They must have been above all trading in luxury goods such as spices and pepper, plus raw cotton, and, of course, grain and salt for the city's own food supply. This gives us an indication not only of the geographical spread of the city's trade, but also of its limits. When it came down to the important commodities, notwithstanding the wide range of goods in the 1130s toll lists, the Genoese carrying trade would seem to have been largely dominated, into the mid-twelfth century, by high-cost products, with the exception—which we will come back to—of Sicilian cotton.

If not in 1157, however, at least very soon after, the communal oath would have been out of date. The notarial register of Giovanni Scriba, with its 1,300-plus transactions covering the years 1154–64, a good third of which concern overseas trading, gives us an idea of scale for the first time, and some information about the goods as well. This register has been discussed and unpicked a dozen times. It would overload this chapter to do so again, and it is unnecessary to do so, given the main focus of study by previous historians, which has been, indeed, the direction and scale of transactions, as well as their legal nature, and the structure of partnerships.[176] I will to an extent rely on them for that, while also paying

contemporary copy for Venice; see *CDGE*, 1, n. 76 (a. 1136). The Fāṭimids in Egypt do not appear in this set, but a fragment of what looks very like a Fāṭimid treaty survives among the last folios of Giovanni Scriba's register, *Giovanni Scriba*, 2, p. 259n; see Rustow, *The lost archive*, pp. 78, 306–7 (cf. n. 178 below).

[175] *LI*, 1, n. 162 (*CDGE*, 1, n. 238), *CDGE*, 1, n. 285 (pp. 354–5). For the cloth colours, see Poloni, *Lucca nel Duecento*, p. 44; for Lucca, see further pp. 581–5 below.

[176] The *commenda*, in which the sedentary merchant provided all or most of the capital (but most typically two-thirds) and divided the profits with the travelling merchant, was overwhelmingly the dominant contract by the end of the twelfth century; less so in Giovanni Scriba's time, when slightly

attention to less studied aspects of the text, in particular the goods involved, the artisans mentioned in the text, and the activities of other Italian cities documented there.

First, this is the only complete register surviving before 1190. Is it typical of the period? It can be shown that notaries around 1190 and later had relatively specific clienteles (Guglielmo Cassinese, for example, and above all Oberto da Piacenza in 1197, had much tighter links with trading to northern France than did Oberto Scriba de Mercato).[177] We have to ask the same of Giovanni Scriba. And in fact, he was himself a figure of importance in the city, for he was the official communal scribe. Caffaro mentions him twice in his annals, as registering for the commune the *dies et horas* of the building of the walls in 1159—which he probably did in the first half of that year, in a six-month period when he only wrote fifteen documents—and in 1162 when he was part of the embassy to Frederick Barbarossa in Pavia, just after the fall of Milan, which got for the city a comprehensive set of privileges in early June—and, again, the register has a gap precisely across the period 15 May to 13 June 1162.[178] It is thus quite likely that he was the notary of choice for the urban elite, many of whom, indeed, reappear often in his

different *societas* partnerships were common, plus some sea loans (cf. p. 516 above, pp. 565, 648–9 below). Bach, *La cité de Gênes*, Abulafia, *The two Italies*, Van Doosselaere, *Commercial agreements*, and—still—Schaube, *Handelsgeschichte* (esp. pp. 154–69, 281–6, 465–71) are the main points of reference for an overall economic analysis of Giovanni Scriba and of later twelfth-century registers. For the ships themselves, as well as their commercial context, Krueger, *Navi*, is fundamental.

I cannot here discuss the social history of twelfth-century Genoa, but recent works, based largely on the registers, which are fundamental for the social history of the period, include Bezzina, *Artigiani a Genova*; Guglielmotti, *Donne, famiglie e patrimoni*; Guglielmotti, 'Women, families and wealth'; both authors discuss previous work, among which I would single out Hughes, 'Urban growth and family structure'. Like Van Doosselaere, they focus on the thirteenth century as much as (and more than) the twelfth. I again set aside Greif, *Institutions*, pp. 273–301; his discussion of Giovanni Scriba, comparing it with the *geniza* letters, is vitiated by his simplistic counterposition of a collective culture among the Egyptian Jewish traders and a supposedly individualistic culture in Genoa (and western Europe as a whole), which not only is entirely unsubstantiated, but is directly undermined by his own stress (itself overschematic) on Genoese 'clans'. For aristocratic families, Filangieri, *Famiglie e gruppi dirigenti* and Inguscio, *Reassessing civil conflicts in Genoa*, are basic; for specific families, see Origone, 'Gli Embriaci a Genova'; Musarra, 'Gli Spinola a Genova'.

[177] See p. 553 below for Guglielmo Cassinese. Oberto da Piacenza is partially edited (only for transalpine contracts) in Doehaerd, *Les relations commerciales*, 2, nn. 1–137. Later, in the thirteenth century, distinct notarial clienteles are even clearer, and indeed, some notaries had few links with trading contracts outside Genoa at all: see Filangieri, *Famiglie e gruppi dirigenti*, p. 104n.

[178] *Annali genovesi*, 1, ed. Belgrano, pp. 54, 66. *Giovanni Scriba*, 1, pp. xxxvii–xxxix gives a brief account of Giovanni himself, but mysteriously fails to cite Caffaro. One other issue deserves comment: Giovanni Scriba's register is the first paper documentary text known in Latin Europe, apart from the single Sicilian charter of 1109 (see p. 197 above). Where did he get the paper from? The historiography is hypothetical and contradictory, but Marina Rustow has now shown that the cut-up documents in Arabic reused in the back of the register are almost certainly caliphal decrees from Fāṭimid Egypt (*The lost archive*, p. 306–7). The section of the register which reuses these is not actually Giovanni's own; it is a contemporary fragment by another notary, rebound with that of Giovanni. But, given that, and given that Giovanni uses Egyptian paper sizing (Jessica Goldberg, pers. comm.), Egypt is the most plausible source for his paper—Genoese trade with Islamic Spain was, it can be added, too minor for it to be plausibly Andalusī. See, not very helpfully, Briquet, 'Les papiers', pp. 290–7; *Giovanni Scriba*, pp. ix–x; Doehaerd, *Les relations commerciales*, 1, pp. 35–6; Bloom, *Paper before print*, pp. 209–11.

text. The financial scale of transactions in his register might well, therefore, be higher than the average for the city as a whole. It is also likely that the percentage of transactions relating to sea trading was higher than a notary with a less ambitious or more rural clientele would have registered. But there is no shortage of non-elite figures in his text, all the same, or sales of rural land, and it is not clear to me that the direction of trading, or the goods involved, would necessarily have been greatly different for other notaries, if they registered sea trade at all. The witnesses to the transactions in his register, who were not necessarily part of his clientele, certainly came from a wide range of social roles; these seem to me probably representative of the city as a whole. For our purposes here, except for financial scale, it seems to me that we can trust his typicality.

Erik Bach in 1955 calculated the broad figures for those contracts in Giovanni Scriba's register which specify a first destination (335 agreements, roughly a quarter of all the documents in the register). In descending order of number of contracts, it runs: Sicily 84, North Africa 73, Alexandria 58, the Levant 34, Byzantium 20, southern France 17, Spain 17, Sardinia 14, mainland Italy south of Liguria 12, Lombardy 6. The figures can certainly be adjusted; if, in particular, final destinations are included as well, which probably were in most cases the most important, Egypt comes up to match North Africa; but as a ballpark they stand. The very low figure for inland northern Italy doubtless reflects the fact that land transport (here probably by mule more often than donkey, given the balance of references to them in sales) required less investment, but it is low all the same, a point we will come back to. The number of contracts does not accurately reflect the scale of investment, however, for actually, in Genoese money, some £10,000 was invested in the Levant trade, £9,000 in Alexandria, under £7,000 in Sicily, £6,000 in North Africa, which reshapes the relationship between the top four considerably; the average per contract was £300 for the Levant, £156 for Alexandria, £100 for Byzantium, and only £80 for the western Mediterranean, taken as a whole. The Levantine trade was the preserve of a smallish group of elite families, who had more to invest; already the Egyptian trade involved a wider array of smaller-scale merchants, and this was far more so for the less risky voyages to Sicily and the Ifrīqiyan ports.[179] The figures actually varied very considerably from year to year across the decade of the register, it should be added; David Abulafia established that in 1156 Sicily saw most investment, in 1157 Alexandria, in 1158 Sicily again, in 1160 Byzantium, in 1161 the Levant.[180]

[179] Bach, *La cité de Gênes*, pp. 50–1, 57–9; I actually count 362 such contracts, not 335—the difference may lie in what is defined as a contract. For mule sales, see ibid., p. 101 (they cost slightly more than slaves, p. 98); for examples, see *Oberto Scriba 1186*, n. 306; *Oberto Scriba 1190*, nn. 202, 627. For the Levant, see esp. Musarra, *In partibus ultramarinis*, pp. 309–20; for earlier, see Byrne, 'Genoese trade with Syria'; for Egypt, see Balard, 'Le commerce génois à Alexandrie', pp. 269–75.

[180] For the investment figures, see Abulafia, *The two Italies*, pp. 105–19.

Genoa had no form of established practice regarding directions of voyages. It was down to the decisions of the sedentary investor above all (the *socius stans*), plus the intentions of ships' captains on whose ships individual partnerships put their goods, and then, probably third, the travelling merchant in partnerships (the *socius negotians* or *tractans*)—which may explain the high number of contracts, another 100, where no destination was specified. The basis for such decisions is lost to us, with obvious exceptions such as the embargo on trade with Sicily from 1162, which meant, it should be added, that trade into the eastern Mediterranean, which inevitably went past Sicily, also vanished in 1162–3, although it picked up in August 1164, in the last month of Giovanni's surviving text. At most, we can detect slight preferences for trade with specific locations among a few of the elite, such as the involvement of some of the richest players with the east. Genoese strategic trading decisions were, however, clearly less stable than those of *geniza* merchants, or, indeed, those of Venice: *geniza* merchants could change their trading from Mahdia to Palermo very easily, but these two were most likely to be their choices, year on year; Byzantium was always by far the main focus for Venetians. In Genoa, the choices were far more variable.

The Genoese were seldom career merchants—we cannot track an equivalent to Romano Mairano—but substantial numbers of them invested or travelled in trading at least sometimes. Most of the two dozen or so most powerful families of the city invested in trade, occasionally or often; members of the elite were also, by and large, the most important traders in Giovanni Scriba's register. A few outsiders joined them, Blancardo from (probably) the south of France and Solimano of Salerno being the main ones, both of them, in effect, naturalized into the city—Solimano's wife Eliadar, who was equally active as an investor, was probably herself Genoese.[181] But that de facto naturalization process was in fact quite common at a less elevated level; of medium elite families, Otone *iudex* of Milan and a number of Lucchese traders were examples. The city also formally permitted half a dozen non-Genoese Italians to have trading rights in the city in return for services rendered to it, as with Folco Stretto in 1149, a very active city consul and civic leader in Piacenza who helped facilitate the repayment of the loan to Genoa by his own commune; henceforth, he had the right to invest £200 a year (not so high a figure) in sea trading with the same privileges as the Genoese.[182] Members of the urban elite sometimes also bought the right to exact commercial tolls for

[181] Abulafia, *The two Italies*, pp. 235–54; Pistarino, 'Commercio e comunicazioni', pp. 267–79. On elite families and trade, see Inguscio, *Reassessing civil conflicts in Genoa*, *passim*; cf. Filangieri, *Famiglie e gruppi dirigenti*, pp. 171–9,

[182] For the Lucchesi, see n. 196 below. For Otone, see the refs. in *Giovanni Scriba*, 2, p. 436, s.v. 'Oto'; his will survives, ibid., n. 411, showing that he lived in Genoa; cf. also ibid., n. 1083, his agreement to support the lords of Passano, south-east of Genoa, as their legal representative in everything unless it is against Milan. For Folco Stretto and other non-Genoese with trading rights, see LI, 1, nn. 121, 132 (cf. 178 for the Piacenza deal), 32, 57, 202, 243, 246, 249 (*CDGE*, 1, nn. 198–9, 239–41, 257; 2, nn. 79, 104, 122). For Folco in Piacenza, see Racine, *Plaisance*, 1, pp. 301–4.

given periods, for substantial sums of money.[183] The capital they used must have been initially from landowning, which, indeed, remained at the centre of prosperity and status for most of the elite families, even when they engaged in trading as well. Although we can say rather less about that than we can for Pisa, as Genoa is less well equipped with surviving land documents, it seems clear that for most families it consisted of fragmented estates up and down the Ligurian coast, and especially near the city itself; as with Pisa, almost no Genoese city leader controlled a castle. (Castle lords regularly swore allegiance to the city, with the commitment to live there, but they do not appear as major commercial actors.)[184] This was not a real financial basis for large-scale investment in the first decades of the city's commercial activity. And, indeed, the data we have indicate that it did not match the resources available to a good number of *geniza* merchants.

Genoese contracts for overseas trade for the years around 1160 varied, taking a yearly average, from £287 down to £35, depending on the region traded with (the Levant trade generally saw the highest figures, as already noted). The years around 1190 show us more contracts, but the scale was similar. Around 1160, these two figures seem to have been the equivalent of (very roughly) 631 and 77 Egyptian dinars, based on documented references to exchange rates. Single contracts in Giovanni Scriba's register could, however, be for under £10; at the high end, 3 out of over 450 were for over £800, with another 5 over £700. The largest single figure that I have seen is £950 in 1164 (depending on how we read the text, it could be as much as £1,217), worth roughly 2,090 (or 2,677) dinars. It is highly likely that this was at the very top end of trading contracts, taken as a whole, given the close connection between Giovanni Scriba and the urban elite, one of whom, Baldizzone Usodimare, was, in fact, the *socius stans* here. But we saw in Chapter 2 that, a century earlier, middle-level Jewish Fusṭāṭī/Alexandrian merchants like Nahray b. Nissīm thought that agreements involving up to 3,000 dinars were standard transactions, and one of Ibn ʿAwkal's agents could export 180 bales of flax worth nearly 5,000 dinars (or indeed, more) in a year; nor do these figures include the Muslim merchants with closer links to official patronage, whose scale could well have been even greater.[185] That is to say, it is clear, as we have already seen for

[183] e.g. *LI*, 1, nn. 113, 122 (*CDGE*, 1, nn. 193, 202), for £1,300 and £1,200 respectively.

[184] Examples: the counts of Lavagna promised to live in the city in 1138/9 (*LI*, 1, n. 8 (*CDGE*, 1, n. 87)); they appear as maritime investors in *Giovanni Scriba* only in nn. 627, 1041, 1121. The lords of Passano swore fealty to Genoa in 1144–5 (*LI*, 1, n. 39–41, 80 (*CDGE*, 1, n. 130–1, 60, 153)); they appear as investors in *Giovanni Scriba* only in n. 1184. Krueger, *Navi*, p. 54 (cf. 171), stresses that around 1160 'most of the capital for the construction and fitting-out of ships came from non-commercial sources'; but those non-commercial sources were themselves restricted. Even if by around 1190 more ship-owners were merchants—often, by now, we can assume, using accumulated merchant capital—they were still very involved in land and political power; see ibid., pp. 135–55. Filangieri, *Famiglie e gruppi dirigenti*, e.g. pp. 127–8, further criticizes the tendency of commercially minded historians to assume that commerce was necessarily more important than land for elite families in Genoa.

[185] For Nahray and Ibn ʿAwkal, and also the high official Amīnaddīn, see Chapter 2, nn. 55, 224 above; Goitein, *MS*, 1, pp. 215–17, gives other, parallel figures. The 180 bales appear in T-S 13J17.3

Venice, that the capital available in the chief cities of a powerful tax-based state was substantially more extensive than that available in a single city of some 20,000 people. This, actually, is what we ought to expect; but it deserves attention as a marker of the difficulties Genoa, or any other single Italian city, had with scale, before invested capital generated much more capital. That they got as close to these *geniza* figures as they did deserves respect. But it does mean that the scale of Genoese trading as a whole in the mid- and late twelfth century is likely to have been considerably less than that going out from Alexandria a century before. Put together with Pisan and Venetian trading, it might perhaps have come closer to an equivalence in scale with eleventh-century Egyptian trading, but we have no good reason to think it was more, in the twelfth century at least. This is guesswork, for the Venetian evidence is much less good and the Pisan evidence almost non-existent, but the Venetian figures we have (see pp. 339, 521 above) were lower than those for Genoa, so it seems to me a fair hypothesis; we will come back to the point in Chapter 7.

We saw when looking at Sicily that most Genoese contracts do not mention goods, but only investment and profits in money. Taken as a whole, however, these contracts contain a reasonable number of references to particular types of goods in Giovanni Scriba's register—not enough to offer statistics, but certainly enough for us to use them as rough guides. The Genoese imported spices and dyes on a regular basis; pepper was so common in the city that it was used as an alternative to silver coin in transactions, as was, less often, brazilwood, used for dyeing.[186] Among bulk goods, we have seen (pp. 257–60) that they imported cotton from Sicily on a particularly large scale; this is reinforced by the fact that not only spices, but even, remarkably, bales of raw cotton were also used as currency substitutes in the city; there was evidently a lot of it about, and it was easily resellable internally.[187] By contrast, notwithstanding the emphasis in urban toll regulations on the import of grain and salt, these are only very occasionally cited as

(Gil K181 [S47]); the figure in dinars could indeed be over 6,000; see Chapter 2, n. 55 above. The Genoese yearly figures are tabulated in Abulafia, *The two Italies*, pp. 105, 109, 111, 119, 166, 174, 177. Those for Egyptian dinars follow the exchange rates in *Giovanni Scriba*, nn. 117, 243, 661, 665, 718 (an outlier is 238, which is rather lower). The multiplier there varies between 2.5 and 3.0; I have taken 2.75, and have subtracted 20% to make 2.2, so as to fit typical Genoese interest rates of 25%, which would presumably have been hidden in the stated exchange rates of the documents. There are several untestable suppositions built into this, but it gives us a ballpark figure. For £950, see *Giovanni Scriba*, n. 1261; other contracts over £800 are nn. 130, 1022; over £700, nn. 207, 650, 738, 740, 900. Money paid for the right to exact tolls could be higher, up to £1,300 (see n. 183 above); but these were high-level political deals, and involved little or no risk. Slessarev, 'The pound-value of Genoa's maritime trade', p. 102, further calculated that the whole of the investing for 1160 in Giovanni Scriba's register came to £12,640, this being the highest-value year of the whole register (the other full years came to between £6,200 and £8,400); this would have amounted to some 27,800 dinars, under six times the value of a single year's worth of flax export (only one of the commodities Jewish merchants dealt in, although the largest by far) for only one of Ibn 'Awkal's agents.

186 Examples include *Giovanni Scriba*, nn. 8, 88. That pepper was an alternative quasi-currency in Latin Europe has, of course, long been known; see, e.g., Bloch, *Mélanges historiques*, 2, pp. 869–70.

187 *Giovanni Scriba*, nn. 152, 256, 846, 1064, 1301.

commodities in the contracts, and other bulk goods are no more common; I would assume that this is because they were too normal to be expressly mentioned.[188]

As to exports, the most frequently mentioned was cloth, the classic bulk commodity, on some three dozen occasions. In Giovanni Scriba's register, the most commonly identified cloth was fustian, the linen–cotton mix which was associated above all with the Lombard cities by the thirteenth century, as we shall see, and, indeed, on two occasions the fustian here is explicitly stated to have come from Milan and Piacenza. Given the fall of Milan in 1162, it is unsurprising that these two references come from earlier than that, 1158 and 1160.[189] Linen, hemp, and woollens are also cited, although only occasional examples of each, and silk slightly more often; in one case it was clearly imported from Sicily, in another it probably came from Spain and was re-exported to Egypt. Twice, cloth for export was from St-Riquier in northern France, and Paris cloth is also mentioned once in an inventory, matching the Lucchese cloth imports mentioned in the *Libri iurium* and, for that matter, the reference to dealers from France in the 1130 toll list, but there is no other sign that transalpine goods were involved, and transalpine merchants are also almost absent from Giovanni Scriba's register.[190]

The markets for this cloth were evenly spread among the standard overseas destinations for Genoese shipping; it already went almost everywhere—to Salerno, Sicily, the Levant, Béjaïa, and Spain. But it does have to be stressed, again, that these references are only a small proportion of the surviving contracts, and in many cases the cloth is an add-on to a contract which is otherwise described as above all in money. For this reason, as we saw (p. 259), Abulafia proposed in the context of Sicily that the Genoese were in the years around 1160 usually buying cotton, not with exported cloth or other goods, but with silver. If we were consistent about this argument, we would have to argue it for all the Genoese maritime destinations, which would not make any sense; we would have to hypothesize that ships went out largely empty except for coin, and that only overseas did merchants deal in real commodities. We must conclude that, as we saw for Venice, these calculations of money were for the most part markers of the value of goods. All the same, at least in the documents when cloth or other goods are explicitly an

[188] Salt: *Giovanni Scriba*, nn. 227, 722, appendix 20; wheat: nn. 980, 1004. Oil appears in nn. 165, 341; timber appears in n. 404; cf. also Chapter 3, n. 261 above.

[189] *Giovanni Scriba*, nn. 383, 678 (plus 689, 1095, 1110, appendix 10 for other fustian references). Note that Piacenza cloth, in different colours, was already being sent to Constantinople and Alexandria in the 1130s, but through Pisa, not Genoa; see n. 228 below.

[190] Linen: *Giovanni Scriba*, nn. 141, 849; hemp: n. 848; wool: n. 937. These were all exports of cloth, not thread; linen and wool are cited as imports in *LI*, 1, nn. 123, 131, 134, 139 (*CDGE*, 1, nn. 132, 194, 200), for 1144 and 1149. For St-Riquier and Paris, see *Giovanni Scriba*, nn. 415, 641, 1212. For silk, see nn. 285, 739, 812, 857, 882, 1132, appendix 16. Cf. the lists in Mainoni, 'Le produzioni non agricole', pp. 251–2. Men of transalpine origin only appear, apart from occasional witnessing, as merchants travelling across the sea for Genoese investors; see *Giovanni Scriba*, nn. 210, 638, 641, appendix 26. Schaube, *Handelsgeschichte*, pp. 159–65, gives a helpful conspectus of trade goods between Genoa and the east.

add-on in the contracts, the export of silver seems to me a possible interpretation in some situations, and particularly in the case of one of the main products essential to Genoa's wider reselling activity, that is to say, Sicilian cotton itself, plus the wheat for the city's own consumption.[191] There was clearly a fair amount of cotton-based (i.e. fustian) cloth being made in Italy, above all in Lombardy, by the years around 1160, a fact heralded by the more casual reference to Lombard cloth in the toll lists for 1128–30. Indeed, the quantity of the raw cotton available in Genoa must imply it of itself, for the Genoese were not yet themselves often weavers. But it is likely, as we shall see later, that it was not yet—before the 1180s—being made on such a scale, or sufficiently cheaply with respect to quality, that it could be used as the main basis for Genoese exports in itself. For this reason, plus the fact that by no means all of it was going back to Sicily, it is at least possible that it was sometimes, around 1160, being supplemented by silver.

Where would such silver come from? Often, probably, from trading on, to the Lombard towns or possibly Provence. But Sardinia, such a strong focus of Genoese (as also Pisan) colonial interest, was a known producer and exporter of silver according to al-Idrīsī around 1150, and in fact one document, surviving in the *Libri iurium*, shows the ruler of Arborea in western Sardinia granting to the Genoese half of the *montium in quibus invenitur vena argenti in toto regno meo*, the silver mines of his whole kingdom, in 1131. This would be a securer datum if the silver mines were ever mentioned again in the run of cessions of different types to Genoa by the rulers of Arborea across the century, but the grant fits squarely with the successful Genoese request to King Conrad III for minting rights in 1138, and the immediate (1139) coinage of Genoese silver money. The successive types of Genoese *denarii* and half-*denarii* are not common in hoards until those of the 1170s, but they became at once the standard currency in almost all Genoese documentation.[192] However much the silver available to the Genoese was added to in trading, it at least seems likely that the basic availability of the

[191] Abulafia, *The two Italies*, p. 219; Van Doosselaere, *Commercial agreements*, pp. 70–1, is the recent author who is most cautious about this as a general statement. For cloth exports, examples include *Giovanni Scriba*, nn. 68, 73, 89, 192, 197, 383, 385, 509, 609, 626. Note that the Egyptians did rely on silver imports for their coinage (see Chapter 2, n. 289 above), but we have little evidence as to where they got it from after 1100 (earlier, Ifrīqiya was a standard source).

As to other commodities: Bach, *La cité de Gênes*, p. 54, had already remarked that contracts for Alexandria would not have mentioned iron or timber (for shipbuilding), which Egypt needed (see pp. 146–9 above), as these exports were banned. But we find timber from Genoa mentioned in one Egyptian document in the early twelfth century (P.SternItalianMerchants), plus some elliptic documents in Giovanni Scriba which imply that the Genoese could sell their ships directly to the Egyptians; see Chapter 2, nn. 316–17 above. The earliest Genoese reference to an export ban is from 1151; see *LI*, 1, n. 151 (*CDGE*, 1, n. 224); the Giovanni Scriba texts postdate it.

[192] Al-Idrīsī, *Nuzhat al-mushtaq*, trans. Jaubert and Nef, p. 302; *LI*, 1, n. 42 (*CDGE*, 1, n. 58); *Conradi III. diplomata*, n. 15; *LI*, 1, nn. 25–6 (*CDGE*, 1, nn. 96–7) for rules against false minting a few months later; for the coins, see Day et al., *Medieval European coinage*, 12, pp. 254–9. See Lopez, *Su e giù per la storia di Genova*, pp. 189–92 (reprinting an article of 1936), for a contextualization: rival Sardinian rulers conceded similar rights to Pisa, which had less need of them (see n. 250 below). Lopez, also struck by the absence for a century of later references to these silver concessions, is

metal in the city derived from its Sardinian rights, which had the added advantage of being the property of the city from the start.[193] The quantities were probably not initially high (or else the commune would not have run out of money after its pyrrhic victory in Tortosa in 1148), but they may well have made the city's economy liquid enough to facilitate the long-term acquisition of grain and cotton from the Sicilians, the main bulk imports into the city in Giovanni Scriba's time, and, therefore, the imports which are most of interest to us.

Finally, two absences from Giovanni Scriba's register are worth mentioning. The first, as just implied, is cloth weavers. Some eighty artisans appear in the register. Most are witnesses, with occasional examples of shoemakers and dyers making sea contracts (the shoemaker planned to go himself to Sicily). Once, builders establish a *societas* to make lime; once, tanners make a deal to tan 650 cowhides; once, a cauldron maker makes an agreement with his new son-in-law that the latter will join him in his workshop, 'to make the profit which is [standard] among men of our trade'.[194] We do not otherwise get much of a sense of artisanal work from these. But the important element for us is that thirty of the individuals mentioned worked in metals, and twenty-five in leather. Cloth workers were just nine in number, and they were all finishers of cloth, either dyers or tailors.[195] Whatever the problems of the representativeness of Giovanni's register, and of the uncertainty about how many artisans actually identified themselves by trade for public purposes, the absence of weavers is striking. This absence underpins the argument that Sicilian cotton was not due to stay in the city for long in the mid-twelfth century; there were too few people there to turn it into anything else, at least before it had been woven.

The second absence, however, is much reference, even casual, to the Lombard cities of the Po plain, or those of Tuscany, that is to say, any links with the rest of north-central Italy. Men from some ten cities are attested, it is true, mostly witnessing documents. But the numbers are very small, except for those from Lucca, from where at least one serious trader came, Oberto, who maintained a long-term partnership with the Genoese patrician Baldizzone Usodimare across most of the

inclined to minimize them, but, nonetheless, remarks (p. 191) 'ci sembra che una relazione tra il primo privilegio sulle miniere e il primo impianto della zecca [genovese] sia fuor di dubbio'.

[193] For how silver was appropriated from actual miners and refiners (in Italy almost always by state or signorial actors, as Genoa's commune was, not by property owners), see Francovich and Wickham, 'Uno scavo archeologico'. Such silver would not have needed to be traded back to Genoa, as it belonged to the commune already, so the fact that not so many trading ships went to Sardinia in our Genoese sources is not a problem here. The Genoese were militarily active there throughout the twelfth century, after all, coming, we assume, on the commune's own warships. But the great days of Sardinian mining were in the century after 1250; see Tangheroni, *La città dell'argento*.

[194] *Giovanni Scriba*, nn. 806, 324, 1024, 323 (*consequendi lucri qui est inter homines nostre artis*).

[195] For cloth workers as actors in documents, see *Giovanni Scriba*, nn. 75 (in which the consuls determine that Pagano *tinctor* may have Ottobuono *cordeanerius*'s fugitive Saracen slave, since the slave had killed his own), 116, 452, appendix 2.6, appendix 9.[10]. Pistarino, 'La civiltà dei mestieri in Liguria (sec. XII)', discusses the trades in Giovanni Scriba's register.

period of the register.[196] A handful of Lombards were also involved in sea trading, or else, in the case of men from Piacenza and Lodi, loaned money—and, of course, the city of Piacenza itself loaned money to Genoa in the 1140s.[197] The Milanese and Piacentine fustians mentioned above are the sole references to actual goods coming from there, even if most or all of the other fustians and much of the rest of the cloth, whose origin is unspecified in the contracts, will probably have come from Lombardy too. In a few contracts, unnamed goods went back, once to the Vercelli fair (*feria*), which we know to have been a fairly generalist market; in this case the man who took £15 of goods there was a *speciarius* (spice merchant).[198] Sicilian cotton as yet never appears as part of these deals, even if it must have been going north already in reasonable quantities. It may again be that Giovanni Scriba was atypical in the lack of commercial connection with the north shown by his clients; but we have no grounds, on the basis of this text or any other before the late 1180s, to think that Genoese relationships with Lombardy were as yet complex, or—apart perhaps from cotton going one way and fustian the other—large in scale. So, taken as a whole, Giovanni's register tells about a Genoese commitment to the sea, and to maintaining a complex network of commercial interconnections. These, even if less large-scale than those coming out of Egypt a century earlier, did genuinely, far more than we can say for any other trading centre in this book, stretch into every part of the Mediterranean (apart from the Adriatic, by now Venice's near-exclusive trading domain). It connected all the highly developed economies looked at in earlier chapters, except, apart from on a small scale, al-Andalus. But what Genoa was not, in the years around 1160, was an organic outlet for the complexities of the inland northern Italian economy. We will explore this further later, in the section on Lombardy; but speaking very generally, this is because there was not, as yet, enough of a complex inland northern Italian economy to connect to in an organic way.

After 1164, notarial registers do not survive for fifteen years, and they are fragmentary until 1186, after the period discussed in this book has ended. But in those two decades, despite all the wars and disruption which northern Italy suffered, a step change did occur, in Genoa at least. Let us conclude this section by looking more briefly at some of its aspects, for it shows us what we had been

[196] *Giovanni Scriba*, nn. 559, 740, 976, 1038, 1261; see Poloni, *Lucca nel Duecento*, pp. 37–8. For the Usodimare family, see Inguscio, *Reassessing civil conflicts in Genoa*, pp. 78–81.

[197] For loans by men of Lodi and Piacenza, see *Giovanni Scriba*, nn. 232, 842, 855, 858, 925, 962. For Lombard sea trading, see ibid., nn. 500–1. For Piacenza's communal loan, see n. 170 above. Venice never appears, even though the commune of Genoa did make a very generic agreement with the Venetians in 1177; see *CDGE*, 1, n. 111; but as we have seen, Venetians very rarely came into the western Mediterranean.

[198] Goods to Lombardy: *Giovanni Scriba*, nn. 5, 922, 1243 (the Vercelli fair). For the same fair, see also Oreste et al., *Guglielmo da Sori*, 1, nn. 74–5 (a. 1195); in this case the goods were leather. For discussion of the Vercelli fair and other goods, see Mainoni, 'Un'economia cittadina nel XII secolo', pp. 328–32.

missing up to here. I will here rely in particular on the two least fragmentary early years of the registers of Oberto Scriba de Mercato, which are also the only two so far to be fully published, 1186 and 1190, and on Gugliemo Cassinese's complete run of documents from the last days of December 1190 (the Genoese new year was 25 December; for him this was the start of 1191) to April 1192, when the text breaks off.[199] I shall not go into the late 1190s, when a more continuous run of registers begins; as with other chapters in this book, I have to stop somewhere, and anyway what we learn from the documents from 1186–91 is in itself consistent.

First, the scale of sea trading which Genoa engaged in had by now increased substantially, as Erik Bach already made clear. In 1161, Giovanni Scriba registered investments totalling £7,370; in 1191, Guglielmo Cassinese registered a total of £41,135. This was so even though there was in the latter year a major drop in contracts with Alexandria, to zero, matched by a similar near-absence in Oberto Scriba's 1190 register, although not in those of 1182–6; this was, as for Venice, in the context of Genoese commitment to the Third Crusade and a resultant breakdown of trade with Egypt (see also p. 145 above). The other major players of the years around 1160, Sicily, the Levant, North Africa, and, increasingly, Byzantium, continued, however, and far more than made up.[200]

The second point is that although seagoing contracts around 1190 are in general even less explicit than they had been around 1160 concerning what was being exported from Genoa, the registers tell us far more about cloth. The artisans in Oberto Scriba's registers are overwhelmingly in leather and iron, as with that of Giovanni Scriba; but Guglielmo Cassinese, who had a different clientele, shows us not only around a hundred references to leatherworkers and seventy to metalworkers, but by now over eighty to cloth workers (*taiaor*, *sartor*, *filaor*, *lanerius*, *tinctor*), and an equal number to *draperii*, cloth merchants and perhaps sometimes also weavers, on top of that. The cloth workers were still dyers and finishers in the majority of cases, but the minority of *fila<t>ores* were certainly spinners and, here too, perhaps also weavers. Even if Genoa did not move fully into core cloth production for another half-century, by now it was beginning to.[201] To this

[199] *Oberto Scriba 1186* and *1190*; *Guglielmo Cassinese*. Abulafia, *The two Italies*, pp. 154–63, and Bach, *La cité de Gênes*, appendix, summarize earlier years of Oberto's registers (those for 1180 are edited in *Giovanni Scriba*, appendix 5). Marta Calleri plans an edition of all his contracts; see Calleri, 'Un notaio genovese' for comments on his work. Guglielmo da Sori, the only other early Genoese notary with surviving documents before the late 1190s, is too fragmentary to be useful before 1200.

[200] Bach, *La cité de Gênes*, p. 64, for the figures (Slessarev, 'The pound-value of Genoa's maritime trade', p. 102, has a slightly higher figure for 1161, £8,339). Bach, in fact, concentrates his attention in his book on the 1180s–1190s, and at pp. 91–102 gives us a useful discussion of commodities in this period. Egyptian trading in 1190–1 only appears in *Oberto Scriba 1190*, n. 333, referring to the previous year. A dozen documents in *Guglielmo Cassinese* allow for trading everywhere 'except (*preter*) Alexandria'; ibid., n. 1504 refers to ransoming a Genoese in prison there; only in 1192 does a single reference to trading there reappear (ibid., n. 1581).

[201] Bach, *La cité de Gênes*, pp. 106–9, argues that *draperii* were cloth workers, not just merchants; they certainly could be later. Wool workers were, however, important only from the 1240s onwards; for Genoese production in the thirteenth century, see the still fundamental Lopez, 'Le origini dell'arte

was added a greater specificity about types and colours of cloth and where they came from. By now, a good deal was coming from northern France, and the Champagne fairs are mentioned several times, particularly in Guglielmo Cassinese. (They would still more be in Oberto da Piacenza's 1197 register.)[202] But cloth was coming not only from northern France: in 1186 Milanesi are, on numerous occasions, registered as selling fustian in the city; and in 1191 an illuminating contract concerns five bales of fustians from Pavia *contrafactis de Placentia* (made to look as if they were from Piacenza). French and Italian fabrics were sold together too: a 1192 contract refers to cloth from Ypres and Lille and Montreuil, but also scarlets, and two-coloured cloths of each pair of scarlets, browns, and vermilions, which were almost certainly finished in Italy (Lucca dyed and finished scarlets, as we shall see, pp. 581–2); all of these were destined for Sicily. In return, Sicilian raw cotton was by now sometimes explicitly referred to as being destined for sale in Lombardy.[203] Almost all this cloth, sometimes in the form it came into town, sometimes dyed and finished in Genoa or Lucca, was intended for export; casual references, indeed, imply that much was to go to Sicily, although the Levant and maybe North Africa were alternatives (doubtless, given its own production, not Byzantium). Historians see cloth as Genoa's major export by the years around 1190, with, now, no need to use silver to integrate it; this makes sense to me. It was certainly added to massively in scale in the thirteenth century, but it began here.

This is backed up by a notable increase, especially in Guglielmo Cassinese, in references to people from other Italian cities operating in Genoa, or else to deals in other Italian cities. Lucchesi were again the commonest: some of them were at least semi-professional merchants, working from Genoa, like Coenna and Paxio, investors in a range of trading agreements; others were involved in dyeing, either

della lana', in his *Studi sull'economia genovese*, pp. 65–204. I am grateful for discussion on this point with Denise Bezzina, who stressed to me the unreliability of statistics on the issue, given the widely differing clienteles of notaries. Savona had weavers too (see Pistarino, 'La civiltà dei mestieri in Liguria (sec. XII)', pp. 64–5); a standardized oath of a weaver to work honestly survives from there in the 1180s register of Arnaldo Cumano, the only non-Genoese register to survive in Italy for the twelfth century; see Balletto, *Il cartulario di Arnaldo Cumano*, n. VI.

202 See n. 177 above for Oberto da Piacenza. For detailed lists of French/Flemish cloth types in these texts, see Reynolds, 'The market for northern textiles in Genoa', updated in Krueger, 'The Genoese exportation of northern cloths'. Note that the figures quoted in these articles make it clear that even the cheapest transalpine cloths were four times the price of fustian in Genoa (for which, see Mainoni, 'Le produzioni non agricole', p. 247). So in the twelfth century, at least, the imports over the Alps were still on the luxury end of trading, and so marginal for most of the arguments here. Chorley, 'The cloth exports of Flanders and northern France', demonstrates a large-scale production and export of cheaper cloth from that region in the thirteenth century, but at pp. 353, 361, 368–70, confirms that even cheap French/Flemish cloth in Italy was generally more expensive than the upper end of Italian cloth. John Munro's claim ('Medieval woollens', pp. 228–30) that northern cloth 'predominated' in Italy in this period is misleading. See n. 207 below for some of the references to the Champagne fairs.

203 *Oberto Scriba 1186*, nn. 63, 86, 95, 154, 186, 218, 269, 297; *Guglielmo Cassinese*, nn. 250, 1565. For cotton to Lombardy, see *Oberto Scriba 1190*, n. 183; *Guglielmo Cassinese*, n. 395; Oreste et al., *Guglielmo da Sori*, 1, n. 64.

in Genoa or at home in Lucca; a couple were involved in silk deals.[204] Men from Verona appear several times in 1190, selling copper; this may well have come from Germany, as two other contracts refer to German copper (one refers to buying a substantial quantity in Como for £91½, plus alum, cinnamon, and silk), and both Como and Verona are close to Alpine passes.[205] An isolated reference mentions Pisan iron too; Pisans were never very common in Genoese documents, but there was peace between the cities in the years around 1190, and ships by now sometimes stopped off there on their way to the east.[206] Many contracts now referred to debts which were contracted in Genoa but would be repaid in inland towns: sometimes at the Champagne fairs (these were often contracted by men from the towns of Piemonte, Alba, Asti, and Tortona, on the route to the Alpine passes into France), but also, and more commonly, in Milan and Verona (in particular), plus Piacenza, Pisa, Lucca, Corneto (modern Tarquinia), and Rome. Some of them involved pledges; these were regularly in cloth.[207] And by now there were crossovers too: in 1186 a loan by a Lucchese to two Romans, to be repaid in either Rome or Paris; in 1190 a loan by a man from Languedoc to a German, to be repaid in Milan.[208]

We cannot simply rely on numbers when looking at this material. Even given that Genoese data are an order of magnitude greater than those for Venice, and vastly higher than those for anywhere else in the twelfth century, we would need a complete set of notarial registers to do that; even in the thirteenth century that would not be possible. But when we see the evidence as, rather, being about relationships between individuals, the patterning I have just set out has its own significance. This interplay of people and cities shows that we have moved on, in fact, sharply on, from the world of Giovanni Scriba. There, the Genoese story was one of a commitment to Mediterranean trade between regions which, for the most part, had economies of much greater complexity than Italy did, trade which, indeed, had little to do with the Italian mainland on which the Ligurian city actually sat—apart from the steady flow, of as yet uncertain dimensions, of exchange of Sicilian cotton for Lombard fustians. Now we are on the edge of the multivalent commercial world of thirteenth-century northern Italy, looking north

[204] For Coenna and Paxio, see Poloni, *Lucca nel Duecento*, pp. 39–41. Dyeing: *Oberto Scriba 1186*, n. 317, *1190*, n. 444, *Guglielmo Cassinese*, nn. 1193, 1700; silk: *Guglielmo Cassinese*, nn. 256, 1352.

[205] Verona: *Oberto Scriba 1190*, nn. 430, 557, 579, 622, 625–6, 638, 668; German copper: nn. 200 (Como), 489.

[206] *Guglielmo Cassinese*, n. 1559 (iron; it has, however, been confiscated in Pisa); for the stopover, see ibid., nn. 37 (probably), 178, 205, 210, 215.

[207] Piemonte and the Champagne fairs: *Guglielmo Cassinese*, nn. 630, 936, 1358, 1385, 1445. Other debts to be repaid elsewhere: *Oberto Scriba 1190*, n. 587, *Guglielmo Cassinese*, nn. 689, 735, 794–5, 801, 1146 (Milan); *Oberto Scriba 1190*, nn. 191, 297, 318, 469–70 (Verona); *Oberto Scriba 1186*, nn. 189, 204, *1190*, nn. 200, 239, *Guglielmo Cassinese*, nn. 69, 167, 170, 299, 338–9, 687–8, 1327, 1354 (other locations). For the Piacentini at Genoa, dealing in leather as well as cloth, see Racine, *Plaisance*, 1, pp. 316–21.

[208] *Oberto Scriba 1186*, n. 319; *1190*, n. 587.

as much as south, which has long been, and still is, the main focus of historians of the Genoese economy—who tend, indeed, to roll the twelfth century into the thirteenth and later as one single triumphal march.[209] But the point for us is that it took a long time for us to get here, and why that is needs explanation too. We will return to the issue when we look at Lombardy.

As stated earlier, Genoa is a city whose archaeology for this period does not match up to the information we can obtain from written sources. But what we know, above all of the distribution of fine wares, fits the patterns we have just seen fairly well, with some interesting nuances. In the eleventh century, Islamic ceramics from Sicily and Ifrīqiya were already available in Genoa and along the Ligurian coast more generally (see p. 228 above), alongside (as usual) a majority of local coarse and common wares. Savona has a particularly important excavation, in the fortress of the Priamàr, in which Kairouan/Ṣabra glaze is found as early as around 1000, very early for mainland Italy. But fine-ware imports are much more visible in the twelfth century. Alongside such wares from the central Mediterranean, Spanish glaze is very occasionally found from the beginning of the century, as in the excavated tower of the Embriaci family in Genoa; eastern glazed wares, particularly from Syria (Raqqa ware), but also Egyptian lustre are sometimes found by now too, as in twelfth-century levels of the Palazzo Ducale in Genoa, S. Silvestro in Genoa, and the Priamàr in Savona. Liguria was also the only part of northern Italy, apart from Pisa and Venice (plus its hinterland), to receive significant imports from twelfth-century Byzantium—even though Genoa as yet had a far weaker presence in the Aegean than Venice did—including in rural castle sites like Rivarola (prov. Genova) and Andora (prov. Savona). These were usually red wares from the Greek production centres, but also amphorae (in this case already in the eleventh). Then, at the end of the twelfth century, we find substantial imports of cobalt and manganese glaze from Tunis, and also more Byzantine imports, notably Zeuxippus ware. These two were the result of new productive developments in their respective regions of origin, not new extensions of Genoese trading, but it is nonetheless significant that they both appear almost immediately after the type was first produced.[210]

[209] e. g. Balard, *La Romanie génoise*; Jehel, *Les Génois*, esp. pp. 321–68. For a stimulating recent survey, see Poloni, 'Italian communal cities and the thirteenth-century commercial revolution', esp. pp. 354–9, whose thirteenth century begins, more convincingly, after 1180, although I am less sure that the model of Genoese economic development set out there can be easily extended to other cities.

[210] See in general de Vingo, 'La céramique d'importation islamique dans la Ligurie médiévale', which summarizes previous work. For Byzantine wares, see Chapter 4, n. 235 above; for Spain, see Chapter 5, n. 215 above. For specific sites, see Cabona et al., 'Nuovi dati' (Palazzo Ducale); Pringle, 'La ceramica dell'area Sud' (S. Silvestro); Benente, 'Ceramica d'importazione'; Benente, 'Mediterranean and Ligurian ceramics' (Embriaci tower), and various contributions to Melli, *La città ritrovata*. For local productions, the point of reference is still Mannoni, *La ceramica medievale*, even though it was written before any of these sites were excavated. (It should be noted that we are here taking our data directly from excavations; *bacini* on churches, which, as we saw earlier, pp. 358, 455, show a less quotidian use for imported fine wares, are rarer in Liguria, and the only major example before the late twelfth

One site deserves particular notice, the just-mentioned coastal castle of Andora, which only has an interim publication, but a clear one. This was a hilltop site in the eleventh century, with copper-working (with non-local copper), and no ceramics except local coarse wares, plus *pietra ollare* from the central Alps. But in the twelfth century, when its stone castle was built, there is a sharp change, for a full 38 per cent of the total ceramics found, a far higher percentage than normal, were by then fine-ware imports—roughly a third each from Sicily/Ifrīqiya, the eastern Mediterranean, and Byzantium. Genoa and Savona so far have not matched this in any excavated site, but it shows how open Liguria—or to be exact, elite sites in Liguria—could be to imported ceramics.[211] We shall see that, as with Byzantine wares in Venice, this openness did not extend to sites in Lombardy, just over the low Appennine passes; Sicilian cotton did not bring Sicilian ceramics with it in its inland progression. But Genoa and the Ligurian coast in general fit the patterns we have seen in the rest of the Mediterranean, just as well as Venice and (as we shall see) Pisa do: once trade was established with the main glazed-ware producer regions, the Genoese were as happy to buy fine wares—a fairly cheap commodity, as we have abundantly seen—as they were to buy cotton and luxury goods. They hardly mentioned this in their documents; as has long been known, the only citation is a reference in an inventory of 1156, registered by Giovanni Scriba, to *unam scutellam pictam de Almaria*, a painted bowl from Almería. People have wondered whether this was actually booty from the Genoese sack of the town in 1147, rather than obtained commercially; given the fact of Genoese rule there until 1157, the distinction is only a very fine one. It is, anyway, entirely usual that ceramics flew under the documentary radar, so a single reference is not a problem for us. But it is interesting that this inventory also lists a copper bowl and other copper receptacles; in the other detailed inventory in the register, from 1164, the two listed bowls likewise appear to be metal, for one is cut (*scissa*)—one might keep damaged metalwork, as it was resellable, but one would scarcely keep 'cut' pottery.[212] The Ligurians may have been only too happy to use imported glazed wares when they could get them, but they did not only use ceramics for the table.

Not Genoa, but Savona, was the focus for the next step change here: the development of fine-ware production in Liguria itself. In the final decades of the twelfth century, we begin to find *graffita arcaica tirrenica*, probably influenced by Byzantine sgraffito types, which was, given wasters found there, certainly made in Savona. Shortly after, from as yet unidentified production sites, we also find tin-glazed *protomaiolica ligure*, which, like other early maiolicas, partially imitates Islamic glazes. It is significant that *graffita arcaica tirrenica* immediately appeared

century is the eleventh-century church of S. Paragorio at Noli; but this does again show Sicilian and Ifrīqiyan glazed wares.)

[211] Varaldo et al., 'Il castello di Andora'. Note, however, that not all castle sites, particularly in eastern Liguria, had many imported wares at all; see Cagnana et al., 'Castelli e territorio', pp. 35, 41–4.

[212] *Giovanni Scriba*, nn. 47b, 1212.

on all major Ligurian sites, and, across the early thirteenth century, in most of the western Mediterranean and even in the Black Sea; both the exchange network and Savona's productive capacity were, clearly, fully ready for it.[213] This can be seen as the material counterpart to the fact that Genoa by the 1190s was beginning to do its own weaving, and it also goes further than that; for this is the first Ligurian-made artisanal product known to have been sold widely. So, by the end of the twelfth century, Genoa and its hinterland were not just reflecting a world in which there was more artisanal production and commercialization across the Italian north, but also directly contributing to it. It is again significant that one area which *graffita arcaica tirrenica* hardly reached was Lombardy itself, where the rest of that production and commercialization was taking place; we will explore that significance later. But the fact that Liguria had in this respect become a producer area, not simply a transit area, still matches what we have seen for cloth.

This archaeological survey adds less to what we can say from the written sources for Genoa than similar discussions added for the other regions discussed in this book, and also less than the equivalent surveys for Venice and (especially) Pisa and Tuscany. But one thing it does do, as we also saw for Venice, is establish that ceramic distributions in Genoa and Liguria fitted, pretty well, the general patterns of the Mediterranean in our period, in which ceramics and cloth were commercialized in similar ways. This in its turn, however, makes the evidence we have for inland northern Italy exceptional, for we cannot find such a fit there. It is hard to be sure why, as we shall see; but attempting to explain it will also help us to see what was actually going on, not just in Lombardy, but in north-central Italy as a whole, as its economic system came to change gear in the very late twelfth century in particular. Let us move, then, back to the problematic of local and regional economies, to try to find out what was going on: first to Tuscany, where Pisa had some of the same role as Venice did for the eastern Po plain, and then to Lombardy, to look as closely as we can at the changes which the central Po plain experienced in the last decades of our period.

6.5 Pisa and Tuscany

What we can say about the economy of Pisa and its hinterland has many parallels with what we have just seen for Venice and Genoa, but the way we can talk about it is profoundly different. It is clear that Pisa, as a maritime city, was active in the Mediterranean in just the same way as Venice and Genoa were; but we have neither the S. Zaccaria archive nor the Genoese notarial registers to give us detailed documentary evidence for it. Conversely, we are dealing with Tuscany here, which

[213] See Varaldo, 'La graffita arcaica tirrenica'; Varaldo, 'Graffita arcaica tirrenica'.

has the densest archaeology of all in Italy. So archaeological data will here be stressed. After a discussion of the political and maritime activity of Pisa, I will set out what the archaeology can tell us about Pisa, and Tuscany in general. I will then compare this with what can be said about Pisa's closest neighbour and enemy, Lucca, and also Florence, a second-rank city in our period but far from that a century later.

Venice, as we have seen, was, in effect, independent of the Byzantine Empire by the mid-eleventh century, and autonomous for two centuries before that. Genoa was part of the Kingdom of Italy, but politically marginal until the late eleventh century, as far as we can see, and geographically fairly separate for a long time. But Pisa was an integral part of the March of Tuscany, the part of the kingdom which stayed organizationally coherent for longest, and was one of the march's two most important centres, along with Lucca, the political capital. Florence, sometimes also a centre for the march, was much smaller as yet; the other major future economic hub, Siena, on a hilltop farther from the Arno river network, seems to have been relatively isolated until the late twelfth century. Northern and central Tuscany was unified by the Arno, which linked all of its major lowland areas except for those stretching down the coast—including the plain of Lucca, for the Lucchese river, the Serchio, ran into the Arno at Pisa in our period, as well as having its own separate river mouth (see Map 21). Pisa sat and sits close to the mouth of the Arno, on the edge of what was then the marshes and lagoons of the delta; its harbour, the Portus Pisanus, some 15 kilometres to the south on the other side of the marshes, was Tuscany's main link to the sea throughout the middle ages.[214] (Only in the early modern period did Livorno take over Pisa's role as Tuscany's port; it is, in fact, just beside the now silted-up Portus Pisanus, but was only a castle in our period.) Pisa thus looked both ways, towards the politics of the march and towards the sea, controlling, as it did, Tuscany's maritime access even more completely than Venice did for the Po plain. And between the marshes which half-surrounded it, the city and its inhabitants controlled rich agricultural lands along the Arno and Serchio; Pisa's immediately accessible agricultural resources were, as a result, rather more substantial than those of either Venice or Genoa. Although it expanded rapidly as an urban centre, it did not face the food supply difficulties which the other main ports (particularly Genoa) had to confront.[215]

[214] For the port, see in general Ceccarelli Lemut et al, *I sistemi portuali*, pp. 77–80, 88–9, 101–3, 118–25.

[215] There are, all the same, some references to the import of food: grain from Corneto in 1173 (Carmignani, *Le pergamene*, n. 31; cf. also Maragone, *Annales pisani*, ed. Lupo Gentile, p. 21), salt from Sardinia in 1103 and 1109 (Banti, *I brevi dei consoli*, p. 113; Guastini, *Le pergamene*, n. 27), even though, in the case of salt, Pisa controlled the salt pans at Vada at the southern end of the Pisan diocese (e.g. Ghignoli, *Carte dell'Archivio arcivescovile*, 1, n. 124, a. 1052). The Pisan law code also envisaged that grain ships would come straight up the Arno to the city, bypassing the Portus Pisanus; see *Constitutum Usus*, ch. 28 (in Vignoli, *I Costituti*, pp. 246–7).

Of all Italy's maritime cities, Pisa is the one which made most noise in the eleventh century. It engaged in naval wars with other western Mediterranean powers: it fought (presumably Sicilian) Arabs at Reggio Calabria in 1005 and Mujāhid of Denia in Sardinia in 1014–15, and then raided Annaba in Algeria in 1034, Palermo in 1064, Mahdia in 1087, Tortosa in 1092, before moving to the Levant with the First Crusade in 1098–9. In the next century, the Pisans also sacked Mallorca in 1113–14 and Amalfi in 1134, although its major sea wars were by now against Genoa (in 1118–33 and especially 1162–75), in particular over rival claims to Corsica and Sardinia. Earlier, as we have seen, the Genoese were with them for some of the eleventh-century attacks, in Sardinia, Mahdia, and the Crusade, but Pisa seems to have dominated up to the 1090s. And not least, it celebrated it in, unusually, inscriptions and poetic texts, some of them—that for Mahdia and especially that for Mallorca, the *Liber Maiorichinus*—very lengthy. The inscriptions, including the poem celebrating the Palermo attack, are still there on the facade of Pisa's cathedral, built in part with the booty from Palermo, and embellished by similar spoils which came later.[216] Together with S. Marco in Venice, this was the most innovative—and expensive—building which we know to have been built in Italy in the later eleventh century, and here it was explicitly associated with war.

Pisa began all this when it was still part of the kingdom and the march. Some of its most committed early attacks were at the request of, or at least with the support of, the marquis and/or the pope, although they were equally to the city's direct benefit. But this protagonism also meant that it could be fast off the mark when the March of Tuscany collapsed in the civil wars of the 1080s and onwards, and, after a brief resurgence in Matilda of Canossa's last years, following her death in 1115. Pisa already had consuls by the beginning of the century (they are first documented *c.*1100, and first named in 1109), at more or less the same time as Genoa; and, more importantly, in the years around 1110 the two cities were by far the earliest in Italy to develop communal government in any organized sense. The communal ruling group was coherent in Pisa; it contained few or no castle-holding families, much as in Genoa, and—here very unlike in Genoa—it ran the city with relatively few conflicts for 150 years, from the mid-eleventh century, well before the commune, onwards.[217]

From the start of the twelfth century, Pisa engaged in border wars with Lucca, matching in this respect every city in the kingdom, as we have seen. But rather

[216] There are many accounts of these wars; for a good example, see Salvatori, 'Lo spazio economico di Pisa', with extensive bibliography; see also Tangheroni, 'La prima espansione di Pisa'. For the texts, see Banti, *Monumenta epigrafica pisana*, nn. 46–7, 51; Scalia, 'Il carme pisano'; *Liber Maiorichinus*, ed. Scalia; and for the twelfth century, see Maragone, *Annales pisani*, ed. Lupo Gentile. Note when using texts such as Maragone that Pisan dating was nine months ahead of modern dating: the year '1150' began there on what is now 25 March 1149.

[217] Wickham, *Sleepwalking*, pp. 67–117, which cites the substantial earlier bibliography; see further Cortese, *L'aristocrazia toscana*, pp. 307–14.

more than most, it also succeeded in expanding the lands under its direct control some way beyond its own diocese, both inland and down the coast. Most significantly, it very soon controlled the coastal lands and the hills above them around Campiglia and Piombino, southwards from the diocesan boundary. Part of the castle of Piombino was already in Pisan hands by 1115, and the rest followed in the next decades; by 1139 part of Campiglia, with other neighbouring castles, was formally conceded to the archbishop of Pisa by the Gherardeschi counts, and Pisan control over it was, in effect, complete shortly after.[218] This direction of expansion, into lands far from any city, was important because behind Campiglia were the Colline Metallifere, the hills which have the widest range of exploitable metals in the whole of the Italian peninsula south of the Alps, and opposite Piombino was the island of Elba, which was, in particular—and had been since Roman times—a major source of iron. How and when Elba itself came into Pisan hands we cannot tell; there are no early documents for the island, and it is most likely that it was almost entirely public land. Although Matilda ceded some of her strategic lands to Pisan churches and citizens (Livorno being an example), she did not give up Elba. Nevertheless, by 1162 at the latest, it was fully under Pisan control, for by then one of the tasks of the annually incoming consuls of the city was, precisely, to choose the consuls of the island. I would suppose that Pisa took it over de facto early in the twelfth century, perhaps in the very year 1115, when Matilda died and Piombino started to be transferred to the city's rule.[219]

So Pisa was aggressively exerting its armed dominance on the sea across the eleventh and twelfth centuries, and also, usually less violently, taking over a metal-rich section of the coast. Its early projection was essentially military, more than commercial. It was, certainly, also laying the grounds for the sort of intense commercial activity which both Venice and, most relevantly here, Genoa were establishing in the same years.[220] But we can say far less about this. If Venice has hundreds of commercial contracts in our period and Genoa thousands, Pisa has precisely two, with four more in the 1180s–1190s.[221] As noted earlier, historians

[218] For the Pisans in Piombino and Campiglia, see Ceccarelli Lemut, 'La Maremma populoniese', pp. 60–2, 74–7; Volpe, *Studi*, the earliest and still the best general history of the early commune of Pisa, discusses Piombino and Elba at pp. 86–92.

[219] For Elba, see n. 218 above; for 1162, see Banti, *I brevi dei consoli*, pp. 51, and cf. 81–2. For Matilda ceding Livorno (in 1103), see *Die Urkunden und Briefe der Markgräfin Mathilde von Tuszien*, n. 74.

[220] Petralia, 'Le "navi" e i "cavalli"', pp. 207–12, as we have seen already, makes the clearest case for the Pisan (and Genoese) Mediterranean projection being essentially military at the outset. There was already trading in the eleventh century as well, though; see, e.g., Amato of Montecassino, *Storia de' Normanni*, ed. de Bartholomaeis, 7.13, 8.4, pp. 305–6, 346–7, for traders in southern Italy from both cities (although Malaterra's parallel comments are more problematic: see Chapter 3, nn. 138, 257 above); and see n. 228 below for some Pisan elite families.

[221] For the commercial contracts, see Cortesini, *Le pergamene*, n. 33 (a. 1169); Pellegrini, *Le pergamene*, n. 7 (a. 1179); Orlandi, *Carte dell'Archivio della Certosa di Calci*, 3, n. 108 (a. 1181), 131 (a. 1189); Blanda, *Le pergamene*, n. 20 (a. 1185); Venturini, *Pergamene*, n. 35 (a. 1191). For comment, see Abulafia, 'Pisan commercial colonies'. I thank Paolo Tomei for finding the 1185 document for me.

sometimes tacitly assume that it cannot have really matched Genoa, and this absence is the major reason why—plus the fact that Genoa largely wiped out the Pisan navy at the battle of Meloria much later, in 1284—but we have no grounds for saying that this was the case until well into the thirteenth century. Pisa after all fought Genoa to a standstill in the 1160s and 1170s, doubtless spending quite as much money as it did so as, for example, in 1166, when it took on a very large £36,000 debt to build forty-seven war galleys. (Indeed, the Pisan public debt began as an institution in this period, as we know from a substantial set of documents registering pledges and repayments, and from early references to an official responsible for communal debt, the *cognitor debiti et crediti communis*, in the 1170s.)[222] And there are many other signs of the intensity of Pisan maritime activity in our texts too, some of them without equivalents in Venetian and Genoese sources, such as the unique set of accounts for the fitting out of one or more ships (probably galleys) written in early Italian, the earliest-known full text in Tuscan *volgare*, from the early to mid-twelfth century: 'Anrigo had 20 *solidi* given to the ropemaker, £3 to Oghicione and Pisanello, 20 *denarii* in foodstuffs, 34 *denarii* to Pilotto for the sawing of the tiller', etc. Warships in this period were always galleys, *galee*, as opposed to ordinary *naves*, without oars, which were commercial; but some galleys were commercial too, so we cannot assume that this is necessarily a military account. Whether the text had a military purpose or not, however, it is strikingly careful and systematic, betraying a firm familiarity with how to carry out the task, and its accounting expertise will not have differed from that needed for commercial vessels.[223]

This brings us to the direct evidence for Pisan trading in our period which we do have. The first is a long list of treaties, often several each, with Byzantium, the Crusader rulers, Egypt, the independent rulers of Valencia, Mallorca, and Tunis,

[222] For the1166 debt, see Maragone, *Annales pisani*, ed. Lupo Gentile, p. 38. For the public debt, see Violante, *Economia società istituzioni*, pp. 67–100. Galley-building was a serious and expensive operation in Pisa, but it was essentially locally based, for the timber could, except for the very largest-scale expeditions, be cut by the city's *galeioti* from the forest on the coastal dunes, as witnesses to a hard-fought court case of 1155 concerning that forest made clear; see Sgherri, *I documenti*, nn. 1–6, referring to ship timbers for the 1110s–1120s wars against Mallorca and Genoa. For the case, see Wickham, *Courts and conflict*, pp. 144–50.

[223] 'Anrigo fece dare alo restaiolo solidos xx, intra Oghicione e Pisanello libras iii, inn amschcre [d]enarios xx, serratura di timone a Pilotto denarios xxxiiii.' ('Amschcre' is doubtless to be read 'amiscere'. Note that 'serrare' means 'to saw' in Latin, not in Italian, where it means 'to lock', and has done since Dante (e.g. *Purgatorio*, 9, l. 128); but 'sawing' seems to me to makes more sense here.) The first edition of the text is Baldelli, 'La carta pisana di Filadelfia'; but I follow here Ciaralli, 'Alle origini del documento mercantile', which has the fullest discussion and a wide bibliography (reflecting the fact that this is one of the first texts in Italian). Ciaralli is in my view too certain that this is a military and perhaps even communal document. He would also (p. 45) like to push its date later on non-palaeographical grounds; this seems to me unnecessary. For non-military galleys, see, e.g., Maragone, *Annales pisani*, ed. Lupo Gentile, p. 39; D'Amia, *Diritto e sentenze*, n. 12 (a court case of 1171); cf. Pryor, *Geography, technology and war*, pp. 32–6. Krueger, *Navi*, p. 24, sets out the statistics for Genoese commercial ships in the time of Giovanni Scriba around 1160: *naves* set against galleys were 50 to 6 or 7.

the Almohads, the Norman kings of Sicily, the judge-kings of Sardinia, the towns of southern France, and also with competitor cities, Amalfi, Genoa, Lucca, and Venice; almost all of them are from the twelfth century (1080–1 is the earliest date known, for the Sardinian judge-king of Torres). They resemble those for Genoa, and in nearly every case they are explicitly concerned with, above all, commercial rights. They do not in themselves indicate scale, nor do they mention many goods traded, but they certainly show that the Pisans were international players. The first set of Egypt treaties, from 1154, is notable for its references to Pisan *funduqs* not only in Alexandria but in Fusṭāṭ (*Babillonia*) as well; both that and the second, with Saladin in 1173, are explicit about one element in Egyptian trade which is usually hidden elsewhere, the import to Alexandria of iron, arms and timber, plus pitch for caulking ships (cf. pp. 146–7 above), as well as the export of alum, which we have seen for Venice and Genoa too.[224] Pisans undoubtedly moved about to trade, in the framework of these sets of agreements; the Pisan *Annals*, for example, record, slightly surprisingly perhaps, a Pisan ship coming from Venice to Alexandria in 1174, only to be captured by the king of Sicily in an attack on the latter port.[225] And traders came to Pisa in return. Even if Donizone's invocation, in his verse biography of Matilda, of Turks, Libyans, Parthians and Chaldeans on the shore of Pisa, was the rhetorical condemnation of a too cosmopolitan city, the first-person account by the Icelandic pilgrim Nikulás Bergsson in the early 1150s of ships coming into Pisa from Byzantium, Sicily, Egypt, Syria, and Africa, seems a more neutral witness, at least to international shipping of some kind.[226]

At home too, texts implying forms of commercial activity appear in our evidence. For a start, references to credit are frequent, from the first decades of the

[224] See Müller, *Documenti*, most of nn. 1–33, for Levant treaties up to the Third Crusade; ibid., n. 34 is the main one for Byzantium, from 1192, incorporating an earlier one from 1111; n. 18 is for Venice. For treaties with Egypt, Mallorca, Valencia, Tunis, and the Almohads, see Amari, *I diplomi arabi*, 2ª serie, nn. 1–17 (nn. 2–3 for *funduqs*; nn. 7–10 for Egyptian trade items), 1ª serie, nn. 1–5, 46 (n. 1, plus 2ª serie, n. 6, also deal with the export of alum to Pisa, this time from Tunis; n. 14 complains about the rules against the export of leather from Béjaïa to Pisa). Leonardo Pisano, *Liber abbaci* (in *Scritti*, ed. Boncompagni, 1), pp. 117–18, also comments on leather and alum exports from Béjaïa; anyway, the sometimes alarming complexities of his calculations of different percentages of commodities in ships (ibid., esp. pp. 83–132), clearly show the range, both in geography and in products, of Pisan trading shortly after our period, in 1202. For Genoa, see n. 174 above; for Amalfi, see Nardi, *Le pergamene*, n. 43 (= Bonaini, 'Due carte pisane-amalfitane'); for Lucca, see Caroti, *Le pergamene*, n. 67 (= Bonaini, 'Diplomi pisani', pp. 28–34); for Sardinia there are too many to list, but early ones are edited in Banti, *I brevi dei consoli*, pp. 107–8, 113–14 (the first of these is dated more tightly, to 1080–1, in Ronzani, *Chiesa e "civitas"*, pp. 190–9); for southern France, see Salvatori, *Boni amici et vicini*. For Sicily, see Maragone, *Annales pisani*, ed. Lupo Gentile, pp. 11, 49 (brief references only); 9, 45, 54, 69, 72 mention other treaties. For food trading, see n. 215 above. Schaube, *Handelsgeschichte*, pp. 135–7, 211–12, 292–8, 325–6, 461–3, is probably still the fullest discussion of all this, but presented in a very fragmented and descriptive way.

[225] Maragone, *Annales pisani*, ed. Lupo Gentile, p. 61; this contradicts the detail of Saladin's reported letter about the (unsuccessful) attack, which supposedly included Pisans as Sicilian allies; see Chapter 2, n. 314 above. But we have seen that all the Italian port cities were torn when their trading partners attacked each other, and Pisans had helped the king of Jerusalem in his own attack on Alexandria in 1167; see ibid., p. 45, with Cortesini, *Le pergamene*, n. 21 (= Müller, *Documenti*, n. 11).

[226] Donizone, *Vita Mathildis*, ed. Simeoni, 1, ll. 1370–2; Nikulás Bergsson, *Leiðarvísir*, ed. and trans. Simek, pp. 481, 486.

eleventh century until the end of our period and beyond; here, they tended to take the form of land sales with a buy-back clause, and probably survive because they were not bought back, but the clauses included interest-paying on a regular basis, called *prode*, as in Venice. The levels of interest were rather less regular than the Venetian *de quinque sex*, but 15–25 per cent was common. The Pisan economy was not yet as fluid as that of Venice, for these were not visibly short-term loans, but our evidence for them starts in the same period, earlier than for most other Italian cities.[227] We saw in Chapter 5 that the Casapieri family, one of the most prominent and influential in the city, had links with Mallorca which perhaps went back to the 1010s, and this family is particularly likely to have gained most of its wealth from trade. The Casalei family, slightly less prominent, were descended from a man called Leone 'de Babillonia', active in or before the 1070s; Babillonia, which here must be a nickname, was the standard Pisan name for Fusṭāṭ-Cairo, as we have just seen, and we can conclude that either Leone or his father had an association with Egypt of some kind already at this date. The Ebriaci, for their part, were involved in sending cloth from Piacenza to Constantinople and Alexandria in the 1130s, as a chance-surviving letter tells us. So at least some of the city's political elite were active traders, even if we cannot say anything about most of the others; and they seem to have begun at an early date, well predating the treaties.[228] This was institutionalized in some places in our period; documents reflecting the activities of the Pisan colony in Constantinople begin to survive from the 1140s, and we have seen that there were Pisan colonies or *fundūq*s in Messina, Egypt, and Béjaïa. It can be added that the *Vita S. Raynerii*, a contemporary life of a Pisan lay saint written around 1170, includes numerous miracles about shipwrecks and the freeing of captives from ships bound for Byzantium, Sicily, Sardinia, and Tunis. The 'consuls of the merchants' of what would become the *ordo mercatorum*, which in the thirteenth century linked together nearly all Pisa's artisan guilds as well, are first documented in the *breve* of the consuls of the city in 1162.[229]

[227] There are too many such contracts to cite up to 1180, but the eleventh-century ones are Scalfati, *Carte dell'Archivio della Certosa di Calci*, 1, nn. 4 (a. 1019, the first of all), 52–3, 141; Falaschi, *Carte dell'Archivio capitolare*, 2, n. 4; Tirelli Carli, *Carte dell'Archivio Capitolare*, 3, n. 13; Sirolla, *Carte dell'Archivio di Stato*, 2, nn. 5, 32, 42; Ghignoli, *Carte dell'Archivio arcivescovile*, 1, n. 199. Unlike in Venice and Genoa, levels of interest remained unregularized: the 1164 consular oath, ed. Banti, *I brevi dei consoli*, p. 90, has the consul state that he will not, when loaning money for the commune, take *maiores usuras... quam maior pars creditorum Pisanorum tunc exiget* ('greater interest than the majority of Pisan creditors do'). In 1173, two brothers fell out over usurious loans (*usuria, profitus*), which here imply fraud; arbiters split the difference (Carmignani, *Le pergamene*, n. 27).

[228] For the Casapieri, see pp. 459–60 above. For Leone *de Babillonia*, see Manaresi, *I placiti*, 3, n. 433 (for the family, see Rege Cambrin. *La famiglia dei Casalei*). For Ebriaci, see Beyer, *Die lombardische Briefsammlung*, nn. 56–7 (for the family, see Ceccarelli Lemut, 'Pisan consular families', pp. 128–39; these texts have been sometimes taken to be for the Genoese Embriaci family, but wrongly).

[229] For the Constantinople colony, see the texts edited in Müller, *Documenti*, nn. 2, 7, 8, 10, 16, 17, 41–4, 46–7, 51. For Messina and Béjaïa, see pp. 256, 265 above. For the miracles, see *Vita S. Raynerii*, ed. Zaccagnini, chs 43, 77, 84–5, 90, 103, 111, 113, 162, 168. For the *consules de negotiatoribus*, see

Conversely, references to sea commerce do not appear in our private documents before the second half of the twelfth century. Even then, they are so few that they are worth listing. In rough chronological order, up to 1180: in 1151, a man gives his son four *carra* of Valencia wine and envisages that the son will go *ultra mare pro negotio*; in the 1160s, there are two references to Pisans in or about to go to Sicily; in 1171, a court case over the unhappy conclusion of a *societas galee*, a shipping partnership, deals with disputes over the rent of the ship and its sails; before 1173, a Pisan is in Saint-Gilles, near Arles; in a will of 1176, a man gives the tutorship over his son to his *socius*, presumably in a *compagnia* or *societas maris*—both terms were used in Pisa; in 1179, two men agree with the commune of Pisa to look after the possessions of a third, who may well be away trading, for they include ship's equipment and commercial goods, including cloth (one piece is from Douai in northern France) and, almost uniquely in this period, four *folia de cartulis de bambace*, cotton-based paper.[230] *Compagniae* and sea loans begin, as already noted, to appear as well. The very small number of twelfth-century voyages which we have actual contracts for do not seem to have gone far (two are for Sardinia, one for Montpellier and Messina, and one for *Bola*, possibly Pula just south of Cagliari in Sardinia); nor are they usually for large sums of money (they vary from £4 to £300, plus once, interestingly, 250 Almohad *massemutini*, on the Montpellier voyage). But they do show a particular Pisan style of characterizing merchandise: the agreed commercial payload of a *compagnia/societas* on a ship is called a *hentica* or *emtica*, a loanword from Greek (*enthēkē*, meaning 'store' or 'capital'). This is not a word used in Venice (which, as we have seen, used *habere* instead) or Genoa (which used *laboratum*), but it was standard in Pisa, and also appears in references in documents to outstanding debts *in hentica*—one for £69, in a will of 1179, also mentions cotton worth £41 sitting in a *botheca* (shop) in the city.[231]

These bitty references are however then tied together, and can be seen as a coherent whole, thanks to the one thing which marks Pisa out from every other Italian city in the twelfth century—its early and ambitious law code. This was promulgated in December 1160, and had many subsequent revisions; the earliest text we have dates to January 1186. It is well known for the part it played in turning Pisa into a city ruled by Roman law, but the section of the code which treats

Banti, *I brevi dei consoli*, p. 50, and in general, for the whole history of the *ordo mercatorum*, Ticciati, *L'Ordine dei Mercanti a Pisa*.

[230] See, respectively, Caroti, *Le pergamene*, n. 28; Cortesini, *Le pergamene*, n. 32; Archivio Capitolare di Pisa, n. 763, '*c.*1200' (the text is cut, removing the date; *c.*1160 is more likely); D'Amia, *Diritto e sentenze*, n. 12; Carmignani, *Le pergamene*, n. 27; Benedetti, *Le pergamene*, nn. 24, 55. See also p. 519 above for a Venetian dying on a Pisan commercial ship in or just before 1176.

[231] The contracts are cited in n. 221 above (the Montpellier text is Orlandi, *Carte dell'Archivio della Certosa di Calci*, n. 131). For debts *in hentica*, see ibid., nn. 94 (a. 1179), 102. Genoese texts used *massemutini* on occasion too; see, e.g., *Giovanni Scriba*, nn. 910, 958 (both for Almohad-ruled Ceuta), 961.

commercial dealings is the more custom-based (if still Roman-influenced) *Constitutum Usus*.[232] *Societates* are here dealt with in considerable detail, along with a wider law of the sea, which deals with hiring ships, or else what to do when goods of some passengers but not others are thrown off the ship during a storm to lighten it, and so on—issues faced in Byzantine and Islamic law, and, indeed, in Roman law itself, as well as being ever-present concerns in the *geniza* letters; we will come back to the point in Chapter 7. It emerges from the discussions of *societates* that these are, indeed, as in Venice and as with the *commenda* of Genoa, partnerships in which the sedentary merchant, the [*socius*] *stans*, generally puts in two-thirds of the capital and the travelling merchant, here called a *tractator*, a third; the whole is then called the *hentica*, and can either be in goods or money. The legislation, when it discusses problem after problem concerning this, tends simply to state that parties have to abide by the terms of the contract, but the concrete examples allow us to see that Pisan sea trading had much the same rules as we can deduce from contracts elsewhere. For example, if the contract says that the *tractator* can go on any *tassedium* (cf. Venetian *taxidium*), and does not specify a place ('such as Alexandria', the text says later), then he can go where he likes; but the contract can also require his return on the first *tassedium* back, in the Pisan version of the 'Venetian business model'.[233]

Sea loans are also discussed. Here, the text sets out, among other things, what profit/interest (*proficuum*, *lucrum*, or *prode*) an investor has the right to expect from a successfully returning ship if the contract does not specify it. I drew on this when discussing Sicily (p. 251 above), for it lists a range of Sicilian ports, but the overall picture is worth characterizing as well: the lowest interest, of 8 *denarii* in the pound (3.3 per cent), is for a journey just along the coast to the Vada salt flats at the southern end of the diocese, with the figure going up slowly as a ship goes farther down the Italian coast, or to France or Sardinia; then, a journey to Spain or Sicily or most of North Africa would render 25 per cent, whereas one to Byzantium, Syria, or Egypt would render 7 *solidi* in the pound, 35 per cent. This list overthinks the issue somewhat, for the Italian contracts that I have seen never fail to specify what the investor expected at the end, but it is at least a neat representation of the minimum scale of profit that different parts of the Mediterranean might be expected to offer, and it is the best source we have for that. Furthermore,

232 See in general Storti Storchi, *Intorno ai Costituti pisani*; Wickham, *Courts and conflict*, pp. 108–67; Vignoli, *I Costituti* (pp. lxxviii–lxxix for the 1186 date).

233 *Constitutum Usus*, chs 4, 21–3, 27–31 (in Vignoli, *I Costituti*, pp. 145–7, 195–25, 235–53—as can be seen, substantial quantities of law-making); ch. 22, the longest, is the main text on *societates* (pp. 208 for ⅔–⅓, 209, 212, 218 for *hentica*, 210–11 for rules about *tassedia*, 214 for Alexandria); ch. 28 is for hiring ships; ch. 29 is for throwing goods off a ship. For earlier law on the last, see Chapter 7, n. 38 below. These chapters of Pisan law have not been commented on as much as one would expect, but one early example is, surprisingly, Max Weber's doctoral thesis, translated as *The history of commercial partnerships*, esp. pp. 129–37, very legalist in its formulations.

it was copied, only slightly changed, into the third and largest version of the code which survives, that of 1233, so it was clearly thought to have value.[234]

If we put all these separate data together, then we have fairly clear evidence that Pisa was more or less exactly like Venice and Genoa in its commitment to sea trading and in its understanding of how that trading worked across every part of the Mediterranean. What we have no idea of, however, and not for the first time, is scale. No elements of quantification exist at all, except the simple fact that the Pisans were respected players in all Mediterranean regions, and that, in simple military terms, they were the equals of Genoa in our period. We can only get any further by comparing rough impressions, built up over this chapter and also all those preceding, focussing on the twelfth-century data.

We saw in Chapter 4 that the Venetians were overwhelmingly dominant among the Italian cities trading inside the Byzantine Empire, with Pisa a distant second, and Genoa very much third. (In all these regions I am here only comparing the Italian cities with each other, not with the mercantile communities of the regions themselves, who remained active, as we have seen in other chapters.) Similarly, the Genoese dominated in Sicily, over Pisa, with the Venetians barely present; and al-Andalus was open above all to Pisans, with the Genoese here a long way behind. Genoa and Pisa were both active in North Africa, possibly equally. In the Levant and Egypt, all three cities were active; the Venetians had less commitment to the Levant, but seem to have been the most prominent of the three in Egypt. These look fairly even, taken as a whole, but al-Andalus, the region where Pisans seem to have been particularly present, was the least involved in Mediterranean trade. Genoa and Pisa both had a wider geographical range than Venice, and, importantly, the scale of individual Genoese maritime investments was greater than that of Venice; but Venice was dominant or particularly prominent in two of the most important trading regions, Byzantium and Egypt, and the Genoese only dominated in one, Sicily. I tentatively concluded earlier (p. 521) that Genoa, taken overall, had a larger-scale trading commitment than Venice in our period, but it is very difficult to be sure of that, even when we have a great deal of data to work with. Pisa is far harder to place, in the absence of those data. My sense is that it came third, given the relative unimportance of sea trading with Italy in the one region, Islamic Spain, where Pisans were the main Italian players. But it was not a distant third; and this tentative ranking did not take away from the fact that it must have gained a great deal of wealth from trading, just as the other two cities did. And here at least, we can be sure, as we could not be for the other two cities, what Pisa had to sell in bulk: iron, from the mines down the coast. Pisan iron is, indeed, mentioned not only in the Egypt treaties but also in smaller-scale accords with central Italian trading cities, Corneto and Rome, and occasionally in the

[234] *Constitutum Usus*, chs 24–5 (in Vignoli, *I Costituti*, pp. 225–31); cf. Bonaini, *Statuti inediti*, 2, pp. 905–6.

Genoese records too. Although the Arab geographers are by and large fairly vague about north-central Italy, one of them, al-Zuhrī (active in al-Andalus in the 1140s), also stresses Pisan iron, particularly weapon-making.[235] That was a core starting point for Pisa's substantial and enthusiastic maritime activity. The next question for us, however, must now be how much effect this had on the economic coherence of Tuscany as a whole. And for that we need to turn to the archaeology.

* * *

Pisa as a city has some of the best—and best-published—archaeology in Italy for our period. Only Rome and, outside the mainland, Palermo have similar numbers of sites. Florence and Siena both have a few significant excavations as well, and other cities have smaller ones. In the countryside of northern and central Tuscany, the greatest density of excavation concerns a large set of castles, that is to say, fortified villages, excavated by Riccardo Francovich and then his pupils and successors at the University of Siena across the last forty years; this set extends from Siena in the centre of Tuscany to the coast, including many of the rural metal-working sites which came under Pisan control. In the Arno valley, closer to the main cities, San Genesio is worth highlighting as a site as well; it was a market centre, lying beneath the later hilltop village of San Miniato, close to the major Arno river crossing of Fucecchio and to the main pilgrim road from France, the via Francigena, up an important Arno tributary, the Elsa, towards Siena and eventually Rome. These are the excavations which give sense and context to over 200 other sites, large and small, in Tuscany. Here, it seems most important to characterize what has been found in Pisa, and then to look at two main topics in more detail: the changes in the ways rural buildings were constructed across our period, and—as in every chapter of this book—the ceramic distributions, which have been established for Tuscany with an unusual level of exactness across urban and rural sites alike.

The main sites in Pisa include two excavated in the 1990s in the centre of the early medieval city north of the Arno, piazza Dante and piazza dei Cavalieri, and a substantial set of more recent sites. The latter are located all over the city, and several of them are south of the Arno, the new urban quarter then and now called Chinzica or Kinzica, which seems to have expanded rapidly from a small core in the late eleventh and twelfth centuries.[236] Indeed, Pisa spread in these centuries

[235] For iron, see Carmignani, *Le pergamene*, nn. 30, 42; for Genoa, see n. 206 above. For al-Zuhrī's account of Pisa, see *Kitāb al-ja'rāfiyya*, trans. Bramón, p. 136; cf. Renzi Rizzo, '*Pisarum et Pisanorum descriptiones*'. Note that the so-called letter of Berta of Tuscany to Caliph al-Muktafī in 906, mentioning gifts of weapons, slaves, and luxury cloth, is a fantasy, probably written in Iraq; see Christys, 'The queen of the Franks offers gifts'. Al-Idrīsī, unfortunately, only gives us generic details for most of north-central Italy (although Pisa—as also Genoa—does get some sort of write-up, unlike Venice and Milan): *Nuzhat al-mushtāq*, trans. Jaubert and Nef, pp. 371–2; cf. 364, 370.

[236] See esp. Bruni, *Pisa: piazza Dante*; Bruni et al., *Ricerche di archeologia medievale a Pisa*, 1; Anichini and Gattiglia, 'Nuovi dati'; Cantini and Rizzitelli, *Una città operosa*. Gattiglia, *Pisa medievale*,

north of the river as well; when the commune decided to build a new set of walls in 1155 (those which largely still stand), they came to include urban areas both north and south of the Arno, and the city's walled area was extended massively, from some 40 hectares in the tenth century to 185 hectares by the end of the twelfth, when Chinzica's walls, begun later, were mostly completed. Even though the space was not all filled, this must reflect a considerable demographic increase. Inside the walls, tower houses for the city's elite families began to be built by the mid-eleventh century, and their height was regulated in 1081 and *c.*1090, as in Genoa a few decades later, as we saw; here their maximum height was to be 21 metres, a little lower than in Genoa.[237] Tower houses from the eleventh century indeed survive in the city, as do those from later centuries. The city was in many places densely inhabited, with houses built straddling streets well before 1200—some of these survive too. Walls and tower houses, like the cathedral, are obvious markers of urban wealth.[238] From 1050 at the latest, this was becoming materially visible in buildings, and it developed more and more clearly across the next century.

The cathedral was, at least initially, paid for by successful warfare, as we have seen; but the rest of this has to have come from a more widespread economic prosperity. Whether agriculture and its profits were the most important element here, or urban production, or overseas trade, cannot easily be said, but all three were developing after 1050. The territory of Pisa was perhaps the main part of Tuscany to have seen serious land clearance in our period, with steady marsh drainage on the edge of the settled land. The immediate hinterland of Pisa was less affected by the growth of rural signorial power than almost anywhere in north-central Italy, and we cannot easily show that landlords took higher rents and dues from peasant cultivators; but the steady increase in land area must have had an effect on overall surplus, and land prices inland from Pisa went up substantially at the end of our period, which indicates increased urban demand.[239] As to overseas trade, we have already seen that it was capable of producing considerable wealth, even if we cannot easily get a sense of its true scale, including in our archaeological evidence, which we will come to shortly. But it is urban

gives an overview up to 2013. For the expansion of Chinzica, see Garzella, *Pisa com'era*, pp. 92–102, 148–52; Baldassarri, 'Da *villa* a *civitas*'.

237 Garzella, *Pisa com'era*, pp. 62–3, 103–207; for the regulation of height, see *Heinrici IV. diplomata*, n. 336; Rossetti, 'Il lodo del vescovo Daiberto'.

238 Redi, *Pisa com'era*, pp. 177–303.

239 For one context of land clearance, the communal marshlands which were part of the public lands known as *guariganga*, see Giardina, 'Le "guariganga"', which is, however, an institutional, not an economic analysis. Pisan estate management has not been systematically studied for our period, but from the thirteenth century, fixed rents and partiary rents in kind were normal; the latter, although variable, were most commonly a third of the crop, as elsewhere in Italy (see p. 492 above). For an overview, see Luzzati, 'Contratti agrari'. For land prices, see Tognetti, 'Produzioni, traffici e mercati', p. 128.

production which is to me the element which allows us to say most, so let us focus on that.

Pisans worked iron throughout the early and central middle ages. The piazza dei Cavalieri site, in the very middle of the early medieval town, showed considerable evidence for iron smelting, probably using Elba iron, between the seventh century and the end of the twelfth (when the area was redeveloped), with a high point in the tenth and eleventh centuries. By the time the site went out of use, other workshops had appeared, including on the nearby piazza Cavallotti, via Consoli del Mare, and via dei Mille sites, the last of which was a bronze-working workshop in the twelfth century but then, by the end of the century, switched to iron. Over the bridge in Chinzica, via Toselli had ironworking (and also leatherworking) by 1100, and by 1200 larger-scale metal workshops, for iron and bronze, appeared too. The latter, found under a former pharmaceutical factory, the Laboratori Gentili, existed in association with glassmaking by the end of the twelfth century, and probably again leatherworking. A substantial textile workshop also existed by the early thirteenth century behind the via dei Mille.[240] By 1150 at the latest, this artisanal world, long in existence, had properly taken off. By then too, the core of the city north of the Arno had expanded so far east that the old edge of town leading down to the Arno bridge had become the main commercial zone (as it still is); beside that was a major artisanal area, to match that in Chinzica (see Map 26).

We also know from excavation that Pisa made its own pottery; early twelfth-century kiln wasters have been found in the 2010s on the via La Tinta site in eastern Chinzica. But in fact, many archaeologists had already assumed it. We do not have any other evidence of kilns for Pisa in our period—the closest are 10–15 kilometres out of town—but the eleventh- and twelfth-century ceramics found there are very close to Pisan types, and are best seen as peri-urban spin-offs of urban production, which is likely to have been active from the eleventh century at the latest. It is, in fact, in the early eleventh century that the undecorated *acroma depurata* ceramic types found in the city, mostly mugs and pitchers, improve markedly in their fabrics, and show signs of large-scale production; it may be then that the city came to dominate the top end of local ceramics in its territory.[241] The ground was here laid for the next step, Pisan *maiolica arcaica*, Tuscany's first decorated glazed ware, made from the 1210s/1220s onwards (see Fig. 18); its glaze

[240] See in general Gattiglia, *Pisa medievale*, pp. 162–72, 176–9. For sites, see Corretti, 'L'attività metallurgica', with Corretti, 'Piazza dei Cavalieri' (p. 68 for Elba iron); Alberti and Giorgio, 'Nuovi dati', p. 31; Meo, 'Archeologia della produzione'; Toscani, 'La produzione di vetro'; Carrera, 'La lavorazione dei metalli'.

[241] For via La Tinta, see Alberti and Giorgio, 'Nuovi dati', pp. 33–4 (the whole article is a valuable recent survey). For peri-urban sites, see Grassi, *La ceramica, l'alimentazione*, pp. 5, 145–6; for Pisa, see ibid., pp. 4, 29–30. For local Pisan pottery, see also in general, among others, Cantini, 'Ritmi e forme', pp. 114, 120; Gattiglia, *Pisa medievale*, pp. 187–92; Giorgio, 'Ceramica e società'; Fatighenti, *La ceramica bassomedievale*; Baldassarri, 'La ceramica a Pisa'.

Fig. 18 *Maiolica arcaica pisana*

techniques are so close to those of al-Andalus that it is likely that the glazing specialists came from there, but the basic pottery-making skills were well honed already. The main production area, Barattularia ('the quarter of the glazed-ware potters') in eastern Chinzica, documented from the 1240s, seems to have been the same—at any rate, the via La Tinta site is located there.[242] Both unglazed and glazed wares were widely marketed, as we shall see in a moment. This, like the iron, shows scale, for Pisan production and distribution alike.

It is this archaeological material which gives context to the documentary citations of artisans which begin to appear in slightly greater numbers in the twelfth century. Broadly, in our casual references, *fabri* are the commonest artisans; although this, as we have seen, is a very generic word (it was here also used for the workers on the cathedral, who were certainly by no means predominantly metalworkers), one, Riccio di Martino, at the end of the 1180s, was explicitly a *ferrarius* or ironsmith, and in Pisa most probably were. Second were leatherworkers, and then a wide range of trades including weavers, dyers, and one *tegularius*, a potter or tile maker (who fails to repay a loan in 1181 and loses his workshop (*domus tegularum*)).[243] We cannot get any sense of scale from these, but the balance of citations favouring iron and leather is consistent with the archaeology—it is

[242] The point of reference for the substantial bibliography on Pisan *maiolica arcaica* remains Berti, *Pisa: le 'maioliche arcaiche'*, from 1997; see ibid., pp. 277, 283 for Spanish models. More recently, see, e.g., Giorgio, 'La maiolica arcaica'; Giorgio, 'Una rivoluzione tecnologica'. For Barattularia, see Berti and Renzi Rizzo, 'Ceramiche e ceramisti', esp. pp. 499, 506–11.

[243] For *fabri* and the cathedral, see, e.g., Ghignoli, *Carte dell'Archivio arcivescovile*, 1, n. 198. Riccio di Martino: Orlandi, *Carte dell'Archivio della Certosa di Calci*, nn. 132, 134, 138, 171; for the *tegularius*,

worth repeating that references to potters are relatively rare in documents. The first (and for a long time the only) written text which gives us a good guide as to scale is a Pisan oath of peace to other Tuscan towns dating to 1228, well after our period, which lists 4,300 names, probably reflecting, as noted earlier, a population of 24–27,000 for the city as a whole at that moment. Of those names, 326 were leatherworkers, 251 metalworkers, 125 textile workers, all of them with a considerable range of specialisms, showing a developed division of labour—in the textile sector, for example, which was not so prominent in Pisa until well into the thirteenth century, there were cotton, wool, and hemp workers, ropemakers, combers, weavers, dyers, tailors, and more again. Even this large set is not complete, as only two *tegularii* were listed, which, even if the word did not simply mean 'tile maker' here, is far fewer than the number of artisans who would have been needed by now to make *maiolica arcaica*, let alone Pisa's other ceramics. All the same, put together with food sellers and smaller groups of artisans, nearly a third of the adult males of the city claimed a trade of some kind in 1228, and the real figure was evidently higher.[244] The scale of our archaeological evidence for iron and ceramics allows us to say that this was probably true by 1150 at the latest, and that it had begun to develop before 1100.

So Pisa was not just an import–export town; in our period, it had rather more of an artisanal base than Venice or Genoa did, even if Venice made iron too (see p. 524 above). The archaeology of ceramic imports can be set against that. They started early enough. The Sicilian amphorae discussed in Chapter 3, probably above all for wine, appear from the late tenth century, and then continue throughout our period. As to tablewares, Sicilian and Tunisian glazed bowls have a similar trajectory, although they are more common after the mid-eleventh century; in the late twelfth, Sicilian glaze is less visible, but cobalt and manganese glaze from Tunis becomes very prominent on the urban sites. The date of the arrival of Andalusī glaze has been disputed, but it is likely that imports into the city in general began a little later, from the late eleventh century, and continued and developed after that. In the twelfth century, the quantities of these imports on Pisan sites increase markedly, and a few Egyptian, Byzantine, and south Italian—and, eventually, Ligurian—glazed wares are added too; they then drop back a little once Pisan *maiolica arcaica* begins to be an acceptable import substitute, well into the thirteenth century.[245] It can be added that imports are found on all sites. Tower

see ibid., n. 107. See further Garzella, *Pisa com'era*, pp. 204–7 for the dominance and urban locations of iron and leather artisans in the twelfth century.

[244] See Salvatori, *La popolazione pisana*, pp. 116–23 for the total figures for the city, 141–78 for trades. I have cut out white-collar occupations such as notaries from the calculation of 'nearly a third'. For the next century, Herlihy, *Pisa*, pp. 128–61, is still empirically valuable.

[245] For Sicilian amphorae, see Chapter 3, nn. 189–91, above; for al-Andalus, see Chapter 5, nn. 108, 218 above. For imports in general, to cite only relatively recent works from the substantial bibliography, see Cantini, 'Ritmi e forme', pp. 115–16, 118–19, 121; Gattiglia, *Pisa medievale*, pp. 187–202; Baldassarri, 'La ceramica a Pisa'; Baldassarri and Giorgio, 'La ceramica di produzione

houses, owned by elites, had more polychrome and tin-glazed wares; but workshops used imported wares too, this time, however, with a higher percentage of monochrome glaze, presumably cheaper, and fewer imports from the eastern Mediterranean, although Tunisian cobalt and manganese tin glaze by the end of the twelfth century reached every type of site.[246] The amphorae mean that Pisa was importing wine from another region, presumably on grounds of quality, since its territory made its own; and from 1000 and into the thirteenth century, it was also getting its fine tableware from many different sectors of the maritime commercial network. This is a striking set of imports. It has parallels to what we saw for Genoa and Venice too, so, if we take into account local variations, the range was evidently typical for Italian ports. But as the archaeology is better for Pisa, we can also say that this fine ware was simply a complementary addition to what was an active ceramic production inside the city itself. It was a higher-quality adjunct to what Pisa could provide, and, indeed, imports were the only ceramic tablewares (apart from drinking vessels) until *maiolica arcaica* came in after the end of our period; but the city produced its own wares on a substantial scale too.

I would assume that this reflects what else Pisa produced as well. We at least know that Pisa not only did not need to import ironwork, but exported it widely—it could well have paid for all the imports into the city we know about, plus those we do not; it was often matched by copper and bronze-working as well. In terms of leather too, it very likely had enough production to export. Cloth is less clear, but the absence of signs of cloth-making on a major scale implies more imports in this arena in the twelfth century, when all other aspects of Pisa's economy were picking up fast. If so, they would perhaps not yet often be from northern Italy, given the city's frequently poisonous relationship with Genoa, the main outlet for cloth from Lombardy after 1150, even if we do see Pisans themselves once or twice linked to the north. It would be tempting to wonder whether the Pisans actually bought some of their cloth from Egypt, the most obvious cloth-making region it traded with regularly, as the Venetians did, but we have no evidence for that at all; by the thirteenth century, it is most likely that it also bought from Lucca, and maybe this was true earlier too.[247] Anyway, if we take these guesses together, we might suppose that imports and local productions roughly balanced, probably more than they did in Venice and Genoa. The ceramic patterns thus seem a good guide to the nature of that balance: Pisan ceramics were not grand as

mediterranea'; Giorgio, 'Circolazione e consumo'; Fatighenti, 'I corredi ceramici'; Meo, 'L'ordinario e l'eccezione'. For *bacini*, see most recently Berti and Giorgio, *Ceramiche con coperture vetrificate*, with the just-cited Meo article. The fullest publication of imports from a single site remains Bruni, *Pisa: piazza Dante*, pp. 535–88.

[246] For status differences, see Gattiglia, *Pisa medievale*, pp. 198–201; Baldassarri and Giorgio, 'La ceramica di produzione mediterranea', pp. 48–9; Giorgio, 'Ceramica e società', pp. 590–1. For cobalt and manganese on artisanal sites, see, e.g., Fatighenti, 'I corredi ceramici', pp. 283–4.

[247] For Venice, see p. 519 above; for Lucca, see p. 584 below. For Pisan links to the north, see n. 228 above, n. 272 below; this, however, used a longer land route, via Lucca and San Donnino (cf. also n. 37 above).

yet, but were functional, and were simply set against, rather than being dominated by, tablewares from outside.

We can say more about the city's links with the rest of Tuscany, however (see Map 21). Pisan iron came in to be worked from Elba, above all; it probably always had done, but once the city took control of the island, it was that much easier. And we have good evidence for a set of metalworking settlements in and beside the Colline Metallifere opposite Elba too. They too started early. Vetricella, founded on public (i.e. royal) land on the plain near the coast south of Campiglia, an unusual site, because it was defended by three concentric banks and ditches already in the ninth century, was a major ironworking centre in the ninth to eleventh centuries, using iron from Elba. It seems to have made horse-riding equipment more than anything else, presumably for the army, on a large scale for nearly two centuries, plus cloth and leather, although it became steadily less active after 1000, and was abandoned by 1100.[248] A set of fortified hilltop settlements picked up metalworking thereafter; in Cugnano and Rocchette Pannocchieschi it began in the tenth century, elsewhere a little later, but on these sites as a set, both closer to the coast and farther inland, iron production reached its height in the eleventh and twelfth.[249] And other metals were added to this, reflecting the resources of the hills—including effectively limitless supplies of wood for smelting. The most striking example is Rocca San Silvestro, near Campiglia, another iron site, which, however, also developed rapidly from the eleventh century onwards as a silver- and copper-producing centre. It or other sites in the Colline Metallifere were the sources for the silver currency of Lucca and, doubtless, Pisa by the twelfth century at the latest, as analysis of the metal of the coins shows; Pisa is, indeed, one of the few Italian cities in which coins are plentiful on sites before 1200.[250]

[248] See in general Bianchi and Hodges, *The nEU-Med project*, esp. Marasco and Briano, 'The stratigraphic sequence'; Agostini, 'The metal finds'; and the earlier Bianchi and Hodges, *Origins of a new economic union*, esp. Bianchi and Collavini, 'Public estates', p. 154 for Elba and local iron; and now Bianchi, *Archeologia dei beni pubblici*, the new synthesis for Vetricella and the sites in n. 249 below.

[249] For recent overviews, see Bianchi and Dallai, 'Le district minier des Collines Métallifères', and Bianchi, *Archeologia dei beni pubblici*; see also Benvenuti et al., 'Studying the Colline Metallifere mining area'; Bianchi, 'Recenti ricerche'. For Cugnano, see Belli et al., *Archeologia di un castello minerario*; Bruttini et al., 'Un insediamento a vocazione mineraria'; Benvenuti et al., 'Studying the Colline Metallifere mining area', p. 264. For other sites, see, e.g., Grassi, *L'insediamento medievale*, esp. pp. 178–82 (Rocchette Pannocchieschi, which had less iron than other metals); Valenti, *Miranduolo*, esp. pp. 215–19; Bianchi, *Campiglia II*, pp. 189–97—that site apparently being a less important metalworking centre in itself, however.

[250] Francovich, *Rocca San Silvestro*; Francovich and Wickham, 'Uno scavo archeologico'. For Lucca's coins, see Benvenuti et al., 'Studying the Colline Metallifere mining area', p. 284 (Pisan coins have not been studied in the same way); for the frequency of coins on Pisan excavations, see Baldassarri, 'Monete, associazioni'. (Only Verona offers a good parallel: see the summaries in Day et al., *Medieval European coinage*, 12, p. 688, nn. 87–8. In both cities, the coins found were from the local mints, Lucca/Pisa and Verona.) Pisa had at least potential access to silver from Sardinia too; see the cessions by Sardinian judge-kings in Bonaini, *Statuti inediti*, 1, pp. 282–4; Viviani, *Le pergamene*, n. 12; this access was indeed sometimes real, as *Vita S. Raynerii*, ed. Zaccagnini, ch. 90, implies. For the early Pisan mint, see Ceccarelli Lemut, 'L'uso della moneta'.

These metal sites were by no means in competition with Pisa, as the city developed across the eleventh and twelfth centuries. The proof is that they were all consumers of Pisan ceramics, throughout our period and after, so must have sold metal and other goods to Pisa to get them. The Tuscan coast had its own local productions, particularly of coarse wares, and some of it also had access to ceramics from an inland site, Roccastrada, which was a major pottery production centre from the late Roman period to the eleventh century; but Pisan products were always available too. The city's wares, indeed, came to be prominent in these coastal sites by the twelfth century, extending inland as far as Miranduolo, 40 kilometres from the sea, and by no means just in the houses of local elites; and later, Pisan *maiolica arcaica* was available in most of them very soon after its production began.[251] So were imports. The small port beside Vetricella had relatively few: low numbers of Byzantine globular amphorae of the eighth and ninth centuries and their tenth- and eleventh-century successors. But after 1100, in particular, the hilltop sites regularly had at least some imported glazed wares, by now probably coming via Pisa. In return, much of the only Tuscan glazed ware before maiolica, the Sparse Glaze ware of the ninth to twelfth centuries, was made near Donoratico, one of the main coastal castles, and exported to Pisa; but we can still assume that metal ores, half-finished metal, and metalwork were the main trading items coming up the coast to the city.[252] What we see here, in fact, is an integrated commercial and productive network, stretching from Pisa more than 100 kilometres down the coast, operative by 1000 at the latest and intensifying in the twelfth century.

This in itself brought greater wealth. Italian rural housing was overwhelmingly in wood in the early middle ages, and even walled sites had at the outset only wooden palisades; the villages of the Tuscan coast are no exception. But from the tenth century the hilltop sites began to be walled in stone (and are called *castra* or *castella* in texts); in the early twelfth century the major buildings in the centres of these castles began to be built in stone too.[253] This development marked an elite commitment to displaying status, initially, and elite rather than more widely spread wealth. The years around 1100 were those in which signorial rights began to crystallize in Tuscany, later than in the Po plain; *signorie* were close to unknown around Pisa, and weak across the lowlands and hill country along and around the Arno valley, but in the southern half of Tuscany, which included these mining

[251] See in general Grassi, *La ceramica, l'alimentazione*, pp. 14–60, and *passim* for individual sites; for Miranduolo, I am grateful for the help of Cristina Menghini. A good specific example is Boldrini et al., 'I reperti ceramici', for Campiglia.

[252] See Vaccaro, 'Long-distance ceramic connections', pp. 90–5, for the port near Vetricella; for the hilltop sites, see Grassi, *La ceramica, l'alimentazione*, pp. 35–6. For Donoratico, see ibid., 19–20, 115; Briano, *La ceramica a vetrina sparsa*, pp. 147–57; Briano and Sibilia, 'Progetto nEU-Med'.

[253] For overviews of this process, see Bianchi, 'Dominare e gestire un territorio'; Bianchi, 'Recenti ricerche'; for an Italy-wide context, see Carocci, 'Nobiltà e pietrificazione', esp. pp. 86–104.

areas, lords were very strong and their lordships exacting.[254] The stone central buildings reflected that. But Rocca San Silvestro, the most fully excavated of these sites, shows stone building spreading throughout the castle village in the twelfth century and later, very well constructed for the most part—the site is now a museum, and is arguably the best-preserved village from this period in Europe, with walls and second storeys still standing to up to 4 metres and more in height—with Pisan pottery found widely in the village houses. In Rocca San Silvestro, the layout of workshops inside the village shows that signorial control over the working of iron and silver was tight, but prosperity was by no means restricted to the lords; buying power spread from them down to the peasants/miners who did the work.[255] Rocca San Silvestro was special in the quality of its building, but not atypical in the move to stone. By the end of our period it was common across the villages that have been excavated in central-southern Tuscany, reflecting a wider prosperity—as well as a serious boost for experienced workers in the building trade. And the peasant buying power which is particularly clear from ceramic finds in Rocca San Silvestro is also, as already stated, by the twelfth century visible in the other villages as well.

Some of these villages did not specialize in metals. The farther inland one goes, towards Siena, the farther one is from the mining areas, and the more one has to assume that excavated castle village sites were essentially agricultural. But some of the same processes can be seen, even if not all. The appearance of stone is again an important guide; stone towers appeared on the summits of hilltop villages such as Montarrenti, some 10 kilometres from Siena, not long after 1100, much as they did on the coast, although here, by contrast, stone did not take over across the whole village for another century. Here, pottery remained rather more local too, even if of good quality, plausibly coming from the nearby city but anyway undecorated, until Siena's own *maiolica arcaica* began to be produced at the end of the thirteenth century.[256] We can assume here, and in parallel inland sites, that this greater ambition in construction was above all a spin-off of lordly control over agricultural surplus, through rents, and, increasingly, signorial dues. But the building expertise necessary to construct the networks of central towers in these inland villages was just as great as on the coast, and the sophisticated stonework which appears in the eleventh- and twelfth-century rebuildings of inland Tuscany's major rural churches attests to similar expertises; ceramics and metals were not the only artisanal traditions which were developing across this period.

[254] See in general Wickham, 'La signoria rurale in Toscana'. For the *signoria* and the move to stone (*pietrificazione* in Italian), see Bianchi et al., 'Rappresentazioni ed esercizio dei poteri signorili'; Bianchi and Collavini, 'Risorse e competizione per le risorse'. A specific example is Valenti, *Miranduolo*, pp. 164–228. That it had as much cultural as economic causes is stressed by Carocci, 'Nobiltà e pietrificazione', pp. 83–4, 92–4.

[255] See n. 250 above. For the pottery, see Grassi, *La ceramica, l'alimentazione*, pp. 126–35.

[256] Cantini, *Il castello di Montarrenti*, esp. pp. 45–53, 217–24; 159–63 for a survey of the pottery. For Siena, see Grassi et al., 'La maiolica arcaica senese'.

In 1155, the powerful Guidi counts began to build the fortified settlement of Podium Bonizi, on the hill overlooking the late medieval and modern town of Poggibonsi, north of Siena, which has also been excavated; this was nothing less than a new small town, built to urban-quality building specifications. Only rural families as powerful as the Guidi could make such interventions as yet (even city communes rarely founded new towns from scratch until the next century); but they could not have done it at all if the expert builders had not already been available. They doubtless in this case came from cities, but travelling construction experts, urban- or rural-based, must have been a common sight in the Tuscany of the twelfth century.[257]

We can see here a double movement. The increased economic power of lords led to greater building expenditure in the countryside, particularly in the south of Tuscany, irrespective of any other changes in the sophistication of the economy. (Poggibonsi was not in the south, and signorial power and the concentration of land in aristocratic hands were in general weaker in the area around it, but the Guidi were exceptional in their rights and resources.) But productive developments, at least along the coast, added further to that; the move to stone was faster here, and it was backed up by wider networks of exchange in ceramics and metals. This was true for urban centres in the north of Tuscany as well. Nearly every city was developing ambitious building programmes by the twelfth century, sometimes starting in the eleventh. In Florence, the cathedral was partially reshaped in the mid-eleventh century and its ambitious baptistery, still standing, dates to around and after 1100. Tower houses, some of which survive, began in the late eleventh century too, and excavation shows a dense process of urbanization in the area of the modern piazza Signoria/Palazzo Vecchio, starting in the twelfth; a new wall circuit was built in, probably, the 1170s, enclosing half the area of that of Pisa but still multiplying the size of the former walled city by four.[258] As for Lucca, its new wall circuit, dating to around 1200, enclosed slightly less, and in this case did not quite double the size of the Roman city, but settlement outside the Roman walls is, all the same, documented early, and more piecemeal excavation (plus an extensive documentary record) shows the same building density that one can see in cities elsewhere.[259] So Florence and Lucca were showing greater material wealth inside the city after 1100, and in Florence even before, than they had in earlier centuries, and a larger population by the late twelfth at the latest. I will come back to these two cities shortly, for they pose problems which are distinct in

[257] For churches, see, e.g., Moretti and Stopani, *Architettura romanica religiosa nel contado fiorentino*, pp. 29–113. For Podium Bonizi, see Francovich and Valenti, *Poggio Imperiale*, pp. 151–73.

[258] See Scampoli, *Firenze*, pp. 196–203. 218–48; for the Palazzo Vecchio site, see Bruttini, *Archeologia urbana a Firenze*.

[259] A recent rapid discussion of archaeology and urbanism in twelfth-century Lucca is Ciampoltrini and Saccocci, 'Dalla città marchionale a quella comunale'. For extramural settlement up to 1100, see Belli Barsali, 'La topografia di Lucca', pp. 505–6, 516–18, 548, 551–2.

each, but in both their demographic increases and greater building ambition seem to me to reflect the same double movement, of the concentration of agricultural wealth and (subsequently) the increase in production, which we have seen both in Pisa and in the south Tuscan castle villages.

But here the pattern is incomplete. The point can be made most clearly by looking at the distribution of ceramics inland from Pisa, along the Arno and its tributaries. The ceramics made at Pisa and its peri-urban sites were available up the Arno to San Genesio, which had been a major market and route centre since the ninth century, but no farther. Similarly, imports from the rest of the Mediterranean reached past Pisa to Lucca and a handful of sites in its vicinity in smaller quantities, and again to San Genesio, extending from there up the Elsa valley (though only as *bacini* on churches); but they too are effectively absent in Florence, only 30 kilometres upstream from San Genesio, until the thirteenth century. Indeed, although after *c.*1220 Pisan *maiolica arcaica* was the only Tuscan glazed ware, until Florence, Siena, and Volterra followed suit much later in the century, it again hardly reached upstream to Florence.[260] The Pisan exchange area extended easily down the coast, but inland it only reached Lucca and San Genesio for the whole of our period, and, even after it, not all that much farther. It is true that east and south-east of Florence there are, so far, rather fewer sites; but they do exist, and do not show imports of any kind. On the other hand, the hinterland of Florence, stretching north-west to Pistoia and south-east to Arezzo, developed a new form of coarse ware in the twelfth century, which became more common in the thirteenth, and was probably made in Florence: *paioli* (cauldrons), possibly a style imported from Romagna; significantly, these are not found along the Arno downstream from San Genesio.[261]

We have to be cautious about proposing a general picture here, for Pisa's hinterland, the lower Valdarno and the coast, is as yet far more clearly visible than the rest of Tuscany. We can at least assume that Pisan iron was marketed in inland Tuscany, given its active production in the city and its hinterland, and given the absence of equivalent sources of iron in the territories of Florence and neighbouring cities—this could be shown by metallurgical analysis of iron finds, although that is work which remains to be done. All the same, it looks as if there were at the end of our period three main material culture areas in Tuscany, delineated by ceramics, looking to Pisa, Florence, and Siena respectively (for Siena seems to have been developing its own productions too, which hardly reached the

[260] For surveys, see Cantini, 'Ritmi e forme'; and Cantini and Grassi, 'Produzione, circolazione e consumo', which puts together both of their monographic studies into a short synthesis with important maps. For the absence of non-local ceramics in Florence in our period, see Cantini et al., *Firenze prima degli Uffizi*, pp. 293–8; Bruttini, *Archeologia urbana a Firenza*, pp. 93–180.

[261] For *paioli*, see Bruttini, *Archeologia urbana a Firenze*, pp. 106–13, 171–4; Cantini, 'Ritmi e forme', pp. 119–21, 123. For one well-studied east Tuscan rural site, Montecchio (prov. Arezzo), in which ceramics stayed local into the late thirteenth century, when maiolica begins to appear, see Orecchioni, *Dopo la peste*, pp. 40–50.

coast), of which Pisa's was by far the most complex. In this respect, up to the end of our period and beyond, Tuscany was very far from unified as an economic region; Pisa was a real focus, but for little more than a third of Tuscany. Inside that area, economic relationships were much more tightly articulated than we saw for the hinterland of Venice, but the actual area covered by Pisa's hinterland was even smaller. This would change substantially later in the thirteenth century, when goods of all kinds were funnelled down the Arno to Pisa from the inland towns; but that had not yet started on a large scale by 1180, or, indeed, probably, for two or three decades after that.[262]

* * *

It is worth looking briefly at both Florence and Lucca, to bring out the differences here. Florence presents a fascinating conundrum. We certainly have to abandon hindsight; Florence may by 1300 have become the second largest city in Italy, after Milan, with a hugely developed woollen-cloth industry and banking capacity, but there is little sign of this in our period. It may have made ceramics; there is also some archaeological signs of bone- and ironworking; but in excavation there is nothing parallel to the density known for Pisa, even if we take into account that there has been less archaeological work done here. The 'rinnovata vivacità' of the city in the twelfth century, to quote Jacopo Bruttini, was, so far, in a fairly low key.[263] Robert Davidsohn a century ago and Enrico Faini more recently, working from the documents, have similarly not found so very much reference to an artisanally focussed Florence in the twelfth century. The 150-odd casual references to artisans in Florence and its territory, that is, urban and rural combined, for the eleventh and twelfth centuries give quite a range of trades; *fabri*, here possibly—but far from certainly—smiths, are the commonest in both centuries, although textile workers and then leatherworkers are prominent too. This is not a trivial number; it is more than we saw in, for example, Padua. It shows that Florence did, indeed, have a certain level of artisanal activity, which it could build on. And the city was clearly expanding demographically in the twelfth century, given its housing and new walls. A similar developing productive centre was nearby Prato, a rising small town some 15 kilometres away, which would also become a cloth centre in the thirteenth century; its earliest attested fulling mill is from 1107, and, here too, from the mid-eleventh century onwards artisans, both generic *fabri* and some specifically characterized cloth workers, are cited in our documentary sources and are sometimes visibly prosperous, although again we cannot say more than that before the 1190s.[264] But we have very little evidence of a commercial

[262] For an indicative survey of Siena, see Cantini and Grassi, 'Produzione, circolazione e consumo', pp. 135–6. For the Valdarno later in the thirteenth century, see Tognetti, 'Produzioni, traffici e mercati'.

[263] For the archaeology, see Scampoli, *Firenze*, pp. 240–3; Bruttini, *Archeologia urbana a Firenze*, p. 171.

[264] For Prato, see Fantappiè, 'Nascita d'una terra di nome Prato', pp. 238–41; for the fulling mill, see Fantappiè, *Le carte*, n. 103; cf. ibid., n. 143 and Piattoli, *Le carte... di Montepiano*, n. 205, for later in

projection towards the sea. Florence had political links with Pisa, plus a treaty in 1171 which included trade provisions, but as we have seen, they were not getting ceramics from the coast.[265] There is nothing here which distinguishes the city from a dozen other slowly expanding Italian towns with a localized economy.

Florence, more than most cities in Tuscany, saw its urban aristocracy move out of the city into the countryside in the years around 1100. The leading families remaining in the city were very much second-level figures, so the city was not getting as rich on agrarian rents and dues.[266] Conversely, several of the rural families had substantial numbers of castle estates, so were wealthy, and thus had potential buying power.[267] So did Florence's strong network of rural monasteries, which were increasing their landowning and thus wealth in this period. The city had relatively little political influence in much of its large *contado* before the thirteenth century; all the same, we can conclude from this network of data that Florence at least remained the focus for artisanal production aimed at satisfying, outside the city itself, the demand of the now ruralized aristocracy of its own territory, even if it as yet did not have many wider links to markets and buyers.

It is quite possible that the eventual step change in the Florentine economy occurred in the opposite direction to the sea. Florentines were indeed, at least intermittently, looking farther afield inland. Merchants from the city were already active in the Po plain around 1100, for both Lucca and Bologna tried to get emperors to limit their rights, although as usual we have no idea of scale here. This continued, as we would expect, for Florentines could cross the Appennines to Bologna relatively easily, even if not as easily as they could reach the sea at Pisa. By the thirteenth century, we have treaties with towns beyond the Appennines; the city's merchants (including cloth traders) were by now welcome there. A fragmentary but fascinating set of accounts in early Italian, dating to 1211, for a Florentine money-changing and credit association (it was probably a *societas*; we might call it a banking company, as the word *bankiere* is used in the text, but that

the century. One *faber*, Megliorello di Teuzo, is quite prominent in Prato in the decades around 1100; see Fantappiè, *Le carte*, thirteen documents from n. 31 (a. 1079) to n. 104 (1108), esp. n. 93. A *marmorarius* in 1163 (n. 181) is a creditor of the local church for the relatively substantial sum of £86. For the archaeology of Prato's urban expansion, see Vannini et al., 'Prato'.

[265] For artisans, see the lists in Davidsohn, *Forschungen*, 1, pp. 152–7, developed in very upbeat (but also generic) ways by Davidsohn, *Storia di Firenze*, 1, pp. 1173–98—he had in mind, of course, the very different picture of the decades around 1300, discussed by him in great detail in vol. 6 of the same work, as also by many later writers. See, much more cautiously, Faini, *Firenze*, pp. 118–25, developed in Faini, 'Prima del fiorino', where he tends to prefer the last quarter of the twelfth century for the date of the Florentine upturn; I would be more cautious still. For 1171, see Santini, *Documenti*, pp. 5–6. It needs to be added that Florentine cloth measures were sometimes used in sea trading by the years around 1200; see Leonardo Pisano, *Liber abbaci* (*Scritti*, ed. Boncompagni, 1), pp. 97–9, 102–3, 117–20, which hints at some maritime visibility for the city by then; but the text is isolated, and anyway says nothing about Florentine goods themselves.

[266] Cortese, *Signori, castelli*, esp. pp. 209–58; Cortese, *L'aristocrazia toscana*, pp. 289–99; Faini, *Firenze*, pp. 127–65; rural lords began to come back into the city only at the end of the twelfth century.

[267] For the pattern of castles, see Cortese, *Signori, castelli*, pp. 153–75; they were also owned by urban churches.

would as yet be anachronistic), shows several debts being contracted by Florentines at the S. Procolo fair in Bologna, plus some in Pisa, although the great bulk of those mentioned were inside the city.[268] Some of these credit agreements concerned cloth too; all the same, evidence for an upturn for Florence's woollens outside the city territory is otherwise only fragmentary until after 1220. North Italian customs tariffs and other documentation, indeed, hardly mention them at all until after 1250. The striking economic and demographic take-off which Florence experienced thus seems to have begun only in the second quarter of the thirteenth century.[269] It has never properly been explained, but at least its late date frees us from having to solve the problem here. In our period, what we can say with most certainty is that Florence (with Prato) was the economic centre of an inland micro-region, reasonably active but mostly cut off from the coast; any potential for major future expansion is hidden from us here. But we will come back to the issue at the end of this section, for we can identify some elements which at least make that major expansion less difficult to comprehend.

Lucca is problematic for almost the opposite reasons to Florence. It never took off as Florence did after *c.*1225 (few cities managed that, indeed), but it had international links unusually early for a city which was not a port. It was a coherent commune by the 1130s, rather earlier than Florence, but here too, the older local aristocracy became less involved in the city in the twelfth century, after the end of the centralizing power of the march of Tuscany, although not as markedly as in Florence. Urban expansion was also relatively limited, even if the quality and cost of urban building certainly went up in the twelfth century.[270] We have already seen the city being very tentative in its land-based commercial projection in the eleventh century, with little reference to trading farther away than Parma, just beyond the Appennines (p. 485 above); its main exchange links up to 1150 or so seem to have been via Pisa, notwithstanding their perennial enmity. Its artisans, however, show a change that cannot be seen in Florence. Between 1050 (when casual references to them begin again after a two-century break) and 1140 nearly all are *fabri*, which here certainly did not mean only 'smiths', for one of them in 1075 owned a fulling mill, *mulino et folle*. That is to say, the city did not yet have an active enough artisanal sector to be too bothered about technical vocabulary.

[268] For Lucca and Bologna around 1100, see n. 37 above. For after 1200, esp. for the agreements, see Day, *The early development of the Florentine economy*, pp. 296–310. The account book is edited in Santini, 'Frammenti di un libro di banchieri fiorentini'; for Bologna, see ibid., pp. 170–4; for Pisa, 174–6; for the (Pisan) *bankiere*, 175.

[269] Raw data in Davidsohn, *Storia di Firenze*, 6. For discussion, see Hoshino, *L'arte della lana*, pp. 37–40, 66, for northern Italy; Day, *The early development of the Florentine economy* (pp. 205–37 for textile manufacturing; cf. also n. 278 below for references to Florentine cloth in Lucca in the 1220s); for demography, see Day, 'The population of Florence'.

[270] See Tomei, *Milites elegantes*, for the aristocratic families and their long back history; see ibid., pp. 383–93 and Cortese, *L'aristocrazia toscana*, pp. 299–307, for their new extra-urban foci. For the commune, see Savigni, *Episcopato e società*, pp. 47–97; Wickham, *Courts and conflict*, pp. 19–40. See n. 259 above for some evidence for urban building.

After 1140, by contrast, we see a diversification, with relatively large numbers of leatherworkers appearing, and also numerous dyers, with some other cloth workers too—and fewer metalworkers, unlike in Florence and especially Pisa, which reinforces the vagueness of the term *faber* in Lucca a century earlier.[271] It is likely that this indicates a shift in scale as far as local production is concerned.

This shift, as in Florence, might not have necessarily implied more than the development of a local demand network. But we have other evidence that the Lucchesi were looking, by 1150, well beyond the city's territory. A treaty with Pisa of *c.*1158 assumes that Lucca, which was on the via Francigena (as we have seen, the long-standing pilgrim route from France to Rome), was the natural stopping place for any *Lumbardi* who wished to come to Pisa; the treaty also envisages that French and German merchants (*Franceschi et Tedeschi et omnes Ultramontani*) should have eight days to sell their wares in Lucca before coming on to Pisa—these being concessions not to Lucca but to Pisa, which would get such merchants next, without being prevented; in return, the Pisans would not impede Lucca's use of the sea route.[272] And indeed, the Lucchesi did go by sea too; we have already looked at the 1153 treaty with Genoa which established that city as a focus for Lucchese cloth-trading activities in France, and Lucchese merchants visibly used Genoa as a base, already around 1160 but still more around 1190 (see pp. 542, 550–1, 553–4 above). Lucca had its own harbour, at Motrone, north of Pisa; the Pisans destroyed it when they could, but more to force the Lucchesi to use the Portus Pisanus than to prevent them from having access to the sea at all. We have seen that Lucca could, unlike Tuscan cities farther from the coast, buy imported ceramics which came via Pisa; similarly, although in the twelfth century Pisa began to compete with Lucca's five-century-old dominance of the minting of coin in Tuscany, Lucchese silver by now came from Pisan-controlled silver mines on or near the coast. But it remains significant that Lucchesi used Genoa, not Pisa, as a commercial base; this certainly reflected long-standing political alliances and enmities.[273]

Lucca's trading in France included, and was probably dominated by, the import of cloth. When this got back to Lucca, almost certainly more often via Genoa and the sea rather than along the via Francigena, it was dyed and finished (which fits the references to dyers in our documents), and then, as far as we can see, re-exported from Genoa, for Lucchese scarlet (*scarlata* or *vermilio*) was, in a few

[271] See Wickham, 'Gli artigiani nei documenti italiani', pp. 432–4; for the fulling mill, see Archivio di Stato di Lucca, diplomatico S. Ponziano, 22 sett. 1075, registered in degli Azzi Vitelleschi, *Reale archivio di Stato in Lucca. Regesti*, 1, n. 256.

[272] Bonaini, 'Diplomi pisani', n. 15B, pp. 28–34.

[273] For Motrone, see, e.g., the narrative in Volpe, *Studi*, pp. 159, 193, 214–16; see further Del Punta, *Mercanti e banchieri lucchesi*, pp. 21–30, with 99–106 for trading with France. The Genoese also offered the Lucchesi alternative ports in eastern Liguria in 1159 if they ran into trouble (*guerra*) with Pisa, at least for salt (*CDGE*, 1, nn. 296–7). For Lucchese silver coming from the Pisan mining area, see n. 250 above.

Genoese notarial records in the 1180s and 1190s, sold through there.[274] It was sufficiently complicated to ship French/Flemish cloth (which was already not cheap) from Genoa to Lucca to be dyed and finished and then back to Genoa to be sold that we are certainly here dealing with the top end of the market, that is to say, the luxury end; Lucca was, indeed, probably the main luxury cloth producer in Italy by the end of the twelfth century. This also helps to explain why such a dyeing and finishing specialization could, as has been frequently argued, lie at the origin of the development in Lucca of a particular expertise in the production of silk cloth in the thirteenth century—getting off the ground after *c.*1210—which, with ups and downs, marked the city out for the rest of the middle ages. The raw silk was imported from or via the Byzantine lands, not in this case Spain or Sicily (Lucca's mulberry trees, and thus its own raw silk, are not attested before 1300), and the cloth specialists in the city were used to working on imports; but, for this material, the weaving process happened in Lucca from the start. Alma Poloni comments, when discussing this development, that the silk dealers of the first decades of the thirteenth century were, unlike the merchants in the twelfth, from prominent families of Lucca—not the older urban elite, but the leaders of the future *popolo*—and that it is only now that the dyeing and weaving commitment of the city stepped up in scale. With a monopoly of silk-making, as far as mainland Italy was concerned, Lucca now had something of value to sell back to the French and Flemish markets too.[275]

The availability in thirteenth-century Lucca of raw silk from or through the Byzantine or ex-Byzantine provinces shows that the Genoese, who must have been the intermediaries here, were becoming more committed to Aegean trade than they had been during our period. This in itself locates most of these developments on the other side of the great watershed in Byzantine history, the fall of Constantinople in 1204, and well away from the main arguments of this book. They are relevant here, all the same, for an opposite reason: Lucca's particular contribution to the thirteenth-century Italian take-off was in a luxury commodity, not in bulk production and commercialization. It is for this reason, I think, that when Florence itself took off, in this case in wool production, Lucca could not compete in scale; and the city never expanded demographically as Florence did. It was much more connected to the coastal world than Florence was until the 1220s and perhaps even later; but what access to the maritime commercial network brought Lucca was a niche position in luxury production, not a contribution to the economic upturn in bulk goods.

[274] See n. 204 above, and Poloni, *Lucca nel Duecento*, pp. 43–6.

[275] Ibid., pp. 46–55 (and see the rest of the book for the real flowering of Lucchese silk in the later thirteenth century); Del Punta, *Mercanti e banchieri lucchesi*, pp. 39–61, with 66–76 for the overwhelming dominance of raw silk coming from the Byzantine lands or the coasts of the Caspian Sea in the thirteenth century; and for a wider Italian context, see Mainoni, 'La seta in Italia'.

Lucca's notarial records appear from the 1220s, second only to Genoa itself, and associated above all with *ser* Ciabatto, by far the best-documented notary of the whole first fifty years of Lucca's registers. They are very late indeed for us, but they provide—and for the first time—such a clear snapshot of the city's economy that it is worth looking at them at least briefly. In their first decade, the over 900 surviving documents in the early paper registers confirm the picture I have just drawn, and also nuance it.[276] The first point to make is that they are quite different from those in the early Genoese registers. They show, it is true, as in Genoa, a very large number of short-term credit agreements, or else the registration of sales with delayed payments, in both cases temporary contracts. But much of their content also concerned transactions which could belong to any Italian collection of parchment documents, such as agrarian leases or the internal affairs and disputes of churches—Ciabatto had his base close to the cathedral, which explain some of the latter. In Ciabatto's early registers, there are no contracts for *societates* to engage in external commerce. There is hardly any reference to external commerce at all, in fact: a handful of loans in 1227 which are to be repaid in Genoa, plus a casual reference in 1231 to a man absent in Sicily *pro mercadantia facienda*, complete the list. The two *societates de arte negotiandi* which are documented in these registers, in 1230–1, are in fact for urban shops, one for the sale of grain, one for the sale of mattresses (*cultricis*) and other *mercadantiis*. (Another *societas*, from 1225, was, very atypically, for the exploitation of war booty, in iron and steel.)[277] There are three references to cloth imported from northern France, from Arras and Ypres, to which we could add, possibly, the half a dozen references to *stanfortes*, probably meaning 'strong-warped cloth', although these could well have been Italian-woven too; but that is not so large a number, given Lucca's visibility in the Genoese records, and it may well show that this visibility was the product of a relatively small scale of trade across the Alps, less than might otherwise appear—which fits the fact that we are mostly dealing here with a luxury trade. Two references to Florentine woollens are the only ones which mention cloth made elsewhere in Italy.[278] Conversely, however, there is no doubt that Lucca's growing commitment to silk production is reflected in the notarial record here. *Seta* and *sendada*, both of them words for 'silk', appear over twenty times,

[276] Only one set of notarial records has been published, the registers of Ciabatto from the years 1222–32; see Meyer, *Ser Ciabattus*, 1. Two notaries, Glandone and Benedetto, have single registers which date to earlier, the first of them fragmentary, 1204 and 1220–1 respectively; see Meyer, *Felix et inclitus notarius*, pp. 193, 199. When looking at Genoa, we saw that we cannot assume that the clients of individual notaries were automatically typical, and the same is true here, but Ciabatto at least had both rich and poor clients. Analysis of the paper has not been undertaken, but *Ser Ciabattus*, n. D170 (a. 1231), refers to a document written on *carta bambacis*, cotton-based paper (cf. the similar citation from Pisa in 1179 at p. 564 above), which might be a guide to what we would find.

[277] Genoa: Meyer, *Ser Ciabattus*, nn. B18, 25, 35, 38; Sicily: D170; *societates de arte negotiandi*: C169, D18; war booty: A1.

[278] Meyer, *Ser Ciabattus*, nn. A7, 33, 46 (Arras and Ypres), A10, 12, 34, 46, 48–9, B86, D180, 351 (*stanfortes*), A30, C158 (Florence). For a good rapid discussion of the *stanfortes* of northern France/Flanders/England and the problems with their etymological association with the town of Stamford in England, see Höfler, *Untersuchungen zur Tuch- und Stoffbenennung*, pp. 35–7.

usually in the context of delayed sales of cloth; and silk-weaving is referred to as well, including in the countryside, for in 1230 an agrarian contract is backed up by a commitment by the contractor's wife to weave enough silk (*texere tot sendada*) to repay a loan of £29.[279] We can, here at least, assume that this silk was largely woven for export, even if the contracts do not ever say so explicitly.

This does not exhaust the references to cloth in these texts. Many other types of *panni* (lengths of cloth) are referred to as being sold here too; these seem to have been above all woollens, and they seem to have been made in Lucca itself, or in the countryside around, as we have other references to spinning and a woollen workshop.[280] Lucca's own wool production was thus clearly developing as well. It was based on a growing sheep-pastoral specialization in the main Lucchese Appennine mountain valley, the Garfagnana, and on a transhumance route from there via Lucca to the coastal plain around Pisa, which is first securely documented in the 1150s and became steadily more important into the middle decades of the thirteenth century.[281] We also have 1240s references to woollen cloth being woven in the countryside, and then bought to be finished in the city and resold in the country. This was a bulk production, certainly. But we are here too close to Florence's own woollen take-off, and the equivalent for Lucca did not have the same future importance—indeed, as we have seen, contracts for woollens already mention Florentine (and by the 1240s, Veronese and Bolognese) cloth as well, so local cloth did not always dominate even the non-luxury market. And we cannot show that any of Lucca's wool production was for sale outside the city's own territory, even if we could well suppose that it went also to neighbouring Pisa, in exchange for that city's iron and ceramics, given the restricted evidence for cloth-making in the port city.[282] So, when it came to Lucca's external economic projection, its speciality remained silk, and it remained a luxury. Its other major role by 1300, banking, was a spin-off of that international projection, certainly, and shows that the city could generate some very wealthy entrepreneurs, but that role involved very few people, and was again generated by the most expensive level of international exchange, not the bulk trade that marked core economic activity.[283] The city's specializations mark a limit to the degree in which access to

[279] Meyer, *Ser Ciabattus*, n. C178; see also D303, 362. For references to *seta* and *sendada*, see ibid., index, s.vv.

[280] See Meyer, *Ser Ciabattus*, index, s.v. *pannus*. Spinning and workshop: ibid., nn. A4, C327. A *banbacarius*, a cotton dealer, appears ibid., n. C296; he also dealt in *pannis de lino*. But fustian, the mix of the two, so important in the Italian north, does not appear (the *barachano* cloth of ibid., nn. A56–7, C231, is probably woollen, as it was in Genoa; see Mainoni, 'Le produzioni non agricole', pp. 244–5).

[281] See n. 50 above for transhumance; cf. also Meyer, *Ser Ciabattus*, n. C323.

[282] For the 1240s, see Blomquist, *Merchant families*, article VI. See p. 571 above for Pisa.

[283] For the beginnings of the Ricciardi banking family in the 1220s–1230s as dyers and silk dealers (and moneylenders, and even counterfeiters), see Del Punta, *Mercanti e banchieri lucchesi*, pp. 141–50; see also Blomquist, *Merchant families*, article V, and other articles in the same book for the situation later in the century; for the Ricciardi in England and elsewhere in the 1270s–1290s, see Del Punta, *Mercanti e banchieri lucchesi*, pp. 151–215; Kaeuper, *Bankers to the Crown*.

maritime commerce could as yet change the economic direction of the Tuscan hinterland, even in a city as close to the sea as Lucca.

So Pisa's hyperactivity only related to its coastal hinterland, and to a relatively short distance up the Arno, apart from its iron products, which almost certainly extended farther. Lucca was reached by it as well, to a smaller degree, and was itself developing a more complex economy in the immediate hinterland of the city by the 1220s, but its wider economic projection was only in luxury cloth production. These clear signs of increasing prosperity and economic activity thus remained relatively localized; they did not extend to the whole of Tuscany, or even to the whole of the Arno valley. In the end, by the second half of the thirteenth century, the Tuscan city which most clearly represented and furthered the great economic take-off of mainland Italy was a hitherto fairly marginal city, Florence—as also a perhaps even more marginal one, Siena, very ill-documented in our period but very active in the 150 years that followed. One conclusion that we have to reach, therefore, is that maritime trade, here just as in the hinterland of Venice, had little or no causal relationship with internal economic development in our period. To finish off this section, then, I will set out some suggestions about what socio-economic relationships in Tuscany were the most likely pointers towards a more complex economic future.

* * *

We have seen that in southern Tuscany castles began to be built of stone in the twelfth century, which certainly indicated greater concentrations of aristocratic wealth. That was an area of quite strong signorial rights, which developed in Tuscany above all after 1100. In the north, the Arno basin saw much weaker signorial powers, for the most part. Even after 1100, some areas, notably the immediate hinterlands of both Lucca and Pisa, saw, in effect, no signorial powers at all, and lords relied only on the rents derived from landowning. But inland too, as, for example, in the well-documented Chianti hills, where signorial lordships were the norm, the dues they exacted were generally relatively light, and such lordships were also often fragmented; only a few major players, such as the Guidi counts, could exercise more control.[284] All the same, northern rural settlements were also beginning to use stone in at least their central areas. There is less dense excavation in the Arno basin than farther south, but we can see this at, for example, San Genesio, and Montecastrese and Gorfigliano (both prov. Lucca). That is to say, there are material signs of the intensification of lordship here as well.[285] Even where signorial dues were light, lords took care to record them, and to formalize their payment. Sometimes they could, indeed, build on this, as with the one-off

[284] Wickham, 'La signoria rurale in Toscana', pp. 352–8, 376–85.
[285] Cantini et al., 'Il borgo di San Genesio', pp. 63–77; Gattiglia and Tarantino, '... *loco ubi dicitur castello*'; Quirós Castillo, *Archeologia e storia*, pp. 77–86.

acattum (arbitrary levy) of over £600 exacted *c.*1200 by the monastery of Passignano, a very large landowner in Chianti, to confront a temporary financial crisis.[286] And in terms of rent-taking they were active too. Lorenzo Tabarrini has shown how, particularly after 1180 and into the thirteenth century, lords in the territories of both Florence and Lucca paid much more attention to how they took rents. Leases were more often written down; lists of rents were more commonly made; around Florence, labour services were converted into rents in produce, sometimes quite high ones, doubtless for sale in the expanding urban market; around both Florence and Lucca, where landlords could get away with it, rents increased as well.[287] In the territory of Florence, we have seen that lay lords had largely moved out of the city after 1100, and rural monasteries were numerous and often rich; in both cases they were thus close or closer to their dependents, and could watch over them more tightly. Urban lords can be found in some places doing the same. That is to say, lords were more pervasive: they exercised more control over the lives of the peasant majority than they had, even when the actual levels of rents and dues which they exacted were not as high as they could have been, and, indeed, this control could contribute to those levels steadily rising.[288] The evidence for lordly intervention in the society of the countryside is substantially greater for the twelfth century than it was in the two preceding centuries.

This went together with increased evidence for marketization. Clearly, selling produce to the city was part of that. But rural markets developed too; in the Florentine territory, lords began to establish markets on a substantial scale in the second half of the twelfth century, and Florence itself followed them when it gained a fuller hegemony in its *contado* in the early thirteenth. The city also encouraged the establishment of more articulated route networks, to link markets together and, more and more, to direct a grain trade towards the city. San Genesio, whose economic links were with Pisa and its political links with Lucca, is a good archaeological example of the way that a market centre could expand; as we have seen, its building switched to stone in the later twelfth century, and it soon increased substantially in size. The Guidi-founded quasi-city of Podium Bonizi, also outside the limits of the direct power of Florence but not far from the city, was built in stone from the start, in the 1150s, and it too was rather larger after 1200. The marketization implied here also fits with the goods which were regularly transported across the neighbouring autonomous territory of San Gimignano a

[286] Archivio di Stato di Firenze, diplomatico, Passignano, 1204, ed. Tabarrini, 'When did clerics start investing?', pp. 423, 425; cf. 407. The *fondo* Passignano, unpublished but available online (www.archiviodigitale.icar.beniculturali.it/it/185/ricerca/detail/82809, accessed 25 September 2022), is one of the largest in Italy for our period; Passignano's lands in Chianti have detailed documentation as a result.

[287] Tabarrini, *Responding to change*, *passim*. See Dameron, *Episcopal power*, pp. 110–18, for resistance to this in the lands of the bishop of Florence.

[288] See n. 72 above for Sandro Carocci's concept of pervasiveness.

little later, by the 1230s, as the records of the town's council in that decade make clear.[289]

And here we can add rural credit as well, which was not only controlled by lords. Soon after the end of our period we can see it operating in the Chianti hills, which had been a relatively remote area in the eleventh century, with few links to Florence. The monastery of Passignano owed *c.*1200 over £1,000 to a host of creditors, particularly urban but also rural. Some of the latter were by no means of high status, such as Borgnolino di Borgno, a medium-level owner from the village of Passignano, who lent to the monastery in the 1190s, when he was not disputing with it. That was true for other monasteries too, as with Salomone di Ubaldino of Montaio, apparently from a family of rich peasants, who lent £310 to the neighbouring monastery of Coltibuono in the far south of the territory of Florence in the 1240s, or Grazia, *conversus* of the same monastery and the monastic representative who repaid Salomone, who was himself a monastic creditor not long after. Indeed, from as early as the 1110s in the same area, the *nepotes Bonizi*, a family some of whose members were *fabri* (smiths or other artisans), are found lending money to local aristocrats. Philippe Lefeuvre has, convincingly, put considerable stress on medium-level figures such as these in his study of Chianti and the upper Arno valley beside it.[290] Of course, more creditors were urban, or else rural lords; credit went with power, in our period as in every other. Credit documents involving interest payments are, indeed, common by the twelfth century everywhere in northern Tuscany, and the powerful were usually the lenders. But the existence of this array of quite small figures who had enough capital to be local players is a marker of the steadily growing fluidity of the economy and society of Chianti, and of the river valleys which penetrated it and surrounded it as well, just as the evidence of markets and roads is a marker for rural commercial infrastructures—and all this, to repeat, in what was previously an area without a close relationship to the urban world.

The point here, in fact, is that lordly power was not the whole story. A good percentage of the lands of Tuscany, particularly its northern half, was in the hands of peasant owners, who were not greatly dependent on lords, and of whom some were prosperous enough to rent out much of their own lands to others—they were the figures who dominated local rural communes, which themselves

[289] For the documentary evidence for markets, see Day, *The early development of the Florentine economy*, pp. 262–83, 445–71. For the archaeology, see Francovich and Valenti, *Poggio Imperiale*, 151–94; see n. 285 above for San Genesio. For San Gimignano, see Muzzi, *San Gimignano: i verbali*, 1. Here too, this was new; the classic survey of the economy of the town, Fiumi, *Storia economica e sociale*, esp. pp. 54–82, has no citations of trading outside its territory before 1215.

[290] For Passignano and the city, see Faini, 'Passignano e i Fiorentini', pp. 139–47; for less high-status creditors of Passignano, see the data in Tabarrini, 'When did clerics start investing?'; for the other examples and further analysis, see Lefeuvre, *Notables et notabilité*, ch. 8.2–3; we can add to these the marble worker who was a major creditor of the main church of Prato (see n. 264 above), as well as, later, the rapidly rising Franzesi della Foresta after 1250 in Figline in the upper Arno valley, discussed in Pirillo, *Famiglia e mobilità*, esp. pp. 30–67.

appeared in the mid- and later twelfth century.[291] The existence of this stratum further limited the power of lords. We find a complex social structure in nearly every part of Tuscany, with lords who owned many castles, monasteries which owned vast estates, and then smaller lords, medium-level owners, and many owner-cultivators, before we reach tenants who were so dependent that they could be regarded as semi-free. This balance meant that however much lords sought to cut tenants out of the market, by, for example, demanding rents in grain which was clearly for urban sale, not all rural inhabitants were tenants; peasants sold to urban markets too, and gained resources from doing so. So, everywhere, substantial concentrations of wealth, urban and rural, coexisted with wider local buying power. Most of our documents tell us little about the buying and selling of goods, but we can manage all the same to find the fluidity set out in the previous paragraph very widely across the north of Tuscany by the 1190s and onwards from there. Indeed, when we reach our first notarial registers in Lucca in the 1220s, which admittedly document an area much closer to that city than most of Chianti was to Florence, rural credit and the sale of agricultural commodities—grain, wine, and oil, not just cloth—force themselves immediately on our attention. Peasants were selling in these documents, as well as urban and rural elites, and such sales once again mean the possibility of widespread peasant buying power.[292] Florence, which came late to this, may simply have become more prominent as time went on because its *contado* was much larger than any other in Tuscany, and the mix of wealthy elites and prosperous peasants could be found widely across it—once market infrastructures came to be denser, allowing goods to be moved more easily, which could allow more substantial commercialization, and once the credit networks, just discussed, developed too.

This is not, however, the answer to 'Why Florence?'. All it does is to make the rise of the city a little bit better than impossible to understand. It is important to stress that I have had to go well into the thirteenth century, fifty years after the end of the period of this book, to find real signs of this level of activity. It is equally important to stress that the picture of the fluid economy of the 1220s in the territories of Florence and Lucca which has been argued for here was, actually, already present in that of Pisa a full century earlier. Furthermore, even when Florence's urban economy and demography rapidly expanded in the middle decades of the thirteenth century, the economic coherence of Tuscany, or even northern Tuscany, was still not a reality, as ceramic distributions clearly show. As William Day has observed, Florence could expand only because it had links with everywhere, which continued to develop, over the Appennines to Bologna and beyond, past Arezzo to central Italy, as well as down the Arno and past Pisa to the sea.

[291] Wickham, *Community and clientele*, esp. pp. 98–131, 177–84, 221–34.

[292] See Meyer, *Ser Ciabattus*, index, s.vv. *granum*, *ordeum*, *oleum*, *vinum*; these references indeed considerably outweigh in number those for cloth, and the sellers were above all village dwellers.

Somehow, it was able, from a nearly standing start, to exploit, not the incompletely integrated economy of Tuscany, but the incompletely integrated economy of the whole of north-central Italy combined. This might have simply been because its cloth was relatively cheap and thus could reach wider markets; but the work has not been done to find out for sure.[293]

Nor, to repeat, is this finding out part of the argument I want to pose here. Rather, what the slow development of commercialization and marketization in Tuscany shows us, both in the north and in the mining areas down the coast, is one basis on which a regional economy in north-central Italy *could* be created. Pisa was obviously first here, in both production and exchange, and the evidence indicates that its links with its hinterland were denser and more comprehensive, well into the thirteenth century, than those of any other Tuscan city. On many levels, it ought to have been Pisa which took off on a really large scale first, not Florence, or even maybe Milan. But its hinterland was too small, and did not get larger. This was not, as was probably the case for Genoa before the 1180s, because its maritime projection looked outwards rather than inland; Pisa was a major producer city in its own right. But all the same, Pisa was not integrated economically with more than a third of Tuscany. What, rather, we can see for Tuscany is the steady development of more integrated economies on the level of single city territories, or at most (as to an extent with Pisa and Lucca) two contiguous ones. Here, one can propose that cities developed productive density steadily, with much the same pacing as their rural hinterlands developed their own demand, through selling food or raw materials (wool, iron) back to cities—demand both at the elite level, and then, even if more slowly, at the level of the peasant majority—so that greater expenditure and, more broadly, economic growth could take place in each in parallel.[294] This was the essential starting point for all future interregional or international projection, for Pisan iron in the twelfth century or Lucchese silk and Florentine woollens in the thirteenth. And it is significant that this was so even for a city such as Pisa which actually did, from 1000 or so, have an international maritime projection, at least a military one; it was iron, not sea raiding, which

[293] Day, *The early development of the Florentine economy*, pp. 284–337. These links also supplied grain, once the city really began to expand, mostly from inland regions, though sometimes, after 1270 in particular, from Sicily and Puglia; see ibid., pp. 330–3. He rightly remarks, p. 263, that all this shows the importance of internal rather than maritime exchange. For Sicily and Puglia, see further Dameron, 'Feeding an Italian city-state', pp. 986–7, 997–1001, 1006–15, for Tuscany as a whole; he shows that such imports tended to be more common in exceptionally bad years for harvest or war. For Florentine cloth as relatively cheap, see the fairly sketchy indicators in Hoshino, *L'arte della lana*, pp. 66–7, 95–7; in those lists, it price-matched local cloth in Genoa and Lucca respectively, that is to say, it was cheap enough to compete with local cloth outside its territory; Verona woollen cloth, from another major productive centre, was cheaper. Hoshino makes little of this, however; cf. n. 32 above. For the incomplete integration of the Tuscan economy until the very end of the middle ages, see Malanima, 'La formazione di una regione economica'; Epstein, 'Cities, regions', pp. 311–13, 36–45.

[294] This dialectic, which we have seen elsewhere and will see again for Lombardy, will be discussed further in Chapter 8.

enabled its bulk export economy really to take off, a century later. Pisa, better than either Genoa or Venice, is thus a guide to a point that I have stressed throughout this book, that local and regional economic links come first, sea commerce on any scale only later. Tuscany remained, all the same, economically less coherent than, in particular, Lombardy came to be; and this contrast helps to explain the differences between the two. So we shall see for Lombardy how the sort of growth we can track for Pisa came to take place on a larger scale, even if farther from the sea, in the next section.

6.6 Milan and Lombardy

Milan, Lombardy's largest city, suffered a catastrophic defeat in 1162 following a long siege directed by Frederick Barbarossa. After this, its new and enlarged walls, dating to 1155, were destroyed, chiefly by vengeful Italian rivals, and its inhabitants were dispersed into settlements in the countryside for five years. Its agricultural hinterland was also damaged in the same war, as we saw at the start of this chapter. But after the alliance of north Italian cities against Barbarossa took shape in 1167, the city was reoccupied (and rapidly redefended by the same wall circuit); not long after the Milanese victory over Barbarossa in 1176, it seems to have already returned to being a centre which was as active economically as it had been politically, which means very active. Milan is thus the type example for the argument which we have looked at for a range of other Mediterranean cities that war and destruction on their own do not adequately account for urban failure in our period. Milan had a wider exchange infrastructure which was not interrupted by the troubles of the 1160s; some of this exchange, indeed, was with the enemy cities which were not confronted by the same level of short-term damage that Milan experienced. It probably also maintained, even in the bad years, at least some of its pre-existing links with the producers of primary materials across Lombardy, such as the iron miners of the Alpine foothills in Milan's own territory and of the valleys north of Bergamo and Brescia, or the wool producers from the pre-Alpine region as a whole; if not, it certainly re-established them soon after. So we might see Lombardy as a subregion of the Italian centre-north which was more coherent than most, and which allowed both the establishment and the re-establishment of a relatively complex production and exchange system which was active by the twelfth century and powerful by the thirteenth. Certainly, many people have seen it that way.

This picture, however, is both true and false. It is based on hindsight: Lombardy was, indeed, a major productive region shortly after our period ends, and remained one for the next four centuries. Historians have supposed, and not unreasonably so, that the antecedents of this must have gone far back into the past; Cinzio Violante traced these roots as far back as the eighth century in his important work on the topic, as we have seen. But the actual evidence for it is very poor. Milanese documents, in particular, give only anecdotal evidence about urban production even in the thirteenth century, and Paolo Grillo's reconstruction of the city's economy in the century after 1180 relies substantially on Genoese notarial records, given that Genoa was, by the end of the twelfth century, unquestionably Milan's and Lombardy's main outlet to the sea and to international markets.[295] But we have already looked at the evidence for Milan in those records in the twelfth century; it only begins to be dense in the years around 1190, and in the years around 1160 it is no more than indicative. The evidence from other Lombard cities is even less clear, with the exception of Piacenza. And the archaeology for this part of Italy, although it is weak by the standards of Tuscany and the Veneto, gives us almost no hint of any productive complexity as yet. We could, in fact, take all our direct economic data for the whole period up to 1180 and conclude that nothing much was obviously going on in Lombardy at all, except the normal rural–urban interchange of products which makes city society possible in the first place. This would be an incorrect conclusion to draw—unlike for Florence and Lucca, which we can see expanding rapidly in different ways after 1200/1220, it really is true that Lombardy's thirteenth-century economy would be impossible to understand if we drew it—but it would be defensible. To get further, therefore, we need to read all the evidence against the grain, more than we have done for any other part of the Mediterranean. We need to approach the problem through a set of data which, each taken alone, are by no means probative, but which, set side by side, do help us to get closer to the explanations we need.

Exactly what 'Lombardy' was in our period needs a few words, for it was wider than the *regione* of Lombardia is today. It was not then clearly defined, except that, on one generic level, it was everything in the north of Italy that was not *Romania*—Romagna and the duchy of Venice. But increasingly *Langobardia* or *Lombardia* did not include the March of Verona, later of Treviso, roughly the modern Veneto; and the less-urbanized west of Piemonte, largely ruled by rural lords, can be excluded too. What remained was the heartland of the old Italian kingdom, the central Po plain, which looked to Pavia as the capital (until the late eleventh century) and Milan as the largest city; this stretched southwards from modern Lombardia to include the Emilian cities of Piacenza and Parma, and to a lesser extent Reggio and Modena, and westwards to include Novara, Vercelli, and Tortona, now in Piemonte. This is the 'Lombardy' I shall discuss.[296]

This territory was linked together by the Po and its tributaries, although split between mountain, prosperous high plain, and low marshy plain, as the Po valley was in general. But it was above all divided politically, pro- and anti-Milan.

[295] See the comments in Grillo, *Milano*, pp. 31–2.

[296] For the geography, see Raccagni, *The Lombard league*, pp. 7–11; Andenna, *Storia della Lombardia medievale*, pp. 3–17.

Milan's allies—including Brescia, Tortona and especially Piacenza—were not its immediate neighbours; the neighbours were its principal enemies, Como, Bergamo, Cremona, Lodi, and Pavia. They had good reasons to be enemies, given the behaviour of the Milanesi in the early twelfth century, both before and after the beginnings of the institutionalization of communes in each city, which in this part of Italy was roughly the 1130s. Milan's destruction of Lodi in 1111 and of Como in 1127 was merciless, in the latter case accompanied by total war in the countryside. Lodi, for its part, was forcibly evacuated to several *burgi* in the countryside, where the inhabitants stayed until Barbarossa built them a new city not far away in 1158—Milan's own destruction and evacuation were directly modelled on that, and the Lodigiani were so keen to destroy Milan's walls in 1162 that they volunteered to take down twice the length assigned to them.[297] It is, indeed, a sort of tribute to the scale of Barbarossa's own oppression that such visceral enemies managed to ally together against him so soon, in 1167 and the years following. But this network of cities was also one which would develop economically and commercially, engaging in mutual exchange which supported that development, particularly after 1200. In addition, as we shall see in more detail shortly, it was integrated by a network of smaller towns, often also called *burgi* in the sources, which were developing in the twelfth century in particular, such as Monza, Vimercate, Meda, Velate, Varese, and Cantù around Milan, or Crema between Cremona and Bergamo, or San Donnino between Piacenza and Parma—towns similar to Monselice outside Padua or Prato outside Florence, but rather more numerous than in the Veneto or Tuscany as yet. And we have already seen that land clearance and a growing interest in irrigation marked the twelfth century and onwards here (pp. 488–90 above), including in the Milanese territory itself, even though it included much less of the lower plain than did its neighbours. This was a direct indicator of economic expansion, which must, among other things, have fuelled a demographic rise sufficient to support the sharp increases in urban populations of the second half of our period, as extended walls show across the whole of Lombardy in the twelfth century, and particularly in Milan. Milan indeed, in the last decades of the twelfth century, as we have also seen, began the canal-building which would link the city, of all the Po plain cities the farthest from a navigable river, to the river systems to both its west and its east.[298]

Whether all this means that we could talk of a single economic subregion in the central Po plain at any time before 1200 is another matter. Cremona, on the

[297] For the general political history of Milan in this period, see *Storia di Milano*, 3. For the Lodigiani and Milan's walls, see Otto and Acerbo Morena, *Historia Friderici I.*, pp. 157–8; for the continuing harsh treatment of Lodi by the Milanesi before that, see also n. 20 above. The Lodigiani remembered their experience of being divided into separate *burgi* into the 1190s: see Grossi, *Il Liber Iurium del Comune di Lodi*, n. 116.

[298] For urban expansion in general, see Hubert, 'La construction de la ville'; Andenna, *Storia della Lombardia medievale*, pp. 21–36; for the canals, see n. 48 above. For a survey of the agrarian history of Milan's territory in the twelfth century in particular, see Occhipinti, 'L'economia agraria'.

Po, is a useful guide here, both for what it shows us and for what it does not. Already in the ninth century, as we have seen, its merchants and its river port were active. A string of imperial privileges into the mid-twelfth century testify to annual markets and port rights, and to the salt trade which was the staple of Po commerce from as early as the eighth century for both Comacchiese/Venetian and Cremonese boats. These rights are repeatedly described as belonging to the bishop—which is not surprising, since our documentation for them comes from the thirteenth-century cartulary of Bishop Sicardo, which was intended to stress the bishop's rights; but, in fact, we also know that the Cremonesi actively contested episcopal control throughout our period, with, as it appears, eventual success by 1115. The confirmation from 1159 is the only one which mentions other goods; they are *sogae*, which could be woollen cloaks, but may simply—the text is ambiguous—be the coverings of the bales of salt.[299] Cremona was certainly expanding in size; it had numerous new suburbs, and a new wall included them in the 1170s. It lay at the centre of a set of subsidiary ports too, Piadena, Guastalla, and Castelnuovo Bocca d'Adda.[300] So an exchange infrastructure was there, for sure, at a major focus of the Po river system, in the twelfth century as already in the ninth, and by implication by now operating on a larger scale, even if salt (plus luxuries) remained at its core, as we also saw when we looked at Venice's inland projection (pp. 508–9 above). This fits other signs of movement along the rivers, which appear casually in narratives.[301]

But whether this really marked a step change in actual *productions* for exchange is much less clear. It probably did not for Cremona itself. Cremona was a fustian-making town by the late thirteenth century, and it has been tempting for historians to propose that it was from the start, but in fact, there is no documentation for this before 1250; at the most, flax-retting is attested from the 1230s. Cremonesi are also attested as buying African wool via Genoa in the 1240s; this was a marker of a new scale for woollen cloth production, which in the thirteenth century came to need more wool that the Po plain in itself could provide.[302] But, as with Florence, that is far later than we need to go for this book. Across our entire

[299] For the whole set of privileges, see most conveniently Falconi, *Le carte cremonesi*, nn. 5, 7, 9–13, 19, 22, 29, 44, 48, 74, 77, 88, 90–1, 95, 97–8, 110, 154–6, 169–70, 185, 262 (a. 1115, redated in *Die Urkunden Heinrichs V.*, n. 143), 381 (a. 1159), 529. They are mostly re-edited in *Privilegia episcopii Cremonensis*, ed. Leoni, an edition of the episcopal cartulary, the *Codex Sicardi*; Bishop Sicardo, significantly, did not include those from 1115 on. *Soga* doubtless relates to *sagum* in Latin, 'woollen cloak' or 'tunic' (*saio* in Italian).

[300] For wall-building in 1172, see Falconi, *Le carte cremonesi*, n. 482; for the ports, see, e.g., nn. 238, 268, 352. For the suburbs and the walls, see in general Astegiano, *Codex diplomaticus Cremonae*, 2, pp. 389–93; Menant, 'La prima età comunale', pp. 202–3.

[301] e.g. Wipo, *Gesta Chuonradi*, ch. 12; Landolfo Seniore, *Mediolanensis historiae*, 2.24, both for the eleventh century.

[302] For thirteenth-century cloth, see Gosi, 'Le origini delle corporazioni tessili' (the fullest guide); Gualazzini, *Inventario dell'Archivio storico camerale*, pp. xxv–xlix; Racine, 'À Cremone, à la fin du XIIIe siècle'; Menant, 'La prima età comunale', pp. 200–2; Menant, 'Un lungo Duecento', pp. 358–60.

period, by contrast, in over 600 documents for the city (fewer than in many cities, but enough to get a clear picture), not many artisans are mentioned. There are certainly some: a few leatherworkers, four tailors and as many dyers, and rather more smiths and bakers; a proto-guild for carpenters in 1143; two references to cotton imports from Piacenza in 1170; and two dyers among the *mercatorum Cremone consules* who made a trade treaty with Venice in 1173. Smiths, a baker, and a leatherworker also figure among the at least informal leaders of the city in the twelfth century, a fact which fits with the unusually contestatory role of the early city commune. We have seen that hardly more artisans are attested for Venice itself, so the small numbers are perhaps not in themselves significant; the range set out here at least shows that Cremona was active as an artisanal centre for its own hinterland, much like, say, Padua, with perhaps a larger role for cloth-finishing than some towns as yet show. But we are nowhere near the activities attested in the late thirteenth century.[303] Cremona, up to 1180, was an entrepôt for exchange along the Po river network for whatever goods went by river, but provides us with no signs that this was a spur to production in the city itself which went much beyond its own territory.

At least we do not see the sharp material separations in the archaeology of Lombardy which we saw in Tuscany between Pisa and Florence; there are, indeed, clear signs of the opposite. The first, and best-attested, is the distribution of vessels made of *pietra ollare* (soapstone), which has already been mentioned (see Fig. 19). *Pietra ollare* was mined in the western and central Alps, and in our period one of its largest producer areas—a large-scale and organized production, as archaeology shows—was in and near Chiavenna, in one of the Alpine valleys north of Milan. The distribution of the cooking and storage vessels which could be made from it can be tracked without a break back to the late Roman Empire, and they can be found on every kind of site in subsequent centuries up to the fifteenth, including villages, all across the Po plain—as also outside it to a smaller extent, farther south in the Italian peninsula along both coasts—with a particular frequency in Lombardy itself. This was not a production and distribution which saw major upturns in our period; but it did represent, and continued to represent, a constant continuity of bulk exchange along the Po river system, adding to the salt attested in the documents. It showed, indeed, given its village

[303] Falconi, *Le carte cremonesi*, nn. 279, 379, 408, 409, 424, 426, 428, 440, 446, 450, 463, 465–6, 471, 483, 488, 493, 495, 498, 506, 509–11, 517, 526, 530, 534, 540, 560, 565–8, 578–9; Orlov et al., *Akty Kremony*, nn. 20, 51, 92 (the last two are rural); Leoni, *Le carte…di S. Cataldo*, n. 11; Leoni, *Le carte…di S. Leonardo*, n. 2; Astegiano, *Codex diplomaticus Cremonae*, 1, p. 114 (a. 1143); Castignoli and Racine, 'Due documenti contabili', p. 50 (a. 1170: this, a Piacenza financial document, simply refers to money taken *pro facto bambasii Cremonensium*, so it could be Cremonese cotton imports to Piacenza, but the opposite is more likely); *CDVE*, 13, n. 2822, 14, n. 2914 (a. 1173). For city leaders, see Menant, 'La prima età comunale', pp. 255, 258. The set of references increases in number after *c.*1160, but not so much as to show a new period of changed productive activity.

Fig. 19 *Pietra ollare* (tenth-century)

Fig. 20 Piadena ware

distributions, a systematic and long-term level of peasant buying power.[304] In the late ninth to eleventh centuries, this was matched by a set of good-quality coarse cooking ware types called Piadena ware, after the first archaeological site where it was properly identified, located beside an important future castle and (as we have just seen) river port near Cremona. Where it was made is as yet unknown, and it may have been several places, although they used very similar fabrics and styles if so. Piadena ware can be found all across the east-central Po plain, as far as Verona, and in western Romagna. If it is less common in the western parts of Lombardy, this is only because there has been much less excavation here; but it can be identified in Milan, Pavia, and Piacenza. (see Map 20 and Fig. 20).[305]

Piadena ware thus backs up *pietra ollare* as a sign of a common distribution network, and a pattern of widespread demand, across the central plain. It seems, all the same, to have become less unified a production from the late eleventh century; coarse wares from here on diverged more, and, although often improved technologically, had more localized distributions. Apart from this significant shift, which will be explored more in the future, site after site in the central plain simply shows coarse wares and *pietra ollare*, with no other ceramics at all.[306] (Note that amphorae are no longer attested on Lombard sites; after the ninth and early tenth century, only a few references to *anfore* as wine containers appear in documents too, and it is likely that in the inland plain at least, barrels had mostly taken over from them.[307]) All this simply reinforces the fact that the central plain remained cut off from the denser economic links, equally visible in the archaeology, which we saw in the eastern plain between Verona, Bologna, and Venice, shown by local glazed jugs and, later, imported glazed bowls—just as it remained as completely cut off from the imports and eventual local productions which are

[304] For the most complete survey, see Maccadanza, *La diffusione della pietra ollare nel nord Italia*, a 2020 *tesi di laurea specialistica*; I am grateful to the author for letting me see it. Earlier surveys include Malaguti and Zane, 'La pietra ollare nell'Italia nord-orientale'. But every site report for the Po plain in our period shows *pietra ollare*, sometimes to the virtual exclusion of ceramics, as, for example, at Pellio Intelvi (prov. Como); see Caimi et al., 'Gli scavi', pp. 132–40.

[305] The core analysis of *ceramica 'tipo Piadena'* and its distribution is Mancassola, 'Le ceramiche grezze di Piadena'; see further Sbarra, 'I materiali ceramici', esp. pp. 152–73, 176–8 (163 for Pavia). For Milan, see Guglielmetti et al., 'Ceramica comune', pp. 241–2, a single sherd; for Piacenza, see Cantatore, *Da Placentia a Placencia*, pp. 259, 316, 342. Kilns have not been found in this part of the Po plain; a very rare example is that of Libarna (prov. Alessandria) in the ninth–tenth centuries, which, however, produced for a local area farther west and south than this: see Filippi et al, 'La produzione di una fornace altomedievale'. The survey of Po plain coarse wares by Brogiolo and Gelichi, 'La ceramica grezza medievale', from as long ago as 1986, is still an essential point of reference.

[306] For this localization, see Maccadanza and Mancassola, 'La ceramica di cucina' (of the monastic site of Leno, prov. Brescia), pp. 314–37, and Nicola Mancassola, pers. comm. For a survey of sites in Lombardy with only coarse wares and *pietra ollare*—and also, to an extent, glass—see Sannazaro et al., 'Manufatti del quotidiano'.

[307] Citations of *anfore*: for the ninth and tenth centuries, see Castagnetti et al., *Inventari*, V and VIII/1–3, *passim*; Merati, *Le carte… di Velate*, 1, n. 5. For after 1000, see ibid., n. 97; Mangini, *Le carte… di S. Ambrogio*, 3.1, nn. 80, 87; Pezzola, *Le carte… di Lenno*, n. 70; Pezzola, *Le carte… dell'Isola Comacina*, n. 8. See n. 139 above for Byzantine wine amphorae reaching inland to Ferrara and Nonantola, but no farther.

visible in Genoa. Indeed, the central plain did not begin to make its own glazed wares until the later thirteenth century, over fifty years later than on the coasts, when Pavia and Bologna began to be productive centres.[308] At least it is clear that there was a cultural difference here, for by then Lombardy was producing plenty of other goods; this was evidently the part of Italy which remained attached for longest to non-ceramic tablewares, wood or metal. But the fact that the central Po plain is the only subregion of the whole of the Mediterranean—or at least the regions of the Mediterranean studied in this book—in which pottery production in no way at all reflected other artisanal developments makes one pause. Coarse wares, in pottery and stone, did, indeed, partially unify the central plain economically, and, indeed, partially link it to the eastern plain as well; but the attitude to fine wares in Lombardy separated it off just as much. It is also likely that, into the late twelfth century, Lombard economic complexity was most marked in Milan and Piacenza, with other towns more peripheral; we will come back to this. But we could simply say, for now, that this subregion had in our period the *potential* to be unified economically—more of a potential than Tuscany had, in fact, even though ceramic productions, at least, were more complex in Tuscany until long past 1200. We will see now how far that potential was realized.

Milan was certainly large. It had been the major city of the Po plain since the Roman Empire, probably without a break. It was systematically expanding in our period; its Roman walls already enclosed 200 hectares, its 1155 walls took that up to 240 hectares, and the city continued, later in the twelfth century, to develop outside the new walls too. It is plausible that Milan was already the largest city in mainland Italy by 1100 or so, overtaking Rome, at a time when (very roughly) 30,000 inhabitants was a likely maximum for the latter, and it certainly increased substantially in population from then on.[309] The exact figures do not matter—and are, anyway, as usual, totally irrecoverable—but the relative scale does: Milan did, indeed, have the human resources to bully Lodi and Como, and plenty of other places. It was an imposing city, with a set of Roman buildings surviving into our

[308] See in general Nepoti, 'La maiolica arcaica nella Valle Padana'. For tiny numbers of imported wares in our period, on a very small number of sites, see, e.g., Lavagna, 'Acqui terme'; Benente, 'Frammenti di ceramica invetriata monocroma'; Sedini, 'Il settore abitativo', p. 135, for Castelseprio; and for a Milan site, see n. 140 above.

[309] For the wall hectarage, see Hubert, 'La construction de la ville', pp. 113–14. See Wickham, *Medieval Rome*, p. 112, for a bald guess about the relative sizes of Rome and Milan in 1100. The figure of 150–200,000 inhabitants in Milan by 1300 or so is often argued for; this was up to twice the size of the then probably second-largest cities in Italy, Florence and Venice; see Grillo, *Milano*, pp. 39–40. Ginatempo and Sandri, *L'Italia delle città*, pp. 74, 78, is a little more cautious. I would be more cautious still; we have seen that Fusṭāṭ-Cairo and Constantinople were hard to feed, with this scale of population, two centuries earlier, and Milan, although landlocked and surrounded by other cities with their own needs, seems to have used the grain resources of the Po plain above all (although this did include, particularly in the western plain, some relatively unurbanized zones): Paolo Grillo, pers. comm. I would myself see 150,000 as a likely outside maximum for the city, given this; but that would still make Milan and Paris the largest cities in Europe by 1300. A shorter version of what follows is published as Wickham, 'The small towns of the territory of Milan'.

period, in some form at least—indeed, some of its very large late Roman churches still do. Its society was complex well before 1100, as was shown by the essentially popular-based protests and (eventually) uprisings of the Pataria movement, opposed to clerical marriage and the selling of church offices, in the 1050s–1070s.[310] And this large and expanding city must have had real productive activities to allow it to develop so systematically and on such a scale, attracting immigrants from the countryside in every period. The trouble is that we cannot tell what activities, particularly across the eleventh century. In the tenth and eleventh centuries (up to around 1050), as we saw earlier, what the documents for the city show is a network of merchants (*negocians/negociator*), plus a smaller number of moneyers, who at least show that the city took its minting rights seriously. Artisans are, like the merchants, better documented around and before 1000 than later in the century, when they are rare and largely located in the countryside. After 1075 or so, there are more ironsmiths (*ferrarius*), still rural, plus bakers (*pistor*, *pristinarius*), attesting to non-household demand, but the figures are too small to be real guides.[311]

That scrappy evidence becomes clearer in the twelfth century. *Ferrarii* by now dominate, with some 90 references in the *c.*1,700 documents for Milan and its territory up to 1180 which I have seen, which is to say over four-fifths of the total documentation. Citations of them outnumber those for all other documented trades combined; the best-attested of the other trades are cloth workers of different types (dyers, weavers, and tailors—in all, around a third as many), and then, in order, bakers and leatherworkers.[312] Milan appears from this to be as clearly an iron town as Pisa, which fits its thirteenth-century fame as an arms manufacturer (indeed, arms from Lombardy are cited in a Genoese text as early as 1128–30, as we have seen, p. 541). The single usable archaeological excavation in the city for this period, of a workshop near the cathedral, found a small forge, which,

[310] We do not know the social composition of the Pataria in detail, despite the detailed narrative sources which describe it from both sides, but its popular base is incontestable. See Violante, 'I laici nel movimento patarino', still fundamental despite the large later bibliography; and most recently Norrie, *Land and cult*. Norrie, ibid., pp. 152–92, gives the best account of the spatial relationships of Milan's eleventh-century buildings, its growing size and building density, and its post-1000 economic activities.

[311] For 1075–1100, see Vittani et al., *Gli atti privati milanesi*, nn. 591–2, 606, 678, 902 for *ferrarii*; 574, 643, 662, 711, 816, 839, 856–7, 885 for other trades.

[312] There are too many *ferrarii* or *ferarii*, or other trades, in the twelfth-century documents to cite here. Milanese documents are largely available in the web-based and searchable *Codice diplomatico della Lombardia medievale* (https://www.lombardiabeniculturali.it/cdlm/, accessed 25 September 2022), which republishes some 80% of the hard-copy *Pergamene milanesi* collection, plus some other editions which are only available online. For the detailed relationship between the two series, see Wickham, *Sleepwalking*, pp. 253–4. I cite all of them here by editor and short title, as with most other documentary collections. Another set of texts for the territory of Milan, unconnected to these in bibliographical terms, is Salemme, *Carte del secolo XII*, for Meda (see esp. n. 47 for rural *ferrarii*); thanks to Riccardo Rao for a copy of this. I further include in my figure some 200 texts for Monza, which are mostly unpublished; see n. 328 below for a description. The only substantial sets of pre-1200 Milanese documents which I have not seen are those of the Monastero Maggiore and some of those of the canonica di S. Ambrogio.

although it does not add much to this evidence, at least fits it. But it equally has to be recognized that, in the twelfth century as the eleventh, only a minority of *ferrarii* were explicitly city dwellers—and those who were mostly lived in extramural *burgi* adjoining city gates, both before and after the expansion of the city's walled area.[313] Other major concentrations were in Velate in the north-western hills of the diocese, and Monza and its immediate hinterland (see Map 20).[314] If we had adequate documentation for the Brianza farther to the north-east, which was Milan's mining area, we would doubtless find them there too; towns and villages there, such as Cantù, were certainly significant metalworking centres in the thirteenth century.[315] So Milan shared its ironworking with its wider territory. It may well be that iron was often finished in the city—this is made more likely by the presence of a few *spadari* (sword makers) and *scudarii* (shield makers) exclusively in the city[316]—so it is very probable that rural iron was sold to the city and sold on, in different forms, from the urban market; but its artisanal work was by no means only city-based. The same was true for artisans working in cloth; the much smaller number of weavers (*textor*) and tailors (*sartor*) were mostly rural. Conversely, the dyers (*tinctor*) were much more urban (the only major rural centre for dyers was Vimercate); one Milanese dyer family, that of the brothers Bombello and Piroto di Bombello, was particularly well off, and in the years around 1130 leased out or pledged sizable collections of land. So cloth too was probably often woven and even sometimes cut rurally, but finished in the city.[317]

It can be added that the early importance for rural ironworking here also fits our information about the rest of Lombardy. We know little about the city of Bergamo in this period, and less still about Brescia, these two being the other Lombard iron centres by the thirteenth century, but a diploma of Henry III shows that the inhabitants of the Val di Scalve above Bergamo were producing large

[313] *Ferrarii* in urban *burgi*: Ambrosioni, *Le pergamene della canonica di S. Ambrogio*, nn. 8, 28, 93, 97; Rapetti, *Le carte...di Chiaravalle*, 1, nn. 73, 111; Ansani, *Le carte...di Morimondo*, 1, n. 117; Baroni, *Le pergamene...di S. Lorenzo*, n. 23. The forge is edited in Andrews, 'Lo scavo di piazza Duomo: età medioevale e moderna', pp. 175–6; for document-based surveys of the same central commercial and productive area around the cathedral, see Spinelli, 'Uso dello spazio e vita urbana'; Salvatori, 'Spazi mercantili e commerciali'. (Contrast, for scale, the 50 horizontal looms found on a fourteenth-century site in the city; see Nepoti, 'Alcuni dati archeologici', pp. 382–9.) For iron production in the thirteenth century, see Grillo, *Milano*, pp. 222–4. Some *ferrarii* were a surnamed family, the influential *de Ferrariis* or Ferrari; all the same, in 1211, they still had a forge; see ibid., pp. 437–9. This may be true elsewhere too, but the frequency of the surname would be equally significant.

[314] For Velate *ferrarii*, see Merati, *Le carte...di Velate*, 1, nn. 48, 90, 109, 111, 123, 125, 129, 146, 148; 2, nn. 1, 5, 9–10, 53, 60, 74, 93, 112; for Monza, see p. 606 below.

[315] Grillo, *Milano*, pp. 226–7.

[316] A group of *spadari* are attested as early as 1066, Vittani et al., *Gli atti privati milanesi*, n. 467; for *scudarii*, see Zagni, *Le pergamene...di S. Margherita*, nn. 9, 11, 13–16, 29; Baroni, *Le pergamene...di S. Maria in Valle*, n. 13. The urban focus for sales is nicely represented by the city family of Pietro and Guilicione Millemerce ('a thousand commodities'); see Martinelli Perelli, *Le pergamene...di Vimercate*, nn. 65, 99; Grossi, *Le carte...di Chiaravalle*, 2, n. 207.

[317] For the Bombello family, see Rapetti, *Le carte...di Chiaravalle*, 1, nn. 2, 7, 13, 18, 22–3, 39, 40, 46, 52–3; Grossi, *Le carte...di Chiaravalle*, 2, nn. 167, 233. For Vimercate, see p. 607 below.

amounts already by 1047 (their rights to mine, and to sell iron across northern Italy, were granted in return for 1,000 pounds of iron a year to the fisc), and nearby Ardesio was doing the same by 1145, when it fought off the claims of the bishop of Bergamo. The silver mines of Ardesio, also important, had been under the control of the bishop since the late eleventh century, but the local inhabitants managed to gain control of most of these too by 1179, buying the bishop out for the low sum of £115. We might thus assume that the city of Bergamo was active in iron- (and silver-) working by then, although, without archaeological evidence, this will remain hypothetical.[318] Against that, in fact, when Bergamo's documentation begins to be relatively dense in the thirteenth century, it is woollen cloth, rather than iron, that tends to be stressed most; so it may well be that the miners of the Bergamasco Alps always supplied Milan and its hinterland (as also, perhaps, Venice; see p. 524 above), as much as Bergamo itself.[319]

It has to be said, once again, that none of the citations in the previous two paragraphs, apart from those for the Val di Scalve and Ardesio, gives us any idea about quantities. There were so many *ferrarii* in the territory of Milan that it would be hyper-suspicious not to see iron as a significant artisanal product of the city and its hinterland, even if we did not know what would happen after 1200. It is also important that the evidence for them is not seriously interrupted by the disaster which befell the city in the 1160s; the number of *ferrarii* documented in that decade halves, but it picks up again at once, and in the 1170s the recorded numbers are even higher than before. These are signs that the city's economy rapidly bounced back. But we cannot say the same for the scale of cloth; we do not have more evidence here than would be consistent with local consumption only, except for dyeing. *Fustaneum* (fustian) and its analogues do not appear as words in the documents for twelfth-century Milan, or, indeed, its immediate neighbours. Nor do our Milanese texts as yet tell us enough about the import of cotton necessary for fustian production, or give us more than occasional references to flax-growing, given that linen was the other component of this cotton–linen cloth mix. Milan's other major thirteenth-century cloth product, woollens, may well not yet have fully developed in our period, given that the evidence for Lombard transhumance of sheep, the best proxy for a wool specialization, only really picks up in the later twelfth century (see p. 490 above). But this absence of documentation cannot really reflect the situation, for fustian in particular; around 1160 we already found a little Milanese fustian in Genoa, and around 1190 it appears much more

[318] *Heinrici III. diplomata*, n. 199; Barachetti, 'Possedimenti del vescovo di Bergamo nella valle di Ardesio', doc. nn. 1–4 for silver before 1100, n. 5 for 1145, and n. 6 for 1179 (this work further edits the best collection of mining documents for the thirteenth century anywhere in Italy). See in general Menant, 'La métallurgie lombarde', and esp. Menant, 'Pour une histoire médiévale de l'entreprise minière'.

[319] Menant, 'Bergamo comunale', pp. 139–47; Mainoni, 'L'economia di Bergamo', pp. 264–9, 283–305; in both cloth and iron, rural production remained more important here.

often there. It was by then, clearly, being produced at scale, and this was emphatically the case for both fustians and woollens in the thirteenth century.[320] That is to say, in general, we can certainly conclude that twelfth-century documents are not giving us an adequate account of Milan's artisanal productions, but we do not yet have any real sense of what they would show us if they did.

Instead, the best guide to what could have been going on in urban cloth production in twelfth-century Milan is probably Piacenza's mercantile statutes. This is not a random comparison, for Piacenza fustian matches that of Milan in the early Genoese registers; as a result, at least as far as that cloth type was concerned, the two cities can in some respects be paralleled with reasonable confidence. When the statutes actually started to be compiled is unclear; the final corpus dates to 1321, but there are many layers to it, and the earliest dated clause is from 1199. The 1967 editors wished to propose that this means that substantial sections of the current text predate 1199; this does not follow (the Pisan law code, which was definitely compiled in 1155–60, has individual dated clauses going back to 1140). The casual references early in the text to the city rulers being *potestas vel consules civitatis* are probably a better guide, for consuls and podestà alternated in Piacenza between 1188 and 1218. I would put the date of the earliest clauses of the text into that period, that is to say, starting in the 1190s.[321] The *mercatores* of Piacenza by then certainly included cloth workers of a wide variety of types; indeed, they appear to have included cloth workers (and cloth merchants) to the exclusion of almost all other artisans. Linen, cotton, and wool are all referred to, and a division of labour in cloth production is clear. Cotton spinners are seen as female, and weavers can be both male and female. There are complex rules about the sizes of long cloth pieces, and of pieces of fustian, and of the proportion of cotton thread in the latter. Workshops seem to be at least in part run on a putting-out system. Fustian and its cotton base are stressed most, and one of the oaths described in the text, dated to 1218, is of fustian weavers. But the 1199 clause concerns woollens: it is the oath of the mercantile consul that he will ensure, at the start of his

[320] For Genoa, see pp. 548–53 above. Barbarossa's army devastated Milan's crops, including flax (*linum*), in 1160 according to the *Gesta Federici I.*, p. 40; but Milanese flax only appears in documents in 1184 and then in 1198 (Grossi, *Le carte…di S. Ambrogio*, 3/2, n. 18; Manaresi, *Gli atti del Comune*, n. 143; Ansani, *Le carte…di Morimondo*, 2, nn. 334–5); and there are only a handful of isolated references to flax elsewhere in Lombardy: for Bergamo, see De Angelis, *Le carte…di S. Sepolcro di Astino*, 1, n. 6; for Lodi, see Grossi, *Le carte della Mensa vescovile*, n. 138. For thirteenth-century cloth production in the city, and also in the countryside, see Grillo, *Milano*, pp. 215–22, 224–8. Note finally Ottone *Zendadarius*, a consul and city official from the 1170s onwards—the first reference in Manaresi, *Gli atti del Comune*, is n. 115 (a. 1178)—whose surname may attest to silk-working in the city, as Paolo Grillo has pointed out to me.

[321] Castignoli and Racine, *Corpus statutorum mercatorum Placentiae*, pp. xciii–xciv for the date; ibid., chs 51–3, 59 for the alternation of consuls and podestà, and Albini, 'Piacenza', pp. 414–18, for the date range for that alternation. The Pisa citation is *Constitutum Legis*, ch. 39 (in Vignoli, *I Costituti*, p. 105). Note that there are no references to production in the first set of statutes for Milan, the 1216 *Liber consuetudinum Mediolani*, ed. Besta and Barni, although they are detailed about other aspects of urban life, and do mention the sale of skins and cloth, as also armour (5.26–7, 29.2; cf. n. 327 below).

mandate, that all male and female wool weavers should weave in the style of the cloth of Monza, with rules against adulteration with cow, donkey, hare, and goat hair.[322]

This is just the sort of regulatory material which a fully developed cloth industry should generate, and the text does, indeed, imply that full development. I would suppose that it would have resembled any text which was being developed in Milan in the same period, including, indeed, the reference to Monza (though such a Milanese text would certainly have said something about metalworking too). The fact that the statutes in effect start in the 1190s seems to me also to fit what we know of Milan's cloth, particularly as it was exported through Genoa. Piacenza has a detailed study, by Pierre Racine; he did not cite any evidence of cloth production in twelfth-century Piacentine documents (again, he relied on the Genoese evidence), but he laid stress on a bas-relief in the cathedral, dating to not long after 1122, one of a set of reliefs depicting urban trades, which shows two women cutting cloth. This at least shows some production for sale, quite early; and 'Lombard' cloth, as well as arms, is referred to in the Genoese regulations for 1128–30, as we have seen. That this cloth came, at least in part, from Piacenza is implied by Genoa's closeness to Piacenza in the 1140s–1150s; even more so is the fact that Genoa's debt to Piacenza in 1155 was repaid in part in raw cotton and dyeing materials. In addition, Piacentine cloth was being exported overseas via Pisa in the 1130s; and a Piacenza contract, surviving in Parma, shows an artisan and his wife giving a pledge in return for cotton (*bambasium*) worth 36 *solidi* in 1146. Cotton imports to Piacenza and, indeed, Milan will have been disrupted not only by the Barbarossa wars, but also by the Sicilian embargo on trade with Genoa in 1162–74 (pp. 256–7 above); but the testimony about the exactions of Barbarossa's officials in Piacenza and its territory which we have from the mid-1160s refers to the taxing of both fustian and its raw materials, flax and cotton, even if these are massively outnumbered in the texts by complaints about the requisitions of agricultural products.[323] Piacenza's large-scale cloth-weaving

[322] Castignoli and Racine, *Corpus statutorum mercatorum Placentiae*, chs 66, 100–4, 136, 158–264 cover cloth; many of the provisions must date far into the thirteenth century, however. See ibid., ch. 188 for female cotton-spinners, chs 179–89 for male and female fustian weavers (ch.184 for the 1218 oath), ch.158 for long cloth, chs 168–9, 202 for fustian rules, ch. 195 for putting out, ch. 248 for the 1199 oath.

[323] Racine, *Plaisance*, 1, pp. 114–24, 293–343; for the late thirteenth century, cf. ibid., 3, pp. 1048–99. I do not agree with all his claims, e.g., at ibid., 1, p. 122, that the Piacentini initially imported cotton though Venice, for which there is no evidence at all. For Genoa, see *LI*, 1, nn. 3, 174, note at p. 250 (*CDGE*, 1, nn. 51, 260); see n. 228 above for Pisa; for the Parma text, see Drei, *Le carte degli Archivi parmensi del secolo XII*, n. 171 (this, however, is the only such reference in over 200 documents from Piacenza in the Parma archives for the twelfth century up to 1180). Piacenza also seems to have exported cotton to Cremona in 1170; see n. 303 above. Note, however, Falconi and Peveri, *Il Registrum Magnum*, 1, n. 30 (a. 1184), a formal Piacenza city consular act witnessed by the leaders, also *consules*, of five guilds, the earliest cited in the *Registrum*: three of the five are for artisanal work, but all are for leather, not cloth. Racine could have mentioned the 1160s testimony about taxation edited in Güterbock. 'Alla vigilia della Lega Lombarda'—for references to the taxing of raw materials and cloth,

could well, given this evidence, have begun a little earlier than that of Milan, although it is fair to add that Milan's dyers were already active by the 1130s as well. The larger city caught up fairly fast, anyway, and matched Piacenza in the Genoese documents already around 1160; by 1190 or so, after the wars, when our evidence properly takes off, they were certainly on a par.

Patrizia Mainoni, in an important article, has sketched the history of twelfth-century cloth-making in northern Italy as a whole. She differentiates sharply between the history of woollens and the history of fustian. Woollens were produced on an increasing scale in many areas of the Po plain across our period, as references to fulling mills show; eastern Lombardy and the western Veneto show references to such mills before 1100, although Milan, in particular, only sees them from the twelfth century. These woollens were in the mid-twelfth century a cheaper alternative to the finer and more expensive cloth by now coming in from Flanders; all the same, the scale of their production, as we have seen, must have been limited until the late twelfth-century developments in transhumance. (It was only some decades after 1200 that northern Italian wool production came to rely on North African imports.) Fustian, however, was cheaper still. Mainoni argues convincingly that it was fustian which was the major production in the mid- to late twelfth century, far more than woollens, which only really developed after 1200, and that it was of fundamental importance in establishing a real export market for Italian cloth for the first time.[324] Fustian relied on local flax, from a variety of places in the Po plain (even if less, as yet, from close to Milan itself), and imported cotton. It, therefore, can only have got off the ground once Sicilian cotton started to come in through Genoa, given that we have no information before the thirteenth century referring to any cotton trade from Byzantium via Venice to Lombardy. This would have happened to some extent by the 1130s (for Piacenza), a little more by around 1160 (for both Piacenza and Milan), and then, after a dip caused by the wars and the Sicilian embargo, massively by around 1190 (probably, by now, for other Lombard cities too). The dialectic between international exchange and regionally based production is thus reasonably clear: Genoese traders made the production of fustian possible at all, from the 1130s; conversely, the cotton trade cannot have begun on any scale before there was enough production in the north to provide a market for it, allowing producers to switch from linen and linen–hemp mixes (there is fragmentary evidence for the

see appendix, pp. 68, 71, 73–4—but did not, which casts doubt on the systematic nature of his work on this subject. I chose not to look at Piacenza's substantial and mostly unpublished documentation, given that Racine had apparently covered the topics discussed here at length, but better-grounded work may well change what I state here.

[324] See in general Mainoni, 'Le produzioni non agricole'. For fulling mills, see ibid., pp. 236–8; Malanima, *I piedi di legno*; for a European context, see also Munro, 'Industrial energy', pp. 245–62. For fulling in the territory of Milan, see Martinelli Perelli, *Le pergamene… di Vimercate*, n. 38 (a. 1143, for Trigerius *fullo*), and see n. 332 below for Monza. For North Africa, see p. 266 above.

latter[325]) to fustian; but its real expansion, nonetheless, had to await the development of a larger-scale productive infrastructure in Lombardy itself, which did not fully appear until around half a century later.

To summarize here, Milan's metalworking was substantial and growing across the whole of the twelfth century, but cloth-weaving in both Milan and Piacenza probably developed more slowly. We could propose that the second quarter of the twelfth century showed a gradual increase in cloth production, picking up in Piacenza in the 1120s–1130s, and in Milan by the mid-century at the latest. But clear evidence for scale for either is only visible in the 1190s, so I would see cloth production in both of them as active, more than in other cities, but only really taking off after the Barbarossa wars—and doubtless, among other things, taking advantage of the relative absence of intercity war in Lombardy as a whole between the establishment of the Lombard League in 1167–8 and the end of the 1190s. That would fit the evidence for both cities, taken as a whole, although, to repeat, it remains weak until the thirteenth century. But, however weak, it is at least stronger than that elsewhere; no other Lombard city has any significant parallel evidence known to me before 1200.[326] If the upward curve for cloth stretched from the 1120s to the 1190s here, with a major upturn only after the 1170s, elsewhere it was later still. Genoa was exporting Lombard cloth already in the 1160s, but I concluded earlier (p. 551 above) that the evidence for this did not yet demonstrate a complex north Italian economy. A fuller development of the subregion as a cloth-producing economy thus dated to after our period, although, as it seems, not long after. This fits, among other things, the tolls attested for Lodi's river port in the 1180s in a set of testimonies from a court case of 1192, which mentions a variety of cloth types (including wool and fustian), as well as dyes, salt, iron, copper, and animals; Lodi, in its new site on the Adda river, was halfway between Piacenza and Milan. This text also tells us little about scale, but the range of goods mentioned at least hints at the complexity of exchange by now.[327]

The Milanese documents do, all the same, give us a guide to at least one aspect of the infrastructure of production and exchange, the relationship between the city and its rural *burgi*; for the documentation for two of the most important,

[325] For *pannis tirlixis*, see Martinelli Perelli, *Le pergamene... di Vimercate*, n. 31 (a. 1138); for the meaning of *tirlixius* and other similar mixes, see Mainoni, 'Le produzioni non agricole', p. 242.

[326] For Bergamo, see n. 319 above; for Cremona, see nn. 302–3 above; for Vercelli, see Mainoni, 'Un'economia cittadina nel XII secolo', esp. pp. 318–22, and Degrandi, *Artigiani nel Vercellese*, pp. 19–23, 35, 49. Fennell Mazzaoui, *The Italian cotton industry*, esp. pp. 29–34, 59–72, 87–93, although she talks up early north Italian cotton (by which she really means fustian) production, does not actually have any further clear evidence until the first decades of the thirteenth century.

[327] Grossi, *Il Liber Iurium del Comune di Lodi*, n. 116, at pp. 235–6. Many of the witnesses remembered back to the 1150s, but the one who lists the tolls is talking about the last decade. A similar set of cloth types appears in the *Liber consuetudinum Mediolani*, ed. Besta and Barni, 29.2, from a generation later.

Monza and Vimercate, is relatively generous, in each case thanks to the survival of the archive of the major local church. Let us look at these two in slightly more detail, as guides to how the countryside was developing, and to how that development related to the city.

First, Monza.[328] Here the local church, S. Giovanni, was old—it was already important, with royal connections, around 600—and rich; it had enough clerics to support an elaborate church hierarchy by the end of our period. It had a castle by as early as 919, and a *castrum novum* already by 1003, which were presumably the basis for the church's occasionally documented territorial *signoria*. The two castles were separate but clearly connected, and had an expanding population; they are associated with housing, which was regularly *solariata* (two-storeyed) from the start of the eleventh century. From 1048 Monza is called a *burgus*, again early for Lombardy, and by then was a small but real urban centre. Merchants are regularly attested as living in Monza, from the mid-tenth century to the mid-eleventh, after which they do not appear in Milanese documents in general, as we have seen. The market is referenced from 1054; and the next village, Concorezzo (also a *burgus* by 1188), three kilometres away, also had a major market by the 1120s, as the verse account of the Milan-Como war makes plain (the Comaschi tried a surprise attack on it, but it was a trap).[329] S. Giovanni was clearly the dominant political force in the town—it had no local aristocrats—but it had a rural commune by 1174, and a set of locally significant elite families. Monza, only

[328] For Monza documents before 1100, see Porro-Lambertenghi, *Codex diplomaticus Langobardiae*; Vittani et al., *Gli atti privati milanesi*. After 1100, three-quarters of the Monza documents are in the Archivio di Stato di Milano, Fondo di religione, pergamene, Capitolo di S. Giovanni di Monza (henceforth ASM, Monza), cartelle nn. 587–8; I cite them by date and number. The others are in the Archivio del Duomo di Monza, and are at present virtually inaccessible; but a copy of Pandolfi, *Regesto documenti monzesi*, a detailed typescript register of the documents there, is available in the Biblioteca civica di Monza, to the helpfulness of whose staff I am very grateful. This shows that all the documents of use to me from that archive are (fortunately) edited in Frisi, *Memorie storiche di Monza*, 2, an eighteenth-century collection. See Norrie, *Land and cult*, pp. 141–7, for a survey of Monzese economy and society in the eleventh century and early twelfth; for the thirteenth century, see n. 331 below. Zaninelli, *Storia di Monza e della Brianza*, 3, *Vita economica e sociale*, pp. 17–21, only provides a very generic account of the Monzese economy, at the end of our period and later.

[329] Church hierarchy: e.g. ASM, Monza, cartella 587, n. 36 (magg. 1132); cartella 588, n. 18 (26 lugl. 1181). *Castrum*, *castrum novum*, *castrum vetus*, and *casa solariata*: Porro-Lambertenghi, *Codex diplomaticus Langobardiae*, nn. 487, 545, 615, 894; Vittani et al., *Gli atti privati milanesi*, nn. 6, 30, 34, 57, 181–2, 199, 326, 375; ASM, Monza, cartella 587, n. 21 (a. 1124); cf. cartella 588, n. 15 (a. 1180, *in burgo in castello veteri*). For the signorial *districtio*, see ASM, Monza, cartella 588, n. 130 (sec. XII); cf. Frisi, *Memorie storiche di Monza*, 2, n. 82, for a very pervasive signorial control by the church of Monza over Calpuno, by Lago Maggiore, in 1196, which we do not see in Monza itself. *Burgus*: Vittani et al., *Gli atti privati milanesi*, n. 329; the terminology is standard after 1150 (see, e.g., ASM, Monza, cartella 587, n. 58 (12 nov. 1155)). Merchants: Porro-Lambertenghi, *Codex diplomaticus Langobardiae*, nn. 613, 619, 809, 894, 900; Vittani et al., *Gli atti privati milanesi*, nn. 6, 65, 199. Market: Vittani et al., *Gli atti privati milanesi*, n. 375, cf. 415; later, e.g. ASM, Monza, cartella 588, n. 38 (13 ago. 1186, a *banco in burgo in mercato*). Concorezzo: *Liber Cumanus*, ed. Stampa, ll. 1608–12; ASM, Monza, cartella 588, n. 43 (4 mar. 1188).

15 kilometres from Milan, was close to the city socio-economically; city dwellers often appear, and prosperous locals moved to Milan in 1096 and 1138.[330]

As noted earlier, Monza made iron, as fits the fact that it is on the edge of the Brianza. *Ferrarii* appear over a dozen times across the twelfth century, and a former forge (*fornax*) is referred to in one 1176 document. No cloth workers appear in the twelfth century, although a couple of dyers do (one was prosperous enough to found a hospital in 1174); this is, however, in this case, a sign of the inadequacy of our documents, given the standing of Monza woollen cloth by the time of the 1199 Piacenza statute.[331] At least we can say that among Monza's very numerous and often large-scale mills (it lies on the river Lambro), fulling mills appear by the 1190s, which is a clear sign of woollen cloth-making; we simply have to conclude that cloth workers did not self-identify as such here. First iron and then cloth are thus documented in this substantial and growing settlement. That was not necessarily their order of importance by the end of our period, but it may represent the chronological ordering of their development.[332]

Vimercate, some 7 kilometres away—it lies just beyond Concorezzo—seems to have matched Monza as a town, and has a parallel density of documentation, thanks to the archive of the church of S. Stefano.[333] It was a market centre from the start, as its Latin name, *vicus Mercato* or *Vicomercato* as one word, first referred to as early as 745, makes transparent; part of the market was granted by King Berengar I to the count of Lodi in the 910s, although the latter does not reappear in the documents for our period. It was a *castrum* by 1053, later than Monza, and a *burgus* by 1079. S. Stefano itself, rebuilt in the tenth and early eleventh centuries, was an unusually large rural church, which is an indicator of its wealth, and its lands were clearly expanding in our period. Vimercate, unlike

[330] Rural commune: Frisi, *Memorie storiche di Monza*, 2, nn. 72, 81, 85; ASM, Monza, cartella 588, n. 43 (29 giug. 1196). The local elites, including the Rabia, Crotta, and Pelluci families, appear throughout the documentation of the twelfth century; they are collectively called *nobiles istius burgi* in 1196; see Frisi, *Memorie storiche di Monza*, 2, n. 81. Moving to Milan: Vittani et al., *Gli atti privati milanesi*, n. 842 (and to Piacenza in n. 80, a. 1016); ASM, Monza, cartella 587, n. 46 (ott. 1138).

[331] *Ferrarii*: ASM, Monza, cartella 587, nn. 8 (mar. 1108), 15 (genn. 1120), 24 (magg. 1125), 51 (genn. 1141), 56 (genn. 1145), 63 (magg. 1148), 116 (mar. 1173), 36 (febb. 1174), 127 (ott. 1175), cartella 588, nn. 80 (16 febb. 1195), 85 (27 giug. 1196), 134–5 (sec. XII); Frisi, *Memorie storiche di Monza*, 2, n. 81. Former *fornax*: ASM, Monza, cartella 588, n. 2 (26 febb. 1176). *Tinctores*: Frisi, *Memorie storiche di Monza*, 2, n. 72 (a. 1174); ASM, Monza, cartella 587, n. 115 (dic. 1173). But two *sarsores* (tailors) are referred to in documents very early in the eleventh century: Vittani et al., *Gli atti privati milanesi*, nn. 6, 80. For thirteenth-century Monza woollens, seen in particular through the Genoese notarial registers, see Grillo, *Milano*, pp. 224–6.

[332] Chiappa Mauri, *I mulini ad acqua nel Milanese*, pp. 32–65, discusses Monza mills in detail; see ibid., pp. 36–7 for fulling mills, which were, when they start to be documented in the 1190s, part of large milling complexes.

[333] Vimercate's documents before 1100 are again edited in Porro-Lambertenghi, *Codex diplomaticus Langobardiae*, and Vittani et al., *Gli atti privati milanesi*; after 1100, almost all in Martinelli Perelli, *Le pergamene… di Vimercate*. Rossetti, 'Motivi economico-sociali e religiosi', esp. pp. 374–405, is the most detailed guide to Vimercate in this period, even if not so much for the material discussed here; see also for some wider remarks Norrie, *Land and cult*, pp. 136–40, 145–6.

Monza, had a local aristocratic family named after the settlement, the *capitanei de Vicomercato*, although they as often lived 20 kilometres to the north in Airuno; they are not documented as having signorial rights in Vimercate, but they were advocates of the church, and controlled many of its tithes.[334] The *burgus* again had several local elite but non-aristocratic families. One, the Trolia, documented from the 1050s (when Vimercate documents start to be numerous) up to nearly the end of our period, was a merchant family, and, indeed, they were among the last merchants who self-identified as such in Milanese documents. After 1100, several members of elite families once again moved to Milan. Prominent among these was the *iudex* Stefanardo, who was actually one of Milan's earliest city consuls, in the 1140s, before he moved back to Vimercate in 1150/3—from then on, he and his heirs had a base in both, well into the thirteenth century. In the 1180s–1190s, indeed, other men from Vimercate appear as consuls in Milan, just as many Milanesi appear in Vimercate; its links with the city seem even closer than those of Monza, although this may simply be a trick of the evidence.[335]

It is clear that Vimercate was developing fast. The town had six churches and an extramural hospital, and also at least three defined quarters by the 1150s; references to houses there are numerous; one of the quarters was extramural in 1087, but incorporated into the expanding town by the middle of the next century. The substantial number of bakers mentioned in texts further confirms its size.[336] Vimercate was a centre for dyeing, as we have seen, and in fact *tinctores* are easily the best-attested artisans—t here are fewer *ferrarii* here. There were a handful of other cloth workers of different types too; and an adult woman in 1197 is, a bit too cutely, named Banbax (Cotton), which hints at fustian rather than Monza's wool.[337] One text from 1138 shows cloth worth £5 being sold between

[334] Schiaparelli, *Codice diplomatico longobardo*, 1, n. 82 (a. 745); Schiaparelli, *I diplomi di Berengario I*, n. 104; Vittani et al., *Gli atti privati milanesi*, nn. 369 (*castro*), 591–2 (*burgo*). For the size of the church (40 metres in length) and some discussion of the whole, see Bairati, 'La collegiata di Santo Stefano protomartire'. For the *capitanei*, see Martinelli Perelli, *Le pergamene... di Vimercate*, nn. 33, 41, 48, 55–8, 70. For other tithe holders, see n. 343 below. Rossetti, 'Motivi economico-sociali e religiosi', pp. 395–403, discusses tithes; her argument, pp. 393–5, that S. Stefano itself held the local signoria is hypothetical.

[335] For the Trolia family, see Vittani et al., *Gli atti privati milanesi*, nn. 355, 393, 408, 456, 499, 597, 873; Martinelli Perelli, *Le pergamene... di Vimercate*, nn. 46–7, 51 (a Trolia daughter moving to Milan), 69; cf. Rossetti, 'Motivi economico-sociali e religiosi', pp. 374–9. For the *iudex* Stefanardo, no more than a medium owner in economic terms, see Wickham, *Sleepwalking*, pp. 47–8. For other people moving to Milan, see Martinelli Perelli, *Le pergamene... di Vimercate*, nn. 43, 68, 107. For other consuls of Milan from Vimercate, see Manaresi, *Gli atti del Comune*, nn. 130, 143, 148, 149.

[336] Quarters: for *Porta S. Damiani*, see Vittani et al., *Gli atti privati milanesi*, nn. 700 (still extramural), 777; Martinelli Perelli, *Le pergamene... di Vimercate*, nn. 53, 82, 87; for *Porta de Moirano*, see ibid., 52, 115; for *Porta de Burgo*, see ibid., 63, 117 (by the latter date, 1199, the *porta* had its own collectivity (*vicinantia*)). Hospital: Martinelli Perelli, *Le pergamene... di Vimercate*, nn. 32, 69; there was, later, also a *scola pauperum* (see ibid., 79), and an early Humiliati house by 1193 (see ibid., 108). Bakers (*pistor*): ibid., 27, 35, 54, 58, 78, 79, 81.

[337] *Tinctor*: Martinelli Perelli, *Le pergamene... di Vimercate*, nn. 25, 28, 30, 40, 56, 65, 86, 110, 117. *Ferrarius*: ibid., 79, 110, 116, 119. Banbax in 1197: ibid., 114 cf. 45 (a. 1150). Other cloth: ibid., 38.

two Milanesi who had a base in the town, plausibly to be dyed there.[338] So Vimercate is actually slightly better documented than Monza as a cloth town, perhaps because fustian production developed earlier than wool production did; and its specialities were, anyway, distinct.

We cannot here get further into the societies of either Monza or Vimercate; interesting though it would be, it would take us too far away from the arguments of this book. But what I have just set out at least shows that they are detailed guides to the way Milan as a city interacted both socially and economically with the growing small towns of its hinterland. Each had artisanal expertises, which complemented each other, as they also complemented those of the city. It is clear from these texts that Milanesi dealt inside the *burgi* as easily as they did at home. The Millemerce family of Milan, for example, already mentioned, had land in Vimercate, and that centre could easily contribute to its multi-trading.[339] There was a settlement hierarchy in the territory of Milan which was based on both artisan production and exchange with the city; the rural network strengthened the coherence of the productive networks of the city itself, and also, doubtless, helped Milan to recover fast from the troubles of the 1160s. This, then, made up the basic exchange infrastructure of the inner territory of Milan, and it doubtless extended farther out, to other *burgi* to the north, whose documentation is for the most part less detailed.

* * *

As I said earlier, these data are incomplete, offering only sideways, indicative insights. But they do point in the same direction, towards a growing complexity of related productions in Milan and its territory, as also in Piacenza, although less clearly in the case of other Lombard towns. This brings us back to the problem of explanation. Here, as with Florence later in time, it should be clear that any explanations will have little to do with Mediterranean trade; that was a result of this growing complexity, not a cause. Almost no non-regional goods can be tracked in the central Po plain as yet, apart from the cotton which came in as a raw material from Sicily. When Piacenza and Milan had enough production for export, Genoa was very ready to act as the intermediary, but the productive scale had to develop internally first. Between Venice and Padua, and in Pisa, we could see a growing fluidity of exchange represented in the growth in the number of documented credit transactions; around Milan too, these begin to appear from the 1020s. From the 1050s some transactions were implicitly at interest, and by the early twelfth century the taking of interest, generally called *servitium* in Milan, could be explicit—by then it was set at 15 or 20 per cent—which is more significant as a sign of exchange activity. The numbers are not large here, however, and

[338] Martinelli Perelli, *Le pergamene... di Vimercate*, n. 31.
[339] For the Millemerce, see n. 316 above.

the formularies are not standardized, which again indicates that the economy was as yet less fluid than in Venice, in particular.[340] There was, nonetheless, certainly a substantial amount of rural exchange by now, as shown by the markets, the expansion of small towns, the rural artisans and, indeed, the bakers.

This again raises the issue of demand. Before 1000, there were certainly major comital families, and already the array of churches and monasteries we have seen across this section, plus a range of examples of rural elite figures, active in our texts in local areas of the countryside.[341] But the rich in Lombardy and, more specifically, in the territory of Milan were getting richer in our period. Castles were beginning to be the norm for any powerful family, and some aristocratic families had dozens (see pp. 494–5 above); this did not in itself show increases in wealth, but it made such wealth more visible, including to us, when we find lists of castle estates in texts. Castles were also by now often foci for *signorie* too, although in the territory of Milan itself, as noted earlier, signorial rights are actually not well documented, unlike (for example) nearby Bergamo; they were often, as far as we can see, not very substantial in scale, and were often fragmented—many villages, indeed, seem to have had no signorial dependence (Vimercate was probably one), and the best evidence we have for coherent and pervasive lordships comes from a few ecclesiastical estates. But we do have some material signs of growing concentrations of wealth. Castle excavations are much less frequent in Lombardy than in Tuscany, but a recent survey by Simone Sestito makes clear that the move to stone in eastern Lombardy, at least, was largely a feature of the twelfth century, as in Tuscany, even if probably slightly later.[342] Rural church-building too, as we saw for S. Stefano di Vimercate, was certainly beginning to be large-scale and costly.

And above all, elites of all kinds were in themselves more numerous than in the early middle ages. By the end of the eleventh century, far more than before, we

[340] For the eleventh century, Violante, 'Prêts sur gage foncier', is basic; see ibid., pp. 149–51 for interest. For the twelfth century, explicit *servitium* can be found in Baroni, *Le pergamene... di S. Lorenzo*, n. 17 (here called *proficuum*, as in other cities); Ansani, *Le carte... di Morimondo*, 1, n. 51; Rapetti, *Le carte... di Chiaravalle*, 1, nn. 21, 46, 50, 60; Grossi, *Le carte... di Chiaravalle*, 2, n. 167. In 1216, the *Liber consuetudinum Mediolani*, ed. Besta and Barni, 9.3, stabilized at 10% the *debitum usurarium* on a loan.

[341] Balzaretti, *The lands of Saint Ambrose*, pp. 299–473; Keller, *Signori e vassalli*, esp pp. 219–31, 269–95.

[342] For castle excavations, see Sestito, 'Dai castelli all'incastellamento'. For signorial rights in Lombardy in general, see Keller, *Signori e vassalli*, pp. 118–36; Menant, *Campagnes lombardes*, pp. 395–485, for eastern Lombardy; Andenna, 'Formazione, strutture', for the territory of Novara. For a Milanese case study, Arosio in the Brianza, see Fonseca, *La signoria del Monastero maggiore*, pp. 29–62, 95–6. The monastery of S. Ambrogio's 1228 regulations for its signorial territory of Origgio, in the plain to the north-west of Milan, give us a model example of a pervasive *signoria*, even if its economic weight is harder to discern; see Berlan, *Statuti di Origgio dell'anno 1228*; cf. also n. 329 above for the *signoria* of the church of Monza over Calpuno. But more recent work on the territory of Milan convincingly shows that strong and fully territorialized *signorie* were rare here: see, e.g., Grillo, 'Le entrate signorili dei Mandelli a Maccagno'; Bernardinello, 'I rapporti tra i "ceti dominanti" e le città padane'; Del Tredici, 'Castelli, mutazione signorile e crescita economica nell'Italia dei secoli XI-XII'. I am grateful here for discussions with Sandro Carocci and Paolo Grillo.

can trace several strata of both urban and rural elites in Milan and its territory, all of them with potential buying power. In the countryside, here as elsewhere, they were often called *milites* (or, at Monza by 1200, even *nobiles*). As to the city, we can see three levels of secular elites in Milan, from *capitanei* with a couple of castles each and some signorial rights to substantial but smaller-scale landowners to prosperous judicial families with less land, but still easily enough to live well from. Outside the cities, there were a few much larger-scale castle-holding families such as the da Besate and the da Carcano on the one side, and on the other a wide set of prosperous smaller landowners with bases in the countryside—in Vimercate, as we have seen, there were a number of such families, set against a local castle-holding family as well, some of whom had or obtained a city base too. In the twelfth and thirteenth centuries, the urban *militia*, as described by Jean-Claude Maire Vigueur, extended to 10–15 per cent of urban populations, and rural figures matched them as well; all these elites, except very rural lords like the da Carcano, will have been part of it. Many of them were also gaining rights to tithes from Milanese churches, urban and rural; this simply redistributed wealth from the church to the elite laity, but tithes could be bought and sold, leased and donated, by lesser elite figures who did not have access to signorial rights, and the process thus widened the range and number of people who could gain wealth this way too.[343] Furthermore, landowning by the best-documented large owners, churches, was itself expanding, as we can see, for example, for S. Giovanni di Monza and S. Stefano di Vimercate, as well as many city churches and monasteries; we can assume that lay elites were as assiduous in their accumulation of property. Urban collective demand was also increasing, simply because all cities were increasing in size, with Milan at their head; and the Vimercate and Monza churches (among others) developed a concern to document rents in kind from the later eleventh century, which, as around Florence, were doubtless for sale to the city as well as for consumption by the church community. Late twelfth-century beginnings for urban taxation would, in the next century, further concentrate wealth in Milan, as in other cities, irrespective of their productive developments.[344]

Elite buying power was thus here, as in Tuscany, increasing in several ways. Indeed, Mainoni has convincingly argued that the production and distribution of fine cloth and furs (and we can add weapons and other metalwork) to elites lay at

[343] For the *militia*, see Maire Vigueur, *Cavaliers et citoyens*, pp. 217–19, 337–62; for the levels of elites in Milan, see Wickham, *Sleepwalking*, pp. 39–50. For tithes, see esp. Violante, 'Pievi e parrocchie', pp. 667–83, 765–78. Tithe holders in Vimercate included several local non-capitaneal elite families; see Martinelli Perelli, *Le pergamene... di Vimercate*, nn. 18, 19, 24, 32, 33. For Monza's *nobiles*, see n. 330 above; for rural *milites*, see the observations in Del Tredici, 'Castelli, mutazione signorile e crescita economica nell'Italia dei secoli XI–XII', § 4.3.

[344] For rents, see, e.g., Norrie, *Land and cult*, pp. 135–44, 209–10. Urban taxation in Milan is, however, not well documented before 1200, and seems to have been based on assessments by local communities, before (after a generation of infighting between urban *milites* and the *popolo*) taxation based on formal *estimi* of property was stabilized in the 1240s, rather later than in many cities; see Biscaro, 'Gli estimi del comune di Milano', pp. 350–73; Grillo, *Milano*, pp. 522–9.

the heart of the take-off in high-end production, which steadily extended to less expensive and larger-scale commodities as well—for elites themselves needed cheaper goods for their own entourages, and cheaper goods could be bought by non-elites too.[345] So growing elite and urban demand lay behind a high percentage of the growing artisanal production of Milan and its territory, and much of the rest of Lombardy, as it did elsewhere. And this concentration of demand was by now sufficiently great that it took Lombardy a serious step up in scale, from the active but relatively simple exchange networks of the tenth century, with sales of salt, coarse pottery, and luxury goods along the Po river network but no real productive complexity, to the major urban productions of the late twelfth and, still more, thirteenth centuries.

If elites were collectively more prosperous, this must have meant, here as elsewhere, that peasant producers were more squeezed. But this did not lead to a widespread immiseration for the peasant majority, at least among those, who remained numerous, who owned some or all their own land. And every large archive, of which there are several for the territory of Milan, shows peasant owners throughout our period. Some were going to the city, others were losing their land to churches, but others continued throughout, right up to the end of our period, and in the thirteenth century as well. Furthermore, we have seen how much agricultural expansion, though land clearance—which was much more substantial in Lombardy than in Tuscany in this period—was the work of peasant actors; such actors, whether landowners or tenants, had more resources as a result.[346] Peasants could thus buy more artisanal goods too, especially when production at scale, which was certainly developing in at least Milan (and its rural *burgi*) and Piacenza—plus the growing density of market relationships, which reduced transaction costs—made professionally made goods, such as iron tools and cloth, cheaper. As we have seen, at least some cloth production at scale has to have preceded the import of cotton through Genoa; but the subsequent development of fustian production meant even cheaper cloth, for a demand base which must have been at least partly peasant-orientated and which could thus extend substantially, given that the great majority of the inhabitants of Lombardy, notwithstanding its increasing levels of urbanization, remained peasants. This sort of dialectic worked for the relationship between aristocratic demand and peasant

[345] Mainoni, 'Le produzioni non agricole', pp. 226–33, 250.

[346] For thirteenth-century peasant landowning in the northern half of the territory of Milan, and its weakening in the south (but only after 1200), see Grillo, *Milano*, pp. 140–2, 162–5; Romeo, *Il comune rurale di Origgio*, pp. 43–5. For twelfth-century examples from Vimercate, see Martinelli Perelli, *Le pergamene...di Vimercate*, nn. 3, 8, 9, 26, all gifts for the soul of a deceased relative of single fields which are then leased back to the family *nomine massaritii* by the church, and 53, a small-scale marriage gift. Peasant owners are still more visible in and around Velate—see Merati, *Le carte...di Velate*, 1 and 2, with Keller, *Signori e vassalli*, pp. 67–74, for the complexity of their social positions—although that area is farther out from Milan, at the start of the hills leading up to the Alps. For agricultural expansion, see n. 52 above.

demand as well: the former allowed production and distribution at scale to develop, which then made metal and cloth goods cheap and accessible enough for peasant demand to fuel production even further, and to create a real mass market. And when that happened, the fact that the river system already linked all the Po plain together made a wider-scale productive complexity easier and faster to achieve than it did in Tuscany, where the coast and the inland were rather more separate.

We have seen this set of developments operating throughout this book. The pacing of them in Lombardy was probably similar to the slightly earlier movements in the eastern Po plain and in western Tuscany; in those two subregions we have the barium meal of developing ceramic distributions to help us, whereas in Lombardy we do not, but there are plenty of parallels all the same. But in all three it was slower than in Sicily, or Byzantium, or, most of all, al-Andalus, because in north-central Italy it was only after 1100 that elites as a whole became sufficiently rich, and numerous, to begin to affect production patterns. Conversely, once this dialectic, moving towards greater and greater productive complexity, began to operate, it pushed inland northern Italy (and then inland Tuscany) consistently onwards, which meant that by the middle decades of the thirteenth century Milan, Florence, and many other cities were, indeed, for the first time, really matching the other great productive regions of the Mediterranean in their scale and complexity. Italy was late to this, but by the later thirteenth century that no longer mattered. And, of course, Genoa and Venice (by now, not so much Pisa) could then export Italian goods all over the Mediterranean, and import goods back again, integrating Italy fully into the maritime network in a way that we cannot show before 1200.

6.7 Mediterranean Projection and Regional Fragmentation

Italian maritime cities were by the late twelfth century highly active in the Mediterranean as traders—and, not least, as armed traders. They are presented by writers on other Mediterranean regions as highly menacing, potentially dominant powers. When they are looked at more directly, however, they can be seen to be more fragile. Italian navies could do a lot of damage, of course. Piracy in the Aegean in the late twelfth century, or attacks on Palermo, Mahdia, Alexandria, Almería, and plenty of other cities, undoubtedly did harm; and we can add the harm Genoa and Pisa could do to each other, given the expense of the ships they captured and destroyed during their wars. But sacked cities could revive quite fast; none of these attacks was as devastating as the depopulation of Milan in 1162–7, which did not by any means ruin that city, even in the short term. Furthermore, all the longer-term changes in the force or prosperity of Mediterranean powers which the Italian port cities had a hand in, most notably the conquest of the

Levant by the Crusaders after 1098 and the destruction of the Byzantine Empire in 1203–4, were the work of much larger armies from the Latin west, which were at best transported or backed up by the Italian port cities. Conversely, the temporary cancellations of Genoese trade with Sicily after 1162 and of Venetian trade with Byzantium after 1171, or the embargoes by Egyptian rulers on Italian trade in the wake of the First and Third Crusades, were potentially destructive to the economies of the cities, without having nearly as much effect on that of the states whose choices these were. The Italian cities were always in trouble when the powers they traded with were at war, if they had to choose sides.

Trade continued; embargoes could often be got around, and were temporary. (The confiscation of Venetian goods in 1171 as well was, beyond doubt, the biggest hit for the island city, although that was in part reversed too.) But it must always be remembered that cities of around 25,000 people or fewer, however determined, were small-scale operators by comparison with the major political systems of the Mediterranean. We have seen that the scale of their transactions, even in the twelfth century, when they were coming into their own for the first time, was not as large as that of the Egyptian *geniza* merchants a century earlier. They did not have the capital to match that of Egypt—even the Ziani in Venice, even the richest handful of families in Genoa (the city which shows the highest investments overall), never mind the others. The breakdown of the Kingdom of Italy allowed cities to go their own way, but it also meant that not only political but economic power was fragmented.

There are some signs in the tenth century that Italian kings or their representatives were capable of putting quite substantial productive operations in place on royal land. The ironwork for horse trappings at Vetricella in Tuscany is one example (see p. 573 above), and Giovanna Bianchi has drawn attention to others, such as the strikingly large-scale production of steatite, for spindle whorls and similar products, in the Appennines above Piacenza around 1000, as markers of economic movement on public estates, especially in the late tenth century.[347] Operations of this kind are so niche that they seem to imply many similar but more mainstream productions for state use as well (maybe on analogy with the iron production for the dukes of Venice in the 1030s; see p. 524 above). All the same, they cannot so far be documented beyond 1050. If they do mark the start of a state-backed set of moves towards production at scale—which is very plausible but as yet only indicative, and that production was not necessarily for commercial

[347] See Bianchi, 'Rural public properties', pp. 189–90, with references to the steatite excavations (one important one is published in Bazzini et al., 'Un'officina per la lavorazione di steatite'). She cites the production of *pietra ollare* at Chiavenna too—this did continue, presumably because it was a straightforward case, here, of mining stone for a large market—and also iron production at Fraore just outside Parma. She further develops the argument in Bianchi, *Archeologia dei beni pubblici*, pp. 215–41. The Val di Scalve iron production, apparently on royal land, documented in 1047 (see p. 600 above), is another example.

purposes—these seem to have ended before the kingdom broke up at the end of the eleventh century.

In terms of scale, then, Italy had to start again after 1100, city by city, with the resources of single cities only. As noted earlier (p. 478), economic actors from one city seldom invested in another; it would have involved the furthering of the profits of rivals, as well as being hazardous in itself. Indeed, cities actively impeded the trading of others, through commercial tolls—even friendly cities, never mind hostile ones. One result was that the build-up of commercial capital, whether deriving from land or, later, from commerce itself, was slow for a long time. Urban landed elites, lay and ecclesiastical, could be wealthy in their own terms, and happy to show it off, already from the late eleventh century onwards; Italian tower houses are unmatched as standing private buildings anywhere else in our regions, except al-Andalus, and the same is true for urban (and rural) churches, some of which were large-scale and richly decorated. They marked a new need for competitive visibility and (for lay elites) private defence which was less important elsewhere. But they did not have the resources which official elites had in Egypt or Byzantium. Commercial capital developed rapidly in the thirteenth century, once the network of internal exchange began to appear, first in the ports and then in inland productive centres; but it had not yet begun to do so by the end of our period. Throughout this chapter we have seen that build-up, but also its slowness, and for that matter its incompleteness.

This incompleteness also meant that city economies as a whole remained fairly separate for a long time. Cities as collectivities often expanded in size and in population, and thus, we can assume, in local productive activity, again from before 1100 onwards; but that economic expansion was, for a long time, largely limited to the production and demand of single city territories, which, here too, restricted its scale. We have seen the lack of integration of the north-central Italian economy throughout our period in several different contexts. The Po plain and Tuscany were separate, certainly; references to Tuscans in the Po plain or Lombards in the Arno valley, although they do exist, are casual and anecdotal before 1200. In Tuscany, the productions of Pisa and the coast southwards from it were tightly interlinked by the twelfth century, and brought in Lucca as well, but there is little sign that they reached inland to Florence, not so far away, and no sign that they got any farther. The inhabitants of the Po plain used its river network to transport goods without a break from the Roman Empire onwards, but for most of our period these were either luxuries or bulk goods such as salt and *pietra ollare* which did not require major productive organization, once the initial technologies for their extraction were mastered (a mastery which, indeed, had already been achieved by the time the Roman Empire ended). Conversely, when it came to more complex productions, the Po plain suddenly appears less united. Coin hoards, which in al-Andalus showed considerable movements of money between cities (see pp. 442–3 above), tend in northern Italy to be dominated by coins from one mint only, the nearest one in nearly all cases.[348] Venice's semi-fine ceramics, attested throughout our period in different forms, did not extend west past Verona and Modena; nor did imported fine wares or wine amphorae. When Milan's iron and Milan and Piacenza's cloth began to develop in the twelfth century, perhaps faster for the iron, more slowly for the cloth, they were exported via Genoa, over the Appennines, rather than down the rivers through Venice. That does have one explanation: it was via Genoa that Sicilian raw cotton came into northern Italy to become part of woven fustian, so it was at least logical that the cloth should go back the same way; but it is still significant that we have no evidence in our period of Venice doing the same with Byzantine cotton. And the link to Genoa was incomplete in other ways, for the Ligurian coast imported and, later, produced, fine ceramics which have not been found in the Po plain cities whose cloth the Genoese traded in. Liguria was thus structurally separate from the Po plain as well; it was not agriculturally rich, but even some of its smaller centres had access to Mediterranean goods which were unavailable, or not wanted, in Milan. So the north-central Italian economy was divided into four or five separate subregions, linked only partially, throughout our period, and each of these subregions had cities with largely independent economic histories. Indeed, this lack of integration extended southwards too: Rome, outside the parts of Italy focussed on here, was in the eleventh century by far the largest and most active city on the Italian mainland, with ranges of artisans which no other city as yet matched, but it had next to no connection to the rest of Italy in economic terms, nor, for that matter, to the Mediterranean.[349] The trend was, beyond doubt, towards more coherent economic interrelationships, but it was slow until well after 1200.

One consequence of this is that the history of the maritime cities is a Mediterranean history, more than it is an Italian one. Only Pisa was really integrated economically with the third of Tuscany closest to it, but that was an even smaller area than the eastern Po plain which intermittently looked to Venice. Venice at least had an economic hinterland, and a near monopoly on northern Italy's salt, but it did not determine the development of neighbouring Padua; and Genoa had very little of one, except its links to subsidiary coastal towns such as Savona. Venice's economic history in our period was, to a large extent, more attached to the Aegean heartland of Byzantium than it was to anywhere in Italy.

[348] Day et al., *Medieval European coinage*, 12, pp. 668–90, provides lists, focussing on hoards from Italy north of the Po. There are some twenty hoards from our period, almost all twelfth-century, which is also the period when mints proliferated, which makes this sort of analysis more productive. The nearest mint turns out to have been Verona or Milan for the most part. Hoards not dominated by the nearest mint are ibid., n. 36 (largely Milanese coins in Naturns (prov. Bolzano), where Verona would be expected), n. 75 (Genoese coins in Verrua Po (prov. Pavia), where Milan and Pavia would be expected), and n. 97 (Parma, coins from Brescia, Cremona, and Milan). I exclude hoards and collections of money on pilgrimage routes, ibid., n. 90 (Lucca), n. 92 (Modena), nn. 101 and 103 (Rome), which have wide ranges of origins.

[349] Wickham, *Medieval Rome*, pp. 111–80.

As for Genoa, its maritime role was as an entrepôt for the whole of the Mediterranean—plus the luxury cloth centres in Flanders and northern France—with, for long, remarkably little linkage to the Italian mainland. Inland northern Italy appears in its economic documents from their start in the second quarter of the twelfth century, but much less prominently than regions on the other side of the sea in every direction, right up to the years around 1190. The economic hyperactivity of the maritime cities had limits in Mediterranean terms, as regards the links of Genoese, Pisans, and Venetians to the internal economies of the other regions they traded with. Their quick-returns business models prevented that in most cases; I will come back to that issue in Chapter 7. But with respect to the rest of north-central Italy, the limits were even stronger. Except for Pisa's relationship with western Tuscany, which had local as much as maritime roots, and apart from one import through Genoa, Sicilian cotton, the economic effervescence of the maritime cities had no significant effect on the early development of the internal Italian economy, and on the beginnings of the take-off which is so visible in the thirteenth century. They are standardly linked together, but as I have stressed several times in this chapter, it is a mistake to do so. In order to discover the bases for Italy's thirteenth-century productive take-off, we have to look elsewhere.

This is what I have tried to do, in particular, in the immediately preceding sections of this chapter on Tuscany and Lombardy. In the latter, we saw that the progressively greater evidence for iron and cloth production, and the development of productive hierarchies in the *burgi* around Milan, which gave these steadily intensifying processes a more solid because diversified base, was linked above all to patterns of higher local demand. Elites were increasing in both numbers and wealth, so they could buy more things; the pre-existing market structures of Lombardy could and did facilitate this. Among the peasant majority, which was itself clearing land, so expanding agricultural production, at least some strata were also prosperous enough to add substantially to local demand—once goods were cheap enough, because produced on a large enough scale, for peasants to buy. Similar processes can be found in Tuscany as well, and ceramic distributions document them directly there. It was this, along with the generalized demographic rise and a linked increase in rural production which we have also seen, which pushed north-central Italy out of the geographically quite wide, but not very complex networks of the early middle ages, as still evidenced by, among other sources, the *Honorantie civitatis Papie* around 1000 (p. 479 above), and into an environment in which urban production and exchange began steadily to develop, each reinforcing the other, and then finally began to connect cities with each other, soon with a considerable dynamism— that is to say, the world of the thirteenth century, with beginnings in the very late twelfth. In both Lombardy and Tuscany, these economic developments were based on a local, not Italy-wide, and not in the least Mediterranean-wide, demand for goods. They were also not uniform; Milan's (or Piacenza's) hinterland, like Pisa's, was economically more complex at the end of our period than were those of most other cities. But from then on they would extend, steadily, outwards—from Pisa to Lucca, from Milan to Como or Bergamo;[350] and other cities, such as Verona and Bologna, Florence and Siena, would later develop their own productive centralities, based again on local demand first, before branching out into wider intra-regional and extra-regional exporting patterns.

In each case, our documentary evidence stresses ironworking, leather, and cloth; archaeology, where it is dense enough, adds ceramics. If one was to be literal about the documentary citations of artisans in private charters, one would conclude that iron was the leading product in many twelfth-century cities, with cloth and leather varying as to which was second-placed. I would be cautious about this; cloth was so important after 1200, after all (and leatherwork, which has been understudied—including, I am sorry to say, here—remained of major importance too). But as a minimum we need to recognize that ironworking, although it is less stressed in modern textbooks, was probably at least as important as cloth-making in our period in north-central Italy, and not only in the great iron towns, Pisa and Milan. And that fits growing peasant demand as well; peasants needed iron as much as cloth or ceramics. More directed archaeological work will add to our understanding of that local demand for iron, in a way that it will never, to the same extent, manage for cloth, although that is for the future.

This was the essential basis for the better-studied world of the thirteenth century. My contribution to that more substantial historiography has been above all to focus on causes. I have also attributed the step change to the last decades of the twelfth century, although the date was certainly different from city to city, as we have seen, with Pisa probably first, given the substantial amount of artisanal activity visible there in the archaeology already in the early twelfth century. Even the documentary evidence before 1200 is far from supportive of the dating and the main characteristics of Lopez's 'commercial revolution'; and that storyline cannot act as a strong competitor, given its evidentiary weakness, to the one constructed, at different moments across this chapter, on the basis of Italy's material culture. From *c.*1190, all the same, there are more and more signs of an economy—or, better, a set of economies—which was gaining complexity quite rapidly. We begin to get casual references to wider arrays of goods being moved about in northern Italy, from Lodi in 1191, Bologna in 1194, or Milan in 1216; and, more significantly for our sense of scale, references in the Genoese registers to many types of goods coming down from the cities of the Po plain also increase very substantially around 1190. References to guilds begin around now too (see p. 467 above, although see also p. 660 below). The *Racio lombardi seu francisci*, a list of

[350] For Milan's widening economic region from the 1190s on, see Grillo, 'Vie di comunicazione'.

customs dues from early thirteenth-century Venice, also shows a substantial set of different types of cloth (plus iron, steel, and other goods) going through the island city, by now coming from Brescia, Como, Cremona, Piacenza, Pavia, Milan, Mantua, the Romagna towns, Lucca, Alexandria in Egypt, several places in France and Flanders, and even England.[351] This text is as unhelpful about scale as any of the one-off texts used in this chapter—even in the thirteenth century, it is still the case that only the Genoese registers really provide that—but it is the first which shows that the Po river network was by now able to join many individual cities together for bulk trading; that would be the next step change. Official documents listing customs dues, which begin in the 1260s, also show us a much greater interconnection between the artisanal goods of different cities.[352] When that happened, the productive hierarchies around Milan, with local *burgi*, and then not too distant rival cities, all making complementary or competitive goods, could extend geographically, and eventually link much more of the Po plain into an economic whole, by 1300 or so, making the whole north Italian economy stronger.[353]

That is to say, this was when the old set of riverine links finally caught up with the developing but localized urban economies we have been looking at, and helped to push them together and further along. That integration was never, as far as I can see, fully complete in the middle ages, but even in its incomplete form it allowed, for the first time, the Po plain to develop a more complex economy than Tuscany. This is also when the complicated associative and credit contracts of the port cities, and now also banking, begin to be found in the inland towns as well, helping to add to the fluidity of exchange. I would put less weight on these than some scholars do, not least because they mark Italy out in the Mediterranean far less than most historians of Europe have supposed—as discussed elsewhere in this book, equivalent contracts were normal in Egypt, and had roots stretching back into the Roman Empire (see pp. 120–1, 128 above and pp. 648–9 below). But at least we can say that, here too, they brought Italy into line with Mediterranean norms.

And the thirteenth-century economic environment for north-central Italy was also the first period in which the Mediterranean dimension came to matter, beyond the smallish hinterlands around the ports. Like Rome in the eleventh century—or for that matter, as we saw in Chapter 5, al-Andalus throughout our

351 Roberti, 'Studi e documenti di storia veneziana', pp. 15–23. For Bologna in 1194, which by now imported iron, cotton, dyes, sugar, and pepper and other spices from Ferrara (i.e., almost certainly, from Venice), see Savioli, *Annali bolognesi*, 2.2, n. 302; for Lodi and Milan, see n. 327 above. See also the attempt by an anti-Milan coalition in 1193 to block trading by Milanese merchants with Genoa and the Ligurian coast, including in cotton (*bunbecium*) and dyestuffs, plus salt (Falconi, *Le carte cremonesi*, n. 748); there is no sign that it succeeded, but this trading was by now explicitly seen as economically significant for Milan.

352 Hoshino, *L'arte della lana*, pp. 37–41, 50–1.

353 I have argued that the absence of a similar hierarchy of productive centres and a weakness in peasant demand in Lazio were the reasons for the absence of a similar take-off in Rome; see Wickham, *Medieval Rome*, pp. 178–80.

period—Milan could grow into a significant economic centre across the twelfth without any major Mediterranean involvement at all. Sicilian cotton did help this growth, but Milanese ironworking did not depend on it, and the city had other cloth types which it could have developed and did develop—hemp and woollens, even in the absence of cotton—as soon as local wool supplies became larger-scale, at least. In the thirteenth century, though, as fustian production expanded still more in different cities in the north, cotton imports became more essential still, and to them were added wool imports from North Africa, as woollen production increased beyond that which even transhumant sheep flocks could supply locally. In return, the Lombard cloth makers had to export as well, and Genoese evidence shows that they indeed did so. Italy, in fact, by now had two substantive cloth productions which were less often made at scale elsewhere in the Mediterranean, fustians and woollens—for we have seen that wool-working was relatively marginal as an urban production in Egypt, Sicily, and Byzantium. (It was more important in Ifrīqiya and al-Andalus, although perhaps not on the scale that it came to have in Lombardy or Verona or Florence by the late thirteenth century.)[354] But, even then, this production for export, however essential to pay for the imports of raw materials, was by a long way second, throughout the middle ages and beyond, to local/regional demand and exchange networks. We will come back to this in Chapter 7.

The ports of Italy became serious Mediterranean trading powers after 1100/1130, but it took separate—and far slower—processes before the inland cities could develop enough to need to and be able to take advantage of this. North-central Italy throughout our period was, in economic terms, playing catch-up with the great political and economic systems of other parts of the Mediterranean, Egypt, Byzantium, or indeed Sicily. This is not a slighting remark; no one could look at the evidence for the Italian economy in 950/1000 and think that it matched those of these other economies, but by 1300 it certainly did. It was a major achievement to do so. It was a slower development than the parallel take-off of al-Andalus, which reached the level of the other Mediterranean states sooner than northern Italy, and from a lower baseline; but northern Italy continued to develop after 1200, whereas al-Andalus faced political disaster. Italy did so even though it did not have an overarching tax-raising state to add substantially to the demand for goods, to lower transaction costs, and to allow larger-scale investment; its decentralization was a disadvantage for its development, but it was a disadvantage which was by now clearly overcome. I would, however, not seek to go further, following many other scholars, and propose that Italy's *force* came to lie in its dramatic decentralization, with every city competing with every other; I can see no grounds for saying so, and the truth seems exactly the opposite.

[354] See the surveys cited in n. 5 above and the collectivity of work in *La crescita economica*.

This decentralization contributed to particular paths for Italian development, all the same; that is certain. Italy in 1300 looked different—still looked different—from other Mediterranean powers. Indeed, with the eclipse of Byzantium and al-Andalus (and also the Crusader states), and given the troubles Sicily was going through from the 1280s onwards, north-central Italy—had it been able to act as a whole—was by then the match of any other Mediterranean power apart from Egypt. But of course, it could not act as a whole; and in the middle ages and for centuries beyond, it never did. This was neither a weakness, by now, nor a strength; it was simply a mark of difference. And anyway, that economic protagonism was still in the future by the end of the period of this book. All we need to say is that, by 1180, we can, dimly, begin to perceive what would come in the next century; the bases had been laid by then.

7

A Brief History of the Mediterranean Economy in the Tenth to Twelfth Centuries

So how did the Mediterranean economy work as a whole? Was there, actually, a Mediterranean economy at all in the long eleventh century? In many ways, the answer to this last question is an easy no. If there was not a single economy in the Po plain of northern Italy, there certainly was not one from Milan to the Fayyūm, Málaga to Thessaloniki. But the different regions of this book were also, in almost every case, more economically complex in 1180 than in 950 (for 'complex', see p. 15 above); we do have to explain why that was, and whether it had common elements—for the six regions we have been looking at did at least have shared features, which need to be explored. I will come back to that at the end of the chapter. They were also all linked together by the sea, strongly or weakly, and their linkage was much more complex in 1180 than it was in 950; this we will look at first.

This chapter, therefore, aims to bring together all the substantive chapters which have gone before, and I will frequently refer to them. But it is not intended to be their culmination, as if, once we have looked at the different regions which make up the Mediterranean (or half of them, at least), we can now more properly appreciate the *real* subject matter of the book, the way they fitted into a Mediterranean whole which was more than the sum of its parts across the years 950–1180. Quite the opposite, in fact. In Chapter 1 of this book, I set out two basic starting points which I intended to use, and have subsequently used, to orientate the argument: bulk exchange was the only guide to economic complexity, for luxuries were by definition economically marginal; and economic structures were local and regional first, which meant that only when two regions had reached a sufficient level of complexity was there likely to be economically significant bulk trading between them, each exporting to the other. Both of these are fundamental to my understanding of medieval economics, and I have discussed the second, in particular, in considerable detail in my regional chapters. Sea trade will never have been more than a very small percentage of the economic activity going on inside each region (cf. pp. 12–13 above). All the same, it did, indeed, connect all the regions of this book, as we have seen in each chapter, to a greater or lesser extent. So it is worthwhile discussing that as well, so that we can set the development of the Mediterranean as a network of commercial routes, as a whole, against what we know of the land-based economies around it—so that we can fairly set the boat beside the donkey.

The Donkey and the Boat. Chris Wickham, Oxford University Press. © Chris Wickham 2023.
DOI: 10.1093/oso/9780198856481.003.0007

We have seen that several of the regional economies of our period did not look to Mediterranean-wide trade to any great degree. The most obvious examples are Byzantium and al-Andalus, which developed considerable levels of economic complexity across our period (in Byzantium, particularly in the twelfth century; in al-Andalus, it started earlier) without participating substantially in Mediterranean-wide exchange at all. The Andalusīs restricted themselves above all to trade inland and around their coastline, with links eastwards largely restricted to semi-luxuries, silk and metals. The Byzantine Empire, of course, had an inland sea at its heart, the Aegean, which not only imperial subjects sailed on; the Venetians, in particular, were active there, but other Italians are attested by the twelfth century as well. But we saw in Chapter 4 that the Venetians only used certain routes, and rarely penetrated beyond the coast towns; they did not integrate the Byzantine economy with the wider sea to more than a small extent. The Aegean was crucial for the coherence and density of the development of the imperial economy—and, indeed, the parts of the empire which were separate from the sea do not seem to have developed in anything like as complex a way—but it did not serve to make that economy more open to the non-Byzantine Mediterranean in our period, except for the routes to southern mainland Italy (itself formerly Byzantine) and northern Syria, and up to (also formerly Byzantine) Venice, routes we will come back to.

It is equally significant that another example of this relative marginality is probably Egypt itself. Egypt was the powerhouse, enormously important to all Mediterranean traders, and more of a focus than any other region in our period, so was far more part of normal Mediterranean-wide trading than was, in particular, Spain. Even outside the great days of the triangular Egypt–North Africa–Sicily trade of flax for oil and cloth (and many other goods) in the eleventh century, it exported sugar and alum on a large scale—it was easily the dominant source for the latter in the Mediterranean before the 1270s[1]—and its own linen cloth; it was also, of course, the main source of luxuries such as spices and dyestuffs from the Indian Ocean, some of them (above all pepper) on the relatively cheap end of the luxury trade. In return, Egypt needed timber and iron, particularly the latter; all the same, the region had presumably managed with fewer imports of these two in the early middle ages, without the density of Egyptian internal production and exchange dropping back much. Egyptians, in this case stretching far down the social hierarchy, were also only too happy to consume, for example, olive oil (from Palestine and, especially in our period, Tunisia), as it was so much better than local oils, but it was not in a strict sense a necessity. In general, the internal Egyptian economy was sufficiently complex and dense that this Mediterranean projection, important as it was for others, was only a sideline for the Egyptians themselves, outside two or three ports.

[1] Cahen, 'L'alun avant Phocée' (although alum came from Tunisia, Morocco, and Castile on a smaller scale; see pp. 136, 149, 264, 453, 461 above).

The two regions most central to the geography of Mediterranean traffic, Sicily and Ifrīqiya, were more structurally involved in it than this. They were, for a start, tightly linked; as we have seen, from the late ninth century at the latest, Sicily–Africa trading was important for each, with wine and sometimes grain (among other goods) going south to the African coast, and oil and gold going north to Sicily, and with ceramics as the marker for this density of interaction in every period. They were both closely involved in the eleventh-century Egypt trade, when their linen industries depended on Egyptian flax; they were also the points of reference for its small-scale western extension to al-Andalus. But all the same, the reason why they could make use of this level of openness to the Mediterranean was that their internal economies were already complex, by 950 at the latest, so that they had products to sell, and donkey-based land routes from the interior to the coast (neither had significant river-based communications) to allow products to be moved around internally—that is to say, solid regional trading systems. These were strong enough both to allow the linen industry to develop in each in the first place, from the late tenth century onwards in all probability, and to weather its fairly rapid eclipse in the decades around 1100, without the rest of the regional economy being affected. In Sicily, indeed, a new trading relationship developed shortly after, based on the export of raw cotton north to Genoa. This did not, however, mean that Sicilians ceased to make their own cloth—far from it, in fact, given the evidence we have in twelfth-century documents for both urban and rural weavers (see pp. 243–6, 253 above).

The regional economies of both Sicily and Ifrīqiya were slightly less internally coherent by the end of our period, with the reappearance of a partial east–west economic separation in the former and a substantial break between the coast and the interior in the latter. But they remained highly active, particularly that of Sicily. The data are much less good for Ifrīqiya, and at best the twelfth century saw the end of any economic expansion there, for various reasons—we will come back to them shortly. But the appearance of a major new ceramic production of cobalt and manganese glazed wares in Tunis at the end of our period, which was widely available in at least the western Mediterranean (as also Alexandria), shows that the region was moving forward in some arenas.[2] The point here is that we can track a greater articulation between the internal economy of both Sicily and North Africa and their Mediterranean projection than we can for Spain, Byzantium, or Egypt; but their internal economies were, all the same, never dependent on that projection. Even in the late middle ages, as we have seen, the exchange of wheat (raw cotton was by now less important) for cloth between Genoa (and other north Mediterranean ports) and Sicily has been calculated at around 5 per cent of the production and consumption of each inside the island; that was very high for

[2] See Chapter 2, n. 290 above; Chapter 3, n. 86 above.

the middle ages, but not high enough to be really significant in economic terms, for this or any region.[3]

Sicily, it has to be added, has suffered, perhaps more than any other region in the Mediterranean, from neocolonial theory as applied to its later medieval (and, indeed, post-medieval) history—by Henri Bresc at the greatest length (see p. 200 above), but by others as well. This is based on the surprisingly entrenched belief that when Region A sold primary products (especially food, and the raw materials for cloth production) to Region B in the middle ages—here, Sicily selling grain to north-central Italy or, by the late middle ages, Catalonia—and bought finished commodities such as the cloth itself in return, then A was in some way economically dominated by B, and that this would mark 'failure' if Region A had exported finished products earlier. These are ideas borrowed from the study of neocolonial relationships today, when the trading and financial power of rich nations is immensely more dominant over the poorer nations of the Global South than could ever have been the case in the middle ages. Indeed, in our period, where import-export was far less than 5 per cent of any regional economy, there is no reason whatsoever to think that such dominations were real. Historians of late thirteenth-century England, which gained almost all its export earnings by selling wool to the Flanders cloth towns, and eventually to Italy as well, certainly do not think so. Region B would have to have been able to control the terms of trade really comprehensively for such a subject relationship to be sustainable, and that was in medieval conditions effectively impossible unless it actually controlled Region A politically.[4] Then, such an economic domination could indeed develop, with Region A required to export certain goods gratis in tax, or prevented from keeping export prices high, or prevented from selling to other regions. This would, however, be a directly *colonial* relationship, not a neocolonial one; and that could certainly be a feature of the middle ages, as, indeed, of the ancient world. Egypt under the Roman Empire was dominated in this way; the Mediterranean islands ruled by Venice or Genoa in the late middle ages were too. But normal exchanges of primary products for finished ones marked no structural subjection, and

[3] See esp. pp. 13, 260–1 above.

[4] Epstein, *An island for itself*, esp. chs 1 and 6, remains the most detailed critique of this argument for Sicily; Sakellariou, *Southern Italy in the late middle ages*, esp. ch. 1, is effective in making similar points for the mainland south. For the general debates on this issue, which have focussed on the late middle ages in Italy, see most recently Galasso, *Alle origini del dualismo italiano* (less helpful) and Mainoni and Barile, *Comparing two Italies* (more helpful). (Italy has been the focus here because the debate has got further confused with the 'southern question' concerning why southern Italy did so much less well economically than the north after mid-nineteenth-century unification; cf. p. 199 above.) One interesting exception to my points here is the twelfth-century agreement by Montpellier not to trade eastwards except via Genoa (see Chapter 6, n. 174 above; see further Reyerson, 'Montpellier and Genoa', pp. 362–4); but that, although an enforced restriction of trade for a few decades, was not any form of neocolonial relationship. For England, see the upbeat tone of Lloyd, *The English wool trade in the middle ages* (although this is a book which offers detail, not any interpretative context), or Bell et al., *The English wool market*. Barile, 'Rethinking "The two Italies"', p. 118, makes the same comparative point.

anyway never showed that any Region A did not produce its own finished goods, for internal sale, as, indeed, Sicily did, on a large scale, which was in itself a far more important process than any external economic relationship.

More or less every economic history of this period, even if it recognizes—as not all do—the driving power of Egypt or Sicily in the eleventh century, sees a step change in the twelfth, and the victory of merchants from the Italian port cities over all competitors from the mid-century at the latest. By 1200, or often well before, we supposedly reach a period in which the routes are essentially Italian ones. There is a partial truth to this, as we have seen, and will see again later. But the picture is misleading all the same, for other reasons, as we saw at length in Chapter 6. The prominence of the Italian port cities—which we really cannot say for sure was an overwhelming one, a point we will also come back to—was only in the sphere of exchange; it was dependent on the productive (and, indeed, the political) choices of other regions. It was not backed up, until the very late twelfth century, by any strong production from inside north-central Italy itself which could be exchanged abroad on any real scale, with the exception of Pisan iron; and Italy was, indeed, less coherent as a regional economy than any other discussed in this book, until 1180 and well after. This is where the weakness of historians who focus on commerce rather than production is most clearly exposed, notwithstanding the fact that such historians have often themselves been Italians. No one can fail to be impressed by the ambition and enthusiastic risk-taking of Italian sea traders in the twelfth century, as is amply demonstrated in Genoese and Venetian commercial documents, and it has been studied in detail for well over a century. But this did not add up to a regionally coherent Italian economy in any kind of dominant role in the Mediterranean; only to the relative dominance of Italian ships, in sea traffic which was itself, as I have stressed, a small percentage of the Mediterranean economy or economies, taken as a whole. Indeed, if we were to suppose that Genoa, Pisa, and Venice together actually did run all or most of that traffic in (say) 1180, we really would have to abandon any ideas that maritime trade was a major element in the economy, for the three cities combined are unlikely as yet to have had more than around 75,000 inhabitants, only a small minority of which (10 per cent of active males? a couple of thousand?) would have been travelling along the 3,500-kilometre length of the Mediterranean Sea in any commercial role—even if they also employed, as they certainly did, sailors from the coasts around them, and even though they were backed up by the capital of plenty of land-based investors.[5] I will come back to these points.

[5] See p. 539 above for guesstimates of population for Genoa and Pisa. The Pisan oath of 1228 gave hardly any weight to professions linked to the sea (cf. Salvatori, *La popolazione pisana*, pp. 142, 174–5); the fact is not statistically significant, for there are so many ways they could have been missed out, but it certainly does not indicate that 10% is too low a guess there. My sense from the Genoese registers is similar. For Venice we have no indications which we can use, and its watery environment might well

For these reasons, the history of Mediterranean exchange, and the Mediterranean economy in general, needs to consist of the way that regions developed internally, and related to each other as a result of that development, rather than focussing first on the merchants who bought and sold the commodities that marked those interrelations. We have looked at this in each of the previous chapters. We have also looked at the underpinnings of regional economic growth, which were various; I sketched them out comparatively at the end of Chapter 5, and will come back to them at the end of this chapter too, when we return to the issue of the root causes of economic development in our period. But to sketch a Mediterranean economic history in a single paragraph, I would see Egypt in the period 800–950 as having the only really complex regional economy among those we have looked at. (And maybe among those we have not looked at, too; the Levant, the only plausible exception, maintained a set of highly articulated economies, but they were more localized than under the Roman Empire, and probably stayed relatively localized throughout our period.[6]) As a result, Egypt would not have been able to maintain dense economic relationships with most other regions, as they would not have had enough artisanal commodities to exchange, or internal routes to get products to ports. We can see some commerce in this early period, but it was only when Sicily and Ifrīqiya came into their own as economically articulated regions, around 950 or a little earlier, that it was possible to have complex exchange relationships with them, and this is, indeed, when these began, facilitated but not caused by Fāṭimid political connections. Al-Andalus was also developing fast from this period onwards; half a century later, so was southern mainland Italy, also not one of our regions;[7] from the late eleventh century, so was the Byzantine heartland—even if two of those three were not closely linked to the wider Mediterranean world. All the main thirteenth-century players were thus in place by 1150 except northern Italy (Catalonia began to be active on the sea even later, after 1250[8]), although this was partially compensated for by the hyperactivity of the Italian port cities, which certainly helped connect all these regions together by 1150. The Italian ports would also eventually help a late-developing northern

have led to a higher percentage of people with maritime experience, but my overall 10% guesstimate still stands.

[6] For the start of the middle ages, see Wickham, *Framing*, pp. 759–80; Walmsley, *Early Islamic Syria*, pp. 49–59. In the eleventh century the southern half of the Levant, Palestine, seems to have been much more linked to Egypt than was northern Syria, which was more distinct as an economic region, and was closer to Byzantium; see Goldberg, *Trade and institutions*, pp. 215–29, and pp. 354, 360–1 above. For the twelfth century, the sharp political separation of the coast from inland areas cannot have helped the economic integration of the region, although, conversely, some external links were wider; see Chapter 2, n. 303 above for Egypt, and Chapter 6 above for Italy. But these are only indicative points of reference, concerning a region I have not studied here.

[7] For Naples as one way into the Italian south, see Feniello, *Napoli*, pp. 163–210 (more upbeat than I would be on some issues); Carsana, 'Anfore altomedievali dall'area portuale di Napoli'; cf. Chapter 3, n. 107 above and pp. 640–3 below for Amalfi.

[8] See, e.g., Bensch, *Barcelona and its rulers*, pp. 277–304 (esp. the table at 288), and the useful overview from 2012 in Ferrer, 'El comerç català'; early thirteenth-century references are few here.

Italian productive economy to have a Mediterranean projection, but in the meantime covered up its absence, at least to the eyes of modern scholars.

Anyone who has read the chapters thus far will not be surprised by the statements in this last paragraph. For the rest of this chapter, I will take that basic outline for granted, and will set out three areas which need to be developed further: the relationship of these basic economic shifts with changes in political systems across our period; a narrative of the main developments in Mediterranean sea trade from the ninth to the twelfth century, with some discussion of the nature of the shared maritime culture of our period; and finally, a discussion of the common features of Mediterranean regional growth.

* * *

The picture set out here of a diversified but steady move towards economic complexity nearly everywhere is quite different from the political history of the same period in the Mediterranean (see Maps 2–4). The late tenth century was a period of considerable strengthening of political systems, both externally and internally. This was the period when al-Andalus reached its peak as a unified state under the Umayyad caliphs, and extended into Morocco; when the Fāṭimids unified most of the southern and eastern Mediterranean, from what is now Algeria to southern Syria; when Byzantium conquered the Balkans, and eastwards into Anatolia as far as Antioch and Armenia; and when the Ottonian Empire united nearly two thirds of continental Italy with Germany. As to internal strength, all of these except the last developed their fiscal structures substantially too. But after that, the eleventh century saw disaster. Al-Andalus broke up into many *ṭāi'fa* statelets; not only did Fāṭimid power become restricted to Egypt (plus, soon, Yemen), but in the west Ifrīqiya and Sicily, now fully autonomous, themselves broke up into small units, paralleling the *ṭāi'fa* kingdoms in their size; and a little later, the Levant fell prey to Crusader attacks and the construction of small polities there too. Byzantium faced new threats from the west, north, and east, and lost, above all, most of the Anatolian plateau; southern Italy, conquered by the Normans after the 1050s, was as yet a set of separate lordships fighting each other; and at the end of the late eleventh-century civil war, the Italian kingdom of north-central Italy, which had been a relatively coherent polity since the seventh century, had more or less ceased to exist—here too, small urban and rural units, some as yet very amorphous, were de facto replacements. By 1100, of the old powers, only Egypt and a reduced Byzantium had any force at all (and the strongest new power, the Almorávids in the west, would be fairly transitory); everywhere, nearly every polity had become smaller and/or weaker. And yet the eleventh century was a period in which the economic coherence of nearly every Mediterranean region remained stable or increased, sometimes substantially. And the reconstructions of the twelfth century—the Almohads in al-Andalus and the Maghreb, the Normans in Sicily and southern Italy, the Komnenoi in Byzantium, eventually Saladin in Egypt and

Syria—although they for sure did not hurt the continuing expansion of the Mediterranean economies in the majority of places, for the most part do not seem to have had a tight causal relation to it either.

Political changes of the types sketched out here have received twenty times more attention from historians than have changes in the economy. I have not left them out of the previous chapters, although readers who seek a detailed account of them will need to look elsewhere. They are relevant here above all, however, because they offer a challenge: what effect did political changes really have on economic changes? One thing is clear to start with: by 1100, they had far less effect than did the break-up of the Roman Empire, in the west in the fifth century, in the east in the seventh. The end of the western empire produced a steady involution of western Mediterranean exchange, which began by 450 at the latest and was close to total by 700/730; and the crisis of the eastern empire in the mid-seventh produced an even more rapid commercial simplification.[9] An entire world system ended when these exchange links went, and had to be built up again, slowly, in successive centuries. This by no means happened when the states existing in 1000 broke down, sometimes dramatically, across the next century.

The Roman Empire was different from its successors in one main respect here, however. As noted in Chapter 1, it took goods in kind as part of its tax system—notably foodstuffs, wheat and olive oil—from the south of the Mediterranean, especially from North Africa and Egypt, and transported them northwards to feed the great capital cities of Rome and Constantinople, and above all the large armies on the northern and eastern frontiers. The scale of state intervention was in itself rather higher in the Roman Empire than in any of its medieval successors; but more important than that is that the geographical range across which the Romans moved state goods was unmatched later. One result of the range of state transport was that large-scale commercial interchanges in the Mediterranean were underpinned by the scale of fiscal movements. These included commercial wine and oil transport, moving in many directions, on a much larger scale than ever in the middle ages, even though there was certainly a significant medieval wine and oil trade. One result of the fiscal underpinning was that when the state collapsed (in the west) and contracted dramatically (in the east), the interregional commerce riding on its back radically weakened.[10] The western successor states could not move goods around like that at all; since they did not tax, such a possibility was unavailable to them even in theory until well after our own period. But the surviving eastern empire, which we call Byzantium, hardly did either. The emperors abandoned the state-backed supply of food to Constantinople as soon

[9] Wickham, *Framing*, pp. 708–824. Some of the text here and in the next three paragraphs is taken, slightly altered, from Wickham, 'Looking back at the eighth century from the eleventh'.

[10] For how the fiscal-commercial relationship worked, see n. 9 above, and McCormick, 'Bateaux de vie, bateaux de mort'.

as they first lost Egypt, in 618–19,[11] and, when the city grew substantially again from the late eighth century onwards, it was always supplied commercially thereafter—even if that commerce was managed carefully by the state. And Byzantine armies, which were still supplied by the state, were by now in large part provided for locally. The fiscal system still made the state effective; indeed, it enabled it to survive the seventh-century crisis; but it did not integrate the different geographical parts of the state to the degree that it did under the Romans.[12] There was, certainly, an east–west exchange system, including in wine, with probable fiscal elements, which linked the scattered Byzantine lands together, something I shall return to in a moment. All the same, commerce, if and when it took advantage of the state's needs, mostly did so inside relatively restricted areas, in particular the Aegean heartland of the empire.[13] This localization was still, to an extent, a feature of the eleventh century, as we saw in Chapter 4, although the state was rather stronger by then, and so, even more, were the local economies, again above all in the Aegean.

The early caliphate was similar to Byzantium in this respect. Each province had its own army under the Umayyads, linked to provincial capitals such as Fusṭāṭ in Egypt or Baṣra in Iraq, and tax went directly to it. Not much taxation got out of each province, to make its way to the caliphs, or to any other location.[14] When the ʿAbbāsids centralized the caliphate, money did, indeed, go to Baghdad from each province, but it was money, not goods, and such movements of money did not underpin much associated commerce, even when that commerce existed, as between Egypt and the Levant, or the latter and Iraq. (This was also one of the most difficult aspects of the relationship between provinces and the state under the second Muslim dynasty; provinces did not want to pay, and revolted so as not to have to pay, such taxation.) So for the caliphate too, the scale and the range of the fiscal system certainly made the state (and its rulers and officials) very rich, and their armies substantial, but the scale of the movement of fiscal goods which had linked the Roman Empire together had gone. Taxation integrated single provinces internally, not the whole state; and it continued to do so when regions detached themselves from central government, as was common in the caliphate after the 860s (and sometimes earlier, in the case of Spain and North Africa). Egypt, indeed, when it separated itself from the ʿAbbāsids in 868, and then again after 935, did not suffer in the least from any economic dislocation, but rather, gained from not having to give surplus to another region (the Ṭūlūnids after 868 and the Ikhshīdids after the 930s did pay some tribute to Baghdad, but far less

[11] *Chronicon Paschale*, ed. Dindorf, p. 711.

[12] See most recently Haldon, *The empire that would not die*, pp. 249–82.

[13] For the Aegean, see Poulou-Papadēmētriou, 'Byzantinē keramikē', and Chapter 4, n. 89 above.

[14] Kennedy, *The armies of the caliphs*, remains the best overview. For an exception, the food supply of Mecca and Madīna from Egypt, see Chapter 2, n. 127.

than before; the Fāṭimids after 969 none at all).[15] Ifrīqiya had also probably gained as much when it established autonomy in 800; here our evidence is too poor to say for sure, but the ninth century is at least more visible there in material terms than the eighth had been (see pp. 169–70, 175–6 above). As in Byzantium, then, the fiscal structures underpinning economies were regionalized; and the increasing and decreasing size of states tended to have relatively little effect on provincial prosperity, or on interregional trade and other forms of exchange. Here is where the lack of a close fit between polities and economies began, and it continued throughout our own period; the Fāṭimids had provincially focussed tax systems run by provincial governors as well.

So, in general, we must recognize that a key underlying structural feature of the second great Mediterranean trade cycle (that is to say, after that of the Roman Empire)—a cycle which had begun by the end of the tenth century, as we have seen, and lasted until at least the Black Death—is that the history of exchange, or at any rate interregional exchange, was not linked directly to the history of state needs, unlike under the Romans. We do not need to think that, in our period, we can make any easy assumption as to the relation between political success or failure and economic success or failure. But this does not mean that there was no relationship at all; it is just that it was more mediated, indeed often more complex, than it had been in the Roman period.

It is not difficult to give examples of major political crises in our period which had little effect, and, in particular, no long-term effect, on economic prosperity and complexity. The *fitna* which destroyed the Umayyad Caliphate in al-Andalus was one; as we saw at length in Chapter 5, the economy of the eleventh century was, if anything, stronger, because more widely based in the *ṭāʾifa*s, than that of the tenth. I have also argued that the military crises of the last third of the eleventh century in Byzantium had equally little effect on the economy of the Aegean heartland, which, indeed, took off from the 1090s, although that of the Anatolian plateau, which we know far less about, doubtless took a much more serious hit. And Sicily, which faced not only political division in the mid-eleventh century but also a violent, although at least fairly rapid conquest by the Normans in, above all, the 1060s, was as complex economically in the twelfth century as it had been in the eleventh, even if some of its economic activities had by now changed substantially, such as the shift from linen to cotton. Evidently, even if some political elites faced destruction and replacement, producers and buyers and the networks of exchange which linked them did not change as much, or in some cases at all.

I would add as an extension of this, as has been argued several times in this book, that war on its own, including the sacking of cities, did not necessarily have a major effect on the future prosperity of regions, or of the unlucky individual

[15] See, e.g., Bianquis, 'Autonomous Egypt', pp. 89, 95, 98, 105.

cities for that matter. The sack of Palermo in 1064, of Mahdia in 1087, of Almería and of Thebes in 1147, of Milan in 1162, or the scorched-earth burning of Fusṭāṭ in 1168 were quickly recovered from, as historians of each (except Almería and sometimes Fusṭāṭ) generally recognize. Essentially, most such destructions were incomplete—cities were large, armies less so, and armies were also more concerned to loot, kill. and burn in ad hoc ways than to destroy whole quarters systematically (as we have seen, Milan is the exception here, for it was not only destroyed but evacuated, but it nevertheless bounced back fast). Fixed capital, to use a partially anachronistic concept, was also far smaller-scale than it became after the Industrial Revolution, so could be replaced more easily—and anyway even in the twentieth century destroyed cities were routinely re-established, as the inhabitants of Rotterdam and Frankfurt and Stalingrad/Volgograd, to name but three out of very many, know well.

All the same, we must not be complacent about this. War and destruction could, indeed, change the economy of a city or region for the worse. The sack of Córdoba in 1013, of Kairouan in 1057, and of Constantinople in 1204 did great and long-term harm to the cities concerned—all, not by chance, capitals. In each case the explanation for it comes down to the fact that states could, indeed, have an effect on the economy, even in the post-Roman world, although in different and varying ways. Córdoba here is the most easily explained; this inland capital, which had expanded hugely in the tenth century, relied on a unitary state to feed it, and the *ṭāi'fa* kingdoms were not going to do that for free; as it lost that size forever, rival Andalusī cities gained in return. But the other two examples show that war could also lead to wider systemic change. As to Kairouan, in the long-standing debate among North Africanists about whether the invasion of the semi-nomadic Banū Hilāl in the 1050s brought about the destruction of the Ifrīqiyan economy itself, not just the capital, I came out on the side of what could be called the moderate continuitists (see pp. 158–67, 263–8 above), but there is no doubt that that economy was much more divided afterwards, with an active and urbanized coast set against an (eventually) increasingly pastoral interior, in which Kairouan was situated. The pastoralism can be associated with specialization for export (North Africa was after 1200 a major exporter of wool), but it marked a considerable change all the same, and as we have seen, Ifrīqiya, alone out of our regions, cannot be said to have had a more complex economy in 1200 than, say, 1000—indeed, although much of it was still highly prosperous, its overall complexity, at the regional level, had very probably dropped back. As to Constantinople in 1204, its closest parallel is the Christian conquest of most of Almohad al-Andalus in the 1230s–1240s; in each case it marked the destruction of the political coherence of a major power. We are not here dealing with ecological shifts, as with agriculture to pastoralism, but both Byzantium and al-Andalus were divided up between conquerors, and substantial parts of them went into economic crisis, even if Seville and Valencia in Spain stayed prosperous, and even if the trade routes in the Aegean actually expanded, with some urban productions there continuing to be highly active. (One example is Zeuxippus ware, the high-end glazed ceramics of the early thirteenth century, which continued to be sold without a break.)[16] The whole basis of the economy in both of these regions changed thereafter, as rule from Castile or Venice (now a genuinely colonial power, and prospering greatly as a result) or Veliko Tărnovo in Bulgaria reorientated long-lasting structural patterns in most of each. Constantinople did not itself recover until the renewed centralization of the Ottomans, when it returned to being a capital of a wide territory. Wars, then, could, indeed, lead to systemic change; and in each of these cases what was destroyed was not so much, or not only, cities and countrysides, but also state systems, whose destruction, in these cases at least, clearly had economic consequences.

So what effect did states have on the economy by now, hundreds of years after the coherence of the Roman state system had gone? Four elements have recurred in this book. The first point is that tax-raising created routes for the movement of goods, even for the most isolated rural societies; central governments took from everyone. When we have detailed documentation for the process—in Egypt and Byzantium above all—it is clear that they did so systematically, on the basis of agrarian surveys and payment receipts. If the tax was in kind (as sometimes in al-Andalus), the routes for its movement laid down a direction of travel for commercial activity too, but if it was in money, it required the sale of goods, usually along the same routes; everywhere, the network of tax-raising helped to integrate economic systems. Al-Andalus is again a specific example here, for the victory of the state and its fiscal system in all or most of the caliphate in the tenth century is matched by the wide distribution of green and manganese fine wares from the capital at Córdoba (see p. 419 above); these cannot have been fiscally distributed for the most part, but they mark the way that, for the first time since the Roman Empire, commercial networks by now stretched across over half the Iberian peninsula. The second is the regularization of customs dues and transaction costs. This may not on one level have had a huge effect, for customs still had to be paid—generally at a standard 10 per cent across the Mediterranean (except in Egypt, where it could vary much more), although also with lower percentages for favoured trading communities. But political unity also helped stability in local interactions. One knew the customs officials who needed to be paid off; and one could often rely on family or friendship connections in other ports inside the same political system, as the *geniza* merchants of Fusṭāṭ and Alexandria visibly did when they went to Mahdia or Palermo.

The third element is state demand. *Geniza* merchants also knew that the Fāṭimid state, or its provincial equivalents, might buy any of their goods by force, at the price previously quoted by the state; but anyway, states always needed

[16] For an overview, see Laiou and Morrisson, *The Byzantine economy*, pp. 166–73, 182–215; for Zeuxippus ware, see Waksman and François, 'Vers une redéfinition typologique et analytique'.

particular sorts of matériel, to supply armies and navies—I have stressed the Egyptian need for timber and iron, which was in part for that precise reason, but, in fact, every other polity needed them too; they were just easier to get elsewhere. The great Egyptian linen factories on the north coast, especially but not only in Tinnīs, were also in part founded for the needs of the state. And where states did not buy directly, they managed supply very considerably; no Egyptian ruler could risk Fusṭāṭ-Cairo running out of food (even if it sometimes happened), nor could any Byzantine emperor risk it for Constantinople—the danger of urban revolt was too great. As we saw earlier (pp. 62, 279–82), they ensured it by fixing prices, fixing legitimate profits (or trying to), controlling supply lines, or selling at times of dearth out of state granaries maintained for the purpose; in each case the supply was still dominated by private merchants, unlike that of the capitals of the Roman Empire, but those private merchants operated under tight state supervision. The Egyptian state was probably always the most directive here (it had not only warehouses for food, but also state-run warehouse complexes, where goods of all kinds could be sold, inspected, and taxed[17]), but plenty of others—the Byzantines, probably the Normans in Sicily, and most rulers of al-Andalus—shared its aspirations, as we can see in the case of al-Andalus in *ḥisba* manuals (see pp. 397–8, 401–2 above). The other side of this coin was embargoes, which the Egyptians, Byzantines, and Normans used against north Italian port cities more than once in the twelfth century for specific political reasons, although these had much less effect on regional economies themselves.

The final, linked element was the fact that the wealth of tax-raising states produced a class of salaried officials, who had movable wealth as a result of that which was often very considerable indeed. They were buyers, of course; they contributed strongly to the fact that every regional state capital in our period (even Pavia, the capital of the weakest regional state) was a major market centre with major buying power; but in particular they were investors in trade. Officials and even rulers owned their own commercial ships, as we saw for Alexandria and Denia, among others (pp. 131, 407). And officials could also themselves be merchants; indeed, many of our most prominent merchants were demonstrably officials, such as Jawdhar, a senior official to the Fāṭimids before the conquest of Egypt, in Ifrīqiya in the mid-tenth century, Michael Attaleiates in eleventh-century Constantinople, and, in Egypt, the Tustarīs in the early eleventh and Amīnaddīn at the end of the twelfth (pp. 44, 109, 188, 282–3 above). These figures varied in their commitment: Attaleiates traded in grain from his own estates and took the rents from shops—he might be better called an entrepreneur than a merchant—but Jawdhar and Amīnaddīn were at the head of their own large-scale commercial enterprises. In Egypt officials invested in cloth manufacturing too (p. 97 above), although that is less easy to see in, for example, Byzantium (p. 331 above). That is to say, what tax-raising states produced here was official figures

[17] See Chapter 2, n. 274 above.

who had a great deal of capital, and who were prepared to risk it in trading, whether inside regions or between them. That was, as we have also seen, the major reason why the scale of documented maritime investment in our period was rather greater in Egypt than in Genoa and Venice (pp. 546–7 above); no Italian port city, whose elites were not rich officials but landowners, and not very large-scale ones either, had any investors as wealthy as these.

States thus produced stability, at least at the crucial regional level, and important concentrations of wealth, which meant both demand and investment. They also directed some trading, in that the supply of the capital was crucial. When they were strong enough, as in Egypt and Byzantium throughout our period, and often but with more breaks in al-Andalus, Ifrīqiya, and Sicily, the structuring of even wholly private trading was strongly influenced by the communications networks and spatial patterning of the state. States could not create regional economies on their own, or else ninth-century Byzantium, notwithstanding some elements of a fiscally backed movement of goods, would have had a more complex economy in other respects than it actually had. Nor were they essential for their creation either, as the belated but eventual appearance, after 1200, of a region-wide economy in northern Italy, in the total absence of a regional state, also shows. All the same, they could have a considerable influence on their forms, once such economies had developed. That influence did not have to be determinant, as the continued prosperity of al-Andalus after the fall of the caliphate makes clear; but it might be, as the very mixed history of the different sections of the former Byzantine Empire showed in the thirteenth century. To summarize in the simplest terms: no regional economy depended on any state in our period for its development, which had different parameters; but states could help further regional complexity and, indeed, prosperity, thanks to the regularity and the concentrations of wealth and demand they could provide. That was a pattern which would have a considerable future in the medieval and modern period.

* * *

The narrative history of Mediterranean trade in our period is probably the aspect of this book which has had the most consistent study. I have criticized the directions and assumptions of previous work sufficiently often in earlier chapters that there is no need to do so again here. Rather, I wish here to simply sketch out that history, as it seems to me to have developed, without arguing with contrary views, even if I sometimes refer to them.

Henri Pirenne famously held that the Mediterranean became closed to trade as a result of the Arab conquests of the seventh century.[18] This at least does not need to be argued with; it is a view that really belongs to the past. Luxuries, which are all Pirenne was concerned with, were in reality always traded in the Mediterranean,

[18] Pirenne, *Mohammed and Charlemagne*, pp. 163–85.

without a break, as we saw, for example, with the *Honorantie civitatis Papie* of around 1000 (p. 479 above). They came and went in every direction, on a small scale—for otherwise they would be too easily accessible to be luxuries—in the hands of Venetians (as we saw in Chapter 6) or Amalfitans (as we shall see shortly), or under any other flag of convenience. They never contributed more than very marginally to the sort of regional and interregional commerce which this book is about, although they sometimes confuse our vision, as chaff confuses radar. They were matched by the connectivity of small-scale cabotage, of boats moving from one port to the next, which across innumerable changes of vessel might, indeed, link the whole of the Mediterranean to some extent, a pattern which had always existed in the inland sea, and which still does sometimes; this certainly contributed rather more to the themes of this book, for it was part of the trading internal to regions which has been discussed here at length.[19] But what we can also see, for the first half of our period, is two separate east–west bulk trading systems, one smaller-scale, linking the provinces of the Byzantine world, the other developing later but operating much more substantially, linking those of the Islamic states. These had separate histories; they were not matched by any significant north–south trade, except in and around Sicily, for a long time. Let us look at each of them in turn, building on what we have seen in previous chapters.

As is well known, the peninsulas jutting into the Mediterranean, Italy and Greece, are in the north; so are the main Mediterranean islands. Most of the mountains of the Mediterranean, visible from the sea and so important navigation points for mariners, are in the north too, plus most of the best harbours; by contrast, the south-east, from Tunisia to Egypt, has only the highlands behind Barqa in Cyrenaica to interrupt nearly 2,000 kilometres of low-lying desert coast, and good harbours are few there. Broadly speaking, as John Pryor has stressed, northern east–west routes are as a result easier to navigate than southern ones,[20] other things being equal, at least—and in fact, for half our period other things were by no means equal, and the Tunisia/Sicily to Egypt route in the eleventh century, notwithstanding its objective difficulties, was far more important than any other in the whole Mediterranean. All the same, the northern route was, indeed, easier. In the earliest middle ages, it was backed up by the fact that the more restricted sectors of the sea which still had small-scale trading systems, after the great trade cycle of the Roman Empire reached its final end in the early eighth century, were all but one in the north, in each case sheltered and facilitated by the patterns of peninsulas and islands there. They were the Tyrrhenian Sea, the

[19] Horden and Purcell, *The corrupting sea*, esp. pp. 133–72. Among semi-luxuries, the availability of eastern glass (and glass cullet) in Italy across the early middle ages is one sign of this continuing commercial connection; see, e.g., Coscarella et al., *Il vetro in transizione*.

[20] Pryor, *Geography, technology and war*, pp. 12–24.

Adriatic, the Aegean, and the south-eastern corner of the Mediterranean. Two decades ago, only the first and third of these were really visible in our mostly archaeological sources; the Comacchio excavations have now illuminated the Adriatic much more clearly, although it was probably the least complex of these systems.[21] The south-eastern system, which is also much more visible now than it was, was the only one to bring in the southern Mediterranean, for it involved a commercial network linking Egypt, Levantine ports such as Caesarea and Beirut, and Cyprus, plus weaker relations with the Byzantine coast. It can be seen both as a continuation of Roman trading patterns, here at least, and as a natural consequence of the fact that Egypt and the Levant were the most complex economies in the Mediterranean in the eighth century; Cyprus's strategic position, and joint rule by the emperors and the caliphs, brought a limited Byzantine economic connection too. The contiguity of these four small networks made it easier to travel between them, and indeed, the route from the Tyrrhenian Sea to the Aegean, with an extension eastwards, was the main early medieval travellers' route identified by Michael McCormick.[22] But by 800 at the latest it was also a route marked by a considerable amphora trade, and it is this which is our best evidence for the Byzantine east–west exchange network (see Map 21).

Written sources tell us very little about this Byzantine network before the twelfth century. In the material record, it was marked, already in the eighth, by globular amphorae, successors of LRA 2 amphorae from the Aegean, probably mostly carrying wine, which have become the principal type fossil for the eighth- and ninth-century Byzantine lands, at least on the coast. We looked at it in Chapter 4, but it needs some reprise here, to make the argument clear. These globular types appear along the Mediterranean coasts of the whole of the empire in fairly standard sizes, extending, in the Adriatic, up to Comacchio and Venice. Fabric analysis shows that they were made in a variety of different places: some in Italy, notably Naples and Otranto; some still in the Aegean. These productions overlapped quite substantially, in that Aegean globular amphorae have been identified in a variety of locations in Italy together with Italian types. They connected, in fact, three of the four smaller networks, extending to Cyprus in the fourth (although not beyond, as far as we yet know); and they were almost all found in Byzantine provinces, with only a few in Lombard-Carolingian Italy. This pattern remained steady

[21] For the end of the Roman trade cycle and the first and third smaller trading sectors, see Wickham, *Framing*, ch. 11, and (for more on the Aegean) Chapter 4, n. 89 above; for Comacchio and the Adriatic, see Chapter 6, n. 82 above. We can now date the final end of the cycle to a generation later than 700, following Bonifay, *Études sur la céramique romaine tardive*, and Reynolds, 'From Vandal Africa to Arab Ifrīqiya', pp. 147–9.

[22] For the eastern Mediterranean exchange area, see Zavagno, *Cyprus*, 162–9; Armstrong, 'Trade in the east Mediterranean in the eighth century'; Reynolds, 'Amphorae in Beirut from the Umayyads to the Crusaders'; Vroom, 'A gentle transition?'; and for the great continuities in Levantine (and Iraqi) production and exchange, see esp. Bessard, *Caliphs and merchants*. For travellers, see McCormick, *Origins of the European economy*, pp. 502–8.

across two centuries.[23] As we saw in Chapter 4, they might have been related to buying wine for army supply; that is to say, the exchange system was not necessarily exclusively commercial at its base, even if it must have been so at least in part. This was, anyway, also the world of the Byzantine *Rhodian Sea Law* of the later eighth century, which envisioned complex commercial agreements between sea captains and merchants, plus rules about apportioning the loss of goods (including luxuries, slaves, and major bulk goods, grain, wine, and oil).[24] Such ships sailed the length of the Byzantine-ruled Mediterranean; Sicily was a major granary for Constantinople in particular, and that city, after a century of population decline, would revive fast after 750.

After 900, globular amphorae were replaced by more varied types and also sizes in the Byzantine world, but the overlapping distributions of each type, almost certainly now fully commercial and again above all used to carry wine, continued. Otranto 1 and 2 amphorae, made in south-east Italy, as their name implies, but elsewhere too, are found generally in the Adriatic and Ionian Seas but also in the Aegean in smaller quantities; conversely, Günsenin 1 wine amphorae of the tenth and eleventh centuries, from Gaziköy in the Sea of Marmara, are found not only very generally in the Aegean but also in the Adriatic. Constantinople's glazed fine ware, in this period GWW 2, is also from the tenth century onwards more often found outside the Aegean than GWW 1 had been, along the same routes.[25]

This pattern of production and distribution, covering the coasts of the Byzantine Empire as a whole, shows substantial continuities from before the beginning of our period to its end. It also seems steadily to have gained in density across the centuries. But outside the network just described, we do not find many signs of similar links. Only in the eleventh century have a small number of Günsenin 1 amphorae been found in the numerous excavations of Fusṭāṭ and Cairo, as also in Venice, although that city could still be seen as in the Byzantine sphere of influence (Otranto types have, less surprisingly, also been found there); isolated examples of Byzantine amphorae have also been seen on some Tyrrhenian coastal sites after 900 too, and in by now Arab-ruled Sicily, including its capital, Palermo.[26] But we are talking about fragments here. Nor are Byzantine glazed wares well attested in northern Italy before 1100 (again on the coasts, plus the eastern Po

[23] For all of this, see Chapter 4, n. 89. The amphorae carried various goods, but wine was certainly a major content; see Pecci, 'Analisi dei residui organici e anfore medievali'. This and the next two paragraphs use some modified text from Wickham, 'Islamic, Byzantine and Latin exchange systems'. The extension to Cyprus is marked by both amphorae and glazed GWW 1 ware from Constantinople (Zavagno, *Cyprus*, pp. 48, 166, 185).

[24] *The Rhodian sea-law*, ed. Ashburner.

[25] For amphorae, see Chapter 4, nn. 28, 94; for GWW 2, see Chapter 4, n. 91.

[26] Monchamp, 'Céramiques fatimides', p. 152; for Sicily, see Chapter 4, n. 233; for Venice, see Chapter 6, nn. 133, 136, 139; for the Tyrrhenian coast, see Meo, 'Anfore, uomini e reti di scambio', pp. 231–2.

plain around Venice), or in Egypt before 1200.[27] This was, then, from the start to the finish, a route above all connecting the Byzantine provinces, with only minor outliers elsewhere (including northern Syria; see pp. 360–1 above). In the twelfth century, this trade reached the Crusader states to a small extent, extending the Syrian link southwards, and also the Italian coasts, to a greater extent than previously; and, of course, by now we know a great deal about the route from the Aegean up the Adriatic to Venice and back again, thanks to Venetian commercial documents. We can be sure that this northern extension of the old east–west trade route was much more active than it had ever been before. But it was still a route which had existed since 800 and earlier, to a city originally under at least nominal Byzantine authority. Byzantine ceramics have been found in Genoa and Pisa, on the west coast of Italy, in the clearest extension of these routes (see pp. 358–60 above); but the scale was less than in Venice, and, conversely, neither city really made an impact inside the Byzantine lands in our period—Venice always dominated over the other two in the Aegean, up to and even after 1204.

So this was both a real east–west route, extending from the Levantine coast to Sicily and up to Venice, and a demonstration that Byzantium's Mediterranean trade still did not really move much beyond the Byzantine lands. And it changed significance across time too. In the ninth century, it was actually a more organized long-distance route than any other, and it showed well the relative coherence of a Byzantine Empire which connected most of the north-eastern Mediterranean. But by the twelfth century, although parts of it were more travelled than before, it simply marked the fact that the Byzantines were not strongly connected—did not need to be strongly connected—to the wider exchange networks which were by then much more active elsewhere in the inland sea.

Those later networks instead developed from the other east–west route of the tenth century and onwards. This was that of the Islamic lands, stretching westwards from Egypt to Sicily and Ifrīqiya and, on a smaller scale, eastwards to Palestine and westwards again to al-Andalus (see Map 23). It was a newer route than the Byzantine one; it is only really attested as operating on any scale from the tenth century. This might be seen as a simple consequence of the fact that tenth- and eleventh-century documentary evidence (including the *geniza*, of course, but not only) is so much better than that from previous centuries, but it is also only really after the first half of the tenth century that a really complex material culture, attesting internal exchange networks, really takes off in any of Sicily, Ifrīqiya, and al-Andalus. Anyway, the Maghreb (and still more so al-Andalus) had been, until the Fāṭimid unification of three-quarters of the north African coast, for the most part fairly marginal to the Islamic world. So although, as we have seen (pp. 186–7), *fatwā*s discussing trade start in the ninth century in Ifrīqiya, it is likely

[27] See Chapter 4, nn. 234–5, Chapter 6, n. 140.

that before the mid-tenth this was still a relatively small-scale operation, still concentrating on luxuries. The *Kitāb akriyat al-sufun*, the discussion of sea law by Muḥammad b. ʿUmar al-Kinānī from the early tenth century, is the first documentary sign of something beginning to move here; the second sign is the trading activities of Jawdhar in Ifrīqiya. After that, the *geniza* dominates our evidence from the end of the century onwards, showing us how the triangular trade between Egypt and the central Mediterranean worked, between the late tenth and the late eleventh century. This is the era which Christophe Picard has called the '"commercial revolution" of the tenth century', in a challenge to, but also an imitation of, Roberto Lopez.[28]

We looked at this trade at length in Chapters 2 and 3, and there is no need to go over it again. But three points are worth repeating, when comparing it with the Byzantine east–west network. First, at least in the eleventh century, it seems to have been far larger in scale than that of the Byzantines—indeed, the scale of investment attested in the *geniza* is, taken as a whole, the largest recorded anywhere in our period. Secondly, what made the scale of this route so substantial was the economic complexity of each of the three regions which were linked by it most tightly. It was the dense network of exchange inside Egypt that made large-scale flax-growing possible there (pp. 99–103), which was then woven into linen in Egyptian factory towns and specialized workshops in Mahdia, Palermo, and elsewhere; and these workshops could only have been sustained by dense internal exchange networks in the central Mediterranean, which had developed in the tenth century itself. Thirdly, and paradoxically, it is less well attested in the material record than that of the Byzantines. Sicilian wine amphorae certainly went to Tunisia, and Ifrīqiyan glazed ceramics can be found in substantial quantities in Sicily, but the east–west part of the route, to Egypt, was mostly one of products which do not survive archaeologically, such as cloth, at least until glazed imports from Tunis begin in the late twelfth century. This does not in itself show a greater range of products for the Islamic route—the *Rhodian Sea Law* shows how many things accompanied wine amphorae on the Byzantine route—but it is a marker of the gaps in our knowledge, even in the brightly lit world of the *geniza*.

This east–west route had a less developed set of links farther west to al-Andalus, as we have seen. The links eastwards were less strong too; it may be that the Jewish merchants whose letters survive had fewer close associations with Syria than their Muslim counterparts did, but they did have relations with Palestine, and these too were relatively unimportant to their commercial activities (see p. 140 above). But what is more significant here is that its links northwards were extremely weak. We have seen how little the Rūm, whether Byzantines or Italians, were involved in *geniza* trading, even though the Byzantines and the Venetians knew the sea

[28] Picard, *La mer des califes*, pp. 324–32.

routes, and both ran a luxury commerce with Alexandria, bringing in high-end cloth in the case of the Byzantines and taking back spices in both cases (pp. 134, 140, 353–6, 506–9 above). The two east–west routes might perhaps have met in Cyprus (it would be logical, but we lack the evidence), but other than that they only really intersected, to a small degree, in Sicily, at the other end of the Byzantine route, although it has to be said that even there, after the Arab conquest, Byzantine finds are commonest in eastern Sicily, whereas the Islamic east–west route followed the Sicilian south-west coast around to Palermo at the other end of the island.

The two east–west routes thus continued in the tenth and eleventh centuries without any significant connection with each other. When a north–south route did begin to appear, with Sicilian exports of wine and glazed wares up the Tyrrhenian coast of Italy after 950, this was a separate development (see p. 228 above). It had antecedents, of course—the Tyrrhenian Sea had had a low-key exchange network without a break—but now it represented the first route between Muslim and Christian lands which carried bulk, not luxury goods. It did not involve *geniza* merchants, and must have been the work of the Sicilians themselves, with maybe some help from the Campanian ports and Pisa, but as yet probably not Genoa. When the Genoese became seriously involved in that route, by the 1110s, although perhaps not on a large scale until the 1150s (see pp. 256, 541–2 above), they were simply following in the Sicilians' footsteps. So north–south bulk trade between the two sides of the Mediterranean really began with the centrality and economic coherence of late tenth- and eleventh-century Sicily, whose associations with Ifrīqiya on the southern coast were already so tight.

The textbooks here all focus on the merchants of Venice and Amalfi as the first people seriously to trade between the north and the south. This seems to me mistaken. We have already looked at the limits of the Venetian evidence; before the late eleventh century they focussed on luxury trade, plus, at least sometimes, the export of wood to the Islamic lands, the sole bulk product associated with them until the 1070s (pp. 507–8). But Amalfi, although it belongs to a region, southern mainland Italy, which I do not discuss here, does need some attention as well. The Amalfitans were, indeed, quite like the early Venetians. Even more than the Venetians, they were everywhere. They had North African political relationships (presumably as traders) by the 870s; popes criticized them for it. There are several references to them in Constantinople in the tenth century, which continue into the late twelfth (they had a waterfront on the Golden Horn beside that of Pisa, plus shops), and included some very rich dealers in the late eleventh—notably Pantaleone and his father Mauro, patrons of (among other places) S. Paolo fuori le mura in Rome, and Montecassino. There was even an Amalfitan monastery on Athos. By 978 they are found in Fusṭāṭ, where they were visible enough to get massacred in a moment of xenophobia in 996, and they were still coming to Alexandria in the time of Benjamin of Tudela in the 1160s. Under the

Normans in Sicily there were Amalfitans in Palermo in the 1170s–1190s and a *ruga Amalfitanorum* in Messina; in the Crusader states there was another such street in Antioch in 1101, which doubtless predated the Crusader conquest of only four years before, as Amalfitans already appear in Jerusalem in the eleventh century. To the north in Italy, they are namechecked in Pavia around 1000 by the *Honorantie*, and had treaty relations with Genoa and Pisa in the 1120s; in 1105, an Amalfitan boat even, unexpectedly, took Sicilian wool up the Adriatic to Ravenna; and to complete the set, Ibn Ḥayyān has them arriving in Córdoba with luxury cloth in 942.[29]

Small wonder that there is a page on Amalfi in every economic survey, as part of the prehistory of the Italian dominance over Mediterranean trade in the twelfth century. And the Amalfitans would be seen as part of that twelfth-century history too, given the frequency of casual reference to them after 1100 too, if it were not for the fact that documents from Amalfi itself barely refer to any of this, and that the Pisans sacked the town in 1135, which is often seen (but actually probably wrongly) as having marked the beginning of its eclipse. In the 1960s there was period of enthusiastic writing up of Amalfitan commerce in the ninth to eleventh centuries, by Armando Citarella in particular, who proposed a large-scale triangular bulk trade of grain, timber, wine, and cloth from Amalfi to North Africa, then gold and olive oil from there (plus spices from Egypt) to Constantinople, and silks back to Amalfi, on the basis of almost no evidence at all.[30] More recent historians, struck by the tiny size of Amalfi's port and, indeed, town, hemmed in by cliffs as it is, have redimensioned this very substantially, and have stressed that 'Amalfitan' might have been a generic term for any Campanian in the eyes of outsiders, and that the various sections of the Amalfitan diaspora might well have had few links at all with the actual town, or with each other, after a generation.[31] This is likely enough, particularly the last, and I certainly belong to those who play down the scale of Amalfitan trading activity in every period.

For me, however, the point is that this is all the same a large number of citations (and I have not listed all of them). And the wealth of some Amalfitans, such as Pantaleone and Mauro, who specialized in paying for bronze doors for prominent Italian churches, is striking. Conversely, what they were actually

[29] The most balanced guide to this huge range is Skinner, *Medieval Amalfi*, pp. 107–9, 203–53, which discusses every example given here. Note that the textbooks also mention a long-distance Jewish 'Radhanite' trade in the pre-*geniza* Mediterranean; a good example of how they can be written up is Gil, 'The Rādhānite merchants'. They are only mentioned in a single source, however, Ibn Khurradādhbih's *Kitāb al-masālik wa al-mamālik*, ed. and trans. Barbier de Meynard, pp. 512–14, in, to me, implausible terms, and I set it aside.

[30] Citarella, 'The relations of Amalfi with the Arab world'; and esp. Citarella, 'Patterns of medieval trade'; see also Balard, 'Amalfi et Byzance'; Cahen, 'Amalfi en Orient' (more nuanced).

[31] Del Treppo and Leone, *Amalfi medioevale*, pp. 8–15, 62–6, 138–40; Figliuolo, 'Amalfi e il Levante nel Medioevo', pp. 578–620 (even then, more upbeat than I would be); Skinner, *Medieval Amalfi*, pp. 247–53; see also Valérian, 'Amalfi e il mondo musulmano'.

trading is very seldom specified, and, when it is, it is almost always silk (we can presumably add bronze); like the Venetians, they were everywhere simply because luxury trade was, and had always been, everywhere. Only two texts show them trading in bulk: they exported timber to Alexandria together with the Genoese in the early twelfth century, and they exported Sicilian wool at scale to Ravenna in 1105. The monastery of Cefalù in Sicily was also permitted in 1132 to send ships to Amalfi and Salerno, nominally to buy necessities, which shows the town linked into a relatively localized Sicilian trading network which was also probably in bulk goods.[32] Again, there are a handful of similar texts for Venice too—starting slightly earlier than this, in fact, before 1100—which show at least some bulk trade from there, which did not prevent the conclusion that they were above all luxury traders before the twelfth century. The same conclusion can be drawn for Amalfi. All that I would add is that this town, together with the other major Campanian ports, Naples and Salerno, was evidently by the twelfth century part of the Sicilian regional bulk trading network, and had probably already participated in the north–south Sicilian trading route of the eleventh century too. It was here, and not in its wide Mediterranean diaspora, that Amalfi was engaged with economically significant exchange.[33]

The Amalfitans can thus simply be added to the pre-twelfth-century Venetians as merchants above all in luxury goods. They may well have been trading with the Islamic world first, as it was nearer, but Byzantium came a close second (like Venice, Amalfi was an ex-Byzantine city). They branched out quite widely from there, more than the Venetians did, but, unlike their Adriatic competitor, seem to have remained luxury traders even after 1100, except along the regional Campania–Sicily routes. After all, most of them were indeed, as far as we can see, deracinated: those widely dispersed colonies could not even have physically fitted back into Amalfi had they returned, and there is no equivalent here of the close association between Venetians in Rialto and Venetians in the Aegean. That is to say, the separate colonies did not create a real Amalfitan commercial network, unlike those of the three main north Italian ports. And had they ever been consistently involved in long-distance bulk trading, it is difficult to see how this fact would have escaped even the poor documentary evidence we have; it is clear in a range of Pisan sources, after all, even though Pisan charters say so little about it until after 1150 (see pp. 560, 564 above). Amalfitans could get rich anywhere, and did, but they were marginal to the arguments of this book, both before and after

[32] See Stern, 'An original document' (P.SternItalianMerchants), for the timber; see *Il Codice Perris*, 1, ed. Mazzoleni and Orefice, n. 96 (cf. Skinner, *Medieval Amalfi*, pp. 204–5), for Ravenna; and see Cusa, *I diplomi*, n. 136 (pp. 489–90; see Chapter 3, n. 246 above), for Cefalù.

[33] If we want good evidence for bulk trading for any of the Campanian cities, it is probably Naples, not Amalfi, that we need to look to. Its linen production, in particular, attested already in the tenth century, was large-scale and must have been in part for export; see Feniello, *Napoli*, pp. 197–202, and Chapter 3, n. 107 above.

1100. They simply show, to repeat, that luxury trade routes could, from the ninth century to the twelfth, go in any direction. The real pioneers in north–south bulk trade were, rather, the Sicilians. And bulk trade ran more predictably; we will now return to that.

The twelfth century, as we have seen, is generally regarded as the century in which Italian ships from the three northern ports really took over Mediterranean bulk-trade shipping. It is certainly the century in which Italian evidence, for the first time, tells us most about that shipping, which privileges our knowledge about, in particular, the Venetians and Genoese, as we saw in Chapter 6. We, however, do still have references to Egyptian, Sicilian, and Byzantine merchants (see pp. 142–3, 255, 356–7, 452–4 above), which in the Egyptian case in particular go beyond the anecdotal, even if the role of Jewish Egyptian merchants, in the Mediterranean at least, had by now substantially dropped. So it is, in fact, impossible that the Italians could really have been the only traders on the inland sea, or even that commerce was by now above all carried in Italian ships, something for which there is occasional evidence.[34] But the Italian cities were certainly far more active and prominent than they ever were before, and quite probably more active than anyone else by the mid-twelfth century, even if it is impossible to establish for certain the degree of their dominance.

Explanations for the rise of Italian merchants and ships have varied. As we have seen, the superior dynamism of the Italian cities and the failing state structures of the Islamic world have often enough been used as unhelpful generic reasons—the first of these being a circular argument as well as self-congratulatory, and the second a thoughtless Orientalist invocation of the long-term 'failure' of Islam. John Pryor has a rather better explanation: the northern east–west trade route was the easiest in the Mediterranean, and it was dominated by Christian powers which were rather more aggressive from the end of the eleventh century onwards than they ever had been before; Italian pirates (who were themselves often merchants on other days of the week) added to that. So Italian boats were henceforth the safest means of travel for any traffic which was not directly between Islamic states, Egypt to Ifrīqiya in particular, plus al-Andalus to Morocco, or inside the Byzantine inland sea (though there were by the end of the twelfth century Italian pirates there too).[35] But even this skips over a step in the argument, for the point about the two east–west routes is not only that the northern one was easier, but also that the southern route was by far the dominant one in the century preceding 1100. We saw earlier (pp. 141–2) that it is by no means certain

[34] For a sensible overview, see Pryor, *Geography, technology and war*, pp. 139–64; as against, out of many, Cahen, *Orient et Occident*, pp. 137–9 (138: after the mid-twelfth century, 'il est certain que ces navires [de commerce] sont désormais exclusivement italiens'). For Italian carriers for non-Italian merchants, see pp. 254, 322 above.

[35] See n. 34 above, with p. 453 above for al-Andalus to Morocco; cf Petralia, 'Le "navi" e i "cavalli"' for Italian violence.

that Italian trading ships were any better protected than Egyptian ships were, and that it would be hard to explain either the decline of the southern route or the rise of Italian ships in purely military terms. It is, however, to an extent true that the Norman conquest of Sicily reorientated that island's commercial interests towards the north rather than towards the east (see pp. 197–8 above), which affected the southern east–west route directly; and above all, as a presumably unintended result, the flax trade failed, which was the most direct hit to the southern route. This would be, here at least, an example of a political change which did have an effect on interregional trade. It is, furthermore, also to an extent true that the Crusader conquest of the Levantine coast meant that there were fewer Islamic sea-facing powers to trade with each other, although we have also seen that there are signs that Egypt's trade with the Levant actually increased in the twelfth century, rather than decreasing; and anyway, the situation was reversed after a century, as the substantial activity of Amīnaddīn between Egypt and Damascus shows around 1200 (see p. 109–10 above). These developments may, indeed, imply that the southern route had become weaker by now. But it had by no means gone away—it is consistently documented in the twelfth century—just as it had not been wholly taken over by the Italians.

Conversely, to counter the endless invocations of Italian commercial dynamism, it must also be remembered, as was stressed in Chapter 6, that the three great Italian port cities were fragile. They were as yet small; they had relatively little to trade which came from their hinterlands, so they were largely still carriers for the strong and economically complex eastern and southern Mediterranean states they traded with; and they were always very exposed to commercial embargoes or outright confiscations of goods by those states, at least up to the fall of Constantinople in 1204. I would, in fact, see that date as the game changer; it was after it that the Venetians, and to a lesser extent the Genoese, obtained fully colonial possessions in the islands in and around the Aegean which gave them a real strategic advantage in the east for the first time. But this book does not deal with the thirteenth century, whose parameters were substantially different from those we have looked at here.

The Italians were violent, without a doubt; Chapter 1 compared them with the Portuguese in the sixteenth-century Indian Ocean, adding themselves to pre-existing networks by force, and for me the parallel holds. But I would argue, as we have also seen in previous chapters, that the rise to prominence of the Italian cities derived above all from a different feature of how they traded: what the Italians did, from the second quarter of the twelfth century onwards, was *unify* the Mediterranean bulk routes (see Map 24). This was their real achievement. It had not been a feature of any trading system since the end of the Roman Empire, but henceforth it was normal. In their eyes, as newcomers, there was no structural difference between the two great east–west routes; they were prepared to trade along both. And they were equally happy to engage in north–south trade too, not just the Tyrrhenian–Tunisia route which the Sicilians had opened up nearly two centuries before, but in every direction. Venetian boats tended to stay with the routes they knew, to Byzantium and Egypt, and continued to prosper along them, trading more in bulk by now, although even they were on occasion happy to use transverse routes, making that a triangular trade, and they dealt with the Levant as well. But the Genoese went almost everywhere, and connected almost everywhere; the Pisans were not far behind. And as a trio—which is a legitimate way to see them, even if they fought each other often enough, especially the Genoese and the Pisans—they linked pretty much every major Mediterranean port with every other, either directly or at one or two removes. This is a different argument from one about Italian 'dominance', and to me a more important one. It is also much easier both to demonstrate and to explain. Precisely because the Italian ports were not acting to any great extent on behalf of productive systems operating in their hinterland, they were flexible enough to connect long-standing trade routes with each other, everywhere, as long as they made a profit out of doing so. So, although the extent of Italian dominance of Mediterranean trade remains an open question, the creation by the Italians of a Mediterranean-wide trading network is much clearer an accomplishment.

That accomplishment is not lessened by two caveats, but both are quite as important, if we want to understand what was really going on in the Mediterranean in the twelfth century. The first, which I have stressed several times, is that the scale of trading of each of the three Italian port cities, taken separately, was substantially less than that attested in Egyptian evidence, both Jewish and Muslim. I hypothesized earlier (p. 547) that with the three Italian ports put together, their twelfth-century trading might perhaps have matched eleventh-century Egyptian trading (that is to say, the trading documented in the *geniza*) in scale; but there is no evidence that it was greater, especially as trading by Muslim officials and, indeed, rulers is likely often to have been a larger operation than that of Jewish merchants, which we know more about. That has one key consequence: if we argue that the Italians entirely took over the maritime trade routes of the twelfth century, we cannot also argue that Mediterranean trading increased in scale as well. That argument is only possible once we recognize that the Italians simply added themselves to, and linked together, groups of sea merchants from other regions who continued to operate in the same way, although less well evidenced in the twelfth century than in the eleventh. This we can, indeed, show, to an extent, even if it is also clear that some of the sea merchants from other regions also became less active. We can, therefore, conclude that the overall scale of trading could well have increased, but rather less than has often been assumed. I will come back to the question of that probable increase in scale at the end of this chapter, for it had other, more important causes too.

The second caveat is one which is as valid for the *geniza* traders of the eleventh century as for the Italian traders of the twelfth: they restricted themselves, almost entirely, to trading in the major ports. They can almost never be seen in any inland trading location, with the occasional exception of capitals, particularly Fusṭāṭ-Cairo and Kairouan. This is essentially because of Jessica Goldberg's '*geniza* business model', which I have several times invoked, and it is equally clear that there was a 'Venetian', a 'Pisan', and a 'Genoese business model' as well, which operated in the same way and with the same constraints: investors in bulk sea trading wished to see returns as rapidly as possible, both to get their investment back quickly and to minimize further risk if the merchants they were financing went farther in their trading than an initial port.[36] So travelling merchants were expected to come back with the first ship or the first flotilla, in a substantial percentage of trading agreements in both Egypt and Italy; in the Italian contracts, only in a minority of cases did the deal leave open where the travelling merchant might trade, or trade after the primary destination, but even then the assumption seems to have been that it would be in other major ports. The only important exception to this concerned the Venetian settlements in the Aegean, where some cabotage and even land trading was envisaged in some contracts; but even then, the Venetians mostly kept to the trunk routes around the edge of the Aegean, and did not operate inside its more complex route variants (see pp. 332–7 above).

These constraints had one important consequence: the sea traders of our period did not get involved, to any serious extent, in the internal regional trading of the products they depended on. That was left to the merchants, big and small, inside each region; but that internal trading was, of course, on a far larger scale than interregional maritime trade. I stressed in Chapter 6 that the economy of the twelfth-century Italian port cities was as yet largely separate from that of the north-central Italian interior, mostly because the latter was as yet not very fully developed. This was not true for Alexandria, Mahdia, Palermo, or Almería, whose links to their hinterlands were tight and organic. But from the standpoint of the sea traders in each of these there was a clear separation, irrespective of the origins of the traders concerned: the merchants who brought goods from inland to the coast were different, and had different trading associations, from those who took them out to sea. Only a small number of specialists did both—the clearest example being the *geniza* merchants who themselves negotiated for the flax, 100 kilometres up the Nile from Fusṭāṭ-Cairo, which they intended to take or send westwards to the central Mediterranean regions. And when it came to sea merchants who brought goods *into* ports (or, occasionally, to inland capitals), exceptions were even fewer; the goods were sold to local dealers, who were the sole people responsible for taking them into the regional economy.

[36] Goldberg, *Trade and institutions*, esp. pp. 279–85 (the *geniza*, however, documents a more complex set of business considerations than Italian contracts do). For discussions of the issue here, see esp. pp. 139, 336, 517, 565 above.

Overall, then, I would see maritime trade in the Mediterranean as increasing considerably in scale in the period 950–1100, particularly on the southern east–west route. After that, it increased in complexity in the twelfth century, in most parts of the sea, and to an extent also in scale, but probably not, in this period, quite as rapidly as it did before 1100; to repeat, we will come back to this. And in both of these time slots, maritime trade was not only much less extensive than the internal trade of the Mediterranean regions, as we have seen, but the former was also not closely connected to the latter. Neither the Egyptian merchants who are so well documented in the eleventh century, nor the Italian merchants who are so well documented in the twelfth, penetrated significantly into any other regional economy; they remained external to it. This is another reason for seeing maritime trade, however interesting, and however much it did, indeed, involve economically significant bulk commodities, as only a small part of the Mediterranean economy (or economies) as a whole.

If we set Egypt against Italy as the place of origin of the two most active groups of long-distance sea traders in the Mediterranean, it seems clear that Egypt was, across our period, easily the more important region of the two. It was the stronger, as regards its internal economy, in each of our centuries. Even if Italian sea traders did become more important than Egyptian ones in the twelfth century, which is likely, they did not displace them; and the Italian traders depended on Egypt far more than Egypt depended on them. (The same was true for the Venetians in Byzantium, the Genoese in Sicily, maybe the Pisans in al-Andalus; but Egypt had this function for all three.) And of course, the internal economy of north-central Italy was hardly as yet connected to the coast at all. So Egypt remained the point of reference for the Mediterranean economy as a whole. In the thirteenth century, the Italian economy caught up, and also extended, helped by now by the development of island colonies, into the Aegean. From perhaps 1250 up to the Black Death, the two regions were operating much more as equals. This is the world Janet Abu-Lughod described in her survey book of 1989, which achieved remarkable insights, given the mediocre quality of so much of the secondary literature she was using.[37] It was, in my view, only because of the plague, which did so much fundamental harm to the Egyptian economy (see p. 126 above), that the roles began to reverse. But these sketchy post-1250 observations must be set out simply as hypotheses: only a detailed study of the thirteenth- and fourteenth-century regional economies of the Mediterranean could confirm or falsify them. And they might, indeed, point in different directions again; after all, given that much of what has been written on the twelfth century and before is unreliable or unbalanced, the same might well be true of that of 1250 and after. That will be for future work, undertaken by others.

[37] Abu-Lughod, *Before European hegemony*.

But on another level, that of Mediterranean sea trade seen as a whole, as a structure, it may also not have mattered so much in any given period which regional origin each set of traders actually had. They had a common culture. They may not have always recognized this; sea wars and sea victories are described in our narratives with all the enthusiastic chauvinism one would expect (Genoa versus Pisa or Norman Sicily versus Byzantium as much as any of them versus 'Saracens'); but when they actually traded, they must have known it. For a start, their practices of trading must have been closely analogous; merchants clearly understood each other as they moved from place to place, once Rūmī merchants got used to Islamic bargaining styles, at least (see p. 134 above). And the rules of the sea were very similar in each. To take one example, the rules for jettisoning cargo when a ship is endangered recur without much change from imperial Roman law (where it is already called the *lex Rodia de iactu* [jettison], and explicitly makes the claim that it is pre-Roman law recognized by early emperors) to the late eighth-century Byzantine *Rhodian Sea Law* and the *Kitāb akriyat al-sufun* of the early tenth to the Pisan *Constitutum Usus* of the late twelfth. They all, although with some hesitation in the Byzantine case, enact that the merchant(s) whose goods are jettisoned should be compensated by the other merchants on the ship according to the relative market prices of the totality of the goods of each group. The only major difference between them is that Roman and (Roman-influenced) Pisan law, when referring to those market prices, assume that they are those of the port of arrival, whereas Islamic jurists, even if with some disagreement, tend to argue that they should be those of the port of departure.[38]

The same substantial similarities and mild differences recur in partnership trading contracts. These are called *qirāḍ* or *muqāraḍa* in Arabic, *ʿeseq* or *ʿisqa* in Hebrew (discussed by Maimonides in late twelfth-century Egypt, among others, although he calls them *qirāḍ* as well), and *commenda*, *collegancia*, *societas*, etc., in Italian Latin. All concern the relationship between one or more sedentary merchants, who put most (often two-thirds) or all of the money into a trading contract, and the travelling merchant, who puts less or none, but who will get a larger percentage of the profits than the money he put in (often a half) when the voyage is successfully concluded. These contracts helpfully allowed the accumulation of commercial capital by even impecunious travelling merchants, and were widely used in the eleventh- and twelfth-century Mediterranean. There is a whole historiography which discusses who invented this contract first, with some arguing that the *qirāḍ* influenced western practice, others seeing the *commenda* as developing independently, and others again locating its ultimate origins in imperial

[38] *Corpus iuris civilis*, 1, *Digesta*, ed. Mommsen and Krueger, 14.2; *The Rhodian sea-law*, ed. Ashburner, 3.9, 43–4 (the least typical of the set); *Kitāb akriyat al-sufun*, trans. in Khalilieh, *Admiralty and maritime laws*, ch. 5 (pp. 299–311)—the differences between the first three are discussed ibid., pp. 150–94; *Constitutum Usus*, ch. 29 (in Vignoli, *I Costituti*, pp. 247–9).

Roman *societas* partnership law, given that this envisages that partners can bring service, including travel, to a partnership rather than money.[39] Some of the arguments here owe more, it has to be said, to rival grand narratives than to the evidence itself, which is weak. To me, however, as also to John Pryor, it is quite likely that the Roman Empire did have a practice resembling medieval *qirāḍs/commendae*, even if its surviving law does not discuss one-voyage contracts at all, and that what developed was a long post-Roman *koinē* of similar maritime practice extending to the Latin-, Greek-, and Arabic-speaking parts of the Mediterranean alike. Conversely, however, the development of Islamic juristic reasoning about *qirāḍ*s was far more complex than that of any other legal or mercantile community, and the *qirāḍ* was more similar to the *commenda* than any of the others were to each other; so, even if the latter was not borrowed from the former, it is plausible that it was influenced by it.

But the real point is that all seagoing merchants in at least the second half of our period had access to capital, using contracts with very similar terms. The only substantial difference between any of them is that the Jewish *ʿisqa*, which Philip Ackerman-Lieberman has shown was, indeed, frequently used by *geniza* merchants (although they used elements of *qirāḍ* procedures too), assigned a share in the risk of the loss of capital to a travelling merchant who lost his investor's goods, for example to shipwreck or piracy, whereas the *qirāḍ* theoretically did not (Italian contracts, in different forms, could do either).[40] This, however, again seems to me simply a detail, even if an interesting one, in a general array of closely analogous maritime legal assumptions. Merchants across the Mediterranean may have spoken different languages, and/or have had different religions, but they borrowed capital and faced trading risks—and indeed, bought and sold—in much the same way. They also faced the same issues of trust in foreign ports, and built up networks of trusted counterparts, in the same way; conversely, they dealt with fraud and deceit in very similar ways.[41] They used similar ships too.[42]

That is to say, when looking at the organization of trade, it is irrelevant where specific merchants came from. Obviously, merchants from Alexandria or Fusṭāṭ took their profits back to Egypt, those from Venice or Genoa took theirs back to Italy, but this was the main difference; and as I have repeatedly argued, the scale of maritime trade was not so great that this would have affected the economies of whole regions (rather than single cities) so very much. The growing complexity of

[39] For good discussions, see esp. Udovitch, *Partnership and profit*, pp. 170–248, with Udovitch, 'At the origins of the western *commenda*' (cf. also Chapter 2, n. 264 above); Pryor, 'The origins of the *commenda* contract'; Khalilieh, *Admiralty and maritime laws*, pp. 224–46, all referring to wider bibliography. For Roman law, see *Corpus iuris civilis*, 1, *Digesta*, ed. Mommsen and Krueger, 17.2.5.1, 17.2.6, 17.2.29.1. *The Rhodian sea-law*, ed. Ashburner, 3.17, also has a brief reference to partnership (*chreokoinōnia*), which is also stressed in the literature, more than the reference merits.

[40] Ackerman-Lieberman, *The business of identity*, pp. 156–71, 191–3.

[41] See Goldberg, *Trade and institutions*, pp. 139–64, 177–84, for trust.

[42] Pryor, *Geography, technology and war*, pp. 25–39, 57–64.

the network of trading when taken as a whole, which is certainly visible in our sources, both documentary and archaeological, seems to me much more important. And so, still more, does the growing complexity of the economies inside each Mediterranean region. I shall finish this chapter with some discussion of that.

* * *

The signs of economic complexity in Egypt in our period are considerable, and in Chapter 2 we tracked them in a wide variety of ways. The Arabic-script merchant letters for Egypt show a dense network of capillary commercial exchange which has no matching evidence for any other region in the Mediterranean, and which not only backs up the better-known material from the *geniza* but also locates it more securely in the towns and villages of Middle Egypt, from Madīnat al-Fayyūm to Ashmūnayn and southwards from there, at the core of the regional economy—with the *geniza* filling this out for the Egyptian Delta too. Although they derive from an evidence base which we could not expect elsewhere, they are backed up by more anecdotal references in narratives and the geographers; and even Egypt's poor archaeological record shows several types of ceramics sold the length of the Egyptian Nile, with visible productive hierarchies operating on a smaller scale, as also a developed urban hierarchy of small, big, and huge towns. We have good evidence of an extensive division of labour, in construction in the capital, in sugar production in the countryside, as also, more generally, in ceramics and cloth-making, and of a very considerable range of trades, from Alexandria up to Aswān. Cloth, in particular, was made and sold in overlapping networks, which are markers of a genuinely complex internal economy; that complexity is further shown by the fact that the great cloth factory towns of the coast, in our period above all Tinnīs, probably up to 1100 or later the largest single-product town anywhere outside China, were not the main foci of interest of the great Jewish flax and cloth merchants evidenced in the *geniza*, who preferred to have their linen woven 1,500 kilometres away. The intensity of flax production is particularly visible in the *geniza*, in fact, and the area around the market at Būṣīr (not obviously a large town, but a highly active one) was such a powerful location for the supply of raw flax, at different stages of preparation, that it was even possible to suppose that peasants there were cash-cropping. Peasants, anyway, had access to cash more or less everywhere in Egypt; not only did they need it to pay taxes, but they were often wage labourers, and were paid in money, not kind, for their labour, as not all rural wage labourers were in the Mediterranean—even where they existed, for in most regions they were uncommon. Peasants were at the mercy of high state taxation, and also exploitative elites lending to them to pay such taxes. But yields in this irrigated landscape were high, and rural workers clearly had buying power, both for primary products which they did not produce themselves and for manufactured goods, including ceramics and cloth; we have the letter and document collection of a peasant entrepreneur, Jirja of Damūya in the Fayyūm, from the 1020s, which shows him doing precisely this. Overall, the patterns of exchange which we see in Egypt depended substantially on peasant and not only elite demand.

This density of economic activity was far greater than that documented in any other Mediterranean region. When I have discussed such patterns in other places, that basic comparator has to be borne in mind: Egypt was the model for what a complex economy could look like in our period, and was unmatched elsewhere. A certain level of complexity had always existed in the economy of Egypt, and it does not seem to have developed further in our period quite as fast as it did in some other regions, but its intensity from the tenth century onwards was, all the same, a step up from previous centuries. One major reason was the end of the colonial relationship during the Roman Empire which had privileged wheat-growing for the needs of Constantinople and the Roman army, plus, in the late ninth and tenth century, the lessening and then end of tax-paying to Baghdad, and the documented investment of Egypt's newly autonomous ruling elites in Tinnīs as a weaving town. Egypt prospered when it was independent, as it would be for all of our period and well beyond, up to 1517, although the Black Death and the breakdown of irrigation networks had halted its prosperity by then.

Ifrīqiya, the part of the North African coast centred on what is now Tunisia, had a less straightforward history, and is also the least well-documented of my chosen regions. All the same, its economy bounces into vision in (in particular) the tenth century, in both the archaeology and the scarce written sources, as we saw in Chapter 3. Its very variegated ecology had been unified by the Romans, and had then lost coherence in the eighth century after the end of the Roman world system—for its economy had been unusually focussed on export—but a solid and active base of agricultural and urban production was re-established after that, in the context of a fiscal reunification under the Aghlabids, and developed further under the Fāṭimids and their Zīrid governors in the tenth and eleventh centuries. The point is that some parts of Ifrīqiya were always rich, notably the wheat lands of the Medjerda valley in the north, the olive forests of the east coast, and the coastal towns, which are well attested as productive centres. A regained political and fiscal coherence by 900 (at the latest) allowed its very different parts to again reinforce each other and to work as a whole; and I see this as the clearest cause of the region's dynamism in our period. These were the great days for linen production using Egyptian flax, and for urban economies more generally, to judge by both archaeology and a variety of written sources (including the *geniza*). But renewed political breakdown in and after the 1050s, with the invasion of the semi-nomadic Banū Hilāl and revolts of the coastal urban centres away from Zīrid rule, ushered in a century of confusion, which visibly undermined Ifrīqiya's economic coherence. Some of the coastal towns at times found it easier to get their wheat from Sicily than from the Medjerda valley. Ceramic production, which is one of our best markers of the region's economic coherence in the century 950–1050, perhaps became (the evidence is not good) more regionalized, until the rise of the cobalt and manganese fine wares of Tunis in the late twelfth century, which had a considerable export penetration. The coastal cities, as a group, seem to have continued to be prosperous across the last half of our period, but they probably had less tight a relationship with their hinterlands, with the exception of Béjaïa on the Algerian coast; nor did this obviously reverse with the Almohad reconquest of the whole region in the 1150s. What, however, we cannot say about Ifrīqiya is what its patterns of internal demand were. We have no usable evidence for peasant prosperity (or its absence), so we cannot be sure how much peasant demand contributed either to the region's overall economic activity or to its coherence. This was an important variable in all our other regions, and its absence here means that Ifrīqiya can contribute less to an overall picture of the economies of the Mediterranean than we would want.

Sicily, discussed in the same chapter because its links with Ifrīqiya were always so tight, is a much easier region to delineate. It had in every period a close exchange relationship between its grain-rich central plateau and its more agriculturally and artisanally variegated coastlands, which acted as the basis for a relatively coherent regional economy without a break, from around 900 to long after 1200. It also, across the same period, had a strong central government whose taxation extended widely (though with far less elaboration than that of Egypt), except for a period of disunity in the 1040s–1060s. The ninth-century Islamic conquest was of an already rich island, even if its western parts were probably not doing well at that moment; and by 950 we can clearly see its economy operating as a single unit, with wine amphorae and glazed ceramics from Palermo reaching nearly every excavated site, a productive dominance of a single city which is very rare in our period. Sicily's grain and wine, its silk (from what is now San Marco in the north-east), and its linen production were particularly clearly commercialized in the eleventh century. This was economic growth, beyond doubt. In the twelfth, the linen factories ended, but cotton exports begin to appear, going north to Genoa. The Norman conquest reorientated the island's external trade to an extent, but the coherence of the regional economy remains clear in ceramic distributions. Rural demand was strong in every part of our period, as those distributions, indeed, indicate; and the documentary evidence we have for the twelfth century indicates that peasants, whether tax-paying (if Muslim) or rent-paying (if Christian)—for the difference, see pp. 239–43 above—were not so very heavily burdened, on an island where wheat yields were unusually high for a dry-farming regime. This probably contrasted with the Byzantine period of the early middle ages, when large estates were common, as they had been under the Roman Empire; it took a long time (until well after our period) for these to build up again. The end of such estates did not mean the end of elites, for sure, but the newly calibrated balance between elite (including tax-based) wealth and peasant buying power was most probably the major underpinning of the rural prosperity and overall growth in economic activity which is documented in our period. In the late twelfth century, the artisanal complexity of the plateau lands to the south of Palermo is particularly clear, with a notable quantity of rural cloth-making, in a period when ceramic links to Palermo—doubtless the market for much of that cloth—are still clearly visible. By now, productions were less centralized than in the tenth century, but this marks, as also in al-Andalus, productive complexity as much as the weakening of a central focus. And many of these patterns continued into the thirteenth century, when, even though the west and east of Sicily had partially different trajectories, Messina's glazed cooking wares begin to appear all over the island, which shows that rural populations, here again, could afford to buy them in preference to cheaper wares made locally.

The Byzantine Empire, discussed in Chapter 4, was more economically divided, and here I focussed above all on the inland Aegean Sea and the coastal territories around it, three-quarters of modern Greece together with the wide western lowlands of modern Turkey. This was another region, like Egypt and Sicily, in which a tax-raising state was continuously strong across our period; the military gains and losses of the empire, which were considerable and complex, did not affect this central economic zone as greatly. The state held the ecologically distinct economies of the whole empire together in every period, but never, outside the Aegean region, integrated them as fully as the most successful regimes in Ifrīqiya (a smaller territory, to be sure) managed. Indeed, in the eighth to early tenth centuries it barely held together even the Aegean as an economic unit, although it at least ensured that it did not break up. But across our period the Aegean steadily gained economic coherence, as increasingly complex amphora distributions show, demonstrating the movement of foodstuffs (still largely wine) around the sea. Constantinople's demand also ensured a seaborne movement of goods in every period, and so did the fiscal system, even though that was much more locally based than it had been under the Roman Empire, as we have also seen earlier in this chapter.

After *c.*1090 at the latest, we can see a take-off. Our archaeological evidence rapidly becomes denser, and Corinth and Thebes/Chalkis, in particular, emerge in both our written documentation and in the archaeology as major centres for the production and distribution of cloth (both linen and silk), wine, and glazed ceramics. The twelfth century also shows a rather more complicated maritime route network than earlier centuries do, given the patterns of the finds of central Greek ceramic types all across the coasts and inland areas of both Greece and Turkey, along with Constantinopolitan types. Byzantium, unlike all the other regions we have looked at apart from northern Italy, has just enough land documents (particularly in northern Greece) for it to be possible, as also in Italy as we shall see, to discern demographic expansion and land clearance. Byzantium also has more archaeological field surveys than most of our regions (particularly in central-southern Greece), which allow us to see that sites both increased in size and accumulated ever larger groups of pottery from major Aegean production centres. These are direct indicators of rural economic growth, and they fit both in their geography and in their chronology with the pacing of the growth in artisanal production. I see them as causally related, with agrarian expansion and thus rural demand fuelling this development, framed by a wider fiscal network which ensured that the main trunk routes around the Aegean never failed. The Byzantine Aegean was another region where we can see an at least partially autonomous—and thus prosperous, even if certainly tax-burdened—peasantry in our written sources, and this too fits directly with our evidence for ceramic imports on rural sites. That is to say, rural buying power was linked directly to urban production here, at least in the period of growth starting at the end of the eleventh century.

Al-Andalus, discussed in Chapter 5, saw the fastest growth of any region of the Mediterranean in our period, including those not studied in this book. Its archaeology shows very simple ceramic types across the eighth century and most of the ninth, but then large-scale glazed productions began, especially in Córdoba in the tenth century, which had wide distributions; when the Umayyad Caliphate broke up, ceramic production was simply decentralized to a dozen productive centres, which, across our period, specialized and often overlapped commercially. Towns grew rapidly across our period, some tripling in size or more. The number of ceramic kilns found by archaeologists is staggering in scale; a single city, Córdoba, has, I think, more excavated kilns than the whole of the rest of the non-Iberian Mediterranean in the early and central middle ages put together. The range of artisans attested in literary and archaeological sources (pottery, metal, and glass stand out in the archaeology; various types of cloth and metal in the written sources) is substantial too. Rural sites had access to wide ranges of ceramics from outside (and on occasion coins from several different mints); that is to say, the interconnectedness of artisanal productions regularly reached rural buyers. But rural society itself was also in many areas getting more prosperous agriculturally, specifically in our period, thanks to a wide extension of often quite complex irrigation networks, whether on flat land beside cities like Valencia and Granada, or on the hill slopes close to villages. Urban and rural expansion must imply demographic growth too, even if it is not documented directly. Rural society was stratified, but many villages were autonomous from outside landowners; rents could be high, but tax was probably less so, which allowed for prosperous peasant elites, who could, and evidently did, buy from these active commercial networks. Islamic Spain and Portugal had, as a result, across the period of this book, developed from being a region with very simple and localized productive systems, simpler than those of any other region studied here, to being on the level of at least Sicily and perhaps nearly reaching that of Egypt in the complexity, specialization, and capillary availability of its commercial goods. This was the product of a level of fiscal centralization which was new in the tenth century and which continued on a more localized scale even in the periods of considerable disunity which followed, plus a considerably increased level of agricultural production in some areas, thanks to irrigation, plus an ability, very visible in the archaeology, for peasants (and, of course, elites) to buy products—all the vectors set out for other regions at once.

North-central Italy, discussed in Chapter 6, was the least typical of these regions in two fundamental respects. First was the absence in any period of a single tax-raising state which might integrate the region economically; even a weak political unity anyway ended by 1100. At the very end of our period, its independent cities were beginning to tax the countryside, paralleling here the *ṭāʾifa* kingdoms of al-Andalus, but it was only beginning then, and would be a systemic feature only of later centuries. This was matched by a considerable localization of archaeologically attested ceramic productions, which were of higher quality than those of al-Andalus around 900, but, unlike there, were not developed and unified to any substantial extent across our period. At most, imports of amphorae and Byzantine or Islamic glazed wares reached the hinterlands of Venice and Pisa, but glazed wares were produced locally only from the very end of the twelfth century onwards. The economic fragmentation of north-central Italy was, then, the second fundamental difference from other regions, and it had hardly even begun to be lessened by the end of our period, except in relatively small areas: more intensively in the hinterland of Pisa, less intensively in the larger hinterland of Venice, and probably in central Lombardy as well, where at least two economically active cities, Milan and Piacenza, were flanked by small towns (*burgi*) with complementary artisanal specializations. The Italian port cities, Genoa, Venice, and Pisa, were highly visible by now in the Mediterranean, but this fact as yet had little impact on the north-central Italian economy in itself. The Italian economy built itself up internally, reflecting, without doubt, the agrarian developments of the same period, which, even more than in Byzantium, visibly involved demographic growth and land clearance. Demand increased as a result; here too, there was peasant demand, as, although rents were high, many peasants were landowners, wholly or in part; but aristocratic domination in the countryside also increased, with the growth of signorial powers in the late eleventh and twelfth century, and with the formation of a wider range of elites whose own buying power was new and competitive—as also with urban expansion, for city-dwellers needed to buy nearly all their goods. The cloth, iron, and leather which were increasingly produced by larger and smaller towns had a ready rural (and urban) market now. This set of developments moved more slowly towards economic complexity than did those in the Mediterranean regions which were more unified by taxation; a north Italian regional economy cannot be said to have existed in any form before the thirteenth century at the earliest. But when it did, it was as strongly based as in Egypt or al-Andalus, and it continued to become more complex well after our period.

We have already seen at the end of Chapter 5 how the basic explanations for economic growth adduced here for each region were different in nearly every case. For that matter, so were the pacing and the extent of each. From a high base, Egypt moved slowly up the curve; Ifrīqiya, Sicily, and al-Andalus moved rapidly up from a lower base around 950, but the first of these hit a plateau (at best) after a century, whereas the second and especially the third continued steadily to develop; Byzantium saw a take-off around 1090, whereas north-central Italy, with some very visible exceptions, only followed suit around a century later. I would add that there were, almost certainly, regions of the Mediterranean which hardly developed economically at all in this period; Sardinia is probably an example—so like Sicily in its resources, but so different.[43] There was nothing inevitable about urban and rural growth in this period, as in every other. For that reason alone, my invocation of different explanations for each region is not in itself a problem. Regional development had in every case very little linkage to developments elsewhere, so it is not surprising that it had different roots from place to place. It would be more surprising, indeed, if the explanations were the same in each.

But the experiences of the regions discussed in this book did, all the same, have features in common. I will list three. The first, and most often repeated across the previous chapters, is that none of them had any significant relationship to the wider networks of Mediterranean trade—as we have amply seen, in this chapter and elsewhere, this was the basis of the prosperity of some individual cities, but never of that of whole regions. The second is that all our regions, with the exception of north-central Italy, were ruled by tax-raising states, with the implications for networks of tax-supported routes, the lowering of some transaction costs along those networks, and state and official foci of large-scale demand and often investment, which again we have already looked at in this chapter. These networks and demand foci were not, in a strict sense, *essential* to the growth of exchange (or else Italy would never have been able to match them), but they greatly helped to underpin a growing fluidity in the economy in each case.

The third is that the roots of growth, of all kinds, were in every case essentially agrarian. They had to be; the great majority of the inhabitants of every region lived in the countryside, and the great majority of the productions of every region were rural-based. It would be hard for towns and thus urban production to grow if agricultural production did not, for they would risk running out of food. So land clearance and/or irrigation and, probably, agricultural specialization would be in general crucial, and was the case in all our regions (although I would guess that Egypt and Sicily had less land clearance, as they were already pretty fully

[43] See, e.g., the interesting recent discussions in Soddu, 'L'aristocrazia fondiaria'; Ferrante and Mattone, 'Le comunità rurali', pp. 169–90; Alias, 'Origini, forme e sviluppi della fiscalità'; plus Day, *La Sardegna*, esp. pp. 27–67, more dated but still intelligent. But none of these really encompasses the problems of understanding the Sardinian economy—above all the problematic lack of fit between an aristocracy (including churches and the judge-kings) with wide lands and an absence of any material signs of concentrations of wealth before the late twelfth century, except a few ceramic imports (see, e.g., Biccone et al, 'La circolazione di ceramiche'; Biccone, 'Invetriate monocrome decorate di stampo'), and some church-building. Thanks to Alex Metcalfe for help here.

occupied). It is quite likely that demographic growth was a feature of all our regions too, as we can say for sure for Byzantium and Italy, and can assume wherever we can see urban expansion. Demographic growth can simply lead to overpopulation and generalized poverty, but in most cases surplus populations tend, instead, to drive denser agricultural production, and/or swell cities and the numbers of urban producers. This is, indeed, what happened to urban societies in al-Andalus and Italy—and doubtless Byzantium as well, although we know much less about how often towns really expanded there in our period; in Sicily too, the rise of Messina or Cefalù in the twelfth century probably has similar implications. And above all, growth in agricultural production led to an increase in rural demand for goods, which would allow for mass artisanal productions for a larger market. Peasants made up, at an open guess, between 75 and 90 per cent of the total population of every one of the Mediterranean regions discussed here in our period, so what goods they wanted to buy, when they had the resources to do so, mattered more than anything else. I have stressed peasant demand in most of the regional summaries just set out, as I also did at length in the chapters they summarize. I see it as one of the main causal elements in all development in our period.

There are both empirical and theoretical problems attached to this last statement. Many historians of the middle ages have in the past assumed that peasant societies were in general too poor, because too oppressed, plus too conservative, to be major players in any medieval market economy. Conversely, a situation in which a peasantry paid low rents, or no rents at all, did not necessarily lead to a more complex economy; it did not always in the early middle ages across much of Europe, for example. These issues are of considerable importance if we want to understand how the medieval economy—economies—worked as a whole. So, indeed, is the much wider issue of what the economic logic of the medieval economy actually was, for this underpins any understanding not only of how development occurred, but even of what it could consist of. I will, therefore, come back to these questions in the final, more theoretical chapter of this book. But there is sufficient evidence in most of our regions in our period (all except Ifrīqiya) for actual peasant buying power, or at least rich-peasant buying power, which indeed means that the first assumption, that one could not expect a mass peasant market in our period, is empirically incorrect in many specific instances. In Egypt, the peasants who sold flax to Fusṭāṭī merchants in Būṣīr must have profited substantially; and Jirja of Damūya was a good example of a peasant who, through trading and the land market, was moving up in the world (see pp. 100–3, 113 above). In Sicily, the rural artisans around Corleone and Jato, on the plateau south of Palermo in the 1180s, were clearly part of a commercial network, although they also remained members of peasant communities; and the wide availability of Palermitan ceramics in the countryside across our period shows clearly the extent of rural buying power (see pp. 221–5, 244–8 above). In Byzantium and al-Andalus, similarly, as also in the hinterland of Pisa in mainland Italy, centrally produced ceramics were widely available on rural sites, and in the last two cases we sometimes find them in every house in a village, which shows that they were not restricted only to elites and richer peasant strata (see pp. 299–301, 426–9, 574–5 above). There are no reasons to believe that these are one-off examples, and, indeed, in all these regions I set out the evidence to argue that combined rents and taxes were not so high that all peasant groups would have found it impossible to buy goods on top of paying dues and subsistence. That is to say, these were indeed mass rural markets, developing steadily across our period. And they make productive developments in towns, often demonstrably on a large scale, less perplexing; there, of course, have to have been buyers for urban-made bulk goods—otherwise no one would have been making them—and in some places we can see where and occasionally even who they were.

So, to summarize, what characterized all our regions, where we have any evidence, is that they were marked both by peasant and by elite buying power. This is the crucial point. Elite (including state) demand created basic minima for the demand of goods which allowed the creation and development of networks, sets of functioning routes for them to be moved around on; peasant demand created the possibility of mass markets for mass production. Both were needed for the economic growth inside each region which is documented at length in this book. And the different structural changes we have tracked in each region, the extension of fiscal systems in some, demographic and agrarian growth in others, each led to the same result, a balance between elite and peasant demand, which was an effective basis for economic growth, taken as a whole. There is not a hard-edged teleology here, for this balance was fragile. Elite and peasant surpluses, of course, came above all from the same source, the land, and the more one class had, the less the other did. Class struggle had to occur over this, and did. It is easy to see that too much demand by rent-taking lords and tax-taking officials/state systems could lead to peasant immiseration and the absence or destruction of a mass rural market (this may have been the case in western Sicily in the age of great estates which preceded the Islamic conquest; see p. 219 above); but also, a possibility discussed less often in our period, a widespread peasant demand could imply weak elites and the resultant lack of an exchange infrastructure which could move goods around (this had been common enough in the early middle ages, however, as already noted; we will come back to the point). All the same, it is at least the case that, other things being equal, if the balance held, economic growth could occur, and, in the regions we have been looking at, did occur. I would here make a stronger claim, indeed: other things being equal, this balance was a general tendency of medieval economic development, part of the logic of growth inside feudalism as an economic system. This will be the core argument of Chapter 8, where I discuss these processes in more generalized terms.

Inside this overarching framework, one extra element certainly pushed economic development along: urban expansion. This is, in part, no more than a redescription of the processes just discussed; urban expansion was simply a sign of demographic growth and greater demand, for it entailed the increase of both rich and poor town dwellers who did not cultivate the land, and thus could only exist because they extracted its surplus in rents and tax, or else bought its products, adding to exchange. That expansion is very visible in our documentation for al-Andalus and north-central Italy, and to an extent in Sicily and Byzantium, as we have seen, and if it did not occur with the same pace in Egypt, it is probably only because towns there were large already. But it also added to the way demand could develop. Urban production itself, of course, did that on its own, for it added materially to the goods which were available to buy in the countryside (as well as inside cities themselves). It also added to the division of labour which we have seen often enough in our case study regions, both in rural and in urban contexts—cloth-working behind Palermo, and in Constantinople, Málaga, and Piacenza; sugar production, ceramics, and construction in Egypt—which added to productive efficiencies in ways well known since Adam Smith, and, indeed, since al-Ghazālī in eleventh-century Iran.[44] And one element which can be added to this, which is important when we can track it, is the development of urban hierarchies, particularly in relatively restricted geographical areas, for the resultant competition in and complementarity of production—plus a linked set of markets, themselves ordered hierarchically—added forcefully to the fluidity of exchange inside given regions. We saw this most clearly for the hinterland of Milan, where we have good evidence for some of the *burgi* around the city (pp. 604–8 above), but the rise of smaller towns elsewhere, which we can sometimes see—the satellite towns of Tinnīs such as Dabīq, Larisa and Edremit in the Byzantine Empire, Cefalù in Sicily, Mértola in Portugal, Lucena and Siyāsa in Spain, Monselice and Prato in Italy—was usually a marker of similar processes. Overall, the infrastructure of artisanal work and its distribution became stronger and more sophisticated in these contexts, adding to the simple tracking of rises in production and demand.

Linked to this, but perhaps less important, simply because there was less of it, was investment. There was less of it because most artisanal production was as yet small-scale, based on single workshops or groups of linked but autonomous—what David Peacock called 'nucleated'—workshops.[45] Most documented investment was in maritime commerce, which could be large-scale, even though it was far less important than regional exchange. It is much harder to pin down

[44] Smith, *The wealth of nations*, Book 1, chs 1, 3; for al-Ghazālī, *Iḥyā' 'ulūm al-dīn*, on the division of labour involved in needle-making, see the summaries in Ghazanfar and Islahi, 'Economic thought of an Arab scholastic', p. 390. For the empirical examples, see pp. 45–6, 73, 82, 244, 323, 402, 601 above .

[45] Peacock, *Pottery in the Roman world*, pp. 9, 38–43.

large-scale investment in artisanal production, except for the development of Tinnīs (see p. 131 above), which was itself a highly atypical specialist cloth town, partly state-backed. Perhaps the most significant investment in this respect was again in infrastructure: walls for defending cities and ports, bridges, dykes in Egypt, transport canals in Italy in the late twelfth century and onwards, and—perhaps above all—the small-scale but cumulative peasant investment in irrigation in al-Andalus. We cannot quantify this, even in the broadest terms, but it certainly contributed to the patterns of infrastructural development discussed in the last paragraph.

Conversely, one element which does not seem to me to have added much to economic development in our period was non-state institutions. I have made very little reference to guilds in the chapters of this book. This is in part because they developed late (in north-central Italy, they are hardly visible until the very end of our period) or never (in most Islamic regions); before 1180, in all the parts of the Mediterranean we have looked at in this book, they are only noticeably active in Byzantium (see p. 318 above). There is no observable correlation in our period between what we can see in our sources about guilds and the development of either production or trade. They evidently had little to do with the causes of economic growth in our period, on simple empirical grounds. Perhaps, indeed, they would not have done anyway; Sheilagh Ogilvie convincingly argues from data for later periods that they never had any positive relationship with such growth. But I would generalize the point in a different way. It is, of course, true that group loyalty can help the success of a productive or commercial community; it can defend against hostile powers, it can police deviant behaviour, and it can act as a safety net for at least some of the temporarily unsuccessful. But this does not have to be, even if it can be, defined by institutions, whether guilds or any other formal procedures, as, indeed, Ogilvie has also argued.[46] I certainly belong with the strand of scholarship which doubts, very greatly indeed, that the apparent (though never really total) reliance on contracts in the mercantile community of Genoa was any stronger or wider a safeguard than the informal *aṣḥābuna* of the equivalent community documented in the *geniza*, which could, anyway, rely on courts for enforcement when necessary (see p. 129 above). In the medieval world (and not only then), informal solidarity was generally, indeed, at least as strong as institutions, even where these were present.

State institutions, however, are another matter. I have argued that they were less dominant in structuring the economy during our period than under the Roman Empire; all the same, at the regional level, the single institution which had most effect on the economy in our period was indeed the state, through its

[46] No positive relationship between guilds and growth: Ogilvie, *The European guilds*, pp. 561–85, Ogilvie, *Institutions and European trade*, pp. 414–34; contract enforcement hardly related to guild structures: ibid., 250–314. Ogilvie, *The European guilds*, p. 32, also criticizes the view that guilds can be called private; hence my use of 'non-state' here.

taxation, its wider bureaucratic structures, the at least potential regularization of transaction costs in its area of rule, and, of course, its buying power, together with that of its officials.[47] This point is at least a nod to New Institutional Economic (NIE) arguments, but I would argue that in our regions state and official demand (plus investment) was rather more important than the lessening of transaction costs and other moves to encourage economic stability and fluidity, which NIE theorists tend to focus on, even if, to be sure, states everywhere helped to underpin contract enforcement and security in market areas, and the regularity of expectations as merchants travelled (as did all medieval powers, in fact, but states were better at it). And state institutions were not determinant either, in the array of explanations for economic development which we have looked at, except insofar as they helped to produce a balance between elite and peasant demand. After all, north-central Italy managed (in the end) to prosper without having any strong state structures, between the fall of the Kingdom of Italy around 1100 and the fuller development of urban (city-state) institutions after 1200, which did, indeed, often focus on the regulation of production and exchange, but were not determinant for its development there either. So could Italy actually have been helped by the informality, rather than by the institutionalization, of its economic practices? It would be a nice way to counter some of the simpler NIE views of medieval economies. I resist this too, however; to repeat, formal and informal economic practices worked in very similar ways, as for that matter they still do today.[48] It is not here that we need to look for explanations of basic economic change; increases in demand still seem to me to be the crucial causal factor. Again, we will come back to the point in Chapter 8.

But the regional economies of the Mediterranean did, indeed, grow across our period, in their complexity and in the volume of bulk goods produced and traded. The basis of their growth was regional only, as I have repeatedly stressed; but it did also lead to Mediterranean-wide trade, as discussed at the end of every preceding substantive chapter and also at the start of this one. So here, finally, we do have a reply to the problem I posed earlier, as to whether the scale of Mediterranean trade increased in the twelfth century, in particular—there being much less question about expansion in the late tenth and eleventh. The answer has to be yes, but not because of the rise in activity of Italian ships, but rather because continued regional growth meant that there could be more to ship. One has to be careful here; the fastest-growing economies in the twelfth century, in

[47] I set aside one, essentially Orientalist reading of medieval Islamic states implicit in much economic history, namely that they were negative for economic development because they menaced the property rights of investors. Such a reading is inaccurate on too many grounds to mention, in its assumptions about both the Islamic and the western European world.

[48] See, e.g., Edwards and Ogilvie, 'Contract enforcement', pp. 438–42. Nor would Douglass North have disagreed (see, e.g., North, *Institutions, institutional change*, pp. 1–10, 36–45), although he made the same mistakes as others when characterizing a somewhat schematic and, again, Orientalist version of the working of 'the suq' and some western comparators, ibid., pp. 123–30.

al-Andalus and the Aegean, were those least linked into the wider patterns of sea trade. But there are enough signs of movement elsewhere to be pretty sure that steadily more bulk commodities were, indeed, available to be moved across the sea. And the new and intensifying commercial shipping of the Italian ports was only too ready to fill the gap. It involved less movement of goods than under the Roman Empire, when far more food products were sold (and otherwise transported) across the sea than was ever the case in the more self-sufficient regional worlds of our period. The central medieval focus on cloth (with ceramics acting so often as a proxy indicator for the cloth trade) was considerable, but did not match that. All the same, its scale did steadily increase, after the first big upswing in the eleventh century, and continued to do so for a long time after our period—until the early fourteenth century at least, probably until the Black Death, in some places after that as well. This is all the 'commercial revolution' was, in the end: the greater linkage between regional economies, which were each growing along their own lines and for their own reasons. This may seem less romantic than the image of Venetian and Genoese argosies and merchant adventurers implicit in an older historiography; but if one wants to be romantic, the growing scale of (among others) Egyptian, Sicilian, and Byzantine cloth production, Andalusī and Ifrīqiyan ceramic production, Pisan iron production, plus the buzz of local markets in places like Būṣīr and Vimercate, nearly all of them more involved with donkeys than with boats, might fill the gap. As they do anyway, whether one wants to be romantic or not.

8
The Internal Logic of Feudal Economies

I have stressed the complementary role of elite and peasant demand in every chapter so far, as bases for economic growth in the tenth to twelfth centuries. I have argued that the framework for serious growth in this period was, empirically, twofold. There needed to be enough elite demand (that is to say, the demand of landowners, state officials, and the state itself, or of towns as collectivities and the urban rich as individuals) to allow productive specializations to develop, in particular in cloth, ironwork, and (the most visible but least important) ceramics—plus some foodstuffs, notably wine and olive oil—and to help establish or maintain the networks which moved goods around, which would make them available at all. And there also needed to be peasant demand for the development of mass markets (by medieval standards), which in turn could allow for the development of mass production (again by medieval standards). These were not only complementary, but necessary for growth on the scale we have seen for some regions to be possible. There must have been a dialectic between them: goods needed to be affordable before peasants could buy, but elite demand and urban development could simply start the process, allowing growing demand from less and less prosperous/powerful strata—who were themselves often gaining in prosperity through agrarian expansion and selling produce to towns—to nudge up the scale of production and the availability of markets, and thus the steady lessening of prices and transport costs; that process is seldom directly observable, but it is highly likely.[1] There also had to be a balance between elites being wealthy enough to be able to sustain their own demand, usually thanks to their exactions from the peasantry in rents and/or taxes, and not being so wealthy that the weight of their exactions made the peasantry too poor to sustain a mass demand. We have, all the same, seen that the growth visible in all our regions, at different times, was sufficiently solid that that balance must have been maintained. These seem to me to be firm conclusions which we can draw from the data presented in the regionally focussed chapters of this book.

In this final chapter, I want to take these conclusions a step further, in order both to widen them chronologically and to make clear the theoretical positions which underlie and (in my view) make best sense of them. So, first, I will look briefly at some earlier aspects of the Mediterranean and also northern European

[1] It has been best tracked in England, from 1150 onwards; see the references in Chapter 1, n. 8. Cf. pp. 587–8, 609–12 above for Italy.

The Donkey and the Boat. Chris Wickham, Oxford University Press. © Chris Wickham 2023.
DOI: 10.1093/oso/9780198856481.003.0008

economy, from the Roman Empire to the twelfth century, to see how my models fit different political and economic environments across a longer period. Then, secondly, I will set out what seems to me to be the economic logic underlying the whole process of exchange in the pre-capitalist world, that is to say, the world dominated by what Karl Marx called the feudal mode of production—which, as I have argued before and argue here, was the dominant form in each regional economy in nearly all class societies across the world before the rise of industrial capitalism[2]—to see in what way this logic fits and explains the patterns we have seen operating across the tenth- to twelfth-century Mediterranean.

The Roman Empire is a real comparator for what I have set out in this book. I have discussed it in this light before, at least for the period after AD 400. In *Framing the early middle ages*, I stressed above all the role of aristocratic elites as buyers, thus emphasizing in particular one side of the balance outlined above. It was, it is true, clear to me twenty years ago that, with apologies for self-citation:

> If élites were rich, then they were more likely to buy artisanal products on a large enough scale to encourage productive complexity, or from further away (and thus more expensively) if products were seen as better there, thus making long-distance transport more normal, perhaps cheaper.... Under these circumstances, peasantries and the urban poor, too, would be able to find good-quality products, sometimes imported from other regions, but still at accessible prices, because the economies of scale had been created already. Often, indeed, goods for the lower end of the market outweighed those for aristocrats and their entourages.

We have amply seen exactly these patterns in our period, including (although no statistics are possible) the probability that mass peasant demand indeed regularly outweighed elite demand. But my focus was then different, all the same, as the immediately succeeding sentences make clear:

> But élite consumption structured these large-scale systems, all the same. Peasantries and the poor were not a sufficiently consistent, prosperous market for these economies of scale to exist just for them, particularly given the absence of sophisticated and responsive structures for the movement of goods. Conversely, if élites were restricted in wealth, then the scale of their demand would be rather less, and élite identity might be simply marked by a few luxuries; the market for bulk goods would then depend more on the peasantry, and would accordingly be much smaller. This was a common feature of our [pre-800] period.[3]

[2] Most recently in Wickham, 'How did the feudal economy work?'.
[3] Wickham, *Framing*, pp. 706–7.

Elite demand thus became the discriminator in that book; the less wealthy elites were, the less exchange there was, as became visible above all in the post-Roman period, and in practice how peasant demand itself worked became less important to the argument. In the present book, it is certainly much more important.

So let us be clear at least about that, as it concerned the Roman Empire: there is ample evidence for the substantial scale of the access by peasants to goods from elsewhere. The wide distributions of Red Slip fine wares in more or less every archaeological field survey for the Roman imperial period which has ever been carried out in the Mediterranean is an immediate heuristic guide. Even if such surveys (in particular in the western Mediterranean, where dispersed settlement was then more often the norm) have always had problems in being entirely sure what the status of individual sites was, it could not be proposed that survey areas where non-local fine wares and amphorae are regularly found on small as well as large sites have somehow missed out the peasantry entirely. To cite only relatively recent examples, this is explicit in the publication of the Tiber Valley survey, north of Rome; and it is equally clear in survey work in Tunisia.[4] And, both in Italy and in Tunisia, it is clearly backed up by the excavation of small rural sites. One example from the latter region, again from recent publications, is Aïn Wassel, in the grain-growing Medjerda valley near the city of Dougga, a seventh-century farmstead with fine wares and amphorae from a variety of Tunisian producer sites (here, one would not expect much pottery from farther away, as North Africa was the largest single fine-ware- and oil-producing region in the empire, but, all the same, one eastern Mediterranean amphora sherd was found too). A second is the important set of, in some cases, extremely simple sites from earlier in the Roman period found by the Roman Peasant Project near Cinigiano in southern Tuscany, almost all of which had at least some ceramics (and sometimes other goods) which came from some way away, including from outside Italy.[5] This generalized availability of commodities, which could only have been bought, shows the same sort of exchange penetration which we have seen throughout this book developing in every region across our period. And this correlates well with the strength of the Roman Empire, which had the largest-scale tax-raising state in ancient or medieval western Eurasia (apart from the caliphate at its height), plus several levels of rich landowners. These provided the basic framework for the demand for agricultural and artisanal products, which became cheap enough to be widely available to peasants too. And it is also clear from Aïn Wassel that the well-documented fiscal harshness of the late Roman state, plus landlordly exactions, did not have to be so extreme that peasants were everywhere cut out of the market through simple immiseration.

[4] Patterson et al., *The changing landscapes of Rome's northern hinterland*, pp. 150–4, 163–4; Dossey, *Peasant and empire in Christian North Africa*, pp. 62–97.

[5] Bowes, *The Roman Peasant Project*, 2, pp. 543–65, 627–9, 632–7. For Aïn Wassel, see de Vos Raaijmakers and Maurina, *Rus africum IV*, esp. pp. 152–8, 239–44, 278–9.

This was the case in the post-Roman world, in some places, as well. Egypt was one; we have seen some of the continuities in the ceramic record already (pp. 71, 83–4), and this again fits the considerable continuities in a strong tax-raising state there and, for a long time, in prosperous landowners too. But we can also see it to an extent in Merovingian and Carolingian northern Francia, where landowning elites (including kings, bishops, and monasteries) were particularly rich, from the late sixth century at the latest. Their demand allowed the maintenance of some networks of exchange extending hundreds of kilometres, along and linking the river systems of the region; Mayen ware, for example, produced near Koblenz, regularly reached villages considerable distances away. That is to say, this network, although here not backed up by a tax-raising state, had a sufficiently solid basis of elite demand that it extended to the peasantry—at least to an extent, for this network, however elaborate by the standards of contemporary Europe, did not match those of the Roman Empire before it.[6] We will come back to northern Francia shortly, for it was not only the stand-out region for early medieval Latin European economic complexity, but also, not entirely by chance, the locus for northern Europe's own productive and commercial take-off, in and around Flanders, from the eleventh century onwards.

The early medieval period in most of the rest of Europe (and still more so north of the old Roman frontier) was much simpler in its economic structures, however. In Spain, Italy, and the whole of northern and eastern Europe, there is a clear empirical correlation between elites whose wealth was relatively restricted (including states which were for the most part also restricted in their power and resources, where these existed at all) and weak exchange systems, as the archaeology shows; this has important structural implications. That is to say, we have to conclude that elites in these regions were not rich enough to act as the demand basis for a productive and communication structure which was sufficiently elaborate to allow large-scale movements of goods which were cheap enough for peasants to buy. The only exceptions were some small areas, such as around Córdoba, where Umayyad *amīr*s were already rich in the late eighth century, and artisanal activity in the Shaqunda suburb was already very great (see p. 395 above), or Rome, for long the largest city in Latin Europe, whose economic activity in the ninth century ranged from ambitious papally sponsored buildings to ceramic productions which were increasingly professionalized.[7] Around

[6] For a starting point, see Wickham, *Framing*, pp. 794–805; I did not in that section stress peasant demand to any significant extent, although the evidence for it was already clear. Theuws, 'Long-distance trade', provides a good critique of that, although he, conversely, underestimates (and even excludes) the structuring role of aristocratic demand before the Carolingians. For Mayen ware, see most recently Grunwald, 'Pottery production'; Grunwald, 'Die "Mayener Ware"'.

[7] For the buildings, see, among many, Goodson, *The Rome of Paschal I*, plus the analysis of Rome's material strengths and weaknesses in Meneghini and Santangeli Valenzani, *Roma nell'altomedioevo*; for other aspects of the economy, see Wickham, *Medieval Rome*, pp. 136–80, although this is focussed on the immediately succeeding period.

Córdoba, we cannot be sure how socially and geographically extended the demand base for local productions was (although it certainly did not yet extend so very far), but we know that it was geographically limited around Rome. Anyway, whether complex or simple, most exchange was highly localized in most parts of early medieval Europe, by contrast with (in particular) Egypt.

When early medieval elites were so weak as to be unable to dominate the peasant majority at all, I have elsewhere argued for a different mode of production entirely, which I called the 'peasant mode', in which material accumulation for most social groups was not a practical prospect. There is no need to characterize it in any detail here, for it was not a feature of any of the regions in this book; indeed, it was always rare south of the old Roman frontier across mainland Europe, and was almost everywhere on the retreat by 900 at the latest. That mode was not in itself incompatible with isolated foci of wealth, as with the major early medieval centre of Gudme in Denmark, but as soon as we begin to see more generalized patterns of exchange and production developing, as in eastern England after 700, for example, then it is likely that we are already dealing with societies in which peasants are by now becoming more subject to lords, and in which feudal relationships (in Marxist terms) become dominant, operating in ways we shall look at later in this chapter.[8] I, however, only raise the peasant mode here as a limiting case, for every economy analysed in this book can be characterized as feudal, whether elites were strong or weak. It was possible for elites in early medieval Europe to be so restricted in their power over the peasant majority that most forms of productive specialization, except for some luxuries, became impossible to sustain, and the logic of the economy itself shifted; that must be set against the fact that it was also possible for them to be sufficiently strong and wealthy that their demand could allow at least some production at scale to develop, as in the Frankish heartland. And in the middle, there were societies, as in Visigothic and emiral Spain and Portugal (up to a little before 950) and Lombard-Carolingian Italy (up to after 1000), in which landowning (and in al-Andalus tax-raising) elites and dependent peasants existed, and characterized the socio-economic patterns of the region as a whole, so these can certainly be described as feudal, but elite wealth was not yet great enough to allow a complex production and exchange system to develop. I described this pattern when discussing north-central Italy in Chapter 6, for it was here, out of our regions, that it lasted longest. When, around 1000, we begin to find more evidence of economic activity in the Po plain and western Tuscany, my reading of the situation is that it was then that Italy was simply coming to match the northern Francia of two centuries earlier in the

[8] Wickham, *Framing*, esp. pp. 535–50, with 368–76 for Gudme. It is necessary to stress that the peasant mode can never have characterized more than small portions of Francia, Italy, and the central-southern Iberian peninsula, for some writers have assumed the contrary. Recent work makes it clear that there was more exchange—and earlier—in seventh- and eighth-century eastern England than was visible 20 years ago; for an overview, see, e.g., Loveluck, *Northwest Europe*, pp. 77–91, 124–31.

capacity of elites to sustain at least some demand, and thus production, and thus commercialization (including, certainly, to some peasant buyers), on a slightly greater scale—but both in Francia earlier and in Italy for longer, no more than that. That is to say, Italy was still operating by early medieval rules, and these rules only began to change in the twelfth century, slowly and patchily.

This is where the contrast between early medieval economies before (say) 950/1000 and the more complex central medieval economies lies. For the regions we have been looking at in this book—including northern Italy by the end of our period—were quite different. We have seen how active urban economies could be in the Mediterranean by now, with complex productions involving, in many cases, elaborate divisions of labour, and geographically wide and overlapping distribution networks, involving, often, large-scale movements of bulk goods. Here, the demand of states, state officials, many-levelled landed elites, and towns allowed a step change in the economy, a take-off, after (all dates are approximate) 900 in Ifrīqiya, 950 in al-Andalus and Sicily, 1090 in Byzantium, and then 1150/80 in northern Italy. An exchange infrastructure came into being, which to an ever greater extent was not only, or even principally, fuelled by that elite demand, but was becoming regularly available to the peasant majority, whose potential demand was so much greater that productions substantially expanded to satisfy it. It was the increasing access that peasants could have to a far wider range of goods which allowed the striking complexities of the regional economies which we have looked at to develop and—eventually—themselves to begin to link together across the sea.

Outside the Mediterranean, the only European region which could match this level of development in our period was Flanders (including parts of what is now northern France, immediately to its south), which, therefore, deserves a short discussion. Here, the eleventh century (and sometimes already the tenth) saw a rapid expansion of a dozen towns, set fairly close together, which by 1100 or so were centres for the production of woollen cloth, plus metalwork and other goods; their spatial and demographic expansion must, here, itself be a proxy for the expansion of artisanal production. We actually know almost nothing about the organization and scale of production in any of them until well after our period, but other external signs of something substantial developing are clear as well: merchants' guild statutes in Valenciennes and Saint-Omer already in the eleventh century, for example. As to distribution, we have anecdotal evidence for wide-ranging sales of Flemish cloth already in the early twelfth century, from England to Novgorod and down (via the fairs of both Flanders itself and Champagne) to Genoa. The scale of such long-distance sales cannot be directly ascertained (the first quantitative evidence is actually the Genoese records of the 1190s, which, as we saw, show a fairly restricted role for Flemish/north French cloth); but closer to Flanders, in the Rhineland or England, they were, as far as we can tell, a substantial operation. Cloth was made in a wide variety of types and qualities. We have no direct data as yet concerning who was buying it, but given that variety, we can suppose that both elites and non-elites were both potential buyers, although elites could also, as elsewhere, have been buying cheaper cloth for their dependants. The peasantry of Flanders itself was more autonomous than were most other peasantries in what had been the Frankish heartland, from the Rhineland across to Paris, and they thus both gave less global surplus to lords and could (we can assume) benefit directly from the possibilities of selling food and raw wool to the towns; they were doubtless buyers of at least some of the cheaper cloth, leaving expensive woollens to elite buyers from the rest of north-west Europe and beyond. But cheaper cloth was sold more widely too, at least in the thirteenth century, by which time the market had built up.[9]

As we have just seen, the Frankish heartland was, by 600 at the latest, the European region with the widest-scale exchange links, as is shown by the distribution of Mayen pottery throughout the early middle ages. Those distribution patterns were continued by later ceramic types as well, often of higher quality; after 1000 the most prominent ones were Pingsdorf ware from just south of Cologne, which spread down the Rhine and along the Flemish coast, and Andenne ware from the Meuse valley, which extended along the Meuse in the eleventh century and throughout the Low Countries in the twelfth. They show that it was easy (thanks above all to the river systems) to take goods, presumably of any kind, across this whole region in every century of the post-Roman period, although, precisely because of that fact, they do not in themselves explain the Flemish take-off in the eleventh and twelfth centuries. But a focussed study by Koen De Groote of the ceramics of the area around Oudenaarde, a small urban centre south of the major Flemish town of Ghent, allows us to get further in characterizing what happened then. He shows that a step change happened there in the late eleventh and early twelfth centuries, when a dominance of Pingsdorf imports was steadily replaced by good-quality local imitations, an 'industrial' production, which developed new glazed types in the later twelfth century as well. Somewhere in the area (Oudenaarde itself?), a critical mass of local artisans had formed, ready to exploit a local demand which equally must have developed (probably both in Ghent and in the countryside). Although we are still in an early stage of our understanding of Flemish ceramics (De Groote's work has no systematic parallels), this would support a similar reading, that is to say, with a major place for local demand, of the Flemish take-off in cloth production too.[10]

[9] A good guide to all this is Verhulst, *The rise of cities in north-west Europe*, pp. 68–148; see further, e.g., the briefer surveys in van Bavel, *Manors and markets*, pp. 153–7, 343–5, and Laleman, 'Ghent'. For peasant autonomy, see, e.g., Thoen and Soens, 'The Low Countries, 1000–1750', pp. 223–30; for cheaper cloth, see Chorley, 'The cloth exports of Flanders and northern France'. But in Genoa such exports remained at the luxury end of the market in our period all the same; see Chapter 6, n. 202 above.

[10] See in turn n. 6 above, for Mayen ware; the surveys in Verhoeven, 'Ceramics and economics', and Loveluck and Tys, 'Coastal societies, exchange and identity'; Sanke, *Die mittelalterliche Keramikproduktion in Brühl-Pingsdorf* (discussing production, not distribution); Challe and de

What probably lay behind the take-off in Flanders was a set of analogous processes to those that we have seen operating in the Mediterranean, an increase in elite demand which allowed a complex productive system to develop, in woollen cloth above all, plus metalwork and ceramics, which was by the twelfth century large-scale enough and cheap enough to be become widely available to non-elites too. I would in general terms attribute this upturn in elite demand, which extended over much of north-west Europe, to the sharp increase in the number of military and castle-holding elite families, to add to older aristocracies who were already major landowners, and the equally sharp rise in seigneurial exactions as a result of the extension of the *seigneurie banale* across much of north-west Europe in (mostly) the eleventh century. Conversely, this 'feudal' or (better) 'seigneurial revolution' was then countered, in the twelfth century, by the extension across northern France and its immediate neighbours of village franchises, fought for (and often paid for) by peasants, which limited lordly powers over peasants and allowed peasants a greater margin of prosperity.[11] As just noted, in Flanders itself lordly power had not developed to the same extent, so peasant buyers were easier to find from the start; but outside Flanders, peasant demand began after 1100 or so to increase as well. This could be added to the elite wealth and demand across a very wide region, which was already fuelling the rapid development of cloth-working towns in Flanders and in Artois to its south, and thus the intensification of the commercial networks which had already stretched across northern Francia since the Carolingian period and before. Take-off at both levels, luxury cloth for elites and more ordinary woollens for peasants, plus their equivalents in other goods, then pushed the productive density of the Flemish towns to heights which had never previously been reached in northern Europe. This was probably a more generalized process than it seems to have been in north-central Italy in and after the twelfth century, where, as we have seen, landowning peasants were more numerous (see pp. 493–4 above), and lordly landed dominance was thus less complete than in much of north-west Europe. But north-central Italy, even if more slowly, came to match Flanders in its economic activity, as it also came

Longueville, 'La céramique médiévale d'Andenelle' (a recent overview of Andenne ware); De Groote, *Middeleeuws aardewerk in Vlaanderen*, esp. pp. 397–402, 412–15, 438–40; Ghent was certainly a buyer of the ceramics described there by the second half of the twelfth century (see ibid., p. 416). For rural demand for Pingsdorf pottery, see, e.g., ibid., p. 324–5, 414 for Moorsel (cf. ibid., p. 346 for Andenne ware), and, more generally, Loveluck and Tys, 'Coastal societies, exchange and identity', p. 159. A large kiln site at Beernem near Bruges shows parallel imitations of Pingsdorf wares, probably in this case for the Bruges market; see Baeyens et al., *Archeologisch onderzoek Alveringem-Maldegem Lot 3*, pp. 391–4, 400–3, 452–60, a reference I owe to Koen De Groote.

[11] For a wider framing for this, see Feller, *Richesse, terre et valeur*. A detailed description of many different seigneurial regimes can be found in Fossier, *Enfance de l'Europe*, pp. 288–601. The 'seigneurial revolution' has been sharply debated, with some denying that it occurred at all; for surveys, all with their own points of view, see Lauranson-Rosaz, 'Le débat sur la mutation féodale'; MacLean, 'Apocalypse and revolution: Europe around the year 1000'; Barthélemy, *The serf, the knight and the historian*, pp. 1–11, 302–13; West, *Reframing the feudal revolution*, pp. 1–9, 255–63. For franchises, see Fossier, 'Les communautés villageoises' and Fossier, *Chartes de coutume*, pp. 25–123; Wickham, *Community and clientele*, pp. 192–231; Bourin and Martínez Sopena, *Pour une anthropologie du prélèvement*, 2, pp. 161–309.

to match the other Mediterranean regions as well, as we have seen in detail in Chapter 6.

The main particularity of the Flemish case is that take-off there was linked, strikingly and interestingly, to a very long-distance luxury and semi-luxury exchange projection across the Rhine river basin, the North Sea, and, soon, even the Baltic. The reason is that Flanders had become, by the late eleventh century, almost unparalleled in the intensity of its productive activity in the whole of northern Europe, and therefore the elites of a very wide range of neighbouring regions wished to buy its goods. (It may perhaps have been matched by economic developments in the neighbouring hinterland of Paris, which was expanding very fast in the twelfth century and later, but the economic development of that region has not been well studied, as was remarked in Chapter 1.) It could extend outwards geographically, very far, above all in the framework of elite demand (non-elite demand remained more regionalized), because for a long time it had no competitors. This is a pattern we have not seen in our own case studies, for the Mediterranean had a larger set of equally economically active regions, whose productions could satisfy most internal needs. It alerts us against putting Flanders and northern Italy into exactly the same explanatory framework, as is done routinely by European historians who are less informed about the economies of the Mediterranean world as a whole. The Flemish example remains, all the same, essentially an extension to the patterns which we have explored in more detail in the rest of this book, even more economically separate from the Mediterranean regions than was al-Andalus, at least in our period. So this is as far as we need go in looking for comparisons for our case studies. What we must now do is look further at how to characterize and explain them.

* * *

Economies have not had the same internal structure across human history. Some of the simplest elements of economics are, of course, found pretty much everywhere, such as the relationship in commercial transactions between supply, demand, and price, as noted at the end of Chapter 1. But there are fundamental differences between, in particular, economic systems that are based above all on the taking of surplus in products, services, or money from peasants and those that are based above all on paying wages or salaries to workers. There are other such systems too, but these two have been the most widespread in recorded history. The first of the two, what Marx called the feudal mode of production, was the most widespread and longest lasting of all; capitalism, the second, has only had a couple of centuries of existence as a dominant mode. But it is capitalism whose internal logic and whose patterns of development and change have been by far the most fully studied, from Marx himself onwards.[12]

[12] This paragraph and the next 10 pages include revised and shortened versions of text first published in Wickham, 'How did the feudal economy work?'. I defend there the use of the word 'feudal' to

These are not particularly controversial statements; all the same, an unevenness in analytical focus has too often meant that the underlying rules of capitalist economics are taken, implicitly or explicitly, to be valid across all time and space. Even the new wave of economic histories of the pre-industrial period outside Europe, which aim to show—and in my view do show—that parts of China and India were as economically complex as the most 'advanced' parts of Europe, up to and into the eighteenth century, do not spend any pages on establishing alternative logics for the economies they are studying.[13] The most systematic challenge to this, of course, comes from Marxism itself, which takes it as axiomatic that capitalist rules are contingent, and can in the future be superseded; but this has remained a challenge on the level of economic and political theory, as actual empirical examples of post-capitalist economies have been hard to establish on any long-term basis so far. The most sustained empirical challenge has, in fact, come from substantivist anthropology, which has identified and theorized the economic practices of relatively egalitarian societies across the globe, dramatically divergent as they generally are from any capitalist logic; but in practice this work has been mostly restricted to societies without classes, and it scales up less well once issues of political and economic dominance come in.[14] So I want in the final section of this book to try to get beyond that, by offering an at least partial analysis of the internal economic dynamic of the feudal mode of production, using the evidence we have already looked at, but drawing in other data as necessary, during the central middle ages and up to the Black Death, although these basic patterns lasted in most regions for several centuries after that too. I will discuss the issue in a very general way first, before coming back to the specific problems offered by our regional case studies.

Marx wrote about this sometimes, of course, above all in his *Formen*, 'Forms which precede capitalist production' in its full title. The problematic posed by Marx in this context is a point of reference for me here—but only his problematic, not his actual conclusions. Marx was writing unpublished notes to himself in this text, not any kind of full discussion; and as Eric Hobsbawm remarked in the

describe the economies of large sections of the globe; an alternative terminology is the 'tributary mode', and, using that terminology, the best discussion of the mode across the world remains Haldon, *The state and the tributary mode of production*. Both 'feudalism' and 'capitalism' will refer from here on to the modes of production as first characterized by Marx, although, as we shall see, I would modify what Marx said about feudal economies. I would add, as we shall also see, that there could well be capitalist elements in feudal economies, including in the regional economies discussed in this book. My aim is, nonetheless, also to be empirically and theoretically convincing to readers who do not use these categories.

[13] See, e.g., Pomeranz, *The great divergence*; Rosenthal and Wong, *Before and beyond divergence*; Parthasarathi, *Why Europe grew rich and Asia did not*; Wong, 'China before capitalism'.

[14] Classics include Godelier, *Rationality and irrationality in economics*, pp. 243–319; Sahlins, *Stone Age economics*. The original substantivist theorist, Karl Polanyi, certainly thought that his categorizations were valid for class societies (see esp. Polanyi et al., *Trade and market in the early empires*); but for me his empirical applications wear considerably less well than his underlying approach.

introduction to Jack Cohen's translation of the text, neither here nor anywhere else did he spend any time discussing the internal dynamic of feudalism—in other words, its economic logic (Marx might have preferred, as with his analyses of capitalism, its 'laws of motion').[15] Plenty of people have tried to guess what Marx would have said, had he actually done this. This is effort wasted; no one working in the 1850s and 1860s knew enough about feudal societies to be able to make any kind of systematic analysis of their underlying economic logic. Probably, I regret to say, this is still true today. In the medieval period, the list of what we do not know about fundamental elements of the economy (or economies) is at least as long as the list of what we know with relative certainty. But we do have a lot more data, and sometimes, in well-studied regions, we have quite a detailed understanding of economic patterns in different medieval centuries; as a result, we can get closer to an analysis of what was going on economically in the period. So we need to confront the issue more explicitly; for to establish a model of feudal economics which can be set against the standard assumptions of capitalist economics is fundamental to any real understanding of how the economies discussed in this book actually operated.

All of this obviously poses the question of what feudalism is, for the word is here being used in a way that evidently extends well beyond medieval western Europe, its traditional location. Here, as stated already, I am using it in its economic sense as a mode of production, derived again from Marx and his contemporaries, but generalizing out from them: in its ideal-type form, it is a socio-economic system based on the exploitative relations of production between peasants, that is to say, subsistence cultivators, and landlords and/or states (I will call both 'lords' in the sketch of the feudal mode that follows). At its core are peasant family units, who work the land and raise animals, usually do some subsistence artisanal work such as weaving, and also, in regions where they are available, mine metals. I here, I need to add, treat the peasant family as a unit, so do not discuss gender; inside the family, work was usually highly gendered—men ploughing and women spinning and weaving was a rhetorical cliché in texts from France to China, and, outside the peasantry, we have seen female spinners and weavers in towns all across the Mediterranean in previous chapters—but that is not my focus here.[16]

[15] Marx, *Pre-capitalist economic formations*, trans. Cohen; see ibid., pp. 41–3 for Hobsbawm's summary of Marx on feudalism, and 62–4 for global feudalism. This book still has to be read for Hobsbawm's introduction, but as a translation it has been superseded by Marx, *Grundrisse*, trans. Nicolaus, pp. 471–514. One of the best descriptions of the feudal mode, Kuchenbuch and Michael, 'Zur Struktur und Dynamik der "feudalen" Produktionsweise im vorindustriallen Europa', does not actually, despite its title, tell us much about its dynamic; see pp. 253–60 of the reprint in Kuchenbuch, *Marx, feudal*, which, however, in its other articles develops the feudal problematic in interesting ways; see, e.g., n. 24 below.

[16] I stress here feudal relations of production; I do not see the other part of the Marxist dyad, technology and productive knowledge (the 'productive forces'), as determinant here. See Wickham, 'Productive forces'. Actually, however, medieval agrarian technology has often been underrated, as we have seen several times in preceding chapters, for example when discussing irrigation in Spain,

Peasants were the vast majority of the inhabitants of the world in any period between the Neolithic and the twentieth century. They controlled and, where peasantries continue to exist, still control the production process, what was actually produced on the land. Not all of them had lords in any period, but in feudal societies most of them did. The main relationship of dominance and system of surplus expropriation here consists of peasants giving surplus, in rent, tax, and services, to lords, in various forms, under the at least implicit threat of violence.[17] The surplus which lords take thus depends on actual or potential class struggle, and is not based directly on the market. Lords can affect the production process by demanding different types of rent or tax, and they frequently do. But they do not have a structural role in production, and their attempts to exercise forms of direct control over it, although these are certainly documented (indeed, quite well documented, as our records tend to be the work of lords), have seldom lasted all that long. They are thus not only external as exploiters, but also very visibly so for the most part—unlike under capitalism, when capitalists dominate the labour process directly, and the exploitation involved is often hidden by the apparently free nature of the wage labour contract. Such external powers can be landlords, extracting rent, or states and other political powers, exacting tax or tribute, or both. In the medieval period, both rent and tax could be in labour, on the lord's directly cultivated land (his demesne) or on public roads, fortifications, or dykes; they could be in produce (the default pattern in all societies); only if exchange was sufficiently developed would they be in money, for peasants would have to be able to sell produce systematically to get the coins to pay money tax/rent.[18] Exchange could, indeed, be highly developed, and peasants could produce substantially for the market, but they had to be sure of their subsistence needs first. Pure cash-cropping, where peasants produce only for sale, and have to buy food in, was almost unknown under feudalism, and, indeed, was rare until the twentieth century even under capitalism; we have only seen even the possibility of it once, on p. 103 above, in Egypt. (Partial cash-cropping was, by contrast, frequent, when markets made it advantageous—for supplying towns with food, in particular—but that was in addition to subsistence needs, not replacing them.) These are patterns that can be found very widely in the history of Eurasia, from well before the Roman Empire up to the present, and extending to much of sub-Saharan Africa and the Americas, although neither of these had many landlords in the strict sense before the Europeans arrived.

pp. 447–8 above. For gender stereotypes, see, e.g., Odo of Cluny, *Vita S. Geraldi Auriliacensis*, ed. Bultot-Verleysen, 1.21; Li, *Agricultural development in Jiangnan, 1620–1850*, p. 143.

[17] Actual violence during rent-taking is less well documented; rent was relatively routinized, and if customary, relatively accepted by peasants. (Tax-taking had much more of a violent aspect in many societies, precisely because it was less accepted.) But it was there as a threat all the same, and the potential for lordly violence was in general very visible, if only because it was used frequently (and often at peasants' expense) in conflicts with other lords.

[18] Cf. also Marx, *Das Kapital*, 3, ch. 47, on forms of pre-capitalist rent.

This is why I have never had any difficulty seeing feudalism as a world system. In AD 100, say, the core of the system was the same from Roman Gaul to Han China, and so it was throughout most of post-Roman and post-Han history. The 'serfdom and labour service' version of this, well known to western medievalists, and thought by many of these historians (as also by Marx) to be *the* feudal economy, was only one variant of the system. And indeed, it had plenty of variants, even in the central middle ages. Tax could be taken directly by states, in money or kind, or else farmed out to intermediaries; tax could be taken together with rent or in entirely separate processes; and it was sometimes impossible to distinguish between the two forms of extraction. Landed estates could have rent-paying tenants, forced slave labour, and wage labour all at once, or move between them; although wage labour is quintessentially part of capitalism as a system, it had plenty of antecedents in feudal economies, certainly in artisanal production in towns, but also in rural society as well, as a minority form of exploitation. The ways rent and tax were presented and justified varied greatly as well. Lords, being so visible as exploiters, needed to justify their claimed rights to take surplus; they risked resistance if they did not, and, even though they had a superiority in weaponry, they were hugely outnumbered by peasants. Some of that justification was in terms of property rights, as, even though peasants possessed the land, they did not always—not usually—have full rights over it. Some derived from claims that a proportion of peasants had an intrinsically subject status, so, as unfree people, were subject to direct control on the part of lords, who extracted 'servile' burdens, which in practice were simply heavier rents, services, and other dues. Related to that, at least in the specific case of western Europe, were the similar seigneurial/signorial dues demanded by many lords as local political powers, justified by claims of lordly protection and local justice, as we have seen for Italy (pp. 496–9); these were sometimes devolved public rights, with lords taking on the local role of the state, but they were also often in competition with the taxation or tribute-taking of rulers. Tax and tribute, widely across Eurasia, were taken by kings, emperors, caliphs, or *amīr*s—or, sometimes, a local city state—as a form of super-lord, deriving from their own political rights of command and dominance, in return, once again, for protection and justice, as we have seen very widely across our regions. In Latin Europe, we can add churches, which developed their own quasi-taxation—tithe—on top of their landowning, to finance their activities.[19] Some unfortunate peasant groups owed dues of all of these kinds at once.

Each of these forms of surplus extraction varied very greatly in scale; taxation could be the main form of surplus extraction, or else hardly visible when compared with rent. It is also important to recognize that, of all of them, taxation, when organized efficiently, could be far and away the most remunerative (even

[19] For tithe, see, e.g., Lauwers, *La dîme, l'église et la société féodale*.

when not the heaviest), and that states based on an effective system of taxation had a wholly different political structure, and far greater stability and power, than the kingdoms or lordships of any king or local lord whose wealth principally derived from the rents from landowning. That was an explicit feature of many of the chapters here, not least Chapter 6, for taxation was absent in north-central Italy until the very end of our period, and the state was always weaker there as a result. Here, however, it is simply necessary to stress that all of these separate institutional forms, each of which had its own history and patterns of development, had in one respect the same essence and purpose, that is to say, to justify taking away agricultural and other surplus from peasants, who could see very well that it had been created by themselves. Peasants were sometimes convinced; interestingly, to judge by what they revolted against (which they did more frequently than historians sometimes claim, at least in some periods and regions), they were convinced most often by landowners' claims to property rights, least often by justifications for taxation and unfreedom, with seigneurial rights in the middle.[20] But peasants were at least quasi-convinced, above all if dues were sanctioned and—crucially—stabilized by custom, which meant that they knew where they were and could make their own forward calculations. Rent and tax were thus just separate institutional forms, and also separate ideological forms, of the same relationship of surplus extraction: peasants having to give their products to lords, with the implicit threat of force. This is what historians like Rodney Hilton meant when they said that the basic feudal 'prime mover' was class struggle over, precisely, these rents, dues, and taxes.[21]

This much is clear, then; but what is rather less clear is how, exactly, the 'struggle for rent' actually did underpin the rest of the economy, including the commercial economy, and its internal logic. Traditional European medieval economic history, both Marxist and non-Marxist, was for a long time unhelpful here. It worked into the 1970s on the general assumption that lords took all disposable surplus from peasants, leaving them little extra to do anything else with—except insofar as peasants had to have access to markets by the twelfth century in much of Europe, for the simple reason that they increasingly had to pay rents in money, which they could not have got hold of any other way. (Analyses of taxation in the Islamic lands would probably have concluded much the same, but the systematic work to do so was seldom done.) As the peasants of Cliviano in the central Italian Appennines said just before 1100, *seniores tollunt omnia:* 'Lords take everything.'[22]

[20] See Firnhaber-Baker and Schoenars, *The Routledge history handbook of medieval revolt*, for recent work; see Cohn, *Lust for liberty*, for the frequency of European peasant revolts after the Black Death (they were less frequent in our period, by contrast).

[21] For the class struggle over rent, a classic formulation is Hilton, 'A comment'; see also, more recently, Haldon, 'Theories of practice'.

[22] See as opposite ends of the arguments, but agreeing on this, Postan, 'Medieval agrarian society in its prime: England', esp. pp. 602–4; Brenner, 'Agrarian class structure', pp. 33–4; Brenner, 'The agrarian roots', pp. 227, 236, 241, 274; Brenner, 'The Low Countries', pp. 176–7, 181, 193. See also Meiksins

So any demand for commodities which could develop into a complex and dynamic exchange sector, such as that of twelfth-century Flanders or thirteenth-century Italy, would have to come from lords. This is, broadly, wrong. Of course, it could sometimes be true; there were plenty of highly oppressive agrarian regimes; and even when there were not, elite demand could often determine the scale of exchange itself, as in most of the European early middle ages, as we have just seen. But I have argued throughout this book that in many environments peasants routinely had disposable surpluses—or at least the richer among them did, and at least in years when crops were good enough—which they marketized wherever there were markets to allow them to do so. In the present century, commercialization theory has had a considerable impact on the later medieval economic history of England, in particular, even though England was far from the most complex economy in this period. Rents in the thirteenth century were much lower than they could have been, giving many peasants considerable flexibility when they decided what to do with surpluses; peasant life cycles allowed for a substantial availability of wage labour, not least among newly adult sons and daughters who had not yet inherited farms and married; and there were hundreds of small rural markets, growing in number in every century but with a sharp upward curve in the thirteenth, in which peasants routinely not only sold produce for money to pay in rent, but also bought artisanal goods, ironwork, and, increasingly, cloth. This English picture, showing a considerable peasant participation in the market by the thirteenth century, fits well that of the rather more developed economies of the tenth- to twelfth-century Mediterranean discussed in previous chapters.[23] The complexities of their high-functioning economies are our best guide to what the logic of the system was.

This brings us to some of the elements of that logic. What is most important here is the longer-term structural dynamic of feudal relations of production. Lords were external to the process of production for the most part, as we have seen. The 'struggle for rent' was, however, usually relatively peaceful because it was structured by custom. This was not immutable, but lords did not always have the resources on the ground necessary to tighten it effectively as the economy changed, or, in some cases, as Christopher Dyer has shown for England, even to police it very

Wood, *The origin of capitalism*, pp. 73–94, a more general version of the same argument. For the quotation, see Giorgi and Balzani, *Il Regesto di Farfa*, n. 1303; this much-cited text is best characterized in Fiore, *The seigneurial transformation*, p. 55.

[23] For all this, see Campbell, 'The agrarian problem in the early fourteenth century'; Dyer, *An age of transition?*, esp. pp. 211–32; Whittle, *The development of agrarian capitalism*, pp. 225–304; Britnell, *The commercialisation of English society*, with the maps in Britnell, *Britain and Ireland*, pp. 162–5; Dyer, *Peasants making history*, pp. 250–62; Dyer, 'Pourquoi les paysans anglais étaient-ils consommateurs', which summarizes recent work. See further, for an England–Germany comparison, Ghosh, 'Rural economies'; p. 278 for mass demand outweighing elite demand in both countries in the sixteenth century; and Petrowiste, 'Le paysan des époques médiévale et moderne est-il un consommateur comme les autres?', for a good guide to the overall problematic.

effectively. Both of these gave a tactical advantage to the peasantry, who were there on the ground, as lords were for the most part not. This, for me, is the key point. As a result—it is a point Guy Bois made particularly clearly in his work on late medieval Normandy—in periods of economic expansion, with the clearance of new land and maybe better yields, plus often (in the case of money rents and taxes) slow inflation, the package of rents and taxes, stabilized by custom, tended steadily to fall in real terms. This, when the economy was expanding, still produced more for landlords and states, but also gave peasants (particularly richer peasants) more surplus to buy things with, or to become small entrepreneurs on their own account; and it did not change back again as fast if and when the economy contracted.[24] Underpayments and non-payments, and the hiding of crops, were also easier to achieve, given that peasants were the primary producers, and knew best what they had produced and where it was. That is to say, other things being equal, there was a general trend towards lower rents and taxes, with the balance tending to favour the peasantry.

Of course, lords could break custom, and increase total surplus extraction by force. This is what happened when newly powerful local lords in France, and then Italy and northern Spain, around 1000 or later, imposed by violence seigneurial levies on woodland, mills, justice and so on, plus outright random payments in some cases, in the 'seigneurial revolution', already discussed. States increased taxation often enough as well; this could happen when new regimes came in, even if sometimes, particularly in the Islamic world, new rulers initially cut taxes to show their greater religious legitimacy, until military and political needs caused them to raise them again (see p. 390 above for al-Andalus). There were many other examples too, of course. But, however numerous, they were all one-offs; and they took a lot of work. As economists would say, such increases were sticky. The rest of the time, lords were not there on the ground, and peasants were; they could more easily erode the proportion of the mostly customary rents and taxes they owed, as the economic environment changed. And class struggle could work in the other direction as well, as when, as also mentioned earlier, peasants in France, Italy, and Spain managed in a long twelfth century to stabilize the arbitrary aspects of seigneurial levies through village franchises, and to turn them into standardized, usually cash payments, which then again steadily lessened as a proportion of total surplus. The same thing happened later, after the Black Death, when a scarcity of people to do the work led to peasant rents and dues dropping markedly in many places, and a more targeted peasant resistance also led to the fading away of the last elements of serfdom, in much of western Europe at least.[25]

[24] Dyer, 'The ineffectiveness of lordship in England, 1200–1400'; Bois, *The crisis of feudalism*, esp. pp. 384–408, with the data at 218–37. Bois's argument survives the criticisms by Robert Brenner in 'The agrarian roots', pp. 231–2, 242–6. It is usefully developed in Kuchenbuch, *Marx, feudal*, pp. 257–60, 275–89, 309–12.

[25] For this resistance, Brenner, 'Agrarian class structure' still stands as a comparative survey.

It is because of this tactical advantage that peasants often had greater disposable surplus in the central middle ages than historians used to think, in good years at least, and in peacetime.

Since feudal relations of production above all channelled surplus to lords, it is not surprising that most commerce was structured by lordly, elite demand *first*. Indeed, as we saw earlier, in the early middle ages in Latin Europe the differing intensity of exchange was almost a direct proxy for differing levels of aristocratic domination. In the Islamic states and Byzantium, this was less of an issue, for states always taxed. Although in the eighth and ninth centuries in Byzantium and al-Andalus, when local societies seem often to have been very simple, the state did not manage to integrate the economy in all respects, in our period the coherence of the state was matched by local demand as well, as we have seen. In Latin Europe too, in regions affected by the 'seigneurial revolution', lordly dominance over essentially all social groups then fully established itself, and from now onwards commerce steadily developed everywhere there as well; but it is also from here on that the ways peasants could use their tactical advantage are most visible, which allowed for local demand to increase as well.

This means that we have a balance. In the period and regions covered by this book, given the dominance of states and landlords, urban and rural economies developed substantially everywhere, to match their demand above all. But conversely, it was also from now onwards that the customary nature and thus the slowly decreasing level of exactions began steadily to favour peasants and peasant buying power too; and increasingly, urban production had a peasant element to its demand base, as we have amply seen. The tenth to thirteenth centuries saw a rapid expansion in demography, agriculture, and urban artisanal activity in most of the Mediterranean world. Nor was that expansion in production reversed later, except in extreme cases such as post-Black Death Egypt.[26] There continued, from now on, to be considerable levels of production, marketization, regional specialization, and international exchange, with some serious regional highs, as in al-Andalus or Egypt or, later, northern Italy. And the context in which this occurred was that of the economic logic of feudalism, based on the fact that the peasant majority was necessary to the basic production process, and lords and states were not; this continued steadily to bring down rents and taxes, except when lords and states put the effort into increasing them, as in the examples we have just seen,

[26] See pp. 126–7 above for Egypt. The possible period of the Malthusian trap of overpopulation after *c.*1290 has had increasing criticism, and was, anyway, insofar as it occurred, dramatically inverted with the mortality of the Black Death in other parts of the Mediterranean (and northern Europe too). For southern Europe, see now esp. Bourin et al., *Dynamiques du monde rural dans la conjuncture de 1300*, with an important critical survey of the English-language debate by the editors in the introduction, pp. 9–101; Grillo and Menant, *La congiuntura del primo Trecento in Lombardia*; Carocci, 'La "crisi del Trecento" e le recenti teorie economiche', equally critical of much recent economic-history modelling, such as NIE theory, which I concur with—although I would except, as he does, some of the more subtle NIE theorists, such as Stephan Epstein and Sheilagh Ogilvie.

which meant that peasants tended to be able to participate in this commercialized world as well—and when they did, a mass market became increasingly possible.

So a general tendency of the economic logic of feudalism was to establish, eventually, reasonably high-functioning production and exchange systems, which could often show considerable dynamism. There were many across time and place in Eurasia; apart from those focussed on in this book, they included different parts of the Roman Empire in the first to sixth centuries, Iraq in the ninth, the Yangzi valley in the eleventh to thirteenth (many people would extend these Chinese dates into the eighteenth), Flanders in the twelfth to fifteenth, north-central Italy in the thirteenth to sixteenth, south Germany in the fifteenth to seventeenth, Bengal and south India in the sixteenth to eighteenth, and Holland and England also in the sixteenth to eighteenth—all these dates are approximate and often contested at the margins—and there were others too.[27] What would happen after that, given that, as is well known, most of these did not transform themselves into an economy dominated by capitalist relations of production? Essentially, there were two directions. One was for elites to intervene by force, to raise rents and taxes, cut peasants out of the exchange system, and take rural profit for themselves. This was, as I have said, a lot of work, but it certainly could happen; images of grinding poverty are hardly uncommon in the historiography of the medieval countryside, as earlier and later too, and some are accurate.[28] In parts of Eurasia where this did not happen, however, what we see instead is the continued role of exchange for a rent- and tax-paying peasantry, which maintained, with ups and downs, reasonable access to surpluses and to buying at markets—at least for the more prosperous peasant strata—which could lead to considerable levels of commercialization, as we have seen. But what this also means is that there was no systemic trend to the impoverishment of the peasantry, its structural weakening, and, eventually, its loss of control over the land. This also means that there was no systemic trend away from the fact that peasants did not, in a strict sense, need to buy most goods in order to subsist, because they could grow their own food and indeed frequently made their own clothes too, from their own wool, cotton, or flax. This was a world which could include richer peasants growing for surplus even if they were rent- and taxpayers, poorer peasants often kept alive and on the land by part-time artisanal work, extending sometimes to proto-industry, and wage labourers for the most part englobed in the long-standing rhythms of peasant production, possessing small plots of land at least, even if not enough to live on, and/or absorbed into family economies as farm servants. This could continue for very long periods

[27] For an insightful global survey of these economies and others, see Findlay and O'Rourke, *Power and Plenty*.

[28] For one good discussion, see Duby, *Rural economy*, pp. 237–86, focussed on the complexities of lordly resource extraction in thirteenth-century France, even though rents were, here too, steadily being eroded.

without changes in the basic agrarian structures of the countryside. There is, indeed, an at least implicit tendency in much recent work to stress the persistence of what I would call a feudal logic for the economy until after 1700, everywhere in Eurasia, including in England, where it is generally supposed to have broken down first.[29] And it makes sense that it should, given that high levels of commercialization did not in themselves undermine that logic.

There are two key elements here, both of which fortified that persistence. First, exchange in this system had a double limit, in that elite demand, the fundamental initial motor for exchange, and capable of considerable growth, was always restricted by the fact that elites were a small minority; and, conversely, that peasant demand was, given that the peasantry's subsistence base was essentially separate from market exchange, finite. We have seen this most explicitly for Byzantium, but it will have been true, as a general rule, for all our regions.[30] The steady trend towards ever greater levels of exchange was, in a feudal economy, not endless, and eventually reached an equilibrium, even though often at a high level, simply because of that limit. Secondly, the more solid peasant demand and thus commercialization were, under normal circumstances, the less likely it would be that most peasants would be forced off their holdings for economic reasons, and potentially proletarianized—that is to say, compelled to work as wage labourers in agriculture or other work, removed from their subsistence base. Lords can, of course, coerce peasants to leave their holdings in some circumstances, or limit peasant economic resources coercively, as with enclosure movements, but these are complex and difficult actions to achieve, and again need a lot of targeted work; normally too, this does not lead to the proletarianization of the peasantry, but, rather, to peasants being forced into new tenures on worse terms. Even in England, proletarianization was mostly a development of the eighteenth century above all, long after the period we are looking at; elsewhere, it did not usually take place before 1850 at the earliest.[31] This is precisely because of that commercial solidity for peasants and lords alike. But conversely, if commercialization slipped back, as it also regularly did, weakening (though seldom entirely cancelling) the dynamism of a given region—as could well happen if taxation or rents rose so far that peasants were cut out of the market, or if lordly demand fell at times of political difficulty, or if there were too many transaction costs attached to trading, or if too much competition from other regions pushed the system out of gear—the result would not be proletarianization either, but simply a return to higher levels

[29] As, for example, in the (otherwise quite different) work of Allen, *Enclosure and the yeoman*, Ogilvie, *State corporatism and proto-industry*, and Ghosh, 'Rural economies', all of them important contributions, plus, implicitly, the work on China cited in n. 13 above.

[30] For Byzantium, see pp. 352–3 above for limits to growth.

[31] See, e.g., Allen, *Enclosure and the yeoman*, pp. 13–21, 204–10, 288–90. For peasants not always being expropriated and forced off the land, see, e.g., Schofield, 'Alternatives to expropriation'; Schofield, 'Impediments to expropriation'; Furió, 'Rents instead of land'.

of peasant production for subsistence.[32] Either direction, that is to say, under normal circumstances would further, rather than undermine, the solidity of a feudal economic system and its resistance to change.

It is for these reasons that a feudal logic for the economy, even in situations of high levels of commercialization, did not ever lead automatically to any other economic mode. And this argument sets my own approach apart from most other Marxist analyses of the economy of our period, for nearly all of them have, either at the front or the back of their minds, the problematic of the transition to capitalism (so have non-Marxist analyses, for that matter, which have, however, been less focussed on the issues which interest me here). This does not need to be my concern, as this book ends well before such a transition could be imagined—and in 1180, had anyone imagined it, northern England would have been one of the last places that anyone would have thought to look for it. But it is not simply an issue of a different periodization; discussions of medieval Eurasia as a whole, even for the period of this book, have regularly been distorted by this concern with what *might* have happened next, and why. So I need briefly to set out my differences from other analysts writing in the same tradition. I have already acknowledged my debt to Guy Bois's theorization of the general tendency for levies from the peasantry to fall, as part of my own economic models. He, at least, as an expert on France, was less driven than many by the teleologies of the transition debate. But I do not follow him in his criticisms of Robert Brenner, whose focus on class struggle as one of the principal motors of economic change after the Black Death seemed too voluntarist for Bois, but seems simply part of the logic of the feudal mode of production to me, as it did to Brenner, and also to Rodney Hilton. Brenner was called a 'political Marxist' by Bois for that, and this phrase has become a term of abuse for some, particularly those theorists who see Brenner's focus on regional development as insufficiently internationally minded (a criticism which seems to me incoherent), and his sharp distinction between feudalism and capitalism as too sharp.[33] Brenner sees that distinction as centring on how coercion works: as extra-economic in the case of pre-capitalist relations, as intrinsic to the labour process in the case of capitalism. As should be apparent from the foregoing, I wholly agree with this. Brenner, however, is not so useful to me as a

[32] See, e.g., Epstein, *Freedom and growth*, pp. 49–88, 127–42, for some of these constraints; see Ghosh, 'Rural economies', for an effective account of the way high-equilibrium systems did not necessarily change into anything else. Van Bavel, *The invisible hand?*, esp. pp. 1–38, 251–87, also stresses that factor markets, as they develop—and often push already complex economies along—tend to operate as a constraint later, creating a cycle which tends to lead to economic involution. This is a powerful additional argument in some cases, even if it is not clear that it is a universal one.

[33] Bois, 'Against the neo-Malthusian orthodoxy', an article which has aged; it now reads as largely rhetorical. Among wholly theory-based critiques of Brenner, whose seminal article for me remains 'Agrarian class structure', see, e.g., Anievas and Nişancıoğlu, *How the West came to rule*, pp. 22–32; Rioulx, 'The fiction of economic coercion'—critiques which left me more sympathetic to the positions criticized than I had been before.

historical model, for he has been very reluctant to recognize that feudal economies are capable of sustained growth, which he would presumably extend to the regions discussed in this book. This has led him to look for capitalist economic relations in rural England rather earlier than the evidence as presented by him seems to merit; his supporter who has done the most actual empirical work (rather than theorizing), Spencer Dimmock, does so too. Agrarian capitalism, for both, was well under way in England by the mid-sixteenth century.[34]

I do not have the expertise to disagree with this on the basis of my own empirical analyses;[35] but the need to look for a dominance of capitalist relations of agrarian production as early as that seems to me unnecessary. The feudal mode allowed a highly active commercial economy in too many regions, including those discussed in this book, without any move to capitalism to be even remotely on the cards in most; nor, given the limits to feudal economic development just discussed, should we expect it. I am resistant to the idea that the special role of England in the Industrial Revolution requires us to backdate that special role into periods when many other economies looked pretty similar.[36] (It is, again, of course, true that that search for the special nature of England, or sometimes England and Holland, has by no means been restricted to Marxists; their singular development has been widely discussed in the last generation, although the grounds claimed for that are, to me, often even more problematic.[37]) But focussing on single regional economies as the basis for an analysis of the transition to capitalism is undoubtedly a better procedure than the invocation of global economic interrelationships as a major cause of that transition, which characterized Immanuel Wallerstein's world systems theory in the 1970s, and which now characterizes that of many theorists keen to avoid Eurocentrism. This keenness is laudable, but the result is that international exchange relations are invested with the sort of explanatory power which this whole book seeks to demolish.[38]

[34] Brenner, 'Agrarian class structure', pp. 46–54; Brenner, 'The agrarian roots', pp. 296–311 (more explicit on dating); Dimmock, *The origin of capitalism*, which contains a long defence of Brenner against every published criticism (though he recognizes some feudal dynamism, e.g. at pp. 58, 163–4).

[35] But I am more convinced by the conclusions of Whittle, *The development of agrarian capitalism*, pp. 15–26, 252–75, 305–15, who puts the development of agrarian capitalist relations of production rather later; cf. Dyer, *An age of transition?*, pp. 40–5, who is very cautious about any early date for a capitalist transition.

[36] For one instance, late medieval and early modern Castile, which by no means moved in the end towards capitalism, see the interesting study of Astarita, *From feudalism to capitalism*, pp. 138–66, 193–222.

[37] Wickham, 'How did the feudal economy work?', p. 16, criticizes that part of the extensive historiography which focusses on comparative wage figures.

[38] Wallerstein, *The modern world-system*, 1; compare, more recently, Anievas and Nişancıoğlu, *How the West came to rule*, alternately highly stimulating and unconvincing. (Other world-historical interpretations, of which there have been several recently, are even less plausible; for criticisms of some of them, see Palombo, 'Studying trade and local economies'.) The resources brought by colonial economic exploitation, invoked by Kenneth Pomeranz in *The great divergence*, among others, are for me more convincing as partial explanations, but Pomeranz is not interested in the social relations of production, which are for me (as for Brenner) the necessary centre of analysis.

I reiterate that medieval (and most post-medieval) economies were never sufficiently dependent on international trade for this to be a helpful starting point for analysis.

Conversely, it is easy to find capitalist relations in the medieval urban world, including before the Black Death. We have here seen them often in mercantile investment, in Egypt and the Italian port cities, and they doubtless existed elsewhere too. Although direct capitalist investment in artisan production is harder to pin down, both because we do not have the right evidence and because single artisan workshops did not actually need much investment, it is far from an inconceivable process either. Jairus Banaji has insisted on this, and rightly.[39] But capitalist investment had the same limits in scale as did the feudal mode itself, in a period in which the latter dominated the economic system, as was the case everywhere in the middle ages. It is not surprising, indeed, that Italian investors, the largest of whom were full-time bankers by the late thirteenth century, and who came to invest in monopolies of whole trading systems, such as the English wool trade to Flanders, found that the next step up was financing royal wars, one of the most classically 'feudal' political enterprises. They could not expand beyond a certain point without becoming wholly imbricated in the feudal political economy which surrounded, and gave form to, their micro-economic environment—and which was also capable of bringing them down, when kings defaulted on debts.[40] Banaji sometimes implies, as I would not, that merchant capital had the power to undermine feudal relations of production, even in the medieval period. He is also unconvinced by the extension of a single feudal (or tributary) mode of production to wide sections of the globe, as John Haldon and I argue for.[41] But Banaji has actually gone and done the empirical work, and he remains less tied to dogmatic interpretations as a result.

I take from all of these writers, in particular, an awareness of the importance of the state in most feudal economies (Haldon), an awareness that class struggle was always involved in the extraction of rents and taxes from the peasantry (Hilton, developed by Brenner), an awareness of the structural differences between the feudal and the capitalist mode (Brenner), and an awareness that, other things being equal, there was a tendency for the levels of peasant payments steadily to fall (Bois), which thus opened up possibilities for peasant demand to underpin and develop the complexity of feudal economies very substantially—without, however, in any way transforming them, in the great majority of instances. These are important insights, which I have drawn on, implicitly, throughout this book,

[39] Banaji, *Theory as history*, pp. 251–76; Banaji, *A brief history of commercial capitalism*. See further Bondioli, *Peasants, merchants and caliphs*, pp. 275–96, for merchant capital in Fāṭimid Egypt.

[40] See Hunt, *The medieval super-companies*, pp. 38–75, for a relatively recent overview.

[41] For the last point, see, e.g., Banaji, *Theory as history*, pp. 354–6. See also Bernstein, 'Historical materialism and agrarian history', the most acute analyst and critic of Banaji's work whom I have read. I would add that Banaji is right in some of his theoretical criticisms of my own prior work (Banaji, *Theory as history*, pp. 2–3); but I do not accept his more empirical disagreements with arguments I have made, ibid., pp. 181–240.

so it is necessary here to make the fact explicit in this more theoretical section. But having done so, let us return to empirical points to conclude. For we need, not only to be theoretically clear, but also to understand how these arguments help us to comprehend the real societies whose economic structures and development have been the heart of this book.

* * *

Growth was agrarian at its core in our period, as in every economy before the Industrial Revolution, so we must here focus on the countryside, and its overwhelming peasant majority. And if one reads the sources for most of the regions of this book, looking for external demands on the peasantry, either by the state or by landowners, one finds that it is comprehensible that historians can easily be convinced that these demands were very oppressive, and often very pervasive. In Egypt, in particular, we have endless sets of tax receipts surviving in our document collections, for, as far as we can see, quite high rates, added to the fact that taxpaying was staggered across the year, so that the tax collectors apparently came out not once but up to nine times, which resulted in the need for peasants to make disadvantageous sales to get the money necessary to pay them at difficult times of the year. We might become, as a result, less surprised at the capacity of fiscal surveyors to identify crop types on individual fields every year after the Nile flood, as described in al-Makhzūmī's fiscal treatise, for the state, here, was apparently all-encompassing.[42] For Byzantium, we have detailed fiscal registers, which were at least sometimes regularly updated, and which show considerable levels of knowledge of rural societies, thus adding to state pervasiveness; and we know, both from hostile legislation and from the Athos archives, that landowners were expanding at the expense of peasantries across our period.[43] In al-Andalus, although we know a great deal less about the actual procedures of the taking of rents and taxes, we have writers like Ibn Ḥazm and ʿAbd Allāh b. Buluqqīn, who are graphic about the fiscal oppression of eleventh-century rulers—and ʿAbd Allāh was one of those rulers himself, so is presumably reliable on this topic; and some share-cropping contracts could be very onerous indeed.[44] In northern Italy, we can show high levels of rent in areas with low grain yields, and we have some explicit complaints by peasants about signorial oppression. Only in Sicily does the evidence show that rents and taxes were relatively low—at least by the twelfth century, for we can say nothing about earlier.[45] (For North Africa we do not have

[42] See pp. 36–7 above; see esp. Bondioli, *Peasants, merchants, and caliphs*, pp. 130–6; for al-Makhzūmī, see *Minhāj*, trans. Frantz-Murphy, *The agrarian administration*, p. 31.

[43] See pp. 303, 343 above; and for the registers, see, e.g., *Actes d'Iviron*, 1, nn. 29, 30; 2, nn. 48, 53.

[44] See Chapter 5, n. 66 above for Ibn Ḥazm, and Chapter 5, nn. 10, 65 above for ʿAbd Allāh; see pp. 392–4 above for share-cropping.

[45] See pp. 492–3 above for northern Italy, pp. 239–43 above for Sicily. For signorial injustice as described by Italian peasants, apart from Cliviano (see n. 22 above), see, e.g., Banti, *I brevi dei consoli*, pp. 105–7, for Casciavola near Pisa *c.*1100.

usable evidence here, so it must be cut out of this final discussion.) So we could well conclude that peasants were very much on the defensive in all these regions, outside Sicily, and that, prima facie, we could not expect to find extensive peasant demand in any of them. But, of course, we have found it in every case, sometimes on a substantial scale, and it visibly fuelled the economic growth of each.

This is where we can legitimately wonder whether we are underestimating the effectiveness of the defensive strategies of peasants themselves—defensive strategies which are going to be ill-documented in every period, for, precisely, they are going to tend to lie outside the bounds of the legal, which is the documented world. Again, let us start with Egypt. States are often seen as far enough away from rural society to be able to impose harsher tax regimes without worrying too much about the ability of peasants to pay, or about the lack of consensus that was the consequence of breaking custom; but the converse of this is that, fiscal surveys or no, it was very difficult to get enough close knowledge of local societies for tax to be accurately exacted. This could have bad effects on the unlucky, but it could allow village communities, which were particularly coherent in Egypt, as they had to run dyke maintenance for the Nile flood, to drag their feet very notably in tax-paying. Nicolas Michel has stressed the effective (although informal) autonomy, and indeed the 'opacity', of village communities in sixteenth-century Egypt, even in the face of a fiscal regime of striking complexity.[46] It was hard to intervene in—even to understand—the practices of each village; and without that, it would be difficult to extract more tax than villagers could easily pay, year by year, in every village of the Nile valley, for at least some cooperation was always needed. It is possible that in other periods, before and after, in which tax-farming was more important in Egypt, local tax-farmers could get inside village structures more effectively (as also could landowners, in earlier periods when private landowning was normal in Egypt, although powerful landowners were also better equipped to drag their feet); that might well have been the case in our own period, when tax-farmers, *ḍāmins*, are well documented. But it is also striking that after the mid-ninth century, rural revolts ceased in Egypt (see p. 36 above), and this may well show that the mediation of tax-farmers, which developed from then on, made the fiscal load easier, rather than harder, to bear—or to evade. Either way, the optimism of al-Makhzūmī that state officials could determine the crop choices on all land, year on year, turns into fantasy; this is how the state would *like to* have controlled rural Egypt, rather than how it actually did. And in that gap between state desire and state practical power, there was a good deal of space for the peasantry to keep enough of their crops for themselves to be able to sell some of it, and buy the goods we know they actually did buy.

[46] Michel, *L'Égypte des villages*, pp. 257–308, 331–9 for village autonomy, 87–208 for fiscal complexity, 339 for opacity.

We get the same sense of rural society being outside the full control of the state, or of landed elites, in Byzantium and al-Andalus. Both of these regions had coherent village collectivities, which in Byzantium could sometimes be aggressive, including against local landowners (see p. 346 above), and in al-Andalus were sufficiently coherent that a substantial historiography has claimed (even if wrongly; see pp. 382–9 above) that Islamic Spain and Portugal had no large landowners at all. The evidence for these two regions is less dense than it is for Egypt, and actual documentation for peasant foot-dragging is certainly no more available, but it is at least likely that the state in neither case extracted as much from the rural population as it would have wished, or maybe even pretended it did. Whether landowners were better able to extract rent is equally unclear—perhaps in the territories most directly controlled by the Athos monasteries, but not necessarily in areas of more fragmented property-holding. The difference between theory and practice here was again evidently enough for there to be firm evidence—above all in the archaeology, in both cases—of the ability of peasants to buy artisanal goods.

In Italy we can get an idea of the same processes. Here the state's capacity to tax is not at issue, for it did not happen until cities started to exact taxes at the very end of our period.[47] We have seen that landed elites were actually increasing their levies on the countryside, in some city territories at least, with the development of the territorial *signoria*. But, conversely, we have at least some documented resistance to rent-paying, often partially successful; and we also have clear documentation of peasant resistance to signorial dues. That was what the franchise movement was all about; and even without formal village franchises, lords had to negotiate with peasant communities in many cases, and were prevented from exacting as much as they had begun to claim at the start. This was piecemeal and inconsistent, but peasants managed in many cases to cut back substantially on arbitrary levies, and anyway, signorial dues in most cases did not match rents—there were limits to what lords could practically claim.[48] Again, peasant buying power does not seem to have been radically undermined, and, indeed, was, as we saw particularly in coastal Tuscany (pp. 574–5), probably higher at the end of the twelfth century than at its beginning, before the 'seigneurial revolution' had really started.

In all these cases, we end with hypotheses, rather than with hard evidence, which is a good place to end a book on a period such as this. We do not have the empirical data to push the point home that rural populations could visibly

[47] And even then, we cannot say that cities taxed as effectively as they might have wanted; the 1427 Florence *catasto*, the most detailed tax register from medieval Europe, which listed and assigned acreage, value, rental value, and ownership to single fields (plus lists of family members and the values of movables) across nearly all the Florentine state, was abandoned after 1434 in the face of mounting arrears. See Herlihy and Klapisch-Zuber, *Tuscans and their families*, pp. 10–26.

[48] For resistance to rent-paying, see, e.g., Wickham, *Courts and conflict*, pp. 79–81, 88–91. For an overview of franchises, see Menant, 'Les chartes de franchise de l'Italie communale'; for negotiation, see Fiore, *The seigneurial transformation*, pp. 187–98.

undermine the full force of tax-raising and rent-collecting simply because of their tactical advantage on the ground, still less that they could continue to do it as time went on, other things being equal. In part, this is because other things were not always equal: landlords and states could increase the pressure on peasantries in ways that are clearly documented, as well as there being periods in which both landlords and states were weaker (periods of war and state breakdown, for example)—there must have been a constant flux in what could actually, in practice, be taken from the land as a result. In part too, as already stated, it is because the ways peasantries could evade levies of different kinds were always likely to be undocumented, as they are even today.[49] But the results of these hypotheses are concretely visible, for all that. Rural populations, in all our regions, could, indeed, buy goods; and their mass demand was capable in each case, from different moments between 950 and 1180, of transforming regional economies in the Mediterranean lands, and making them complex and active, with the expansion of cities and their production, and the regional commercialization of their products, and even some Mediterranean-wide trading, which we have seen nearly everywhere. Whether elites wanted to or not, they were not taking so much from the peasantries of the Mediterranean in our period for this to be made impossible. The balance between elite and peasant demand was established in each region, in shorter- or longer-lasting forms. And the dynamism which we can see across the medieval Mediterranean economy or economies, in our period and up to the Black Death—in some regions after that as well—was the result.

[49] Scott, *Weapons of the weak*, *passim*, but esp. pp. 289–303.

Bibliography

1. Unpublished Sources and Web-Based Source Databases

Arabic Papyrology Database [cited as APD], http://www.apd.gwi.uni-muenchen.de:8080/apd/project1c.jsp.

Archivio Capitolare di Pisa, n. 763, 'c.1200'.

Archivio di Stato di Firenze, diplomatico, fondo Passignano, https://www.archiviodigitale.icar.beniculturali.it/it/185/ricerca/detail/82809/.

Archivio di Stato di Lucca, diplomatico S. Ponziano, 22 sett. 1075.

Archivio di Stato di Milano, Fondo di religione, pergamene, Capitolo di S. Giovanni di Monza [cited as ASM, Monza], cartelle 587, 588.

Archivio di Stato di Venezia, *Codice diplomatico veneziano. Codice Lanfranchi* [cited as *CDVE*].

Archivio di Stato di Venezia, Patrimonio, San Zaccaria, pergamene [cited as ASV, SZ], https://asve.arianna4.cloud/patrimonio/206f5e39-93ac-4549-ae59-12140168499c/001-serie-pergamene.

Cambridge Digital Library, https://cudl.lib.cam.ac.uk/.

Codice diplomatico della Lombardia medievale, https://www.lombardiabeniculturali.it/cdlm/.

DocuMult, http://krc.orient.ox.ac.uk/documult-it/.

Filāḥa Texts Project, www.filaha.org/.

Friedberg Genizah Project, http://fjms.genizah.org/.

Oates, J. F and Willis, W. H. (eds.), *Checklist of editions of Greek, Latin, Demotic, and Coptic papyri, ostraca, and tablets*, https://papyri.info/docs/checklist.

Princeton Geniza Project [cited as PGP], https://genizalab.princeton.edu/pgp-database.

2. Published Primary Sources, Including Secondary Works Consulted Principally for the Editions and Translations in them

'Abd Allāh b. Buluqqīn, *al-Tibyān*, trans. A. T. Tibi (Leiden, 1986).

'Abd al-Tawab, 'A. al-R. M. (ed.), *Stèles islamiques de la nécropole d'Assouan*, 3 vols. (Cairo, 1977–86).

Abraham ibn Daud, *The book of tradition (Sefer ha-qabbalah)*, ed. and trans. G. D. Cohen (Philadelphia, PA, 1967).

Abū al-Khayr, *Kitāb al-filāḥa*, ed. and trans. J. M. Carabaza, *Abū l-Jayr, Kitāb al-filāḥa. Tratado de agricultura* (Madrid, 1990).

Abū Ṣāliḥ, *The churches & monasteries of Egypt and some neighbouring countries*, trans. B. T. A. Evetts (Oxford, 1895).

Abū Shāma, *Kitāb al-rawḍatayn fī akhbār al-dawlatayn*, partial ed. and trans. A.-C. Barbier de Meynard, *Recueil des historiens des Croisades: historiens orientaux*, 4 (Paris, 1898).

Accounts of medieval Constantinople: the Patria, ed. and trans. A. Berger (Cambridge, MA, 2013).

Actes de Docheiariou, ed. N. Oikonomidès, Archives de l'Athos, 4 (Paris, 1968).

Actes de Lavra, 1, ed. P. Lemerle et al., Archives de l'Athos, 5 (Paris, 1970).

Actes de Saint-Pantéléèmôn, ed. G. Dagron et al., Archives de l'Athos, 12 (Paris, 1982).

Actes de Xénophon, ed. D. Papachryssanthou, Archives de l'Athos, 15 (Paris, 1986).

Actes d'Iviron, 1–3, ed. J. Lefort et al., Archives de l'Athos, 14, 16, 18 (Paris, 1985–94).

Actes du Pantocrator, ed. V. Kravani, Archives de l'Athos, 17 (Paris, 1991).

Actes du Prôtaton, ed. D. Papachryssanthou, Archives de l'Athos, 7 (Paris, 1975).

Amari, M. (ed.), *Biblioteca arabo-sicula*, 2 vols. (Leipzig, 1857–87); *versione italiana*, 2 vols. (Turin, 1880–9).

Amari, M. (ed.), *I diplomi arabi del R. Archivio fiorentino* (Florence, 1863).

Amari, M. (ed.), *Le epigrafi arabiche di Sicilia*, 1 (Palermo, 1875).

Amato of Montecassino, *Storia de' Normanni*, ed. V. de Bartholomaeis (Rome, 1935).

Ambrosioni, A. M. (ed.), *Le pergamene della canonica di S. Ambrogio nel secolo XII* (Milan, 1974), https://www.lombardiabeniculturali.it/cdlm/edizioni/mi/milano-sambrogio-can/.

Amico, A. (ed.), *I diplomi della cattedrale di Messina* (Palermo, 1888).

Anna Komnene, *Alexias*, ed. D. R. Reinsch et al. (Berlin, 2001).

Annali genovesi di Caffaro e de' suoi continuatori, 1–2, ed. L. T. Belgrano and C. Imperiale di Sant'Angelo (Rome, 1890–1901).

Ansani, M. (ed.), *Le carte del monastero di S. Maria di Morimondo*, 1–2, https://www.lombardiabeniculturali.it/cdlm/edizioni/mi/morimondo-smaria1/, https://www.lombardiabeniculturali.it/cdlm/edizioni/mi/morimondo-smaria2/.

al-Anṭakī, Yaḥyā, Tārīkh al-Anṭakī, trans. B. Pirone, *Cronache* (Milan, 1998).

Ascheri, M. (ed.), *Antica legislazione della Repubblica di Siena* (Siena, 1993).

Ashtor, E., 'Documentos españoles de la Genizah', *Sefarad*, 24 (1964), pp. 41–80.

Asín Palacios, M., 'Un codice inexplorado del cordobés Ibn Ḥazm', *al-Andalus*, 2 (1934), pp. 1–56.

Astegiano, L. (ed.), *Codex diplomaticus Cremonae, 715–1334*, 2 vols. (Turin, 1896–9).

Astruc, C., 'Un document inédit de 1163 sur l'évêché thessalien de Stagi', *Bulletin de correspondance hellénique*, 83.1 (1959), pp. 206–46.

Attaleiates, Michael, *Historia*, ed. I. Pérez Martín (Madrid, 2002), cited from the reprint in *The history of Michael Attaleiates*, trans. A. Kaldellis and D. Krallis (Cambridge, MA, 2012).

Auvray, L. (ed.), *Les registres de Grégoire IX* (Paris, 1890–1955).

al-Bakrī, *al-Masālik wa al-mamālik*, trans. W. M. de Slane, *Description de l'Afrique septentrionale par el-Bekri*, 2nd edn (Algiers, 1913) [Africa section only]; trans. E. Vidal Beltrán, *Geografia de España* (Zaragoza, 1982) [Iberian section only].

Baldelli, I., 'La carta pisana di Filadelfia', *Studi di filologia italiana*, 31 (1973), pp. 5–33.

Balletto, L. (ed.), *Il cartulario di Arnaldo Cumano e Giovanni di Donato (Savona, 1178–1188)* (Rome, 1978).

Banti, O. (ed.), *I brevi dei consoli del Comune di Pisa degli anni 1162 e 1164* (Rome, 1997).

Banti, O. (ed.), *Monumenta epigrafica pisana saeculi XV antiquiora* (Pisa, 2000).

Barachetti, G. (ed.), 'Possedimenti del vescovo di Bergamo nella valle di Ardesio', *Bergomum*, 73.1–3 (1980), https://www.bdl.servizirl.it//bdl/bookreader/index.html?path=fe&cdOggetto=4977#mode/2up/.

Baroni, M. F. (ed.), *Le pergamene del secolo XII della chiesa di S. Maria in Valle di Milano* (Milan, 1988), https://www.lombardiabeniculturali.it/cdlm/edizioni/mi/milano-smariavalle/.

Baroni, M. F. (ed.), *Le pergamene del secolo XII della chiesa di S. Lorenzo di Milano* (Milan, 1989), https://www.lombardiabeniculturali.it/cdlm/edizioni/mi/milano-slorenzo/.

Becker, J. (ed.), *Documenti latini e greci del conte Ruggero I di Calabria e Sicilia* (Rome, 2013).
Belgrano, L. T. (ed.), 'Il registro della curia arcivescovile di Genova', *Atti della Società ligure di storia patria*, 2.2 (1862).
Belgrano, L. T. and L. Beretta (eds.), 'Il secondo registro della curia arcivescovile di Genova', *Atti della Società ligure di storia patria*, 18 (1887).
Benedetti, L. (ed.), *Le pergamene dell'Archivio di Stato di Pisa dal 1175 al 1179*, tesi di laurea, Università di Pisa, relatore C. Violante, a.a. 1965–1966.
Benericetti, R. (ed.), *Le carte del decimo secolo nell'Archivio arcivescovile di Ravenna*, 3 vols. (Ravenna and Faenza, 1999–2002).
Benericetti, R. (ed.), *Le carte ravennati del secolo undicesimo. Archivio arcivescovile*, 4 vols. (Faenza, 2003–7).
Benericetti, R. (ed.), *Le carte ravennati dei secoli ottavo e nono* (Faenza, 2006).
Benjamin of Tudela, *The itinerary*, ed. and trans. M. N. Adler (London, 1907).
Berlan, F. (ed.), *Statuti di Origgio dell'anno 1228* (Venice, 1868).
Bertolotto, G. and Sanguineti, A. (eds.), 'Nuova serie di documenti sulle relazioni di Genova coll'Impero bizantino', *Atti della Società ligure di storia patria*, 28 (1896), pp. 337–573.
Beyer, H.-J. (ed.), *Die lombardische Briefsammlung* (2010), https://data.mgh.de/databases/lomb/Lo.html.
Blanda, M. L. (ed.), *Le pergamene dell'Archivio di Stato di Pisa dal 1184 al 1188*, tesi di laurea, Università di Pisa, relatore C. Violante, a.a. 1966–1967.
Bonaini, F. (ed.), 'Diplomi pisani e regesto delle carte pisane che si trovano a stampa', *Archivio storico italiano*, 6.2, suppl. 1 (1848–89).
Bonaini, F. (ed.), *Statuti inediti della città di Pisa dal XII al XIV secolo*, 3 vols. (Florence, 1854–70).
Bonaini, F. (ed.), 'Due carte pisano-amalfitane dei secoli XII e XIV', *Archivio storico italiano*, 3 ser., 8.1 (1868), pp. 3–8.
Book of gifts and rarities, Kitāb al-hadāyā wa al-tuḥaf, trans. G. al-Ḥijjāwī al-Qaddūmī (Cambridge, MA, 1996).
Branousē, E. L. et al. (eds.), *Byzantina eggrapha tēs monēs Patmou*, 2 vols. (Athens, 1980).
Brühl, C. R. (ed.), *Rogerii II regis diplomata latina* (Cologne, 1987).
Brühl, C. R. and C. Violante (eds.), *Die 'Honorantie civitatis Papie'* (Cologne, 1983).
Bryennios, Nikephoros, *Histoire*, ed. P. Gautier (Brussels, 1975).
Buenger Robbert, L., 'L'inventario di Graziano Gradenigo', *Studi veneziani*, n.s., 5 (1981), pp. 283–310.
Calleri, M. (ed.), *Le carte del monastero di San Siro di Genova (952–1224)*, 1 (Genoa, 1997).
Calleri, M. (ed.), *Codice diplomatico del monastero di Santo Stefano di Genova*, 1 (Genoa, 2009).
Canard, M., 'Une lettre du calife fāṭimite al-Ḥāfiẓ (524–544/1130–1149) à Roger II', in *VIII Centenario della morte di Ruggero II: Atti del Convegno internazionale di studi ruggeriani* (Palermo, 1955), pp. 125–46.
Carmen de gestis Frederici I. imperatoris in Lombardia, ed. I. Schmale-Ott, *MGH*, *SRG*, 62 (Hanover, 1965).
Carmignani, B. (ed.), *Le pergamene dell'Archivio di Stato di Pisa dal 3 maggio 1172 al 18 marzo 1175*, tesi di laurea, Università di Pisa, relatore C. Violante, a.a. 1965–1966.
Caroti, S. (ed.), *Le pergamene dell'Archivio di Stato di Pisa dal 1145 al 1155/1158*, tesi di laurea, Università di Pisa, relatore C. Violante, a.a. 1965–1966.
Cartolari notarili genovesi (1–149), inventario (Rome, 1956).
Castagnetti, A. et al. (eds.), *Inventari altomedievali di terre, coloni e redditi* (Rome, 1979).
Castignoli, P. and P. Racine (eds.), *Corpus statutorum mercatorum Placentiae (secoli XIV–XVIII)* (Milan, 1967).

Castignoli, P. and P. Racine, 'Due documenti contabili del comune di Piacenza nel periodo della Lega Lombarda (1170–1179)', *Studi di storia medioevale e di diplomatica*, 3 (1978), pp. 35–93.

Castrillo Márquez, R., 'Descripción de al-Andalus según un MS. de la Biblioteca de Palacio', *al-Andalus*, 34 (1969), pp. 83–103.

Cessi, R. (ed.), *Documenti relativi alla storia di Venezia anteriori al Mille*, 2 vols. (Padua, 1942).

Chartae latinae antiquiores, ed. A. Bruckner et al., 118 vols. (Olten and Zurich, 1954–).

Chiaudano, M., 'Una pergamena mercantile veneziana del 1087 nell 'Archivio Storico Comunale di Ravenna', *Felix Ravenna*, 31 (1926), pp. 63–71.

Choniates, *see* Michael and Niketas Choniates.

Christopher of Mytilene, *Poems*, ed. and trans. F. Bernard and C. Livanos, *The poems of Christopher of Mytilene and John Mauropous* (Cambridge, MA, 2018).

Chronica magistri Rogeri de Houedene, ed. W. Stubbs, 4 vols. (London, 1868–71).

Chronicon Paschale, ed. L. A. Dindorf (Bonn, 1832).

Chronicon Romualdi Salernitani, ed. C. A. Garufi (Città di Castello, 1914–35).

Chronique de Michel le Syrien, patriarche jacobite d'Antioche (1166–1199), ed. and trans. J. B. Chabot, 5 vols. (Paris, 1899–1924).

Chronographiae quae Theophanis continuati nomine fertur, liber quo Vita Basilii Imperatoris amplectitur, ed. I. Ševčenko (Berlin, 2011).

Ciaralli, A., 'Alle origini del documento mercantile', *Filologia italiana*, 6 (2009), pp. 21–49.

Collura, P. (ed.), *Le più antiche carte dell'Archivio capitolare di Agrigento (1092–1282)* (Palermo, 1961).

Conradi II. diplomata, ed. H. Bresslau, *MGH*, *Diplomata* (Hanover, 1909).

Conradi III. et filius eius Heinrici diplomata, ed. F. Hausmann, *MGH, Diplomata* (Vienna, 1969).

Constantin VII Porphyrogénète, *Le livre des cérémonies*, ed. G. Dagron and B. Flusin, 5 vols. (Paris, 2020).

Corpus iuris civilis, 1: *Digesta Iustiniani*, ed. T. Mommsen and P. Krueger (Berlin, 1870).

Corpus iuris civilis, 3: *Novellae*, ed. R. Schoell and W. Kroll (Berlin, 1895).

Cortesini, L. (ed.), *Le pergamene dell'Archivio di Stato di Pisa dal 1165 al 1172*, tesi di laurea, Università di Pisa, relatore C. Violante, a.a. 1964–1965.

Cour, A., *Un poète arabe d'Andalousie: Ibn Zaïdoün* (Algiers, 1920).

Cronache Veneziane antichissime, ed. G. Monticolo (Rome, 1890).

Crónica del moro Rasis, ed. D. Catalán and M. S. de Andres (Madrid, 1975).

Cusa, S. (ed.), *I diplomi greci ed arabi di Sicilia* (Palermo, 1868).

D'Amia, A., *Diritto e sentenze di Pisa* (Milan, 1962).

Dante, *Purgatorio*, ed. G. Petrocchi (Milan, 1967).

Das 'Itinerarium Bernardi monachi', ed. J. Ackermann (Hanover, 2010).

al-Dāwudī, *Kitāb al-amwāl*, trans. H. H. Abdul Wahab and F. Dachraoui, 'Le régime foncier en Sicile au Moyen Âge (IXe et Xe siècles)', in *Études d'orientalisme dédiées à la mémoire de Lévi-Provençal*, 2 (Paris, 1962), pp. 401–44.

De Angelis, G. M. (ed.), *Le carte del monastero di S. Sepolcro di Astino*, 1 (2010), https://www.lombardiabeniculturali.it/cdlm/edizioni/bg/bergamo-ssepolcro1/.

de Prémare, A. L. and P. Guichard. 'Croissance urbaine et société rurale à Valence au début de l'époque des royaumes de Taifas (XIe siècle de J.-C.)', *Revue de l'Occident musulman et de la Méditerranée*, 31 (1981), pp. 15–30.

De Simone, A., *Splendori e misteri di Sicilia in un' opera di Ibn Qalāqis* (Messina, 1996).

degli Azzi Vitelleschi, G. (ed.), *Reale archivio di Stato in Lucca. Regesti*, 1, 2 vols. (Lucca, 1903–11).

Der Epitaphios des Nikolaos Mesarites auf sein Bruder Johannes, ed. A. Heisenberg (Munich, 1923).

Die Urkunden Heinrichs V. und der Königin Mathilde, ed. M. Thiel and A. Gawlik, *MGH, Diplomata* (2010), https://data.mgh.de/databases/ddhv/toc.htm.

Die Urkunden und Briefe der Markgräfin Mathilde von Tuszien, ed. E. Goez and W. Goez, *MGH, Diplomata* (Hanover, 1998).

Diem, W. (ed.), *Arabische Geschäftsbriefe*, 2 vols. (Wiesbaden, 1995).

Diem, W. and Edzard, L., 'Ein unhöflicher Brief und liebliche Verse', *Zeitschrift der Deutschen Morgenländische Gesellschaft*, 161 (2011), pp. 265–304.

Doehaerd, R., *Les relations commerciales entre Gênes, la Belgique et l'Outremont* (Brussels, 1941).

Donizone, *Vita Mathildis*, ed. L. Simeoni (Bologna, 1930–40).

Dozy, R. P. A. (ed.), *Scriptorum arabum loci de Abbadidis*, 3 vols. (Leiden, 1846–63).

Drei, G. (ed.), *Le carte degli Archivi parmensi del sec. XII* (Parma, 1950).

Eberwin of Trier, *Vita Sancti Symeonis*, ed. G. Henschen, *Acta sanctorum, Junii*, 1 (Antwerp, 1695), cols. 89–101.

Enzensberger, H. (ed.), *Guillelmi I. regis diplomata* (Cologne, 1996).

Enzensberger, H. (ed.), *Willelmi II regis Siciliae diplomata* (2017), www.hist-hh.uni-bamberg.de/WilhelmII/index.html/.

Falaschi, E. (ed.), *Carte dell'Archivio capitolare di Pisa*, 2 (Rome, 1973).

Falconi, E. (ed.), *Le carte cremonesi dei secoli VIII–XII*, 4 vols. (Cremona, 1979–88).

Falconi, E. and R. Peveri (eds.), *Il Registrum Magnum del comune di Piacenza*, 1 (Milan, 1984).

Falletta, S. (ed.), *Liber privilegiorum Sanctae Montis Regalis Ecclesiae* (2010), http://vatlat3880.altervista.org/.

Fantappiè, R. (ed.), *Le carte della propositura di S. Stefano di Prato* (Florence, 1977).

Farag, W., *The truce of Safar A.H. 359: December–January 969–70* (Birmingham, 1977).

Fossier, R. (ed.), *Chartes de coutume en Picardie: XIe–XIIIe siècle* (Paris, 1974).

Frantz-Murphy, G. (ed.), *Arabic agricultural leases and tax receipts from Egypt 148–427 A.H./765–1035 A.D.* (Vienna, 2001).

Frenkel, M., *'Ha-Ohavim ṿeha-nedivim'* (Jerusalem, 2006).

Friderici I. diplomata, ed. H. Appelt, 5 vols., *MGH, Diplomata* (Hanover, 1975–90).

Friedman, M. A., 'An India trader's partnership in Almería (1139)', *Sefarad*, 76 (2016), pp. 75–96.

Frisi, A.-F. (ed.), *Memorie storiche di Monza e sua corte*, 2 (Milan, 1794).

Garufi, C. A. (ed.), *I documenti inediti dell'epoca normanna in Sicilia* (Palermo, 1899).

Garufi, C. A. (ed.), *Catalogo illustrato del Tabulario di S. Maria Nuova in Monreale* (Palermo, 1902).

Garufi, C. A., 'Le donazioni del conte Enrico di Paternò al monastero di S. Maria di Valle Giosafat', *Revue de l'Orient latin*, 9 (1902), pp. 206–29.

Garufi, C. A., 'Un contratto agrario in Sicilia nel secolo XII per la fondazione del casale di Mesepe presso Paternò', *Archivio storico per la Sicilia orientale*, 5 (1908), pp. 11–22.

Garufi, C. A., '"Memoratoria, chartae et instrumenta divisa" in Sicilia nei secoli XI a XV', *Bullettino dell'Istituto storico italiano*, 32 (1912), pp. 67–127.

Garufi, C. A., 'Censimento e catasto della popolazione servile', *Archivio storico siciliano*, 49 (1928), pp. 1–100.

Gautier, P., 'La diataxis de Michel Attaliate', *Revue des études byzantines*, 39 (1981), pp. 5–143.

Gautier, P. 'Le typikon du sébaste Grégoire Pakourianos', *Revue des études byzantines*, 42 (1984), pp. 5–145.

George Kedrenos, *Synopsis istoriōn*, ed. I. Bekker, 2 vols. (Bonn, 1838–9).

Gesta Federici I. imperatoris in Lombardia, ed. O. Holder-Egger, *MGH, SRG*, 27 (Hanover, 1892).

Ghignoli, A. (ed.), *Carte dell'Archivio arcivescovile di Pisa: fondo arcivescovile*, 1 (Pisa, 2006).
Gil, M. (ed.), *Documents of the Jewish pious foundations from the Cairo Geniza* (Leiden, 1976).
Gil, M. (ed.), *Erets-Yishra'el ba-teḳufah ha-Muslemit ha-rishonah (634–1099)* [cited as Gil P], 3 vols. (Tel Aviv, 1983).
Gil, M. (ed.), *Be-malkhut Yishma'el bi-teḳufat ha-ge'onim* [cited as Gil K], 4 vols. (Tel Aviv, 1997).
Gil, M. and S. Simonsohn, 'More on the history of the Jews in Sicily in the Norman period' (in Hebrew), in M. Rozen et al. (eds.), *Sefer yovel le-Daniyel Ḳarpi* (Tel Aviv, 1996), pp. 23–57.
Giorgi, I. and U. Balzani (eds.), *Il Regesto di Farfa*, 5 vols. (Rome, 1879–92).
Giovanni Diacono, *Istoria Veneticorum*, ed. L. A. Berto (Bologna, 1999).
Giunta, F. (ed.), *Acta Siculo-Aragonensia*, 1.1 (Palermo, 1972).
Gloria, A. (ed.), *Codice diplomatico padovano dal sesto secolo a tutto l'undecimo* (Venice, 1877).
Gloria, A. (ed.), *Codice diplomatico padovano dall'anno 1101 alla pace di Costanza (25 giugno 1183)*, 2 vols. (Venice, 1879–81).
Goitein, S. D., 'A letter from Seleucia (Cilicia): dated 21 July 1137', *Speculum*, 39 (1964), pp. 298–303.
Goitein, S. D., 'Bankers accounts from the eleventh century A.D.', *JESHO*, 9 (1966), pp. 28–66.
Goitein, S. D., *Letters of medieval Jewish traders* (Princeton, NJ, 1973).
Goitein, S. D. and M. A. Friedman (eds.), *India traders of the middle ages* (Leiden, 2008).
Goitein, S. D. and M. A. Friedman (eds.), *India book* IV/B, *Ḥalfon ha-soḥer ha-mashkil ṿeha-nose'a ha-gadol* (Jerusalem, 2013).
González Palencia, A., *Los Mozárabes de Toledo en los siglos XII y XIII* [cited as P.Mozarab], 3 vols. and *Volumen preliminar* (Madrid, 1926–30).
González Palencia, A., 'Documentos árabes de Cenete (siglos XII–XIV)', *al-Andalus*, 5 (1940), pp. 301–82.
Granstrem, E. et al., 'Fragment d'un praktikon de la région d'Athènes (avant 1204)', *Revue des études byzantines*, 34 (1976), pp. 5–44.
Green, M., 'A private archive of Coptic letters and documents from Teshlot', *Oudheidkundige mededelingen uit het Rijksmuseum van Oudheden te Leiden*, 64 (1985), pp. 61–122.
Grégoire, H., 'Diplômes de Mazara (Sicile)', *Annuaire de l'Institut de philologie et d'histoire orientales de l'Université de Bruxelles*, 1 (1932–3), pp. 79–107.
Gregorii VII Registrum, ed. E. Caspar, *MGH, Epistolae selectae*, 2, 2 vols. (Berlin, 1920–3).
Grossi, A. (ed.), *Il Liber Iurium del Comune di Lodi* (Rome, 2004).
Grossi, A. (ed.), *Le carte del monastero di S. Ambrogio*, 3.2 (2005), https://www.lombardiabeniculturali.it/cdlm/edizioni/mi/milano-sambrogio-mon3-2/.
Grossi, A. (ed.), *Le carte del monastero di S. Maria di Chiaravalle*, 2 (2008), https://www.lombardiabeniculturali.it/cdlm/edizioni/mi/chiaravalle-smaria2/.
Guastini, M. (ed.), *Le pergamene dell'Archivio di Stato di Pisa dal 1100 al 1115*, tesi di laurea, Università di Pisa, relatore C. Violante, a.a. 1964–1965.
Guglielmo Cassinese (1190–1192), ed. M. W. Hall et al., 2 vols. [cited as *Guglielmo Cassinese*] (Genoa, 1938).
Guillou, A. (ed.), *Les actes grecs de S. Maria di Messina* (Palermo, 1963).
Guillou, A. (ed.), 'Les archives de S. Maria di Bordonaro', *Zbornik radova*, 8.1 (1963), pp. 135–48.
Guillou, A. (ed.), *Le brébion de la métropole byzantine de Règion (vers 1050)* (Rome, 1974).
Guo, L., *Commerce, culture, and community in a Red Sea port in the thirteenth century: the Arabic documents from Quseir* (Leiden, 2004).

Güterbock, F., 'Alla vigilia della Lega Lombarda', *Archivio storico italiano*, 95 (1937), 2, pp. 188–217, 3, pp. 64–77.

Haldon, J. F. (ed.), *Three treatises on imperial military expeditions* (Vienna, 1990).

Hartmann, L. M., *Zur Wirtschaftsgeschichte Italiens im frühen Mittelalter* (Gotha, 1904).

Heinrici II. et Arduini diplomata, ed. H. Bresslau et al., *MGH, Diplomata* (Hanover, 1900–3).

Heinrici III. diplomata, ed. H. Bresslau and P. Kehr, *MGH, Diplomata* (Hanover, 1931).

Heinrici IV. diplomata, ed. D. von Gladiss and A. Gawlik, 3 vols., *MGH, Diplomata* (Hanover, 1941–78).

al-Ḥimyarī, *Kitāb al-rawḍ al-mi'ṭār*, trans. É. Lévi-Provençal, *La péninsule ibérique au Moyen-Âge* (Leiden, 1938).

Historia ducum Venetorum, ed. L. A. Berto, *Testi storici veneziani (XI–XIII secolo)* (Padua, 2000), pp. 1–83.

History of the patriarchs of the Egyptian church, 2 and 3, ed. and trans. Y. 'Abd al-Masīḥ et al. (Cairo, 1943–70).

Al-Ḥulal al mawshīyya, trans. A. Huici Miranda, *Al-Ḥulal al-mawšiyya: cronica árabe de las dinastias Almorávide, Almohade y Benimerin* (Tetuán, 1951).

Ibn 'Abd al-Ḥakam, *Futūh Miṣr*, trans. A. Gateau, *Conquête de l'Afrique du Nord et de l'Espagne* (Tunis, 1931).

Ibn 'Abd al-Ra'ūf, *Risāla fī ādāb al-ḥisba wa al-muḥtasib*, trans. R. Arié, 'Traduction annotée et commentée des traités de *ḥisba* d'Ibn 'Abd al-Ra'ūf et de 'Umar al-Garsīfī', *Hespéris tamuda*, 1 (1960), pp. 5–38, 199–214, 349–86.

Ibn 'Abdūn, *Risāla fī al-qaḍā' wa al-ḥisba*, trans. É. Lévi-Provençal, *Séville musulmane au début du XII*[e] *siècle* (Paris, 1947).

Ibn al-Athīr, *Kāmil fī al-tārīkh*, partial trans. E. Fagnan, *Annales du Maghreb et de l'Espagne* (Algiers, 1898).

Ibn al-'Aṭṭār, *Kitāb al-wathā'iq wa al-sijillāt*, trans. P. Chalmeta and M. Marugán, *Formulario notarial y judicial andalusí* (Madrid, 2000).

Ibn al-'Awwām, *Kitāb al-filāḥa*, trans. J.-J. Clément-Mullet, *Le livre d'agriculture d'Ibn al-Awam (Kitab el-felahah)*, 2 vols. (Paris, 1864–7).

Ibn al-Dāya, *Kitāb al-mukāfa'a*, trans. E. Panetta, *Kitâb al-Mukâfa'a di Ibn ad-Dâya* (Naples, 1982).

Ibn al-Qalānisī, *al-Ma'rūf bi-Dhayl tārīkh Dimashq*, partial trans. R. Le Tourneau, *Damas de 1075 à 1154* (Damascus, 1952).

Ibn al-Qūṭīyya, *Ta'rīkh iftāḥ al-Andalus*, trans. D. James, *Early Islamic Spain* (Abingdon, 2009).

Ibn al-Ṣayrafī, *al-Ishāra ilā man nāl al-wizāra*, ed. A. Mukhlis, *Bulletin de l'Institut français d'archéologie orientale du Caire*, 25 (1925), pp. 49–112.

Ibn Baṣṣāl, *Kitāb al-qaṣd wa al-bayān*, trans. J. M. Millás Vallicrosa and M. Aziman, *Libro de agricultura* (Tetuán, 1955).

Ibn Bassām, *Anīs al-jalīs fī akhbār Tinnīs*, trans. A. L. Gascoigne and J. P. Cooper, in Gascoigne, *The island city of Tinnīs* (Cairo, 2020), pp. 57–70.

Ibn Baṣṣām, *al-Dhakhīra fī maḥāsin ahl al-Jazīra*, ed. I. 'Abbās, 4 vols. (Beirut, 1978–81).

Ibn Ghālib, *Farḥat al-anfus*, trans. J. Vallvé Bermejo, 'Una descripción de España de Ibn Gālib', *Anuario de filología* (Barcelona, 1975), pp. 369–84; Vallvé Bermejo, 'La descripción de Córdoba de Ibn Gālib', in *Homenaje a Pedro Sáinz Rodríguez*, 3 (Madrid, 1986), pp. 669–79.

Ibn Ḥawqal, *Kītāb ṣūrat al-arḍ*, trans. J. H. Kramers and G. Wiet, *Configuration de la terre*, 2 vols. (Beirut, 1964).

Ibn Ḥayyān, *Muqtabis II.1*, trans. M. Á. Makki and F. Corriente, *Crónica de los emires Alḥakam I y Ábdarraḥmān II entre los años 796 y 847* (Zaragoza, 2001).

Ibn Ḥayyān, *Muqtabis V*, trans. M. J. Viguera and F. Corriente, *Cronica del califa ʿAbdarraḥmān III an-Nāsir entre los años 912 y 942 (al-Muqtabis V)* (Zaragoza, 1981).

Ibn Ḥayyān, *Muqtabis VII*, trans. E. García Gómez, *Anales palatinos del califa de Córdoba al-Hakam II, por ʿĪsā ibn Ahmad al-Rāzī (360–364 H. = 971–975 J. C.)* (Madrid, 1967).

Ibn Ḥazm, *Ṭawq al-ḥamāma*, trans. E. García Gómez, *El collar de la paloma* (Madrid, 1952).

Ibn ʿIdhārī, *al-Bayān al-mughrib*, trans. E. Fagnan, *Histoire de l'Afrique et de l'Espagne intitulée al-Bayano'l-Mogrib*, 1 (Algiers, 1901); F. Maíllo Salgado, *La caída del califato de Córdoba y los reyes de taifas* (Salamanca, 1993); A. Huici Miranda, *al-Bayān al-mugrib fi ijtiṣār ajbār muluk al-Andalus wa al-Magrib: los Almohades* (Tetuán, 1953–4).

Ibn ʿIdhārī, *al-Bayān, Nuevos fragmentos*, trans. A. Huici Miranda, *al-Bayan al-Marrakushi: nuevos fragmentos almorávides y almohades* (Valencia, 1963).

Ibn Jubayr, *Riḥla*, trans. R. Broadhurst, *The travels of Ibn Jubayr* (London, 1952).

Ibn Khaldūn, *Kitāb al-ʿIbar*, trans. W. M. de Slane and P. Casanova, *Histoire des Berbères*, 4 vols. (Paris, 1925–56); introduction trans. F. Rosenthal, *The Muqaddimah*, 3 vols. (London, 1958).

Ibn Khurradādhbih, *Kitāb al-masālik wa al-mamālik*, ed. and trans. C. Barbier de Meynard, 'Le livre des routes et des provinces, par Ibn-Khordadbeh', *Journal asiatique*, 6 ser., 5 (1865), pp. 5–127, 227–96, 446–532.

Ibn Mammātī, *Qawānīn al-dawāwīn*, trans. R. S. Cooper, *Ibn Mammātī's Rules for the ministries*, PhD thesis, University of California-Berkeley, 1973.

Ibn Ṣāḥib al-Salā, *al-Mann bi al-imāma*, trans. A. Huici Miranda (Valencia, 1969).

Ibn Wāfid, *Majmūʿ fī al-filāḥa*, ed. J. M. Millás Vallicrosa, 'La traducción castellana del Tratado de Agricultura de Ibn Wāfid', *al-Andalus*, 8 (1943), pp. 281–332.

al-Idrīsī, *Nuzhat al-mushtāq*, trans. P.-A. Jaubert and A. Nef, in H. Bresc and A. Nef, *Idrîsî: la première géographie de l'Occident* (Paris, 1999).

Il cartolare di Giovanni Scriba, ed. M. Chiaudano and M. Moresco, 2 vols. [cited as *Giovanni Scriba*] (Rome, 1935).

Il Codice Perris, 1, ed. J. Mazzoleni and R. Orefice (Amalfi, 1985).

Imperiale di S. Angelo, C. (ed.), *Codice diplomatico della repubblica di Genova* [cited as *CDGE*], 3 vols. (Rome, 1936–42).

Iohannis Euchaitorum Metropolitae quae in codice Vaticano graeco 676 supersunt, ed. J. Bollig and P. de Lagarde (Göttingen, 1882).

al-Iṣtakhrī, *al-Masālik wa-al-mamālik*, trans. A. D. Mordtmann, *Das Buch der Länder von Schech Ebu Ishak el Farsi el Isztachri* (Hamburg, 1845).

Jamil, N. and J. Johns, 'Four Sicilian documents—three Kalbid and one Norman—from the Qubbat al-Ḫazna in Damascus', in U. Bsees and M. Hradek (eds.), *Proceedings of the 4th Conference on the layout and structure of Arabic documents*, in press, krc.orient.ox.ac.uk/resources/documult/jamil_johns_2021.pdf.

Jean-Léon l'Africain, *Description de l'Afrique*, trans. A. Épaulard, 2 vols. (Paris, 1956).

Jeffreys, E., *Four Byzantine novels* (Liverpool, 2012).

Jeffreys, M., 'Summaries', in M. Jeffreys and M. D. Lauxtermann (eds.), *The letters of Psellos* (Oxford, 2016), pp. 167–416.

John VI Kantakouzenos, *Historiai*, ed. L. Schopen, *Historiarum libri IV*, 3 vols. (Bonn, 1828–32).

John Kaminiates, *De expugnatione Thessalonicae*, ed. G. Böhlig (Berlin, 1973).

John Kinnamos, *Epitome rerum ab Ioanne et Alexio Comnenis gestarum*, ed. A. Meineke (Bonn, 1836).

John Lydos, *On powers*, ed. A. C. Bandy (Philadelphia, PA, 1983).

John Mauropous, *Letters*, ed. and trans. A. Karpozilos, *The letters of John Mauropous metropolitan of Euchaita* (Thessaloniki, 1990).

John Mauropous, *Poems*, ed. and trans. F. Bernard and C. Livanos, *The poems of Christopher of Mytilene and John Mauropos* (Cambridge, MA, 2018).
John Oxites, ed. P. Gautier, 'Diatribes de Jean l'Oxite contre Alexis Ier Comnène', *Revue des études byzantines*, 28 (1970), pp. 5–55.
John Skylitzes, *Synopsis historiarum*, ed. I. Thurn (Berlin, 1973).
John Tzetzes, 'Iambi', ed. P. A. M. Leone, 'Ioannis Tzetzae Iambi', *Rivista di studi bizantini e neoellenici*, 6–7 (1969–70), pp. 127–56.
John Tzetzes, *Epistulae*, ed. P. A. M. Leone (Leipzig, 1972).
Johns, J., 'Arabic contracts of sea-exchange from Norman Sicily', in P. Xuereb (ed.), *Karissime Gotifride* (Msida, 1999), pp. 55–78.
Johns, J., 'The boys from Mezzoiuso', in R. G. Hoyland and P. F. Kennedy (eds.), *Islamic reflections, Arabic musings* (Cambridge, 2004), pp. 243–55.
Johns, J. and A. Metcalfe, 'The mystery at Chùrchuro', *Bulletin of the School of Oriental and African Studies*, 62 (1999), pp. 226–59.
Jüdische Urkundenformulare aus dem muslimischen Spanien, trans. H.-G. von Mutius (Bern, 1997).
Kekaumenos, *Consilia et Narrationes*, ed. and trans. C. Roueché (2013), https://ancientwisdoms.ac.uk/library/kekaumenos-consilia-et-narrationes/.
al-Khushanī, *Kitāb al-quḍā bi-Qurṭuba*, ed. and trans. J. Ribera, *Historia de los jueces de Córdoba por Aljoxani* (Madrid, 1914).
Kitāb al-Istibṣār, partial trans. E. Fagnan, 'L'Afrique septentrionale au XIIe siècle de notre ère', *Recueil des notices et mémoires de la société archéologique du Département de Constantine*, 33 (1899), pp. 1–229.
Koder, J. (ed.), *Das Eparchenbuch Leons des Weisen* (Vienna, 1991).
Kölzer, T. (ed.), *Constantiae imperatricis et reginae Siciliae diplomata (1195–1198)* (Cologne, 1983).
Kurze, W. (ed.), *Codex diplomaticus amiatinus*, 4 vols. (Tübingen, 1974–2004).
La vie de saint Cyrille le Philéote, moine byzantin, ed. É. Sargologos (Brussels, 1964).
Landolfo Seniore, *Mediolanensis historiae libri quatuor*, ed. A. Cutolo (Bologna, 1934).
Lanfranchi, L. (ed.), *Codice diplomatico veneziano*, *see* Archivio di Stato di Venezia.
Lanfranchi, L. (ed.), *Famiglia Zusto* (Venice, 1955).
Lanfranchi, L. (ed.), *S. Giorgio maggiore*, 4 vols. (Venice, 1968–86).
Lanfranchi, L. and B. Strina (eds.), *SS. Ilario e Benedetto e S. Gregorio* (Venice, 1965).
Lanfranchi Strina, B. (ed.), *SS. Trinità e S. Michele arcangelo di Brondolo*, 4 vols. (Venice, 1981–97).
Lanza, E. (ed.), *Le carte del capitolo della cattedrale di Verona*, 2 vols. (Rome, 1998–2006).
Le calendrier de Cordoue, ed. R. Dozy, trans. C. Pellat (Leiden, 1961).
Leges langobardorum, 643–866, ed. F. Beyerle (Witzenhausen, 1962).
Lenel, W., 'Ein Handelsvertrag Venedigs mit Imola vom Jahre 1099', *Vierteljahrschrift für Sozial- und Wirtschaftsgeschichte*, 6 (1908), pp. 228–31.
Leo of Synada, *Letters*, ed. M. P. Vinson, *The correspondence of Leo, metropolitan of Synada and syncellus* (Washington, DC, 1985).
Leo the Deacon, *Historiai*, ed. C. B. Hase, *Leonis diaconi Caloënsis Historia libri decem* (Bonn, 1828).
Leonardo Pisano, *Liber abbaci*, ed. B. Boncompagni, *Scritti di Leonardo Pisano*, 1 (Rome, 1857).
Leoni, V. (ed.), *Le carte del monastero di S. Leonardo 'de capite Mose' di Cremona (1157–1191)* (2003), https://www.lombardiabeniculturali.it/cdlm/edizioni/cr/cremona-sleonardo/.
Leoni, V. (ed.), *Le carte della chiesa di S. Cataldo di Cremona (1119–1200)* (2007), https://www.lombardiabeniculturali.it/cdlm/edizioni/cr/cremona-scataldo/.

Les Novelles de Léon VI le Sage, ed. A. Noailles and P.-B. Dain (Paris, 1944).

Les novelles des empereurs macédoniens concernant la terre et les stratiotes, ed. N. Svoronos (Athens, 1994).

Levtzion, N. and J. F. P. Hopkins (trans.), *Corpus of early Arabic sources for West African history* (Cambridge, 1981).

Liber consuetudinum Mediolani, anni MCCXVI, ed. E. Besta and G. L. Barni (Milan, 1949).

Liber Cumanus, ed. G. M. Stampa, in L. A. Muratori (ed.), *Rerum Italicarum scriptores*, 5 (Milan, 1724), pp. 413–56.

Liber Maiorichinus de gestis Pisanorum illustribus, ed. G. Scalia (Florence, 2017).

Life of Athanasios of Athos, version B, ed. and trans. R. P. H. Greenfield and A. M. Talbot, *Holy men of Mount Athos* (Cambridge, MA, 2016), pp. 128–367.

Life of John and Euthymios, trans. T. Grdzelidze, *Georgian monks on Mount Athos* (London, 2009).

Life of John the Almsgiver, ed. (as *Vie de Jean de Chypre*) in A. J. Festugière and L. Rydén (eds.), *Léontios de Néapolis, Vie de Syméon le Fou, Vie de Jean de Chypre* (Paris, 1974).

Life of Lazaros of Galesion, ed. H. Deleheye, *Acta sanctorum. Novembris*, 3 (Brussels, 1910), cols. 508–88.

Life of Paul the younger, ed. J. Sirmond, 'Vita S. Pauli iunioris in Monte Latro', *Analecta bollandiana*, 11 (1892), pp. 5–74, 136–82.

Lirola Delgado, J. L. (ed. and trans.), *Almería andalusí y su territorio* (Almería, 2005).

Liudprand of Cremona, *Relatio de legatione Constantinopolitana*, ed. P. Chiesa, *Antapodosis; Homelia paschalis; Historia Ottonis; Relatio de legatione Constantinopolitana* (Turnhout, 1998), pp. 187–218.

Lombardo, A. and R. Morozzo della Rocca (eds.), *Nuovi documenti del commercio veneto dei sec. XI–XIII* [cited as *DCV*, N] (Venice, 1953).

Loud, G. A. and T. Wiedemann, *The history of the tyrants of Sicily by 'Hugo Falcandus'* (Manchester, 1998).

Ludovici II. diplomata, ed. K. Wanner, *MGH, Diplomata* (Munich, 1994).

al-Makhzūmī, *al-Muntaqā min kitāb al-minhāj fī 'ilm kharāj Miṣr* [cited as *Minhāj*], partial edns and trans. in Frantz-Murphy, *The agrarian administration* (Cairo, 1986), pp. 19–42, and Cahen, 'Douanes' (1964).

Malaterra, Gaufridus, *De rebus gestis Rogerii Calabriae et Siciliae comitis et Roberti Guiscardi ducis fratris eius*, ed. E. Pontieri (Bologna, 1927–8).

Malloy. A. G. et al., *Coins of the Crusader states 1098–1291*, 2nd edn (Fairfield, CT, 2004).

Manaresi, C. (ed.), *Gli atti del Comune di Milano fino all'anno MCCXVI* (Milan, 1919).

Manaresi, C. (ed.), *I placiti del 'Regnum Italiae'*, 3 vols. (Rome, 1955–60).

Mangini, M. (ed.), *Le carte del monastero di S. Ambrogio*, 3.1 (2007), https://www.lombardiabeniculturali.it/cdlm/edizioni/mi/milano-sambrogio-mon3-1/.

Mansi, G. D. (ed.), *Sacrorum conciliorum nova et amplissima collectio*, 31 vols. (Venice, 1759–98).

al-Manṣūr, *Sīrat al-Ustādh Jawdhar*, trans. M. Canard, *Vie de l'Ustadh Jaudhar* (Algiers, 1958); H. Haji, *Inside the immaculate portal* (London, 2012).

al-Maqrīzī, *Kitāb al-mawā'iẓ wa al-i'tibār bi-zikr al-khiṭaṭ wa al-āthār* [cited as *Khiṭaṭ*], partial trans. U. Bouriant and P. Casanova, *Description topographique et historique de l'Égypte*, 4 vols. (Cairo, 1895–1920).

al-Maqrīzī, *Ighāthat al-umma bi-kashf al-ghumma*, trans. A. Allouche, *Mamluk economics* (Salt Lake City, UT, 1994).

al-Maqrīzī, *Itti'āẓ al-ḥunafā' bi-akhbār al-a'imma al-Fāṭimiyyīn al-khulafā'*, partial trans. S. Jiwa, *Towards a Shi'i Mediterranean empire* (London 2009).

Maragone, Bernardo, *Annales pisani*, ed. M. Lupo Gentile (Bologna, 1930–6).
Marini, G. (ed.), *I papiri diplomatici* (Rome, 1805).
al-Marrākushī, *Kitāb al-mu'jib*, trans. A. Huici Miranda, *Kitāb al-mu'ŷib fī taljīṣ ajbār al-Magrib por Abū Muḥammad 'Abd al-Wāḥid al-Marrākušī* (Tetuán, 1955).
Martinelli Perelli, L. (ed.), *Le pergamene del secolo XII della chiesa di S. Stefano di Vimercate* (Milan, 2001), https://www.lombardiabeniculturali.it/cdlm/edizioni/mi/vimercate-sstefano/.
McGeer, E., *The land legislation of the Macedonian emperors* (Toronto, 2000).
Medina Gómez, A., *Monedas hispano-musulmanas* (Toledo, 1992).
Ménager, L. R. (ed.), *Les actes latins de S. Maria di Messina, 1103–1250* (Palermo, 1963).
Merati, P., 'La rappresentazione dell'esperienza', *MEFRM*, 113 (2001), pp. 453–91.
Merati, P. (ed.), *Le carte della chiesa di S. Maria del Monte di Velate*, 2 vols. (Varese, 2005–7), https://www.lombardiabeniculturali.it/cdlm/edizioni/mi/velate-smaria1/, https://www.lombardiabeniculturali.it/cdlm/edizioni/mi/velate-smaria2/.
Meyer, A. (ed.), *Ser Ciabattus: regesti*, 1 (Lucca, 2005).
Meyer, P. (ed.), *Die Haupturkunden für die Geschichte der Athosklöster* (Leipzig, 1894).
Michael Choniates, *Ta sōzomena*, ed. S. P. Lampros, 2 vols. (Athens, 1879–80).
Michael Choniates, *Epistulae*, ed. F. Kolovou (Berlin, 2001).
Michael Italikos, *Lettres et discours*, ed. P. Gautier (Paris, 1972).
Michael Psellos, *Epistolai*, ed. K. N. Sathas, *Michaēl Psellou istorikoi logoi, epistolai kai alla anekdota* (Venice, 1876).
Michael Psellos, *Epistulae*, ed. E. Kurtz and S. Drexl, *Scripta minora*, 2 (Milan, 1941).
Michael Psellos, *Epistole*, ed. E. V. Maltese, 'Epistole inedite di Michele Psello', *Studi italiani di filologia classica*, 3 ser., 5 (1987), pp. 82–98, 214–23, 6 (1988), pp. 110–34.
Michael Psellos, *Chronographia*, ed. D. R. Reinsch (Berlin, 2014).
Michael Psellus, *Epistulae*, ed. S. Papaioannou (Berlin, 2019).
Migne, J.-P. (ed.), *Patrologiae cursus completus, series latina*, 200 (Paris, 1855).
Miklosich, F. and J. Müller (eds.), *Acta et diplomata graeca medii aevi sacra et profana*, 6 vols. (Vienna, 1860–90).
Mirto, C. (ed.), *Rollus Rubeus* (Palermo, 1972).
Molina López, E., 'El documento árabe de Guadix (s. XII)', in *Homenaje al prof. Jacinto Bosch Vilá*, 1 (Granada, 1991), pp. 271–92.
Monumenta Germaniae historica: Capitularia regum francorum, 2, ed. A. Boretus and V. Krause (Hanover, 1897).
Morozzo della Rocca, R. and A. Lombardo (eds.), *Documenti del commercio veneziano nei secoli XI–XIII*, 2 vols. [cited as *DCV*] (Rome, 1940).
Mouton, J-M. et al. (eds.), *Propriétés rurales et urbaines à Damas au Moyen Âge* (Paris, 2018).
Mubārak Esmail, A., *Cartas de la época almorávide de Ibn Abi-l-Jisal y de Ibn al-Yannan (manuscrito núm. 15 de la Biblioteca General de Rabat con un apéndice), edición, contenido y estudio*, tesis de doctorado, Universidad de Granada, 1986.
Mubārak Esmail, A., 'Cinco cartas inéditas del kātib 'Abd al-Ḥaqq b. al-Ŷannān procedentes del ms. 15 de la Biblioteca General de Rabat (Marruecos)', in *Homenaje al prof. Jacinto Bosch Vilá*, 1 (Granada, 1991), pp. 95–113.
Muḥammad b. 'Umar al-Kinānī, *Kitāb akriyat al-sufun*, ed. M. Ṭāher, 'Kitāb akriyat al-sufun wa al-nizā' bayna ahlihā', *Cahiers de Tunisie*, 123–4 (1983), pp. 5–53, trans. in Khalilieh, *Admiralty and maritime laws* (Leiden, 2006), pp. 273–330.
Müller, G. (ed.), *Documenti sulle relazioni delle città toscane coll'Oriente cristiano e coi Turchi fino all'anno MDXXXI* (Florence, 1879).

al-Muqaddasī, *Aḥsan al-taqāsīm*, trans. A. Miquel, 'L'Égypte vue par un géographe arabe du IVe/Xe siècle', *AI*, 11 (1972), pp. 109–39 [Egypt section only]; B. A. Collins, *The best divisions for knowledge of the regions* (Reading, 1994).

al-Musabbiḥī, *Akhbār Miṣr*, ed. A. F. Sayyid et al., 2 vols. (Cairo, 1978–84).

Muzzi, O. (ed.), *San Gimignano: i verbali dei consigli del podestà 1232–1240*, 1 (Florence, 2010).

Muzzi, O. and D. Nenci (eds.), *Il contratto di mezzadria nella Toscana medievale*, 2 (Florence, 1988).

Nardi, R. (ed.), *Le pergamene dell'Archivio di Stato di Pisa dall'8 novembre 1115 al 13 febbraio 1130*, tesi di laurea, Università di Pisa, relatore C. Violante, a.a. 1964–1965.

Nāṣer-e Khosraw's book of travels (Safarnāma), trans. W. M. Thackston, Jr. (New York, 1986).

Nesbitt, J. W. and N. Oikonomides (eds.), *A catalogue of Byzantine seals at Dumbarton Oaks and in the Fogg Museum of Art*, 6 vols. (Washington, DC, 1991–2009).

Nicol, N. D., *A corpus of Fāṭimid coins* (Trieste, 2006).

Niketas Choniates, *Historia*, ed. J. L. van Dieten (Berlin, 1975).

Nikulás Bergsson, *Leiðarvísir*, ed. and trans. R. Simek, *Altnordische Kosmographie* (Berlin, 1990), pp. 264–80, 478–90.

Nykl, A. R., *Hispano-Arabic poetry* (Baltimore, MD, 1946).

Oberto Scriba de Mercato (1186), ed. M. Chiaudano [cited as *Oberto Scriba 1186*] (Genoa, 1940).

Oberto Scriba de Mercato (1190), ed. M. Chiaudano and R. Morozzo della Rocca [cited as *Oberto Scriba 1190*] (Genoa, 1938).

Ocaña Jiménez, M. (ed.), *Repertorio de inscripciones árabes de Almería* (Madrid and Granada, 1964).

Odo of Cluny, *Vita S. Geraldi Auriliacensis*, ed. A.-M. Bultot-Verleysen (Brussels, 2009).

Oikonomides, N., 'Quelques boutiques de Constantinople au Xe siècle', *DOP*, 26 (1972), pp. 345–56.

Olszowy-Schlanger, J. (ed.), *Karaite marriage documents from the Cairo Geniza* (Leiden, 1998).

Orderic Vitalis, *The ecclesiastical history*, ed. M. Chibnall, 6 vols. (Oxford, 1969–80).

Oreste, G. et al. (eds.), *Guglielmo da Sori*, 1 (Genoa, 2015).

Orlandi, M. L. (ed.), *Carte dell'Archivio della Certosa di Calci (1151–1200)* (Pisa, 2002).

Orlov, A. S. et al. (eds.), *Akty Kremony X–XIII vekov* (Leningrad, 1936).

Otto and Acerbo Morena, *Historia Frederici I.*, ed. F. Güterbock, *MGH*, *SRG*, 57 (Berlin, 1930).

Ottonis III. diplomata, ed. T. Sickel, *Ottonis II. et III. diplomata*, *MGH*, *Diplomata* (Hanover, 1893).

Otto of Freising, *Chronica sive Historia de duabus civitatibus*, ed. A. Hofmeister, *MGH*, *SRG*, 45 (Hanover, 1912).

Otto of Freising and Rahewin, *Gesta Friderici I. imperatoris*, ed. G. Waitz and B. de Simson, *MGH*, *SRG*, 46 (Hanover, 1912).

Pandolfi, P. L. S., *Regesto documenti monzesi* (Monza, 1962) [typescript in the Biblioteca civica di Monza].

Papadopoulos-Kerameus, A. I., *Noctes Petropolitanae* (St. Petersburg, 1913).

Pellegrini, B. (ed.), *Le pergamene dell'Archivio di Stato di Pisa dal 1179 al 1184*, tesi di laurea, Università di Pisa, relatore C. Violante, a.a. 1965–1966.

Peregrinationes tres, ed. R. B. C. Huygens and J. H. Pryor (Turnhout, 1994).

Pérès, H., *Esplendor de al-Andalus* (Madrid, 1983).

Petrucci, A. et al. (eds.), *Lettere originali del Medioevo latino (VII–XI sec.)*, 1 (Pisa, 2004).

Pezzola, R. (ed.), *Le carte dei monasteri di S. Maria dell'Acquafredda di Lenno e di S. Benedetto in val Perlana (1042–1200)* (2011), https://www.lombardiabeniculturali.it/cdlm/edizioni/co/lenno-smaria/.

Pezzola, R. (ed.), *Le carte del monastero di San Faustino dell'Isola Comacina (1011–1190)* (2011), https://www.lombardiabeniculturali.it/cdlm/edizioni/co/comacina-sfaustino/.
Piattoli, R. (ed.), *Le carte del monastero di S. Maria di Montepiano (1000–1200)* (Rome, 1942).
Pirri, R. (ed.), *Sicilia sacra disquisitionibus et notitiis illustrata*, 2, 2nd edn (Palermo, 1733).
Poèmes prodromiques en grec vulgaire, ed. D. C. Hesseling and H. O. Pernot (Amsterdam, 1910).
Porro-Lambertenghi, G. (ed.), *Codex diplomaticus Langobardiae* (Turin, 1873).
Pozza, M. (ed.), *Gli atti originali della cancelleria veneziana*, 1 (Venice, 1994).
Pozza, M. and G. Ravegnani (eds.), *I trattati con Bisanzio, 992–1198* (Venice, 1993).
Privilegia episcopii Cremonensis o Codice di Sicardo (715/730–1331), ed. V. Leoni (2004), https://www.lombardiabeniculturali.it/cdlm/edizioni/cr/cremona-sicardo/.
Prodromos, Theodore, *Historische Gedichte*, ed. W. Hörandner (Vienna, 1974).
Prokopios, *Anekdota*, ed. J. Haury and G. Wirth, *Procopius Caesariensis, Opera omnia*, 3 (Munich and Leipzig, 2001).
Psellos/Psellus, *see* Michael Psellos.
al-Qāḍī al-Nuʿmān, *Iftitāḥ al-daʿwa*, trans. A. Haji, *Founding the Fatimid state* (London, 2006).
Rāġib, Y. (ed.), *Marchands d'étoffes du Fayyoum au IIIe/IXe siècle d'après leurs archives (actes et lettres)*, vols. 1, 2, 3, 5.1 (Cairo, 1982–96).
Rapetti, A. M. (ed.), *Le carte del monastero di S. Maria di Chiaravalle*, 1 (Milan, 2004), https://www.lombardiabeniculturali.it/cdlm/edizioni/mi/chiaravalle-smaria1/.
Rapoport, Y. and I. Shahar, *The villages of the Fayyum* (Paris, 2018).
Richter, T. S., 'Spätkoptische Rechtsurkunden neu bearbeitet (II)' [cited as P.Teshlot], *The journal of juristic papyrology*, 30 (2000), pp. 95–148.
Richter, T. S., 'Ein fatimidenzeitliches koptisches Rechnungsheft aus den Papieren Noël Girons', *Travaux et mémoires*, 20.1 (2016), pp. 381–402.
Richter, T. S. and G. Schmelz, 'Der spätkoptische Arbeitsvertrag. P. Heid. inv. kopt. 541', *The journal of juristic papyrology*, 40 (2010), pp. 185–204.
Roberti, M., 'Studi e documenti di storia veneziana', *Nuovo archivio veneto*, n.s., 8 (1908), pp. 5–61.
Romanin, S. (ed.), *Storia documentata di Venezia*, 1 (Venice, 1853).
Rosada, M. (ed.), *S. Maria Formosa* (Venice, 1972).
Rossetti, G., 'Il lodo del vescovo Daiberto sull'altezza delle torri', in *Pisa e la Toscana occidentale nel Medioevo*, 2 (Pisa, 1991), pp. 25–47.
Rovere, A. et al. (eds.), *I libri iurium della repubblica di Genova*, 1, 8 vols. [cited as *LI*] (Genoa, 1992–2002).
Roy, B. and P. Poinssot (eds.), *Inscriptions arabes de Kairouan*, 3 vols. (Paris, 1950–8, Tunis, 1983).
Ruodlieb, ed. B. K. Vollmann (Darmstadt, 1993).
Salemme, T. (ed.), *Carte del secolo XII nel fondo di San Vittore di Meda* (Milan, 2012).
Santini, P., 'Frammenti di un libro di banchieri fiorentini scritto in volgare nel 1211', *Giornale storico della letteratura italiana*, 10 (1887), pp. 161–77.
Santini, P. (ed.), *Documenti dell'antica costituzione del comune di Firenze* (Florence, 1895).
al-Saqaṭī, *Kitāb fī ādāb al-ḥisba*, trans. P. Chalmeta Gendrón, *al-Andalus*, 32 (1967), pp. 125–62, 359–97; 33 (1968), pp. 143–95, 367–434; P. Chalmeta and E. Corriente, *Libro de buen gobierno del zoco* (Almería, 2014).
Sauvaget, J., 'Sur un papyrus arabe de la Bibliothèque égyptienne', *Annales de l'Institut d'études orientales*, 7 (1948), pp. 29–38.
Savioli, L. V., *Annali bolognesi*, 2.2 (Bassano, 1789).
Sāwīrus ibn al-Muqaffaʿ, *Kitāb miṣbāḥ al-ʿaql*, ed. and trans. R. Y. Ebied and M. L. J. Young, *The lamp of the intellect of Severus ibn al-Muqaffaʿ, bishop of Ashmūnain*, Corpus scriptorum Christianorum orientalium, 365–6 (Louvain, 1975).

Scalfati, S. P. P. (ed.), *Carte dell'Archivio della Certosa di Calci*, 2 vols. (Rome, 1971–7).

Scalia, G., 'Il carme pisano sull'impresa contro i Saraceni del 1087', in *Studi di filologia romanza: scritti in onore di Silvio Pellegrini* (Padua, 1971), pp. 1–63.

Schenke, G., 'Übereignung eines Bäckereianteils', in *Kölner Papyri*, 11 (Paderborn, 2007), pp. 288–300.

Schiaparelli, L. (ed.), *I diplomi di Berengario I* (Rome, 1903).

Schiaparelli, L. (ed.), *Codice diplomatico longobardo*, 1–2 (Rome, 1929–33).

Sgherri, R. (ed.), *I documenti dell'Archivio Capitolare di Pisa dall'agosto 1155 al 18 febbraio 1176*, tesi di laurea, Università di Pisa, relatore O. Bertolini, a.a. 1963–1964.

al-Shaqundī, *Risāla fi faḍl al-Andalus*, trans. E. García Gómez, *al-Šaqundī, Elogio del Islam español* (Madrid, 1934).

Simonsohn, S., *The Jews in Sicily*, 1 (Leiden, 1997).

Sirolla, M. L. (ed.), *Carte dell'Archivio di Stato di Pisa, 2 (1070–1100)* (Pisa, 1990).

Spata, G. (ed.), *Le pergamene greche esistenti nel grande archivio di Palermo* (Palermo, 1862).

Starr, J., 'The epitaph of a dyer in Corinth', *Byzantinisch-neugriechische Jahrbücher*, 12 (1935–6), pp. 42–9.

Stern, S. M., 'An original document from the Fāṭimid chancery concerning Italian merchants', in *Studi orientalistici in onore di Giorgio Levi della Vida*, 2 (Rome, 1956), pp. 529–38.

Stillman, N. A., *East-West relations in the Islamic Mediterranean in the early eleventh century*, PhD thesis, University of Pennsylvania, 1970.

Strehlke, E. G. W. (ed.), *Tabulae ordinis theutonici* (Berlin, 1869).

Suetonius, *De vita caesarum*, ed. R. A. Kaster (Oxford, 2016).

Svoronos, N. G., 'Recherches sur le cadastre byzantin et la fiscalité aux XIe et XIIe siècles'. *Bulletin de correspondance hellénique*, 83 (1959), pp. 1–145, 805–23.

al-Ṭabarī, *Tārīkh al-rusul wa al-mulūk*, partial trans. D. Waines, *The revolt of the Zanj*, The history of al-Ṭabarī, 36 (Albany, NY, 1992).

Tafel, G. L. F. and G. M. Thomas (eds.), *Urkunden zur älteren Handels- und Staatsgeschichte der Republik Venedig*, 1 (Vienna, 1856).

Tanner, N. P. (ed.), *Decrees of the ecumenical councils*, 2 vols. (London, 1990).

al-Tanūkhī, *Nishwār al-muḥāḍara*, trans. D. S. Margoliouth, *The table-talk of a Mesopotamian judge*, vols. 1, 2, 8 (London, 1922, Hyderabad, 1929–32).

The life and miracles of Saint Luke of Steiris, ed. and trans. C. L. Connor and W. R. Connor (Brookline, MA, 1994).

The life of Saint Nikon, ed. and trans. D. F. Sullivan (Brookline, MA, 1987).

The Rhodian sea-law, ed. W. Ashburner, in *Nomos rodiōn nautikos: the Rhodian sea-law* (Oxford, 1909).

The Taktika of Leo VI, ed. and trans. G. T. Dennis (Washington, DC, 2010).

Theophanes, *Chronographia*, ed. C. de Boor, 2 vols. (Leipzig, 1883–5).

Theophanes Continuatus, ed. I. Bekker (Bonn, 1838).

Theophylacti Achridensis epistulae, ed. and trans. P. Gautier (Thessaloniki, 1986).

Thietmar of Merseburg, *Chronicon*, ed. R. Holtzmann, *MGH, SRG*, n.s., 9 (Berlin, 1935).

Thomas, J. and A. Constantinides Hero (trans.), *Byzantine monastic foundation documents* [cited as *BMFD*], 5 vols. (Washington, DC, 2000).

Thung, M. H., 'An Arabic letter of the Rijksmuseum van Oudheden, Leiden', *Oudheidkundige mededelingen uit het Rijksmuseum van Oudheden te Leiden*, 76 (1996), pp. 63–8.

Timarione, ed. R. Romano (Naples, 1974).

Tirelli Carli, M. (ed.), *Carte dell'Archivio Capitolare di Pisa*, 3 (Rome, 1977).

Translatio S. Marci, ed. E. Colombi, '"Translatio Marci evangelistae Venetias" [BHL 5283–5284]', *Hagiographica*, 17 (2010), pp. 73–129.

Trombetti Budriesi, A. L. and T. Duranti (eds.), *I libri iurium del comune di Bologna: regesti*, 2 vols. (Bologna, 2010).

Tzetzes, *see* John Tzetzes.

al-ʿUdhrī, *Tarṣīʿ al-akhbār*, different sections trans. E. Molina López, *La cora de Tudmīr según al-ʿUḏrī* (Granada, 1972); M. Sánchez Martínez, 'La cora de *Ilbira* (Granada y Almería) en los siglos X y XI, según al-ʿUḏrī (1003–1085)', *Cuadernos de historia del Islam*, 7 (1975–6), pp. 5–82; R. Valencia, 'La cora de Sevilla en el *Tarṣīʿ al-ajbār* de Aḥmad b. ʿUmar al-ʿUḏrī', *Andalucía islámica*, 4–5 (1985–6), pp. 107–43.

Ugo Falcando, *Liber de regno*, ed. G. B. Siragusa, *La Historia o Liber de Regno Sicilie e la Epistola ad Petrum Panormitane ecclesie thesaurarium*, 2 vols. (Rome, 1897).

Usāma b. Munqidh, *Kitāb al-iʿtibār*, trans. P. M. Cobb, *The book of contemplation* (London, 2008).

van Berchem, M. (ed.), *Matériaux pour un Corpus inscriptionum Arabicarum*, 1.1 (Paris, 1894).

Venturini, C. (ed.), *Pergamene dell'Archivio Capitolare di Pisa dal 1176 al 1192*, tesi di laurea, Università di Pisa, relatore C. Violante, a.a. 1965–1966.

Vignoli, P. (ed.), *I Costituti della legge e dell'uso di Pisa (sec. XII)* (Rome, 2003).

Villehardouin, Geoffroi de, *La conquête de Constantinople*, ed. E. Faral, 2nd edn, 2 vols. (Paris, 1961).

Vita S. Raynerii, ed. G. Zaccagnini, *La 'Vita' di san Ranieri (secolo XII)* (Pisa, 2008).

Vittani, G. et al. (eds.), *Gli atti privati milanesi e comaschi del sec. XI*, 4 vols. (Milan, 1933–69).

Viviani, G. (ed.), *Le pergamene dell'Archivio di Stato di Pisa dal 18 giugno 1129 al 9 febbraio 1145*, tesi di laurea, Università di Pisa, relatore C. Violante, a.a. 1964–1965.

von Falkenhausen, V., 'I mulini della discordia sul Fiumefreddo', in E. Cuozzo et al. (eds.), *Puer Apuliae*, 1 (Paris, 2008), pp. 227–38.

von Falkenhausen, V. (ed.), 'I documenti greci di S. Maria della Grotta rinvenuti in Termini Imerese', in R. Lavagnini and C. Rognoni (eds.), *Byzantino-Sicula*, 6 (Palermo, 2014), pp. 215–42.

von Falkenhausen, V. et al. (eds.), 'The twelfth-century documents of St. George's of Tròccoli, Sicily', *Journal of Arabic and Islamic studies*, 16 (2016), pp. 1–84.

Wansborough, J. (ed.), 'A Judaeo-Arabic document from Sicily', *Bulletin of the School of Oriental and African Studies*, 30 (1967), pp. 305–13.

al-Wansharīsī, *al-Miʿyār al-muʿrib wa al-jāmiʿ al-mughrib ʿan fatāwī ʿulamāʾ Ifrīqīya wa al-Andalus wa al-Maghrib*, partial trans. and summary in V. Lagardère, *Histoire et société en Occident musulman au Moyen Âge* (Madrid, 1995).

Weiss, G., *Legal documents written by the court clerk Halfon ben Manasse (dated 1100–1138)*, PhD thesis, University of Pennsylvania, 1970.

William of Tyre, *Chronicon*, ed. R. B. C. Huygens, Corpus Christianorum. Continuatio medievalis, 63A (Turnhout, 1986).

Wipo, *Gesta Chuonradi imperatoris*, ed. H. Bresslau, *Wiponis opera*, *MGH*, *SRG*, 61 (Hanover, 1915).

al-Yaʿqūbī, *Kitāb al-buldān*, trans. M. S. Gordon et al., *The works of Ibn Wāḍih al-Yaʿqūbī: an English translation*, 1 (Leiden, 2018), pp. 64–199.

Yāqūt, *al-Muʿjam al-buldān*, trans. G. ʿAbd al-Karīm, 'La España musulmana en la obra de Yāqūt (s. XII–XIII)', *Cuadernos de historia del Islam*, 6 (1974), pp. 11–354.

Zagni, L. (ed.), *Le pergamene del secolo XII del monastero di S. Margherita* (Milan, 1984).

Zeldes, N. and M. Frenkel, 'The Sicilian trade', in N. Bucaria (ed.), *Gli ebrei in Sicilia dal tardoantico al medioevo* (Palermo, 1998), pp. 243–56, translating documents edited and translated into Hebrew by Zeldes and Frenkel in *Michael*, 14 (1997), 89–137.
Zepos, I. D. and P. Zepos (eds.), *Jus graecoromanum*, 8 vols. (Athens, 1931).
Zimmermann, H. (ed.), *Papsturkunden 896–1046*, 2 vols. (Vienna, 1988–9).
al-Zuhrī, *Kitāb al-ja'rāfiyya*, trans. D. Bramón, *El mundo en el siglo XII* (Sabadell, 1991).

3. Secondary Works

Abulafia, D., *The two Italies* (Cambridge, 1977).
Abulafia, D., 'Pisan commercial colonies and consulates in twelfth-century Sicily', *The English historical review*, 93 (1978), pp. 68–81.
Abulafia, D., 'The crown and the economy under Roger II and his successors', *DOP*, 37 (1983), pp. 1–14.
Abulafia, D., 'The Norman kingdom of Africa and the Norman expeditions to Majorca and the Muslim Mediterranean', *Anglo-Norman studies*, 7 (1985), pp. 26–49.
Abulafia, D., 'Asia, Africa, and the trade of medieval Europe', in M. M. Postan and E. Miller (eds.), *The Cambridge economic history of Europe*, 2, 2nd edn (Cambridge, 1987), pp. 402–73.
Abulafia, D., 'Southern Italy, Sicily and Sardinia in the medieval Mediterranean economy', in Abulafia, *Commerce and conquest in the Mediterranean, 1100–1500* (Aldershot, 1993), study I.
Abulafia, D., 'Il contesto mediterraneo e il primo disegno delle due Italie', in Galasso, *Alle origini del dualismo italiano* (Soveria Mannelli, 2014), pp. 11–28.
Abu-Lughod, J., *Before European hegemony* (Oxford, 1989).
Acién Almansa, M., *Entre el feudalismo y el Islam. 'Umar ibn Ḥafṣūn en los historiadores, en las fuentes y en la historia*, 2nd edn (Jaén, 1997).
Acién Almansa, M., 'El final de los elementos feudales en al-Andalus', in Barceló and Toubert, *'L'incastellamento'* (Rome, 1998), pp. 291–305.
Acién Almansa, M., 'Sobre el papel de la ideología en la caracterización de las formaciones sociales: la formación social islámica', *Hispania*, 200 (1998), pp. 915–68.
Acién Almansa, M., 'Poblamiento y sociedad en al-Andalus', in J. I. de la Iglesia Duarte (ed.), *Cristiandad e Islam en la edad medieval hispana* (Logroño, 2008), pp. 141–67.
Acién Almansa, M. et al., 'Excavación de un barrio artesanal de Baŷŷāna (Pechina, Almería)', *Archéologie islamique*, 1 (1990), pp. 147–68.
Ackerman-Lieberman, P. I., *The business of identity* (Stanford, CA, 2014).
Adams, W. Y., *Ceramic industries of medieval Nubia* (Lexington, KY, 1987).
Adamsheck, B., *Kenchreai, 4: the pottery* (Leiden, 1979).
Aerts, W. J., 'Ptochoprodromos', *Byzantinische Zeitschrift*, 34–5 (1991–2), pp. 519–23.
Agostini, A., 'The metal finds from the site of Vetricella (Scarlino, Grosseto)', in Bianchi and Hodges, *The nEU-Med project* (Florence, 2020), pp. 33–47.
Aguirre Sádaba, F. J., 'Notas acerca de la proyección de los "kutub al-waṯā'iq" en el estudio social y económico de al-Andalus', *Miscelánea de estudios árabes y hebraicos*, 49 (2000), pp. 3–30.
Aissani, D. and A. Amara, 'Qal'a des Banī Ḥammād', *Encyclopédie Berbère*, 37–9 (Aix-en-Provence, 2015), pp. 6642–68.
Al-Ándalus: país de ciudades (Toledo, 2008).
Alaimo, R. et al., 'Produzione ceramica nell' insediamento medievale presso la Villa del Casale di Piazza Armerina', in Pensabene, *Piazza Armerina* (Rome, 2010), pp. 39–60.

Alberti, A. and M. Giorgio, 'Nuovi dati sulla produzione di ceramica a Pisa tra XI e XII secolo', in Cantini and Rizzitelli, *Una città operosa* (Florence, 2018), pp. 29–35.

Albini, G., 'Piacenza dal XII al XIV secolo', in J.-C. Maire Vigueur (ed.), *I podestà dell'Italia comunale*, 2 vols. (Rome, 2000), pp. 405–45.

Aleo Nero, C., 'Attività produttive a Palermo nel medioevo', in V. Caminneci et al. (eds.), *La città che produce* (Bari, 2018), pp. 73–83.

Alexiou, M. et al., 'The poverty of écriture and the craft of writing', *Byzantine and Modern Greek studies*, 10 (1986), pp. 1–40.

Alfano, A., 'I paesaggi medievali in Sicilia', *AM*, 42 (2015), pp. 329–52.

Alfano, A., 'La ceramica medievale', in Pensabene and Barresi, *Piazza Armerina, Villa del Casale* (Rome, 2019), pp. 599–628.

Alfano, A. and G. D'Amico, 'La conservazione dei cereali a lungo termine nella Sicilia medievale', *AM*, 44 (2017), pp. 73–91.

Alfano, A. and V. Sacco, 'Tra alto e basso medioevo' (2014), https://www.academia.edu/10181575/Antonio_Alfano_Viva_Sacco_2014_Tra_alto_e_basso_medioevo_Ceramiche_merci_e_scambi_nelle_valli_dello_Jato_e_del_Belìce_Destro_dalle_ricognizioni_nel_territorio_Palermo_.

Alfano, A. and V. Sacco, 'I paesaggi medievali in Sicilia', *AM*, 42 (2015), pp. 329–52.

Alfano, A. et al., 'I nuovi scavi alla Villa del Casale', in Pensabene and Sfameni, *La villa restaurata* (Bari, 2014), pp. 583–94.

Alfano, A. et al., 'Produzione e circolazione presso l'insediamento medievale della Villa del Casale', in P. Arthur and M. Leo Imperiale (eds.), *VII Congresso nazionale di archeologia medievale* (Florence, 2015), pp. 218–22.

Alias, F., 'Origini, forme e sviluppi della fiscalità nella Sardegna giudicale (XI–XIII secolo)', in A. Soddu (ed.), *Linguaggi e rappresentazioni del potere nella Sardegna medievale* (Rome, 2020), pp. 89–144.

Allen, R. C., *Enclosure and the yeoman* (Oxford, 1992).

Almbladh, K., 'The letters of the Jewish merchant Abū l-Surūr Faraḥ b. Ismā'īl al-Qābisī in the context of medieval Arabic business correspondence', *Orientalia Suecana*, 53 (2004), pp. 15–35.

Almenar Fernández, L., 'Why did villagers buy earthenware?', *Continuity and change*, 33 (2018), pp. 1–27.

Amabe, F., *Urban autonomy in medieval Islam* (Leiden, 2016).

Amar, Z. et al., 'The paper and textile industry in the land of Israel and its raw materials in light of an analysis of the Cairo Genizah documents', in B. Outhwaite and S. Bhayro (eds.), *From a sacred source* (Leiden, 2010), pp. 25–42.

Amara, A., 'Retour à la problématique du déclin économique du monde musulman médiéval', *The Maghreb review*, 28 (2003), pp. 2–26.

Amara, A., 'L'organisation foncière du Maghreb central (VIIe–XIVe siècle)', *Al-Mawaqif*, 5 (2010), pp. 53–65.

Amara, A., 'Bône et la littoralisation du pays Kutāma (IXe–XIIe siècles)', *RM2E—Revue de la Méditerranée, édition électronique*, 3.1 (2016), pp. 141–152.

Amari, M., *Storia dei Musulmani di Sicilia*, ed. C. A. Nallino (Catania, 1933–9).

Ampolo, C., 'Lo scarico di fornace arabo-normanna rinvenuto nel peristilio della villa', *MEFR*, 83.1 (1971), pp. 261–73.

Andenna, G. C., 'Formazione, strutture e processi di riconoscimento giuridico delle signorie rurali tra Lombardia e Piemonte orientale (secoli XI–XIII)', in Dilcher and Violante, *Strutture e trasformazioni* (Bologna, 1996), pp. 123–67.

Andenna, G. C., *Storia della Lombardia medievale* (Novara, 2018).

Anderson, G. et al. (eds.), *The Aghlabids and their neighbours* (Leiden, 2018).

Andreolli, B., 'Contratti agrari e patti colonici nella Lucchesia dei secoli VIII e IX', *Studi medievali*, 19 (1978), pp. 69–158.

Andreolli, B., 'L'evoluzione dei patti colonici nella Toscana dei secoli VIII–X', *Quaderni medievali*, 16 (1983), pp. 29–52.

Andreolli, B. and M. Montanari, *L'azienda curtense in Italia* (Bologna, 1983).

Andrews, D., 'Lo scavo di piazza Duomo: età medioevale e moderna', in D. Caporusso (ed.), *Scavi MM3*, 1 (Milan, 1991), pp. 163–209.

Andriollo, L. and S. Métivier, 'Quel rôle pour les provinces dans la domination aristocratique au XIe siècle?', *Travaux et mémoires*, 21.2 (2017), pp. 505–29.

Angold, M., 'Archons and dynasts', in Angold (ed.), *The Byzantine aristocracy, IX to XIII centuries*, BAR, I221 (Oxford, 1984), pp. 231–53.

Anichini, F. and G. Gattiglia, 'Nuovi dati sulla topografia di Pisa medievale tra X e XVI secolo', *AM*, 35 (2008), pp. 121–50.

Anievas, A. and K. Nişancıoğlu, *How the West came to rule* (London, 2015).

Antonaras, A. Ch., 'Artisan production in Byzantine Thessaloniki (4th–15th century)', in F. Daim and J. Drauschke (eds.), *Hinter den Mauern und auf dem offenen Land* (Mainz, 2016), pp. 113–40.

Aparicio Sánchez, L., 'Una estructura de probable uso industrial aparecida en el arrabal califal de el Fontanar (Córdoba)', in A. García Porras (ed.), *Arqueología de la producción en época medieval* (Salobreña, 2013), pp. 129–53.

Aparicio Sánchez, L., 'Los primeros indicios de saturación en los arrabales cordobeses', in M. Retuerce Velasco (ed.), *Actas VI Congreso de arqueología medieval (España–Portugal)* (Ciudad Real, 2021), pp. 227–32.

Archaeology, 'Medieval Egyptian pottery found in Bulgaria', https://www.archaeology.org/news/6549-180417-bulgaria-medieval-murals/.

Arcifa, L., 'Indicatori archeologici e dinamiche insediative nella Sicilia tardo bizantina', in M. Congiù et al. (eds.), *La Sicilia bizantina* (Caltanissetta, 2010), pp. 67–89.

Arcifa, L., 'La Sicilia bizantina agli inizi del IX secolo', in A. Puglisi and M. Turco (eds.), *L'acqua, la roccia e l'uomo* (Nicolosi, 2015), pp. 143–55.

Arcifa, L., 'Contenitori da trasporto nella Sicilia bizantina (VIII–X secolo)', *AM*, 45 (2018), pp. 123–48.

Arcifa, L., '"Insularità" siciliana e Mediterraneo altomedievale', in K. Wolf and K. Herbers (eds.), *Southern Italy as contact area and border region in the middle ages* (Cologne, 2018), pp. 125–48.

Arcifa, L. and A. Bagnera, 'Ceramica islamica a Palermo', in R. M. Carra Bonacasa and E. Vitale (eds.), *Studi in memoria di Fabiola Ardizzone, 3: ceramica* (Palermo 2018), pp. 7–60.

Arcifa, L. and A. Bagnera, 'Palermo in the ninth and early tenth century', in Anderson et al., *The Aghlabids* (Leiden, 2018), pp. 382–404.

Arcifa, L. and R. Longo, 'Processi di diversificazione territoriale nella Sicilia di inizi IX secolo: il contesto di Rocchicella-Mineo (CT)', in P. Arthur and M. Leo Imperiale (eds.), *VII Congresso nazionale di archeologia medievale* (Florence, 2015), pp. 361–6.

Arcifa, L. and F. Maurici, 'Castelli e incastellamento in Sicilia', in A. Augenti and P. Galetti (eds.), *L'incastellamento: storia e archeologia* (Spoleto, 2018), pp. 447–78.

Arcifa, L. and M. Messina, 'La frontiera arabo-bizantina in Sicilia orientale (IX–XI secolo)', in F. Sogliani et al. (eds.), *VIII Congresso nazionale di archeologia medievale* (Florence, 2018), pp. 371–83.

Arcifa, L. and M. Sgarlata (eds.), *From polis to madina* (Bari, 2020).

Arcifa, L. et al., 'Archeologia della Sicilia islamica', in P. Sénac (ed.), *Villa 4* (Toulouse, 2012), pp. 214–74.

Ardizzone, F., 'Rapporti commerciali tra la Sicilia occidentale ed il Tirreno centro-meridionale alla luce del rinvenimento di alcuni contenitori di trasporto', in G. P. Brogiolo (ed.), *II Congresso nazionale di archeologia medievale* (Florence, 2000), pp. 402–7.

Ardizzone, F., 'Le produzioni medievali di Agrigento alla luce delle recenti indagini nella Valle dei Templi', *Atti, XLII Convegno internazionale della ceramica* (Savona, 2009), pp. 275–85.

Ardizzone, F., 'Nuove ipotesi a partire dalla rilettura dei dati archeologici: la Sicilia occidentale', in A. Nef and V. Prigent (eds.), *La Sicile de Byzance à l'Islam* (Paris, 2010), pp. 51–76.

Ardizzone Lo Bue, F., *Anfore in Sicilia (VIII–XII sec. d.C.)* (Palermo, 2012).

Ardizzone, F. et al., 'Il complesso monumentale in contrada "Case Romane" a Marettimo (Trapani)', in S. Patitucci Uggeri (ed.), *Scavi medievali in Italia 1994–1995* (Rome, 1998), pp. 387–424.

Ardizzone, F. et al., 'Lo scavo della chiesa di S. Maria degli Angeli alla Gancia', in Nef and Ardizzone, *Les dynamiques* (Rome and Bari, 2014), pp. 197–223.

Ardizzone, F. et al., 'The role of Palermo in the central Mediterranean', *Journal of Islamic archaeology*, 2 (2015), pp. 229–57.

Ardizzone, F. et al., 'Aghlabid Palermo', in Anderson et al., *The Aghlabids* (Leiden, 2018), pp. 362–81.

Ariza Armada, A., 'El tesorillo almohade de Moncarapacho (Algarbe, Portugal)', *Hécate*, 5 (2018), pp. 64–99.

Armstrong, P., 'Some Byzantine and later settlements in Eastern Phokis', *Annual of the British School at Athens*, 84 (1989), pp. 1–47.

Armstrong, P., 'Byzantine Thebes', *Annual of the British School at Athens*, 88 (1993), pp. 295–335.

Armstrong, P., 'The survey area in the Byzantine and Ottoman periods', in W. Cavanagh et al. (eds.), *The Laconia survey*, 1 (London, 1996), pp. 339–402.

Armstrong, P., 'The Byzantine and Ottoman pottery', in W. Cavanagh et al. (eds.), *The Laconia survey*, 2 (London, 2002), pp. 125–40.

Armstrong, P., 'Merchants of Venice at Sparta in the 12th century', in W. G. Kavanagh et al. (eds.), *Sparta and Laconia from prehistory to pre-modern* (London, 2009), pp. 313–21.

Armstrong, P., 'Trade in the east Mediterranean in the eighth century', in Mundell Mango, *Byzantine trade* (Farnham, 2009), pp. 157–78.

Armstrong, P., 'Greece in the eleventh century', in J. Howard-Johnston (ed.), *Social change in town and country in eleventh-century Byzantium* (Oxford, 2020), pp. 133–56.

Armstrong P. and N. Günsenin, 'Glazed pottery production at Ganos', *Anatolia antiqua*, 3 (1995), pp. 179–201.

Arnold, F., *Elephantine XXX* (Mainz, 2003).

Arnon, Y. D., *Caesarea maritima, the late periods (700–1291 CE)*, BAR, S1771 (Oxford, 2008).

Arthur, P., 'Amphorae for bulk transport', in F. D'Andria and D. B. Whitehouse (eds.), *Excavations at Otranto*, 2 (Galatina, 1992), pp. 197–217.

Arthur, P., *Byzantine and Turkish Hierapolis (Pamukkale)* (Istanbul, 2006).

Arthur, P., 'Byzantine and Turkish glazed ceramics in southern Apulia, Italy', *Byzas*, 7 (2007), pp. 239–54.

Artifoni, E., 'Corporazioni e società di "popolo"', *Quaderni storici*, 74 (1990), pp. 387–404.

Ashtor, E., 'The Kārimī merchants', *The journal of the Royal Asiatic Society of Great Britain and Ireland*, 88.1–2 (1956), pp. 45–56.

Ashtor, E., *Histoire des prix et des salaires dans l'Orient médiéval* (Paris, 1969).
Ashtor, E., *A social and economic history of the Near East in the middle ages* (London, 1976).
Ashtor, E. and C. Cahen, 'Débat sur l'évolution économico-sociale de l'Égypte à la fin du Moyen Âge', *JESHO*, 12 (1969), pp. 102–11.
Astarita, C., *From feudalism to capitalism* (Leiden, 2022).
Athanasoulis, D., 'Corinth', in J. Albani and E. Chalkia (eds.), *Heaven and earth* (Athens, 2013), pp. 191–209.
Athanassopoulos, E. F., 'Landscape archaeology of medieval and pre-modern Greece', in J. Albani and E. Chalkia (eds.), *Heaven and earth* (Athens, 2013), pp. 79–105.
Avissar, M. and E. Stern, *Pottery of the Crusader, Ayyubid and Mamluk periods in Israel* (Jerusalem, 2005).
Avramea, A., 'Land and sea communications, fourth–fifteenth centuries', in Laiou, *The economic history of Byzantium* (Washington, DC, 2002), pp. 57–90.
Azuar Ruiz, R., *Denia islámica* (Alicante, 1989).
Azuar Ruiz, R., *La rábita califal de las dunas de Guardamar (Alicante)* (Alicante, 1989).
Azuar Ruiz, R. (ed.), *El Castillo del Rio (Aspe, Alicante)* (Alicante, 1994).
Azuar Ruiz, R., 'Alfares y testares del Sharq al-Andalus (siglos XII–XIII)', in J. I. Padilla et al. (eds.), *Ceràmica medieval i postmedieval* (Barcelona, 1998), pp. 57–71.
Azuar Ruiz, R., 'Una necesaria revisión de las cerámicas andalusíes halladas en Italia', *ATM*, 12.1 (2005), pp. 175–99.
Azuar Ruiz, R., 'Castillos y espacios marginales de las ciudades en el Šarq al-Andalus (siglos XII–XIII)', in P. Cressier (ed.), *Castrum 8* (Madrid, 2008), pp. 89–108.
Azuar, R., 'Cerámicas en "verde y manganeso", consideradas norteafricanas, en al-Andalus (s. X–XI dC)', *ATM*, 19 (2012), pp. 59–90.
Azuar Ruiz, R., 'Bronces fatimíes de Denia', *Marq, arqueología y museos*, 9 (2018), pp. 61–70.
Azuar Ruiz, R., *Las taifas del Sharq al-Andalus en las rutas y el mercado mediterráneo del siglo XI* (Valencia, 2019).
Azuar, R. and O. Inglese Carreras, 'Contenedores cerámicos de transporte marítimo de al-Andalus en el Mediterráneo occidental (siglos X–XIII)', in P. Petridis et al. (eds.), *12th congress AIECM3 on medieval and modern period Mediterranean ceramics* (Athens, 2021), pp. 355–61.
Bacci, G. M. and G. Tigano, *Da Zancle a Messina* (Messina, 2001).
Bach, E., *La cité de Gênes au XIIe siècle* (Copenhagen, 1955).
Bacharach, J. L. (ed.), *Fustat finds* (Cairo, 2002).
Backman, C. R., *The decline and fall of medieval Sicily* (Cambridge, 1995).
Baeyens, N. et al., *Archeologisch onderzoek Alveringem-Maldegem Lot 3* (Ghent, 2018).
Bagnall, R. S. and B. W. Frier, *The demography of Roman Egypt* (Cambridge, 1994).
Bagnera, A., 'From a small town to a capital', in Nef, *A companion to medieval Palermo* (Leiden, 2013), pp. 61–88.
Bahgat, A., 'Les forêts en Égypte et leur administration au moyen âge', *Bulletin de l'Institut égyptien*, 4 ser., 1 (1901), pp. 141–58.
Bahgat, A. and A. Gabriel, *Fouilles d'al Fousṭâṭ, publiées sous les auspices du Comité de conservation des monuments de l'art arabe* (Paris, 1921).
Bahgat, A. and F. Massoul, *La céramique musulmane de l'Égypte* (Cairo, 1930).
Bahri, F. B. and C. Touihiri, 'Des jarres des IVe–V^{e} s /X^{e}–XIe siècles de Qasr al-Āliya (Mahdiyya)', in S. Sehili (ed.), *L'olivier en Méditerranée*, 2 (Tunis, 2011), pp. 253–80.
Bailey, D. M., 'The pottery from the South Church at el-Ashmunein', *CCE*, 4 (1996), pp. 48–112.
Bailey, D. M., *Excavations at el-Ashmunein*, 5 (London, 1998).

Bairati, E., 'La collegiata di Santo Stefano protomartire', in G. A. Vergani (ed.), *Mirabilia Vicomercati* (Venice, 1994), pp. 139–59.
Bairoch, P., *Commerce extérieur et développement économique de l'Europe au XIXe siècle* (Paris, 1976).
Baker, J., *Coinage and money in medieval Greece 1200–1430* (Leiden, 2020).
Bakirtzis, Ch., 'Imports, exports and autarky in Byzantine Thessalonike from the seventh to the tenth century', in J. Henning (ed.), *Post-Roman towns*, 2 (Berlin, 2007), pp. 89–118.
Bakourou, A. et al., 'Argos and Sparta', in Ch. Bakirtzis (ed.), *VIIe congrès international sur la céramique médiévale en Méditerranée* (Athens, 2003), pp. 233–6.
Balard, M., 'Amalfi et Byzance (X^e–XIIe siècles)', *Travaux et mémoires*, 6 (1976), pp. 85–94.
Balard, M., *La Romanie génoise (XIIe–début du XVe siècle)* (Rome, 1978).
Balard, M., *Les Latins en Orient (X^e–XVe siècle)* (Paris, 2006).
Balard, M., 'Le commerce génois à Alexandrie (XIe–XIVe siècle)', in Décobert et al., *Alexandrie médiévale*, 4 (Cairo, 2011), pp. 125–44.
Baldassarri, M., 'Monete, associazioni e processi formativi nei contesti medievali degli scavi urbani di Pisa', in F. Redi and A. Forgione (eds.), *VI Congresso nazionale di archeologia medievale* (Florence, 2012), pp. 746–51.
Baldassarri, M., 'La ceramica a Pisa dal Mille al Duecento, tra produzioni locali e importazioni mediterranee', in Baldassarri (ed.), *Pisa città della ceramica* (Pisa, 2018), pp. 91–102.
Baldassarri, M., 'Da *villa* a *civitas*', in F. Cantini (ed.), *"Costruire lo sviluppo"* (Florence, 2019), pp. 21–32.
Baldassarri, M. and M. Giorgio, 'La ceramica di produzione mediterranea a Pisa tra XI e fine XIII secolo', in S. Gelichi and M. Baldassarri (eds.), *Pensare/classificare* (Florence, 2010), pp. 35–51.
Ballet, P. and M. C. Guidotti, 'Identificazione e analisi delle discariche domestiche e industriali della città di Antinoe', in R. Pintaudi (ed.), *Antinoupolis II* (Florence, 2014), pp. 165–221.
Balog, P., 'History of the dirhem from the Fāṭimid conquest until the collapse of the Mamlūk empire', *Revue numismatique*, 6 ser., 3 (1961), pp. 109–46.
Balzaretti, R., *The lands of Saint Ambrose* (Turnhout, 2019).
Banaji, J., *Theory as history* (Leiden, 2010).
Banaji, J., *A brief history of commercial capitalism* (Chicago, 2020).
Banti, O., *Scritti di storia, diplomatica ed epigrafia*, ed. S. P. P. Scalfati (Pisa, 1995).
Banti, O. (ed.), *Amalfi, Genova, Pisa e Venezia* (Pisa, 1998).
Barceló, C., '¿Galgos o podencos?', *al-Qanṭara*, 11 (1990), pp. 429–60.
Barceló, C. and A. Heidenreich, 'Lusterware made in the Abbadid taifa of Seville (eleventh century) and its early production in the Mediterranean region', *Muqarnas*, 31 (2014), pp. 245–76.
Barceló, M., *El sol que salió por Occidente* (Jaén, 1997).
Barceló, M., 'Un estudio sobre la estructura fiscal y procedimientos contables del emirato omeya de Córdoba (138–300/755–912) y del califato (300–366/912–976)', in Barceló, *El sol que salió* (Jaén, 1997), pp. 103–36.
Barceló, M., '*Al-Mulk*, el verde y el blanco', in Barceló, *El sol que salió* (Jaén, 1997), pp. 187–94.
Barceló, M. and P. Toubert (eds.), '*L'incastellamento*' (Rome, 1998).
Barceló, M. et al., *Les aïgues cercades* (Palma de Mallorca, 1986).
Barceló, M. et al., *El agua que no duerme* (Granada, 1996).
Bargigia, F., 'I Pavesi e la prassi bellica nella prima età sveva', *Bollettino della società pavese di storia patria*, 105 (2005), pp. 111–34.

Barile, N. L., 'Rethinking "The two Italies"', in Mainoni and Barile, *Comparing two Italies* (Turnhout, 2020), pp. 117–38.
Barnéa, I., 'La céramique byzantine de Dobroudja, X^{e}–XIIe siècles', in V. Déroche and J.-M. Spieser (eds.), *Recherches sur la céramique byzantine* (Athens, 1989), pp. 131–42.
Barresi, P., 'I risultati delle campagne di scavo 2004–2005', in Pensabene and Bonanno, *L'insediamento medievale* (Galatina, 2008), pp. 133–57.
Barthélemy, D., *The serf, the knight and the historian* (Ithaca, NY, 2009).
Bartusis, M. C., *Land and privilege in Byzantium* (Cambridge, 2012).
Basileiou, *see also* Vassiliou.
Basileiou, A., *Byzantinē ephyalōmenē keramikē apo to Argos (10os–a' miso 13ou ai.)*, 2 vols. (Athens, 2021).
Bass, G. F. and J. W. Allen (eds.), *Serçe Limanı*, 2 vols. (College Station, TX, 2004–9).
Bauden, F., 'Maqriziana XII', in B. Craig (ed.), *Ismaili and Fatimid studies in honor of Paul E. Walker* (Chicago, 2010), pp. 33–85.
Bazzana, A., 'La céramique verde e morado califale à Valence', in *A cerâmica medieval no Mediterrâneo ocidental* (Mértola, 1991), pp. 349–58.
Bazzana, A., *Maisons d'al-Andalus*, 2 vols. (Madrid, 1992).
Bazzana, A. and J. Bedia García, *Excavaciones en la isla de Saltés (Huelva)* (Seville, 2005).
Bazzana, A. and N. Trauth, 'Minéralurgie et métallurgie à Saltés et dans son arrière-pays (Huelva)', in Canto García and Cressier, *Minas y metalurgía* (Madrid, 2008), pp. 209–43.
Bazzana, A. et al., *Les châteaux ruraux d'al-Andalus* (Madrid, 1988).
Bazzini, M. et al., 'Un'officina per la lavorazione di steatite (XI–XII secolo)', *AM*, 35 (2008), pp. 453–89.
Beale-Rivaya, Y. C., 'Shared legal spaces in the Arabic language notarial documents of Toledo', in Y. C. Beale-Rivaya and J. Busic (eds.), *A companion to medieval Toledo* (Leiden, 2018), pp. 221–37.
Beasley, W. G. and E. G. Pulleyblank (eds.), *Historians of China and Japan* (London, 1961).
Bejaoui, F., 'Une nouvelle église d'époque byzantine à Sbeïtla', *L'Africa romana*, 12 (1998), pp. 1173–83.
Belke, K. and N. Mersich, *Phrygien und Pisidien* (Vienna, 1990).
Bell, A. R. et al., *The English wool market, c.1230–1327* (Cambridge, 2007).
Belli, M. et al., *Archeologia di un castello minerario* (Florence, 2005).
Belli Barsali, I., 'La topografia di Lucca nei secoli VIII–XI', in *Atti del V Congresso internazionale di studi sull'alto medioevo* (Spoleto, 1973), pp. 461–554.
Beltrán de Heredia Bercero, J., '*Barcino*, de colònia romana a sede regia visigoda, medina islàmica i ciutat comtal', *Quaderns d'arqueologia i història de la ciutat de Barcelona*, 9 (2013) pp. 17–118.
Beltrán de Heredia Bercero, J. and N. Miró i Alaix, 'Los contactos comerciales en Barcelona a través de la cerámica', *Quaderns d'arqueologia i història de la ciutat de Barcelona*, 13 (2017) pp. 113–35.
Ben Amara, A. et al., 'Distinction de céramiques glaçurées aghlabides ou fatimides (IXe–XIe siècles, Ifriqiya) par la mise en évidence de différences de texture au niveau de l'interface glaçure–terre cuite', *ArcheoSciences*, 29 (2005), pp. 35–42.
Benaboud, M., 'La economía', in Viguera Molins, *Historia de España*, 8.1 (Madrid, 1994), pp. 231–72.
Benaboud, M. and M. Bensbaa, 'Privatisation and inheritance in Andalusian documents during the period of the Murābiṭūn', *al-Qanṭara*, 14 (1993), pp. 259–74.
Benassi, F. and G. Bosi, 'Modena, corso Duomo, Palazzo Arcivescovile', *AM*, 38 (2011), p. 378.

Benente, F., 'Ceramica d'importazione islamica e bizantina', in C. Varaldo (ed.), *Archeologia urbana a Savona*, 2.2 (Savona, 2001), pp. 167–98.
Benente, F., 'Mediterranean and Ligurian ceramics in Genoa in the XII and XIII centuries', *Medieval ceramics*, 31 (2011), pp. 27–33.
Benente, F., 'Frammenti di ceramica invetriata monocroma ad impasto siliceo', in M. Sannazaro et al. (eds.), *1287 e dintorni* (Mantua, 2017), pp. 264–5.
Bennison, A. and M. Á. Gallego, 'Jewish trading in Fes on the eve of the Almohad conquest', *Miscelánea de estudios árabes y hebraicos. Sección hebreo*, 56 (2007), 33–51.
Bensch, S. P., *Barcelona and its rulers, 1096–1291* (Cambridge, 1995).
Benvenuti, M. et al., 'Studying the Colline Metallifere mining area in Tuscany', *IES* [*Institute Europa Subterranea*] *Yearbook* (2014), pp. 261–87.
Benvenuti, M. et al., 'Metals and coinage in medieval Tuscany', in Bianchi and Hodges, *Origins of a new economic union* (Florence, 2018), pp. 135–45.
Bercher, H. et al., 'Une abbaye latine dans la société musulmane', *Annales E. S. C.*, 34 (1979), pp. 525–47.
Bergemann, J. (ed.), *Der Gela-Survey*, 3 vols. (Munich, 2010).
Bergemann, J., 'Funde der islamischen Phase im Gebiet von Gela und im Hinterland von Agrigent', in Nef and Ardizzone, *Les dynamiques* (Rome and Bari, 2014), pp. 373–8.
Bernardinello, S., 'I rapporti tra i "ceti dominanti" e le città padane (metà XI–metà XII secolo', *Studi di storia medioevale e di diplomatica*, n.s., 3 (2019), pp. 5–42.
Bernwieser, J., *Honor civitatis* (Munich, 2012).
Berque, J., 'Du nouveau sur les Banî Hilâl?', *Studia islamica*, 36 (1972), pp. 99–111.
Bertelé, T., 'Moneta veneziana e moneta bizantina', in A. Pertusi (ed.), *Venezia e il Levante fino al secolo XV*, 1.1 (Florence, 1973), pp. 3–146.
Berti, G., *Pisa: le 'maioliche arcaiche': secc. XIII–XIV* (Florence, 1997).
Berti, G. and A. García Porras, 'A propósito de "Una necesaria revisión de las cerámicas andalusíes halladas en Italia"', *ATM*, 13.1 (2006), pp. 155–95.
Berti, G. and S. Gelichi, 'La ceramica bizantina nelle architetture dell'Italia medievale', in Gelichi, *La ceramica nel mondo bizantino* (Florence, 1993), pp. 125–99.
Berti, G. and M. Giorgio, *Ceramiche con coperture vetrificate usate come "bacini"* (Florence, 2011).
Berti, G. and C. Renzi Rizzo, 'Ceramiche e ceramisti nella realtà pisana del XIII secolo', *AM*, 24 (1997), pp. 495–524.
Bertrand, M. and J. R. Sánchez Viciana, 'Production du fer et peuplement de la région de Guadix (Grenade) au cours de l'Antiquité tardive et du haut Moyen Âge', in Canto García and Cressier, *Minas y metalurgía* (Madrid, 2008), pp. 123–57.
Bessard, F., *Caliphs and merchants* (Oxford, 2020).
Bezzina, D., *Artigiani a Genova nei secoli XII–XIII* (Florence, 2015).
Bianchi, G. (ed.), *Campiglia II* (Florence, 2001).
Bianchi, G., 'Dominare e gestire un territorio', *AM*, 37 (2010), pp. 93–103.
Bianchi, G., 'Recenti ricerche nelle Colline Metallifere ed alcune riflessioni sul modello toscano', *AM*, 42 (2015), pp. 9–26.
Bianchi, G., 'Rural public properties for an economic history of the Kingdom of Italy (10th and 11th centuries)', in Bianchi and Hodges, *The nEU-Med project* (Florence, 2020), pp. 185–94.
Bianchi, G., *Archeologia dei beni pubblici* (Florence, 2022).
Bianchi, G. and S. Collavini, 'Risorse e competizione per le risorse nella Toscana dell'XI secolo', in V. Loré et al. (eds.), *Acquérir, prélever, contrôler* (Turnhout, 2017), pp. 171–88.

Bianchi, G. and S. Collavini, 'Public estates and economic strategies in early medieval Tuscany', in Bianchi and Hodges, *Origins of a new economic union* (Florence, 2018), pp. 147–59.

Bianchi, G. and L. Dallai, 'Le district minier des Collines Metallifères (Toscane, Italie) durant la période médiévale', in N. Minvielle Larousse et al. (eds.), *Les métaux précieux en Méditerranée médiévale* (Aix-en-Provence, 2019), pp. 29–39.

Bianchi, G. and R. Hodges (eds.), *Origins of a new economic union (7th–12th centuries)* (Florence, 2018).

Bianchi, G. and R. Hodges (eds.), *The nEU-Med project* (Florence, 2020).

Bianchi, G. et al., 'Rappresentazioni ed esercizio dei poteri signorili di XII secolo nella Toscana meridionale', in G. Volpe and P. Favia (eds.), *V Congresso nazionale di archeologia medievale* (Florence, 2009), pp. 412–17.

Bianquis, T., 'Une crise frumentaire dans l'Égypte fatimide', *JESHO*, 23 (1980), pp. 67–101.

Bianquis, T., 'Autonomous Egypt from Ibn Ṭūlūn to Kāfūr, 868–969', in C. F. Petry (ed.), *The Cambridge history of Egypt*, 1 (Cambridge, 1999), pp. 86–119.

Biccone, L., 'Invetriate monocrome decorate di stampo dallo scavo del palazzo giudicale di Ardara (SS)', *Atti, XXXVII e XXXVIII Convegno internazionale della ceramica* (Albisola, 2006), pp. 251–64.

Biccone, L. et al., 'La circolazione di ceramiche da mensa e da trasporto tra X e XI secolo', in S. Gelichi (ed.), *Atti del IX Congresso internazionale sulla ceramica medievale nel Mediterraneo* (Florence, 2012), pp. 124–30.

Bintliff, J. et al., *Testing the hinterland* (Cambridge, 2007).

Biscaro, G., 'Gli antichi "Navigli" milanesi', *Archivio storico lombardo*, 35 (1908), pp. 285–326.

Biscaro, G., 'Gli estimi del comune di Milano nel secolo XIII', *Archivio storico lombardo*, 55 (1928), pp. 343–495.

Bjelalac, L., 'Byzantine amphorae in the Serbian Danubian area in the 11th–12th centuries', in V. Déroche and J.-M. Spieser (eds.), *Recherches sur la céramique byzantine* (Athens, 1989), pp. 109–18.

Björnesjö, S., 'Approche archéologique d'une céramique "de luxe"', in G. Démians d'Archimbaud (ed.), *La céramique médiévale en Méditerranée* (Aix-en-Provence, 1997), pp. 271–5.

Blake, H., 'Ceramiche romane e medievali e pietra ollare dagli scavi nella Torre Civica di Pavia', *AM*, 5 (1978), pp. 141–70.

Blake, H. and F. Aguzzi, 'I bacini ceramici della Torre Civica di Pavia' in E. Gabba (ed.), *La Torre Maggiore di Pavia* (Milan, 1989), pp. 209–68.

Blanco Guzmán, R., 'Córdoba y el califato almohade: una lectura arqueológica', in P. Cressier and V. Salvatierra (eds.), *Las Navas de Tolosa, 1212–2012* (Jaén, 2014), pp. 499–508.

Blanco-Guzmán, R., 'Vivir en la Córdoba islámica', in D. Vaquerizo Gil (ed.), *Los barrios en la historia de Córdoba*, 1 (Córdoba, 2018), pp. 351–97.

Blázquez Cerrato, C. and A. Martín Esquivel, 'Conjunto de *dírhams* califales hallado en Zamora', *Archivo español de arqueología*, 92 (2019), pp. 287–306.

Bloch, M., *Feudal society* (London, 1961).

Bloch, M., *Mélanges historiques*, 2 vols. (Paris, 1963).

Blomquist, T., *Merchant families, banking and money in medieval Lucca* (Aldershot, 2005).

Bloom, J. M., 'Five Fatimid minarets in Upper Egypt', *Journal of the Society of architectural historians*, 43 (1984), pp. 162–7.

Bloom, J. M., *Paper before print* (New Haven, CT, 2001).

Boato, A., 'La torre degli Embriaci e le sue trasformazioni', in M. E. De Minicis e E. Guidoni (eds.), *Case e torri medievali*, 3 (Rome, 2005), pp. 82–98.
Bocchi, F., 'Città e mercati nell'Italia padana', *Settimane di studio del Centro italiano di studi sull'alto medioevo*, 40 (1993), pp. 139–85.
Böhlendorf-Arslan, B., *Glasierte byzantinische Keramik aus der Türkei*, 3 vols. (Istanbul, 2004).
Böhlendorf-Arslan, B., 'Die mittelbyzantinische Keramik aus Amorium', in F. Daim and J. Drauschke (eds.), *Byzanz*, 2.1 (Mainz, 2010), pp. 345–71.
Böhlendorf-Arslan, B., 'Das bewegliche Inventar eines mittelbyzantinischen Dorfes', *Byzas*, 15 (2012), pp. 351–68.
Böhlendorf-Arslan, B., 'Pottery from the destruction contexts in the enclosure', in C. S. Lightfoot and E. A. Ivison (eds.), *Amorium reports*, 3 (Istanbul, 2012) pp. 153–79.
Böhlendorf-Arslan, B., 'Surveying the Troad', in J. Vroom (ed.), *Medieval and post-medieval ceramics in the eastern Mediterranean* (Turnhout, 2015), pp. 47–75.
Böhlendorf-Arslan, B., 'Boğazköy', in Niewöhner, *The archaeology of Byzantine Anatolia* (Oxford, 2017), pp. 361–7.
Bois, G., *The crisis of feudalism* (Cambridge, 1984).
Bois, G., 'Against the neo-Malthusian orthodoxy', in T. H. Aston and C. H. E. Philpin (eds.), *The Brenner debate* (Cambridge, 1985), pp. 107–18.
Boldrini, E. et al. 'I reperti ceramici', in Bianchi, *Campiglia II* (Florence, 2001), pp. 275–361.
Bolens, L., 'La révolution agricole andalouse du XIe siècle', *Studia islámica*, 47 (1978), pp. 121–41.
Bolens, L., *Agronomes andalous du Moyen Âge* (Geneva, 1981).
Bolens, L., *L'Andalousie du quotidien au sacré* (Aldershot, 1990).
Bon, A., *Le Peloponnèse byzantin jusqu'en 1204* (Paris, 1951).
Bonacasa Carra, R. M. and F. Ardizzone (eds.), *Agrigento dal tardo Antico al Medioevo* (Todi, 2007).
Bonanno, C. et al., 'Da Henna a Qasryannah', in Arcifa and Sgarlata, *From polis to madina* (Bari, 2020), pp. 193–204.
Bondioli, L., *Peasants, merchants and caliphs*, PhD thesis, University of Princeton, 2020.
Bondioli, L. M., 'The Sicilian tithe business', *Medieval worlds*, 14 (2021), pp. 208–28.
Bondoux, C. R., 'Les villes', in B. Geyer and J. Lefort (eds.), *La Bithynie au Moyen Âge* (Paris, 2003), pp. 377–409.
Bonfiglio Dosio, G., 'Le arti cittadine', in Cracco and Ortalli, *Storia di Venezia*, 2 (Rome, 1995), pp. 577–625.
Bonifay, M., *Études sur la céramique romaine tardive d'Afrique*, BAR, I1301 (Oxford, 2004).
Bonifay, M., 'Africa: patterns of consumption in coastal regions vs. inland regions', in L. Lavan (ed.), *Local economies?* (Leiden, 2015), pp. 529–66.
Bonifay, M., 'Marqueurs céramiques de l'Afrique byzantine tardive', in R. Bockman et al. (eds.), *Africa-Ifriqiya: continuity and change in North Africa from the Byzantine to the early Islamic age* (Rome, 2019), pp. 295–313.
Bonneau, D., *La crue du Nil, divinité égyptienne, à travers mille ans d'histoire (332 av.–641 ap. J.-C.) d'après les auteurs grecs et latins, et les documents des époques ptolémaïque, romaine et byzantine* (Paris, 1964).
Bonnéric, J. and A. Schmitt, 'Tinnîs', *CCE*, 9 (2011), pp. 95–139.
Bora, F., *Writing history in the medieval Islamic world* (London, 2019).
Bordone, R., 'Le origini del comune di Genova', *Atti della Società ligure di storia patria*, 42.1 (2002), pp. 237–59.
Borisov, B. D., *Djadovo*, 1, ed. A. Fol et al. (Tokyo, 1989).

Borisov, B., 'Settlements of northeast Thrace: 11–12 centuries', *Archaeologia bulgarica*, 5.2 (2001), pp. 77–92.

Borsari, S., 'Il commercio veneziano nell'impero bizantino nel XII secolo', *Rivista storia italiana*, 76 (1964), pp. 982–1011.

Borsari, S., 'Per la storia del commercio veneziano nel mondo bizantino nel XII secolo', *Rivista storia italiana*, 88 (1976), pp. 104–26.

Borsari, S., *Venezia e Bisanzio* (Venice, 1988).

Borsari, S., 'Pisani a Bisanzio nel XII secolo', *Bollettino storico pisano*, 60 (1991), pp. 59–75.

Borsch, S. J., 'Environment and population', *Comparative studies in society and history*, 46 (2004), pp. 451–68.

Borsch, S. J., *The Black Death in Egypt and England* (Austin, TX, 2005).

Borsch, S., 'Plague depopulation and irrigation decay in medieval Egypt', *The medieval globe*, 1 (2014), pp. 125–56.

Bortolami, S., 'Monselice "oppidum opulentissimum"', in A. Rigon (ed.), *Monselice: storia, cultura e arte di un centro "minore" del Veneto* (Monselice, 1994), pp. 101–71.

Bortolami, S., *Urbs antiquissima et clara* (Padua, 2015).

Bortoletto, M. et al., 'Laguna di Venezia', in R. Fiorillo and P. Peduto (eds.), *III Congresso nazionale di archeologia medievale* (Florence, 2003), pp. 220–3.

Bosanquet, A., 'Maritime trade from 3rd/9th-century Ifrīqiya', *Medieval worlds*, 16 (2022), pp. 108–28.

Bosch Vilá, J., *La Sevilla islámica 712–1248* (Seville, 1980).

Bouchaud, C. et al., 'Fuelwood and fuel supplies in the Eastern Desert of Egypt during Roman times', in J. P. Brun et al. (eds.), *The Eastern Desert of Egypt during the Greco-Roman period* (Paris, 2018), pp. 406–45.

Bougard, F., 'Entre Gandolfingi et Obertenghi', *MEFRM*, 101.1 (1989), pp. 11–66.

Bougard, F., *La justice dans le royaume d'Italie de la fin du VIIIe siècle au début du XIe siècle* (Rome, 1995).

Bougard, F. and V. Loré (eds.), *Biens publics, biens du roi* (Turnhout, 2019).

Bouras, Ch., 'Aspects of the Byzantine city, eighth to fifteenth centuries', in Laiou, *The economic history of Byzantium* (Washington, DC, 2002), pp. 497–528.

Bouras, Ch., *Byzantine Athens, 10th–12th centuries* (Abingdon, 2018).

Bourin, M. and P. Martínez Sopena (eds.), *Pour une anthropologie du prélèvement*, 2 vols. (Paris, 2004–7).

Bourin, M. et al. (eds.), *Dynamiques du monde rural dans la conjuncture de 1300* (Paris, 2014).

Bowes, K. (ed.), *The Roman Peasant Project 2009–2014* (Philadelphia, PA, 2021).

Bowman, A. K., 'Agricultural production in Egypt', in A. K. Bowman and A. I. Wilson (eds.), *The Roman agricultural economy* (Oxford, 2013), pp. 219–53.

Bramoullé, D., 'La Sicile dans la Méditerranée fatimide (X^e^–XIe siècle)', in Nef and Ardizzone, *Les dynamiques* (Rome and Bari, 2014), pp. 25–36.

Bramoullé, D., *Les Fatimides et la mer (909–1171)* (Leiden, 2020).

Bramoullé, D. et al., 'Le mobilier céramique dans la Méditerranée des Xe–XIIe siècles', *AI*, 51 (2017), pp. 191–221.

Braudel, F., *La Méditerranée et le monde méditerranéen à l'époque de Philippe II*, 2nd edn (Paris, 1966), trans. S. Reynolds, *The Mediterranean and the Mediterranean world in the age of Philip II* (London, 1973).

Brenner, R., 'Agrarian class structure and economic development in pre-industrial Europe', in T. H. Aston and C. H. E. Philpin (eds.), *The Brenner debate* (Cambridge, 1985), pp. 10–63.

Brenner, R., 'The agrarian roots of European capitalism', in T. H. Aston and C. H. E. Philpin (eds.), *The Brenner debate* (Cambridge, 1985), pp. 213–328.

Brenner, R., 'The Low Countries in the transition to capitalism', *Journal of agrarian change*, 1 (2001), pp. 169–241.
Bresc, H., *Un monde méditerranéen* (Rome, 1986).
Bresc, H., 'Limites internes de la Sicile médiévale', in J.-M. Poisson (ed.), *Castrum 4* (Rome, 1992), pp. 321–30.
Bresc, H., 'Le marchand, le marché et le palais dans la Sicile des Xe–XIIe siècles', *Settimane di studio del Centro italiano di studi sull'alto medioevo*, 40 (1993), pp. 285–325.
Bresc, H., 'La propriété foncière des Musulmans dans la Sicile du XIIe siècle', in B. Scarcia Amoretti (ed.), *Del nuovo sulla Sicilia musulmana* (Rome, 1995), pp. 69–97.
Brett, M., 'Fatimid historiography', in D. O. Morgan (ed.), *Medieval historical writing in the Christian and Islamic worlds* (London, 1982), pp. 47–59.
Brett, M., 'Muslim justice under infidel rule', *Cahiers de Tunisie*, 43 (1991), pp. 325–68.
Brett, M., 'The flood of the dam and the sons of the new moon', in *Mélanges offerts à Mohamed Talbi à l'occasion de son 70e anniversaire* (Tunis, 1993), pp. 55–67.
Brett, M., 'The armies of Ifriqiya, 1052–1160', *Cahiers de Tunisie*, 48 (1995), pp. 107–25.
Brett, M., 'The origins of the Mamluk military system in the Fatimid period', in U. Vermeulen and D. de Smet (eds.), *Egypt and Syria in the Fatimid, Ayyubid and Mamluk eras*, 1 (Leiden, 1995), pp. 39–52.
Brett, M., 'The way of the nomad', *Bulletin of the School of Oriental and African Studies*, 58 (1995), pp. 251–69.
Brett, M., *The rise of the Fatimids* (Leiden, 2001).
Brett, M., *The Fatimid empire* (Edinburgh, 2017).
Briano, A., *La ceramica a vetrina sparsa nella Toscana altomedievale* (Florence, 2020).
Briano, A. and E. Sibilia, 'Progetto nEU-Med', *AM*, 45 (2018), pp. 357–65.
Bridgman, R., 'Potting histories', in *34th international symposium on archaeometry* (Zaragoza, 2006), pp. 419–26.
Bridgman, R., *Potting histories*, PhD thesis, University of Southampton, 2007.
Bridgman, R., 'Re-examining Almohad economics in south-western al-Andalus through petrological analysis of archaeological ceramics', in G. D. Anderson and M. Rosser-Owen (eds.), *Revisiting al-Andalus* (Leiden, 2007), pp. 143–65.
Bridgman, R., 'Contextualising pottery production and distribution in south-western al-Andalus during the Almohad period', in S. Gelichi (ed.), *Atti del IX Congresso internazionale sulla ceramica medievale nel Mediterraneo* (Florence, 2012), pp. 95–100.
Briquet, C. M., 'Les papiers des Archives de Gênes et leurs filigranes', *Atti della Società ligure di storia patria*, 19 (1888), pp. 269–394.
Britnell, R. H., 'Commercialisation and economic development in England, 1000–1300', in R. H. Britnell and B. M. S. Campbell (eds.), *A commercialising economy* (Manchester, 1995), pp. 7–26.
Britnell, R. H., *The commercialisation of English society, 1000–1500*, 2nd edn (Cambridge, 1996).
Britnell, R. H., *Britain and Ireland 1050–1530* (Oxford, 2004).
Brogan, O. and D. J. Smith, *Ghirza* (Tripoli, 1984).
Brogiolo, G. P. and S. Gelichi, 'La ceramica grezza medievale nella pianura padana', in *La ceramica medievale nel Mediterraneo occidentale* (Florence, 1986), pp. 293–316.
Brogiolo, G. P. and S. Gelichi, *La città nell'alto medioevo italiano* (Bari, 1998).
Brogiolo, G. P. and B. Portulano, *La Rocca di Manerba* (Mantua, 2011).
Broise, H. and Y. Thébert, *Recherches archéologiques franco-tunisiennes à Bulla Regia*, 2.1 (Rome, 1993).
Browning, R., 'The city and the sea', in S. Vryonis (ed.), *The Greeks and the sea* (New Rochelle, NY, 1993), pp. 97–112.

Bruand, O., *Voyageurs et marchandises aux temps des Carolingiens* (Brussels, 2002).

Brubaker, L. and C. Wickham, 'Processions, power and community identity', in W. Pohl and R. Kramer (eds.), *Empires and communities in the post-Roman and Islamic world, c.400–1000 CE* (New York, 2021), pp. 121–87.

Bruce, T., 'The politics of violence and trade', *Journal of medieval history*, 32 (2006), pp. 127–42.

Bruce, T., 'Piracy as statecraft', *Al-Masāq*, 22 (2010), pp. 235–48.

Bruce, T., *La Taifa de Denia et la Méditerranée au XIe siècle* (Toulouse, 2013).

Bruce, T., 'The taifa of Denia and the Jewish networks of the medieval Mediterranean', *Journal of medieval Iberian studies*, 10 (2018), pp. 147–66.

Brugnoli, A., 'Dal Mediterraneo all'Europa', *Settimane di studio del Centro italiano di studi sull'alto medioevo*, 54 (2007), pp. 107–54.

Brühl, C. R., *Fodrum, gistum, servitium regis* (Cologne, 1968).

Bruni, S. (ed.), *Pisa: piazza Dante* (Pisa, 1993).

Bruni, S. et al. (eds.), *Ricerche di archeologia medievale a Pisa*, 1 (Florence, 2000).

Bruning, J., *The rise of a capital* (Leiden, 2018).

Bruning, J., 'Slave trade dynamics in Abbasid Egypt', *JESHO*, 63 (2020), pp. 682–742.

Bruno, B. and N. Cutajar, 'Imported amphorae as indicators of economic activity in early medieval Malta', in D. Michaelides et al. (eds.), *The insular system of the early Byzantine Mediterranean*, BAR, I2523 (Oxford, 2013), pp. 15–29.

Brunschvig, R., *La Berbérie orientale sous les Ḥafṣides des origines à la fin du XV siècle* (Paris, 1940–7).

Bruttini, J., *Archeologia urbana a Firenze* (Florence, 2013).

Bruttini, J. A. et al., 'Un insediamento a vocazione mineraria nella Toscana medievale', in G. Volpe and P. Favia (eds.), *V Congresso nazionale di archeologia medievale* (Florence, 2009), pp. 306–12.

Buenger Robbert, L., 'Twelfth-century Italian prices', *Social science history*, 7 (1983), pp. 381–403.

Bugalhão, J., 'The production and consumption of Islamic ceramics in Lisbon', *Al-Masāq*, 21 (2009), pp. 83–104.

Bugalhão, J. and S. Gómez Martínez, 'Lisboa, uma cidade do Mediterrâneo islâmico', in M. J. Barroca and I. C. F. Fernandes (eds.), *Muçulmanes e Cristãos entre o Tejo e o Douro (sécs. VIII a XIII)* (Palmela, 2005), pp. 227–62.

Bugalhão, J. et al., 'La production céramique islamique à Lisbonne', in J. Zozaya et al. (eds.), *Actas del VIII Congreso internacional de cerámica medieval en el Mediterráneo* (Ciudad Real, 2009), pp. 373–98.

Bulliet, R. W., *The patricians of Nishapur* (Cambridge, MA, 1972).

Bulliet, R. W., *The camel and the wheel* (Cambridge, MA, 1975).

Bulliet, R. W., *Conversion to Islam in the medieval period* (Cambridge, MA, 1979).

Burgmann, L., 'Lawyers and legislators', in M. Mullett and D. Smythe (eds.), *Alexios I Komnenos*, 1 (Belfast, 1996), pp. 185–98.

Burke, K. S., *Archaeological texts and contexts on the Red Sea*, PhD thesis, University of Chicago, 2007.

Buzzo, G., 'La ceramica invetriata in monocottura', in F. Saggioro (ed.), *Nogara* (Rome, 2011), pp. 225–39.

Byrne, E. H., 'Genoese trade with Syria in the twelfth century', *The American historical review*, 25 (1920), pp. 191–219.

Cabella, R. et al., 'Il contributo delle analisi di laboratorio allo studio delle ceramiche nordafricane', in Cressier and Fentress, *La céramique maghrébine* (Rome, 2011), pp. 221–32.

Cabona, D. et al., 'Nuovi dati sulla circolazione delle ceramiche mediterranee dallo scavo di Palazzo Ducale a Genova (sec. XII–XIV)', in *La ceramica medievale nel Mediterraneo occidentale* (Florence, 1986), pp. 453–82.

Cacciaguerra, G., 'La ceramica a vetrina pesante altomedievale in Sicilia', *AM*, 36 (2009), pp. 285–300.

Cacciaguerra, G., 'Cultura materiale e commerci nella Sicilia bizantina', in M. Congiù et al (eds.), *La Sicilia bizantina* (Caltanissetta, 2010), pp. 25–42.

Cacciaguerra, G., 'Anfore altomedievali nell'area megarese', in F. Redi and A. Forgione (eds.), *VI Congresso nazionale di archeologia medievale* (Florence, 2012), pp. 613–17.

Cacciaguerra, G., 'L'area megarese tra il IX e l'XI secolo', in Nef and Ardizzone, *Les dynamiques* (Rome and Bari, 2014), pp. 379–87.

Cacciaguerra, G., 'Città e mercati in transizione nel Mediterraneo altomedievale', *AM*, 44 (2018), pp. 149–73.

Cacciaguerra, G., 'Commerci e sistemi di scambio nella Sicilia altomedievale', in M. Giorgio (ed.), *Storie [di] ceramiche*, 6 (Florence, 2020), pp. 21–8.

Cacciaguerra, G., 'Siracusa nel contesto socio-economico del Mediterraneo tardoantico e altomedievale', in Arcifa and Sgarlata, *From polis to madina* (Bari, 2020), pp. 55–86.

Cacciaguerra, G. and V. Sacco, 'Due "capitali", due storie? Siracusa e Palermo', *MEFRM*, 134.1 (2022), pp. 27–66.

Cagnana, A., 'Residenze vescovili fortificate e immagine urbana nella Genova dell'XI secolo', *Archeologia dell'architettura*, 2 (1997), pp. 75–100.

Cagnana, A. and R. Mussardo, 'Le torri di Genova fra XII e XIII secolo', *Archeologia dell'architettura*, 17 (2012), pp. 94–110.

Cagnana, A. et al., 'Castelli e territorio nella Repubblica di Genova (secoli X–XIII)', *AM*, 37 (2010), pp. 29–46.

Cahen, C., 'L'évolution de l'*iqta*' du IXe au XIIIe siècle', *Annales E. S. C.*, 8 (1953), pp. 25–52.

Cahen, C., 'L'alun avant Phocée', *Revue d'histoire économique et sociale*, 41 (1963), pp. 433–47.

Cahen, C., 'Douanes et commerce de l'Égypte médiévale d'après le *Minhādj* d'al-Makhzūmī', *JESHO*, 7 (1964), pp. 217–314.

Cahen, C., 'Amalfi en Orient à la veille, au moment et au lendemain de la Première Croisade', in *Amalfi nel Medioevo* (Salerno, 1977), pp. 269–83.

Cahen, C., *Orient et Occident au temps des Croisades* (Paris, 1983).

Cahen, C., *Makhzūmiyyāt* (Leiden, 1997).

Caimi, R. et al., 'Gli scavi nel sito fortificato di Pellio Intelvi (CO)', in G. P. Brogiolo (ed.), *Dai Celti ai castelli medievali* (Mantua, 2001), pp. 123–52.

Calleri, M., 'Un notaio genovese tra XII e XIII secolo', in *Ianuensis non nascitur sed fit*, 1 (Genoa, 2019), pp. 303–24.

Camacho Cruz, C., 'Evolución del parcelario doméstico y su interacción con la trama urbana', *ATM*, 25 (2018), pp. 29–65.

Cammarosano, P., *Italia medievale* (Rome, 1991).

Cammarosano, P., 'I *libri iurium* e la memoria storica delle città comunali, in *Il senso della storia nella cultura medievale italiana (1100–1350): Atti del 14° Convegno internazionale di studio* (Pistoia, 1995), pp. 309–25.

Cammarosano, P., *Economia politica classica e storia economica dell'Europa medievale* (Trieste, 2020).

Campbell, B. M. S., 'The agrarian problem in the early fourteenth century', *Past and present*, 188 (2005), pp. 3–70.

Campopiano, M., 'The evolution of the landscape and the social and political organisation of water management', in E. Thoen et al. (eds.), *Landscapes or seascapes?* (Turnhout, 2013), pp. 313–32.

Campopiano, M. and F. Menant, 'Agricolture irrigue: l'Italia padana', in *I paesaggi agrari d'Europa (secoli XIII–XV)* (Rome, 2015), pp. 291–322.

Canard, M., 'Le riz dans le Proche Orient aux premiers siècles de l'Islam', *Arabica*, 6 (1959), pp. 113–31.

Cano Piedra, C., *La cerámica verde manganeso de Madīnat al-Zahrā* (Granada, 1996).

Cantatore, M. F. A., *Da Placentia a Placencia*, tesi di dottorato di ricerca, Università di Bologna, 2021.

Cantero Sosa, M. and J. J. Egea Gonzáles, 'Aportación al estudio de la producción local de cerámica califal en Almería', in *IV Congreso de arqueología medieval española*, 3 (Alicante, 1994), pp. 807–15.

Cantini, F., *Il castello di Montarrenti* (Florence, 2003).

Cantini, F., 'Ritmi e forme della grande espansione economica dei secoli XI–XIII nei contesti ceramici della Toscana settentrionale', *AM*, 37 (2010), pp. 113–27.

Cantini, F., 'Produzioni ceramiche ed economiche in Italia centro-settentrionale', in M. Valenti and C. Wickham (eds.), *Italia, 888–962: una svolta* (Turnhout, 2013), pp. 341–64.

Cantini, F. and F. Grassi, 'Produzione, circolazione e consumo della ceramica in Toscana tra la fine del X e il XIII secolo', in S. Gelichi (ed.), *Atti del IX Congresso internazionale sulla ceramica medievale nel Mediterraneo* (Florence, 2012), pp. 131–9.

Cantini, F. and C. Rizzitelli (eds.), *Una città operosa* (Florence, 2018).

Cantini, F. et al., 'Il borgo di San Genesio tra XI e metà XIII secolo', in F. Cantini (ed.), *"Costruire lo sviluppo"* (Florence, 2019), pp. 49–79.

Canto García, A., 'La moneda', in Viguera Molins, *Historia de España*, 8.1 (Madrid, 1994), pp. 273–87.

Canto García, A. J., 'Numismática taifa y economia', in Zozaya Stabel-Hansen and Kurtz Schaefer, *Bataliús III* (Badajoz, 2014), pp. 135–56.

Canto García, A. and P. Cressier, *Minas y metalurgía en al-Andalus y Magreb occidental* (Madrid, 2008).

Capelli, C. et al., 'Caractérisation des céramiques glaçurées et importées en Provence aux XIIe et XIIIe s.', in J. Zozaya et al. (eds.), *Actas del VIII Congreso internacional de cerámica medieval en el Mediterráneo* (Ciudad Real, 2009), pp. 937–46.

Cara Barrionuevo, L. (ed.), *Ciudad y territorio en al-Andalus* (Granada, 2000).

Cara Barrionuevo, L., 'Ciudades portuarias, alquerías y comercio en el sudeste peninsular', *Arqueología medieval*, 9 (2005), pp. 125–37.

Cara Barrionuevo, L. et al., 'Arqueología urbana e historia de la ciudad', in Cara Barrionuevo, *Ciudad y territorio* (Granada, 2000), pp. 167–92.

Carbonell, A., 'La minería y la metalurgia entre los musulmanes en España', *Boletín de la Real Academia de ciencias, bellas letras y nobles artes de Córdoba*, 8 (1929), pp. 179–217.

Carbonetti Vendittelli, C., '"Sicut inveni in thomo carticineo iam ex magna parte vetustate consumpto exemplavi et scripsi atque a tenebris ad lucem perduxi"', in C. Braidotti et al. (eds.), *Scritti in memoria di Roberto Pretagostini*, 1 (Rome, 2009), pp. 47–69.

Carbonetti Vendittelli, C., 'I supporti scrittorii della documentazione: l'uso del papiro', in J.-M. Martin et al. (eds.), *L'héritage byzantin en Italie (VIIIe–XIIe siècle)*, 1 (Rome, 2011), pp. 33–48.

Cardon, D., *La draperie au Moyen Âge* (Paris, 1999).

Carli, F., *Il mercato nell'alto medioevo* (Padua, 1934).

Carli, F., *Il mercato nell'età del Comune* (Padua, 1936).
Carloni, C. and M. Ventura, 'Il *calidarium* e il riutilizzo degli ambienti in età islamica', in Pensabene and Barresi, *Piazza Armerina, Villa del Casale* (Rome, 2019), pp. 535–45.
Carocci, S., 'Le libertà dei servi', *Storica*, 37 (2007), pp. 51–94.
Carocci, S., 'La "crisi del Trecento" e le recenti teorie economiche', in D. Chamboduc de Saint Pulgent and M. Dejoux (eds.), *La fabrique des societés médiévales méditerranéennes* (Paris, 2018), pp. 129–40.
Carocci, S., *Lordships of southern Italy* (Rome, 2018).
Carocci, S., 'Nobiltà e pietrificazione della ricchezza fra città e campagna (Italia, 1000–1280)', in *XLVII semana de estudios medievales* (Pamplona, 2022), pp. 81–142.
Carocci, S., 'The pervasiveness of lordship (Italy, 1050–1500)', *Past and present*, 256 (2022), pp. 3–47.
Carpentier, E. and M. Le Mené, *La France du XIe au XVe siècle* (Paris, 1996).
Carrera, F. M. P., 'La lavorazione dei metalli delle botteghe artigianali degli Ex Laboratori Gentili', in Cantini and Rizzitelli, *Una città operosa* (Florence, 2018), pp. 55–63.
Carsana, V., 'Anfore altomedievali dall'area portuale di Napoli', *AM*, 45 (2018), pp. 193–204.
Carvajal López, J. C., *La cerámica de Madīnat Ilbīra (Atarfe) y el poblamiento altomedieval de la Vega de Granada* (Granada, 2008).
Carvajal López, J. C. et al., 'Combinación de análisis petrográfico y químico de contenedores de agua y cerámicas vidriadas de la Vega de Granada altomedieval (siglos VII–XII d.C.)', in Grassi and Quirós Castillo, *Arqueometría de los materiales cerámicos de época medieval en España* (Bilbao, 2018), pp. 193–205.
Carver, M. and A. Molinari, 'Sicily in transition research project: investigations at Castronovo di Sicilia' (2016), https://www.fastionline.org/docs/FOLDER-it-2016-352.pdf.
Casal García, M. T., 'Caracteristicas generales del urbanismo cordobés de la primera etapa emiral', *Anejos de Anales de arqueología cordobesa*, 1 (2008), pp. 109–34.
Casal García, M. T., 'Contextos arqueológicos en el arrabal omeya de Šaqunda', in C. Doménech and S. Gutiérrez (eds.), *El sitio de las cosas* (Alicante, 2020), pp. 235–54.
Casal, M. T. et al., 'Aproximación al estudio de la cerámica emiral del arrabal de *Šaqunda* (*Qurṭuba*, Córdoba)', *ATM*, 12 (2005), pp. 189–235.
Cassis, M., 'Çadır Höyük', in T. Vorderstrasse and J. Roodenberg (eds.), *Archaeology of the countryside in medieval Anatolia* (Leiden, 2009), pp. 1–23.
Cassis, M., 'The Cide-Senpazar region in the Byzantine period', in B. S. Düring and C. Glatz (eds.), *Kinetic landscapes* (Berlin, 2015), pp. 294–363.
Castagnetti, A., *Mercanti, società e politica nella Marca veronese-trevigiana (secoli XI–XIV)* (Verona, 1990).
Castagnetti, A., *La società ferrarese (secoli XI–XIII)* (Verona, 1991).
Castagnetti, A., 'Il primo comune', in Cracco and Ortalli, *Storia di Venezia*, 2 (Rome, 1995), pp. 81–130.
Castagnetti, A. (ed.), *La vassalità maggiore del regno italico* (Rome, 2001).
Castagnetti, A., *Il processo per Ostiglia* (Verona, 2016).
Castagnetti, A., *Mercanti a Verona nel secolo XII* (Verona, 2021).
Castillo Armenteros, J. C., 'Los alcázares de Jaén entre los siglos VIII–XIII', in P. Cressier (ed.), *Castrum 8* (Madrid, 2008), pp. 223–49.
Castillo Galdeano, F. and R. Martínez Madrid, 'La vivienda hispanomusulmana en Bayyâna-Pechina (Almería)', in *La casa hispano-musulmana* (Granada, 1990), pp. 111–28.
Castillo Galdeano, F. and R. Martínez Madrid, 'Producciones cerámicas en Baŷŷāna', in A. Malpica Cuello (ed.), *La cerámica altomedieval en el sur de al-Andalus* (Granada, 1993), pp. 69–116.

Catalioto, L., *Il vescovato di Lipari-Patti in età normanna, 1088–1194* (Messina, 2007).

Catarino, H. et al., 'La céramique islamique du Ġarb al-Andalus', in S. Gelichi (ed.), *Atti del IX Congresso internazionale sulla ceramica medievale nel Mediterraneo* (Florence, 2012), pp. 429–41.

Cazelles, R., *Nouvelle histoire de Paris de la fin du règne de Philippe Auguste à la mort de Charles V (1223–1380)* (Paris, 1972).

Ceccarelli Lemut, M. L., 'L'uso della moneta nei documenti pisani dei secoli XI e XII', in B. Casini et al., *Studi sugli strumenti di scambio a Pisa nel medioevo* (Pisa, 1979), pp. 47–127.

Ceccarelli Lemut, M. L., 'Pisan consular families in the communal age', in T. W. Blomquist and M. F. Mazzaoui (eds.), *The 'other Tuscany'* (Kalamazoo, MI, 1994), pp. 123–52.

Ceccarelli Lemut, M. L., 'La Maremma populoniese nel medioevo', in G. Bianchi (ed.), *Campiglia I* (Florence, 2003), pp. 1–116.

Ceccarelli Lemut, M. L. et al. (eds.), *I sistemi portuali della Toscana mediterranea* (Pisa, 2011).

Chalandon, F., *Histoire de la domination normande en Italie et en Sicile* (Paris, 1907).

Challe, C. and S. de Longueville, 'La céramique médiévale d'Andenelle dans son contexte régional', in E. Goemaere (ed.), *Terres, pierres et feu en vallée mosane* (Stavelot, 2010), pp. 65–72.

Chalmeta, P., *El "señor del zoco" en España* (Madrid, 1973).

Chaudhuri, K. N., *Trade and civilisation in the Indian Ocean* (Cambridge, 1985).

Chavarría Arnau, A. (ed.), *Padova: architetture medievali* (Mantua, 2011).

Chavarría Arnau, A. (ed.), *Ricerche sul centro episcopale di Padova* (Mantua, 2017).

Cherry, J. F. et al., *Landscape archaeology as long-term history* (Los Angeles, 1991).

Cheynet, J.-C., *Pouvoir et contestations à Byzance (963–1210)* (Paris, 1990).

Cheynet, J.-C., 'Fortune et puissance de l'aristocratie (X^e^–XIIe siècle)', in V. Kravari et al. (eds.), *Hommes et richesses dans l'empire byzantin*, 2 (Paris, 1991), pp. 199–213.

Cheynet, J.-C., 'L'époque byzantine', in B. Geyer and J. Lefort (eds.), *La Bithynie au Moyen Âge* (Paris, 2003), pp. 311–50.

Cheynet, J.-C., 'La société urbaine', *Travaux et mémoires*, 21.2 (2017), pp. 449–82.

Chiappa Mauri, L., *I mulini ad acqua nel Milanese (secoli X–XV)* (Rome, 1984).

Chiappa Mauri, L., 'Riflessioni sulle campagne lombarde del Quattro-Cinquecento', *Nuova rivista storica*, 69 (1985), pp. 123–30.

Chiappa Mauri, L., *Paesaggi rurali nella Lombardia: secoli XII–XV* (Rome, 1990).

Chiappa Mauri, L., *Terra e uomini nella Lombardia medievale* (Bari, 1997).

Chiappa Mauri, L., 'Tra consuetudine e rinnovamento', in R. Comba and F. Panero (eds.), *Aziende agrarie nel medioevo* (Cuneo, 2000), pp. 59–91.

Chiarelli, L. C. C., *A history of Muslim Sicily* (Sta Venera, 2011).

Chittolini, G., 'Alle origini delle "grandi aziende" della Bassa lombarda', *Quaderni storici*, 39 (1978), pp. 828–44.

Chorley, P., 'The cloth exports of Flanders and northern France during the thirteenth century: a luxury trade?', *Economic history review*, 40 (1987), pp. 349–79.

Christ, G., 'Eine Stadt wandert aus', *Viator*, 42 (2011), pp. 145–68.

Christ, G., *A king of the two seas?* (Berlin, 2017).

Christys, A., *Christians in al-Andalus, 711–1000* (Abingdon, 2002).

Christys, A., 'The queen of the Franks offers gifts to the caliph al-Muktafi'', in W. Davies and P. Fouracre (eds.), *The languages of gift in the early middle ages* (Cambridge, 2010), pp. 149–70.

Christys, A., 'Did all roads lead to Córdoba under the Umayyads?', in M. J. Kelly and M. Burrows (eds.), *Urban interactions: communication and competition in late Antiquity and the early middle ages* (Binghampton, NY, 2018), 47–62.

Ciampoltrini, G. and A. Saccocci, 'Dalla città marchionale a quella comunale', in F. Cantini (ed.), *"Costruire lo sviluppo"* (Florence, 2019), pp. 9–19.
Cirelli, E., 'Leptis Magna in età islamica', *AM*, 28 (2001), pp. 432–40.
Cirelli, E., 'Anfore medievali rinvenute a Ravenna e nell'area centroadriatica (VIII–XII secolo)', *AM*, 45 (2018), pp. 35–46.
Cirelli, E. et al., 'Insediamenti fortificati nel territorio di Leptis Magna tra III e XI secolo', in P. Galetti (ed.), *Paesaggi, comunità, villaggi medievali* (Spoleto, 2012), pp. 763–77.
Citarella, A. O., 'The relations of Amalfi with the Arab world before the Crusade', *Speculum*, 42 (1967), pp. 299–312.
Citarella, A. O., 'Patterns of medieval trade', *The journal of economic history*, 28 (1968), pp. 531–55.
Clapés Salmoral, R., 'Un baño privado en el arrabal occidental de Madinat Qurtuba', *ATM*, 20 (2013), pp. 97–128.
Clapés Salmoral, R., 'La actividad comercial de Córdoba en época califal a través de un edificio hallado en el arrabal de poniente', *Anales de arqueología cordobesa*, 25–6 (2014–15), pp. 225–54.
Clapés Salmoral, R., 'La formación y evolución del paisaje suburbano en época islámica', *ATM*, 26 (2019), pp. 311–54.
Clément, F., *Pouvoir et légitimité en Espagne musulmane à l'époque des Taifas, V^e/XIe siècle* (Paris, 1997).
Cohen, M. R., *The voice of the poor in the Middle Ages* (Princeton, NJ, 2005).
Cohen, M. R., 'Geniza for Islamicists', *Harvard Middle Eastern and Islamic review*, 7 (2006), pp. 129–45.
Cohen, M. R., *Poverty and charity in the Jewish community of medieval Egypt* (Princeton, NJ, 2009).
Cohen, M. R., *Maimonides and the merchants* (Philadelphia, PA, 2017).
Cohen, Z., *Composition analysis of writing materials in Cairo Genizah documents* (Leiden, 2022).
Cohn, S. K., *Lust for liberty* (Cambridge, MA, 2006).
Colangeli, F., *Il riflesso di vetri e metalli: oltre alla ceramica per la comprensione dei mutamenti culturali ed economici*, tesi di dottorato di ricerca, Università di Roma 'Tor Vergata', 2020/2021.
Colangeli, F. and N. Schibille, 'Glass from Islamic Sicily', in *Le forme del vetro*, conference held at the École française de Rome, 21–22 October 2021.
Coll Conesa, J. and A. García Porras, 'Tipología, cronología y producción de los hornos cerámicos en al-Andalus' (2010), www.arqueologiamedieval.com/articulos/125/.
Coll Conesa, J. et al., 'La alfarería musulmana del carrer de Botons, Palma de Mallorca', in S. Gelichi (ed.), *Atti del IX Congresso internazionale sulla ceramica medievale nel Mediterraneo* (Florence, 2012), pp. 236–45.
Collavini, S., *"Honorabilis domus et spetiosissimus comitatus"* (Pisa, 1998).
Collavini, S., 'Le basi materiali della contea dei conti Guidi tra prelievo signorile e obblighi militari (1150 *c.*–1230 *c.*)', *Società e storia*, 115 (2007), pp. 1–32.
Colomban, P. et al., 'Identification par microscopie Raman des tessons et des pigments de glaçures de céramiques de l'Ifriqiya (Dougga, XI–XVIIIèmes siècles)', *Revue d'archéometrie*, 25 (2001), pp. 101–12.
Constable, O. R., 'Genoa and Spain in the twelfth and thirteenth centuries', *The journal of European economic history*, 19 (1990), pp. 635–56.
Constable, O. R., *Trade and traders in Muslim Spain* (Cambridge, 1994).
Constable, O. R., 'Cross-cultural contracts', *Studia Islamica*, 85 (1997), pp. 67–84.

Constable, O. R., *Housing the stranger in the Mediterranean world* (Cambridge, 2003).
Conte, E., *Servi medievali* (Rome, 1996).
Conti, E., *La formazione della struttura agraria moderna nel contado fiorentino*, 1 (Rome, 1965).
Cooper, J. P., *The medieval Nile* (Cairo, 2014).
Corretti, A., 'L'attività metallurgica', in S. Bruni et al. (eds.), *Ricerche di archeologia medievale a Pisa*, 1 (Florence, 2000), pp. 83–100.
Corretti, A., 'Piazza dei Cavalieri: scavo 1993', in Cantini and Rizzitelli, *Una città operosa* (Florence, 2018), pp. 65–9.
Corretti, A. and L. Chiarantini, 'Contessa Entellina (Palermo)', in C. Ampolo (ed.), *Sicilia occidentale* (Pisa, 2012), pp. 137–50.
Corretti, A. et al., 'Tra Arabi, Berberi e Normanni', *MEFRM*, 116.1 (2004), pp. 145–90.
Corretti, A. et al., 'Entella (Contessa Entellina, PA)', in G. Volpe and P. Favia (eds.), *V Congresso nazionale di archeologia medievale* (Florence, 2009), pp. 602–8.
Corretti, A. et al., 'Frammenti di medioevo siciliano', in Pensabene, *Piazza Armerina* (Rome, 2010), pp. 147–96.
Corretti, A. et al., 'Contessa Entellina (PA)', in Nef and Ardizzone, *Les dynamiques* (Rome and Bari, 2014), pp. 341–9.
Cortese, M. E., *Signori, castelli, città* (Florence, 2007).
Cortese, M. E., *L'aristocrazia toscana* (Spoleto, 2017).
Cortese, M. E., 'Rural *milites* in central and northern Italy between local élites and aristocracy (1100–1300)', in S. Carocci and I. Lazzarini (eds.), *Social mobility in medieval Italy (1100–1500)* (Rome, 2018), pp. 335–52.
Cortese, M. E., 'Sui sentieri del sale', *Reti medievali rivista*, 23.1 (2022), www.serena.unina.it/index.php/rm/article/view/9080/9725.
Cortonesi, A. and M. Montanari (eds.), *Medievistica italiana e storia agraria* (Bologna, 2001).
Cortonesi, A. and L. Palermo, *La prima espansione economica europea* (Rome, 2009).
Cortonesi, A. and S. Passigli, *Agricoltura e allevamento nell'Italia medievale* (Florence, 2016).
Cortonesi, A. and G. Piccinni, *Medioevo delle campagne* (Rome, 2006).
Coscarella, A. et al. (eds.), *Il vetro in transizione (IV–XII secolo)* (Bari, 2021).
Cottica, D., 'Micaceous White Painted Ware from insula 104 at Hierapolis/Pamukkale, Turkey', *Byzas*, 7 (2007), pp. 255–72.
Couleurs de Tunisie: 25 siècles de céramique (Paris, 1994).
Coulton, J. J., *The Balboura survey*, 2 vols. (London, 2012).
Cracco, G., *Società e stato nel medioevo veneziano (secoli XII–XIV)* (Florence, 1967).
Cracco, G., 'Santità straniera in terra veneta (secc. XI–XII)', in *Les fonctions des saints dans le monde occidental (IIIe–XIIIe siècle)* (Rome 1991), pp. 447–65.
Cracco, G. and G. Ortalli (eds.), *Storia di Venezia*, 2 (Rome, 1995).
Cracco Ruggini, L. (ed.), *Storia di Venezia*, 1 (Rome, 1992).
Crespo Pascual, A., 'Cerámica esgrafiada: estado de la cuestión', *Anales de arqueología cordobesa*, 12 (2001), pp. 353–70.
Cressier, P., 'Agua, fortificaciones y poblamiento', *Aragón en la edad media*, 9 (1991), pp. 403–47.
Cressier, P., 'Ville médiévale au Maghreb', in P. Sénac (ed.), *Histoire et archéologie de l'Occident musulman (VIIe–XVe siècle)* (Toulouse, 2012), pp. 117–40.
Cressier, P. and E. Fentress (eds.), *La céramique maghrébine du haut Moyen âge (VIIIe–Xe siècle)* (Rome, 2011).
Cressier, P. and S. Gutiérrez Lloret, 'Al-Andalus', in B. J. Walker et al. (eds.), *The Oxford handbook of Islamic archaeology* (Oxford, 2020), pp. 311–34.

Cressier, P. and A. Nef (eds.), 'Les Fatimides et la Méditerranée centrale (X^{e}–XIIe siècle)', *Revue des mondes musulmans et de la Méditerranée*, 139 (2016), pp. 13–166.
Cressier, P. and M. Rammah, 'Ṣabra al-Manṣūriya', *Comptes rendus des séances de l'Académie des Inscriptions et Belles-Lettres*, 150 (2006), pp. 613–33.
Cressier, P. and M. Rammah, 'Sabra al-Mansûriya (Kairouan, Tunisie)', *MEFRM*, 119 (2007), pp. 468–77.
Cressier, P. and M. Rammah, 'Sabra al-Mansūriyya', in N. Boukhchim et al. (eds.), *Kairouan et sa région: Actes du 3ème colloque international du Département d'Archéologie* (Manouba, 2013), pp. 287–99.
Creswell, K. A. C., *The Muslim architecture of Egypt*, 1 (Oxford, 1952).
Crouzet-Pavan, É., 'La conquista e l'organizzazione dello spazio urbano', in Cracco and Ortalli, *Storia di Venezia*, 2 (Rome, 1995), pp. 549–75.
Curta, F., *Southeastern Europe in the middle ages, 500–1250* (Cambridge, 2006).
d'Acunto, E., 'Mercato, mercati e mercanti a Milano', in *La rinascita del mercato nel X secolo* (Pistoia, 2012), pp. 21–33.
D'Amico, E., *Byzantine finewares in Italy (10th–14th centuries AD)*, PhD thesis, Durham University, 2011.
D'Amico, E., 'Circolazione di ceramiche a Messina nel basso Medioevo', in M. Giorgio (ed.), *Storie [di] ceramiche*, 6 (Florence, 2020), pp. 29–36.
D'Angelo, F., 'La monetazione di Muḥammad ibn 'Abbād emiro rebelle a Federico II di Sicilia', *Studi magrebini*, 7 (1975), pp. 149–53.
D'Angelo, F., 'La protomaiolica di Sicilia e la ricerca delle sue origini', *AM*, 22 (1995), pp. 456–60.
D'Angelo, F., 'Le produzioni di ceramiche invetriate dipinte in Sicilia nei secoli X–XII', *Mediaeval sophia*, 8 (2010), pp. 108–40.
Dachraoui, F., *Le califat fatimide au Maghreb (296–365 H./909–975 JC.)* (Paris, 1981).
Dagron, G., 'Poissons, pêcheurs et poissonniers de Constantinople', in C. Mango and G. Dagron (eds.), *Constantinople and its hinterland* (Aldershot, 1995), pp. 57–73.
Dagron, G., 'The urban economy, seventh–twelfth centuries', in Laiou, *The economic history of Byzantium* (Washington, DC, 2002), pp. 393–461.
Dagron, G., *Emperor and priest* (Cambridge, 2003).
Daim, F. and S. Ladstätter (eds.), *Ephesos in byzantinischer Zeit* (Mainz, 2011).
Dameron, G. W., *Episcopal power and Florentine society, 1000–1300* (Cambridge, MA, 1991).
Dameron, G., 'Feeding the medieval Italian city-state', *Speculum*, 92 (2017), pp. 976–1019.
Danys-Lasek, K., 'Pottery from Deir el-Naqlun (6th–12th century)', *Polish archaeology in the Mediterranean*, 23.1 (2014), pp. 543–642.
Daouatli, A., 'La céramique médiévale en Tunisie', *Africa*, 13 (1995), pp. 189–204.
Dark, K. R., 'Houses, streets and shops in Byzantine Constantinople from the fifth to the twelfth centuries', *Journal of medieval history*, 30 (2004), pp. 83–107.
Dark, K. R., 'Pottery production and use in Byzantine Constantinople', *Byzantinoslavica*, 68 (2010), pp. 115–28.
Darley, R., 'Who ate all the pepper?', in press.
Darmstädter, P., *Das Reichsgut in der Lombardei und Piemont, 568–1250* (Strassburg, 1896).
Dartmann, C., *Politische Interaktion in der italienischen Stadtkommune (11.–14. Jahrhundert)* (Ostfildern, 2012).
Davidsohn, R., *Forschungen zur älteren Geschichte von Florenz*, 4 vols. (Berlin, 1896–1908).
Davidsohn, R., *Storia di Firenze*, 8 vols. (Florence, 1956–78).
Davies, W., 'Notions of wealth in the charters of ninth- and tenth-century Christian Iberia', in J.-P. Devroey et al. (eds.), *Les élites et la richesse au Haut Moyen Âge* (Turnhout, 2010), pp. 265–84.

Davis-Secord, S., *Where three worlds meet* (Ithaca, NY, 2017).

Day, J., *La Sardegna sotto la dominazione pisano-genovese* (Turin, 1987).

Day, W. R., *The early development of the Florentine economy, c. 1100–1275*, PhD thesis, London School of Economics, 2000.

Day, W. R., 'The population of Florence before the Black Death', *Journal of medieval history*, 28 (2002), pp. 93–129.

Day, W. R. et al., *Medieval European coinage*, 12 (Cambridge, 2016).

de Amores Corredano, D., 'Las alfarerías almohades de la Cartuja', in Valor Piechotta, *El último siglo de la Sevilla islámica* (Seville, 1995), pp. 303–6.

De Giorgi, A. U. and A. A. Eger, *Antioch* (Abingdon, 2021).

De Groote, K., *Middeleeuws aardewerk in Vlaanderen* (Brussels, 2008).

de Lange, N., 'Byzantium in the Cairo Genizah', *Byzantine and Modern Greek studies*, 16 (1992), pp. 34–47.

de Roover. R., 'The commercial revolution of the thirteenth century', *Bulletin of the Business Historical Society*, 16 (1942), pp. 34–9.

De Simone, A., '*Al-zahr al-bāsim* di Ibn Qalāqis e le vicende dei musulmani nella Sicilia normanna', in B. Scarcia Amoretti (ed.), *Del nuovo sulla Sicilia musulmana* (Rome, 1995), pp. 99–152.

De Simone, A., 'Ruggero II e l'Africa islamica', in G. Musca (ed.), *Il Mezzogiorno normanno-svevo e le Crociate* (Bari, 2002), pp. 95–129.

De Simone, A., 'Ancora sui "villani" di Sicilia', *MEFRM*, 116.1 (2004), pp. 471–500.

de Souza, G. et al., 'The Islamic pottery from Senhora do Barrocal (Satão, Central-Northern Portugal', in S. Prata et al. (eds.), *Paisajes, espacios y materialidades* (Oxford, 2022), pp. 272–7.

de Vingo, P., 'La céramique d'importation islamique dans la Ligurie médiévale', in R.-P. Gayraud et al. (eds.), *Héritages arabo-islamiques dans l'Europe méditerranéenne* (Paris, 2015), pp. 281–99.

de Vos, M. (ed.), *Rus africum* (Trento, 2000).

de Vos Raaijmakers, M. and B. Maurina (eds.), *Rus africum IV: la fattoria bizantina di Aïn Wassel, Africa Proconsularis (Alto Tell, Tunisia)* (Oxford, 2019).

Décobert, C. et al. (eds.), *Alexandrie médiévale*, 4 vols. (Cairo, 1998–2011).

Degrandi, A., 'Vassalli cittadini e vassalli rurali nel Vercellese del XII secolo', *Bollettino storico-bibliografico subalpino*, 91 (1993), pp. 5–45.

Degrandi, A., *Artigiani nel Vercellese dei secoli 12. e 13.* (Pisa, 1997).

Degrassi, D., *L'economia artigiana nell'Italia medievale* (Rome, 1996).

Dekker, R., 'The development of the church at Dayr Anba Hadra', in G. Gabra and H. Takla (eds.), *Christianity and monasticism in Aswan and Nubia* (Cairo, 2013), pp. 105–15.

Del Punta, I., *Mercanti e banchieri lucchesi nel Duecento* (Pisa, 2005).

Del Tredici, M., 'Castelli, mutazione signorile e crescita economica nell'Italia dei secoli XI–XII', *Reti medievali rivista*, 24 (2023), in press.

Del Treppo, M. and A. Leone, *Amalfi medioevale* (Naples, 1977).

Delattre, A. et al., 'Écrire en arabe et en copte', *Chronique d'Égypte*, 87 (2012), pp. 170–88.

Déléry, C., *Dynamiques économiques, sociales et culturelles d'al-Andalus à partir d'une étude de la céramique de cuerda seca (seconde moitié du Xe siècle—première moitié du XIIIe siècle)*, thèse de doctorat, Université de Toulouse II-Le Mirail, 2006.

Déléry, C., 'Using *cuerda seca* ceramics as a historical source to evaluate trade and cultural relations between Christian-ruled lands and al-Andalus, from the tenth to thirteenth centuries', *Al-Masāq*, 21 (2009), pp. 31–58.

Déléry, C. et al., 'Contribution à l'étude de l'évolution technologique et du commerce des céramiques de *cuerda seca* en al-Andalus (X^e^–XIIe siècles)', in J. Zozaya et al. (eds.),

Actas del VIII Congreso internacional de cerámica medieval en el Mediterráneo (Ciudad Real, 2009), pp. 571–98.
Dellaporta, A. P., 'The Byzantine shipwreck at Pelagonnesos-Alonessos', in Papanikola-Bakirtzi, *Byzantine glazed ceramics* (Athens, 1999), pp. 122–42.
Delumeau, J.-P., *Arezzo, espace et sociétés, 715–1230* (Rome, 1996).
Demus, O., *The mosaics of San Marco in Venice*, 2 vols. (Chicago, 1984).
den Heijer, J., *Mawhūb ibn Manṣūr* (Leuven, 1989).
Desrosiers, S., *Soieries et autres textiles de l'Antiquité au XVIe siècle* (Paris, 2004).
Deutsches Archäologisches Institut, *Deir Anba Hadra excavations*, https://www.dainst.org/projekt/-/project-display/63443/.
Devisse, J., 'Trade and trade routes in West Africa', in M. El Fasi and I. Hrbek (eds.), *General history of Africa*, 3 (Berkeley, CA, 1988), pp. 367–435.
Devroey, J.-P., *Économie rurale et société dans l'Europe franque (VIe–IXe siècles)* (Paris, 2003).
Di Muro, A., *La terra, il mercante e il sovrano* (Potenza, 2020).
Didioumi, S., 'Local pottery production in the island of Cos, Greece, from the early Byzantine period', in N. Poulou-Papadimitriou (ed.), *LRCW 4*, BAR, I2616 (Oxford, 2014), pp. 169–80.
Diem, W., *Arabischer Terminkauf* (Wiesbaden, 2006).
Diem, W., 'Philologisches zu arabischen Dokumenten der Österreichischen Nationalbibliothek in Wien', *Wiener Zeitschrift für die Kunde des Morgenlandes*, 101 (2011), pp. 75–140.
Dietz, S. et al., *Africa proconsularis*, 3 vols. (Aarhus, 1995–2000).
Dilcher, G. and C. Violante (eds.), *Strutture e trasformazioni della signoria rurale nei secoli X–XIII in Italia e Germania durante il medioevo (1000–1250)* (Bologna, 1996).
Dimmock, S., *The origin of capitalism in England, 1400–1600* (Leiden, 2014).
Dimopoulos, I., 'Trade of Byzantine red wares, end of the 11th–13th centuries', in Mundell Mango, *Byzantine trade* (Farnham, 2009), pp. 179–90.
Dinnetz, M., 'Iron and steel in Islamic Spain', *Madrider Mitteilungen*, 45 (2004), pp. 532–60.
Discarded history, Cambridge University Library exhibition guide, available on site.
Ditchfield, P., *La culture matérielle médiévale* (Rome, 2007).
Dixneuf, D., *Amphores égyptiennes* (Alexandria, 2011).
Djellid, A., 'La céramique islamique du haut Moyen Âge en Algérie (IXe–Xe siècles)', in Cressier and Fentress, *La céramique maghrébine* (Rome, 2011), pp. 147–58.
Dochev, K., 'Tŭrnovo, sixth–fourteenth centuries', in Laiou, *The economic history of Byzantium* (Washington, DC, 2002), pp. 673–8.
Doğer, L., 'Byzantine ceramics', *Byzas*, 7 (2007), pp. 97–122.
Dölger, F., *Beiträge zur Geschichte der byzantinischen Finanzverwaltung, besonders des 10. und 11. Jahrhunderts* (Berlin, 1927).
Dols, M. W., *The Black Death in the Middle East* (Princeton, NJ, 1977).
Doménech Belda, C., *Dinares, dirhams y feluses* (Salamanca, 2003).
Doménech-Belda, C., 'Fatimíes y taifas', *al-Qanṭara*, 37 (2016), pp. 199–232.
Doménech-Belda, C., 'The Fāṭimid coins from Sicily in al-Andalus', in B. Callegher and A. D'Ottone Rambach (eds.), *5th Simone Assemani symposium on Islamic coins* (Trieste, 2018), pp. 197–211.
Dorigo, W., *Venezia origini*, 2 vols. (Milan, 1983).
Dorin, R., 'Adriatic trade networks in the twelfth and early thirteenth centuries', in Morrisson, *Trade and markets* (Washington, DC, 2012), pp. 235–79.
Dossey, L. *Peasant and empire in Christian North Africa* (Berkeley, CA, 2010).
Drieu, L. et al., 'Chemical evidence for the persistence of wine production and trade in Early Medieval Islamic Sicily', *PNAS*, March 9, 2021 118 (10). doi: 10.1073/pnas.2017983118.

Duby, G., *Rural economy and country life in the medieval West* (London, 1968).

Duby, G., *The early growth of the European economy* (London, 1974).

Dunn, A., 'The rise and fall of towns, loci for maritime traffic, and silk production', in E. Jeffreys (ed.) *Byzantine style, religion and civilization* (Cambridge, 2006), pp. 38–71.

Durand, M. and S. Rettig, 'Un atelier sous contrôle califal identifié dans le Fayoum: le ṭirāz privé de Ṭuṭūn', in M. Durand (ed.), *Égypte, la trame de l'histoire: textiles pharaoniques, coptes et islamiques* (Paris, 2002), pp. 167–70.

Durliat, J., *De la ville antique à la ville byzantine* (Rome, 1990).

Duval, N., 'L'urbanisme de Sufetula', in *Aufstieg und Niedergang der römische Welt*, 2.10.2 (Berlin, 1982), pp. 596–632.

Dyer, C., *Standards of living in the later Middle Ages* (Cambridge, 1989).

Dyer, C. *An age of transition?* (Oxford, 2005).

Dyer, C. 'The ineffectiveness of lordship in England, 1200–1400', in C. Dyer et al. (eds.), *Rodney Hilton's middle ages*, Past and present supplement, 2 (Oxford, 2007), pp. 69–86.

Dyer, C. 'Pourquoi les paysans anglais étaient-ils consommateurs (XIIIe–XVe siècle)?', in G. Ferrand and J. Petrowiste (eds.), *Le nécessaire et le superflu* (Toulouse, 2019), pp. 127–46.

Dyer, C., *Peasants making history* (Oxford, 2022).

Eastwood, W. J. et al., 'Integrating palaeoecological and archaeo-historical records', in T. Vorderstrasse and J. Roodenberg (eds.), *Archaeology of the countryside in medieval Anatolia* (Leiden, 2009), pp. 45–69.

Edwards, J. and S. Ogilvie, 'Contract enforcement, institutions and social capital', *Economic history review*, 65 (2012), pp. 421–44.

Eger, C., 'Guarrazar (Provinz Toledo)', *Madrider Mitteilungen*, 48 (2007), pp. 267–305.

Eiroa Rodríguez, J. A., 'Arqueología de los espacios agrarios andalusíes en el Sureste peninsular', in H. Kirchner (ed.), *Por una arqueología agraria*, BAR, I2062 (Oxford, 2010), pp. 107–21.

Eiroa Rodríguez, J. A., 'Representations of power in rural communities in south-eastern al-Andalus (tenth–thirteenth centuries)', in A. Fábregas and F. Sabaté (eds.), *Power and rural communities in al-Andalus* (Turnhout, 2015), pp. 85–111.

Eiroa Rodríguez, J. A. et al., 'Nuevas investigaciones arqueológicas en el arrabal de la Arrixaca (Murcia)', in M. Retuerce Velasco (ed.), *Actas VI Congreso de arqueología medieval (España–Portugal)* (Ciudad Real, 2021), pp. 55–62.

El Faiz, M., 'L' Aljarafe de Séville', *Hespéris tamuda*, 29 (1991), pp. 5–25.

Elbendary, A., 'The worst of times', in N. Hanna (ed.), *Money, land and trade* (London, 2002), pp. 67–83.

Ellenblum, R., *The collapse of the eastern Mediterranean* (Cambridge, 2012).

Encyclopaedia of Islam, 2nd edn [cited as *EI*^{2}] (Leiden, 2012), s.v. al-Ḳulzum (E. Honigmann and R.Y. Ebied); al-Ṣaḳāliba (P. B. Golden et al.); sharika (M. Y. Izzi Dien); al-Ushmūnayn (A. F. Sayyid).

Engemann, J., *Abū Mīnā VI* (Wiesbaden, 2016).

Epstein, S. A., *Wage labour and guilds in medieval Europe* (Chapel Hill, NC, 1991).

Epstein, S. A., *Genoa and the Genoese, 958–1528* (Chapel Hill, NC, 1996).

Epstein, S. R., 'The textile industry and the foreign cloth trade in late medieval Sicily (1300–1500)', *Journal of medieval history*, 15 (1989), pp. 141–83.

Epstein, S. R., 'Cities, regions and the late medieval crisis', *Past and present*, 130 (1991), pp. 3–50.

Epstein, S. R., *An island for itself* (Cambridge, 1992).

Epstein, S. R., 'A reply', *Revista d'historia medieval*, 5 (1995), pp. 133–80.

Epstein, S. R., *Freedom and growth* (London, 2000).

Ertl, T. and K. Oschema, 'Les études médiévales après le tournant global', *Annales H. S. S.*, 76 (2021), pp. 787–801.

Escribà, F., *La ceràmica califal de Benetússer* (Valencia, 1990).

Espinar Cappa, A. et al., 'La producción de cerámica verde y manganeso en Málaga', *Mainake*, 36 (2016), pp. 65–82.

Esquilache Martí, F., *Els constructors de l'Horta de València* (Valencia, 2018).

Estangüi Gómez, R., 'Richesses et propriété paysannes à Byzance (XIe–XIVe siècle)', in O. Delouis et al. (eds.), *Le saint, le moine et le paysan* (Paris, 2016), pp. 171–212.

Estangüi Gómez, R. and M. Kaplan, 'La société rurale au XIe siècle', *Travaux et mémoires*, 21.2 (2017), pp. 531–59.

Fábregas García, A., 'Almería en el sistema de comercio de las repúblicas italianas', in A. Suárez Márquez (ed.), *Almería, puerta del Mediterráneo (ss. X–XII)* (Almería, 2007), pp. 136–59.

Faini, E., 'Passignano e i Fiorentini (1000–1266)', in P. Pirillo (ed.), *Passignano in Val di Pesa*, 1 (Florence, 2009), pp. 129–52.

Faini, E., *Firenze nell'età romanica (1000–1211)* (Florence, 2010).

Faini, E., 'Prima del fiorino', in T. Verdon (ed.), *Firenze prima di Arnolfo* (Florence, 2016), pp. 93–103.

Faini, E., 'Il comune e il suo contrario', in G. Cariboni et al. (eds.), *Presenza-assenza* (Milan, 2021), pp. 259–300.

Fantappiè, R., 'Nascita d'una terra di nome Prato', in *Storia di Prato*, 1 (Prato, 1980), pp. 97–359.

Fatighenti, B., 'I corredi ceramici di fabbri e vetrai nella Pisa medievale (fine XII–XIV secolo)', *AM*, 42 (2015), pp. 281–95.

Fatighenti, B., *La ceramica bassomedievale a Pisa e a San Genesio (San Miniato-PI)* (Oxford, 2016).

Faust, D. et al., 'High-resolution fluvial record of late Holocene geomorphic change in northern Tunisia: climatic or human impact?', *Quaternary science reviews*, 23 (2001), pp. 1757–75.

Federico, R., 'Il saggio nord-ovest nel settore medievale a sud della Villa del Casale', in Pensabene and Barresi, *Piazza Armerina, Villa del Casale* (Rome, 2019), pp. 289–325.

Fees, I., *Reichtum und Macht im mittelalterlichen Venedig: die Familie Ziani* (Tübingen, 1988).

Fees, I., *Le monache di San Zaccaria a Venezia nei secoli XII e XIII* (Venice, 1998).

Fehérvári, G. et al., *The Kuwait excavations at Bahnasa/Oxyrhynchus (1985–1987)* (Kuwait City, 2006).

Feller, L., *Les Abruzzes médiévales* (Rome, 1998).

Feller, L., *Richesse, terre et valeur dans l'Occident médiéval* (Turnhout, 2021).

Felloni, G., 'Note sulla finanza pubblica genovese agli albori del comune', *Atti della Società ligure di storia patria*, 42.1 (2002), pp. 329–51.

Fenech, K., *Human-induced changes in the environment and landscape of the Maltese Islands from the Neolithic to the 15th century* AD, *as inferred from a scientific study of sediments from Marsa, Malta*, BAR, I1682 (Oxford. 2007).

Feniello, A., *Napoli, società ed economia (902–1137)* (Rome, 2011).

Fennell Mazzaoui, M., 'The emigration of Veronese textile artisans to Bologna in the thirteenth century', *Atti e memorie della Accademia di agricoltura scienze e lettere di Verona*, 6 ser., 19 (1968–9), pp. 275–321.

Fennell Mazzaoui, M., *The Italian cotton industry in the later middle ages 1100–1600* (Cambridge, 1981).

Fentress, E., 'Reconsidering Islamic houses in the Maghreb', in S. Gutiérrez Lloret and I. Grau Mira (eds.), *De la estructura doméstica al espacio social* (Alicante, 2013), pp. 237–44.

Fentress, E. et al., 'Prospections dans le Belezma: rapport préliminaire', in *Actes du colloque international sur l'histoire de Sétif* (Algiers, 1993), pp. 107–27.

Fenwick, C., 'From Africa to Ifrīqiya', *Al-Masāq*, 25 (2013), pp. 9–33.

Fenwick, C., 'The fate of the classical cities of North Africa in the Middle Ages', in R. Bockmann et al. (eds.), *Africa—Ifriqiya: continuity and change in North Africa from the Byzantine to the early Islamic age* (Rome, 2019), pp. 137–56.

Fenwick, C., *Early Islamic North Africa* (London, 2020).

Fernandes, I. C. et al., 'O comércio da corda seca no Gharb al-Andalus', in M. J. Gonçalves and S. Gómez-Martínez (eds.), *Actas do X Congresso internacional, A cerâmica medieval no Mediterrâneo* (Silves, 2015), pp. 649–66.

Ferrandis Torres, J., 'Tesorillo de dinares almorávides hallado en la Alcazaba de Almería', *al-Andalus*, 4 (1941), pp. 327–37.

Ferrante, C. and A. Mattone, 'Le comunità rurali nella Sardegna medievale (secoli XI–XV)', *Studi storici*, 45 (2004), pp. 169–243.

Ferrer, M. T., 'El comerç català a la baixa edat mitjana', *Catalan historical review*, 5 (2012), pp. 159–93.

Ferri, M., 'Le strutture produttive di Comacchio', in Coscarella et al., *Il vetro in transizione* (Bari, 2021), pp. 229–36.

Fialho Silva, M., *Mutação urbana na Lisboa medieval: das Taifas a D. Dinis*, tese doutoral, Universidade de Lisboa, 2017.

Fierro, M., 'La obra histórica de Ibn al-Qūṭiyya', *al-Qanṭara*, 10 (1989), pp. 485–512.

Fierro, M., 'Cuatro preguntas en torno a Ibn Ḥafsūn', *al-Qanṭara*, 16 (1995), pp. 221–57.

Fierro, M., 'El conde Casio, los Banū Qasī y los linajes godos en al-Andalus', *Studia historica, Historia medieval*, 27 (2009), pp. 181–9.

Fierro, M., 'Les généalogies du pouvoir en al-Andalus', in D. Valérian (ed.), *Islamisation et arabisation de l'Occident musulman médiéval (VIIe–XIII siècle)* (Paris, 2011), pp. 265–94.

Figliuolo, B., 'Amalfi e il Levante nel Medioevo', in G. Airaldi and B. Z. Kedar (eds.), *I comuni italiani nel regno crociato di Gerusalemme* (Genoa, 1986), pp. 573–664.

Filangieri, L., *Famiglie e gruppi dirigenti a Genova (secoli XII–metà XIII)*, tesi di dottorato di ricerca, Università degli Studi di Firenze, 2010.

Filipe, V. et al., 'Cerâmica de importação no arrabalde ocidental de Luxbuna (Lisboa)', in M. J. Gonçalves and S. Gómez-Martínez (eds.), *Actas do X Congresso internacional, A cerâmica medieval no Mediterrâneo* (Silves, 2015), pp. 711–18.

Filippi, F. et al., 'La produzione di una fornace altomedievale per ceramica da Libarna (AL)', in G. Pantò (ed.), *Produzione e circolazione dei materiali ceramici in Italia settentrionale tra VI e X secolo* (Mantua, 2004), pp. 57–83.

Findlay, R. and K. H. O'Rourke, *Power and plenty* (Princeton, NJ, 2007).

Fiore, A., *Signori e sudditi* (Spoleto, 2010).

Fiore, A., *The seigneurial transformation* (Oxford, 2020).

Fiorilla, S., 'Considerazioni sulle ceramiche medievali della Sicilia centromeridionale', in S. Scuto (ed.), *L'età di Federico II nella Sicilia centromeridionale* (Agrigento, 1991), pp. 115–69.

Fiorilla, S., 'Ceramiche medievali della Sicilia centromeridionale', in R. El Hraîki and E. Erbati (eds.), *Actes du Vè colloque international: la céramique médiévale en Méditerranée occidentale* (Rabat, 1995), pp. 205–15.

Fiorilla, S., *Gela* (Messina, 1996).

Fiorilla, S., 'Primi dati sulle produzioni ceramiche di Siracusa', in J. Zozaya et al. (eds.), *Actas del VIII Congreso internacional de cerámica medieval en el Mediterráneo* (Ciudad Real, 2009), pp. 193–306.

Firnhaber-Baker, J. and D. Schoenars (eds.), *The Routledge history handbook of medieval revolt* (London, 2016).
Fiumi, E., *Storia economica e sociale di San Gimignano* (Florence, 1961).
Flecker, M., 'A ninth-century Arab shipwreck in Indonesia', in Krahl et al., *Shipwrecked* (Washington, DC, 2011), pp. 101–19.
Flores Escobosa, I., 'La fabricación de cerámica islámica en Almería: la loza dorada', *Tudmīr*, 2 (2011), pp. 9–28.
Flores Escobosa, I. et al., 'Las producciones de un alfar islámico en Almería', *ATM*, 6 (1999), pp. 207–39.
Flors, E. and D. Sanfeliu, 'Los materiales cerámicos', in E. Flors Ureña (ed.), *Torre la Sal (Ribera de Cabanes, Castellón)* (Castellón, 2009), pp. 269–352.
Fonseca, C. D., *La signoria del Monastero maggiore di Milano sul luogo di Arosio (secoli XII–XIII)* (Genoa, 1974).
Foss, C., *Byzantine and Turkish Sardis* (Cambridge, MA, 1976).
Foss, C., 'Late antique and Byzantine Ankara', *DOP*, 31 (1977), pp. 29–87.
Foss, C., *Ephesus after Antiquity* (Cambridge, 1979).
Foss, C., 'The cities of Pamphylia', in Foss, *Cities, fortresses and villages of Byzantine Asia Minor* (Aldershot, 1996), study IV.
Foss, C. and J. A. Scott, 'Sardis', in Laiou, *The economic history of Byzantium* (Washington, DC, 2002), pp. 617–22.
Fossier, R., *Enfance de l'Europe* (Paris, 1982).
Fossier, R., 'Les communautés villageoises en France du nord au moyen âge', in *Les communautés villageoises en Europe occidentale du Moyen Âge aux temps modernes* (Auch, 1984), pp. 29–53.
Fozzati, L. (ed.), *Ca' Vendramin Calergi* (Venice, 2005).
Franceschi, F., 'La crescita economica dell'Occidente medievale', in *La crescita economica* (Pistoia, 2017), pp. 1–24.
Franceschi, F. and L. Molà, 'Regional states and economic development', in I. Lazzarini and A. Gamberini (eds.), *The Italian Renaissance state* (Cambridge, 2012), pp. 444–66.
Franceschi, F. and I. Taddei, *Le città italiane nel Medioevo, XII–XIV secolo* (Bologna, 2012).
François, V., 'Céramiques importées à Byzance: une quasi-absence', *Byzantinoslavica*, 58 (1997), pp. 387–404.
François, V., *Céramiques médiévales à Alexandrie* (Cairo, 1999).
François, V., 'Cuisine et pots de terre à Byzance', *Bulletin de correspondance hellénique*, 134 (2010). pp. 317–82.
François, V., *La vaisselle de terre à Byzance* (Paris, 2017).
Francovich, R. (ed.), *Rocca San Silvestro* (Rome, 1991).
Francovich, R. and M. Valenti (eds.), *Poggio Imperiale a Poggibonsi* (Cinisello Balsamo, 2007).
Francovich, R. and C. Wickham, 'Uno scavo archeologico e il problema dello sviluppo della signoria territoriale', *AM*, 21 (1994), pp. 7–30.
Frankopan, P., 'Byzantine trade privileges to Venice in the eleventh century', *Journal of medieval history*, 30 (2004), pp. 135–60.
Frankopan, P., 'Land and power in the middle and later period', in J. Haldon, *A social history of Byzantium* (Oxford 2009), pp. 112–42.
Frantz-Murphy, G., 'A new interpretation of the economic history of medieval Egypt', *JESHO*, 24 (1981), pp. 274–97.
Frantz-Murphy, G., *The agrarian administration* of *Egypt from the Arabs to the Ottomans* (Cairo, 1986).
Frendo, J. D. C., 'The *Miracles of St. Demetrius* and the capture of Thessaloniki', *Byzantinoslavica*, 58 (1997), pp. 205–24.

Frenkel, M., 'Medieval Alexandria: life in a port city', *Al-Masaq*, 26 (2014), pp. 5–35.

Frenkel, M., 'Review of Ackerman-Lieberman, *The business of identity*', *Journal of the American oriental society*, 136 (2016), pp. 640–3.

Frenkel, M. and A. Lester, 'Evidence of material culture from the Geniza', in D. Talmon-Heller and K. Cytryn-Silverman (eds.), *Material evidence and narrative sources* (Leiden, 2014), pp. 147–87.

Fuertes Santos, M. del C., 'Aproximación al urbanismo y la arquitectura doméstica de época califal del yacimiento de Cercadilla', *ATM*, 9 (2001), pp. 105–26.

Fuertes Santos, M. del C., *La cerámica califal del yacimiento de Cercadilla, Córdoba* (Seville, 2001).

Fuertes Santos, M. del C., 'El Sector Nororiental del arrabal califal del yacimiento de Cercadilla', *ATM*, 14 (2007), pp. 49–68.

Fujita, M. et al., 'On the evolution of hierarchical urban systems', *European economic review*, 43 (1999), pp. 209–52.

Fumagalli, V., *Le origini di una grande dinastia feudale: Adalberto-Atto di Canossa* (Tübingen, 1971).

Fumagalli, V., *Coloni e signori nell'Italia settentrionale, secoli VI–XI* (Bologna, 1978).

Fumagalli, V., 'L'evoluzione dell'economia agraria e dei patti colonici dall'alto al basso Medioevo', in B. Andreolli et al. (eds.), *Le campagne italiane prima e dopo il Mille* (Bologna, 1985), pp. 13–42.

Furió, A., 'Rents instead of land', *Continuity and change*, 36 (2021), pp. 177–209.

Galasso, G. (ed.), *Alle origini del dualismo italiano* (Soveria Mannelli, 2014).

Galliker, J., *Middle Byzantine silk in context*, PhD thesis, University of Birmingham, 2015.

Gamberini, A. and F. Pagnoni (eds.), *La signoria rurale nell'Italia del tardo medioevo*, 1 (Milan and Turin, 2019).

García Porras, A., 'La ceramica smaltata spagnola nella Liguria di Ponente', *Rivista di studi liguri*, 74 (2008), pp. 223–50.

García Porras, A., 'La producción de cerámica en Almería entre los siglos X y XII', in L. Cara Barrionuevo (ed.), *Cuando Almería era Almariyya* (Almería, 2016), pp. 273–92.

García Sánchez, E., 'Agriculture in Muslim Spain', in S. K. Jayyusi (ed.), *The legacy of Muslim Spain* (Leiden, 1992), pp. 987–99.

García Sánchez, E., 'Los cultivos en al-Andalus', in *El agua en la agricultura de al-Andalus* (Madrid, 1995), pp. 41–55.

García, E., 'Las plantas textiles y tintóreas en al-Andalus', in M. Marín (ed.), *Tejer y vestir* (Madrid, 2001), pp. 417–51.

García Sanjuán, A., 'El concepto tributario y la caracterización de la sociedad andalusí', in García Sanjuán (ed.), *Saber y sociedad en al-Andalus* (Huelva, 2006), pp. 81–152.

García Sanjuán, A., *Till God inherits the earth* (Leiden, 2007).

Garcin, J.-C., 'Remarques sur un plan topographique de la grande mosquée de Qûs', *AI*, 9 (1970), pp. 97–108.

Garcin, J.-C., *Un centre musulman de la Haute-Égypte médiévale: Qūṣ* (Cairo, 1976).

Garcin, J.-C., 'Habitat médiéval et histoire urbaine à Fusṭāṭ et au Caire', in Garcin et al., *Palais et maisons du Caire*, 1 (Paris, 1982), pp. 145–216.

Garcin, J.-C. et al., *États, sociétés et cultures du monde musulman médiéval, Xe–XVe siècle*, 3 vols. (Paris, 1995–2000).

Gardini, A., 'La ceramica bizantina in Liguria', in Gelichi, *La ceramica nel mondo bizantino* (Florence, 1993), pp. 47–77.

Garland, L., 'Political power and the populace in Byzantium prior to the Fourth Crusade. *Byzantinoslavica*, 53 (1992), pp. 17–52.

Garufi, C. A., 'Gli Aleramici e i Normanni in Sicilia e nelle Puglie', in E. Besta et al. (eds.), *Centenario della nascita di Michele Amari*, 1 (Palermo, 1910), pp. 67–83.
Garver, E. L., *Byzantine amphoras of the ninth through thirteenth centuries in the Bodrum Museum of underwater archaeology*, MA thesis, Texas A&M University, 1993.
Garzella, G., *Pisa com'era* (Pisa, 1990).
Gascoigne, A., *The impact of the Arab conquest on late Roman settlement in Egypt*, PhD thesis, University of Cambridge, 2002.
Gascoigne, A. L., 'Dislocation and continuity in early Islamic provincial urban centres: the example of Tell Edfu', *Mitteilungen des Deutschen Archäologischen Instituts, Abteilung Kairo*, 61 (2005), pp. 153–89.
Gascoigne, A., 'Amphorae from Old Cairo', *CCE*, 8 (2007), pp. 161–83.
Gascoigne, A. L., *The island city of Tinnīs* (Cairo, 2020).
Gascoigne, A. and G. Pyke, 'Nebi Samwil-type jars in medieval Egypt', in D. Aston et al. (eds.), *Under the potter's tree* (Leuven, 2011), pp. 417–31.
Gasparri, S., 'Dagli Orseolo al comune', in Cracco Ruggini, *Storia di Venezia*, 1 (Rome, 1992), pp. 791–826.
Gasparri, S., 'Mercanti o possessori?', in Gasparri and C. La Rocca (eds.), *Carte di famiglia* (Rome, 2005), pp. 157–78.
Gasparri, S., 'The formation of an early medieval community', in V. West-Harling (ed.), *Three empires, three cities* (Turnhout, 2015), pp. 35–50.
Gattiglia, G., *Pisa medievale* (Rome, 2013).
Gattiglia, G. and G. Tarantino, '*...loco ubi dicitur castello*', *AM*, 40 (2013), pp. 233–57.
Gayraud, R.-P., 'Tebtynis', in C. Décobert (ed.), *Itinéraires d'Égypte* (Cairo, 1992), pp. 31–44.
Gayraud, R.-P., 'Les céramiques égyptiennes à glaçure, IXe–XIIe siècles', in G. Démians d'Archimbaud (ed.), *La céramique médiévale en Méditerranée* (Aix-en-Provence, 1997), pp. 261–60.
Gayraud, R.-P., 'Fostat', in Gayraud (ed.), *Colloque international d'archéologie islamique* (Cairo, 1998), pp. 435–60.
Gayraud, R.-P., 'Pauvreté et richesse de l'Égypte médiévale', in J.-P. Pascual (ed.), *Pauvreté et richesse dans le monde musulman méditerranéen* (Paris, 2003), pp. 173–81.
Gayraud, R.-P., 'La réapparition des céramiques à glaçure en Égypte', in B. Mathieu et al. (eds.), *L'apport de l'Égypte à l'histoire des techniques* (Cairo, 2006), pp. 101–16.
Gayraud, R.-P. and J.-C. Tréglia, 'Amphores, céramiques culinaires et céramiques communes omeyyades d'un niveau d'incendie à Fustat—Istabl 'Antar (Le Caire, Égypte)', in N. Poulou-Papadimitriou et al. (eds.), *LRCW* 4 (Oxford, 2014), pp. 365–75.
Gayraud, R.-P. and L. Vallauri, *Fustat II* (Cairo, 2017).
Gayraud, R.-P. et al., 'Iṣṭabl 'Antar (Fostat) 1992: rapport des fouilles', *AI*, 28 (1994), pp. 1–27. [Other preliminary reports for the French Fusṭāṭ expedition appear in *AI*, 22 (1986), pp. 1–26, 25 (1991), pp. 57–87, 27 (1993), pp. 225–32, 29 (1995), pp. 1–24.]
Gayraud, R.-P. et al., 'Assemblages de céramiques égyptiennes et témoins de production, datés par les fouilles d'Istabl Antar, Fustat (IXe–Xe siècles)', in J. Zozaya et al. (eds.), *Actas del VIII Congreso internacional de cerámica medieval en el Mediterráneo* (Ciudad Real, 2009), pp. 171–92.
Gelichi, S., 'La ceramica bizantina in Italia e la ceramica italiana nel Mediterraneo orientale tra XII e XIII secolo', in Gelichi, *La ceramica nel mondo bizantino* (Florence, 1993), pp. 9–46.
Gelichi, S. (ed.), *La ceramica nel mondo bizantino tra XI e XV secolo e i suoi rapporti con l'Italia* (Florence, 1993).
Gelichi, S., 'Ceramiche "tipo Santa Croce"', *AM*, 20 (1993), pp. 229–301.

Gelichi, S. (ed.), 'Comacchio e il suo territorio tra la tarda antichità e l'alto Medioevo', in F. Berti (et al.), *Genti nel Delta: da Spina a Comacchio* (Ferrara, 2007), pp. 365–683.

Gelichi, S., 'Nuove invetriate alto-medievali dalla laguna di Venezia e di Comacchio', in S. Lusuardi Siena et al. (eds.), *Archeologia classica e post-classica tra Italia e Mediterraneo* (Milan, 2016), pp. 297–317.

Gelichi, S., 'Islamic pottery in the neighbourhood of the Venetian lagoon', in T. Nowakiewicz et al. (eds.), *Animos labor nutrit* (Warsaw, 2018), pp. 115–28.

Gelichi, S., 'Jumping on the dunes: Venice and the myth of origin', in V. Ivanišević et al. (eds.), *Svet srednjovekovnich utvrdjenja, gradova i manastira* (Belgrade, 2021), pp. 35–43.

Gelichi, S. and G. Berti, 'La ceramica bizantina nelle architetture dell'Italia medievale', in Gelichi, *La ceramica nel mondo bizantino* (Florence, 1993), pp. 125–99.

Gelichi, S. and R. Hodges (eds.), *From one sea to another* (Turnhout, 2012).

Gelichi, S. and M. Milanese, '*Uchi maius*', in M. Khanoussi and A. Mastino (eds.), *Uchi Maius*, 1 (Sassari, 1997), pp. 49–94.

Gelichi, S. and F. Sbarra, 'La tavola di San Gerardo', *Rivista di archeologia*, 27 (2003), pp. 119–41.

Gelichi, S. et al., 'Importare, produrre, consumare nella laguna di Venezia dal IV al XII secolo', in S. Gelichi and C. Negrelli (eds.), *Adriatico altomedievale (VI–XI secolo)* (Venice, 2017), pp. 23–113.

Gelichi, S. et al. (eds.), *Nonantola 6* (Florence, 2018).

Gelichi, S. et al. (eds.), *Un emporio e la sua cattedrale* (Florence, 2021).

Gellner, E., *Muslim society* (Cambridge, 1981).

Georgacas, D. J., 'Greek terms for "flax", "linen", and their derivatives', *DOP*, 13 (1959), pp. 253–69.

Georgieva, S., 'Keramikata ot dvoretsa na Tsarevets', in *Tsarevgrad Tărnov*, 2 (Sofia, 1974), pp. 7–186.

Gerolymatou, M., 'L'aristocratie et le commerce (IXe–XIIe siècles)', *Byzantina symmeikta*, 15 (2002), pp. 77–89.

Gerolymatou, M., *Agores, emporioi kai emporio sto Byzantio (9os–12os ai.)* (Athens, 2008).

Gerousi, E., 'Rural Greece in the Byzantine period in the light of new archaeological evidence', in J. Albani and E. Chalkia (eds.), *Heaven and earth* (Athens, 2013), pp. 13–43.

Gerstel, S. E. J. et al., 'A late medieval settlement at Panakton', *Hesperia*, 72 (2003), pp. 147–234.

Getzov, N. et al., *Ḥorbat 'Uẓa*, 2 vols. (Jerusalem, 2009).

Ghazanfar, S. M. and A. A. Islahi, 'Economic thought of an Arab scholastic', *History of political economy*, 22 (1990), pp. 381–403.

Ghosh, S., 'Rural economies and transitions to capitalism', *Journal of agrarian change*, 16 (2016), pp. 255–90.

Giannitrapani, E. et al., 'Nuovi dati provenienti dalle indagini archeologiche presso la Rocca di Cerere a Enna', in Arcifa and Sgarlata, *From polis to madina* (Bari, 2020), pp. 173–92.

Giardina, C., 'Le "guariganga"', in Giardina, *Storia del diritto*, 1 (Palermo, 1963), pp. 135–85.

Gil, M., 'The Rādhānite merchants and the land of Rādhān', *JESHO*, 17 (1974), pp. 299–328.

Gil, M., 'Supplies of oil in medieval Egypt', *Journal of Near Eastern studies*, 34 (1975), pp. 63–73.

Gil, M., 'References to silk in Geniza documents of the eleventh century A.D.', *Journal of Near Eastern studies*, 61 (2002), pp. 31–8.

Gil, M., 'The Jewish merchants in the light of eleventh-century Geniza documents', *JESHO*, 46 (2003), pp. 273–319.

Gil, M., 'The flax trade in the Mediterranean in the eleventh century A.D. as seen in merchants' letters from the Cairo Geniza', *Journal of Near Eastern studies*, 63 (2004), pp. 81–96.

Gil, M., *Jews in Islamic countries in the Middle Ages* (Leiden, 2004).

Gilotte, S., *Aux marges d'al-Andalus* (Helsinki, 2010).
Gilotte, S. and Y. Cáceres Gutiérrez (eds.), *Al-Balât* (Cáceres, 2017).
Gilotte, S. et al., 'Un ajuar de época almorávide procedente de Albalat (Cáceres, Extremadura)', in M. J. Gonçalves and S. Gómez-Martínez (eds.), *Actas do X Congresso internacional, A cerâmica medieval no Mediterrâneo* (Silves, 2015), pp. 763–76.
Ginatempo, M. A., 'I prelievi non fondiari', in S. Carocci (ed.), *La signoria rurale nel XIV–XV secolo*, 4 (Florence, 2023).
Ginatempo, M. and L. Sandri, *L'Italia delle città* (Florence, 1990).
Giorgio, M., 'La maiolica arcaica e le invetriate depurate di Pisa', in G. Volpe and P. Favia (eds.), *V Congresso nazionale di archeologia medievale* (Florence, 2009), pp. 569–74.
Giorgio, M., 'Ceramica e società a Pisa nel medioevo', in F. Redi and A. Forgione (eds.), *VI Congresso nazionale di archeologia medievale* (Florence, 2012), pp. 590–4.
Giorgio, M., 'Circolazione e consumo di vasellame di importazione mediterranea a Pisa e nel contado nel Bassomedioevo (XI–XIV secolo)', in Giorgio (ed.), *Storie [di] ceramiche*, 3 (Florence, 2017), pp. 31–41.
Giorgio, M., 'Una rivoluzione tecnologica', in M. Baldassarri (ed.), *Pisa città della ceramica* (Pisa, 2018), pp. 103–13.
Gisbert Santonja, J. A., *Cerámica califal de Dénia* (Murcia, 2000).
Gisbert Santonja, J. A., 'La ciudad y la cocina' (2014), https://lamarinaplaza.com/2014/12/21/el-paraiso-culinario-de-daniya/.
Gisbert Santonja, J. A., 'Cerámicas del siglo XI, presentes en la Qalʿa de los Banū Ḥammād (Argelia) y procedentes del entorno de Cairuán, Sabra y Cartago (Túnez), en Denia y en al-Andalus. Grupos 1 y 2', in Sarr, *Ṭawā'if* (Granada, 2018), pp. 275–305.
Gisbert Santonja, J. A. et al., *La cerámica de Daniya-Dénia* (Valencia, 1992).
Glick, T. F., *From Muslim fortress to Christian castle* (Manchester, 1995).
Glick, T. F., *Islamic and Christian Spain in the early middle ages*, 2nd edn (Leiden, 2005).
Glidden, H. W. and D. Thompson, 'Ṭirāz fabrics in the Byzantine Collection, Dumbarton Oaks. Part one: Ṭirāz from Egypt', *Bulletin of the Asia Institute*, 2 (1988), pp. 119–39.
Gobbo, V., 'Treviso, ex Ospedale dei Battuti', *AM*, 40 (2013), p. 306.
Godelier, M., *Rationality and irrationality in economics* (London, 1972).
Goitein, S. D., 'The oldest documentary evidence for the title *alf laila wa-laila*', *Journal of the American oriental society*, 78 (1958), pp. 301–2.
Goitein, S. D., *A Mediterranean society* [cited as *MS*], 6 vols. (Berkeley, CA, 1967–93).
Goitein, S. D., 'Two Arabic textiles', *JESHO*, 19 (1976), pp. 221–4.
Goitein, S. D., 'A mansion in Fustat', in H. A. Miskimin et al. (eds.), *The medieval city* (New Haven, CT, 1977), pp. 163–78.
Golb, N. et al., 'Legal documents from the Cairo Genizah', *Jewish social studies*, 20 (1958), pp. 17–46.
Goldberg, J. L., 'On reading Goitein's *A Mediterranean Society*', *Mediterranean historical review*, 26 (2011), pp. 171–86.
Goldberg, J. L., 'Choosing and enforcing business relationships in the eleventh-century Mediterranean', *Past and present*, 216 (2012), pp. 3–40.
Goldberg, J. L., *Trade and institutions in the medieval Mediterranean* (Cambridge, 2012).
Goldberg, J. L., 'Mercantile letters', *Jewish history*, 32 (2019), pp. 397–410.
Goldberg, J. L., 'Writing history from the Geniza', *Jewish history*, 32 (2019), pp. 497–523.
Goldberg, J. L. and E. Krakowski (eds.), *Jewish history*, 32, 2–4 (2019).
Goldthwaite, R. A., *The economy of Renaissance Florence* (Baltimore, MD, 2009).
Golvin, L., *Le Magrib Central à l'époque des Zirides* (Paris, 1957).
Golvin, L., *Recherches archéologiques à la Qalʿa des Banû Hammâd* (Paris, 1965).

Golvin, L., 'Les céramiques émaillées de période hammâdide', in *La céramique médiévale en Méditerranée occidentale Xᵉ–XVᵉ siècles* (Paris, 1980), pp. 203–17.

Gómez Martínez, S., 'New perspectives in the study of al-Andalus ceramics, Mértola (Portugal) and the Mediterranean maritime routes in the Islamic period', *Al-Masāq*, 21 (2009), pp. 59–82.

Gómez Martínez, S., *Cerámica islámica de Mértola* (Mértola, 2014).

Gómez Martínez, S., 'La cultura material del Garb al-Andalus en el siglo XI', in Sarr, *Ṭawā'if* (Granada, 2018), pp. 141–76.

Gómez Martínez, S. and J. R. Santos, 'Évora y Mértola (Ptg)', in Y. Hazırlayan and F. Yenişehirlioğlu (eds.), *XIth congress AIECM3 on medieval and modern period Mediterranean ceramics proceedings* (Ankara, 2018), pp. 145–50.

Gómez Martínez, S. et al., 'A cidade e o seu território no Gharb al-Andalus através da cerâmica', in M. J. Gonçalves and S. Gómez-Martínez (eds.), *Actas do X Congresso internacional, A cerâmica medieval no Mediterrâneo* (Silves, 2015), pp. 19–50.

Gómez, S. et al., 'El verde y morado en el extremo occidental de al-Andalus (siglos X al XII)', in Y. Hazırlayan and F. Yenişehirlioğlu (eds.), *XIth congress AIECM3 on medieval and modern period Mediterranean ceramics proceedings* (Ankara, 2018), pp. 21–30.

Gonçalves, M. J., 'Objectos de troca no Mediterrâneo Antigo', *Arqueologia medieval*, 11 (2010), pp. 25–41.

Gonçalves, M. J., 'Evidências do comércio no Mediterrâneo antigo', in S. Gelichi (ed.), *Atti del IX Congresso internazionale sulla ceramica medievale nel Mediterraneo* (Florence, 2012), pp. 181–4.

González Gutiérrez, C. and Clapés Salmoral, R., 'La ciudad islámica', in M. Retuerce Velasco (ed.), *Actas VI Congreso de arqueología medieval (España–Portugal)* (Ciudad Real, 2021), pp. 71–6.

González Jiménez, M., 'Repartimientos andaluces del siglo XIII', in *De al-Andalus a la sociedad feudal* (Barcelona, 1990), pp. 95–117.

Goodson, C., *The Rome of Paschal I* (Cambridge, 2010).

Goodson, C., 'Topographies of power', in Anderson et al., *The Aghlabids* (Leiden, 2018), pp. 88–105.

Goodson, C., *Cultivating the city in early medieval Italy* (Cambridge, 2021).

Gordon, M. S., *Ahmad ibn Tulun* (London, 2021).

Gordon, M. S., 'Ibn Ṭūlūn's pacification campaign', in press.

Gosi, F., 'Le origini delle corporazioni tessili e l'espansione del commercio cremonese nel XIII secolo', *Bollettino storico cremonese*, 2 ser., 6 (1941), pp. 28–51.

Gragueb Chatti, S., 'L'apport d'Oudhna à la connaissance de la céramique islamique en Tunisie', in H. Ben Hassan and L. Maurin (eds.), *Oudhna (Uthina), colonie des véterans de la XIIIᵉ légion* (Brussels, 2004), pp. 245–58.

Gragueb Chatti, S., 'La céramique vert et brun à fond blanc de Raqqāda', in Cressier and Fentress, *La céramique maghrébine* (Rome, 2011), pp. 181–95.

Gragueb Chatti, S., 'La céramique islamique de la citadelle byzantine de Ksar Lemsa (Tunisie centrale)', *Africa*, 23 (2013), pp. 263–300.

Gragueb Chatti, S., 'Le vert et le brun de Sabra al-Mansūriyya', in N. Boukhchim et al., *Kairouan et sa région: Actes du 3ème colloque international du Département d'Archéologie* (Manouba, 2013), pp. 317–30.

Gragueb Chatti, S., 'La céramique aghlabide de Raqqada et les productions de l'Orient islamique', in Anderson et al., *The Aghlabids* (Leiden, 2018), pp. 341–61.

Gragueb Chatti, S., 'Note sur un matériel céramique rare en Ifrīqiya', *Arqueología y territorio medieval*, 27 (2020), pp. 79–92.

Gragueb Chatti, S. and C. Tréglia, 'Un ensemble de céramiques fatimides provenant d'un contexte clos découvert à Sabra al-Mansūriya (Kairouan, Tunisie)', in S. Gelichi (ed.), *Atti del IX Congresso internazionale sulla ceramica medievale nel Mediterraneo* (Florence, 2012), pp. 518–20.

Gragueb Chatti, S. et al., 'Jarres et amphores de Ṣabra al-Manṣūriya (Kairouan, Tunisie)', in Cressier and Fentress, *La céramique maghrébine* (Rome, 2011), pp. 197–220.

Gragueb Chatti, S. et al., 'Le mobilier céramique en Ifriqiya et Sicile de la fin du IXe jusqu'au XIe siècle', in M. R. Hamrouni and A. El Bahi (eds.), *Villes et archéologie urbaine au Maghreb et en Méditerranée* (Tunis, 2019), pp. 281–310.

Granara, W., *Narrating Muslim Sicily* (London, 2019).

Grañeda Miñón, P., 'La explotación andalusí de la plata en Córdoba', in Canto García and Cressier, *Minas y metalurgía* (Madrid, 2008), pp. 19–36.

Grassi, F., *La ceramica, l'alimentazione, l'artigianato e le vie di commercio tra VIII e XIV secolo*, BAR, I2125 (Oxford, 2010).

Grassi, F. (ed.), *L'insediamento medievale nelle Colline Metallifere (Toscana, Italia): il sito minerario di Rocchette Pannocchieschi dall'VIII al XIV secolo*, BAR, I2532 (Oxford, 2013).

Grassi, F. and J. A. Quirós Castillo (eds.), *Arqueometría de los materiales cerámicos de época medieval en España* (Bilbao, 2018).

Grassi, F. et al., 'La maiolica arcaica senese', in R. Fiorillo and P. Peduto (eds.), *III Congresso nazionale di archeologia medievale* (Florence, 2003), pp. 665–70.

Greci, R., *Corporazioni e mondo del lavoro nell'Italia padana medievale* (Bologna, 1988).

Greif, A., *Institutions and the path to the modern economy* (Cambridge, 2006).

Greif, A., 'The Maghribi traders: a reappraisal?', *Economic history review*, 65 (2012), pp. 445–69. [Also available, greatly expanded, at https://papers.ssrn.com/sol3/papers.cfm?abstract_id=2029327.]

Grillo, P., *Milano in età comunale (1183–1276)* (Spoleto, 2001).

Grillo, P., 'Vie di comunicazione, traffici e mercati nella politica intercittadina milanese fra XII e XIII secolo', *Archivio storico italiano*, 159 (2001), pp. 259–88.

Grillo, P., *Legnano 1176* (Rome and Bari, 2012).

Grillo, P., 'Le entrate signorili dei Mandelli a Maccagno', in Gamberini and Pagnoni, *La signoria rurale*, 1 (Milan and Turin, 2019), pp. 157–68.

Grillo, P. and F. Menant (eds.), *La congiuntura del primo Trecento in Lombardia (1290–1360)* (Rome, 2019).

Grob, E. M., *Documentary Arabic private and business letters on papyrus* (Berlin, 2010).

Grohmann, A., 'Contributions to the topography of al-Ushmûnain', *Bulletin de l'Institut d'Égypte*, 21 (1939), pp. 211–14.

Grossi Bianchi, L. and E. Poleggi, *Una città portuale del medioevo* (Genoa, 1980).

Grunwald, L., 'Die "Mayener Ware" zwischen Produktion, Handel und Distribution (4. bis 14. Jahrhundert)', in M. Schmauder and M. Roehmer (eds.), *Keramik als Handelsgut* (Bonn, 2019), pp. 37–47.

Grunwald, L., 'Pottery production for the European market—the Roman and early medieval potter's workshops of Mayen', in M. Herdick et al. (eds.), *Pre-modern industrial districts* (Heidelberg, 2020), pp. 27–37.

Gualazzini, U., *Inventario dell'Archivio storico camerale, con un saggio su la Mercadandia nella vita cremonese* (Milan, 1955).

Guarnieri, C. and M. Librenti, 'Ferrara, sequenza insediativa pluristratificata', 1–2, *AM*, 23 (1996), pp. 275–307, 24 (1997), pp. 183–206.

Guglielmetti, A. et al., 'Ceramica comune', in D. Caporusso (ed.), *Scavi MM3*, 3.1 (Milan, 1991), pp. 133–257.

Guglielmotti, P., 'Lopez, Roberto Sabatino', *Dizionario biografico degli Italiani* (2017), https://www.treccani.it/enciclopedia/roberto-sabatino-lopez_%28Dizionario-Biografico%29/.

Guglielmotti, P. (ed.), *Donne, famiglie e patrimoni a Genova e in Liguria nei secoli XII e XIII* (Genoa, 2020).

Guglielmotti, P., 'Women, families and wealth in twelfth- and thirteenth-century Liguria', in Mainoni and Barile, *Comparing two Italies* (Turnhout, 2020), pp. 167–87.

Guichard, P., *Structures sociales "orientales" et "occidentales" dans l'Espagne musulmane* (Paris, 1977).

Guichard, P., *Al-Andalus frente a la conquista cristiana* (Madrid, 2001).

Guichard, P., 'Sur quelques sites "castraux" du Haut Tell algéro-tunisien', in P. Sénac (ed.), *Histoire et archéologie de l'Occident musulman (VIIe–XVe siècle)* (Toulouse, 2012), pp. 141–55.

Guichard, P. and B. Soravia, *Les royaumes de taifas* (Paris, 2007).

Günsenin, N., *Les amphores byzantines (Xe–XIIIe siècles)*, thèse de doctorat, Université de Paris-I, 1990.

Günsenin, N., 'La typologie des amphores Günsenin', *Anatolia antiqua*, 26 (2018), pp. 89–124.

Gutiérrez, A. et al., 'The earliest Chinese ceramics in Europe?', *Antiquity*, 95 (2021), pp. 1213–30.

Gutiérrez, S., *La cora de Tudmīr de la antigüedad tardía al mundo islámico* (Madrid and Alicante, 1996).

Gutiérrez Lloret, S., 'La mirada del otro', in A. Molinari et al. (eds.), *L'archeologia della produzione a Roma (secoli V–XV)* (Rome, 2015), pp. 583–95.

Gutiérrez Lloret, S., 'The case of Tudmīr', *Early medieval Europe*, 27 (2019), pp. 394–415.

Gyllensvärd, B., 'Recent finds of Chinese ceramics at Fostat', 1–2, *Bulletin of the museum of Far Eastern antiquities*, 45 (1973), pp. 91–119, 47 (1975), pp. 93–117.

Hahn, M., 'The Berbati-Limnes project: the early Byzantine to modern periods', in B. Wells and C. Runnels (eds.), *The Berbati-Limnes archaeological survey 1988–90* (Stockholm, 1996), pp. 345–451.

Haldon, J. F., *The state and the tributary mode of production* (London, 1993).

Haldon, J. F., *Warfare, state and society in the Byzantine world, 550–1204* (London, 1999).

Haldon, J. F., 'Commerce and exchange in the seventh and eighth centuries', in Morrisson, *Trade and markets* (Washington, DC, 2012), pp. 99–124.

Haldon, J., 'Theories of practice', *Historical materialism*, 21 (2013), pp. 36–70.

Haldon, J. F., *The empire that would not die* (Cambridge, 2016).

Haldon, J. F. et al., 'Euchaïta', in Niewöhner, *The archaeology of Byzantine Anatolia* (Oxford, 2017), pp. 375–88.

Haldon, J. F. et al. (eds.), *Archaeology and urban settlement in late Roman and Byzantine Anatolia* (Cambridge, 2018).

Halm, H., *The empire of the Mahdi* (Leiden, 1996).

Hartmann, F., 'Heinrich V. im Diskurs Bologneser Gelehrter', in G. Lubich (ed.), *Heinrich V. in seiner Zeit* (Vienna, 2013), pp. 191–213.

Harvey, A., 'Economic expansion in central Greece in the eleventh century', *Byzantine and Modern Greek studies*, 8 (1982), pp. 21–8.

Harvey, A., *Economic expansion in the Byzantine Empire, 900–1200* (Cambridge, 1989).

Harvey, A., 'The middle Byzantine economy: growth or stagnation?', *Byzantine and Modern Greek studies*, 19 (1995), pp. 243–62

Harvey, A., 'Risk aversion in the eleventh-century peasant economy', in S. Lampakēs (ed.), *Ē Byzantinē Mikra Asia (6os–12os ai.)* (Athens, 1998), pp. 73–82.

Hayes, J. W., *Excavations at Saraçhane in Istanbul*, 2 (Princeton, NJ, 1992).

Heidenreich, A., *Islamische Importkeramik des hohen Mittelalters auf der Iberischen Halbinsel* (Mainz, 2007).

Heidenreich, A., 'La loza dorada temprana en el ámbito mediterráneo y la implementación de la nueva técnica en la Península Ibérica: una aproximación', in *I Congreso internacional Red europea de museos de arte islámico: actas* (Granada, 2012), pp. 271–97.

Hellenkemper, H. and F. Hild, *Lykien und Pamphylien* (Vienna, 2004).

Helmecke, G., 'Textiles with Arabic inscriptions', *Polish archaeology in the Mediterranean*, 16 (2004), pp. 195–202.

Henderson, J. and M. Mundell Mango, 'Glass at medieval Constantinople', in C. Mango and G. Dagron (eds.), *Constantinople and its hinterland* (Aldershot, 1995), pp. 333–56.

Hendy, M. F., 'Byzantium, 1081–1204', *Transactions of the Royal Historical Society*, 5 ser., 21 (1971), pp. 31–52.

Hendy, M. F., *Studies in the Byzantine monetary economy, c.300–1450* (Cambridge, 1985).

Hendy, M. F., 'Byzantium, 1081–1204: the economy revisited, twenty years on', in Hendy, *The economy, fiscal administration and coinage of Byzantium* (Aldershot, 1989), study III.

Herlihy, D., *Pisa in the early Renaissance* (New Haven, CT, 1958).

Herlihy, D., *Opera muliebria* (Philadelphia, PA, 1990).

Herlihy, D. and C. Klapisch-Zuber, *Tuscans and their families* (New Haven, CT, 1985).

Herrin, J., 'Realities of Byzantine provincial government', *DOP*, 29 (1975), pp. 253–84.

Heyd, W., *Histoire du commerce du Levant au Moyen-Âge* (Leipzig, 1936).

Heynen, R., *Zur Entstehung des Kapitalismus in Venedig* (Stuttgart, 1905).

Hilton, R. H., 'A comment', in *The transition from feudalism to capitalism* (London, 1978), pp. 109–17.

Hitchner, R. B., 'The Kasserine archaeological survey 1987', *Antiquités africaines*, 26 (1990), pp. 231–59.

Hitchner, R. B., 'The Kasserine archaeological survey 1982–1985', *Africa*, 11–12 (1992–3), pp. 158–98.

Hobson, M. S., *The North African boom* (Portsmouth, RI, 2015).

Hocquet, J.-C., *Le sel et la fortune de Venise* (Lille, 1978–9).

Hocquet, J.-C., 'Le saline', in Cracco Ruggini, *Storia di Venezia*, 1 (Rome, 1995), pp. 515–48.

Hodges, R., 'Excavating away the "poison"', in I. L. Hansen et al., *Butrint 4* (Oxford, 2013), pp. 1–21.

Hodges, R. et al., *Byzantine Butrint* (Oxford, 2004).

Hoffman, T., *Ashkelon 8* (University Park, PA, 2019).

Höfler, M., *Untersuchungen zur Tuch- und Stoffbenennung in der französischen Urkundensprache* (Tübingen, 1967).

Holmes, C., *Basil II and the governance of empire (976–1025)* (Oxford, 2005).

Holmes, C. and N. Standen (eds.), *The global middle ages*, Past and Present supplement, 13 (Oxford, 2018).

Holod, R. and E. Cirelli, 'Islamic pottery from Jerba (7th–10th century)', in Cressier and Fentress, *La céramique maghrébine* (Rome, 2011), pp. 159–79.

Holod, R. and T. Kahlaoui, 'Jerba of the ninth century', in Anderson et al., *The Aghlabids* (Leiden, 2018), pp. 451–69.

Hopley, R., 'Aspects of trade in the western Mediterranean during the eleventh and twelfth centuries', *Mediaevalia*, 32 (2011), pp. 5–42.

Horden, P. and N. Purcell, *The corrupting sea* (Oxford, 2000).

Hoshino, H., *L'arte della lana in Firenze nel basso Medioevo* (Florence, 1980).

Howard-Johnston, J., 'Le commerce à Byzance (VIIIe–XIIe s.)', *Journal des savants*, 2 (2018), pp. 289–355.

Huarte Cambra, R. and P. Lafuente Ibáñez, 'Los siglos X y XI en Isbilia', in *V Congreso de arqueología medieval española* (Valladolid, 2001), pp. 547–57.

Hubert, É., 'La construction de la ville', *Annales H. S. S.*, 59 (2004), pp. 109–39.

Hudson, P. J., 'La ceramica medievale', in G. Cavalieri Manasse (ed.), *L'area del Capitolium di Verona* (Verona, 2008), pp. 469–89.

Hughes, D. O, 'Urban growth and family structure in medieval Genoa', in *Past and present*, 66 (1975), pp. 3–28.

Humphreys, M. T. G., *Law, power, and imperial ideology in the Iconoclast era, c.680–850* (Oxford, 2015).

Hunt, E. S., *The medieval super-companies* (Cambridge, 1994).

Idris, H. R., *La Berbérie orientale sous les Zīrīdes* (Paris, 1959).

Idris, H. R., 'Commerce maritime et ḳirāḍ en Berbérie orientale: d'après un recueil inédit de fatwās médiévales', *JESHO*, 4 (1961), pp. 225–39.

Idris, H. R., 'De la réalité de la catastrophe hilâlienne', *Annales E. S. C.*, 23 (1968), pp. 390–6.

Inguscio, A., *Reassessing civil conflicts in Genoa, 1160–1220*, DPhil thesis, University of Oxford, 2012.

Íñiguez Sánchez, M. C., 'Arqueología de los Ḥammūdíes', in Sarr, *Ṭawā'if* (Granada, 2018), pp. 323–85.

Íñiguez Sánchez, M. C. and J. F. Mayorga Mayorga, 'Un alfar emiral en Málaga', in A. Malpica Cuello (ed.), *La cerámica altomedieval en el sur de al-Andalus* (Granada, 1993), pp. 119–38.

Innemée, K. C., 'The monastery of St. Macarius, survey and documentation work 2009–2012', in P. Buzi et al. (eds.), *Coptic society, literature and religion from Late Antiquity to modern times*, 2 (Leuven, 2016), pp. 1463–77.

Ioannidaki-Dostoglou, E., 'Les vases de l'épave de Pelagonissos', in V. Déroche and J.-M. Spieser (eds.), *Recherches sur la céramique byzantine* (Athens, 1989), pp. 157–91.

Irwin, R., *The Arabian nights: a companion* (London, 1994).

Irwin, R., 'Under western eyes', *Mamlūk studies review*, 4 (2000), pp. 27–51.

Isler, H. P., 'Monte Iato', in C. A. Di Stefano and A. Cadei (eds.), *Federico e la Sicilia* (Palermo, 1995), pp. 121–50.

Italiano, S., 'I reperti ceramici dai contesti medievali', in G. Tigano (ed.), *Mylai II* (Messina, 2009), pp. 151–6.

Izdebski, A. et al., 'Exploring Byzantine and Ottoman history with the use of palynological data', *Jahrbuch der österreichischen Byzantinistik*, 65 (2015), pp. 67–110.

Izquierdo Benito, R., *La ciudad hispanomusulmana de Vascos, Navalmoralejo (Toledo)* (Toledo, 2000).

Izquierdo Benito, R., 'Vascos', in Canto García and Cressier, *Minas y metalurgía* (Madrid, 2008), pp. 71–93.

Jacoby, D., 'La population de Constantinople à l'époque byzantine', *Byzantion*, 31 (1961), pp. 81–109.

Jacoby, D., 'Italian privileges and trade in Byzantium before the Fourth Crusade', *Anuario de estudios medievales*, 24 (1994), pp. 349–69.

Jacoby, D., 'Les Italiens en Égypte aux XIIe et XIIIe siècles', in M. Balard and A. Ducellier (eds.), *Coloniser au Moyen Âge* (Paris, 1995), pp. 76–89, 102–7.

Jacoby, D., 'Byzantine Crete in the navigation and trade networks of Venice and Genoa', in L. Balletto (ed.), *Oriente e Occidente tra medioevo ed età moderna*, 1 (Genoa, 1997), pp. 517–40.

Jacoby, D., 'Silk crosses the Mediterranean', in G. Airaldi (ed.), *Le vie del Mediterraneo* (Genoa, 1997), pp. 55–79.

Jacoby, D., 'Silk in western Byzantium before the Fourth Crusade', in Jacoby, *Trade, commodities and shipping* (Aldershot, 1997), study VII.

Jacoby, D., *Trade, commodities and shipping in the medieval Mediterranean* (Aldershot, 1997).

Jacoby, D., 'What do we learn about Byzantine Asia Minor from the documents of the Cairo Genizah?', in S. Lampakēs (ed.), *Ē Byzantinē Mikra Asia (6os–12os ai.)* (Athens, 1998), pp. 83–95.

Jacoby, D., 'Byzantine trade with Egypt from the mid-tenth century to the Fourth Crusade', *Thesaurismata*, 30 (2000), pp. 25–77.

Jacoby, D., 'Diplomacy, trade, shipping and espionage between Byzantium and Egypt in the twelfth century', in C. Scholz and G. Makris (eds.), *Polypleuros nous* (Munich, 2000), pp. 83–102.

Jacoby, D., 'Jews and the silk industry of Constantinople', in Jacoby, *Byzantium, Latin Romania and the Mediterranean* (Aldershot, 2001), study XI.

Jacoby, D., 'The supply of war materials to Egypt in the Crusader period', *Jerusalem studies in Arabic and Islam*, 25 (2001), pp. 102–32.

Jacoby, D., 'Seta e tessuti in seta nella Sicilia araba e normanna', in M. Andaloro (ed.), *Nobiles officinae*, 2 (Catania, 2006), pp. 133–43.

Jacoby, D., 'The Greeks of Constantinople under Latin rule 1204–1261', in T. F. Madden (ed.), *The Fourth Crusade* (Aldershot, 2008), pp. 53–73.

Jacoby, D., 'Venetian commercial expansion in the eastern Mediterranean, 8th–11th centuries', in Mundell Mango, *Byzantine trade* (Farnham, 2009), pp. 371–91.

Jacoby, D., 'Mediterranean food and wine for Constantinople', in E. Kislinger (ed.), *Handelsgüter und Verkehrswege* (Vienna, 2010), pp. 127–47.

Jacoby, D., 'Commercio e navigazione degli amalfitani nel Mediterraneo orientale', in B. Figliuolo and P. F. Simbula (eds.), *Interscambi socio-culturali ed economici fra le città marinare d'Italia e l'Occidente dagli osservatorî mediterranei* (Amalfi, 2014), pp. 89–128.

Jacoby, D., 'Byzantine maritime trade, 1025–1118', *Travaux et mémoires*, 21.2 (2017), pp. 627–48.

Jameson, M. H. et al., *A Greek countryside* (Stanford, CA, 1994).

Janssen, M. C. and M. D. Lauxtermann, 'Authorship revisited: language and metre in the *Ptochoprodromika*', in T. Shawcross and I. Toth (eds.), *Reading in the Byzantine Empire and beyond* (Cambridge, 2018), pp. 558–83.

Jarrett, J., 'Outgrowing the Dark Ages', *Agricultural history review*, 67 (2019), pp. 1–28.

Jefferson, R. W., 'The Cairo Genizah unearthed', in B. Outhwaite and S. Bhayro (eds.), *From a sacred source* (Leiden, 2010), pp. 171–99.

Jeffery, H., *The archaeology of Middle Byzantine Aphrodisias*, DPhil thesis, University of Oxford, 2019.

Jeffreys, M., 'Michael Psellos and the monastery', in M. Jeffreys and M. D. Lauxtermann (eds.), *The letters of Psellos* (Oxford, 2016), pp. 42–58.

Jehel, G., *Les Génois en Mediterranée occidentale (fin XIème—début XIVème siècle)* (Amiens, 1993).

Jenkins, M., 'Medieval Maghribi luster-painted pottery', in *La céramique médiévale en Méditerranée occidentale Xe–XVe siècles* (Paris, 1980), pp. 335–42.

Jiménez Castillo, P. and M. Pérez Asensio, 'Cerámicas emirales y califales de Murcia, calle Pascual (siglos IX–XI)', *ATM*, 25 (2018), pp. 67–106.

Jiménez Castillo, P. and J. L. Simón García, 'El poblamiento andalusí en las tierras de secano', *al-Qanṭara*, 38 (2017), pp. 215–59.

Jiménez Castillo, P. et al., 'El campesinado andalusí del secano manchego (s. XI)', *ATM*, 28 (2021), pp. 45–90.

Jiménez Puertas, M., *El poblamiento del territorio de Loja en la edad media* (Granada, 2002).
Joel, G., 'Céramique glaçurée d'époque islamique trouvées à Tōd', *AI*, 26 (1992), pp. 1–18.
Johns, J., 'I re normanni e i califfi fāṭimiti', in B. Scarcia Amoretti (ed.), *Del nuovo sulla Sicilia musulmana* (Rome, 1995), pp. 9–50.
Johns, J., *Arabic administration in Norman Sicily* (Cambridge, 2002).
Johns, J., 'Arabic sources for Sicily', *Proceedings of the British Academy*, 132 (2007), pp. 341–60.
Johns, J., 'Paper versus parchment' (2018), https://drive.google.com/file/d/12-sWbCXcfZsY6AP6WnbyVAYVKMFvhE80/view.
Jones, A. H. M., *The later Roman empire, 284–602* (Oxford, 1964).
Jones, P. J., 'An Italian estate, 900–1200', *Economic history review*, 2 ser., 7 (1954), pp. 18–32.
Jones, P. J., 'La storia economica', in *Storia d'Italia*, 2 (Turin, 1974), pp. 1469–810.
Jones, P. J., 'Economia e società nell'Italia medievale: la leggenda della borghesia', in *Storia d'Italia: Annali*, 1 (Turin, 1978), pp. 187–372.
Jones, P. J., *The Italian city-state* (Oxford, 1997).
Kaeuper, R. W., *Bankers to the Crown* (Princeton, NJ, 1973).
Kaldellis, A., *The argument of Psellos'* Chronographia (Leiden, 1999).
Kaldellis, A., *The Byzantine republic* (Cambridge, MA, 2015).
Kaldellis, A., *Streams of gold, rivers of blood* (New York, 2017).
Kaplan, M., *Les hommes et la terre à Byzance du VIe au XIe siècle* (Paris, 1992).
Kaplan, M., *Byzance: villes et campagnes* (Paris, 2006).
Kaplan, M., 'Les élites rurales byzantines', *MEFRM*, 124 (2012), pp. 299–312.
Kaplan, M., 'Monks and trade in Byzantium from the tenth to the twelfth centuries', in Magdalino and Necipoğlu, *Trade in Byzantium* (Istanbul, 2016), pp. 55–64.
Kaplony, A., 'Scribal traditions in documentary Arabic', *Jewish history*, 32 (2019), pp. 311–33.
Kaptijn, E. and M. Waelkens, 'Before and after the eleventh century AD in the territory of Sagalassos', in J. Howard-Johnston (ed.), *Social change in town and country in eleventh-century Byzantium* (Oxford, 2020), pp. 76–97.
Karlin-Hayter, P., 'Notes sur les archives de Patmos comme source pour la démographie et l'économie de l'île', *Byzantinische Forschungen*, 5 (1977), pp. 189–215.
Karpozelos, A., 'Realia in Byzantine epistolography X–XIIc', *Byzantinische Zeitschrift*, 77 (1984), pp. 20–37.
Katzara, E., 'Byzantine glazed pottery from Sparta (12th to 13th centuries A.D.)', in Y. Hazırlayan and F. Yenişehirlioğlu (eds.), *XIth congress AIECM3 on medieval and modern period Mediterranean ceramics proceedings* (Ankara, 2018), pp. 297–310.
Kawatoko, M., 'Multi-disciplinary approaches to the Islamic period in Egypt and the Red Sea Coast', *Antiquity*, 79 (2005), pp. 844–57.
Kazhdan, A. P., 'Some questions addressed to the scholars who believe in the authenticity of Kaminiates' "Capture of Thessalonica"', *Byzantinische Zeitschrift*, 71 (1978), pp. 301–14.
Kazhdan, A. P. and G. Constable, *People and power in Byzantium* (Washington, DC, 1982).
Kazhdan, A. P. and S. Ronchey, *L'aristocrazia bizantina* (Palermo, 1997).
Kazhdan, A. P. and A. Wharton Epstein, *Change in Byzantine culture in the eleventh and twelfth centuries* (Berkeley, CA, 1985).
Kedar, B., 'Mercanti genovesi in Alessandria d'Egitto negli anni sessanta del secolo XI', in *Miscellanea di studi storici*, 2 (Genoa, 1983), pp. 21–30.
Keller, H., *Signori e vassalli nell'Italia delle città (secoli IX–XII)* (Turin, 1995).
Kelley, A. C., *Commodity, commerce and economy*, PhD thesis, University of Birmingham, 2018.
Kelley, A. C., 'Searching for professional women in the mid to late Roman textile industry', *Past and present*, 258 (2023).

Kennedy, H., *Muslim Spain and Portugal* (London, 1996).
Kennedy, H., *The armies of the caliphs* (London, 2001).
Kennet, D. et al., 'Uno scavo urbano a Vico Infermiera, Marsala', *AM*, 16 (1989), pp. 613–36.
Khalilieh, H. S., *Admiralty and maritime laws in the Mediterranean Sea (ca. 800–1050)* (Leiden, 2006).
Khéchine, T. and S. Gragueb Chatti, 'Contribution à l'histoire de la ville de Kairouan au haut Moyen Âge', *Revue tunisienne d'archéologie*, 3 (2016), pp. 107–79.
King, M., 'The sword and the sun', *Al-Masāq*, 29 (2017), pp. 221–34.
King, M., 'Reframing the fall of the Zirid dynasty, 1112–35 CE,' *Mediterranean Studies*, 26 (2018): 1–25.
Kirchner, H., *Étude des céramiques islamiques de Shadhfīlah* (Lyon, 1990).
Kirchner, H. (ed.), *Por una arqueología agraria*, BAR, I2062 (Oxford, 2010).
Kislinger, E., 'Verkehrsrouten zur See im byzantinischen Raum', in Kislinger (ed.), *Handelsgüter und Verkehrswege* (Vienna, 2010), pp. 149–74.
Kiyohiko Sakurai and Kawatoko Mutsuo, *Ejiputo Isurāmu toshi aru Fusutāto iseki*, 2 vols. (Tokyo, 1992).
Klein, J., *The Mesta* (Cambridge, MA, 1920).
Koder, J., 'Fresh vegetables for the capital', in C. Mango and G. Dagron (eds.), *Constantinople and its hinterland* (Aldershot, 1995), pp. 49–56.
Koder, J., 'Regional networks in Asia Minor during the Middle Byzantine period (seventh–eleventh centuries)', in Morrisson, *Trade and markets* (Washington, DC, 2012), pp. 147–75.
Koder, J., 'Salt for Constantinople', in Magdalino and Necipoğlu, *Trade in Byzantium* (Istanbul, 2016), pp. 91–103.
Koilakou, Ch., 'Byzantine Thebes', in A. Drandaki et al. (eds.), *Heaven and earth* (Athens, 2013), pp. 181–91.
Koleva, R., 'Byzantine sgraffito pottery from northern Thrace', in P. Petridis et al. (eds.), *12th congress AIECM3 on medieval and modern period Mediterranean ceramics* (Athens, 2021), pp. 433–8.
Kondyli, F., *Rural communities in Late Byzantium* (Cambridge, 2021).
Kondyli, F., 'The view from Byzantine archaeology', in F. Kondyli and B. Anderson (eds.), *The Byzantine neighbourhood* (Abingdon, 2021), pp. 44–69.
Konstantinidou, K. P. and K. T. Raptis, 'Archaeological evidence of an eleventh-century kiln with rods in Thessaloniki', in M. J. Gonçalves and S. Gómez-Martínez (eds.), *Actas do X Congresso internacional, A cerâmica medieval no Mediterrâneo* (Silves, 2015), pp. 589–95.
Kontogiannis, N. D., 'A tale of two cities', in F. Kondyli and B. Anderson (eds.), *The Byzantine neighbourhood* (Abingdon, 2022), pp. 214–44.
Kostova, R., 'Polychrome ceramics in Preslav, 9th to 11th centuries', in Mundell Mango, *Byzantine trade* (Farnham, 2009), pp. 97–117.
Kotel'nikova, L. A., *Mondo contadino e città in Italia dall'XI al XIV secolo* (Bologna, 1975).
Koukoulis, T., 'Medieval Methana', in C. Mee and H. Forbes (eds.), *A rough and rocky place* (Liverpool, 1997), pp. 92–100.
Koutsouflakis, G., 'The transportation of amphorae tableware and foodstuffs in the Middle and Late Byzantine period', in S. Y. Waksman (ed.), *Multidisciplinary approaches to food and foodways in the medieval eastern Mediterranean* (Lyon, 2020), pp. 447–81.
Kraemer, J. L., 'Women speak for themselves' in S. C. and S. Reif (eds.), *The Cambridge Genizah collections* (Cambridge, 2002), 178–216.
Krahl, R. et al. (eds.), *Shipwrecked* (Washington, DC, 2011).
Krakowski, E., *Coming of age in medieval Egypt* (Princeton, NJ, 2017).

Krallis, D., *Michael Attaleiates and the politics of imperial decline in eleventh-century Byzantium* (Tempe, AZ, 2012).
Krallis, D., 'Popular political agency in Byzantium's villages and towns', *Byzantina symmeikta*, 28 (2016), pp. 11–48.
Kritzas, Ch., 'To byzantinon nauagion Pelagonnēsou-Alonnēsou', *Archaiologika analekta ex Athēnōn*, 4 (1971), pp. 176–82.
Krueger, H. C., 'Genoese trade with northwest Africa in the twelfth century', *Speculum*, 8 (1933), pp. 377–95.
Krueger, H. C., *Navi e proprietà navale a Genova* (Genoa, 1985).
Krueger, H. C., 'The Genoese exportation of northern cloths to Mediterranean ports, twelfth century', *Revue belge de philologie et d'histoire*, 65 (1987), pp. 722–50.
Kubiak, W., 'The burning of Miṣr al-Fusṭāṭ in 1168', *Africana bulletin*, 25 (1976), pp. 51–64.
Kubiak, W., 'Alexandria. Kom el-Dikka', *Polish archaeology in the Mediterranean*, 8 (1996), pp. 32–9.
Kubiak, W. and G. T. Scanlon, 'Fusṭāṭ expedition: preliminary report, 1971', 2, *Journal of the American research center in Egypt*, 17 (1980), pp. 77–96.
Kubiak, W. and G. T. Scanlon, *Fusṭāṭ expedition final report*, 2 vols. (Winona Lake, IN, 1986–9).
Kuchenbuch, L., *Marx, feudal* (Berlin, 2022)
Kuchenbuch, L. and B. Michael, 'Zur Struktur und Dynamik der "feudalen" Produktionsweise im vorindustriallen Europa', in L. Kuchenbuch and B. Michael (eds.), *Feudalismus—Materialen zur Theorie und Geschichte* (Frankfurt am Main, 1977), pp. 694–761. [Reprinted in Kuchenbuch, *Marx, feudal* (Berlin, 2022), pp. 206–51.]
Kühnel, E. and L. Bellinger, *Catalogue of dated tiraz fabrics* (Washington, DC, 1952).
La crescita economica dell'Occidente medievale (Pistoia, 2017).
La protomaiolica e la maiolica arcaica dalle origini al Trecento: Atti, XXIII Convegno internazionale della ceramica (Albisola, 1990).
La rinascita del mercato nel X secolo (Pistoia, 2012).
Labib, S. Y., *Handelsgeschichte Ägyptens im Spätmittelalter* (Wiesbaden, 1965).
Ladstätter, S. (ed.), *Die Türbe im Artemision* (Vienna, 2016).
Lafuente Ibáñez, P., 'La cerámica almohade en Sevilla', in Valor Piechotta, *El último siglo de la Sevilla islámica* (Seville, 1995), pp. 285–301.
Lagardère, V., *Campagnes et paysans d'Al-Andalus (VIIIe–XVe s.)* (Paris, 1993).
Lagardère, V., 'Structures étatiques et communautés rurales: les impositions légales et illégales en al-Andalus et au Maghreb', *Studia Islamica*, 80 (1994), pp. 57–95.
Laiou, A. E., 'The festival of "Agathe"', in N. A. Stratos (ed.) *Byzantium*, 1 (Athens, 1986), pp. 111–22.
Laiou, A. E., 'Byzantium and the commercial revolution', in G. Arnaldi and G. Cavallo (eds.), *Europa medievale e mondo bizantino* (Rome, 1997), pp. 239–53.
Laiou, A. E., 'Byzantine trade with Christians and Muslims and the Crusades', in A. E. Laiou and R. P. Mottahadeh (eds.), *The Crusades from the perspective of Byzantium and the Muslim world* (Washington, DC, 2001), pp. 157–96.
Laiou, A. E., 'The Byzantine economy: an overview', in Laiou, *The economic history of Byzantium* (Washington, DC, 2002), pp. 1145–64.
Laiou, A. E., 'Economic thought and ideology', in Laiou, *The economic history of Byzantium* (Washington, DC, 2002), pp. 1123–44.
Laiou, A. E., 'Exchange and trade, seventh–twelfth centuries', in Laiou, *The economic history of Byzantium* (Washington, DC, 2002), pp. 697–770.
Laiou, A. E. (ed.), *The economic history of Byzantium*, 3 vols. [cited as *EHB*] (Washington, DC, 2002).

Laiou, A. E., 'Regional networks in the Balkans in the Middle and Late Byzantine periods', in Morrisson, *Trade and markets* (Washington, DC, 2012), pp. 125–46.
Laiou, A. E., 'The Byzantine city: parasitic or productive?' in Laiou, *Economic thought and economic life in Byzantium*, ed. C. Morrisson and R. Dorin (Aldershot, 2013), study XII.
Laiou, A. E. and C. Morrisson, *The Byzantine economy* (Cambridge, 2007).
Laleman, M.-C., 'Ghent (East Flanders, Belgium) in the discussion about early towns and artisan production', *Medieval and modern matters*, 4 (2013), pp. 109–18.
Lambourn, E., *Abraham's luggage* (Cambridge, 2018).
Lambourn, E. and P. Ackerman-Lieberman, 'Chinese porcelain and the material taxonomies of medieval Rabbinic law', *The medieval globe*, 2.2 (2016), pp. 199–238.
Lapidus, I. M., *Muslim cities in the later Middle Ages* (Cambridge, MA, 1967).
Latham, D. J., 'Some observations on the bread trade in Muslim Malaga (ca. A.D. 1200)', *Journal of Semitic studies*, 29 (1984), pp. 111–22.
Lauranson-Rosaz, C., 'Le débat sur la mutation féodale', in P. Urbanczyk (ed.), *Europe around the year 1000* (Warsaw, 2001), pp. 11–40.
Lauwers, M. (ed.), *La dîme, l'église et la société féodale* (Turnhout, 2012).
Lavagna, R., 'Acqui terme', *AM*, 23 (1996), p. 549.
Lazzarini, L. and E. Canal, 'Ritrovamenti di ceramica graffita bizantina in laguna e la nascita del graffito veneziano', *Faenza*, 69 (1983), pp. 19–58.
Lazzarini, L. and E. Canal, 'Altra ceramica graffita bizantina dalla laguna veneta', in Gelichi, *La ceramica nel mondo bizantino* (Florence, 1993), pp. 79–92.
Le Goff, J., *Marchands et banquiers du Moyen Âge* (Paris, 1956).
Le marchand au Moyen Âge (Paris, 1988).
Lecuyot, G. and G. Pierrat, 'À propos des lieux de production de quelques céramiques trouvées à Tôd et dans la Vallée des Reines', *CCE*, 3 (1992), pp. 173–80.
Lefeuvre, P., *Notables et notabilité dans le contado florentin des XIIe–XIIIe siècles* (Rome, 2023).
Lefort, J., 'The rural economy, seventh–twelfth centuries', in Laiou, *The economic history of Byzantium* (Washington, DC, 2002), pp. 231–310.
Lefort, J., *Société rurale et histoire du paysage à Byzance* (Paris, 2006).
Lefort, J. et al. (eds.), *Les villages dans l'empire byzantin* (Paris, 2005).
Legendre, M., *La Moyenne-Égypte du VIIe au IXe siècle*, thèse de doctorat, Université de Paris-4, 2014.
Legendre, M., 'Perméabilité linguistique et anthroponymique entre copte et arabe', in A. Boud'hors et al. (eds.), *Coptica argentoratensia* (Paris, 2014), pp. 325–440.
Lemerle, P., *Cinq études sur le XIe siècle byzantin* (Paris, 1977).
Lemerle, P., *The agrarian history of Byzantium* (Galway, 1979).
Leo Imperiale, M., 'Anfore e reti commerciali nel Basso Adriatico tra VIII e XII secolo', *AM*, 45 (2018), pp. 45–64.
León Muñoz, A. and R. Blanco, 'La fitna y sus consecuencias', in D. Vaquerizo Gil and J. F. Murillo Redondo (eds.), *El anfiteatro romano de Córdoba y su entorno urbano*, 2 (Córdoba, 2010), pp. 699–726.
Lerma, J. V. (ed.), *La cerámica islámica en la ciudad de Valencia*, 2 (Valencia, 1990).
Lesnes, E. and J.-M. Poisson (eds.), *Calathamet* (Rome, 2013).
Lev, Y., *State and society in Fatimid Egypt* (Leiden, 1991).
Lev, Y., 'Tinnīs', in M. Barrucand (ed.), *L'Égypte fatimide* (Paris, 1999), pp. 83–96.
Lev, Y., 'Coptic rebellions and the Islamization of medieval Egypt 8th–10th century', *Jerusalem studies in Arabic and Islam*, 39 (2012), pp. 303–44.
Levine Melammed, R., 'He said, she said', *Association for Jewish studies review*, 22 (1997), pp. 19–35.
Lévi-Provençal, É., *Histoire de l'Espagne musulmane*, 3 vols., 2nd edn (Paris, 1950).

Lewicka, P. B., *Food and foodways of medieval Cairenes* (Leiden, 2011).

Li Bozhong, *Agricultural development in Jiangnan, 1620–1850* (Basingstoke, 1998).

Liard, F. and F. Kondyli, 'Pottery traditions "beyond" Byzantium', paper given at the International Medieval Congress, University of Leeds, July 2018.

Librenti, M. and C. Negrelli, 'Le indagini archeologiche 1990–1991 a Ferrara', in M. Valenti and R. Francovich (eds.), *IV Congresso nazionale di archeologia medievale* (Florence, 2006), pp. 111–13.

Lightfoot, C. S., 'Amorium', in Niewöhner, *The archaeology of Byzantine Anatolia* (Oxford, 2017), pp. 333–41.

Lilie, R.-J., *Handel und Politik zwischen dem byzantinischen Reich und den italienischen Kommunen Venedig, Pisa und Genua in der Epoche der Komnenen und der Angeloi (1081–1204)* (Amsterdam, 1984).

Little, L. K., *Religious poverty and the profit economy in medieval Europe* (London, 1978).

Livingston, D., 'Life in the Egyptian valley under Ikhshīdid and Fāṭimid rule', *JESHO*, 61 (2018), pp. 426–60.

Lloyd, T. H., *The English wool trade in the middle ages* (Cambridge, 1977).

Lo Cascio, E., 'Le procedure di *recensus* dalla tarda repubblica al tardo antico e il calcolo della popolazione di Roma', in *La Rome impériale* (Rome, 1997), pp. 3–76.

Lombard, M., *Espaces et réseaux du Haut Moyen Âge* (Paris, 1972).

Lombard, M., *Les textiles dans le monde musulman du VIIe au XIIe siècle* (Paris, 1978).

Lombard, M., *Les métaux dans l'Ancien Monde du Ve au XIe siècle* (Paris, 2001).

Lopez, R. S., *Genova marinara nel Duecento* (Milan, 1933).

Lopez, R. S., 'Le origini dell'arte della lana', in Lopez, *Studi sull'economia genovese*, pp. 65–204.

Lopez, R. S., *Studi sull'economia genovese nel medio evo* (Turin, 1936).

Lopez, R. S., 'Silk industry in the Byzantine empire', *Speculum*, 20 (1945), pp. 1–42.

Lopez, R. S., *The Commercial revolution of the middle ages, 950–1350* (Englewood Cliffs, NJ, 1971).

Lopez, R. S., *Su e giù per la storia di Genova* (Genoa, 1975).

Lopez, R. S., 'The trade of medieval Europe: the south', in M. M. Postan and E. Miller (eds.), *The Cambridge economic history of Europe*, 2, 2nd edn (Cambridge, 1987), pp. 306–401.

Lopez, R. S. and I. W. Raymond, *Medieval trade in the Mediterranean world* (New York, 1955).

López Chamizo, S. et al., 'La industria de la alfarería en Málaga', in *Atti, XLII Convegno internazionale della ceramica* (Savona, 2009), pp. 77–85.

López Elum, P., *La alquería islámica en Valencia* (Valencia, 1994).

López Martínez de Marigorta, E., 'Acuñaciones monetarias de al-Andalus en la primera mitad del siglo V/XI', *al-Qanṭara*, 36 (2015), pp. 69–106.

López Martínez de Marigorta, E., *Mercaderes, artesanos y ulemas* (Jaén, 2020).

Lorenzo Jiménez, J., *La dawla de los Banū Qasī* (Madrid, 2010).

Loud, G. A., *The Latin church in Norman Italy* (Cambridge, 2007).

Louhichi, A., 'La céramique fatimide et ziride de Mahdia d'après les fouilles de Qasr al-Qaïm', *Africa*, 15 (1997), pp. 123–38.

Louhichi, A., 'La céramique d'Ifriqiya du IXe au XIe siècle d'après une collection inédite de Sousse', *Africa*, 18 (2000), pp. 141–65.

Louhichi, A., 'La céramique islamique d'*Ammaedara*', in *Actes du 4ème colloque international sur l'histoire des steppes tunisiennes* (Tunis, 2006), pp. 211–25.

Louhichi, A., 'Un mode de cuisson de céramique du Bas Moyen Âge inédit en Ifriqiya', *Africa*, 21 (2007), pp. 167–78.

Louhichi, A., *Céramique islamique de Tunisie* (Tunis, 2010).
Louhichi, A. and M. Picon, 'Importation de matériel céramique ifriqiyen en Mauritanie', *Revue d'archéometrie*, 7 (1983), pp. 45–58.
Louhichi, A. and C. Touhiri, 'La céramique de Mahdiya du Xe au XIIe siècle', in Cressier and Fentress, *La céramique maghrébine* (Rome, 2011), pp. 233–49.
Louvi-Kizi, A., 'Thebes', in Laiou, *The economic history of Byzantium* (Washington, DC, 2002), pp. 631–8.
Loveluck, C., *Northwest Europe in the early Middle Ages, c.* AD *600–1150* (Cambridge, 2013).
Loveluck, C. and D. Tys, 'Coastal societies, exchange and identity along the Channel and southern North Sea shores of Europe, AD 600–1000', *Journal of maritime archaeology*, 1 (2006), pp. 140–69.
Lunardon, G., 'Protomaioliche savonesi', in C. Varaldo (ed.), *Archeologia urbana di Savona*, 2.2 (Savona, 2001), pp. 199–205.
Lusuardi Siena, S. and C. Giostra, 'Archeologia a San Benedetto Po', in *Matilde di Canossa* (Spoleto, 2016), pp. 645–63.
Luzzati, M., 'Contratti agrari e rapporti di produzione nelle campagne pisane dal XIII al XV secolo', in *Studi in memoria di Federigo Melis*, 1 (Naples, 1978), pp. 569–84.
Luzzatto, G., *Studi di storia economica veneziana* (Padua, 1954).
Luzzatto, G., 'Capitale e lavoro nel commercio veneziano dei sec. XI e XII', in Luzzatto, *Studi sull'economia veneziana* (Padua, 1955), pp. 89–116.
Łyżwa, A., 'Naqlun 2001: glazed pottery', *Polish archaeology in the Mediterranean*, 13 (2001), pp. 185–9.
Maccadanza, E., *La diffusione della pietra ollare nel nord Italia*, tesi di laurea, Università Cattolica del Sacro Cuore, relatore F. Saggioro, a.a. 2019–2020.
Maccadanza, E. and N. Mancassola, 'La ceramica di cucina', in F. Saggioro et al. (eds.), *Il monastero di S. Benedetto di Leno* (Florence, 2019), pp. 311–51.
Maccari Poisson, B., 'La céramique médiévale', in Pesez, *Brucato* (Rome, 1984), pp. 247–450.
Macías, S., *Mértola islâmica* (Mértola, 1996).
Mackie, L. W., 'Textiles', in Kubiak and Scanlon, *Fusṭāṭ expedition final report*, 2, pp. 81–97.
MacLean, S., 'Apocalypse and revolution: Europe around the year 1000', *Early medieval Europe*, 15 (2007), pp. 86–106.
Macrides, R. J., 'Justice under Manuel I Komnenos', in D. Simon (ed.), *Fontes minores*, 6 (Frankfurt am Main, 1984), pp. 99–204.
Magdalino, P., *The empire of Manuel I Komnenos 1143–1180* (Cambridge, 1993).
Magdalino, P., 'The grain supply of Constantinople, ninth–twelfth centuries', in C. Mango and G. Dagron (eds.), *Constantinople and its hinterland* (Aldershot, 1995), pp. 35–47.
Magdalino, P., *Constantinople médiévale* (Paris, 1996).
Magdalino, P. and N. Necipoğlu (eds.), *Trade in Byzantium* (Istanbul, 2016).
Maggi Bei, M. T., 'Sulla produzione del sale nell'alto medio evo in zona romana', *Archivio della società romana di storia patria*, 101 (1978), pp. 354–66.
Mahfoudh, F., *Architecture et urbanisme en Ifriqiya médiévale* (Tunis, 2003).
Mahfoudh, F., 'La Grande Mosquée de Kairouan', in Anderson et al., *The Aghlabids* (Leiden, 2018), pp. 163–89.
Mahjoubi, A., *Recherches d'histoire et d'archéologie à Henchir el-Faouar (Tunisie)* (Tunis, 1978).
Maíllo Salgado, F., 'Fuentes árabes escritas para historiar los reinos de taifas', in Sarr, *Ṭawā'if* (Granada, 2018), pp. 25–67.
Mainoni, P., *Economia e politica nella Lombardia medievale* (Cavallermaggiore, 1994).

Mainoni, P., 'L'economia di Bergamo tra XIII e XV secolo', in G. Chittolini (ed.), *Storia economica e sociale di Bergamo*, 2 (Bergamo, 1999), pp. 257–338.

Mainoni, P., 'La seta in Italia fra XII e XIII secolo', in L. Molà (ed.), *La seta in Italia* (Venice, 2000), pp. 365–400.

Mainoni, P., 'A proposito della "rivoluzione fiscale" nell'Italia settentrionale del XII secolo', *Studi storici*, 44 (2003), pp. 5–42.

Mainoni, P., 'Un'economia cittadina nel XII secolo: Vercelli', in *Vercelli nel secolo XII* (Vercelli, 2005), pp. 310–52.

Mainoni, P., 'Sperimentazioni fiscali e amministrative nell'Italia settentrionale', in G. C. Andenna (ed.), *Pensiero e sperimentazioni istituzionali nella 'Societas Christiana' (1046–1250)*, (Milan, 2007), pp. 705–59.

Mainoni, P., 'Le produzioni non agricole', in *La crescita economica* (Pistoia, 2017), pp. 221–54.

Mainoni, P. and N. L. Barile (eds.), *Comparing two Italies* (Turnhout, 2020).

Maire Vigueur, J.-C., 'Les "casali" des églises romaines à la fin du Moyen Âge (1348–1428)', *MEFRM*, 86 (1974), pp. 63–136.

Maire Vigueur, J.-C., *Cavaliers et citoyens* (Paris, 2003).

Majcherek, G., 'Alexandria: Excavations and preservation work, preliminary report 2006/2007', *Polish archaeology in the Mediterranean*, 19 (2007), pp. 31–48.

Malaguti, C. and A. Zane, 'La pietra ollare nell'Italia nord-orientale', *AM*, 26 (1999), pp. 463–79.

Malamut, É., *Les îles de l'Empire byzantin* (Paris, 1988).

Malanima, P., 'La formazione di una regione economica', *Società e storia*, 6 (1983), pp. 229–69.

Malanima, P., *I piedi di legno* (Milan, 1988).

Malanima, P., *La fine del primato* (Milan, 1998).

Malczycki, M., 'The papyrus industry in the early Islamic era', *JESHO*, 54 (2011), pp. 185–202.

Malfitana, D. and M. Bonifay, *La ceramica africana nella Sicilia romana*, 2 vols. (Catania, 2016).

Malfitana, D. and G. Cacciaguerra (eds.), *Priolo romana, tardo romana e medievale*, 1 (Catania, 2011).

Malpica Cuello, A., *Granada, ciudad islámica* (Granada, 2000).

Malpica Cuello, A. and A. Gómez Becerra, *Una cala que llaman La Rijana* (Granada, 1991).

Mancassola, N., 'Le ceramiche grezze di Piadena', in S. Gelichi (ed.), *Campagne medievali* (Mantua, 2005), pp. 143–69.

Mancassola, N., *L'azienda curtense tra Langobardia e Romania* (Bologna, 2008).

Mancassola, N., *Uomini senza storia* (Spoleto, 2013).

Mancassola, N., 'Le ceramiche da cucina dal castello di Terrossa', in F. Saggioro (ed.), *Il castello di Terrossa* (Florence, 2021), pp. 139–46.

Mangiaracina, C. F., 'La ceramica invetriata nella Sicilia islamica e normanna (X–XII secolo)', in F. Berti and M. Caroscio (eds.), *La luce del mondo* (Florence, 2013), pp. 89–105.

Mangiaracina, C. F., 'La Sicilia islamica', in M. J. Gonçalves and S. Gómez-Martínez (eds.), *Actas do X Congresso internacional, A cerâmica medieval no Mediterrâneo* (Silves, 2015), pp. 667–80.

Mango, C. A., *Byzantium: the empire of the new Rome* (London, 1988).

Maniatis, G. C., 'The domain of private guilds in the Byzantine economy, tenth to fifteenth centuries', *DOP*, 55 (2001), pp. 339–69.

Mannoni, T., *La ceramica medievale a Genova e nella Liguria* (Genoa, 1975).

Manolova, M., 'Medieval ceramics with a micaceous coating from Plovdiv (11th–12th century)', *Archaeologia bulgarica*, 3.2 (1999), pp. 77–82.
Manolova-Voykova, M., 'Import of Middle Byzantine pottery to the Western Black Sea coast', in Y. Hazırlayan and F. Yenişehirlioğlu (eds.), *XIth congress AIECM3 on medieval and modern period Mediterranean ceramics proceedings* (Ankara, 2018), pp. 93–105.
Mansouri, T., 'Produits agricoles et commerce maritime en Ifrīqiya aux XIIe–XVe siècles', *Médiévales*, 33 (1997), pp. 125–39.
Manzano Martínez, J., 'Aproximación a la estructura de la propiedad musulmana de la tierra en la huerta de Murcia (siglo XIII)', in A. Bazzana (ed.), *Castrum 5* (Madrid, 1999), pp. 61–75.
Manzano Moreno, E., *La frontera de al-Andalus en época de los Omeyas* (Madrid, 1991).
Manzano Moreno, E., 'El asentamiento y la organización de los *ŷund*-s sirios en al-Andalus', *al-Qanṭara*, 14 (1993), pp. 327–59.
Manzano Moreno, E., 'Relaciones sociales en sociedades precapitalistas', *Hispania*, 200 (1998), pp. 881–913.
Manzano Moreno, E., *Conquistadores, emires y califas* (Barcelona, 2006).
Manzano, E., 'Circulation des biens et richesses entre al-Andalus et l'Occident européen aux VIIIe–Xe siècles', in L. Feller and A. Rodríguez (eds.), *Objets sous contrainte* (Paris, 2013), pp. 147–80.
Manzano Moreno, E., '"Desde el Sinaí de su arábiga erudición"', in M. Marín (ed.), *al-Andalus/España: historiografías en contraste* (Madrid, 2017), pp. 213–30.
Manzano Moreno, E., *La corte del califa* (Barcelona, 2019).
Manzano Moreno, E., '¿Existieron comunidades rurales autosuficientes en al-Andalus?', in A. García Porras and A. Fábregas García (eds.), *Poder y comunidades campesinas en el Islam occidental (siglos XII–XV)* (Granada, 2020), pp. 53–74.
Marano, Y., *Le fortune di un patriarca* (Rome, 2022).
Marasco, L. and A. Briano, 'The stratigraphic sequence at the site of Vetricella (Scarlino, Grosseto)', in Bianchi and Hodges, *The nEU-Med project* (Florence, 2020), pp. 9–20.
Marchand, S. and D. Laisney, 'Le survey de Dendara (1996–1997)', *CCE*, 6 (2000), pp. 261–97.
Marchandin, P., *Moulins et energie à Paris du XIIIe au XVIe siècle*, thèse de doctorat, PSL Université Paris/École des chartes, 2021.
Margariti, R. E., *Aden and the Indian Ocean trade* (Chapel Hill, NC, 2003).
Margariti, R. E., '*Aṣḥābunā l-tujjār*: our associates, the merchants', in A. E. Franklin et al. (eds.), *Jews, Christians, and Muslims in medieval and early modern times* (Leiden, 2014), pp. 40–58.
Margariti, R. E., 'Mercantile networks, port cities, and "pirate" states', *JESHO*, 51 (2008), pp. 543–77.
Marín, M., *Mujeres en al-Ándalus* (Madrid, 2000).
Marques, J. A. et al., *Povoamento rural no troço médio do Guadiana entre o Rio Degebe e a Ribeira do Álamo (Idade do Ferro e períodos medieval e moderno)* (Évora, 2013).
Martí, J. and J. Pascual, 'El desarrollo urbano de Madīna Balansiya hasta el final del califato', in Cara Barrionuevo, *Ciudad y territorio* (Granada, 2000), pp. 500–36.
Martin, J.-M., *La Pouille du VIe au XIIe siècle* (Rome, 1993).
Martín Civantos, J. M., 'Working in landscape archaeology', *Early medieval Europe*, 19 (2011), pp. 385–410.
Martínez-Gros, G., *L'idéologie omeyyade* (Madrid, 1992).
Martínez Salvador, C. and J. Bellón Aguilera, 'Consideraciones sobre la simbologia, tradición y materialidad del vino en al-Andalus', *Revista murciana de antropología*, 12 (2005), pp. 159–73.

Marx, K., *Pre-capitalist economic formations*, ed. E. J. Hobsbawm, trans. J. Cohen (London, 1964).

Marx, K., *Grundrisse*, trans. M. Nicolaus (Harmondsworth, 1973).

Marx, K., *Das Kapital*, 3, ed. G. Hubmann et al. (Berlin, 2017).

Mason, R. B., 'Medieval Egyptian lustre-painted and associated wares', *Journal of the American research center in Egypt*, 34 (1997), pp. 201–42.

Mason, R. B., *Shine like the sun* (Costa Mesa, CA, 2004).

Mason, R. B. and M. S. Tite, 'The beginnings of Islamic stonepaste technology', *Archaeometry*, 36 (1994), pp. 77–91.

Mason R. B. and M. S. Tite, 'The beginnings of tin-opacification of pottery glazes', *Archaeometry*, 39 (1997), pp. 41–58.

Masschaele, J., *Peasants, merchants, and markets* (New York, 1997).

Masschaele, J., 'Economic take-off and the rise of markets', in C. Lansing and E. D. English (eds.), *A companion to the medieval world* (Oxford, 2009), 89–110.

Masson, A. et al., 'Overview of the ceramic productions from the Luxor town mound', *Bulletin de liaison de la céramique égyptienne*, 23 (2012), pp. 125–45.

Matilde di Canossa e il suo tempo (Spoleto, 2016).

Maurici, F., *Castelli medievali in Sicilia* (Palermo, 1992).

Maurici, F. et al., 'Il "Castellazzo" di Monte Iato in Sicilia occidentale (PA)' (2016), https://www.fastionline.org/docs/FOLDER-it-2016-360.pdf.

Mayerson, P., 'The role of flax in Roman and Fatimid Egypt', *Journal of Near Eastern studies*, 56 (1997), pp. 201–7.

Mazza, R., *L'archivio degli Apioni* (Bari, 2001).

Mazzoli-Guintard, C., *Villes d'al-Andalus* (Rennes, 1996).

Mazzoli-Guintard, C., 'Quand, dans le premier tiers du XI siècle, le peuple cordouan s'emparait de la rue…', *al-Qanṭara*, 20 (1999), pp. 119–35.

Mazzoli-Guintard, C., *Vivre à Cordoue au Moyen Âge* (Rennes, 2003).

Mazzoli-Guintard, C., 'Almería, ¿ciudad-mundo en los siglos XI y XII?', in J. R. Molina et al. (eds.), *Carolus* (Alcalá la Real, 2016), pp. 241–9.

McCartney, E., 'The use of metaphor in Michael Psellos' *Chronographia*', in J. Burke et al. (eds.), *Byzantine narrative* (Melbourne, 2006), pp. 84–91.

McCormick, M., 'Bateaux de vie, bateaux de mort', *Settimane di studio del Centro italiano di studi sull'alto medioevo*, 45 (1998), pp. 35–122.

McCormick, M., *Origins of the European economy* (Cambridge, 2001).

McCormick, M., 'Movements and markets in the first millennium', in Morrisson, *Trade and markets* (Washington, DC, 2012), pp. 51–98.

McDermott, J. P. and Shiba Yoshinobu, 'Economic change in China, 960–1279', in J. W. Chaffee and D. Twitchett (eds.), *Cambridge history of China*, 5.2 (Cambridge, 2015), pp. 321–436.

McDonald, W. A. et al., *Excavations at Nichoria in southwest Greece*, 3 (Minneapolis, MI, 1983).

McNally, S. and I. D. Schrunk, *Excavations in Akhmīm, Egypt*, BAR, I590 (Oxford, 1993).

Meiksins Wood, E., *The origin of capitalism* (London, 2002).

Mélanges de l'École française de Rome: Moyen-Âge, 116.1 (2004).

Melero Serrano, M. et al., 'La ceramica del siglo XIII en Calatrava la Vieja (Ciudad Real)', in J. Zozaya et al. (eds.), *Actas del VIII Congreso internacional de cerámica medieval en el Mediterráneo* (Ciudad Real, 2009), pp. 759–72.

Menant, F., 'Pour une histoire médiévale de l'entreprise minière en Lombardie', *Annales E. S. C.*, 42 (1987), pp. 779–96.

Menant, F., 'La métallurgie lombarde au Moyen Âge', in P. Benoit, D. Cailleaux (eds.), *Hommes et travail du métal dans les villes médiévales* (Paris, 1988), pp. 127–61.
Menant, F., *Campagnes lombardes du Moyen Âge* (Rome, 1993).
Menant, F., 'Bergamo comunale', in G. Chittolini (ed.), *Storia economica e sociale di Bergamo*, 2 (Bergamo, 1999), pp. 15–182.
Menant, F., 'La prima età comunale (1097–1183)', in G. C. Andenna (ed.), *Storia di Cremona: dall'alto medioevo all'età comunale* (Cremona, 2004), pp. 198–281.
Menant, F., 'Un lungo Duecento', in G. C. Andenna (ed.), *Storia di Cremona: dall'alto medioevo all'età comunale* (Cremona, 2004), pp. 282–363.
Menant, F., 'Les chartes de franchise de l'Italie communale', in Bourin and Martínez Sopena, *Pour une anthropologie du prélèvement*, 1 (Paris, 2004), pp. 239–67.
Menant, F., *L'Italie des communes (1100–1350)* (Paris, 2005).
Meneghini, R. and R. Santangeli Valenzani, *Roma nell'altomedioevo* (Rome, 2004).
Menéndez Fueyo, J. L., 'La cerámica de la rábita califal', in R. Azuar Ruiz (ed.), *El ribāṭ califal* (Madrid, 2004), pp. 89–130.
Meo, A., 'Anfore, uomini e reti di scambio sul "mare pisano" (VIII–XII secolo)', *AM*, 45 (2018), pp. 219–38.
Meo, A., 'Archeologia della produzione *prope ecclesia Sancte Frasse*', in Cantini and Rizzitelli, *Una città operosa* (Florence, 2018), pp. 37–46.
Meo, A., 'L'ordinario e l'eccezione', in Y. Hazırlayan and F. Yenişehirlioğlu (eds.), *XIth congress AIECM3 on medieval and modern period Mediterranean ceramics proceedings* (Ankara, 2018), pp. 59–73.
Meouak, M., *Ṣaqāliba, eunuques et esclaves à la conquête du pouvoir* (Helsinki, 2004).
Merores, M., 'Die venezianischen Salinen der älteren Zeit in ihrer wirtschaftlichen und sozialen Bedeutung', *Vierteljahrschrift für Sozial- und Wirtschaftsgeschichte*, 13 (1916), pp. 71–107.
Mesqui, J. and J. Martineau, *Césarée Maritime* (Paris, 2014).
Messina, A., 'Uomini e mestieri della Sicilia normanna', *Quellen und Forschungen aus italienischen Bibliotheken und Archiven*, 73 (1993), pp. 19–51.
Messina, A. et al., 'Islamic pottery production in eastern Sicily (10th–11th centuries)', *Mediterranean archaeology and archaeometry*, 18 (2018), pp. 207–23.
Metalla, E., 'Les données céramiques sur le commerce dans la ville de Durrës pendant IXe–XVe s.', *Proceedings of the international congress of Albanian archaeological studies* (Tirana, 2014), pp. 599–612.
Metalla, E., 'La céramique médiévale en Albanie', in M. J. Gonçalves and S. Gómez Martínez, *Actas do X Congresso internacional, A cerâmica medieval no Mediterrâneo* (Silves, 2015), pp. 807–18.
Metcalfe, A., *Muslims and Christians in Norman Sicily* (London, 2003).
Metcalfe, A., *The Muslims of medieval Italy* (Edinburgh, 2009).
Metcalfe, A., 'Historiography in the making', in J. H. Drell and P. Oldfield (eds.), *Rethinking Norman Italy* (Manchester, 2021), pp. 46–92.
Meyer, A. *Felix et inclitus notarius* (Tübingen, 2000).
Michel, N., 'Devoirs fiscaux et droits fonciers', *JESHO*, 43 (2000), pp. 521–78.
Michel, N., *L'Égypte des villages autour du seizième siècle* (Paris, 2018).
Miholjek, I. et al., 'The Byzantine shipwreck of Cape Stoba (Mljet, Croatia)', in S. Gelichi and C. Negrelli (eds.), *Adriatico altomedievale (VI–XI secolo)* (Venice, 2017), pp. 229–46.
Mikami, T., 'Chinese ceramics from medieval sites in Egypt', in Mikasa no Miya Takahito (ed.), *Cultural and economic relations between East and West* (Wiesbaden, 1988), pp. 8–44.

Mikhail, M. S. A., *From Byzantine to Islamic Egypt* (London, 2014).

Milani, G., 'Contro il comune dei *milites*', in M. T. Caciorgna et al. (eds.), *I comuni di Jean-Claude Maire Vigueur* (Rome, 2014), pp. 235–58.

Milliot, L., *L'association agricole chez les musulmans du Maghreb (Maroc, Algérie, Tunisie)*, (Paris, 1911).

Milwright, M., 'Pottery in the written sources of the Ayyubid-Mamluk period (*c*.567–923/1171–1517)', *Bulletin of the School of Oriental and African Studies*, 62 (1999), pp. 504–18.

Mineo, I., *Nobiltà di stato* (Rome, 2001).

Mitchell, P., *The donkey in human history* (Oxford, 2018).

Mitchell, S., 'Aşvan Kale', *Anatolian studies*, 23 (1973), pp. 121–51.

Modéran, Y., *Les Maures et l'Afrique romaine (IVe–VIIe siècle)* (Rome, 2003).

Mohamedi, A., E. Fentress et al., *Fouilles de Sétif 1977–1984* (Algiers, 1991).

Moine, C. et al., *Paesaggi artificiali a Venezia* (Florence, 2017).

Molera, J. et al., 'Lead frits in Islamic and Hispano-Moresque glazed productions', in A. J. Shortland et al. (eds.), *From Mine to Microscope: Advances in the study of ancient technology* (Oxford, 2009), pp. 11–22.

Molera, J. et al., 'Vidriados, colorantes y decoraciones en cerámicas vidriadas de época islámica de la Vega de Granada (siglos IX–XII d.C.)', in Grassi and Quirós Castillo, *Arqueometría de los materiales cerámicos de época medieval en España* (Bilbao, 2018), pp. 223–40.

Molina López, E., 'Noticias geográficas y biográficas sobre Tudmīr en el "Iqtibās al-anwār" de al-Rušāṭī', in *Homenaje al profesor Juan Torres Fontes*, 2 (Murcia, 1987), pp. 1085–98.

Molina López, E., 'Economía, propiedad, impuestos y sectores productivos', in Viguera Molins, *Historia de España*, 8.2 (Madrid, 1997), pp. 213–300.

Molinari, A., 'La produzione e la circolazione delle ceramiche siciliane nei secoli X–XIII', in R. El Hraîki and E. Erbati (eds.), *Actes du Vè colloque international: la céramique médiévale en Méditerranée occidentale* (Rabat, 1995), pp. 191–204.

Molinari, A., *Segesta II* (Palermo, 1997).

Molinari, A., 'La ceramica siciliana del X e XI secolo tra circolazione interregionale e mercato interno', in S. Gelichi and M. Baldassarri (eds.), *Pensare/classificare* (Florence, 2010), pp. 159–70.

Molinari, A., 'La ceramica siciliana di età islamica tra interpretazione etnica e socio-economica', in Pensabene, *Piazza Armerina* (Rome, 2010), pp. 197–228.

Molinari, A. (ed.), 'Mondi rurali d'Italia', *AM*, 37 (2010), pp. 9–281.

Molinari, A., 'Paesaggi rurali e formazioni sociali nella Sicilia islamica, normanna e sveva (secoli X–XIII)', *AM*, 37 (2010), pp. 229–45.

Molinari, A., 'La ceramica altomedievale nel Mediterraneo occidentale islamico', in Cressier and Fentress, *La céramique maghrébine* (Rome, 2011), pp. 267–91.

Molinari, A., 'La Sicilia tra XII e XIII secolo', in G. Vannini and M. Nucciotti (eds.), *La Transgiordania nei secoli XII e XIII e le 'frontiere' del Mediterraneo medievale*, BAR, I2386 (Oxford, 2012), pp. 345–60.

Molinari, A., '"Islamisation" and the rural world', in S. Gelichi and R. Hodges (eds.), *New directions in early medieval European archaeology: Spain and Italy compared* (Turnhout, 2015), pp. 187–221.

Molinari, A., 'La Sicilia e le trasformazioni delle reti di scambio mediterranee', in S. Gasparri and S. Gelichi (eds.), *I tempi del consolidamento* (Turnhout, 2017), pp. 349–68.

Molinari, A., 'Riflessioni sulle economie dei secoli X e XI', in R. Balzaretti et al. (eds.), *Italy and medieval Europe* (Oxford, 2018), pp. 155–70.

Molinari, A., 'Sicily from Late Antiquity to the early middle ages', in M. Á. Cau Ontiveros and C. Mas Florit (eds.), *Change and resilience* (Oxford, 2019), pp. 87–110.

Molinari, A. and D. Cassai, 'La Sicilia e il Mediterraneo nel XIII secolo', *Atti, XXXVII e XXXVIII Convegno internazionale della ceramica* (Albisola, 2006), pp. 89–112.
Molinari, A. and A. Meo (eds.), *Mazara/Māzar* (Florence, 2022).
Molinari, A. and I. Neri, 'Dall'età tardoimperiale al XIII secolo', *MEFRM*, 116.1 (2004), pp. 109–27.
Mölk, N., *Giato/Jāṭū*, Dissertation, Universität Innsbruck, 2019.
Monchamp, J., 'Céramiques fatimides de Bāb al-Naṣr, murailles du Caire', *Bulletin de liaison de la céramique égyptienne*, 26 (2016), pp. 143–65.
Montanari, M., *L'alimentazione contadina nell'alto medioevo* (Naples, 1979).
Montanari, M., 'Rese cerealicole e rapporti di produzione', *Quaderni medievali*, 12 (1981), pp. 32–60.
Morena Narganes, J. M., 'Tejiendo en casa', in M. Retuerce Velasco (ed.), *Actas VI Congreso de arqueología medieval (España–Portugal)* (Ciudad Real, 2021), pp. 429–33.
Moretti, I. and R. Stopani, *Architettura romanica religiosa nel contado fiorentino* (Florence, 1974).
Morgan, C. H., *Corinth XI* (Cambridge, MA, 1942).
Morimoto, K., 'Land tenure in Egypt during the early Islamic period', *Orient*, 11 (1975), pp. 109–53.
Morimoto, K., *The fiscal administration of Egypt in the early Islamic period* (Kyoto, 1981).
Morley, N., 'Population size and social structure', in P. Erdkamp (ed.), *The Cambridge companion to ancient Rome* (Cambridge, 2013), pp. 29–44.
Morris, R., 'The powerful and the poor in tenth-century Byzantium', *Past and present*, 73 (1976), pp. 3–27.
Morris, R., 'Dispute settlement in the Byzantine provinces in the tenth century', in W. Davies and P. Fouracre (eds.), *The settlement of disputes in early medieval Europe* (Cambridge, 1986), pp. 125–47.
Morris, R., *Monks and laymen in Byzantium, 843–1118* (Cambridge, 1995).
Morris, R., 'The "life aquatic" on Athos in the tenth and eleventh centuries', in R. Balzaretti et al. (eds.), *Italy and medieval Europe* (Oxford, 2018), pp. 372–83.
Morrisson, C., 'La Sicile byzantine', *Numismatica e antichità classiche*, 27 (1998), pp. 307–34.
Morrisson, C. (ed.), *Trade and markets in Byzantium* (Washington, DC, 2012).
Morrisson, C., 'Trading in wood in Byzantium', in Magdalino and Necipoğlu, *Trade in Byzantium* (Istanbul, 2016), pp. 105–27.
Morrisson, C., 'Coins', in Niewöhner, *The archaeology of Byzantine Anatolia* (Oxford, 2017), pp. 71–81.
Morrisson, C., 'Revisiter le XIe siècle quarante ans après', *Travaux et mémoires*, 21/2 (2017), pp. 611–26.
Morrisson, C. and J.-C. Cheynet, 'Prices and wages in the Byzantine world', in Laiou, *The economic history of Byzantium* (Washington, DC, 2002), pp. 815–78.
Motos Guirao, E., *El poblado medieval de 'El Castellón' (Montefrío, Granada)* (Granada, 1991).
Mouton, J.-M., 'La société villageoise au Fayyoum de 900 à 1100', in C. Gaubert and J.-M. Mouton, *Hommes et villages du Fayyoum dans la documentation papyrologique arabe (Xe–XIe siècles)* (Geneva, 2014), pp. 165–271.
Müller, C., 'Us, coutumes et droit coutumier dans le *fiqh* malikite', in A. Nef and É. Voguet (eds.), *La légitimation du pouvoir au Maghreb médiéval* (Madrid, 2012), pp. 35–54.
Müller-Mertens, E., *Karl der Grosse, Ludwig der Fromme, und die Freien* (Berlin, 1963).
Müller-Wiener, M., *Eine Stadtgeschichte Alexandrias von 564/1169 bis in die Mitte des 9./15. Jahrhunderts* (Berlin, 1992).
Müller-Wodarg, D., 'Die Landwirtschaft Ägyptens in der frühen 'Abbāsidenzeit'', *Islam*, 31 (1954), pp. 174–227, 32 (1957), pp. 14–78, 141–67, 33 (1958), pp. 310–21.

Mullett, M., *Theophylact of Ochrid* (Aldershot, 1997).

Mundell Mango, M. (ed.), *Byzantine trade, 4th–12th centuries* (Farnham, 2009).

Muñoz Martín, M. del M. and I. Flores Escobosa, 'La cerámica medieval en los intercambios comerciales mediterráneos', in A. Suárez Márquez (ed.), *Almería, puerta del Mediterráneo (ss. X–XII)* (Almería, 2007), pp. 52–84.

Munro, J. H., 'Medieval woollens', in D. Jenkins (ed.), *The Cambridge history of western textiles*, 1 (Cambridge, 2003), pp. 228–324.

Munro, J. H., 'Industrial energy from water-mills in the European economy, 5th to 18th centuries', in S. Cavaciocchi (ed.), *Economia e energia secc. XIII–XVIII* (Florence, 2003), pp. 223–69.

Munzi. M. et al., 'La Tripolitania rurale tardoantica, medievale e ottomana alla luce delle recenti indagini archeologiche territoriali nella regione di Lepcis Magna', *AM*, 40 (2014), pp. 215–45.

Musarra, A., 'Genova e il mare nell'Alto Medioevo', *Bullettino dell'Istituto storico italiano per il medio evo*, 119 (2017), pp. 109–47.

Musarra, A., *In partibus Ultramaris* (Rome, 2017).

Musarra, A., 'Gli Spinola a Genova nel XII secolo', *Atti della società ligure di storia patria*, 57 (2017), pp. 5–65.

Nacib, Y., *Une geste en fragments* (Paris, 1994).

Navarro, C., 'Los espacios irrigados rurales y el tamaño de sus poblaciones constructoras en Al-Ándalus', *Arqueología medieval*, 3 (1995), pp. 171–86.

Navarro Palazón, J., *La cerámica esgrafiada andalusí de Murcia* (Madrid, 1986).

Navarro Palazón, J., 'Murcia como centro productor de loza dorada', in *La ceramica medievale nel Mediterraneo occidentale* (Florence, 1986), pp. 129–43.

Navarro Palazón, J., 'La cerámica con decoración esgrafiada', in Lerma, *La cerámica islámica*, 2 (Valencia, 1990), pp. 117–35.

Navarro Palazón, J., 'Los materiales islámicos del alfar antiguo de San Nicolás de Murcia', in F. Arrigues and A. Bazzana (eds.), *Fours de potiers et "testares" médiévaux en Méditerranée occidentale* (Madrid, 1990), pp. 29–43.

Navarro Palazón, J. and P. Jiménez Castillo, 'La producción cerámica medieval de Murcia', in C. M. Gerrard et al., *Spanish medieval ceramics in Spain and the British Isles*, BAR, I610 (Oxford, 1995), pp. 185–215.

Navarro Palazón, J. and P. Jiménez Castillo, *Siyāsa* (Murcia, 2005).

Navarro Palazón, J. and A. Robles Fernández, *Liétor* (Murcia, 1996).

Nef, A., 'La Sicile dans la documentation de la Geniza cairote (fin X^e^–XIIIe siècle)', in D. Coulon et al. (eds.), *Espaces et réseaux en Méditerranée VIe -XVIe siècle*, 1 (Paris, 2007), pp. 273–91.

Nef, A., 'La déportation des musulmans siciliens par Frédéric II', in C. Moatti et al. (eds.), *Le monde de l'itinérance en Méditerranée de l'Antiquité à l'époque moderne* (Brussels, 2009), pp. 455–77.

Nef, A., 'La fiscalité en Sicile sous la domination islamique', in A. Nef and V. Prigent (eds.), *La Sicile de Byzance à l'Islam* (Paris, 2010), pp. 131–56.

Nef, A., 'Michele Amari ou l'histoire inventée de la Sicile islamique', in B. Grévin (ed.), *Maghreb-Italie* (Rome, 2010), pp. 285–306.

Nef, A., *Conquérir et gouverner* (Rome, 2011).

Nef, A. (ed.), *A companion to medieval Palermo* (Leiden, 2013).

Nef, A., 'Islamic Palermo and the dār al-Islām', in Nef, *A companion to medieval Palermo* (Leiden, 2013), pp. 39–59.

Nef, A., *L'état imperial islamique*, Habilitation à diriger les recherches, Université Paris 1-Panthéon Sorbonne, 2018.

Nef, A., 'Reinterpreting the Aghlabids' Sicilian policy (827–910)', in Anderson et al., *The Aghlabids* (Leiden, 2018), pp. 76–87.

Nef, A. and F. Ardizzone (eds.), *Les dynamiques de l'Islamisation en Méditerranée centrale et en Sicile* (Rome and Bari, 2014).

Negrelli, C, 'Modelli di scambio e di consumo tra VII e XII secolo', *AM*, 45 (2018), pp. 11–27.

Nepoti, S., 'La maiolica arcaica nella Valle Padana', in *La ceramica medievale nel Mediterraneo occidentale* (Florence, 1986), pp. 411–18.

Nepoti, S., 'Alcuni dati archeologici sulle manifatture tessili bassomedievali', in S. Patitucci Uggeri (ed.), *Scavi medievali in Italia, 1996–1999* (Rome, 2001), pp. 381–400.

Neri, E., 'Produzione e circolazione del vetro nell'alto medioevo', in Coscarella et al., *Il vetro in transizione* (Bari, 2021), pp. 19–31.

Neville, L., *Authority in Byzantine provincial society, 950–1100* (Cambridge, 2004).

Neville, L., *Anna Komnene* (New York, 2016).

Nicholson, P. and H. Patterson, 'Pottery making in upper Egypt: an ethnoarchaeological study', *World Archaeology*, 17.2 (1985), pp. 222–39.

Niermeyer, J. F. (ed.), *Mediae Latinitatis lexicon minus* (Leiden, 1976).

Niewöhner, P., 'Neue spät- und nachantike Monumente von Milet und der mittelbyzantinische Zerfall des anatolischen Städtewesens', *Archäologischer Anzeiger*, 2 (2013), pp. 165–233.

Niewöhner, P., 'The Byzantine settlement history of Miletus and its hinterland—quantitative aspects', *Archäologischer Anzeiger*, 2 (2016), pp. 225–90.

Niewöhner, P. (ed.), *The archaeology of Byzantine Anatolia* (Oxford, 2017).

Nigro, G., *Francesco di Marco Datini* (Florence, 2020).

Nilsson, J., *Aristocracy, politics and power in Byzantium, 1025–1081*, DPhil thesis, Oxford University, 2017.

Nixon, S. (ed.), *Essouk-Tadmekka* (Leiden, 2017).

Nobili, M., 'L'equazione città antica-città comunale', *Società e storia*, 10 (1980), pp. 891–907.

Norrie, J., *Land and cult: society and radical religion in the diocese of Milan c.990–1130*, DPhil thesis, University of Oxford, 2017. [Forthcoming as *Urban change and radical religion: medieval Milan, c.990–1140* (Oxford)].

North, D. C., *Institutions, institutional change and economic performance* (Cambridge, 1990).

Northedge, A., 'Les origines de la céramique à glaçure polychrome dans le monde islamique', in G. Démians-Archimbaud (ed.), *La céramique médiévale en Méditerranée* (Aix-en-Provence, 1997), pp. 213–23.

Noth, A., 'I documenti arabi di Ruggero II di Sicilia', in C. R. Brühl, *Diplomi e cancelleria di Ruggero II* (Palermo, 1983), pp. 189–222.

Nouschi, A., *Enquête sur le niveau de vie des populations rurales constantinoises, de la conquête jusqu'en 1919* (Paris, 1961).

O'Brien, P., 'European economic development', *Economic history review*, 35 (1982), pp. 1–18.

Occhipinti, E., 'L'economia agraria in territorio milanese tra continuità e spinte innovative', in *Atti dell'11° Congresso internazionale di studio sull'alto medioevo* (Spoleto, 1989), pp. 245–63.

Ogilvie, S. C., *State corporatism and proto-industry* (Cambridge, 1997).

Ogilvie, S. C., *Institutions and European trade* (Cambridge, 2011).

Ogilvie, S., *The European guilds* (Princeton, NJ, 2019).

Ohlhoff, R., *Von der Eintracht zur Zwietracht?* (Hildesheim, 1999).

Oikonomidēs, N., 'Oi byzantinoi douloparoikoi', *Byzantina symmeikta*, 5 (1983), pp. 295–302.

Oikonomidēs, N., 'Ē Peira peri paroikōn', in V. Kremmydas et al. (eds.), *Afierōma ston Niko Svorōno*, 1 (Rethymno, 1986), pp. 232–41.

Oikonomidès, N., 'Le kommerkion d'Abydos', in V. Kravari et al. (eds.), *Hommes et richesses dans l'empire byzantin*, 2 (Paris, 1991), pp. 232–48.

Oikonomidès, N., *Fiscalité et exemption fiscale à Byzance (IXe–XIe s.)* (Athens, 1996).

Oikonomides, N., 'The role of the Byzantine state in the economy', in Laiou, *The economic history of Byzantium* (Washington, DC, 2002), pp. 973–1058.

Olstein, D. A., *La era mozárabe* (Salamanca, 2006).

Ordóñez Frías, A., 'La formación de nuevas entidades poblacionales durante el siglo XI en el Valle de Río Grande (Málaga)', in Sarr, *Ṭawā'if* (Granada, 2018), pp. 387–408.

Orecchioni, P., *Dopo la peste* (Florence, 2022).

Origone, S., 'Gli Embriaci a Genova fra XII e XIII secolo', in *Serta antiqua et mediaevalia*, 5 (Rome, 2001), pp. 67–81.

Ortalli, G., 'Il ducato e la "civitas Rivoalti"', in Cracco Ruggini, *Storia di Venezia*, 1 (Rome, 1992), pp. 725–90.

Ortega Ortega, J. M., 'Una gobernanza poscalifal', in Sarr, *Ṭawā'if* (Granada, 2018), pp. 449–71.

Ortenberg, *see also* West-Harling.

Ortenberg West-Harling, V., '"Venecie due sunt"', in M. Valenti and C. Wickham (eds.), *Italia, 888–962: una svolta* (Turnhout, 2013), pp. 237–64.

Ortiz-Ospina, E. and D. Beltekian, 'Trade and globalization', https://ourworldindata.org/trade-and-globalization#two-centuries-of-trade-country-by-country.

Ortíz Soler, D. et al., 'Ámbitos ocupacionales y áreas residenciales en la Alcazaba de Almería', in *IV Congreso de arqueología medieval española*, 2 (Alicante, 1994), pp. 103–13.

Ostrogorsky, G., *History of the Byzantine state*, 2nd edn (Oxford, 1968).

Ouerfelli, M., *Le sucre* (Leiden, 2008).

Ousterhout, R. G., *A Byzantine settlement in Cappadocia*, 2nd edn (Washington, DC, 2011).

Ousterhout, R. G., *Visualising community* (Washington, DC, 2017).

Öztaşkin, M., 'Byzantine and Turkish glazed pottery finds from Aphrodisias', in S. Bocharov et al. (eds.), *Glazed pottery of the Mediterranean and the Black Sea region, 10th–18th centuries*, 2 (Kazan, 2017), pp. 165–88.

Palombo, C., 'Studying trade and local economies in early Islamicate societies', *Cromohs*, 24 (2021), https://oajournals.fupress.net/index.php/cromohs/article/view/13571/12723.

Panero, F., *Terre in concessione e mobilità contadina* (Bologna, 1984).

Panero, F., *Schiavi, servi e villani nell'Italia medievale* (Turin, 1999).

Panero, F., 'Rese cerealicole e tecniche agrarie nell'Italia nord-occidentale (secoli XII–XV)', *Bullettino dell'Istituto storico italiano per il medio evo*, 107 (2007), pp. 197–215.

Pantůček, S., *Das Epos über den Westzug der Banū Hilāl* (Prague, 1970).

Papanikola-Bakirtzi, D. (ed.), *Byzantine glazed ceramics* (Athens, 1999).

Papanikola-Bakirtzi, D., 'Ergastēria ephyalōmenēs keramikēs sto byzantino kosmo', in *VIIe Congrès international sur la céramique médiévale en Méditerranée* (Athens, 2003), pp. 45–66.

Papanikola-Bakirtzi, D., 'Byzantine glazed ceramics on the market', in Morrisson, *Trade and markets* (Washington, DC, 2012), pp. 193–216.

Papavassiliou, E. et al., 'A ceramic workshop of the early Byzantine period on the island of Lipsi in the Dodecanese (Greece)', in N. Poulou-Papadimitriou (ed.), *LRCW 4*, BAR, I2616 (Oxford, 2014), pp. 159–68.

Parker, M. E., '*Papa et pecunia*', *Mediterranean history review*, 32 (2017), pp. 1–23.

Parman, E., 'The pottery from St John's basilica at Ephesos', in V. Déroche and J.-M. Spieser (eds.), *Recherches sur la céramique byzantine* (Athens, 1989), pp. 277–89.

Parthasarathi, P., *Why Europe grew rich and Asia did not* (Cambridge, 2011).

Pascual, J., et al., 'València i el seu territori', *Arqueo Mediterrània*, 2 (1997), pp. 179–203, 326–8.

Pasquali, G., *Sistemi di produzione agraria e aziende curtensi nell'Italia altomedievale* (Bologna, 2008).

Patitucci Uggeri, S., 'Protomaiolica: un bilancio', in *Atti, XXIII Convegno internazionale della ceramica* (Albisola, 1990), pp. 7–39.

Patlagean, É., 'Byzance et les marchés du grand commerce, vers 830–vers 1030', *Settimane di studio del Centro italiano di studi sull'alto medioevo*, 40 (1993), pp. 587–632.

Patterson, H. and D. B. Whitehouse, 'The medieval domestic pottery', in F. D'Andria and D. B. Whitehouse (eds.), *Excavations at Otranto*, 2 (Galatina, 1992), pp. 87–195.

Patterson, H. et al., *The changing landscapes of Rome's northern hinterland* (Oxford, 2020).

Peacock, D. P. S., *Pottery in the Roman world: an ethnoarchaeological approach* (London, 1982).

Pecci, A., 'Analisi dei residui organici e anfore medievali', *AM*, 45 (2018), pp. 275–80.

Pecci, A. et al., 'Residue analysis of medieval amphorae from the eastern Mediterranean', in S.Y. Waksman (ed.), *Multidisciplinary approaches to food and foodways in the medieval eastern Mediterranean* (Lyon, 2020), pp. 417–28.

Pederzoli, G., *I poteri signorili in un'area di confine*, tesi di dottorato, Università degli Studi di Trento, 2012–2015.

Penet, H., 'Les communautés marchandes de Messine à la fin du Moyen Âge (*c.*1250–*c.*1500)', in T. Jäckh and M. Kirsch (eds.), *Urban dynamics and transcultural communication in medieval Sicily* (Paderborn, 2017), pp. 227–50.

Pensabene, P. (ed.), *Piazza Armerina* (Rome, 2010).

Pensabene, P., 'Villa del Casale e il territorio di Piazza Armerina tra tardoantico e medioevo', in Pensabene, *Piazza Armerina* (Rome, 2010), pp. 1–32.

Pensabene, P., 'Il contributo degli scavi 2004–2014 alla storia della Villa del Casale di Piazza Armerina tra IV e XII secolo', in Pensabene and Barresi, *Piazza Armerina, Villa del Casale* (Rome, 2019), pp. 711–57.

Pensabene, P. and P. Barresi (eds.), *Piazza Armerina, Villa del Casale* (Rome, 2019).

Pensabene, P. and C. Bonanno (eds.), *L'insediamento medievale sulla Villa del Casale di Piazza Armerina* (Galatina, 2008).

Pensabene, P. and C. Sfameni (eds.), *La villa restaurata e i nuovi studi sull'edilizia residenziale tardoantica* (Bari, 2014).

Pérez Alvarado, S., *Las cerámicas omeyas de Marroquíes Bajos (Jaén)* (Jaén, 2003).

Pérez Macías, A., 'La producción metalúrgica en el suroeste de al-Andalus', in Canto García and Cressier, *Minas y metalurgía* (Madrid, 2008), pp. 179–207.

Peri, I., 'La questione delle colonie "lombarde" in Sicilia', *Bollettino storico-bibliografico subalpino*, 57 (1959), pp. 255–80.

Peri, I., 'Per la storia della vita cittadina e del commercio nel medio evo', in *Studi in onore di Amintore Fanfani*, 1 (Milan, 1962), pp. 531–616.

Peri, I., *Villani e cavalieri nella Sicilia medievale* (Rome, 1993).

Perry, C. A., *The daily life of slaves and the global reach of slavery in medieval Egypt, 969–1250 CE*, PhD thesis, Emory University, 2014.

Perry, C. et al. (eds.), *The Cambridge world history of slavery*, 2 (Cambridge, 2021).

Peschlow, U., 'Ancyra', in Niewöhner, *The archaeology of Byzantine Anatolia* (Oxford, 2017), pp. 349–60.

Pesez, J.-M. (ed.), *Brucato*, 2 vols. (Rome, 1984).

Peters-Custot, A., *Les Grecs de l'Italie méridionale post-byzantine* (Rome, 2009).

Peters-Custot, A., '*Plateae* et *anthrôpoi*', in J.-M. Martin et al. (eds.), *L'héritage byzantin en Italie (VIIIe—XIIe siècle)*, 4 (Rome, 2017), pp. 293–317.

Petralia, G., 'La nuova Sicilia tardomedievale', *Revista d'historia medieval*, 5 (1995), pp. 137–62.

Petralia, G., 'Le "navi" e i "cavalli"', *Quaderni storici*, 103 (2000), pp. 201–22.

Petralia, G., 'La "signoria" nella Sicilia normanna e sveva', in C. Violante and M. L. Ceccarelli Lemut (eds.), *La signoria rurale in Italia nel medioevo* (Pisa, 2006), pp. 233–70.

Petralia, G., 'Economia e società del Mezzogiorno nelle Giornate normanno-sveve', *Giornate normanno-sveve*, 20 (Bari, 2014), pp. 237–68.

Petrowiste, J., 'Le paysan des époques médiévale et moderne est-il un consommateur comme les autres?', in G. Ferrand and J. Petrowiste (eds.), *Le nécessaire et le superflu* (Toulouse, 2019), pp. 7–26.

Peyer, H. C., *Zur Getreidepolitik oberitalienischer Städte im 13. Jahrhundert* (Vienna, 1950).

Pezzini, E. and V. Sacco, 'Le produzioni da fuoco a Palermo (IX–XI secolo)', in Y. Hazırlayan and F. Yenişehirlioğlu (eds.), *XIth congress AIECM3 on medieval and modern period Mediterranean ceramics proceedings* (Ankara, 2018), pp. 347–56.

Pezzini, E. et al., 'La ceramica', in A. Bagnera and A. Nef (eds.), *Les bains de Cefalà* (Rome, 2018), pp. 353–457.

Philon, H., *Early Islamic ceramics, ninth to late twelfth centuries* (Athens, 1980).

Pianel, G., 'La céramique de Négrine (IXe siècle)', *Hespéris*, 38 (1951), pp. 1–30.

Picard, C., *L'océan atlantique musulman* (Paris, 1997).

Picard, C., *Le Portugal musulman: VIIe–XIIIe siècle* (Paris, 2000).

Picard, C., 'Pechina-Almeria aux IXe–Xe siècles', in É. Malamut and M. Ouerfelli (eds.), *Villes méditerranéennes au Moyen Âge* (Aix-en-Provence, 2014), pp. 163–75.

Picard, C., *La mer des califes* (Paris, 2015).

Pierrat, G., 'Essai de classification de la céramique de Tôd de la fin du VIIe siècle au début du XIIIe siècle ap. J.-C.', *CCE*, 2 (1991), pp. 145–204.

Pini, A. I., 'Energia e industria tra Sàvena e Reno', in *Tecnica e società nell'Italia dei secoli XII–XVI* (Pistoia, 1987), pp. 1–22.

Pirenne, H., *An economic and social history of medieval Europe* (London, 1936).

Pirenne, H., *Mohammed and Charlemagne* (London, 1939).

Pirillo, P., *Famiglia e mobilità sociale nella Toscana medievale* (Florence, 1992).

Pispisa, E., 'Messina, Catania', *Giornate normanno-sveve*, 10 (Bari, 1993), pp. 147–94.

Pistarino, G., 'Commercio e vie marittime nell'epoca di Ruggero II', in *Giornate normanno-sveve*, 3 (Bari, 1979), pp. 239–58.

Pistarino, G., 'Commercio e comunicazioni tra Genova e il Regno normanno-svevo', in *Giornate normanno-sveve*, 4 (Bari, 1981), pp. 231–90.

Pistarino, G., 'La civiltà dei mestieri in Liguria (sec. XII)', in Pistarino (ed.), *Saggi e documenti*, 2.1 (Genoa, 1982), pp. 9–74.

Pistarino, G., 'Genova e il Maghreb', in R. H. Rainero (ed.), *Italia e Algeria* (Milan, 1982), pp. 23–68.

Pitarakis, B. 'Témoignage des objets métalliques dans le village médiéval (Xe–XIVe siècles)', in Lefort et al., *Les villages dans l'empire byzantin* (Paris, 2005), pp. 247–65.

Poblome, J., *Sagalassos Red Slip ware* (Turnhout, 1999).

Polanyi, K. et al., *Trade and market in the early empires* (Glencoe, IL, 1957).

Polemis, D., *The Doukai* (London, 1968).

Poliak, A. N., *Feudalism in Egypt, Syria, Palestine, and the Lebanon, 1250–1900* (London, 1939).

Polica, S., 'Basso Medioevo e Rinascimento', *Bullettino dell'Istituto storico italiano per il medio evo*, 88 (1979), pp. 287–316.

Poloni, A., *Lucca nel Duecento* (Pisa, 2010).

Poloni, A., *Potere al popolo* (Milan, 2010).

Poloni, A., 'Una società fluida', *Storica*, 21 (2015), pp. 164–90.

Poloni, A., 'Italian communal cities and the thirteenth-century commercial revolution', in S. Carocci and I. Lazzarini (eds.), *Social mobility in medieval Italy (1100–1500)* (Rome, 2018), pp. 353–71.
Polonio, V., 'Da provincia a signora del mare', in D. Puncuh (ed.), *Storia di Genova* (Genoa, 2003), pp. 111–231.
Polvorinos del Río, A. et al., 'Estudio arqueométrico de la loza dorada de Madinat al-Zahra, Córdoba', *Cuadernos de Madīnat al-Zahrā'*, 6 (2008), pp. 165–79.
Pomeranz, K., *The great divergence* (Princeton, NJ, 2000).
Poncet, J., 'Le mythe de la "catastrophe hilalienne"', *Annales E. S. C.*, 22 (1997), pp. 1099–120.
Popović, M., 'Importation et production locale de céramique à Ras (fin XIe–début XIIIe siècle)', in V. Déroche and J.-M. Spieser (eds.), *Recherches sur la céramique byzantine* (Athens, 1989), pp. 119–30.
Popović, M. and V. Ivanišević, 'Grad Braničevo u srednjem veku', *Starinar*, 39 (1988), pp. 125–79.
Postan, M. M., 'Medieval agrarian society in its prime: England', in Postan (ed.), *The Cambridge economic history of Europe*, 1, 2nd edn (Cambridge, 1966), pp. 548–632.
Poulou-Papadēmētriou, N., 'Byzantinē keramikē apo ton ellēniko nēsiōtiko chōro kai apo tēn Peloponnēso (7os–9os ai.)', in E. Kountoura-Galakē (ed.), *Oi skoteinoi aiōnes tou Byzantiou (7os–9os ai.)* (Athens, 2001), pp. 231–66.
Poulou-Papadimitriou, N., 'Middle Byzantine pottery from Eleutherna', in E. Gabrilakē and Gi. Z. Tziphopoulos (eds.), *O Mylopotamos apo tēn archaiotēta ōs sēmera*, 6 (Rethymno, 2006), pp. 77–92.
Poulou-Papadimitriou, N. and E. Nodarou, 'Transport vessels and maritime trade routes in the Aegean from the 5th to the 9th C. AD', in Poulou-Papadimitriou (ed.), *LRCW 4*, BAR, I2616 (Oxford, 2014), pp. 873–83.
Poulou, N., 'Transport amphorae and trade in the Aegean from the 7th to the 9th century AD: containers for wine or olive oil?', *Byzantina*, 35 (2017), pp. 195–216.
Poulou, N., 'Sailing in the dark', in S. Esders et al. (eds.), *The 8th century* (Berlin, 2023).
Powell, J. M., *Anatomy of a crusade, 1213–1221* (Philadelphia, PA, 1986).
Pozza, M., *I Badoer* (Abano Terme, 1982).
Pradines, S. et al., 'Excavations of the archaeological triangle', *Mishkah: the Egyptian journal of Islamic archeology*, 4 (2009), pp. 177–222.
Preiser-Kapeller, J., 'A collapse of the eastern Mediterranean?', *Jahrbuch der österreichischen Byzantinistik*, 65 (2015), pp. 195–242.
Prigent, V., 'Les empereurs isauriens et la confiscation des patrimoines pontificaux d'Italie du sud', *MEFRM*, 116.2 (2004), pp. 557–94.
Prigent, V., *La Sicile byzantine (VIe–Xe siècle)*, thèse de doctorat, Université de Paris IV-Sorbonne, 2006.
Prigent, V., 'Monnaie et circulation monétaire en Sicile du début du VIIIe siècle à l'avènement de la domination musulmane', in J.-M. Martin et al. (eds.), *L'héritage byzantin en Italie (VIIIe–XIIe siècle)*, 2 (Rome, 2012), pp. 455–82.
Prigent, V., 'Palermo in the eastern Roman empire', in Nef, *A companion to medieval Palermo* (Leiden, 2013), pp. 11–38.
Prigent, V., 'L'évolution du réseau épiscopal sicilien (VIIIe–Xe siècle)', in Nef and Ardizzone, *Les dynamiques* (Rome and Bari, 2014), pp. 89–102.
Primavera, M., 'Introduzione di nuove piante e innovazioni agronomiche nella Sicilia medievale', *AM*, 45 (2018), pp. 439–44.
Pringle, D., 'La ceramica dell'area Sud del Convento di San Silvestro a Genova', *AM*, 4 (1977), pp. 100–61.

Prinzing, G., 'Zur Intensität der byzantinischen Fern-Handelsschiffahrt des 12. Jahrhunderts in Mittelmeer', in E. Chrysos et al. (eds.), *Griechenland und das Meer* (Mannheim, 1999), pp. 141–50.

Prinzing, G., 'Sklaven oder freie Diener im Spiegel der "Prosopographie der mittelbyzantinischen Zeit" (PmbZ)', in A. D. Beihammer et al. (eds.), *Prosopon Rhomaikon* (Berlin, 2017), pp. 129–73.

Provero, L., 'Forty years of rural history for the Italian middle ages', in I. Alfonso (ed.), *The rural history of medieval European societies* (Turnhout, 2007), pp. 141–72.

Provero, L., *L'Italia dei poteri locali* (Rome, 2010).

Pryor, J. H., 'The origins of the *commenda* contract', *Speculum*, 52 (1977), pp. 5–37.

Pryor, J. H., *Geography, technology and war* (Cambridge, 1988).

Pucci Donati, F., 'Ravitaillement en céréales et marché urbain à Bologne au XIIIe siècle', in A. Knaepen et al. (eds.), *Approvisionner la ville* (Brussels, 2018), pp. 13–25.

Pulak, C. et al., 'Eight Byzantine shipwrecks from the Theodosian harbour excavations at Yenikapı in Istanbul, Turkey', *The international journal of nautical archaeology*, 44 (2015), pp. 39–73.

Putnam, R. D. et al., *Making democracy work* (Princeton, NJ, 1993).

Puy, A. and A. L. Balbo, 'The genesis of irrigated terraces in al-Andalus', *Journal of arid environments*, 89 (2013), pp. 45–56.

Pyke, G., 'The ceramic material from Tinnīs', in Gascoigne, *The island city of Tinnīs* (Cairo, 2020), pp. 179–251.

Qin, D. and J. C. Ho, 'Chinese ceramic exports to Africa during the 9th–10th centuries', in H. Nol (ed.), *Riches beyond the horizon* (Turnhout, 2021), pp. 95–128.

Quirós Castillo, J. A. (ed.), *Archeologia e storia di un castello apuano* (Florence, 2004).

Quirós Castillo, J. A., 'Castillo de Pancorbo y recinto de Santa Marta' (2019), www.fastionline.org/excavation/micro_view.php?fst_cd=AIAC_4806&curcol=sea_cd-AIAC_10321.

Rabie, H., *The financial system of Egypt* (London, 1972).

Rabinowitz, A. et al., 'Daily life in a provincial late Byzantine city', in F. Daim and J. Drauschke (eds.), *Byzanz*, 2.1 (Mainz, 2010), pp. 425–78.

Raccagni, G. L., *The Lombard league, 1167–1225* (Oxford, 2010).

Racine, P., 'À Cremone, à la fin du XIIIe siècle', in *Studi in memoria di Federigo Melis*, 1 (Naples, 1978), pp. 527–41.

Racine, P., *Plaisance du Xème à la fin du XIIIème siècle* (Lille, 1979).

Racine, P., 'Associations de marchands et associations de métiers en Italie de 600 à 1200', in B. Schwineköper (ed.), *Gilden und Zünfte* (Sigmaringen, 1985), pp. 127–49.

Ragheb, Y., 'Marchands d'Égypte du VIIe au IXc siècle d'après leur correspondance et leurs actes', in *Le marchand au Moyen Âge* (Paris, 1988), pp. 25–33.

Rāğib, Y., Reviews of books by W. Diem, *Bulletin critique des Annales islamologiques*, 14 (1998), pp. 171–9; 15 (1999), pp. 195–7; 16 (2000), pp. 185–6.

Ragia, E., 'The circulation, distribution and consumption of marine products', *Journal of maritime archaeology*, 13 (2018), pp. 449–66.

Randazzo, M., 'The evidence of Byzantine *sgraffito wares* in 12th-century Sicily', in M. Ivanova and H. Jeffery (eds.), *Transmitting and circulating the late Antique and Byzantine worlds* (Leiden, 2020), pp. 227–50.

Randazzo, M. G., 'Middle Byzantine glazed wares in Sicily (12th to mid-13th century)', in P. Petridis et al. (eds.), *12th congress AIECM3 on medieval and modern period Mediterranean ceramics* (Athens, 2021), pp. 689–96.

Randazzo, M. G., 'La transizione bizantino-islamica in Sicilia (VIII–X secolo)', *AM*, 48 (2021), pp. 127–60.

Rao, R., *I paesaggi dell'Italia medievale* (Rome, 2015).
Rao, R., 'Cavalieri, mercanti e consoli a Savona', *Archivio storico italiano*, 176 (2018), pp. 4–38.
Rapetti, A., *Campagne milanesi* (Cavallermaggiore, 1994).
Rapetti, A., *La terra degli uomini* (Rome, 2012).
Rapoport, Y., 'Invisible peasants, marauding nomads', *Mamluk studies review*, 8.2 (2004), pp. 1–22.
Rapoport, Y., *Marriage, money and divorce in medieval Islamic society* (Cambridge, 2005).
Rapoport, Y., 'Reflections of Fatimid power in the maps of island cities in the "Book of curiosities"', in I. Baumgärtner and M. Sterken (eds.), *Herrschaft verorten* (Zurich, 2012), pp. 183–210.
Rapoport, Y., *Rural economy and tribal society in Islamic Egypt* (Turnhout, 2018).
Rapoport Y. and I. Shahar, 'Irrigation in the medieval Islamic Fayyum', *JESHO*, 55 (2012), pp. 1–31.
Raptis, K. T., 'Seeking the marketplaces of Byzantine Thessalonike', in *Niš and Byzantium, Thirteenth symposium* (Niš, 2015), pp. 237–50.
Recchia, V., *Gregorio Magno e la società agricola* (Rome, 1978).
Redi, F., *Pisa com'era* (Naples, 1991).
Redlak, M., 'Syro-Palestinian underglaze painted ceramics from Kom el-Dikka, 13th–15th century', *Polish archaeology in the Mediterranean*, 15 (2003), pp. 46–52.
Rege Cambrin, L., *La famiglia dei Casalei dalle origini alla metà del XIII secolo*, tesi di laurea, Università di Pisa, relatore M. L. Ceccarelli Lemut, a.a. 1988–1989.
Reif, S. C., *A Jewish archive from Old Cairo* (London, 2000).
Renzi Rizzo, C., '*Pisarum et Pisanorum descriptiones* in una fonte araba della metà del XII secolo', *Bollettino storico pisano*, 72 (2003), pp. 1–29.
Retamero, F., *La contínua il·lusió del moviment perpetu* (Bellaterra, 1998).
Retamero i Sarralvo, F., 'Sobre els ocultaments de peces almoràvits', in *Actes II Jarique de numismàtica hispano-àrab* (Lleida, 1998), pp. 222–41.
Retuerce Velasco, M., 'El templén', *Boletín de arqueología medieval*, 1 (1987), pp. 71–7.
Retuerce Velasco, M., *La cerámica andalusí de la Meseta* (Madrid, 1998).
Retuerce Velasco, M. and A. de Juan García, 'La cerámica almohade en verde y manganeso de la meseta', *ATM*, 6 (1999), pp. 241–60.
Retuerce Velasco, M. et al., 'La cerámica islámica de Calatrava la Vieja y Alarcos', in J. Zozaya et al. (eds.), *Actas del VIII Congreso internacional de cerámica medieval en el Mediterráneo* (Ciudad Real, 2009), pp. 729–58.
Reyerson, K. L., 'Montpellier and Genoa', *Journal of medieval history*, 20 (1994), pp. 359–72.
Reynolds, P., 'The medieval amphorae', in Hodges et al., *Byzantine Butrint* (Oxford, 2004), pp. 270–7.
Reynolds, P., 'The pottery', in J. Rossiter et al. (eds.), 'A Roman bath-house and a group of Early Islamic middens at Bir Ftouha, Carthage', *AM*, 39 (2012), pp. 245–82, at 250–73.
Reynolds, P., 'Amphorae in Beirut from the Umayyads to the Crusaders', *AM*, 45 (2018), pp. 91–110.
Reynolds, P., 'From Vandal Africa to Arab Ifrīqiya', in J. P. Conant and S. T. Stevens (eds.), *North Africa under Byzantium and early Islam* (Washington, DC, 2018), pp. 129–72.
Reynolds, R. L., 'The market for northern textiles in Genoa 1179–1200', *Revue belge de philologie et d'histoire*, 8 (1929), pp. 831–52.
Rheidt, K., *Die byzantinische Wohnstadt* (Berlin, 1991).
Ricci, M., 'Ceramica acroma da fuoco', in L. Saguì and L. Paroli (eds.), *Archeologia urbana a Roma: il progetto della Cripta Balbi*, 5 (Florence, 1990), pp. 215–49.

Ricci, R., *La marca della Liguria orientale e gli Obertenghi (945–1056)* (Spoleto, 2007).
Richarté-Manfredi, C., 'Navires et marchandises islamiques en Méditerranée occidentale durant le Haut Moyen Âge', *MEFRM*, 129.2 (2017), pp. 485–500.
Richarté-Manfredi, C., 'Céramiques glaçurées et à décor vert et brun des épaves islamiques de Provence (Fin IXe–début Xe siècle)', *ATM*, 27 (2020), pp. 63–77.
Richarté, C. et al., 'Céramiques et marchandises transportées le long des côtes provençales, témoignages des échanges commerciaux entre le domaine islamique et l'Occident des IXe–Xe siècle', in R.-P. Gayraud et al. (eds.), *Héritages arabo-islamiques dans l'Europe méditerranéenne* (Paris, 2015), pp. 209–27.
Richter, T. S., *Rechtssemantik und forensische Rhetorik*, 2nd edn (Wiesbaden, 2008).
Richter, T. S., 'Coptic papyri and juristic papyrology', *The journal of juristic papyrology*, 43 (2013), pp. 405–31.
Rio, A., *Slavery after Rome, 500–1100* (Oxford, 2017).
Rioulx, S., 'The fiction of economic coercion', *Historical materialism*, 21 (2013), pp. 92–128.
Rippe, G., *Padoue et son contado (X[e]–XIIIe siècle)* (Rome, 2003).
Ritter, M., 'Panegyric markets in the Byzantine Empire and their role in the pilgrimage economy (5th–12th centuries)'. in D. Ariantzi and I. Eichner (eds.), *Für Seelenheil und Lebensglück* (Mainz, 2018), pp. 367–82.
Ritter-Lutz, S., *Monte Iato—die mittelalterliche Keramik mit Bleiglasur* (Zurich, 1991).
Rizzo, M. S. and D. Romano, 'Le butte del villaggio rurale di Colmitella (Racalmuto, Agrigento)', *Archeologia postmedievale*, 16 (2012), pp. 99–107.
Rizzo, M. S. et al., 'L'insediamento rurale nel territorio di Agrigento', in Nef and Ardizzone, *Les dynamiques* (Rome and Bari, 2014), pp. 351–63.
Rizzo, M. S. et al., 'Il villaggio di Colmitella (Racalmuto, AG)', in P. Arthur and M. Leo Imperiale (eds.), *VII Congresso nazionale di archeologia medievale* (Florence, 2015), pp. 442–7.
Rodríguez, A., 'À propos des objets nécessaires', in L. Feller and A. Rodríguez (eds.), *Objets sous contrainte* (Paris, 2013), pp. 63–89.
Rodziewicz, E., *Bone carvings from Fustat-Istabl 'Antar* (Cairo, 2012).
Rodziewicz, M., *La céramique romaine tardive d'Alexandrie, Alexandrie I* (Warsaw, 1976).
Rognoni, C., 'Au pied de la lettre?', in A. Nef and V. Prigent (eds.), *La Sicile de Byzance à l'Islam* (Paris, 2010), pp. 205–28.
Rognoni, C., 'Disposer des hommes dans la Sicile du XIIe siècle', *Nea Rōmē*, 9 (2012), pp. 133–52.
Romeo, R., *Il comune rurale di Origgio nel secolo XIII* (Assisi, 1970).
Ronzani, M., *Chiesa e "civitas" di Pisa nella seconda metà del secolo XI* (Pisa, 1996).
Rösch, G., *Venezia e l'impero, 962–1250* (Rome, 1985).
Rösch, G., *Der venezianische Adel bis zur Schliessung des Grossen Rats* (Sigmaringen, 1989).
Rösch, G., 'Lo sviluppo mercantile', in Cracco and Ortalli, *Storia di Venezia*, 2 (Rome, 1995), pp. 131–51.
Rosenthal, J.-L. and R. B. Wong, *Before and beyond divergence* (Cambridge, MA, 2011).
Rosselló Bordoy. G., *Ensayo de sistematización de la cerámica árabe en Mallorca* (Palma de Mallorca, 1978).
Rosselló Pons, M., *Les ceràmiques almohades del carrer de Zavellà, ciutat de Mallorca* (Palma de Mallorca, 1983).
Rosser-Owen, M., '"From the mounds of Old Cairo"', in *I Congreso internacional Red europea de museos de arte islámico: actas* (Granada, 2012), pp. 163–87.
Rossetti, G., 'Motivi economico-sociali e religiosi in atti di cessione di beni a chiese del territorio milanese nei secoli XI e XII', in *Contributi dell'Istituto di storia medioevale*, 1 (Milan, 1968), pp. 349–410.

Rossini, E., 'La tecnica nell'alto medioevo (Le gualchiere del Tramigna nel 985)', in *Scritti in onore di mons. Giuseppe Turrini* (Verona, 1973), pp. 723–36.
Rossini, E. and M. Fennell Mazzaoui, 'Società e tecnica nel medioevo', *Atti e memorie della Accademia di agricoltura scienze e lettere di Verona*, 6 ser., 21 (1969–70), pp. 571–624.
Rouighi, R., *The making of a Mediterranean emirate* (Philadelphia, PA, 2011).
Rousset, M.-O. and S. Marchand, 'Secteur nord de Tebtynis (Fayyoum). Mission de 1999', *AI*, 34 (2000), pp. 387–436.
Rousset, M.-O. et al., 'Tebtynis 1998', *AI*, 33 (1999), pp. 185–262.
Rousset, M.-O et al., 'Secteur nord de Tebtynis (Fayyoum). Mission de 2000', *AI*, 35 (2001), pp. 409–89.
Roveda, E., *Uomini, terre e acque* (Milan, 2012).
Rovelli, A., 'Coins and trade in early medieval Italy', *Early medieval Europe*, 17 (2009), pp. 45–76.
Rowlandson, J., *Landowners and tenants in Roman Egypt* (Oxford, 1996).
Rustow, M., 'Karaites real and imagined', *Past and present*, 197 (2007), pp. 35–74.
Rustow, M., *Heresy and the politics of community* (Ithaca, NY, 2014).
Rustow, M., *The lost archive* (Princeton, NJ, 2020).
Saccardo, F., 'Contesti medievali nella laguna e prime produzioni graffite veneziane', in Gelichi, *La ceramica nel mondo bizantino* (Florence, 1993), pp. 201–39.
Saccardo, F., 'Contributo alla conoscenza della ceramica invetriata veneziana "tipo Santa Croce"', in S. Gelichi (ed.), *I Congresso nazionale di archeologia medievale* (Florence, 1997), pp. 409–15.
Saccardo, F. et al., 'Ceramiche importate a Venezia e nel Veneto tra XI e XIV secolo', in Ch. Bakirtzis (ed.), *VIIe congrès international sur la céramique médiévale en Méditerranée* (Athens, 2003), pp. 395–420.
Sacco, V., *Une fenêtre sur Palerme entre le IXe et la première moitié du XIIe siècle*, thèse de doctorat, Université de Paris-Sorbonne, 2016.
Sacco, V., 'Le ceramiche invetriate di età islamica a Palermo', *AM*, 44 (2017), pp. 337–66.
Sacco, V., 'Ceramica con decorazione a *splash* da Palermo (fine X–prima metà XI secolo), in Y. Hazırlayan and F. Yenişehirlioğlu (eds.), *XIth congress AIECM3 on medieval and modern period Mediterranean ceramics proceedings* (Ankara, 2018), pp. 433–47.
Sacco, V., 'Produzione e circolazione delle anfore palermitane tra la fine del IX e il XII secolo', *AM*, 45 (2018), pp. 175–91.
Sacco, V., *Dalla ceramica alla storia economica: il caso di Palermo islamica* (Rome 2023).
Sacco, V. et al., 'Islamic ceramics and rural economy in the Trapani mountains during the 11th century', *Journal of Islamic archaeology*, 7 (2020), pp. 39–77.
Saggioro, F. and G. M. Varanini (eds.), *Il castello di Illasi* (Rome, 2009).
Saggioro, F. et al., 'Insediamento ed evoluzione di un castello della Pianura Padana', *AM*, 31 (2004), pp. 169–86.
Sahlins, M., *Stone Age economics* (Chicago, 1972).
Sakellariou, E., *Southern Italy in the late middle ages* (Leiden, 2012).
Salinas Pleguezuelo, M. E., *La ceramica islámica de Madinat Qurtuba de 1031 a 1236*, tesis doctoral, Universidad de Córdoba, 2012.
Salinas Plegezuelo, E., 'Producciones cerámicas de un alfar del siglo XII en Córdoba (España)', in S. Gelichi (ed.), *Atti del IX Congresso internazionale sulla ceramica medievale nel Mediterraneo* (Florence, 2012), pp. 353–8.
Salinas, E., 'Ceramica vidriada de época emiral en Córdoba', *ATM*, 20 (2013), pp. 67–96.
Salinas, E., 'Revisando Pechina y el antecedente de las cerámicas vidriadas islámicas en al-Andalus', in C. Fernández Ibáñez (ed.), *al-Kitāb* (Madrid, 2019), pp. 299–306.
Salinas, E. and T. Pradell, 'The introduction of the glaze in al-Andalus', *Libyan studies*, 51 (2020), pp. 87–98.

Salinas, E. and T. Pradell, 'Madīnat al-Zahrā' or Madīnat Qurtuba?', *Archaeological and anthropological sciences*, 12 (2020), 207.

Salinas, E. and T. Pradell, 'Primeras evidencias de producción de cerámica verde y manganeso califal en un alfar de Córdoba', in M. Retuerce Velasco (ed.), *Actas VI Congreso de arqueología medieval (España–Portugal)* (Ciudad Real, 2021), pp. 409–14.

Salinas, E. and J. Zozaya, 'Pechina', in M. J. Gonçalves and S. Gómez-Martínez (eds.), *Actas do X Congresso internacional, A cerâmica medieval no Mediterrâneo* (Silves, 2015), pp. 573–6.

Salinas, E. et al., 'From tin- to antimony-based yellow opacifiers in the early Islamic Egyptian glazes', *Journal of archaeological science: reports*, 26 (2019), 101923.

Salinas, E. et al., 'Glaze production at an early Islamic workshop in al-Andalus', *Archaeological and anthropological sciences*, 11 (2019), pp. 2201–13.

Salinas, E. et al., 'Polychrome glazed ware production in Tunisia during the Fatimid-Zirid period', *Journal of archaeological science: reports*, 34 (2020), 102632.

Salinas, E. et al., 'The beginnings of glaze technology in Garb al-Andalus (south-west of the Iberian peninsula) during the 9th–10th centuries', in P. Petridis et al. (eds.), *12th congress AIECM3 on medieval and modern period Mediterranean ceramics* (Athens, 2021), pp. 263–8.

Salinas, E. et al., 'From glass to glaze in al-Andalus', *European journal of archaeology*, 25 (2022), pp. 22–41.

Salvatierra Cuenca, V., *El Alto Guadalquivir en época islámica* (Jaén, 2006).

Salvatierra Cuenca, V., 'Crecimiento y transformación urbana: Jaén en época almohade', in *Al-Ándalus: país de ciudades* (Toledo, 2008), pp. 177–96.

Salvatierra, V., 'Algunas cuestiones sobre el urbanismo almohade en al-Andalus', in P. Cressier and V. Salvatierra (eds.), *Las Navas de Tolosa, 1212–2012* (Jaén, 2014), pp. 445–63.

Salvatierra Cuenca, V. and E. M. Alcázar Hernández, 'A 12th-century urban project', *AM*, 43 (2016), pp. 187–97.

Salvatori, E., *La popolazione pisana nel Duecento* (Pisa, 1994).

Salvatori, E., 'Spazi mercantili e commerciali a Milano nel medioevo', in A. Grohmann (ed.), *Spazio urbano e organizzazione economica nell'Europa medievale* (Perugia, 1994), pp. 243–66.

Salvatori, E., *Boni amici et vicini* (Pisa, 2002).

Salvatori, E., 'Lo spazio economico di Pisa nel Mediterraneo: dall'XI alla metà del XII secolo', *Bullettino dell'Istituto storico italiano per il medio evo*, 115 (2013), pp. 119–152.

Sanders, G. D. R., 'Medieval pottery', *Annual of the British School at Athens*, 88 (1993), pp. 251–86.

Sanders, G. D. R., *Byzantine glazed pottery at Corinth to c.1125*, PhD thesis, University of Birmingham, 1995.

Sanders, G. D. R., 'Byzantine Polychrome pottery', in J. Herrin et al. (eds.), *Mosaic* (London and Athens, 2001), pp. 89–103.

Sanders, G. D. R., 'Corinth', in Laiou, *The economic history of Byzantium* (Washington, DC, 2002), pp. 647–54.

Sanders, G. D. R., 'An overview of the new chronology for 9th to 13th century pottery at Corinth', in Ch. Bakirtzis (ed.), *VIIe Congrès international sur la céramique médiévale en Méditerranée* (Athens, 2003), pp. 35–44.

Sanders, G. D. R., 'Recent developments in the chronology of Byzantine Corinth', in *Corinth XX* (Athens, 2003), pp. 385–99.

Sanders, G. D. R., *Recent finds from Ancient Corinth* (Leiden, 2016).

Sanders, P., *Ritual, politics, and the city in Fatimid Cairo* (Albany, NY, 1994).
Sanke, M., *Die mittelalterliche Keramikproduktion in Brühl-Pingsdorf* (Mainz, 2002).
Sannazaro, M. et al., 'Manufatti del quotidiano', in Sannazaro et al. (eds.), *1287 e dintorni* (Mantua, 2017), pp. 129–59.
Santoro, S., 'Pantellerian ware', *L'Africa romana*, 13 (2002), pp. 991–1004.
Sanz García, F. J. et al., *Intervención arqueológica integral en el solar de la sede del Consejo Consultivo de Castilla y León en la ciudad de Zamora (Plaza de la Catedral c/v Calle Obispo Manso y Calle Infantas* (Valladolid, 2019).
Sapori, A., 'I beni del commercio internazionale nel Medioevo', *Archivio storico italiano*, 113 (1955), pp. 3–44.
Sapori, A., *Il mercante italiano nel Medio Evo* (Milan, 1983).
Sarr, B., *La Granada zirí (1013–90)*, tesis doctoral, Universidad de Granada, 2009.
Sarr, B. (ed.), *Ṭawā'if* (Granada, 2018).
Sarris, P., *Economy and society in the age of Justinian* (Cambridge, 2006).
Sarris, P., 'Large estates and the peasantry in Byzantium *c.* 600–1100', *Revue belge de philologie et d'histoire*, 90 (2012), pp. 429–50.
Sato Tsugitaka, *State and rural society in medieval Islam* (Leiden, 1997).
Sato Tsugitaka, *Sugar in the social life of medieval Islam* (Leiden, 2014).
Savigni, R., *Episcopato e società cittadina a Lucca da Anselmo II (+1086) a Roberto (+1225)* (Lucca, 1996).
Sayyid, A. F., *La capitale de l'Égypte jusqu'à l'époque fatimide* (Beirut, 1998).
Sbarra, F., 'I materiali ceramici', in S. Gelichi et al. (eds.), *Un villaggio nella pianura* (Florence, 2014), pp. 146–78.
Scales, P., 'A proletarian revolution in 11th century Spain?', *al-Qanṭara*, 11 (1990), pp. 113–25.
Scales, P., *The fall of the caliphate of Córdoba* (Leiden, 1994).
Scampoli, E., *Firenze, archeologia di una città, secoli I a.C.–XIII d.C* (Florence, 2010).
Scanlon, G. T., 'Excavations at Fustat, 1964', *Journal of the American Research Center in Egypt*, 4 (1965), pp. 6–30.
Scanlon, G. T., 'Fusṭāṭ expedition: preliminary report, 1965', 2, *Journal of the American Research Center in Egypt*, 6 (1967), pp. 65–86.
Scanlon, G. T., 'Fusṭāṭ expedition: preliminary report, 1972', 1, *Journal of the American Research Center in Egypt*, 18 (1981), pp. 57–84. [Other preliminary reports for the US-led Fusṭāṭ expedition appear in *Journal of the American Research Center in Egypt*, 5 (1966), pp. 83–112; 10 (1973), pp. 11–25; 11 (1974), pp. 81–91; 13 (1976), pp. 69–89; 16 (1979), pp. 103–24; 17 (1980), pp. 77–96; 19 (1982), pp. 119–29; 21 (1984), pp. 1–38; and *AI*, 17 (1981), pp. 407–36.]
Scanlon, G. T., 'Fayyumi pottery', in N. Swelim (ed.), *Alexandrian studies in memoriam Daoud Abdu Daoud* (Alexandria, 1993), pp. 295–330.
Scanlon, G. T., 'Fustat Fatimid Sgraffiato', in M. Barrucand (ed.), *L'Égypte fatimide* (Paris, 1999), pp. 265–83.
Schaube, A., *Handelsgeschichte der romanischen Völker des Mittelmeergebiets bis zum Ende der Kreuzzüge* (Munich and Berlin, 1906).
Schibille, N., *Islamic glass in the making* (Leuven, 2022).
Schibille, N. et al., 'Chronology of early Islamic glass compositions from Egypt', *Journal of archaeological science*, 104 (2019), pp. 10–18.
Schofield, P. R., 'Alternatives to expropriation', *Continuity and Change*, 36 (2021), pp. 141–48.
Schofield, P. R., 'Impediments to expropriation', *Continuity and Change*, 36 (2021), pp. 211–32.

Schreiner, P., 'Untersuchungen zu den Niederlassungen westlicher Kaufleute im Byzantinischen Reich des 11. und 12. Jahrhunderts', *Byzantinische Forschungen*, 7 (1979) pp. 175–91.

Schuster, G., *Die Beduinen in der Vorgeschichte Tunesiens* (Berlin, 2006).

Schweizerische Institut für ägyptische Bauforschung und Altertumskunde in Kairo, Aswan excavations, http://swissinst.ch/html/forschung_neu.html/.

Scibona, G., 'Messina XI–XII secc.', in R. Fiorillo and P. Peduto (eds.), *Atti del III Congresso nazionale di archeologia medievale* (Florence, 2003), pp. 504–7.

Scott, J. C., *Weapons of the weak* (New Haven, CT, 1985).

Scranton, R. L., *Corinth XVI* (Princeton, NJ, 1957).

Sedini, E., 'Il settore abitativo in prossimità delle mura sud-occidentali', in P. M. De Marchi (ed.), *Castelseprio e Torba* (Mantua, 2013), pp. 125–42.

Semenova, L. A., *Salakh ad Din i Mamlyuki v Egipte* (Moscow, 1966).

Sénac, P., *La frontière et les hommes, VIIIe–XIIe siècle* (Paris, 2000).

Sénac, P., 'Le califat de Cordoue et la Méditerranée occidentale au XIe siecle: le Fraxinet des Maures', in J.-M. Martin (ed.), *Castrum VII* (Rome and Madrid, 2001), pp. 113–26.

Sénac, P. and P. Cressier, *Histoire du Maghreb médiéval, VIIe–XVe siècle* (Paris, 2012).

Serjeant, R. B., 'Material for a history of Islamic textiles up to the Mongol conquest', *Ars Islamica*, 13 (1948), pp. 75–117.

Serrano-Piedecasas Fernández, L., 'Elementos para una historia de la manufactura textil andalusí (siglos IX–XII)', *Studia historica: historia medieval*, 4 (1986), pp. 205–27.

Sestito, S., 'Dai castelli all'incastellamento', in F. Troletti (ed.), *Castelli e fortificazioni dalla Valcamonica alla Franciacorta* (Capo di Ponte, 2019), pp. 11–38.

Settia, A. A., *Castelli e villaggi nell'Italia padana* (Naples, 1984).

Settia, A. A., '"Per foros Italie"', *Settimane di studio del Centro italiano di studi sull'alto medioevo*, 40 (1993), pp. 187–237.

Sevilla almohade (Seville and Rabat, 1999).

Shatzmiller, M., *Labour in the medieval Islamic world* (Leiden, 1994).

Shatzmiller, M., 'Economic performance and economic growth in the early Islamic world', *JESHO*, 54 (2011), pp. 132–84.

Shatzmiller, M., 'The adoption of paper in the Middle East, 700–1300 AD', *JESHO*, 61 (2018), pp. 461–90.

Sheppard Baird, W., 'The distribution of tin (casseritite)' (2013), https://www.minoanatlantis.com/Tin_Distribution.php/.

Shoshan, B., 'Fatimid grain policy and the post of the *muḥtasib*', *International journal of Middle East studies*, 13 (1981), pp. 181–9.

Sigalos, L., 'Housing people in medieval Greece', *International journal of historical archaeology*, 7 (2003), pp. 195–221.

Sigalos, E., *Housing in medieval and post-medieval Greece*, BAR, I1291 (Oxford, 2004).

Sijpesteijn, P. M., 'Profit following responsibility', *Journal of Juristic Papyrology*, 31 (2001), pp. 91–132.

Sijpesteijn, P. M., *Shaping a Muslim state* (Oxford, 2013).

Simonsen, J. B., *Studies in the genesis and early development of the caliphal taxation system* (Copenhagen, 1988).

Simpson, A. J., *Niketas Choniates* (Oxford, 2014).

Skartsē, S. S. and G. Baxebanēs, 'Ē Chalkida kata tous Mesobyzantinous chronous kai tēn epochē tēs Latinokratias', in Ž. Tankosić et al. (eds.), *An island between two worlds* (Athens, 2017), pp. 593–612.

Skinner, P., *Medieval Amalfi and its diaspora, 800–1250* (Oxford, 2013).

Skoblar, M. (ed.), *Byzantium, Venice and the medieval Adriatic* (Cambridge, 2021).
Slessarev, V., 'The pound-value of Genoa's maritime trade in 1161', in D. Herlihy et al. (eds.), *Economy, society and government in medieval Italy* (Kent, OH, 1969), pp. 95–111.
Smit, T. J., *Commerce and coexistence*, PhD thesis, University of Minnesota, 2009.
Smith, A., *The wealth of nations* (London, 1802).
Smyrlis, K., *La fortune des grands monastères byzantins (fin du Xe–milieu du XIVe siècle)* (Paris, 2006).
Smyrlis, K., 'Trade regulation and taxation in Byzantium, eleventh–twelfth centuries', in Magdalino and Necipoğlu, *Trade in Byzantium* (Istanbul, 2016), pp. 65–87.
Smyrlis, K., 'Social change in the countryside of eleventh-century Byzantium', in J. Howard-Johnston (ed.), *Social change in town and country in eleventh-century Byzantium* (Oxford, 2020), pp. 62–75.
Soddu, A., 'L'aristocrazia fondiaria nella Sardegna dei secoli XI–XII', in J.-M. Martin et al. (eds.), *L'héritage byzantin en Italie (VIIIe–XIIe siècle)*, 4 (Rome, 2017), pp. 145–206.
Sombart, W., *Der moderne Kapitalismus*, 3 vols., 2nd edn (Munich, 1916–27).
Soravia, B., 'Ibn Ḥayyān, historien du siècle des taifas', *al-Qanṭara*, 20 (1999), pp. 99–117.
Soravia, B., 'A portrait of the *'ālim* as a young man: the formative years of Ibn Ḥazm, 404/1013–420/1029', in C. Adang et al. (eds.), *Ibn Ḥazm of Córdoba* (Leiden, 2013), pp. 25–49.
Soriano Sánchez, R. and J. Pascual Pacheco, 'Aproximación al urbanismo de la Valencia medieval', in R. Azuar Ruiz et al. (eds.), *Urbanismo medieval del País Valenciano* (Madrid, 1993), pp. 333–51.
Soriano Sánchez, R. and J. Pascual Pacheco, 'La evolución urbana de Valencia desde época visigoda hasta época taifa: siglos V–XI', in *IV Congreso de arqueología medieval española*, 2 (Alicante, 1994), pp. 67–75.
Spatafora, F., *Da Panormos a Balarm* (Palermo, 2005).
Spatafora, F. et al., 'Ceramica da mensa nella Palermo di XI secolo', *Archeologia postmedievale*, 16 (2012), pp. 23–33.
Spieser, J.-M., *Die byzantinische Keramik aus der Stadtgrabung von Pergamon* (Berlin, 1996).
Spinelli, M., 'Uso dello spazio e vita urbana a Milano tra XII e XIII secolo'. in *Paesaggi urbani dell'Italia padana nei secoli VIII–XIV* (Bologna, 1988), pp. 253–73.
Sprandel, R., 'Die oberitalienischen Eisenproduktion im Mittelalter', *Vierteljahrschrift für Sozial- und Wirtschaftsgeschichte*, 52 (1965), pp. 289–329.
Spufford, P., *Money and its use in medieval Europe* (Cambridge, 1988).
Spufford, P., *Power and profit* (London, 2002).
Spufford, P. et al., *Handbook of medieval exchange* (London, 1986).
Squatriti, P., *Water and society in early medieval Italy: AD 400–1000* (Cambridge, 1998).
Steffy, J. R., 'Construction and analysis of the vessel', in Bass and Allen, *Serçe Limanı*, 1 (College Station, TX, 2004), pp. 153–70.
Stephenson, P., *Byzantium's Balkan frontier* (Cambridge, 2000).
Stern, E. J. et al., *'Akko 1* (Jerusalem, 2012).
Stern, S. M., 'The constitution of the Islamic city', in A. H. Hourani and S. M. Stern (eds.), *The Islamic city* (Oxford, 1970), pp. 25–50.
Stevens, S. T., 'Carthage in transition', in S. T. Stevens and J. P. Conant (eds.), *North Africa under Byzantium and early Islam* (Washington, DC, 2016), pp. 96–103.
Stevens, S. T., 'Not just a tale of two cities', in R. Bockmann et al. (eds.), *Africa—Ifriqiya: continuity and change in North Africa from the Byzantine to the early Islamic age* (Rome, 2019), pp. 245–63.
Stevens, S. T. et al., *Bir Ftouha* (Portsmouth, RI, 2005).

Stillman, N. A., 'The eleventh-century merchant house of Ibn 'Awkal (a Geniza study)', *JESHO*, 16 (1973), pp. 15–88.

Stillman, N. A., 'A case of labor problems in Medieval Egypt', *International journal of Middle East studies*, 5 (1974), pp. 194–201.

Storia di Milano, 3 (Milan, 1954).

Stories from the hidden harbor (Istanbul, 2013).

Storti Storchi, C., *Intorno ai Costituti pisani della legge e dell'uso (secolo XII)* (Naples, 1998).

Svoronos, N. G., 'Remarques sur les structures économiques de l'empire byzantin au XIe siècle', *Travaux et mémoires*, 6 (1976), pp. 49–67.

Symeonoglou, S., *The topography of Thebes from the Bronze Age to modern times* (Princeton, NJ, 1985).

Tabacco, G., *The struggle for power in medieval Italy* (Cambridge, 1989).

Tabales Rodríguez, M. A., *El Alcázar de Sevilla* (Seville, 2010).

Tabales Rodríguez, M. A., *Excavaciones arqueológicas en el Patio de Banderas, Alcázar de Sevilla* (Seville, 2015).

Tabarrini, L., 'When did clerics start investing?', *Annali della scuola normale superiore di Pisa: classe di lettere e filosofia*, 10 (2018), pp. 399–434.

Tabarrini, L., *Responding to change: estate management around Florence and Lucca (1000–1250)* (Oxford, 2023).

Takayama, H., *The administration of the Norman kingdom of Sicily* (Leiden, 1993).

Takayama, H., 'Classification of villeins in medieval Sicily', in Takayama, *Sicily and the Mediterranean* (London, 2019), pp. 218–38.

Takayama, H., *Sicily and the Mediterranean in the middle ages* (London, 2019).

Talbi, M., *L'émirat aghlabide, 184–296/800–909: histoire politique* (Paris, 1966).

Talbi, M., 'Law and economy in Ifrīqiya (Tunisia) in the third Islamic century', in A. L. Udovitch (ed.), *The Islamic Middle East, 700–1900* (Princeton, NJ, 1981), pp. 209–49.

Tanabe, S. et al., *Excavation of a sunken ship found off the Syrian coast* (Tokyo, 1990).

Tangheroni, M., *La città dell'argento* (Naples, 1985).

Tangheroni, M., *Commercio e navigazione nel medioevo* (Bari, 1996).

Tangheroni, M., 'La prima espansione di Pisa nel Mediterraneo', in G. Rossetti and G. Vitolo (eds.), *Medioevo, Mezzogiorno, Mediterraneo*, 1 (Naples, 2000), pp. 3–23.

Tartari, F., 'Amforat e muzeut arkeologjik të Durrësit', *Iliria*, 12.2 (1982) pp. 239–79.

Taylor, R. et al., 'La secuencia arqueológica andalusí (siglos XI–XII) de la Cueva de la Dehesilla (Sierra de Cádiz, España)', *ATM*, 25 (2018), pp. 107–43.

Thayer, J., 'In testimony to a market economy in Mamlūk Egypt', *Al-Masāq*, 8 (1995), pp. 45–55.

Theuws, F., 'Long-distance trade and the rural population of northern Gaul', in B. Effros and I. Moreira (eds.), *The Oxford handbook of the Merovingian world* (Oxford, 2020), pp. 883–915.

Thiriet, F., *La Romanie vénitienne au Moyen Âge* (Paris, 1959).

Thiry, J., *Le Sahara libyen dans l'Afrique du Nord médiévale* (Leuven, 1995).

Thoen, E. and T. Soens, 'The Low Countries, 1000–1750', in Thoen and Soens (eds.), *Struggling with the environment: land use and productivity* (Turnhout, 2015), pp. 221–60.

Thonemann, P., *The Maeander valley* (Cambridge, 2011).

Throckmorton, P., 'Exploration of a Byzantine wreck at Pelagos Island near Alonessos', *Archaiologika analekta ex Athēnōn*, 4 (1971), pp. 182–5.

Ticciati, L., 'Strategie familiari della progenie di Ildeberto Albizo—i Casapieri—nelle vicende e nella realtà pisana fino alla fine del XIII secolo', in *Pisa e la Toscana occidentale nel Medioevo*, 2 (Pisa, 1991), pp. 49–150.

Ticciati, L., *L'Ordine dei Mercanti a Pisa nei secoli XII–XIII* (Pisa, 1992).
Till, W., *Datierung und Prosopographie der koptischen Urkunden aus Theben*, Österreichische Akademie der Wissenschaften, philosophisch-historische Klasse, Sitzungsberichte, 240.1 (Vienna, 1962).
Tillier, M., 'Du pagarque au cadi', *Médiévales*, 64 (2013), pp. 19–36.
Tillier, M., 'The qadis' justice according to papyrological sources (seventh–tenth centuries CE)', in M. van Berkel et al. (eds.), *Legal documents as sources for the history of Muslim societies* (Leiden, 2017), pp. 39–60.
Tite, M. et al., 'Revisiting the beginnings of tin-opacified Islamic glazes', *Journal of archaeological science*, 57 (2015), pp. 80–91.
Tobias, N., *Basil I, founder of the Macedonian dynasty* (Lewiston, NY, 2007).
Todorova, E., 'Policy and trade in the northern periphery of the eastern Mediterranean', in M. J. Gonçalves and S. Gómez-Martínez (eds.), *Actas do X Congresso internacional, A cerâmica medieval no Mediterrâneo* (Silves, 2015), pp. 637–48.
Todorova, E., '"Dark Age" amphorae from present-day Bulgaria', *AM*, 45 (2018), pp. 65–76.
Tognetti, S., 'Produzioni, traffici e mercati secoli XIII–XIV', in A. Malvolti and G. Pinto (eds.), *Il Valdarno Inferiore, terra di confine nel medioevo (secoli XI–XV)* (Florence, 2008), pp. 127–50.
Tognetti, S., 'Attività mercantili e finanziarie nelle città italiane dei secoli XII–XV: spunti e riflessioni sulla base della più recente storiografia', *Ricerche storiche*, 48.2 (2018), pp. 23–44.
Tomasi di Lampedusa, G., *Il gattopardo* (Milan, 1959).
Tomei, P., *Milites elegantes* (Florence, 2019).
Tomei, P., 'Il sale e la seta', in G. Salmeri and P. Tomei (eds.), *La transizione dall'antichità al medioevo nel Mediterraneo centro-orientale* (Pisa, 2020), pp. 21–38.
Torró Abad, J., *La formació d'un espai feudal: Alcoi de 1245 a 1305* (Valencia, 1992).
Toscani, C., 'La produzione di vetro a Pisa tra XII e XIV secolo', in Cantini and Rizzitelli, *Una città operosa* (Florence, 2018), pp. 47–53.
Touati, N., 'Mines et peuplement en Ifrīqiya', in S. Gilotte and É. Voguet (eds.), *Terroirs d'al-Andalus et du Maghreb* (Saint-Denis, 2015), pp. 119–38.
Toubert, P., *Les structures du Latium médiéval* (Paris, 1973).
Toubert, P., *Dalla terra ai castelli* (Turin, 1997).
Toussoun, O., *La géographie de l'Égypte à l'époque arabe*, 1 (Cairo, 1926).
Trading Economics, 'Greece: agricultural land (sq. km)' (2022), https://tradingeconomics.com/greece/agricultural-land-sq-km-wb-data.html/.
Travaini, L., *La monetazione nell'Italia normanna* (Rome, 1995).
Tréglia, J.-C. et al., 'Importations d'amphores médiévales dans le sud-est de la France (Xe–XIIe s.)', in S. Gelichi (ed.), *Atti del IX Congresso internazionale sulla ceramica medievale nel Mediterraneo* (Florence, 2012), pp. 205–7.
Tsanana, A., 'The glazed pottery of Byzantine Vrya (Vrea)' in Ch. Bakirtzis (ed.), *VIIe congrès international sur la céramique médiévale en Méditerranée* (Athens, 2003), pp. 245–50.
Türker, A. Ç., 'A Byzantine settlement in Kalabaklı valley in the Hellespontus: Kepez', *Höyük*, 5 (2014) pp. 69–82.
Turnator, E. G., *Turning the economic tables in the medieval Mediterranean*, PhD thesis, Harvard University, 2013.
Udovitch, A. L., 'At the origins of the western *commenda*', *Speculum*, 37 (1962), pp. 198–207.
Udovitch, A. L., 'Formalism and informalism in the social and economic institutions of the medieval Islamic world', in A. Banani and S. Vryonis (eds.), *Individualism and conformity in classical Islam* (Wiesbaden, 1977), pp. 61–81.

Udovitch, A. L., 'A tale of two cities', in H. A. Miskimin et al. (eds.), *The medieval city* (New Haven, CT, 1977), pp. 143–62.
Udovitch, A. L., *Partnership and profit in medieval Islam* (Princeton, NJ, 1977).
Udovitch, A. L., 'Time, sea and society', *Settimane di studio del Centro italiano di studi sull'alto medioevo*, 25 (1978), pp. 503–46.
Udovitch, A. L., 'Merchants and *amīrs*, government and trade in eleventh-century Egypt', *Asian and African Studies*, 22 (1988), pp. 53–72.
Udovitch, A. L., 'New materials for the history of Islamic Sicily', in *Di nuovo sulla Sicilia musulmana* (Rome, 1995), pp. 183–210.
Udovitch, A. L., 'Medieval Alexandria', in K. Hamma (ed.), *Alexandria and Alexandrianism* (Malibu, CA, 1996), pp. 273–84.
Udovitch, A. L., 'International trade and the medieval Egyptian countryside', *Proceedings of the British Academy*, 96 (1999), pp. 267–85.
Vaccaro, E., 'Re-evaluating a forgotten town using intra-site surveys and the GIS analysis of surface ceramics', in P. Johnson and M. Millett (eds.), *Archaeological survey and the city* (Oxford, 2013), pp. 107–45.
Vaccaro, E., 'Sicily in the eighth and ninth centuries AD', *Al-Masāq*, 25 (2013), pp. 34–69.
Vaccaro, E., 'Long-distance ceramic connections', in Bianchi and Hodges, *Origins of a new economic union* (Florence, 2018), pp. 81–99.
Vaccaro, E. and G. F. La Torre, 'La produzione di ceramica a Philosophiana (Sicilia centrale) nella media età bizantina', *AM*, 42 (2015), pp. 53–91.
Valenti, M. (ed.), *Miranduolo* (Florence, 2008).
Valérian, D., *Bougie, port maghrébin, 1067–1510* (Rome, 2006).
Valérian, D., 'Amalfi e il mondo musulmano', *Rassegna del Centro di cultura e storia amalfitana*, 39–40 (2010), pp. 199–212.
Valérian, D., 'Conquêtes normandes et commerce maritime en Ifrīqiya', in P. Baudouin et al. (eds.), *Sur les pas de Lanfranc, du Bec à Caen* (Caen, 2018), pp. 429–39.
Vallauri, L. and G. Démians d'Archimbaud, 'La circulation des céramiques byzantines, chypriotes et du Levant chrétien en Provence, Languedoc et Corse du Xe au XIVe s.', in Ch. Bakirtzis (ed.), *VIIe congrès international sur la céramique médiévale en Méditerranée* (Athens, 2003), pp. 137–52.
Vallejo, A., *La ciudad califal de Madīnat al-Zahrā'* (Córdoba, 2010).
Valor Piechotta, M. (ed.), *El último siglo de la Sevilla islámica (Seville, 1147–1248)* (Seville, 1995).
Valor Piechotta, M., *Sevilla almohade* (Madrid, 2008).
Valor, M. and A. Gutiérrez González, *The archaeology of medieval Spain 1100–1500* (Sheffield, 2014).
Valor Piechotta, M. and P. Lafuente Ibáñez, 'La Sevilla 'abbādí', in Sarr, *Ṭawā'if* (Granada, 2018), pp. 179–220.
Valor Piechotta, M. and P. Lafuente Ibañez, 'La arqueología medieval en el Aljarafe sevillano', in M. Retuerce Velasco (ed.), *Actas VI Congreso de arqueología medieval (España–Portugal)* (Ciudad Real, 2021), pp. 151–8.
Valor Piechotta, M. et al., 'Espacio rural y territorio en el Aljarafe de Sevilla', in C. Trillo (ed.), *Asentamientos rurales y territorio en el Mediterráneo medieval* (Granada, 2002), pp. 337–72.
van Bavel, B., *Manors and markets* (Oxford, 2010).
van Bavel, B., *The invisible hand?* (Oxford, 2017).
van der Veen, M., *Consumption, trade and innovation* (Frankfurt am Main, 2011).
Van Doosselaere, Q., *Commercial agreements and social dynamics in medieval Genoa* (Cambridge, 2009).

Van Staëvel, J. P. V., 'La foi peut-elle soulever les montagnes?', *Revue des mondes musulmans et de la Méditerranée*, 135 (2014), pp. 49–76.

Vanacker, C., 'Géographie économique de l'Afrique du Nord selon les auteurs arabes, du IXe siècle au milieu du XIIe siècle', *Annales E. S. C.*, 28 (1973), pp. 659–80.

Vannini, G. et al., 'Prato', in F. Cantini (ed.), *"Costruire lo sviluppo"* (Florence, 2019), pp. 89–97.

Varaldo, C., 'La graffita arcaica tirrenica', in G. Démians d'Archimbaud (ed.), *La céramique médiévale en Méditerranée* (Aix-en-Provence, 1997), pp. 439–51.

Varaldo, C., 'Graffita arcaica tirrenica', in Varaldo (ed.), *Archeologia urbana a Savona*, 2.2 (Savona, 2001), pp. 167–98.

Varaldo, C. et al., 'Il castello di Andora (SV)', in R. Fiorillo and P. Peduto (eds.), *III Congresso nazionale di archeologia medievale* (Florence, 2003), pp. 191–200.

Vasileiadou, S., 'Glazed tableware from the Middle Byzantine workshops of Thessaloniki', in P. Petridis et al. (eds.), *12th congress AIECM3 on medieval and modern period Mediterranean ceramics* (Athens, 2021), pp. 747–55.

Vassi, O., 'An unglazed ware pottery workshop in twelfth-century Lakonia', *Annual of the British School at Athens*, 88 (1993), pp. 287–93.

Vassiliou, *see also* Basileiou.

Vassiliou, A., 'Measles ware', in Y. Hazırlayan and F. Yenişehirlioğlu (eds.), *XIth congress AIECM3 on medieval and modern period Mediterranean ceramics proceedings* (Ankara, 2018), pp. 267–70.

Vassiliou, A., 'Early Green and Brown Painted ware from Middle Byzantine Argos', *Deltion tēs Christianikēs archaiologikēs Etaireias*, 40 (2019), pp. 373–400.

Veikou, M., *Byzantine Epirus* (Leiden, 2012).

Vera Reina, M. and P. López Torres, *La cerámica medieval sevillana (siglos XII al XIV)*, BAR, I1403 (Oxford, 2005).

Verhoeven, A. A. A., 'Ceramics and economics in the Low Countries AD 1000–1300', in J. C. Besteman et al. (eds.), *Medieval archaeology in the Netherlands* (Assen, 1990), pp. 265–81.

Verhulst, A., *The rise of cities in north-west Europe* (Cambridge, 1999).

Verhulst, A., *The Carolingian economy* (Cambridge, 2002).

Versteegh, K., 'The Arab presence in France and Switzerland in the 10th century', *Arabica*, 37 (1990), pp. 359–88.

Vezzoli, V., *La céramique islamique d'Apamée de Syrie* (Brussels, 2016).

Viguera Molins, M. J., *Los reinos de taifas y las invasiones magrebíes* (Madrid, 1992).

Viguera Molins, M. J. (ed.), *Historia de España*, 8.1–2 (Madrid, 1994–7).

Villanueva, O. et al., 'Burgos en torno al año mil', in *Al-Ândalus, espaço de mudança* (Mértola, 2006), pp. 256–65.

Vince, A., 'Medieval and post-medieval Spanish pottery from the City of London', in I. Freestone et al. (eds.), *Current research in ceramics: thin-section studies* (London, 1982), pp. 135–44.

Violante, C., *La società milanese nell'età precomunale* (Bari, 1953).

Violante, C., 'Les prêts sur gage foncier dans la vie économique et sociale de Milan au XIe siècle', *Cahiers de civilisation médiévale*, 5 (1962), pp. 147–68, 437–59.

Violante, C., 'I laici nel movimento patarino', in *I laici nella "societas christiana" dei secoli XI e XII* (Milan, 1968), pp. 597–697.

Violante, C., 'Una famiglia feudale della "Langobardia" nel secolo XI', in *Studi filologici, letterari e storici in memoria di Guido Favati*, 2 (Padua, 1977), pp. 653–710.

Violante, C., 'Pievi e parrocchie nell'Italia centro-settentrionale durante i secoli XI e XII', in *Le istituzioni ecclesiastiche della "societas christiana" dei secoli XI–XII: diocesi, pievi e parrocchie* (Milan, 1977), pp. 643–799.

Violante, C., *Economia società istituzioni a Pisa nel medioevo* (Bari, 1980).

Violante, C., 'I transpadani in Tuscia nei secoli VIII e IX', in *Studi di storia economica toscana nel Medioevo e nel Rinascimento in memoria di Federigo Melis* (Pisa, 1987), pp. 403–48.

Violante, C., 'La signoria rurale nel secolo X', *Settimane di studio del Centro italiano di studi sull'alto medioevo*, 38 (1991), pp. 329–85.

Vionis, A. K., 'Current archaeological research on settlement and provincial life in the Byzantine and Ottoman Aegean', *Medieval settlement research*, 23 (2008), pp. 28–41.

Vionis, A. K., 'The Byzantine to early modern pottery from Thespiai', in J. Bintliff et al. (eds.), *Boeotia project*, 2 (Cambridge, 2017), pp. 351–74.

Vionis, A. K., 'Understanding settlements in Byzantine Greece', *DOP*, 71 (2017), pp. 127–73.

Vionis, A. K., 'Island responses in the Byzantine Aegean', in J. Crow and D. Hill (eds.), *Naxos and the Byzantine Aegean* (Athens, 2018), pp. 61–80.

Vionis, A. K., 'Bridging the early medieval "ceramic gap" in the Aegean and eastern Mediterranean (7th–9th C.)', *Herom*, 9 (2020), pp. 291–325.

Vionis, A. K. et al., 'Ceramic continuity and daily life in medieval Sagalassos, SW Anatolia (ca. 650–1250 AD), in T. Vorderstrasse and J. Roodenberg (eds.), *Archaeology of the countryside in medieval Anatolia* (Leiden, 2009), pp. 191–213.

Vionis, A. K. et al., 'A middle-late Byzantine pottery assemblage from Sagalassos', *Hesperia*, 79 (2010), pp. 423–64.

Vitelli, G., *Islamic Carthage* (Tunis, 1981).

Vogt, C., 'Les céramiques ommeyyades et abbassides d'Istabl'Antar-Fostat', in G. Démians d'Archimbaud (ed.), *La céramique médiévale en Méditerranée* (Aix-en-Provence, 1997), pp. 243–60.

Voguet, É., *Le monde rural du Maghreb central, XIV*e*–XV*e *siècles* (Paris, 2014).

Volpe, G., *Studi sulle istituzioni comunali a Pisa*, 2nd edn (Florence, 1970).

von Pilgrim, C. and W. Müller, 'Report on the ninth season of the Joint Swiss-Egyptian Mission in Syene/Old Aswan (2008/2009)', https://www.swissinst.ch/downloads/Report%209th%20Season_2008-2009.pdf.

von Pilgrim, C. et al., 'The town of Syene', *Mitteilungen des Deutschen Archäologischen Instituts, Abteilung Kairo*, 66 (2010), pp. 179–224.

von Pilgrim, C. et al., 'Report on the 16th season of the Joint Swiss-Egyptian Mission in Syene/Old Aswan (2015/2016)', https://www.swissinst.ch/downloads/Report%2016th%20season%202015_16.pdf.

von Pilgrim, C. et al., 'Report on the 19th season of the Joint Swiss-Egyptian Mission in Syene/Old Aswan (2018/2019)', https://www.swissinst.ch/downloads/Report%20Swiss_Egyptian%20Mission%20ASWAN%202019.pdf.

von Rummel. P. and H. Möller, 'Chimtou médiévale', in R. Bockmann et al. (eds.), *Africa—Ifriqiya: continuity and change in North Africa from the Byzantine to the early Islamic age* (Rome, 2019), pp. 185–215.

von Wartburg, M.-L. and Y. Violaris, 'Pottery of a 12th-century pit from the *Palaion Demarcheion* site in Nicosia', in J. Zozaya et al. (eds.), *Actas del VIII Congreso internacional de cerámica medieval en el Mediterráneo* (Ciudad Real, 2009), pp. 249–64.

Vorderstrasse, T., 'Reconstructing houses and archives in Islamic Egypt', in A. Regourd (ed.), *Documents et histoire* (Geneva, 2013), pp. 281–311.

Vorderstrasse, T., 'Terms for vessels in Arabic and Coptic documents and their archaeological and ethnographic correlates', in A. T. Schubert and P. M. Sijpesteijn (eds.), *Documents and the history of the early Islamic world* (Leiden, 2015), pp. 195–234.

Vroom, J., *After Antiquity* (Leiden, 2003).

Vroom, J., 'The medieval and post-medieval finewares and cooking wares from the Triconch Palace and the Baptistery', in Hodges et al., *Byzantine Butrint* (Oxford, 2004), pp. 278–92.
Vroom, J., 'The medieval pottery', in A. Johnston et al., '*Kythera* forty years on', *Annual of the British School at Athens*, 109 (2014), pp. 3–64, at pp. 45–61.
Vroom, J., *Byzantine to modern pottery in the Aegean*, 2nd edn (Turnhout, 2015).
Vroom, J., 'Byzantine sea trade in ceramics', in Magdalino and Necipoğlu, *Trade in Byzantium* (Istanbul, 2016), pp. 157–77.
Vroom, J., 'Bright finds, big city', in Y. Hazırlayan and F. Yenişehirlioğlu (eds.), *XIth congress AIECM3 on medieval and modern period Mediterranean ceramics proceedings* (Ankara, 2018), pp. 383–96.
Vroom, J., 'On the trail of the enigma amphora', *AM*, 45 (2018), pp. 77–90.
Vroom, J., 'Shifting Byzantine networks', in E. Fiori and M. Trizio (eds.), *Proceedings of the plenary sessions, 24th International congress of Byzantine studies* (Venice, 2022), pp. 453–87.
Vroom, J., 'A gentle transition?', in S. Esders et al. (eds.), *The 8th century* (Berlin, 2023).
Vroom, J. et al., 'Exploring daily life in the Byzantine empire: pottery from Chalkis (Euboea, Greece), ca. 10/11th–13th c.', in P. Petridis et al. (eds.), *12th congress AIECM3 on medieval and modern period Mediterranean ceramics* (Athens, 2021), pp. 449–58.
Vryonis, S., 'The will of a provincial magnate, Eustathius Boilas', *DOP*, 11 (1957), pp. 263–77.
Vryonis, S., 'Byzantine *dēmokratia* and the guilds in the eleventh century', *DOP*, 17 (1963), pp. 287–314.
Vryonis, S., *The decline of medieval Hellenism in Asia Minor* (Berkeley, CA, 1971).
Vryonis, S., 'The panēgyris of the Byzantine saint', in S. Hackel, *The Byzantine saint* (London, 1981), pp. 196–226.
Wagner, E.-M., *Linguistic variety of Judaeo-Arabic in letters from the Cairo genizah* (Leiden, 2010).
Wagner, E.-M., 'Register and layout in epistolary Judeo-Arabic', *Jewish history*, 32 (2019), pp. 335–49.
Waksman, S. Y., *Les céramiques byzantines des fouilles de Pergame*, thèse de doctorat, Université Louis Pasteur de Strasbourg, 1995.
Waksman, S. Y., 'Ceramics of the "Serçe Limanı" type and Fatimid pottery production in Beirut', *Levant*, 43 (2011), pp. 201–12.
Waksman, S. Y., 'Medieval ceramics from the Türbe', in Ladstätter, *Die Türbe im Artemision* (Vienna, 2016), pp. 293–311.
Waksman, S. Y., 'Defining the main "Middle Byzantine Production" (MBP)', in Y. Hazırlayan and F. Yenişehirlioğlu (eds.), *XIth congress AIECM3 on medieval and modern period Mediterranean ceramics proceedings* (Ankara, 2018), pp. 397–407.
Waksman, S. Y., 'Byzantine pottery production in Constantinople/Istanbul', in N. D. Kontogiannis et al. (eds.), *Glazed wares as cultural agents in the Byzantine, Seljuk and Ottoman lands* (Istanbul, 2021), pp. 65–81.
Waksman, S. Y. and V. François, 'Vers une redéfinition typologique et analytique des céramiques du type Zeuxippus Ware', *Bulletin de correspondance hellénique*, 128–9 (2004–5), pp. 629–724.
Waksman, S. Y. et al., 'The main "Middle Byzantine Production" and pottery manufacture in Thebes and Chalkis', *Annual of the British School at Athens*, 109 (2014), pp. 379–422.
Waksman, S. Y. et al., 'Investigating the origins of two main types of Middle and Late Byzantine amphorae', *Journal of archaeological science: Reports*, 21 (2018), pp. 1111–21.

Waldbaum, J. C., *Metalwork from Sardis* (Cambridge, MA, 1983).
Wallerstein, I. M., *The modern world-system*, 1 (New York, 1974).
Walmsley, A., *Early Islamic Syria* (London, 2007).
Wasserstein, D., *The rise and fall of the party-kings* (Princeton, NJ, 1985).
Wasserstein, D., *The caliphate in the west* (Oxford, 1993).
Wasserstein, D. J., 'Inventing tradition and constructing identity', *al-Qanṭara*, 23 (2002), pp. 269–97.
Watson, O., 'Fritware: Fatimid Egypt or Saljuq Iran?', in M. Barrucand (ed.), *L'Égypte fatimide* (Paris, 1999), pp. 299–307.
Weber, M., *The history of commercial partnerships in the middle ages* (Lanham, MD, 2003).
Weitz, L., 'Islamic law on the provincial margins', *Islamic law and society*, 27 (2020), pp. 5–52.
West, C., *Reframing the feudal revolution* (Cambridge, 2013).
West-Harling, *see also* Ortenberg.
West-Harling, V., *Rome, Ravenna, and Venice, 750–1000* (Oxford, 2021).
Whitcomb, D., 'Excavations in the site of medieval 'Aqaba', in Y. Rāġib (ed.), *Documents de l'Islam médiéval* (Cairo, 1991), pp. 123–30.
White, H. E., *An investigation of production technologies of Byzantine glazed pottery from Corinth, Greece in the eleventh to thirteenth centuries*, PhD thesis, University of Sheffield, 2009.
Whittle, J., *The development of agrarian capitalism* (Oxford, 2000).
Whittle, J., 'Tenure and landholding in England 1440–1580', in B. J. P. van Bavel and P. C. M. Hoppenbrouwers (eds.), *Landholding and land transfer in the North Sea area (late middle ages–19th century)* (Turnhout, 2004), pp. 237–49.
Whittow, M., *The making of Orthodox Byzantium, 600–1025* (London, 1996).
Wickham, C., *The mountains and the city* (Oxford, 1988).
Wickham, C., *Land and power* (London, 1994).
Wickham, C., '*Manentes* e diritti signorili durante il XII secolo: il caso della Lucchesia', in *Società, istituzioni, spiritualità* (Spoleto, 1994), 1067–80.
Wickham, C., 'La signoria rurale in Toscana', in Dilcher and Violante, *Strutture e trasformazioni* (Bologna, 1996), pp. 343–409.
Wickham, C., 'Aristocratic power in eighth-century Lombard Italy', in A. Murray (ed.), *After Rome's fall* (Toronto, 1998), pp. 153–70.
Wickham, C., *Community and clientele* (Oxford, 1998).
Wickham, C., *Courts and conflict in twelfth-century Tuscany* (Oxford, 2003).
Wickham, C., *Framing the early middle ages* (Oxford, 2005).
Wickham, C., 'The early middle ages and national identity', in N. Fryde et al. (eds.), *Die Deutung der mittelalterlichen Gesellschaft in der Moderne* (Göttingen, 2006), pp. 107–22.
Wickham, C., 'Fonti archeologiche e fonti storiche: un dialogo complesso', in A. Barbero (ed.), *Storia d'Europa e del Mediterraneo*, 9 (Rome, 2007), pp. 15–49.
Wickham, C., 'La cristalización de la aldea', in *XXXIV semana de estudios medievales* (Pamplona, 2008), pp. 33–51.
Wickham, C., '*Iuris cui existens*', *Archivio della società romana di storia patria*, 131 (2008), pp. 5–38.
Wickham, C., 'Productive forces and the economic logic of the feudal mode of production', *Historical Materialism*, 16.2 (2008), pp. 3–22.
Wickham, C., 'Problems in doing comparative history', in P. Skinner (ed.), *Challenging the boundaries of medieval history* (Turnhout, 2009), pp. 5–28.

Wickham, C., 'La struttura della proprietà fondiaria nell'agro romano, 900–1150', *Archivio della società romana di storia patria*, 132 (2009), pp. 181–238.

Wickham, C., 'Comacchio and the central Mediterranean', in Gelichi and Hodges, *From one sea to another* (Turnhout, 2012), pp. 503–10.

Wickham, C., *Medieval Rome* (Oxford, 2014).

Wickham, C., 'Gli artigiani nei documenti italiani dei secoli XI e XII', in A. Molinari et al. (eds.), *L'archeologia della produzione a Roma (secoli V–XV)* (Rome, 2015), pp. 429–38.

Wickham, C., *Sleepwalking into a new world* (Princeton, NJ, 2015).

Wickham, C., 'Sulle origini del comune di Bologna', *Bullettino dell'Istituto storico italiano per il medio evo*, 119 (2016), pp. 209–37.

Wickham, C., 'Administrators' time', in B. Sadeghi et al. (eds.), *Islamic cultures, Islamic contexts* (Leiden, 2017), pp. 430–67.

Wickham, C., 'Prima della crescita: quale società?', in *La crescita economica* (Pistoia, 2017), pp. 93–106.

Wickham, C., 'The power of property', *JESHO*, 62, 1 (2019), pp. 67–107.

Wickham, C., 'How did the feudal economy work?', *Past and present*, 251 (2021), pp. 3–40.

Wickham, C., 'Informal and formal trading associations in Egypt and Ifrīqiya, 850–1150', in M. van Berkel and L. Osti (eds.), *The historian of Islam at work* (Leiden, 2022), pp. 171–82.

Wickham, C., 'Islamic, Byzantine and Latin exchange systems in the Mediterranean, 750–1050', in S. Heidemann and K. Mewes (eds.), *The reach of empire* (Berlin, 2023).

Wickham, C., 'Looking back at the eighth century from the eleventh', in S. Esders et al. (eds.), *The 8th century* (Berlin, 2023).

Wickham, C., 'The small towns of the territory of Milan in the twelfth century, 1075–1180', in M. Dejoux et al. (eds.), *Les fruits de la terre* (Paris, 2023).

Wiesner, J., 'Mikroskopische Untersuchung der Papiere von el-Faijûm', *Mittheilungen aus der Sammlung der Papyrus Erzherzog Rainer*, 1 (1887), pp. 45–8.

Wiesner, J., 'Die Faijûmer und Uschmûneiner Papiere', *Mittheilungen aus der Sammlung der Papyrus Erzherzog Rainer*, 2/3 (1887), pp. 179–260.

Williams, G., *"Fayyumi" ware*, MA thesis, American University in Cairo, 2013.

Williams, G., 'Medieval ceramics from Aswan', *Bulletin de liaison de la céramique égyptienne*, 28 (2018), pp. 297–306.

Williams, G., *Syene VI* (Gladbeck, 2022).

Wong, R. B., 'China before capitalism', in L. Neal and J. G. Williamson (eds.), *The Cambridge history of capitalism*, 1 (Cambridge, 2014), pp. 125–64.

Wrigley, E. A., *Continuity, chance and change* (Cambridge, 1988).

Yangaki, A. G., 'Céramique glaçurée provenant de Nauplie et d'Argos (XIIe–XIIIe siècles)', *Bulletin de correspondance hellénique*, 132 (2008), pp. 587–616.

Yangaki, A. G., 'Observations on the glazed pottery of the 11th–17th centuries A.D. from Akronauplia', in S. Gelichi (ed.), *Atti del IX Congresso internazionale sulla ceramica medievale nel Mediterraneo* (Florence, 2012), pp. 276–81.

Younes, K. M., 'Textile trade between the Fayyūm and Fusṭāṭ in the IIIrd/IXth century according to the Banū 'Abd al-Mu'min archive', in A. Regourd (ed.), *Documents et histoire* (Geneva. 2013), pp. 313–34.

Zaninelli, S., *Storia di Monza e della Brianza*, 3: *vita economica e sociale* (Milan, 1969).

Zavagno, L., *Cyprus between late antiquity and the early middle ages (ca. 600–800)* (Abingdon, 2017).

Zavagno, L., *The Byzantine city from Heraclius to the Fourth Crusade, 610–1204* (Basingstoke, 2021).

Zeller, B. et al., *Neighbours and strangers* (Manchester, 2020).

Zhang, R., *An exploratory quantitative archaeological analysis and a classification system of Chinese ceramics trade in the western Indian ocean: AD c.800–1500*, PhD thesis, Durham University, 2016.

Zinger, O., *Women, gender and law*, PhD thesis, University of Princeton, 2014.

Zinger, O., 'Finding a fragment in a pile of Geniza', *Jewish history*, 32 (2019), pp. 279–309.

Zozaya Stabel-Hansen, J. and G. S. Kurtz Schaefer (eds.), *Bataliús III* (Badajoz, 2014).

Zupko, R. E., *Italian weights and measures from the middle ages to the nineteenth century* (Philadelphia, PA, 1981).

Żurek, M., 'Two pottery deposits from building AA in Naqlun', *Polish archaeology in the Mediterranean*, 15 (2003), pp. 165–72.

Zurndorfer, H., 'Cities and the urban economy', in D. Ma and R. von Glahn (eds.), *The Cambridge economic history of China*, 1 (Cambridge, 2022), pp. 522–59.

Index

Note: names beginning 'al-' are indexed according to the attached word. Placenames are linked to countries; they are always the modern countries. The main discussions of the regions which are the focus of study in this book are **bolded**.